THE ENCYCLOPEDIA OF
STAGE PLAYS
INTO FILM

THE ENCYCLOPEDIA OF STAGE PLAYS INTO FILM

JOHN C. TIBBETTS AND JAMES M. WELSH

Associate Editor:
JOHN STANIUNAS

Contributing Editors:
REV. GENE PHILLIPS, S.J.; RICHARD VELA
TONY WILLIAMS; ROBERT F. WILLSON, JR.

Foreword by
STEVE ALLEN

Facts On File, Inc.

This book is dedicated to
Kevin Brownlow
and
David Shepard
who taught us how to preserve
and protect our film heritage.

❋ ❋ ❋

The Encyclopedia of Stage Plays into Film

Facts On File, Inc.
132 West 31st Street
New York NY 10001

Library of Congress Cataloging-in-Publication Data

Tibbetts, John C., 1946 Oct. 6–
The encyclopedia of stage plays into film / John C. Tibbetts, James M. Welsh
p. cm.
Includes bibliographical references and index.
ISBN 0-8160-4155-5 (alk. paper)
1. Film adaptations—Catalogs. 2. Drama—Bibliography—Catalogs.
I. Welsh, James M. II. Title
PN1997.85 .T544 20001
016.79143'6—dc21   00-063622

Facts On File books are available at special discounts when purchased in bulk
quantities for businesses, associations, institutions, or sales promotions.
Please call our Special Sales Department in New York at
(212) 967-8800 or (800) 322-8755.

You can find Facts On File on the World Wide Web at
http://www.factsonfile.com

Text design by Cathy Rincon
Cover design by Nora Wertz

Printed in the United States of America

VB FOF 10 9 8 7 6 5 4 3 2 1

This book is printed on acid-free paper.

Contents

Foreword

BY STEVE ALLEN

It is so obvious that it goes without saying, I suppose—but I will say it anyway: Movies can bring plays and musicals to a much wider audience than could ever see them on stage. Even if you live in a small town without a theatre house, you can see the movie on television and purchase the video. It is the indisputable fact that justifies their existence. Yet it is also true that these film versions need not be accepted as definitive versions. This book, *The Encyclopedia of Stage Plays into Film*, addresses that problem. Often we are too lazy to go ahead and read the original book or see the play. My recollection of a film like *Amadeus*, for example, is of the movie, and not the stage version, which I have not seen. Conversely, I saw *Equus* on stage but have not seen the film. It is too easy to form wrong conclusions when you have not bothered to get all the data available. I wrote at length in my book, *Dumbth* (Prometheus Books, 1999), that this sort of neglect and ignorance is increasing. For example, our schools should direct students to read the original Shakespeare texts before or after seeing the movie versions. Having several angles of vision on anything enlarges the experience.

The subject of this book is enormous. Plays, teleplays, novels, musicals, all shift back and forth from one medium to another. The simple fact is that it *has all been done*, countless times. I could even argue that there is a sense in which it doesn't really matter where the original story comes from. You have to make up your own rules in each case. There's wisdom in the old jazz song, "It Ain't What You Do, It's the Way How You Do It." Certainly it is true that in translating a short story or one-set play into a movie, you have more freedom for the creative screenwriter to inject his or her own thoughts and opinions. But it is also true that when you have a very complete and self-contained work like *Who's Afraid of Virginia Woolf?*, a faithful rendering on screen is really all that is needed. Too much embellishment may ruin it. This brings up the issue of "opening up" a play so that the players won't be restricted to the same couch, the same chair, the same breakfast table. Even if the world's greatest actors are in the movie version, it will not be enough; you still are obliged to open

up the property in a spatial and visual sense, to move your players around, to write in scenes with them on bicycles or swimming in the ocean or whatever. The movie version of *Driving Miss Daisy* certainly opened up the play, but it did so in ways appropriate to the actions already implied in the play. Right now I am working on a film treatment of my own play, *The Wake*, which also obliges me to "open up" activities surrounding the central action—insert exterior sequences and perhaps employ some flashback scenes.

There are instances, however, where a screen translation of a play has been just wrong-headed. Most of the movie versions of Neil Simon's delightful plays have not worked for me. It should not be difficult to turn a very funny play into a very funny movie, but the film versions have sometimes lost the compactness of their original play texts. When the screen adaptation of James Hilton's novel, *Lost Horizon*, was remade into a musical in the early 1970s, it was not successful, perhaps because they hired Burt Bacharach, who was then very popular—and deservedly so—to write the music. Although he has enormous talent, he was not right for that particular project. They would have had much better luck with somebody like Michel Legrand or Henry Mancini. It was an object lesson that it is very hard to fail with a film that contains solid and well-known songs. That was an advantage enjoyed by the Benny Goodman movie [*The Benny Goodman Story*] or the *The Glenn Miller Story*, with Jimmy Stewart and June Allyson. The same holds true with the Rodgers and Hammerstein and Cole Porter and Irving Berlin movie adaptations.

A fascinating problem that sometimes comes up is that on stage an actor can suddenly burst into song, with a full orchestral accompaniment, and nobody is bothered by it. But on screen, the effect might be especially odd. I poked fun at that in a comedy sketch on my Sunday night television show when Esther Williams was a guest. You'll recall that in her movies she would usually be in the pool with someone like Fernando Lamas, and suddenly their romantic dialogue would be interrupted by violin music coming out of nowhere. Well, on our show, Esther and I splashed around in a big swimming pool we had built on the stage. Suddenly, violin music is heard and about nine violinists with dripping instruments rise up out of the water! Mel Brooks lampooned that sort of thing in *Blazing Saddles*, when he has Count Basie's band suddenly appearing in the desert wastes to provide musical accompaniment to the action.

Another problem in filming musical scenes is the necessity of lip-synching a song to a playback that was recorded earlier on a sound stage. It's not the easiest thing in the world to do. The more creative you are as a singer, the more "takes" you have to do because new ideas keep occurring to you. That's a no-no. You must do it the exact way you recorded it in the studio. It's even more of a problem if you're lip-synching to somebody else's voice, where you must imitate a performance that is not your own. I had to do a lot of lip-synching for the big production numbers in my television shows. Close-ups were difficult, because you had to match those m's and b's and p's right on the button. It was not so much of a problem as long as we could keep the scenes in medium-to-long shot, where your errors of lip movement may not be detectable.

Many of our favorite musical films may seem *theatrical*, but in actuality they did not come from the stage at all. My favorite movie musical is *The Umbrellas of Cherbourg*, a wholly original screen conception. I had no idea what it was all about when I went to see it. As the first song was heard under the opening credits, I thought, what a brilliant idea. And it was only a moment later that I realized that the music was not going to stop. It was total music, all the way, one great melody after another, a story that was musical and a musical that was a story. Michel Legrand has that marvelous ability to create sweeping, old-fashioned romantic music. Everything complemented it and sustained it—even down to the photography and the scenic details of the wallpaper. It was like an opera, in its own way.

Whether I am writing a short story, song, novel, play, or screenplay, I always have a visual image in my mind. I don't think I could ever confine myself to one medium. Versatility is necessary if you are to survive in this multi-media age. A person does not decide to be versatile, by the way. It is just the way you are stamped out by the universal cookie cutter. But the problems later come from being involved in too many things. Mel Brooks wrote me several years ago with this complaint about his busy schedule: "I'm so busy doing everything, I don't have time to do anything."

In a way, I have always been a stage performer. That comes, I suppose from those early years working in radio and television studios, where there were studio audiences to "play" to and where we were confined to relatively cramped spaces. Experience in "live" television writing has helped me to understand how the limited playing area of a stage can be put to work, how to get characters on and off stage as needed, that sort of thing. Like a small stage, the television studio space allows only for a central set and an adjacent playing area, say, for a living room and an adjoining kitchen. Or variations on that. You see that sort of studio layout in series like *Home Improvement.*

Many important playwrights came out of that kind of television writing experience—like Paddy Chayevsky, Horton Foote, Stirling Silliphant, and Rod Serling—and their scripts fell into the hands of such talented directors and producers as John Frankenheimer, Delbert Mann, Fred Coe, Sidney Lumet, and Martin Manulis. To be sure, we had problems arise from the fact that everything was "live." There were breakdowns and mishaps. In my book, *Hi-Ho, Steverino* [1992], I take the time to describe some of them.

Another difficulty we encountered in playing to an audience, as we did on live television, was that we had to connect with studio audiences through a jungle of cameras, lights, microphone dollies, three camera operators, and several stagehands creeping around in the darkness. Sometimes it seemed as if we were playing to *three* audiences at the same time—the technical crew, the studio audience, and the viewers at home.

My short stories have encountered few problems on their way to the stage. Five of my stories written around 1960 were staged for a couple of weeks at the Pasadena Playhouse in the L.A. area. We just transferred the dialogue from the stories to the stage, and that was about all there was to it. I attended a number of rehearsals and was pleased with the general production. Another story, *The Wake*, was written in the early 1970s and later brought to the stage. It was an autobiographical drama about a wake held for my maternal grandmother, Bridget Scanlon Donohue, who had been born in Ireland. We situated the action in a specific apartment at 4911 Cottage Grove Avenue on Chicago's South Side. The coffin was situated right in the living room, center stage, surrounded by flowers and candles. People come in sniffling and crying, but pretty soon they begin telling funny family stories. After the refreshments, however, they get drunk and quarrelsome. I had assumed that they loved each other, and it was shocking to hear them arguing and screaming. *The Wake* is both a comedy and a tragedy. Every year the Los Angeles drama critics nominate several plays for their "Best Play" category, and one year *The Wake* was nominated.

Another of my stories, "The Public Hating," which appeared in my story collection, *Fourteen for Tonight*, has also been staged at the Pasadena Playhouse. It has also been frequently anthologized. It is a fantasy about a day when executions will become public spectacles, held in sporting arenas, as in olden times. Orson Welles once wrote me that if the play ever became a film, he wanted one of the roles.

Some of the most rewarding dramatic writing I have done for television was the *Meeting of Minds* series that aired on PBS, beginning in 1977. These were stage dramas, disguised as television talk shows; dramatized discussions among famous historical figures from politics, the sciences, religion, and the arts—figures who could never have met in real time and space. Abraham Lincoln might speak with Julius Caesar, or George Washington might debate an important question with Freud or Lenin. I was very careful to attribute to these people only those views they actually held—and, in as many cases as possible, do so using their actual words. One of my favorite shows in the series had a distinctly theatrical bent. Several years before the series aired, I had considered an experiment where I confronted William Shakespeare with three of his characters—Hamlet, Romeo, and Othello—to talk about that greatest of subjects, love. I thought it would be interesting to see what might happen if reality and fiction were brought together face to face. The "Dark Lady" of the sonnets was chosen as the discussion "host." Inevitably, I was forced to write transition lines for the characters that were not in Shakespeare but which *sounded* like Shakespeare. That particular program, "Shakespeare in Love," was staged by the Shakespeare Society of America at a theatre in Los Angeles in 1975; and it finally was televised years later, with myself as host, Jayne Meadows as Desdemona and Juliet, William Marshall as Othello, Anthony Costello as Hamlet, Charles Lanyer as Romeo, and Harris Yulin as Shakespeare.

Writing musical shows is another outgrowth of my television years. My first musical, *The Bachelor*, starring Hal March and Carol Haney, was written for NBC-TV in 1952 at the behest of producer Gilbert Cates. It must have been one of the very first such productions written especially for television. Here the challenge was to compress within the small space of a song all the emotions that a scene might demand. One of my best songs came from that experience. I knew I had to write a number conveying the frustrations of being a bachelor, so one night I fell asleep and dreamed the song, "This Could Be the Start of Something Big." Usually we forget our dreams, but fortunately, I had this one just before I woke up. I took a pad and pencil beside my bed and simply wrote down several lines of the lyric. It became the main song in the score. I also wrote another

number, "Impossible," for that score.

Another show was *Sophie*, which I wrote and composed for the Broadway stage in 1964. It was about Sophie Tucker, a star in vaudeville in the 1920s—a tough broad, as they say, who did semi-naughty songs (but tame compared to today's vulgarity!). One of the show's ballads, "I'll Show Them All," which closed the first act, really stopped the show. It was about the fact that Sophie had been told by everybody to forget show business, that she wasn't good looking enough, that she was overweight. She sings it in response to all those nay-sayers. It was quite dramatic. Judy Garland later performed it on her CBS television show. Unfortunately, *Sophie* was not a success. Its failure was an object lesson in the importance of casting. The producers made a fatal error in casting a slender blonde actress named Libby Steiger for the gutsy, heavy-set Tucker. I told the producers the casting did not make sense, but that is what they wanted. Barbra Streisand could have done it, witness her work later in *Funny Girl* as Fanny Brice.

Still another musical show was *Belle Star*, based on the life of a notorious character in the Old West. I only saw one production of it, in Las Vegas. The producer cast Betty Grable in the title role, and it toured the British Isles.

My most recent show, for which I wrote the book, music, and lyrics, is an adaptation of Charles Dickens' *A Christmas Carol*. As yet unrealized is another project that has always intrigued me, a musical version of *Miracle on 34th Street*. When I first considered it, I discovered that Meredith Willson already had control of the rights to the property. So that was that, at least for the time being.

One of my early films was *College Confidential*, a movie that I later regretted getting trapped in. It was based on an actual case about a professor at the University of Illinois who was fired because he had started a class about sex (a perfectly responsible course, by the way). But he was fired. Such was the mood of the times. A producer commissioned a script and asked me to play the role of the professor. A worthwhile movie could have been done, but in actuality, it was cheapened up, with Mamie Van Doren walking around the campus in tight skirts. That sort of thing.

Then there was *The Benny Goodman Story*, of course. That was a straight dramatic assignment. I had to keep things very restrained and quiet, quite a contrast to my television antics. Nobody knew much about Benny, except for his music. Part of the reason for that is that Benny was one of the most colorless people you ever would meet, shy and inarticulate and, on occasion, rather unpleasant to boot. As a result, the biographical material in the film was pretty flimsy. The *real* challenge was to learn how to finger the clarinet and simulate the breathing for the close-up scenes. I studied with a longtime Goodman admirer, a good player and teacher. The most fun was hanging around with musicians whom I had idolized as a teenager, like Teddy Wilson, Lionel Hampton, and Gene Krupa. It was directed by Valentine Davies, who I later found out had written the original novel, *Miracle on 34th Street*.

I do not fear for the future of quality plays, musicals, and films. Creative people will always come along. And they will continue to cross-pollinate their works among all the various media. Yes, talented people will continue to work, despite the increasing vulgarity of our media culture and today's audiences' willing participation in this descent into the gutter. I can only remind you that new ideas and cultural shifts invariably come as a surprise. The week before Elvis showed up, nobody knew he was coming. Same with the Beatles, and the Bossa Nova, Bebop, and the Charleston. Nobody predicted them. That's a hopeful note. It means there will always be new things, and some of them will be valuable and admirable, no matter what medium in which they appear.

(Note: Steve Allen completed this Foreword on 28 October 2000, just a few days before his death, on 31 October.)

Steve Allen (John Tibbetts)

Acknowledgments

The editors of this volume wish especially to thank the following for their invaluable assistance and contributions in the preparation of this encyclopedia: first and foremost, to editor James Chambers of Facts On File, whose patience and consistent good humor helped us over many rough spots. To Paul Scaramazza, longtime friend and boon companion, whose painstaking attention to the manuscript enabled us to correct more errors than we care to admit. To the members of the Literature/Film Association, founded in 1988 by the editors of *Literature/Film Quarterly*. This organization's annual national conferences, activities, and publications have in large measure both inspired this book and brought it to completion. We are grateful to Professor Peter C. Rollins, editor of *Film and History*, who allowed us to promote this project in the regional Popular Culture Association Conference organized in Albuquerque in February 2000. Thanks are also due to Anne Welsh, for her understanding and continued support; and the contributing editors of *Literature/Film Quarterly*, who participated in the writing of many entries—particularly, Father Gene D. Phillips, S.J., of Loyola University of Chicago, Tom Erskine, Salisbury State University, Tony Williams, Southern Illinois University, and the redoubtable Frank Thompson, a freelance writer of kaleidoscopic talents, Burbank, California. For many years we have enjoyed the close friendship and continuing support of many friends and colleagues at the University of Kansas, including Katherine Giele, former director of Student Union Activities (who also generously assisted in the organization of the KU Film Society), and Chuck Sack, friend and collaborator on many film projects; Professors Harold Orel, Marilyn Stokstad, Charles M. Berg, Joe Anderson, Edward Small, Catherine Preston, and the late Edward L. Ruhe; and, finally, John Gronbeck-Tedesco, former chair of the Department of Theatre and Film and editor of *Journal of Dramatic Theory and Criticism*, and Mary-Karen Dahl, present chair of that department. Lastly, a grateful tip of the hat is due to Richard Dyer MacCann, professor emeritus of the University of Iowa, formerly of the University of Kansas, whose pioneering efforts on behalf of academic film studies have been and continue to be an inspiration to us and to many other students and teachers of cinema studies.

Many of the photos in this book were originally distributed to publicize and/or promote films made or distributed by the following companies, to whom we gratefully offer acknowledgment: Argos/Comei/Pathe/Daiei; Artcraft; Cinema Center Films; Columbia Pictures; Dino De Laurentiis Cinematographica S.P.A.; Elmer Enterprises; Eon; Epoch; Famous Players-Lasky; Fantasy Films; Films du Carrosse/SEDIF; Filmways; Fox Film Corporation; Gainsborough; General Production; Island Alive; Kino International; Landau-Unger; Long Road Productions; Mary Pickford Foundation/Timeline Films/Milestone Films; Metro; MGM; Newdon Company; NSW Film Corporation; Omni Zoetrope; Orion; Palomar/Chartoff-Winkler-Pollack; Panorama/Nordisk/Danish Film Institute; Picnic Productions; Paramount Pictures; Polaris; Prana; RKO; Samuel Goldwyn; Saul Zaentz Company; David O. Selznick; Speva/Cine Alliance/Filmsonor; SRO; TCF-Rockley-Cacoyannis; Twentieth Century-Fox; UFA; United Artists; Universal; Vanadas; Warner Bros.; World Entertainment.

—*John C. Tibbetts*, The University of Kansas
—*James M. Welsh*, Salisbury State University

Theatrical Films: The New Proscenium

Like freebooters of yore, filmmakers have long plundered the stores of the stage and the novel. They have grabbed the swag with brutish fists. They have picked it over with delicate fingers. They have held it hostage. They have purchased its freedom. They have appropriated, adapted, rejected, mangled, and transformed it. Some of the treasure they buried, nowhere to be found; and some they exchanged for common currency, coin of the realm. The fate of these bandit chieftains is yet to be decided. Pronounce them guilty of heinous crimes against Art and hang 'em from the highest yardarm? Or exonerate them all and honor their names?

This book, confronted with these two choices, chooses to follow the advice of Yogi Berra, who said that when we come to a fork in the road—take it. The sheer volume of literary adaptations—that is the polite word—leaves us no choice. The majority of all feature-length films released to a mainstream audience betray their literary sources. It is necessary to "round up the usual suspects"—don't forget that *Casablanca* was based on a stage play—and ask some tough questions.

For example, is it easier to transform novels or stage plays into film? Since both plays and films dramatize situations and involve actors performing written dialogue, the stage play would seem to be the more adaptable, but is this only an educated guess?

Consider the relatively recent example of Willy Russell's *Educating Rita*, a simple, sparsely staged drama translated into a big-budget Hollywood film with an all-star cast. The eponymous Rita was a working-class hairdresser in England who wanted to broaden her horizons, improve her station in a class-bound society, and change her life. She called herself "Rita" because she had read a liberating book by Rita Mae Brown. She enrolled in Britain's Open University and was assigned to Frank, a cynical tutor who, although he initially did his best to drive her away, was, to their mutual astonishment, eventually charmed by her innocence and determination. The relationship they ultimately develop is one of mutual respect and tolerance for each other's differences and limitations.

Because *Educating Rita* was written for the stage, dialogue rather than action functioned as the most important way to define character and situation. Not a very promising concept to put on the movie screen, at first blush, but film director Lewis Gilbert "opened up" the play and propelled much of the action out of the tutor's office. He also visualized the "back stories" of Rita and the tutor, and added many more voices to the ongoing chorus of her "education" process. By placing actors Julie Walters (who reprised her original stage role) and Michael Caine in a shifting context of scenes and situations barely alluded to in the play, they emerged as more fully realized characters and, hence, more believable for American audiences, especially those viewers more accustomed to movies than stage plays.

For purposes of the book you are holding in your hands, Rita's "education" can be regarded as a paradigm of the "education" playwrights and filmmakers have gained in over a century of struggle to bring the contrasting media of theatre and film into some sort of harmony—or, as Edward Albee might have termed it, a "delicate balance." Rita, like the emerging film medium at the turn of the century, was brash, untried, vulgar, opportunistic, yet full of possibilities and potential. Her tutor, Frank, symbolized a theatrical establishment fully formed, yet tied to formulas and practices that, by contrast, seemed stuffy and outmoded. Thus, theatre and film, like Rita and Frank, regarded each other with suspicion, alarm, and fascination. The symbiotic relationship that is gradually forged between the two—like the "education" that both Rita and Frank gain—is, by turns, problematic and productive. What it has been and where it is going is yet to be determined.

Hence this book.

The long and complicated saga of stage-film "education" may be conveniently broken up into four periods, or "lessons." In the first, proto-filmmakers in

America and Europe at the turn of the century borrowed heavily from vaudeville acts and performers for their short peep-show films. Second, the rise of the feature-length film in 1912–15 encouraged the translation of "legitimate" plays, melodramas, and farces into films that were exhibited in legitimate theatre houses and movie palaces. Third, the introduction of sound technology to the movies in 1926–30 brought a resurgence of theatre and film interaction—including an influx of stage stars and the movies' adoption of a variety of theatrical forms, from the well-made play to the farce and vaudeville turn—that has remained unabated to this day. And fourth, the appearance in the last two decades of a number of directors and actors who work with equal facility in both camps, and who have introduced new and innovative approaches to the ongoing challenge of adaptation from stage play to film.

At the outset, the term "theatrical film" should be clarified. In the broadest sense, the term is used to designate any film that has a theatrical source, such as a stage play, vaudeville revue, or musical show. More specifically, it refers to any film that, to one degree or another, either directly imitates or in some way utilizes the subjects, processes, and effects of the stage in a visible and prominent way. At one extreme this is seen most clearly in the works of Georges Méliès in France and Edwin S. Porter in America in the latter 1890s and early 1900s. These films, typically derived from French *faerie* pantomimes, magic shows, and popular melodramas, transformed the movie screen into a "new proscenium"—i.e., a simulacrum of the playing space within a stage proscenium, where the action occurs within a frame, the stage space is shallow, a shot constitutes a scene, entrances and exits are guided into lateral directions, the viewer's vantage point is fixed, artificial scenery is utilized. At the other extreme are recent films like David Mamet's *The Winslow Boy*, which demonstrates how even a film that is wholly "cinematic" in its sophisticated manipulations of space, time, and montage techniques may still support and convey a primarily "theatrical" experience.

From the very beginning, filmmakers working in America for the Edison, Biograph, Essanay, Vitagraph, Kalem, and Kleine studios and in France for the Méliès and Pathé studios began to adopt and/or imitate theatrical models of entertainment and organization. It has been exaggerated that this upstart new medium was commonly regarded as crude and vulgar, that few theatre actors were willing to trust their talents to them, few theatrical producers and playwrights saw profitable opportunities on celluloid, few drama critics considered them in a serious light, and few filmmakers had even a modestly sophisticated idea of the range of theatrical activity available to them. This view needs revising.

The fact is that the film medium was from the very first presumed to be a suitable recording medium for theatrical events. As early as 1894, a writer in *The Critic* predicted that Edison's kinetoscope peepshow device would enable the viewer to "witness and hear shadow plays in which the only real performer will be the electro-magnetic motor behind the scenes."[1] A year later Edison himself was quoted as saying that by linking the phonograph and the kinetoscope the movies could preserve and disseminate theatrical events so that, for example, grand opera could be presented "without any material change from the original, and with artists and musicians long since dead."[2] Thus, many short films displayed in his peep-show machines were simply photographed variety turns, their length varying from mere seconds to a few minutes. Meanwhile, at its peak between 1890 and 1913, vaudeville reached mass audiences in 37 houses in New York alone, extending to an estimated 2,000 smaller theatres outside the big cities. The length of these short turns proved them to be ideal subjects for early film shorts, and the vaudeville houses were appropriate settings for the first exhibitions of these films as part of the variety program. Tumbling, dancing, marching, and cavorting across the screen were strong men, jugglers, knockabout comedians, exotic dancers, and headliner performers like Annabelle, Dolorita, Carmencita, the Gaiety Girls, and "legit" players like John Drew and May Irwin.

Vaudeville also held out to the movies the concept of the excerpted play. By 1903, brief scenes from plays began finding their way to the screen—from Edison's 1894 short, *The Band Drill* (from Charles Hoyt's *A Milk White Flag*) and Biograph's 1903 *Ten Nights in a Barroom* (a series of excerpts from William S. Pratt's popular melodrama). Other films condensed entire plays into one reel. Literally hundreds of popular plays reached audiences in this way. In France, Méliès reduced the melodramas of Guilbert de Pixerecourt—including *Robinson Crusoe* and *The Thousand and One Nights*—to a one-reel format. In America, too, many plays and operas were abbreviated into scant minutes of running time. Porter's *Jack and the Beanstalk* and *Uncle Tom's Cabin* (both 1903) were presented in a series of brief tableaux, scenes recorded in an unbroken shot from a fixed camera position. D.W. Griffith managed to smelt the opera *Rigoletto* and Shakespeare's *The Taming of the Shrew* down into one reel each.

Commentators took notice. The *New York Daily Tribune* observed that the motion picture "had its stage machinery, its wings, its properties, its lights, its makeups, its exits, and its entrances."[3] In his article, "The Nickelodeons," written for *The Saturday Evening Post* in

1907, Joseph Medill Patterson noted that each film studio had its painted scenic flats, a property-room, dressing rooms, and a completely equipped stage. "The studio manager orders rehearsals continued until his people have their parts 'face-perfect,' then he gives the word, the lens is focused, the cast works rapidly for twenty minutes while the long strip of celluloid whirls through the camera, and performance is preserved in living, dynamic embalmment (if the phrase may be permitted) for decades to come."[4] Actors faced the challenge of working in a silent medium that reduced a play to one reel of pantomimed action. Writing in 1911, Montrose Moses dubbed this new, shorthand kind of gesture "strenuous acting in a mechanical age."[5] Of course, at this time it was not yet possible to photograph a theatrical event in an indoor theatre because the use of artificial light was as yet limited. The solution was to build stages in accordance with standard theatre houses and leave the roofs off (or build walls of glass) to permit the sunlight. Examples include Méliès' Théâtre de prises de vues, a glass studio at Montreuil, France; Robert Paul's studio in England; and the Edison "Kinetographic Theatre," the so-called "Black Maria," which was a stage that revolved 360 degrees on a pivot with its roof open to the sunlight.

Story structure, too, was to be patterned after dramatic models, particularly the "unities" inherent in the standard "well-made play" paradigm. As early as 1904, just as the nickelodeons were growing in popularity and one-reel theatrical films were appearing, one writer described the formula: "There should be no lagging in the story which it tells; every foot [of film] must be an essential part, whose loss would deprive the story of some merit; there should be sequence, each part leading to the next with increasing interest, reaching its most interesting point at the climax, which should end the film."[6] Standard theatrical story formulas, like those formulated by Eugene Scribe a half-century previously, should be imitated: "the authors and experts employed by the [motion picture] producer should be primarily familiar with the technique of the acted drama."[7]

The results on screen, predictably, resembled a kind of "canned" theatre. Intertitles approximated the cues in a printed program, and dialogue titles abbreviated the text of the play. Just as the viewer in a theatre house sat in a fixed position at an unchanging distance from the stage, films by directors like Edwin S. Porter simulated similar effects by means of a fixed camera, protracted takes, medium-distance shots, and the players' frontal presentation to the lens, as if addressing an audience. "Here Mr. Porter works on a large stage," observed a commentator in *Moving Picture World*, "and places his camera at a considerable distance from his actors. The result is that he avoids abnormality of size, and when you see the pictures on the screen, they express the proper sensuous impression of size. . . ."[8] Moreover, many players in films "play to the front, thus betraying unconsciously that they know they are being pictured, and giving the impression to the spectators that they are going through their parts before an audience which is not seen in the picture but which appears to be located in front of the scene."[9]

Even the film industry's organization of production, distribution, and exhibition was patterned after the business practices of the theatrical establishment. Motion pictures had been first presented in public exhibitions in the years 1895–96, precisely at the time that the legitimate theatre and vaudeville in America and abroad were being standardized into popular formulas of production, story, and distribution. The New York–based theatrical Syndicate was a centralized authority, conducted almost tyrannically through the offices of men like Sam Nixon, Fred Zimmerman, Charles Frohman, Al Hayman, Marc Klaw, and Abraham Erlanger, that enforced commercial standards of production and exhibition in thousands of theatre houses throughout the country. It exploited the star system, determined what particular kinds of theatrical events would be presented, how they would be presented, and along what routes they could best reach the widest cross section of audiences, both urban and rural. The vaudeville equivalent of the Syndicate was the United Booking Office, which promoted its own brands of standardized entertainment through the circuits of theatres controlled by Keith, Pantages, Sullivan and Considine, Martin Beck, Gun Sun, and the Western Vaudeville Association.

Before 1910 the American film industry had itself become similarly standardized with the Motion Picture Patents Company and its General Film Exchange. As historian Gertrude Jobes has demonstrated, the Patents Company—while initially unwilling to adopt the theatre's star system (a position that would soon change)—did imitate many of the Syndicate's business practices. For example, just as the Syndicate established and maintained standards of quality for the houses in which touring companies played, so did the Patents Company improve conditions under which movies were shown. Improved film stocks were developed, better projection systems installed, admission prices standardized, and the cleanliness of the houses brought under the guidelines of local fire laws. Moreover, films were now distributed along organized routes, from the metropolitan houses to the small-town theatres (in many cases along the self-same routes followed by the touring theatrical road shows).[10]

Of course, there was a reverse impact of the film medium on the practices of the stage. For example, as early as 1896 films were not only becoming a part of the variety and revue bills, but were also being incorporated into actual theatrical presentations. An article in the *North American Review* in 1896 speculated that projected films could replace a theatre house's artificial scenic backdrops. By projecting a film from behind a screen on stage, it was argued, scenic backdrops of, say a waterfall or a storm at sea, could be effected. "The Vitascope [Edison's projection device] would represent these things, taken absolutely from life, with a thousandfold more effectiveness and pleasure to the audience than anything in the line of the most skillful stage device with which we are now acquainted." Battle scenes for a Shakespearean spectacle could be enhanced by such methods: "Imagine how much more brilliant and veracious the effect might be with Vitascope figures for auxiliaries!"[11] Sure enough, within the next decade Georges Méliès was incorporating films into his stage programs. Historian John Frazer has cited many examples, like Méliès use of filmed footage of a "celestial carriage" in his stage play, *The Devil's Pills*, presented at the Théâtre Municipal du Châtelet in 1905; and a filmed "North Pole" sequence used in his ballet, *Near the Stars*, presented at the Olympia Theatre a year later (which became the basis for one of his last films, *The Conquest of the Pole* (1912).[12]

In addition to the many attractions filmmakers found in theatrical events—the stories, performers, built-in popularity, and audience identification—there was also the issue of their accessibility. Copyrights of plays did not protect them from being photographed on celluloid. When Vitagraph made a condensed version of the Broadway hit, *Raffles, the Amateur Cracksman*, the filmmakers gained the rights merely by acknowledging the name of the stage producer on the screen titles. Other filmmakers were not so open about their thievery. Reporting in 1911, Robert Grau noted, "Recently, some of the unprincipled moving picture producers have been pirating copyrighted dramatic compositions, and resorting to changing the titles and scenes to escape detection."[13] This problem persisted until 1912 when one such theft led to a new copyright law, one that placed the motion picture under the copyright restrictions formerly reserved only to still photographs and printed words.[14]

These short theatrical films did not constitute a tiny percentage of the total output of movies during these years. Quite to the contrary, theatrical films may be safely estimated as constituting over one-third of the output. Valuable sources in gaining this sense of proportion include *The American Film Institute Catalogue: Film Beginnings, 1893–1910*, and Kemp R. Niver's compendium, *Motion Pictures from the Library of Congress Paper Print Collection, 1894–1912*. These comprehensive listings of all films made or presented in America contain short summaries and descriptions of plots and scenic effects. Of the thousands of titles listed and described, over one-third are derived from specific theatrical events or in some way devoted to simulating the effect of witnessing a theatrical event. Typical descriptions include, "This was photographed as if from the audience at a theatre"; or, "all the scenes were photographed from a single camera position and all activity parallels the camera plane"; or, "the set is a backdrop painted as an ocean scene"; or, "the action consists of the participants being introduced to the audience." One such film, titled *The Critic* (Biograph, 1906), went to extraordinary lengths to simulate a theatrical event: "The camera, placed as though in the audience, shows several seats with spectators in the immediate foreground and a box to the right. The stage acts are burlesques of regular vaudeville acts."[15]

The second critical period of theatrical filmmaking transpired in 1912–15, precisely at the time when feature-length film formats from Europe, particularly Italy, were influencing Americans like D.W. Griffith and Thomas Ince to experiment with longer films. At last, full-length plays could be brought to the screen in at least some semblance of their original state. In July 1912 film entrepreneur Adolph Zukor and stage impresario Daniel Frohman combined their resources to form the Famous Players company. Their first release was imported from France, the Sarah Bernhardt film of her stage success, Emile Moreau's *Queen Elizabeth*. The *New York Dramatic Mirror* reported at the time that the ambition of Zukor and Frohman was avowedly to bring the legitimate stage and the motion picture together:

> The men back of this movement have become fully convinced that the time for the amalgamation of the legitimate stage and the motion picture has come. . . . It is felt that the last barrier has been removed between the picture and the stage. . . . The films will comprise for the most part past and present successes of the European and American stage.[16]

The model for Famous Players was the Film d'Art company in France, which had been formed four years earlier by the Laffite brothers. They recruited actors and designers from the Comédie Française and Théâtre Français with the express purpose of making feature-length films from popular and prestigious stage plays—an agenda quickly copied by other European studios, like Pathé, Gaumont, and Eclair. In America, too, rivals to Famous Players sprang up, studios that brought together stage entrepreneurs and playwrights with filmmakers—notably, the Protective Amusement Company (an amalgamation of Biograph Film and the Klaw/Erlanger stage properties), the World Film Corporation (film promoter Lewis J. Selznick and theatrical entrepreneurs William A. Brady and the Shubert brothers), the Jesse L. Lasky Feature Play Company (Lasky and stage impresario David Belasco), and the Triangle Film Corporation (leading actors of the stage and film directors D. W. Griffith, Thomas Ince, and Mack Sennett).[17]

To a considerable degree, as with the short theatrical films already cited, these feature-length theatrical films quite intentionally simulated on the screen the illusion of a theatrical event. The shallow-depth staging, the use of artificial scenery and props, the exaggerated acting styles, and the prevailing sense of a proscenium boundary—elements common to late-19th-century stagecraft—were all imitated on film. Writing in March 1912 a critic for the *New York Dramatic Mirror* described some of these effects he perceived on the screen: "Characters will enter a scene in the background and walk deliberately down to the front to carry on a conversation that would naturally have occurred where they first met." Moreover, when the characters converse, "they will in many cases keep their faces turned fully or partly to the front instead of looking at each other as people do when they hold conversations in real life."[18] And, finally, there was a noticeable exaggeration of gesture and pose characteristic of the declamatory school of stage acting, implying that the actor on film was still "playing direct to the front and for a supposed audience." Another writer noted that in theatrical films like *Martin Chuzzlewit* (1912), only a few outdoor scenes were enacted in natural locations, "most of the exteriors as well as interiors being studio made."[19]

While this approach to filmmaking might seem strange in hindsight—considering that other, more cinematically advanced films, like chase and news actualities, were being produced at the same time—it should be remembered that film and theatre entrepreneurs were trying to reach the same audiences that formerly had been exposed only to stage presentations. The cinematic techniques filmmakers like D. W. Griffith had been developing since 1909 were out of place in these contexts. Historian Kevin Brownlow concurs with this point:

> Far from being the move of an industry that did not know what it was doing, the theatrical films were deliberately planned to reproduce the experience of the stage. After all, almost all the cinematic devices

existed by the time Bernhardt made *Queen Elizabeth*. But Porter, Zukor, and the others kept them out of their early theatrical films. They knew that the theatrical "carriage trade" did not appreciate violent changes of scene, moving cameras, or closeups of gargantuan proportions.[20]

Alone among these companies the Jesse L. Lasky Feature Play Company sought to expand the limited boundaries of the proscenium. Its theatrical films contained more location photography, depth staging, and intra-scene cutting than was customary at the time. There are several reasons for this. For one thing, the Lasky films were based on plays by luminaries like David Belasco that had western locations and implied physical action—as opposed to the standard interior

David Belasco

settings and reported action of most parlor dramas of the day. Moreover, recognizing that the rise of the feature-length film could have an audience appeal beyond the carriage trade, Lasky noted in 1914 that, unlike Zukor, "we can do novel and unusual things on the screen that are impossible on the stage. And anything that is original has an appeal for a vaudeville audience." Like taking the camera out of doors:

> We have adopted the motto, "The World Is Our Studio." As an earnest of that, we are sending the present company to Southern California and Wyoming for the atmosphere of the story. We will not hesitate to go wherever the best interests of any production require. If necessary, we will send companies abroad. We intend to erect outdoor stages in different part of the country.[21]

Thus, when tyro director Cecil B. DeMille was dispatched to locales around San Diego County in California to make film versions of Edwin Milton Royle's *The Squaw Man*, Owen Wister/Kirke La Shelle's stage play, *The Virginian*, and David Belasco's *The Girl of the Golden West* in 1913–14, he responded to the natural locales in ways that would have been impossible had he been filming inside a studio or on a stage.[22] "Imagine the horizon is your stage limit," he wrote in *The New York Dramatic Mirror* in January 1914:

> No height limit, no close-fitting exits, no conserving of stage space, just the whole world open to you as a stage and a thousand people in a scene does not crowd your accommodations. . . . I felt lost at first. I could not get the stage idea out of my head at first. I looked skyward for sets of lines, borders and drops.[23]

Thus, commentator Robert Grau praised the cinematic achievement of these films, noting, "The realities of life . . . prove the most compelling attractions with the public."[24]

The story of the Lasky company exemplifies what the researches of historians like A. Nicholas Vardac and John Fell have revealed—that many popular novels came to the screen via stage dramatizations, particularly during the first 15 years of the century.[25] For example, it is a mistake to assume that the film version of Thomas Hardy's *Tess of the d'Urbervilles* (1913) was based on the novel; rather, it was derived from the popular stage production of actress Minnie Maddern Fiske. Similarly, *The Count of Monte Cristo* and *The Prisoner of Zenda* (both in 1913) derived not from the novels, but from their stage adaptations by, respectively, James O'Neill and James K. Hackett.[26] Significantly, these film versions featured the same stage stars who had made the plays famous, and they "toured" the country's theatres along the same routes customarily taken by theatrical road show companies.[27] It was a reasonable calculation on the part of filmmakers to choose properties that resembled the shows the public had already accepted and supported.

The second major wave of theatrical filmmaking transpired during the transition to sound, 1926–30. Just as the Film d'Art presentation of Sarah Bernhardt's *Queen Elizabeth* had inspired a host of American feature-length theatrical films, so now did the element of sound inaugurate a new burst of theatrical film activity among the major studios: Paramount, Fox, Warner Bros., RKO, Universal, Columbia, and United Artists. Leading off this second wave was the premiere in New York on November 16, 1928, of Paramount's first all-talking feature-length film, *Interference*. Like *Queen Elizabeth*, *Interference* was released by Adolph Zukor and Daniel Frohman (whose Famous Players company by now had merged with Lasky to form Paramount Pictures). It too was based on a current stage play, was staged in a standard proscenium style, and stimulated a new wave of feature-length films (the feature-length format had been temporarily interrupted the year before by the spate of experimental, synchronized-sound short films derived from vaudeville turns and opera scenes). In his filmed, spoken prologue to *Interference*, Frohman reaffirmed the philosophy and agenda of his earlier Famous Players productions:

> It was only last winter that this play [*Interference*] we are about to see tonight was enacted on the boards of the Lyceum Theatre. It was presented by the company which was founded by my brother, the late Charles Frohman. Tonight, carrying on the Frohman tradition, I once more welcome you on behalf of the greatest era in entertainment—an era made possible through this miraculous invention, the talking picture. No more will our best plays be confined to the few big cities. These plays, with their stirring drama enhanced by the richness of the human voice, will go to the whole world.[28]

Of course, many theatrically oriented synchronized-sound films had appeared in the year or so immediately prior to *Interference*—*The Jazz Singer, Glorious Betsy, The Lion and the Mouse*, to name a few—but they were part-talkies containing only a few sound sequences injected into otherwise silent films. But *Interference* was the first film to translate an entire stage play into a feature-length, all-talking format. It was, in short, a film completely representative of a new technology, indicative of how that technology translated and processed theatrical events onto celluloid. As historian Ron Haver noted, the play itself had been an ideal property for the early talkies: "It was suspenseful, had a small cast, and only three main sets, which could be easily confined within the confines of the crude sound stage."[29] Many all-talking theatrical features quickly followed within a few months; among the dramas were Universal's *The Last Warning* (play by Thomas F. Fallon), MGM's *The Bellamy Trial* (play by Frances Noyes Hart), Fox's *The Ghost Talks* (play by Max Marcin and Edward Hammond), United Artists' *Coquette* (play by George Abbott and Ann Preston Bridgers), and Paramount's *The Letter* (play by Somerset Maugham). Among the Broadway musical shows and revues were Warner Bros.' *The Desert Song* and RKO's *Rio Rita*. In general, the major studios were predicting in March 1929 that approximately two-thirds of their future features would have synchronized sound. Many of these would draw from theatrical origins.

In 1927–28 alone the studios collectively bought the rights to nearly 40 plays and musicals.[30] The movie studios quickly developed a system for "scouting" new Broadway shows. Representatives would attend out-of-town tryouts and opening nights on Broadway, assessing a production solely on its potential to be a motion picture. They applied the following rules: First, they would write synopses of the action and a detailed report of the play, including its merits and faults as possible film material, and rush the reports to the story editors back in Hollywood. If interested, the studio would obtain a copy of the playscript and, if a purchase was decided upon, the property would be bought for as little as $35,000 or as much as $225,000.

As always, the prestige these plays and, most particularly, their players brought to the Hollywood product was highly desirable. George Arliss, the eminent stage actor who appeared in several Warner Bros. film versions of his plays in 1929–31—including *The Green Goddess* and *Disraeli*—recalled in his autobiography that attracting "respectable" audiences was a primary reason behind Warner Bros.' securing his services:

> I believe that the plays I was doing in the theatre might be looked upon as "high-brow," and I was regarded as an actor devoted to that exalted plane of the drama. This was the time when everybody didn't go to the movies—the prehistoric days. . . . There is no doubt that a considerable percentage of the people that came to see me in the theatre never went to the movietones [sic] at all. . . . The Warner Brothers realized that these lost sheep must be collected and brought into the fold. . . . And that was why they came to think of me, Harry Warner told me afterwards.[31]

Other prominent and respected stage stars followed Arliss' example. Hal Skelly's characterization of "Skid"

in Watters and Hopkins' *Burlesque* (1927) was repeated for the Paramount cameras in *The Dance of Life* (1929); Dennis King duplicated his appearance in *The Vagabond King* (1925) for Paramount in 1930; James Gleason and Lucille Webster re-created their roles in *The Shannons of Broadway* (1927) for United Artists in 1929; Eddie Cantor followed Florenz Ziegfeld to Hollywood in 1929 to reprise his role (and sing the title song) in *Whoopee!*; Herbert Marshall and Minna Gombell converted their success in *The Great Power* (1928) into a film for MGM in 1929; Mary Lawlor repeated her success in *Good News* for MGM in 1930; Leslie Howard and Beryl Mercer brought their *Outward Bound* to Warner Bros. in 1930; and, on a less "elevated" plane, perhaps, the Marx Brothers filmed their stage production of *The Cocoanuts* for Paramount in 1929.

What is most immediately apparent about these filmed plays, like their predecessors in the 1912–15 period, is their relative fidelity to their theatrical origins. For example, while preparing his film version of James M. Barrie's playlet, *Half an Hour*, William C. de Mille announced that he would faithfully preserve the action and dialogue of the stage play; that he would *not* "add situations, sequences, or elaborations" to further the story.[32] When Paramount released Somerset Maugham's *The Letter* in 1929, with stage star Jeanne Eagels in her screen debut, *Variety* praised it for its fidelity to the original production: "Any summary of the picture must record that the merits of the screen production belong to the original play, written for and played on the stage." Moreover, the production was "entirely a transcription of a stage work and the cinema version does little to make the subject matter its own."[33] Again and again, other theatrical features were singled out for this fidelity. Released in April 1929 by the William Fox studios, *Thru Different Eyes*, a courtroom drama by Milton E. Gropper and Edna Sherry, "follows the play in every detail. . . ."[34] MGM's *The Trial of Mary Dugan* (March 1929), based on the popular courtroom melodrama by Bayard Veiller, was described by Mordaunt Hall in the *New York Times*: "With the exception of a few scenes, this is virtually a reproduction of the play."[35] And *Disraeli*, a starring vehicle for George Arliss, from Warner Brothers, was described in the New York *Morning Telegraph* as "no more than an audible photograph of the stage piece."[36]

More often than not, however, this degree of fidelity was regarded as a mixed blessing. Just as the use of written intertitles in early, silent theatrical films had all too often overwhelmed the visual dimension of the filmed play, now the use of protracted, statically filmed dialogue sequences limited the potential of the film medium for a dynamic interplay of image and sound. In

The Doctor's Secret, complained Herbert Cruikshank in *Motion Picture*, there was nothing but "long photographic discussions between characters."[37] When George M. Cohan's *The Home Towners* reached the screen in a Warner Bros. production late in 1928, the characters "just grouped in front of the microphone and wished they were on the stage. . . ."[38] Referring to the Fox production in 1929 of Henry Arthur Jones's playlet, "The Knife," *Variety* noted that "people stand still and talk" with "never a raised voice or a spirited gesture."[39] And *Coquette* was criticized that it had "a repeated tendency to become too talky and motionless."[40] In sum, reported *Variety* in March 1929, "progress comes out of the spoken word instead of from essential action, which is strictly an attribute of the stage."[41]

Based on statistics gathered from *The American Film Institute Catalogue, 1921–1930*, the *Library of Congress Copyright Entries, 1912–1939*, and the series of "Best Plays" volumes compiled by Burns Mantle, during the 1928–30 period, it can be determined that the major studios produced 511 films, of which 141 were based on stage plays and musical shows. One may conclude that at least 28 percent of all the feature-length talkies during this period were based on theatrical properties. This is a high percentage, especially when it is remembered that all of the studios included within their total output a substantial body of "programmer" material like westerns and serials (in 1930 alone Universal produced 11 westerns out of a total of 35 talkies).

OUT OF THE PAST TO THE PRESENT

We began with Willy Russell's *Educating Rita* as a convenient metaphor for the process by which filmmakers became "educated" to meet the challenges of transforming stage plays into film, resulting in entertainments that establish a "delicate balance" between the prime virtues and potentials of both stage and screen. In fact, such transformations are magical, but rare. Let us consider another, particularly challenging example, by playwright Russell and film director Gilbert. After collaborating on the theatrical film of *Educating Rita*, they worked together again on the scenario of an even more challenging play, *Shirley Valentine* (1986), starring Pauline Collins.

Whereas *Educating Rita* was a two-hander, *Shirley Valentine* was a one-woman show, an extended monologue in which Shirley shares her thoughts with the audience while cooking her husband's supper in Act One. She has been a good housewife and mother, but she has been taken for granted for years by her husband and children. Now that her children are grown, Shirley wants to be her own person and desires to escape to the Greek islands (represented on stage by a minimal set conception, namely, a single large rock).

A bare stage with one woman delivering a monologue was quite adequate to the stage, but how would it "play" on celluloid? Russell's solution in the screenplay is to dramatize and illustrate Shirley's monologue (Pauline Collins reprising her stage role and addressing herself directly to the camera) with flashbacks that provide a more detailed backstory leading to Shirley's desire to escape from dreary England to sunny Greece—to find herself, as it were, and become the woman she was before she got married (resuming her maiden name, Valentine).

It would seem that in both stage and screen versions Shirley breaks through the so-called fourth wall to connect with the audience. For movie audiences the film is like a confessional, a gossip session with a woman who could be a neighbor, confiding her most intimate secrets. In approximating on film the theatrical convention of the broken fourth wall, filmmakers are respecting the fact that something so unlikely as an extended monologue can work on film without unduly testing the patience of an audience, so long as the delivery is idiomatic and relaxed and apparently authentic.

The film entertainingly visualizes Shirley's recounting of her history, which allows the viewer to relive the experience with her. In order to understand her motives and frustrations, it certainly helps to see and understand the behavior of her family and friends: her husband, who has taken her for granted for too long; her ungrateful children, who still make demands on her, even though they should be grown up; and her former classmate, now a well-to-do prostitute, who asks her, after a chance meeting, "Didn't you used to be Shirley Valentine?" Ultimately, what results is a motion picture that leads unsuspecting viewers to think this is a wholly cinematic experience, but which in actuality commingles elements that are both theatric and cinematic.

ACTORS AND DIRECTORS ON STAGE AND SCREEN

It has been said that theatre is an actor's medium in which the actor is the creator, whereas film is a director's medium, wherein the actor is the created. But the actor can still "create" a performance in front of the camera. Italian neo-realist directors demonstrated amazing results with non-professionals, for example, working creatively with amateur actors, and not only in films that came out of the documentary tradition.

But more often than not, cinema, like theatre, depends on trained actors. Film, like theatre, is a performance medium, and the better, the more gifted the actor, the better the picture is likely to be. Star charisma was what powered the studio system. In those days (up to the 1950s and the advent of television) no one would automatically assume that movie stars were actors, though some certainly were, and the weaker the studio system became, the more that trained stage actors began to infiltrate the industry. Marlon Brando and Paul Newman, for example, were serious actors of their generation who established their credentials on stage, Brando breaking through as a Broadway star by playing Stanley Kowalski in Tennessee Williams's *A Streetcar Named Desire*, and Newman, trained at the Yale Drama School and New York's Actors Studio, in William Inge's *Picnic*. Although she was a certifiable superstar, Marilyn Monroe desperately wanted to be taken seriously as an actor and went to Lee Strasberg's Actors Studio for professional training.

Gradually throughout the 1970s and 1980s, more and more film actors began to see the advantages of stage training and experience, a common path to cinema careers in Britain, but not so common in America under the studio system. Some stars have gone on to become directors—notably Ida Lupino, trained at London's Royal Academy of Dramatic Art, Robert Redford, Paul Newman, Barbra Streisand, and, more recently, Tim Robbins, Tim Roth, and Sean Penn. Such crossovers are likely to become more common as more actors take their craft seriously.

During the first century of cinema, as was pointed out earlier in this essay, filmmakers and entrepreneurs did indeed come from a variety of backgrounds, such as cartoonists, inventors, salesmen, and painters. However, there is no question that the stage was a prime influence upon a majority of artists. Important directors like David Wark Griffith in America and Abel Gance in France came to filmmaking from a theatrical background. So did Sergei Eisenstein in the Soviet Union, after he realized that the cinema could overcome the space limitations of the stage and that it certainly could be used far more efficiently to propagate the ideals of the revolution in such groundbreaking films as *Strike* (1924) and his masterpiece, *The Battleship Potemkin* (1925). In Scandinavia pioneers Mauritz Stiller and Victor Seastrom both came from the theatre, while Sweden's greatest filmmaker, Ingmar Bergman, has never faltered in his allegiance to his first love, the stage. He has continued to direct plays by Strindberg, for example (*The Dance of Death*, Parts One and Two), and operas (Mozart's *The Magic Flute*), while creating films such as *The Seventh Seal* and *Wild Strawberries* (in which Victor Seastrom gave one of the greatest per-

formances ever recorded on film), films that established Bergman's international reputation.

Of course, film directors traditionally have come from several different crafts and avocations. In Hollywood, Robert Wise began as a film editor, for example, as did Mark Robson (with whom Wise worked as editor on *Citizen Kane*), and Kevin Brownlow in England; William Cameron Menzies began as a production designer, and, later in the century, David Lynch was a trained artist before he turned to film directing, as was Peter Greenaway in England and Sergei Paradjanov in the Soviet Union. Tim Burton began as a trained animator. Nicolas Roeg started as a cinematographer. All of these latter talents had an acute sense of visual design; their films tended to be far more off-beat, imaginative, and challenging than the work of more traditionally trained directors. Though all of them managed to make interesting films, only the work of Lynch and Burton was successfully mainstreamed for a mass audience.

It is appropriate to consider briefly several case studies of important directors who have worked successfully in the arenas of both theatre and film—indeed, who have invested in their work the best of their experience and expertise in both realms. The cinema has served as a magnet for talent from all areas, but artists trained in theatre have had an edge since the advent of the talking picture. With the coming of sound, theatre people were suddenly in demand, voice coaches, actors with stage experience, and, of course, theatre directors such as Rouben Mamoulian, who had trained as an actor with Stanislavsky at the Moscow Art Theatre. Mamoulian went on to organize his own company in Tbilisi in his native Georgia, then toured with the Russian Repertory Theatre before directing in London and New York and then being lured to Paramount to make the film *Applause* in 1929 at the studio's facilities in Astoria, New York. Thereafter, Mamoulian helped to transform Hollywood's approach to making talking pictures.

Another transformative talent and, arguably, America's greatest film director, Orson Welles, began as a gifted theatre director before becoming a screen actor and film producer. He had collaborated with John Houseman's Phoenix Theatre Group and directed for the Federal Theatre Project before originating the Mercury Theatre in 1937, the gateway to his direction of *Citizen Kane* for RKO in 1941. *Citizen Kane* proved to be extremely controversial and was boycotted by the Hearst chain of newspapers since the main character, Charles Foster Kane, was modeled upon news magnate William Randolph Hearst. Welles was proclaimed a genius, but his innovative and groundbreaking film was taken out of circulation, and from that point forward he had to struggle to protect his integrity against studio control. Unfortunately, Welles was ahead of his time in the industry, and generally regarded as an outsider and a maverick. The man was considered a "difficult" and extravagant, "risky" talent. In other words, Welles was born to be an independent long before the industry was congenial to independent filmmakers.

George Cukor established his credentials on Broadway before being recruited as a dialogue director for Lewis Milestone's *All Quiet on the Western Front* in 1930. He later became famous for being an "actor's director"—more specifically as a "woman's director"—but, as Ephraim Katz notes, this label shortchanges Cukor's contribution to the cinema: "True, he was essentially a man of the theatre and much of his film style is attributable to the influence of the stage." Even so, "while his material was often adapted from the stage, and even his characters were frequently theatre people, most of his films look nothing like photographed stage plays."[42]

In the next generation, Sidney Lumet may also be said to have suffered the critical curse of being considered simply an "actor's director." Born into a theatrical background, Lumet performed as a child actor in New York's Yiddish Art Theatre before moving on to Broadway. By 1950 he was directing television drama for CBS. His breakthrough feature film was skillfully adapted from Reginald Rose's teleplay *Twelve Angry Men* (1957), which earned him Academy Award nominations for best picture and best director and won for him the Directors Guild Award. Though other theatrical films were to follow—most notably, adaptations of Eugene O'Neill's *Long Day's Journey into Night* (1962), *The Sea Gull* (1968), *Equus* (1977), and *Deathtrap* (1982)—Lumet's achievements include many mainline successes, from *Fail-Safe* (1964) to *Prince of the City* (1981). Though perhaps not popular with trendy *auteur* critics, Lumet was surely one of the very best directors of the latter half of the century.

In Britain, in contrast to America, there has been a far more intimate and creative connection between stage and screen. In Britain actors are actors, not stars, and directors direct, no matter the medium. Likewise, writers write, and sometimes direct, but it is not necessarily their ambition to become film directors.

Harold Pinter, for example, arguably Britain's foremost playwright, has written for the screen as well as the stage and even directed the American Film Theatre production of *Butley* (1974), curiously enough, because that play was written by Simon Gray, not by Pinter himself.

David Hare adapted his own play *Plenty* to the screen for director Fred Schepisi in 1985, and then went on to direct original filmscripts he had written, *Wetherby* (1985), *Paris by Night* (1989), *Strapless* (1990), and *The Designated Mourner* (1997), but such work did not interfere with his playwriting career. Tom Stoppard, another outstanding playwright, also has written his share of screenplays and directed one of his own plays, *Rosencrantz and Guildenstern Are Dead* (1990).

The American playwright who comes closest to paralleling the careers of Pinter, Stoppard, and Hare is David Mamet, who has dedicated his work to Pinter and has imitated Pinter's verbal mastery in an American idiom. Like Pinter and Hare, Mamet has not directed his own plays for the screen but has directed from his own original screenplays, *House of Games* (1987), *Things Change* (1988), *Homicide* (1991), *Oleanna* (1994), and *The Spanish Prisoner* (1998). And like David Hare, Mamet has continued to write for the stage, even though writing and directing for Hollywood might be more lucrative.

Sam Mendes was a theatrical talent before he demonstrated a flair for cinema in his first feature, *American Beauty*, a film that swept the Academy Awards for 1999. Also, Julie Taymor moved from *Lion King*, a stage musical, to her distinctively stylized film adaptation of Shakespeare's *Titus Andronicus*, completing a 10-year continuous run of Shakespeare adaptations that followed upon the success of Kenneth Branagh's *Henry V* in 1989. A new generation of theatrically trained directors and actors, undaunted by the restrictions of the proscenium stage and wholly cinematic in their vision of theatrical translation to film, is poised at the end of the first century of the cinema to carry forward the tradition of intelligent dramatic adaptation, and in that resides a host of new challenges that will define adaptation in the next century.

—John C. Tibbetts
—James M. Welsh

NOTES

1. "The Fine Arts: The Kinetoscope," *The Critic*, 24: 638 (May 12, 1894), 330.

2. Quoted in Antonia and W.K.L. Dickson, *Edison's Invention of the Kineto-Phonograph* (Los Angeles: Pueblo Press, 1939). When Edison formed the American Talking Picture Company in 1912, he put his vision to the test. This early experiment in synchronized-sound films, in partnership with the Keith-Albee vaudeville chain, produced a series of celluloid "turns" and play excerpts for distribution in 1,500 theatres across the country. Although short-lived, the enterprise produced theatrical films like *Wolsey's Soliloquy* from Shakespeare's *Henry VIII*, and *The Deaf Mute*, a Civil War drama by Rupert Hughes.

3. Quoted in Marshall Deutelbaum, ed., *"Image" on the Art and Evolution of the Film* (New York: Dover Press, 1979), 32.

4. Joseph Medill Patterson, "The Nickelodeons: The Poor Man's Elementary Course in the Drama," *The Saturday Evening Post*, 180: 21 (November 23, 1907), 10–11.

5. Montrose J. Moses, *The American Dramatist* (Boston: Little, Brown, 1911), 201.

6. "About Moving Picture Films," in *Complete Illustrated Catalog of Moving Picture Films, Stereopticons, Slides, Films, 1904*, quoted in George C. Pratt, ed., *Spellbound in Darkness* (New York Graphic Society, 1973), 37.

7. Rollin Summers, "The Moving Picture Drama and the Acted Drama," *The Moving Picture World*, September 19, 1908, quoted in Stanley Kauffmann, ed., *American Film Criticism* (New York: Liveright, 1972), 9–10.

8. "Too Near the Camera," *The Moving Picture World*, 8: 12 (March 25, 1911), 633–634.

9. "Spectator's Comments," *The New York Dramatic Mirror*, May 14, 1910, quoted in Stanley Kauffmann, ed., *American Film Criticism*, 39–40.

10. Gertrude Jobes, *Motion Picture Empire* (Hamden, Conn.: Archon Books, 1966), 44–110.

11. George Parsons Lathrop, "Stage Scenery and the Vitascope," *North American Review*, 163 (September 1896), 379.

12. John Frazer, *Artificially Arranged Scenes* (Boston: G.K. Hall, 1979), 8.

13. Robert Grau, *The Stage in the Twentieth Century* (New York: Broadway Publishing Company, 1912), 273.

14. The case involved the Kalem Film Company's one-reel version in 1908 of the stage adaptation of Lew Wallace's novel, *Ben Hur*, which was made without any consultation or permission of either the author's estate or the stage producers. A suit was initiated against Kalem that was settled in 1912 when the higher courts decided that movie producers could not use copyrighted literary or dramatic material without the consent of the owner.

15. See Kemp R. Niver, *Motion Pictures from the Library of Congress Paper Print Collection, 1894–1912* (Berkeley and Los Angeles: University of California Press, 1967).

16. "Theatrical Stars in Pictures," *The New York Dramatic Mirror*, July 10, 1912, 34.

17. For an account of the formation of Film d'Art and its American imitator, Famous Players, see John C. Tibbetts, *The American Theatrical Film* (Bowling Green, Ohio: The Popular Press, 1985), 53–71. The only detailed history of the Protective Amusement Company can be found in Kemp R. Niver, *Klaw and Erlanger: Famous Plays in Pictures* (Los Angeles: Locare Research Group, 1976). For information on the World Film and Jesse L. Lasky ventures, see ongoing reports in the trades and journals of the day, particularly *Moving Picture World* and *The New York Dramatic Mirror*. The story of the Triangle Film Corporation is chronicled in Kalton Lahue, *Dreams for Sale: The Rise and Fall of the Triangle Film Corporation* (Cranbury, N.J.: A.S. Barnes, 1971).

18. "Spectator," *The New York Dramatic Mirror*, April 10, 1912, 26.

19. "Spectator," *The New York Dramatic Mirror*, July 3, 1912, 31.

20. Letter from Kevin Brownlow to John C. Tibbetts, November 16, 1979.

21. "Jesse L. Lasky in Pictures," *Moving Picture World*, January 3, 1914, 1412.

22. For a detailed account of DeMille's 1914 production of *The Virginian*, see John C. Tibbetts, "The Stage Goes West: Routes to *The Virginian*," *Indiana Social Studies Quarterly*, 34: 2 (Autumn 1981), 26–39.

23. Cecil B. DeMille, "Making a Picture Director," *The New York Dramatic Mirror*, January 14, 1914, 62.

24. Robert Grau, *The Theatre of Science* (New York: Benjamin Blom, 1969; reprint), 104.

25. See John Fell, *Film and the Narrative Tradition* (Norman: University of Oklahoma Press, 1974); and A. Nicholas Vardac, *Stage to Screen* (Cambridge: Harvard University Press, 1949). Both of these invaluable volumes contain numerous discussions concerning the popularity and staging of such literary classics as Harriet Beecher Stowe's *Uncle Tom's Cabin*, Charles Dickens' *Oliver Twist*, Dumas' *The Count of Monte Cristo* and many other 19th-century novels.

26. *Tess of the d'Urbervilles* was dramatized by Lorimer Stoddard in 1897 and first presented at the Fifth Avenue Theatre in New York on March 2, 1897, starring Minnie Maddern Fiske. The Famous Players film version, also starring Miss Fiske, was released in September 1913. *The Count of Monte Cristo* was first dramatized by Alexandre Dumas in 1848 and first presented in New York and London that year. There were several other dramatizations that subsequently appeared: James O'Neill first appeared in what became known as the "Fechter Version" in 1883 and continued to play the role of Edmund Dantes the rest of his life, for an estimated 6,000 performances. The Famous Players film version brought the O'Neill production to the screen in December 1912. *The Prisoner of Zenda* was first dramatized by Edward E. Rice and first presented by Daniel Frohman at the Lyceum Theatre in New York on September 4, 1895, starring E.H. Sothern. James K. Hackett took over the role from Sothern in

1896 and performed it periodically the rest of his life. The Famous Players film version brought Hackett and his production company to the screen in December 1912.

27. For an informal history of the American theatrical "road" system, see Philip C. Lewis, *Trouping: How the Show Came to Town* (New York: Harper and Row, 1973). And two excellent business histories include Robert McLaughlin, *Broadway and Hollywood: A History of Economic Interaction* (New York: Arno Press, 1974), 1–30; and Jack Puggi, *Theatre in America: Impact of Economic Forces, 1870–1967* (Ithaca, N.Y.: Cornell University Press, 1968), 25–41.

28. Quoted in Mordaunt Hall, "Interference" [review], *The New York Times*, November 17, 1928, 23.

29. Ron Haver, *David O. Selznick's Hollywood* (New York: Knopf, 1980), 49.

30. See Robert McLaughlin, *Broadway and Hollywood: A History of Economic Interaction*, 115–116.

31. George Arliss, *My Ten Years in the Studios* (Boston: Little, Brown, 1940), 12.

32. William C. de Mille, "No Stage Director or Writer Required for Talkers," *Variety*, October 17, 1928, 4.

33. "The Letter" [review], *Variety*, March 13, 1929, 14.

34. "Thru Different eyes" [review], *Variety*, April 17, 1929, 22.

35. "The Trial of Mary Dugan" [review], *The New York Times*, March 29, 1919, 21.

36. Quoted in "Disraeli Speaks," *Literary Digest*, April 12, 1930, 19.

37. Quoted in Alexander Walker, *The Shattered Silents: How the Talkies Came to Stay* (New York: William Morrow, 1979), 127.

38. Robert Herring, "Twenty-Three Talkies," *Close Up*, February 1930, 119.

39. "The Knife" [review], *Variety*, May 29, 1929, 26.

40. "Coquette" [review], *Variety*, April 10, 1929, 25.

41. "The Letter" [review], *Variety*, March 13, 1929, 14.

42. Ephraim Katz, *The Film Encyclopedia*, 3rd ed. (New York: Harper Perennial, 1998), 313–314.

Introduction

HOW TO USE THIS BOOK

The Encyclopedia of Stage Plays into Film is intended to be a convenient reference for those seeking basic information about significant plays and their screen adaptations; and about significant film adaptations of plays that may be of secondary importance as literature but have nonetheless achieved a certain popularity on their own, or as a consequence of their being filmed.

The entries are distributed in three sections—Standard Dramatic Adaptations, Shakespearean Adaptations, and Musical Theatre Adaptations—each of which alphabetically lists the titles under which plays were published and each of which contains its own bibliography. In instances where the film title differs from the title of the play—*10 Things I Hate About You*, for example, was adapted from Shakespeare's *The Taming of the Shrew*—the film title has been cross-referenced for easy access. Head notes provide production information that relates to the process of film adaptation, listing the director and screenwriter(s) in all instances, the date of the film's release, and the production and/or the releasing company. This is followed by a plot synopsis of the play and an assessment of the play's standing and importance. The latter half of the entry details the particular problems of adapting the work—length, point of view, stagecraft, censorship, for example—and a description of the changes or modifications made to film the play and to deliver it within the time limitations of a typical feature film (90 minutes to two hours, ordinarily). Finally, there is a brief list of "references" to direct the user to further reading.

We have endeavored to make the writing as clear and readable as possible and to banish the foolish and obscure jargon that all too often students in film schools and film departments are obliged to use. This is a book for the common reader, not for a small tribe of narrow specialists. For the most part we have not attempted full coverage of made-for-television adaptations. Not only

are many of them of inferior quality, but also they are usually difficult to obtain (either for general viewers or for researchers). Nonetheless, we have occasionally cited a few, and for specific reasons: Viewers seeking information about *Death of a Salesman*, for example, will want to know that there was a fine adaptation made for CBS television in 1985, starring Dustin Hoffman as Willy Loman.

It is worth noting, lamentably, that there are at least a half-dozen books treating film adaptations of novels (including our own *Encyclopedia of Novels into Film*, 1998), but there is a singular dearth of scholarship pertaining to filmed adaptations of plays—i.e., examinations, title by title, of the transfer process from stage to screen. Surprisingly neglected are studies of classical drama on film (the lone exception extant is Kenneth MacKinnon's *Greek Tragedy into Film*, a 200-page monograph printed in England in 1986 and not readily available in America). Clearly, more work needs to be done in these areas. On the other hand, the field of Shakespeare on film has been extensively mined over the last 25 years. Since most of these books were studies published by university presses and intended for specialists, we have drawn extensively on that scholarship in order to make it available to the general reader.

Meanwhile, our selection here of titles has been ambitious and eclectic. There are the obligatory "classic" plays and films, to be sure—Sophocles' *Oedipus the King* and Euripides' *Medea*; the Shakespearean dramas; the major works of G.B. Shaw, Oscar Wilde, Eugene O'Neill, Henrik Ibsen, Tennessee Williams, Rodgers and Hart, and Arthur Miller, for example; and the more recent works of Edward Albee, Harold Pinter, David Mamet, Robert Anderson, and Sam Shepard. The musical films range from such classics as the early talking-picture adaptation of *Whoopee!* in 1929 to *Evita* in 1997. Among the lesser-known playwrights and titles, the editors, for a variety of reasons, have included plays and films from works by Terence Rattigan (*The Browning Version* and *The Winslow Boy*), Shelagh Delaney (*The Taste of Honey*), John Osborne (*Look Back in Anger* and *Entertainer*), David Hare (*Plenty*), and Kaufman and Hart (*You Can't Take It With You* and *The Man Who Came to Dinner*). Virtually forgotten today are titles that in their day were landmarks in the history of the theatrical film, e.g., Sarah Bernhardt's *Queen Elizabeth* (1912), which stimulated the acceptance and proliferation of the feature-length film in America; Cecil B. DeMille's adaptation of Edwin Milton Royle's *The Squaw Man* (1913), which spearheaded feature film production in Hollywood; Victor Seastrom's adaptation of Leonid Andreyev's *He Who Gets Slapped*, which brought expressionist techniques to the Hollywood mainstream; and Eleanor Gates' *Poor Little Rich Girl*, which gave Mary Pickford the archetypal "little girl" role that she would exploit for the rest of her career. More plays, Shakespearean dramas, and musical show adaptations could have been covered had we enjoyed the luxury of more space for a larger book. In fact, more entries were collected than we were able to use, but we feel that a worthy assortment of plays and films is represented here.

The encyclopedic entries are followed by an appendix, "Backstage with the Bard," that considers those theatrical films that do not precisely fall within the three major categories of filmed adaptations. Films like Kenneth Branagh's *A Midwinter's Tale*, Marcel Carné's *Children of Paradise*, and Mike Leigh's *Topsy-Turvy*, for example, are not, strictly speaking, filmed adaptations of plays—*Hamlet*, *Othello*, and *The Mikado*, respectively—so much as they are films *about* plays and about theatrical life.

Finally, there is a list identifying the many scholars and writers who have contributed to this project. Although the book may not be as comprehensive as we could wish, we believe it to be a responsible selection and one of the only reference works of its kind extant.

—John C. Tibbetts and
James M. Welsh

PART I
Standard Dramatic Adaptations

ABE LINCOLN IN ILLINOIS (1938)

ROBERT E. SHERWOOD (1896–1955)

Abe Lincoln in Illinois (1940), U.S.A., directed by John
Cromwell, adapted by Grover Jones; RKO Radio
Pictures.

Television Productions of *Abe Lincoln in Illinois* were
mounted in 1945, 1950, 1957, and 1964.

The Play

Robert E. Sherwood's poignant retelling of the Lincoln story opened in October 1938 and was an immediate and enormous success on the Broadway stage.
Raymond Massey, who starred in both the play and the
film based upon it, remembered that Sherwood had
mentioned working on the play at least six years earlier.
"Long after the play opened," Massey wrote, "Bob told
me that it had been the most difficult project he had
ever attempted. He felt he had engaged in a collaboration, a task he had always avoided, and that Lincoln
himself had written some of the play."

Sherwood's Abraham Lincoln, rather like John
Drinkwater's before him (see ABRAHAM LINCOLN), was
a Lincoln of the poet, rather than of the historian.
Over those six years, Sherwood meticulously
researched Lincoln's life, studying biographies by Ida
Tarbell, Carl Sandburg, and Albert Bushnell Hart, as
well as the memoirs of those who had known Lincoln:
John Nicolay, William Herndon, and others. Having
gathered as much factual information as he could, the
writer then began to shape his own portrait of Lincoln,
feeling free to alter history whenever he felt it suited a
greater dramatic purpose. "The playwright's chief
stock in trade is feelings, not facts," Sherwood wrote.
"When he writes of a subject out of history, or out of
today's news, he cannot be a scholarly recorder or a
good reporter; he is, at best, an interpreter."

Carl Sandburg wholeheartedly approved Sherwood's approach. "It may be that sometime we shall
have a Lincoln drama employing entirely speeches and
situations authenticated by documents and evidence,"
Sandburg wrote, "but whether it will be a drama that
people will go to see and value as drama is another
question.

"Having seen Sherwood's play, and having noticed
how the audience itself participated, I believe it carries
some shine of the American dream, that it delivers
great themes of human wit, behavior and freedom,
with Lincoln as mouthpiece and instrument."

Abe Lincoln in Illinois captures a young Lincoln on
the verge of greatness, beginning with his days in New
Salem where he passionately pursues his education and
falls desperately in love with Ann Rutledge. It details
his stormy relationship with Mary Todd—and his
extreme reluctance to marry her—and ends as he is
leaving Springfield for Washington, D.C., the presidency, and destiny.

Curiously, Sherwood chose to stage Ann's death offstage, concentrating on Abe's grief afterward, instead of creating a tearful deathbed scene. The loss of Ann Rutledge, in Sherwood's eyes, is not the source of Lincoln's sadness (as it is in so many other Lincoln films and plays) but just one more component. It is also one of the reasons that Abe's relationship with firebrand Mary Todd is so tentative. Sherwood suggests that Abe can never again know true romantic love—that's a part of his dead past—and his next partner will fuel the ambitious side of his nature, not the sentimental side. He resists becoming involved with Mary, even to the point of running away, out into the wilderness, in the hope that she will just forget about him.

But, to Sherwood, Mary is not just a wife; she is Lincoln's destiny. His fear of marrying her reflects his reticence to immerse himself in political life, a career that, he senses, will take him down a dark road. While out in the wilderness, he happens to run across two friends who are moving on to settle in Oregon. Their child is ill and—a preacher not being handy—they ask Abe to pray for him. Reluctantly he begins praying, and as he does, he begins to see the responsibility before him and starts to accept his place in history. Sherwood knows, and the audiences knows—and more important, Lincoln knows—that Abe himself will be compelled to "die on the cross to set men free" and it is in this moment on the plains that he comes to accept his dark future.

When the play opened in New York, a *Times* critic wrote, "In the chief part Raymond Massey gives a glorious performance—rude and lazily humorous on the surface, but lighted from within. He suffuses the simplicity of Mr. Sherwood's writing with the luminous beauty of inspired acting. Fortunately, the entire performance, under Elmer Rice's illuminating direction, is all of one piece, and *Abe Lincoln in Illinois* is a profoundly moving portrait of our human lore and our spiritual heritage."

The Film

No sooner had the play opened than RKO Radio Pictures began planning a motion picture version, despite the fact that John Ford also had a Lincoln film currently in the works, written by Lamar Trotti and starring Henry Fonda. The usual Hollywood way of doing things when adapting a hit Broadway play was to replace the stage star with a more bankable Hollywood star, but Raymond Massey had become so thoroughly identified with Sherwood's Lincoln that he himself was brought to Hollywood to re-create his role on film. Richard Gaines replaced Massey on Broadway with the

agreement that, after filming was completed, Massey would rejoin the company for a national tour.

Sherwood's play was adapted for the screen by veteran script writer Grover Jones and actor-turned-director John Cromwell was chosen to direct the film. Interiors were filmed in Hollywood, but the beautiful exteriors, standing in for New Salem and Springfield, were shot in Eugene, Oregon. In the inevitable expansion that takes place in all such translations from stage to screen, at least two key elements were changed. First, Abe and Ann Rutledge got the tearful deathbed scene they had been denied in the play. The scene works beautifully on film, adding an extra dimension of emotion that helps to more sharply define Abe's later actions.

But Raymond Massey was not pleased at another change. The prayer in the prairie—to Massey, the heart of the play—had been excised. "Without it," Massey wrote, "the story had become a documentary, a procession of episodes."

Massey did indeed rejoin the touring company of *Abe Lincoln in Illinois* after filming was completed and went on to play Lincoln many more times throughout his long and distinguished career on stage, screen, and television. Interestingly, he often portrayed other characters who had some connection with Lincoln—Junius Brutus Booth, the father of Edwin and John Wilkes Booth in *Prince of Players* (1955); and that fiery abolitionist John Brown in *Santa Fe Trail* (1940) and *Seven Angry Men* (1955). In fact, in the stage production of Stephen Vincent Benet's poem *John Brown's Body*, Massey read the parts of both Lincoln *and* John Brown. In 1950, Massey brought his performance from *Abe Lincoln in Illinois* to television, with Betty Field costarring as Mary Todd.

As early in the life of television as this was, it was not the first production of *Abe Lincoln in Illinois* ever televised. Stephen Courtleigh had starred in an adaptation of the play, broadcast over three nights in 1945. Now apparently lost, this production was highly praised for its excellence, and also for the depth of its ambition; it was a big task for a very primitive medium. A critic for *Variety* singled out the production's strongest element: its star. "Just as the legit [stage] version of Sherwood's great drama will be forever associated with the name of Raymond Massey, so television's greatest play to date must be tied in with the name of the man who grew before your eyes and insinuated himself into your heart—Stephen Courtleigh."

In the years since, *Abe Lincoln in Illinois* has been revived countless times. Both Hal Holbrook and Sam Waterston have had great success with the role on Broadway, and Jason Robards, Jr., performed it in a stagebound—but attractive—production for television in 1964. Robert Sherwood's deceptively simple and poetic treatment of Lincoln's life makes the play an enduringly moving and inspiring experience. The full beauty of its language and emotion didn't quite translate to the only motion picture production (to date) but there are still stage productions to come, and new actors to find the determined and melancholy heart of Abraham Lincoln through the perceptive and sympathetic words of Robert E. Sherwood.

REFERENCES

Massey, Raymond, *A Hundred Different Lives* (New York: Little, Brown, 1979); Sandburg, Carl, "Foreword," in the published edition of the play *Abe Lincoln in Illinois* (New York: Charles Scribner's Sons, 1939); Sherwood, Robert E., "The Substance of 'Abe Lincoln in Illinois,'" in the published edition of the play *Abe Lincoln in Illinois* (New York: Charles Scribner's Sons, 1939); Thompson, Frank, *Abraham Lincoln: Twentieth-Century Popular Portrayals* (Dallas: Taylor Publishing Co., 1999).

—*F.T.*

ABIE'S IRISH ROSE (1922)

ANNE NICHOLS (1892–1966)

Abie's Irish Rose (1928), U.S.A., directed by Victor Fleming, adapted by Jules Furthman; Paramount.

Abie's Irish Rose (1946), U.S.A., directed by Edward A. Sutherland, adapted by Anne Wigton and Rip Van Ronkel; United Artists/Bing and Harry Crosby.

The Play

In the theatre, there has frequently been a mighty gulf separating critical acclaim and popular success. That gulf has seldom been wider, or more treacherous, than in the case of Anne Nichols' comedy *Abie's Irish Rose*. When *Abie's Irish Rose* opened on Broadway on May 23, 1922, the reviews were beyond merciless—they were downright savage. Several critics—Percy Hammond, Robert Benchley, and Heywood Broun, among them—made a gleefully vicious personal vendetta out of hounding and pounding the show, week after week. As it turned out, they had plenty of time to stalk their prey. *Abie's Irish Rose* became an enormous box office hit, running for a remarkable 2,327 performances over the next five years. It wasn't until the debut of *Tobacco Road* in 1933 that its record was broken. The play was translated into many languages and performed all over

the world. Will Rogers saw it in China with an all-Chinese cast. And Adolph Hitler saw it—and didn't like it one bit—when it played in Berlin.

Anne Nichols earned between $5 million and $10 million for the play—originally titled *Marriage in Triplicate*—that took her about three days to write and, in 1927, added over a quarter of a million dollars to that amount for the movie rights in a deal that would return the copyright to her in a mere nine years.

She claimed that she based the play on a story told at one of her parties by Irish comedian Fiske O'Hara who had recounted an amusing tale about two friends of his—a Jewish man and an Irish woman—who married secretly and concealed from his parents the fact that she was a Gentile. After her guests left, Nichols sat down and began writing a play about the difficulties facing a similar young couple. In *Abie's Irish Rose*, young Rosemary Murphy (Marie Carroll) and Abie Levy (Robert B. Williams) meet in France during the First World War. They fall in love and marry but then come face to face with racial and social intolerance from both their families. Only after the birth of Abie and Rosemary's twins, do their fathers reconcile with them and with each other. Perhaps significantly, this joyful reunion takes place on Christmas Eve.

The play was not only successful, it was also quite influential. In no time, plays and films with similar themes began cropping up. Nichols took most of this imitation as the sincerest form of flattery, but a few of the more blatant copies got under her skin; in 1930, she sued Universal Pictures over their comedy *The Cohens and the Kellys*, claiming that it was an out-and-out theft of her work. The courts disagreed, arguing that both works relied on such stereotypical, one-dimensional characters that Nichols could hardly claim to have invented them. She lost the case and had to pay Universal's court costs. A modern assessment of the play by Howard Taubman is scathing: "Its plot is childish, its characters puerile, and even its ear for Jewish and Irish dialects monstrously false."

The Film

Sitting comfortably on the millions earned from the play's theatrical rights, Nichols was soon happily accepting a stunning offer from Paramount Pictures, which purchased the screen rights for a record $300,000. Columnist Louella O. Parsons nominated Eddie Cantor and Clara Bow for the leads in the film, which was to be shot at Paramount's Astoria Studios on Long Island. Instead, Charles "Buddy" Rogers and Nancy Carroll were awarded the roles, to be directed by the vigorous Victor Fleming. Fleming would later make some of the masterworks of the cinema—including *Gone With the Wind* and *The Wizard of Oz*—but there was nothing much he could do with the simplistic and overly familiar story of *Abie's Irish Rose*. After a beautifully atmospheric opening, which goes from the melting pot of a New York ghetto to the battlefields of France, the film becomes nothing more than a by-the-numbers restaging of the play, enlivened only by the charm of the two young leads.

Abie's Irish Rose was filmed as a 12-reel silent film, which was released to marginal box office success early in 1928. However, in the wake of the new mania for sound, Paramount decided to pull it out of release, shoot some new sequences, and turn it into a talkie, complete with a Kaddish sung by Jean Hersholt and a few bouncy numbers performed by Nancy Carroll. The new version—a full 49 minutes shorter than the "roadshow" print—opened at Christmas of 1928. Even sound didn't save it. The movie of *Abie's Irish Rose*—in stark contrast to the blockbuster status awarded the play—was never more than a moderate hit.

However, its life was far from over. Anne Nichols had already novelized her play in 1927. In 1942, she decided to bring her characters to the world of radio with a weekly series starring Julie Stevens as Rosemary and Richard Coogan as Abie. In 1946, Nichols and Rip Van Ronkel, the director of the radio series, updated the story for a new film version, produced by Bing Crosby and starring Joanne Dru as Rosemary and Richard Norris as Abie.

Where the first film was set in the years during and following World War I, the remake, directed by Edward A. Sutherland in 1946, took place during the Second World War. The play itself hadn't changed much in the intervening two decades, but the attitudes of audiences had. The remake was roundly lambasted by critics and clergy, not for its slight story and easy emotions, but for its racial content that now, after the horrors of the forties, doesn't seem very quaint any more. *Variety*'s "Abel" wrote, "Many 'Hebe comics' once enjoyed applause and approbation. The Tad comic and 'Irish Justice' were surefire and potently valuable for laughs. But circumstances have long since altered the situation—it just doesn't figure that this screen version of *Abie's Irish Rose* will make popular entertainment."

Theatrical revivals of *Abie's Irish Rose* became less frequent as time wore on. Although the radio series was popular, it did not spin off into early television, as happened with many radio hits. However, in 1972, the basic situation of *Abie's Irish Rose* did come to television under the title *Bridget Loves Bernie*. Instead of the slightly patronizing sermon-of-tolerance tone of the play and the film versions of *Abie's Irish Rose*, *Bridget Loves Bernie* came from the perspective of a new comedic freedom regarding ethnicity on television, as pioneered on such biting situation comedies as *All in the Family* and *Sanford and Son*. The series was popular, but was cancelled after a single season. The subject of inter-racial marriage—even treated with high comedy—was still one that made the public uncomfortable—even if it did make Anne Nichols very, very wealthy.

REFERENCES

"Abel," review of *Abie's Irish Rose*, *Variety*, November 27, 1946; Brownlow, Kevin, *Behind the Mask of Innocence* (New York: Alfred A. Knopf, 1990); Hanson, Patricia King, exec. ed., *American Film Institute Catalog of Motion Pictures Produced in the United States: Feature Films, 1941–1950* (Berkeley and Los Angeles: University of California Press, 1999); Nemcek, Paul, *The Films of Nancy Carroll* (New York: Lyle Stuart, 1969); Thompson, Frank, *The Star Film Ranch: Texas' First Picture Show* (Plano: Republic of Texas Press, 1996); Thompson, Frank, ed., *Between Action and Cut: Five American Directors* (Metuchen, N.J.: Scarecrow Press, 1985).

—*F.T.*

ABRAHAM LINCOLN (1919)

JOHN DRINKWATER (1882–1937)

Abraham Lincoln (1924), U.S.A., directed by J. Searle Dawley; DeForest Phonofilm Co.

Abraham Lincoln (1930), U.S.A., P.C. Pictures.

Westinghouse Studio One: Abraham Lincoln (1952), U.S.A., directed by Paul Nickell, adapted by David Shaw.

The Play

John Drinkwater was perhaps not the most obvious playwright to bring this quintessential American story to life. Born at Leytonstone, Essex, England, and educated at Oxford High School, Drinkwater served as an insurance clerk for 12 years, during which time he developed a reputation as a poet and a critic. In 1913 he became manager-producer of the Pilgrim Players, which developed into the Birmingham Repertory Theatre. *Abraham Lincoln* was his most successful play and he followed it with many more plays on historical themes: *Mary Stuart* (1921), *Oliver Cromwell* (1921), and many others.

Drinkwater approached the subject of Abraham Lincoln, he wrote, "not [as] the historian but [as] the dramatist. While I have, I hope, done nothing to traverse history, I have freely telescoped its events, and imposed invention upon its movement, in such ways as I needed to shape the dramatic significance of my subject."

The play begins with the line, "Abraham. It's a good name for a man to bear, anyway." It is the spring of 1860 in Lincoln's Springfield home as he meets with a delegation from the Republican Party, which has come to invite him to be their nominee for president. The play ends with a single shot at Ford's Theatre followed by Edwin Stanton's solemn declaration, "Now he belongs to the ages." In between is a simple, rather straightforward account of some of the crucial moments in Lincoln's life, from the beginning of the war, to his troubles with his generals, to his pardon of a condemned sentry, to Lee's surrender at Appomattox.

But the effect that Drinkwater created was anything but simple and straightforward. His Lincoln is already encased in myth, serious and deliberate, with little trace of the man's jocular wit. Indeed, Drinkwater's Lincoln is not only *encased* in myth, but also aware of it, and this foreknowledge of history—this realization of his own doom and destiny—weighs heavily upon him.

Abraham Lincoln was originally produced by the Birmingham Repertory Theatre and was, to nearly everyone's surprise, an enormous hit with both critics and the public. St. John Irving wrote in the *North American Review*, "*Abraham Lincoln* was performed in London at an obscure and ugly theatre in a distant suburb by an unknown management with a cast which did not contain the name of a single player of reputation. There was not an actor in the cast with sufficient popularity to draw sixpence in the theatre, the scenic effects were so slight as to be negligible, there was no orchestra . . . and yet the play was an enormous success."

That first production ran for some 466 performances. The title role was played by Irish actor William J. Rea who was, wrote Arnold Bennett, "merely great. The audience cried, and I should have cried myself, but for my iron resolve not to stain a well-earned reputation for callousness."

"John Drinkwater was not a dramatist of genius," wrote theatre historian Ernest Short, "but he was poet enough to reach the heart of the matter. He knew that this meant cutting out non-essentials in any given recension of history. He was also actor enough to know what players needed if they were to lay down the broad lines of a character and an epoch. Lastly, he was philosopher enough to realize the need for some such device as a Chorus, which would lift his play above mere realism."

On December 15, 1919, *Abraham Lincoln* opened in New York at the Cort Theatre. Here, Lincoln was portrayed by Frank McGlynn, a little-known character actor who bore an uncanny resemblance to the president. McGlynn's success in the role would, quite literally, change his life. The acclaim that greeted his performance in Drinkwater's play would cement him in the public eye as the very personification of the Great Emancipator.

Critic Alexander Woolcott, a man known for his iconoclastic views and caustic wit, was completely won over by McGlynn's performance. He wrote in the *New York Times*, ". . . That there should have been found for Mr. Drinkwater's play a native actor who resembled Lincoln, who could play him with eloquence and understanding, and who would trail into the production no clouds of former glories—well that was merely one of the miracles that have attended this play's progress from its inception. An astonishing thing, if you will, but, after all, not more astonishing than the fact that American audiences are now, and for years will be, sitting enraptured at a Lincoln play written by an insurance clerk from Birmingham, England."

The Films

Frank McGlynn, Sr., again performed in *Abraham Lincoln* in the 1929 New York revival at the Forrest Theatre. Critics believed that it captured the mood of the earlier production, and the *New York Times* praised Drinkwater's "splendid control and poetic clarity." McGlynn had already portrayed Lincoln in an Edison film, *The Life of Abraham Lincoln* (1915), but his second cinematic appearance as the Great Emancipator was in a film almost certainly adapted from the Drinkwater play: *Abraham Lincoln*, a one-reel DeForest Phonofilm (1924). Little is known of this early sound production, nor do any prints seem to survive of McGlynn's next appearance as Lincoln, in a 1930 two-reel film, also based on Drinkwater's play. McGlynn went on to appear as Lincoln in at least a dozen more films throughout the thirties.

In 1952, *Abraham Lincoln* was adapted for television by David Shaw and starred Robert Pastene as Lincoln, Judith Evelyn as Mary Todd Lincoln, and a young James Dean as William Scott, the sentry who is pardoned by Lincoln. Shortened considerably—quite understandably, Shaw excised the Greek chorus that introduced in blank verse each act in the play—this spare television production offered only a flavor of the power and poetry of the original play that proved so moving to so many theatregoers.

REFERENCES

Drinkwater, John, and Arnold Bennett, introductions to the published version of *Abraham Lincoln* (Boston: Houghton Mifflin, 1919); Harwell, Richard, *King Linkum the First*, Sources & Reprints Series IV (Atlanta, Ga.: Emory University Publications, 1947); Lewis, Lloyd, *Myths After Lincoln* (New York: The Press of the Readers Club, 1929); Thompson, Frank, *Abraham Lincoln: Twentieth Century Popular Portrayals* (Dallas: Taylor Publishing Co., 1999).

—F.T.

AGNES OF GOD (1978)

JOHN PIELMEIER (1949–)

Agnes of God (1985), U.S.A., directed by Norman Jewison, adapted by John Pielmeier; Columbia Pictures.

The Play

John Pielmeier's two-act play, written and copyrighted in 1978, was first produced professionally at the Actors Theatre of Louisville in 1980 after its premiere at the Eugene O'Neill Playwrights Conference in 1979. A Broadway production was mounted at the Music Box Theatre in 1982 featuring a strong cast: Elizabeth Ashley as Dr. Martha Livingston, Geraldine Page as the Mother Superior, and Amanda Plummer as Sister Agnes, a novitiate nun at a convent in Quebec who somehow turns up pregnant, even though she claims not to have had any contact with men. Agnes hears voices and bears the stigmata, suggesting a saintliness that contrasts sharply with the disturbing fact that she has murdered her baby. Court-appointed psychiatrist Dr. Martha Livingston is assigned to interview Agnes and plumb the mystery of her pregnancy. The title of the play and film echoes the Latin ritual of the Roman Catholic Church: *Ecce Agnus Dei* ("Behold the Lamb of God"). But Sister Agnes appears to be more than simply a Holy Innocent sacrificed to appease the cynicism of the modern world. She appears to be saintly; she has visions and she hears voices; but the modern world, represented by Dr. Livingston, an apostate Catholic, seeks scientific explanations for such mysterious occurrences as Agnes claims to have experienced, which are symptomatic of mental illness.

A conflict is therefore established between secular-rational Dr. Livingston and Mother Superior Miriam Ruth, who attempts to protect Agnes, whom she believes was "touched by God" in some mysterious and potentially miraculous way that science cannot explain. The cynical Dr. Livingston cannot accept the "miraculous" explanation that is offered and is primarily interested in healing her patient's shattered mind. The play resembles Peter Shaffer's *Equus*, which it seems to imitate. The framing situation is almost exactly the same for both plays: A young person (an unstable stable boy in *Equus*, a novitiate nun in *Agnes of God*) who has been subjected to peculiar religious influences is accused of an unspeakable crime in both instances. Since motivation is difficult to determine, a psychiatrist is brought in to examine the suspect and to solve the psychological mystery. The parents in the one case, the Mother Superior in the other, are reluctant to cooperate. Finally, the psychiatrist seeks to unlock the mystery through hypnosis. In a hypnotic state, then, the patient relives the disturbing experience and is able to come to grips with it. Both cases involve a confusion of religion and sexuality.

The problem is that Shaffer's Alan Strang is a more interesting patient than Sister Agnes, and that Shaffer's Dr. Martin Dysart, an overworked psychiatrist with problems of his own that need to be resolved and a man who has professional doubts about the ethics of "healing" his patient, is far more complicated than Dr. Livingston. Dysart's monologues and self-doubts are simply better written and more interesting. *Equus* is a unique paradigm, and Pielmeier's imitative play is bound to suffer by comparison.

The Film

Norman Jewison's adaptation was an ambitious movie, graced by star power (Anne Bancroft as Mother Miriam Ruth, Jane Fonda as Dr. Martha Livingston, and Meg Tilly as Sister Agnes), and certainly a woman's film. The opening sequence, introducing the viewer to convent life, showing rows of nuns devoutly at their prayers, is affectingly captured by Sven Nykvist's camera and beautiful to watch. The problem here is dramatic. The main conflicts of *Equus* were between the concerned doctor and his patient and between the doctor and himself. The main conflicts of *Agnes of God* are between the psychiatrist and the Mother Superior and between the psychologist and her patient, sensitively played by Meg Tilly, who gives the film's best performance, despite strong competition, and even though her bizarre behavior is never appropriately explained.

Agnes has led a sheltered life and has suffered sexual abuse at the hands of an alcoholic mother. She has heard voices and claims to have been visited by a mysterious "Lady," presumably the Blessed Virgin. She sings God's praises with the visionary Lady's voice. She has even experienced the stigmata, but all of this supernatural apparatus is for naught, providing an astonishing spectacle, but leading nowhere.

Anne Bancroft is also impressive as the Mother Superior, worldly-wise and married for 23 years before entering the convent. One of the script's surprises is that Agnes's mother was the Mother Superior's natural sister, but this revelation proves nothing, ultimately. Mother Superior Miriam Ruth sees the psychiatrist as a secular threat. She sees herself competing for the young woman's soul, while the Jane Fonda character is trying to pull the girl away from God. That conflict is a worthy one and makes sense in context, but Jane Fonda's lines are simply not good enough to make her seem a worthy opponent.

The "mystery" at the core of this play turns out to be more mundane than metaphysical: Was Agnes raped or seduced and, if so, how? Because of her worldly background before entering the convent, it seems odd that Mother Superior seems content to accept the pregnancy as a religious mystery, unless one assumes that she is orchestrating a cover-up in order to avoid scandal for the Order. The play seems to want to have it both ways and gives the girl a squirting stigmata under hypnosis that suggests that the Mother Superior might be right. But the facts are these: A baby was born and a baby was murdered, either by Agnes or by one of the other nuns. That is the mystery that is logically solved, but the mystery of her conception is more difficult to deal with. There were natural causes, no doubt, but the film presents them in a subjective and visionary way that is misleading, with images of flapping doves that clearly suggest the Holy Ghost. That is not only ambiguous but potentially blasphemous.

Ultimately, Jane Fonda was defeated by her role. Audiences were used to seeing her play strong, liberated women, but this role is curiously empty. Fonda does her best with inferior lines, but her performance cannot compensate for the apparent weaknesses of the script. At the end of the year both of her co-stars fared better than Fonda. Anne Bancroft was nominated for a best actress Academy Award and Meg Tilly earned a best supporting actress nomination. Opening to mixed reviews, the film was only a modest commercial success.

REFERENCES

Andersen, Christopher, *Citizen Jane: The Turbulent Life of Jane Fonda* (New York: Henry Holt, 1990); Bonavoglia, Angela, "Agnes of God," *Cineaste*, 14:3 (1986), 41–42; Welsh, James M., "Dream Doctors as Healers in Drama and Film," *Literature & Medicine*, 6 (1987), 117–127.

—*J.M.W.*

AH, WILDERNESS! (1933)

EUGENE O'NEILL (1888–1953)

Ah, Wilderness (1935), U.S.A., directed by Clarence Brown, adapted by Frances Goodrich and Albert Hackett; MGM.

Summer Holiday (1948), U.S.A., directed by Rouben Mamoulian, adapted by Frances Goodrich and Albert Hackett, music by Harry Warren and lyrics by Ralph Blane; MGM.

The Play

Considered Eugene O'Neill's only comedy, *Ah, Wilderness!* sought to depict the spirit of American family life at the turn of the century. Rather than the deep, probing psychological studies that are characteristic of much of O'Neill's work, this four-act "comedy of recollection" is primarily aimed at developing a more subtle mood or atmosphere. In a letter to his son, Eugene O'Neill, Jr., the playwright wrote of the comedy that he wanted ". . . more the capture of a mood, an evocation [of] the spirit of a time that is dead now with all its ideals and manners & codes."

The play is set on July 4, 1906, in a small New England town modeled after New London, Connecticut (the town where O'Neill grew up). The plot revolves around the Miller family. Richard, Nat Miller's son, is an exuberant socialist-radical-romantic wannabe who has a passion for decadent poetry and prose, a la Swinburne and Wilde, and also harbors a youthful ardor for Muriel McComber. Upon finding some letters to Muriel from Richard, which have snatched fragments of Swinburne's poetry included in them, Muriel's father demands that Richard stay away from his daughter. The youth seeks solace in a local bar and, in the company of a prostitute, Richard gets drunk. The morning after, having arrived to a waiting, concerned family late that evening, Richard is admonished by his father, Nat Miller, who also unsuccessfully tries to instruct him about "a certain class of women" like the one he was with the night before. The play ends with Richard's agreeing to go to Yale in the fall and the Miller household reminiscing about youth.

Ah, Wilderness! was originally produced by the Theatre Guild in December 1933, directed by Philip Moeller and with sets designed by Robert Edmund Jones. The production starred George M. Cohan as Nat Miller and Elisha Cook as Richard. The play ran for 289 performances and the West Coast productions included Will Rogers and Harry Carey essaying the role of Nat Miller.

The Films

Clarence Brown seemed the appropriate choice to direct the film version of *Ah, Wilderness!* Not only had he directed the silent adaptation of *Anna Christie*, but he also shared many things in common with O'Neill himself. Brown was two years younger than O'Neill, having been born in 1890. Brown, like O'Neill, was a New Englander, born in Clinton, Massachusetts (much of *Ah, Wilderness!* was filmed in the town of North Grafton, Massachusetts, which is close to Clinton). And of the 36 sound films Brown directed for MGM in the 1930s, *Ah, Wilderness!* was his only comedy. Brown's film captures both the spirit and mood of O'Neill's idealized portrait of turn-of-the-century American life, thereby preserving the playwright's original intent. This is accomplished through Brown's skillful direction and the adroit screenplay by Albert Hackett and Frances Goodrich.

Rather than confining the setting to the July 4th weekend, the film begins with a high school cotillion preceding graduation that is not in the play. This extended sequence allows for the creation of atmosphere as well as some backstory concerning the romance between Richard and Muriel (in the play Muriel does not appear until the fourth act). It also develops the character of the bibulous Uncle Sid (portrayed by Wallace Beery, who received star billing in the film). Brown highlights the romance of Richard and Muriel throughout the film, which provides a bit more motivation for Richard's escapade at the hotel saloon than O'Neill gives. The cotillion also furnishes an insight into Richard's character, which is considerably softened in Hackett and Goodrich's screenplay. An example of this is when Richard, who has been talking to Muriel, is offered some cakes by a hostess. "Man does not live by bread alone!" Richard exalts (one of many aphorisms he proclaims throughout the film). As she turns to leave, Richard immediately snatches some of the pastries off of the tray. The hypocrisy of Richard's actions undermines his original remarks. This opening sequence ends with Muriel's promise to go with Richard on a canoe ride during the Fourth of July picnic.

The film's second act (which is O'Neill's first act) opens quietly in the early morning hours of July 4. The serenity is soon broken by the eruption of fireworks which increase in intensity in a montage sequence that is played out as if it were a battle scene.

Brown then cuts to the Miller household, where much of O'Neill's play is set. Brown's effective editing allows O'Neill's dialogue to proceed naturally within the scene in a slice-of-life manner. Clarence Brown was noted for his handling of actors, and the performances in the film are consistent as well as accomplished. Lionel Barrymore plays Nat Miller and Spring Byington, his wife. Richard is played by Eric Linden and Muriel by Cecelia Parker. All of the performances create an ensemble that adheres to O'Neill's script. Consistency of performance and style are important in creating an adaptation whose intent is faithful, if not exact, to its source.

Rouben Mamoulian's 1948 Technicolor musical *Summer Holiday* presents a different set of circumstances in regard to the adaptation process. The primary problem here is that it is an adaptation of an adaptation. It also represents an attempt to exploit another past success from MGM, *Meet Me in St. Louis* (1944). According to John Orlandello, "Mamoulian's musical is clearly based on the scenario of the earlier 1935 adaptation rather than being a new and direct adaptation of O'Neill's play. It utilizes all of the structuring and focal changes made in the Hackett/Goodrich scenario . . . the fact remains that it is less an adaptation of O'Neill's play than a twice-removed creation." The music and lyrics by Harry Warren and Ralph Blane seem to be an attempt to replicate the style of their past musical effort *Meet Me In St. Louis*. The song "The Stanley Steamer" is highly reminiscent of "The Trolley Song" made famous by Judy Garland in Minnelli's musical. The miscasting of Mickey Rooney as Richard only adds to the faults in this production. Rooney's clownish antics are simply a carryover from his numerous Andy Hardy films. It is interesting to note here that MGM had a special affinity for nostalgic portraits of small-town America, which may have been instigated by the success of Clarence Brown's *Ah, Wilderness!* Two years after that film was made, in 1937, MGM utilized most of the original cast members in *A Family Affair*, which began the Andy Hardy series.

REFERENCES

Bogard, Travis, ed., *Selected Letters of Eugene O'Neill* (New Haven, Conn.: Yale University Press, 1988); Leiter, Samuel L., *The Encyclopedia of the New York Stage, 1930–1940* (New York: Greenwood Press, 1989); Orlandello, John, *O'Neill on Film* (Rutherford, N.J.: Fairleigh Dickinson University Press, 1982).

—*R.W.*

ALFIE (1963)

BILL NAUGHTON (1910–1992)

Alfie (1966), U.K./U.S.A., directed by Lewis Gilbert, adapted by Bill Naughton; Sheldrake Films/Paramount Pictures.

The Play

Bill Naughton adapted his 1962 radio play, *Alfie Elkins and His Little Life*, for the stage in 1963. The 1950s world of London "wideboys" is transformed and updated in the stage play to the swinging 1960s of the Beatles. The play retains its working class protagonist, Alfie, whose life-style revolves around conquests of married and single "birds," as Alfie is fond of calling women. Alfie addresses the audience directly, and these various asides allow him to expound on a hedonistic and cynical philosophy of life. Alfie impregnates two women. Gilda chooses a loveless marriage to a steady, dull man, Humphrey, who helps raise her illegitimate son. Rather than face disgrace, Lily, a married lover, elects for an illegal abortion procured by Alfie and performed in his apartment. Devastated by the sight of the aborted fetus, Alfie decides to settle down with his older, wealthy lover, Ruby. In an ironic twist, Alfie discovers another man in Ruby's bedroom when he arrives at her apartment unannounced.

Ultimately, Alfie's selfish behavior and amoral life leaves a devastating mark on all those he encounters. Naughton pulls no punches in showing the emptiness of this pleasure-seeking loner, but he does so with a sympathetic wit, avoiding any heavy-handed sermonizing in his treatment of modern moral behavior.

The Film

Bill Naughton adapted his play for the screen in 1966, keeping closely to the feel of the stage play, including the device of having Alfie directly address the audience (camera). He opened up the play by introducing London street scenes and adding a barroom brawl. Jazz arrangements by Sonny Rollins and a title song, performed by Cher, capture the upbeat backdrop and giddy mood of '60s London.

Like the play, the film depicts Alfie's inability to commit to a single woman, leaving him with a series of short flings and failed relationships. Although Alfie is both selfish and deceptive, Michael Caine plays him as a charming rogue. Alfie is tender and affectionate with his young, illegitimate son and genuinely remorseful over Lily's abortion. The film is a tale of human foibles

and develops sympathetic, yet flawed characters who live with the dire consequences of their choices. Millicent Martin gives a dignified performance as a lonely, married woman caught in a horrible predicament of aborting an unwanted pregnancy or facing her ailing husband with the truth of her unfaithfulness.

With a slight change in the film's ending Naughton emphasizes Alfie's philandering life-style as ultimately pathetic and lonely. On stage, Alfie and a married former lover, Siddie, end the play as it opened with an illicit romp. In the film, however, Siddie is off to meet her husband and obviously no longer interested in Alfie, leaving no doubt that Alfie is completely alone.

An American/British production, the film was Paramount's most successful venture in Great Britain. In a movie that was saturated with sexual liaisons, there is no nudity or explicit sexuality on-screen, in keeping with the conventions of much Hollywood filmmaking under the standards of the Production Code. The graphic depiction of abortion, which was banned under the Code, was quite controversial for the American release. In order to receive a Production Code seal for its American distribution, the Motion Picture Producers Association required several cuts and, only on appeal, issued a special exception for *Alfie*, labeling it Suggested for Mature Audiences, to limit the audience to those over 18. Nevertheless, the film was popular and nominated for several Academy Awards, including best picture, best actor, best supporting actress, and best screenplay.

REFERENCES

Murphy, Robert, ed., *The British Cinema* (London: BFI Publishing, 1997); Murphy, Robert, *Sixties British Cinema* (London: BFI Publishing, 1992); Vizzard, Jack, *See No Evil: Life Inside a Hollywood Censor* (New York: Simon and Schuster, 1970).

—D.H.

AMADEUS (1979)

PETER SHAFFER (1926–)

Amadeus (1984), U.S.A., directed by Milos Forman, adapted by Peter Shaffer; Orion Pictures.

The Play

When *Amadeus* opened at Britain's National Theatre in November of 1979, it was a sensational success, according to Peter Hall, director of both the production and the National Theatre. But the playwright was not satisfied and kept revising the play for its American premiere—first in Washington, D.C., followed by its opening at the Broadhurst Theatre in New York—compelled by what Shaffer called "a nearly obsessive pursuit of clarity, structural order, and drama" and trying to find a way to put Mozart's antagonist, the Court composer Antonio Salieri, "at the wicked center of the action." Because Shaffer continued to revise his play, as was his habit, it is difficult to say what the definitive version should be. The motion picture gave him an opportunity for further revision, as he worked with director Milos Forman to transform the play into cinema.

The Broadway version is probably the most "authoritative," however, with a revised and more active Salieri functioning as a surrogate father, actively working to damage Mozart's career in Vienna and encouraging him to betray the secrets of the Freemasons in his opera *The Magic Flute*, which would alienate him from his most powerful ally at the Hapsburg Court, Baron Gottfried Von Swieten, prefect of the Imperial Library. The play begins and ends with Kapellmeister Antonio Salieri, the former Court composer and the dominant character of the drama, a figure of evil and vengeance, corrupted by envy and intent upon destroying the more talented composer, Wolfgang Amadeus Mozart, whom Salieri regards as an unworthy vulgarian. Wolfgang Amadeus Mozart, "beloved of God" and amazingly gifted, is not the main subject of the play but the object of Salieri's corrosive envy. This is not a biographical drama but a moral allegory and a reflection on the nature of evil, embodied by Salieri, who narrates the play in November of 1823, recalling the events in Vienna of 1781 to 1791, the year of Mozart's death.

The play starts with a chorus made up of the "Venticelli," purveyors of fact, gossip, and rumor throughout the play. It is rumored that mad Salieri begs forgiveness for having murdered Mozart 32 years before. In the next scene Salieri introduces himself and what he calls his last composition, entitled "The Death of Mozart; or, Did I Do It?" At the end of this scene Salieri slips off his robe to reveal himself as a younger man, as the scene shifts back into the 18th century, into the Imperial Court, where influential Masons were in power, under Baron Von Swieten. In the following scene Salieri encounters Mozart for the first time, and his music, a "solemn Adagio in E Flat," and realizes that this "obscene child" speaks with "the voice of God." When Emperor Joseph II of Austria first meets Mozart, Salieri composes a "March of Welcome," which Mozart arrogantly presumes to improve by improvising on the spot. Salieri is humiliated, and infu-

riated. In the play the emperor has exited before this humiliation; in the film, the emperor witnesses Salieri's humiliation, which makes it all the worse.

Salieri works behind the scenes to hinder Mozart's financial advance. When Mozart's wife Constanze comes to him to enlist his aid for her husband, Salieri, a married man in the play, attempts to seduce her, then, when she starts to undress, he rejects her, as if by humiliating Constanze, he also humiliates her husband. Salieri does nothing to advance Mozart's career, though he fully recognizes his rival's talent. Mozart has middling success with operas—*The Marriage of Figaro*, for example—and *The Magic Flute*, described as a "vaudeville," which is damaging for Mozart because Salieri has persuaded him to draw upon the secret rituals of the Masonic Lodge, which alienates him from Von Swieten. Mozart confides in Salieri that a mysterious masked figure (a symbolic Messenger of God later identified as a servant of Count Walsegg, who wanted to take the credit) has commissioned him to write a Requiem Mass. Salieri disguises himself as that "messenger" and appears below the window of Mozart's apartment. Mozart dies apparently out of nervous exhaustion, though perhaps due to kidney failure, and Salieri tells him in their last encounter that he has poisoned him over 10 years. At the end, the scene shifts ahead to 1823. Salieri proclaims himself "The Patron Saint of Mediocrities," then slits his throat, but he does not die, and the Venticelli inform the audience that no one believes him responsible for Mozart's premature death.

The Film

As stated above, the film adaptation could more accurately be described as a transformation, since the play was essentially reinvented for the screen. Salieri (F. Murray Abraham) becomes even more active in the demise of Mozart and his faltering career, though the Masonic betrayal is removed from the film. As played by Tom Hulce, Mozart is a paradigm of vulgarity in the film, fond of pink wigs and possessed of a hideous cackling laugh that is still heard echoing as the film credits begin to roll at the end, after Mozart's burial. Since the audience sees Mozart from Salieri's demented point of view, the distorted and cartoonish vulgarity are psychologically justified. Mozart's adolescent sexual advances toward Constanze (Elizabeth Berridge) are witnessed by Salieri in the film, but moved forward so that Salieri has this negative impression before he first hears Mozart's "miraculous" Adagio in E Flat.

Though the "Venticelli" chorus is absent from the film, Shaffer adds the character of a maid Salieri hires to work for Mozart and spy on him. Shaffer also adds Leopold (Roy Dotrice), Mozart's father, who comes to Vienna to live with his son, until Constanze drives him away, making Mozart feel all the more guilty later on, when he learns that his father has died. The most helpful addition is the young priest (Herman Meckler), who comes to hear Salieri's confession, after Salieri attempts to slit his throat at the beginning of the story, not at the end, as in the play. Thus old Salieri tells his story to this priest, who becomes increasingly horrified as Salieri reveals his evil intent. The play is reimagined in such a way that the film is able to present an impressive musical spectacle, enriched by operatic performances. The film also provides a lavish visual spectacle as director Milos Forman takes full advantage of the ancient city of Prague in his native Czechoslovakia to double for Mozart's Vienna. In the film Salieri's hatred and dementia are amplified significantly.

Shaffer had seen two of his earlier plays (*The Royal Hunt of the Sun* and *Equus*) unsuccessfully adapted to the screen, but soon realized that director Milos Forman was willing to work harder than others had done to do justice to his work and to get it right. This is a rare example of a playwright working patiently with a gifted director not only to adapt but also to reinvent and perfectly transform an original play for the benefit of a mass audience. The motivation is sharpened and the action clarified but not necessarily simplified, so that the film arguably improves the play. The film swept the Academy Awards with 11 nominations, winning eight Oscars, including best actor (Abraham), best director, best adapted screenplay, and best picture.

REFERENCES

Eberle, Thomas, *Peter Shaffer: An Annotated Bibliography* (New York: Garland, 1991); Forman, Milos, and Jan Novak, *Turnaround: A Memoir* (New York: Villard Books, 1994); Gianakaris, C.J., *Modern Dramatists: Peter Shaffer* (New York: St. Martin's, 1992).

—*J.M.W.*

AMERICAN BUFFALO (1975)

DAVID MAMET (1947–)

American Buffalo (1997), U.S.A., directed by Michael Corrente, adapted by David Mamet; Samuel Goldwyn.

The Play

This play, originally directed by Gregory Mosher for the Goodman Theatre in Chicago, launched David Mamet's dramatic career. It later opened at the Ethel Barrymore Theatre on February 16, 1997, for a run of 135 performances. The play is remarkable for its sparseness and deceptive simplicity as well as its cynical take on the American dream, reduced here to the rubble of an urban junkshop. Mamet's three lowlife characters talk "business," the word they use to describe petty larceny. The plot turns on the themes of friendship and betrayal. Don Dubrow (Kenneth McMillan in the New York production) owns Don's Resale Shop, cluttered with junk. The action is set during a single day: Act One begins in the morning and Act Two takes place that same evening, about 11 P.M. Don is angry because he thinks a coin collector has bilked him into selling a rare buffalo-head nickel for much less than he later imagines it was worth—though he doesn't seem to know exactly what it *was* worth and he isn't clever enough to find out—and Don is obsessed with the notion of payback, revenge to soothe his wounded pride. He knows where the client lives, and he plans to have Bobby (John Savage), his 15-year-old gofer, steal back the coin. The problem is, he is not smart enough to have a well-developed plan. When his poker buddy Walter "Teach" Cole (Robert Duvall) gets wind of the plan, he wants a piece of the action and is determined to squeeze Bob out of the caper. Teach persuades Don to tell Bob that the theft will not take place that night as planned; but Bob is smart enough to sense a double-cross. In Act Two Teach comes back that evening with a revolver, which would notch the theft up to armed robbery. Don also wants to enlist the help of another poker-buddy, Fletch, who would be able to crack a safe, if it turns out the mark has one. Bob turns up that evening and tells the other two that Fletch cannot be reached because Fletch has been hospitalized by a mugger, which puts the planned robbery on hold. Teach loses his temper and hits Bob, making his ear bleed. As the angry Teach later admits, "We all live like the cavemen." The play is about frustrated losers who are incapable of achieving their goals. The robbery never takes place. The play ends with Teach going to his car so they can take Bob to the hospital.

The Film

The vanishing American buffalo seems to be an extended metaphor for a contemporary America that has become urbanized, dehumanized, and made cynical after the disappearance of the Frontier—a very differ-

David Mamet adapted his American Buffalo *to the screen, with Dennis Franz as Donny (left) and Sean Nelson as Bobby.* (COURTESY SAMUEL GOLDWYN COMPANY)

ent place from what was imagined a century earlier. Likewise, the generally slow-witted characters are "buffaloed" and incapable of taking decisive action. Mamet's forte is his ability to capture the nuances of everyday speech. The play won an Obie Award and the Drama Critics' Circle Award, but since nothing happens in Don's Resale Shop but hyper-inflated, angry talk, this play is clearly not a very promising vehicle for the screen. It is therefore understandable that 20 years would pass before it was adapted to film, on the heels of the critical success of another Mamet adaptation, *Glengarry Glen Ross*, in 1992. Mamet himself rewrote the latter play for the screen adaptation directed by James Foley, whereas *American Buffalo* is little more than an exercise in filmed theatre, as directed by Michael Corrente. Most of the action still takes place in the Resale Shop, though the camera ventures out to the curbside on two occasions, and viewers are given a shot of the disordered hotel room in which Teach lives.

The casting works well enough, with 14-year-old Sean Nelson as Bob, Dennis Franz as Donny, and an explosive Dustin Hoffman as a menacing and volatile Teach. The confining atmosphere of the Resale Shop makes perfect sense for the stage, since it serves as an extension of Donny's disordered and jumbled mind; but at no point does the film viewer lose sight of the fact that this is merely a filmed play. The adaptation fails to work as a film and is of little more than academic interest, despite superior performances from a talented cast and the rough vernacular poetry of Mamet's text.

REFERENCES

Pawelczak, Andy, "American Buffalo," *Films in Review*, 48:2 (January–February 1997): 67; Savran, David, *In Their Own Words: Contemporary American Playwrights* (New York: Theatre Communications Group, 1988).

—*J.M.W. AND J.C.T.*

ANDROCLES AND THE LION (1912)

GEORGE BERNARD SHAW (1856–1950)

Androcles and the Lion (1952), U.K., directed by Chester Erskine, adapted by Erskine and Ken Englund; RKO.

The Play

After forays in the 1880s into novel writing (*Cashel Byron's Profession* and *An Unsocial Socialist*) and stints for newspapers as a music critic, George Bernard Shaw turned to the *Piece bien faite* type of "thesis play" in the 1890s with *Widower's Houses* (1892), *Arms and the Man* (1893), and *Mrs. Warren's Profession* (1899). Noted for his injection of issues and polemics into his work, he achieved his greatest critical and popular successes with later plays, notably *Man and Superman* (1903), *Major Barbara* (1905), *Pygmalion* (1913), and *Saint Joan* (1923). Less substantial, perhaps, but no less popular, was *Androcles and the Lion* (1912). This "Fable Play" in two acts and a prologue was first produced in London in 1913. In a lengthy preface, "On the Prospects of Christianity," Shaw commented on the differing Gospel narratives of Christ and mankind's 2,000-year rejection of Him, whose teachings "are not turning out to be good sense and sound economics."

In the Prologue, Androcles has been expelled from home by his shrewish wife, Megaera, because of his obsession with animals and with Christianity. He encounters a lion suffering from a thorn in its paw. He extracts it and departs with the grateful lion by his side. Act One transpires in the Roman Coliseum, where a Roman captain unsuccessfully urges the beautiful Christian Lavinia to save her life by paying symbolic homage to the gods, "if only as a matter of good taste, to avoid shocking the religious convictions of the Romans." Joining the group are Androcles, the powerful warrior Ferrovius, and the debauched Spintho, who earnestly hopes that martyrdom will gain him entrance to Heaven. In Act Two Androcles and Lavinia prepare themselves to be thrown to the lions. But the lion confronting them turns out to be the beast Androcles had assisted earlier. Androcles is allowed to walk off unmolested, a free man. Ferrovius joins Caesar's Pretorian Guard. And Lavinia agrees to let her captain come to visit her and argue about religions. In a terminal note to the play, Shaw commented on the Roman persecutions, describing them as "an attempt to suppress a propaganda that seemed to threaten the interests involved in the established law and order, organized and maintained in the name of religion and justice by politicians who are pure opportunist Have-and-Holders."

The Film

G.B. Shaw was no fan of the movies, particularly American movies. "The huge polynational audience makes mediocrity compulsory," he asserted in 1924. "Many of them are full of the stupidest errors of judgment. Overdone and foolishly repeated strokes of expression, hideous make-ups, close-ups that an angel's face would not bear. . . . Conceit is rampant among your film makers; and good sense is about non-existent." Indeed, before the movies learned to talk, Shaw refused to allow any of his plays to be adapted to the screen. "I repeat that a play with the words left out is a play spoiled; and all those filmings of plays written to be spoken as well as seen are boresome blunders. . . ."

Yet, Shaw had long been interested in photography, and he was willing to admit that he saw the film medium as a potentially revolutionary social force. With the advent of the talking picture in the late 1920s—he appeared in a Fox Movietone short in 1927 to address his public through the medium of the camera—he saw the possibility of bringing his plays to the screen. "My shop is open," he told the public in 1928, "and people can come and negotiate with me." However, he insisted that a cinematic adaptation should be nothing more than a filmed play—it was the dialogue that mattered, not the techniques of editing and camera.

Accordingly, the first Shavian adaptation to hit the screen was *How He Lied to Her Husband* (1931), directed by Cecil Lewis in a virtually unaltered piece of canned theatre. Both it and the next venture, *Arms and the Man* (1932), were tediously static, and they flopped at the box office. But the arrival of one Gabriel Pascal, a self-styled film producer, would change all that. He met Shaw in 1935 and, by his own admission, talked Shaw into allowing him to produce his plays on film. "I said that I would make no picture with box-office compromises. And I think the old man believed in my love of art, that's all. There's no mystery about it." Shaw later admitted he had been quite taken with Pascal's charm: "A delightful creature, but quite outside all ordinary rules." At any rate, Pascal's three adaptations of Shaw's work—*Pygmalion* (1938), *Major Barbara* (1941), and (to a lesser degree) *Caesar and Cleopatra* (1944) for his own production company, General Films (examined exhaustively in Donald Costello's invaluable study of the subject, *The Serpent's Eye* [1965]—would not only be successes, but would also represent a more enlightened attitude on Shaw's part toward the recognition of a more "cinematic" union of play, text, and camera.

Pascal did produce one more Shavian adaptation, although it was without the active collaboration of Shaw, who died before the project was completed. The adaptation rearranges the sequence of events. With the financial backing of RKO, Pascal hired Jean Simmons (who had become a popular star since her tiny role in *Caesar and Cleopatra*) as Lavinia and Victor Mature (then at the peak of his sword-and-sandal career in Hollywood) as the captain. The action is located in Rome in 161 A.D. As a security measure, the authorities decide to arrest a number of Christians, including Androcles. As he flees the soldiers, he encounters Tommy the lion (played by Tommy the Lion), who is afflicted with a thorn in his paw. In the Colosseum, the romance between Lavinia and the Roman captain is considerably expanded, pushing the Androcles plot into a secondary position. Pascal claimed to have been pleased with the finished product, calling it "an important improvement over the original play." The critics, however, wickedly charged that Pascal "had thrown Shaw to the lions of RKO." Pascal never made another movie.

REFERENCES

Costello, Donald P., *The Serpent's Eye: Shaw and the Cinema* (Notre Dame, Ind.: University of Notre Dame Press, 1965); Dukore, Bernard F., ed., *Bernard Shaw on Cinema* (Carbondale: Southern Illinois Press, 1997); Pascal, Valerie, *The Disciple and His Devil* (New York: McGraw-Hill, 1970).

—*J.C.T.*

ANGEL STREET (GASLIGHT) (1938)

PATRICK HAMILTON (1904–1962)

Gaslight (1940), U.K., directed by Thorold Dickinson, adapted by A.R. Rawlinson, Bridget Boland; British National.

Gaslight (1944), U.S.A., directed by George Cukor, adapted by John Van Druten, John L. Balderston, and Walter Reisch; MGM.

The Play

The setting is a four-storied house in an unfashionable section of Victorian London in the 1880s. Several years before the play's opening a murder had been committed in that house. Now, Jack Manningham is trying to drive his nervous and insecure wife, Betty, insane by hiding things and then accusing her of forgetfulness or theft. When her husband is out of the house, the wife is further tormented by the inexplicable dimming of the gaslight in her room. Is she imagining things? Is she really going mad? It turns out that the husband had murdered an old lady in this house several years before in an attempt to steal her precious jewels. It is his continuing secret search in the attic for the missing jewels that is causing the dimming of the lights. His motive for trying to drive Mrs. Manningham insane is that she has discovered a letter that might link him to the murder. Fortunately, he has been recognized by an ex-policeman, Sergeant Rough, who was on the original case. During his investigation, Rough uncovers the husband's plan and rescues the wife. The last scene is a tour-de-force in which Mrs. Manningham gives her husband a dose of his own medicine: She torments him by pretending to help him escape; but then, at the last minute, she lapses into a feigned madness and incompetence. As he is taken away to the gallows, she luxuriates in her triumph.

Gaslight opened in Richmond on December 5, 1938, and then relocated to the Apollo Theatre in London's West End, where it had a run for four months. Later in 1941 producer Shepard Traube opened it in New York under the title of *Angel Street*, with Judith Evelyn and Vincent Price in the main roles. It was a celebrated success, running for 1,295 performances, making it the longest-run foreign drama in Broadway history. Commentator John Chapman notes, "The most admirable thing about Mr. Hamilton's play is its economy—its economy of characters, of action, of words. There are five players and there is one set. There is a murder, all right—but it happened years ago. The action is such slight stuff as the dimming of the gas mantles, the lock picking of a desk. Anything resembling violent action is avoided until the triumphant finale."

The Films

Thorold Dickinson's 1940 film version stars Anton Walbrook and Diana Wynyard as Mr. and Mrs. Manningham. It begins with a reconstruction of the original murder, followed by an exciting montage of the unidentified killer's frantic search for the jewels. Two later scenes also open out the action—at a concert, when the wife embarrassingly breaks down under her husband's whispered accusations; and at a music hall, where the husband accompanies his flighty housemaid. In the main, however, the film preserves the play's confinement of the action to the house, climaxing with the famous confrontation between husband and wife. Manningham, now bound to a chair while waiting to be taken to prison, begs his wife to cut him free. The wife now torments him by enacting the very "madness" he has tried to provoke in her. In Dickinson's film, brooding close-ups and distorted camera angles emphasize the twisted psychology at work here—murder is in the air and, at this stage, both husband and wife seem on a borderline between sanity and insanity. Finally, it is the husband who steps over the edge and the wife who steps back from the brink.

MGM not only bought the rights to the play, it also acquired the rights to Dickinson's film in order to suppress it. This provoked considerable hostility from British critics, which subsequently fed into their disparaging responses to Cukor's version (which appeared in Britain under the title *Murder in Thornton Square*). While Cukor's film retains many of the features of the play and the Dickinson adaptation, there are important differences. First of all, Cukor's version is over 20 minutes longer due to its dramatization of the backstory of how the Manninghams first met: The murdered woman was the future Mrs. Manningham's aunt, an opera star for whom Mr. Manningham had been an accompanist. Attempting unsuccessfully to follow in her aunt's operatic footsteps, Betty is seen performing an aria from Donizetti's *Lucia de Lammermoor*—significantly, an opera about a heroine driven mad by men—accompanied on the piano by her future husband. Moreover, Manningham's motivation for the original murder seems more complex than in either the play or Dickinson's film, since he is aware that the jewels are so famous that he could never hope to sell them (it is as if they symbolize for him the aunt's feminine power, which he is trying to possess). His relationship with Mrs. Manningham has similar implications—he is trying to exploit her vulnerability and draw power away from her. The theme is extended in a superb piece of parallel editing where, on the one hand, Manningham is enraptured by the Crown Jewels in the Tower of London (counterpointed by a voice-over describing the physical tortures endured by the Tower's unfortunate victims and inmates), and, on the other hand, Mrs. Manningham is undergoing her psychological torture as she searches for a missing brooch that her husband has maliciously secreted.

In sum, if Dickinson's film is a stylish slice of Victorian Gothic, Cukor's is a powerful critique of patriarchy in the guise of a period thriller. It is brilliantly performed by Ingrid Bergman, Charles Boyer, and, in her first film role, Angela Lansbury as the maid. Bergman won a best actress Oscar, and Cedric Gibbons and William Ferrari won for their art direction of the superbly sinister Victorian mansion.

REFERENCES

French, Sean, *Patrick Hamilton* (London: Faber and Faber, 1993); Richards, Jeffrey, *Thorold Dickinson and the British Cinema* (London: Scarecrow Press, 1997); Wood, Robin, *Sexual Politics and Narrative Film: Hollywood and Beyond* (New York: Columbia University Press, 1998).

—*N.S.*

ANNA CHRISTIE (1921)

EUGENE O'NEILL (1888–1953)

Anna Christie (1923), U.S.A., directed by John Griffith Wray, adapted by Bradley King; Thomas H. Ince/First National.

Anna Christie (1930), U.S.A., directed by Clarence Brown, adapted by Frances Marion; MGM.

The Play

Although it was to become one of his most successful plays, Eugene O'Neill's *Anna Christie* failed in its original version, *Chris Christopherson*, starring Lynn Fontanne as Anna. However, on November 2, 1921, under its new title and with a new cast it premiered at the Vanderbilt Theatre in New York and ran for an impressive 177 performances. Despite O'Neill's later cavil that the play was too commercial and had "employed all the Broadway tricks which I had learned in my stage training," critic Burns Mantle recognized its essential greatness, calling it "one of the big dramas of the day, soundly human, impressively true in characterization and, in its bigger moments, intensely dramatic." The story, most of which is set in Johnny-the-Priest's waterfront saloon, chronicles Anna's regeneration under the influence of the sea and the love of a man. After years as a prostitute, Anna (Pauline Lord) reunites with her father, Christopher Christopherson (George Marion), the grizzled captain of a coal barge. Life on the coastal waters of Massachusetts brings her a sense of rebirth, and she falls in love with Matt Burke (Frank Shannon), a roistering Irishman whom she has saved from a shipwreck. But when she turns down Matt's proposal of marriage and confesses to her illicit past, both men reject her. In the play's final act, she reconciles with Matt and agrees to his demand that she pledge to him an oath of loyalty and purity.

The Films

Blanche Sweet starred as Anna in the first screen version, released through First National Pictures in 1923. Determined to keep his daughter, Anna, away from the sea, Chris Christopherson (George Marion, repeating his stage role) has her brought up by cousins on a Minnesota farm. Because she is abused by her relatives, Anna runs away to Chicago where she becomes a prostitute. Later, after visiting her father on a coal barge on the New York docks, she meets and falls in love with a sailor, Matt Burke (William Russell). Her father disapproves of the match and quarrels with Burke. When she reveals her past to the two men, there is a row and the men leave. Upon returning, however, they reconcile with Anna. Anna prepares for a successful marriage with Matt. The film was hailed as "one of the most striking achievements of the year in motion pictures," by the critic in *Exceptional Photoplays*. "It courageously lifts the screen to the level of the best on the contemporary stage and will stand as a landmark in the photodrama's coming of age." *Photoplay* also applauded the film, singling out George Marion's "masterly performance" as Christopherson and Blanche Sweet's portrait of Anna ("Miss Sweet does the finest work of her career and leaves nothing to be desired"). "While it may not be a picture for the children," concluded the critic, "no adult should miss it."

MGM's 1930 remake was a vehicle for Greta Garbo's talking debut. George F. Marion again recreated his stage role as Christopherson, Charles Bickford took on the part of Matt, and Marie Dressler played Old Marthy Owen, Christopherson's seedy mistress. Despite favorable critical and popular acceptance, the picture suffered from the stagy, proscenium-bound nature of so many early-sound era theatrical films. Director Brown and scenarist Marion chose to retain most of the substance and flavor of O'Neill's text, at the expense of achieving a more "cinematic" film. For example, Anna's soliloquies about her past were retained without benefit of flashbacks or the inclusion of a visualized prologue (which would become a standard practice in theatrical films within the next few years). Medium shots, static camera placements, and studio sound-stage sets predominated, although a few added scenes "opened up" the play a bit, including exterior shots of the barge docking at the Provincetown port and Anna and Matt's outing at the Coney Island amusement park. Today the film is regarded as a relic of the early talking picture era, whose main claim to fame is Garbo's first screen utterance: "Gimme a whiskey—ginger ale on the side. And don't be stingy, baby." Writing in *Cinema*, critic James

Shelley Hamilton noted its chief value lay in its being a vehicle for outstanding performances by Garbo, Marion, and Dressler; otherwise, it was marred by a stagebound quality: "There is simply no cinematic movement in it. Each fade out and time-lapse title has the effect of a curtain falling and an entr'act, and each episode is as distinctly a set and separate scene as if it were being done on a stage."

At the same time a German-language version utilizing the same cast and sets was directed by Jacques Feyder. It is purportedly less stagy than the Clarence Brown picture, and, because censorial restrictions were not as severe in Europe, Anna's past history as a prostitute is more frankly depicted.

REFERENCES

"Anna Christie," *Photoplay*, 25:2 (January 1924), 68; "Anna Christie," *Exceptional Photoplays*, 4:1–2 (October–November 1923), 1–2; Clark, Barrett H., *Eugene O'Neill: The Man and His Plays* (New York: Dover Publications, 1947); Hamilton, James Shelley, "Anna Christie," *Cinema*, 1:3 (April 1930), 37; Tibbetts, John C., *The American Theatrical Film* (Bowling Green, Ohio: Bowling Green State University Press, 1985).

—*J.C.T.*

ANNE OF THE THOUSAND DAYS (1948)

MAXWELL ANDERSON (1888–1959)

Anne of the Thousand Days (1969), U.S.A., directed by
　　Charles Jarrott, adapted by Bridget Boland and
　　John Hale; Universal.

The Play

Maxwell Anderson wrote poetic dramas that succeeded to a remarkable degree in the Broadway commercial theatre. Writing in verse and prose, he produced romances, fantasies, social protest dramas, tragedies, comedies, and histories. His many verse histories included *Elizabeth the Queen* (1930), *Mary of Scotland* (1933), *Valley Forge* (1934), and *Anne of the Thousand Days* (1948). This two-act drama premiered in New York at the Shubert Theatre on December 8, 1948, and it ran for a successful 288 performances. The historical outlines of the story are well known: The setting is England during the years 1526 to 1536. The action begins as Anne Boleyn, Henry's second wife, awaits her execution. Flashbacks recount her experiences: Henry VIII (Rex Harrison) is weary of both his wife, Queen Catherine, and his mistress, Mary Boleyn.

Preferring Mary's younger sister, Anne (Joyce Redman), he determines to divorce Catherine and marry Anne, even if he must split from the Church of Rome to do so. His most stubborn opponent, however, is not the Church, but Anne herself. She prefers to marry Percy, earl of Northumberland (Robert Duke). Henry removes Percy from his way by forcing him to marry someone else; and Anne, somewhat to her astonishment, finds herself falling in love with Henry. But upon the birth of a daughter, Elizabeth, the ever-fickle king decides that Jane Seymour would give him a male heir. Confronted with the choice of exile or death, Anne elects to die. Henry is stricken with remorse. "It would have been easier," he realizes, "to forget you living than to forget you dead." The blank-verse drama was a theatrical history play characterized by gusto, humor, and tragedy. However, as historian Antonia Fraser has noted, of any historically accurate political significance there was little (a few murmurs about the dissolution of the monasteries have to stand in for the whole process of the Reformation). Anne's own commitment to reformist Protestant doctrines, which made her a female of noted independence and originality in her own time, is entirely omitted.

The Film

The circumstances concerning Henry VIII's infamous serial marriages have been the stuff of many films, most notably Alexander Korda's *The Private Life of Henry VIII* (1933) and *A Man for All Seasons* (1966). *Anne of the Thousand Days*, as derived from the Anderson play, concentrates only on the relationship between Henry and Anne Boleyn. The screen adaptation by Bridget Boland and John Hale lays heavy emphasis throughout on the king's need of a son "to give the land peace after I am gone," as he observes more than once. However, Henry is assumed *already* to be searching for a son when he falls in love with Anne Boleyn (a presumption for which there is no historical evidence). Likewise, there is no historical evidence that Henry sees his marriage to the darkly melancholy Irene Pappas (her Greek accent standing in for a Spanish accent) as "accursed." The screenplay makes drastic cuts in the play's long speeches and dispenses with prologues and epilogues to each act. It begins with Henry (Richard Burton) reluctantly signing Anne's death warrant. The rest of the action is related in a series of flashbacks.

Anne (Genevieve Bujold) is portrayed as a skilled politician, who states that "power is as exciting as love." Catherine of Aragon (Irene Pappas), who does not appear in the play, here appears to refuse Henry his divorce—a decision that parallels Anne's similar refusal

Richard Burton

later in the play. After their marriage and Anne's failure to provide Henry with a son, Henry turns to Jane Seymour (Lesley Paterson) at court; and Anne, as Catherine had done at the beginning of the film, leaves Henry in disgust. These two parallel events function to tighten the plot structure, and they also suggest that Henry's actions are ultimately futile—that "what goes around comes around." Additional screen time is devoted to the efforts of Cromwell (John Colicos) to frame Anne and to the trial scenes. At the film's end Henry is hunting outside London while Anne approaches the execution site. When he learns of Anne's death, Henry and his party head for Jane Seymour's home. In an ironic footnote the young Elizabeth (Katharine Blake) is seen posing before a mirror and pretending to be queen of England.

Producer Hal B. Wallis's taste for historical epics (*Mary, Queen of Scots*) is everywhere in evidence. The set re-creations of Hampton Court and Hever Castle are lavish and majestic, and the choice of Genevieve Bujold was an inspiration. Her appearance carefully matched extant portraits of Anne and her French accent was correct because the real Anne had been educated in France (a distinction, says historian Antonia Fraser, that gave her an additional allure in the eyes of the English court). Of Richard Burton's performance, however, critic Pauline Kael had substantial reservations: "Burton's performance is colorless. It's as though he *remembered* how to act but couldn't work up much enthusiasm or involvement."

The film received many Oscar nominations, including best picture, best screenplay, best musical score (Georges Delerue), best actor, and best actress.

REFERENCES

Bragg, Melvyn, *Richard Burton: A Life* (Boston: Little, Brown, 1988); Fraser, Antonia, *Past Imperfect: History According to the Movies* (New York: Henry Holt, 1995).

—*J.C.T.*

ANTIGONE (c. 442 B.C.)

SOPHOCLES (496?–406 B.C.)

Antigone (1961), Greece, directed and adapted by George Tzavellas; Finos.

The Cannibals [*I Cannibali*] (1970), Italy, directed by Liliana Cavani, adapted by Cavani and Italo Moscati; Doria Films/San Marco Films.

The Play

Antigone is the final increment in the cycle of Theban plays that began with *Oedipus the King*. From *Oedipus at Colonus*, the second play in the cycle, those familiar with the Oedipus story will recall that his sons, Polyneices and Eteocles, waged war against each other for control of Thebes, a power struggle dramatized by Aeschylus in his play *Seven Against Thebes* (467 B.C.), and that the brothers killed each other in battle. Creon has become king and rules that Eteocles, the defender of Thebes, shall have an honorable burial, but that Polyneices, who led the invading army, will be left to rot.

The play is built upon a conflict between Antigone and King Creon concerning burial rites for Antigone's

brother, Polyneices. Since Creon regards Polyneices as a traitor and has decreed that he should not be properly buried as a consequence of his insurrection, Antigone is outraged because, according to Greek belief, she knows that the soul of her brother will not immediately enter the underworld without the requisite burial rites. She regards Creon's decree as a sacrilege.

At the beginning of the play Antigone tells her sister Ismene that she intends to perform the burial rites herself, in defiance of Creon. Ismene, a dramatic foil to her strong-willed sister, attempts to persuade Antigone not to go forward with her plans, saying "we were both born women, who should not strive with men" and it is "foolish to meddle" in such affairs. Ismene is frightened and will not cooperate in this burial scheme, but she promises to keep it a secret. Antigone sprinkles dirt over the body to release her brother's soul. When Creon learns of the ritual burial, he is incensed and vows recriminations.

Unbending in her idealism and self-righteous stance, Antigone is captured and brought before Creon. Even though Antigone is betrothed to his own son, Haemon, Creon condemns Antigone to death. Haemon argues with Creon to spare her life, but Creon is as unbending as Antigone was, no doubt because he fears that his authority may be undercut if he reverses his decree. Antigone is taken to an underground cell, where she will be left to die. The seer Tiresias sides with Antigone and advises Creon that the gods require the burial of Polyneices and prophesies that Creon will suffer in retribution for his crime and that members of his family will die.

Creon finally decides to reverse his decree, to bury Polyneices, and then intends to free Antigone, but his reversal comes too late. A messenger reports that when Creon went to release Antigone after the burial, he found that she had hanged herself. Mourning her death, Haemon curses his father and attempts to kill him, then falls on his sword. Grieving the death of Haemon and blaming her husband, Creon's wife Eurydice kills herself, leaving Creon devastated.

The Films

The first adaptation of *Antigone* was made in 1961 by George Tzavellas, who later served as director of the Greek Film Center until his death in 1976. The film was shot in black and white, in and around Athens, in keeping with the director's intention to "naturalize" the stylized action of ritual drama. The first challenge was to make the Chorus as unobtrusive as possible. The problem is that his solution tended to fragment the choric function. Reports of the terrible consequences of Creon's stubbornness that Sophocles designated to a messenger are cut, and this off-stage action is dramatized and filmed. Reviewer Penelope Gilliatt praised the way Tzavellas "put a gag on the Chorus without sacrificing anything interesting that it had to say," but, as Kenneth MacKinnon objected, "interesting" is the key word here, and for Gilliatt it appears only "to signify elements that relate to [the film's] narrative thrust." It is, of course, the function of the Chorus to comment on the obvious in guiding the audience through the action, the Chorus being one of the central components of Greek ritual drama.

Adapting Greek drama involves more than mere visual storytelling. Writing for *The Sunday Times* of London (April 14, 1963), Dilys Powell described the problem posed for any director attempting to film Greek tragedy. A choice has to be made between "complete liberation from the conventions of the theatre" and "performance in the manner of the classical stage." If a play is wrenched too far out of its theatrical context and ritualistic imperatives, the nature of the dramatic experience is likely to be transformed. As MacKinnon defined the problem in his book *Greek Tragedy into Film*, the fundamental question "is whether showing something by visual means is equivalent to verbal description." The messenger in *Antigone* speaks from a distinctive point of view and that component will be lost if his report is simply filmed.

Liliana Cavani's *The Cannibals* is more a derivative than an adaptation of Sophocles' play, but the director held a degree in classics and no doubt fully understood what she was doing. This is not a faithful reproduction of the play, but rather, in the words of unfriendly critics such as Derek Elley, who reviewed the film for *Films and Filming*, a "distortion" that was "unforgivable." Piles of corpses litter the streets of Milan, and the carnage seems not to bother the middle-class citizens. With the help of Tiresias (Pierre Clementi), Antigone (Britt Ekland) takes her brother's body to the beach for the symbolic burial, then returns to remove a second and then a third corpse. Her concern goes beyond mere kinship, as MacKinnon points out, "replaced with a broader concern for human dignity." In this adaptation Tiresias is not blind, nor is he fluent in Italian. There is a muted quality to this production, which depends on significant, silent cinematic exchanges. Antigone's confrontation of Haemon's father (Francesco Leonetti), for example, strips away the eloquent rhetoric of Sophocles. "There is no pleading, not even an explanation," MacKinnon explains, adding: "Only in the confrontation between

Haemon (Thomas Milian) and his father are echoes of the Sophoclean argument permitted to be heard," making this exchange the "most powerful, and Sophoclean, scene in the film." After this exchange, Haemon is imprisoned and degenerates into madness.

Though he fully understands that *The Cannibals* is not really *Antigone*, MacKinnon defends the film, interpreting it as an allegory about political action and bourgeois indifference to death and suffering. There are so many corpses to be buried that the task that Antigone and Tiresias undertake is absurd, but they do what they can, setting a moral example. After they have been executed, others who were considered lunatics "begin to gather up corpses, climbing up a hillside with the bodies in the same dogged, defiant manner" as the young people had done. The events of May 1968 and the protesting of the war in Vietnam inform the film's presentation of Antigone, herself the well-bred daughter of bourgeois parents, who revolts against them and their middle-class values: "While there are bourgeois cannibals," MacKinnon concludes, "the state, even as repressive as it is represented to be here, is not beyond rescue," offering "a glimmer of hope through the resistance of the devout to secular and secularizing authority."

REFERENCES

Elley, Derek, "The Cannibals," *Films and Filming*, 22:4 (1974), 35; Gassner, John and Edward Quinn, *The Reader's Encyclopedia of World Drama* (New York: Thomas Y. Crowell, 1969); MacKinnon, Kenneth, *Greek Tragedy into Film* (London: Croom Helm, 1986); Schuster, Mel, *The Contemporary Greek Cinema* (Metuchen, N.J.: Scarecrow Press, 1979).

—*J.M.W.*

ARSENIC AND OLD LACE (1941)

JOSEPH KESSELRING (1902–1967)

Arsenic and Old Lace (1942), U.S.A., directed by Frank Capra, adapted by Julius J. and Philip G. Epstein; Warner Bros.

The Play

Of his dozen or so plays, Joseph Kesselring's *Arsenic and Old Lace* (1941) is by far his most popular. He originally conceived it as a serious thriller, entitled *Bodies in Our Cellar*. It premiered in New York at the Fulton Theatre on January 10, 1941, and ran for a spectacular 1,444 performances. The venerable team of Howard Lindsay and Russel Crouse (*Life with Father*, 1939; *State of the Union*, 1945) produced the play, and it is they who were responsible for converting it into a madcap dark comedy. Two nice, sweet old ladies, Abby Brewster (Josephine Hull) and her sister Martha (Jean Adair), occupy their time by murdering lonely old men. They invite them to their home and then lace their elderberry wine drinks with a little arsenic. They bury the bodies in the cellar with the aid of their dotty brother, Teddy (John Alexander), whose resemblance to Teddy Roosevelt has developed into an obsession (he periodically leads an imaginary "charge" up the stairway, believing it to be San Juan Hill). He believes his cellar excavations to be preparations for the digging of the Panama Canal. One day the Brewsters' nephew Jonathan (Boris Karloff) arrives, accompanied by the mysterious Dr. Einstein (Edgar Stehli). They are both murderers, and the corpse of their latest victim is deposited in the sisters' window seat. Meanwhile, another nephew, Mortimer (Allyn Joslyn), a drama critic engaged to marry Elaine Harper and who appears to be the only sane member of the family, learns of these activities and determines to commit the family to a mental institution. However, when he learns that he in reality is not a family member but an adopted child, Mortimer departs in obvious relief. The sisters, meanwhile, are left alone with a representative from the asylum, and the play ends as they offer him a glass of their elderberry wine. Writer/critic Richard Lockridge of the *New York Sun* wrote that the play was a "noisy, preposterous, incoherent joy," adding, "You wouldn't believe that homicidal mania could be such great fun."

The Film

After the relative box-office disappointment of *Meet John Doe*, Frank Capra looked for a more commercial property, and he signed a deal with Jack Warner to direct an adaptation of the phenomenally successful *Arsenic and Old Lace*. On the one hand, it might seem an odd choice from a man whose socially conscious work, like *Mr. Deeds Goes to Town* (1936) and *Mr. Smith Goes to Washington* (1939), had become his trademark; but when one considers that Capra had also directed another theatrical adaptation, *You Can't Take It With You* (1938), about another eccentric family, the zany Sycamores—not to mention the "pixilated" sisters in *Mr. Deeds*—the chance to direct another comedy about a homicidally inclined family does not seem so inappropriate. "Hell, I owe myself a picture like this," he declared. "I'm not going to try to reform anybody. It'll be a picture without a sermon, and I'm going to have a lot of fun. . . . For a long time now I've been preaching

one thing or another. Why, I haven't had a real good time since *It Happened One Night*." Biographer Joseph McBride sees other, darker motives behind Capra's decision. Perhaps he saw yet another chance to poke fun at Yankee society in the guise of the "respectable" Brewsters. Moreover, perhaps he enjoyed the story's implications of insanity in the Roosevelt lineage: "Teddy Brewster, who thinks he is President Theodore Roosevelt, confides that he is planning to run for a third term, like his distant relative FDR, 'if the country insists'; Mortimer even tells him, 'the name Brewster is code for Roosevelt.'" At any rate, *Arsenic and Old Lace* was to be Capra's last theatrical film until after the war. He enlisted in the army a few days after Pearl Harbor.

Due to the original play's extraordinary long run, the film, which had been shot between October 20 and December 16, 1941, was held up until 1943 when it was released to the military around the world. It did not receive a theatrical release until September 1944. Reprising their stage roles were Josephine Hull and Jean Adair as the sisters, and John Alexander as the bugle-blowing Teddy. Because Boris Karloff's continued presence in the stage play was deemed necessary, Capra had to content himself with casting Raymond Massey in the role of Jonathan. The film opens with the title, "This transpires in Brooklyn, where anything can happen and usually does." Frantic farce replaces the play's saucy satire, and the action is propelled at an exhausting pace. Much of the underlying frenzy turns on Mortimer's (Cary Grant) fear of inheriting his family's psychoses. In a significant alteration from the play, Mortimer has already married Elaine (Priscilla Lane), and a resulting undercurrent of sexual frustration runs through the film, since he cannot enjoy his honeymoon until he resolves the problems in his family and establishes his own state of (in)sanity. "Insanity runs in my family," he says, "—it practically gallops!" The play's ambiguous ending is also cleaned up—Teddy, Abby, and Martha are all duly committed, and Mortimer prepares to enjoy his honeymoon at last. Unfortunately missing from the film—due to censorship—was the play's funniest line, when Mortimer, relieved upon learning he is illegitimate (and not the inheritor of the Brewster insanity), declares to Elaine, "Darling, I'm a bastard!" Instead, he says in the film, "I'm not really a Brewster, *I'm the son of a sea cook!*"

Critics and biographers, then and now, are divided about the film's merits. "Under Capra's tutelage," opined Herb Sterne in *Rob Wagner's Script* at the time of the film's release, "the players comport themselves as though they were appearing in a Deep South touring troupe of *The Bat*. No holds are barred in corning the comedic capers, and poor Cary Grant has been wheedled into providing a mugfest the likes of which hasn't affronted a camera since Wally Beery ceased delineating Swedish serving maids for dear old Essanay." By contrast, biographers Charles Maland and Joseph McBride find much to admire in the picture.

REFERENCES

Maland, Charles J., *Frank Capra* (Boston: Twayne, 1980); McBride, Joseph, *Frank Capra: The Catastrophe of Success* (New York: Simon and Schuster, 1992); Sterne, Herb, "Arsenic and Old Lace," reprinted in Anthony Slide, ed., *Selected Film Criticism: 1941–1950* (Metuchen, N.J.: Scarecrow Press, 1983), 7–8.

—*J.C.T.*

ATTACK!

See *FRAGILE FOX*

BAREFOOT IN THE PARK (1963)

NEIL SIMON (1927–)

Barefoot in the Park (1967), U.S.A., directed by Gene Saks, adapted by Neil Simon; Paramount.

The Play

Neil Simon's second full-length play (and one of his most popular) premiered in New York at the Biltmore Theatre on October 23, 1963, and ran for a spectacular 1,530 performances. Coming after the success of *Come Blow Your Horn*, it confirmed Simon's mastery of character-driven comedy. The story focuses on newly-weds Corie (Elizabeth Ashley) and Paul Bratter (Robert Redford), characters trying to cope with their unheated walkup apartment, a scatterbrained mother-in-law, and a romantically disreputable neighbor. Corie is "lovely, young, and full of hope for the future." Paul, on the other hand, is a sedate, rather stuffy young man trying to make a start as a lawyer. Corie and Paul appear to be madly in love, doting on each other after a glorious honeymoon at the Plaza Hotel. However, complications ensue when Corie inadvertently invites her mother, Mrs. Banks (Mildred Natwick), and Mr. Velasco (Kurt Kasznar), a neighbor, to dinner on the same night. The affair is a fiasco, and it accounts for most of the dramatic action. Unable to cook dinner after discovering that the oven doesn't work, the quartet ends up in a crazy Albanian restaurant in Staten Island. Paul is the only one who doesn't enjoy the evening. Corie becomes frustrated with Paul, accuses him of being unable to loosen up, and decides that she wants a divorce. However, after she witnesses a drunken Paul dancing barefoot in the park and her mother arriving in Mr. Velasco's bathrobe the next morning, she comes to appreciate her new husband's quiet demeanor and realizes that she truly loves him.

Most critics found the play mild and disposable, noting Simon's witty, acerbic one-liners as the major strength of an otherwise forgettable situation comedy. Many jokes are mined from the apartment's location, six flights up by stairway. The gags deriving from cramped city living can be appreciated by anyone who has had a similar experience in modern urban sprawl. Commentator Sheila Ennis Geitner observes that "beneath Simon's delightful craftsmanship is the writer's statement: successful relationships are built upon compromise and tolerance."

The Film

The play was transferred to film relatively intact. Simon adapted his own play, Robert Redford and Mildred Natwick reprised their roles, and Gene Saks directed. Jane Fonda, still something of a newcomer to film, took on the role of Corie. Unlike the play, the film depicts the Bratters' honeymoon, and treats view-

Neil Simon

ers to a tour of New York City. When Paul finally goes back to work, we begin to appreciate how different these newlyweds really are (apart from a shared enthusiasm for sex). The slow pacing of these opening scenes quickens with the appearance of Corie's mother (Natwick), whose difficulties in negotiating the apartment's six flights of stairs provide some genuinely funny gags ("I thought I'd died and gone to heaven, but I had to climb the stairs"). Fonda and Redford acquit themselves admirably, especially as their marital situation grows more complicated. Both learn to compromise to make their marriage work. Unfortunately, the story's rather naïve worldview would soon be rendered obsolete in the 1960s by the renegade realism of New Hollywood films such as *Easy Rider* and *Bonnie and Clyde*.

REFERENCES

Geitner, Sheila Ennis, "Neil Simon," in John MacNicholas, ed., *Twentieth-Century American Dramatists* (Detroit: Gale Research Company, 1981); McGovern, Edyth M., *Neil Simon: A Critical Study* (New York: Frederick Ungar, 1978).

—*J.A.*

BECKET, OR THE HONOR OF GOD (1959)

JEAN ANOUILH (1910–1987)

Becket (1964), U.S.A., directed by Peter Glenville, adapted by Edward Anhalt; Paramount.

The Play

The action of the play centers on the character and career of Saint Thomas à Becket, the archbishop of Canterbury murdered in his cathedral by four knights of the court of King Henry II on December 29, 1170. Anouilh, well aware of T. S. Eliot's handling of the same story in his *Murder in the Cathedral* and not a religious man, treats the story as personal and political rather than as religious and moral, choosing to emphasize the friendship between Henry and Becket over the martyr's internal struggle. The issue for Henry is love, not power, while Becket's primary motive is to play his social role well, which means to serve his master, whether Henry or God. Besides its representation of a compelling historical conflict, the play and the film made from it are appealing because they directly address the question of homosocial male love at a time when most men on stage or in films were required to be laconic and stoic.

Anouilh based his understanding of the conflict between king and archbishop on an old-fashioned history book, *The Conquest of England by the Normans*, by Augustin Thierry, which he happened to buy from a Parisian *bouquiniste*. Only after the play was completed did Anouilh discover that his source had misled him on a crucial point: According to Thierry, Becket was a Saxon and thus one of the native races conquered by the Normans in 1066, when in fact Becket was more Norman than Henry II. Because the Saxon-Norman tensions in England at the time made the relationship between the two men—to each other and to their society—more fraught (and because the specter of collaboration had a deep resonance for the French), Anouilh left it in. The play's other historical inaccuracies, most strikingly its representation of Henry's wife and mother, have presumably been introduced to heighten the drama and provide a basis for Henry's bond to Becket by showing how unsatisfying his other relationships are. Anouilh answered those who criticized his infidelity to history by saying, "I didn't look in any book to find out who Henry II really was, nor even Becket. I created the king I needed, and the ambiguous Becket I needed."

Becket is one of three plays Anouilh called "costume dramas"; the others deal with Joan of Arc and with Napoleon's 100 days. All three plays emphasize the conflict between one's ideals and one's desire for worldly comfort and happiness. In *Becket* friendship is unable to survive the clash between ideals and political realities. It is much too simple to link Henry to political necessity and Becket to noble idealism: Each is marked by a hope to create a perfect world in which his desires can be balanced, and each man is disappointed. Henry becomes a hardened cynic, and Becket becomes a martyr and a saint.

The Broadway version of the play starred Anthony Quinn as Henry and Laurence Olivier as Becket. After 200 performances, Quinn left the play, Arthur Kennedy took over the role of Becket, and Olivier switched to playing Henry. Olivier's interpretation of Henry introduced the idea that Henry had a homosexual attraction for Becket, and this interpretation influenced that of Peter O'Toole, who played Henry in the film.

Becket begins as Henry is about to undergo penance at the site of Becket's tomb. His conversation with Becket's ghost sets up a flashback that introduces us to Becket as Henry's friend and adviser, sketches out the conflict between church and state, shows us how Becket tries to serve his prince once he has been made chancellor, and the cost of that service, as Henry exercises his power to take Becket's mistress, a Welsh woman who commits suicide. In the second act, Henry makes Becket archbishop, seeking to resolve the conflict by investing his friend with the highest civil and ecclesiastical authority in the land. Becket warns Henry that this idea will not work, but happily reinvents himself as a cleric. In the third act, Becket resigns as chancellor. Henry, feeling betrayed, conspires with Becket's enemies to force Becket's removal as archbishop by charging him with embezzlement and fraud. Here the action widens to include the court of Louis VII of France, who gives Becket asylum, and Pope Alexander III, who plays Becket and Henry off against each other. The act ends when Becket decides that he can serve God best by leaving his harsh exile at a French convent and returning to England.

In the final act, Louis brokers a peace between Henry and Becket. At a poignant but tense meeting, Becket agrees to most of Henry's conditions, but refuses to give up the major prerogatives of his posi-

tion. Although these key issues remain unresolved, Henry permits Becket to return to England. Shortly thereafter, the Queen Mother's needling about his unwholesome love for Becket drives Henry into a drunken fit of temper during which he incites four of his barons to "rid him of this meddlesome priest." The play ends cynically, as Henry accepts a whipping as his penance, declares his desire to secure sainthood for Becket, and appoints one of the murderers to investigate the crime.

The Film

The adaptation of *Becket* is very faithful, as might be expected, since Peter Glenville, who directed the film, also directed the Broadway play. The screenplay, which won an Oscar for adaptation for Edward Anhalt, is intelligent and witty. In general it is less talky than the play and rearranges the order of its episodes to simplify the plot and heighten dramatic tension. It also makes Becket's motives less opaque than the play does and presents Henry as more manly, more kingly, and somewhat less cynical.

For example, two key events in the play—Becket's appearance at his trial and his resignation as chancellor—are merely reported to Henry (and thus to us) secondhand by pages and messengers. In the film, Becket's challenge to Henry's justice is directly presented to us. His resignation as chancellor is made much more moving because he returns the Great Seal of England directly to Henry, which allows Henry the opportunity to express his feelings of betrayal and rejection directly to Becket's face while simultaneously allowing us to see that Becket's choices have painful consequences for him as well. While several different churchmen in the play criticize Becket's behavior as chancellor and as archbishop, the film gives most of those speeches to the bishop of London, which positions him as a more powerful antagonist and makes Henry's use of him as an ambassador, and as a participant in his scheme to use false charges of embezzlement to force Becket to resign his office, more dangerous. As the end of the story approaches, the film, unlike the play, makes it clear that Henry stays in France when Becket returns to England. Becket's death is slow and graphic, but not as violent as in the play, where the stage directions say that the knights "hack at his body, grunting like woodcutters."

At the very end, the film tries to soften the audience's feelings toward Henry. He looks sternly at the four barons and says "We will *all* have to do penance," instead of appointing them to investigate their own crime. Finally his announcement to the Saxon peasants that the pope has made Becket a saint is followed, rather than preceded, by Henry's taking a quiet moment alone by Becket's tomb to ask, "Is the honor of God washed clean enough? Are you satisfied now, Thomas?" Instead of ending with Henry in front of cheering Saxon crowds, having used Becket's death to strengthen his hold on the English peasantry, a hold that we have already seen is far from advantageous to the peasants, the film ends with Henry walking alone through the huge, dark, and empty cathedral.

The film also presents a gentler picture of the other power players in the story. Louis VII does not state his weather-vane sense of political expediency as openly as the French king in the play does. The pope seems much less Machiavellian since the suspicions of insincerity and cynical political tactics that mark the character in the play are expressed in the film by his cardinals.

The casting of the film presented two towering British actors at a time when America was rediscovering its awe of the British stage tradition. Both Richard Burton, who played Becket, and Peter O'Toole, who played Henry II, were at the height of their beauty and fame: Burton had just stolen Elizabeth Taylor from Eddie Fisher and sailed down the Nile with her, and O'Toole had just emerged from T.E. Lawrence's desert. Burton and O'Toole became fast friends, and their pleasure in each other's company off the set gave an added sparkle to their scenes together. Both the film and the play cast the taller of the two actors as Henry while in reality Becket would have been the taller man, probably because the size difference was a good analogue to the political power held by each man. Both the play and the film used actors of approximately the same age, although Becket in reality was 16 years older than Henry, to strengthen the bond between them and to emphasize the men's youthful friendship.

The film was beautifully photographed (its cinematographer, Geoffrey Unsworth, received an Oscar nomination and a BAFTA award), and its use of the castles and landscape of Northumberland was one of the pleasures of the film. Anouilh was far from being a realist, and the sketchy set design of the play, in which columns stand for all the settings, becomes much more weighty in the film, which is set in real buildings. These large settings allow the film to emphasize the spectacle of court and cathedral life, and we have several scenes of rituals and processions that do not appear in the play and that make tangible the weight and power of these two great medieval institutions. For example, while Henry has only to point his finger to make Becket a nobleman and creates him chancellor simply by giving him a ring, Becket's consecration as primate of England and his excommunication of one of Henry's barons are both shown at length. We are also shown crowds of people—Saxon peasants, chapters of monks, groups of barons—that continually remind us that the loves and hatreds of Henry and Becket have application outside themselves in a way that the play was not always able to do.

Despite its rather dry historical theme *Becket* was a critical and commercial success. The film's popularity kicked off a 1960s vogue for high drama in the Middle Ages, and its release was followed by three other films that, like *Becket*, combined colorful spectacle, manly conflict based on principle and expressed through elevated language rather than through arms, and high intelligence and wit: *A Man for All Seasons* (1966), about the conflict between Thomas More and Henry VIII; *The Lion in Winter* (1968), a continuation of Henry's story focusing on his family relationships toward the end of his reign in which O'Toole played Henry again; and *Anne of the Thousand Days* (1969), a life of Anne Boleyn in which Burton played Henry VIII.

REFERENCES

Falb, Lewis W., *Jean Anouilh* (New York: Frederick Ungar, 1977); Harvey, John, *Anouilh: A Study in Theatrics* (New Haven: Yale University Press, 1964); Jones, Thomas M., *The Becket Controversy* (New York: John Wiley, 1970); Vandromme, Pol, *Jean Anouilh: Un auteur et ses personnages* (Paris: La Table Ronde, 1965).

—*S.C.*

BELL, BOOK, AND CANDLE (1950)

JOHN VAN DRUTEN (1901–1957)

Bell, Book, and Candle (1958), U.S.A., directed by Richard Quine, adapted by Daniel J. Taradash; Columbia.

The Play

London-born John Van Druten is best known for his comedies *I Remember Mama* (1944), *Bell, Book, and Candle* (1950), and *The Voice of the Turtle* (1943), in addition to his more serious plays, including *I Am A Camera* (1951). The three-act *Bell, Book, and Candle* premiered in New York at the Ethel Barrymore Theatre on November 14, 1950, and ran for a successful 234 performances. The action is set entirely in Gillian Holroyd's (Lili Palmer) apartment. When a young

BENT

publisher, Shep Henderson (Rex Harrison), accosts Gillian to complain about the behavior of her eccentric Aunt Queenie, he does not realize that Gillian and Queenie, and Gillian's brother Nicky, are witches. Gillian instantly is attracted to Shep and uses her powers to eliminate any rivals for her suit, including a woman named Merle. She casts a spell on Shep, and he promptly falls in love with her and cancels his wedding plans with Merle. Shep, in the meantime, suspects something downright infernal in his girl friend, and he is aghast when Nicky reveals the family's witcherly attributes. Disturbed by the news, Shep determines to leave. But Gillian contracts with another witch, Mrs. De Pass, to be "cured" of her powers. When she blushes and cries, Shep is convinced that she is no longer a witch and that she genuinely does love him. The *New York Times* described the play as "completely enchanting . . . a wonderfully suave and impish fancy." Subsequent road shows toured successfully with Rosalind Russell and Dennis Price, and with Joan Bennett and Zachary Scott.

The Film

While the film adaptation retains most of the play's dialogue, it also opens up the action to include scenes in Shep's office, Mrs. De Pass' "haunted house," and the Zodiac Club, where the witches hold their meetings. The character of Merle (Janice Rule), who does not appear on stage in the play, is also added to the cast. James Stewart portrays Shep, Kim Novak is Gillian, Jack Lemmon is Nicky, Elsa Lanchester is Queenie, Hermione Gingold is Mrs. De Pass, and Ernie Kovacs plays Sidney Redditch, a self-promoting "expert" on witchcraft. Despite what *Variety* called a "dream cast," this entertaining comedy fell short of box-office expectations. The pairing of Jimmy Stewart and Kim Novak after their successful roles in Alfred Hitchcock's *Vertigo* (1958) caused *Variety* to predict "hefty box-office returns," but, *Variety* added, "the light mood of comedy occasionally becomes as heavy as a witch's curse," perhaps because Novak was not "equipped for light comedy," even though *The Motion Picture Herald* considered this film her "best effort."

REFERENCES

Widener, Don, *Lemmon: A Biography* (New York: Macmillan, 1975); Gow, Gordon, *Hollywood in the Fifties* (New York: A.S. Barnes, 1971); Kleno, Larry, *Kim Novak on Camera* (San Diego: A.S. Barnes, 1980).

—*J.C.T. AND J.M.W.*

BENT (1979)

SHERMAN, MARTIN (1938–)

Bent (1997), U.K./Japan, directed by Sean Mathias, adapted by Martin Sherman; Channel Four Films/Nippon Film Development and Finance/ Goldwyn Entertainment Co./MGM Distribution Co.

The Play

Considering the fact that by 1994 only 15 testimonies of surviving gay witnesses from Nazi concentration camps had been collected, Martin Sherman deserves much credit for bringing to public attention the fact that thousands of gay men were persecuted and killed by the Nazis. A conservative estimate suggests that in the concentration camps 10,000 to 15,000 gay men wore the pink triangle designating them as homosexuals. The numbers persecuted may have run into the hundreds of thousands.

The action begins on the Night of the Long Knives, June 30, 1934, when Hitler purged Ernst Roehm, leader of the SA, the Storm Troopers. Roehm was a known and blatant homosexual, and while he was being murdered in southern Germany, hundreds of his followers were killed or arrested in Berlin. Max, an emotionally shallow gay man from a rich family, is targeted in the persecution, for he has just picked up at a bar a handsome SA trooper. Unable to get help from Grete, the club owner and a transvestite, Max flees with his roommate and lover, Rudy. Living on the run, Max refuses to leave Germany alone when his rich uncle Freddie offers a passport to Amsterdam for him only but not Rudy. The two gay men are arrested and taken on a train to Dachau. To save his own life Max assists the Nazis' murder of Rudy. He is befriended by Horst, a kind gay man who wears the pink triangle. In Dachau concentration camp, Max refuses to wear the pink triangle, claiming to be Jewish and wearing the Jewish yellow star instead.

Max is assigned the demoralizing job of hauling rocks. To keep from going crazy, he manages to get Horst to share the job with him. The men fall in love, and there is an extraordinary scene in which during their three minute "stand at attention" break they make love to each other only by whispered words. They each ejaculate without even touching themselves. Later Max has sex with a camp guard to get medicine for the sickly Horst. Horst is killed when he runs into the electric wire fence while retrieving his hat. Moved by Horst's example of love and dignity, Max finally assumes a gay identity. He places Horst's pink triangle on his chest and then commits suicide by running against the fence.

The Film

Although the film did not find general release in theatres in the United States, most of the reviews in cities where it was shown were positive. Playwright Sherman rewrote the play for the screen during a month-long rehearsal workshop with the film's director and cast. The challenge was to find the dramatic connection between Act One's setting of prewar Berlin and Act Two's setting of the concentration camp. "Most plays are claustrophobic," Sherman explained, "and that's why they are so hard to turn into films." Above all, he did not want to approach the drama simply as filmed theatre, because, he claimed, "if it is done really well, with impeccable acting, it can look like a definitive production of a play; and then, why would anybody want to do the play on stage again?" The director was stage director Sean Mathias—who is both gay and Jewish—in his first film project. (In 1990 he revived the play for the National Theatre in London with Ian McKellen as Uncle Freddie.) Clive Owen was cast as Max and Brian Webber as Rudy. Also in the cast were Mick Jagger, as the transvestite Grete (performing the unforgettable "The Streets of Berlin" while swinging on a trapeze), Sir Ian McKellen, who was a closeted Royal Shakespeare Company actor before he starred in the initial British stage production, as Uncle Freddie, Jude Law as a Nazi storm trooper, and Lothaire Bluteau, who stole the film as Horst. Music was by Philip Glass, whose minimalist repetitions were appropriate for the mindless repetitions of labor in the Dachau sequence. Glasgow locations in an abandoned power station served as the concentration camp setting.

Both film and play remain controversial for several reasons. Some have claimed that Sherman's play suggests that gays must be persecuted to death before they find the meaning of love and acceptance of gay identity—perhaps a wake-up call to urban gays of the 1970s who chose the sex and drugs circuit. Moreover, the AIDS crisis from 1980 onward gives the prison sex scene a totally different connotation today, since it is hard not to think of the scene as an unusual example of "safe sex."

REFERENCES

Bandon, Alexandra, "Thinking Past the Barriers to Making a Movie of 'Bent,'" *The New York Times*, November 30, 1997, sec. 2, 17–18; Clum, John, *Acting Gay: Male Homosexuality in Modern Drama* (New York: Columbia University Press, 1992); de Jongh, Nicholas, *Not in Front of the Audience: Homosexuality on Stage* (London: Routledge, 1992); Hammermeister, Kai, "Inventing History: Toward a Gay Holocaust Literature," *German Quarterly*, 70:1 (Winter 1997), 18–26; Heger, Heinz, *The Men with the Pink Triangle: The True, Life-and-Death Story of Homosexuals in the Nazi Death Camps*, rev. ed., trans. David Fernback (Boston: Alyson, 1994); Kimberly, Nick, "Review of *Bent*," *Sight and Sound*, n.s. 8:3 (March 1998), 39–40.

—P.C.

BETRAYAL (1978)

HAROLD PINTER (1930–)

Betrayal (1982), U.S.A./U.K., directed by David Jones, adapted by Harold Pinter; Horizon Pictures/20th Century-Fox International Classics.

The Play

Betrayal was the first play Harold Pinter wrote after the breakup of his marriage to Antonia Fraser. According to Michael Billington's biography of Pinter, it is based "even down to the general chronology and specific incidents—on an affair between Pinter and the greatly admired TV presenter and journalist Joan Bakewell that long predated his meeting with Antonia Fraser and lasted from 1962 to 1969." Pinter succinctly described the play as being "about a nine-year relationship between two men who are best friends."

In November of 1978 the play premiered in London in the National's Lyttelton Theatre production directed by Peter Hall and starring Michael Gambon and Penelope Wilton as the adulterous lovers, Jerry, a writer and agent, and Emma, who is married to Jerry's friend and publisher, Robert (David Massey). The action begins in 1977, when Jerry and Emma meet, two years after their affair has ended. The chronology of the play then moves backward in time to 1968 when a tipsy Jerry flirted with Emma while a party was in progress at Robert's house. The affair develops gradually until Jerry rents a flat for their assignations. After her betrayal has pretty well wrecked her marriage with Robert, the illicit romance fades and Emma distances herself from Jerry, perhaps because she begins to realize that Robert is far more subtle than Jerry. Organized into nine symmetrically arranged and interlocked scenes, the play is a marvel of construction.

Pinter explained that the play is "about various different kinds of betrayal," concerning "two friends, two

Harold Pinter's Betrayal *reached the screen with Jeremy Irons and Patricia Hodge.* (COURTESY TWENTIETH CENTURY-FOX)

men who have known each other for years and the wife of one of them who has had an affair with the friend of her husband. We see the story move from the point where it's all over right back to the point where they first met and the lover first declared his love for the lady." Of course, Pinter added, "you only see selected scenes because obviously you can't show everything that took place."

The Film

Producer Sam Spiegel saw the Broadway production of the play in New York (featuring Blythe Danner, Roy Scheider, and Raul Julia) early in 1980 and began negotiations with Pinter about filming a play that had only three characters "locked into an emotional situation which has taken control of their lives." Spiegel had known Pinter for over 20 years, and Pinter had written the screenplay for *The Last Tycoon*, which Spiegel had produced, so he offered Pinter the job of adapting his own play to film. Pinter approved of

Spiegel's choice of David Jones to direct the film. Born in Poole, Dorset, and educated at Christ's College, Cambridge, Jones had also taken a television training course with the British Broadcasting Corporation in London before becoming producer and editor of over 40 programs for the *Monitor Arts Magazine* television series. In 1964 Jones joined the Royal Shakespeare Company, where he worked for 13 years, first assisting Peter Hall. Jones later became company director of the Aldwych Theatre, the RSC London headquarters before RSC moved to the Barbicon Arts Centre, and finally was appointed artistic director of the Aldwych.

The film was shot on location in London and at Twickenham Studios in England. Robert's home was shot in St. Peter's Square, Hammersmith; for Jerry's home, a house in Kentish Town was chosen; Jerry and Emma's rented flat was on the top floor of a house in Kilburn; an appropriate pub was found in Shepherd's Bush, near Hammersmith. The cast consisted of top theatrical talents: Ben Kingsley (Robert), Patricia Hodge (Emma), Jeremy Irons (Jerry). David Jones had directed Jeremy Irons in a play Pinter adapted for BBC in 1977, *Langrishe Go Down*, and he later directed Ben Kingsley in Shakespeare's *Cymbeline* in 1979.

Despite the innovative design of the play, the direction is straightforward, even though the film closely follows the play's chronological reversals. The film adaptation of *Betrayal* begins with a shot outside the apartment where Robert and Emma live. After the guests leave, the camera, still outside the window, catches Emma cleaning up. No dialogue can be heard. Standing in the doorway, drink in hand, Robert apparently baits her. She moves toward him and slaps him; he slaps her back, hard. A little boy is seen in the kitchen, witnessing this reciprocal violence. The next scene takes the viewer to a pub outside city center (Shepherd's Bush), where Emma meets Jerry to tell him she is separating from her husband. "He's betrayed me for years. He told me everything, and I told him everything. It's all all over," she says, meaning her marriage, the friendship, and, presumably, the betrayal. In the next scene, however, Robert tells Jerry "she didn't tell me last night; she told me four years ago." When Jerry asks "Why didn't you tell me?" Robert answers: "Because you were my friend."

Although the film follows the text quite closely, Pinter added two scenes, one involving a telephone conversation between Robert and Jerry, with Robert inviting Jerry to lunch on the day Jerry is to meet Emma, and another in which Jerry and Emma examine the flat they are about to rent. Pinter took an active interest in the film production, visiting the sets and examining the rushes while the film was made. "I come to the sets and I watch and listen," Pinter told Alan Arnold. "I go to rushes almost every day. I've always been very closely involved in the films I've written. I suppose, in a sense, I'm not just a writer but a man of the theatre in a broad sense. For many years I've been involved both as an actor and director." Jones and Spiegel obviously valued Pinter's presence, and the screenplay, which Pinter himself reshaped, is as authoritative as any adaptation could be.

"It's the same work," Pinter told Leslie Bennetts: "Essentially I don't think it differs at all." But there are subtle differences in the film that deepen the texture of the play. David Jones's goal was to make the film "more human and more humorous" than the play had been. For example, the film opens up family situations and includes the children who are betrayed by their parents. "During the course of her affair," Bennetts noticed, "the woman has another baby; she tells her lover and later her husband that it is her husband's child," but Pinter leaves room for speculation and "corrosive doubt." At one point after Emma takes a telephone call from Jerry, she lies to her five-year-old child about who was calling.

The film is also effective in its technique, especially in the way it uses close-ups to punctuate the script's "Pinter pauses," when the playwright purposely uses silence to heighten emotional effect or irony. David Jones explained: "Fifty percent of the emotional impact of this piece is when people are not speaking; 50 percent of the actors' performances are on what their eyes are doing throughout." Ben Kingsley is especially masterful in his ability to convey such silent, semiotic nuances.

Pinter considered the play "dangerously cynical" and a "rather immoral piece." Sam Spiegel believes the film is less cynical and more moral in what it suggests about married love: "The trick is to convert love into some lasting friendship that overcomes the fading of passion," Spiegel told the *New York Times*. "But that requires an honest attitude on all parts, and since this was based on dishonesty, everyone betrayed the very nature of what love is about."

Pinter himself "felt we should try to put the center of gravity in the film on human feelings rather than philosophical attitudes." He saw the film as a morality play that would show "more anguish than the play does. You didn't see the pain on the stage. It was glib; we removed the glibness from it." Pinter wanted the audience to come out of the film thinking: "There but for the grace of God; this could have happened to me, my best friend, my wife." In the way the filmscript reinvented the play and in the way the actors performed it, the film can arguably be seen as an improvement as well as a splendid adaptation.

REFERENCES

Bennetts, Leslie, "On Film. Pinter's 'Betrayal' Displays New Subtleties," *The New York Times*, February 27, 1983, sec. 2, 1, 23; Billington, Michael, *The Life and Work of Harold Pinter* (London: Faber and Faber, 1996); Brown, John Russell, *A Short Guide to Modern British Drama* (London: Heinemann, 1982).

—*J.M.W.*

BIG KAHUNA, THE

See *HOSPITALITY SUITE*

THE BIG KNIFE (1949)

CLIFFORD ODETS (1906–1963)

The Big Knife (1955), U.S.A., directed by Robert Aldrich, adapted by James Poe; United Artists/Aldrich and Associates.

The Play

"Method" doyen Lee Strasberg directed the first stage production of *The Big Knife* at New York's National Theatre on February 24, 1949. It lasted for 108 performances. It had been eight years since Odets had last written for Broadway, in *Clash By Night* (1941). Featuring John Garfield in the role of actor Charlie Castle, *The Big Knife* was obviously based on the real-life experiences of its leading actor and playwright in the duplicitous world of Tinseltown. Castle lives in luxury in Beverly Hills, but his marriage is in trouble and his career is threatened by a scandal that is about to be spilled by a gossip columnist, Patty Benedict. Benedict threatens Castle's publicity agent, Buddy Bliss, with exposure of a past indiscretion unless he helps her confirm the Castle story. Meanwhile, Castle is struggling to decide whether to renew a contract with studio head Marcus Hoff, or to return to the New York stage. He decides to remain in Hollywood, to the disgust of his wife, Marion. Bad news quickly follows: It is revealed that Castle is, in fact, the author of the indiscretion that had been hitherto blamed on his agent, Buddy Bliss. In order to hide his guilt, he is advised by the studio to murder an incriminating witness, a lowly starlet. Castle, now riddled with guilt, commits suicide.

The play's critique of Hollywood mores aroused harsh criticism from columnist Hedda Hopper, after whom the character of Patty Benedict may have been modeled. Other critics accused Odets of sour-grapes recriminations against a Hollywood that he had grown to despise.

The Film

Perhaps because of its damning indictment of the Hollywood studio system, *The Big Knife* was not filmed by a major studio but by an independent production company under director Robert Aldrich. Since John Garfield had died of a heart attack in 1952 subsequent to continuing harassment by the House Un-American Activities Committee, director Robert Aldrich attempted in vain to interest several Hollywood stars, including Burt Lancaster, to play his role of Charlie Castle. It finally went to Jack Palance.

Like the play, the film interrogates the crisis of conscience afflicting popular Hollywood star Charlie Castle, who has betrayed his original talents by appearing in several mediocre films produced by the monstrous Stanley Hoff (Rod Steiger), a figure modeled on Louis B. Mayer and Harry Cohn. As in the play, Charlie wishes to avoid signing another long-term studio contract and instead to act in New York stage productions. However, the studio forces him to sign another 14-year contract by playing on his guilty feelings following a drunken hit-and-run accident involving the death of a child. The studio has covered up Charlie's involvement and arranged for his friend and associate Buddy Bliss to take the blame and go to jail on his behalf. When Charlie signs the contract Marion feels betrayed and plans to leave town with Hank Teagle, a writer and old friend. After experiencing further evidence of Hollywood inhumanity, Charlie commits suicide.

Although Aldrich and scenarist James Poe followed the original play closely, they had to tone down several politically sensitive subjects. Excised, for example, is Charlie's devotion to a number of artistic "rebels," ideologically taboo authors such as Jack London, Victor Hugo, Henrik Ibsen, and Upton Sinclair. Charlie's critical speech about postwar America in the play also disappears from the film version: "When I came home from Germany'. . I saw most of the war dead were here, not in Africa and Italy. And Roosevelt was dead . . . and the war was last week's snowball fight." Also absent from the film is the play's brief reference to Bel Air racism, involving a store's refusal to supply the Castles' black maid with the correct-size uniform. And due to Production Code

morality, Charlie's sexual liaison with Connie Bliss is barely suggested.

The film opens with shots of Bel Air accompanied by Richard Boone's voice-over commentary. "This is Bel Air, luxurious retreat of the wealthy and powerful. If you work in the motion picture industry and are successful, this is where you will probably make your home. Failure is not permitted here." This leads to a helicopter shot of Charlie training like a boxer (an obvious reference to John Garfield's role in *Body and Soul*, on which Aldrich acted as assistant director). The subsequent action is located, for the most part, in the interior of Charlie's home. Working under the pressure of a strict 16-day shooting schedule, Aldrich and cameraman Ernest Laszlo photographed the action in long takes with relatively little cutting.

Aldrich's biographers acclaim the film as "one of the most effective and biting satires yet made on Hollywood, more so than Odets' play, which today seems too serious and self-satisfied. Aldrich adds the necessary anger and outrageousness to bring the satire off." Odets also acclaimed the film as the best film version of any of his plays. However, commentator Gerald Weales contends that Odets had by now softened his attitudes toward Hollywood and was attempting to disclaim its more obviously satirical attacks. "This new play of mine is about certain moral facts," Odets said, "written as objectively as possible. It's not necessarily about Hollywood." Shortly before his death, Odets admitted, "At that time I had had California up to the neck and could never make peace with the place. Now I've learned to make peace with it."

REFERENCES

Arnold, Edwin T., and Eugene L. Miller, *The Films and Career of Robert Aldrich* (Knoxville: University of Tennessee Press, 1986); Silver, Alain, and James Ursini, *What Ever Happened to Robert Aldrich? His Life and His Films* (New York: Limelight Editions, 1995); Weales, Gerald, *Clifford Odets: Playwright* (New York: Pegasus, 1971); Wertheim, Albert, "Hollywood's Moral Landscape: Clifford Odets' *The Big Knife*," *American Drama*, 7:1 (1997), 67–81.

—*T.W.*

BIRDCAGE, THE

See *LA CAGE AUX FOLLES*

THE BIRTHDAY PARTY (1958)

HAROLD PINTER (1930–)

The Birthday Party (1968), U.K., directed by William Friedkin, adapted by Harold Pinter; Palomar.

The Play

Early plays by Harold Pinter, like *The Room* (1957) and *The Birthday Party* (1958), attest to the influence of writers like Luigi Pirandello and Samuel Beckett. Their evocation of terror, allied with farcical incidents and dialogue, have led reviewers to dub them "comedies of menace." *The Birthday Party* premiered in London at the Lyric Theatre in 1958. His first full-length play, it is a modern allegory that bears a resemblance to Beckett's *Waiting for Godot*. It has been interpreted, variously, as a man's descent into deadly conformity, and as a depiction of a man being "delivered" from life into death. In Act One we meet pianist Stanley Webber, who lives alone at a boardinghouse operated by old-age pensioner Petey Boles and his wife, Meg. Stanley confesses that he has been so traumatized after bad reviews of one of his concerts that he has now retreated from the world, convinced there is a conspiracy against his career. When two strangers, Nat Goldberg and Seamus McCann, arrive, they behave in a sinister, vaguely menacing way toward Stanley. Their wish to organize a birthday party for him is met with suspicion. In Act Two Goldberg and McCann use incessant and nonsensical word games to browbeat Stanley into submission, and he remains inarticulate for the rest of the play. The ensuing party is a rowdy, drunken affair, attended by Lulu, a flirtatious neighbor. Although he seems interested in Lulu, Stanley remains generally oblivious to everything.

Act Three begins the next morning. Goldberg and McCann report that Stanley has had a nervous breakdown and that they are going to take him away. Stanley appears, clean-shaven and nattily dressed in striped trousers, black jacket, white collar, and carrying a bowler hat. They leave in Goldberg's big, black car. "You'll be adjusted," says Goldberg enigmatically. "You'll be a success," adds McCann. They leave, despite the protests of the proprietor. Boles and his wife sit down and resume the small talk that had opened the play. "Wasn't it a lovely party last night?" the old woman asks. *The Birthday Party* opened to nearly unanimous popular denunciation (one performance played to only six people in the audience). The critics treated the play with enthusiasm. Henry Hobson wrote in the London *Sunday Times* that Pinter "possesses the most original, disturbing, and arresting talent in theatrical London." And Ronald Hayman regarded the play's "moments of terror and violence . . . the best Pinter has contrived."

The Film

Film director William Friedkin had seen the play in 1962 and declared, "It changed my life." He was determined to bring it to the screen, but at that time financing was difficult, since few people knew the names of either Pinter or Friedkin. The two young men met in New York and decided to form a company of their own to make the film. Independent producer Max Rosenberg of Palomar Pictures International then stepped in to finance the project. Pinter was a stickler for the verbatim reading of his scenario text. During rehearsals he made strenuous objections to *any* changes, even of a single word. His adaptation removes any references to Stanley's retreat to the boarding house, his sexual interest in Lulu, and any background information about McCann and Goldberg. The effect of this void is to render the film even more enigmatic than the original play. "Devoid of the back story," writes commentator Nat Segaloff, "Stanley's victimization is seen as an act of pure persecution, with the even darker presumption of guilt. In this sense, the play is about mankind's ultimate responsibility and desire to escape from its consequences."

While the play was redolent with layered resonances, the film suppressed them. By pruning the specifics, the results are less a mystery than what one critic called "a brooding essay on pure paranoia." Nonetheless, the trajectory of Stanley's deterioration is clear enough—from a whining child carping about corn flakes, to an adolescent boy playing with toys, to a libidinous teenager toying with sex, to a senile old man lost in a trance-like oblivion. The finished film was everything Friedkin's previous pictures—notably, *The Night They Raided Minsky's*—had not been, i.e., confined and claustrophobic rather than open and kinetically dynamic. Unfortunately, few people saw the independent release in 1968. Even today, it is available only on cable television. While many critics praised its acting and staging, they objected to it as too talky, too realistic, too dissipated in its tensions. Still, Friedkin's experience with this stage adaptation provided him with the confidence and credentials to essay another theatrical adaptation two years later, Matt Crowley's *The Boys in the Band*.

REFERENCES

Hayman, Ronald, *Harold Pinter* (New York: Frederick Ungar, 1973); Segaloff, Nat, *Hurricane Billy: The Stormy Life and Films of William Friedkin* (New York: William Morrow, 1990).

—*J.C.T.*

BLOOD WEDDING (BODAS DE SANGRE, 1933)

FEDERICO GARCIA LORCA (1898–1936)

Blood Wedding (1981), Spain, directed by Carlos Saura, adapted by Alfredo Manas and Emiliano Piedra.

The Play

Federico Garcia Lorca's experimental plays freely combined elements of farce, vaudeville, folk tragedy, puppet show, and surrealistic extravaganza. His fusion of poetry and drama remains, according to commentator Haskell M. Block, "among the unique theatrical achievements of our time." Like *Yerma* (1934) and *The House of Bernarda Alba* (1936), *Blood Wedding* (1933) belongs to the late period of the Spanish playwright. It abandons the partisan politics of his early works and concentrates on the collision between erotic passion and societal constraint. Told in three acts and seven scenes, *Blood Wedding* combines stylized diction and song-poetry with a fantasy world of the supernatural and the surreal. The hot, yet stark language of the drama is closely akin to Lorca's most famous collection of poetry, *Romancero Gitano* (Gypsy ballads). The human and the symbolic move side by side. *Bodas de sangre* begins in the Andalusian countryside on the eve of an arranged wedding between a young man and a woman who was formerly betrothed to another, Leonardo, whose family had murdered the groom's father and brother. The marriage ceremony is interrupted when the bride bolts with Leonardo. The groom and his friends leap onto their horses and pursue them through the forest. Surreal elements dominate the chase sequence in Act Three, Scene One, with symbolic characters appearing who represent the light of the moon and the darkness of death. The knife fight that leaves both men dead transpires offstage before the beginning of Act Three, Scene Two. The anguished bride returns to the slain groom's mother and offers to end her life with the same knife that killed her son.

Although Lorca's play was an instant international success, he had little time to enjoy his celebrity. His life was cut tragically short when he was executed in August 1936 by a Fascist firing squad. His *Bodas de sangre* remains a lyric testament to the violence that eventually ended his own life.

The Film

A participant in the New Spanish Cinema movement of the 1960s, Carlos Saura was one of the first Spanish filmmakers to deal openly with the Spanish Civil War and its aftermath. Despite the censorship imposed by the Franco regime, he made films like *La caza* (The hunt, 1964), which through allusion and allegory dealt with the emotional, physical, and psychological damage of Spain's repressive postwar dictatorial regime. After Franco's death in 1975, Saura moved into a simpler, more direct, almost documentary style that explored Spain's cultural past. *Bodas de sangre* is, with *Carmen* (1983), an example of his examination and virtual dissection of classic ballets. With the assistance of Antonio Gades, Spain's leading dancer-choreographer and former director of the National Ballet of Spain, Carlos Saura filmed a pantomime flamenco ballet version of the Lorca play. This was a bold move, considering the play is so verbally rich in poetic dialogue and songs. Yet Gades' superb choreography, complemented by Teo Escamilla's virtuoso camerawork, conveys the essential spirit, if not the literal text, of the play.

The film begins in the dressing rooms as Gades' dance troupe prepares for a dress rehearsal. While the dancers apply their makeup and don their costumes, their interior voices provide monologues about their past experiences as performers. Out on the dance floor, after Gades leads the assembled troupe through a few practice steps, the ballet proper begins. The action is conveyed entirely through dance pantomime; the only words heard are the song texts performed by offstage singers to the accompaniment of two flamenco guitars. There is no scenery and no props, just the bare stage with three illuminated windows deployed symmetrically across the back wall. Scene divisions are eschewed, and there is only a brief respite midway while the ensemble and the musicians pause for a group photograph (the same photograph that begins and ends the film). The highlight of the performance is the knife fight (which occurs offstage in the original play) between the groom and his rival. The entire scene is choreographed—*not* photographed—in slow motion as the two men warily circle each other and finally lunge toward each other in their fatal thrusts. They fall to the ground in a maddeningly slow descent. . . . The image of the wedding photograph reappears over the concluding credits.

Saura and Gades have achieved in this dance film what Lorca had intended all along, what commentator Allan Lewis describes as "a musical orchestration of changing rhythms, folk songs, and lamentations . . . in which there is no concern with psychological motivation but with pagan forces in a primitive pageant of revolt, vengeance, and death."

REFERENCES

Adams, Mildred, *Garcia Lorca: Playwright and Poet* (New York: George Braziller, 1977); Block, Haskell M., and Robert G. Shedd, eds., *Masters of Modern Drama* (New York: Random House, 1962); Lewis, Allan, *The Contemporary Theatre: The Significant Playwrights of Our Time* (New York: Crown Publishers, 1971).

—*J.C.T.*

BORN YESTERDAY (1946)

GARSON KANIN (1912–)

Born Yesterday (1950), U.S.A., directed by George Cukor, adapted by Albert Mannheimer and Garson Kanin [uncredited]; Columbia.

Born Yesterday (1993), U.S.A., directed by Luis Mandoki, adapted by Douglas McGrath; Hollywood Pictures/Buena Vista.

The Play

Judy Holliday made her mark on Broadway in Garson Kanin's play *Born Yesterday*, which premiered at the Lyceum Theatre in New York on February 4, 1946. Jean Arthur was originally cast in the role of Billie, but she bowed out during the play's tryout. As Billie, Holliday stepped in at the 11th hour and rendered an archetypal portrayal of a beautiful but dumb blonde. An ex-chorine, Billie is the mistress of a wealthy junk dealer, Harry Brock (Paul Douglas), who is determined to buy his way into Washington politics. Harry engages Paul Verrall (Gary Merrill) to give the scantily educated Billie an elementary course in political science, so that she will not embarrass him when he is entertaining the politicians he hopes to bribe. Proving that she was not born yesterday after all, Billie learns enough from Paul to know that what Harry is doing is vile; and she threatens to expose his plans unless he abandons them. As one critic wittily summed up the situation, Billie's behavior is an illustration of the old maxim that, if you lead a whore to culture, you can make her think.

The play scored a huge success and ran on Broadway for four years and 1,643 performances.

The Films

Columbia Pictures purchased the screen rights for 1 million dollars, an enormous sum for those days. The first draft of the script was prepared by Albert Mannheimer, who presumably worked on the assumption that a screenwriter is not exercising his own creativity unless he makes significant alterations in the work that he is adapting for the screen. Director George Cukor recalled taking one look at this version of the screenplay and turning it down flat, because the writer had jettisoned some excellent material in Kanin's play. He then asked Garson Kanin to take a hand in fashioning the script.

Kanin, who received no screen credit for composing the final shooting script, did more than simply restore some of the material that Mannheimer had excised from the play. Taking his cue from references in the original dialogue to several Washington landmarks that Billie (Judy Holliday, reprising her Broadway role in an Oscar-winning performance) mentions visiting, he opened out the play for the screen by constructing a number of scenes that were filmed on location at these very sites.

"We shot scenes at places like the Jefferson Memorial and the Capitol," Cukor told this writer, "and this gave the picture greater mobility." These scenes also served to dramatize more vividly than was feasible within the confines of the stage the manner in which Billie's systematic tour of the city's historic monuments with Paul (William Holden) enables her for the very first time in her life to discover for herself America's rich and meaningful past; and consequently to see the crass attempts of Harry (Broderick Crawford) to manipulate elected government officials for his own aggrandizement as a perversion of the democratic principles on which America was founded.

The main interior set in the film was Harry's huge Washington hotel suite, and Cukor's camera explored virtually every inch of this elaborate set as the action moved from room to room. Conversely, Cukor had no qualms about shooting the celebrated gin rummy game sequence with a stationary camera from a single angle, in acknowledgment of Holliday's power to hold the moviegoer's attention, as Billie repeatedly bests Harry in hand after hand. "The quiet, blank-faced assurance of the girl," writes critic Gordon Gow, "and the riffling of the cards in her deliberate hands reduced her opponent to a jelly of nervous frustration." Commenting on this scene, Cukor explained, "My rule of thumb is this: unless moving the camera is going to contribute something to the scene in question, let it remain at rest."

Throughout the movie Judy Holliday demonstrates her ability to make us laugh at Billie's dim-witted remarks, at the very same time that she is stirring our compassion for Billie's vulnerable stupidity. In one scene the apelike Harry becomes so exasperated with

Billie that he strikes her savagely across the face. As she whimpers and cries softly, we realize just how deeply the actress has made us care for Billie.

Released in 1993, the second version of *Born Yesterday* starred Melanie Griffith as Billie, Don Johnson as Paul, and John Goodman as Harry. Despite Luis Mandoki's competent direction and a serviceable cast, the remake lacked the panache and verve of Cukor's tough, affectionate treatment of the same story. The movie sags after a while, largely because the comic timing is off, the romance between Billie and Paul is hardly developed, and—most importantly—Melanie Griffith lacks Judy Holliday's unmatched gift for comic vulnerability.

REFERENCES

Gow, Gordon, *Hollywood in the Fifties* (New York: Barnes, 1971); Levy, Emmanuel, *George Cukor, Master of Elegance: Hollywood's Legendary Director and His Stars* (New York: Morrow, 1994); McGilligan, Patrick, *George Cukor: A Double Life* (New York: St. Martin's Press, 1997).

—G.D.P.

BRIEF ENCOUNTER

See *STILL LIFE*

THE BROWNING VERSION (1948)

TERENCE RATTIGAN (1911–1982)

The Browning Version (1951), U.K., directed and adapted by Anthony Asquith; GFD/Javelin.

The Browning Version (1994), U.K., directed by Mike Figgis, adapted by Ronald Harwood; Paramount Pictures.

The Play

Although Terence Rattigan represented to a new breed of British playwrights in the late 1950s all that was contrived and artificial in drama, his work nonetheless repays fresh scrutiny. Indeed, young filmmakers like Mike Figgis and David Mamet are rediscovering his work, to the delight of a new generation of theatre and filmgoers. Rattigan's first theatrical success came in 1936, when he was only 25, in *French without Tears*. With *The Winslow Boy* and *The Browning Version* in the late 1940s and early 1950s, he seemingly had secured his position as Britain's master of the well-made play.

Yet, timely as they seem today, his plays were dismissed in the next five years by the "Angry Young Man" generation of playwrights emerging after 1956, led by John Osborne. Today, however, Rattigan's great theme of the irrationality of love, seems more timely than ever.

First produced in 1948, *The Browning Version* derived from a one-act play Rattigan wrote at the behest of John Gielgud. It is a drama of wintry discontents that transpires in a single room in little more than an hour's running time. Cloistered buildings, hallowed halls, a game of cricket, a book of poetry, and the retirement of a prep school master constitute the setting and incidents. Andrew Crocker Harris is facing several crises: Once a brilliant academic, he is now a desiccated pedant, held in contempt by his colleagues, and derided by his pupils as "the Himmler of the Lower Fifth." His wife, Millie, is openly flaunting an affair with a younger master, Frank Hunter. The headmaster informs him that the school governors have decided not to grant him a badly needed pension, and he asks Harris to forego his right to speak last at the next day's prize-giving ceremony, in favor of the school's victorious cricket master. Crocker Harris placidly assents to these indignities. "You can't hurt Andrew," sniffs his wife to her lover, "he's dead." The one ray of light in this miserable existence is the respect and affection of one of his pupils, John Taplow, who gives Crocker Harris a copy of Robert Browning's version of Aeschylus' *Agamemnon* (hence the play's title). Crocker Harris suffers an epiphany. Here is the one success that "can atone and more than atone for all the failures of the world." Newly inspired, Crocker Harris comes to terms with his wife and with himself. He defies the authorities and refuses to defer his speech at the leaving ceremony.

Rattigan has confessed that the boy, Taplow, is modeled after himself as a student at Harrow, and Crocker Harris was patterned after his own Greek master, Coke Norris. The *Agamemnon*, moreover, was Rattigan's favorite play while a student. Biographers Michael Darlow and Gillian Hodson regard *The Browning Version* as an authentic masterpiece: "The theme of deceit and falsity in relations between people pervades the play. Characters who hide their feelings, relationships which are not as they appear, bonhomie which hides pain, all have been much in evidence throughout Rattigan's writing. Yet in *The Browning Version* the full destructive force of these elements is revealed for the first time. He shows how deceit in personal relationships, the pursuit of popularity and emotional repression all lead to tragedy; not just to personal unhappiness but to a betrayal of integrity."

The Films

Two film adaptations have been made. Anthony Asquith directed the 1951 film version, adapted by Rattigan himself and starring Michael Redgrave as Crocker Harris. Asquith, the son of Herbert Asquith, first earl of Oxford and prime minister of Britain (1908–15), was a veteran of the British cinema since the silent days and enjoyed a long and fruitful collaboration with playwright Rattigan. In 1945, with Rattigan, he formed International Screenplays, and in succeeding years he made several films from Rattigan's original scripts (*The Way to the Stars*, 1945; *The VIPs*, 1963; *The Yellow Rolls-Royce*, 1964) and from his plays (*While the Sun Shines*, 1947; *The Winslow Boy*, 1948; *The Browning Version*, 1951). Rattigan himself adapted *The Winslow Boy*. Although he did not adapt *The Browning Version* himself, Rattigan participated in story conferences and had a hand in the casting. His was the decisive vote in favor of Michael Redgrave as Crocker Harris, a role for which Rattigan had lobbied long and hard.

The play's compression into one set and an hour's running time is here expanded to the more explicit detail and variety of settings appropriate to a feature-length film. The backstory of Crocker Harris's marriage is fleshed out, as is his wife's affair, and the activities of the other staff members of the school. Among the added scenes is one in which a group of masters' wives discuss Crocker Harris and his wife: "Yes, a marriage of mind and body. It never has worked since the world began." This reinforces Crocker Harris' speech in both play and film in which he pleads for compassion toward him and his wife: "Both of us needing from the other something that would make life supportable for us, and neither of us able to give it. Two kinds of love. Hers and mine. Worlds apart. . . ." Also added is Crocker Harris' prize-day speech. He movingly confesses his failures and apologizes to the boys for having let them down. Lapsing into silence at last, he is greeted finally by the cheers of the boys.

The Mike Figgis/Ronald Harwood version updates the play to the 1990s and casts Albert Finney as Crocker Harris. Although photographed on location amid the lush colors of the Dorset County countryside, the film remains true to the rather bleak tone of the play. Finney's flint-hard face and chunky body have the texture and substance of the school's stone-and-ivy walls. His best scenes occur when he reads passages from Aeschylus' *Agamemnon* to his students. Then, as the lurid tale unfolds of Clytemnestra's infidelity to her husband and her subsequent cold-blooded murder of him (a tale with more than a few parallels to his own troubled marriage), he shakes off his inertia and comes

Terence Rattigan

alive. *That* is the Crocker Harris to which young Taplow pays tribute when he presents him Browning's translation. "From a distance God looks down kindly upon such a gentle man," reads the boy's inscription in the book. No matter that Mrs. Crocker Harris (here renamed "Laura")—glacially portrayed by Greta Scacci—tries to spoil the moment. It remains a benediction that graces the rest of the movie, a tiny blaze from which we (and Crocker Harris) can warm our cold hands. To the movie's credit, it remains true to Rattigan's insistence that none of these characters is entirely likable. Unfortunately, a jarring note (as it were) comes from Mark Isham's music score, which tends to underscore dramatic moments with a sledgehammer emphasis, marring the otherwise restrained quality of the performances.

REFERENCES

Darlow, Michael, and Gillian Hodson, *Terence Rattigan: The Man and His Work* (London: Quartet Books, 1979).

—*J.C.T.*

BUFFALO BILL AND THE INDIANS

See *INDIANS*

BUS STOP (1955)

WILLIAM INGE (1913–1973)

Bus Stop (1956), U.S.A., directed by Joshua Logan, adapted by George Axelrod; 20th Century-Fox.

The Play

Expanded from *People in the Wind*, Inge's one-act play about several bus passengers stranded in a blizzard, *Bus Stop* is primarily a romantic comedy that foregrounds the courtship of Montana cowboy Bo Decker and Cherie, a nightclub singer he met in Kansas City while performing at a rodeo. The rambunctious and naive Bo has abducted Cherie and intends to take her to Montana despite her own naive protestations that she wants to go to Hollywood and become a star, and despite the urgings of his older friend and mentor, Virgil Blessing, to let her go. The action takes place in the single setting of a Kansas bus stop where the travelers must wait until the blizzard passes. Cherie's resistance to Bo's clumsy attempts to bully her into acquiescence provides several humorous scenes that juxtapose their respective Ozark and cowboy hick qualities. But after Bo is humiliated in a fight with the local sheriff, he apologizes to Cherie and tells her he still wants her to marry him. Touched by Bo's transformation and probably aware that her Hollywood dreams are even more improbable than happiness with Bo in Montana, she decides to go with him after all.

Although the romantic comedy is central, Inge has peopled this play with an ensemble cast of interesting characters for whom romance proves much more complex and elusive, and for whom enduring loneliness is more likely. Among these are Grace, the proprietress of the bus stop, who trysts with Carl, the bus driver, but wants no lasting relationship with any man; Virgil, Bo's companion who is essentially supplanted in Bo's life by Cherie and who is, at play's end, "left out in the cold"; and especially Professor Lyman, a lonely, drunken, unemployed schoolteacher who decides not to follow up on his earlier inappropriate attentions toward Elma, the naive young waitress, and whose observations on life seem to be most consistent with those of Inge himself.

The Film

Bus Stop was given the "big movie" Cinemascope treatment from the outset by producer Buddy Adler, who chose Joshua Logan to direct Marilyn Monroe as Cherie (Harold Clurman had directed Kim Stanley in that role on Broadway). Logan's reputation was at its peak because he had co-written and directed both the stage and screen versions of *Mr. Roberts* and also directed the stage and screen versions of Inge's Pulitzer Prize–winning *Picnic*. Monroe had the largest box-office appeal of any mid-1950s film actress, and an attractive newcomer, Don Murray, was cast as Bo, rather than Albert Salmi, who had been Bo on stage. Established character actors Arthur O'Connell and Betty Field appeared as Virgil and Grace; a pretty young "starlet," Hope Lange, played Elma, and Robert Bray played Carl, the bus driver. In keeping with the commercial ambitions of the project, Logan had Ken Darby write "A Paper of Pins," a catchy main title song that was performed by the Four Lads, a popular group of the day, assuring repeated radio play time that would help promote the film.

Logan and screenwriter George Axelrod "opened out" Inge's play considerably, changing the setting from Kansas to Arizona and adding Cinemascope scenes of Bo and Virgil traveling through rugged mountain and desert locales enhanced by DeLuxe color. There also are scenes of Bo performing at the rodeo, Cherie singing at the nightclub, Bo abducting Cherie at the bus station, and more. The scenes in which Monroe performs histrionic renditions of "That Old Black Magic" in the nightclub and then later at the bus stop became among the most famous in Monroe's career. Although many key scenes still occur in and just outside the bus stop, and the central romantic plot unwinds as it does in the play, with Virgil still "out in the cold" at the end, Logan and Axelrod omit Professor Lyman and the sheriff altogether (Carl defeats Bo in the film's fight scene) and add Vera (played by Eileen Heckart), Cherie's co-worker and friend. These changes heighten the romantic comedy but lessen Inge's more complex subtheme of loneliness.

The film proved very popular, as did the main-title song, and many critics, such as the *Saturday Review*'s Arthur Knight, praised Monroe's acting, claiming that she now deserved to be taken seriously as an actress rather than a "sex symbol." Others praised Logan's added scenes showing Bo and Virgil on their Montana ranch and on their way to Phoenix, Bo quieting the rowdy patrons at the nightclub while Cherie sings, and Bo literally roping Cherie in the bus station.

REFERENCES

Crowther, Bosley, "Bus Stop," *The New York Times*, September 1, 1956; Knight, Arthur, "SR Goes to the Movies," *Saturday Review*, September 15, 1956; Voss, Ralph F., *The Strains of Triumph: A Life of William Inge* (Topeka: University Press of Kansas, 1989).

—*R.F.V.*

CAESAR AND CLEOPATRA (1899)

GEORGE BERNARD SHAW (1856–1950)

Caesar and Cleopatra (1945), U.K., directed by Gabriel Pascal, adapted by George Bernard Shaw; General Films/J. Arthur Rank.

The Play

George Bernard Shaw developed "thesis plays" in the 1890s with *Widower's Houses* (1892), *Arms and the Man* (1893), and *Mrs. Warren's Profession* (1899). He achieved his greatest critical and popular successes with later plays, notably *Man and Superman* (1903), *Major Barbara* (1905), *Pygmalion* (1913), and *Saint Joan* (1923). *Caesar and Cleopatra* was a five-act "history" play that premiered in London in 1899 and later in New York in 1906. In the preface to *Three Plays for Puritans*, which included this play, Shaw declared that his "real" characters were superior to the "love-obsessed" ones of Shakespeare's drama. He also stated how he intended to view history in terms of his own philosophy and in modern-day contexts.

Shaw provided two prologues from which a given production might choose. In one, the Egyptian god Ra exposits Rome's historical background and some details about that "great man" Caesar and the 16-year-old Cleopatra. In the other, a conversation between two Egyptian soldiers tells of the Roman invasion of Egypt and the disappearance of Queen Cleopatra. In Act One Caesar meets Cleopatra at the base of the Sphinx. She does not know who he is at first, and they go back to her palace, where he instructs her in the art of ruling. When the Roman troops enter, she realizes his identity and falls into his arms, sobbing in relief. In Act Two Cleopatra's brother, Ptolemy of Alexandria, refuses to allow Cleopatra and Caesar to take his throne from him. Caesar arrives and finds his troops under siege by Ptolemy's soldiers. In retaliation, he orders the seizure of the Alexandrian lighthouse. Act Three opens as Cleopatra, stowed away in a carpet, secrets herself out of the palace to visit Caesar at the lighthouse. Caesar's loyal officer, Britannus, is shocked at Cleopatra's ruse. When Egyptian troops suddenly arrive to surround the lighthouse, Caesar dives into the sea with Cleopatra on his back. Act Four transpires six months later. Caesar is warned that once Cleopatra has her crown, she will turn her back on him. Horrified at her actions in ordering the death of Ptolemy's guardian, Pothinus, Caesar declares prophetically: "And so, to the end of history, murder shall breed murder, always in the name of right and honor and peace, until the gods are tired of blood and create a race that can understand." Sure enough, a mob from the city is up in arms against their queen. Act Five begins after Caesar has defeated Ptolemy's army. Cleopatra is dressed in mourning because of the death of her old nurse, Ftatateeta. But when Caesar promises to send her young Mark

Antony from Rome, she is amused. The play ends as Caesar sails away.

Commentator Eric Bentley notes that a striking aspect of Shaw's history plays was his debunking of heroes. To a degree, he was a pioneer of the "fictional biography," in which the so-called great man is revealed to be an ordinary chap after all. In truth, however, writes Bentley, "He *did* bring the hero off his pedestal, but only to demonstrate that the flesh-and-blood man was much more of a hero than the statue and the legend." Moreover, Caesar here is a teacher to Cleopatra more than a man of action and romance.

The Film

No fan of the movies, Shaw insisted that a cinematic adaptation should be nothing more than a filmed play; claiming that it was the dialogue that mattered, not the techniques of editing and camera. The first Shavian film adaptation *How He Lied to Her Husband* (1931), directed by Cecil Lewis, was little more than canned theatre. Both it and the tediously static next venture, *Arms and the Man* (1932), failed at the box office. Self-styled film producer, Gabriel Pascal would change all that after he met Shaw in 1935 and talked Shaw into allowing him to produce his plays on film. Pascal's three adaptations of Shaw—*Pygmalion* (1938), *Major Barbara* (1941), and (to a lesser degree) *Caesar and Cleopatra* (1944)—for his General Films production company represent a more enlightened attitude on Shaw's part toward the recognition of a more "cinematic" union of play text and camera.

Unlike Shaw, who had reservations about the choice of *Caesar and Cleopatra* for a film, Pascal liked its potential for spectacle and color. Besides, Vivien Leigh and Claude Rains were both available, which sealed the deal. Shaw himself picked up enthusiasm at last and wrote the screenplay, and maintained vigilance over the production. Pascal functioned both as producer and director. He began filming on June 12, 1944, just six days after D-day, at a time when equipment and skilled craftsmen were scarce or unobtainable. Rocket bombing of London, and a pregnancy and subsequent miscarriage on the part of Vivien Leigh, further added to the delays and difficulties. What resulted was the least cinematic of the three Shaw-Pascal collaborations (Shaw enjoined Pascal not to "change the play into an exhibition of camera conjuring"). In addition to retaining most of the dialogues of Caesar and Cleopatra, Shaw created 16 new scenes—amounting to 13 minutes out of a total playing time of 128 minutes—to show events that took place offstage in the play and to smooth out the gaps between the acts. Most of these new scenes were lavishly spectacular, but, says commentator Costello, they "did little except provide a lovely backdrop for the talk. . . . Shaw and Pascal substituted sheer spectacle for the more dynamic and functional cinematic methods which had crept into their two previous films."

The film opts to begin with a shortened version of the prologue in which the soldiers relate the story's background. Immediately following is one of Shaw's new scenes, an elaborate, wholly visual depiction of the presence of Caesar's soldiers in Egypt. This then dissolves into an eerie moonlit desert as Caesar hails the Sphinx and compares it with himself. Other visual additions include the Roman troops' scattering of the Alexandrian citizens, a wordless moment with Caesar in the King's Room in the Palace, and a montage of the Roman victory mentioned in the play's Act Five. An additional dialogue between Cleopatra and the faithful nurse, Ftatateeta, suggests some of the romantic attachment between Caesar and Cleopatra. The concluding scene suggests far more of Cleopatra's anticipation of the arrival of Marc Antony than of her sorrow over the departure of Caesar. Ultimately, spectacle won out over Shavian wit and satire. Pascal outdid himself—and his financiers—in exploiting the advantages of a huge budget and a Technicolor palette. Costello reports that some of the critics even suggested later that the real star of the film was set designer Oliver Messel. Moreover, Pascal's rigorous historical research had grown excessive. He even hired an astronomer to reproduce the exact location of the stars in the sky at the time of the story's events. "Far from helping the film, all this extreme historical accuracy merely blurred the fun of Shaw's play," says Costello. "Shaw's vision of ancient Egypt was, of course, extremely personal, full of paradox and anachronism. He got his fun by showing us that the people and situations of Caesar's day are exactly like the people and situations of our own day. Pascal, instead, showed the viewer an exotic and very explicitly Egyptian Egypt."

The film opened on December 13, 1945, a year and a half after filming began, at the Odeon Theatre. Queen Mary was in attendance. Despite a promising opening and press headlines that boasted the picture was "The Motion Picture Event of the Century" and was "A Sensational Spectacle of Seductive Beauty," it proved to be a miserable failure at the box office. An associate of the releasing company, J. Arthur Rank, declared it to be a "disastrous loss." An American critic in *The Commonweal* summed up the prevailing opinion of the film's generally uncinematic qualities: "Regardless of the heights GBS may have reached as a playwright, this film shows that motion picture writing is not one of his talents."

REFERENCES

Bentley, Eric, *Bernard Shaw*, rev. ed. (New York: Limelight Editions, 1985); Costello, Donald P., *The Serpent's Eye: Shaw and the Cinema* (Notre Dame, Ind.: University of Notre Dame Press, 1965); Pascal, Valerie, *The Disciple and His Devil* (New York: McGraw-Hill, 1970).

—*J.C.T.*

LA CAGE AUX FOLLES (1973)

JEAN POIRET (1926–1992)

La Cage aux Folles (aka *The Mad Cage; Birds of a Feather*) (1978/released in U.S.A., 1979), France/Italy, directed by Edouard Molinaro, adapted by Edouard Molinaro, Francis Veber, Marcello Danon, and Jean Poiret; Les Productions Artistes Associés-DaMa Produzione.

The Birdcage (1997), U.S.A., directed by Mike Nichols, adapted by Elaine May; United Artists.

The Play

La Cage aux Folles, Jean Poiret's 1973 French farce, was a popular play, running more than seven years before it was made into the highly successful 1978 film. This entertaining satire blends social commentary with engaging character studies of two gay men, Renato and Albin. Renato runs the Cages aux Folles drag club in St. Tropez, where he presents shows featuring Albin as the popular "Zaza." During a drunken lapse years before, Renato had fathered a son, whom he and Albin have brought up into young manhood. When the son, who is "straight," announces he is getting married, Renato and Albin have to pretend they are "normal" in order to meet the intended bride's conservative parents. The results, played out over a dinner party, are comically disastrous. The sympathies of the audience are adroitly manipulated toward a compassionate and warm understanding of the life of this gay couple. The jolting collision between the gay and "straight" lifestyles is accomplished with amenable jesting, physical trumpery, and sexual humor. Poiret later helped write the screenplay.

The Films

There are two film versions of *La Cage aux Folles:* the 1978, French/Italian production and the 1996 American update, *The Birdcage*. The 1978 movie stars Ugo Tognazzi, as Renato, and Michel Serrault, as Albin, in the roles that they each played on the stage. Both actors make the transition to the screen with an ease and flair that repeatedly make credible the vitality and durability of their characters' relationship. Their union is an affinity of opposites, where Renato is dependable and unflappable and Albin is emotional and dramatic, acting the difficult diva "ZaZa," onstage and off. Unlike *La Cage* as seen on stage, the movie screen is able to show us the close-up details of Albin and Renato's world. Theirs is an ostentatious life, and we meet it in every comic detail: in where and how they live and in the trappings of the nightclub that they not only own, but also love through each new headache it entails. Even Jacob (Benny Luke), their household assistant, adds to the humor enhanced by the camera. He mugs in close-up and cavorts, in long shots, through his chores. Whether he is dressing in the "uniform" of a French maid or in hot pants, Jacob ostentatiously and provocatively costumes himself in delightfully scanty apparel that form ongoing and ongoingly funny sight gags. The humor of the movie *La Cage aux Folles*, throughout, is amplified by the minutiae the camera can show us; and, just as in the play, in the film we see that despite the surface outlandishness of their lives, Renato and Albin experience problems that, generally speaking, could befall any couple—the everyday difficulties of living together and the lengths to which parents are willing to go in serving the needs of their children.

Their child, Laurent, is the offspring of a dalliance Renato had had years earlier. Now an adult, Laurent is engaged to Andrea, the daughter of the secretary-general of the Union of Moral Order. Andrea's parents want to meet Laurent's parents; and, knowing that a homosexual couple will not be well received by the Moral Order's secretary-general, Albin reluctantly agrees to be absent from the dinner, yielding his seat to Laurent's biological mother. Albin does so, at what he feels to be great personal sacrifice, because he loves Laurent as a son. However, when the mother fails to show up to dinner, Albin, drag-dressed as "Laurent's mother," plays her part. In contrast to Renato and Albin, Andrea's parents are social-climbers, outwardly reserved and excessively priggish. Since Laurent has misleadingly described his parents as occupying a well-heeled position in "Cultural Affairs," Andrea's parents are hoping that their social footing will be raised through the union of families created by the wedding. Comic mayhem follows when Laurent's actual mother arrives. The scene ends in great farce: Andrea's pompously intolerant father must dress in drag to avoid recognition by the press.

La Cage aux Folles opened with excellent reviews, and for several years ranked as the highest grossing foreign-language feature released in the United States. The director (Edouard Molinaro) and the screenwriter (Francis Veber) were both nominated for Oscars. The National Board of Review voted *La Cage* "Best Foreign Film of 1979" and the Foreign Press Association's Golden Globe chose it as "Best Picture of the Year." Molinaro went on to direct the sequel, *La Cage aux Folles II* (1980), which was moderately successful. A second sequel, *La Cage aux Folles 3: The Wedding* (1985), was far less popular.

In 1983 the musical *La Cage aux Folles* (music and lyrics by Jerry Herman and book by Harvey Fierstein) opened on Broadway to impressive reviews. Unlike the film, it showcased the nightclub drag queen show; the musical's defining number, "I Am What I Am," became the widely recorded stuff of popular culture.

The last version of *La Cage aux Folles* is the 1996 American film, *The Birdcage*. Directed by Mike Nichols, from a script by the legendary Elaine May, the movie starred Robin Williams as Armand Goldman, the Renato character, and Nathan Lane as Albert, the Albin character. Set in contemporary Miami, the film uses its revised setting for humorous effect. We see the collisions of contrasting cultures: Miami's wealthy jet-setters, the restricted-income retirees, the vividly gay, open world of the "Birdcage" nightclub, and the bigoted, tight-laced members of "The Coalition for Moral Order." Armand is preparing a dinner party in honor of his 20-year-old son, who is bringing over his fiancee and her parents (Gene Hackman and Dianne Wiest as Senator and Mrs. Keeley). Keeley is an ultra-right-wing Republican conservative, the cochairman of a watchdog committee in public morals, who thinks Billy Graham is too liberal. A scandal involving his cochair and a hooker has just broken, and the tabloid press is hounding him. All the senator needs right now are a gay man and a drag queen for in-laws. "I feel like a psychotic horse galloping toward a burning barn," quips Armand. Indeed, the movie wears its liberal bias right on its sleeve ("We Are Family" sing the strutting drag queens as they prance about the nightclub). The set piece of the film is the hilarious dinner party, in which even the staid senator and his wife fling their repressions to the winds. In sum, *The Bird-*

Mike Nichols cast Nathan Lane opposite Robin Williams in The Birdcage, *a remake of* La Cage aux Folles. (COURTESY UNITED ARTISTS)

cage is a gentle, winning portrait of two gay men struggling under the tyranny of the expectations of conventional society. The point is clearly made: It is not their life-style that is problematic (they are quite happy in their relationship); rather, it is the tyrannical expectations of others (particularly the demands of Armand's heterosexual son) that they conform to society norms that creates the problems. The film is a rarity—it elicits laughter at first, but more serious reflection later.

REFERENCES

Kael, Pauline, *Taking It All In* (New York: Holt, Rinehart and Winston, 1984); Magill, Frank N., ed., "La Cage aux Folles," *Magill's Survey of Cinema* (Englewood Cliffs, N.J.: Salem Press, 1981).

—*L.C.C.*

THE CARETAKER (1960)

HAROLD PINTER (1930–)

The Caretaker (1963), U.K., directed by Clive Donner, adapted by Harold Pinter; Caretaker Films (Michael Birkett)/United Artists.

The Play

Harold Pinter's first big theatrical success, *The Caretaker*, opened at the Arts Theatre, London, on April 27, 1960, transferring to the Duchess Theatre a month later and ran for 444 performances. A tramp named Davies is rescued from a mugging by a rather mysterious and taciturn man, Aston, who invites him back to his cluttered room in a house in West London. Davies tells him he has been going around under an assumed name, but that everything will be resolved once he gets down to Sidcup for his belongings and his papers, which will establish his identity. The following morning, when Aston is out of the house, Davies unexpectedly encounters a young man, Mick, who turns out to be Aston's brother and the landlord of the premises. He offers Davies the job of redecorating the house. (Aston had already offered him the same job, but since Aston revealed that he had once been confined to a mental hospital, Davies sided with Mick in an attempt to play off brother against brother.) This is precisely what Mick has intended in order to drive Davies away. With his brother's approval, Mick denounces the tramp. Rejected now by both brothers, Davies is left staring into an uncertain future—unless perhaps he can get down to Sidcup for his papers.

The Film

First shown at the 1963 Berlin Festival, where it took the Silver Bear, Clive Donner's film of *The Caretaker* was shot by cinematographer Nicolas Roeg on location in a derelict, unheated house in Hackney. The budget was £30,000, which was largely raised by individual donations from admirers of the play within the film and theatrical community, such as Noel Coward, Peter Sellers, Richard Burton and Elizabeth Taylor, Peter Hall and Leslie Caron. Donald Pleasence as Davies and Alan Bates as Mick were repeating the roles they had played on stage. Peter Woodthorpe had played Aston on the London stage, but the part had been taken to New York by Robert Shaw, who now played the role on screen.

Although he remained generally faithful to his original text, playwright Pinter took advantage of the film medium to open it out in ways that clarified some of the offstage action. Amused and bemused by some of the more fanciful allegorical and Freudian readings of the play, he took care to establish a literal reality. For example, when Aston talks of building a shed in the back garden, he is talking about a reality rather than a symbol. There are some witty inventions for the film, like the moment when Mick picks up Davies at one stage in his van and says he will drive him to Sidcup but instead drives him in a circle and drops him where he started (a visual correlative to the verbal rings he runs round him in the course of the action). Pinter also cut out some sections of the play, mainly from the opening of Act Three. Director Donner introduces some cinematic effects, particularly the startling shock-cut that introduces Mick's first encounter with Davies.

The basic themes remain intact. Both play and film are about the struggle for emotional and territorial advantage in relationships; the bonds of fraternity; the protective illusions that people build around themselves to sustain their lives; and the whole issue of "taking care"—not only in terms of being caretaker of the property, but also in Mick's taking care of his brother, and of Davies *not* taking sufficient care of what he says. The performances are all superb, though special mention must be given to the rich detail of Pleasence's characterization, from the tramp's violent punching into his hand when he is angry or frustrated to the way he lifts his coat tails like a concert pianist before sitting down (as if these are his last vestiges of gentility). "He was born to play the part," Pinter said of him. "His ferocity, vitality and bewilderment as an actor allowed him to give a great performance."

REFERENCES

Billington, Michael, *The Life and Work of Harold Pinter* (London: Faber and Faber, 1996); Klein, Joanne, *Making Pictures: The Pinter Screenplays* (Columbus: Ohio State University Press, 1985); Taylor, John Russell, *Anger and After: A Guide to the New British Drama* (London: Methuen, 1962).

—N.S.

CASABLANCA

See *EVERYBODY GOES TO RICK'S*

CAT ON A HOT TIN ROOF (1955)

TENNESSEE WILLIAMS (1911–1983)

Cat on a Hot Tin Roof (1958), U.S.A., directed by Richard Brooks, adapted by Richard Brooks and James Poe; Metro-Goldwyn-Mayer.

The Play

Tennessee Williams often dealt with homosexuality in his work; and it is interesting to see how this theme was allowed gradually to creep into film versions of his plays, since at the time that most of his plays were filmed homosexuality was a taboo subject for Hollywood films. The screen adaptation of *Cat on a Hot Tin Roof* is a case in point, since the homosexual implications of the relationship between Brick, the hero, and his old school buddy Skipper were obscured in the film.

In the play, which premiered at the Morosco Theatre in New York on March 24, 1955, Brick (Ben Gazzara), a latent homosexual suffering from impotence, has ruined his marriage to Margaret Politt (Barbara Bel Geddes) because he is still in love with his former football chum, Skipper. But when Skipper confesses his feelings for him, Brick cruelly rejects him. This total rejection by the one person to whom Skipper looked for understanding and compassion precipitates his suicidal leap from a hotel window. (It was all too typical of plays of this period that when a character was revealed to be homosexual, he had to go offstage and kill himself.)

At all events, Big Daddy (Burl Ives), Brick's overbearing father, suspects that Brick's relationship with Skipper was latently homosexual and that Brick is taking his fears about his sexual identity and his marriage to his wife Maggie and drowning them in alcohol. What's more, Big Daddy tells his immature son in the long and painful confrontation scene that climaxes the play that he must face himself and confront the past if he is to save his marriage. *Cat on a Hot Tin Roof* not only became Williams's longest-running play (694 performances), but also won him a Pulitzer Prize and a New York Critics Prize.

The Film

At the time that *Cat on a Hot Tin Roof* was adapted to the screen, homosexuality was, as already mentioned, all but a forbidden topic in American cinema; therefore it had to be downplayed in the picture. In Richard Brooks's film, Big Daddy (Burl Ives in a reprise of his stage role) does not contend that the continued emotional involvement of his son with his old school chum brands Brick (Paul Newman) as a latent homosexual, as in the play. Rather, Big Daddy

accuses him of being an immature and irresponsible 30-year-old who still refuses to relinquish adolescence—the world that he and Skipper created for themselves to stave off the responsibilities of adult life. Thus, although the suggestion of Brick's latent homosexuality is still present in the movie, it is ruled out as the decisive motivating factor in his relationship with Skipper and with his wife Maggie (Elizabeth Taylor).

While in no way a substitute for the homosexual theme of the play, Brick's arrested emotional development—his prolonged adolescence—is the primary focus of Big Daddy's vociferous criticism of Brick in the film. In their confrontation scene, Big Daddy hammers at Brick to grow up. Unwilling to listen, incapable at this moment of facing reality, Brick stumbles out of the house into a rainstorm and gets into his car, hoping to escape his father's pursuit and continuing harangue. But Big Daddy won't let him drive off. A close-up of the wheels of Brick's car spinning in the mud underscores the impasse that he and his father have reached at this moment. As the scene continues, Big Daddy matches the elements with a torrent of words, accusing his son of being a grown man who is still stuck in adolescence. At the scene's conclusion, Brick is prepared to acknowledge that there is some truth in his father's criticism; and they reach a tentative reconciliation.

Although Brooks stayed as close as possible to the text of the play in his film version, he did add one important location sequence to the story. The film begins with a scene that is not in the play, but was suggested in the play's dialogue. The hero is drunkenly trying to recapture his long-lost days as a star athlete. He does so by attempting to jump hurdles in a dark, deserted stadium, lit only by his car's headlights. As he jumps, an imaginary crowd can be heard on the sound track, roaring the approval he still craves. Then he stumbles and breaks his leg. This prologue was intended to establish the problem underlying Brick's character at the start of the story; a grown man with an adolescent's dream of acceptance on a mass scale—the crowd.

John Baxter observes that "Brooks's literary adaptations are sustained by their bravura performances"; indeed, he coaxes high passion from Elizabeth Taylor as Maggie fights to save her marriage to an alcoholic and guilt-ridden husband. And he elicits strong performances from Newman and Ives, particularly in their powerful quarrel scene. All in all, given the pressures and taboos that existed in the film industry at the time that Brooks made the film, he did a conscientious job of adapting *Cat* to the screen.

REFERENCES

Baxter, John, "Richard Brooks," in *International Dictionary of Films and Filmmakers: Directors*, vol. 2, ed. Laurie Hillstrom (Detroit: St. James Press, 1997), 117; Tyler, Parker, *Screening the Sexes: Homosexuality in the Movies* (New York: Da Capo, 1993), 307.

—*G.D.P.*

CEILING ZERO (1935)

FRANK WEAD (1894–1947)

Ceiling Zero (1935), U.S.A., directed by Howard Hawks, adapted by Frank "Spig" Wead; Warner Bros./Cosmopolitan.

The Play

Ceiling Zero premiered at New York's Music Box Theatre on April 10, 1935. Directed by Antoinette Perry, the play featured John Litel and Osgood Perkins in the roles of Dizzy Davis and Eastern Division Superintendent Jake Lee. The entire action takes place over a four-day period in the New Jersey Hadley Field Operations Office of Federal Air Lines at Newark. The play contrasts the lure of irresponsibility with the necessity of recognizing the responsibilities of age and maturity. Dizzy Davis and Jake Lee have been close friends ever since their flying days in World War I. But now their situations have changed. Jake has settled into a comfortable marriage and a desk job as supervisor of the Eastern Division of Federal Air Lines, while Dizzy retains his wartime behavior patterns of disregarding regulations and chasing women (unbeknownst to Jake, Dizzy has had an affair with his wife many years before). Other cast members include Dizzy's former roommate, Texas Clark, a pilot, and Mike, a victim of a flying accident that has left him brain-damaged. Wishing to bed a female pilot named Tommy, Dizzy rearranges his flying schedule by claiming a heart condition, so Texas takes his place. His irresponsibility leads to the death of his friend. In the meantime, the federal authorities ground Dizzy. However, feeling responsible for the death of his friend, Dizzy overpowers Tommy's boyfriend, Tay Lawson, who represents the educated generation of postwar college-trained pilots and flies a dangerous mission in his place. Although Tommy temporarily yields to Dizzy's suggestion to take his key and wait for him in his room, she returns to the control room intending to give it back when he lands. The play ends with Dizzy's voice over

the intercom advising Jake about adjustments to the plane's de-icer before he crashes. Finally, a loudspeaker announces the weather conditions signifying the play's title: "Visibility Zero. Ceiling Zero."

The Film

Director Howard Hawks saw the play during its modest 13-week Broadway run and was delighted to see in its cast his former *Scarface* friend, actor Osgood Perkins. Moreover, a former flyer himself in the Army Air Corps, Hawks was sympathetic to the story, especially since it was written by a fellow aviator. He may even have seen it as a sequel to his first sound film, another aviation picture called *The Dawn Patrol* (1930), with Dizzy and Jake Lee representing peacetime versions of Captain Courtney and Major Brand. Indeed, as critic Andrew Sarris has observed, aviation was Hawks' favorite subject, ideally suited to "dramatize the conflicts between the pioneer spirit of the old carefree, ne'er-do-well pilots and the mechanized modern aircraft industry supervised by government bureaucracy." It also has obvious affinities with other Hawks films about professional groups, like his earlier racing car film, *The Crowd Roars* (1932), also starring James Cagney. And it must be noted that it was envisaged as a perfect vehicle for those Warners stalwarts, James Cagney and Pat O'Brien as Dizzy and Jake, respectively.

Hawks brought in Pulitzer Prize–winning playwright Morrie Ryskind, coauthor of *Of Thee I Sing* and frequent Marx Brothers scenarist, to prune Wead's own 142-page screenplay. Hal Wallis also granted Hawks an unprecedented (for Warner Brothers) four-day rehearsal period. The film was finished after six weeks at a total cost of $375,000. Hawks opened out the play by setting scenes in an Italian restaurant to develop the romance between Dizzy and Tommy. Female characters such as air hostess Jane and Dizzy's common-law wife Birdie are missing. Also, Hawks eliminated Dizzy's sporadic advances toward Tommy and conflated them into one long seduction scene. Hawks may have helped future theatrical productions of Wead's play by removing several long speeches, including one in which Dizzy articulates Wead's theme that the real days of airplane pioneering are over, and another wherein Jake manipulates Dizzy's return to Newark to confirm the suspicions he has over him and Mary.

The vitality of *Ceiling Zero* as a film owes much to Hawks's direction. It deals not only with the lure of irresponsibility affecting Hawks's characters such as Dude in *Rio Bravo* and Robert Mitchum's sheriff in *El*

Dorado but also with the noble heroism characteristic of other figures in the Hawksian canon, such as *The Dawn Patrol's* Courtney and Thomas Mitchell's "The Kid" in *Only Angels Have Wings*. Like "The Kid," Dizzy's time in the professional arena is fast drawing to a close due to a heart condition (emphasized in the film but not in the play). However, both play and film stress the humanitarian aspects of Hawks's male professional group by showing Jake's care for Mike who is past his prime. Despite Dizzy's reaction at seeing an image of what he may become, Jake keeps Mike on as a janitor so he can still feed his family. Mike himself also parallels figures such as "The Kid" after his grounding and Walter Brennan's Stumpy in *Rio Bravo*. *Ceiling Zero* also touches on Hawks's fascination with the triangle theme of two men involved in past and present entanglements with the same woman. However, although Dizzy makes the noble sacrifice like Courtney, *Ceiling Zero* is one of the last Hawks films to embody the suicide concept, which the director later would regard as too convenient a solution to avoid high-pressure situations, as well as a ploy to avoid responsibility.

REFERENCES

McBride, Joseph, ed., *Focus on Howard Hawks* (Englewood Cliffs, N.J.: Prentice-Hall, 1972); McCarthy, Todd, *Howard Hawks: The Grey Fox of Hollywood* (New York: Grove Press, 1997).

—*T.W.*

LA CELESTINA (COMEDIA O TRAGICOMEDIA DE CALISTO Y MELIBEA) (1499)

FERNANDO DE ROJAS (15TH CENTURY)

La Celestina (1995), Spain, directed and adapted by Gerardo Vera; Sogetel/Lola Films/Sogepaq.

The Play

La Celestina is the common name by which most readers know the *Comedia o Tragicomedia de Calisto y Melibea* (The comedy or tragicomedy of Calisto and Melibea). It is a late medieval work that marks the beginning of the Spanish Renaissance. *La Celestina* enjoyed popularity from its first 16-act edition in 1499, enlarged in successive editions up to the 21 acts of the 1514 edition. This has been considered the standard version for subsequent editions and the one chosen for the 1995 film. Because of the success of the work and the popularity of the character of the go-between, the

tragicomedy began to be known by her name and even in present-day Spanish, "celestina" is a synonym of "pander."

The work is written as a dramatic dialogue, but it is difficult to consider it as a play suitable for the stage. Its 21 acts and the frequent changes in location present problems for a theatre performance. The story comes from a Latin medieval play, *Pamphilus*, which in turn was taken from Plautus. Calisto meets Melibea and falls in love with her. Since she rejects the nobleman, his servant Sempronio persuades him to hire Celestina. The servants make an arrangement with the old woman to share whatever they may obtain for bringing the lovers together. Calisto and Melibea begin their meetings but Celestina refuses to share her payment, and Calisto's servants Sempronio and Pármeno stab her, are caught and sentenced to death. Pármeno's lover, Areusa, holds Calisto responsible for the deaths of her friends and persuades Centurio, an official, to kill him. Instead, Centurio sends some men to give Calisto a beating, but he accidentally falls off Melibea's garden wall and dies. Melibea cannot endure the pain of having lost her lover and commits suicide by throwing herself off a tower.

La Celestina deals with those themes basic to the Middle Ages: love, fate, and death. Characters strive to achieve their particular goals regardless of their birth or social rank, and the portrait of society is one of restlessness and passions. Calisto and Melibea are derived from the paradigms of courtly love but they become the archetypes of Renaissance sentimental poetry. Celestina is the central character of the play because of her cunning and intelligence and desire for a pleasurable life. Her fate will be largely a consequence of her avarice, rather than her skill as a matchmaker. Nevertheless, the theme of sin and retribution is present.

The dialogue in *La Celestina* is considered an early masterpiece of Castilian dramatic prose. It achieves a balance between the scholarly and the realistic tradition, between rhetorical elaboration and popular language. Thus, erudite allusions are matched by sayings, irony, and humor. Dialogues emphasize the feelings and personalities of characters: the passion of lovers, the slyness and cowardice of servants, the individualism of Celestina and her friends, or the grief of parents.

The Film

Gerardo Vera is a well-known theatre director-turned filmmaker who adapted *La Celestina* for his second film outing. Although his first film, *Una mujer bajo la lluvia* (Woman in the rain, 1992) failed at the box office, *La Celestina*, released in 1995, was a success. The film adaptation follows the order of the events in the play closely. A more demanding task was the rendering of elaborate, 16th-century Spanish into contemporary dialogue. The original dialogue would have been an almost impossible challenge for spectators due to the difficulties of the language and the cryptic nature of many allusions. Thus, the screenplay cuts and adjusts the dialogue in a number of ways. Speeches are reduced to the portrayal of characters, to the presentation of the theme, and to the establishment of some facts of the past. The ability to present this contrast between the aristocracy and the common people has been one of the best achievements of Vera's adaptation. Extra care was taken with additional dialogues, which were written by Francisco Rico, a university specialist in Spanish medieval and Golden Age literature.

The most difficult and probably the least accomplished aspect of the film are the parts played by Calisto and Melibea. Although the realism of the dialogue in *La Celestina* has been praised by scholars of all periods, it often verges on exaggeration. In the screenplay, such rhetorical speeches have been cut but the elevated expression is still maintained. Strictly, the challenge was not to make Calisto and Melibea sound natural. Any spectator can accept a degree of artifice as a mark of their noble rank, but they should also speak passionately. Therefore, such shortcomings of the dialogue are due less to the lack of verisimilitude than to the lack of feeling.

The mise-en-scène and photography successfully contrast the worlds of aristocrats and common people. Early scenes in the film cross-cut between Calisto, filmed in static long shots alone in his bed chamber, and the servants, who, in dynamic editing and shot variety, rejoice in food and drink. There is comedy in the way Celestina pushes Pármeno into Areusa's bed and passion in the cross-cutting montage between Pármeno and Areusa's erotic scene, and Celestina's conjuration before a blazing fire. By contrast, the love scenes of Calisto and Melibea unfold in a more stylized and chaste manner. Such editing strategies are particularly effective at displaying the two plot lines and reinforcing other meanings derived from the language. The remarkable music track also contributes to the overall effect. It includes pieces that convey the Renaissance atmosphere, particularly the recurring guitar theme from *Fantasía para un gentilhombre*, composed by Joaquín Rodrigo in the style of a collection of courtly dances written by Gaspar Sanz in 1640.

Although this filmed version has kept all the major events of the plot, the moral purpose has been played down and Vera achieves a balance between the individuals' capacity to control their destiny and the inevitability of fate. Writing in *El pais*, A. Torres noted, "It is a faithful adaptation of the play by Fernando de Rojas, richly and accurately set."

REFERENCES

Gilman, Stephen, *The Art of La Celestina* (Madison: University of Wisconsin Press, 1956); Rojas, Fernando de, *Celestina*, tr. J. Mabbe (1631), ed. Dorothy S. Severin (Warminster: Aris & Phillips, 1987 [bilingual edition]); A. Torres, "La Celestina," *El pais*, November 11, 1997.

—*M.M-C.*

UN CHAPEAU DE PAILLE D'ITALIE (THE ITALIAN STRAW HAT) (1851)

EUGÈNE LABICHE (1815–1888)/MARC MICHEL

Un Chapeau de paille d'Italie (1927), France, adapted and directed by René Clair; Films Albatros.

The Play

First staged at the Palais-Royal vaudeville theatre, Labiche's fast-moving farce was laced with inventive wordplay, songs, and comic routines. It was an immediate success, much to the relief of the manager Dormeuil, who had considered the highly inventive satire of contemporary middle-class manners impossible to stage. The brilliantly constructed plot with its heady cocktail of improbable coincidences, deceptions, misunderstandings, and eccentric individuals proved a perfect vehicle for exposing bourgeois pretense and hypocrisy.

The action takes place in Paris. On his wedding day, Fadinard becomes embroiled with a cavalry officer (Emile) and his adulterous partner (Anaïs) when his horse eats her straw hat, a present from her husband (Beauperthuis). Fearing the ruined hat will alert the cuckolded husband, the couple threaten to destroy Fadinard's furniture if an immediate replacement is not found. The wedding guests take Fadinard to the ceremony, but, preoccupied with the hat, he slips into a milliner's shop, which the confused guests assume to be city hall. Fadinard learns that a baroness has bought an identical straw hat for her godchild and, as soon as the marriage formalities are over, he hurries to her mansion. She mistakes him for the tenor hired for her banquet, while the pursuing guests assume they have arrived at the reception and enjoy the meal. Fadinard slips away to the home of the godchild who is none other than the adulterous Anaïs. He innocently confides in the cuckolded husband who in turn demands to know his wife's whereabouts. Meanwhile, the pursuing wedding guests settle down in the house assuming it to be Fadinard's. All ends happily when a straw hat given as a wedding present is passed off as the missing hat. The cuckolded husband is persuaded of his wife's innocence and Fadinard is free to start his married life.

The Film

For this silent version of the vaudeville play, René Clair, who had already distinguished himself with avant-garde films like *Paris qui dort* (1924) and *Entr'acte* (1924), made several changes, replacing verbal humor with visual gags and introducing minor characters with well-worked comic routines. "To remain faithful to the spirit of the original," he contended, "I wrote the scenario as Labiche would have done had he been writing for the cinema." Few explanatory or prefatory titles are required in this highly visual reworking for the screen.

The action is transposed to the turn of the century with sets designed by Lazare Meerson and costumes by Souplet caricaturing the bourgeois love of ornamental furnishings and elegant dress, while a prewar theatrical acting style completes the sense of period. The whole is conceived as a frenetic Mack Sennett or Jean Durand chase, with the film medium adroitly used to provide a parallel montage of the double plot involving the wedding ceremonies and the search for the hat. Some plot elements are changed so that the episode involving the baroness and the banquet with Fadinard mistaken for a tenor is replaced by a sequence in a restaurant that sets the formal pattern of the Lancers' quadrille against Fadinard's imagined destruction of his property. As he miserably performs the dance, his worst fears are made concrete: Chairs fly from his windows; elegant mirrors are smashed; the nuptial bed careers down the street; finally the house itself explodes. The visualization of real events is also used when Fadinard innocently tells Beauperthuis about the eating of the hat and the embarrassment of the lovers emerging from the bushes. Other successful sequences include the mayor's interminable speech with guests first falling asleep, then leaving while he still drones on, and the episode of the distraught Beauperthuis chasing Fadinard with a gun. Further additions involve street scenes as characters rush from location to location in their carriages, often mocked by bystanders; slapstick episodes in the milliner's where confusion reigns over hats and hat boxes; comic routines with trousers and shoes at Beauperthuis's home; and a sequence involving various objects thrown from Fadinard's house (a clock and a

chair gratefully collected by a passing rag-and-bone man). A series of running jokes involving the secondary puppet-like characters constantly enlivens the narrative: shoes that pinch; a missing glove; a bow tie out of place; an irritating dress pin; a blocked ear-trumpet. Although not an immediate commercial success the film earned critical acclaim and initiated an important artistic relationship between Clair and Lazare Meerson, while the excellent performances of Albert Préjean (Fadinard), Paul Olivier (Vesinet, the deaf uncle), and Jim Gerald (Beauperthuis) confirmed their positions as leading comic actors of the day.

REFERENCES

Dale, R. C., *The Films of René Clair*, 2 vols. (Metuchen, N.J.: Scarecrow Press, 1986); McGerr, Celia, *René Clair* (Boston: Twayne, 1980); Mitry, Jean, *René Clair* (Paris: Editions Universitaires, 1960).

—*R.F.C.*

CHILDREN OF A LESSER GOD (1980)

MARK MEDOFF (1940–)

Children of a Lesser God (1986), U.S.A., directed by Randa Haines, adapted by Mark Medoff and Hesper Anderson; Paramount.

The Play

Mark Medoff had two off-Broadway successes behind him, *When You Comin' Back, Red Ryder?* (1973), about the brutalizing effects of a bully, and *The Wager* (1974), about the seduction of gambling, when he turned to *Children of a Lesser God* (1980). This two-act play premiered in New York at the Longacre Theatre on March 30, 1980, where it ran for a spectacular 887 performances. It concerns an instructor at a school for the deaf, James Leeds (John Rubinstein), who is assigned the task of teaching Sarah Norman (Phyllis Frelich) lip reading and speaking skills (she uses only sign language). Older than most of the other students, she is a difficult, even hostile student. However, James and Sarah fall in love and marry. But the marriage falls apart because of Sarah's fears that they might have a deaf child. The play was conceived in expressionist terms, i.e., it takes place in James' mind, and the characters step forth from his memory to perform on a bare stage, with only a bench and a blackboard for props. Actress Phyllis Frelich was herself born deaf. The Tony Award–winning play was universally praised. Critic

Otis L. Guernsey, Jr., declared it to be the best of the season and described it as "an outcry for a group which, it insists, speaks more eloquently for itself in signs than hearing people are able to manage with mere words."

The Film

When director Randa Haines and playwright Mark Medoff adapted *Children of a Lesser God* for the screen, they abandoned the original expressionist conception and added realistic interior and exterior scenes. Accordingly, it is no longer a memory play but a third-person view of real events. Only the nude scenes in the swimming pool may be interpreted in a subjective way. There are also significant changes in the plot and the characters. Eliminated entirely is the dorm counselor Orin, a deaf person who speaks and reads lips, who is James' rival for Sarah's affections. Also gone is Orin's lawsuit against the school. Another character who didn't make the cut, as it were, is Lydia, another deaf student who is in love with James. Laid bare is the main business between James and Sarah. She has been emotionally damaged as a result of adolescent sexual encounters, and she fears commitment. James' desire to help her may be only a thinly disguised attempt to control her. When she confronts him about his Pygmalion-like behavior, he gains a deeper understanding of her problems and his own motivations. Their struggle is resolved when he understands that she wants to be an "I" rather than a "we." Their discussion of "connection" becomes clearer, and they are able to be "joined" as equals. A secondary focus in the film is James' work with his students. These scenes achieve a peculiar poignancy in the film's superb use of close-ups to depict the graceful gestures of the signers. Hands and fingers achieve an almost balletic quality as they describe words—and meanings—in the air. William Hurt portrayed James and Marlee Matlin made her film debut in an Oscar-winning performance as Sarah.

REFERENCES

Erben, Rudolf, *Mark Medoff* (Boise, Idaho: Boise State University Press, 1995).

—*J.C.T.*

THE CHILDREN'S HOUR (1934)

LILLIAN HELLMAN (1905–1984)

These Three (1936), U.S.A., directed by William Wyler, adapted by Lillian Hellman; Samuel Goldwyn/ United Artists.

The Children's Hour (1961), U.S.A., directed by William Wyler, adapted by Lillian Hellman and John Michael Hayes; United Artists.

The Play

One of America's most important playwrights in the 1930s, Lillian Hellman combined in her plays chilling portraits of the workings of evil with tacked-on moral preachments. Born into a middle-class Jewish family in New Orleans, Hellman attended New York University and Columbia University, where she wrote her first short stories. After a stint as a book reviewer for the *New York Herald Tribune*, she became a play reader for the Broadway producer Herman Shumlin. It was through her association with novelist Dashiell Hammett that she first became acquainted with an early 19th-century Scottish lawsuit, "Great Drumsheugh Case," which she transformed into her first stage success, *The Children's Hour*. It was produced by Herman Shumlin in New York at Maxine Elliott's Theatre on November 20, 1934, where it ran for a spectacular 691 performances.

The setting is the Wright-Dobie School, a boarding school in a converted farmhouse. In Act One we meet Mary Tilford (Florence McGee), a sullen, 14-year-old student who is in the habit of spreading vicious lies. Her teacher, Karen Wright (Katherine Emery), who is about to be married, tries to discipline her. Mary, in retaliation, overhears gossip concerning Karen's affectionate relationship with her friend and colleague, Martha Dobie (Anne Revere). Mary decides to run away and brutally abuses a schoolfriend to obtain some travel money. Act Two transpires in Mary's home, where she tells her grandmother horrendous lies about the "strange" relationship between Karen and Martha. The grandmother calls her friends, and they all withdraw their children from the school. Karen and her fiancé, a local doctor, are appalled and try to reason with Mary's grandmother. "We're human beings, see? It's our lives you're fooling with." Karen's fiancé exposes Mary's lies, but the child is undaunted. "Everybody is yelling at me," she cries; "I don't know what I'm saying with everybody mixing me all up." Mary even extorts a schoolfriend into backing up her story. Act Three takes up the action seven months later. The Wright-Dobie School is no more. Karen realizes that her fiancé is not quite sure about her relationship with Martha. Indeed, Martha confesses that

50

perhaps she had indeed harbored lesbian longings for her friend. "I love you that way," she says, "maybe the way they said I loved you." Blaming herself for the disaster, Martha goes into an adjoining room and shoots herself. A few minutes later Mrs. Tilford, the grandmother of the wicked Mary, arrives and admits she is sorry about the destruction she and her grandchild had caused. After begging Karen to go ahead and marry the doctor, she begs forgiveness. As the old woman leaves, Karen stands at the window, quietly watching.

The Children's Hour was the sensation of the season, but it was banned in London, Boston, and Chicago. It brought Hellman fame and money and won her the newly established New York Drama Critics Award. It was revived, with somewhat lesser success, in 1952. Critic Brooks Atkinson upbraided Hellman for the use of several melodramatic clichés: "Please, Miss Hellman," he wrote, "conclude the play before the pistol shot and before the long arm of coincidence starts wobbling in its socket. Leave them the dignity of their hatred and despair." Eight years later, in her introduction to *Four Plays*, Hellman agreed, declaring, "The play probably should have ended with Martha's suicide; the last scene is tense and over-burdened." Hellman observed that the play's most important concern was not its lesbian theme but the more general subject of lying. "The bigger the lie the better, as always," she wrote, adding that it was lies that made the neurotic child "the utterly malignant creature which audiences see in her." Hellman's later works included *The Little Foxes* (1939), *Watch on the Rhine* (1941), *Another Part of the Forest* (1946), *The Autumn Garden* (1951), and *Toys in the Attic* (1960). Her work has been generally characterized as belonging to the Ibsenesque *Pièce bien faite* school of drama, i.e., combining the contrivances of the thriller with social messages about the role of the individual in society.

The Films

The success and controversy of *The Children's Hour* brought Hellman to the attention of Hollywood and Sam Goldwyn, who hired her in 1935 as a screenwriter at $2,500 a week. After scripting *Dark Angel* in 1935—a shameless tearjerker—she signed on to adapt *The Children's Hour* to the screen. The result, *These Three*, directed by William Wyler (in the first of his many associations with Goldwyn and with cinematographer Gregg Toland), is almost unrecognizable from the original. It abandoned the lesbian theme, which ran afoul of the film industry's Production Code Administration, and substituted a heterosexual love triangle in which Mary (Bonita Granville) spies

Martha (Miriam Hopkins) in an embrace with Karen's (Merle Oberon) fiancé, Dr. Cardin (Joel McRea). A slander suit is brought to court and dismissed. Martha subsequently admits to Karen her affection for Cardin; and Cardin loses his post at the hospital. There is a happy ending, however, as Karen and Cardin are reunited in Vienna. Among Hellman's additions to the story are an extended prologue in which the triangular relationship among the three principal characters develops.

It has been suggested by commentators Bernard Dick and John Baxter that Hellman's script subtly suggests the lesbian theme. Biographer Michael Anderegg, disagrees. Although he flatly declares there is no lesbian subtext, he does admit that the film retains some of the play's powerful moral statement: "*These Three* condemns sexual hypocrisy at the same time that the circumstances of its creation exemplify the very hypocrisy. The film suggests—but never directly states—that an open attitude toward sexual curiosity and desire among the young as well as the old might have prevented misunderstanding and conclusions." Anderegg also singles out for praise the performance of Miriam Hopkins as Martha, who provides the character "with a genuine complexity, and revealing a core of insecurity and loneliness in her that explains how she could turn to either Joe or Karen for affection."

Director William Wyler regretted he could not shoot the original play, so in 1960, after the Production Code had considerably weakened, he returned to the story. Besides, he welcomed the opportunity to film a small-scale drama after the exhausting work he had just completed on *Ben Hur*. He asked Hellman once again to adapt her play. She began a new script, but when Dashiell Hammett died in 1960, she lost all interest. Wyler turned to John Michael Hayes, who had scripted several of Alfred Hitchcock's most successful films, including *Rear Window* and *The Man Who Knew Too Much*. Audrey Hepburn portrayed Karen, Shirley MacLaine was Martha, Karen Balkin was Mary, and James Garner was Dr. Cardin. Miriam Hopkins was back, this time in the role of Martha's aunt, Mrs. Lily Mortar. Initially titled *Infamous*, the picture went into rehearsals in May 1961 at the Goldwyn Studios. The results, for Wyler at least, were disastrous. The problem, he admitted, was that the film was too respectful to the original play: "Miss Hellman was busy at the time," he said, "and couldn't work on the second script, and I adhered too closely to the original play, which had dated badly. By the time I remade the story, so what if two lady school teachers had an affair? Who cared?" Critic Bosley Crowther likewise tagged the film and the play as a "cultural antique." Perhaps Wyler and Crowther's opinions were misguided. Allegations of homosexuality among teachers is indeed a volatile issue, as today's newspaper headlines continue to attest. *The Children's Hour* closely followed the original play, but, in the opinion of Anderegg, it strengthened it through characterization and directorial emphasis. Martha, for example, no longer was in any way stereotypically lesbian; rather, Shirley MacLaine's performance lends the role a sympathy and vulnerability it had lacked. A new scene is added in which a conversation between Mrs. Tilford and Martha's aunt gives new credibility to the little girl's lies. Moreover, a new ending makes it clear that Joe and Karen will never be reconciled in the future.

The atmosphere of the school is claustrophobic with its low ceilings and arches enveloping the characters. Care is taken in the camera placements and deep-focus photography to keep the slyly watchful Mary in the frame, a chilling presence in the otherwise adult world. Long shots, as opposed to the expected close-ups during intimate moments, tend to underplay the drama, never allowing the action to descend into mawkish melodrama. Ironically, even though PCA censorship was on the wane in Hollywood, the word "lesbian" is never used in the film (nor was it ever uttered in Hellman's play). "It would no doubt have helped both Wyler's reputation and the box office," opines Anderegg, "if everyone involved had been willing to go beyond Hellman's frequently unconvincing theatrics to a genuine struggle with the implications of homosexuality, though it seems unlikely that, in 1962, such a film could have been made. As it is, *The Children's Hour* now seems a very hesitant step into virtually uncharted waters."

REFERENCES

Anderegg, Michael, *William Wyler* (Boston: Twayne, 1979); MacNicholas, John, *Twentieth-Century American Dramatists* (Detroit: Gale Research Company, 1981); Stern, Richard G., "Lillian Hellman on Her Plays," *Contact*, 3 (1959), 113–119.

—*J.C.T.*

CLASH BY NIGHT (1940)

CLIFFORD ODETS (1906–1963)

Clash by Night (1952), U.S.A., directed by Fritz Lang, adapted by Alfred Hayes; RKO.

The Play

Clifford Odets was the leading playwright of 1930s left-wing social protest. His work with the Group Theatre resulted in his best-known plays, *Waiting for Lefty* (1935), about a taxi drivers' union strike, *Awake and Sing!* (1935), about a troubled, poor Jewish family, and *Golden Boy* (1937), about an Italian-American musician who abandons his talent for a career as a prizefighter. In later plays, like *Clash by Night* (1940) and *The Country Girl* (1950), he seemingly abandoned his political leanings for the more commercially viable trappings of romance and melodrama. *Clash by Night* opened in Detroit on October 27, 1941. Set in Staten Island during a hot summer season, it involves a love triangle among Jerry Wilenski (Lee J. Cobb), a poor day laborer, Mae (Tallulah Bankhead), his wife (who dreams of "big, comfortable men"), and Earl (Joseph Schildkraut), a movie projectionist. At Jerry's insistence, Earl moves in with him and Mae. Soon, the trusting Jerry discovers Earl and Mae are sleeping together. Encouraged by his alcoholic Uncle Vince, Jerry strangles Earl to death in the theatre projection booth. At the play's end, Mae mounts the steps to the projection booth, heading toward a fate that is undisclosed. In contrast to the love triangle is the relationship of Joe Doyle, a responsible young man (who serves as Odets' spokesman), and Peggy, his patient girlfriend. Their marriage appears to be imminent at the play's conclusion. Odets hinted that behind the melodrama of the characters' discontents was a political statement: "Part of the theme of this play is about how men irresponsibly wait for the voice and strong arm of Authority to bring them to life, to shape and working disciplines. So can come fascism to a whole race of people."

By the time the play opened in New York at the Belasco Theatre on December 27, 1941, dissension among cast members and fallout from the Pearl Harbor disaster 20 days before may have influenced the unfavorable press notices. Biographer Gerald Weales reports that most critics treated the play "simply as a sordid triangle." It closed after only 49 performances.

The Film

Beginning with *Fury* in 1935, émigré director Fritz Lang produced a notable series of American films interrogating the closed reality of the delusional American Dream. Like other *films noir* of the time, Lang exposed the existence of suppressed dreams and desires in the world around him. He pursued this theme not only in tough gangster films like *The Big Heat* (1952) and thrillers like *The Ministry of Fear* (1944) but also in mordant romance melodramas like *Scarlet Street* (1945) and *The Woman in the Window* (1944). As Alfred A. Appel, Jr., has observed, Lang is the "classicist" of the *film noir*, "an economical and precise craftsman whose carefully controlled effects are all the more powerful for the compression of their means." However, his adaptation of *Clash by Night* softens his typically acerbic and trenchant vision. It minimizes the tensions among the characters created by their economic and class disparities and by the omnipresent effects of the crushing summer heat. Here, the setting is a fishing village, and Jerry (Paul Douglas) is the captain of a fishing boat. The film begins when Mae (Barbara Stanwyck) meets Jerry in the fishing village and, despite her warnings that she is not right for him (a caveat not in the original play), marries him and bears him a child. Upon discovering her infidelity with Earl (Robert Ryan), Jerry intends to kill Earl. But he cannot carry out the threat. Instead, he takes away the baby to his boat. Mae, in turn, dismisses Earl and joins Jerry. This absurd ending savages what some critics have described as Odets' "most despairing" play. The characters themselves are softened—Jerry is no longer a pitiful loser; Mae now has a conscience; and Earl is not the sleazy cad Odets had envisioned. Also altered are the secondary characters of Joe Doyle and Peggy. As a result of Marilyn Monroe's performance, Peggy is now a flamboyantly sexy character and Joe (Keith Andes) is a violent chauvinist.

On the whole, the drama was an uphill challenge for the cast. The always reliable Barbara Stanwyck struggled with overwrought scenes like the one where she confronts Earl: "What kind of animal am I? Do I have fangs, do I purr? What jungle am I from?" And Paul Douglas' emasculated Jerry has to enact a scene where he hugs his baby and makes baby-talk in the moonlight. "Unlike the play," opines commentator Patrick McGilligan, "the film version of *Clash by Night* had to abide by the cautious atmosphere of 1950s America. For the first time in any Fritz Lang film (disregarding the feebly comic *You and Me*), not a single person expires. Everyone turns apologetic. . . . The message was contrition and redemption." True, the wobbly, uneven characterizations and tone are a far cry from Lang's standard. However, Nicholas Musuraca's cinematography nicely captures the moody atmosphere of the Monterey locations.

As a footnote to all this, shortly before the film's release in May 1952, Odets became a "combative informer" before the House Un-American Activities Committee's investigations into alleged communist infiltrations in Hollywood. Perhaps, as commentator McGilligan alleges, the fate of *Clash by Night* and Odets' future in Hollywood were at stake, for he named six names—"all dead or expendable people in his view"—and as a result was "passed" by HUAC. "He was guaranteed work as script doctor in Hollywood for the rest of his short, haunted life."

REFERENCES

Appel, Jr., Alfred, "Fritz Lang's American Nightmare," *Film Comment*, 10:6 (November–December 1974), 12–17; Jensen, Paul M., *The Cinema of Fritz Lang* (New York: A.S. Barnes, 1969); Weales, Gerald, *Clifford Odets: Playwright* (New York: Pegasus Books, 1971).

—*J.C.T.*

COME BACK, LITTLE SHEBA (1949)

WILLIAM INGE (1913–1973)

Come Back, Little Sheba (1952), U.S.A., directed by Daniel Mann, adapted by Ketti Frings; Paramount.

The Play

In a very real sense, William Inge never strayed far from his roots in the American Midwest. Born in Independence, a little town in southeast Kansas, he was educated at the University of Kansas, taught drama at Stephens College in Missouri, and worked as a dramatic critic for the *St. Louis Star-Times*. Almost all of his work reflects his midwestern roots, especially his sensitivity to the frustrations, sexual repressions, and thwarted opportunities of small-town people. *Come Back, Little Sheba* (1950) was his second play, and his first to reach the Broadway stage. It premiered at the Booth Theatre on February 15, 1950, and, although it received sharply divided critical notices, it ran for a respectable 190 performances. Doc Delaney (Sidney Blackmer) is a failed physician struggling with alcoholism and a dysfunctional marriage to his fat and smothering wife, Lola (Shirley Booth). When Lola encourages their attractive lodger, Marie (Joan Lorring), to entertain her lover in her room, the sexually frustrated Doc hits the bottle and, in a fit of violence, smashes up the apartment and tries to kill Lola. He "dries out" in a hospital and, upon returning home, reconciles with Lola. She, in turn, realizes that her daydreaming (including laments over her lost baby and her long-lost puppy, Sheba) has jeopardized the relationship. Doc and Lola prepare to get on with their marriage.

Sheba placed second in the balloting for the New York Drama Critics Circle's "best new play of the 1949–1950 season," losing out to Carson McCullers' *Member of the Wedding*. In her study of small-town American plays, Ima Honaker Herron notes the play's special qualities: "As a bare, almost clinical characterization of a middle-aged and intellectually mismated couple, the play exhibits a young playwright's genuine concern for hapless people, beset by secret frustrations and dreams of a better life—for small-town natives who, transplanted to a small midwestern city, live lives 'of quiet desperation,' knowing in themselves that their narrow world will not improve, yet clinging to hope."

The Film

There was no question at the start that the Tony Award–winning Shirley Booth would be the choice of film producer Hal Wallis to repeat her stage role of Lola and that the play's original director, Daniel Mann, would bring it to the screen. Despite the prestige of the play and the actress, however, the Paramount brass were appalled at what was perceived as the sordid nature of the story itself. "Prepared to accept glamorous men and women in melodramas of the seamy side of life, they were shocked at the thought of making a picture with beaten, unkempt, depressing people," reports Wallis. Perhaps that's why young Burt Lancaster, fresh from his triumph in the swashbuckling *The Crimson Pirate*, was signed on to replace the stage's Sidney Blackmer and portray the sixtyish Doc. It was Lancaster's idea to transform the weakling Doc into a strong man debilitated by his wife over a period of years. Lancaster padded out his trim physique with a shapeless sweater, he wore baggy trousers to make him appear wide at the hips, and he adopted a stoop in his posture. Otherwise, Ketti Frings's screenplay made no major changes in the play and characterizations. It won "Best Picture" at the Cannes Film Festival, and the Motion Picture Academy voted Shirley Booth the best actress Oscar for 1952.

REFERENCES

Herron, Ima Honaker, *The Small Town in American Drama* (Dallas: Southern Methodist University Press, 1969); Voss, Ralph F., *A Life of William Inge: The Strains of Triumph* (Lawrence: University of Kansas Press, 1989); Windeler, Robert, *Burt Lancaster* (New York: St. Martin's Press, 1984).

—*J.C.T.*

THE CONNECTION (1959)

JACK GELBER (1932–)

The Connection (1962), U.S.A., directed by Shirley Clarke, adapted by Jack Gelber; The Connection Co.-Allen-Hidgdon/Films Around the World.

The Play

When *The Connection*, the first play by 27-year-old Jack Gelber, opened off-Broadway in 1959, it became a theatrical cause célèbre. Directed by Judith Malina, Gelber's unflinching probe into the nether world of solipsistic junkies was pilloried by the New York press as an apologia for drug use. Louis Calta of the *New York Times* dismissed it as "a farrago of dirt, small-time philosophy, empty talk and extended runs of 'cool music'." Despite such broadsides, *The Connection* won a loyal following. Writing for *The New Republic*, Robert Brustein described it as "the first hipster drama to be seen in New York . . . the only honest and balanced work ever created by a Beat Generation writer." *The New Yorker*'s Donald Malcolm added that it was the "first really interesting new play to appear off-Broadway in a good long time."

For adventurous theatregoers, there were numerous attractions. First, *The Connection* was a production of the Living Theatre, at the time, the most influential experimental theatre troupe of the period. Second, it upped the naturalistic ante of playwrights Arthur Miller, Tennessee Williams, and William Inge by presenting a galvanizing slice-of-life stripped of virtually all theatrical artifice. Third, it dealt forthrightly with the then largely taboo subject of heroin addiction. Fourth, it featured a quartet of noted jazzmen who provided a half-hour's worth of sizzling bebop for each of the play's two acts. In fact, *The Connection* was given a boost by the soundtrack album released by the connoisseur Blue Note label and featuring the play's onstage foursome of pianist/leader Freddie Redd, alto saxophonist Jackie McLean, bassist Michael Mattos, and drummer Larry Ritchie. Finally, Gelber's interracial casting, in contrast to the prevailing social and theatrical attitudes of the late 1950s, suggested that skin color was of little consequence.

Gelber's play takes place in "Leach's pad" where several addicts wait nervously for Cowboy, the ostensible "connection" of the title. Before Cowboy finally returns with the heroin at the play's end, Gelber's characters, to cite Kenneth Tynan, explore the meaning of life as "absentees from the daytime universe" whose relationship to society is not one of enmity, but rather of truancy. Presented as a reflexively self-conscious play-within-a-play, the addicts, including Leach (Warren Finnerty) and Cowboy (Carl Lee), occasionally step out of character to respond to Jim Dunn, the fictive producer of the "play" contained within Gelber's drama, and Jaybird, the fictive author and, to a degree, Gelber's alter-ego. Opening on July 15, 1959, *The Connection* enjoyed a run of 722 performances at New York's Living Theatre. The production won a number of awards in New York, and subsequently, in 1961, at the Théâtre des Nations in Paris.

The Film

In the faithful adaptation of the play, there were few changes except for substituting a film-within-a-film structure for Gelber's original play-within-a-play format. Significantly, instead of "opening up" the play, the usual procedure in cinematic adaptations of stage works, director Shirley Clarke restricted her camera to the claustrophobic confines of Leach's pad. The junkies, in order to help subsidize their heroin "buy," agree to let documentary filmmaker Jim Dunn and his cameraman, J.J. Burden, film them for a fee. As they kill time, as in the play, they reveal themselves through small talk and philosophical quips. Interludes of spirited jazz in the argot of bebop pioneer Charlie Parker are played by the jazz quartet of Redd, McLean, Mattos, and Ritchie, who had opened with the play in 1959. Other holdovers are actors Warren Finnerty (Leach), Jerome Raphel (Solly), Garry Goodrow (Ernie), Henry Proach (Harry), Barbara Winchester (Sister Salvation), and Carl Lee (Cowboy). Added for the film are William Redfield (Jim Dunn, the filmmaker), Roscoe Lee Browne (J.J. Burden, Dunn's cinematographer), and James Anderson (Sam). Toward the end of the film, when Cowboy returns to the pad, the men file one-by-one into the dingy bathroom for their brief moments of injected ecstasy. At the conclusion, Dunn deems his documentary film experiment a failure.

Reviews were mixed. Dwight Macdonald praised the Clarke adaptation's depiction of junkies as individuals, while Stanley Kauffmann found the film a flawed exercise in overwrought naturalism. As a low-budget independent feature, the 110-minute *The Connection* received only limited distribution. And because "shit" is uttered as a junkie synonym for heroin, *The Connection*'s New York opening was delayed by censors until successfully litigated by the film's distributor. As a result, the Clarke-Gelber collaboration film never had a real chance to win an art house following. Today, while having significant historical value as a glimpse into the late 1950s' worlds of drugs, jazz, and experi-

mental theatre, *The Connection* "plays" as dated as the jargon of its hipster-junkies.

REFERENCES

Gelber, Jack, *The Connection* (New York: Grove Press, 1960), includes Kenneth Tynan's insightful "Introduction"; Kauffmann, Stanley, *A World on Film* (New York: Harper and Row, 1966); Macdonald, Dwight, *On Movies* (Englewood Cliffs, N.J.: Prentice-Hall, 1969).

—*C.M.B.*

COQUETTE (1927)

GEORGE ABBOTT (1887–1995)/ANN PRESTON BRIDGERS (1900–1967)

Coquette (1929), U.S.A., directed by Sam Taylor, adapted by Taylor and John Grey; United Artists.

The Play

Playwright Ann Preston Bridgers had worked with theatrical impresario George Abbott on several plays when she came up with the idea for *Coquette*. Originally titled *Norma's Affairs*, it was conceived as a comedy with a happy ending. However, producer Jed Harris demanded changes in tone and structure, and the final version emerged as a satire with tragic implications. Under its new title, *Coquette*, it premiered in New York at Maxine Elliott's Theatre on November 8, 1927, and ran for a spectacular 366 performances. The title character, Norma Besant (Helen Hayes), is a beautiful, flirtatious, and conniving daughter of a gallant of the Old South, Dr. John Besant (Charles Waldron). One of her admirers is young Michael Jeffrey (Eliot Cabot), who, because of his relative poverty and lack of social connections, is discouraged by Dr. Besant. When Jeffrey persists in his attentions, Besant shoots him dead. At Besant's subsequent murder trial, Norma conceals the fact that she is pregnant with Jeffrey's child. Rather than allow this revelation to come out in court, thus weakening her father's defense case and staining her own honor, she commits suicide. The critic for the *Evening Post* called the play "a fragile and exquisite tragedy, a truly rare and touching evening in the theatre."

The Film

After making her last silent film, *My Best Girl* (1927), Mary Pickford sought a vehicle for her first talking picture. Weary of her "little girl" and plucky ingenue

Mary Pickford won a Best Actress Oscar for her first talkie, Coquette, *in 1929.* (COURTESY MARY PICKFORD FOUNDATION)

roles, she was attracted by the dramatic implications of the tragic Norma, a chaste yet coquettish Southern belle trapped between the restrictions of her social code and by her own sexual awakening. However, the limitations imposed upon filmmakers by the censorial Hays Office required major changes in the screenplay. The world's "imperfections" might be the stuff of good drama, writes author Greg Black in his history of Hollywood censorship, *Hollywood Censored,* but the Hollywood censors "saw no reason why films should not show simple and direct solutions to complex moral, political, economic, and philosophical issues." Thus, scenarists Sam Taylor and John Grey side-stepped her pregnancy, keeping Norma's character essentially chaste and restricting her encounters with Jeffrey (John Mack Brown) to a few tepid kisses and lines like "I love you more than anything in the world; I love you even more than my Daddy." Norma could never be

permitted to commit suicide at the conclusion of the courtroom scene, so the censors demanded that her father (John Sainpolis) take on that burden. Although suicide was generally rejected by movie censors, Dr. Besant's self-destruction could be construed as an act of reparation and expiation for his murder of Jeffrey.

The film's production values strongly reflect the proscenium-bound nature of the original play, as well as the restrictions imposed upon filmmakers by the new sound technology. Entire scenes from the play are transferred virtually intact, and the blocking of the action is limited to shallow-depth interior sets (designed by William Cameron Menzies). Entrances and exits use the right and left sides of the frame as if they were the wings of a stage. Cinematographer Karl Struss shot the courtroom scenes in a flat light with six cameras running simultaneously, permitting a modicum of cutting. Moreover, John Mack Brown's performance as Jeffrey (originally played on stage by Eliot Cabot) is all too typical of the stiffness associated with actors unaccustomed to the microphone. While Pickford's performance is hardly any better—marred by a thin voice and an insistently declamatory style—it did earn her a best actress Oscar, winning over heavy competition, including Ruth Chatterton in *Madame X*, Betty Compson in *The Barker*, Bessie Love in *Broadway Melody*, and Jeanne Eagels in *The Letter*. That her Oscar triumph may have been more an acknowledgment of her lifetime achievement than an individual performance was suggested by the critic for *Photoplay*, who admitted it was "a creditable first try" for her, but complained that "few could be found who could agree with the Academicians that it was last year's outstanding labor before the microphone." Nonetheless, *Coquette* grossed over $1.3 million domestically, establishing it as one of her most successful pictures.

REFERENCES

Black, Gregory, *Hollywood Censored* (New York: Cambridge University Press, 1994); Eyman, Scott, *Mary Pickford: America's Sweetheart* (New York: Donald I. Fine, 1990); Tibbetts, John, "*Coquette*: Mary Pickford Finds a Voice," *Films in Review*, 48:1–2 (January–February 1997), 61–66.

—*J.C.T.*

CORN IS GREEN, THE (1938)

EMLYN WILLIAMS (1905–1987)

The Corn Is Green (1945), U.S.A., directed by Irving Rapper, adapted by Casey Robinson and Frank Cavett; Warner Bros.

The Play

Emlyn Williams was Wales' first successful dramatist. His most notable plays, written in English, include the murder thriller, *Night Must Fall* (1935), and the coming-of-age drama, *The Corn Is Green* (1938). The latter play is largely autobiographical, and it draws from his experiences as a boy in a Welsh mining town, whose education is stimulated by a devoted English teacher, and who subsequently attends Oxford. The three-act play premiered in London on September 20, 1938, and starred Williams himself as the young man, Morgan Evans, and Sybil Thorndike as Miss Moffat. The play went to Broadway in the 1940–41 season and featured Ethel Barrymore as Miss Moffat. It ran for a spectacular 236 performances.

In the play, confined entirely to a schoolroom, Miss Moffat is an educated spinster of 40 who comes to Glensarno, Wales, with her cockney housekeeper, Mrs. Watty, and Mrs. Watty's teenage daughter, Bessie. When she discovers the town's appalling rate of illegitimacy, she establishes a school for the children. She even pays the children's parents what they would have earned working in the mines. "These nippers are to be cut off from [an education]," she angrily declares, "because they happen to be born penniless in an uncivilised countryside, coining gold down there in that stinking dungeon for some beef-headed old miser!" Because the local squire, a coal mine owner, objects to her establishing a school building, she converts her own home to a classroom. Her "star" pupil is Morgan Evans, who has written an essay comparing the darkness of the mines with the fields "where the corn is green." She determines to get him a scholarship at Oxford University. Despite her avowed feminist views, she cons the squire into helping her. Morgan, meanwhile, begins to resent her overbearing influence on him, and he is teased by his friends for his newly acquired skills at spoken English. He also enters into a brief affair with Bessie Watty. Finally, he passes the scholarship exam, successfully interviews for the Oxford scholarship, and returns to Glensarno in triumph. "Everything I have ever learned from those books, and from you," he tells Moffat, "was lighted up—like a magic lantern. . . . Everything had a meaning." When Miss Moffat learns that Morgan and Bessie have had a child—and that Bessie expects Morgan to marry her—she agrees to adopt the baby, freeing Bessie to marry a new admirer and Morgan to go to school. Morgan's duty, she says, "is to the world," to free other children like him from the coal mines.

The Film

After serving an apprenticeship with Warner Bros. star director, Michael Curtiz, Irving Rapper scored with his first films, *One Foot in Heaven* (1941) and *Now, Voyager* (1942). He brought his scenarist of choice, Casey Robinson, and his favorite actress, Bette Davis, to the adaptation of *The Corn Is Green*. The film closely parallels the play and retains much of the dialogue. In secondary roles, Rhys Williams, Rosalind Ivan, Mildred Dunnock, and Gene Moss reprised their Broadway performances. In the leads were newcomer John Dall as Morgan Evans and Joan Lorring as Bessie. The action is confined to Miss Moffat's schoolroom, with an occasional glimpse of the surrounding areas. These exterior scenes depict Bessie's seduction of Morgan, Miss Moffat's drive to town to inquire about the rental of a school building, and Morgan's being taunted in a bar because he speaks English rather than Welsh (the film omits the play's sequences that are spoken entirely in Welsh). In his screen debut John Dall was nominated for an Oscar for his role of Morgan. While some critics objected to the disproportionate screen time devoted to the singing of Welsh songs and hymns, there were no quibbles regarding the screenplay's fidelity to the play. James Agee, however, found much to object to in Bette Davis' performance. "I like and respect Miss Davis as a most unusually sincere and hard-working actress, and I have seen her play extremely well; but I did not find much in this performance to bring one beyond liking, respect, and, I am afraid, a kind of sympathy which no healthily functioning artist needs. It seems to me she is quite limited, which may be no sin but is a pity, and that she is limiting herself beyond her rights by becoming more and more set, official, and first-ladyish in mannerism and spirit. . . ."

REFERENCES

Agee, James, *Agee on Film* (Boston: Beacon Press, 1968); Findlater, Richard, *Emlyn Williams* (London: Rockliff, 1956); Ringgold, Gene, *Bette Davis: Her Films and Career* (Secaucus, N.J.: Citadel Press, 1985).

—*J.C.T.*

COUNSELLOR AT LAW (1931)

ELMER RICE (1892–1967)

Counsellor at Law (1933), U.S.A., directed by William Wyler, adapted by Elmer Rice; Universal.

The Play

After earlier successes such as *The Adding Machine* (1923) and the Pulitzer Prize–winning *Street Scene* (1929), *Counsellor at Law* consolidated Elmer Rice's standing as one of the most important American dramatists of his day. His particular strength lay in his gift for exploring sensitive social issues such as class snobbery and anti-Semitism within the format of the well-made play. *Counsellor at Law* premiered at the Plymouth Theatre in New York on November 6, 1931, and ran for 397 performances. Soon, it was having simultaneous productions in Chicago, Los Angeles, and San Francisco. The eponymous hero is George Simon (Paul Muni), an aggressive Lower East Side Jew, the most successful lawyer in New York, who has made his way to the top of his profession from an impoverished upbringing. However, a rival is now threatening him with disbarment for unprofessional conduct; earlier in his career, Simon falsified an alibi in order to save a young man from a lengthy confinement in prison. His dilemma is intensified by the lack of support from his socialite wife, who fears the scandal that the revelation will bring. Although Simon effectively counters the accusation when he discovers some unsavory scandal about his opponent's private life, his joy is short-lived: his wife has departed on a European cruise with another man. On the point of suicide, Simon is rescued by his secretary, Regina (Anna Kostanat), who is secretly in love with him. At the end they are excitedly pursuing a lucrative new case. The play was successfully revived in 1942.

The Film

Carl Laemmle, Jr., purchased the screen rights for the play for $150,000 and, with Rice (a former attorney himself) adapting his own text, success seemed assured, particularly with Paul Muni reprising the leading role of George Simon. However, he did not wish to repeat the part on screen out of a fear of being typecast in Jewish roles. (He had yet to rocket to screen stardom through his performances in Howard Hawks' *Scarface* in 1932 and Mervyn LeRoy's *I Was a Fugitive from a Chain Gang* in 1933.) Somewhat unexpectedly, the part went instead to John Barrymore. He gave what is widely regarded as his finest screen performance, which Pauline Kael later would call "one of the few screen roles that reveal his measure as an actor." Particularly commendable was his deft disclosure of the insecurity and despair lurking beneath Simon's swaggering and self-confident façade. In addition to a strong supporting cast that included Bebe Daniels as the loyal secretary Regina, Dorothy Kenyon as Simon's wife, Melvyn Douglas as her smooth admirer, and Thelma Todd as a grasping client, there were fine performances by two young men who were later to become accomplished directors: Vincent Sherman as the doomed anarchist, who reminds Simon of his roots and social passion; and Richard Quine as Simon's snobbish stepson, emblematic of a society Simon both covets and despises.

By confining the action to a back room, a front office, a secretary's office, and an elevator lobby, William Wyler preserved the play's tight structure and adhered closely to the original text. (He even put back in some parts of the text that Rice was planning to jettison for the screen.) At the same time, his adroit framing sustained visual interest, particularly when building to the film's most powerful moment as Simon, at his lowest ebb, swivels round in his chair and toward the office window and contemplates the prospect of self-annihilation. It was to be Wyler's first big critical success and the first of several theatrical adaptations he was to undertake. Also, his sympathetic observation of class antagonism and unrequited love revealed concerns that were to recur in his later work. Commentator Francis M. Nevins lauds the film as the "finest law-related film of the decade." It is precisely the absence of conventional courtroom sequences, continues Nevins, "that enables Wyler to dodge the bullet that maims or kills most lawyer movies of the time and to portray the practice in a manner still vivid and compelling sixty years later."

REFERENCES

Denvir, John, ed., *Legal Reelism: Movies As Legal Texts* (Urbana and Chicago: University of Illinois Press, 1996); Herman, Jan, *A Talent for Trouble: William Wyler* (New York: Da Capo Press, 1997); Kael, Pauline, *Kiss, Kiss, Bang, Bang* (New York: Little, Brown, 1968); Rice, Elmer, *Minority Report: An Autobiography* (New York: Simon and Schuster, 1963).

—N.S.

COUNTRY GIRL, THE (1950)

CLIFFORD ODETS (1906–1963)

The Country Girl (1954), U.S.A., directed and adapted by George Seaton; Paramount.

The Play

Thanks to his associations with the Group Theatre and the prestige of his early plays *Waiting for Lefty* (1935), *Awake and Sing!* (1935), and *Golden Boy* (1937), Clifford Odets was regarded as the most promising American playwright of the 1930s. After a relatively fallow period during the wartime years, when he wrote screenplays (*None But the Lonely Heart*, 1943), he regained commercial theatrical success with *The Country Girl* in 1950. It was his only play in which he abandoned outright social protest. Premiering in New York in 1950, *The Country Girl* is set in a theatrical milieu and features Frank Elgin, once a famous actor but now a drunkard, and his younger wife, Georgie ("the country girl"). Frank is given a last chance to redeem his career when he is given the lead in a play. With the help of a friend, Bernie, a stage director, he is a success when the play opens in New York. But

Bernie in the meantime has fallen in love with Georgie. The affair ends when Georgie declares her renewed loyalty to Frank. At the heart of the play is the strained relationship between Georgie and Frank, who unfairly blames his alcoholism on her. After rejecting Bernie's attentions, Georgie counsels Bernie: "Stay unregenerate. Life knocks the sauciness out of us soon enough."

Despite his failure to fulfill his early promise, Odets' legacy is secure. He had a decided impact on Arthur Miller and Tennessee Williams, and in plays like *Waiting for Lefty* transformed "agitprop" drama into a commercially viable theatre. But it is in his dramatization of Depression-era America, particularly the Jewish-American milieu, that he truly made his greatest contributions.

The Film

Director George Seaton wrote the scripts for most of his films (*A Day at the Races*, 1937; *The Song of Bernadette*, 1943). He had already won an Oscar for his script of *Miracle on 34th Street* (1947) when he turned to *The Country Girl*. He transformed the character of Frank from a dramatic actor into a musical performer, doubtless in acknowledgment of the casting of Bing Crosby. Thus, Crosby's singing talent is utilized, and in one of his songs he refers to his drinking addiction and the loss of his self-esteem. A flashback is added, prompted by Frank's hearing one of his early recordings, in which we learn the circumstances of his son's death, for which Frank blames himself. We realize that he has been using his son's death to legitimize his drinking. References to this incident recur repeatedly throughout the film. It is when Frank later hears the same song, without the triggering of his remorse, that we know he is recovering from his alcoholism. The simmering affair between Georgie and Bernie is amplified in the screenplay, and Frank addresses their mutual attraction in several key speeches. Grace Kelly won an Academy Award for her performance as Georgie. Seaton's screenplay also received an Oscar. Other Oscar nominations included best picture and Crosby's surprisingly effective performance as Frank, which won critical and popular plaudits.

REFERENCES

Bookbinder, Robert, *The Films of Bing Crosby* (Secaucus, N.J.: Citadel Press, 1977); Miller, Gabriel, *Clifford Odets* (New York: Ungar, 1989).

—J.C.T.

THE CRADLE WILL ROCK (1937)

MARC BLITZSTEIN (1905–1964)

Cradle Will Rock (1999), U.S.A., directed and adapted by Tim Robbins; Touchstone Pictures.

The Play

Author-composer Marc Blitzstein described *The Cradle Will Rock*, which he wrote in 1936, simply as "a play with music." Producer John Houseman claimed its "prime inspiration" was *The Threepenny Opera* and bits of Gilbert and Sullivan, with "recitatives, arias, revue patters, tap dances, suites, chorales, silly symphonies, continuous incidental commentary music, [and] lullaby music." He described it, variously, as "an opera, a labor opera, a social cartoon, a marching song, and a propagandistic tour de force." *Cradle Will Rock* started with a dramatic sketch Blitzstein wrote in 1935 to a song entitled "The Nickel Under the Foot." It was Bertolt Brecht who advised Blitzstein to expand the sketch into a full-blown agitprop "play with music," a hymn for the rights of the American labor movement.

The play was to have been produced by the Federal Theatre Project, headed by Hallie Flanagan, who in turn delegated the production (#871) to Orson Welles and John Houseman. Will Geer was cast to play Mr. Mister, the Lord of Steeltown, against Howard da Silva's proletarian hero, Larry Foreman. Mr. Mister battles the labor-agitating Foreman for the industrial and social salvation of the town. During the play's four-month rehearsal period, labor unrest was building in the country at large. The great sit-down strike in Flint, Michigan, mobilized the United Auto Workers, who demanded union recognition and a 30-hour week. Seven auto plants were closed in the Midwest, and, as Houseman remembers, the very day *The Cradle Will Rock* went into rehearsal, "there were riots in Akron and Pontiac as strikes halted work in the Chrysler and Hudson auto plants," as well as at General Motors. Then John L. Lewis announced his intention "to unionize the steel industry," which led to strikes and riots in Chicago, where both strikers and policemen were injured and killed.

Thus, the stage was set for a pro-union play to run squarely into political fallout. Budgets were cut as news reached Washington about Blitzstein's "dangerous" play. But Houseman was still determined, as he recalls in his memoir, *Run-Through*, "to get Marc Blitzstein's play with music onto the stage of Maxine Elliott's Theatre against a variety of odds." To build support in New York, hundreds of guests were invited to the play's final run-through, but the next day armed guards took over the theatre. An obvious solution was to move the production to another theatre, but Actors' Equity members were then forbidden to perform the piece "on any stage or for any management other than . . . the Federal Theatre of the WPA." At the last minute, a kind of solution was found as the Venice Theatre on 59th Street was engaged. "The entire cast and the entire first-night audience marched twenty-one blocks up Broadway to the other theatre," recalls Stanley Kauffmann, "with no scenery and with Blitzstein at the piano." The cast members performed from their seats in the audience in a kind of quasi-impromptu manner. After a number of special matinees, the play had its official premiere at the Windsor Theatre on January 3, 1938, and ran for 108 performances. It has been revived several times, but it has never reached a large audience.

The Film

Stanley Kauffmann considers the Tim Robbins film "a mess." Certainly there is no questioning its ambitious agenda, as it attempts to reproduce not only *Cradle Will Rock*'s first performance but also the backstage shenanigans behind that performance and the complex sociopolitical context of the time. Against the backdrop of the Depression and political turmoil in Spain, Italy, and Germany, Robbins assembles a crazy-quilt pastiche to accompany the behind-the-scenes preparations by the players and producers—most notably Marc Blitzstein (Hank Azaria), Orson Welles (Angus Mcfayden), John Houseman (Carey Elwes), and Hallie Flanagan (Cherry Jones). The screenplay incorporates numerous distracting subplots involving the artist Diego Rivera (Reuben Blades) in a wholly invented incident; Nelson Rockefeller (John Cusack); a poor starving starlet (Emily Watson) who gets the role of the prostitute; a Russian art collector (Susan Sarandon) who buys up DaVinci paintings for William Randolph Hearst (John Carpenter); a daffy socialite (Vanessa Redgrave) who tries to lend a hand to save the show; a talented Italian actor (John Turturro) with a wife and family to support; and a wholly invented, mentally unstable, lovelorn vaudeville ventriloquist named Tommy Crickshaw (Bill Murray). While one might expect to find Bertolt Brecht (Steven Skybell) in the cast, why Rockefeller, Rivera, Hearst, and Marion Davies (Gretchen Mol)? Among these impersonations, Kauffmann opined that only Hallie Flanagan, as portrayed by Cherry Jones, "takes on any reasonable life."

So intent is Robbins at establishing a densely textured, contextual tapestry of events surrounding the production of *Cradle Will Rock*, that the story of the

Tim Robbins directed a backstage portrait of the legendary premiere of Marc Blitzstein's Cradle Will Rock. (COURTESY TOUCHSTONE PICTURES)

play itself gets lost in the process. Too many cooks have spoiled this broth. After almost two hours, the film finally lumbers to its finale—the march of the players up Broadway and into the Venice Theatre for the actual production. What transpires is indeed a compelling recreation of that miraculous performance as, one by one, the cast members rise from their seats to join in the performance. However, irritating and intrusive cross-cutting to digressive subplots again mars the dramatic thrust. One watches in bewilderment the wretched business with Bill Murray, who loses his mind as his dummy crumples to the stage floor. The final scenes of *Cradle Will Rock* are given over to shots of the dummy's funeral procession. What this all means is up for grabs, although one might surmise that the procession symbolizes the death of vaudeville and the birth of guerrilla theatre.

REFERENCES

Houseman, John, *Run-Through: A Memoir* (New York: Simon and Schuster, 1972); Kauffmann, Stanley, "Listening Again," *The New Republic* (January 10, 2000): 26–27; Robbins, Tim, *Cradle Will Rock: The Movie and the Moment* (New York: Newmarket Press, 2000).

—*J.C.T. AND J.M.W.*

CRAIG'S WIFE (1925)

GEORGE KELLY (1887–)

Craig's Wife (1928), U.S.A., directed by William C. de Mille, adapted by Clara Beranger; Pathe Exchange.

Craig's Wife (1936), U.S.A., directed by Dorothy Arzner, adapted by Mary McCall, Jr.; Columbia.

Harriet Craig (1950), U.S.A., directed by Vincent Sherman, adapted by Anne Froelick; Columbia.

The Play

Craig's Wife opened at New York's Morosco Theatre on October 12, 1925, and ran for 360 performances, garnering author George Kelly a Pulitzer Prize. It was successfully revived on February 12, 1947. Playwright Kelly directed both versions. His admiration for the works of Ibsen and Strindberg—especially Ibsen's *Hedda Gabler* and *A Doll's House*—is apparent. (Kelly later came to the conclusion that *Craig's Wife* was really *A Doll's House* in reverse, since it dealt with the liberation of a husband from a selfish, oppressive wife.) The play's three acts are set in Harriet Craig's living room between 5:30 P.M. and 9:00 A.M. the following morning. It is a character study of a domineering woman (Chrystal Herne) who is obsessed with her home and possessions and prioritizes them far above Walter her husband (Charles Trowbridge), whom she has symbolically castrated into domestic subordination. Harriet's maiden aunt, Miss Austen (Anne Sutherland), warns her that her obsession will cost her her friends and family: "Other people will not go on being made miserable indefinitely for the sake of your ridiculous idolatry of house furnishings." Things come to a crisis when Harriet selfishly refuses to help in the investigation of a neighbor's suicide. The furious Walter wreaks the ultimate revenge—he wrecks some of Harriet's furniture. After enjoying a well-earned cigarette, he and the aunt leave Harriet alone and in sole possession of the house. The play's somber theme represented a striking departure for playwright Kelly, who previously had written stage works satirizing backstage theatre life. Many of his later plays, particularly *Daisy Mayme* (1926), *Maggie the Magnificent* (1929), and *Reflected Glory* (1936), also centered around strong female characters. Alexander Woolcott described *Craig's Wife* as "a thorough, unsmiling, patiently detailed and profoundly interesting dramatic portrait of a woman whom every playgoer will recognize with something of a start and yet whose prototype has never before appeared in any book or play that has passed my way."

The Films

Hollywood made three versions of Kelly's play. The first version was a 1928 silent production starring Irene Rich and Warner Baxter. The director was William C. de Mille, and the scenarist was Clara Beranger (de Mille's wife), one of the silent era's most noted screenwriters. The harsh social satire of the original play has been supplanted here by a standard Hollywood melodrama. In addition to the bare bones of the plot, a subplot is added involving Harriet Craig's younger sister, Ethel, who falls in love with a college professor. Harriet goes to Ethel and does all she can to end the affair. Upon her return home, she discovers her husband has been implicated in a murder. Although Mr. Craig is eventually cleared, Harriet in the meantime has fully demonstrated her own selfishness in trying to avert a scandal. Mr. Craig leaves his wife, and he takes Ethel with him, encouraging her to return to college and her lover.

Dorothy Arzner's 1936 version, starring Rosalind Russell, brings a feminist sensibility to the project. In almost every way it is strikingly different in situation and tone from both the Kelly play and the de Mille 1928 version. Whereas the play had attacked Harriet's behavior, the Arzner film allows her a more sympathetic nature. As a young girl, Harriet witnesses her mother losing her husband and home due to the machinations of another woman. Although her later marital conduct is certainly inexcusable, it is seen to be the result of childhood trauma rather than deliberate malice. Arzner suggests that Harriet's behavior originates from her psychic entrapment by a patriarchal society structured by factors later described by Adrienne Rich as "compulsory heterosexuality" as well as by the stifling confines of monogamy and possessiveness. The play is also opened out to reveal that men, as well as women, are victims of such a society. Scenes are added that reveal how Walter's friends, Brinkmeyer and Fergus, are also the victims of marital misery. One scene shows Brinkmeyer taking his father out for a night on the town. The old gentleman is clearly pleased at enjoying a "boys' night out" away from his domineering wife. As for Fergus, he is just as obsessed with a possessive mania as Harriet is. Marriage has made him a neurotically dependent male who will murder his wife in a fit of possessive jealousy.

Arzner adds another scene not in the play, showing Harriet attempting to warn her niece, Ethel, about the dangers of romantic love and the necessity for all women to have economic security (a carry-over from the 1928 film). There is an ambivalence to the film's closing images that marks a departure in tone from the play's climax. Harriet is left alone in her house, a "punishment" that is reinforced by the closing caption, "People who live for themselves are usually left to themselves." But her prolonged stare—captured from a low-angle view that for commentator Molly Haskell reveals her "as awesome in her loneliness"—begins to suggest that she is not so much a prisoner of her house as a character who has gained a measure of independence and who may achieve solidarity with other solitary women, such as the kindly Mrs. Frazier (Billie Burke) who offers her flowers at the end. Indeed, it could be argued that by slightly changing Kelly's original focus and inserting a feminist attitude toward the material, Arzner has made a film version of Virginia Woolf's *A Room of Her Own*.

The Vincent Sherman version of 1950 was retitled *Harriet Craig*, and it starred Joan Crawford and Wendell Corey as Harriet and Arthur Craig. For her first film for the Columbia studio, Crawford brought to the selfish and tyrannical Harriet a nasty psychotic undertone that rendered the character unsympathetic to audiences. Corey's weak and spineless Arthur is just as problematic. Like the Arzner film version, *Harriet Craig* chooses to concentrate on the crippling influences on Harriet of an emotionally and psychologically damaging childhood. She reveals that as a child she had been abandoned by her father; now as a result, she clings with fanatic desperation to husband and home. Her jealousy and possessiveness of Arthur lead to her interference in his social life and career. She even lies to him that she cannot have children. Finally, Arthur declares he is leaving her and the house to seek a job in Japan. Harriet is left alone, after lying to a neighbor that her husband has merely left to get a newspaper.

REFERENCES

Hirsch, Foster, *George Kelly* (Boston: Twayne, 1974); Haskell, Molly, *From Reverence to Rape* (New York: Holt, Rinehart and Winston, 1974); Houston, Beverle, "Missing in Action: Notes on Dorothy Arzner," *Wide Angle*, 6:3 (1984), 24–31; Mayne, Judith, *Directed by Dorothy Arzner* (Bloomington: Indiana University Press, 1994).

—*J.C.T.*

THE CRIMINAL CODE (1929)

MARTIN FLAVIN (1883–1967)

The Criminal Code (1931), U.S.A., directed by Howard Hawks, adapted by Seton I. Miller; Columbia.

Penitentiary (1938), U.S.A., directed by John Brahm, adapted by Seton I. Miller and Fred Niblo, Jr.; Columbia.

Convicted (1950), U.S.A., directed by Henry Levin, adapted by Seton I. Miller and William Bowers; Columbia.

The Play

Still hailed by many critics as the best of all American prison dramas, *The Criminal Code* premiered in New York at the National Theatre on October 2, 1929, and ran for a respectable 174 performances. It won the Theatre Club Trophy of America in 1929 as the year's best play. Written in response to several recent prison riots, it exposed not only the appalling nature of prison conditions but also indicted the "criminal code" that operates on both sides of the law: the "eye for an eye" dictum that forms the basis for a harsh criminal justice system, and the silence that criminals adopt to protect each other from incrimination. In the prologue Robert Graham (Russell Hardie) is convicted on a charge of second degree murder by an unscrupulous and politically ambitious district attorney, Martin Brady (Arthur Byron). Brady admits that he could have pleaded mitigating circumstances and absolved Graham of the charge had he been his defense lawyer. The first act begins six years later. Graham now suffers from an advanced form of mental deterioration. Feeling some responsibility for Graham, Brady, now the prison warden, gives him an easy assignment as the chauffeur of his daughter Mary (Anita Kerry). When a failed prison break results in the murder of an inmate by a convict named Ned Galloway, Graham finds himself unjustly accused of the crime. Although he knows the real circumstances, Graham remains true to the "criminal code" of silence and refuses to incriminate Galloway. Graham is thrown into solitary confinement. After being beaten by a cruel prison officer, Gleason (Leo Curley), Graham kills him in reprisal. Now any possibility of parole is gone, and Graham must spend the rest of his life in prison. "It's just the way things break sometimes," says Brady to his daughter. *The Criminal Code* was hailed by critic Burns Mantle as "a thoughtful study, not only of our methods of prison conduct and corrective punishments, but also of the normal reactions, of both prisoners and keepers, to the law, to the system, and to their respective codes." The play ends pessimistically with the potential romantic relationship between Graham and Mary over for good and Graham facing life imprisonment for the murder of Gleason.

The Films

The Criminal Code opened in New York on January 31, 1931. It is an unjustly neglected early talkie from director Howard Hawks. Playwright Flavin had made four unsuccessful attempts to translate the play to the screen before Hawks and collaborator Seton I. Miller took it on. It came on the heels of a spate of prison pictures, notably *The Big House* (1930) and *The Last Mile* (1931). The prologue is "opened up" as two policemen leave their card game to visit a nightclub where the murder occurs. Brady (Walter Huston) then manipulates Graham (Phillips Holmes) into accepting a guilty plea for second degree murder. The rest of the film transpires within the walls of the prison. Characteristically, Hawks was more concerned with the relationships among the prisoners and keepers than with exposing penal injustice. The play's original downbeat ending is transformed into a happy conclusion. Galloway clears Graham and kills the sadistic Gleason before being shot himself. Graham and Mary are reunited. In this fashion the play's thesis—that a harsh prison system could turn a basically innocent man into a hardened killer—was undermined. Commentator Carlos Clarens has noted that for Hawks "prison could not possibly be the worst of all possible worlds if it still allowed for fierce commitments of fraternity and silence to be made within. There is no real feeling of wasted lives in Hawks' penitentiary, nor of real outrage. He was an Emersonian, a man-to-man idealist rather than a New Deal pragmatist: the reform of institutions took second place to the moral evolution of man himself."

A few imaginative uses of sound and at least one striking example of casting enliven this otherwise stagebound film. Hawks uses overlapping dialogue in the opening police station scene when one cop is on the phone while two others play cards. Montages of sound and image depict the dreary nature of convict life. Dynamic editing is employed in the scene where Galloway (Boris Karloff) kills a prison informer (the murder itself takes place behind a closed door, with only the sounds of prisoners' shouts as an aural counterpoint). A highlight of the film is Boris Karloff's taciturn, hulking Galloway. Karloff had played the role for seven months in the West Coast production of the play. Here, his performance is a masterpiece of understated menace and made such an impression that it led directly to his being cast in *Frankenstein* that year.

Columbia remade the film as *Penitentiary* (1938) and *Convicted* (1950). John Howard and Walter Connolly portrayed Graham and Brady in the former, and Glenn Ford and Broderick Crawford played their roles in the latter. Neither was successful as an adaptation, but *Convicted*, directed by Henry Levin, was arguably the better film, praised for its sincerity.

REFERENCES

Clarens, Carlos, *Crime Movies* (New York: W.W. Norton, 1980); McCarthy, Todd, *Howard Hawks: The Grey Fox of Hollywood* (New York: Grove Press, 1997); Parish, James Robert, *Prison Pictures from Hollywood* (Jefferson, N.C.: McFarland, 1991).

—*T.W.*

THE CRUCIBLE (1953)

ARTHUR MILLER (1915–)

The Crucible (1997), U.S.A., directed by Nicholas Hytner, adapted by Arthur Miller; Twentieth Century Fox.

Les Sorcières de Salem [Witches of Salem] (1957), France, directed by Raymond Rouleau, adapted by Jean-Paul Sartre; Gaumont.

The Play

A graduate of the Federal Theatre Project, Arthur Miller wrote his three most famous plays in the late 1940s through the early 1950s—*All My Sons* (1947), about a veteran who learns that his father has sold defective airplane parts to the government; *Death of a Salesman* (1949), a character study of the life and death of an aging commercial traveler; and *The Crucible* (1953), a thinly veiled indictment of McCarthyism. There is no question that *The Crucible* implies that the HUAC investigations of a presumed communist infiltration of Hollywood deployed the same rituals of ruthless interrogation, extortion, and confession. "I wrote [*The Crucible*]," Miller has recounted, "because I was being surrounded by a feverish flood of accusations of Communism coming from everywhere. There was no way to deal with that in ordinary conversation, because if you cast any doubt on the veracity of the accusations you might well be linked to the Devil, which at that time was Communism."

The Crucible premiered in New York at the Martin Beck Theatre on January 22, 1953, and ran for a successful 197 performances. The setting is Salem, Massachusetts, in the year 1692. Act One begins with the discovery by Reverend Samuel Parris (Fred Stewart) that his beautiful young niece, Abigail Williams (Madeline Sherwood), has joined other village girls in "dancing like heathen in the forest." To escape being punished, Abigail soon "confesses" that she and the other girls have been trafficking with spirits. She then accuses Elizabeth Proctor (Beatrice Straight), the wife of stalwart John Proctor (Arthur Kennedy), of being a witch. Abigail's motives are clear—she has been carrying on an affair with John while working for the family and has been fired by the suspicious Elizabeth. When Abigail tries to entice John to be her lover again, he rejects her, even after she threatens to "Name" him. Meanwhile, a neighboring minister, a demonologist renowned for his fire-and-brimstone sermons, arrives and hears Abigail's confession. She also names others she saw "with the Devil."

In Act Two Elizabeth and John Proctor receive news of the ongoing witch trials in the town court, and they are appalled to learn of the arrest of a much-respected old grandmother. Meanwhile, suspicion of Elizabeth results in the demonologist coming to their home to interrogate her. She is arrested when a rag doll with a needle in it is discovered in the house (the doll actually belongs to the Proctors' servant). As John watches his wife being carried away, he vows to save her. But when he demands that the servant girl tell the truth about the doll, she refuses, threatening him with Abigail's schemes to incriminate him, too.

Act Three is taken up with the trial. Proctor comes to his wife's defense and organizes a petition by the townspeople confirming the innocence of the accused. Deputy-governor Danforth (Walter Hampden) demands that Proctor drop the petition, but he refuses. Danforth then orders the arrest of the signers. The demonologist, who has had a change of heart by now—"Nothing's left to stop the whole green world from burning"—objects to these proceedings, but to no avail. During her testimony, Abigail pretends to be bewitched. Angrily, Proctor discloses their affair, saying, "She thinks to dance with me on my wife's grave! It is a whore's vengeance, and you must see it." Ironically, Elizabeth Proctor, who has never been known to lie, denies his adultery, unwittingly consigning him to death. Proctor is denounced and sentenced to hang. "I say—God is dead!" Proctor says, and warns of vengeance for "them that quail to bring men out of ignorance, as I have quailed, and you quail now when you know in all your black hearts that this be fraud." Act Four transpires in the Salem jail cell, where John Proctor and others await their hanging. The Salem minister is full of doubt. His daughter and Abigail have stolen his money and run away. Proctor is pressured by Danforth to give his confession and save himself. He finally does so, but at the last minute he recants and tears up the paper. He embraces Elizabeth passionately and goes out to the gallows. The minister urges Elizabeth to run out and save him. "He has his goodness now," she weeps; "God forbid I take it from him!" Drum rolls announce his death.

Because of the play's basic theme of the conflict between social order and individual freedom, its use of historical notes, and its scenes of trial and martyrdom, it has been likened to Shaw's *Saint Joan*.

Playwright Miller was subpoenaed in 1956 by the House Committee on Un-American Activities, where he refused to inform on other writers and artists regarding alleged communistic activities. However, he

Arthur Miller

did testify about his own activities and beliefs, which resulted in a fine and a contempt citation. He was subsequently acquitted on an appeal. In all his work Miller has attempted to create tragic drama out of the peoples and contexts of the common man and the modern world. In his essays, as well as in his plays, he has grappled with vital contemporary issues like universal guilt in the Nazi genocide, the threat of the atomic bomb, and artistic freedom and personal integrity in the face of social and political conformity.

The Film

A French film adaptation was made in the late 1950s, directed by Raymond Rouleau, starring Simone Sig-

A moment of reckoning for Daniel Day-Lewis as John Proctor, accused of witchcraft in Arthur Miller's screen adaptation of his own play The Crucible. (COURTESY TWENTIETH CENTURY-FOX)

noret and Yves Montand as Elizabeth and John Proctor. In his autobiography, *Timebends*, Arthur Miller reports his dissatisfaction with it: "Jean-Paul Sartre's screenplay seemed to me to toss an arbitrary Marxist mesh over the story that led to a few absurdities. Sartre laid the witchcraft outbreak to a struggle between rich and poor peasants, but in reality victims . . . were of the class of relatively large landowners, and the Proctors and their like were by no means poor. It amused me to see crucifixes on the farmhouse walls, as they would be in French Catholic homes but never, of course, in a Puritan one." In his note to his own screenplay of *The Crucible*, released in 1997, Arthur Miller admitted his biases against the film medium, accusing it of producing "wonderfully trivial entertainment things," by contrast to the stage medium, which is a "more difficult art to master." Furthermore, he stated, "I have successfully resisted making screenplays of my plays because the adaptation process most often seems to make less of the original, something I cannot get myself to get enthusiastic about." Nonetheless, Miller did write the screenplay and collaborated actively with director Nicholas Hytner, a renowned British stage director

who had made his feature film debut a few years before with another theatrical adaptation, *The Madness of King George*. Both apparently felt that *The Crucible*'s theme had gained more topicality in the 1990s than ever. "As Arthur and I prepared to shoot the movie, we were struck time and again by its alarming topicality," Hytner says. "It spoke directly about the bigotry of religious fundamentalists across the globe, about communities torn apart by accusations of child abuse, about the rigid intellectual orthodoxies of college campuses—there is no shortage of contemporary Salems ready to cry witchcraft."

The film is no photographed play. Less than a third of the play's text is retained. "Anybody seeing *The Crucible* now would never dream that it had been a play," Miller said. "[Hytner's] idea was that it was a hurricane moving through this tight little village—a man-made hurricane built of mysticism and a complete misunderstanding of nature. And he made it work." Thus, the film visualizes much that is only reported action in the play. For example, the powerful opening sequence visualizes the teenage girls' sexual fantasies in the midnight forest—complete with the sight of Abigail

Williams' (Winona Ryder) face covered with blood from a sacrificed chicken—before Reverend Parris (Bruce Davison) induces the hysteria that eventually brings the witch-hunters to Salem.

Although the play is enacted entirely indoors, much of the film's action is transferred to the open fields and the windswept seacoast of Hog Island off the coast of Cape Ann, within shouting distance of Salem—places where many of the historical characters lived and where some of the incidents actually took place. During the trial scene, the camera assumes the swooping vantage point and actions of the imaginary birds conjured up by the hysterical girls. Moments of grisly violence abound, as in the scene when Giles Cory is convicted of contempt of court and pressed to death by granite blocks laid upon him. Powerful close-ups—the Russian concept of *typage* comes to mind—lend power to the actors' impersonations. Judge Danforth is portrayed by Paul Scofield, who, in the words of commentator Linda Holt, "is a study in living portraiture: minutely calibrated facial and verbal inflections express his lugubrious majesty . . . His face fills the screen as if it means to swallow the world. . . ." Miller himself added two new scenes involving the sexual tensions between Proctor (Daniel Day-Lewis) and Abigail, and visualizes the scene at the scaffold, during which Proctor now is permitted the glow of martyrdom and a recitation of the Lord's Prayer. That Miller permitted this brush with sentimentality comes as a surprise, inasmuch as he admitted in 1957 that *The Crucible* could be rightly criticized for not being tough enough on its subject: "We are so intent upon getting sympathy for our characters that the consequences of evil are being muddied by sentimentality under the guise of a temperate weighing of causes."

In addition to a truly terrifying performance by Paul Scofield as Danforth, other performances were outstanding. Winona Ryder's sensuously twisted Abigail was truly frightening, Daniel Day-Lewis' Proctor appropriately stalwart and impassioned, and Joan Allen's Elizabeth Proctor a model of restrained pathos. Memorable lines were in abundance, like John's rebuke to his unforgiving wife, "There's a funeral marching around in your brain!" and Judge Danforth's heavily ironic, "No person pure in heart ever needed a lawyer."

The film was greeted with mixed reactions. Commentator Edmund S. Morgan objected to the depiction of Proctor's martyrdom as somehow connected with the subsequent end to the witch hunts. "It was not the stubborn dignity of people like John Proctor but political expediency that ended the terror." Moreover, Morgan complained that both play and film reduced the Salem tragedy to the premise, in director Hytner's

words, that "the source of the girls' destructive energy is their emergent sexuality." Morgan argues that the historical record refutes that: "A few of the girls in the bewitched group who demonized their elders were old enough to be driven by emergent or already emerged sexuality. But most of them were probably prepubescent. Abigail, whose age Miller acknowledges he has advanced, was no more than twelve. It seems unlikely that she could actually have had an affair with John Proctor several months or perhaps years earlier." Nonetheless, Morgan calls *The Crucible* "a powerful version of a powerful play" that successfully "overcomes the restraints laid on it in transformation from the stage."

REFERENCES

Holt, Linda, "Bleeding Love Again," *Times Literary Supplement*, March 21, 1997: 20; Miller, Arthur, *Timebends* (New York: Grove Press, 1987); Morgan, Edmund S., "Bewitched," *The New York Review of Books*, January 9, 1997, 4–6; Span, Paula, "Miller's Dialogue with the World," *The Washington Post*, December 15, 1996: G1, G6; Wolf, Matt, "No Thorns in Hytner's Hollywood," *The Times* (London), January 21, 1997, 34.

—*J.C.T. AND J.M.W.*

CYRANO DE BERGERAC (1897)

EDMOND ROSTAND (1868–1918)

Cyrano de Bergerac (1950), U.S.A., directed by Michael Gordon, adapted by Carl Foreman and Brian Hooker; Allied Artists.

Roxanne (1987), U.S.A., directed by Fred Schepisi, adapted by Steve Martin; Columbia.

Cyrano de Bergerac (1990), France, directed by Jean-Paul Rappeneau, adapted by Rappeneau and Jean-Claude Carriere (from an English adaptation by Anthony Burgess); Hachette Premiere/Camera One Films.

The Play

Apart from the swashbuckling sword fights, the real glory of Edmond Rostand's play was its poetically charged language, which critic Max Beerbohm described as "gusts of rhetoric," featuring lines "loaded and encrusted with elaborate phrases and curious conceits." Appearing as Cyrano in the original stage production was the legendary French actor,

The latest version of the oft-filmed Rostand's Cyrano de Bergerac *featured Gerard Depardieu in the title role.*
(COURTESY ORION CLASSICS)

Coquelin. Rostand's five-act comedy opened in Paris in 1897. The character of Cyrano not only excels at fencing, philosophizing, and rhyming verse, but he also boasts an extraordinarily large nose. Thus, despite his poetic inventiveness and ardently romantic nature, he is reluctant to declare his love for the beautiful Roxanne. Besides, she loves the handsome Baron Christian de Neuvillette. Unselfishly, Cyrano assists the inarticulate Christian in wooing Roxanne; and he promises Roxanne to protect Christian while on the battlefield. When Christian is killed, the heartbroken Roxanne retires to a convent, where the faithful Cyrano visits her until his death 15 years later. It is only then that she discovers, too late, who her real lover has been.

The familiar story is full of wonderful paradoxes. It is about the world's ugliest man falling in love with the loveliest woman. This man, moreover, wields his eloquent love lyrics not on his own behalf but secretly in the service of another swain, who is as handsome as he

is dull. Thus it is with eloquence sometimes—it is veiled, like the night. It is elbowed aside. It is invisible.

The Films

Cyrano de Bergerac has been filmed many times, most notably in versions by Stanley Kramer, Fred Schepisi/Steve Martin, and Jean-Paul Rappeneau. Also worthy of note is an experimental, short talking picture in the "Chronophone" sound-on-disc process in 1904, starring the legendary Coquelin duplicating the eponymous stage role. Decades later, after Alexander Korda and Orson Welles successively considered, then discarded, plans to make a full-length film version, producer-director Stanley Kramer obtained the rights and completed his own adaptation in 1950. Screenwriter Carl Foreman made extensive cuts in Brian Hooker's English translation of the play, which lasted more than three hours on stage. "I found it necessary to perform major surgery on the beginnings of each of the five acts," recalled Foreman, "for in every instance Rostand had paused to recapitulate and set the stage anew. Surgery and suture were necessary, we felt, for space, tempo, and cinematic movement." The action is paced zestfully and the dueling beautifully choreographed, particularly in the first half of the film, highlighted by Cyrano's duel with an overbearing nobleman (while composing a poem on the spot) and his tussle with a gaggle of villains. The sets by Rudolph Sternad—the theatre, Roxanne's garden, the pastry shop, the streets, and the plains of Arras—strike a perfect equipoise between cinematic naturalism and theatrical stylization. Composer Dimitri Tiomkin's musical score nicely preserves the flavor of 17th-century French balladry.

And best of all is Jose Ferrer, who reprised his Broadway role and won a best actor Oscar. His rich bass voice and athletic agility are quite up to the role's special demands. The makeup on his nose was exaggerated even further by the use of cinematographer Franz Planer's new wide-angle "Garutso Lens," which kept both the nose, in the foreground, and Cyrano's antagonists, in the background, in perfect focus. "Around and through Rostand's arch romanticism," declares historian Donald Spoto, "[Ferrer] creates a deeply human soul who in fact lives in a decaying and grotesque society that seems to have concentrated all its cruelties into his dreadful deformity."

Roxanne, released in 1987, is an updated adaptation by actor Steve Martin and director Fred Schepisi. The action has been transferred from Paris in the 17th century to a modern-day small town in the American Northwest. Martin's Cyrano (here called "C. D. Bales") is a miracle of physical agility. We knew all along that behind Steve Martin's foolish pratfalls and humor lay the grace of a dancer. And here it is, at last, a fireman who sings love lyrics to Roxanne Kowalski (Daryl Hannah) as he jogs, dances, and twirls his way to work. He dispatches his enemies—those who ridicule his nose—not with a sword, but with a tennis racket. Although he may be frustrated in love, his body is at least in harmony with the physical universe. Appropriately, his current love, Roxanne, is an astronomer. She perches high on her rooftop, a crown of stars above her. She's looking for a comet, but she finds Cyrano instead. Rostand notwithstanding, happy endings are permitted here. When the two lovers finally embrace at the end, the sought-for comet slides by, but now it is unnoticed.

Edmond Rostand's 1897 tragicomedy receives its most sumptuous treatment to date in Jean-Paul Rappeneau and Jean-Claude Carriere's 1990 adaptation, which returns to Paris in the 17th century. For his Cyrano, Gerard Depardieu won a Cannes best actor award in 1990; indeed, his is the first Cyrano whose schnozzola needed only minimal enhancement! The film, in general, is a wholly cinematic conception, from the opening scenes in a Paris theatre, where Cyrano (Gerard Depardieu) denounces a piece of phony stage histrionics, to the duel with the Vicomte de Valvert (when Cyrano declaims couplets between thrusts and parries), to the brooding, moonlit balcony scenes to the breathless pursuit of Cyrano by a hundred men, to the penultimate battle scenes. The film is equally effective when language, not action, demands our attention. For example, the pastry cook-poet Ragueneau steals some of the best moments when he supervises his assistant cooks with a philosophical line or two, and when he wraps his rolls and buns in papers ripped out of his poetry books. And Cyrano, after refusing to work as a paid poet, broods by a window, alone, in a static shot—soliloquizing about the choices he makes, to look at the moon, to be alone.

Indeed, the moon itself is omnipresent; it flies ahead of Cyrano as he strides purposefully along the city's walls to Roxanne's wedding; and it hovers like a benediction above the convent walls at the end as the dying Cyrano announces his intention to travel there at last. The famous balcony scene is splendidly staged and edited: Cyrano stands below, hidden in shadows, while his puppet, the lover Christian de Neuvillette (Vincent Perez) declaims the words to the rapt Roxanne (Anne Brochet). A restless camera circles and surrounds the scene, while the editing slices up the action with the deftness of Cyrano's sword. Unfortunately, a stagy, static quality prevails in the climactic sequence, when it takes Cyrano entirely too long to die. Suffering from an attack by an assassin, he slumps, revives, slumps again, revives again, etc. As for Roxanne, it takes her an eternity to realize this dying man is the author of the precious love letters she presumed to have been penned by Christian. The viewer feels, with some sympathy, that neither the filmmakers nor the cast members were willing to give up this delicious entertainment.

REFERENCES

Base, Ron, and David Haslam, *The Movies of the Eighties* (New York: Portland House, 1990); Beerbohm, Max, *Around Theatres* (New York: Greenwood Press, 1978); Hinson, Hal, "Roxanne," *Washington Post*, June 19, 1987; Howe, Denson, "Cyrano de Bergerac," *The Washington Post*, December 21, 1990; Spoto, Donald, *Stanley Kramer: Filmmaker* (New York: G.P. Putnam's Sons, 1978).

—*J.C.T.*

DANCING AT LUGHNASA (1990)

BRIAN FRIEL (1929–)

Dancing at Lughnasa (1998), U.S.A./U.K., directed by
Pat O'Connor, adapted by Frank McGuinness;
Capitol Films/Sony Pictures Classics/Channel
Four Films/Ferndale Films.

The Play

Dancing at Lughnasa was first performed at the Abbey
Theatre, Dublin, on April 24, 1990, then moved to
the National Theatre in October 1990 with essentially
the same Irish cast, excepting three changes: Alec
McCowen in the role of Father Jack, the returned missionary; Stephen Dillane as Gerry, the suitor of one of
the Mundy sisters; and Rosaleen Linehan as Kate
Mundy, the role later played by Meryl Streep in Pat
O'Connor's film adaptation. After its premiere at the
Abbey Theatre, *Dancing at Lughnasa* was an immediate
hit in London, where it won the Olivier Award in
1991, and on Broadway. Even so, it was a long time
coming to the screen.

Brian Friel has been regarded as a sort of latter-day
Celtic Chekhov. In 1981 he translated Chekhov's *Three
Sisters* and became acutely aware of subtle differences
between English as it is spoken in Ireland and as it is
spoken in Britain. His goal was to produce an *Irish* version of Chekhov rather than one "redolent of either

Edwardian England or the Bloomsbury set. Somehow
the rhythms of these versions do not match with the
rhythms of our own speech patterns." As he assimilated Chekhov's language to the cadences of Irish
speech, he also assimilated Chekhov's dramatic methods. As a consequence, Friel developed a talent for
presenting the microcosm of rural Ireland with great
economy of detail. He has referred to Ireland "as being
inbred and claustrophobic" and Northern Ireland as "a
schizophrenic community." English literature he considers "foreign" and different from Irish literature: "It
is the literature of a different race."

Set in 1936, the play tells the story of the five poor,
unhappy, unmarried Mundy sisters in County Donegal, Ireland. The play is narrated by Michael, the son
of Chris Mundy, youngest of the sisters, 26 years old.
Michael also speaks the lines of himself as a boy, age
seven. Friel describes the other sisters as follows: Kate,
40, a school-teacher; Maggie, 38, housekeeper; Agnes,
35, knitter; and Rose, 32, knitter. They live in a village
called Ballybeg, which resembles the village of Glenties, where the playwright's mother lived, before her
marriage, with her four sisters and their brother, a
priest who returned from Africa and entertained the
family with exotic stories of native life and pagan rituals. As a boy Friel would visit his aunts, and as a man
he dedicated his play to the "memory of those five
brave Glenties women."

The closely knit Mundy family is disturbed by the
arrival of two men, their brother, Father Jack, burnt-

out after years of missionary work in Africa, and Gerry Evans, a Welshman who visits the youngest sister, Christina, and is the father of the son she bore out of wedlock. Father Jack, the eldest at 53 years old, considers himself an outsider: "I couldn't name ten people in Ballybeg now," he says, and he is unable to "recollect the lay-out of this home." After 25 years of service at a leper colony in "a remote village called Ryanga in Uganda," he has returned home, suffering from malaria and dementia, to die, and the climate of Ireland seems cold to him, Michael informs the audience. Jack brings to Donegal a sense of mystery and of primitive paganism. He believes in "ancestral spirits" and speaks of ritual sacrifices of roosters and goats to appease the spirits: "You have a ritual killing. You offer up sacrifice. You have dancing and incantations."

In Africa Jack was known as the "Irish Outcast" who had "gone native." Jack readily accepts Michael as a "love child," saying, "In Ryanga women are eager to have love-children." Not so, however, in Catholic Ireland, as Kate Mundy reminds him. Elder sister Kate, a self-righteous spinster schoolteacher, regards Christina's behavior with skepticism, as conflict builds. The other sisters are the unpredictable and vulnerable Rose, Maggie, the resident wit, and Agnes, the hardworking leader who holds them all together. But things are changing, and Michael predicts that Kate will "wake up one morning in September" to find that both Rose and Agnes "would have left for ever." The times are changing and the family is breaking up.

The play consists of a series of wonderfully realized vignettes in a warmly Irish setting. The "Dance" of the title celebrated in the woods is a local pagan festival dedicated to Lugh, the Celtic god of light. Kate does not approve and lays down the law: "You do not dance!" she says, when the others express interest in going to the harvest festival. Kate does not think it appropriate for "mature women" to dance, though she later admits to being a "sanctimonious bitch." Michael explains that his Aunt Kate was wrong about his father, "Because he did come back in a couple of weeks as he said he would. And although my mother and he didn't go through a conventional form of marriage, once more they danced together, witnessed by the unseen sisters. And this time it was a dance without music; just there, in ritual circles round and round that square and then down the lane and back up again; slowly, formally, with easy deliberation." They dance before Gerry goes off to fight with the International Brigade. Their ritual dancing is the very essence of theatre, not the sort of spectacle that would be easily transformed to cinema. Arguably, the play is too good for the cinema.

The Film

The film was gorgeously photographed by Kenneth MacMillan to show off the wonderfully atmospheric Irish landscape. It opens with the boy Michael flying a kite, as off-screen narrator Gerard McSorley reads the play's opening exposition in abbreviated form. Michael trips, falls, and loses hold of the string. The kite that he had is gone, just as the summer he is to spend with his mother and father and aunts and uncle will be gone, a passing idyll he will remember the rest of his life. Pat O'Connor's film does an excellent job of capturing that idyll, and the gradual awareness that the world is changing around the Mundy sisters. Christina (Catherine McCormack) is briefly reunited with the man she loves, whom she has not seen in 18 months; but Gerry (Rhys Ifans) intends to tilt at windmills in Spain, fighting for democracy against Franco. Because Jack (Michael Gambon) is considered an "Irish Outcast" who has taken up pagan ways, the local priest tells Kate (Meryl Streep) that "the numbers are falling" and she is likely to lose her job as schoolteacher. "But I am a teacher, Father," she protests. "What will I do if I stop teaching?" The heartless priest leaves the room without answering her. Moreover, a woolen mill is opening in Donegal that will do machine knitting, and that will have a serious impact on the family income.

The film opens up the play coherently. The sisters and Michael walk into town to meet the bus that is bringing Father Jack home. The camera follows Kate into town shopping and to the schoolhouse. Gerry arrives on a motorbike and treats both Christine and Michael to rides into the countryside. Much of the play's dialogue is preserved, despite these visual excursions. The dancing motif is visualized as frequently as possible. When Gerry arrives, he tells Christina that he has been teaching ballroom dancing in Dublin and dances with her on the lawn while singing "The Isle of Capri." Father Jack, awakened by a rooster, comes outside confused and performs a pagan dance while beating out an African tattoo with sticks on a bucket. The radio, which Jack considers "a miracle" (Kate corrects him by pointing out "It's not a miracle; it's science") also provides music to dance by. All of the sisters, excepting Kate, are excited about the forthcoming harvest dance. Simpleminded Rose (Sophie Thompson, the sister of Emma Thompson) dances in the house, until Kate stops her. Rose has fallen in love with a married man whose wife left him and asks Father Jack to marry them. Obviously Kate does not approve. When Father Jack wants to dance, Kate informs him: "You are an ordained priest, and priests do not dance." There is enough repression going on here to make the film seem authentically Irish. Agnes Mundy, considered "deep," is played by Brid Brennan, who introduced the character at the Abbey Theatre and later in London. Kathy Burke plays Maggie. In short, this is an entirely respectable cast. Novelist Maeve Binchy was gratified by the movie because "It makes us Irish women realize what a long and triumphant journey we have taken. If those Mundy sisters had lived in the '90s rather than the '30s, they could have conquered the world."

The film was far better than the reviews indicated. Owen Gleiberman of *Entertainment Weekly*, for example, who admitted that he had never seen the play, understands that "Friel was obviously going for a Chekhovian flavor" but thought the film somehow missed "Chekhov's underlying life force—the dramatic charge of people reconnecting, however tragically, to the emotions that have been stomped out of their lives." Mike Clark of *USA Today* protested that there were "too many characters" and claimed it was "irritating to have a voice-over spoon-feeding us the ins and outs of local history and relationships." Perhaps, however, the film suffers from the curse of great, language-intoxicated Irish drama that is resistant to screen treatment. Though fortified by outstanding pictorial cinematography and a gifted cast, the glory of the language gets lost or displaced in the cinematic treatment, no matter how good the film, and this one was in many ways outstanding.

REFERENCES

Binchy, Maeve, "Five Sisters Alone Against Their World," *New York Times*, September 13, 1998, sec. 2, pp. 41, 64; Clark, Mike, "Also Opening," *USA Today* (November 13, 1998): E6; Dantanus, Ulf, *Brian Friel: A Story* (London: Faber and Faber, 1988); Gleiberman, Owen, *Entertainment Weekly*, 460 (November 27, 1998), 54; Maslin, Janet, "5 Unmarried Sisters in Postcard Ireland," *The New York Times*, November 13, 1998, E1, E29; Owen, Michael, "A Woman of Donegal, at Least by Adoption," *The New York Times*, November 15, 1998, sec. 2, 30, 35.

—*J.M.W.*

DANGEROUS LIAISONS

See *LES LIAISONS DANGEREUSES*

THE DARK AT THE TOP OF THE STAIRS (1957)

WILLIAM INGE (1913–1973)

The Dark at the Top of the Stairs (1960), U.S.A., directed by Delbert Mann, adapted by Harriet Frank, Jr., and Irving Ravetch; Warner Bros.

The Play

The Dark at the Top of the Stairs is a revision of *Farther Off from Heaven*, William Inge's autobiographical first play, enhanced by fuller characterization and deeper psychological understanding in its newer treatment. The play's protagonists are the members of the Flood family, who reside during the 1920s in a small Oklahoma town that is quite similar to Inge's hometown of Independence, Kansas. The four Floods—father Rubin, mother Cora, daughter Reenie, and son Sonny—strongly correspond to Luther, Maude, Helene, and William Inge. The "dark" in the title sym-

William Inge

bolizes the various fears that beset all the Floods. Rubin fears that the changing times and his recent loss of his traveling job selling harness, a loss he has kept secret from Cora, will eclipse his role as a virile bread-winner. Because he doesn't want to "settle down" to a job in town, Cora fears she'll lose Rubin, who philanders when on the road. She also fears that Reenie's pathological shyness will doom her to spinsterhood, and that Sonny, who shares her bed in Rubin's absence, has become a hopeless "sissy" that she has drawn too close to her. The play's action involves the resolution of these fears.

After a quarrel between Rubin and Cora that begins with Cora's buying Reenie an expensive dress for a party but quickly escalates into a confrontation about Rubin's job and Cora's suspicions of his sexual infidelity, Rubin strikes her and leaves. Cora summons her sister and brother-in-law, Lottie and Morris Lacey, to ask if she and the children can move in with them in Oklahoma City. Lottie, a bigoted shrew who long ago reduced Morris into a quiet cipher, refuses to help, but in the process causes Cora to realize there's no solution in running from her problems. When Lottie relents and tells Cora she may move in after all, Cora declines and states her determination to fight for her marriage. She also talks with Sonny, forbidding him to come to her bed at night anymore despite his fear of the dark, and suggesting that he must no longer fear the boys who tease him.

With proficient plotting, Inge also causes Reenie to confront her paralytic shyness. In action that takes place entirely offstage, Reenie cowers in the powder room while her blind date to the party, Sammy Goldenbaum, is banished from the country club because he is Jewish. Without finding Reenie, he flees to Oklahoma City, where he commits suicide. When Reenie hears about Sammy's fate the next day, she realizes that if she had been at his side they could have left the party together and the suicide could have been avoided. She resolves to overcome her shyness, which she now sees as a kind of selfishness. Thus Cora, Sonny, and Reenie are ready for the play's conclusion when Rubin apologetically returns with a new traveling job selling oilfield equipment. When Rubin explains his fears caused by losing his previous job, Cora forgives him and accepts him as he is. The play ends with Sonny grabbing a stick and dispersing the boys who tease him, then taking Reenie to a movie while Rubin and Cora climb toward their bedroom at the top of the stairs, now bathed in warm light. Most critics praised the play despite its fortuitous plotting and soap-opera tendencies.

The Film

Saint Subber produced and Elia Kazan directed the stage play, but the film was produced by Michael Garrison and directed by Delbert Mann. To attract movie audiences, Robert Preston, fresh from his triumph as Harold Hill in the film version of *The Music Man*, was cast as Rubin Flood, and he brought some of his familiar fast-talking charm to the role that had been played on stage by Pat Hingle. Teresa Wright played Cora on Broadway, but Dorothy McGuire took the film role, and Eve Arden took Eileen Heckart's role as Lottie Lacey. Charles Saari and Judith Robinson's stage roles as Sonny and Reenie were taken in the film by Robert Eyer and Shirley Knight, whose luminous performance earned her an Academy Award nomination for best supporting actress.

Screenwriters Ravetch and Frank remained quite faithful to Inge's play script, though Mann "opened up" the film to show scenes from downtown stores, walks along streets, and rides in period automobiles. More importantly, Mann added scenes that depict the banishment of Sammy (Lee Kinsolving) from the country club and his subsequent suicide and death. Another significant addition to the film is a scene featuring Mavis Pruitt (Angela Lansbury), a beautician who shares a mutual attraction with Rubin, but who serves to help make Cora appreciate what she has in her marriage and children with Rubin. Eve Arden portrays Lottie with relish splendidly counterposed to Frank Overton's Morris; if Robert Preston weren't so winning as Rubin, Arden's Lottie would nearly steal the film.

The film reinforces the small-town prejudices and attitudes that so richly inform Inge's play. In the 1950s Inge wrote plays and screenplays that fit well with the "Revolt from the Village" poetry and prose of America's 1920s; and Delbert Mann, along with cinematographer Harry Stradling, Sr., and art director Leo K. Kuter give this film an authentic look of those times.

REFERENCES

Gill, Brendan, "The Current Cinema: False Faces," *The New Yorker*, October 1, 1960; Knight, Arthur, "SR Goes to the Movies," *Saturday Review*, September 17, 1960; Voss, Ralph F., *The Strains of Triumph: A Life of William Inge* (Topeka: University Press of Kansas, 1989).

—R.F.V.

DAYS OF WINE AND ROSES (1958)

J. P. MILLER (1919–)

The Days of Wine and Roses (1962), U.S.A., directed by Blake Edwards, adapted by J. P. Miller; Warner Bros.

The Play

Beginning as a live television play on *Playhouse 90* on October 2, 1958, it was directed by John Frankenheimer and starred Cliff Robertson. It begins at an Alcoholics Anonymous meeting, where Joe Clay, a public relations executive, confesses to his alcoholism and describes his life in a series of flashbacks. It all began at a party for a client, where he met Kirsten, his boss's secretary. Indulging their mutual tastes for drink and good times, they soon marry. With the birth of their child, Kirsten ceases her drinking; but she eventually acquiesces to Joe's urging to resume the habit. By now Joe is a full-blown alcoholic, and he loses a series of jobs as a result. He and Kirsten are eventually reduced to selling Kirsten's book collection and to drinking vanilla extract. Although Joe manages to sober up, with the help of Jim Hungerford, an AA member, Kirsten falls deeper into her own alcoholism. At the end of the play a sober Joe rejects Kirsten, who by now is hopelessly addicted to drink.

The Film

Having gotten his start creating several television series in the 1950s—*Peter Gunn, Mr. Lucky, Dante's Inferno*—Blake Edwards had his first theatrical film success with the celebrated *Breakfast at Tiffany's* in 1961. Although his most popular films have been comedies, notably the "Pink Panther" series, his occasional forays in the early 1960s into serious drama resulted in such standouts as *Experiment in Terror* (1962) and *The Days of Wine and Roses*. His adaptation of the teleplay, with the assistance of playwright J. P. Miller, involved numerous changes. The flashback technique was dropped and the location was transplanted from Long Island to California. As portrayed by Jack Lemmon, Joe's character is more insecure and immature: He buries his head in Kirsten's (Lee Remick) lap, assumes a fetal position when he drinks, and holds a liquor bottle as a baby holds a bottle. Although he eventually achieves sobriety, he pays a heavy price for his drinking. His pimping duties for parties, for example, make him "feel like a eunuch in a harem," and his drunkenness reduces his interest in sex. As a result, Kirsten challenges his manhood, and in his bouts of delirium tremens he sees "a green man with shears"—indicative of threats to his masculinity. At the end of the film, like the play, he is alone. As is

the case with many of Edwards's films, there is no likelihood of positive heterosexual coupling. It is the "wine" and not the "roses" that symbolizes the life and times of this married couple. Both Remick and Lemmon were nominated for Oscars; and composer Henry Mancini won an Oscar for his title song.

REFERENCES:

Lehman, Peter and William Luhr, *Blake Edwards* (Athens: Ohio University Press, 1981); Stelzer, Dick, *The Star Treatment* (Indianapolis: Bobbs, Merrill, 1977).

—*J.C.T.*

DEAD END (1935)

SIDNEY KINGSLEY (1906–1995)

Dead End (1937), U.S.A., directed by William Wyler, adapted by Lillian Hellman; United Artists/Goldwyn.

The Play

Sidney Kingsley's social protest drama about juvenile delinquency, *Dead End*, opened on Broadway in October 1935 to rave reviews and a successful run of 65 weeks. One of the things that impressed the critics about the Broadway production was the elaborate set that designer Norman Bel Geddes had constructed on the stage of the Belasco Theatre: A narrow tenement street reached a dead end at the East River and ran up against a swanky new high-rise. As film historian Gregory Black notes, "A sturdy masonry wall, guarded by a row of spikes on top, separates the wealthy residents of the East River Terrace apartment building from the squalid tenement buildings that line the other side of the street. Into this environment are thrust the characters whose lives will be, or have been, determined by which side of the wall they live on."

A former inhabitant of the riverfront slum, Baby Face Martin (Joseph Downing), comes back for a nostalgic visit to his old stomping grounds. He is now a major figure in the New York underworld, and the members of the youth gang, led by Tommy (Billy Halop), idolize him. Martin has come home to see his mother (Marjorie Main) and his old girlfriend, but his meetings with both women prove to be a disaster. His encounter with Francie, his erstwhile girlfriend, is particularly painful. He happens upon her on the street and invites her to rekindle their old relationship. She replies, pathetically, "Look at me good—I'm not what

I used to be." Whereupon she steps out of the doorway and reveals herself to be a shabby, diseased prostitute. Stunned, Martin slips her a few bills and turns away. His sidekick, Hunk, who has accompanied him on his trip to the old neighborhood, advises Martin: "Never go back; always go forward."

Like many other critics before her, Pauline Kael endorses the play because it radiates the ambiance of the "Broadway social consciousness of the Thirties," and has a "beautifully engineered plot" that is "highly entertaining."

The Film

Producer Samuel Goldwyn assembled an impressive team to film the play, including veteran director William Wyler, designer Richard Day, and ace cinematographer Gregg Toland. He chose Lillian Hellman, with whom he had worked earlier on *These Three*, an adaptation of her play, *The Children's Hour*, to write the script. Since the drama dealt with crime, violence, prostitution, and other lurid subjects, Hellman recalled later that Goldwyn told her to "clean up the play." But what he really meant, Hellman continued, was "to cut off its balls." Accordingly, details of the diseased prostitute (whose illness was changed from syphilis to tuberculosis), the married man's mistress, the brutal killing of the policeman, the vulgar language had to be expunged. Nonetheless, Hellman managed to preserve a modicum of the play's integrity, while still satisfying Goldwyn and the Hollywood censors.

Fearful that too much realism might yet find itself into the film, Goldwyn insisted on building an elaborate $100,000 set rather than shooting the film on location in the New York slums. He even ordered the set to be cleaned up of garbage and litter, declaring, "Well, this slum cost a lot of money; it should look better than an ordinary slum."

The film begins with an elaborate camera movement, beginning with a panoramic shot of the glitzy New York skyline, followed by a tilt down to the waterfront below, and concluded with a move in closer to the film's elaborate principal setting, a slum street that comes to a dead end at the waterfront. The tenement here is where the members of the local juvenile gang live. Moreover, the tenement is located on a dead end street, which symbolizes how the boys have already reached a dead end; that is, they have no prospects for a promising future, and will probably wind up pursuing a life of crime. (The film was advertised as "Dead End, Cradle of Crime.")

The sole satisfaction that Baby Face Martin (Humphrey Bogart) finds while he is back in the old

neighborhood is to bask in the adulation of Tommy's gang of tough kids on the block, who admire him for making good in the rackets uptown. Tommy Gordon (Billy Halop in a reprise of his stage role), the ring leader of the gang, looks up to Martin more than the others. The plot thickens when the wealthy Mr. Griswald accuses Tommy of beating up his boy; Tommy impulsively stabs Griswald's hand with a knife and makes his getaway. Drina Gordon, who constitutes the only family he has, is distraught when she learns that her kid brother is being pursued by the police at Mr. Griswald's behest.

Dave Connell (Joel McCrea), Drina's boyfriend, has a confrontation with Martin in an alley shortly afterward. Dave warns the mobster to stay away from the neighborhood kids because he is a bad influence on them. The pair get into a scuffle; Martin then pulls a gun on Dave and retreats down the alley. Dave, in turn, grabs another gun and pursues Martin up a fire escape; Dave fires upward at Martin, who falls into the alley below and soon dies. The image of Martin's ignominious fall from the top of the fire escape to the ground below symbolizes that he has been knocked off the pedestal on which Tommy and the other boys had placed him. As the film draws to a close, Dave assures Drina that he will bail Tommy out of jail with the reward money that is his due for bringing down Baby Face Martin, who had a price on his head. He thereby saves Tommy from going to reform school—in contrast to the play, where Tommy's future remains in doubt.

Lillian Hellman's script was praised by most reviewers for retaining much of the play's unvarnished realism. Commentator Greg Black notes that despite the censorial excisions, "the film still gives an overriding sense of hopelessness": "There is no mention of venereal disease, but only the very young and the extremely naive would fail to understand what Francey suffered from and what repelled Baby Face. The kids neither curse nor seem quite as bad in the film as in the play, yet it is clear that they have little education and no skills and are destined to live in the slums; only a miracle will save them from a life of crime. . . . Nor does the film lapse into the saccharin ending it might have had, with the courts forgiving Tommy, and Drina and Dave marrying and moving to the suburbs."

Like the play before it, *Dead End* is a riveting picture of the environmental influences on crime and poverty. There simply had been nothing in a Depression film before it like the high voltage theme of social protest seen in *Dead End*. For the record, the young actors who played the delinquents—Leo Gorcey, Huntz Hall, Gabriel Dell, Bernard Punsley, Bobby

Jordan, and Billy Halop—were billed as the "Dead End Kids" in the films they made together after *Dead End*, to cash in on the movie's huge success.

REFERENCES

Black, Gregory, *Hollywood Censored: Morality and the Movies* (New York: Cambridge University Press, 1994); Kael, Pauline, "Dead End," *The New Yorker*, September 11, 1995, 28; Youqinto, Marilyn, *Pump 'Em Full of Lead: Gangsters on Film* (New York: Simon and Schuster, 1998).

—G.D.P.

DEATH AND THE MAIDEN (1992)

ARIEL DORFMAN (1942–)

Death and the Maiden (1994), directed by Roman Polanski, adapted by Ariel Dorfman and Rafael Yglesias; Fine Line Features.

The Play

This political play by Ariel Dorfman, who fled Chile after the fall of Salvador Allende in 1973, is set in "a country in South America, after the fall of a dictatorship" and involves only three characters: Paulina Escobar, her husband Gerardo, and Dr. Roberto Miranda, a motorist who pays them a call at their country house on a dark and stormy evening, assisting Gerardo, whose automobile had had a flat tire. The action begins with Paulina, who has learned by listening to the radio that her husband has accepted a presidential appointment under the new government to chair a committee that will investigate terrorism under the previous regime. When an unfamiliar car approaches the house, she fetches a gun. The driver, Dr. Miranda, has done a good deed by picking up Gerardo and bringing him home. Later, Dr. Miranda returns with the repaired tire and is invited in for a cognac. The problem is that Paulina thinks that she recognizes Miranda as the doctor who had tortured and raped her 14 times under the old regime, while playing Schubert's "Death and the Maiden." She was tortured as a political prisoner because she would not disclose information about her husband, who, as a dissenting student, had edited an underground newspaper that was critical of the government. She had been blindfolded, but she thinks she recognizes his voice, and when she discovers the music tape in his car, she is convinced. Miranda, who has got pleasantly drunk with Gerardo, is knocked unconscious, captured, and tied up at gun-

Roman Polanski adapted Death and the Maiden *to the screen, with Sigourney Weaver as Paulina Escobar.* (COURTESY FINE LINE FEATURES)

point. Paulina intends to put Miranda on trial, with her husband as judge and the audience as jury. Paulina is hell-bent for revenge and is determined that Miranda should confess his wrongdoings. The point of the mystery is not whether Miranda is guilty, but whether he will admit his guilt, as he finally does at the end. Georgia Brown recalled in *The Village Voice* that the 1992 Broadway production of the play, starring Glenn Close, Richard Dreyfuss, and Gene Hackman, and directed by Mike Nichols, was a fiasco that attempted to transform this political-psychological thriller into a domestic comedy—Broadway's "first escapist entertainment about political torture," as Frank Rich described it for the *New York Times*—but the play had been far more successful in London, as directed by Lindsay Posner.

The Film

Death and the Maiden may be based upon a stage play, but the adaptation by Ariel Dorfman and Rafael Yglesias is so smooth and seamless that audiences may not notice that, apart from the opening and closing sequences in a concert hall, the film has a single setting—the seaside country home—and only three players. The film, expertly directed by Roman Polanski, begins with the Amadeus Quartet playing the Schubert composition from which the drama takes its title and ends back in the same concert hall, with Schubert's

String Quartet in D Minor. At the beginning Paulina Escobar (Sigourney Weaver) is transfixed and disturbed by the music. At the end, the viewers perfectly understand the reason for her disturbance.

Polanski is a master of the perverse and has specialized in designing a distinctive cinema of cruelty. The situation recalls other, earlier Polanski films, such as *Repulsion* (1965), which told the story of a woman who was utterly mad and dangerous. Paulina, driven by hatred, seems almost equally dangerous in her quest for revenge, especially as played by Sigourney Weaver as the wronged and embittered victim. Likewise, Ben Kingsley seems perfectly cast as the potentially charming but sinister Miranda, as he responds to his plight with outraged dignity and protests his innocence to Gerardo (Stuart Wilson), a trained lawyer forced by Paulina to interrogate him. The uncomprehending Gerardo is inclined to believe that Miranda is innocent, but Paulina controls the situation. The notion of people held captive in an isolated house recalls *Cul-de-Sac* (1966), which has been called Polanski's absurdist masterpiece. It may be absurd, but it is also absolutely creepy, and the perverse and shifting power games played in *Cul-de-Sac* have resonance in *Death and the Maiden*.

Though he did not take writing credit, Polanski controls this adroit adaptation; as Georgia Brown explained, "He's mercilessly pared the text, speeded up the opening, and dealt with the play's various implausibilities, making events more logical in some instances, the characters more compulsive in others." Polanski told *Movieline* that what "intrigued" him about the play was Paulina, who had been "tortured, violated [and] abused. And now she has a chance to face her torturer. But maybe it's not him. It's about vengeance and retribution, about the relativity of truth. And what is she capable of, how much degradation and pain is she willing to put him through? What they did to her was unspeakable yet she wants to talk about it."

The action is riveting, and the suspense could be killing.

REFERENCES

Brown, Georgia, "Arms and the Woman," *Village Voice*, December 20, 1994, 60; Frankel, Martha, "Roman Holiday," *Movieline* (January 1995), 59–63; Gleiberman, Owen, "With a Vengeance," *Entertainment Weekly* (February 3, 1995), 32–33.

—*J.M.W.*

DEATH OF A SALESMAN (1949)

ARTHUR MILLER (1915–   )

Death of a Salesman (1951), U.S.A., directed by Laslo Benedik, adapted by Stanley Roberts; Columbia.

Death of a Salesman (1985), U.S.A., directed and adapted by Volker Schlondörff; Bioskop/CBS.

The Play

Arthur Miller had studied drama at the University of Michigan before writing his first plays, including *The Man Who Had All the Luck* (1944) and *All My Sons* (1947). The latter, a painful indictment of a manufacturer who sold defective airplane parts to the government, won the New York Drama Critics Circle Award. His next major play, *Death of a Salesman* (1951), won both the Circle Award and the Pulitzer Prize. Subtitled "Certain Private Conversations in Two Acts and a Requiem," it had its first public performance at the Locust Street Theatre in Philadelphia, and its New York premiere was at the Morosco Theatre on February 10, where it ran for a spectacular 742 performances.

In Act One we learn that Willy Loman (Lee J. Cobb) is a 63-year-old salesman living in Brooklyn who is reluctant to admit to his family—wife Linda (Mildred Dunnock) and two sons, Happy (Cameron Mitchell) and Biff (Arthur Kennedy)—that he is down on his luck. Other tensions smolder in the family. "All I have done is waste my life," Biff confesses to his brother. Rather than pursue a career "outdoors," as he says, he has squandered his years drifting in and out of dead-end jobs. His brother, Happy, too, while generally satisfied with his independence—"my own apartment, a car, and plenty of women"—admits he is lonely and worried about their father's current depressed state. The scene shifts to the past, where Willy enjoys happier times horsing around with his boys, boasting of Biff's success in football, and bragging of his own success on the road. A burst of laughter from his wife triggers another of Willy's memories—a liaison in a hotel room with a prostitute. Back in the present, Willy refuses a job offer from his neighbor, Charley. Instead, he grows preoccupied with thoughts of his brother, Ben, a successful prospector in Alaska who died a few weeks before. Another flashback, this time to a conversation between Ben and Biff, wherein Ben tells young Biff that success in life comes only when you break the rules: "Never fight fair with a stranger, boy. You'll never get out of the jungle that way."

Back in the present, Willy's wife worries about the bad feelings between Willy and their sons. She confesses further to them that she knows Willy is no longer on salary, is only pretending to receive commissions but all the while planning suicide in the basement with a rubber hose. "I don't say he's a great man," she says, "but he's a human being, and a terrible thing is happening to him." Willy comes in and for a few minutes it seems as if he and the sons are reconciling. Excitedly, they consider plans for staking Biff to opening a sporting goods store and promise each other they will talk it over the next night at dinner. But later Linda can't help asking her husband what it is that has caused tension for so long between him and Biff. Willy is evasive. Elsewhere in the house, Biff finds the rubber tube Willy has prepared for his suicide, and he takes it away.

Act Two begins the next morning as Willy promises his wife that he will go to his boss to ask for an advance in money. He is also looking forward to dining that night with his sons. The interview with his boss, a young man more preoccupied with the novelty of his new dictaphone machine than with Willy, is a disaster. Despite his pathetic pleadings, Willy is fired. He slips into a flashback wherein he replays the day of Biff's big football game. Back in the present, he visits neighbor Charley and gets a loan (although he is too proud to accept a job from him). At the restaurant, while the boys and their dates wait for their father, Biff tells Happy that he failed in his attempt to get seed money for a sporting goods store. Instead, he stole a fountain pen and ran out. Willy appears. Distraught, and unable to concentrate on his sons, he slips again into the past, where he revisits a hotel room where Biff had inadvertently discovered him with a prostitute. This traumatizes young Biff, who rebukes Willy: "You phony little fake!" The sons leave. Back in the present, Linda excoriates her sons for having left their father in the restaurant. Meanwhile, Willy, now clearly insane, is planting a garden with seeds and talking to the dead and departed Ben. Biff comes to his father and breaks down in his arms, sobbing, "I'm nothing, Pop. Can't you understand that?" Determined that his "boy is going to be magnificent" with the $20,000 insurance money to back him, Willy rushes out and in offstage action drives his car into a tree, killing himself.

The *Requiem* transpires at Willy's gravesite. "Nobody dast blame this man," says Charley. "A man way out there in the blue, riding on a smile and a shoeshine . . . A salesman has got to dream." Biff, now reconciled to his past and present failures, gets ready to leave. "I know who I am, kid," he tells Happy. Linda, meanwhile, sits alone by the grave. "I made the last payment on the house today," she says. "Today, dear. And there'll be nobody home."

Critic John Mason Brown noted the play "is the most poignant statement of man as he must face himself to have come out of our theatre." He added, "Mr. Miller's play is a tragedy modern and personal, not classic and heroic. Its central figure is a little man sentenced to discover his smallness rather than a big man undone by his greatness."

Jo Mielziner's stage settings were merely suggestive of a house and garden. The skeletal walls afford full view into each of the rooms, allowing, with the aid of lighting changes, for instantaneous transitions between present and past, objective and subjective reality. This fluidity of time, space, and mind in the play's 17 scenes was what Miller had wanted all along: "I had known all along that this play could not be encompassed by conventional realism, and for one integral reason: in Willy the past was as alive as what was happening at the moment, sometimes even crashing in to completely overwhelm his mind. I wanted precisely the same fluidity in the form. . . ."

The Films

Arthur Miller sold the film rights to Stanley Kramer. This would be his third theatrical adaptation, after *Home of the Brave* and *Cyrano de Bergerac*. "Plays are a safe commodity," recalled Kramer, "and that's why I chose to produce lots of them in their screen versions. I knew what they were, and the screenplays turned out to be, basically, just adaptations." Retained from the original cast were Cameron Mitchell and Mildred Dunnock. The role of Biff was assigned to Kevin McCarthy. The lead role, however, went to Fredric March rather than Lee J. Cobb. It was decided not to "open up" the play, but rather to rely upon the performances and the fine cinematography of Franz Planer to bolster what was essentially "canned drama." The flashback scenes were designed by set designer Rudolph Sternad and editor Harry Gerstad, to exploit juxtaposed sets, elongated perspectives, and shifts in lens focal lengths. For example, when Willy's mind goes back 20 years, the camera dollies close to his face and, after an imperceptible cut, the camera reverses back to reveal a different scene. In another example, when Willy enters his kitchen for a night snack, the flick of the light switch illuminates a scene in the back yard in the past. These transitions, claims Kramer biographer Donald Spoto, "are handled with unusual skill, each cut matched so flawlessly that when the film is studied at an editing table, it's necessary to watch the sequences frame by frame to appreciate just how seamlessly the changes are made, and how slightly the camera angles change the angle of the person photographed, so that the background and setting seem to alter magically!"

In the second filmed adaptation of Death of a Salesman, *Dustin Hoffman portrayed Willy Loman.* (COURTESY NATIONAL FILM SOCIETY ARCHIVES)

As for the performances, March, who had originally been considered for the stage role, interpreted Willy as if he were psychotic, rather than pathetically muddled. The effect, complained Miller, was to draw "the teeth of the play's social contemporaneity, obliterating its very context. If he was nuts, he could hardly stand as a comment on anything." Mildred Dunnock's role of Linda Loman, by contrast, has received universal acclaim. "The simple nobility of Linda Loman lingers in the mind long after the film ends," enthuses Spoto. "It is a performance that deserves to be ranked with Sara Allgood's Mrs. Boyle in Hitchcock's *Juno and the Paycock* and Jane Darwell's Ma Joad in Ford's *The Grapes of Wrath*."

Miller's sole participation, he recalled later in his memoir, *Timebends*, "was to complain that the screenplay had managed to chop off almost every climax of the play as though with a lawnmower, leaving a flatness that was baffling in view of the play's demonstrated capacity for stirring its audiences in the theatre." Incidentally, Miller recalls that officials at Columbia were so nervous about the film and about Miller's own avowed leftist political associations that he was called to a screening room to view a short film that was to precede the feature—a sort of disclaimer of the film's social relevance. Interviews with professors at the Business School of New York's City College assured viewers that Willy Loman was a throwback to a past time when salesmen did indeed have problems, but that selling was now an admirable profession. "At the bottom I was being asked to concur that *Death of a Salesman* was morally meaningless, a tale told by an idiot signifying nothing," wrote Miller. The outraged playwright threatened a lawsuit and, as far as anyone knows, the short film was never screened in the theatres.

Volker Schlondörff's 1985 adaptation cast Dustin Hoffman as Willy, Kate Reid as Linda, John Malkovich as Biff, Stephen Lang as Happy, and Charles Durning as Charley. Miller's text is transferred virtually intact. The sets, while more realistic than those of the stage, shifted in and out of time and place by means of simple dissolves and lighting changes. A significant departure from the play is the film's opening, when Willy emerges from a near-fatal car crash, a device used to foreshadow his later deliberate attempt to end his life. The film was first shown on the CBS television network in June 1985.

REFERENCES

Griffen, Alice, *Understanding Arthur Miller* (Columbia: South Carolina University Press, 1996); Miller, Arthur, *Timebends: A Life* (New York: Grove Press, 1987); Spoto, Donald, *Stanley Kramer, Filmmaker* (New York: G.P. Putnam's Sons, 1978).

—*J.C.T.*

DEATH TAKES A HOLIDAY (1929)

ALBERTO CASELLA (1891–1957)

Death Takes a Holiday (1934), U.S.A., directed by Mitchell Leisen, adapted by Maxwell Anderson, Gladys Lehman, and Walter Ferris; Paramount.

Meet Joe Black (1998), U.S.A., directed by Martin Brest, adapted by Ron Osborn, Jeff Reno, Kevin Wade, Bo Goldman; Universal Studios.

The Play

Alberto Casella's play, *La Morte in vacanza*, rewritten for the American stage by Walter Ferris in 1929, is set entirely in the Great Hall of the castle of Duke Lambert. The duke and his guests are discussing the miracle that spared their lives in a near automobile accident. Moments later a stranger appears to the duke and identifies himself as Prince Sirki, an assumed name that hides his real identity of Death. He is taking a three-day holiday to learn why people fear him and to discover the meaning of human love. After warning the duke not to reveal his identity, he meets the guests: Alda, Rhoda, and Grazia. His attentions to Grazia anger the duke's son, Corrado, to whom Grazia is affianced. When Alda and Rhoda make advances to Sirki, he directs them to look deep into his eyes. Both recoil at the intimations of mortality they see there. Meanwhile, Grazia, who has grown hesitant to marry Corrado, is clearly attracted to Sirki. When he discovers that Sirki wants Grazia to go with him, the duke reveals Sirki's identity to his guests and demands that Sirki disclose his true nature to Grazia. But Grazia replies that she will go with him anyway. "There *is* a love which casts out fear," says Sirki, "and I have found it." The play ends at the stroke of midnight, as the stage dissolves into darkness.

The Films

Mitchell Leisen had been a costume designer for Douglas Fairbanks and Mary Pickford, and an art director for Cecil B. DeMille before he turned to directing at Paramount in 1933. *Death Takes a Holiday* was his first major success. Always a stickler for fashion and design, he hired Ernst Fegte as his art director to design the Florentine palazzo that encloses most of the action. Charles Lang handled the impressionistic photography. "[Leisen] had a tremendous feel for the cameras," reported Lang; "I guess it was because of his experience as an art director. He always placed the cameras himself. I'd give him the finder and he'd tell me what angles he wanted." The screen version was originally entitled *Strange Holiday* and had been in the planning stages since 1930. By the time of its release more than three years later, Fredric March had replaced Dick Powell in the lead, and Guy Standing appeared as Duke Lambert, Katherine Alexander as Alda, Evelyn Venable as Grazia, Kent Taylor as Corrado, and Gail Patrick as Rhoda. Most of the stage action and dialogue were transferred intact. Several added scenes amplify events. The opening scene visualizes the near-accident from which Lambert and his guests escape. Other scenes depict Sirki at the gaming tables, and there are vignettes from the outside world establishing that no deaths are occurring during Sirki's three-day "leave of absence." Finally, anguished at having to leave his newfound humanity behind, Sirki confesses his identity to Grazia. She confesses that she already knows his secret and will not leave him. Joyfully, they depart together.

Several admirable photographic effects enhance the sense of Sirki's other-worldliness. In some scenes he seems semi-transparent, thanks to the use of mirrors and black draping. And in one memorable moment, his face dissolves into the semblance of a skull. The secret of the effect was to apply red makeup to March's face. "Under red light, the make-up didn't show and he looked normal," explained Leisen. "Then by dissolving the red light out and bringing the green light in, the make-up slowly began to show until his face became a skull." Critic John Baxter has found the results "a strange film . . . skating the delicate line between poetry and comedy."

Martin Brest's updated version, released in 1998, is only tangentially related to its source materials. It casts Anthony Hopkins as media tycoon William Parrish, who awakes in the middle of the night suffering chest pains, only to meet Death (Brad Pitt) in the guise of Joe Black. Death has "taken over" Black's body after his recent death and is now curious to experience what it is like to be human. Before he takes Parrish away with him, Death wants him to be his companion and guide; and Parrish, desperate to prolong his life by any means, agrees. Accordingly, Joe accompanies Parrish everywhere, even to work, where he falls in love with Parrish's daughter, Susan (Claire Forlani). As Joe experiences mortal love with Susan, Parrish begins to appreciate the things he has taken for granted in his life, such as his relationship with his daughters and son-in-law, Quince (Jeffrey Tambour). Director Brest worked on the script for 10 years. His vision of Death, by contrast to the magnetic impersonation by Fredric March in the 1934 version, is as an angelic figure who maintains an enigmatic façade, like a blank slate. Critic James Sterngold deplored the film's padded length and called the results "The Education of Death."

REFERENCES

Chierichetti, David, *Hollywood Director: The Career of Mitchell Leisen* (New York: Curtis Books, 1973); Gleiberman, Owen, "Reaper Madness," *Entertainment Weekly*, 459 (November 20, 1998), 89–92; Quirk, Lawrence J., *The Films of Fredric March* (New York: Citadel, 1971); Sterngold, James, "At the Movies: Death and Life," *New York Times*, August 14, 1998, B9.

—*J.C.T.*

A DELICATE BALANCE (1966)

EDWARD ALBEE (1928–)

A Delicate Balance (1973), U.S.A., directed by Tony Richardson, adapted by Edward Albee; American Film Theatre.

The Play

Edward Albee's Pulitzer Prize–winning three-act play was first produced at the Martin Beck Theatre in New York on September 22, 1966, and ran for 132 performances. The production featured Hume Cronyn and Jessica Tandy. The play takes place in the living room of a "large and well-appointed suburban house" over the course of a weekend. Sitting in their living room after dinner Agnes confides to her husband that she sometimes worries that she may one day "go mad." Her husband, Tobias, assures her that he knows no saner woman. Living with them is Agnes's younger sister, Claire, a bitter, malicious alcoholic. The couple are visited that same evening by Tobias's best friend and the friend's wife, Harry and Edna, who, for some unexplained reason, are frightened by something they cannot identify. It becomes apparent that Edna and Harry have every intention of staying indefinitely. The next day Julia, Agnes and Tobias' much married daughter, arrives after breaking up with her fourth husband. She finds her room occupied by Edna and Harry.

These events produce a crisis for all six characters in the play. The crises force the characters, especially Agnes and Tobias, to reevaluate their relationships and to recognize that they must maintain a "delicate balance" between love and hate. According to John Mac-Nicholas, Albee's play concerns itself with loss, "not loss which occurs in one swift traumatic stroke, but that which evolves slowly in increments of gentle and lethal acquiescence." Much of the initial criticism of the play concerned the repetitiveness of themes (similarities between Zoo Story and Who's Afraid of Virginia Woolf) and the stilted nature of the dialogue, such as, "I apologize that my nature is such to bring out in you the full force of your brutality." Albee's language was compared to the ultra-poetic musings of T. S. Eliot's The Cocktail Party. Tobias's monologue at play's end is described by the author as "an aria" and is modulated in a fashion comparable to such. In 1973, when the film version of the play was released, it was considered by many a curious choice for both Tony Richardson, the film's director, and the American Film Theatre, which produced the film.

The Film

A Delicate Balance was the third feature film released by Ely Landau's American Film Theatre, a distribution company intent on bringing theatre culture to the multitudes. The eight-feature subscription series was released for two-day runs in the United States in 1973 and 1974. A planned third season of filmed plays was

canceled. Tony Richardson, the acclaimed British theatre and film director, had been offered the choice of either John Osborne's Luther or Eugene Ionesco's Rhinoceros to direct for American Film Theatre. Richardson opted for Albee's A Delicate Balance when it was offered after he turned down the other two. Most critics of the film considered it a statically filmed stage play, even though Richardson lensed it on actual locations rather than on a studio or stage set. By 1973 as well, the play itself seemed outdated to some. This, in addition to the fact that it followed on the heels of Harold Pinter's The Homecoming, a very successful American Film Theatre presentation directed by Peter Hall, severely biased its critical reception.

There would seem to be a method in the director's madness, however. Tony Richardson's film, as Albee's play, is set entirely in the Tobias/Agnes household. Richardson insisted on using locations in order to "create a stronger sense of reality" thereby "creating a situation in which quarters were cramped and cast and crew were often restricted and uncomfortable." This confined sense of space is in keeping with other film versions of plays set in interior locations, most notably John Frankenheimer's The Iceman Cometh (1973) and Sidney Lumet's Long Day's Journey Into Night (1962). The use of location shooting also contributed to the photographic style of cinematographer David Watkin. The Time review noted that Watkin "uses a kind of embellished natural light. His uncluttered compositions can shock the eye with a shaft of light from a table lamp or lull it with a suggestion of the dark distances between night and morning. His craftsmanlike photography, at least, makes the film worth watching." Visual correlatives are often utilized to suggest the delicate balance of the characters in Albee's play. As Edward T. Jones notes, "Lights from lamps and white shades on lamps are often used for dramatic effect with the most notable example being the substantial slash of a white lampshade that divides the frame with Claire who concludes the first act, saying 'I was wondering when it would begin . . . when it would start.'" Characters are often "balanced" on either side of the frame with an object, such as a piece of sculpture or furniture, between them.

The casting of Richardson's film was a notable and worthy one. Paul Scofield plays Tobias, and his monologue concerning his beloved cat who one day stopped liking him, is one of the emotional highlights of the film. The venerable Katharine Hepburn was cast as Agnes, and her performance was one of the most cited among film critics. Lavish praise was also afforded to Kate Reid as Claire, a character that could easily become caricatured but is given some depth through

Reid's performance. It is curious to note that Kim Stanley was Richardson's first choice for the role, but Stanley was an alcoholic herself, and it became obvious during rehearsals that it would not work out. Lee Remick plays Julia, and Joseph Cotten and Betsy Blair portray Harry and Edna. Richardson's exceptional skill with actors and his compositional style make this film well worth a critical reassessment.

REFERENCES

MacNicholas, John, "Edward Albee," *Dictionary of Literary Biography*, vol. 7 (Detroit: Gale Research Company, 1981); Radovich, Don, *Tony Richardson: A Bio-Bibliography* (Westport, Conn.: Greenwood Press, 1995); Welsh, James M. and John C. Tibbetts, *The Cinema of Tony Richardson* (New York: State University of New York Press, 1999).

—*R.W.W.*

DESIRE UNDER THE ELMS (1924)

EUGENE O'NEILL (1888–1953)

Desire Under the Elms (1958), U.S.A., directed by Delbert Mann, adapted by Irwin Shaw; Paramount.

The Play

The play was first produced by the Theatre Guild, opening at the Greenwich Village Theatre on November 11, 1924. The production was both directed and designed by Robert Edmond Jones, and featured Walter Huston as Ephraim Cabot and Charles Ellis as Eben. The play, which was almost closed by the police due to its salacious subject matter, ran for 208 performances.

O'Neill's three-part drama is set in and immediately outside the Cabot family farmhouse in New England around 1850. Ephraim Cabot, the puritanical, hard-driven father has left the farm, two months earlier, "t'learn God's message . . . like the prophets done." In his absence, Eben Cabot convinces his half-brothers, Simeon and Peter, to sign over to him their share in the farmland. He pays them with money he has taken from Ephraim's hiding place. Eben believes that the farm rightfully belongs to him because his mother willed it to him. The brothers agree to the transaction once they learn that Ephraim has taken a young wife whom he is bringing back to the farm. Simeon and Peter decide to leave for the gold fields in California, taunting Ephraim and his young wife Abbie Putnam as they leave. Eben realizes that his stake in the farm is now in jeopardy with this new rival.

In order to keep control over both Ephraim and the farm, Abbie suggests the possibility of conceiving a son. Ephraim ecstatically promises her anything should she give birth to a son. Abbie asks him to will her the farm. At first quarreling with Eben over her motives in marrying Ephraim, soon both are in each other's arms. Abbie seduces Eben in his mother's parlor, replacing his dead mother with herself—as his obsession.

Abbie bears a son, but it is Eben's not Ephraim's. Ephraim throws a celebration in honor of his accomplishment and invites several of the townfolk, who are all too aware of what is suspected. Ephraim and Eben get into a fight and Ephraim reveals Abbie's motive to get possession of the farm. Eben threatens to disclose the real father of their child to his father and plans to leave for the West. Abbie, in order to prove that she really loves Eben, kills the child. When she reveals this to Eben, he goes to get the sheriff. Abbie tells Ephraim what she has done as well as the truth of the child's father. The sheriff and Eben arrive and Eben tells Abbie that he knows that she is in love with him and falsely admits to the sheriff that he was an accomplice to the murder. The play closes with the sheriff looking over the farm and saying, "It's a jim-dandy farm, no denyin'. Wished I owned it!"

The Film

Delbert Mann's film version of O'Neill's play suffers from two glaring shortcomings: the disparate acting styles of the performers and the ineffective use of a widescreen format. Perhaps if Mann had been more attentive to casting and had utilized a regular aspect ratio the film could have worked. As it is, Paramount's VistaVision version of *Desire Under the Elms* only hints at the stark drama of O'Neill's play. According to John Orlandello, "The whole film is rather like the bizarrely manic dance that old Cabot does during the christening scene—potentially powerful, but exaggerated ludicrously."

Bosley Crowther suggested, in his review of the film for the *New York Times*, that there was "something curiously missing . . . that should charge with electricity the terrible events of this drama and give force to its obvious tragedy." Much of this lack of "electricity" can be attributed to the performers themselves. Anthony Perkins's portrayal of Eben Cabot seems wooden and unemotional in his initial scenes. Although he is physically well suited to the role, as described by O'Neill, Perkins lacks much of the emotional intensity and determination of the character. His Oedipal obsession with his mother is totally absent in the film, thereby weakening the seduction scene in his mother's parlor. The relationship with Abbie/Anna is considerably more romanticized than it is in O'Neill's play.

Sophia Loren is surprisingly good as Anna; the character has been changed to an Italian immigrant, to justify the casting. She is able to characterize the sultry, seductive qualities of the role. Her scenes with Perkins work well for the most part, with the exception that the role has been significantly modified to downplay the maternal qualities of the character. Loren is also able to capture the scheming and feeling sides of the role.

Burl Ives, however, brings a theatrical quality to the part of Ephraim that stands in contrast to the other performances. Both physically and emotionally, Ives is not suited to the part. Most of his lines are delivered in a monotone and O'Neill's effective use of New England dialect is simply not used at all in the film. Ives' broad, stylized manner is more in keeping with one of his previous screen credits, Big Daddy in Tennessee Williams' *Cat on a Hot Tin Roof.* The use of stage character makeup is also quite noticeable on Ives, especially a prosthetic nose that seems to change in many scenes.

Irwin Shaw's screenplay, though it retains the basic plot line, fails to preserve the poetry and tragic atmosphere of O'Neill's drama. The absence of the New England vernacular is one reason. But Shaw includes scenes, not in O'Neill's play, that do not add to the drama, but, if anything, detract from it. A prologue introduces the theme of greed and avarice, by showing Eben and his mother spying on Ephraim as he hides his money in the woods near the farmhouse. Although this ostensibly shows the relationship between mother and son against father—the Oedipal connection in O'Neill's play—the approach is abandoned in the rest of the film. Likewise, Shaw adds a scene where Simeon and Peter return to the farm with their wives, coincidentally enough, during the christening celebration. There is no reason or motivation for this addition, which adds nothing to the play.

The *Time* review for the film faulted the VistaVision format as a major weakness, "the atmosphere is dissipated in the irrelevant vastness of the VistaVision screen, and almost all the emotional pressure is lost." In many ways the widescreen process is a handicap to Delbert Mann's television aesthetics through which he attempts to frame the action. The majority of scenes in the film were shot on a sound stage; Mann's background work in television is quite evident here. But the problem lies in trying to accommodate the staging of actors with the widescreen format. VistaVision was Paramount's answer to Twentieth Century-Fox's Cinemascope. Much of the staging for VistaVision films was relegated to the middle plane, which was the area of focus. The location shots, which were filmed in Santa Monica, and the studio shots are not carefully matched. Orlandello states that with O'Neill adaptations, "Either the whole work must be treated in terms of fluid film space, as in *Long Voyage Home*, or the confined physical space of the drama must be dynamized through entirely filmic devices (such as camera angles, flatness or depth of field, camera movement, effective close-ups), as in *Long Day's Journey into Night*." The emotional and physical intensity of *Desire Under the Elms* is severely debilitated by the inconsistencies of the performances as well as the design.

REFERENCES

Belton, John, *Widescreen Cinema* (Cambridge: Harvard University Press, 1992); Leiter, Samuel L., *The Encyclopedia of the New York Stage, 1920–1930* (Westport, Conn.: Greenwood Press, 1985); Orlandello, John, *O'Neill on Film* (Rutherford, N.J.: Fairleigh Dickinson University Press, 1982).

—R.W.W.

THE DEVIL'S DISCIPLE (1897)

GEORGE BERNARD SHAW (1856–1950)

The Devil's Disciple (1959), U.S.A., directed by Guy Hamilton, adapted by Roland Kibbee and John Dighton; Hecht-Hill-Lancaster/United Artists.

The Play

George Bernard Shaw turned to the *Pièce bien faite* type of "thesis play" in the 1890s with *Widower's Houses* (1892), *Arms and the Man* (1893), and *Mrs. Warren's Profession* (1899). His greatest critical and popular successes came with later plays, such as *Man and Superman* (1903), *Major Barbara* (1905), *Pygmalion* (1913), and *Saint Joan* (1923). *The Devil's Disciple*, while popular with audiences, was never a favorite of Shaw himself. In the preface to *Three Plays for Puritans*, of which this was the first, he ridiculed critics who called the play advanced. He insisted that it was hackneyed in structure and plot, and that its only novelty was its realistic presentation of the character of Dick Dudgeon, a Puritan, as a reprobate and an outcast. The play was performed just once, for copyright purposes, in London in 1897 and was not seen again until it was later staged in New York City.

The story is set in Websterbridge, New Hampshire, in 1777. Against the backdrop of the struggle between the British and rebellious colonists, news arrives that the British have hanged as rebels two Dudgeon brothers. The family gathers for the reading of the will, which leaves most of the property to Dick Dudgeon, a dissolute wastrel—self-styled as a "devil's disciple"—who is disliked by the rest of the family. Fearing that the British intend to hang Dick as well, Anthony Anderson, a Protestant minister, warns him. But it is Anderson who has been targeted, and the British arrive to make the arrest. In the confusion, Dick is mistaken for Anderson and led away to jail. Refusing to reveal his true identity (for reasons that remain unclear), Dick remains in jail, where he is comforted by Judith, Anderson's wife, who confesses her love for him. At the trial, Dick is openly scornful of the British, and he is duly convicted. Anderson arrives at the gallows at the last minute to save Dick. It seems that Anderson has doffed his cleric's robes and has at last found his true calling as a soldier. He now offers to exchange occupations with Dick (who in the meantime has promised Judith that he will not reveal to Anderson her infatuation for him). He predicts that the idealist Dick "will start presently as the Reverend Richard Dudgeon, and wag his brow in my old pulpit, and give good advice to this silly sentimental little wife of mine." A "fool" in his own eyes but a "hero" to the townsfolk and to Judith, Dick vows never to reveal her romantic interest in him.

The play abounds in the sort of external action usually absent in Shaw, including violent confrontations, pursuits, crises, and escapes. Commentator Eric Bentley regards it as a rather "crude," uncharacteristic example of Shavian satire. "Every incident in the play," he writes, "—from the announcement of the legacy to the last-minute rescue at the scaffold—is a standard item of Victorian melodrama; so is every character from the dashing hero to the little orphan child Essie. When Shaw himself calls the play 'threadbare melodrama' he means presumably that it is melodrama insufficiently Shavianized, insufficiently transformed into a satire upon melodrama."

The Film

G. B. Shaw considered American movies "full of the stupidest errors of judgment. . . . Conceit is rampant among your film makers; and good sense is about nonexistent." Indeed, before the movies learned to talk, Shaw refused to allow any of his plays to be adapted to the screen. "I repeat that a play with the words left out is a play spoiled; and all those filmings of plays written to be spoken as well as seen are boresome blunders. . . ." Yet, Shaw had long been interested in photography, and he was willing to admit that he saw the film medium as a potentially revolutionary social force. However, he insisted that a cinematic adaptation should be nothing more than a filmed play; he insisted that it was the dialogue that mattered, not the techniques of editing and camera.

Accordingly, the first Shavian adaptation to hit the screen was *How He Lied to Her Husband* (1931), directed by Cecil Lewis in a virtually unaltered piece of canned theatre. Both it and the next venture, *Arms and the Man* (1932), were tediously static, and they flopped at the box office. But the arrival of one Gabriel Pascal, a self-styled film producer, would change all that. He met Shaw in 1935 and, by his own admission, talked Shaw into allowing him to produce his plays on film. "I said that I would make no picture with box-office compromises. And I think the old man believed in my love of art, that's all. There's no mystery about it." Shaw later admitted he had been quite taken with Pascal's charm: "A delightful creature, but quite outside all ordinary rules." At any rate, Pascal's three adaptations of Shaw—*Pygmalion* (1938), *Major Barbara* (1941), and (to a lesser degree) *Caesar and Cleopatra* (1944) for his own production company would not only be successes, but would also represent a more enlightened attitude on Shaw's part toward the recognition of a more "cinematic" union of play text and camera.

The Devil's Disciple has a less satisfying history on screen. Ironically, it was one of the first Shaw plays to be considered for adaptation. In 1927 Shaw decided to release the screen rights to the play to a British company *only* if he retained control over the production. He emphatically did *not* want it to be turned into a love story. The project lapsed, but it was taken up again five years later when the American studio, RKO, petitioned Shaw for the rights. He rejected the offer, and when he was asked for a reason, he declared: "Tell [them] I've seen an RKO picture." RKO persisted, however, and when John Barrymore joined the negotiations, Shaw relented. But again, fearing "Hollywood sobstuff," Shaw insisted that the character of Dick Dudgeon *not* be portrayed as being in love with Judith, who, after all, was merely "a snivelling little goody-goody, as pathetically pretty as she pleases, and spoilt and conceited enough to imagine that Dick has faced the gallows for her sake instead of 'by the law of his own nature.'" This project also fell through. It was not until Gabriel Pascal entered Shaw's life that he finally decided to have a crack himself at a screen adaptation. Although no film of the play was ever completed during his lifetime, Shaw wrote two introductory scenes, one showing a fussy King George III unconcerned about the "Colonies," and the other a foppish Lord Germain failing to send a vital military dispatch to General Howe in America.

Shaw was safely dead when Hollywood's Hecht-Hill-Lancaster company decided to film *The Devil's Disciple* in 1959. The cast featured Burt Lancaster as Anderson, Kirk Douglas as Dick Dudgeon, Janette Scott as Judith, and Sir Laurence Olivier as General Burgoyne. Although the company was offered Shaw's own introductory scenes, it refused them, producing instead what commentator Donald P. Costello calls "the mutilation and murder which Shaw feared—a love story, a traditional adventure romance, which, as he had once prophetically warned, would some day be 'presented to the public with my name attached,' and an assurance that nobody need fear that it had any Shavian quality whatever, and was real genuine Hollywood." Scenarists John Dighton and Roland Kibbee provided a historical context through several animated sequences; and there are additional scenes depicting the American guerillas' frustrations of the British and Anderson's evolution from minister to soldier. Another addition occurs at the end of the film, when Anderson reclaims his wife by riding after her and sweeping her up into his arms. Thus, the sanctity of marriage is preserved for film audiences.

REFERENCES

Bentley, Eric, *Bernard Shaw*, rev. ed. (New York: Limelight Editions, 1984); Costello, Donald P., *The Serpent's Eye: Shaw and the Cinema* (Notre Dame, Ind.: University of Notre Dame Press, 1965); Dukore, Bernard F., ed., *Bernard Shaw on Cinema* (Carbondale: Southern Illinois Press, 1997).

—*J.C.T.*

DIAL M FOR MURDER (1952)

FREDERICK KNOTT (1918–)

Dial M for Murder (1954), U.S.A., directed by Alfred Hitchcock, adapted by Frederick Knott; Warner Bros.

The Perfect Murder (1998), U.S.A., directed by Andrew Davis, adapted by Patrick Smith Kelly; Warner Bros.

The Play

Dial M for Murder debuted at New York's Plymouth Theatre on October 29, 1952. The setting is London.

Sheila Wendice is married to ex-tennis-star Tony, now a sporting goods salesman. When Sheila's former lover, Max, a writer of television murder mysteries, shows up, Tony immediately conspires to murder her. His motivation is not entirely one of jealousy; rather, he wants to inherit her money. He calls upon one Captain Lesgate and blackmails him into a plot to break into the apartment and stab Sheila. But the plan goes wrong and Sheila stabs Lesgate to death. Tony tries to turn his failed plot to his advantage by making it look as though Sheila had murdered a blackmailer. This would make her culpable of murder and result in her being hanged. However, the dogged efforts of Inspector Hubbard, combined with the murder story expertise of Max, eventually clear Sheila.

The Films

After the lukewarm reception of *I Confess*, Alfred Hitchcock cast about for a more conventional murder thriller. Frederick Knott's commercially proven *Dial M for Murder* was available, and he chose it as his next project. Hitchcock generally believed that film versions of stage plays should emphasize their dramatic origins and refrain from adding too many exterior scenes and added bits of business. He had employed this tactic particularly in his film versions of *Juno and the Paycock* (1930) and *Rope* (1948). With *Dial M for Murder* he put his theory to the additional test by filming it in 3-D, thereby enhancing on screen the dynamics of theatrical space.

Playwright Frederick Knott wrote his own screen adaptation, and it cleaves closely to the spare theatricality of his original play. It was shot in just 36 days, primarily in one apartment set, and with an absolute minimum of action carried on outside. However, this is not to say that Hitchcock doesn't add a few additional settings, like the Wendice bedroom and the club dining room area where Tony phones Margot to lead her to her death; and he does employ various cinematic techniques such as close-ups, low angle shots, and a dominating high-angle-shot visual scheme. He also exploits the 3-D process to foreground several mise-en-scène elements, such as a lamp, flower vase, and the scissors Margot grabs prior to her stabbing her assailant in the back. The most striking use of three-dimensional space occurs when Lesgate pushes forward Margot's body onto Tony's desk while attempting to strangle her. Her reaching to the audience breaks the normal voyeuristic barriers between a screen character and the audience and serves to involve the spectator in the fate of the characters. Her gesture represents a plea for help to an audience accustomed to the usual cinematic pleasures of "harmless entertainment" and spectacular pleasure. Since the viewer cannot intervene to help Margot, her accompanying gesture of seizing the scissors and stabbing Lesgate in self-defense is the only action available to her. The viewer thus will be deeply empathetic to her predicament.

Ray Milland portrayed the charming villain, Tony Wendice, and Grace Kelly filled the role of his wife, Margot. Robert Cummings portrayed the assassin, and John Williams appeared as Inspector Hubbard. Although Hitchcock was purportedly preoccupied with the planning of his *next* picture, *Rear Window*, he did prepare carefully for certain scenes, notably the stabbing scene. According to biographer Donald Spoto, he staged and executed this action with characteristic erotic implications: "The finished scene, like other scenes of violence in Hitchcock's work, has clear references to sexual struggle; with its separate inserted shots of the actress's legs pushing against her oncoming attacker, and in the frenzied ambiguity of the strangling, it reveals a care delineated even more vividly in his later, longer murder scenes."

Because audiences were already tiring of the novelty of 3-D by 1954, *Dial M for Murder* was generally released in a conventional flat version. However, in 1981, Warner Brothers gave permission for the brief rerelease of the original 3-D version in America and England. In the latter country, it played at the Institute of Contemporary Arts in London, a venue generally noted for exhibiting avant-garde art films. The relatively unseen 3-D version is really Hitchcock's "director's cut," since it represents the way the film was intended to be seen. Biographer John Russell Taylor applauds the finished product: "The film improves on the play in intensity and concentration, and seems to give everything an extra neurotic edge which is not totally explicable in rational terms."

Andrew Davis' remake, titled *The Perfect Murder*, is only loosely based on the Knott/Hitchcock production, but it is a solid, no-nonsense, tautly paced, and beautifully acted thriller. Here, Michael Douglas plays Stephen Taylor, a corporate investor who, upon learning of the infidelity of his wife Emily (Gwyneth Paltrow), confronts her lover, a talented painter named David Shaw (Viggo Mortensen) and blackmails him into a plan to murder her. The plan, which follows closely the original scheme of the play, fails, of course, and Emily stabs the hitman Shaw has hired with a stiletto-like meat thermometer. Now it is Shaw who attempts to blackmail Taylor—and he is murdered for his efforts. In the end, his wife learns of Taylor's treachery and, in her turn, kills him. The movie ends

with her being interrogated by an extremely sympathetic detective. Every detail counts in this intricately crafted plot—a missing key, a tape recording, a wedding ring. And while Paltrow and Mortensen are competent enough, it is Michael Douglas, with those beady eyes, knife-edge temper, and menacing manner, who dominates the affair.

REFERENCES

Rothman, William, *Hitchcock: The Murderous Gaze* (Cambridge, Mass.: Harvard University Press, 1982); Spoto, Donald, *The Dark Side of Genius: The Life of Alfred Hitchcock* (Boston: Little, Brown, 1983); Taylor, John Russell, *Hitch* (New York: Pantheon Books, 1978); Truffaut, François, *Hitchcock* (London: Panther, 1999).

—*T.W.*

DINNER AT EIGHT (1932)

GEORGE S. KAUFMAN (1889–1961) AND EDNA FERBER (1887–1968)

Dinner at Eight (1933), U.S.A,, directed by George Cukor, adapted by Herman J. Mankiewicz and Frances Marion; MGM.

The Play

Playwright/satirist George S. Kaufman was not dubbed "The Great Collaborator" for nothing. In his long and distinguished career he teamed up with many writers, including Marc Connelly, Herman Mankiewicz, Morrie Ryskind, and Moss Hart. The relationship with novelist Edna Ferber was especially productive. Beginning with *Minick* in 1924, a story of an elderly widower disrupting the home life of his son and daughter-in-law, they wrote six plays together. *The Royal Family* (1927) affectionately lampooned the Barrymore dynasty, *Dinner at Eight* (1932) the world of cosmopolitan socialites, *Stage Door* (1936) the backstage activities of wannabe actors, *The Land Is Bright* (1941) the saga of a western robber baron and his descendants, and *Bravo!* (1948) the fortunes of European refugees in America.

Dinner at Eight opened in New York at the Music Box Theatre on October 22, 1932, and ran for a successful 243 performances. Hostess Millicent Jordan attempts the social coup of the season by inviting to her dinner party a variety of social notables. A series of separate scenes introduce each of them: Lord Ferncliffe is a member of the visiting British nobility, Dan

Packard is a Montana millionaire, Dr. Talbot is Jordan's physician, and Carlotta Vance and Larry Renault are two actors past their prime. Expository dialogue reveals unexpected connections among them all. Packard is scheming with Ferncliffe to take over the business interests of Mr. Jordan, whose health and fortune are failing. Talbot has two secrets: He has had a clandestine affair with Montana's wife, Kitty, and he alone knows that Jordan is dying. Renault has seduced the Jordans' daughter, Paula. And Carlotta Vance is considering selling her interests in Jordan's business. In the second half of the play, Millicent's careful party plans are smashed. Each of the characters meets with some kind of disaster. When the Ferncliffes cancel out at the last minute, Packard's takeover plans are dashed. Dr. Talbot decides to end his affair with Kitty Packard and return to his wife. Renault commits suicide. And Carlotta learns that she has inadvertently aided in the planned takeover of the Jordan business. As commentator Ina Rae Hark notes, *Dinner at Eight* is sharply biting in its social comedy: "[It] balances its criticism of pretension and double-dealing with little affirmation of the eventual triumph of common sense and decency."

The Film

MGM was having a stellar season in 1932–33, when it released two of its most prestigious ensemble pictures, *Grand Hotel* and *Dinner at Eight*. The studio's $8 million profit margin in 1932 stood out in sharp contrast to the failing fortunes of the other major studios. Its stable of stars was the finest in Hollywood. And the two aforementioned pictures topped the list of its successful releases. In a successful attempt to out-do *Grand Hotel*, producer David O. Selznick and director George Cukor assembled a star-studded cast for an adaptation of *Dinner at Eight*. Former Ziegfeld Follies girl Billie Burke and the redoubtable Lionel Barrymore were Millicent and Oliver Jordan, Madge Evans was their daughter, Wallace Beery (late of *The Champ*) and Jean Harlow (whose recent *Red-Headed Woman* and *Red Dust* had aroused censorship controversies) were Dan and Kitty Packard, and Marie Dressler (late of *Min and Bill*) and John Barrymore (*Grand Hotel*) rounded out the cast as Carlotta Vance and Larry Renault. "What a challenge!" screenwriter Mankiewicz sarcastically said to Cukor: "I can't imagine you will ever get Jean Harlow to play a tart. And I sympathize with you, trying to take the edge off Wallace Beery's sophistication. Although nothing can compare with your problem in getting Jack Barrymore to understand the part of a fading matinee idol. . . ." Indeed, in the

opinion of Cukor's biographer, Patrick McGilligan, "Barrymore's bleak study of a drink-doomed Lothario anchored the film somberly." The caustic bitterness of the Kaufman-Ferber play was transferred intact, with little softening. All the characters here face disaster of some sort. Oliver Jordan is dying, his business fortunes doomed; his wife's dinner party is a catastrophe; the dissolute actor commits suicide; and his mistress, Paula Jordan, is forced to contemplate marriage with someone she doesn't love. At the same time, it has its hilarious moments, particularly in the exchanges between Harlow and Dressler. *Dinner at Eight* launched the career of Selznick at MGM, and he went on in the next few years to helm *Dancing Lady*, with Joan Crawford, *Viva Villa*, with Wallace Beery, *A Tale of Two Cities*, with Ronald Colman, and *David Copperfield* with Freddie Bartholomew and W.C. Fields.

REFERENCES

McGilligan, Patrick, *George Cukor: A Double Life* (New York: St. Martin's Press, 1991); Pollack, Rhoda-Gale, *George S. Kaufman* (Boston: Twayne Publishers, 1988).

—D.S. AND J.C.T.

DOG IN THE MANGER, THE

See *EL PERRO DEL HORTELANO*

A DOLL'S HOUSE (ET DUKKEHJEM) (1879)

HENRIK [JOHAN] IBSEN (1828–1906)

A Doll's House (1917), U.S.A., directed and adapted by Joseph De Grasse, Bluebird Photoplay.

Ee Zertva [*Her Sacrifice*] (1917), Russia, directed and adapted by Ceslav Sabinskij, Tovariscestvo.

A Doll's House (1918), U.S.A., directed and adapted by Maurice Tourneur, Artcraft Photoplay.

A Doll's House (1922), U.S.A., directed by Charles Bryant, adapted by Peter M. Winters; Nazimova Productions.

Nora (1922–23), Germany, directed by Berthold Viertel, adapted by Georg Froschel and Berthold Viertel; Projections-AG Union.

Nora (1944), Germany, directed by Harald Braun, adapted by Harald Braun and Walter Lutz; Ufa.

A Doll's House (1973), U.K./France, directed by Joseph Losey, adapted by David Mercer; World Film Services/Les Films la Boetie.

A Doll's House (1973), U.K., directed by Patrick Garland, adapted by Christopher Hampton; Elkins Productions/Freeward Films.

The Play

Henrik Ibsen's controversial masterpiece, *A Doll's House*, which premiered at the Royal Theatre in Copenhagen on December 21, 1879, was not his first indictment of the conventions of marriage and the institutionalization of gender roles in the household. One of his early verse plays, *Love's Comedy* (1862), about the doomed relationship between a poet and his fiancee, Svanhild, was attacked by critics as immoral and lacking in taste. The play was far removed from his previous historical dramas and folklore poetics. Subsequent plays like *Brand* (1866) and *Peer Gynt* (1867) marked his developing interests in philosophical and psychological drama; and the eight plays written between 1877 and 1890—inaugurated by *Pillars of Society* and culminating with *Hedda Gabler*—carried forward his preoccupations with realism and social satire. Without question, *A Doll's House*, the second in that sequence, remains the best known and most notorious. In its day many theatrical producers refused to stage it, primarily due to its shocking conclusion, and feminist groups embraced it as one of the first important dramatic statements of their cause. Another leading radical of the day, August Strindberg, attacked it on the grounds that it exalted those creatures he considered to be man's enemy, women. His *The Father* (1887) presented a side of the domestic tangle that had not been told by Nora. Today, commentators like Oscar Brockett and Robert Findlay regard it as "the first important modern drama, both because of qualities within the work and because of the powerful impression it made on the public consciousness."

Aside from its thematic material, *A Doll's House* established a pattern subsequently adopted by Ibsen and many other playwrights of the current schools of realism and naturalism, i.e., it deliberately limited the scope of the action to one or two rooms, concentrating upon a mere handful of characters caught up in the toils of escalating events and falling victim to both their environment and their own character flaws. As Brockett and Findlay note, "[It] treats only the end of

Henrik Ibsen

a long chain of events, all interconnected but whose significance is unclear until the past recoils on the present and creates crisis and catastrophe." A full decade elapsed before the play was presented in English in London—the first time, noted George Bernard Shaw, that an Ibsen play was presented in an English theatre exactly as the author wrote it. Shaw's remarks convey just a touch of judicious irony: "[The play] set women thinking hard in Norway, and it will set them thinking equally hard here, where the breakup of the doll's-house conception of woman's sphere has gone further than in Norway."

A Doll's House tells the story of a woman, Nora, entrapped by circumstances. She is the trophy wife of a smug lawyer, Torvald Helmer, who has just been appointed manager of a bank. He treats his wife condescendingly and considers her a spendthrift. As Ibsen wrote in his "Notes for the Tragedy of Modern Times," there are "two kinds of spiritual laws, two kinds of conscience, one for men and one, quite different, for women," as the play demonstrates. "A woman cannot be herself in modern times," Ibsen concluded, and will be "judged by masculine law."

Torvald had earlier fallen ill, and Nora was advised that he needed to go to a warmer climate to be healed. At the time Nora was torn between her sick husband and her dying father but none the less managed to finance a year's stay in Italy. Helmer believes Nora paid for the trip with her father's inheritance, but in fact she borrowed money from an unscrupulous lawyer named Krogstad (his name echoes the Norwegian word *krokstav*, which means "crook"). Nora broke the law by giving her father's name on the contract, three days after her father's death. Torvald is a more highly trained lawyer than Krogstad, whom he dislikes and intends to fire from his subordinate position at the bank. Nora petitions Torvald to hire her friend, Christine Linde, a widow who needs work, to replace Krogstad. Krogstad attempts to blackmail Nora with the forged contract in order to persuade Nora to intercede with Torvald on his behalf, but Torvald refuses to listen to her. Nora is therefore in a very awkward position.

Nora approaches a close family friend, Dr. Rank, who is dying of an inherited disease, for help, but after Rank confesses his love for her, Nora decides not to confide in him. At a Christmas party, Nora dances the Tarantella with wild abandon, because she knows Torvald will soon read Krogstad's letter in which he threatens to create a scandal by making the forgery known. Enraged, Torvald calls Nora an unfit mother, but later forgives her when Krogstad sends a second letter, withdrawing the threat. By that time Torvald has already revealed his true nature to Nora as an egotistical fool who cares only about appearances. Nora therefore decides to leave him and her children. She knows full well she is transgressing societal conventions. When her husband accuses her of ignorance of "the society in which you live," she replies: "But now I shall try to learn. I must make up my mind which is right—society or I." Helmer insists on his status as patriarch, saying, "But no man sacrifices his honor, even for one he loves." She replies in words that shocked and aroused a generation: "Millions of women have done so. . . . It burst upon me that I had been living here these eight years with a strange man, and had borne him three children—Oh, I can't bear to think of it! I could tear myself to pieces." She then departs by the hall door,

leaving Helmer alone. At the last moment he thinks she may have decided to return. But no, the last sound he hears is the slam of the front door downstairs. As Egil Törnquist notes, "the play ends on a note of climactic disruption" instead of attempting to reinstate a sense of equilibrium.

It is worth noting that so controversial was this ending that Ibsen was forced to write an alternative ending when it became clear that in no other form would the play be produced. Many audiences of the day first saw the play with an ending involving reconciliation between Nora and Helmer.

The Films

In discussing the play adaptations, Törnquist notes that the play had been filmed a dozen times by 1978, most notably with Nazimova as Nora in the American silent film directed by Charles Bryant in 1922, which incorporated much of the off-stage action. In this adaptation Alan Hale played Torvald; Nigel De Brulier, Dr. Rank; Florence Fisher, Mrs. Linde; and Wedgewood Nowell, Krogstad. The earliest adaptations were American, made in 1911 (Thanhouser), 1915 (directed by Allan Holubar), and 1917, directed by Joseph De Grasse and featuring Lon Chaney as Krogstad, Dorothy Phillips as Nora, and William Stowell as Torvald. A Russian version of 1917 was entitled *Her Sacrifice*, and was followed by Maurice Tourneur's adaptation of 1918, featuring Elsie Ferguson as Nora, Holmes E. Herbert as Torvald, Alex K. Shannon as Krogstad, and Warren Cook as Dr. Rank.

Of the two film adaptations made from the play in 1973, the one directed by Patrick Garland is by far the more faithful to the play and the better acted, "based on the Broadway play by Christopher Hampton," the credits state. Hampton's adaptation follows Ibsen's three-act structure exactly. Act One is set on Christmas Eve, Act Two on Christmas Day, as Nora awaits the dreaded delivery of Krogstad's letter, rehearsing the Tarantella while Mrs. Linde leaves to go to Krogstad to plead for Nora, and Act Three on Boxing Day. The action is almost entirely confined to Nora's house, though it begins with an outdoor establishing shot of a horse-drawn sleigh bringing Nora home with presents, including a doll's bed. Claire Bloom plays a vivacious Nora, so ready to assume the role of Helmer's "little squirrel" that she uses her hands to feign cleaning her imagined whiskers. Anthony Hopkins makes a fine Torvald. Sir Ralph Richardson plays a weary Dr. Rank, and Denholm Elliott a stuffy and sinister Krogstad. Dame Edith Evans as the nurse Anne-Marie rather eclipses Anna Massey's Christine Linde. While Nora dances the Tarantella, Garland cross-cuts to shots of Mrs. Linde's meeting with Krogstad, suggesting that as Nora and Torvald are being drawn apart, Krogstad and Christine are being drawn together. Bloom's Nora is the more subtle rendering psychologically. In the Rank seduction scene Bloom's Nora seems possibly receptive as, faithful to the play, she lights Rank's cigar. Rank thanks her for "the fire." In Garland's film Nora seems about to give in to Torvald's lovemaking before the interruption of Rank's knocking at the door as he delivers his calling card. As Nora leaves, the film ends with a slow zoom that isolates Torvald and ends with a close-up of his face, as he whispers his last line in disbelief while the outer door is heard closing.

Joseph Losey's film, adapted by David Mercer, is far more cinematic than Garland's. It begins with a Prologue that goes back in time to show Nora (Jane Fonda) and Christine (Delphine Seyrig) before their marriages at a restaurant on an ice-skating outing. After Nora leaves, Krogstad (Edward Fox) enters and approaches Christine and challenges her: "Christine, your rejection of me is heartless, and yet you do care for me, don't you?" She answers that she does. Thus the film labors to create a backstory for Krogstad, Christine, and Nora, who is seen with her dying father and with her sick husband, as Dr. Rank (Trevor Howard) recommends a warmer climate in the interest of Torvald's health. This film is atmospheric in the way the mining town of Roros, Norway, is used as a setting. In this adaptation, Krogstad is seen quarreling with a co-worker at the bank. He later apologizes to his colleague, whom he meets by chance while taking his children sledding. Nora's first exchange with Krogstad also takes place out of doors. Delphine Seyrig is excellent as Christine, and Edward Fox is more interesting as Krogstad than David Warner is as Helmer. Trevor Howard is outstanding as Rank. Jane Fonda's Nora is more sexy than subtle. She plays the role of a woman betrayed before her time with a great deal of energy and animation. The film gives no evidence of the tension that apparently existed on location between Fonda and Losey, the director. Fonda was convinced that she understood Ibsen better than Losey ever could.

Fonda arrived in Roros not only with Tom Hayden, the most radical of her husbands, but also with her own screenwriter, Nancy Dowd, who helped her to redefine Nora, working counter to David Mercer, Losey's screenwriter. As Fred Lawrence Guiles claims, Fonda's Nora is more noble and less reprehensible for the crime of forgery. She only wants to save the life of her "charmless and tyrannical" husband. Fonda constantly upstages David Warner, whose Helmer seems weak, foolish, and far more "actorish" than Anthony Hopkins

in the Garland adaptation. The strongest performances, beyond Fonda's, are those of Edward Fox as Krogstad and Trevor Howard as Dr. Rank. In Patrick Garland's film Krogstad and Mrs. Linde recede into the background, whereas in Losey's they seem to be more important than David Warner's Torvald. Fonda dismissed the work of David Mercer ("an alcoholic misogynist English playwright," she claimed), who "built up" the "somewhat shadowy" male characters, while reducing the women and, in her metaphor, tied Nora's tubes. Fonda claimed that Ibsen's "whole thesis was being acted out" on location, since she "had to become Nora with Losey," batting her eyelashes to get her way. The film's many exterior shots are effectively atmospheric and cinematic, but the play is distorted as lines are added and Fonda's more noble Nora's predicament seems far less claustrophobic.

REFERENCES

Bloom, Claire, *Leaving A Doll's House: A Memoir* (Boston: Little, Brown, 1996); Brockett, Oscar G. and Robert R. Findlay, *Century of Innovation* (Englewood Cliffs, N.J.: Prentice-Hall, 1973); Ciment, Michel, *Conversations with Losey* (London: Methuen, 1985); Guiles, Fred Lawrence, *Jane Fonda: The Actress in Her Time* (Garden City, N.Y.: Doubleday, 1982); Hansen, Karin Synnove, *Henrick Ibsen, 1828–1978: A Filmography* (Oslo: Norsk Filminstitutt, 1978); Hirsch, Foster, *Joseph Losey* (Boston: Twayne, 1980); Törnquist, Egil, *Ibsen's: A Doll's House* (Cambridge, U.K.: Cambridge University Press, 1995); Wisenthal, J.L., *Shaw and Ibsen* (Toronto: University of Toronto Press, 1979).

—J.M.W.

DRACULA: THE VAMPIRE PLAY IN THREE ACTS (1927)

HAMILTON DEANE AND JOHN L. BALDERSTON (1889–1954)

Dracula (1931), U.S.A., directed by Tod Browning, adapted by Garret Fort; Universal Studios.

Dracula (1979), U.S.A., directed by John Badham, adapted by W. D. Richter; Universal Studios.

The Play

Interestingly enough, the first stage version of Bram Stoker's *Dracula* reached the public a few days before the novel was published. For this, and other reasons, the four-hour dramatization (by Stoker himself), which premiered at London's Lyceum Theatre on

May 17, 1897, puzzled its audiences and failed at the box office.

A decade after Stoker's death, the play was trimmed and restructured by Hamilton Deane, with the consent of Stoker's widow. In order to simplify the story, Deane removed Stoker's opening at Castle Dracula and the concluding chase scene when the Count is thwarted in his attempt to return to Transylvania. This version of the play opened at the Grant Theatre, in Derby, in 1924, then later in London at the Little Theatre on February 14, 1927, where it was a runaway success. Deane transformed Stoker's pagan prince into the sophisticated, world-weary, and elegant figure in evening dress, costumed in a tuxedo and cape and with a stand-up collar, that the public has ever since come to expect. The play was further rewritten and tuned for American audiences by John L. Balderston for its New York premiere at the Fulton Theatre in October 1927, where it ran for 33 weeks, followed by two separate touring companies the following year. In the cast was Bela Lugosi, born Bela Ferenc Dezso Blasko, in the Banat region of Transylvania (now a part of Romania). Lugosi brought a distinctive styling and voice to the role and was later to be cast for the Tod Browning film (the *New York Post* noted that "Mr. Lugosi performs Dracula with funereal decorations suggesting . . . an operatically inclined but cheerless mortician"). After playing a year on Broadway, the Balderston production toured the country successfully for two years. As horror historian David Skal writes, "It was one of those jazz-age thrill-machines that audiences couldn't resist, sort of a theatrical equivalent to the Coney Island Cyclone, another 1927 invention that was attracting record crowds."

The plot was further simplified as follows: Lucy Seward suffers from apparent anemia and is wasting away. Her father, a physician in charge of a sanatorium near London, sends for Dr. Van Helsing, a specialist in obscure diseases. Van Helsing soon suspects Dr. Seward's new foreign neighbor, Count Dracula, as being the cause of Lucy's ill health and reveals him to be a blood-sucking vampire. After Van Helsing drives a stake through the vampire's heart, both Lucy and the sanatorium patient Renfield begin to recover.

The action is structured in three acts involving eight characters. Lucy Seward becomes Dr. Seward's daughter and Mina, already dead, is not in the cast, though she is referred to as the "Bloofer Lady" of the novel who terrorizes children. The play adds Miss Wells, a maid, and Mr. Butterfield, a hospital attendant who looks after the demented Renfield. The main characters are Abraham Van Helsing, the "metaphysician and scientist from Amsterdam," Count Dracula,

and Lucy. Jonathan Harker is Lucy's suitor, but is merely a secondary character in the play.

The action is set entirely in England—the library in Dr. Seward's sanatorium in Purley (Act One), Lucy's boudoir (Act Two), and "A Vault [at Carfax Abbey], just after sunrise." Alarmed over the state of his daughter Lucy's health, Dr. Seward sends for Van Helsing, "a man of resourceful action," to exorcise her demons. Dracula is "polished and distinguished," elegant and Continental in appearance and manner. Renfield and Butterworth provide comic relief. Dracula does not escape to Transylvania, but is dispatched at Carfax, where Van Helsing discovers his coffin at the end of Act Three and drives a stake through his heart. The novel was streamlined and re-imagined for the stage production, but at the expense of some of the novel's best moments in Transylvania.

The Films

Before the Universal talkie, *Dracula*, was released in 1931, the Dracula legend had reached the screen many times (although variants of the legend, as well as several adaptations of the novel, were the primary source materials). Most notably, F.W. Murnau's *Nosferatu* (1922), an unauthorized adaptation of Stoker, and Tod Browning's *London After Midnight* (1927), a pastiche of vampire lore, should be mentioned. Credit for the first true talkie adaptation of the stage *play*, however, goes to Universal Pictures, which bought the rights to the Balderston-Deane stage version. Universal chief Carl Laemmle was initially reluctant to authorize the purchase. Only when his son, Carl, Jr., insisted on it, did the old man relent and give the project the green light (he may also have wanted to deprive rival MGM of the rights). Lon Chaney was to portray Dracula, but his death from throat cancer forced the studio to look elsewhere. Despite Lugosi's stage success in the role, it was his very *unfamiliarity* to movie audiences that eventually won him the part. The film was a spectacular hit. Societal changes, explains historian Skal—not the least of which included a worsening Depression—helped explain its success: "Horror films served as a kind of populist surrealism, rearranging the human body and its processes, blurring the boundaries between Homo sapiens and other species, responding uneasily to new and almost incomprehensible developments in science and the anxious challenges they posed to the familiar structures of society, religion, psychology, and perception."

Garrett Fort's screenplay also borrowed from the original novel, sending Renfield (Dwight Frye) rather than Jonathan Harker to Transylvania, and generally following the design of the play. Except for cinematographer Karl Freund's wonderfully atmospheric opening depicting the visit to Castle Dracula, most of the Tod Browning–directed film is awkwardly stage-bound (historian Skal alleges that Freund actually directed major portions of the film). The acting is stiff and postured, and the action is photographed from the perspective of a viewer in the third row of the center stalls. Supporting Lugosi's Count were Helen Chandler (Mina) and Edward Van Sloane (Dr. Van Helsing).

The film does not fully exploit the potential of the medium. For example, Dracula's supernatural transformations into vampires and other beasts are not magically represented, as they are in Francis Ford Coppola's *Bram Stoker's Dracula*, which, it should be stressed, was adapted from the original novel and not the stage version. Much of the action transpires offstage, even Dr. Van Helsing's final impalement of the Count. As was seen in the play, the climactic action takes place at Carfax Abbey.

Ironically, it is the Mexican version of the film, shot at night on the same sets and from the same script, but with a Spanish-language cast and a different director (George Melford), that is visually superior to the Browning film. Its richness of detail and chiaroscuro lighting and fluid camera movements remove the film from its stagy context and establish it as a wholly cinematic achievement.

In 1977 the Balderston-Deane play was revived on Broadway with Frank Langella in the lead. This stage revival led to another Universal Studios adaptation written by W.D. Richter and directed by John Badham, with Frank Langella following in Lugosi's footsteps from stage to screen, playing against Sir Laurence Olivier's Van Helsing. This stage revival had a sense of humor, and the film presented Langella as a romantically charged, caped, Byronesque lover not to be taken lightly.

REFERENCES

Glut, Donald R., *The Dracula Book* (Metuchen, N.J.: Scarecrow, 1975); Skal, David J., *The Monster Show: A Cultural History of Horror* (New York: W.W. Norton, 1993); Wolf, Leonard, *Dracula: The Connoisseur's Guide* (New York: Broadway Books, 1997).

—*J.M.W. AND J.C.T.*

DREAM OF PASSION, A

See *MEDEIA*

THE DRESSER (1980)

RONALD HARWOOD (1934–)

The Dresser (1983), U.K., directed by Peter Yates, adapted by Ronald Harwood and Peter Yates; Columbia Pictures.

The Play

The Dresser, an outstanding backstage drama about loyalty, love, friendship, and the theatre, first premiered at the Royal Exchange Theatre in Manchester, before its transfer to the Queen's Theatre, London, where, after a successful run, it won the *New Standard* and Drama Critics' awards for best play of 1980. When it was produced on Broadway in 1981, it was nominated for a Tony Award. It was autobiographically based on the experience Ronald Harwood had after moving from his native South Africa to England, where, after studying at the Royal Academy of Dramatic Art, he joined Donald Wolfit's Shakespeare Company at the King's Theatre, Hammersmith, in 1953.

Set in a provincial English theatre in 1942 during the German bombings of World War II, the play concerns a troupe of generally decrepit Shakespearean actors struggling to perform in the British countryside. The main focus, however, involves the relationship between a famous Shakespearean actor, referred to only as "Sir," and his loyal servant and "dresser," Norman. Sir is on his last legs, forgetful of his lines and hardly able to manage his personal affairs, let alone manage his supporting actors, most of them also past their prime. The actor is sick and apparently not able to perform without Norman's coaxing and encouragement. Norman's challenge in the second act is to prepare the actor for King Lear, Shakespeare's most demanding role. With Norman's help, Sir rises to the occasion and gives the performance of a lifetime, but when the curtain comes down after Lear's death scene, the actor dies, leaving a grief-stricken Norman alone, to face an uncertain future. "What about me?" he says, despairingly.

The play followed Harwood's biography, *Sir Donald Wolfit C.B.E., His Life and Work in the Unfashionable Theatre* (1971), but in his Foreword to the play Harwood advised that the play's egotistical actor, referred to only as "Sir," was not exactly a portrait of the great actor-manager Sir Donald Wolfit, but a dramatic creation, possibly with certain similarities: "Lear was Wolfit's greatest performance—so is it Sir's; the grand manner both on and off the stage which Wolfit often employed is also Sir's way; the war did not stop Wolfit from playing Shakespeare in the principal provincial cities and in London." Moreover, as Wolfit's business manager, Harwood "witnessed at close quarters a great actor preparing for a dozen or more major classical roles," including Shakespeare's King Lear, and remembered, as a member of the crew, attempting to create a theatrical tempest for the play's storm scene that "was never loud enough for Wolfit, as it never is for Sir." Finally, the character of Norman was "in no way autobiographical," but "an amalgam of three or four men I met who served leading actors as professional dressers."

The Film

The film introduces Sir (Albert Finney) giving an extravagant performance of Othello, declaiming in the distance while Norman (Tom Courtenay) busies himself in the dressing room. During his curtain call, Sir advises the audience that their next performance will be at the Alhambra Theatre, Brantford, then upbraids Geoffrey Thornton (Lockwood West) for overacting his final line after Othello dies and the younger Oxenby (Edward Fox) for upstaging him. Backstage, Sir talks with Norman about the autobiography he intends to write. "I've begun my life," he says, ironically, because he says this at the very point his life is about to end. Literally in this play, Sir lives to act.

Because the play has only two settings, film director Peter Yates opens it up a bit, extending the action outside the theatre to show one of the actor's bouts with dementia in the wrecked setting of a bombed-out provincial town. Sir has lost his bearings and has no idea of where he is when Norman finds and rescues him. Because the actor is clearly ill, Madge, the troupe's manager (Eileen Atkins), decides to cancel the forthcoming performance of *King Lear*, but Norman convinces her that he can get the old man in shape to perform, even though the actor is inclined to scramble together lines from several plays and cannot even remember Lear's opening lines. When this distinguished actor takes the stage and the performance begins, however, Sir is in his element. After the storm scene Sir rants "I want a tempest, not a drizzle!" Encouraged, Norman proclaims, "he is himself again!"

Shakespeare's Lear becomes the dominant metaphor for Harwood's play. "There, there, it's only a play," an older man tells a wounded soldier moved to tears by the performance during the play's intermission. But *Lear* is not "only a play." It is a play about a world gone mad,

Albert Finney (right) and Tom Courtenay starred in a screen adaptation of Ronald Harwood's play The Dresser. (COURTESY COLUMBIA PICTURES)

like the world of England under attack. "The agony was in the moment of acting created," Sir proclaims grandly, between scenes. Ultimately, Sir manages to give the performance of a lifetime, mainly because the state of the actor's mind is nearly as disturbed as that of King Lear in the play. As art and nature coincide, a magical performance is created. The same can be said of Albert Finney's bravura performance as Sir, which is second only to Tom Courtenay's rendering of Norman, who is to Sir as the Fool is to Lear, a care-giver and a loving and comforting presence. Both Tom Courtenay, who originated the role of Norman on stage, and Albert Finney, two actors at the top of their form, were nominated for Academy Awards, and the film was rightly nominated for best picture.

REFERENCES

Ansen, David, "Fools of Fortune," *Newsweek* (December 5, 1983), 125; Billington, Michael, "All the Stage Is a Movie," *New York Times*, June 26, 1983, sec. 2, p. 17; Canby, Vincent, "Ronald Harwood's 'Dresser,'" *The New York Times*, December 6, 1983, C19; Geist, William E., "For Albert Finney, Risk Is Everything," *The New York Times*, December 4, 1983, sec. 2, pp. 1, 18; Harwood, Ronald, *Sir Donald Wolfit, C.B.E., His Life and Work in the Unfashionable Theatre* (London: Secker & Warburg, 1971).

—*J.M.W.*

DRIVING MISS DAISY (1987)

ALFRED UHRY (1937–)

Driving Miss Daisy (1990), USA, directed by Bruce Beresford, adapted by Alfred Uhry; Warner Bros.

The Play

Originally produced Off-Broadway by Playwrights Horizons in 1987, Alfred Uhry's Pulitzer Prize–winning play is set in Atlanta during the years 1948 to 1973. There are only three characters: Daisy Werthan, a widow, 72 years old when the play begins; her son Boolie (who ages from 40 to 65); and Hoke Coleburn, 60 years old when Boolie first hires him to be Miss Daisy's chauffeur and 85 years old at the end of the play. Miss Daisy is a wealthy Jewish lady and Hoke is an African American, both of them outsiders in the Deep South, though it takes Miss Daisy years to discover exactly what she and Hoke may have in common. At first, Hoke has to demonstrate his usefulness to Miss Daisy, who refuses his services, even though he is on salary (paid by her son, Boolie). Their relationship is grounded on the comic antipathy that the self-sufficient mistress establishes between them. Hoke, by con-

Driving Miss Daisy *cast Jessica Tandy as Daisy, Morgan Freeman as Hoke, and Dan Aykroyd as Boolie.*
(COURTESY WARNER BROS.)

trast, is defined by his good nature, his patience and tolerance, and his constant consideration, since he takes his job seriously.

As southern society changes over the years they spend together, so does their relationship. Miss Daisy is a very independent-minded lady and her pride is wounded when her son arranges a chauffeur for her after she demonstrates that she is no longer able to drive safely. At first she treats Hoke like a servant but over the years a friendship gradually develops. She is shocked when a synagogue is bombed in Atlanta, but Hoke has a broader perspective on hate crimes and explains to her, "A Jew is a Jew to them folks. Jes' like light or dark we all the same nigger." (Hoke's language might not be considered politically correct, but seems to capture the proper inflection for a southern black of his years and education. The film was criticized for its racial stereotyping.) Finally sensitized to the plight of oppressed minorities in the South, Miss Daisy attends a lecture by Martin Luther King Jr. She buys tickets for Boolie and his wife Florina, but is shocked when Boolie decides not to go because, as he explains to her, "A lot of the men I do business with wouldn't like it." Boolie suggests that she be escorted by Hoke, but Hoke refuses because she asked him to go only at the very last minute, and Hoke knows that she has had the invitation for a month. Hoke has a discerning sense of dignity and will not be taken advantage of.

Miss Daisy, who refuses to think of herself as prejudiced, remarks, "Isn't it wonderful the way things are changing?" Hoke replies, "Things changin', but they ain't change all dat much." In the next scene, Hoke calls Boolie because he notices that Miss Daisy's mind and memory seem to be confused, the first evidence of her oncoming senility, which marks a shift in the play. But her mind comes and goes, and in a moment of coherence, she has an epiphany, when she realizes Hoke is trying to keep her from being sent to an "asylum." She says to him, stating the obvious, "You're my best friend." Finally, Miss Daisy has to be sent to a nursing home, and the play ends with Hoke visiting her. He is 85 years old; she is 97. Boolie has continued to keep Hoke on his payroll after his mother has left home, but, clearly, Hoke is visiting her on Thanksgiving (a symbolic holiday) out of love and friendship. What is Daisy Werthan "driven" to? A more complete understanding of her place in society and of the meaning of friendship and compassion, as she is drawn into the New South of the 20th century, the South of Martin Luther King and the civil rights movement. At the very least, she learns to become a more considerate and tolerant human being.

The Film

Bruce Beresford's film adaptation obviously needed to extend the action and to open up the play. The film begins by showing Daisy (Jessica Tandy) having an accident with her Chrysler (rather than a LaSalle, as in the play). Other changes are not terribly substantial. Boolie owns a textile plant in the film, for example, rather than a printing plant, and Hoke first visits him at the plant. An elevator gets stuck between floors, and Hoke (Morgan Freeman) is resourceful enough to fix it, giving Boolie (Dan Aykroyd) the confidence to hire him. Characters who are simply mentioned in the play, such as Idella (Esther Rolle), Daisy's maid, and Florine (Patti Lupone), Boolie's wife, are brought into the action of the film, to good effect, especially with regard to Idella, who can commiserate with Hoke over Miss Daisy's surliness. The film also shows Hoke "driving Miss Daisy" places, to the Piggly-Wiggly (grocery) store, to the synagogue, to Boolie's house, and to the Biltmore Hotel for the Martin Luther King event, for example. Hoke stays in the car and listens to the speech on the radio, while Daisy sits in the banquet hall next to an empty chair, as Dr. King's words drive home the point: "The greatest tragedy of this period of social transition are not the vitriolic words and violent actions of the bad people," he says, "but the appalling silence and indifference of the good people." In this instance Dr. King is quoting Edmund Burke.

The film contains many time cues to keep the viewers on track chronologically. For the year 1948, Hoke is driving a Hudson, for example, and is still driving it when he listens to radio news about war breaking out in Korea. Later, one notices a "Christmas 1953" card on Boolie's mantle, while Eartha Kitt sings "Santa Baby" on the radio. Later still, Boolie's woolen mill is modernized and Boolie is recognized as Man of the Year 1966 in Atlanta. Also in the film Florine becomes a foil for Daisy, when we see Florine criticizing her black maid in a way that Daisy would never do, despite her cantankerousness. Idella's presence in the film, moreover, creates a whole new plot line, showing her kinship with Hoke, her death in Daisy's kitchen while shelling peas, and her funeral, attended by Hoke, Daisy, Boolie, and Florine.

Alfred Uhry insisted on writing the screenplay himself. "A movie like this could easily be oversentimental," he told the *New York Times*, "so I made it clear I wanted to write the screenplay, and nobody seemed to mind that, which I found surprising because I had never written one." Although the text is extended for the film, this is not simply a matter of padding, but a successful attempt to give the play a wider social and visual context. And the extension is done with the highest "authority," since Uhry himself refashioned the play. The film is not merely a simplification, but a clarification and an elaboration of the original text. It drives home the lesson of prejudice and civil rights far better by the invented sequences, the words of the Martin Luther King speech, for example, and the incident when Hoke is stopped by two redneck state policemen in Alabama, who scoff at the notion of a Negro driving a Jewish lady. The film is realistically in tune with a world that is potentially nasty and brutal. And that, in union with the excellent and gifted cast, is what makes *Driving Miss Daisy* such a remarkable and entertaining adaptation.

REFERENCES

Forsberg, Myra, "'Daisy' Blossoms Once More in Atlanta," *The New York Times*, June 4, 1989, sec. 2, pp. 13–17; Vann, Helen and Jane Caputi, "*Driving Miss Daisy:* A New 'Song of the South,'" *Journal of Popular Film and Television*, 18:2 (1990), 80–82; Welsh, J.M., "Driving Miss Daisy," *Films in Review*, 41:4 (1990): 231; Witchel, Alex, "Remembering Prejudice, Of a Different Sort," *The New York Times*, February 23, 1997, sec. 2, 5, 27.

—*J.M.W.*

EAST IS EAST (1996)

AYUB KHAN-DIN (C.1960–   )

East Is East (2000), U.K., directed by Damien O'Donnell, adapted by Ayub Khan-Din; Film Four/Miramax.

The Play

East Is East was Ayub Khan-Din's first effort as a playwright. It was produced at the Royal Court Theatre in 1996. After a successful run, it went on a national tour before returning to London at the Theatre Royal Stratford East and the Royal Court at the Duke of Yorks. Ayub won the Writer's Guild of Great Britain awards for best West End play and best new writer; and he was nominated for the Laurence Olivier Award for best new writer. Largely autobiographical, Ayub's play told the story of the Khans, a mixed-race family of seven "swinging" Brits living in Manchester whose life-styles clash with their sternly traditional Pakistani father's plans for their marriages and careers. "The parents in *East Is East* are drawn directly from my parents," says Ayub. "My father's generation was an immigrant one. They had to fit into an alien environment. So he kept holding up a thing in front of us and saying 'this is what you should be,' but of course, we weren't that at all. . . . The big irony, of course, is that our spark of rebelliousness came from my father. He'd

done basically the same thing we wanted to do. He abandoned his culture by coming to settle in England." Spurred by the success of his first play, Ayub wrote a second play, *Last Dance at Dum-Dum*, which opened in the West End in July 1999.

The Film

Producer Leslee Udwin saw Ayub's hit play and instantly resolved to bring it to the screen. First-time feature director Damien O'Donnell—neither a Pakistani nor an Englishman—was chosen to helm the project because of the quirky humor he had displayed in a short film, *35 Aside*. O'Donnell in turn selected a cast of young unknowns from England's burgeoning Asian community to portray the Khan children. However, for the roles of fearsome George Khan and his wife Ella, the legendary Indian actor Om Puri and the veteran English actress Linda Bassett were chosen, respectively.

Ayub Khan-Din's script fleshes out the reported action of his play and freewheels the action into numerous locations in and around the Khan household. Opening titles explain that in 1937 George Khan, a Muslim from Pakistan, met an Englishwoman, Ella. Ten years later they married. Twenty-five years later, in 1971, the story proper begins in Manchester, England. The Khan family now numbers six sons and a daughter, and they live in a nondescript, crowded red-brick row house. A Muslim wedding procession is in place.

The marchers get to the church only after dodging around an English marriage procession. At the altar, the groom takes one look at the bride and silently imagines the world he is getting into—and bolts. After declaring his wayward son "dead," George Khan now sets his sights on marrying off his next two eldest sons to the daughters of another Muslim family. No matter that the prospective mother-in-law is a snob and the daughters fat and ugly. No matter that the prospective grooms rebel. And no matter that George's wife, Ella, herself objects. George will force his way. Even if it means brutalizing the boys and abusing his own wife.

This seriocomic story abounds in contrasts of locations and life-styles. During the day, the Khans operate a fish-and-chips shop ("George's Chippies"). At other times, their household is an oasis of Muslim tradition in the midst of the grimy Manchester street. George Khan rules his roost with an iron hand. Nonetheless, while one son dutifully observes Muslim traditions, the other boys have their own ambitions. The one who ran away from the wedding has gone on to become a fashionable clothier downtown and to live with his male lover. Another is a self-styled sculptor who creates plastic models of female vaginas; another has eyes on the bleach-blonde next door; and the youngest, an odd, silent child, gazes out at the world from within the parka he wears morning, noon, and night. The daughter's character is less well defined, but she's not happy that old dad wants her to wear a customary sari on Sundays.

At the center of it all is George Khan, a brute, a despot who uses his fists to enforce what he sees as a dying Muslim tradition. He does love his long-suffering wife, but he won't brook any interference, even from her. And when his two eldest sons object to the planned marriages—one of the boys trashes the chest of marriage clothes and headdresses—he flies into a towering rage and inflicts a beating on his wife and sons. George gets his way, of course, and preparations are in order to entertain the prospective in-laws.

The Khans' reception of the in-laws is the set piece of the film, a sustained scene that is by turns hilarious and sad. There the guests sit, the stiffly traditionalist father, the shrewish wife, and the cow-like daughters. Father Khan tries to entertain them, and Ella, despite her bruises, does her best to be obliging. But the guests' petty critiques of their cramped house, clothes, and life-style begin to tell. Tensions simmer. A polite question about what the youngest Khan wants to do when he grows up elicits the following response: "I don't want to be told who to marry." Pandemonium erupts when the guests react in horror to the appearance of the notorious vagina sculpture. Outraged herself, Ella nonetheless decides it is time to protect her brood. She rebukes

her snobbish guests and orders them out of the house. Ultimately, the whole Khan family unites against the outraged father and restrains him. Sobbing, he claims that he wants only what is best for his family against the corrupting influences of Western life-styles. In the epilogue, he sits alone in the fish shop. Ella silently arrives. After a moment, she takes his hand. He is obviously contrite. Cut to the crowded streets outside. The camera lifts up and away as life goes on.

The contrasts between sharp-eyed satire, occasional slapstick, and brutal melodrama are extreme. But that is the way the Pakistani and English cultures themselves collide. If George Khan is a brute, we must remember he sees himself as a self-styled bastion of morality in a murky world. He lives next to bigoted neighbors who openly support a politician who would turn Pakis out of England. George has had to be tough to survive. But he has his blind spots. For example, he outrages his wife when he confesses his scorn and contempt for English women (she has to remind him that he married an English woman). In sum, George's tough-mindedness has led to his inability to adjust to changing times and cultures. This is ironic, considering that he himself must once have been quite a rebel to leave his country in the first place. Meanwhile, if Ella seems a passive victim, she also emerges as ultimately a restraining influence on George. She is right when she accuses him not just of upholding his traditions but also of imposing prejudices against his children. They are, after all, not Muslim so much as inevitably English in temper and upbringing.

"If I had to sum up where the heart of *East Is East* resides, I'd say it is a plea to parents that the most unique gift you can give to a child is the freedom to be different," says producer Leslee Udwin. "The extraordinary thing is how this story unifies audiences . . . I was shocked and moved and thrilled by the familiarity of what I was seeing, and felt that same reaction, that echo, in the other people around me, all laughing together. What resonates is a universality, a rebellion against parental authority which speaks to everyone."

Following the film's release in Europe, playwright/scenarist Ayub Khan-Din was nominated for a European Film Award for best screenplay.

REFERENCES

David Denby, "Devoted," *The New Yorker* (April 24 & May 1, 2000), 221–223; Desson Howe, "All in the Anglo-Asian Family," *Washington Post*, April 16, 2000, G1, G8. Stewart Klawans, "On Tyson vs. Downey," *The Nation* (May 15, 2000), 34–36. Pressbook for *East Is East*, Miramax Pictures.

—*J.C.T.*

EASY VIRTUE (1925)

NOËL COWARD (1889–1973)

Easy Virtue (1927), U.K., directed by Alfred Hitchcock, adapted by Eliot Stannard; Gainsborough.

The Play

Noël Coward's acerbic social drama, his 13th play, received its New York premiere in December 1925 and bowed in London the following June. Coward intended to undermine the premises of the popular drawing-room plays that dominated the British stage from the late 1800s to the beginning of World War I. These works usually focused upon the intense psychological and social, personal dilemmas faced by various representatives of the English upper classes, the chief examples being Arthur Wing Pinero's *The Second Mrs. Tanquery* and John Galsworthy's *Loyalties*. Like them, *Easy Virtue* deals with the social isolation of a fallen woman (here, the survivor of a singularly nasty divorce) by a hypocritical society. Unlike them, it does not conclude with the heroine dying as a sacrificial victim for her "past sins." Instead, Coward's Larita Filton realizes her mistake in marrying a younger husband who proves both unsupportive and morally weak. She ends the play by walking away from a repressive British class society to return to France. The action occurs entirely in the country house of the Whittakers, a wealthy English upper-class family.

The Film

Released in 1927 as a silent film, between the popular *Downhill* and the boxing picture, *The Ring, Easy Virtue* is probably Hitchcock's least known feature film. The suspense hinges on our own speculation as to how the other characters will react when they learn what Hitchcock has already privileged us to know about Larita's shadowed past. The film begins with the opening caption, "Virtue has its own reward, they say, but easy virtue is society's reward for a slanderous reputation." Cut to a courtroom, where a judge adjusts his monocle to focus his vision on Larita (Isabel Jeans). Her image changes from a blur to sharp focus, a cinematic metaphor foreshadowing the enlightenment that comes to the Whittaker family regarding the truth of Larita's past. As the courtroom proceedings continue, Hitchcock supplies the viewer with flashbacks showing Larita suffering abuse from a brutal husband, Filton, and by her devoted artist admirer Claude (Eric Bransby-Williams). Claude's suicide anticipates the

Alfred Hitchcock

similar "betrayal" of her lover, John Whittaker (Robin Irvine), later in the film when he proves inadequate to defend Larita from patriarchal assault.

After she is pronounced culpable in Filton's divorce proceedings, Larita goes to Cannes where she meets John Whittaker. (Hitchcock makes his cameo appearance at this point; and, significantly, he is carrying a walking stick, perhaps symbolic of Larita's castration by a vicious social system.) As in the play, Larita falls victim to the hidebound morality of the Whittaker family. After the marriage to John fails, Larita leaves the Whittaker home with her past exposed and the marriage over. At this point, Hitchcock interjects with an epilogue that represents, according to historian Maurice Yacowar, his most personal touch in the film. Larita faces a firing squad of cameras as she leaves the divorce court. She confronts them with a world-weary gesture: "Shoot . . . there's nothing left to kill." As Christopher Morris remarks, her lines "establish an analogy between camera and weapon—one that Hitchcock would explore more explicitly in later films like

Foreign Correspondent and *Rear Window*." Hitchock thus ends his version in a more pessimistic manner than Coward by showing that his heroine can never escape unjust victimization by patriarchal law.

REFERENCES

Barr, Charles, *Hitchcock's English Films* (London: Cameron and Hollis, 1999); Cole, Stephen, *Noël Coward: A Bio-Bibliography* (Westport, Conn.: Greenwood Press, 1993); Gottlieb, Sidney, "Alfred Hitchcock's *Easy Virtue* (1927): A Descriptive Shot List," *Hitchcock Annual 1993*, 41–95; Kuhns, J.L., "Comments on 'Alfred Hitchcock's *Easy Virtue* (1927): A Descriptive Shot List'," *Hitchcock Annual 1995–96*, 126–133; Morris, Christopher, "*Easy Virtue*'s Frames," *Hitchcock Annual 1998–1999*, 20–30; Yacowar, Maurice, *Hitchcock's Silent Films* (Hamden, Conn.: Archon Books, 1977).

—*T.W.*

Julie Walters reprised on screen her stage role in Educating Rita, *costarring Michael Caine.* (COURTESY COLUMBIA PICTURES)

EDUCATING RITA (1980)

WILLY RUSSELL (1947–)

Educating Rita (1983), U.K., directed by Lewis Gilbert, adapted by Willy Russell; Columbia Pictures.

The Play

The play, called a "two-hander" because it involves only two actors, was successfully launched by the Royal Shakespeare Company in London's West End on June 10, 1980, and soon became popular throughout Britain. It centers upon the relationship between a 26-year-old hairdresser from Liverpool who calls herself Rita (a literary affectation and a tribute to the novelist Rita Mae Brown), though her real name is Susan White, and her Open University tutor, Frank Bryant, a failed poet turned alcoholic, who at first has no interest in being her tutor, though he is gradually won over by her enthusiasm and her genuine desire to become educated. Frank is at first cynical, then charmed, and finally infatuated as he witnesses the gradual transformation of crude Rita into sophisticated Susan. His mentoring soon turns to affection, but Frank's personal life is a mess, and in this regard Rita is superior to him. The tutor learns a lesson in life from his student. Education is not a one-way street here.

Frank is akin to the burned-out Dr. Dysart in Peter Shaffer's *Equus*. He knows he has the power to change and transform his student, just as Dysart knows he is capable of changing the life of his patient, Alan Strang, but, like Dysart, Frank questions whether or not he has the ethical right to do so, even though Rita demands an education. In a way Frank is a foolish idealist, glamorizing in his mind the folk wisdom of the working class, but in a way he is right. As Rita becomes educated, she loses touch with her husband Denny, who wants only to see her obedient and pregnant, and when she takes charge of her life and decides to take birth-control pills to avoid pregnancy, he divorces her. On her own, then, Rita reforms her life and moves in with a pseudo-sophisticate flatmate named Trish, whose learning is superficial and who is so depressed that she finally attempts suicide at the time Rita is to sit for her comprehensive exams. Though the timing of this personal crisis is awkward, Rita takes time to look after Trish and still passes her exams. The poetry of William Blake is a dominant metaphor in the play, as Rita moves from innocence to experience. Following the advice of her mother, Rita is determined to find a "better song" to sing. By this time Rita is so well educated that she no longer needs Frank, and she knows it. She has learned to think for herself. She has learned that she can truly change herself only from the inside out.

The irony of the play is that Rita is finally more mature than her tutor. When Frank attempts to pawn her off on another tutor, Rita reminds him of his responsibility: "you are my teacher—an' you're gonna Bleedin' well teach me." She discovers that Frank has split up with his wife and that he has "stopped writing altogether." Frank now lives with a graduate student, but that relationship is not going well, either. Frank has given up on himself. Though he teaches Rita, he hardly notices the changes taking place in her. He can think of her only as Rita the hairdresser, long after she has taken employment elsewhere and is now known to her friends as Susan. During the course of Rita's education, Frank's drinking brings him up on charges of drunk and disorderly conduct in the classroom, after his students report him. The administration advises that he take a year-long sabbatical to Australia to reconsider his priorities. When Rita (now Susan) comes to thank Frank at the end of the play, he offers to take her with him to Australia, but she is too smart to link herself to a lost cause and a man twice her age. Instead, she offers to give him a haircut. The Royal Shakespeare Company production of *Educating Rita* was voted best comedy of 1980, and by 1983, the year it was adapted to cinema, it was rated the fourth most popular play on the British stage.

The Film

In order to turn this play into a motion picture Willy Russell had to reinvent the play for director Lewis Gilbert. The action had to be extended beyond Frank's office at the university and is opened up to show an effective contrast between working-class Liverpool and the university setting. Thus the camera follows Rita home and shows her at work as well, both at the hair salon early on, and later at the restaurant. Gilbert shows her at summer school discovering Blake at the library and participating in regular class discussions, as well as Frank's drunken performance in his own classroom. Julie Walters, who created the role on the London stage (800 performances over a two-year span), brilliantly demonstrates Rita's transformation, as her language improves and as her appearance, her wardrobe, and her hairstyle change gradually to reflect her change in station and class. On stage Walters had won the London Critics' Award as "Best New Actress" and the Variety Club of Great Britain voted her the "Most Promising New Artiste of 1980." She first met Russell at the Everyman Theatre in Liverpool, and he told her that he had written the play with her in mind.

Characters merely referred to in the play are dramatized for the film adaptation, notably Rita's husband Denny (Malcolm Douglas), her classmate Tiger (Philip Hurdwood), her disturbed flatmate Trish (Maureen Lipman), her mother and father, Frank's live-in girlfriend Julia (Jeananne Crowley), and his sneaky Dean Brian (Michael Williams), a smirking Judas who is the most hollow stereotype in the film. Michael Caine, who had earlier been the star of Lewis Gilbert's *Alfie*

(1966), is memorable as Rita's infatuated tutor, whose own life shows more promise of being reformed in the film as a result of his relationship with Rita. He is debauched enough that he might be coaxed into lechery if given some encouragement, but none is forthcoming. Although the play ends simply and decisively with Rita giving Frank a haircut; the film ends with an emotional leave-taking at the airport, leaving open the possibility that Rita might one day join him in Australia. When making *Educating Rita*, Russell has written, "I tried very hard to write a love story." He is trying even harder in revising the play for the screen, though the characters are still separated, avoiding a sentimental conclusion.

REFERENCES

Godfrey, Stephen, "I Like to Think of Myself as Cary Grant," *Toronto Globe and Mail*, September 16, 1983, E5; Johnston, Sheila, "Educating Rita," *Monthly Film Bulletin*, 50 (May 1983): 130; Magill, Marcia, "Educating Rita," *Films in Review*, 34:9 (November 1983), 569; Russell, Willy, "Educating the Author," in *Educating Rita*, ed. Richard Adams (Harlow, Essex: Longman Study Texts, 1985).

—*J.M.W.*

EDWARD II (1592)

CHRISTOPHER MARLOWE (1564–1593)

Edward II (aka *Queer Edward II*) (1991), U.K., directed and adapted by Derek Jarman and Ken Butler; Working Title Productions.

The Play

Written in 1592, *Edward II* is a typically brutal play from the author of *Tamburlaine the Great* (1587), *Dr. Faustus* (1588), and *The Jew of Malta* (1589). A major figure in Elizabethan drama, Marlowe's plays usually depict characters destroyed by their own weakness or ambition. *Edward II* is certainly no exception to this paradigm. It was first performed in London in December 1592 by the theatrical troupe Pembroke's Servants. The plot and numerous subplots are too complex for a detailed explication, and the following bare summary will have to suffice: The year is 1307 and Edward II, age 23, an openly gay man, begins his reign as king of England by rejecting his queen, Isabella (with whom he has fathered a son, Edward III), for the affections of his male lover, Gaveston. His consequent neglect of his duties of state outrages the court, but when Edward demands that Gaveston be allowed to rule as his equal, side by side on the throne of England, open rebellion breaks out. The barons, led by young Mortimer, force Edward to sign a decree that sends Gaveston into exile. Furious, Edward turns to Isabella and forces her to assist him in recalling Gaveston to England. The reconciliation between Edward and Gaveston is short-lived, however. Mortimer, now in league with Isabella, arranges for Gaveston's execution. In revenge, Edward wages a battle campaign against Mortimer and the barons. After Edward is captured and imprisoned, Mortimer and Isabella deliver him into the hands of Lightborn the executioner, who murders Edward by forcing a red-hot poker into his rectum. Edward III, the boy king, now claims the throne and avenges his father's death.

The Film

The late Derek Jarman was a pioneering gay film-maker whose earlier works, such as *Sabastianne* (1976), *Caravaggio* (1986), *The Last of England* (1987), *War Requiem* (1989), and *The Garden* (1990), defined and mirrored the new gay consciousness in England in the 1980s and 1990s. He was already seriously ill with complications due to HIV/AIDS when he began shooting *Edward II*. Only by ingesting a variety of drugs to boost his immune system was he able to stay on his feet during the filming. His assistant, Ken Butler, helped him write the screenplay and direct the actors on those days when Jarman was too ill to work. *Edward II* is a curious blend of stark spareness and colorful sumptuousness. It reflects both Jarman's debilitating illness and his fury at the "straight" establishment in England, particularly the infamous "Section 28" of the British Penal Code, which made it a crime to create openly gay works that espoused and celebrated the gay life-style.

The film concentrates almost exclusively on Edward (Steven Waddington), Gaveston (Andrew Tiernan), Isabella (Tilda Swinton), Mortimer (Nigel Terry), and Lightborn (Kevin Collins). To an extent, Jarman treats Marlowe's play with a characteristically cavalier attitude: "How to make a film of a gay love affair and get it commissioned?—find a dusty old play and violate it." Nonetheless, his adaptation cuts to the very core of the play, and it demonstrates that homosexuality is still seen as a threat to the prevailing social order throughout most of the world. Much of the action is staged on minimally decorated sets and performed in modern dress (with only the barest suggestion of period costuming to frame the piece). As in all of his work, Jarman's love of fabrics, light, and color is evident throughout. Contemporary music is juxtaposed with period compositions—and Annie Lennox, late of the Eurythmics, makes a brief appearance to sing "Everytime We Say Goodbye" after Gaveston and Edward are separated. The film was shot at Bray Studios, the home of Hammer horror films in the 1950s and 1960s. In 1991 Jarman published a shooting diary of the film, *Queer Edward II*.

REFERENCES

Jarman, Derek, *Queer Edward II* (London: BFI Publishing, 1991); Wollen, Roger, ed., *Derek Jarman: A Portrait* (London: Thames and Hudson, 1996).

—*W.W.D.*

84 CHARING CROSS ROAD (1970)

HELENE HANFF (1916–1997) AND JAMES ROOSE-EVANS (1927–)

84, Charing Cross Road (1987), U.S.A., directed by David Jones, adapted by Hugh Whitemore; Columbia Pictures.

The Play

The title suggests a London address, a collection of letters, a stageplay extrapolated from a popular and sentimental memoir, and, finally, a motion picture. Thus the play has an unlikely provenance. It began as an epistolary memoir, mainly involving two kindred spirits, the writer Helene Hanff in New York City and the antiquarian bookseller Frank Doel at Marks & Co., a London bookstore located at 84 Charing Cross Road, a street famous for its book trade. The two had in common a wry sense of humor and an intense love of books. Unable to complete her education at Temple University, Hanff became a devoted autodidactic, determined to buy the books on the reading list of Sir Arthur Quiller-Couch, a professor of English at Cambridge University, referred to as "Q." Hanff answered an advertisement she noticed in *The Saturday Review of Literature* on October 5, 1949, beginning a correspondence with Doel and his staff and family that lasted until October 1969. After the death of Frank Doel in December 1968, Hanff continued to correspond with Doel's widow Nora and obtained the family's permission to publish the letters.

The book could be considered an epistolary romance, but the correspondents never met and were separated by the Atlantic Ocean. Even so, a close friendship developed by transatlantic mail over 20 years. Doel was charmed by Hanff, but his marriage in England was safe and secure, since he and his correspondent were mainly in love with books. Hanff's own book was popular enough to spawn two memoir-sequels, *Q's Legacy* and *The Duchess of Bloomsbury Street*, which became fodder for the dramatization of *84 Charing Cross Road*. The letters were chatty and conversational, so once the book became a best-seller, Hanff and James Roose-Evans adapted it to the stage. Hanff had studied playwrighting at the Theatre Guild and had worked as a writer for *The Hallmark Hall of Fame* and for the *Ellery Queen* television series.

The Film

The film begins with Helene on a plane to London—she did eventually get there after the death of Frank Doel—and ends with her standing in the empty, abandoned shop, for Marks & Co. had closed its doors. She tells a fellow passenger she is going to London to attend to "unfinished business." The award-winning screenwriter Hugh Whitemore had already written a teleplay for the BBC production of *84 Charing Cross Road* when he undertook writing the screenplay for David Jones. The film is splendidly cast, with Anne Bancroft playing Helene Hanff and aging gracefully. A young looking Anthony Hopkins plays Frank Doel, with the same kind of reserve he would later bring to *Remains of the Day* (1993), and he is supported by Judi Dench as his wife, Nora. How does one adapt an epistolary narrative to stage or screen: by rewriting the story using the letters as a reference source, or by actually incorporating the letters into the story? The mixture of action, dialogue, and narration used as a solution works quite well. Eventually Helene and Frank talk to each other, as if they were in the same room while composing their letters. In her last latter to Frank, Helene speaks directly to the camera, and Frank answers her paragraph by paragraph, also addressing the camera, all of which serves to emphasize the intimacy of the letters. There were 24 letters left out of the film that were in the book; other letters were edited, shortened, or combined in the interest of economy. The film opens up the action, as when in London Frank and his wife go out on the town, or when Frank visits fellow clerk George Martin in the hospital before he dies. In the film, "Q" is mentioned, but the film neglects to explain the significance of Quiller-Couch to Helene. Perhaps the film was intended for an audience "slightly suspicious of movies," as one reviewer suggested, but it certainly is

Anne Bancroft starred in a romance of books in David Jones's adaptation of 84 Charing Cross Road. (COURTESY COLUMBIA PICTURES)

true to the spirit of the book and intelligently directed.

REFERENCES

Billington, Michael, "Calm: Key to a Stormy Actor," *The New York Times*, March 15, 1987, sec. 2, pp. 21, 29; Hinson, Hal, "'Charing Cross': Tidy but Tired," *The Washington Post*, June 6, 1987, G1, 9; Kauffmann, Stanley, "On Film," *The New Republic* (February 23, 1987), 24.

—J.M.W.

ELECTRA [ELEKTRA] (413 B.C.)

EURIPIDES (480?–406? B.C.)

Electra (1961), Greece, directed and adapted by Michael Cacoyannis; Finos.

Elektreia [*Elecktra Szerelmem*] (1975), Hungary, directed by Miklós Jancsó, adapted by Laszlo Gyurko and Gyula Hernadi, based on the play by Laszlo Gyurko, also adapted by Miklos Vasarhelyi; Hunnia Studio Mafilm.

The Play

The legend has been dramatized by Aeschylus and Sophocles as well as Euripides. While Agamemnon, king of Mycenae, is leading his army to Troy, his wife Clytemnestra takes a lover, Aegisthus, who conspires with her to kill Agamemnon after his triumphant return from the Trojan Wars. Aegisthus also intends to kill Agamemnon's son, Orestes, who is saved by a servant who takes him to safety, and his daughter Electra, whom Clytemnestra manages to protect. To protect his reign against future claims, Aegisthus sees that Electra is married to a farmer. A son born of such a union would pose no threat to Aegisthus, but because the farmer respects her virginity, no children are conceived. As the play begins, the grown Orestes returns to Mycenae with his friend, Pylades, and plots with his sister the murder of their mother and her lover. Electra lures her mother to her hut while Orestes kills Aegisthus; then, encouraged by Electra, he kills Clytemnestra. In the Euripides dramatization of the story, it is Electra who kills her mother. She hates her almost as much for her adultery as for her involvement in the murder of her father. In the final confrontation, when Orestes hesitates, Electra takes his sword and kills Clytemnestra. She is the fearsome embodiment of the lust for revenge.

The Film

The story of Electra and Orestes was dramatized by Aeschylus, Sophocles, (perhaps as late as 410 B.C.), and by Euripides (413 B.C.). The Sophocles play was done as a modern production within an ancient theatre in 1938, directed by A. Meletoupolos, and as a public performance on film in 1961 in Epidaurus by Ted Zarpas. Both of these Sophoclean productions were done in what Kenneth MacKinnon calls the "theatrical mode." By contrast, the Michael Cacoyannis film, the first increment of what was to become his Euripidean Trilogy, was shot in the "realistic mode" in 1961, using the ancient site of Mycenae for the prologue and shooting the rest of the action on the road between Athens and Sounion. Although "realistic," the approach taken is also very stylized.

The film's Prologue visualizes through a wordless montage the murder of Agamemnon by Aegisthus (Phoebus Rhaziz) and Clytemnestra (Aleka Catselli) and its subsequent effect upon Electra (Irene Pappas). The style of this montage is, as MacKinnon describes it, "synecdochic, allusive, [and] metaphorical." The women of the countryside sing in chorus, but are grouped in stylized patterns. MacKinnon criticizes Cacoyannis's treatment for being "closer to Aeschylus's conception of tragedy than Euripides's." The director contends his approach is Aristotelian: "the basic purpose of Greek drama," according to Cacoyannis, "is *to move*. To serve both the original author and his audience, the director must eliminate the distance between them." But MacKinnon believes that Cacoyannis misses the distinctions Euripides makes to separate his drama from that of Aeschylus. "Electra and Orestes (Yannis Fertis) are made sympathetic, Clytemnestra insincere even when she appears to have a point in her favor, Aegisthus licentious even when he could be thought pious." Some critics praised Cacoyannis for "removing the stagy prologue by the farmer and the *deus ex machina* ending." MacKinnon contends that Cacoyannis made this "puzzling play far more obviously tragic than the original could have been."

In the Hungarian adaptation *Elektreia*, directed by the structuralist Miklós Jancsó in 1975, fidelity to the text is not a prime consideration, since this is an adaptation of an adaptation. The most immediate source is the play *Szerelmem Elecktra*, written by Laszlo Gyurko partly as a response to the Hungarian rebellion that the Soviets suppressed in 1956. The death of the tyrant Aegisthus seemed to reflect allegorically upon the death of Stalin and the play has been seen as a defense of the liberalization movement of Janos Kadar in Hungary. Gyurko portrayed Electra (Mari Torosic) as an avenger oppressed by Aegisthus (Jozsef Madaras) who, according to Peter Day, becomes "a militant revolutionary who overthrows Aegisthus's rule and frees the people from his tyranny."

Like such other Jancsó films as *Agnus Dei* (1970) and *Red Psalm* (1971), which had nothing to do with Greek tragedy, the setting is a barren Hungarian plain. True to his structuralist inclinations, Jancsó concentrates on long takes and choreographed action. According to one source, the director boasted that "the whole picture consists of no more than ten sequences," but Graham Petrie mentions a more likely 12 shots, while Peter Day counts 13 takes. Critics, however, seemed even more mystified by the film's meaning than by the exact number of takes Jancsó used to film it.

MacKinnon finds links to both Sophocles and Euripides here, but admits that "what is basically a revenge tale has been invested with a new political, and specifically East European political, significance by the play and that, in turn, has been converted into a parable about the necessity of perpetual revolution by the film." Graham Petrie complained about the "total incomprehensibility of the plot, the aimless scampering of the characters from place to place, the solemn banality and even childishness of the political discussions," and admits that even sympathetic critics might conclude that Jancsó's work "appears to have reached a stage of self-parody and empty visual pyrotechnics." After mulling over the mystification, he hedges all bets by saying that *Elektreia* may be "a flawed masterpiece, but a masterpiece nonetheless." Most viewers are likely to be more skeptical.

REFERENCES

Day, Peter, "*Elektreia*," *Sight and Sound*, 44:4 (1975), 258–259; Gassner, John, and Edward Quinn, *The Reader's Encyclopedia of World Drama* (New York: Thomas Y. Crowell, 1969); MacKinnon, Kenneth, *Greek Tragedy into Film* (London: Croom Helm, 1986); Petrie, Graham, "Style as Subject: Jancsó's 'Electra,'" *Sight and Sound*, 11:5 (1975), 50–53.

—*J.M.W.*

ELIZABETH THE QUEEN (1930)

MAXWELL ANDERSON (1888–1959)

The Private Lives of Elizabeth and Essex (1939), U.S.A., directed by Michael Curtiz, adapted by Norman Reilly Raine and Aeneas MacKenzie; Warner Bros.

The Play

It was Maxwell Anderson's desire to create contemporary drama using verse that was supple and clear; he believed, according to scholar Laurence Avery, "that through skillful use of such elements as rhythm and imagery and allusion the playwright could increase the impact of a play on its audience." The first of Anderson's verse tragedies, *Elizabeth the Queen* was inspired by Lytton Strachey's *Elizabeth and Essex: A Tragic History*. While Strachey uses the two figures to represent a clash between the feudal and the Renaissance eras, seeing Essex as an exemplar of the older age, Anderson focuses on Elizabeth's internal conflict between her desires and her duty to her throne. The play premiered at the Theatre Guild, New York, with Lynn Fontanne and Alfred Lunt as Elizabeth and Essex, on November 3, 1930, and ran for 147 performances. It was revived in 1961 with Eva Le Gallienne in the title role and again in 1966 with Judith Anderson.

The first act of the play introduces the passionate but competitive relationship between Elizabeth and Robert Devereaux, earl of Essex, just returned from his military adventure in the Spanish port of Cádiz. In the second act, Essex's enemies maneuver him into leading a disastrous expedition against the Irish rebel leader Tyrone. They then hinder the exchange of letters between Elizabeth and Essex, until the discontented earl returns to England and leads his abortive rebellion against Elizabeth, who has him arrested. Essex awaits execution in the third act, and meets with his queen for a final time, choosing death in spite of her desperate offer to surrender her throne to him.

The Film

Bette Davis twice played Elizabeth I, first in *The Private Lives of Elizabeth and Essex*, and 16 years later in *The Virgin Queen*. She said, "I always felt a great propinquity to the character of Elizabeth. In many ways we were very alike. But the power to roll heads—this she had over me." Davis wanted to play Elizabeth with as much verisimilitude as possible, and collaborated with Perc Westmore to design her distinctive makeup, including the shaving of her hairline a few inches to give the impression that she was bald beneath her bejewelled red wig.

Conflict arose initially over the title of the film. Because the title of Anderson's play ignored Essex, the studio first intended to christen the film *The Knight and the Lady*; this in turn appalled Davis, who objected to Jack Warner. Another alternative, *Elizabeth and Essex*, would have required a substantial payment to Lytton Strachey's estate, leading to the eventual choice, with its echo of the earlier *Private Lives of Henry VIII* (1933).

The dispute over the title was only the first sign of the considerable discord that would ensue during filming. Davis, as she would frequently remark in interviews later in her life, wanted Laurence Olivier to play Essex; instead, she said, "I was stuck with that beautiful ass, Errol Flynn," cast by the film's producer, Hal Wallis. The relationship between the two stars during the filming was hostile and contentious.

Norman Reilly Raine and Aeneas MacKenzie's adaptation of the original play preserves some of Anderson's verse dialogue, particularly in the scenes between Elizabeth and Essex, and generally compresses the action effectively. The screenplay increases the focus on the two stars and their scenes together, and wisely eliminates such features as the queen's Fool and an interpolated performance by actors from Shakespeare's company. The nervous, neurotic performance given by Davis is powerful; throughout the film, Elizabeth is visibly racked by strong emotions and opposing desires, and these are translated into physical gestures by Davis, who is virtually never still—compulsively fidgeting or playing with her fan or her necklace in every scene. The film is greatly weakened, however, because no chemistry emerges in her scenes with Flynn. His performance has frequently been criticized. The *New York Times* review when the film premiered asserted that going up against Davis, he "had as much chance as a beanshooter against a tank." Flynn's Essex does not differ perceptibly from his title role in *Captain Blood*, or his Geoffrey Thorpe in *The Sea Hawk*, and since the film lacks the swashbuckling excitement of those roles, he is at a distinct disadvantage. The fine supporting cast includes Olivia de Havilland as Penelope, a lady-in-waiting to the queen and in love with Essex, Vincent Price as Sir Walter Raleigh, Donald Crisp as Francis Bacon, Henry Stephenson as Lord Burghley, Henry Daniell as Sir Robert Cecil, and a cameo by Alan Hale as the Irish rebel Tyrone.

Like so many works of historical fiction, both play and film are historically inaccurate. Though it is perhaps too harsh to call the film, as Charles Higham has, "a stiff and awkward pageant, dead under its lavish trappings," neither is it truly successful. It remains most worth watching for Davis' intense performance and a memorable score by Eric Wolfgang Korngold. The film was nominated for Academy Awards for best color cinematography, best score, and best special effects.

REFERENCES

Avery, Laurence, "Maxwell Anderson" in *The Dictionary of Literary Biography*, vol. 7 (Detroit: Bruccoli Clark Layman, 1981); Higham, Charles, *Bette: The Life of Bette Davis* (New York: Dell, 1981); Pigeon, Renée, "Gloriana Goes Hollywood: Elizabeth I on Film, 1937–1940," in *Reinventing the Middle Ages and The Renaissance* (Turnhout, Belg.: Brepols Press, 1998), 107–126; Stine, Whitney, with Bette Davis, *Bette Davis: Mother Goddam* (New York: Berkley Books, 1974); Stine, Whitney, *"I'd Love to Kiss You . . .": Conversations with Bette Davis* (New York: Pocket Books, 1990).

—*R.P.*

THE EMPEROR JONES (1920)

EUGENE O'NEILL (1888–1953)

The Emperor Jones (1933), U.S.A., directed by Dudley Murphy, adapted by DuBose Heyward; United Artists.

The Play

Eugene O'Neill's restless early years included stints at Princeton, prospecting in Honduras, acting in a theatrical touring troupe, sailing as a ship's hand to South America, and recuperating from tuberculosis in a sanatorium. During this latter time, he resolved to be a playwright; and he began his professional career when he joined the Provincetown Players in 1916. After writing a series of one-act maritime dramas, and after the reception of a Pulitzer Prize for *Beyond the Horizon* (1920), his *Emperor Jones* premiered at the Neighborhood Playhouse on November 1, 1920, and ran for a spectacular 204 performances. Both *Jones* and the later *The Hairy Ape* (1924) reveal how profoundly he was influenced by the techniques of German Expressionist stagecraft and effects. Like the German prototypes of Ernst Toller's *Man and the Masses* and Georg Kaiser's *Gas Trilogy*, *The Emperor Jones* is structured as a series of eight episodes, flashbacks, and dream visions—in this instance, chronicling the adventures of Brutus Jones (Charles S. Gilpin), an African-American Pullman car attendant who killed a man in a dice game, served time in a prison chain gang, and escaped to a small West Indian island, where he assumed the mantle of "Emperor." Because he has plundered the island, a native uprising forces him to escape to the rain forest. He loses his way, encountering several phantoms and memories from his racial heritage and his past before being shot and killed by four silver bullets. A steadily accelerating crescendo of drum beats underpins the final sequences. Critic George Jean Nathan hailed it as a compelling drama "touched by a visionary ecstasy." Not so much a satire or critique of the black man in America, *The Emperor Jones* was a more general representation of the predicament of modern man, trapped between the modern civilization and the "jungle" of primitive instincts.

The Film

The play was retooled for the screen as a more overt statement on the status of the black man in a racist society. Two white men—independent filmmaker Dudley Murphy (who three years before had directed two important black two-reelers, *St. Louis Blues* and *Black and Tan Fantasy*) and Dubose Heyward, author of *Porgy* (the basis for Gershwin's later *Porgy and Bess*) confronted the challenge of making a feature film about the black experience that would still have an appeal to major American distributors and exhibitors. A key to that accomplishment was the signing of Paul Robeson, who had appeared as Jones in a 1925 revival of the play, and who was riding a wave of success with his "Joe" in the London production of *Show Boat*. With O'Neill's blessing, Murphy and Heyward fashioned a prologue depicting Brutus' backstory as a railway porter and chain-gang victim, adding for good meas-

Paul Robeson reprised his stage role as Brutus in the 1932 screen adaptation of Eugene O'Neill's The Emperor Jones. (COURTESY JOHN C. TIBBETS)

ure scenes of life in jazzy Harlem. The "haunts" that afflict Jones during his jungle flight are provided by means of effects superimpositions—creating a result that, for many viewers, has the unsettling effect of representing too literally the abstractions of Jones' inner vision. The score, by black composer J. Rosamond Johnson, represented four categories of musical motifs—African, Gullah, Harlem jazz, and, finally, voodoo. The film's reception, reports Thomas Cripps in *Slow Fade to Black*, was generally favorable: "It was an impressive debut of blacks into independently produced and financed feature films outside the confines of Hollywood and crafted with finer stuff than that of the race movies."

REFERENCES

Thomas Cripps, *Slow Fade to Black* (New York: Oxford University Press, 1977); Lahr, John, "Eugene O'Neill," in *Automatic Vaudeville* (New York: Alfred A. Knopf, 1984), 63–88; Valgemae, Mardi, *Accelerated Grimace: Expressionism in the American Drama of the 1920s* (Carbondale: Southern Illinois University Press, 1972).

—*J.C.T.*

THE ENTERTAINER (1957)

JOHN OSBORNE (1929–   )

The Entertainer (1960), U.K., directed by Tony Richardson, adapted by John Osborne and Nigel Kneale; Woodfall Films/Warner Bros.

The Play

The discovery at London's Royal Court Theatre of a struggling 27-year-old playwright named John Osborne is one of those benchmark moments in the history of modern British theatre. His first two plays produced at the Court in 1956–57, *Look Back in Anger* and *The Entertainer*, changed the face of contemporary drama and established him within months as a member of that generation derisively dubbed as "Angry Young Men." If the first play introduced that emblem of his "angry" generation, Jimmy Porter, the second presented an even more colorful character, Archie Rice, a fading song-and-dance man who epitomized a vanishing tradition of music hall theatre. Osborne began working on the play before *Look Back* was completed. When Laurence Olivier came to the Court to see *Look Back* he was handed the unfinished draft of *The Entertainer*, and he took to it immediately. "Sir Laurence was suddenly 'available,'" recalled Osborne, "and eager in the way of prized actors who come into season with occasional surprising suddenness and have to be accommodated while the bloodstock is raring." Olivier himself remembered that the role offered him something fresh: "I was going mad, desperately searching for something suddenly fresh and thrillingly exciting. . . . In many ways it showed the worst side of me, and that felt good too: something like a confession, a welcome and beneficial expulsion of filth."

The play premiered at the Royal Court on April 10, 1957, and ran for 36 performances. Later it played six months at the Palace in London and six months on Broadway at the Royale Theatre, debuting on February 12, 1958. The story is set in 1956 in the backstreets of an English coastal resort—an area, Osborne notes in his scene description, "full of dirty blank spaces, high black walls, a gas holder, a tall chimney, a main road that shakes with dust and lorries." Most of the action transpires in the living room of Archie Rice (Olivier), a down-and-out vaudevillian. A series of prolonged arguments reveal the bitter schisms that divide his family: the debt-ridden Archie is estranged from his wife, and he spends his nights performing in a sleazy nudie club. His alcoholic wife, Phoebe (Brenda de Banzie), is resentful of his philandering; his stepdaughter Jean (Dorothy Tutin) is a disillusioned art teacher; a son, Frank (Richard Pasco), has just been released from jail (another son, Mick, has joined the army and is away at the Suez conflict); and Billy (George Relph),

Archie's father, is a retired vaudevillian lost in his befuddled memories of the good old days. Surveying this familial wreckage, Archie laments, "We don't get on with anything. We don't ever succeed in anything. We're a *nuisance*, we do nothing but make a God almighty fuss about anything we ever do." Indeed, by curtain's fall, the absent son, Mick, has died in the Suez, Jean abandons plans to marry, Billy collapses and dies in a "come-back" attempt; and Archie abandons plans to finance a new show with his mistress' money. Archie is left alone in the spotlight, singing his theme song, an anthem of resignation and futility:

> Why should I care?
> Why should I let it touch me,
> Why shouldn't I sit down and try
> To let it pass over me?

His final words are addressed directly to the audience: "You've been a good audience. Very good. A very *good* audience. Let me know where you're working tomorrow night—and I'll come and see *you*." Stage director Tony Richardson regarded Olivier's performance as Archie to be a seminal event: "He transcended himself, and, as with *Henry V,* became the embodiment of a national mood. . . . Archie was the future, the decline, the sourness, the ashes of old glory, where Britain was heading."

The action plays out on a divided stage, scenes alternating between the Rice living room upstage—a relatively naturalistic set—and the more stylized music hall set downstage where Archie performs his "turns" and declaims his monologues. In Alan Tagg's original Royal Court design, the front curtain was replaced by a music-hall advertisement cloth, and fake red-plush stage boxes were installed for Archie's "audience."

The Film

In bringing Osborne's *Look Back in Anger* and *The Entertainer* to the screen, Tony Richardson (who had directed them both at the Royal Court) wanted to attain nothing less than the revitalization of what he regarded as a moribund British cinema: "I should certainly like British films to be different from what many of them have been in the past. . . . It is absolutely vital to get into British films the same sort of impact and sense of life that, what you loosely call the Angry Young Man cult has had in the theatre and literary worlds. It is a desperate need." Accordingly, Richardson helped form the Woodfall Films production company, the name deriving from the street off King's Road where Osborne had rented a little house. Yet although he had had little difficulty translating *Look*

Back to the screen in 1959, *The Entertainer* presented challenges. In hindsight, he complained that the "totally realistic medium" of film was ill-suited to the metaphoric resonances of Archie's character and the performance of his third-rate routines. On the Royal Court stage, those routines had served as a commentary in Brechtian fashion on Archie's character and, by extension, his world. However, the very specificity of film would only emphasize the condition of this particular man. Richardson accepted this limitation, rationalizing that "our only entry to [Archie] is through understanding his own vulnerability and squalor so deeply that we can empathize with the individual without extending the character to thoughts about society. The detail of the performance was what had to count, not the leaps to beyond." Nonetheless, several critics, including John Russell Taylor, complained that the resulting film was "totally misconceived" because it "tries to transplant the least realistic sections unchanged into a setting of documentary realism."

In the cast were Olivier and Joan Plowright reprising their roles as Archie and Jean (Plowright had taken over on stage from Dorothy Tutin), Brenda de Banzie also reprising her role of Phoebe, Roger Livesey as Billy, Alan Bates as Frank, and Albert Finney as Mick (a role fleshed out for the film). The script by Osborne and Nigel Kneale burst the confines of the Rice apartment and relocated much of the action to seaside locations at Morecambe. Gone is the scaffolding device of the music-hall turns; rather, they are more naturally interpolated into the essentially linear narrative. The sketchy character development and reported action of the play are elaborately amplified. An extended flashback early in the film depicts Jean's work in the art school, her relationship with Graham, and her farewell to Mick as he leaves for the Suez. Numerous added scenes fill out the roles of Frank (he now works backstage with Archie) and Billy (who sings a "British Navy" song at his club and takes his "comeback" play to London). Scenes of Archie's adulterous affairs—incidents only briefly alluded to in the play—are interwoven throughout the film, such as his emceeing of the "Miss Great Britain" beauty pageant and his seduction of a contestant with the aim of persuading her parents to underwrite his new show. Several of composer John Addison's original songs remain, including Archie's comic turns, "The Old Church Bell Won't Ring Tonight, as the Vicar's Dropped a Clanger" and "Now I'm Just an Ordinary Bloke." Archie's signature song, "Why Do I Care?" which attracted little attention during the original stage production, is heard everywhere in the film, either as a leitmotif on the soundtrack— over the opening credits, during Jean's flashback, and during Billy's comeback scene—or as a performed stage routine (after Archie's hopes for a new show are dashed).

Although Olivier's first appearance as Archie is startling, almost cartoonish—with his white grease-painted mask of a face, dark-limned eyes, sharp nose, and slash of a mouth—he soon emerges as an entirely more sympathetic character than in the play. He no longer works in a sleazy nudie club but gets top billing—"Television and Radio's Sauciest Comic" blares the billboard next to a cut-out caricature of his face—in a rather ornate resort theatre.

REFERENCES

Findlater, Richard, *At the Royal Court* (Derbyshire: Amber Lane Press, 1981); Gomez, Joseph, "*The Entertainer:* From Play to Film," *Film Heritage,* 8 (1973), 19–26; Osborne, John, *Almost a Gentleman: An Autobiography* (London: Faber and Faber, 1991); Richardson, Tony, *The Long Distance Runner: A Memoir* (New York: William Morrow, 1993); Welsh, James M., and John C. Tibbetts, eds., *The Cinema of Tony Richardson: Essays and Interviews* (Albany: State University of New York Press, 1999).

—*J.C.T.*

EQUUS (1973)

PETER SHAFFER (1926–)

Equus (1977), U.S.A., directed and adapted by Sidney Lumet; United Artists.

The Play

Brilliantly designed by John Dexter for Britain's National Theatre in London, the play premiered at the Old Vic Theatre on July 26, 1973, and was an immediate success. The action is set in southern England at the Rokesby Psychiatric Hospital, where a burnt-out psychiatrist, Dr. Martin Dysart (Alec McCowen) has been asked by Magistrate Hesther Salomon (Gillian Barge) to treat an adolescent boy, Alan Strang (Peter Firth), who has blinded six horses with a metal spike for no apparent reason. Through a series of therapy sessions probing the young man's past and home environment, Dr. Dysart unravels the mystery. The stage was designed as an arena, with the actors seated on benches surrounding the stage and entering the arena as needed to dramatize the past events.

Most remarkable is the boy's fascination with horses, transformed in Alan's disturbed mind to objects of worship. Alan's disturbance and confusion has resulted from mixed signals from his religious, middle-class mother and his working-class father, an atheist and socialist. After Alan takes a job as a stable hand caring for Harry Dalton's thoroughbred horses, he devises a peculiar midnight ritual, taking one of the horses, Nugget, out at night and riding, naked, so as to achieve an orgasm. In his mind sexuality and worship are intertwined and confused. On stage, this bizarre ritual was enacted by actors wearing masks and "track suits of chestnut velvet" carrying naked Alan piggy-back. Though describing the stage spectacle makes it sound ridiculous, the representation was oddly effective. The crisis comes one night when his coworker at the stables, Jill Mason, attempts to seduce him. Unable to perform, Alan becomes terribly agitated because he believes the horses have seen the attempted seduction and he feels that he has betrayed them. This awareness drives Alan to his act of mutilation, tearing out the eyes that have witnessed his shame.

The main conflict of the play is between Dr. Dysart and his patient and between Dr. Dysart and himself. Dysart first has to win over the boy's confidence, for initially Alan is unwilling to talk at all. By functioning as a father figure, Dysart eventually encourages Alan to confide in him. Dysart later tricks Alan into remembering and reliving his traumatic experience by means of hypnosis and by using what Alan thinks is a "truth drug," until Alan is finally "cured." But Dysart is conflicted, for he respects and admires Alan's ability to tap into a mysterious world of primitive instincts and invented rituals. He is even envious of his patient. Finally, Dysart questions his right to change an extraordinary boy into an ordinary one. At the end, after Alan has been "cured," Dysart appears to have taken over his patient's demons. Dysart's final monologue, which spirals into the monologue that begins the play is nearly incoherent. The doctor himself seems a candidate for therapy.

The Film

Because of its entirely abstract theatrical design, *Equus* is essentially unfilmable. "Any literalism which could suggest the cosy familiarity of a domestic animal," Shaffer wrote in his "notes" for the play, "should be avoided." But cinema is defined by its "literalism," and director Sidney Lumet, faced with the challenge of filming Shaffer's play, was not about to have the horses represented by actors and decided, reasonably enough, to use real horses, even if it meant changing the essential nature of the play and its peculiar spectacle. The spectacle of the blinding, however, is made utterly grotesque as a consequence. The film further violates the play by "opening-up" the action to out-door settings. What works especially well, understandably, is the film's ability to dramatize the past through the use of flashbacks. Despite the film's realistic transformation, Shaffer's dialogue is faithfully preserved, and Dysart's long monologues remain intact.

This play is surely an actor's vehicle, and the film offers several strong performances. Peter Firth first played Alan in the Old Vic stage premiere. Richard Burton had played the role of Martin Dysart on stage as well, and his disturbed monologues, though stage-bound, effectively hold the film together. Critics had objected to an alleged homosexual subtext in the play, since Dysart is unusually attracted to Alan and has lost all interest in his wife, but Lumet's film suggests a cozy and intimate relationship between Dysart and Hesther Salomon (Eileen Adkins), who brings Alan to Dysart's office and whom Dysart later visits at her home. The film therefore presents Dysart as an exhausted professional but a relatively "normal" heterosexual, who becomes a father-figure for Alan. Joan Plowright and Colin Blakely strike just the right chord of guilt and embarrassment in their portrayals of Alan's parents. Jenny Agutter is convincing enough as the seductive Jill Mason, who has a nervous breakdown after the horses are blinded, and Harry Andrews is brilliant at the enraged Harry Dalton, whose horses are mutilated. Lumet might be faulted for not finding a truly "cinematic" approach, but given the difficulty of the play, this is about as successful a film adaptation as one could hope for.

REFERENCES

Bowles, Stephen E., *Sidney Lumet: A Guide to References and Resources* (Boston: G.K. Hall, 1979); Cunningham, Frank R., *Sidney Lumet: Film and Literary Vision* (Lexington: University Press of Kentucky, 1991); Welsh, J.M., "Dream Doctors as Healers in Drama and Film," *Literature and Medicine*, 6 (1987): 117–127.

—*J.M.W.*

EVERYBODY GOES TO RICK'S (CASABLANCA) (1943)

MURRAY BURNETT (1911–1997) AND JOAN ALISON (D. 1992)

Casablanca (1942), U.S.A., directed by Michael Curtiz, adapted by Julius J. Epstein, Philip G. Epstein and Howard Koch; Warner Bros.

The Play

Murray Burnett, a public school teacher and would-be playwright, and Joan Alison, who also aspired to a career in theatre, coauthored a play that would eventually become one of the most famous movies ever produced. *Everybody Comes to Rick's* had a less than stellar history as a play—it was produced only once, in Rhode Island in 1946. Countless historians have repeated *The Nation*'s film critic James Agee's comment that the film was "obviously an improvement on one of the world's worst plays." The film *was* an improvement, but it owes much to the original work of Burnett and Alison.

The play's origins grew out of a summer vacation that Burnett and his wife took to Europe in 1938. In Austria, they witnessed a flood of refugees fleeing from the Nazis. In the south of France, Burnett encountered an African-American entertainer at a small café where refugees from all over Europe gathered trying to escape to freedom.

By 1940 Burnett and Alison had completed the play, which was now set in a café in Casablanca run by an expatriate American, Rick. The play has much in common with its more famous celluloid version. Rick, the owner of the café, is an embittered expatriate. The city is full of refugees, corrupt officials, political intrigue, and the requisite number of slimy underworld figures, con-men, and prostitutes. In the second scene of the first act, Ugarte, a local tough, tells Rick he has murdered two German couriers and has "two letters of transit that cannot be rescinded or questioned." He gives the letters to Rick for safekeeping.

The local French prefect of police, Captain Rinaldo, uses his position for graft and sex—bedding every pretty woman trying to escape the Germans. He does much of his business at Rick's and is surprised to discover that Victor Laszlo, a famous underground leader, is also there, seeking an exit visa. He has come with a striking woman, Lois Meredith, who just happens to be the woman with whom Rick had a torrid affair in Paris. The Germans, represented in Casablanca by General Strasser, are determined to keep Laszlo in Casablanca.

As Act Two opens it is clear that Rick and Lois have taken up where they left off in Paris. Lois has slept with Rick hoping that he will give her the two exit visas. Much of the second act is given over to whether or not Lois will use the exit visas to run away with Laszlo or stay with Rick in Casablanca.

As the third act opens, the question is still up in the air. Lois decides she wants to stay with Rick. She pleads with him: "You fool, I'm in love with you again." But Rick will have none of it. He tells her: "You're going,

Lois. There's nothing here for you. Victor's still fighting, and he needs you, Lois." When General Strasser bursts into the room to arrest Laszlo, Rick pulls a gun on him and allows Laszlo and Lois to escape. After they have gone, Rick surrenders to Strasser and the curtain falls.

Clearly, the core of the movie plot is present in the play. Casablanca is a city teeming with refugees and political corruption. Rick is a cynical American running from a broken love affair. He employs a black piano player who is his friend. His ex-love returns as the mistress of a famed underground leader. General Strasser, Police Prefect Rinaldo, Victor Laszlo, and Rick all represent differing political philosophies. There is even a scene in Rick's where the Germans sing the "Horst Wessel" song and the French counter with "La Marseillaise." In fact, there is little in the movie that is not in the play.

The Film

Casablanca is one of the most famous movies to emerge from World War II. For example, the film has contributed some of the most famous lines of dialogue in the history of the movies. Bogart's: "Of all the gin joints in all the towns in all the world, she walks into mine." "Go ahead and shoot, you'll be doing me a favor." And, of course, "Here's looking at you, kid"—have become part of the American lexicon.

The play remained unproduced when Warner Bros., desperate for good war material, optioned it for $20,000 in January 1942. Producer Hal Wallis assigned veteran screenwriters Philip and Julius Epstein to adapt the play to the screen. Wallis inked Michael Curtiz to direct and eventually signed an all-star cast to the project. Humphrey Bogart was cast as Rick, Ingrid Bergman as Ilsa Laszlo, Paul Henreid as Victor Laszlo, Claude Rains as Captain Louis Renault, Conrad Veidt as General Strasser, Sydney Greenstreet as Señor Ferrari, Peter Lorre as Ugarte, Dooley Wilson as Sam, and a solid cast of Warner Bros. character actors.

The Warner Bros. publicity department would later claim that 34 different nationalities were represented in the cast. The two most famous were Paul Henreid (Victor Laszlo), an ardent anti-Nazi from Austria, and Conrad Veidt (General Strasser), who fled Nazi Germany in the mid-1930s and was also an outspoken opponent of the fascist regime.

The movie plot follows that of the play rather closely, but the politics of the film are much sharper than the play. The biggest difference is that the characters are more sharply defined in the film. Wallis hired playwright/screenwriter Howard Koch, who wrote Orson Welles's radio script for *War of the Worlds*, to inject politics into the screenplay. Koch made Humphrey Bogart/Rick Blaine a much more forceful person. It was clear, despite his cynicism, that he was an anti-fascist. He had fought for the Loyalists in Spain and run guns in Ethiopia. He was wanted in Paris by the Germans and had to flee before they occupied the city. While he told General Strasser that his occupation was a drunkard, in truth everyone knew that Rick hated the Germans.

All of the refugees and many of the French soldiers and civilians clearly despise the Germans. Captain Renault's position is unclear—he seems to cooperate with the Germans but in the end he is clearly anti-fascist. As the film opens, a narrator tells the audience that a flood of refugees trying to escape the Nazi terror have come to Casablanca. In Casablanca they must wait until they can get an exit visa to Lisbon and then to America. A man is stopped by the French police and asked for his identity papers. He runs and is shot underneath a poster of Marshal Petain—a handbill for the French resistance in his hand. Casablanca is dangerous.

The most popular place in the city is Rick's Café Americain. Everybody, it seems comes to Rick's. Ugarte, the thief who has killed the German couriers, comes to Rick with the two visas. He asks Rick to hide them until he can sell them later that same night. Rick reluctantly agrees and hides them in Sam's piano.

Then the Laszlos enter—Victor and Ilsa. General Strasser, who is in the café with Captain Louis Renault, sees Laszlo and demands a meeting with him. Then Ilsa sees Sam. She now knows that Rick is the owner of the café. She asks Sam to play "As Time Goes By." When he finally begins to play the song, Rick is furious. He starts to berate Sam and then sees Ilsa, the love of his life and the reason he has turned away from liberal causes to run a gambling joint in Casablanca.

From this point the film uses a flashback to Paris to explain to the audience why Rick and Ilsa split up. They were very much in love and were about to leave the city together just as the Germans were about to occupy Paris. But Ilsa stood up Rick at the train station when she was told that Victor, whom she believed dead, was alive and hiding in Paris.

Now that the audience understands why Rick is so bitter and why Ilsa left him, the film returns to Casablanca. Ilsa attempts to explain to him why she left him in Paris and to convince him that she still loves him. But Rick is too drunk and too stubborn to listen. The next morning General Strasser and Renault met with Laszlo. They attempt to bribe him by offering him visas in exchange for the names of the underground leaders. Laszlo dismisses their offer. Later that evening one of the most memorable scenes in film history takes place. The setting is Rick's café. Laszlo has come to beg Rick for the letters of transit. But Rick refuses. Suddenly, they hear the German "Wacht am Rhein" playing. Laszlo is furious. He demands that the band play "La Marseillaise." When Rick nods his approval, the band plays it and everyone in the café, except the Germans, begins singing an emotional tribute to freedom. This act of defiance so infuriates Strasser that he orders the café closed.

From this point, the film rushes toward its conclusion. Rick sells his café to Senor Ferrari and makes plans to leave Casablanca. He tricks Renault into thinking that he is going to give Laszlo the exit visas so that Renault can arrest him. Instead, he forces Renault to take him and the Laszlos to the airport where he tells Ilsa to leave with her husband on the plane to Lisbon. But Renault has a trick of his own. He alerts General Strasser who rushes to the airport and attempts to stop the plane from leaving. When Strasser goes for his gun, Rick kills him. When the French police arrive, Renault tells his men: "General Strasser's been shot. Round up the usual suspects." Rick and Renault walk off the tarmac headed for a Free French outpost. They are going to resume their fight against fascism.

Timing is everything and Warner Bros.' timing was perfect. The film opened on Thanksgiving Day of 1942, just weeks after the Allies landed at Casablanca. When the film went into general release in early 1943 Americans were reading about the meeting between Churchill and Roosevelt at Casablanca—a fact Warner Bros. capitalized on in their publicity for the film.

Because *Casablanca* was produced during the war it was subjected to review and evaluation by the Office of War Information. The American propaganda agency judged the film to be an "excellent picture" on the importance of the underground movement, the misery that fascism brings to ordinary people, and on the worldwide reputation of America as a haven for the oppressed. But the OWI was disappointed that Rick did not verbalize his conversion to the fight against fascism, and the agency worried that American attitudes toward Free and Vichy France were confused. The reviews were positive. "Splendid anti-Axis propaganda," wrote *Variety*. Bosley Crowther wrote in the *New York Times* that the film makes the "spine tingle." *Film Daily* raved that the film was "extremely gripping entertainment." Manny Farber in *The New Republic* called it pure "hokum" but even he admitted it was "good hokum."

And it *was* hokum. The Germans would never have allowed Victor Laszlo to leave Casablanca. They would have arrested him on the spot and tortured him until he told them what they wanted. Nor was the ending really in doubt. The PCA censors would not have allowed Ilsa to desert her husband and fly off to Lisbon with Rick. Had they gotten on the plane, it would have crashed because the PCA demanded that sinners be punished. But hokum or not audiences loved it. So did the Academy of Motion Picture Arts and Sciences. It was nominated for eight Academy Awards. It won best picture, best director for Michael Curtiz, and best screenplay for Julius and Philip Epstein and Howard Koch. It is an American classic.

REFERENCES

Miller, Frank, *Casablanca: As Time Goes By* (Atlanta: University of Georgia Press, 1993); Rosenzweig, Sidney, *Casablanca and Other Major Films of Michael Curtiz* (Ann Arbor, Mich.: UMI Research Press, 1982).

—*G.B.*

THE FARMER'S WIFE (1928)

EDEN PHILPOTS (1862–1960)

The Farmer's Wife (1928), U.K., directed by Alfred Hitchcock, adapted by Eliot Stannard; British International Pictures.

The Play

Eden Philpotts based his *The Farmer's Wife* on his phenomenally successful novel, *Widecombe Fair*. It premiered at the Birmingham Repertory Theatre on November 11, 1916, and then moved to the West End, where it ran for some 1,400 performances. Recently bereaved farmer Samuel Sweetland seeks a new wife. He has three women in mind: independent fox-hunting devotee Louisa Windeatt; spinster Thirza Tapper; and plump, hysterical Mary Hearn. Despite his confidence in his own virtues, Sweetland is rejected by all three. He later decides to marry his devoted housemaid Araminta Dench. A subplot involves the romantic problems affecting his two daughters, Petronell and Sibley, which are also resolved at the climax.

The Film

Alfred Hitchcock already had the spectacularly successful *The Lodger* (1926) behind him when he took on a silent-screen adaptation of Philpotts' play. No proj-ect could have been further away from *The Lodger*'s dark shadows and intrigue. Uncharacteristic as it seems today, and despite Hitchcock's virtual lack of interest when discussing this film with François Truffaut (describing it as "largely a title film"), *The Farmer's Wife* is not completely without interest. Indeed, historian Maurice Yacowar regards it as his most underrated work. Its camera and lighting style are derivative of Hitchcock's apprentice years at Germany's UFA studios, where he learned to emulate the rich chiaroscuro and mobile camera of the German master, F.W. Murnau. Moreover, because *The Farmer's Wife* was a play heavily dependent upon dialogue, with the subplot involving Sweetland's daughters echoing the main themes, Hitchcock eliminates most of the dialogue and attempts to make his adaptation as cinematic as possible. As Yacowar notes, his economy is effective: He omits one daughter completely and, with it, the romantic tangle of two courtships, two suitors, a legacy, and much accompanying community gossip.

An air of rural landscape and rustic community pervades the film. The opening shots reveal a quiet valley of verdant forests and meadows. After the death of his wife, Tibby, and the marriage of his daughter, Samuel Sweetland (Jameson Thomas) determines to seek a new mate from among the village's available prospects. But, willful and arrogant as he is, he does everything wrong: He either arrives too late or too early; his proposals are rough and unflattering; and each time he is rejected, he loses his temper. His struggles are counterpointed by delicious titles that perfectly capture the rustic spirit of place and situation, such as "Holy matrimony's a proper steam-roller for flattening the hope out of a man and the joy out of a woman." At last, humbled, he settles upon his devoted and modest housekeeper, Araminta Dench (Lilian Hall-Davis)—or "Minta," for short.

There are numerous Hitchcockian touches. When Minta promises to "air out" her husband's underpants, Hitchcock includes several shots of Sweetland's underpants being washed, aired, and put on his bed—anticipating a similar scene in *Vertigo*, when Madeleine's underwear is hung up to dry. During the nuptial meal for Sweetland's daughter Petronell, the aged bucolic Henry Coaker suggestively pokes Petronell with his walking stick, a gesture needing no titles. Great emphasis is placed upon the fireside chair that Sweetland's wife used to occupy. At times it serves to wordlessly symbolize her absence; at other times it is occupied by each of the prospective wives (and, finally, by Minta herself).

Far from a trivial rural farce, *The Farmer's Wife* has been reexamined by commentators like Raymond Durgnat and declared a diamond in the rough: "A sense of clumsy contacts, of loneliness, infiltrates the film, until every outgoing gesture, however clumsy, however stupid, seems cherished. The mixture of warmth and solitudes, of pomposities and uneasinesses . . . is a pleasure to watch."

REFERENCES

Yacowar, Maurice, *Hitchcock's British Films* (Hamden, Conn.: Archon Books, 1977).

—*T.W.*

FEATHERTOP

See *SCARECROW*

A FEW GOOD MEN (1989)

AARON SORKIN (1961–)

A Few Good Men (1992), U.S.A., directed by Rob Reiner, adapted by Aaron Sorkin; Columbia.

The Play

A Few Good Men first appeared at the Virginia Heritage Repertory Theatre in 1989, and its promising reception led to its performance at New York's John F. Kennedy Center for the Performing Arts on November 15, 1989. It later ran for 449 performances on Broadway. As is the case with most successful stage productions, it was immediately signed up by Hollywood, with an all-star cast and screenplay by the original dramatist who (unusually) received sole credit. The original play was a two-act performance with individual scenes melding into each other rather in the fashion of an expressionist play. The subject was the court-martial of two marines for their culpability in the death of a fellow soldier on the American military base at Guantánamo Bay, located in Cuba. An inexperienced defense attorney, Daniel Kaffee, eventually uncovers the true culprit, base commander Col. Jessep. The play uses many "cinematic" techniques, such as flashbacks and parallel narratives on a split stage.

The Film

Rob Reiner's film version is primarily linear in its chronology, with the exception of a few flashbacks. Lt. Kaffee (Tom Cruise) is a brash young lawyer just putting in his time before retiring into what surely will be a lucrative civilian career. He is assigned to defend two young marines, formerly stationed at Guantánamo Bay, who are accused of the murder of another soldier. Certain of their guilt at first, Kaffee is convinced by an Internal Affairs officer (Demi Moore) that irregularities in the case implicate their commanding officer, Col. Jessep (Jack Nicholson), in a cover up. It seems the two men are indeed guilty, but they had been ordered to harrass the victim by Jessep because of the dead man's violation of military codes of behavior. This essentially vigilante form of justice, operating outside conventional codes of conduct, is euphemistically designated "Code Red." Kaffee must decide whether or not to have his clients plead guilty, in which case they will serve a minimal prison term, or plead not guilty and risk having his clients incarcerated for the rest of their lives. Deciding on the latter course, Kaffee must prove that it was Col. Jessep who ordered the "Code Red." Ultimately, Jessep breaks down on the stand and rants about how society needs people like him to operate outside the bounds of an ineffective civil justice system. The defendants are declared "not guilty" on all counts, except that of "behavior unbecoming a marine."

The film simplifies the play by reducing the role of the murdered marine, Private Santiago, to a brief appearance in the pre-credit sequence and in the flashbacks. In sum, it is less a critique of an inhumane militaristic system than a *Bildungsroman* narrative of Lt.

Kaffee's coming of age. Although Jessep's responsibility for the death of Santiago is revealed in the courtroom, Reiner follows traditional, conservative Hollywood patterns by assuring the audience that the prevailing system is still all right as long as "a few good men" (and a token woman played by Demi Moore!) are around to see that democratic justice is done. Apart from some lively performances by Cruise, Nicholson, Kevin Bacon, and J.T. Walsh, the film is merely routine and formulaic. It may have inspired the television naval courtroom drama, *J.A.G.*

REFERENCES

Britton, Andrew, "Blissing Out: The Politics of Reaganite Entertainment," *Movie*, 31/32 (1986), 1–42; Newman, Kim, "A Few Good Men," *Sight and Sound*, 3:1 (1993), 46.

—*T.W.*

FIVE STAR FINAL (1930)

LOUIS WEITZENKORN (1893–1943)

Five Star Final (1931), U.S.A., directed by Mervyn LeRoy, adapted by Robert Lord and Byron Morgan; Warner Bros.

The Play

Five Star Final opened at the Cort Theatre in New York on December 30, 1930, with Arthur Byron in the role of Joseph Randall, Merle Maddern as Nancy Voorhees Townsend, Malcolm Duncan as Michael Townsend, Frances Fuller as Jenny Townsend, King Calder as Philip Weeks, Berton Churchill as Hinchecliffe, and Alexander Onslow as the Reverend T. Vernon Isopod. Also in the cast was future Hollywood veteran Allen Jenkins as Ziggie Feinstein. The story is set in 1930. Bernard Hinchecliffe, editor of the *New York Evening Gazette*, desperately wants to boost circulation for his sleazy tabloid newspaper. He bullies city editor Joseph Randall into digging up an old scandal, a 20-year-old murder case in which a pregnant Nancy Voorhees shot her lover, went to prison, and was subsequently released. Although Nancy's new husband, Michael Townsend, knows all about her past, her daughter Jenny knows nothing of the case. When Jenny gets engaged to young Philip Weeks, son of a socially prominent family, Randall sends over the "Reverend" T. Vernon Isopod (actually a defrocked clergyman now on the payroll of the *Gazette*) to get more information on the Voorhees case, by posing as

the priest who will conduct the wedding ceremony. The good "Reverend" dutifully obtains pictures and enough inside information to give the *Gazette* a tremendous scoop, but the horror of having her past dredged up again is too much for poor Nancy, who kills herself. Her husband, Michael, discovers her body, but keeps the news from Jenny and Philip, who are on their way to the church to be married. He then kills himself. Moments after the double suicide, the bodies of Nancy and Michael are found by two of the *Gazette* reporters, and the case is splashed all over the front page.

The outraged Jenny and Philip confront Randall and Hinchecliffe at the *Gazette* offices. While Hinchecliffe tries to justify the paper's actions, Randall, disgusted, admits to Jenny that the *Gazette* "killed your mother and Michael Townsend for purposes of circulation. . . . That's the answer—that's the only answer there is." Jenny pulls a revolver and tries to kill Hinchecliffe, but is prevented by Philip. Randall quits the paper, but Hinchecliffe simply installs another editor who is willing to do his bidding. It seems the scandal-sheet *Gazette* will continue its campaign to exploit news and gossip for the sake of selling papers.

Playwright Louis Weitzenkorn was writing from experience. He had served as editor of the *New York Graphic*, one of the most notorious scandal-sheets in the history of American journalism. Disgusted with the experience, Weitzenkorn quit the *Graphic* and turned to writing plays. *Five Star Final* was his second attempt, and it was a smash hit.

The Film

One of the most uncompromising of the early 1930s social problem films from Warner Bros., *Five Star Final* was Mervyn LeRoy's follow-up to the gangster classic he directed the year before, *Little Caesar*. LeRoy had seen the play in New York and immediately wired Jack Warner to purchase the screen rights. He recast the film with Edward G. Robinson as Randall, the tough-talking city editor, H.B. Warner and Frances Starr as the appropriately pathetic couple Michael and Nancy Voorhees Townsend, ingenue Marian Marsh as the starry-eyed daughter Jenny, and Boris Karloff as the unctuous and corrupt "Reverend" Isopod. The dialogue-driven action of this pre-Code film is characteristically tough and terse. When the greedy publisher asks his secretary her opinion about a scandalous story, she cynically responds, "I think the part about the illegitimate child is not made quite clear enough." When the contest editor stages a taxi race across the city, he declares, "I'm going to let an Irishman, a Jew, and a

Wop win." And when Jenny and Philip confront Randall at the end, Philip delivers a memorable attack on yellow journalism: "You'll go on hunting down little people who can't fight back. You'll go on with your filthy newspaper, pulling the clothing off women and selling their naked souls. You've grown rich off filth—and no one's ever dared rise up and crush you out."

Moments later, as Randall himself excoriates his profession, he refers to his boss, saying, "Tell him to shove it up his—"and a crash of glass drowns out the offending last word (a technique used in another newspaper film of the period, *The Front Page*). The issue of suicide—a subject that in a few years would be expressly forbidden by the Production Code Administration censorial policies—is handled discreetly: Nancy walks into her bathroom and takes up a bottle of poison. As the door closes behind her, we hear a moan and the sound of a body falling to the floor. When her husband arrives, we see him enter the room and close the door; seconds later we hear the sound of his body falling to the floor.

Taking its cue from the play, LeRoy and screenwriters Robert Lord and Byron Morgan confine most of the action to two sets, the *Gazette* offices and the Townsend apartment. Exceptions include the exciting opening montage of shots of rolling presses, banner headlines, and newsboy shouts of "Extra!"; and the split-screen effects employed in several crucial scenes involving telephone conversations. In the most famous example, a triptych reveals Nancy in the center of the frame, trying to contact Randall to stop the presses; and on either side of her are images of the switchboard operators. As her attempt to connect fails, the left and right sides of the frame go dark, leaving her alone in the darkness. The cumulative dramatic effect is stunning. Robinson's performance is generally regarded as one of the finest screen performances of the day. "The playing of Robinson as Randall, the overworked, dishonest editor still capable of seeing the truth, was magnificent," notes commentator Charles Higham, "brilliantly right for the new camera techniques of the period, laying down the whole foundation of movie acting technique in the talkies for forty years to come."

REFERENCES

Doherty, Thomas, *Pre-Code Hollywood* (New York: Columbia University Press, 1999); Higham, Charles, *Warner Brothers* (New York: Charles Scribner's Sons, 1975); LeRoy, Mervyn, as told to Dick Kleiner, *Mervyn LeRoy: Take One* (New York: Hawthorn, 1974).

—*W.W.D.*

LA FOLLE DE CHAILLOT (1945)

JEAN GIRAUDOUX (1882–1944)

The Mad Woman of Chaillot (1969), U.K., directed by Bryan Forbes, adapted by Maurice Valency and Edward Anhalt; Commonwealth United Productions.

The Play

Jean Giraudoux's posthumous allegorical play about the struggle between good and evil opened in December 1945 at the Théâtre de l'Athénée to ecstatic reviews and ran for nearly 300 performances. The action takes place in Paris at the turn of the century: Chez Francis on the Place de l'Alma and in the basement belonging to Countess Aurélia, the so-called Mad Woman of Chaillot. A syndicate of hard-nosed businessmen, concerned only with profit, plot to exploit putative oil reserves beneath Paris. Pierre, blackmailed by the group over a financial indiscretion, is rescued from suicide and reveals their sinister plans to Aurélia who summons her friends to defend their beloved Paris. Her so-called mad companions from other districts of Paris—Constance from Passy, Gabrielle from Saint-Sulpice, and Joséphine from Concorde—assemble with angry locals in her basement to stage a mock trial of the unscrupulous businessmen, defended with masterful irony by the local ragpicker. Inevitably found guilty, they are tricked by Aurélia into testing for oil in her cellar, only to find themselves imprisoned forever in the sewers.

Contemporary Parisian audiences readily identified the evil businessmen as the occupying German forces, though Giraudoux may also have had in mind French wartime profiteers. His allegory presents humble and so-called mad people as the defenders of human and environmental values against the destructive power of vested interests, whether these are expressed as invading military powers or international capitalism. The opposing camps are sharply drawn through colorful characters, but none is more colorful that the Countess herself, dressed in gaudy clothes and constantly fantasizing about her lost lover. Her companions also live harmlessly in their own fantasies and though mad they are deemed saner than the syndicate whose ruthless self-interest would destroy Paris. The role of the scathing ragpicker was memorably played by Giraudoux's lifelong collaborator Louis Jouvet, doubling as director. Exceptional too was Marguerite Moréno as an inimitable Aurélia, bedecked in the extraordinary costumes designed by the artist Christian Bérard, who also created the atmospheric sets. Translated by Maurice Valency, Giraudoux's play has been performed twice on Broadway; initially in 1948, as *Madwoman* with Martita Hunt in the lead, and subsequently as the musical *Dear World*.

The Film

Edward Anhalt provided the original script from Maurice Valency's translation, but Bryan Forbes, having replaced John Huston as the director after only three weeks, decided to rework Anhalt's adaptation to produce a shooting script with greater cinematic treatment. He opened up the play by truncating the early, lengthy monologues and provided character associated locations only alluded to in the text. He also updated the action to sixties Paris with student riots and topical references to France's place in Europe and Russian missiles. Roderick (Giraudoux's Pierre), for example, becomes a left-wing activist duped by the syndicate into attempting to blow up the city planner's office he has been told is the headquarters of military intelligence. Topicality may draw in the spectator, but this switch to contemporary realism militates against Giraudoux's more allusive conception in which his larger-than-life characters exist more comfortably as allegorical figures.

The film has excellent visual qualities with a mood of nostalgia evoked in lyrical establishing shots of a Paris under threat from commercial interests. This exquisite color portrait of the photogenic French capital was principally the work of Claude Renoir, but contractual commitments meant that after 10 weeks he relinquished his role to Burnett Guffey (*Bonnie and Clyde*). The film's languid mood is completed by Michael Lewis's wistful score conjuring up a bygone period untainted by modern commercial pressures. In adopting this more sentimental, less cerebral, approach, Forbes plays down Giraudoux's harsher critique and in so doing runs counter to less flattering film portraits of sixties Paris, notably Godard's bleak presentations in *Alphaville* or in *Deux ou trois choses que je sais d'elle*. However, a suitably sharper edge persists in sequences unmasking the would-be developers: at the café where the menacing evil of the unscrupulous businessmen is revealed in the tough performances of Yul Brynner and Donald Pleasence and at the mock trial where Danny Kaye—returning to the screen after a six-year absence—excels as the ironical ragpicker defending the shameless self-interest of the syndicate. In the principal role, Katharine Hepburn, magnificently attired in outrageous hats, strikes the right note of lucid eccentricity, but the most memorable cameo performances belong to her companions: Margaret Leighton, confiding in her nonexistent dog, Dickie, and the splendid Edith Evans, haunting the corridors of the American Embassy and demanding an interview with Woodrow Wilson.

REFERENCES

Cohen, Robert, *Giraudoux: Three Faces of Destiny* (Chicago: University of Chicago Press, 1968); Knapp, Bettina L., *French Theatre 1918–1938* (London: Macmillan, 1985); Lemaitre, Georges, *Jean Giraudoux: The Writer and His Work* (New York: Frederick Ungar, 1971).

—R.F.C.

FOOL FOR LOVE (1983)

SAM SHEPARD (1943–)

Fool for Love (1986), U.S.A., directed by Robert Altman, adapted by Sam Shepard; Cannon Group.

The Play

Shepard's play came at a turning point in his career. Having portrayed pilot Chuck Yeager in the film *The Right Stuff*, he was on the cusp of widespread recognition and fame, being touted in some circles as a new Redford or Newman. Whatever his growing appeal as a leading man, *Fool for Love* remained loyal to many of Shepard's trademark themes and styles as a playwright; it is of a piece with *Buried Child* and *True West*, concerned with ideas such as the destructiveness of passionately felt love and the interplay between reality and illusion. The play opens with the reunion of Eddie and May, sometime lovers, at a motel in the middle of the Mojave Desert. May is preparing for a date with the hapless Martin, while Eddie has been courting a flamboyant and mysterious woman called the "Countess." Eddie and May collide in alternating arguments and seductions, all the while observed by an "Old Man" who may or may not be a figment of their joint imagination. Martin is subjected to abuse by Eddie and the Countess blows up Eddie's pickup truck in retribution, as Eddie reveals that the Old Man is actually the father of him and May by different mothers.

The Film

By the mid-1980s, Robert Altman had retreated from mainstream filmmaking to focus on cinematic adaptations of stage plays. His production of *Fool for Love*

Sam Shepard

pickup truck—that the play was forced to merely imply.

The film adaptation of *Fool for Love* marked the first time that a Shepard play had been transferred to the screen. Based on its lack of success and Shepard's unhappy experience with it, he became hesitant to allow any further adaptations. Perhaps trading in on his own recent success as an actor, Shepard portrayed Eddie in the adaptation, while Kim Basinger (replacing Shepard's pregnant wife, Jessica Lange) played May. Stanton handled the role of the Old Man, with Randy Quaid playing Martin. The film was for the most part badly received. David Denby of *New York* magazine declared that Shepard's own portrayal ended any speculation about his status as an up-and-coming leading man, and the performances by Basinger and Stanton were roundly criticized. Shepard himself criticized Altman, saying that the venerable director had "no respect for actors." Shepard followed the film version of *Fool for Love* with several more film performances, making his own feature film directing debut in 1988 with *Far North*. Altman subsequently returned to more mainstream productions with *Vincent and Theo* (1990) and *The Player* (1992).

REFERENCES

DeRose, David J., *Sam Shepard* (New York: Twayne Publishers, 1992); Keyssar, Helene, *Robert Altman's America* (Oxford: Oxford University Press, 1991); Shewey, Don, *Sam Shepard* (New York: DeCapo Press, 1997).

—C.M.

came toward the end of this cycle and was characteristic of the adaptations he directed in this period: using a screenplay written by the playwright, utilizing relatively modest production values, and exhibiting, for the most part, a "stagy" presentation. In this case, Altman did make some significant changes to the Shepard play. For one, he exercised the standard tactic used in cinematic adaptations of plays and "opened up" the action; whereas Shepard's play had taken place in the stylized set of a motel room, much of the action in the film occurs outside the motel, in a parking lot that, by the account of one critic, has "more neon . . . than on 42nd Street and Broadway." Second, the film seems to have settled the question of the Old Man's reality, as the character is presented by Altman and actor Harry Dean Stanton as a fully human and nonimaginary (if still enigmatic) person. Finally, the film takes advantage of the opportunity to portray some of the action—such as the Countess' explosive destruction of Eddie's

FRAGILE FOX (1955)

NORMAN BROOKS

Attack! (1956), U.S.A., directed by Robert Aldrich, adapted by James Poe; United Artists.

The Play

Norman Brooks's *Fragile Fox* is a three-act play set during the Battle of the Bulge, which occurred during the last winter of World War II in Europe. Staged in New York, the play was unsuccessful due to its grim view of corruption in the military, contradicting both the cold war ethos as well as Hollywood's glamorized view of World War Two. Staged with a cast of 13, the action takes place in Fox Company C.P., with the exception of Act Two, Scene One, which occurs in a farmhouse recently occupied by the Americans. The first act opens in Fox Company headquarters situated in the Belgian village of Plainveux. Inexperienced, alcoholic Captain Cooney awaits the arrival of his Georgia buddy and commanding officer, Colonel Shehan, for a card game with himself and his fellow officers. Despite Lt. Joseph's resentment of Cooney's incompetence (whom he blames for the loss of his men in combat), the diplomatic Lt. Woodruff insists on his participation. Although he knows Cooney's failings, Shehan keeps him in a commanding position to further his future political career with the aid of Cooney's powerful father. Although Shehan refuses Woodruff's request to remove Cooney by assuring him the war is virtually over, an unexpected German advance sends the company back into battle. Lt. Joseph threatens to kill Cooney if he loses any more men due to the latter's incompetence. Former history instructor Woodruff admonishes Joseph and assures him of military support. Cooney later refuses to give artillery support to Joseph's platoon when they take a farmhouse.

Act Two is set in the farmhouse. The platoon discovers two German soldiers hiding in the basement. Joseph shoots the German sergeant to extract information from the other soldier about a German division lurking nearby. Realizing Cooney's lack of support, the men make a run for it. Scene two opens in Fox Company headquarters when the captured German informs the Americans that the division is an S.S. unit. Despite Cooney wishing to flee, Shehan arrives and forces him to stay and defend the company position. While Woodruff deals with a drunken, cowardly Cooney, an injured Joseph arrives. Despite Woodruff's objections, he is about to kill Cooney when news of an S.S. tank threatening the company position sends him outside with a bazooka.

Act Three depicts Fox Company surrounded by the Germans. Despite having an injured Jewish private and knowing S.S. practices of never rescuing wounded prisoners, Cooney intends to surrender. A mortally wounded Joseph arrives and attempts to kill him but dies in the attempt. Realizing Cooney still intends to surrender, Woodruff shoots him. Although Woodruff intends to take full responsibility for his actions, all his men fire bullets into Cooney's body thus taking collective responsibility for their actions. When the S.S. retreat Shehan arrives. Guessing the circumstances, he informs Woodruff of awarding Cooney a posthumous distinguished service cross to impress his father. When Woodruff objects, Shehan threatens him with an investigation. Despite Woodruff revealing the truth, Shehan leaves the scene intending to call his bluff as in a card game. "I've lost hands, but never two in a row." The play ends with an uncertain Woodruff weeping convulsively as the grave detail removes Cooney's body.

The Film

After unsuccessfully trying to purchase the rights to *The Young Lions* and *The Naked and the Dead*, Robert Aldrich finally achieved his wish to make an "angry" war film by acquiring *Fragile Fox*. Aldrich intended to contradict the contemporary image of a "positive" war movie represented by *To Hell and Back, Mr. Roberts,* and *Strategic Air Command*. However, despite Pentagon refusal to cooperate on the film, Aldrich eventually shot a low-budget version of Brooks's play on the back lot of RKO with purchased (or rented) war equipment. The film is generally faithful to the spirit of the original play with some minor exceptions. Lt. Joseph and Col Shehan now become Jack Palance's Lt. Costa and Lee Marvin's Colonel Bartlett. The captured German sergeant now becomes an officer to make stage parallels to Cooney more explicit. Although *Attack!* anticipates Vietnam War imagery of soldiers "fragging" incompetent officers, certain modifications also occur. Costa does not shoot Peter Van Eyck's German officer on the spot but throws him outside to be killed by his fellow S.S. Despite the final scene showing Woodruff phoning headquarters and intending to denounce Bartlett, Aldrich concludes the shot with the camera craning to a pessimistic high-angle position, dwarfing the lieutenant against the surrounding darkness.

Although censorship requirements necessitated the film concluding with Woodruff "doing the right thing," Aldrich shoots it in such a way as to keep faith with the bleak nature of the original theatrical conclusion. Aldrich also "opens out" the original stage play to accommodate cinematic conventions. The pre-credit sequence reveals the decimation of Costa's men due to Cooney's incompetence. We do not see Cooney fully at this time. Also, the sequence ends with a helmet coming to a complete stop next to a single flower following a shell blast. As Silver and Ursini note, "The image is held as the main titles begin, accompanied by the clattering, martial music of the film's score by Frank DeVol." Costa's arm is also crushed by a tank in the film. Palance's death grimace derived its inspiration from the faces of dead miners he saw in his youth. Also, Aldrich depicts Cooney breaking down and reenacting memories of parental abuse. This associates him with the director's other victims of family trauma, seen in *Autumn Leaves* (1956), *The Last Sunset* (1961), *What Ever Happened to Baby Jane* (1962), and *Hush . . . Hush Sweet Charlotte* (1965).

REFERENCES

Arnold, Edwin T., and Eugene L. Miller, *The Films and Career of Robert Aldrich* (Knoxville: University of Tennessee Press, 1986); Brooks, Norman, *Fragile Fox* (New York: Dramatists Play Service, 1955); Silver, Alain, and James Ursini, *What Ever Happened to Robert Aldrich?* (New York: Limelight Editions, 1995)

—T.W.

FRANKENSTEIN (1823)

RICHARD BRINSLEY PEAKE AND PEGGY WEBLING

Frankenstein (1931), U.S.A., directed by James Whale, adapted by John L. Balderston and Garrett Fort; Universal.

The Play

If we know the Frankenstein story at all, it is doubtless through Mary Shelley's original novel, *Frankenstein; or, The Modern Prometheus* (published anonymously in 1818), or through the numerous film adaptations that have appeared from 1910 until the present. However, the translation of the story into a stage play—actually a series of stage plays—is crucial to any understanding of those films. The novel had been in print less than six years when several stage adaptations appeared in 1823 in London. No less than three versions were burlesques, one of which featured a tailor named "Frankenstitch," who applied his skills to sew together body parts from nine dead men. The most significant adaptation that year was a three-act "opera" entitled *Presumption; or, The Fate of Frankenstein*, which premiered on July 28, 1823. Playwright Richard Brinsley Peake confronted here the same problems that would bedevil all future adapters to stage and film: how to dramatize a complex narrative that was told from multiple points of view, that spanned a vast geographical compass, and was fraught with fantastic effects and action, from laboratory transformations to chases across mountains and ice floes.

Peake's stage version would serve as a blueprint for most future adaptations. It constructed a chronologically linear plotline, reduced the many scenes into a few key situations (the creation scene, the bridal night, the climactic destruction of the Monster), eliminated other scenes (notably the Monster's education at the De Lacey household), stripped the dialogue of philosophical and scientific musings, introduced a new character, Fritz, Frankenstein's servant, and exploited the hideousness of the Monster. Portraying Victor

Frankenstein was James Wallack, and, as the monster, Thomas Potter Cooke (who would be typecast in the role for the rest of his life). Prophetically, Cooke's visualization of the Monster was for pure gory effect—yellow and green greasepaint on the face, black lips, a tangled wig of unkempt hair, and blue makeup on the arms and legs. The big moment in the action came at the end of Act One, when the Monster appears, throttles his maker, and escapes out a window. Like so many Hollywood incarnations to come, the Monster did not speak the eloquent phrasings of Mary Shelley's original, but merely grunted inarticulately. Responding to outraged moralists, the play's producer, S.J. Arnold, protested: "The striking moral exhibited in this story, is the fatal consequence of that presumption attempts to penetrate, beyond prescribed depths, into the mystery of nature." As for Mary Shelley, she saw the play and applauded the impersonation of the Monster, adding, "I was much amused and it appeared to excite a breathless eagerness in the audience."

A century later, after many other subsequent dramatizations, Peggy Webling's 1927 stage adaptation was still following Peake's basic story formula. Her *Frankenstein* premiered in London at the Preston Theatre. In the role of the Monster was Hamilton Deane, who had himself previously adapted to the stage another horror classic, Bram Stoker's *Dracula*. Webling's play added a few new story elements that would prove greatly influential to the James Whale Universal film adaptation to come: Victor Frankenstein's name change from "Victor" to "Henry" Frankenstein; the Monster's accidental drowning of a little girl; his fascination with sunlight; and his attempted rape of Frankenstein's fiancee. The production was a sensation. Writing in *The Graphic*, a critic noted: "It would be idle to pretend that *Frankenstein* is a very noteworthy play. Written with romantic confidence and great volubility, there are times when we wish that the authoress would cut the cackle and come to the monster."

It is worth noting that allusions to the Frankenstein monster dotted Joseph K Kesselring's play, *Arsenic and Old Lace*, which opened on Broadway in 1941. Portraying the murderer, Jonathan Brewster—a character referred to in the dialogue as looking like Boris Karloff—was none other than Boris Karloff himself. The play went on to a spectacular run of 1,444 performances and several radio dramatizations (all featuring Karloff). However, when Columbia adapted the play to the screen, it was not Karloff but Raymond Massey who impersonated the evil Jonathan. Many subsequent dramatizations have appeared—including Julian Beck's 1965 version for the Living Theatre. However, since they do not have a direct bearing on the Universal motion picture, they will not be considered here.

The Films

There have been three silent film versions of *Frankenstein*. The first *Frankenstein* on film came from the Edison Studios in 1910. According to the script, the film, directed by J. Searle Dawley, was "A Liberal Adaptation of Mrs. Shelley's Famous Story." Charles Ogle's creature was a hunchbacked and shaggy-chested rascal who emerged from a vat of blazing chemicals. The film is apparently now lost. In 1915 another version appeared, *Life Without Soul*, directed by Joseph W. Smiley and starring Percy Darrell Standing as the Monster. Oddly, Standing appeared sans makeup. The third silent version was made in Italy in 1920 as *Il Mostro di Frakestein*, directed by Eugenio Testa and adapted by Giovanni Drovetti. This film is also lost.

Only *Dracula* rivals *Frankenstein*'s enduring success as *the* quintessential horror film from Universal Studios in the 1930s. When Universal decided to follow up its successful *Dracula* (which itself was adapted from a stage play rather than the original novel) with *Frankenstein*, writers John L. Balderston and Garrett Fort were called in to adapt Webling's play. But while Webling's basic outline and overly talky drawing-room sequences were transferred intact, there were a few significant changes: The primitive, garret-like laboratory customarily designed for the stage became a spectacular set designed by Herman Rosse; and its bizarre electrical apparatus, designed by Kenneth Strickfaden, sparked, fizzed, and hummed alarmingly. The climactic search-and-destroy operation by the outraged villagers proved an exciting way to end the story, and has been an established ingredient of the Frankenstein legend ever since.

From director James Whale, who took over the project from director Robert Florey, came the suggestion that the Monster's violent nature was to be explained away by the fact that he had been given the brain of a criminal. Moreover, makeup ace Jack Pierce contributed a new "look" to the creature. The flat-topped head, surgical scars, and neck electrodes all suggested the procedures that had stitched him together and brought him to life. "I made him the way the textbooks said he should look," explained Pierce. "I spent three months of research in anatomy, surgery, medicine, criminology, ancient and modern burial customs, and electro-dynamics." (The face was coated with a ghastly green makeup for the sake of the desired ashen hue on black-and-white film.) Other departures

from the play included the deletion of a scene in which the Monster demands a bride and a change in the circumstances of his death—from a fire in an old mill rather than from a lightning bolt in the laboratory. The casting of the Monster resulted, in large part, from director Whale's seeing Boris Karloff (William Henry Pratt) in the Los Angeles stage presentation of a play called *The Criminal Code*, in which he had portrayed a murderous convict.

The Hollywood censors played their part in the finished product. Although, after discussion, they allowed Frankenstein's line, "In the name of God, now I know what it feels like to *be* God!" to remain, they demanded excision of several other scenes, including the Monster's hanging of the unfortunate Fritz and his tossing of the little girl into the lake. There were the inevitable sequels, but only *The Bride of Frankenstein* need concern us, since it developed the idea in Shelley's original novel of Frankenstein's fashioning of a mate for the Monster. Unlike the novel, however, wherein the mate was destroyed before it could come to life, the Bride (Elsa Lanchester) lived long enough to scare the hell out of the startled Monster. (Lanchester also appears in the film's Prologue as Mary Shelley.)

Regardless of the many alterations and departures from Shelley's original novel in this and other "Frankenstein" films—whether the Frankenstein story be told in prose or on stage and screen—the basic thesis has remained intact: As commentator Albert J. LaValley has noted, "In each [the Monster] carries the burden of similar conflicts: endowed with superhuman strength, he is also highly vulnerable, the crucible in which the struggle of joy and suffering, sympathy and revenge, passivity and destructiveness most clearly is worked out."

REFERENCES

Forry, Steven Earl, *Hideous Progenies: Dramatizations of* Frankenstein *from Mary Shelley to the Present* (Philadelphia: University of Pennsylvania Press, 1990); Glut, Donald F., *The Frankenstein Legend* (Metuchen, N.J.: Scarecrow Press, 1973); Lavalley, Albert J., "The Stage and Film Children of *Frankenstein*: A Survey," in George Levine and U.C. Knoepflmacher, *The Endurance of Frankenstein: Essays on Mary Shelley's Novel* (Berkeley: University of California Press, 1979), 243–289.

—*J.C.T.*

FRANKIE AND JOHNNY IN THE CLAIRE DE LUNE (1987)

TERRENCE MCNALLY (1939–)

Frankie & Johnny (1991), U.S.A., directed by Garry Marshall, adapted by Terrence McNally; Paramount.

The Play

Set in present-day New York City, the play premiered in New York City on June 2, 1987, with established actors Kathy Bates as Frankie and F. Murray Abraham as Johnny, with the Voice of the Radio Announcer done by Dominic Cuskern. In October, as the venue changed, Kenneth Welsh replaced Abraham as Johnny. This two-act play, set entirely in a "quite cramped" apartment in the "west 50's," presents the action of one night between two characters who show "a comic clash between sharply opposed attitudes toward romantic love." Johnny, a short-order cook who is also an ex-con, and Frankie, a tough waitress who is emotionally closed off, spend their time relating their past experiences and arguing over Johnny's desire for emotional attachment. Frankie spends much of her time trying to get Johnny out of her apartment, and Johnny, having convinced himself that he loves her, ardently persuades Frankie to make a commitment to a relationship. The play ends with the two characters lying in bed, hopeful of a future without emotional "armor."

The Film

Aware that viewers would not flock to a film set entirely in a small apartment with two characters, McNally expanded the play drastically and rearranged parts of the story to fit the conventions of a romantic comedy. Also conscious of the graphic dialogue and subject matter in the play, he cut some of the explicit language and reinforced the loneliness of the main characters. For example, instead of beginning with the two characters reaching sexual climax together, the movie presents a lengthy exposition of Frankie and Johnny before they even meet. The movie starts with the depiction of Frankie going to see her family in Altoona, Pennsylvania, and her lonely behavior back in New York, compared with Johnny's release from prison and his acquisition of an apartment. Using short and energetic scenes, the movie exhibits a sit-com quality that producer Garry Marshall was both lauded and panned for.

Essentially, the movie opens up the play by letting viewers see the streets of New York, the apartments of the two main characters, and the Apollo Café where both Frankie and Johnny work and where much of the verbal sparring and courtship presents itself. The movie places the characters in a diversity of settings to extend the narrative into a more tightly constructed plot, while also showcasing new characters and providing further material that fosters sympathy for Frankie and Johnny. For example, accentuating the sentimental quality of Johnny's character, we see him pay a prostitute to lie with him in the "spoon position" as they sleep together, showing his desire for the warmth of female companionship and sweetening his image away from the obsessive nature some see in him from the play. In Frankie's case, we see her observation of an abused woman across the street, and she confronts the woman in a grocery store about escaping the abusive relationship (all alluded to in the play). As the movie reaches closure, Frankie views the abusive husband searching closets to verify the woman's flight. This is done to reinforce Frankie's past experience and to also provide an image of hope for a future without pain.

In the movie, the star power of Al Pacino and Michelle Pfeiffer replaced the Broadway actors, and McNally created a host of new characters. Frankie and Johnny no longer argue in solitude but in a "densely populated world." Because so much of the movie is set in the restaurant, most of the new characters are associated with the café. Hector Elizondo plays the good-natured Greek owner whose various relatives help out at the cash register for comic relief. Kate Nelligan plays Cora, a flirtatious waitress looking for love from numerous men. Nedda, played by Jane Morris, is an old maid who serves as a contrast to Cora but also provides a picture of what Frankie may turn into if she gives up on relationships. Various cooks and busboys provide the energy and comedic elements of a New York diner, most notably Tino (Greg Lewis), a cook who is indelibly linked to the phone. Outside of the Apollo Café, the most important new character is Tim, Frankie's homosexual neighbor played by Nathan Lane. This character is Frankie's confidant who also provides comedic one-liners in the sit-com tradition.

Structurally, the film moved many of the play's dialogue sections from the apartment into the outside world via the coffee shop, a bowling alley, a going-away party, and the streets and park benches of New York. The movie ends much like the play, with Frankie and Johnny snuggling on her sofa bed, but before this closing scene we see various characters in their bedrooms at this time of the morning. The ending emphasizes that the main characters have a realistic hope for happiness though the film's "celebration of cautious optimism."

REFERENCES

Alleve, R., "Two too cute," *Commonweal*, 118:20 (November 22, 1991); Ansen, David, "Love Over Easy, Hold the Mayo,"

Newsweek, 118:16 (October 14, 1991); Kaufmann, Stanley, "Finding Themselves," *The New Republic*, 205:20 (November 11, 1991); Rafferty, Terrence, "Boundless Love," *The New Yorker*, 67:35 (October 21, 1991); Simon, John, "Urban Plight, Slightly Varnished," *The National Review*, 43:22 (December 2, 1991); Travers, P., "Love in a Greasy Spoon," *Rolling Stone*, 616 (October 31, 1991); Welsh, James M., "Frankie & Johnny," *Films in Review*, 43:1–2 (January–February 1992).

—*T.N.T.*

THE FRONT PAGE (1928)

BEN HECHT (1893–1964) AND CHARLES MACARTHUR (1895–1956)

The Front Page (1931), U.S.A., directed by Lewis Milestone, adapted by Bartlett Cormack (uncredited) and Ben Hecht and Charles Lederer; United Artists.

His Girl Friday (1940), U.S.A., directed by Howard Hawks, adapted by Charles Lederer; Columbia.

The Front Page (1974), U.S.A., directed by Billy Wilder, adapted by Wilder and I.A.L. Diamond; Universal-International.

Switching Channels (1988), U.S.A., directed by Ted Kotcheff, adapted by Jonathan Reynolds; J. Arthur Rank/Martin Ransohoff.

The Play

This most famous of all American newspaper plays premiered in New York at the Times Square Theatre on August 14, 1928, and ran for 276 performances. Unlike *Five Star Final* (1931), arguably its closest rival, it continues to be revived, and has seen recent productions in 1969 and 1990 with Bert Convy and John Lithgow, respectively, as Walter Burns. Ben Hecht's own newspaper experiences at the *Chicago Daily Journal*, circa 1910, invested the play with an unmistakable ring of authenticity. "*The Front Page*, with its rowdy virility, its swift percussion of incident, its streaks of Gargantuan derision, is as breath-taking an event as ever dropped . . . on Broadway," rejoiced a critic in the *New York World*.

All the action of the three-act play is set in the pressroom of the Chicago Criminal Courts Building. A group of reporters have gathered to cover the hanging of Earl Williams (George Leach), whose execution for the murder of a policeman has been stage-managed to promote the law-and-order agenda of the mayor, who is up for reelection. Williams escapes and, due to the ineptitude of Sheriff Hartman (who gave him a gun so he could reenact the crime), enters the press room and surrenders to Hildy Johnson (Lee Tracy), star reporter for Walter Burns's (Osgood Perkins) newspaper. Hildy, who had been planning to leave his job and retire to a more comfortable world of marriage and advertising, realizes this is the scoop of his reporting life. He conceals Williams in a rolltop desk. Eventually, Williams is found, and both Hildy and Burns, who have been trying surreptitiously to remove the desk from the building, are arrested for harboring a fugitive. But because they have incriminating evidence on the sheriff's nefarious activities, they are released. Hildy resumes his plans to leave the newspaper, but Burns plants a watch on him and reports to the police that it was stolen. In the play's famous closing line, Burns orders the police to arrest Hildy—"The son of a bitch stole my watch!"

The Films

The Front Page has been filmed four times, by Lewis Milestone, Howard Hawks, Billy Wilder, and Ted Kotcheff. The Milestone version, adapted by the playwrights, was one of a cycle of buccaneering newsman sagas—including *Gentlemen of the Press* (1929), *Scandal Sheet* (1930), *Five Star Final* (1931), and *The Great Edition* (1932)—that introduced the character type of the enterprising, wisecracking street reporter to the screen. "Like the gangster, another fast-talking, disreputable denizen of the urban underworld," writes historian Thomas Doherty, "the newspaperman was ethnic and déclassé, chatty and cynical, hard-drinking and insubordinate. Trafficking on his Boldini-bold byline, he gained access to all levels of society, from lowlife snitches to high-class debutantes." Director Milestone, fresh from his masterpiece, *All Quiet on the Western Front* (1930), was recruited to helm the project by Howard Hughes, who had acquired the rights. Milestone's initial choice of James Cagney as Hildy was rejected in favor of stage actor Pat O'Brien in his screen debut. Walter Menjou's Walter Burns was more debonair than his rougher, tougher stage counterpart.

While the film could not entirely escape its stage-bound origin, it succeeded by virtue of its staccato, rapid-paced dialogue. "The true romance of the newspaper film," continues Doherty, "was in the delirious love of talk." Without question, this version loves to talk, and it delivers the dialogue faster than any succeeding version. It opens with a cross-cutting sequence between the boys in the press room and the executioner testing the gallows. Street scenes further "open out" the play, such as when Burns pulls the fire alarm to delude Hildy into thinking there is a fire in progress. Burns' own role is expanded, and added scenes have him giving Hildy counterfeit money and enlisting an accomplice to kidnap the mother of Hildy's fiancée. The cutting is rapid throughout and the camera is constantly in motion, not only in the introductory tracking shot of the desks and telephones of the pressroom, but also in the numerous pans that circle and enclose the action. As if in anticipation of the subsequent Howard Hawks version, this film foregrounds the relationship between Hildy and Walter, at the expense of Hildy's pursuit of his girlfriend, Peggy (Mary Brian). Indeed, there is more than a hint of misogyny in Burns' advice to reporters, "Tell her nothing; she's a woman"; and the reporters' cruel taunting of the prostitute, Molly (Mae Clarke), who loves Earl Williams. Inasmuch as the film was released before the tightening of the Hollywood Production Code, Milestone was able to retain the play's notorious final line. The film was nominated by the Academy as Best Picture of 1930–31, and Milestone headed the list of "Ten Best Directors of 1930–31."

Director Howard Hawks thought *The Front Page* had "the finest modern dialogue that had been written." His film version, retitled *His Girl Friday*, released in 1940, contains some of the most dazzlingly virtuosic, contrapuntal interplay of speakers and telephone conversations ever recorded on screen. Moreover, after hearing his secretary read aloud the part of reporter Hildy Johnson, Hawks discovered that the part could be effectively played by a woman. In addition to changing Hildy's gender, Hawks and scriptwriter Charles Lederer made considerable alterations in the material. They added a 20-minute sequence opening the film that tracks the camera through the newspaper offices, introducing Hildy (Rosalind Russell), Burns (Cary Grant), and her fiancé, Bruce Baldwin (Ralph Bellamy). Dialogue is added between Hildy and the escaped Earl Williams (John Qualen) concerning the use of an insanity plea to escape the gallows.

Of course, the presence of a female Hildy changes the dynamics of the plot. Whereas Hecht-MacArthur explored the newspaper world for its own sake, Hawks examines the impact of a woman on such a world. Now the original play's critique of unscrupulous journalistic tactics is replaced by an emphasis on a misbegotten love triangle, as a jealous Burns attempts to deep-six Hildy's choice of a lackluster rival suitor. Critic Robin Wood observes that not much of a choice is to be made between either Burns' "slick, cynical brilliance," or Baldwin's "life of unadventurous respectability." Hildy herself comes across as a force of nature, able to keep these two rascals at bay while saving a demented, innocent man from the gallows. For historian Gerald Mast, whose analysis of the film is definitive, this shift in plot dynamics is the film's finest attribute: "The film's psychological entanglement of Walter's and Hildy's personal and professional lives makes it, like *Twentieth Century* (1934), a very curious and complex romantic comedy in which love is expressed through work and work is expressed as love." As in the play and the Milestone film version, *His Girl Friday* concludes with the business of the watch and the final punchline.

The Billy Wilder-I. A. L. Diamond adaptation, released in 1974, follows the basic plot and observes the original time period of the play. Wilder had long been fascinated by the world of journalism, as evidenced in his earlier films, *The Big Carnival* (1951) and *Sunset Boulevard* (1950). And here he was able to return to the volatile, ragtime world of 1929, the time period of his *Some Like It Hot* (1959). He retains the play's double plot, which paralleled Burns' efforts to keep Hildy from getting married and with a prostitute's attempt to save her anarchist boyfriend from the gallows. But unlike *His Girl Friday*, as biographer Bernard Dick points out, "what is truly unusual about the film is the fact that, without altering the plot, Wilder transformed the play into a screwball comedy featuring not the battle of the sexes but an ongoing battle between two members of the same sex." At the same time, in the vulgarization of its dialogue and in the more cynical and sexually ambiguous characterization of its players, the tone seems more modern. For example, the first attempt by Walter Burns (Walter Matthau) to break up Hildy's (Jack Lemmon) romance consists of his impersonating one Otto Fishbein, Hildy's supposed probation officer. "Otto" tells Hildy's fiancée that he is on probation for flashing young girls. In another scene, Dr. Eggelhoffer, the Freudian psychologist who examines Earl (Austin Pendleton) and allows him to escape, provides a graphic phallic analysis of his subject. And in the film's postscript, the good doctor is described as having written something called *The Joys of Impotence*. This sort of coarse cynicism is further demonstrated at the end of the picture when the viewer is informed about subsequent events in the characters' lives—that when Hildy split up with his girlfriend, she married and named one of her children "Hildy"; and that the amoral Walter Burns teamed up with Hildy to give university lectures on the Ethics of Journalism.

Less directly related to the Hecht-MacArthur play is Ted Kotcheff's *Switching Channels*, released in 1988. Like *His Girl Friday*, the character of Hildy (here renamed Christy) suffers a gender change. Christy Colleran (Kathleen Turner) is the star anchorwoman for a cable news station owned by John L. Sullivan IV (Burt Reynolds), her former husband. She intends to quit her job and marry billionaire Blaine Bingham (Christopher Reeve), a sporting goods magnate. The Earl Williams character, Ike Roscoe (Henry Gibson), is charged with the death of a drug-dealing policeman responsible for his son's death. The crooked mayor of Chicago is now Roy Ridnitz (Ned Beatty), a law-and-order candidate who uses race riots as justification for hastening Ike's execution. Ike escapes from the electric chair as the result of a power outage, and Christy hides him in a photo-copying machine. At its best, the film's updating of the play into the world of electronic journalism is timely. The results, by turns, are funny—instead of reporters kicking their typewriters to get them to work, they kick the satellite dish to improve the signal—and grim—the reporters intend to bring their cameras into the death chamber, a controversial issue hotly debated (and unresolved) to this day. Not so successful, perhaps, are the scenes with Christy and the two men in her life. Actors Turner and Reynolds seem uncomfortable with the requisite rapid-fire delivery of their exchanged quips. Finally, there is a witty commentary on the profanity that first sparked controversy in the original Hecht-MacArthur play: When Ned Beatty's despicable district attorney launches into a storm of invectives, the camera moves in close to his mouth and the dialogue track goes silent. The viewer's imagination likely conjures up more imaginative and profoundly awful words than anything in the characters' vocabulary.

REFERENCES

Canby, Vincent, "Film: Turner in *Switching Channels*," *The New York Times*, March 4, 1988, C10; Dick, Bernard F., *Billy Wilder* (Boston: Twayne, 1980); Doherty, Thomas, *Pre-Code Hollywood* (New York: Columbia University Press, 1999); Mast, Gerald, *Howard Hawks: Storyteller* (New York: Oxford University Press, 1982); Parker, David L., and Burton J. Shapiro, "Lewis Milestone," in John Tuska, ed., *Close Up: The Contract Film Director* (Metuchen, N.J.: Scarecrow Press, 1976), 299–350.

—*J.C.T.*

GASLIGHT

See *ANGEL STREET*

GEORGE WASHINGTON SLEPT HERE (1940)

GEORGE S. KAUFMAN (1889–1961) AND MOSS HART (1904–1961)

George Washington Slept Here (1942), U.S.A., directed by William Keighley, adapted by Everett Freeman; Warner Bros.

The Play

The team of Kaufman and Hart was the most successful writing duo on the Broadway stage in the 1930s. The caustic Kaufman and the amiable Hart co-wrote nine plays, beginning with *Once in a Lifetime* in 1930 (the subject of Hart's memoir, *Act One*), a Hollywood spoof that was adapted to the screen in 1931; and including *Merrily We Roll Along* (1934), which told the story of a playwright in reverse chronology; *You Can't Take It With You* (1936), which won the 1936 Pulitzer Prize; *I'd Rather Be Right* (1937), which brought the semiretired George M. Cohan back to the stage as President Franklin D. Roosevelt; *The Man Who Came to Dinner* (1939), written for and about Alexander

Woollcott, and filmed in 1941 with Monte Woolley; and *George Washington Slept Here* (1940), brought to the screen a year later with Jack Benny and Ann Sheridan. Although they wrote no more plays together after 1941, they remained close friends. They died within a few months of each other in 1961.

George Washington Slept Here, the last of the Kaufman-Hart collaborations, was eagerly anticipated on Broadway. The three-act comedy premiered at the Lyceum Theatre on October 18, 1940, and ran for 173 performances. The objects of the satire were city folk who longed to live in the country and who subsequently found themselves in over their heads with Mother Nature and the local yokels. City-dweller Newton Fuller (Ernest Truex) buys a decrepit country home in which George Washington reputedly slept. Fuller's wife (Jean Dixon) is unimpressed, saying, "Martha wasn't a very good housekeeper." After they move in, a series of problems arise: The old well has long since run dry. Their daughter, Madge (Peggy French), begins going around with a married man, an actor in a local summer stock company. Relatives like Uncle Stanley (Dudley Digges) show up, flat broke and boring as ever. Worst of all, the Fullers learn that it was not George Washington who visited the place, but Benedict Arnold! In the end, when foreclosure threatens, it is an unlikely hero who comes to the rescue—Uncle Stanley. The critics found the play mild fare after the preceding Kaufman and Hart blockbuster hits. Malcolm Goldstein, Kaufman's biographer, carped, "The play proceeds with intermittent merriment, but without a display of true wit. The characterization is slight and the twists of plot improbable, excessive, and dull."

The Film

After scoring a success with *The Man Who Came to Dinner* early in 1942, Warner Bros. again assigned director William Keighley to helm a Kaufman and Hart comedy, *George Washington Slept Here*. What emerged was a cross between the later television sitcom, *Green Acres*, and the Tom Hanks theatrical film, *The Money Pit*. Headliner Benny Kubelsky, better known to radio listeners as "Jack Benny," had flirted with movie stardom since 1929, when he appeared in MGM's *Hollywood Revue of 1929*. Whereas he had hoped to fashion a career as a leading man in light comedies, producers persisted in casting him as—well, as Jack Benny. But in two pictures in the early 1940s, he almost broke the stranglehold of typecasting. In *Charley's Aunt* (1941) he appeared in feminine attire through most of the film; and in Ernst Lubitsch's comedy classic, *To Be or Not to Be* (1942), he played a Polish actor who joins the Resistance against invading Nazis. However, in *George Washington Slept Here* (1942), as the hapless houseowner, Bill Fuller, he seemed to slip back into type. As his biographer notes, "Lubitsch had proved that Jack was indeed an actor, and these two movies had tried to capitalize on this talent, but either through uncertainty or a desire to get easy laughs, the producers [of *George Washington Slept Here*] had him slipping back into the well-known airwaves image of Jack Benny." Scenarist Everett Freeman reversed the dynamics of the play. Instead of Newton Fuller buying an abandoned farmhouse in Bucks County, Pennsylvania, to the dismay of his wife, Annabelle, it is the wife (here named Connie, played by Ann Sheridan) who buys the house for her husband (here named Bill). Benny employed his matchless talent at double-takes as indignities piled up around him—including a collapsed floor, leaking roof, obnoxious nephew (Douglas Croft), and phony rich uncle (Charles Coburn). The neighbor who threatens to foreclose the mortgage was played by Charles Dingle. What saves the Fuller family is the miraculous unearthing of a valuable letter from George Washington, which enables them to raise the necessary money. Stealing the show was Percy Kilbride, who reprised his stage role as the taciturn caretaker, Mr. Kimber, who is always on hand to announce yet another deficiency in the house.

REFERENCES

Josefsberg, Milt, *The Jack Benny Show* (New Rochelle, N.Y.: Arlington House, 1977); Sennett, Ted, *Lunatics and Lovers* (New Rochelle, N.Y.: Arlington House, 1973).

—*J.C.T.*

GERTRUD (1907)

HJALMAR SODERBERG (1869–1941)

Gertrud (1964), Denmark, directed and adapted by Carl-Theodor Dreyer; Palladium Films.

The Play

Based on events in the life of the singer, Maria von Platen, *Gertrud* was written by Hjalmar Soderberg (1869–1941) in 1906. The first production took place on February 13, 1907, in Stockholm, with a rotating cast that included Betty Nansen and Gerda Lundequist as Gertrud, Poul Reumert and Axel Hanson as Jansson, and August Lindberg as Lidman. The story begins in the early 1900s. Gertrud, an operatic diva, is an avowed atheist and a staunch advocate of self-expression. Her intellectual questionings are encouraged by a friend, Axel Nygren, who tells Gertrud that she must go to Paris to find herself. Gertrud subsequently allows her career to be sidetracked by a love affair with Gabriel Lidman, a poet, and is stunned when she realizes Gabriel's dedication to poetry comes before his love for her. Despite Lidman's pleas for understanding, Gertrud leaves him. Shaken by the experience, Gertrud seeks refuge in a marriage to Gustav Kanning, a lawyer whose growing political ambitions soon leave little room for romance. When Gustav is about to be named to an important government post, Gertrud realizes that his passion for his career is ruining their marriage. Though Gustav insists that he still loves her, Gertrud leaves him and begins a tempestuous love affair with musician and composer Erland Jansson. But he betrays their love by bragging about the affair to his friends. It seems he is also involved with another woman, who had used her influence to help him in the early stages of his career. Now, this woman is pregnant with his child, and Jansson refuses to leave her. When he urges Gertrud to accept his complicated situation, she abandons him. Realizing that true love—at least as she imagines it—is not to be found in this world, she departs for Paris, determined to spend the rest of her life in study and contemplation.

The Film

In his early films—including *The Parson's Widow* (1921) and *The Passion of Joan of Arc* (1927)—Danish director Carl-Theodor Dreyer produced a series of challenging and compelling films that relied on intensely edited and photographed sequences in the manner of Sergei Eisenstein's *Strike* (1925) and *Potemkin* (1925). However, as Dreyer's career progressed into the sound era with films like *Day of Wrath* (1943), *Two People* (1944), *Ordet* (1954), and his final film, *Gertrud* (1964), Dreyer became much more interested in the mise-en-scène of the "long take" and the mobile camera. This change in style from reliance on montage to an almost religious faith in the camera's uninterrupted gaze reaches its zenith in *Gertrud*, which consists of a series of lengthy, dreamlike takes lasting many minutes each (somewhat akin to what Eisenstein himself embraced in his final works, *Ivan the Terrible*, Parts One and Two (1945–1946). "Camera movement has a fine soft rhythm," Dreyer once remarked; and *Gertrud*, which received a disastrous initial reception, is now seen as a forerunner of the work of Jean-Marie Straub, Rainer Werner Fasssbinder, Andy Warhol, Chantal Akerman, and others who rely on the "long take" to structure their films. Indeed, although *Gertrud* took three months to shoot, it was edited in just three days—a testament to the stark simplicity of his mise-en-scène conception.

To accentuate the theatricality of the film's source, Dreyer stages his scenes in such a way that his actors (Nina Pens Rode as Gertrud, Bendt Rothe as Gustav, Ebbe Rode as Gabriel, Baard Owe as Erland, and Axel Strobye as Axel) move and gesture as if in a dream on a bare stage. They seem to face an audience rather than each other, and they move with a slow, stylized deliberation. Beneath this formal, rather stiff presentation, the raw emotional undercurrents stand out in sharp relief. "What I have tried to do in *Gertrud* is to have the camera follow the actors," Dreyer said, "The idea has been to have the actors' faces in focus all the time so that the audience can read their thoughts."

Dreyer remained faithful to Soderberg's play, although he shortened the third act and added an epilogue set in Paris in 1942, in which Gertrud is visited by her friend Axel Nygren, who had first encouraged Gertrud's artistic ambitions. In this scene the two old friends discuss their lives and the different possible outcomes had their ambitions led them down alternate paths. At the end of the film, Gertrud seems resigned, even peaceful in her exile. As she leaves her home for Paris, the impassive camera moves from one empty room to the next, her husband's farewell words,

"Gertrud . . . Gertrud" sounding out in the empty stillness. Commentator Tom Milne describes the final effect: "As Gertrud lives her uninspired life with a dull husband, fends off an appeal from her former lover, and suffers her affair with the callow musician, the whole film echoes like a counterpoint for two voices— 'I love you' and 'Come with me'—which never quite coincide. Appeals ring out, never answered, crying their fears, their solitude, their need for love." Indeed, in the dreamy world of flashbacks and protracted camera movements that form the emotional and physical texture of Dreyer's *Gertrud*, we realize perhaps that only the knowledge of love as an unrealized possibility is all that one can ever hope for.

REFERENCES

Bordwell, David, *The Films of Carl-Theodor Dreyer* (Berkeley: University of California Press, 1981); Milne, Tom, *The Cinema of Carl Dreyer* (New York: A.S. Barnes, 1971); Rein, Sten, *Hjalmar Soderberg's Gertrud* (Stockholm: Bonniers, 1962).

—*W.W.D.*

THE GLASS MENAGERIE (1945)

TENNESSEE WILLIAMS (1911–1983)

The Glass Menagerie (1950), U.S.A., directed by Irving Rapper, adapted by Tennessee Williams and Peter Berneis; Warner Bros.

The Glass Menagerie (1987), U.S.A., directed by Paul Newman, adapted by Tennessee Williams; Cineplex.

The Play

In Tennessee Williams' first Broadway play, which premiered in New York at the Playhouse on March 31, 1945, Tom Wingfield (Eddie Dowling), an idealistic young man, seeks escape from his stifling home, where Amanda (Laurette Taylor), his faded, genteel mother, worries about the marriage prospects of her reclusive, crippled daughter Laura (Julie Haydon). Amanda cajoles Tom into bringing home Jim (Anthony Rosso), a fellow employee at the shoe factory where he works, in order to meet Laura. It is Amanda's desperate hope that Jim in due course will become Laura's "gentleman caller" and see her regularly.

But the evening is an unqualified disaster, since the extrovert Jim could never be seriously taken with the introvert Laura. After Jim beats a hasty retreat from the Wingfield flat, Amanda utters her heartbreaking line, "Things have a way of turning out so badly." The central image of the play is the one enshrined in its title. Laura collects glass ornaments to make her little room in the Wingfields' shabby apartment a private sanctuary from the unpleasant realities of life in a St. Louis slum. Williams describes Laura's glass menagerie as comprising "all the small and tender things that relieve the austere pattern of life and make it endurable" for a fragile, sensitive girl like Laura. *The Glass Menagerie* ran a year and a half on Broadway, 561 performances in all, and won the New York Critics Award for Williams. Its success placed Williams in the front rank of contemporary American dramatists.

The Film

Though Tennessee Williams is credited as coauthor of the screenplay of the 1950 film adaptation of his play, he actually contributed only a few scenes to the script; moreover, the screenplay was revised during shooting by producer Jerry Wald and other interested parties, including director Irving Rapper. The ill-advised alterations of the play when it was filmed were epitomized by the studio-imposed happy ending.

In addition, there was a misguided attempt to enlarge the scope of the movie by including a flashback that depicted Amanda (Gertrude Lawrence) as a youthful southern belle. It was inserted into the film primarily to allay Lawrence's misgivings about playing the role of a woman several years her senior. This flashback is based on Amanda's monologue in the play, in which she describes how she received 17 "gentlemen callers" in one day and had to quell their jealous quarrels over her. The sequence, which portrays Amanda dancing at an elegant cotillion, first with one young man and then another, caused Williams to comment that such a scene belonged in an epic of the Old South like *Gone with the Wind*, not in a small and intimate film like *The Glass Menagerie*.

The highpoint of the film, as in the play, comes about when Tom (Arthur Kennedy), at the behest of his mother, brings home to dinner Jim (Kirk Douglas), to meet Laura (Jane Wyman). For her part, Laura is completely captivated by Jim's slick and superficial charm; but that says more about her naiveté than it does about Jim's suitability as a suitor for her. Jim literally sweeps Laura off her feet by dancing with her to the music that intrudes into the Wingfield living room from the Paradise Dance Hall across the alley. Admittedly, Jim's attempt to bring into her life a little of the glamour of the outside world, which the Paradise represents, is a nice gesture on his part—but that is all that it is, a gesture. In reality, Jim is a smoothie who can

adroitly talk his way out of any situation—and he glibly talks his way out of the Wingfield apartment, when he realizes that Amanda has targeted him as a promising suitor for Laura.

Still, after Jim's hasty departure, Laura tells her mother, "I've had a lovely evening; I danced for the first time." Her observation is very likely intended to pave the way for the movie's happy ending. Laura expresses no such positive sentiments in the play, where it is evident that Jim has left Laura to retreat into her world of glass once more.

In the film, however, Richard, a new gentleman caller, comes down the alley toward Laura and Amanda on their fire escape "terrace." Laura introduces Richard to her mother and Tom's voice-over on the sound track refers to him as "the long delayed but always expected something we lived for." When Williams uses this expression in the play, he means just the opposite of what the line is made to mean here: Most of us have a cherished desire that we know in our more realistic moments will never be fulfilled, "a long delayed but always expected something" that never comes. Yet, like Amanda, we go on hoping against our better judgment because all of us need something to look forward to.

This happy ending in the movie, in which Laura finds her eligible bachelor, was conceived by the studio front office in deference to the Hollywood taboo of the period, which stated that downbeat endings were box-office poison. Williams told the present writer that the film's happy ending—which represents a complete reversal of the intent of the play—simply infuriated him: "The worst film ever made of any of my plays was that made of *The Glass Menagerie*—where a happy ending was provided by bringing in another, eligible Gentleman Caller for Laura. The play deserved better." Michael Barson sums up the film more benignly when he writes that Irving Rapper's film was "a respectable if uninventive transcription" of its literary source.

Tennessee Williams did not live to see the 1987 remake of *The Glass Menagerie* directed by Paul Newman (who earlier starred in two Williams films, *Cat on a Hot Tin Roof* and *Sweet Bird of Youth*). Williams would have been pleased that Newman adhered to the playscript as the basis for his screenplay. Joanne Woodward appeared as Amanda, John Malkovich as Tom, Karen Allen as Laura, and James Naughton as Jim. As a matter of fact, Woodward, Allen, and Naughton had appeared in two regional stage productions of the play prior to committing their performances to film.

Of course, Newman's film excludes the opulent flashback to Amanda's youth, which was so intrusive in the earlier movie; and there is no new Gentleman

Tennessee Williams

Caller named Richard waiting in the wings to replace Jim in Laura's life at the final fadeout this time around. In the last analysis, Newman's remake is a faithful, well-acted screen adaptation of Williams's masterwork.

REFERENCES

Barson, Michael, "Irving Rapper," in *Hollywood Directors of the Sound Era* (New York: Farrar, Straus, and Giroux, 1995),

348–349; Phillips, Gene, *The Films of Tennessee Williams* (Cranbury, N.J.: Associated University Presses, 1980).

—G.D.P.

GLENGARRY GLEN ROSS (1983)

DAVID MAMET (1947–   )

Glengarry Glen Ross (1992), U.S.A., directed by James Foley, adapted by David Mamet; New Line Cinema.

The Play

The play premiered on September 21, 1983, at the Cottesloe Theatre in the British National Theatre's South Bank Complex. The American premiere was at the Goodman Theatre of the Arts Institute of Chicago on February 6, 1984. Mamet dedicated the play to the British playwright Harold Pinter, no doubt because it attempts to translate Pinter's dexterity with dialogue into an American idiom. According to C. W. E. Bigsby, Mamet "worked for a year in what he called 'a fly-by-night operation' which sold tracts of undeveloped land in Arizona and Florida to gullible Chicagoans," confessing that "I sold worthless land to elderly people who couldn't afford it."

The action is set in two acts, the first in a Chinese restaurant where shady real estate agents gather to discuss business, the second in the real estate office where they work. Between Act One and Act Two the office is burglarized, and the prime "leads" the salesmen are competing for in Act One are stolen. All of the salesmen are angry and frustrated because of the pressure put on them by sales manager John Williamson. Only Ricky Roma, the top salesman at the moment, seems to be secure in his job. Because Dave Moss puts pressure on George Aaronow to steal the leads in Act One, the audience is led to believe Moss is responsible for the burglary, especially since former top salesman Shelley Levene has apparently closed a contract worth $80,000 during the intervening evening. Levene is therefore cheerful and upbeat in Act Two, having regained his self-confidence, but he overreaches himself after one of Roma's clients, James Lingk, comes to the office wanting to cancel the contract he had signed with Roma. Roma tells Lingk his check has not gone to the bank. Williamson, overhearing the conversation, assures him that it has. Roma, who was manipulating the client, is furious and berates Williamson after Lingk has left the office. Shelley, who dislikes the younger Williamson, amplifies Roma's abuse, saying "You're going to make something up, be sure it will *help* or keep your mouth closed." Williamson then asks Shelley how he knew Williamson had "made something up," since only the thief would know that Williamson lied about the check being taken to the bank. The play ends with Levene being taken to Detective Baylen for interrogation.

In Mamet's own words, the play is about "a society with only one bottom line: How much money you make. It concerns how business corrupts, how the hierarchical business system tends to corrupt. It becomes legitimate for those in power in the business world to act unethically. The effect on the little guy is that he turns to crime."

The Film

The film is more varied in its setting and opens up the play to a degree, following Levene (Jack Lemmon) as he visits one possible client, for example, and shifting the action of Act One between the Chinese restaurant and the office, where a new character named Blake (Alec Baldwin) is introduced, a man sent from "Mitch and Murry downtown" to intimidate the salesmen and give them a pep talk, which is quite the opposite, since Blake is so crude, brutal, and ruthless. In fact, he breaks down their self-esteem, telling them that they either have to produce or they will be fired. The character appears out of nowhere as an impersonal agent of business and commerce. His appearance certainly manages to clarify the film's message about inhuman business practices.

The film isolates Levene and sets him apart from the others, disturbing (or at least changing) the balance of the play. Levene and Roma (Al Pacino) dominate the film, perhaps because two star actors were cast in these roles. The film adds more detail to make Levene sympathetic. In the film he has a very ill daughter in the hospital, which adds to his desperation because he needs to pay her medical expenses. This emphasis helps to establish motivation, but the newly imagined Levene becomes merely pathetic and seems out of place in Mamet's black "comedy." Certainly there is a better balance among the characters of the play, which paired Aaranow (Alan Arkin) with Moss (Ed Harris) and Roma with Lingk (Jonathan Pryce), than with Levene. Since the film gives more weight to Levene by giving him a backstory and a motive he lacked in the play, the balance of the play's ensemble is disturbed. The very nature of the play is changed, edging it toward the melodramatic, if not the tragic, and away

from the bitter satire of the original. Mamet's play was concerned with heartless capitalism and greed during the Reagan era, whereas Mamet's film, made 10 years later, transforms the play into a sort of personal tragedy of a salesman close to retirement, struggling to hold his own and maintain his dignity in the workforce. Although intelligently designed and competently directed, the film never entirely escapes its theatrical origins, for there is hardly any opportunity in the play to make the action cinematic. The adaptation is distinguished by a gifted cast, however, that makes the film an unforgettable experience.

REFERENCES

Bigsby, C.W.E., *David Mamet* (New York: Methuen, 1985); Kane, Leslie, *David Mamet: A Casebook* (New York: Garland, 1992); Lahr, John, "Fortress Mamet," *The New Yorker* (November 17, 1997), 70–82; Ryan, James, "Playing Mamet's Music," *The Boston Sunday Globe*, September 27, 1992, B34–35.

—*J.M.W.*

GOLDEN BOY (1937)

CLIFFORD ODETS (1906–1963)

Golden Boy (1939), U.S.A., directed by Rouben Mamoulian, adapted by Lewis Meltzer/Daniel Taradash, Sarah Y. Mason; Columbia.

The Play

Clifford Odets, who got his start in the famous Group Theatre of Lee Strasberg and Harold Clurman, was the foremost playwright of left-wing social protest in the 1930s. He is best known for his 1930s dramas, *Waiting for Lefty* (1935), about a taxi drivers' union strike, *Awake and Sing!* (1935), about a poor, troubled Jewish family, and *Golden Boy*, about an Italian-American boy who abandons his talents in music for a career in prizefighting. The three-act *Golden Boy* premiered in New York at the Belasco Theatre on November 4, 1937, where it ran for a successful 250 performances. Purportedly, Odets wrote it to reunite members of the Group Theatre, who had recently dispersed to Hollywood.

The setting is New York City, 1937. Despite his talents as a classical violinist, and despite his father's urgings that he pursue a music career, Joe Bonaparte (Luther Adler) knows that the best way out of the slums is with his fists. He begins his professional boxing career by stepping in at the last minute to replace an injured boxer. He wins the bout. His father, who has just bought him an expensive violin for his 21st birthday, sadly puts the instrument away. "I want to do what I want," declares Joe. "I proved it tonight I'm good—I went out to earn some money and I earned!" After some indecision, due to his reluctance to injure his hands, Joe determines to continue to pursue boxing. He does regret leaving music, but he reasons, "You can't get even with people by playing the fiddle. If music shot bullets I'd like it better. Artists and people like that are freaks today." More professional victories behind him—during which Joe breaks his hand, and shouts, "Hallelujah! It's the beginning of the world!"—Joe becomes coarse and arrogant, the friend of gangsters and the object of scorn from his girlfriend, Lorna (Frances Farmer). When he kills a man in the ring, Joe is stunned: "I murdered myself, too! I've been running around in circles. Now I'm smashed!" Lorna returns and comforts him, urging him to give up fighting and return to music: "We'll find some city where poverty's no shame—where music is no crime!—where there's no war in the streets—where a man is glad to be himself, to live and make his woman herself!" In the final scene, Joe's brother, a union organizer, receives a telephone call announcing that Joe and Lorna have been killed in an auto accident. "What a waste," moans the brother.

Golden Boy is Odets's most popular play. Joe's sacrifice of art and sensitivity for the brutal game of material success has been interpreted both as an indictment of the seductiveness of crass American commercialism and as a contemporary allegory in the *Faust* mold. Its "pungent, flashy story" was marred, complained critic Brooks Atkinson in the *New York Times*, by "an unwillingness to be simple in style."

The Film

A graduate of the Second Studio at the Moscow Art Theatre, Rouben Mamoulian went to America to organize and help direct the American Opera Company in Rochester, New York. Moving on to the Theatre Guild in New York City, he directed Dubose Heyward's *Porgy* in 1927. He made the transition from the stage to talking pictures seemingly effortlessly, and his *Applause* (1929) and *Dr. Jekyll and Mr. Hyde* (1931) and *Love Me Tonight* (1933) were all critical and popular successes. With the musicals *The Gay Desperado* (1936) and *High, Wide and Handsome* (1937) recently behind him, Mamoulian turned to Odets to adapt *Golden Boy* to the screen. He had directed Odets as an actor in the old days at the Theatre Guild in 1929 for a production of Karel Kapek's *R.U.R.*, but conflicts

Clifford Odets

between the two resulted in Odets's angry refusal of the assignment to adapt *Golden Boy* ("You tell [him] that he is the only director I loathe and won't work with"). Nonplussed, Mamoulian found two fledgling writers, Daniel Taradash and Lewis Meltzer to strip the play down to a workable script. Newcomer William Holden was cast as Joe, Barbara Stanwyck as Lorna, Lee J. Cobb as Mr. Bonaparte (reprising his role in the West Coast stage production), Adolphe Menjou as Joe's fight manager, and Joseph Calleia as the gangster who tries to buy "a piece" of Joe. Gone was the character of the labor organizer, Frank, and with him most of the philosophizing over the struggle between Capital and Labor that lay behind Joe's choice of careers. Instead, as commentator Tom Milne notes, the film makes Joe's decision "largely a moral and personal one, with its real climax the murderous championship fight rather than Joe's *crise de conscience*."

Also gone were many of Odets's sententious lines, like Lorna's declamation, "We'll find some city where poverty's no shame. . . ." Stanwyck's Lorna is not the sloppy, tarnished girl of the original play, but a tough dame who melts into the arms of her golden boy, and who says to the disappointed boxer at the end, "Be glad . . . you're free. . . . Now you can go back to yourself, to your music. . . . Nothing can stop you when you do what's in your heart." Meanwhile, the film's mise-en-scène dutifully depicts the Bonaparte home down to what Milne calls its "every monstrous detail," floral wallpaper, fringed lampshades and antimacassars, and a perfect fury of Victorian bric-a-brac. The New York street scene is just as vivid—flickering neon signs illuminating a conversation between Joe and his father in their backyard, a love scene between Joe and Lorna atop a skyscraper, and moments between the two lovers while gazing at the Brooklyn Bridge in the moonlight. The climactic boxing match is a tough, unsparing slugfest, effectively photographed by veterans Nicholas Musuraca and Karl Freund. The ending, predictably, is a happy one, with Joe and Lorna reunited.

Despite critical cavils about the film's exploitation of the already shopworn boxing milieu, Odets defended the film in the *New York Times*. He called the motion picture medium "the folk theatre of America," which had "great talent for picking important American types and interesting and vital themes."

REFERENCES

Milne, Tom, *Rouben Mamoulian* (Bloomington: Indiana University Press, 1969); Weales, Gerald, *Clifford Odets: Playwright* (New York: Pegasus Books, 1971).

—*J.C.T.*

THE GREAT WHITE HOPE (1967)

HOWARD SACKLER (1929–1982)

The Great White Hope (1970), U.S.A., directed by Martin Ritt, adapted by Howard Sackler; Twentieth Century-Fox.

The Play

This blank-verse version of the career of boxer Jack Johnson premiered in Washington at the Arena Stage on December 12, 1967, and later opened in New York at the Alvin Theatre on October 30, 1968, where it ran for an impressive 556 performances. It won the Pulitzer Prize, the Antoinette Perry Award, and the New York Drama Critics' Circle Award for the 1968–69 Broadway season. James Earl Jones won a Tony Award for best dramatic actor, and Jane Alexander was named best supporting actress.

Jack Johnson fought 113 recorded fights, the first in 1897 when he was 19, the last in 1945, a year before his death from a car crash, when he was 67. He won the world championship in Sydney, Australia, on December 16, 1908, by beating defender Tommy Burns so badly that the fight was called in the 14th round. The victory set off national race riots. Johnson assumed a flamboyant, highly visible celebrity; beyond his race, his notoriety was enhanced by his taste for fast cars, flashy clothes, and beautiful women. Those who were offended by the reality of a black boxing champion searched for a "white hope"—like Jim Jeffries or Jess Willard—to defeat him. In 1913 Johnson was forced to flee the country after being convicted of violating the Mann Act. He lived openly with a white mistress in Europe for the next seven years. At last he returned to America and served a 10-month prison sentence in the Leavenworth federal penitentiary.

In his autobiography, *Jack Johnson–In the Ring–and Out* (1927), Johnson wrote, "My life, almost from the very start, has been filled with tragedy and romance, failure and success, poverty and wealth, misery and happiness. All these conflicting conditions that have crowded in upon me and plunged me into struggles with warring forces have made me somewhat of a unique character in the world today."

For legal reasons playwright Howard Sackler named his boxer Jack Jefferson. He gave him a black mistress, Clara (who represented several African-American women in his life) and a white mistress, Eleanor (also representative of several white mistresses). The play is set just before and during World War I, when Jefferson has become heavyweight champion of the world. Already the target of angry racists, Jefferson's arrogance and flamboyance, not to mention his flaunting of a white girlfriend, Ellie (Jane Alexander), bring about his downfall. To the joy of his enemies, Jack is toppled by a white fighter, but not before he pounds his opponent to a pulp. Ellie commits suicide. Jefferson remains unapologetic about either his race or his ambition: "Man, Ah ain't runnin' for Congress! Ah ain't fightin' for no race, ain't redeemin' nobody! My momma tole me Mr. Lincoln done that—ain't that why you shot him?!" Thirty-seven-year-old actor James Earl Jones, son of a boxer-actor, relates in his autobiography that he was living in France in 1967 when he first read the play. "I knew immediately that this was a role I had to play," he recalled. "Here was explosive drama, and poetry, and complex tragedy. Beautifully drawn on the page was a role of a lifetime." After months of grueling physical training and hours spent watching documentary films of Johnson's fights, Jones stepped onstage to perform what would become his signature role. "The acting is dominated by James Earl Jones, who is magnificent as Jefferson," wrote Clive Barnes in the *New York Times*. "With head shaved, burly, huge, Mr. Jones stalks through the play like a black avenging angel. Even when corrupted by misery, his presence has an almost moral force to it, and his voice rasps out an agony nearly too personally painful in its nakedness."

Now forgotten, by the way, is the fact that Jack Johnson himself appeared in several films in the 1920s. He plays a fugitive-turned-prize-fighter in *For His Mother's Sake* (1922) and himself in *As the World Rolls On* (1921). The former film was banned in the state of Ohio because of Johnson's conviction on a "white slavery" charge. Johnson died in 1946 from injuries resulting from a car crash.

The Film

When playwright Sackler adapted his play to the screen, he simply expanded its episodic outline into a series of more richly developed scenes. Actors James Earl Jones and Jane Alexander were retained to reprise their stage roles. As a black boxing champion with a white mistress, Jack is a threat to racist America. But he is also hated by the "Uncle Toms" of the black community. After he and Ellie cross the state line, a federal agent uses the Mann Act as an excuse to arrest him. After being fined and sentenced to three years in prison, he escapes and flees to England and France. Unable to legally fight there, he is reduced to playing the eponymous character in stage productions of *Uncle Tom's Cabin*. He refuses to accept a reduced prison sentence in exchange for returning to America, and he retires to Mexico, where he and Ellie sink into de-gradation. When he rejects her, she drowns herself. Finally, in Havana, he agrees to take a fall in a fight with a new "white hope." He takes a beating before he decides to fight, after all. But, ultimately, he is knocked out.

The failure of this decidedly downbeat film at the box office can be attributed, claims historian Daniel J. Leab, to the fact that black audiences of the day preferred the upbeat tone and heroism of contemporary films like *Shaft* and *Sweet Sweetback's Baadasssss Song*. In his autobiography, James Earl Jones offers a different opinion: "The screenplay eliminated every poetic aspect that the stage play had conjured, so that the stage characters who were mythic, gothic, larger

Jane Alexander costarred with James Earl Jones in Martin Ritt's screen adaptation of The Great White Hope. (COURTESY MARTHA SWOPE PHOTOGRAPHY)

than life, were reduced in the film to mere social entities. The black mistress became little more than a shrew; the conjure man became just another street protestor; that giant oak on stage, Captain Dan, the head of the clique of white American boxing officials, became another dirty trickster." The film emerged a mere "crime scenario," concluded Jones, "about criminal behavior instead of the depth of human behavior."

REFERENCES

Jackson, Carlton, *Picking up the Tab: The Life and Movies of Martin Ritt* (Bowling Green, Ohio: Bowling Green University Popular Press, 1994); Jones, James Earl, *Voices and Silences* (New York: Charles Scribner's Sons, 1993); Roberts, Randy, *Papa Jack: Jack Johnson and the Era of White Hopes* (New York: Free Press, 1983); Sampson, Henry T., *Blacks in Black and White: A Source Book on Black Films* (Metuchen, N.J.: Scarecrow Press, 1977).

—*J.C.T.*

HARRIET CRAIG

See *CRAIG'S WIFE*

HEDDA

See *HEDDA GABLER*

HEDDA GABLER (1890)

HENRIK [JOHAN] IBSEN (1828–1906)

Hedda Gabler (1917), U.S.A., directed by Frank Powell.

Hedda Gabler (1919), Italy, directed by Piero Rosco (Giovanni Pastrone); Itala Films.

Hedda Gabler (1924), Germany, directed by Franz Eckstein, adapted by Rosa Porten and Franz Eckstein; National-Film AG.

Hedda Gabler (1963), U.S.A., directed by Alex Segal, adapted by Philip H. Reisman, Jr.

Hedda (1975), U.K., directed and adapted by Trevor Nunn; Bowden/Brut.

The Play

Hedda Gabler was published in 1890 before it was first produced in 1891. Set in the late 19th century at a villa in west Oslo, the four-act play is primarily a dramatic character sketch of a selfish, complex, potentially neurotic, and dangerous woman, married to a scholar, Jürgen (George) Tesman, who is in line for a university fellowship in cultural history. Hedda, considered an emerging "new woman," retains her maiden name in the title because of her close attachment to her aristocratic father, General Gabler, and the military traditions of her family. She has no interest at all in the scholarship that dominates the life and thought of her husband. Trapped in a marriage of convenience, Hedda is destructive and "demonic," to use Ibsen's description.

Having just returned from her honeymoon, Hedda shows contempt for both her husband, whom she considers (with reason) an unimaginative, pedantic bore, and his kindly maiden aunt, Juliane Tesman. Family friend Judge Brack, a cynic not to be trusted and who is keenly interested in Hedda, informs Tesman that he will have to compete for the university fellowship that Tesman thought would be automatically given to him. His competitor is Ejlert Lövborg, an unstable young man who has just completed a brilliant book manuscript with the help and encouragement of Mrs. Thea Elvsted, who left her husband to devote herself to Lövborg and his work. Brack, who manages Tesman's financial affairs and made the arrangements for the villa in which Hedda now lives, warns Tesman that he will have to economize.

Judge Brack invites both Lövborg and Tesman to a stag party, where Lövborg reverts to his old irresponsible habits, gets drunk, and loses his manuscript. The envious Tesman, who has seen the work and regards it as "one of the most remarkable books ever written," finds this "precious, irreplaceable manuscript" in the gutter and brings it home rather than giving it to the addled Lövborg, who then goes on to a soirée at the salon of Mademoiselle Diana, whom he later accuses of stealing the manuscript. Lövborg creates such a row that he is taken to the police station. Lövborg has thoroughly disgraced himself: "From now on every decent house will be closed to Ejlert Lövborg," Judge Brack speculates.

The next day, Lövborg pays Hedda a visit and tells Mrs. Elvsted in her presence that he has ripped up his manuscript and torn it to shreds and that "it's all over between us now." Horrified, Mrs. Elvsted says, and Lövborg agrees, "It was like killing a child." As the desperate and suicidal Lövborg leaves, Hedda gives him one of her father's pistols and tells him to "use it well." Wanting him to die a "beautiful" death, Hedda fantasizes the creative Lövberg into some kind of Dionysian ideal, but she herself is not creative, merely destructive. After he leaves, Hedda takes the manuscript from her husband's desk drawer, goes to the stove, and burns it up, page by page, whispering to herself, wickedly, "I'm burning your child."

In Act Four Tesman intends to return the manuscript to Lövborg, but Hedda admits that she "burnt it up," adding that she did it for her husband's sake in order to improve his chances for the fellowship. Tesman is astonished, but stupidly grateful. Judge Brack then arrives to say that Lövborg has shot himself and is in hospital, mortally wounded. Mrs. Elvsted is beside herself with grief and concern, but she tells Tesman that she still has the notes Lövborg dictated to her. Excitedly, Tesman then expresses an interest in working with her to reconstruct the text, and the two of them begin to examine the notes.

Meanwhile, Judge Brack advises Hedda, who wants to believe that Lövborg died nobly, that the pistol discharged accidentally in Lövborg's breast pocket, wounding him fatally in the abdomen. Brack also knows that Lövborg was shot with Hedda's pistol but insinuates that Hedda may avoid an "unpleasant scandal," so long as he maintains his silence. Realizing that she is now in Brack's power and what the price of his silence may involve, the independent-minded Hedda takes the other pistol from its case, withdraws to an inner room, and shoots herself in the temple. Astonished by her suicide at the end, Judge Brack exclaims, "People don't *do* such things!"

The Films

There were three silent-cinema adaptations of the play. Nance O'Neil played Hedda for the 1917 American adaptation directed by Frank Powell, which also featured Aubrey Beattie as George Tesman, Einar Linden as Lövberg [sic], and Alfred Hickman as Judge Brack. Powell opened up the play to include scenes at the salon, as is indicated by his casting Edith Campbell Walker as "Miss Diana." Asta Nielsen played Hedda in the 1924 German adaptation directed by Franz Eckstein, which also included Diana (Olga Limburg). Paul Morgan was cast as Tesman, Grigori Chmara as Lövborg, and Albert Steinruck as Brack. In 1963 Alex Segal directed a made-for-television adaptation that boasted a remarkable cast: Ingrid Bergman as Hedda, Trevor Howard as Lövborg, Michael Redgrave as Tesman, and Ralph Richardson as Judge Brack. Twelve years would pass before the next film adaptation, a stage-to-film transfer of a Royal Shakespeare Company production, offering an offbeat but nonetheless distinctive Hedda.

Trevor Nunn's *Hedda* (1975) was derived from his Royal Shakespeare Company production staged at the Aldwych Theatre in London. Glenda Jackson played Hedda as a shallow, cowardly woman, trapped in "a society held together by kinship and class," as David Nathan described her, having no claims "to intellectual or moral superiority." Jackson did not consider Hedda "a calculating, ruthless woman," but merely a "rather stupid" one: "She has no courage and she's none of the things that she has been told she is. She's always bewailing being stuck in that awful little town, but her husband had taken her all over Europe and she hadn't set Paris on fire and nobody had told her that she was the most remarkable woman they had ever met." Jackson saw all the characters as second-rate, "with pretentions [sic] to being first-rate."

Hedda's only admirable trait for Jackson was her realization that "there is no way out for her. She could not become any of the things that were expected of her and she chooses not to conform. It's the only element of choice she has." Peter Hall thought Jackson's Hedda was "rather wrong-headed." For Hall, the character "should initially be vital, full of joy. Glenda's Hedda was glum from the word go, bent on a course of self-destruction." Jackson took satisfaction in playing "a character that everybody thinks they know and you don't conform to their expectations."

For Neil Sinyard the highlight of the film was Hedda's scene with Mrs. Elvsted (Jennie Linden), "who has risked her reputation," as Hedda has not. "Hedda is both envious and contemptuous, wanting not to serve and sacrifice like her friend, but to be and to do." Sinyard found the film more competent than inspired, "but it faithfully treasures Miss Jackson's fine performance," he concluded. John Simon, on the other hand, sneered at Trevor Nunn's "mere transfer, not adaptation" of his stage production, especially Peter Eyre's "excessively absurd and sniveling Tesman" and Patrick Stewart's "brash and boring Lövborg." Though Simon approved of Timothy West's "persuasive Judge Brack," he objected to Glenda Jackson's "vastly infelicitous Hedda," whose "amusing bitchiness" had "nothing to do with what Ibsen wrote."

Nunn's direction was not especially cinematic, Simon opined, but even a sparse "transposition to the screen that in no way 'opens up' and pads or dissipates the work is bound to be disastrous." The "basic problem" for Simon was "that a great stage work belongs to the stage alone. Its space, time, and dialogue are inextricably wedded to the dimensions and expectations of the playhouse, and any kind of tampering can only upset the delicate balances involved." This may be the assessment of an insufferable theatre snob, but is essentially on target.

REFERENCES

Gassner, John, and Edward Quinn, eds., *The Reader's Encyclopedia of World Drama* (New York: Thomas Y. Crowell, 1969); Hansen, Karin Synnove, *Henrik Ibsen, 1828–1978: A Filmography* (Oslo: Norsk Filminstitutt, 1978); Matlaw, Myron, *Modern World Drama* (New York: E.P. Dutton, 1972); Nathan, David, *Glenda Jackson* (Tunbridge Wells, Kent: Spellmount Ltd., 1984); Simon, John, *Something to Declare* (New York: Clarkson N. Potter, 1983); Sinyard, Neil, *Filming Literature: The Art of Screen Adaptation* (London: Croom Helm, 1986).

—*J.M.W.*

HE WHO GETS SLAPPED (1915)

LEONID ANDREEV (1871–1919)

He Who Gets Slapped (1924), U.S.A., directed by Victor Seastrom, adapted by Seastrom and Carey Wilson; MGM.

The Play

Virtually forgotten today, Russian playwright Leonid Andreev was once famed for his plays combining natu- ralistic and symbolistic modes. Trained as a lawyer, he gave up the profession and turned to writing at the turn of the century. With *The Life of Man* (1906) and *Anathema* (1909) he established his reputation as a playwright. *He Who Gets Slapped* remains his best-known play. Unlike Gorky, who supported the October Revolution of 1917, Andreev fled the Soviets and went to Finland, where he died two years later. *He Who Gets Slapped* was first produced in 1915. Like most of his works, it reflects Andreev's gloomy, morbid outlook on life (he attempted suicide three times.)

The setting is the anteroom of a circus in a large French city early in the 20th century. In the first act circus performers are rehearsing in the adjoining hall as the lustful Count Mancini tries to extort money from the circus manager, "Papa" Louis Briquet. If he is refused, Mancini threatens to take away Briquet's daughter, Consuelo, "The Equestrian Tango Queen." Meanwhile, a stranger appears and begs to join the circus. He says he doesn't know his name, and he admits he has no talent. But when he sees Consuelo, he decides on the spot that he will henceforth be known as "He Who Gets Slapped"—"Slap me, I want to play my part. Perhaps it will awaken love in my heart, too." In the second act, He learns that Consuelo may marry a wicked suitor, a baron. Posing as a palm reader, He mesmerizes Consuelo and warns her that such a marriage will kill her and that she really loves another suitor, the dashing equestrian rider. Later, a visitor appears to He, and it is revealed that the visitor was a former friend who betrayed He by appropriating his philosophical theories for his own and subsequently eloping with He's wife.

In Act Three He accuses his traitorous friend of stealing his love and his life: "With the art of a great vulgarizer, a tailor of ideas, you dressed my Apollo in a barber's jacket, turned my Venus into a whore, pinned ass ears on my bright hero—and your career is made." In the last act it is announced that Consuelo is to marry the baron. Refusing to listen to He's warnings, she does agree to have a farewell drink with him. But He has poisoned it, and as she breathes her last, He consoles her, saying she is not dying, but will find eternal life. Disappointed and maddened by this turn of events, the groom, the baron, shoots himself. As he lies dying, He, who is also on the verge of death after finishing Consuelo's drink, tells him that they will be fighting over Consuelo in the next life: "We shall fight it out there, whose she is to be—forever. . . . " He falls dead.

The Film

Victor Seastrom and his friend Mauritz Stiller were regarded as Sweden's finest film directors when

Seastrom came to Hollywood in 1923 (actually, he had spent his youth in America, in Brooklyn). Having finished *The Phantom Chariot* that year, he accepted an offer by Louis B. Mayer to come to America precisely at the time that the Goldwyn Pictures Corporation was merging with the Mayer and Metro companies to form the conglomerate of Metro-Goldwyn-Mayer. Seastrom stayed on for six years, directing nine films, the most famous of which were *The Scarlet Letter* (1926), an adaptation of Nathaniel Hawthorne's novel; *The Wind* (1928), a fable of love and murder in the Mojave Desert; and *He Who Gets Slapped* (1924), a vehicle for MGM's new star, Lon Chaney, who had the year before scored a tremendous success with *The Hunchback of Notre Dame*. *He Who Gets Slapped* was MGM's first released feature film, and it stands out as one of the most remarkable commercial features of the twenties. Seastrom wrote the adaptation in Swedish, and Carey Wilson gave it a final polish in English. Thanks largely to Seastrom's bent for fatalistic themes and Chaney's psychologically insightful performance, with its distinctly sadomasochistic implications, the film occupies a unique position among the masterpieces of the silent cinema.

Taking its cue from the Andreev play, naturalism and expressionism exist side by side. On the one hand, it is a gritty drama of sawdust and tinsel, with a restrained performance by Chaney and superbly realized circus sets by designer Cedric Gibbons. On the other, there are sequences—particularly He's performances—that suggest He's deranged subjective vision of the world (a subtle image distortion is imparted by cinematographer Milton Moore's clever use of extreme "long" lenses). Moreover, through the use of parallel editing, the circus audience is linked in He's mind to the "audience" of scientists that years before had come to jeer his downfall in the science lecture room. A visual metaphor is employed throughout—a spinning globe of the world that dissolves into a circus ring—to imply the inexorable turning of fate. A prologue has been added, suggested by the reported dialogue of the original play, which details the circumstances of He's betrayal at the hands of Baron Regnard, a rival scientist who plagiarizes his life's work, "The Origins of Mankind," and presents it as his own before a conference of esteemed scientists. The victimized scientist challenges his tormentor and is slapped down to the derision of the crowd. And when he learns that his wife is leaving him for Regnard, he suffers a second slap from her. Clearly insane, he decides to lose himself in a sadomasochistic circus act in which He is slapped continuously by a group of clowns. His only link with his former humanity and sanity is the love He feels for the beautiful Consuelo (Norma Shearer), a bareback rider. But even she turns away from him since she is in love with Bezano (John Gilbert), her riding partner. In a radical departure from the play's conclusion, He, upon learning that Consuelo's father, the wicked Count Mancini (Tully Marshall), plans to marry her off to Regnard, releases a lion, which kills both men. But He incurs fatal injuries to himself, and the wounded clown staggers around the circus ring, to the gales of audience laughter. He dies in the arms of the now contrite Consuelo.

The most memorable aspects of the film lie in the fantasy scenes and in the depictions of He's circus act. The film opens with a close-up of a revolving globe of the world. The camera pulls back to reveal that a grotesque clown in white is spinning the globe on the tips of his fingers. The globe then dissolves into a circus ring. This image of the clown and the globe recurs several times throughout the picture. In one variation on this motif, we see a group of tiny clowns lowering themselves by ropes onto the rim of the globe. As they sway back and forth, the image dissolves into several clowns seated around the ring.

He's act is overtly surreal, a nightmare in white. His entrance into the ring is heralded by a phalanx of clowns, grotesquely swaying back and forth as they walk. When He appears, they ask him a series of questions; but no matter how He responds, they strike him hard across his face. The slaps get rougher and more frequent, until finally the clowns pass by him, each slapping him in turn. The audience members laugh hysterically. He gazes out at them, and in his mind's eye, their hideously grinning faces transform into the faces of the scientists who had derided him years before, each of whom now in his imagination wears a silly clown hat. Later, as He lies motionless in the sawdust, one of the clowns (Ford Sterling) reaches down and tears away the cloth heart that has been stitched to his costume and grinds it into the sawdust. Then the clowns procure a stretcher and attempt to carry him away in a mock funeral procession. However, the stretcher breaks and He is left alone in the sawdust. By this time, the onlookers are in hysterics of laughter. At the end, He is alone in the center of the ring, with only a small spotlight picking out his white, bruised face, accentuating his loneliness and pain. These moments, disturbing and pathetic and brutal, by turns, are still painful to watch, even by the standards of today's more callous taste.

Seastrom was pleased with the results. "It was like making a picture back home in Sweden," he said. "I wrote the script without any interference, and the actual shooting went quickly and without any complications." The MGM producers were impressed that he brought it in for the unusually low budget of $140,000. The picture was released on November 3, 1924, at the Capitol Theatre in New York. It was a box-office success and set a one-day world's record business with $15,000, a one-week's record with $71,900, and a two-week record with $121,574. Critics of the time applauded. *Photoplay* magazine praised Chaney's work as the best of his career, and Seastrom's directorial work as placing him in the front rank of directors. "Andreyev's [sic] play was elusive behind the footlights," opined the critic. "Enmeshed in celluloid by Seastrom, it gains immeasurably in clarity. The director has taken liberties with the original story, but they seem to us logical and in the spirit of the Russian dramatist's original theme."

REFERENCES

Pensel, Hans, *Seastrom and Stiller in Hollywood* (New York: Vantage Press, 1969); "He Who Gets Slapped," reprinted in Anthony Slide, ed., *Selected Film Criticism, 1921–1930* (Metuchen, N.J.: Scarecrow Press, 1982).

—*J.C.T.*

HIS GIRL FRIDAY

See *FRONT PAGE, THE*

HOLIDAY (1928)

PHILIP BARRY (1896–1949)

Holiday (1930), U.S.A., directed by Edward H. Griffith, adapted by Horace Jackson; Pathé.

Holiday (1938), U.S.A., directed by George Cukor, adapted by Donald Ogden Stewart and Sidney Buchman; Columbia.

The Play

Philip Barry wrote successful plays in a wide variety of styles and genres: murder mysteries, stark human dramas, allegories, and even a tragedy about John the Baptist. But he was best known for his sparkling comedies like *Holiday* (1928), *The Human Animal* (1932) and *The Philadelphia Story* (1939). However, even these comedies were usually supported by serious underpinnings. He was particularly fascinated by the dilemmas of wealth versus freedom, comfort versus nonconformity.

The play premiered in New York at the Plymouth Theatre on November 26, 1928, and ran for a successful 230 performances.

Holiday is the story of a man who prefers freedom to privilege and his encounters with a family condemned by their wealth to a life of smug dullness. As the play begins, Johnny Case is visiting the home of Julia Seton, the woman he has met and fallen in love with on vacation. He is stunned to find that she is a member of a rich and powerful family. At the palatial Seaton home he meets Julia's older sister Linda and alcoholic brother Ned. These two have rebelled against the confinement brought on by riches and family obligation, but Julia revels in her pampered life. Johnny is a successful businessman himself, having worked since childhood to escape a deprived and unhappy childhood. Now, on the verge of a minor stock market killing, he wants to retire while he's still young, to enjoy his freedom while he can. Julia and her stuffy father are appalled at the notion, but Linda, who is falling in love with Johnny, sees him as a kindred spirit and supports him wholeheartedly. The conflict nearly fractures the family as Johnny discovers that he has been in love with the wrong sister. He leaves to sail around the world, and Linda, once she gets Julia to admit that she is relieved to get this rebel out her life, leaps into a taxi to follow him.

The Broadway cast of *Holiday* included Hope Williams as Linda, Barbara White as Julia, Ben Smith as Johnny, and writer Donald Ogden Stewart as Ned. Hope Williams' understudy was a young actress named Katharine Hepburn.

The Films

When Pathé announced that it would film *Holiday* in 1930, Hepburn auditioned for the role of Linda. She had not yet appeared in a film and, since Pathé preferred a star in the role, Ann Harding was cast. Significantly, when Hepburn auditioned for director George Cukor's *A Bill of Divorcement* (1932), her film debut, she did so with a scene from *Holiday*.

Pathé's film was directed by Edward H. Griffith. Barry's play was adapted almost word for word, with only a few minor scenes deleted and nothing added. Many early talkies—especially those based upon theatrical works—were hampered by a certain stagebound quality, but *Holiday* was brought to the screen with a lively informality that perfectly translates Barry's witty play from one medium to another. Although the 1938 version directed by George Cukor is usually considered the classic, Griffith's film is nearly as good and the casting is sometimes better. In the Cukor film there is never any question in the viewer's mind that Cary Grant and Katharine Hepburn will end up together; their star power makes any other conclusion unthinkable. But in the 1930 version, Julia Seton is played by the bright and sexy Mary Astor; as appealing as Ann Harding is, it is no foregone conclusion that Robert Ames's Johnny Case will choose her over her more sophisticated sister. And Monroe Owsley brings a haunted despair to poor, drunken Ned, the brother who would like to rebel against his father but doesn't have the courage to do so. Lew Ayres in the same role in 1938 is effective but callow; he lacks Owsley's priceless hangdog air of defeat.

Curiously, the engaging Edward Everett Horton plays the same role in both versions of *Holiday*, that of Johnny's friend Ned Potter. He is, as ever, supremely effective in each film, but he delivers a hilarious monologue in the 1930 version that is unaccountably missing from the remake.

Cukor's direction in 1938 is flawlessly elegant and more effortlessly cinematic than Griffith's. (Cukor, of course, was working with far superior technology for the production of sound movies, a fact that makes Griffith's style even more impressive on its own.) Donald Ogden Stewart, who had appeared in the Broadway production in 1928, adapted the script, adding a few scenes and slightly deepening the characters. Interestingly, he was almost cast in the film as Ned—but Cukor wanted the role to be played by Robert Benchley, whose sweet goofiness would certainly have thrown off the balance of Barry's witty, bitter world.

Cukor's *Holiday* was released just after the infamous "box-office poison" list was issued by the Independent Theatre Owners Association. Katharine Hepburn headed that list and the public rejected her even in this sparkling adaptation of Barry's play. Audiences came around eventually, embracing *Holiday* as one of the classics of sophisticated comedy. Hepburn, Grant, and Cukor would interpret Barry to even greater success in 1940 when they made *The Philadelphia Story*, which earned an Academy Award for James Stewart. This work was later turned into a musical, *High Society* (1956) starring Frank Sinatra, Bing Crosby, and Grace Kelly.

Holiday was turned into a musical for the stage too. Renamed *Happy New Year*, the story of the Setons and Johnny Case was put to music by Cole Porter (including 14 previously unpublished songs) in 1980. But where Barry's play and the two film versions placed the dilemma squarely in the present, confronting a realistic, only slightly idealized world, the producers of *Happy New Year* were going strictly for nostalgia: "It is

a love song to a way of life that no longer exists," said producer Leonard Slowly, "and it is a nice, clean, old-fashioned musical."

There have been in recent years several announcements of a new movie remake of *Holiday*, but so far none has been produced. Such an undertaking seems futile. Few plays are fortunate enough to have one adequate motion picture adaptation. *Holiday* has two, each with distinct charms, but almost equally witty, charming, dramatic, and thought provoking. Both of these *Holidays* do full justice to the original—*very* original—work of Philip Barry.

REFERENCES

Astor, Mary, *A Life on Film* (New York: Delacorte Press, 1971); Blum, Daniel, *A Pictorial History of the American Theatre 1860–1970*, 3rd ed., rev. and enlarged John Willis (New York: Crown Publishers, 1969); Hanson, Patricia King, exec. ed., *American Film Institute Catalog of Motion Pictures Produced in the United States, Feature Films, 1931–1940* (Berkeley: University of California Press, 1993); Munden, Kenneth W., exec. ed., *American Film Institute Catalog of Motion Pictures Produced in the United States, Feature Films, 1921–1930* (New York: R.R. Bowker, 1971).

—F.T.

THE HOMECOMING (1965)

HAROLD PINTER (1930–)

The Homecoming (1973), U.S.A., directed by Peter Hall, adapted by Harold Pinter; American Film Theatre.

The Play

The Homecoming was first performed by the Royal Shakespeare Company at the Aldwych Theatre on June 3, 1965, and premiered in America at the Music Box Theatre, New York, on January 5, 1967. The setting is a house in North London, presided over by the domineering Max, whose power is beginning to fail. He is hostile toward his brother Sam, a chauffeur, and antagonistic toward his two sons, Lenny, a pimp, and Joey, a novice boxer. Max reminisces about the old days when he was a butcher and when, with his best friend MacGregor, he was "one of the worst hated men in the West End of London." He also recalls his dead wife Jessica, of whom he talks with a mixture of love and hate.

The tense atmosphere in the household is inflamed by the unexpected homecoming of Max's other son, Teddy, with his wife, Ruth, whom the family has never met. Now a doctor of philosophy and teaching at a prestigious American university, Teddy is on a European tour with his wife in what appears to be an attempt to salvage a disintegrating marriage. What follows is a battle for psychological and emotional supremacy within the family, with Ruth as the target. With Teddy as inactive bystander, she will be treated as a whore by Lenny and by Joey; but, ironically, this seems to offer her an escape from the marriage. By the end of the play, she has seized the initiative from the men, with Joey in thrall, Lenny upstaged, Max impotent, Sam unconscious, and Teddy departed. The father's power has been supplanted: "mother" has returned.

The Film

The Homecoming was one of eight plays made in the American Film Theatre Series in the 1970s, produced by Ely Landau, with the twin aim of providing a market for a more thoughtful kind of film entertainment and giving people outside New York an opportunity to see prestigious theatrical productions that otherwise might not come their way. Because of these aims, the adaptations stayed mainly faithful to the originals, and this is no less true of *The Homecoming*. Most of the action is confined to interiors, save Teddy and Ruth's arrival by taxi, Ruth's walk outdoors (viewed from a window by the anxious Teddy), and Joey's exercising outdoors in the morning. The film's tightly framed shots function to emphasize the battle for territorial supremacy in the house; particularly, a compressed shot of four men in unison puffing at their cigars is an unforgettable image of suffocating masculinity.

The film's cast was mainly the same as in the original stage production: Paul Rogers as Max, Ian Holm as Lenny, Terence Rigby as Joey, and Vivien Merchant as Ruth. Significantly, however, the part of Teddy was played by a different actor in the British, New York, and film versions (respectively, by Michael Bryant, Michael Craig, and Michael Jayston). "They were all good," said the director Peter Hall, but the casting changes probably reflected his view that the role of Teddy was the most difficult to understand and interpret: "He's the biggest bastard in the play—absolutely fireproof. He has no intention of letting any human feeling get to him or alter him." Pinter was more equivocal. "I don't find myself more critical of any one character than another," he said; "I love and detest the lot of them." Critics particularly disagreed over the role of Ruth—whether she was an exploited victim, left to the mercy of his rapacious family by the appalling Teddy; or whether, by contrast, she was the victor, the woman usurping the power of the patriarch and, at the end, commanding center stage by taking over father's

chair. Few viewers are left unmoved by the play's violent dissection of male/female relationships and its vision of a hostile domestic jungle in which the family that stays together, preys together.

REFERENCES

Billington, Michael, *The Life and Work of Harold Pinter* (London: Faber and Faber, 1996); Cahn, Victor L., *Gender and Power in the Plays of Harold Pinter* (Basingstoke: Macmillan, 1994); Esslin, Martin, *Pinter: A Study of His Plays* (London: Eyre Methuen, 1973); Klein, Joanne, *Making Pictures: The Pinter Screenplays* (Columbus: Ohio State University Press, 1985).

—*N.S.*

HOOK

See *PETER PAN*

HOSPITALITY SUITE (1991) (THE BIG KAHUNA)

ROGER RUEFF

The Big Kahuna (1999), U.S.A., directed by John Swanbeck, adapted by Roger Rueff; Trigger Street Productions/Lion's Gate Films.

The Play

Playwright Roger Rueff's *Hospitality Suite* is a three-character drama set in the 16th floor hospitality suite of a Wichita hotel. Three salesmen from a company called Lodestar Laboratories, a manufacturer of industrial lubricants, converge on the site for an annual sales convention. Larry Mann is a brisk, aggressive, albeit cynical salesman in his forties. Phil Cooper is a newly-divorced, sadder, wiser man on the far side of middle age. Bob Walker is the new kid on the block, just married, fresh-faced and idealistic. Their goal at the convention, explains Larry, is to snare a potentially big buyer, one "Mr. Fuller" ("El Grande Kahuna" is his slang expression for him) for their product. Securing him as a client could make their careers; but failure to do so could result in the loss of all their jobs. It's a make or break opportunity. But the "Kahuna" fails to show up at the cocktail reception. At least, that's what everyone thinks, until young Bob casually reveals that he has indeed had a conversation with the man, who was wearing someone else's name tag. Excited that a contact has been made, Larry and Phil demand that Bob return to Fuller and make the sale. But when Bob returns later that night, he confesses he had not discussed business at all; rather, they had talked about dogs and religion. Topics like God are more important than business, explains Bob. Larry is so outraged that he threatens physical violence. After he leaves, Phil patiently explains to Bob that his "born-again" smugness has dehumanized him. "Only when you have made mistakes, and admit that you have made mistakes," Phil says, "will you become a mature man." Bob departs into the night, leaving Phil alone in the suite. The phone rings. Phil answers, listens silently for a moment, and then softly says, "I love you, too." The play ends on this ambiguous note.

The Film

Fresh from his Oscar-winning performance in *American Beauty*, actor Kevin Spacey chose to film *Hospitality Suite* to inaugurate his new production company, Trigger Street Productions. As co-producer, he secured playwright Roger Rueff to adapt it to the screen and veteran stage director John Swanbeck to make his film debut as director. In the central roles are Spacey as Larry Mann, Danny DeVito as Phil Cooper, and Peter Facinelli as Bob Walker. With the exception of a main-title montage depicting the arrivals of the three salesmen at the Wichita hotel and the use of occasional cut-aways to the cocktail reception where Bob converses with the "Kahuna," the film restricts the action to the hospitality suite. The entire text has been transferred virtually intact to the screen. The contrasts among the three characters are instantly drawn: No sooner has Larry arrived in the room than he's complaining about the tacky appointments—no closet, a nondescript view out the window, and a cheap setting of hors d'oeuvres. While the world-weary Phil quietly takes his ease on the couch, Larry spars with the wide-eyed Bob. Bob, it seems, has just gotten married. Not only has he never been with another woman, but his religious morality and conservative values render him unsympathetic to his companions. Something of a "Jesus freak," he later arouses Larry's explosive ire at his failure to secure the sale with the Kahuna. His confrontation with Larry and his subsequent conversation with Phil are depicted in screen-filling close-ups in the half-light of the room. As performed by Facinelli, who at times bears a startling resemblance to the young Tom Cruise, Bob emerges as something of a monster, a self-appointed Bible-thumper with little sense of the practical demands of his job. While the work of the bland, baby-faced Facinelli might be undervalued in comparison with the slick charisma of

Spacey and the intensity of DeVito, it should not be ignored. Facinelli's superb characterization quietly builds to a smug superiority, and it is quite understandable that violence would break out between him and Spacey.

While not as pointed as other dramas about the desperate lives of salesmen, notably *Death of a Salesman* and *Glengarry Glen Ross*, *The Big Kahuna* nonetheless shares with them concerns about self-identity, faith, moral codes, and the onset of age and mortality. Moreover, in its quiet intensity, it emerges with an identity all its own. More overtly philosophical than the other plays, it concentrates on just three characters to show three different attitudes and temperaments—or is it just one salesman split into three stages of his life?

REFERENCES

Kauffmann, Stanley, "Out of the Ordinary," *The New Republic*, May 1, 2000, 24–25; Loos, Ted, "During a 16-Day Sprint Instinct Takes Charge," *The New York Times*, April 23, 2000, II:26.

—*J.C.T.*

THE HOUSE OF BERNARDA ALBA (1936)

FEDERICO GARCIA LORCA (1898–1936)

La casa de Bernarda Alba (1987), Spain, directed by Mario Camus; adapted by Mario Camus and Antonio Larreta.

The House of Bernarda Alba (1991), U.K., staged by Nuria Espert and directed for television by Stuart Burge.

The Play

Though extremely popular and often staged outside of Spain, Lorca's plays were considered taboo within Spanish borders during the Franco dictatorship (1939–75). The 38-year-old poet and playwright was assassinated in his Andalusian home town of Fuente Vaqueros (Granada) just days after the outbreak of the Spanish Civil War in 1936, an event that contributed a greater tragic aura to the third play of a dramatic trilogy, including the earlier *Blood Wedding* (1933) and *Yerma* (1934). *The House of Bernarda Alba* picks up a common theme in Lorquian theatre, i.e., frustrated love and the instinctive, magical power it has to prompt characters to resist traditional morality and social order. The play traces the destruction of

Bernarda Alba's family—her aged mad mother and five spinster daughters—after the death of her husband. Angustias, the eldest daughter, attracts a proposal of marriage, which arouses the jealousy of her sisters. Adela, the youngest, begins a clandestine affair with Angustias' fiancé. Bernarda pretends to have him killed in order to shock Adela, but the plan miscarries when the frustrated Adela commits suicide. "My daughter has died a virgin," Bernarda hypocritically states upon finding Adela's body.

The Films

It comes as no surprise that the first attempt to adapt it to the screen would be by Lorca's friend, Luis Buñuel, who was working in Mexico and France in 1946. Lorca himself had saluted Buñuel's influence on him in the original subtitle of the play, which advises the reader that "these three acts have the intention of a photographic documentary." However, because the Lorca family had already sold the rights of the play, the Buñuel enterprise came to naught. Another thwarted attempt occurred in 1954, when French producer M. Thuillier proposed the project with screenwriter/director Roger Leenhardt. A portion of the unrealized script was published in the Spanish film journal, *Cinema Universitario* (no. 8).

By 1987, Marios Camus had directed 18 feature-length films, including commercially successful adaptations of famous Spanish novels such as *Fortunata y Jactinta* (1979), *La colmena* (The Beehive, 1982) and *Los santos inocentes* (The Holy Innocents, 1984). Nevertheless, most critical sources concur that Camus fails to transpose the dramatic impact of Lorca's play to the cinematic medium. Camus prompts the camera to burst the proscenium and depict scenes outside the claustrophobic confines of Bernarda's house, whereas Lorca's intent clearly was to concentrate on the interior, not the exterior world. Commentator Peter Podol deplores this strategy: "Keep in mind that in *The House of Bernarda Alba* it is almost more important 'what one does not see' as what is really represented." Thus, the film version seems ponderous and inflated by contrast to the austerity of the play. For example, Lorca's simple use of the sound of bells to represent the role of the Catholic Church in the oppression of the daughters is replaced here by an opening sequence set in the vast space of a Catholic cathedral. Scenic contrasts between a stark light-and-dark lighting scheme are muted by Camus' flat lighting. And, surprisingly, Camus alters the verbal bracketing of the play with Bernarda's (Irene Gutierrez Caba) uttering of the word "Silence!" at the beginning and end of the play by employing instead the visually metonymic device of a close-up of Bernarda's gnarled hand, resting on her cane. Near the story's end, Camus adds a scene that transpires just before the discovery of Adela's (Ana Belen) suicide: Adela's sisters, mother, and the maid, Poncia, clad only in nightshirts and shawls, frantically search for her, fluttering from room to room, opening and closing doors, all the while a pounding Flamenco beat counterpointing their anxiety. But, again, Camus manages to deflate the effect by pulling the camera back to a wideshot, revealing in the background Adela's hanging body. Thus, "what is not seen" on stage is revealed all too graphically in the film medium.

Stuart Burge's production for television of Nuria Espert's 1986 London stage version suitably conveys in its thick-walled sets and tightly framed shots the oppressive claustrophobia of Lorca's original conception. Despite the obvious drawbacks of translation, Glenda Jackson as Bernarda and Joan Plowright as the maid, La Poncia, work brilliantly to convey their mutual antagonism; and Espert's staging magnifies the individual personality of each daughter. Lorca's injunction to suggest, not depict, crucial exterior events and settings is respected here. This is most apparent in the final scene, in which Bernarda utters "Silence!" three times. Glenda Jackson finds a different intonation for each utterance. The first time is throaty and firm. When she shouts the word for the second time, it is less controlling, more uncertain. Then, finally, when the full import of Adela's tragic death and Pepe's escape infiltrates her consciousness, her final "silence" is merely whispered, communicating a clear sense of defeat and pain. Examples like this of the production's nuanced verbal text are indicative of the superior quality of this television adaptation.

REFERENCES

Galan, Eduardo, *Claves de "La case de Bernada Alba"* (Madrid: Ciclo Editorial, 1989); Podol, Peter L., "La casa de Bernarda Alba in Performance: Three Productions in Three Media," *Estreno*, 21:2 (1995); Taylor, Diana, "Interiority and Exteriority in Garcia Lorca's *La casa de Bernarda Alba*," *Estreno*, 15:1 (1989); Utrera, Rafael, *Garcia Lorca y el cinema* (Sevilla: Edisur, 1982).

—*M.V.L.*

HURLYBURLY (1984)

DAVID RABE (1940–)

Hurlyburly (1998), U.S.A., directed by Anthony Drazan, adapted by David Rabe; Fine Line Features.

The Play

David Rabe first came to national attention in 1971 with Joseph Papp and the American Place Theatre in a series of plays—including *The Basic Training of Pavlo Hummel* (1970) and *Sticks and Bones* (1971)—dealing with the Vietnam War. In most of his work, then and now, Rabe is concerned with territorial space, both private and familial, which is frequently violable or nonexistent. According to commentator Dennis Carroll, the motif of the family is an ongoing concern, "especially the way that an artificial or 'extended' family may be turned to as a substitute for a nuclear family that has failed one of its members. But without exception the 'extended' family, too, fails to nurture." Rabe's characters often speak in the form of "arias," or soliloquies, replete with nonstop effusions and nonsense phrases and words ("blah-blah-blah"), which signal their unwillingness (or inability) to open themselves up to deeper insights and personal revelations.

Hurlyburly was Rabe's dissection of the morally bankrupt world of Hollywood. It premiered in 1984 in New York City at the Promenade Theater. Directed by Mike Nichols, it featured an all-star cast, including Harvey Keitel, Christopher Walken, Judith Ivey, William Hurt, and Sigourney Weaver. Restricted to the claustrophobic confines of a casting office and a Hollywood Hills residence, the male rivalries and interior tensions among four friends explode into scenes of violence, anguish, and self-loathing. Here is Rabe's "family" motif, men all shell-shocked by marriages or destroyed by their own instability. Eddie and Mickey, a casting director and his associate, respectively, are living together in a Hollywood Hills condo. Their friends include Artie, a struggling screenwriter, and Phil, an out-of-work actor. Two incidents trigger episodes of confrontation and violence among the four—Phil's frustrations over his damaged career, broken marriage, and past record of physical abuse; and the rivalry between Eddie and Mickey over the affections of a woman named Darlene. In the end, Eddie loses Darlene and, after an abortive suicide attempt, consoles himself with the dubious company of a prostitute, Donna; Phil is killed in an auto "accident" that may have been suicide; and Artie is perpetually lost in a cocaine haze. Only the cool, suave Mickey manages to remain above the fray. Accused of having no emotions, Mickey sardonically remarks that he does indeed have feelings—at least "enough to get by." In the play's "Afterword," Rabe emphasizes his feeling that accident and destiny may well be the same: "Because always under the little we could will and then attain there was some unknown immensity on which we stood and all utterly beyond us."

The Film

In bringing his play to the screen, playwright Rabe (who has also adapted John Grisham's *The Firm*) explodes the proscenium and relocates many of the monologues and conversations in locations like Mulholland Drive and Beverly Hills. Eddie's climactic suicide attempt has also been altered from a pill-popping episode to an elaborately staged sequence in his swimming pool. As the self-flagellating Eddie, Sean Penn pulls out all the stops and indulges himself in a succession of over-the-top harangues and self-recriminations (Penn won the best actor prize at the 1998 Venice Film Festival). As Artie, Gary Shandling is, for the most part, muffled in a drug-induced haze. Chazz Palminteri, on the other hand, is a ticking bomb just waiting to explode, a bristling collection of brutish tics and quirks. Best of all is Kevin Spacey as the unflappable Mickey. Of all the characters, Mickey is the most frightening, for, unlike the anguished Eddie who persists in trying to find the "pattern" in the quagmire of life that threatens to engulf him, Mickey has most successfully accommodated himself to situational ethics of his times. While Eddie is still searching for answers to life's enigmas, Mickey has long since given up the quest. And while Eddie tortures himself with the presumption that Phil's mysterious suicide note possesses an interior meaning, Mickey coolly dismisses it out of hand. It is Eddie who is obviously Rabe's tool to question the workings of a pernicious society, and it is Mickey who, ultimately, becomes that society's chief emblem—and victim.

A major problem, however, is that the abstract nature of the characters' problems, which may have played well on a stark stage platform, is defeated by the specificity of the camera. Against this very real and concretized world, the fuzzy existentialism just hovers like a dirty cloud. On the plus side, Rabe's screenplay has kept relatively intact the play's dazzling verbal virtuosity and the characters' ongoing semantics gamesmanship. Each character has his own sound, his own mantra—from Eddie's whine to Mickey's urbane verbal chic. "Language is something people use to create realities," says Rabe, "to create truth and systems and inflict them on other people, or try to coerce others into agreeing with their reality or submitting to it. That's what happens in the world. It happens in our own minds, with the words we think. The words create reality, rather than reflecting it."

REFERENCES

Carroll, Dennis, "Not-Quite Mainstream Male Playwrights: Guare, Durang and Rabe," in Bruce King, ed., *Contemporary American Theatre* (New York: St. Martin's Press, 1991); Clements, Marcelle, "A Dispatch from the War Against Women," *New York Times*, November 23, 1998; Savran, David, *In Their Own Words* (New York: Theatre Communications Group, 1988).

—*J.C.T.*

I AM A CAMERA (1951)

JOHN VAN DRUTEN (1901–1957)

I Am a Camera (1955), U.K., directed by Henry Cornelius, adapted by John Collier; Romulus Films.

The Play

Based on the *Goodbye to Berlin* (1939) stories of Christopher Isherwood (and particularly the character of Sally Bowles), John van Druten's *I Am a Camera* premiered in New York at the Empire Theatre on November 28, 1951, and played for 262 performances. Heading the cast as Sally Bowles, an amoral *chanteuse*, was Julie Harris, and as the young writer Christopher Isherwood, William Prince. They live together in two rooms in Fraulein Schneider's Berlin boarding house in 1930, on the eve of the Nazi assumption of power. Sally's boyfriend Klaus has abandoned her after impregnating her. She has an abortion so she can continue her current affair with Clive, a rich American who plans to take Chris and Sally on a world tour. But Clive eventually leaves Sally, and she departs Berlin with a new lover, a Yugoslav. The play also concerns the relationship between Fritz, a gigolo, and Chris' English pupil, Natalia, the daughter of a wealthy Jewish department store owner. When Fritz reveals his Jewish identity to Natalia, the two marry. The anti-Semitic abuse the pair endures prefigures the Nazi terrors to come. Meanwhile, Chris observes it all and sets out to write a series of stories about life in Berlin. "I am a camera with its shutter open," he says of his recording of the city's impressions all around him, "quite passive." Although the play was perceived by many critics as a loosely strung together, albeit theatrically effective, series of scenes, there was no doubting the triumphant impression left by the incandescent performance of Julie Harris.

The Film

When scenarist John Collier adapted the play to film, he made some radical alterations. Now the story begins and ends at a cocktail party for writer Sally Bowles (Julie Harris reprising her stage role), attended by Christopher Isherwood (Laurence Harvey), now a successful writer. As he tells Bowles story to his fellow journalists, the story flashes back to the events of 25 years before. Sally's background as a cabaret performer is outlined, and scenes of Nazi brutality are detailed, particularly a fight between Chris and several Nazi thugs. The political message is more pronounced here than in the play. At the same time, Collier's script makes several concessions to the film censors, including the elimination of any reference to Sally's abortion (her presumption that she is pregnant proves to be false). At the end of the flashback Chris leaves the party with Sally.

The play and film were both sources for the popular musical show, *Cabaret*, by John Kander and Fred Ebb, which opened on Broadway in 1966.

REFERENCES

Mizejewski, Linda, *Divine Decadence: Fascism, Female Spectacle, and the Makings of Sally Bowles* (Princeton: Princeton University Press, 1992); Prince, Hal, *Contradictions: Notes on Twenty-Six Years in the Theatre* (New York: Dodd, Mead, 1974).

—*J.C.T.*

THE ICEMAN COMETH (1939)

EUGENE O'NEILL (1888–1953)

The Iceman Cometh (1973), U.S.A., directed by John Frankenheimer, adapted by Ely Landau; American Film Theatre.

The Play

Often called the American *Lower Depths*, like Maxim Gorki's drama, O'Neill's four-act play concerns a group of people (in this case the inhabitants of Harry Hope's saloon and rooming house) who escape reality by continually musing over their individual "pipe dreams." The play was originally written in 1939, but O'Neill, judging that a wartime audience would not be receptive to his pessimistic blending of symbolism and realism, delayed production until 1946. This production staged by the Theatre Guild under the direction of Eddie Dowling featured James Barton as Hickey and Dudley Digges as Harry Hope. Opening to mixed reviews the play closed after 136 performances. It wasn't until a 1956 revival at the Circle in the Square Theatre in New York directed by Jose Quintero and starring Jason Robards, Jr., that the drama received the critical acclaim it deserved. This production, which began the Eugene O'Neill revival of the late fifties, under the direction of Jose Quintero, ran for 565 performances.

The drama is set in "a cheap ginmill of the five-cent whiskey, last-resort variety situated on the downtown West Side of New York" and owned by Harry Hope. The action of the play covers two days and nights in the early summer of 1912. A collection of misfits and miscreants that make up the clientele of the bar are eagerly awaiting the arrival of Hickey, a traveling salesman and fellow drinking companion, in order to begin their annual birthday "blowout" for Harry Hope. Among them is Larry Slade, "the old foolosopher," a 60-year-old disenchanted anarchist who cultivates a detached attitude from life. His recognition of the fact that "the lie of a pipe dream is what gives life to the whole misbegotten mad lot of us, drunk or sober" is the philosophical underpinning for the entire play. Hickey arrives and to the surprise of everyone announces that he has given up drink. He begins to extol to the group a new philosophical outlook: Truth. His new sales pitch, claiming a desire to make converts of all present, is "Honesty is the best policy—honesty with yourself, . . . Just stop lying about yourself and kidding yourself about tomorrows." In the past Hickey has always regaled the group with stories and jokes, especially one concerning his wife in bed with the iceman. Now Hickey's demeanor has changed and he preaches the "new hope."

In each act a little more information is provided concerning the death of his wife, Evelyn. In Act Two, Hickey reveals that she is dead, in Act Three he tells the group that "it was a bullet in the head that killed her," leading many to believe she committed suicide. And finally in Act Three during Hickey's extended monologue and confession, he reveals that he killed her. The police arrive and arrest him, and the group, now adhering to a new "pipe dream," that Hickey will not go to the chair because he was insane, settle back into their sheltered nonexistence at Harry Hope's "End of the Line Cafe." With the exception of Hickey's sole convert, Larry Slade, who finally realizes, "Be God, there's no hope! I'll never be a success in the grandstand—or anywhere else! . . . I'll be a weak fool looking with pity at the two sides of everything till the day I die!"

As can be discerned from the brief synopsis there is very little action in O'Neill's drama; instead, it primarily relies on characterization and dialogue to provide its dramatic impact. The meaning of the play has been variously interpreted by scholars as a religious allegory or an autobiographical drama. O'Neill uses repetitious words and phrases throughout the four-act four-hour-long play. During the original production of *Iceman* by the Theatre Guild, Lawrence Langner, producer and founding member of the Guild, complained to O'Neill that a character repeated the same point 18 times. O'Neill replied, "I *intended* it to be repeated eighteen times." Langner later suggested that the true greatness of the work would be discovered only when it was possible to make cuts in the text. *The Iceman Cometh* provides, then, a distinct challenge for any intended stage production, let alone a filmic one.

The Film

The Iceman Cometh was the premiere film for the 1973 season of Ely Landau's American Film Theatre. The purpose of the American Film Theatre was to present a "national theatre on film" by distinguished casting in screen adaptations of modern stage plays. The American Film Theatre survived for two seasons, 1973–74 (*The Iceman Cometh, Rhinoceros, The Homecoming, A Delicate Balance, Luther, Butley, Lost in the Stars,* and *Three Sisters*) and 1974–75 (*The Maids, The Man in the Glass Booth, Galileo, Jacques Brel is Alive and Well and Living in Paris,* and *In Celebration*), through subscription audiences in much the same manner as live theatre. Problems with theatrical distribution—many theatres did not want a two- to three-day AFT run to interrupt their more profitable bookings—led to its discontinuance after the 1974 season.

The film version of *The Iceman Cometh* was directed by John Frankenheimer, who gathered an exceptional cast, including Fredric March (Harry Hope), Robert Ryan (Larry Slade), and Lee Marvin (Hickey). Frankenheimer's direction relies primarily on confining the screen space to the interior of the bar and utilizing deep-focus photography (Ralph Woolsey was the film's cinematographer) to provide several planes of interest. Early on during the production Frankenheimer outlined three central problems in adapting O'Neill's drama to film: "first, the extraordinary length of the original; second, the fact that the entire action takes place in one room; and third, the fact that the impact of the play comes from the cumulative effect of the ensemble playing." Frankenheimer cut about an hour and a quarter of dialogue and resisted the temptation to open up O'Neill's play to exterior shots (such as showing the outside of Harry Hope's bar and the suicide of one of the characters). By confining the action, as O'Neill does, to the inside of the bar and utilizing deep-focus shots, Frankenheimer allows "the important overall atmosphere of the bar to be maintained at all times." John Orlandello notes a similarity to Gregg Toland's deep-focus photography in *Citizen Kane* (1941). This is particularly true in shots that include foreground and background planes of objects and characters. "This photographic style," Orlandello states, "uncramps and visually dynamizes confined space, helps to maintain the sense of ensemble playing, and allows for an interesting dramatic play between objects or people in the foreground and the background of a shot."

Many critics have agreed that another one of the strengths of this film is in its exceptional ensemble casting. This was both Fredric March and Robert Ryan's last film, and both performers create characters that are multilayered. Orlandello observes that Harry Hope is "an assemblage of contradictions—he is doddering and willfully powerful; he is good-natured and

cantankerous; he is weak and self-defeated, yet possessed of such pride and dignity as the landlord of the lower depths." March's performance skillfully captures these qualities as well as other "subtleties and inconsistencies." Ryan's Larry Slade was also singled out by Pauline Kael as having penetrated "the mystery of O'Neill's gaunt grandeur." Lee Marvin's Hickey, however, received mixed reviews. Many faulted the actor as lacking the bravura and the spellcaster qualities needed for the role. Orlandello defends the performance, stating that much of the negative criticism stemmed from the fact that Marvin was playing against type. "There is a certain monotony in Marvin's delivery, but this is suitable to the character who . . . harps on a single issue throughout the film." Moreover, Marvin captures the well-meaningness of the character's self-appointed mission. He is really trying to convince himself, especially in his lengthy monologue, to accept the truth of life. Above all, Frankenheimer's film maintains the integrity of O'Neill's play by confining it to a self-enclosed world where the playwright's poetic language forcefully reveals the existential situation of the denizens of the "Bottom of the Sea Rathskeller" and of life itself.

REFERENCES

Orlandello, John, *O'Neill on Film* (Rutherford, N.J.: Fairleigh Dickinson University Press, 1982); Ranald, Margaret Loftus, *The Eugene O'Neill Companion* (Westport, Conn.: Greenwood Press, 1984); Slide, Anthony, *The American Film Industry: A Historical Dictionary* (New York: Limelight Editions, 1990).

—*R.W.W.*

AN IDEAL HUSBAND (1895)

OSCAR WILDE (1854–1900)

An Ideal Husband (1947), U.K., directed by Alexander Korda, adapted by Lajos Biro; London Films/20th Century-Fox.

An Ideal Husband (1999), U.K./U.S.A., directed and adapted by Oliver Parker; Icon Entertainment/Miramax.

The Play

Premiered at the Theatre Royal, Haymarket, on January 3, 1895, just after the success of *Lady Windemere's Fan* and mere weeks before the spectacular success of *The Importance of Being Earnest, An Ideal Husband* marks

Oscar Wilde at the height of his public celebrity. Lewis Waller appeared as Sir Robert Chiltern, Charles Hawtrey as Lord Goring, Julia Neilson as Lady Chiltern, and Florence West as Mrs. Cheveley. Although the play's brittle wit is quite characteristic of Wilde at his best, there is a deeper seriousness of purpose here—if not elements of hoary melodrama—that, in the opinion of biographer St. John Irvine, reflects Wilde's growing anxiety about the likely exposure of certain aspects of his controversial private life. The secrets that lie hidden in the breast of the character of Sir Robert Chiltern may be but the symbol of the great secret in Wilde's own private life, i.e., his homosexual activities, which within the year would destroy his career and reputation and result in his imprisonment.

The first act opens at a dinner party at the home of Sir Robert Chiltern, under-secretary for foreign affairs, and his young wife, Gertrude. Making her entrance is the scheming Mrs. Cheveley, just arrived from Vienna. In a private interview with Sir Robert she quickly outlines a wicked blackmail scheme: Unless Sir Robert relinquishes his plans to denounce in Parliament the illegal transactions of the Argentine Canal Company, in which she has a vital interest, she will produce an incriminating letter regarding his dubious business practices in his past. Not only would this revelation ruin Sir Robert's hitherto unstained public career, it would also break up his marriage with his primly proper wife, Lady Gertrude. Distraught and confused, he withdraws his objections and takes his troubles to his cynical bachelor friend, Lord Arthur Goring. Lady Gertrude, meanwhile, having learned of her husband's indiscretions, also seeks advice from Lord Goring. It so happens that Goring is the ex-fiancé of Mrs. Cheveley, and now he too finds himself the target of her scheming. She offers to give up Sir Robert's incriminating letter if Goring will marry her. Ultimately, her blackmailing tactics fail in the face of Lady Chiltern's devotion to her husband and the loyalty of Goring. Sir Robert regains his moral authority by confessing his past: "I began my career with an act of low dishonesty. . . . I would to God I had died before I had been so horribly tempted, or fallen so low." Thinking that he has lost his wife and his career, he denounces the Argentine Canal scheme in Parliament. As a result, however, his marriage is restored and a cabinet post is offered him. Goring falls in love with Sir Robert's sister, Mabel, and announces their engagement.

Commentator Philip K. Cohen declares that *An Ideal Husband* is a tragicomedy that "attempts a rapprochement between Christian morality and the legitimate claims of society." Sir Robert will not have to subject himself to a life of either penitential self-sacrifice or public disgrace. As his friend, Goring—surely Wilde's spokesperson here—says, "Self-sacrifice is a thing that should be put down by law. It is so demoralizing to the people for whom one sacrifices oneself. They always go to the bad." It is Sir Robert's ultimate reconciliation of love and ambition, individual needs and society pressures, that makes him the "ideal husband" of Wilde's title. As for Wilde, he described his play as "exquisitely trivial, a delicate bubble of fancy, and it has its philosophy!"

The Films

Alexander Korda chose the Wilde play as the last film he was to direct personally. Elaborately staged by his brother Vincent (with a reconstructon of Hyde Park Corner in the 1890s), it was beautifully dressed by Cecil Beaton and photographed by Georges Perinal. The cast included Paulette Goddard as Mrs. Cheveley, Michael Wilding as Goring, Hugh Williams as Sir Robert, Diana Wynyard as Lady Childtern, and Glynis Johns as Mabel. Trade reviewers described it as "a lavish production that never ceased to dazzle the eyes." Later commentators, however, have been unimpressed by its stagy qualities. Charles Oakley, for instance, complained that the coincidences in Wilde's plot "became embarrassingly apparent in the cinema." Except with select audiences, concluded Oakley, *An Ideal Husband* was a comparative failure in this country as well as overseas."

Oliver Parker's second film version stars Jeremy Northam and Cate Blanchett as Robert and Gertrude Chiltern, Julianne Moore as Mrs. Cheveley, and Rupert Everett and Minnie Driver as Goring and Mabel. The basic plot elements are intact and most of the key dialogue exchanges are transcribed verbatim—including the first-act exchange between Cheveley and Sir Robert during which her blackmail plan is laid out; the complex third-act scene in Goring's apartment that climaxes in Sir Robert's denunciation of him and Mrs. Cheveley's attempts to bargain with Goring for his hand in marriage (absent is some rather tedious business about a bracelet Mrs. Cheveley had stolen years before); and the various fourth-act misunderstandings that lead to Sir Robert's initial rejection of the cabinet post and his refusal to sanction Mabel's marriage to Goring.

It is in the characterizations and some of the thematic considerations that the film departs from its original material. For example, much of Sir Robert's inner conflicts and contradictions are simplified. Here, he is never allowed to defend his past actions (as he does in the play). His wife's strict puritanism, which in the play leads her to demand Sir Robert give up his career, is softened here, and she rallies more readily to her husband's side. Moreover, the sexist aspect of her conversion, so clearly stated in Wilde—she forgives him out of her sense of a woman's inferiority and necessary obeisance to a man—is dropped. It is compassion more than a conviction of feminine inferiority that guides her forgiveness. As for the union between Goring and Mabel, it lacks the essential superficiality Wilde envisioned; rather, it is seen here as a quite sincere romantic conclusion.

Oscar Wilde himself makes an appearance. When Sir Robert and his friends attend a performance of Wilde's *The Importance of Being Earnest*, the playwright (enacted in a cameo by actor Michael Culkin) delivers his famous curtain speech. But there is a howler that is unforgivable, and that is when Lord Goring attends Sir Robert's speech in the House of Commons (a *Lord* in the House of Commons?). Sir Robert's speech, by the way—a scene not in the original play—is replete with references to the responsibilities of meeting a new century, implications perhaps more meaningful to today's audiences than those of a century ago.

REFERENCES

Cohen, Philip K., *The Moral Vision of Oscar Wilde* (Rutherford, N.J.: Fairleigh Dickinson University Press, 1978); Irvine, St. John, *Oscar Wilde: A Present Time Appraisal* (New York: William Morrow, 1952); Oakley, Charles, *Where We Came In* (London: George Allen and Unwin, 1964); Tabori, Paul, *Alexander Korda: A Biography* (New York: Living Books, 1966).

—*J.C.T.*

IDIOT'S DELIGHT (1936)

ROBERT SHERWOOD (1896–1955)

Idiot's Delight (1939), U.S.A., directed by Clarence Brown, adapted by Robert Sherwood; MGM.

The Play

As a young man in 1917 Robert Sherwood was caught up in the patriotic fervor of a world at war and left Harvard to join the Canadian Expeditionary Force after being rejected by the U.S. Army. Gassed and wounded in France, he returned to the United States determined to oppose future wars. Sherwood drifted in and out of Hollywood during the late '20s and early '30s. In 1935 he captured national attention with his play *The Petrified Forest*, and in 1936 he was awarded the first of four Pulitzer Prizes for his antiwar *Idiot's Delight*.

Idiot's Delight opened at the National Theatre in Washington, D.C., on March 9, 1936, and moved to the Shubert Theatre in New York in April. Its timeliness and controversial content guaranteed considerable attention. The Senate investigation in 1934 and 1935 of the role of the munitions industry in World War I, led by Senator Gerald Nye, Republican from North Dakota, was still fresh in the minds of most Americans. While Nye failed to prove his case, millions of Americans agreed with him when he claimed we fought "to save the skins of American bankers who had bet too boldly on the outcome of the war and had two billions of dollars of loans to the Allies in jeopardy." Sherwood certainly believed it.

The play takes place in a small Italian hotel near the Swiss border. This idyllic setting is suddenly disrupted when the Italians close the border and launch a surprise air attack on Paris. World War II has begun. The hotel is suddenly packed with people desperate to cross the border: a young English artist on his honeymoon, a French communist, a German scientist, an American entertainer (Alfred Lunt) traveling with "Les Girls," a group of six chorus girls, and an American munitions manufacturer (Sidney Greenstreet) traveling with his "Russian" mistress (Lynn Fontanne).

The war is a tragedy for everyone except the American munitions manufacturer. The English artist decides to return home and join the army. A French communist taunts several Italian soldiers and is arrested and shot by a firing squad, becoming the first senseless casualty in the war. The German scientist, who was working on a cure for cancer, is forced to make poison gas for war. The American arms merchant is unaffected. He not only expected the war, he also conspired to start it and will profit handsomely from it. His treachery continues when he forces the Italians to refuse an exit visa for his "Russian" mistress, Irene, because she knows too much about his role in starting the war.

The American entertainer, Harry Van, is unfazed by the war. He is apolitical, dead broke, and his only concern is how to get to his next engagement so he and his girls can get back to the United States. But Van is fascinated by the beautiful "Russian." She strikes him as someone from his past whom he cannot quite remember. Irene is deserted by her lover and finally admits to Van that they had a brief, but passionate, love affair in Omaha many years ago. When the Italians open the border everyone leaves. Van and Irene are the only ones left at the hotel. While they drink champagne and make plans for the future, the French launch a counterattack against the Italians. The play ends when a stray bomb smashes into the hotel and the two lovers are killed. War is an idiot's delight.

Sherwood's drama was anti-Italian, anti-Mussolini, as well as antiwar. The hotel was once a sanatorium but "the Fascisti—they don't like to admit that anyone can be sick," says one character. When seven out of 18 Italian pilots return after a sneak attack on Paris, one character notes sardonically: "Not bad, for Italians." In case anyone missed the point Sherwood added a postscript: "The megalomaniac, to live, must inspire excitement, fear and awe. If, instead, he is greeted with calmness, courage and ridicule, he becomes a figure of supreme insignificance. . . . By refusing to imitate the Fascists in their policies of heavily fortified isolation, their hysterical self-worship and psychopathic hatred of others, we may achieve the enjoyment of peaceful life on earth, rather than degraded death in the cellar."

The critics loved the play. James P. Cunningham, theatre critic for *Commonweal*, called the play "admirable." *The Nation* told its readers that "the horror of war has been conveyed about as effectively as it has ever been on the stage." The *New Republic* labeled it "a delightful play, witty, inventive, full of theater." This was confirmed when Sherwood was awarded the Pulitzer Prize for his play.

The Film

The combination of the Senate investigations and the rise of fascism in Europe and the Pulitzer made the play attractive for Hollywood. But it was also very controversial and Hollywood hated controversy. When two studios asked PCA director Joseph Breen for an evaluation, he told them that he doubted *Idiot's Delight* could be filmed because it "would be banned widely abroad and might cause reprisals against the American company distributing it. The play is fundamentally anti-war propaganda, and contains numerous diatribes against militarism, fascism and the munitions ring."

Interest in Sherwood's play dwindled until MGM inquired about the feasibility of making a film version of the play in December 1936. The censor warned MGM that he considered the play to be dangerous and cited "industry policy" as a reason for not making a motion picture version.

Despite Breen's warning, MGM decided to forge ahead with the project. Throughout the spring of 1937 discussions continued on both coasts over the future of *Idiot's Delight*. The Italian ambassador threatened MPPDA president Will Hays that the film, along with all other MGM products, would be banned in Italy. The ambassador claimed Robert Sherwood was "anathema" to the Italian government and any project with which he was associated would be "hissed off the screen" in Italy. Hays, determined to keep the Italian market open for American films, ordered Breen to use the Italian consul in Los Angeles, Mr. R. Caracciolo, as a "technical" adviser. Given final script approval, the Italian government agreed to cooperate on the production of *Idiot's Delight*.

Hunt Stromberg, the film's producer, and director Clarence Brown recast the film as a love story not a political statement against Italian fascism. To stress this emphasis, MGM assigned heartthrob Clark Gable to play the irresistible Harry Van and Norma Shearer as the beautiful and flirtatious "Russian." The film, Stromberg wrote, "will not say, as the play did, that Italy started the new war, nor will we hold her Government responsible for hostile or secret intrigue, breaking treaties, or any other such acts." To ensure that the politics would be written out of the film, MGM hired Robert Sherwood to turn his stormy political tract into a steamy Hollywood love story.

The film finally reached American screens in February 1939. Joining Gable and Shearer were Edward Arnold as the evil munitions maker and Charles Coburn as the German scientist. But even a cast as powerful as this one could not transform a silly love story set in Central Europe into an interesting film. While some of the antiwar flavor remained in the first reel, the central focus of the film was not the folly of war, but whether the "Russian" Irene was the same woman with whom Harry Van had a brief affair in Omaha. Once that was established, the point switched to whether the two lovers would pick up where they left off. They did, and in the grand finale bombs again destroy the quaint little hotel, but, of course, they miraculously miss the lovers. *Idiot's Delight* not only was shorn of its political punch, it also gave audiences a happy ending.

The critics had a field day with the film. *Newsweek* wondered why Hollywood leaned "over backward" to keep Italy happy. "The Italy of the stage set becomes an Alpine never-never land in celluloid, and its people speak that international language, Esperanto." Otis Ferguson wrote in *The New Republic* that the screen version of *Idiot's Delight* was "no more antiwar than a few squads of well-meaning and offended citizens, pelting a nasty old caterpillar tank with chocolate eclairs." The *North American Review* charged the Hays Office with hypocrisy in turning an antiwar play into "an adventure in obscurantism." Why, the NAR asked its readers, was it impossible to have "entertainment, information, or any combination of the two that is clear, sincere, and well told . . . seen on the American screen?" The answer, the NAR wrote, was "the Hays Office." Even Sherwood was disappointed. He thought that Shearer was "beautiful" as Irene and Gable "very funny" as Van. But, after seeing the screen version, the writer lamented that "so much was cut from the play it seems confusing." While the film was popular in America, it was on the whole a disappointment at the box office.

REFERENCES

Brown, John Mason, *The Worlds of Robert E. Sherwood; Mirror to His Times, 1896–1939* (New York: Harper & Row, 1965); Meserve, Walter J., *Robert Sherwood: Reluctant Moralist* (New York: Pegasus, 1970).

—G.B.

IMPORTANCE OF BEING EARNEST, THE (1895)

OSCAR WILDE (1854–1900)

The Importance of Being Earnest (1952), U.K., directed and adapted by Anthony Asquith; J. Arthur Rank.

The Play

Among Oscar Wilde's seven plays, *The Importance of Being Earnest* is the most highly regarded. It marked the crest of his public acclaim as a playwright, which had begun in 1892 with *Lady Windermere's Fan*, and continued unabated with *A Woman of No Importance* (1893) and *An Ideal Husband* (1895). Subtitled "a trivial comedy for serious people," *Earnest* successfully maintained a combination of brittle wit, dazzling wordplay, and offhand absurdity. Wilde had not long to bask in its glow, however; before the year was out he would find himself disgraced and imprisoned for two years on morals charges. Indeed, commentator Philip K. Cohen finds in the dual identities in the play allusions to Wilde's own "double life": "His literary transformations of these personal elements exemplify his intent to trivialize the serious, and thus to escape his anxieties." These darker implications notwithstanding, *Earnest* justifies the boast he later made in *De Profundis:* "I took the drama, the most objective form known to art, and made of it as personal a mode of expression as the lyric or the sonnet; at the same time, widened its range and enriched its characterization." Because of the notoriety of Wilde's imprisonment, *Earnest* was not published until 1899.

Oscar Wilde

Act One begins as Algernon (Algy) Moncrieff, an unrepentant playboy, entertains his friend, Ernest. Ernest has been leading a double life as "Ernest" in town and "Jack Worthing" in the country. As Jack he maintains a high moral tone for the sake of his ward, Cecily Cardew. For his city debauches, Jack pretends to Cecily that he has to look after a ne'er-do-well brother, Ernest. Algy confesses that he, too, is conducting a similar game: He pretends to have an out-of-town invalid friend, Bunbury, who serves as a convenient pretext for his own escapades. Ernest declares that he wants to marry Algy's cousin, Gwendolen Fairfax. Gwendolen arrives at that moment with her mother, Lady Bracknell. Left alone with Ernest,

Gwendolen assists him in his proposal: "I think it only fair to tell you quite frankly beforehand that I am fully determined to accept you." She further disconcerts him by declaring that she can only love someone named "Ernest"—a name like "Jack" would never do. Lady Bracknell is at first sympathetic to the proposed match, until she learns that Ernest is a foundling who as a baby was left in a handbag in the cloakroom at Victoria station. Considering this "to display a contempt for the ordinary decencies of family life that reminds one of the worst excesses of the French Revolution," Bracknell leaves in a huff. Unless Ernest can produce at least one parent, his suit is doomed. Algy, in the meantime, upon learning of his friend's ward, determines that a trip to the country may be in order.

Act Two transpires in the country home of "Jack Worthing." Algy arrives, posing as Uncle Jack's reprobate brother, "Ernest." Of course, he immediately falls in love with Cecily. While the two are out walking, the real Jack appears with a plan in mind to woo Gwendolen. Dressed in deep mourning, he announces to Cecily's spinster governess, Miss Prism, that his brother Ernest has just died. "What a lesson for him! I trust he will profit by it," she sniffs. Further, Jack plans to be christened "Ernest" in recognition of Gwendolen's predilections toward that name. He is appalled to hear Cecily's news that "Ernest" has arrived earlier. As soon as he is alone with his "brother," Jack insists that Algy leave. During Algy's farewell, he learns from Cecily that she has always hoped to marry someone named "Ernest." She has even written to herself badly spelled letters from her fantasy suitor, Ernest. "The three you wrote me after I had broken off the engagement are so beautiful," she tells him, "and so badly spelled, that even now I can hardly read them without crying a little." Now Algy is off to arrange for *his* rechristening. But things get even more complicated when Gwendolen arrives. At once she and Cecily—united in their common adoration of the name "Ernest"—are fast friends. But when they realize they are both engaged to "Ernest," they draw apart. When Jack and Algy return to clear up the misunderstanding, the women resume their friendship and sorrowfully leave the men behind to sup with their misery: "I refuse everything except food and drink," moans the disappointed Algy.

Act Three begins as Cecily and Gwendolen return to resolve the complications with Jack and Algy. Although they decide to accept the men's protests of affection—"In matters of grave importance, style, not sincerity, is the vital thing"—there is still the sticky wicket of the "Ernest" dilemma. Both Jack and Algy declare they will accept the name. Enter Lady Brack-

nell, who still harbors a bias against the foundling, Jack. Playing his trump card, Jack challenges Bracknell that he will not consent to the marriage between Algy and Cecily unless Bracknell allows him to marry Gwendolen. Bracknell refuses. At that moment, someone mentions the name of Cecily's governess, Miss Prism. "Is this Miss Prism a female of repellent aspect, remotely connected with education?" asks Bracknell. In the ensuing revelations, Prism turns out to be the governess who had once lost a baby, Bracknell's nephew, in a handbag. Thus, Jack realizes he is in reality Algy's elder brother, Ernest. "It is a terrible thing," he says, "for a man to find out suddenly that all his life he has been speaking nothing but the truth." The two couples embrace, and Jack concludes, "I've now realized for the first time in my life the vital Importance of Being Earnest."

The Importance of Being Earnest eludes easy classification. It contains elements of romantic comedy, social satire, farce, parody, and burlesque. Above all, it happily breaks free of reality and triumphs over the problems of modern life—not to mention Wilde's own personal turmoils. The serious and the trivial are kept in a kind of suspension, like so many balls kept aloft by the hands of a juggler. "We should treat all the trivial things in life seriously," Wilde said in an interview in January 1895, "and all the serious things in life with sincere and studied triviality." And, as the character of Algy points out in the play, "One must be serious about something, if one wants to have any amusement in life."

The Film

Anthony Asquith, a veteran of the British cinema since the silent days, enjoyed a reputation in the 1930s and 1940s second only to Alfred Hitchcock. He directed the esteemed *Pygmalion* (1938) in collaboration with Gabriel Pascal and George Bernard Shaw, and enjoyed a long and fruitful collaboration with playwright Terence Rattigan, including adaptations of his plays, *While the Sun Shines* (1947), *The Winslow Boy* (1948), and *The Browning Version* (1951). Capable of visual experimentation in his work, Asquith intentionally steered clear of any stylistic affectations in his adaptation of *The Importance of Being Earnest*. He streamlined the play and eliminated much of the repetition, the conversations among the peripheral characters, and allusions to contemporary topics. Otherwise, as Asquith made it clear, he intended to preserve Wilde's text and "allow Oscar Wilde to speak with his own voice." Accordingly, the cinematography is limited, for the most part, to recording a relatively frontal presentation and maintaining character relationships in a series of two-shots. The film's theatricality declares itself, literally, as an audience arrives at a theatre before the rise of a curtain and, at the end, leaves after the final curtain. The credits are presented in the form of a theatre program. The cast is exemplary. Edith Evans reprised her stage role as Lady Bracknell, Michael Redgrave portrays Jack Worthing, Michael Denison is Algy, Joan Greenwood is Gwendolyn, Dorothy Tutin is Cecily, and Margaret Rutherford is Miss Prism. There is an obvious chemistry between Redgrave and Denison, and their badinage is brilliant in the best Wildean manner. Not surprisingly, the two grande dames, Evans and Rutherford, steal the show. Rutherford's Miss Prism woos the country rector with all her patented tongue-in-cheek style, and Evans is properly imperious as the redoubtable Bracknell. Her lines are delicious. Upon finding Redgrave on his knees proposing to her niece, she declaims, "Mr. Worthing! Rise, sir, from this semi-recumbent posture!" And later, when she learns that Worthing is an orphan, she exclaims, "To lose one parent is a misfortune; to lose both is a carelessness!"

REFERENCES

Asquith, Anthony, "The Importance of Being Faithful," *Theatre Arts*, 37 (April 1953), 72–74; Cohen, Philip K., *The Moral Vision of Oscar Wilde* (Rutherford, N.J.: Fairleigh Dickinson University Press, 1978).

—*J.C.T.*

INDIANS (1969)

ARTHUR KOPIT (1937—   )

Buffalo Bill and the Indians, or, Sitting Bull's History Lesson (1976), U.S.A., directed by Robert Altman, adapted by Alan Rudolph; United Artists.

The Play

Arthur Kopit is a native New Yorker who began writing plays while a student at Harvard. His first success, *Oh Dad, Poor Dad, Mamma's Hung You in the Closet and I'm Feelin So Sad* (1962, a grotesquerie about a dominating widow who revenges herself on her evil husband by preserving his corpse in her apartment), played in both London and Off-Broadway. Subsequent New York productions included *Sing to Me through Open Windows* and *The Day the Whores Came Out to Play Tennis* (1965). His most important play, and one of the most important American dramas of the 1960s, is *Indi-*

Arthur Kopit's Indians *was freely adapted by Robert Altman for his* Buffalo Bill and the Indians, *starring Paul Newman.* (COURTESY UNITED ARTISTS)

ans (1969). It was first staged in London in 1968 before coming to the Arena Stage a year later. It is an elegant satire that focuses on America's greed and racism during the 19th century. There were no scenic backdrops, just three glass cases housing effigies of Buffalo Bill, Sitting Bull, and a bloodstained Indian shirt, suggesting that Native American culture has been reduced to the status of quaint artifacts. Oppression of the Indians, moreover, has been an institutionalized tragedy. A series of scenes, or vignettes, contrast the romantic dream with the sordid reality, suggesting that the exploits of Buffalo Bill, dime-novel heroes, and Hollywood movies have all participated in shaping America's acceptance of what was nothing less than genocide. Moreover, the play serves as a critique of the Vietnam conflict. In one of the ensuing scenes, the parallels with recent Vietnam war history become clear. Echoing a speech by General Westmoreland, the character of Colonel Forsyth says, "Of course innocent people have been killed. In war they always are. And of course our heart go out to the innocent victims of this." The play ends on a note of pathos. Commentator Carol Harley notes that "the play itself has been a series of impasses between two alien systems. . . . *Indians* reveals the tragic consequences of incomprehensible exchanges between people speaking different languages. And the complexity of communicating through language has continued to obsess the American dramatist."

The Film

During the year of the American bicentennial, Robert Altman's adaptation of Kopit's play continued his inclination to skewer patriotic stereotypes and beliefs. Targeted specifically are America's obsession with celebrity and the oppression of Native Americans. The film's credits suggest that the film is "suggested by" the stage play. Paul Newman, a celebrity icon himself, portrays Buffalo Bill Cody, and Joel Grey plays his producer. Stripped of the starkly expressionist staging of Kopit's original, the movie is amplified and padded with real-life exteriors and opulent reenactments of moments from Buffalo Bill's Wild West shows. The film opens with Cody in his winter camp planning his Wild West Show with Chief Sitting Bull (Frank Kaquitts) as his prized attraction. The old chief has joined the show for the sole purpose of meeting President Grover Cleveland to argue the case of his dispossessed people. As Kopit had done, Altman opposes the Native Americans' beliefs about their traditions with Cody's "better sense of history," as he puts it. Thus, Sitting Bull refuses to surrender his perception of history to Cody's egotistical, imperialist scenarios. Failing in his agenda, the old man walks away into the wilderness. Alone among Cody's troupe is Annie Oakley, who sympathizes with the plight of the Indians. After Sitting Bull's death, Cody is haunted by his spirit, which he confronts, saying, "Truth is whatever gets the loudest applause."

The film concludes with a Wild West Show reenactment of Cody's triumph over Sitting Bull (now portrayed by the chief's interpreter). Cody is now no longer a human being so much as he is a caricature created by Ned Buntline (Burt Lancaster) come to life. Biographer Daniel O'Brien suggests that he is an inversion of other Altman heroes, like McCabe, Popeye, and Philip Marlowe: "These people may seem bumbling, incompetent and decidedly unheroic, but prove themselves when tested. Bill is a 'hero' only on the surface, carefully groomed for stardom. Underneath he is weak and feeble." The film's box-office reception was likewise feeble. Its drab visual style and plodding pace are partially responsible, as surely were its political sentiments. It was cut by 20 minutes before its overseas' release. Altman's own career, recently boosted by the success of *Nashville*, took a plunge that would not recover for years, until *Popeye* brought him back to public favor in 1980.

REFERENCES

Harley, Carol, "Arthur Kopit," in John MacNicholas, ed., *Twentieth-Century American Dramatists* (Detroit: Gale Research Company, 1981); McGilligan, Patrick, *Robert Altman: Jumping Off the Cliff* (New York: St. Martin's Press, 1989); O'Brien, Daniel, *Robert Altman: Hollywood Survivor* (New York: Continuum, 1995).

—*D.S. AND J.A. AND J.C.T.*

INHERIT THE WIND (1955)

JEROME LAWRENCE (1915–)/ROBERT E. LEE (1918–1994)

Inherit the Wind (1960), U.S.A., directed by Stanley Kramer, adapted by Nathan E. Douglas and Harold Jacob Smith; United Artists.

The Play

Hailed by many critics as one of the most noteworthy plays of the 1950s, *Inherit the Wind* was a thinly veiled fictionalization of the notorious "Scopes Monkey Trial" in Tennessee in 1925, which pitted Fundamentalist Christianity against Darwinian evolutionary theory. Premiering at the National Theatre on April 21, 1955, it ran for a spectacular 806 performances. Playwrights Jerome Lawrence and Robert E. Lee recast defense attorney Clarence Darrow as "Henry Drummond" (Paul Muni), prosecutor William Jennings Bryan as "Matthew Harrison Brady" (Ed Begley), the defendant Henry Scopes as "Bertram Cates" (Karl Light), and journalist H.L. Mencken as "E.K. Hornbeck" (Tony Randall). The action is transferred from Dayton, Tennessee, to the midwestern town of Hillsboro, where Cates is being tried for breaking a state criminal statute barring the teaching of evolution in public schools. In the climactic scene between the two attorneys, the wily Brady forces Drummond to admit that the Bible can be interpreted in a non-literal fashion, thus making it possible to argue that a theory of evolution is not necessarily inconsistent with the biblical account of creation. Although Cates is found guilty, the judge imposes only a token fine. The humiliated Brady dies on the spot of a heart attack. Drummond surprises Hornbeck at the end by coming to the defense of Brady: "He was looking for God too high up and far away."

In his book, *Summer for the Gods*, Edward J. Larson declares that *Inherit the Wind* has all but replaced the actual trial in the nation's memory. Moreover, the play's authors were interested in the Scopes trial not so much as historical fact but as "a metaphor for the blacklisting of their day," i.e., as a commentary on the anticommunist witch hunts of the late 1940s and early 1950s, with the Bryan character as a "mindless, reactionary creature of the mob" and the Darrow character as an advocate of tolerance.

The Film

Independent producer/director Stanley Kramer intended his film version to be the conclusion of a trilogy of pictures, beginning with *The Defiant Ones* (1958) and *On the Beach* (1959), that dealt with controversial racial and religious issues: "Enjoy them or not—agree with them or not—these are motion pictures that hit people hard," said Kramer, "that force people to see them, to think and to take a stand." In order to ensure the film version's commercial appeal, however, Kramer replaced the original Broadway stage actors with established movie stars: Ed Begley's Brady with Fredric March, Paul Muni's Drummond with Spencer Tracy, and Tony Randall's Hornbeck with Gene Kelly. Like the play, the film did not mention certain real-life facts, i.e., that the ACLU participated in stage-managing the trial; that the accused teacher was really a sports coach and had never formally taught evolutionary theory; and that although the trial's outcome loosened restrictive teaching practices in some states, the Tennessee statute in question remained in effect for many years.

The screenplay by Nathan E. Douglas and Harold Jacob Smith added many scenes to "open out" the courtroom-bound play. For example, the arrivals in town of Drummond and Brady are separately depicted in order to establish their respective characters: Drummond arrives anonymously on a community bus, while Brady arrives in an entourage amid the hoopla of the cheering crowd. Other additions include a full-scale revival meeting, incidents among the demonstrators picketing in the town square outside the courtroom, a romance between Cates and his fiancée, Rachel (Donna Anderson), and several episodes in the boarding house where Drummond and Brady are staying.

As if to counteract negative criticisms by fundamentalists that the film was "anti-Christ," Kramer persistently layers the soundtrack with hymns and folk songs, including "Gimme that Old-Time Religion" and, at the very end, a full-scale choral rendition of "The Battle Hymn of the Republic" (with soloist Leslie Uggams). Nonetheless, the film's script pro-

voked the Hollywood censors, who felt it violated that portion of the Production Code that held that "no film . . . may throw ridicule on any religious faith." Geoffrey Shurlock, spokesperson for the Code, declared, "Nearly all the Christians portrayed in this story seem to be described as near-fanatic, Old Testament fundamentalists. In addition, there is a tendency to create a considerable amount of sympathy against the Christian Bible and to misrepresent certain facts regarding Christian dogma. This all adds up to the ridicule of a religious faith, thus rendering this story unacceptable." Accordingly, recommendations were issued to screenwriters Nathan Douglas and Harold Smith that the script use the characters of Hornbeck and Drummond to distinguish "this one narrow-minded community from the Christian world as a whole." Moreover, Drummond's attack was to be seen not as an attack on the Christian Bible per se, "but rather on the obtuse literal interpretation of the Old Testament clung to by the citizens of this town."

REFERENCES

Bergman, Paul, and Michael Asimov, *Reel Justice: The Courtroom Goes to the Movies* (Kansas City, Mo.: Andrews and McMeel, 1996); Gardner, Gerald, *The Censorship Papers* (New York: Dodd, Mead, 1987); Harris, Thomas J., *Courtroom's Finest Hour in American Cinema* (Metuchen, N.J.: Scarecrow Press, 1987); Larson, Edward J., *Summer for the Gods: The Scopes Trial and America's Continuing Debate over Science and Religion* (Boston: Harvard University Press, 1998); Spoto, Donald, *Stanley Kramer: Film Maker* (New York: G.P. Putnam's Sons, 1978).

—*J.C.T.*

THE INNOCENTS (1950)

WILLIAM ARCHIBALD (1924–1970)

The Innocents (1961), U.K., directed by Jack Clayton, adapted by William Archibald and Truman Capote; Twentieth Century-Fox.

The Play

William Archibald's dramatization of Henry James' 1897 short novel, *The Turn of the Screw*, was retitled *The Innocents* because of the central position of the two children in the story. They are either the "innocent" victims of possession by the ghosts of two dead servants who once inhabited Bly House, or they are victimized by a neurotic, repressed governess who projects onto them her own disturbed fantasies. James, of course, would not tell, and his story remains to this day the most baffling of all modern ghostly tales. Archibald's play version premiered in New York at the Playhouse Theatre on February 1, 1950. The two-act drama featured Beatrice Straight as Miss Giddens, the governess, David Cole and Iris Mann as the children, Miles and Flora, and Isobel Elsom as Mrs. Grose, the housekeeper.

Generally faithful to the plot and characters of James's book, Act One opens as eight-year-old Flora and Mrs. Grose, the housekeeper, greet the new governess, Miss Giddens (for that is the name playwright Archibald gives the unnamed character in James's book), who has come to Bly House to take charge of Flora and her older brother, Miles. In a departure from the Jamesian original, in which James scrupulously withholds all background knowledge of the governess and of recent past incidents at Bly, there is a substantial amount of expository dialogue between Giddens and Grose that establishes at once the circumstances of Giddens's cramped, repressive upbringing (an important clue to her possible neuroses) and the recent history of activities at Bly House. Later, Giddens sees the shadow of a man appear against the curtain, then fade away. Little Flora seems oblivious to the sight. The next day, Giddens admits to Mrs. Grose that while out walking she saw a man staring at her from a distance. "Even though there was that distance between us, I could feel his eyes on me—bold, insolent—" confesses Giddens. "He stared at me as though *I* were the intruder!" A letter arrives revealing that Miles has been expelled from school and will be returning home soon. Upon his arrival, Miles refuses to answer any questions about the nature of his expulsion. In a scene lifted right out of the novella, the figure of a man reappears—this time at the window—and Giddens goes outside after it. Seconds later, Mrs. Grose enters the room and screams at the sight of Giddens's face framed in the window. (This is an important moment, since it prefigures the interpretation that Giddens is the real haunter of the house, rather than a couple of spooks.) Increasingly distraught by the apparitions, Giddens forces Grose to admit that the man she has been seeing resembles one Peter Quint, the former valet, who had died the year before. Grose explains that Quint had been an "evil" man who had "used his position here to do what he wanted." Act One ends as Giddens hears Miles singing a sinister little song, and she is now convinced that he is falling under the influence of the spirit of the wicked Peter Quint.

Act Two opens as Giddens and Grose discuss the possibly sinister impact Quint might have had on Miles in the past. While Grose admits that Quint frequently spoke to him furtively during long walks, she refuses to

believe there was any harm in it. Giddens is unconvinced. Later that night both children sneak downstairs to play. Giddens sees the figure of a woman dressed in black on the landing. Flora turns, sees the woman, and stretches out her arms toward her. Rushing to Flora's side, Giddens fails to force her to admit she has actually seen the apparition. The children adopt a mocking attitude toward Giddens; moreover, they protest her over-protective manner. "But is it the best thing?" asks Miles sarcastically, "being with a governess all the time? A boy wants other things, you know—." Grose admits to Giddens that Quint and the former governess, Miss Jessel, had indulged in indecent relations. Giddens wonders if the children were aware of that relationship, and if Quint had used and abused them to conceal those activities. Giddens decides on the spot to send Flora and the housekeeper away. She will remain with Miles to extract an admission of his collusion with Quint and thereby exorcise the evil in Bly House. "All that was base in Quint lives in Miles," argues Giddens. "He lives with the memory, the longing for all that Quint taught him. I must free him of it. Even if I must hurt him." Finally, alone with Miles, Giddens forces him to confess why he was expelled from school (he had said "bad things") and to confront the image of Quint that has reappeared at the window. She demands that Miles "reject" him. Finally, Miles shouts out, "Peter Quint!" He turns to the window and screams, "Leave me!" The figure at the window gestures menacingly. Miles crumples to the floor. Giddens rushes to him and embraces him. "You are safe," she repeats several times, rocking him back and forth. "You won back goodness and kindness. You are free—you're free—you're free." Realizing at last that Miles is dead, Giddens releases the body. Alone, she sobs again, "You are free. . . ." The curtain falls.

While retaining much of the ambiguity of James' novel—are there ghosts or are the apparitions merely the result of a deranged woman's imagination?—Archibald's play necessarily tips the scales toward the possibility of authentic ghosting. The play's restriction of all action to Bly House's ground floor rooms—eliminating James' frequent use of locations outside the house, like a pond, a church, and a wooded field—creates a pressure-cooker tension among the characters that effectively generates a sense of threat and terror. Much of the riddle of James' ghosts depended upon the dubious reliability of the governess' first-person testimony. James carefully distanced the reader from the narrative by utilizing a complex triple-framing device: An unnamed narrator relates the circumstances of an eyewitness tale that is told many years after the fact in the form of a document that is in turn presented at a dinner party. Archibald's play enjoys no such framing device to filter our apprehension of events. Quint and Jessel are real, corporeal presences who appear on stage in full view of everybody (the children on several occasions obviously are aware of their presence). The six-month time span of the novel, which afforded James plenty of leisure to complicate the story, enhance the suspense, and provoke confusion in the reader, is here confined to four days of dramatic time. Thus, the two acts and eight scenes inevitably compress events into a much swifter narrative, and delineate the characters in broad strokes. Dialogue must bear the entire burden of mood, action, and characterization, robbing the story of James's delicate subtlety, converting it at times into a more coarsely textured melodrama.

Music and sound effects, which, of course, were unavailable to James, are extensively employed in the play to enhance an evil atmosphere, pointing toward the possibility of authentic ghosting. Several songs and children's rhymes are introduced that seem to embody, by turns, the sweet innocence of childhood and the darker implications of perverse maturity. While Flora's songs seem harmlessly simple—"O bring me a bonnet of bright rosy red"—Miles' lyrics carry a sinister foreboding:

> Enter! My Lord! Come from your prison!
> Come from your grave!
> For the moon is arisen!

This might point toward either a genuine possession by spirits, or at least to the children's culpability in ensuing events. But it should be remembered that music's affective properties are perversely ambiguous. Perhaps Flora's little song contains a deceptively darker poignancy. And perhaps Miles's song is no more bitter or ghastly than hundreds of other children's songs and folk lyrics. More overtly sinister, however, is the background music that is everywhere in evidence to inflect key scenes and to effect transitions from one scene to another. The sounds of chiming clocks, heartbeats, and "vibrations" (as the script denotes them) underscore words and actions with an appropriately ominous emphasis. All appearances by Quint and Jessel are accompanied by aural cues. This is particularly flagrant in the final scene, when a steadily rising crescendo of sounds announces Quint's presence at the window.

The Film

Film director Jack Clayton had directed only one major feature film, *Room at the Top* (1958), before taking on a movie version of *The Turn of the Screw* in 1961. Assisted by the noteworthy cinematography of Freddie Francis, it was also his first film in Cinemascope. The subsequent film reveals that it was Archibald's dramatic version, as much as James's original novel, that influenced the final product. Indeed, Archibald was called in to write the scenario (he was later assisted by Truman Capote, with whom he shares co-billing). Clayton immediately announced he was concerned that the film, like the novel and the play, should have a "dual life," i.e., on the one hand, the ghosts could be interpreted as projections of the governess, and on the other, that "there are the ghosts and they are after the children." And, following James's example, Clayton was careful not to box himself in on the issue of supernatural events versus psychological projections. He went on record as blaming Giddens's repressed sexual attraction for the children's uncle—and perhaps, by extension, for Miles—for the disaster at Bly. But he also insisted that Giddens did indeed see ghosts—or at least was convinced she did. "This is what I love about the story," he said in an interview. "There is nothing black and white about it; it's full of question marks and possibilities. I don't want, you know, to say absolutely what the picture means. There should be an aura of uncertainty; that's what I think James intended. I want the audience to exercise its intelligence."

In a scene borrowed from James, the film begins as Giddens (Deborah Kerr) is being interviewed by the children's uncle (Michael Redgrave), during which it is learned that the former governess had died. Attending her arrival at Bly House and first meetings with Flora (Pamela Franklin) and Miles (Martin Stephens) are a series of strange incidents, including sightings of a man standing atop the tower of Bly House and a black-clad woman flitting about the hallways and rooms of the house. After learning from Mrs. Grose details about the unholy relationship between Quint and Jessel, she speculates that the children may have been "contaminated" by them and are now vulnerable to their malicious presence. More sightings confirm her resolve to intervene, if possible—the image of Quint at a window and the figure of Jessel in the children's schoolroom. Most disturbing, perhaps, is the silent apparition of Jessel standing in the reeds across the lake. The children, in the meantime, are behaving strangely. They disappear at intervals and go wandering alone in the woods. Both display a rude attitude toward the protective governess and accuse her of stifling them. For her part, and despite Mrs. Grose's protests, Giddens is now convinced that the children are "playing some monstrous game [that is] secretive, whispery, and indecent."

They are being "used" by Quint and Jessel as the vehicles by which the ghosts can be reunited in their mutual lust.

Flora by now has become hysterical. She and Mrs. Grose quit the house, leaving Giddens alone with Miles. Their climactic confrontation "opens up" the scene as it was staged in the play. It now begins in the house interior, continues to the pavilion outside, and concludes in the adjoining statuary park. After forcing Miles to admit that he "said things" in school, Giddens sees Quint's face at the rain-smeared window behind him. Miles then breaks into hysterical laughter and accuses Giddens of being a "damned hussey" and a "dirty-minded hag." In a tight two-shot Miles' contorted face addresses the camera, while behind him Quint's face breaks into silent laughter (unlike the staging of the play, where they face each other). Suddenly, Miles breaks away and races into the statuary park, where Quint's form reappears among the standing statues. At length, Miles utters the name "Peter Quint." In a startling overhead shot, Quint's gesturing hand appears in the foreground, hovering over the form of Miles. The child crumples to the ground. Giddens rushes to him and clutches him in her arms, murmuring she "has him" now. She leans forward and kisses him full upon the lips. After several moments, her head arches backward, and she and the boy fall away from each other, leaving only a dark void on the screen.

The controversial kiss—actually, the second time the two have kissed; the first transpired in Miles's bedroom halfway through the film—is the best-remembered detail of the film. It confirms what James had only suggested, that there is an erotic charge to the relationship between Miles and Giddens. Witnesses of Archibald's play swear they saw a kiss on stage, too; however, close examination of the play reveals no such scene. Instead, the kiss is derived from a scene in James's novel and subsequently repeated at the film's conclusion.

If anything, according to Clayton's pre-production notes, Archibald's first-draft screenplay was *too* close to the play. It relied too much on dialogue, provided too few characters, and was too restrictive in limiting the action to the house. "This was all right on stage," said Clayton, "but [it] does not give us the opportunities that one normally has in a film for constantly varying the tempo, atmosphere and tension by going from one scene to another scene . . . usually with fresh characters." It was Clayton who restored some of James's original locations, including the country church and the area of the pond. To Clayton also must go the credit of adding a statuary garden as a location for the final confrontation of Giddens, Miles, and Quint.

Maintaining a character's specific point of view, as James had done in the novel, is notoriously difficult in the film medium, but Clayton does convey a sense of that in his choice of camera angles and strategies of editing. Usually, when the apparitions appear, they are presented either from Giddens' foregound point of view in a deep-focus two-shot, or via the simple means of eyeline cutting. Either way, the viewer shares her point of view. When the camera angle shifts to a more omniscient angle, however, the phantom vanishes. For example, the scene wherein she sees Miss Jessel sitting at the schoolroom desk foregrounds Giddens, allowing the viewer to look past her shoulder toward the black-clad woman. However, when the vantage point changes to a reverse angle and the camera dollies with her as she walks toward the desk, the figure vanishes. If Clayton were entirely consistent throughout with this strategy, Giddens's subjective inflection of events would be confirmed. But there are significant variations in this schema. In the schoolroom scene, Giddens finds a teardrop on the desk seconds after witnessing Jessel. In another scene, early in the film, Quint appears at the window *behind* Giddens. Because he sees her and she at first does not see him, his objective presence is implied. This is confirmed during the film's conclusion at the moment of Miles's death. Giddens has raced breathlessly after Miles as he flees to the garden. A subjective camera simulates her disorientation with a 360-degree pan, coming to rest momentarily on the figure of Quint, standing atop one of the statue pedestals. But then, in a startling and unexpected break from Giddens's point of view, an overhead shot reveals her and the boy in the middle distance while in the foreground Quint's gesturing hand dominates the frame in the same gesture that playwright Archibald had used in the last moments of his play. Miles crumples to the ground, lifeless. The effect is extremely disconcerting, because for the first time in the film, the viewer sees the action from *Quint's* point of view. Moments like these seem to be carefully calculated disruptions of the otherwise carefully calculated subjective strategy of much of the rest of the film. Perhaps the ghosts are real, after all?

A significant carryover from Archibald's play is the emphasis on music, sound effects, and songs. As in the play, the film contains two songs, each associated with innocence and/or morbidity. A tune called "Willow Waylee" is a leitmotif for the entire film. It is first heard in Flora's sweet voice,

> We lay, my love and I,
> Beneath the weeping willow

But now alone I lie. . . .
Oh Willow, I die.
Oh Willow, I die.

Who has died? Is it just a children's innocent folk song, or does it suggest the death of someone in the film—perhaps Quint and/or Jessel? Flora also plays it as a simple tune on the piano, and she hums it softly to herself on several occasions—as she gazes out her bedroom window, picks flowers at the moment Giddens first sees Quint on the tower, and at the lake just before the appearance of Miss Jessel. The song is also heard several times from a music box found in the attic among Miss Jessel's effects. And it is omnipresent on the film's background music track (composed by Georges Auric).

Miles has his own song, the same song he declaimed in Archibald's play during the scene when he and Flora play a "dress-up" game:

Enter my Lord. Come from your prison.
Come from your grave
For the moon is arisen.

Not just a death is suggested, now, but a *return.* . . .

This sound and music plot is, according to commentator Jeanne Thomas Allen, "in many ways more upsetting than the visuals." The use of echo chambers and electronic effects throughout—which includes distortions of Flora's song—is "generally ambiguous" and suggestive either of the apparitions or of Miss Giddens's deranged mind. For example, we may ask, are the echo effects "a sign of passing from objectively heard sound into an inner chamber of subjective haunting sound," or just simply an aural game inherited from decades of melodramatic claptrap?

Clayton employs an unusual method of dissolving in and out of scenes, which lends its own ambiguity to the action. Rather than simply juxtaposing two shots, exiting from one and entering into another, an intermediate image is insinuated between them. Images of clouds, trees, rain, and faces materialize in the brief seconds before one shot has entirely yielded to the succeeding shot. "*The Innocents* is completely mood-oriented," Clayton explained, "and it gave me opportunities to explore this field, which I had never done before; to create, in those multiple dissolves, images which hang there, and have a meaning which applies both to the end of the last scene and the beginning of the next."

That Clayton's film succeeded in conveying at least some of the ambiguity of James's novel and Archibald's play is borne out by the contradictory critical reactions. Alexander Walker judged it a "study in erotic obsessions rather than supernatural events." Ivan But-

ler, however, writes that the film means us to take the ghosts literally: Both Archibald and Clayton show us the ghosts and thus indicate their opinion of the governess' stage of mind. Commentator Don G. Smith would have it both ways: "I believe Miss Giddons [sic] *is* emotionally disturbed. She *is* sexually repressed, and she *is* a pederast. I also believe that the ghosts *are* real and they *are* indeed attempting to possess the children. . . . Both interpretations are defensible, and they are not mutually exclusive. Indeed, both are necessary if we are actually to reconcile what we see and hear."

Operating at a distinctly lower level of intent and achievement is Michael Winner's *The Nightcomers* (1971), which has nothing whatever to do with William Archibald's play. Arguably, it has little to do with James's novel, either. It insists on explaining away all the ambiguities that novelist James, playwright Archibald, and filmmaker Clayton had hitherto worked so strenuously to promote. Marlon Brando as Quint and Stephanie Beacham as Jessel gleefully induct the children into perverse practices. When they try to leave, the kids kill them. At the end, a newly recruited governess arrives, unaware of the dangers awaiting her.

REFERENCES

Allen, Jeanne Thomas, "*The Turn of the Screw* and *The Innocents*: Two Types of Ambiguity," in Gerald Peary and Roger Shatzkin, eds., *The Classic American Novel & the Movies* (New York: Frederick Ungar, 1977), 132–142; Butler, Ivan, *Horror in the Cinema* (New York: A.S. Barnes, 1970); Gow, Gordon, "The Way Things Are," *Films and Filming*, April 1974, 11–14; "The Innocents," *Show Magazine*, January 1962, 30; Seitz, Hunter, "Haunted Cinema: *The Innocents*," *All Hallows*, 19 (October 1998), 37–40; Smith, Don G., "*The Innocents*," in Gary J. and Susan Svehla, eds., *Cinematic Hauntings* (Baltimore: Midnight Marquee Press, 1996).

—*J.C.T.*

INSIGNIFICANCE (1982)

TERRY JOHNSON

Insignificance (1985), U.K., directed by Nicolas Roeg, adapted by Terry Johnson; Zenith Productions/Recorded Picture Company.

The Play

Terry Johnson's play was originally performed at London's Royal Court Theatre in 1982, with Judy Davis playing the sexy but intellectually insecure "Actress," inspired by Marilyn Monroe, who had among her possessions a photograph signed by Albert Einstein, represented in the play by a character defined simply as "The Professor." The Actress is in New York filming what in Roeg's film is clearly *The Seven Year Itch*, accompanied by a jealous "Baseball Player" (Joe DiMaggio is the model) and also pursued by a predatory "Senator" (a Joe McCarthy clone), who wants the Professor to testify before Congress, expecting to discover some manner of communist affiliation. The Senator is a publicity hound, searching out celebrities to exploit.

The action is set in New York City in 1954. After completing her shoot on the film, the Actress stops by a drug store and buys a peculiar assortment of items, which she will later use when she visits the Professor in his hotel room to demonstrate to him that she understands the theory of relativity. She is followed there by the jealous Baseball Player, who hardly expects to find an elderly, ironic, bemused intellectual. The Professor has been badgered and threatened by the Senator, who is a natural bully, first attempting to intimidate the physicist, and then returning later with a subpoena.

People make unreasonable demands on the Professor because he is famous, but there is something sweet and genuine about the Actress, and that brings out a parallel sweetness in him. "Because of being famous," he tells the Actress, "everywhere I go people fall over themselves to be with me," and "because of fame, everything I do develops into a ridiculous comedy." The Actress tells him he is lucky: "Everything I do develops into a nightmare." Put the two together and you have a comic nightmare. The characters appear to be detached, from each other and from "reality," but the Actress and the Professor can appreciate each other's existential loneliness and have perhaps a fleeting moment of mutual understanding. "It was always meant to be a play about the era, about fame," playwright Terry Johnson explained, and "what these people stood for, the fact that this was different from what they are."

The Film

This was the first time Nicolas Roeg had adapted a play to the screen. A difficult and challenging cinematographer turned director—previous films like *Bad Timing* (1980) and *Eureka* (1982) had seemed arbitrarily abstract and abstruse to some tastes—Roeg was a master of ambiguity and something of a mystic. He wanted his film to be "a Real, Mythical, Melodramatic Farce." As Roeg explained (none too clearly) in the published screenplay, "To me the characters were

mythic, not invented by any single person, not the public or the press, probably not even by the characters themselves. Familiar but strange, living or dead people made up from stories, fictions, gossip. Truly fictional people, but their fiction was made up of so many other fictions that they could represent something to everyone."

According to Neil Sinyard's book on Roeg, the director opens the play "out not so much spatially as laterally," or, as Terry Johnson put it, "he opened it backwards." Sinyard traces image patterns of clocks and watches, the most important of which is the Professor's watch, "which is permanently stuck at 8:15, the time at which the bomb went off in Nagasaki," marking the time the nuclear era and the cold war began. Since then time has stood still for the Professor (Michael Emil is the Einstein look-alike). Roeg asked Johnson to rethink and shorten the play, stretching out the images: "There are two watches in the play [but] there are about a half-a-dozen in the film."

Following the time cues in the play, the action is set in New York in 1954. The Actress (Theresa Russell) is hounded by celebrity seekers throughout the film as a consequence of her beauty and her fame. She is also watched by the technicians below the grill who operate the fan that blows up her dress during the shoot. She is watched by the jealous Ball Player (Gary Busey) and by the Senator (Tony Curtis), who fixes her as the object of his lustful "gaze," but attempts to have sex with a prostitute who is a Marilyn look-alike (to no avail, since he is impotent). The name of the actress playing the prostitute is listed as Desiree Erasmus; the name would seem to be an oxymoron and a joke that links the emotional with the intellectual. All of the main characters have achieved celebrity status, which complicates their lives. They are well known, but can they have true significance in a world that may be headed for self-destruction?

The Professor is haunted by the memory of Nagasaki, and an apocalyptic nuclear wind blows through the film's final frames. Nonetheless, there are some charming, if arbitrarily contrived moments, as when the Actress explains to the Professor his own relativity theory as they both push toy trucks around the apartment floor; and when the Professor and the Ball Player discuss their appearances on bubblegum cards. Or Roeg commented that maybe people could be better if they cultivated "a sense of their own insignificance in the scheme of things." *Insignificance* has been called Roeg's funniest film, but Roeg is not noted for his sense of humor. What lingers most vividly in the mind is not the farcical subtext, but the nuclear one—

a kind of incendiary cocktail—combined with feelings of guilt, frustration, and anxiety over political persecution, a marriage on the rocks, and the continuing motif Neil Sinyard described as "the death of children, both individually (the Actress's miscarriage) and globally." Johnson's adaptation is inventive, even ingenious, and entertaining, far more accessible than most of Roeg's films, but it is likely to be puzzling on first viewing.

REFERENCES

Lanza, Joseph, *Fragile Geometry: The Films, Philosophy, and Misadventures of Nicolas Roeg* (New York: PAJ Publications, 1989); Norman, Neil, and John Barraclough, *Insignificance: The Book* (London: Sidgwick and Jackson, 1985); Sinyard, Neil, *The Films of Nicolas Roeg* (London: Charles Letts and Co., 1991).

—*J.M.W.*

IPHIGENIA IN AULIS (c. 405 B.C.)

EURIPIDES (480?–406? B.C.)

Iphigenia (1976), Greece, directed and adapted by Michael Cacoyannis; Greek Film Centre/United Artists.

The Play

Euripides probably left *Iphigenia in Aulis* unfinished. It was produced after his death, and the finale seems to have been added by another hand. There are two versions of the first scene, moreover. The high priest Calchas has told the Greeks that their fleet cannot sail for Troy from Aulis unless Agamemnon agrees to sacrifice his daughter, Iphigenia. The mother, Clytemnestra, and her daughter both plead for her life, as does Achilles, who is threatened by the Greek army for defending her. Pressured by his brother Menelaus and the other generals Agamemnon reluctantly agrees, and the dutiful Iphigenia, who freely offers herself up at last, is led away to be sacrificed.

The Film

The film by the "New Wave" Greek director Michael Cacoyannis is part of the Euripidean trilogy—including *Electra* (1961) and *The Trojan Women* (1971)—shown at the National Film Theatre (London) in 1981 in reverse order so as to establish narrative coherence. In 1968 Cacoyannis mounted a stage production in New York City, eight years before he was to film the adaptation on location at Haidari, near Athens. As noted above, the text of the play is problematic and probably not entirely the work of Euripides. The language is not considered appropriate for the heroic characters, and Iphigenia's change of heart at the end seems to be an unexpected reversal, damaging the logic of the piece. Are there any assurances, moreover, that Iphigenia's sacrifice will effect a change in the weather to put wind in the sails of the Greek fleet, for example, or is this to be taken as a matter of faith?

The film's opening rehearses events alluded to in the play's opening dialogue between Agamemnon (Costa Kazakos) and his loyal slave and other events mentioned later. A tracking shot reveals idle soldiers and a row of beached ships. There is no wind and they are running short of food. In the film Calchas (Dimitri Aronis) approaches Agamemnon with Menelaus (Costa Carras) and Odysseus (Christos Tsangos), presenting him with a demand from Artemis calling for the sacrifice of Iphigenia, a departure from the play text. The film "makes it clear that Agamemnon refuses to countenance the sacrifice of his daughter until the army's enthusiasm for him forces him to think again," according to Kenneth MacKinnon, whereas in the play the army's attitude and "particularly Agamemnon's psychology are more elusive."

MacKinnon nails home the adaptation's shortcomings as follows: "The principal difference between film and play in this area is that inconsistency and ambiguity seem to be eliminated in the film's account of [the] events." Moreover, in the film "Menelaus pleads for Iphigenia, while Agamemnon claims that her fate is sealed." MacKinnon singles out the "sequences in which Iphigenia listens appalled to [the] discussion and makes a vain attempt at flight and where Odysseus harangues the army," because these sequences "are entirely new." The film was both a critical and popular success and was nominated for an Academy Award as best foreign film of 1978.

REFERENCES

MacKinnon, Kenneth, *Greek Tragedy into Film* (London: Croom Helm, 1986); Schuster, Mel, *The Contemporary Greek Cinema* (Metuchen, N.J.: Scarecrow Press, 1979).

—*J.M.W.*

ITALIAN STRAW HAT, THE

See *UN CHAPEAU DE PAILLE D'ITALIE*

THE JAZZ SINGER (1925)

SAMSON RAPHAELSON (1896–1983)

The Jazz Singer (1927), U.S.A., directed by Alan Crosland, adapted by Alfred A. Cohn; Warner Bros.

The Play

Playwright Samson Raphaelson had seen Al Jolson in *Robinson Crusoe Jr.* in 1917 and had never forgotten the impact of the volatile performer. "I shall never forget the first five minutes of Jolson," Raphaelson recalled 10 years later, "his velocity, the amazing fluidity with which he shifted from a tremendous absorption in his audience to a tremendous absorption in his song." Only in cantors in synagogues had Raphaelson seen a comparable spirit and intensity. The energy of Jolson and the duality of entertainer and cantor so intrigued Raphaelson that he wrote a short story, "The Day of Atonement," about the conflicts between a cantor and his rebellious son. He then adapted it into a three-act play, *The Jazz Singer,* which premiered in New York at the Fulton Theatre on September 24, 1925, where it ran for an impressive 303 performances. Although Raphaelson had approached Jolson to take on the role of Jakie Rabinowitz, the singer refused the part because the play was a drama rather than a musical. Instead, George Jessel took on the part.

The story is simple: Young Jakie is so obsessed with jazz music that he runs afoul of his traditionalist cantor father (Howard Lang). He runs away from home, takes on the stage name of "Jack Robin," and becomes a success as a popular singer. On the eve of his big break headlining a major Broadway revue, he learns his father is dying. Rushing to his father's bedside, Jakie is persuaded to return to the synagogue and follow in his father's footsteps. Despite critical cavils that it was "hokum" and a "garish and tawdry Hebrew play," the show received great word of mouth and drew a steady business. Historian Scott Eyman notes that the play's theme of the eternal conflict between the demands of a father and the dreams of a son "could never be outdated, that [it] would have a hard nugget of reality so long as the siren call of freedom lures children to embrace values their immigrant parents find objectionable."

The Films

Bringing *The Jazz Singer* to the screen was largely the brainchild of Sam Warner. He secured the screen rights for $50,000 and pushed it into production in the summer of 1927 as a Vitaphone synchronized-sound feature to be shot on the new Warners lot on Sunset Boulevard in Hollywood. George Jessel was supposed to re-create his role of Jakie, but he chose instead to make another film, *Private Izzy Murphy,* a variation on the popular play, *Abie's Irish Rose.* Al Jolson, who in a sense had started it all, was signed instead (he had already appeared in several Vitaphone short sound films). Alan Crosland, who had directed Warners' first Vitaphone release, *Don Juan*, the year before, was assigned to direct. Whereas Raphaelson's play was a sincere portrait of a time of crisis in a Jewish family, and a play whose most melodramatic elements—the jazz singing, the old cantor's death, the religious pageantry—had occurred offstage, the Warners' film dragged them center stage, as it were, and bathed them in the most flagrant eyewash, with mother-love the dominating emotion. Audiences today find Eugenie Besserer's performance as Jakie's mother unwatchable, and Raphaelson himself described Jolson's acting as "lousy" (Jolson's vaunted "improvised dialogue" was probably, in actuality, planned in advance; and his line, "You ain't heard nothin' yet," had become his signature tag years before). In true Hollywood fashion, Jakie gets to have it both ways in the end, leaving opening night to sing the "Kol Nidre" for his father but returning to the Winter Garden stage to resume his Broadway career and sing "Mammy."

The Jazz Singer premiered at the Warner Theatre on Broadway and 52nd Street just a day after the death of Sam Warner. Although it was a spectacular success in New York, it was the silent version of the picture that played at most theatres on its first run. That was because its synchronized sound-on-disk system precluded its showing in theatres not equipped for sound. Yet, it singlehandedly launched the talking picture revolution that in just a few months would turn Hollywood topsy-turvy. And the importance of Jolson's involvement in the new technology could not be underestimated. As critic Richard Watts, Jr., wrote at the time, "The important thing was that this device for synchronizing sound with cinema proved capable of catching all of that distinctive quality of voice and method, all of that unparalleled control over the emotions of his audience that is Al Jolson." But playwright Raphaelson, while acknowledging that the finished product had some attractive location shots of New York's East Side, bitterly attacked everything else: "The whole damned thing—the dialogue, whatever they had taken from my innocent play was either distorted or broken up. I had a simple, corny, well-felt little melodrama, and they made an ill-felt, silly, maudlin, badly timed thing of it."

In retrospect, the film is all about the Warner brothers themselves. "*The Jazz Singer* implicitly celebrates the ambition and drive needed to escape the *shtetls* of Europe and ghettos of New York," concludes historian Scott Eyman. "Jack, Sam, and Harry let Jack

Robin have it all: the satisfaction of taking his father's place *and* of conquering the Winter Garden. They were, perhaps unwittingly, dramatizing some of their own ambivalence about the debt first-generation Americans owed their parents." *The Jazz Singer* has been remade and updated twice, by Michael Curtiz in 1952, starring Danny Thomas in the Jolson role; and by Richard Fleischer in 1980, starring Neil Diamond.

The 1980 remake was flat and lifeless, even though Laurence Olivier was cast to play Jack's father and turned into a Holocaust survivor in the updated story. In this instance the Warner's sound classic becomes an uninspired, sentimental, and even laughable vehicle to showcase Neil Diamond's singing.

REFERENCES

Carringer, Robert L., ed., *The Jazz Singer* (Madison: University of Wisconsin Press, 1979); Eyman, Scott, *The Speed of Sound: Hollywood and the Talkie Revolution, 1926–1930* (New York: Simon and Schuster, 1997); Higham, Charles, *Warner Brothers* (New York: Charles Scribner's Sons, 1975).

—*J.C.T.*

JEZEBEL (1933)

OWEN DAVIS (1874–1956)

Jezebel (1938), U.S.A., directed by William Wyler, adapted by Clement Ripley, Abem Finkel, and John Huston; Warner Bros.

The Play

Owen Davis was one of the American theatre's great eclectics. His plays embraced musical spectacles like *The Battle of Port Arthur* (1908), social problem topics like *Sinners* (1915), and family melodramas like *The Detour* (1921) and the Pulitzer Prize–winning *Icebound* (1923). He wrote quickly and easily, always with an eye toward the box office. "One of the first tricks I learned was that my plays must be written for an audience who, owing to huge, uncarpeted, noisy theaters, couldn't always hear the words and who, a large percentage of them having only recently landed in America, couldn't have understood them in any case." *Jezebel* opened in New York on December 19, 1933, at the Ethel Barrymore Theatre. The play was to star Tallulah Bankhead as Julie Kendrick, but when she became sick during rehearsals, Miriam Hopkins came in at the last minute. The story takes place in Louisiana in 1853, and young and pretty Julie has returned from Europe with the intention of marrying her cousin Preston Kendrick, whose advances she had earlier rejected. Unknown to Julie, Preston, in the interval, has married. Feeling slighted, Julie seeks revenge. She provokes a duel, in which Preston's own brother, Ted, kills Preston, then dramatically throws the fatal pistol in Julie's lap. Shunned now by her society and overcome with guilt, Julie volunteers as a nurse during the Yellow Fever plague. The play ends with the assumption that she will die a redemptive death. Sumptuous scenery and costumes contributed to making this a costly production, a Broadway casualty that ran for only 32 performances.

The Film

The production route of this film is interesting. William Wyler, working then at Universal, tried to persuade that studio to purchase the rights to Davis's play, *Jezebel*. Wyler intended his wife, Margaret Sullavan, to star in the leading role. However, Universal turned down the project, and Wyler eventually moved to Warner Brothers, which ended up producing the movie, with Wyler as director. In casting the leading role, Warner Brothers decided against both Margaret Sullavan and Miriam Hopkins (despite Hopkins's favorable Broadway reviews) and, instead, chose Bette Davis, who, a short while earlier, had been turned down by David O. Selznick for the role of Scarlett O'Hara. Warner Brothers saw *Jezebel* as their marketing response to *Gone With the Wind;* and they were resolute in doing everything they could to have their film open first. They succeeded; and, while the film was expensive—$1 million—*Jezebel* was decidedly successful, financially and critically. Reviews of Bette Davis's performance were especially favorable. Critics also lauded the movie's strong writing and direction. Davis won an Oscar for best actress (her second) and Fay Bainter (Aunt Belle Massey) was given the Oscar for best supporting actress.

Like *Gone with the Wind, Jezebel* opens in the pre–Civil War South. Set in New Orleans, the story focuses on Julie Morrison (Davis), a Southern belle, as beautiful as she is willful. Young, fiery, and unmarried, Julie decides to wear a scarlet-red gown to the Olympus Ball, an act that she knows is brazen in its defiance of social custom, a custom that plainly required young women of her class and situation to wear only modest, white gowns. In consequence of this act, New Orleans society judges her harshly and Julie's fiancé, Preston (Henry Fonda), calls off their engagement and moves to Philadelphia. Julie, who loves Preston deeply, waits in patience and relative

solitude for his return home. Three years later, Pres does come back, and a transformed Julie, in a decorous gown of white, kneels before him and speaks her kindhearted and imploring apology. The moment is melodramatic loveliness, and, true to melodrama's formula, the apology proves fruitless. Preston is already married, to a mild and mannerly Northerner. In short time, a fatal yellow-jack epidemic breaks out, and Preston becomes infected with the deadly fever. His only chance of survival is to be brought to a quarantined island, where someone must nurse him, if he is to survive. Julie Morrison, risking contracting the fever herself, selflessly accompanies Pres and hopes to nurture him back to health and subsequently and altruistically return Pres safely home to his wife. This plot is an extreme departure from Davis's play, in which Julie snubs her fiancé Preston by moving to Europe for three years, fully expecting him to wait for her; but on returning, she discovers he has married a Northerner.

While both the stage and screen versions of *Jezebel* are highly melodramatic, the movie *Jezebel* embraces the Hollywood version of this genre by making the woman's love (i.e., Julie's) ennoblingly long-suffering and self-denying. However, the film dislodges itself from melodrama's conventions, in a manner that the play does not, in creating an ending that lacks closure. It is unclear whether Press and/or Julie survive the too-often-fatal yellow-jack fever.

In the Warner Brothers' *Jezebel* we see an elegant instance of classic Hollywood cinema. The acting is appropriately stylized, almost high-toned. Handsome balance continuously defines the frame's composition. The story drives the viewer's attention. Lighting, while almost radiant, is also beautifully subtle, as is the continuity editing. Most surprisingly, Max Steiner's music, notoriously inflated and distracting in other movies, underscores *Jezebel* in a complementary and appropriate way.

In addition to Bette Davis, Henry Fonda, and Fay Bainter, the cast also incudes George Brent (Buck Cantrell), Henry O'Neill (General Bogardus), and Margaret Lindsay (Amy Dillard).

REFERENCES

Bordman, Gerald, *American Theater: A Chronicle of Comedy and Drama, 1930–1969* (New York: Oxford University Press, 1996); Herman, Jan, *A Talent for Trouble: The Life of Hollywood's Most Acclaimed Director, William Wyler* (New York: Putnam, 1996); Ringgold, Gene, *The Complete Films of Bette Davis* (New York: Citadel Press, 1990).

—*L.C.C. AND S.C.C.*

JOHNNY BELINDA (1940)

ELMER HARRIS (1878–1966)

Johnny Belinda (1948), U.S.A., directed by Jean Negulesco, adapted by Irmgard von Cube and Allen Vincent; Warner Bros.

The Play

Elmer Blaney Harris was a Chicago-born playwright whose first produced play was *Sham* (1909). Apart from *Johnny Belinda*, his best-known plays include a collaboration with Oliver Morosco on *So Long Letty* (1916) and a comedy, *Young Sinners* (1929). *Johnny Belinda* aroused considerable controversy over its content, which included a rape, the birth of an illegitimate child, and a murder. The three-act drama was first produced at the Belasco Theatre on September 18, 1940, and ran for a successful 321 performances. The story is set in 1900 on Prince Edward Island, one of Canada's maritime provinces. Belinda McDonald (Helen Craig) is a deaf-mute who is brutally raped by Locky McCormick (Willard Parker), a drunken bully. Because he has befriended Belinda and taught her sign language, Dr. Jack Davidson (Horace McNally) is suspected of the act. The town gossip results in the loss of his practice and his banishment to another location. After Belinda's child is born, McCormick attempts to take it from her. She kills him. At her trial for murder, she is defended—and then acquitted—by Dr. Davidson. She agrees to marry him. Despite critical cavilings that the action was melodramatic and "overwrought," the play was a great success.

The Film

Warner Brothers paid an estimated $65,000 for the film rights to the play. Delmer Daves was originally scheduled to direct, but was replaced by Jean Negulesco, who had already made such classics of atmosphere and melodrama as *The Mask of Dimitrios* (1944) and *Humoresque* (1947). The film adaptation by Jean Negulesco and Irmgard von Cube and Allen Vincent retained the play's basic scenes and key dialogues, while opening out the three interior sets to include exterior scenes capitalizing on the Canadian locations. The action is set on Cape Breton Island, near Nova Scotia. Scenes between Belinda (Jane Wyman) and Dr. Davidson—here renamed Robert Richardson—(Lew Ayres) are expanded to emphasize their romantic attachment, such as when Dr. Richardson takes her to a big-city doctor to diagnose her mute condition (and learns that she is pregnant). Other added scenes enhance the villainy of McCormick (Stephen [Horace] McNally, reprising his stage role), as when he fights Belinda's father (Charles Bickford) and tosses him off a cliff to the rocks below. Moreover, the trial scenes are considerably augmented. Purportedly, when Jack Warner first saw the film, he disliked it so intensely that he refused to renew director Negulesco's contract. Yet the picture went on to become a huge critical and commercial hit, earning $4.25 million and nine Oscar nominations. Jane Wyman, who hitherto had performed principally comic roles, won an Academy Award for best actress, and Charles Bickford and Agnes Moorehead were nominated for best supporting actor and best supporting actress, respectively. Director Negulesco was also nominated for best director. Other Oscar nominations included best picture, screenplay, art direction, cinematography, film editing, music (Max Steiner), and sound recording. "With such lurid material to deal with," opined a critic in *Fortnight*, "it is horrible to think what might have evolved. But *Johnny Belinda* has been made with tenderness. The sombre little story has been given enormous poignancy and yet has been told with just the right restraint, so that it is neither crude melodrama nor shameless tearjerker, rather a warm, intensely human, impassioned tragedy."

REFERENCES

Negulesco, Jean, *Things I Did and Things I Think I Did* (New York: Simon and Schuster, 1984); Quirk, Lawrence J., *Jane Wyman: The Actress and the Woman* (New York: Dembner Books, 1986).

—T.W.

JOURNEY'S END (1928)

R.C. SHERRIFF (1896–1975)

Journey's End (1930), U.S.A./U.K., directed by James Whale, adapted by Joseph Moncure March; Gainsborough-Welsh-Pearson (U.K.)/Tiffany Studios-Stahl (U.S.A.).

The Play

Journey's End: A Play in Three Acts was first produced in 1928 at London's Apollo Theatre, December 10; published in 1929; and adapted to the cinema in 1930. Both the London stage production and the film were directed by James Whale, who also designed the sets (simply involving "A dug-out in the British trenches before St. Quentin in France," on March 18, 1918). Whale also directed the American production that opened in New York at the Henry Miller Theatre on March 22, 1929. Critic Hannen Swaffer of the London *Daily Express* called it "the greatest of all war plays." It has also been revived in Britain and the United States, and in Canada at the Stratford, Ontario, Festival during the 1990s.

Act One begins with the arrival of Lieutenant James Raleigh (Maurice Evans, in the London production), just out of school, who asked to be assigned to "C" Company, commanded by Captain Dennis Stanhope (Laurence Olivier), his old schoolmate and idol who came to France straight from school when he was 18 and has served there for three years. Raleigh is greeted by Lieutenant Osborne, a 45-year-old former schoolmaster, who describes Stanhope as battle-fatigued: a hard drinker whose "nerves have got battered to bits" as a result of his wartime service. Stanhope is engaged to Raleigh's sister, but he is not pleased that Raleigh has been assigned to his company. Stanhope is ashamed of what he has become, a cynic who cannot face the enemy without being fortified with whiskey.

The next morning in Act Two, Stanhope tells his men that the Germans are expected to attack within two days. Later that afternoon Osborne and Raleigh are to be sent on a mission to capture a German soldier for interrogation. The English want to know where the Germans are concentrated. The German front line is "only about seventy yards" away, "about the breadth of a Rugger field." Two officers and 10 men will be sent into No Man's Land. The colonel suggests that Stanhope send Osborne and Raleigh. It's a suicide mission, and Stanhope knows it but is unable to protect either Raleigh or his friend and comrade Osborne. The Germans will concentrate their fire as soon as the British break through the barbed-wire barrier. As 2nd Lieutenant Trotter tells Osborne, "It's damn ridiculous making a raid when the Boche are expecting it." The raid commences in Act Three. A young German soldier is captured, but seven men, including Osborne, are killed. Raleigh survives the raid but is mortally wounded the next day during the German attack, and dies.

According to filmmaker George Pearson's memoir, *Flashback*, the play was autobiographical. Robert Sherriff had served his country in France during the Great War. Back in England after the war he became an insurance clerk and was captain of the Kingston Rowing Club. The club wanted him to find a play that could be inexpensively produced as a fund-raiser, so Sherriff wrote his war play based on his own experi-

ences at St. Quentin. The club rejected the play, but a friend took it to James Whale, "a young Stage Director who had served through the war and was now a member of the London Stage Society."

Laurence Olivier first played Captain Stanhope at the Apollo Theatre in 1928, but when the play was moved to the Savoy in 1929, Colin Clive played the lead, with popular and critical acclaim. In both productions, Maurice Evans played Raleigh. In New York, Colin Keith-Johnson starred as Stanhope, supported by Derek Williams as Raleigh and Leon Quartermaine as Lt. Osborne.

The Film

Because the play was successful and because there had been a string of popular World War I films—*What Price Glory?* (1926), *The Big Parade* (1925), and *Wings* (1929)—Hollywood took immediate interest in Sherriff's play, which was less ribald than *What Price Glory?* and also more grim. *Journey's End* influenced Howard Hawks's *The Dawn Patrol* (1930), so much so that Sherriff unsuccessfully sued Hawks for plagiarism. In England the first film script was written by Gareth Gundry, "an ex-army officer who had served in the war and was now an expert film-director with Gainsborough," Pearson recalled, but since Whale rejected Gundry's script, George Pearson was given "instructions to take over the responsibility of arranging for the writing of the film-script version of the play" and "to supervise the filming by James Whale," then an inexperienced film director, and "to see that no distortion of Sherriff's work was attempted by America."

Gundry's script was technically well made, but Pearson realized "it over-elaborated much that needed the utter simplicity of the play" and its "stark realism." In New York, producer Maurice Browne agreed and sent Pearson on to Hollywood to meet Whale at Tiffany Studios. Moncure March was finally commissioned on loan from Howard Hughes to complete the screenplay. James Whale cast Colin Clive, who played a very popular Stanhope at the Savoy, but Whale and Pearson struggled mightily to get the actor for the movie role, since, as R.C. Sherriff had written, "So far as London was concerned, Colin Clive was *Journey's End*" and the London stage production would suffer if Clive took the film assignment. The Shakespearean actor Ian MacLaren was cast as Lt. Osborne and the Canadian actor David Manners as Raleigh.

Reviewing the film for *Cinema* (June 1930), James Shelley Hamilton wrote that the adaptation to the screen was "amazingly good," adding that "the text has been almost literally transposed from the stage to the screen, with additions of action in the trenches and in No Man's Land that prevent the monotony that might come from always watching one set." But the most authoritative praise came from the playwright himself: "I did not detect a single false note throughout the whole picture," R.C. Sherriff wrote Pearson. "The scenario is true to the play [and] the scenes outside the dug-out are brilliantly conceived."

Although *Journey's End* made several "Ten Best" lists, it was ultimately eclipsed by another war film, *All Quiet on the Western Front*, which was nominated for two top Academy Awards—best picture and best director—instead of *Journey's End*. As a play, however, *Journey's End* has had the better track record on the revival circuit. Moreover, it launched the career of James Whale, who went on to direct *Frankenstein* with Colin Clive in 1931.

REFERENCES

Curtis, James, *James Whale* (Metuchen, N.J.: Scarecrow Press, 1982); Hamilton, James Shelley, *Cinema*, 1:5 (June 1930), 38; Matlaw, Myron, *Modern World Drama: An Encyclopedia* (New York: E.P. Dutton, 1972); Pearson, George, *Flashback: An Autobiography of a British Film-maker* (London: George Allen and Unwin, 1957).

—*J.M.W.*

KEY LARGO (1939)

MAXWELL ANDERSON (1888–1959)

Key Largo (1948), U.S.A., directed by John Huston, adapted by Huston and Richard Brooks; Warner Bros.

The Play

In his day, playwright Maxwell Anderson was lauded as the rightful successor to Eugene O'Neill. "Almost alone in the American theatre since O'Neill, he has attempted to rise beyond the pedestrian realistic drama," wrote theatre critic John Gassner. "He has tried to scale the forbidding peaks of poetic composition by means of a pliant and free blank verse, and he has even leaped into the stratosphere of fantasy. He has, above all, striven to make tragedy prevail in the modern theatre despite the untragic psychological and photographic viewpoints of the age." Granted, there were noticeable incongruities in his blend of poetry and realism. In *Winterset*, for example, slum inhabitants speak in an unduly forced and decorative blank verse. More preferable was his ability to capture the muck of war and the foul-mouthed bluster of Sergeant Quirt and Captain Flagg in *What Price Glory?* (1924).

Key Largo combined both the best and the worst of Anderson's method and viewpoint. It premiered at the Ethel Barrymore Theatre on November 27, 1939, and ran for a respectable 105 performances. The story is about King McCloud (Paul Muni), an American who is fighting Fascists in the Spanish Civil War. After concluding that his side has lost, he urges his men to desert. They refuse, and they die fighting. Later, back in America, King attempts to expiate his guilt by visiting the families of his fallen comrades. One such family is the D'Alcalas, who run a small hotel in the Florida Keys. He finds himself in a struggle between the family and a group of gangsters. In the ensuing battle he is killed.

The Film

John Huston's adaptation sacrifices the psychological complexities of the play for a narrative that relies on physical conflict and gunplay for its impact. Wisely, except for a few exterior scenes—notably the climactic showdown at sea between McCloud and Rocco—Huston retains the play's claustrophobic atmosphere by confining the action to the hotel interiors. The tense atmosphere, which includes an impending hurricane, is enhanced by the superb photography of Karl Freund and the evocative music of Max Steiner. Producer Jerry Wald rounded up the cast of the usual Warner Bros. suspects: Humphrey Bogart as King McCloud; Lionel Barrymore as the wheelchair-bound hotel proprietor James Temple; Edward G. Robinson as the gangster leader, Johnny Rocco, who, accompanied by his moll, Gaye Dawn (Claire Trevor), has come to sell stacks of counterfeit bills that he has imported from Cuba; and Lauren Bacall as the widow of the slain soldier and the target of the lascivious Rocco. Ex-soldier Bogart enters the scene not to seek atonement, as in the play, but merely to convey the news to Temple of the death of his son in Spain. Essentially a passive observer throughout most of the story, his eventual decision to kill Rocco seems more an individual act of courage rather than an acknowledgment of the play's theme that democracy must defeat fascism anywhere and everywhere it arises.

Critics found the picture rather lackadaisical in its narrative energy. "On the whole the picture rambles endlessly—and unavoidably—and is not very exciting," opined the critic in *Fortnight*. "There are, though, some quite effective scenes. Besides Robinson, who is in top form, Barrymore excels himself, and Thomas Gomez and Claire Trevor impress favorably." *Key Largo* was Huston's last film for Warner Bros. and the last film to pair Bogart and Bacall. Claire Trevor garnered a best supporting actress Oscar for the role of Gaye Dawn.

REFERENCES

Hammen, Scott, *John Huston* (Boston: Twayne, 1985); McCarty, John, *The Films of John Huston* (Secaucus, N.J.: Carol Publishing, 1987).

—J.C.T.

THE KILLING OF SISTER GEORGE (1965)

FRANK MARCUS (1928–   )

The Killing of Sister George (1969), U.S.A., directed by Robert Aldrich, adapted by Lukas Heller; ABC Palomar International.

The Play

The Killing of Sister George was originally a three-act theatrical production with a four-woman cast headed by Beryl Reid in the title role. It opened at London's Duke of York Theatre on June 17, 1965, and proved an instant success both in Britain and America. The original play is set in the London apartment shared by middle-aged radio actress June Buckridge and her companion Alice "Childie" McNaught. It is loosely based on the firing of actress Ellis Powell from BBC Radio's long-running afternoon series *Mrs. Dale's Diary* and her replacement by former British musical

star Jessie Matthews. After finding employment in the incongruous role of a London night-club hostess, Powell eventually committed suicide.

In the play, June Buckridge has performed the role of country nurse "Sister George" from the very beginning of a long-running radio series very much like the original inspiration for the play, Ellis Powell. Alcoholic and insecure about her position in the series, June suspects that the BBC management intends to write her out of the show. After a drunken assault on a group of nuns in a London cab, BBC executive Mercy Croft visits June's apartment and witnesses a life-style that conflicts with the typical moral standards the corporation expected of its employees at the time. June wallows in self-pity and constantly abuses her dependent roommate "Childie." Eventually, June is written out of the series via a convenient road accident. She is offered the role of "Clarabelle Cow" as compensation in a new children's program. June returns to find that Mercy Croft has seduced "Childie." Both women leave the tragic June alone. She realizes her new situation and ends the play practicing "Clarabelle Cow's" somber moos.

The Film

Film director Robert Aldrich bought the rights to *The Killing of Sister George* in April 1967 and intended it to be his first Aldrich Studios production following the success of *The Dirty Dozen*, which enabled him to fulfil his dream of owning his own studio (a dream that collapsed in 1971). Although the director is usually associated with inaccurately labeled "macho" films such as *Kiss Me Deadly* and *The Dirty Dozen*, both his films and personality were much more complex, and his work deserves more detailed examination than it has received heretofore. Although related to the New York Rockefellers, Aldrich always disassociated himself from this privileged background and aligned himself with many of the blacklisted talents and ideas that became taboo in the era he worked in. His films often revealed empathy toward excluded elements in society such as aging females, non-whites, and those having different sexual orientation. Aldrich's first film as director, *World for Ransom* (1954), originally contained a lesbian theme, but it was altered by censorship. The director's first Aldrich Studio film, *The Legend of Lylah Clare* (1968) also contained a lesbian element in its plot. Aldrich never sensationalized the theme and described George and her fellow lesbians as merely individuals just trying "to make it through the night."

Aldrich opens up Marcus's play to extend its location beyond the original stage confines in order to show the relationship of George's dilemma to the world outside. He inserts a pre-credit sequence showing June's mild public persona as "Sister George" (Beryl Reid reprising her stage role) in a London pub before revealing the more destructive side of her personality. But, unlike the play, Aldrich reveals how the outside world of society is often responsible for causing these personal defects. As the credits roll, Aldrich pans across George as she successively walks down several walled-in paths. In several films, such as *Attack!* and *Autumn Leaves* (both 1956), *What Ever Happened to Baby Jane?* (1962), and *Hush Hush Sweet Charlotte* (1964), Aldrich often points to the culpability of outside social forces for the character flaws and traumas suffered by various individuals. Despite her self-destructive behavior, June is at least more direct in her dealings with others than the people she encounters in her personal and professional life.

Aldrich and scenarist Lucas Heller also changed the original BBC radio show to a television soap opera in line with media critiques often appearing in other films such as *The Legend of Lylah Clare* and *What Ever Happened to Baby Jane?* Like the problematic family upbringing suffered by Aldrich characters such as Captain Cooney in *Attack!* the media often construct false worlds of representations for those caught within their traps. Heller also includes BBC studio scenes not in the original play to reveal both George's contempt for the artificial world in which she exists, as well as to show her concern when she gradually realizes she is being written out of the script. He also removes the play's farcical fortune teller Madame Xenia and includes instead the sympathetic prostitute Betty Thaxter (Beryl Reid), who supports George in her darkest moments. The presence of this character also reveals Aldrich's continual sympathy toward outsiders alienated by a dehumanizing social structure.

Unlike the play, Aldrich included an explicit lesbian seduction scene between Mercy Croft and Childie (Susannah York), if only to emphasize the traumatic nature of June's betrayal by her long-term companion. Despite the sensationalist nature of the scene for the time, Aldrich shoots it in such a manner as to engage the audience's attention voyeuristically and highlight the dark nature of a betrayal practiced both by June's employer and lover. Aldrich cloaks the scene with oblique shadows and shafts of light cutting across both characters to emphasize their complicit role in destroying June's professional and personal life. However, this scene gained the film an X rating, resulting in poor box-office returns.

Aldrich later explained that George's offensive traits had nothing to do with her lesbianism. The director also gained permission to film an additional interior location at a lesbian Chelsea night club, which had never allowed cameras in before. Aldrich shot the scene with the same sympathy he showed toward June whom Russo describes as "the only multifaceted woman in the film" who is also a "more complete human being" than either organization woman Mercy Croft or opportunistic Childie. As in *The Big Knife* (1955) and *Attack!* Aldrich concludes the film by craning out from a vulnerable character to a high-angle shot as the screen darkens. As June practices her tragic "moos," the screen encloses her dwarfed figure in a small square.

REFERENCES

Arnold, Edwin T., and Eugene L. Miller, *The Films and Career of Robert Aldrich* (Knoxville: University of Tennessee Press, 1986); Russo, Vito, *The Celluloid Closet: Homosexuality in the Movies* (New York: Harper and Row, 1981); Silver, Alain, and James Ursini, *What Ever Happened to Robert Aldrich?: His Life and His Films* (New York: Limelight Editions, 1995).

—*T.W.*

LADY WINDERMERE'S FAN

OSCAR WILDE (1854–1900)

Lady Windermere's Fan (1925), U.S.A., directed by Ernst Lubitsch, adapted by Julien Josephson; Warner Bros.

The Play

Oscar Wilde's first popular play is uncharacteristically serious. The four-act drama premiered in London in 1892. While the situation and the sentimentality are Victorian, the wit and epigrammatic dialogue are entirely Wilde's. Act One opens just before the 21st birthday party of the prim and proper Lady Windermere. She scolds a young gallant, Lord Darlington—who considers "life far too important a thing ever to talk seriously about"—for his intentions. At the same time, she is upset at the news that her husband is paying a lot of attention to the mysterious, notorious Mrs. Erlynne. She is further pained when he insists that Mrs. Erlynne be invited to the party. Although Windermere insists that there are good reasons for Erlynne to attend, Lady Windermere retorts that if she shows up, she will strike her with her new fan, Windermere's birthday present. In Act Two her appearance at the party further arouses Lady Windermere's jealousy. In a pique, she accepts Darlington's request to leave with him. Meanwhile, a conversation between Windermere and Erlynne reveals that she is Lady Windermere's mother, who had abandoned husband and baby for a lover who had subsequently left her. Erlynne now threatens to blackmail Windermere for enough money to establish herself in society.

As Act Three opens, Lady Windermere has come to Darlington's rooms to wait for him. Mrs. Erlynne arrives to persuade her daughter to return to her husband. At that moment, Darlington and friends arrive, and the two women barely have enough time to conceal themselves. The men's banter is interrupted when Lady Windermere's fan is discovered on the sofa. In order to save her daughter the notoriety that she herself has endured for so many years, Mrs. Erlynne steps forward to save the day and claim she had taken the fan by mistake. In Act Four the penitent Lady Windermere is thwarted in her desire to confess all to her husband by the arrival of Mrs. Erlynne. Alone with Lord Windermere, Mrs. Erlynne promises him never to reveal her identity to her daughter. His contempt at the discovery of her in Darlington's rooms leads to his refusal to pay her the blackmail money. No matter, she announces that she and an elderly suitor will soon be married and will leave England (taking as a present the infamous fan). Her defiance of conventional morality bespeaks Wilde's own contempt for the standard forms of melodrama, with a final telling twist: "I suppose, Windermere, you would like me to retire into a convent, or become a hospital nurse, or something of that kind, as people do in silly modern novels. That is stu-

Ernst Lubitsch

pid of you, Arthur; in real life we don't do such things—not as long as we have any good looks left, at any rate." As commentator Philip K. Cohen points out, Wilde has reversed our attitude toward Mrs. Erlynne, initially a target of intense dislike, and toward Lady Windermere, at first the very emblem of idealized virtue. In the end they—and our sympathies—have traded places.

The Film

After making a name for himself in Germany with historical epics like *DuBarry* (1919) and *Anne Boleyn* (1920), Ernst Lubitsch came to Hollywood to make *Rosita* (1923) for Mary Pickford. But it was not until he signed a five-picture contract with Warner Bros. in 1924 that he hit his stride as a director of sophisticated

social satires. In quick succession, he made *The Marriage Circle*, *Three Women*, the lost *Kiss Me Again*, *Lady Windermere's Fan*, and *So This Is Paris*. For *Lady Windermere's Fan* members of Lubitsch's stock company were deployed—Irene Rich as Mrs. Erlynne, Ronald Colman as the suave Lord Darlington, May McAvoy as Lady Windermere, and Bert Lytell as Lord Windermere. No respecter of theatrical texts, Lubitsch immediately decided to jettison Oscar Wilde's witty epigrams; indeed, only two lines of the play's dialogue were directly transposed. "Playing with words is fascinating to the writer and afterward to the reader," Lubitsch said in a newspaper interview, "but on the screen it is impossible." (Nonetheless, some of the intertitles do capture the Wildean irony: "Lady Windermere was facing a grave problem: of seating her dinner guests."). In stripping away Wilde's verbal wit, Lubitsch effectively reduced the material to a succession of trenchant images and to a bare narrative—the coming to terms of a mother with a scandalous past and the daughter who thinks she is dead.

Commentator Sabine Hake notes that Lubitsch's tightly composed images "take up Wilde's fascination with the rituals of social intercourse and use them to criticize the hypocrisy that lies behind such obsession with form." For example, to depict the various kinds of reception accorded Mrs. Erlynn by London's high society, Lubitsch concocts a scene at the horse races at Ascot: Mrs. Erlynne is seated in the stands with other members of high society. The shots alternate between a group of society ladies who observe her jewelry through their binoculars and several men who scrutinize her body with frankly erotic interests. "Social interaction in high society, the Ascot sequence seems to suggest, is structured around relationships of looking and, consequently, privileges two kinds of feelings: sexual desire and sexual rivalry." At Lady Windermere's birthday party, when Wilde's characters offer gossipy observations about Mrs. Erlynne, Lubitsch satisfies himself with a single shot of the salon wall, where several women's heads appear and disappear at intervals, each facial expression registering the requisite interest, curiosity, disapproval. To some commentators, the absence of Wilde's *mots* makes the film seem more serious than the play. While commentator Scott Eyman admits that the film is "well directed," he adds that "it's also nominal silent film material amounting to little more than well-dressed tailor's dummies exchanging significant glances over teacups." However, there is no quarreling with Harold Grieve's superbly spare set design: A few columns, some drapes, a staircase, a few tall doors, and polished floors sufficiently suggest the larger confines of a spacious manorial house.

REFERENCES

Cohen, Philip K., *The Moral Vision of Oscar Wilde* (Cranbury, N.J.: Associated University Press, 1978); Eyman, Scott, *Ernst Lubitsch: Laughter in Paradise* (New York: Simon and Schuster, 1993); Hake, Sabine, *Passions and Deceptions: The Early Films of Ernst Lubitsch* (Princeton, N.J.: Princeton University Press, 1992).

—*J.C.T.*

THE LETTER (1927)

W. SOMERSET MAUGHAM (1874–1965)

The Letter (1929), U.S.A., directed and adapted by Jean de Limur; Paramount.

The Letter (1940), U.S.A., directed by William Wyler, adapted by Howard Koch; Warner Bros.

The Play

Somerset Maugham adapted *The Letter* for the stage from a short story he had written in 1924 and published in the collection *The Casuarina Tree* in 1926. Its inspiration was a true story that had scandalized Malaya in 1911 when Ethel Proudlock, the English wife of a headmaster in Kuala Lumpur, had shot the manager of a tin mine, William Steward, on her veranda. Sentenced to hang for murder, she had gained a reprieve after pressure from the European community. Maugham's play was first performed at London's Playhouse Theatre in 1927 and ran for 338 performances. The author's preferred actress for the role, Gladys Cooper, scored a personal triumph as the heroine, Leslie Crosbie, who shoots a family friend, Hammond, in self-defense after, she claims, he had tried to rape her. Her lawyer, Howard Joyce, is puzzled by the fact that Leslie had kept on shooting after it was clear Hammond was dead. But when it is discovered that Hammond had been living with a Chinese woman, his character is sufficiently diminished in the eyes of the English community that Leslie's acquittal from the murder seems a foregone conclusion.

However, Joyce's legal assistant, Ong Chi Seng, has come into possession of a letter from Leslie to Hammond on the day of the murder that seems to imply a different relationship from the one she has described, i.e., that she and Hammond have been lovers. Questioned by Joyce, Leslie confesses she has shot Hammond in a jealous rage when he told her their affair was

W. Somerset Maugham

over. Joyce makes arrangements to buy the letter. The evidence is suppressed and Leslie is found not guilty. After the trial, Leslie's husband Robert finds out about the letter but resolves to forgive her. However, Leslie confides to Joyce, "with all my heart I still love the man I killed."

The Films

The Letter was first filmed in 1929 with Jeanne Eagels making her screen debut in the leading role (she had earlier created a sensation on Broadway in the role of Sadie Thompson in Maugham's *Rain*). Confirming its fidelity to the stage version, *Variety* noted, "Any summary of the picture must record that the merits of the screen production belong to the original play, written for and played on the stage. . . . [It] is entirely a transcription of a stage work and the cinema version does little to make the subject matter its own." Eagels and director de Limur teamed up again a few months later for another film, *Jealousy*.

The Letter was filmed again in 1940, reuniting Bette Davis with William Wyler, who had previously directed her Oscar-winning performance in *Jezebel* (1938). Wyler and his screenwriter Howard Koch made a number of significant changes and additions to Maugham's text. The film opens with a famous panning shot across the rubber plantation compound, which both establishes setting and builds up a tension that is finally broken by the sound of gunshots. Because the killing is committed during a full moon, subsequent shots of the moon interpolated into the action serve to remind Leslie of Hammond's death; and the bar-like pattern of shadows thrown across her white blouse evoke the prison where she ought to be (or the emotional prison she feels she is actually in). Unlike the play, a scene is added in which Joyce sums up the case for the jury, and we see that his defense of the accused is inextricably linked to the compromising of his own professional integrity (James Stephenson's performance superbly conveys Joyce's stress). Also added is a tense scene wherein Leslie must collect the letter in person from Hammond's widow (Gale Sondergaard), and the wordless confrontation crackles with hatred. The famous final line of the play is delivered by Leslie—not to Joyce, as in the play, but to her husband (Herbert Marshall). Wyler and Davis purportedly argued about the staging of this scene. Davis felt no wife could make such an admission directly to her husband's face; Wyler insisted that the drama required it, since an audience, perhaps previously deceived by Leslie's evasiveness, must at this juncture be in no doubt of her honesty. "I lost the argument," said Davis, "but at least I lost to a genius."

The film's ending is problematic. Maugham had revised the play's ending to incorporate a flashback to Hammond and Leslie's final meeting. Wyler omitted that but the Hays Code demanded that Leslie be punished for her transgression: She is stabbed to death but the murderers are instantly caught. (Curiously, the real-life equivalent to Leslie also suffered moral retribution: cleared by the court, she was to return to England without her husband and die in an asylum.) It is a weak conclusion to a film that elsewhere invests moral hypocrisy with the tension of a thriller.

REFERENCES

Anderegg, Michael A., *William Wyler* (Boston: G.K. Hall, 1979); Calder, Robert, *Willie: The Life of W. Somerset Maugham* (London: Heinemann,1989); Davis, Bette, *The Lonely Life* (London: Macdonald, 1962); Tibbetts, John C., *The American Theatrical Film* (Bowling Green, Ohio: Popular Press, 1985).

—N.S.

LES LIAISONS DANGEREUSES (1985)

CHRISTOPHER HAMPTON (1946–)

Dangerous Liaisons (1988), U.S.A., directed by Stephen Frears, adapted by Christopher Hampton; Warner Bros.

The Play

A multiple process of adaptation is in evidence in Christopher Hampton's play, crossing media, language, and culture. The inspiration for his play was the French epistolary novel by Pierre-Ambroise-François Choderlos de Laclos (1741–1803), first published in 1782. During the French Revolution, the shadow of which hangs over the decadent aristocrats of Hampton's play, he was a Jacobin and a friend of Danton, as well as secretary to the king's cousin, the Duc d'Orleans. Though imprisoned twice during the Terror, he escaped execution and was ultimately made a general by Napoleon. He wrote his novel before the Revolution, while stationed as a career soldier on an island in the Bay of Biscay.

The play opened in Stratford-upon-Avon at the Other Place on September 24, 1984, in a production designed by Bob Crowley and directed by Howard Davies, starring Alan Rickman as the Vicomte de Valmont and Lindsay Duncan as his partner in crime, the Marquise de Merteuil. This Royal Shakespeare Company production transferred to the Music Box Theatre in New York on April 30, 1987, with Rickman and Duncan still playing the leads. It ran for five years in London at the Ambassador Theatre on West Street, racking up over 1,200 performances and winning four best play awards, including the prestigious Laurence Olivier Award for 1986. The RSC Broadway production was later nominated for seven Tony Awards.

To say simply that this story is sexy is rather like saying that the Empire State Building is tall, that is, merely suggesting a basic tendency without taking into account its proper magnitude. The action begins on a warm August evening in the salon of Mme. la Marquise de Merteuil, playing cards with her cousin Mme. de Volanges, whose 15-year-old daughter looks on. The game is interrupted by the arrival of Monsieur le Vicomte de Valmont, of whom Volanges says "no one has the slightest respect for him; but everyone is very nice to him" because they are afraid of provoking his malice. He takes great pride in his seductive skills. Merteuil is a malicious busybody and troublemaker, intent on getting even with Valmont, her ex-lover whom she seeks to control, and also with M. le Comte de Bastide, who has abandoned Merteuil for a younger woman, a convent girl, whom Bastide intends to marry. Merteuil will have her revenge.

The play's central conflict, then, is between these two characters, Merteuil and Valmont. Playing upon his vanity, she challenges the libertine Valmont to deflower the convent girl, 16-year-old Cecile de Volanges, who secretly loves the Chevalier Danceny. Valmont is insulted because he senses that the challenge would be too easy for him. For Valmont a more worthy challenge for a libertine of his reputation would be to seduce a virtuous married woman respected for her religious and moral scruples who firmly believes in the sanctity of marriage, Madame de Tourvel. A bargain is struck: If Valmont succeeds, Merteuil will reward him with a night of lust, so long as he also does her bidding with Cecile. Madame de Volanges, the mother of the virgin Merteuil wants seduced, complicates Valmont's intended affair with Madame de Tourvel by constantly warning her about his wicked character and evil intentions. Finally, Valmont seduces Cecile, partly to have his revenge on her mother, who hates him because she was one of his conquests, years earlier.

Valmont's conquest of Madame de Tourvel becomes very complicated when Valmont realizes, to his astonishment, that he is falling in love with her. A master of deception, Valmont wins the love of Madame de Tourvel, but Merteuil then challenges him to drop his newly won conquest, at the expense of breaking Tourvel's heart. Merteuil puts Valmont in a position of choosing between his heart (atrophied through years of cynicism and hateful indulgence) and his reputation. Naturally, his pride and vanity govern his decision. He breaks her heart, and her health fails thereafter. He is responsible, and knows it.

Dangerous Liaisons is a sort of morality play involving generally immoral characters. Merteuil and Valmont first seem to be locked into abstract stereotypes, he representing Deceit, she representing Cruelty; but as they both come to grief, they are humanized by their suffering and become objects of pity. Valmont finally has to pay for his double-dealings with his life, as he is killed in a duel with the virgin's younger lover, Danceny, but in his dying moment he grieves only for the woman he loved but shunned. Merteuil, who collects *billet deux* as insurance for blackmail and reprisal, is finally betrayed by her own letters, which document her cruel designs and are made public, revealing her for the villainess she is. Thereafter, she is shunned. Ultimately, then, the play is about Justice. This cynical and repulsive story of multiple deceits and debauchery, this comedy of bad manners, is set on the eve of the French Revolution. All of these vain, double-dealing, reprehensible hedonists will stand to lose when the Revolution comes. The shadow of the guillotine falls across the set at play's end, a portent of things to come.

The Film

The film, directed by Stephen Frears and adapted by Hampton himself, Anglicized the title as a concession to its English-speaking audience. Hampton agreed with director Stephen Frears that the film should not simply follow the play but should be drawn directly from the novel. Although the story is set just before the French Revolution, Hampton believed that it had contemporary relevance: "Recently, both in England and America, institutionalized selfishness has been encouraged," Hampton claimed, "so the heartlessness of the characters' behavior seems to strike a chord. People recognize the greed—not for money, since the characters are unbelievably rich—but for power." Frears, who had already lambasted Thatcherite greed in his previous film *Sammy and Rosie Get Laid* (1987), noted succinctly: "People behaving badly is quite familiar."

Frears was determined that the adaptation should be cinematic: "People tell stories in plays," he observed. "In film, you show it. Plays are always too long. Films are often too long, but it's worse in the theatre." Hampton managed to shorten his play by 40 minutes for the film version, going back to the novel and re-imagining the dramatization. "The story is more from the book," Frears explained. "The dialogue is from the play." Frears successfully opened up the

Christopher Hampton's drama, Les Liasons Dangereuses, *reached the screen in Stephen Frears'* Dangerous Liasons, *with John Malkovich as Valmont and Michelle Pfeiffer as Madame de Tourvel.* (COURTESY WARNER BROS.)

one-set play, achieving the illusion of historical reconstruction on a budget of $12 million, about half the average Hollywood budget during the late 1980s. But what is most remarkable about the film was not the splendid art direction or the extravagant costumes, but the tone, which seemed to capture the very soul of the 18th century—haughty and aristocratic, lecherous and debauched, by turns comic, satiric, and tragic. Part lusty romp and part drawing-room comedy of manners, it is mainly a spoiled love story. It is certainly satiric in the way it holds vanity and affectation up to ridicule, but the satire finally melds into tragedy.

The film was cast with recognizable Hollywood stars, including Glenn Close (Marquise de Merteuil), John Malkovich (Vicomte de Valmont), Michelle Pfeiffer (Madame de Tourvel), Swoosie Kurtz (Madame de Volanges), Keanu Reeves (Chevalier Danceny), Mildred Natwick (Mademe de Rosemonde), and Uma Thurman (Cecile de Volanges). The focus, then, is upon American actors and accents. Pfeiffer is especially fine as the wronged Tourvel, as is Glenn Close as the malevolent Merteuil, left, at the end, studying her aging face in the mirror, confronting her emptiness. Even Keanu Reeves gets by, on such talent as he has, as does the more gifted John Malkovich as Valmont. *Variety* criticized Malkovich's "blatant American accent" in particular, however, and the film's "Americanized, deformalized performances," in general, because they "serve to dilute delectation of [the] material's delicious decadence." Critics argued that the coming French Revolution should have been more in the forefront, as in the play.

However, the film was not without its advocates. The Motion Picture Academy nominated Glenn Close and Michelle Pfeiffer for best actress and best supporting actress. The film was also nominated for five other Academy Awards, including best adapted screenplay (Christopher Hampton), best art direction (Stuart Craig and Gerard James), and best costume design (James Acheson). No doubt the adaptation will do as a parallel text. Valmont is punished, and, like Edmond in *King Lear*, means to do some good in the service of his malice by exposing Merteuil, either to her peers, as in the film, or to the mob and the guillotine, as at the end of the play. These characters are cut from the same mold, and Justice is surely done.

Other films have treated the story, notably Roger Vadim's *Les Liaisons Dangereuses* (1959), which updated the story to a contemporary French ski resort and is therefore beyond the scope of our consideration here, and Milos Forman's *Valmont* (1989), which kept the original setting and was adapted by Jean Claude Carriere, but both of these were adapted straight from the novel, not from Christopher Hampton's play. The novel's influence extends even to a teenpix spin-off, *Cruel Intentions* (2000).

Interestingly enough, in his memoir *Turnaround*, Forman recalls seeing Hampton's play adaptation in London and being shocked at the liberties Hampton had taken in adapting the novel to the stage. He felt that Hampton had completely distorted the story. But when Forman then re-read the book, he discovered that "Hampton had been as faithful to the original as you can be when you condense a long novel into a play. He had gotten all the facts right and had captured the spirit of the book." Forman saw the play again and set up a meeting with Hampton to discuss "the possibility of a film collaboration," but that meeting never took place, and Forman went forward with his own independent adaptation of the novel. Curiously, Michelle Pfeiffer was Forman's first choice to play Merteuil, but by the time Forman contacted her, she had already signed with Stephen Frears. Even so, Forman was just as happy to have Meg Tilly for the role, with Colin Firth playing Valmont, her opposite. Forman's film was quite eclipsed by *Dangerous Liaisons*, however, and was not a commercial success. On the other hand, since Hampton himself went back to the novel when he re-imagined his play as a film, arguably his film may have more in common with *Valmont* than might first be apparent. As noted above, the process of adapting the novel to the stage to the film was extremely complicated.

REFERENCES

Ansen, David, "Boudoir Battleground," *Newsweek* (December 26, 1988): 63; Cart., "*Dangerous Liaisons*," *Variety*, December 21–27, 1988, 12; Forman, Milos and Jan Novak, *Turnaround: A Memoir* (New York: Villard Books, 1994); Hoberman, J., "Age of Reason," *Village Voice*, December 27, 1988, 65; Hunter, Mark, "Marquise de Merteuil and Comte de Valmont Get Laid," *American Film*, 14:3 (December 1988), 26–31; Kael, Pauline, "The Comedy of Evil," *The New Yorker* (January 9, 1989): 78–80; White, Edmund, "Before the Revolution," *Premiere*, 2:5 (January 1989): 50–54.

—*J.M.W.*

LIFE WITH FATHER (1939)

HOWARD LINDSAY (1889–1968) AND RUSSEL CROUSE (1893–1966)

Life with Father (1947), U.S.A., directed by Michael Curtiz, adapted by Donald Ogden Stewart; Warner Bros.

The Play

Life with Father opened at New York's Empire Theatre on November 8, 1939, and went on to a spectacular run of 3,224 performances (a record-setting run). Howard Lindsay and Russel Crouse (who wrote *State of the Union* in 1945, later filmed by Frank Capra) based it on a series of best-selling family sketches written for *The New Yorker* in 1935 by Clarence Day, Jr., Co-playwright Howard Lindsay played the role of Clarence Day, Sr., in the original Broadway production. Set in a Madison Avenue residence in New York City during the late 1880s, the three-act play occurs entirely inside the Day household. Like the original stories, the play consists of a number of comedy sketches strung together around the paterfamilias of the Day household. Clarence Day, Sr., attempts to run his house on business lines. But his wife Vinnie (Dorothy Stickney) and numerous children usually manage to defeat his scheme. Clarence Day, Jr., the oldest son, encounters his first romantic interest in the figure of Mary Skinner, whom he will later marry. When Father announces that he was never baptized, Vinnie conspires to ensure that her reluctant husband will undergo the necessary social propriety. He finally capitulates at the end of the play, bellowing "I'm going to be baptized, damn it!"

The Film

Although Jack Warner purchased the screen rights from the surviving members of the Day family in 1945, Day's widow Mary and the original playwrights exercised a limiting contractual stranglehold on the film version, which prevented director and scenarists from creatively diverging from the original text. As a result, the type of innovations Curtiz brought to purchased properties such as Jack London's *The Sea-Wolf* and James M. Cain's *Mildred Pierce* became impossible under this arrangement. Warner Brothers and Curtiz underwent several frustrating situations when dealing with the copyright holders of the original play. For example, no mention is made of the color of the Day family's hair in the original play. But Mary Day and the playwrights insisted that the entire Day family were to have red hair. This led to some redundant stereotypical scenes in which each male member of the Day family individually appears with prominent red hair. Scenarist Stewart even included a comment by an Irish maid who notices this and remarks on this fact to the audience. However, despite dealing with the irritating demands of the copyright holders, who even insisted on casting Irene Dunne when Curtiz wanted Bette Davis for the role of Vinnie, Curtiz not only made the best of a bad job but also attempted to make the play as cinematic as possible, using the best resources of the Hollywood studio system in which he achieved many significant works in his screen career.

Curtiz opens out the play so events do not occur exclusively within the Day household. For example, after credit scenes showing stereoscopic views of period photographs of old New York, he begins the film by showing the street outside the Day residence. The audience also witnesses the baptism service, referred to in the play, when the minister delivers a baptism sermon aimed at Father's unwillingness to undergo this social ritual. Also, unlike the play when Clarence and Mary talk privately within the confines of the home, the camera follows them as they go onto the porch. Curtiz also includes a street scene when Cora and Mary depart in an awaiting cab. One scene written specially for the film depicts Father visiting an employment agency to replace a servant. Finally, both Curtiz and Stewart include a visit to an upper-class store, utilizing both meticulous studio set design techniques as well as crane and tracking shots. These cinematic methods make the film less visually claustrophobic than the stage version.

Curtiz also creatively uses the mobile camera to depict events inside, as well as outside, the home. For example, when Father and Vinnie debate the baptism issue in their bedroom, the camera tilts down a vent to reveal the two younger sons listening outside in the yard below. One brother teases the other concerning Father's predestined journey to Hell unless he undergoes baptism. This replaces the original scene statically set in the Day living room, a scene whose effectiveness relies entirely upon dialogue. Curtiz also frequently employs the moving camera to follow characters through different rooms of the household. He thus overcame the frustrating barriers placed upon the film version by the copyright holders of the original play.

Although the film ran 30 days over schedule, it became a major box-office success for Warners subsequent to its delayed release in August 1947. Curtiz scholar James C. Robertson aptly remarks, "Despite the tense off-screen atmosphere, the film does credit to all concerned, but Curtiz's skill is crucial."

REFERENCES

Lindsay, Howard, and Russel Crouse, *Clarence Day's Life with Father Made into a Play* (New York: Alfred A. Knopf, 1949); Robertson, James C., *The Casablanca Man: The Cinema of Michael Curtiz* (London: Routledge, 1993).

—*T.W.*

THE LION IN WINTER (1966)

JAMES GOLDMAN (1927–1998)

The Lion in Winter (1968), U.K., directed by Anthony Harvey, adapted by James Goldman; Haworth Productions/Embassy Pictures.

The Play

Like *Becket* (q.v.), *The Lion in Winter* represents medieval English history inflected through intense personal relationships. The main characters are Henry II; his queen, Eleanor of Aquitaine; and their three sons: Richard, afterward the Lionheart; Geoffrey, Count of Brittany; and John, afterward John Lackland, the signatory of Magna Carta. Through this cluster of titanic characters is represented the major theme of the play: power politics as determined by personal emotions rather than by intellectual policy. As Henry says: "We are the world in small. A nation is a human thing; it does what we do, for our reasons." Since the family relationships presented in the play are highly dysfunctional, the prognosis for the world is bleak.

The plot is complex, since its roots lie in the family's own complicated history. Eleanor has been locked up in Salisbury Tower for the past 10 years because she encouraged Richard, her favorite, to rebel against Henry's authority. In her absence, Henry has begun an affair with Alais, the sister of Philip, king of France. Alais was sent to England as a child to become the bride of the heir to the English throne, who had been Richard but is now John. Geoffrey suffers from a classic case of middle-child syndrome and shifts his allegiance from John. Henry needs to appoint a successor in order to avoid a civil war after his death and the breakup of his empire, which includes England, Ireland, and half of France. This necessity creates an awkward situation for Henry, who, as reigning monarch, is unwilling to give any of his sons, even his chosen heir, any real power. The inevitable result is resentment and jealousy, a fertile breeding ground for betrayal and conspiracy. The overall tone of the play is intensely vicious; the lines are delivered as if they were knives. No one, except Alais, can be trusted to mean what they say, and the hateful revelations follow fast and hard. *The Lion in Winter* resembles a medieval version of *Who's Afraid of Virginia Woolf*, with wider political implications.

The action of the play takes place at a Christmas Court held at Chinon in Normandy, in 1183. While such an event never took place, the action of the play is based on much historical research, and, except for the occasional anachronism, one believes it could have happened. The selection of the Christmas holidays for the play's action is, of course, ironic, considering the flawed relationships in this powerful but damaged family.

The play is in two acts; Act One has six scenes and Act Two has three. Act One, Scene One is exposition; the real action of the play begins in Act One, Scene Two, when the family arrives and the sparring begins. Philip of France, only 17 years old, arrives to demand that Alais's marriage take place or that Henry return her dowry, a county near Paris called the Vexin. Henry's style of negotiating involves bluster, bluff, and outright lying, and he is very good at it. We see Eleanor's skill and ruthlessness in Act One, Scene Three, when she breaks through Richard's shell of reserve and resentment to win him back to her side. In Act One, Scene Four, since Richard's star appears to be rising, Geoffrey and John make a deal with Philip to declare war on Henry. Meanwhile, intense negotiations between Henry and Eleanor end in an aborted wedding between Alais and Richard, an event stage-managed by Henry. In Act One, Scene Five, for reasons having as much to do with jealousy as with power, Eleanor is in despair at her inability to maneuver Henry into giving Alais and the Crown to Richard, until John reveals his conspiracy with Philip. Energized, Eleanor sends Richard off to woo Philip. Aware that Richard is a homosexual, she tells him to promise Philip "anything" to get his support. The intense and emotional action of the first act builds to a climax in Act One, Scene Six, when the breadth of betrayal and conspiracy within his family is revealed to Henry, along with Richard's homosexual relationship with Philip, a relationship that Philip swears he began only so that he could later hurt Henry by telling him about it. Henry staggers out, a broken man: "I've lost my boys," he wails.

As Act Two begins, however, he has recovered and grimly announces his intention to go to Rome and annul his marriage to Eleanor (despite their having been married 31 years and her having borne him 11 children). Eleanor reminds him that a new son would give his three quarreling sons common ground against him, and so Henry has the three of them locked in the castle wine cellar. In Act Two, Scene Two, he formally proposes marriage to Alais, and she adds to his misery by reminding him that, once he locks up Richard, Geoffrey, and John, he can never let them out because, if they were free, they would kill any offspring she and Henry had. In the final scene, Henry finds himself unable to be his sons' executioner and sets them free, knowing that he will have to fight them. He and

Eleanor are both distraught at the failure of their plans, but console each other with the thought that "there's everything in life but hope" and the wish that the two of them might live forever.

The play opened in New York City on March 3, 1966. Despite its sharp, witty dialogue and excellent cast (Robert Preston as Henry, Rosemary Harris as Eleanor, and Christopher Walken as Philip), the play got poor reviews and closed after only 83 performances.

The Film

Ironically, the critical and commercial success of the movie version of *The Lion in Winter* drew renewed attention to the play. The film is a splendidly mounted production, starring Peter O'Toole as Henry (the same role he played in *Becket*), Katharine Hepburn in an Academy Award–winning performance as Eleanor, and Anthony Hopkins as Richard. The film also won an Oscar for best adapted screenplay, and, since that award-winning screenplay was written by the playwright, James Goldman, the film is nearly a verbatim copy of the play.

In the play we meet Henry's family all at once, but in the film we are introduced to them individually as William Marshal, Henry's lieutenant, comes to summon them to Chinon. In addition to showing us what these characters are like outside of Henry's sphere, this device emphasizes how distant the members of the family are from each other. Richard is shown jousting and has to be shocked out of his fighting mood to respond to his father's summons. Geoffrey watches two troops of his cavalry ambush a rival's foot soldiers, and, while absorbed in the battle, he knows before Marshal speaks that Henry wants to see him. The final visit is to Eleanor's prison in Salisbury Tower, an isolated and rough setting that arouses our sympathy for her as well as our admiration, since she also intuits the message that Marshal has come to deliver. These three formidable people will be arrayed against Henry and John. While John in the play's directions is described as "sweet-faced and totally adorable," he is played by Nigel Terry in the film as a dolt, a change that suggests that Eleanor and Richard are right to resent Henry's choice of John as his successor.

Minor changes include a new scene that clarifies Geoffrey's role in the conspiracy by having him tell Eleanor in advance that he intends to set John up. Another series of scenes showing William Marshal arresting each of the sons in turn (a bookend to the scenes in which they were introduced) is also added, making their plight more poignant and desperate than

it seems in the play, but, in the main, the dialogue in the film is that of the play, somewhat tightened in most cases and rearranged in others. The handling of the dialogue in Henry's scenes with Eleanor in particular keeps the film from being too "talky" and allows more variation in their interactions, which can range in the same scene from teasing, to direct conflict, to admiration, to sentiment, and then to threats. The film also cuts several speeches given to Henry and Eleanor in the play that speak to their intellectual achievements. The result is to shift the balance that the play maintains between the intellectual and the emotional elements in their makeup much more heavily on the side of the emotional reasons for their behavior. Other key cuts take the edges from Alais's character and make her weaker and more vulnerable, particularly in her relationship to Henry. The film is also much harder on Henry and Eleanor as parents. As in the play, Eleanor shares a loving scene with Richard, though her motives are suspect, and she and Henry share a couple of scenes of unsuccessful communication with Geoffrey. But the two scenes in which each of them interacts with John in what might be a sincerely loving way have been cut in the film.

The film deromanticizes the Middle Ages, using an approach not taken from the play: the action of the film proper (after a brief exposition and the introductions of the main characters), opens with an extreme long shot of a white castle in the mist, like a picture out of a storybook. However, the film then cuts to a shot of the mud, straw, and dogs in the castle yard and shots of peasants going out to the fields. The sequence ends as a man's hands, revealed to be those of the king, break the ice that has formed over the water basin during the night. These images effectively shatter the stereotypical notions of the elegance of the medieval courtly tradition, a tradition ironically associated directly with Eleanor of Aquitaine. The Middle Ages in *The Lion in Winter* are a hard, tough era demanding hardness and toughness in those who survive it.

In 1183, when the film is set, Henry is already 50 years old, quite elderly in medieval terms, yet he is remarkable for his dynamic energy. One major group of changes in the film is designed to emphasize Henry's robust vitality. While the stage play necessitates restricted motion, the film is full of scenes of Henry's dashing here and there: "When the King is off his ass, nobody sleeps," as he says. Several scenes emphasize his forcefulness by opening with shock cuts to his close-up as he gives an order, an effect impossible on the stage. Unlike the play, which begins as Henry and Alais wake and prepare for the "jungle of a day" to come, the film opens with the clang of broadswords, as Henry spars outdoors with John and vanquishes him, a fitting bookend to his final contact with his sons: His last-second refusal to use a sword to kill Richard. In addition to visually representing the subtext of Henry's puzzling preference for John over the "constant soldier" Richard, this opening scene immediately impresses us with Henry's energy and vigor. The issue of Henry's physical power is important because one of the themes in the play contrasts Henry's age and need for a successor with his holding on to his kingdom with his preternatural strength of body as well as with his intellect and his will. While the play provides little direct evidence of Henry's physical power, the film insists on it and presents plenty of proof that Henry's "paint's not peeling off" yet.

The feeling at the end of the play is that these two defeated people are supporting each other in despair by whistling in the dark together. The final images of Henry and Eleanor in the film, however, emphasize their buoyant resolution to fight on as long as there is life in their bodies. The film closes with Henry, laughing, arms outstretched to embrace whatever life has to offer, as the camera, mounted on Eleanor's barge, takes her (and us) away from him.

REFERENCES

Kael, Pauline, *Going Steady* (Boston: Little, Brown, 1970); Simon, John, *Movies into Film: Film Criticism 1967–1970* (New York: Dial Press, 1971).

—S.C.

LITTLE FOXES, THE (1939)

LILLIAN HELLMAN (1906–1984)

The Little Foxes (1941), U.S.A., directed by William Wyler, adapted by Lillian Hellman; Samuel Goldwyn/RKO.

The Play

One of America's most important playwrights in the 1930s, Lillian Hellman combined in her plays chilling portraits of the workings of evil with tacked-on moral preachments. Born into a Jewish middle-class family in New Orleans, Hellman attended New York University and Columbia University, where she wrote her first short stories. After a stint as a book reviewer for the *New York Herald Tribune*, she became a play reader for the Broadway producer Herman Shumlin. It was through her association with novelist Dashiell Hammett that she became acquainted with an early 19th-

century Scottish lawsuit, "Great Drumsheugh Case," which she transformed into her first stage success, *The Children's Hour*. Compared to it, her next big success, *The Little Foxes*, was, in the words of critic Richard Watts, Jr., "a grim, bitter and merciless study, a drama more honest, more pointed and more brilliant."

The title was suggested to Hellman by Dorothy Parker, citing the text from Song of Solomon, 2:15: "Take us the foxes, the little foxes, that spoil the vines, for our vines have tender grapes." The setting is a turn-of-the-century southern town dominated by the Hubbards, a rapacious family torn by inner conflicts. Oscar (Carl Benton Reid) has married Birdie Bagtry (Patricia Collinge) for her money. But he and his older brother Ben (Charles Dingle) need more cash to buy a controlling interest in a new cotton mill, so they offer their sister Regina (Tallulah Bankhead) a one-third interest in the mill in return for a $75,000 loan. When Regina's husband, Horace Giddens (Frank Conroy), balks, the scheming Oscar persuades his timid son, Leo (Dan Duryea), to steal Horace's bonds. Frictions, in the meantime, have increased between Regina and Horace. "I hope you die," she declares maliciously. "I hope you die soon. I'll be waiting for you to die soon." Her words are prophetic: During an argument, he succumbs to a heart attack. Refusing to bring him his medicine, Regina coldly witnesses his death throes as he struggles up the stairs. She then turns to her brothers and extorts a three-quarters interest in the business in exchange for her silence about the theft. But the closing scene suggests that her victory may ultimately spell her defeat. When Regina asks her daughter, Alexandra, if she would sleep with her that night, Alexandra replies, "Are you afraid, Mama?" Regina pauses in silence, then slowly mounts the stairs, alone, as the final curtain falls.

The play has been described as an allegory of the threat to the virtues of the Old South, represented by Birdie and Horace, from industrial greed, personified by Regina and her brothers. Those who construed it as an attack on the free-enterprise system labeled Hellman as a communist sympathizer, a "fellow traveler." At its core, however, commentator Carol MacNicholas regards it essentially as a fable of "sibling rivalry due to greed for power and wealth among members of a single family and the way such vicious infighting destroys love, loyalty, generosity, and concern for others." Moreover, it expresses one of Hellman's recurring themes—especially prevalent in another of her plays, *Watch on the Rhine* (1941)—the danger of ignoring social responsibilities. As the Hubbards' family servant, Addie, observes: "Well, there are people who eat the earth and eat all the people on it like in the Bible with the locusts. Then there are the people who stand around and watch them eat it. Sometimes I think it ain't right to stand and watch them do it."

The Little Foxes has been revived regularly, notably in 1967 by the Repertory Theatre of Lincoln Center. Composer Mac Blitzstein drew from it for his opera, *Regina* (1949).

The Film

The success and controversy of *The Children's Hour* brought Hellman to the attention of Hollywood and Sam Goldwyn, who hired her in 1935 as a screenwriter at $2,500 a week. After scripting *Dark Angel* in 1935—a shameless tearjerker—she signed on to adapt *The Children's Hour* to the screen. The result was *These Three* (1936). After adapting Sidney Kingsley's play, *Dead End*, to the screen a year later, she turned to writing the scenario of *The Little Foxes* for director William Wyler and producer Samuel Goldwyn.

It was Wyler's third collaboration with Bette Davis, following *Jezebel* (1938), an adaptation of a play by Owen Davis, and *The Letter* (1940), deriving from a story and play by W. Somerset Maugham. Wyler and Davis was surely one of the greatest director-star relationships in the history of American cinema. At the outset, however, things were tense between director and star regarding the interpretation of Regina's character. Wyler preferred a warmer, more appealing character than Davis wanted. "We fought bitterly," Davis recalled. "I had been forced to see Tallulah Bankhead's performance. . . . It was Willie's intention that I give a different interpretation of the part. I insisted that Tallulah had played it the only way it could be played. Miss Hellman's Regina was written with such definition that it could only be played one way." Evidence on screen proves that Davis won the argument. She was joined in the cast by several actors reprising their original stage roles, Charles Dingle, Carl Benton Reid, Patricia Collinge, and Dan Duryea.

Hellman, with the assistance of her friend Dorothy Parker, kept the play's outline and most important dialogues intact, while opening up the story and muting the unrelenting pessimism of the play by introducing a love interest, David Hewitt (Richard Carlson) for Alexandra (Teresa Wright). This allowed for some expansion of Alexandra's character, which Goldwyn may have ordered to build up his new actress, Wright. Wyler, teamed up again with camera ace Gregg Toland, contributed his own impeccable sense of camera and staging. He either traps characters in the frame with no room to move, or uses the camera's viewfinder as a variable proscenium, as it were, positioning his characters in deep space and breaking up extended scenes into visual units of two- and three- and four-shots. Horace's death scene stands out in its stark simplicity. Davis' implacably cold face is kept in screen closeup while in the distance behind her, the suffering Horace staggers up the stairs. More complex is the scene in which Horace and Leo converse about Leo's theft of Horace's bonds. They shave as they talk, Oscar before one mirror and Leo, across the room, at another. The dominant shot is a close-up of Oscar, while over his shoulder can be seen both the reflection of Leo as well as the reflection of a reflection of Leo in the other mirror. The point is that not only is Leo a "reflection" of Oscar in a literal and metaphoric way, but that the two men talk without ever directly looking at each other—as deceitful toward each other as toward people outside the family. Some scenes are kept in deep focus, like the early dinner party, allowing us to make our own decisions about where to direct our attention. And other scenes are restrictive in their focus, like Horace's death scene, where his out-of-focus figure does not distract us from Davis' close-up in the foreground.

"*The Little Foxes*," writes Charles Affron, "is a film of duets, trios, quarters, and small ensembles, which fully exploits an enviably collaborative cast." To critical charges that Wyler's mise-en-scène is too calculated and mechanistic, Wyler biographer Michael Anderegg responds: "*The Little Foxes* is after all about calculation, its substance the constant talk of who will get how much, of how many ways a pie can be divided, of how far one is willing to go to achieve one's goal. Wyler chose to emphasize rather than soften Hellman's mechanistic structure: his manipulation of her characters reflects their manipulation of each other." In the opinion of Anderegg, the film "is not so much an adaptation as a realization of Hellman's play." So pleased was she with the results that she considered the movie version to be superior to the stage original.

REFERENCES

Anderegg, Michael A., *William Wyler* (Boston: Twayne Publishers, 1979); MacNicholas, Carol, "Lillian Hellman," in John MacNicholas, ed., *Twentieth-Century American Dramatists* (Detroit: Gale Research, 1981).

—D.S. AND J.C.T.

LITTLE MURDERS (1967)

JULES FEIFFER (1929–)

Little Murders (1972), U.S.A., directed by Alan Arkin, adapted by Jules Feiffer; 20th Century-Fox.

The Play

Before he turned to playwrighting, Jules Feiffer had studied at the Art Students League in New York, worked for various cartoon syndicates, served in a cartoon animation unit in the Army Signal Corps, and drawn political cartoons for the *Village Voice*. His first play was *The Explainers*, produced in 1961. He also wrote the screenplay for Mike Nichols' *Carnal Knowledge* in 1971. *Little Murders* premiered in New York at the Broadhurst Theatre on April 25, 1967, and ran for a mere seven performances. However, it was a hit in London with the Royal Shakespeare Company and after playing for two years returned to New York for a successful off-Broadway revival at the Circle in the Square, where it ran for 400 performances. Set entirely in the Newquist apartment in New York City, the black comedy concerns a family of misfits: Carol (Heywood Hale Broun), a successful photographer who dislikes his effeminate name; his wife, Marjorie (Ruth White), who dislikes her family in general; a son Kenny (David Steinberg), who wants to change his gender; and Patsy, who is unwisely in love with a thin-skinned liberal, Alfred Chamberlain (Elliott Gould). When Patsy is shot dead by random gunfire, the Newquists decide to fight back. Alfred brings firearms into the Newquist apartment, and soon he and Mr. Newquist and Kenny are taking potshots at passersby outside their window. After an investigating officer, Lieutenant Practice, is killed, the Newquists hold a celebratory dinner. The target of the dark satire is America's paranoia and frustration with the spate of assassinations and violence that marked the 1960s.

The Film

Feiffer himself adapted the play. In order to open up the action, he adds an introductory sequence in which Patsy (Marcia Rodd) observes a beating on the streets, calls the police (who fail to respond), and herself repels the attackers. The victim, Alfred Chamberlain, escapes; but for her efforts, Patsy is roughed up. Despite this inauspicious introduction to Alfred, she decides to marry him. Other added scenes include a visit by Patsy to Alfred's parents in Chicago and an interview between Carol and Lieutenant Practice (Alan Arkin) The most interesting addition features Donald Sutherland as the hippie minister of the First Existential Church, who, after declaring that most of the people

he's married are now divorced, watches as the wedding ends in a pitched battle. As in the play, Patsy is killed by gunfire, and a distraught Alfred returns to the Newquist apartment, prepared to indulge in some wholesale slaughter of his own. Finally, everyone sits down to a big dinner prepared by Mrs. Newquist (Elizabeth Wilson), who asserts that it is good to hear the family laughing again.

REFERENCES

Arkin, Alan, *Halfway through the Door: An Actor's Journey Toward the Self* (New York: Harper and Row, 1979); Kael, Pauline, "Varieties of Paranoia," in *Deeper into Movies* (Boston: Little, Brown, 1973), 253–259.

—*T.L.E. AND J.C.T.*

LONG DAY'S JOURNEY INTO NIGHT (1939–41)

EUGENE O'NEILL (1888–1953)

Long Day's Journey into Night (1962), U.S.A., directed by Sidney Lumet, adapted by Ely Landau, Jack Dreyfus, Jr., and Joseph E. Levine; Embassy Pictures.

The Play

Eugene O'Neill's autobiographical four-act naturalistic drama, written between 1939 and 1941, was first performed at the Royal Dramatic Theatre in Stockholm, Sweden, on February 2, 1956. It received its American premiere at the Helen Hayes Theatre in New York City on November 7, 1956, under the direction of Jose Quintero, with Fredric March as James Tyrone, Florence Eldridge as Mary, and Jason Robards, Jr., as Jamie. In 1957 Eugene O'Neill posthumously received the Pulitzer Prize (his fourth) for the play. Originally, O'Neill stipulated that the play would not be published, let alone produced, until 25 years after his death. Saxe Commins, O'Neill's editor at Random House, claimed that the playwright wished to withhold publication "until everyone involved, particularly the members of his family, was dead or old enough not to be hurt or even disturbed by it." It was through the efforts of O'Neill's widow Carlotta O'Neill that the play was eventually published by Yale University Press and subsequently produced theatrically. Ironically, of the entire O'Neill canon, *Long Day's Journey into Night* is the most frequently produced of his works. In addition to the film version, there have been to date four television adaptations of the play, including one with an African-American cast.

O'Neill's "play of old sorrow, written in tears and blood" observes the Aristotelian unities of time and place by being set entirely in the living room of James Tyrone's summer home on an August day in 1912. The play begins on a sunny morning, around 8:30, and ends after midnight. During the day the audience witnesses the tortured lives of the "four haunted Tyrones," as O'Neill himself referred to his characters. James Tyrone, a former matinee idol, regrets having abandoned his artistic success for a "damned play" that earned him a fortune, but limited his artistic range by permanently identifying him with a particular role. His wife, Mary, who has become a morphine addict, yearns for a happier innocence, before her marriage 36 years ago, when she considered joining a convent. Their two sons, Jamie and Edmund, are also dysfunctional through alcohol abuse. Edmund has recently been diagnosed with consumption and plans to go to a sanatorium. Little physical action occurs in the drama. O'Neill instead relies entirely on the psychological conflict among the four major characters, who through self-exculpatory monologues reveal their tormented, anguished lives. The Tyrones' home becomes a prison, metaphorically encapsulated by fog, in which they have lost their bearings and cannot escape save only through liquor or morphine.

The Film

Sydney Lumet's film version of *Long Day's Journey into Night* is primarily noted for its stellar performances by Katharine Hepburn as Mary Tyrone, Ralph Richardson as James, Jason Robards, Jr., as Jamie (repeating his Broadway role), and Dean Stockwell as Edmund. The ensemble cast was even awarded a joint best-acting award at the Cannes Film Festival. Because of the length of the work and the amount of confrontational dialogue and confessional monologues within it, the acting is of paramount importance. Screenwriter Dudley Nichols (*Stagecoach*, *The Long Voyage Home*, *Bringing Up Baby*) has suggested that the theatrical stage is a "medium of action" whereas the cinema is "the medium of reaction," in which "the audience identifies with the person *acted upon* on the screen, and not with the person acting." Lumet stresses this importance by remaining faithful to O'Neill's intent and allowing the action and characters to emerge from the Tyrones' prison-like existence. Although Lumet's film has been criticized as being nothing more than a filmed staged

Eugene O'Neill

play, on closer examination one finds that Lumet takes full and subtle advantage of the technical capacities of the film medium.

The idea of spatial confinement is extremely important in Lumet's visualization of O'Neill's drama. According to John Orlandello, "Throughout the film Lumet insists that the four characters are not only confined but metaphorically imprisoned within the walls of the house and within their own problematic egos." The film's composition allows Lumet to fully explore this design of imprisonment. The walls and narrow corridors of the Tyrone house are filled with bric-a-brac and furniture that clutter the interior of the house. The staircase, which leads, most importantly, to the spare room where Mary frequently confines herself, also contributes to the sense of imprisonment in the film. The bars of the stair railing further enhance this image in several scenes where Mary ascends the staircase. Lumet also begins the film by setting it outdoors in natural sunlight; as the film progresses the audience is brought inside the house, underscoring O'Neill's metaphoric movement from light to darkness and the image of imprisonment.

Both Sidney Lumet and his cinematographer, Boris Kaufman, sought visual equivalents for the characters of O'Neill's play through lighting, lens selection, and camera angles. Both developed a "lens plot" for the film—Katharine Hepburn's Mary Tyrone, for example, was shot with increasingly longer lenses and the subsequent loss of depth further isolated her within the film's composition. Jamie and Tyrone were shot with wider lenses, creating a greater depth of field as well as some distortion to the image. This image underlined "an increased hostility, an increased violence, and increase in the change of emotions the two characters were feeling." Edmund was kept "objective" by utilizing few lens changes. Camera angles helped to "dynamize" the film's composition. Mary is filmed from increasingly high angles, thereby diminishing her screen size as she is further isolated from reality. Both Jamie and Tyrone are shot from low angles, magnifying both the size and nature of their conflicts. Edmund is shot from an eye-level angle, further enhancing his "objectivity."

One of the tour de force technical images in the film occurs at the end with Mary's lengthy monologue. Lumet changes the film's compositional style from a naturalistic one to an expressionistic style. Mary is sitting at the kitchen table with the other characters and as O'Neill's stage direction reads, "She speaks aloud to herself, not to them." Kaufman slowly pulls the camera back until "the characters at the table become isolated in a single shaft of light; the entire space surrounding them becomes black, except for the lighthouse lights slowly flashing across the windows of the room." This image accentuates the theme of isolation and imprisonment. According to Orlandello, "The image of the four seen from above at great distance, with blackness totally surrounding them, visually reinforces the idea both of their isolation from the world, and of their confinement with each other." Lumet has skillfully realized O'Neill's dark vision through cinematic means.

REFERENCES

Bordman, Gerald, *The Oxford Companion to American Theatre* (New York: Oxford University Press, 1992); Nichols, Dudley, "The Writer and the Film," in *Film: A Montage of Theories*, ed. Richard Dyer MacCann (New York: Dutton, 1966); Orlandello, John, *O'Neill on Film* (Rutherford, N.J.: Fairleigh Dickinson University Press, 1982); Ranald, Margaret Loftus, *The Eugene O'Neill Companion* (Westport, Conn.: Greenwood Press, 1984).

—R.W.W.

THE LONG VOYAGE HOME (1917)

EUGENE O'NEILL (1888–1953)

The Long Voyage Home (1940), U.S.A., directed by John Ford, adapted by Dudley Nichols; Argosy Corporation/United Artists.

The Play

The quartet of one-act plays known collectively as the "S.S. *Glencairn* cycle" was first produced separately by the Provincetown Players at the Provincetown Theatre in New York. They were later combined to form a single work (1924) and, when produced in tandem, are generally performed in the following order (dates given are the years of composition): *The Moon of the Caribees* (1918), *In the Zone* (1917), *The Long Voyage Home* (1917), and *Bound East for Cardiff* (1916). The group of one-acts concerns the seamen aboard the British tramp steamer, S.S. *Glencairn*. Each of the four plays revolves around a central situation and a recurring assemblage of characters who make up the crew of the *Glencairn*. The primary characters are: Yank, Driscoll, Smitty, Olson, Cocky, Davis, and Ivan.

O'Neill was particularly fond of *Moon of the Caribees*, which depicts the *Glencairn* anchored off the coast of a West Indies island on a moonlit night. Rum is smuggled aboard the ship by some visiting island women. A fight breaks out and one of the crew receives a knife wound. The short play has little action and relies instead on the evocation of mood through the offshore chanting of the natives and the individual musings of the ship's crew. *In The Zone* is a melodramatic wartime play in which the action is limited to a confined interior space, the forecastle of the S.S. *Glencairn*. The ship has taken on a cargo of ammunition from the United States to England. Entering the war zone the crew become highly suspicious of one of its own members who, they have reason to believe, may be a spy. A small black box, which is believed to be a bomb, is revealed to contain only a package of love letters. The death of a crew member, Yank, constitutes the plot of *Bound East for Cardiff*, a revision of an earlier unproduced O'Neill one-act titled, *Children of the Sea* (1913–14). The play is actually a dialogue between Yank and Driscoll as they reflect on their lives as seamen. The stage production at the Provincetown Players' Wharf Theatre in Provincetown, Massachusetts, on July 28, 1916, is noted as the first production of an O'Neill play. A London waterfront dive is the setting for *The Long Voyage Home*, the only one-act in the series located on shore. Driscoll, Cocky, Ivan, and Olson ("Ollie") have been paid off by the S.S. *Glencairn* and are celebrating at Fat Joe's. Ollie, who is planning to return home to Stockholm and take up farming, is shanghaied by members of the *Amindra*, a notorious "hell-ship" that is in dock looking for a crew.

According to Margaret Loftus Ranald, "the basic theme of the series is that mankind, represented by the complement of the S.S. *Glencairn*, is the plaything of an unalterable destiny. While there are isolated acts of free will or attempted rebellion against fate, the seamen (the voyagers) are unsuccessful, for the sea always wins and takes its own." This theme is best represented in the musings of Smitty and the Donkeyman in *Moon of the Caribees*; the death of Yank in *Bound East for Cardiff*; and the shanghaiing of Olson in *The Long Voyage Home*. O'Neill uses dialect extensively in the series: Swedish, Cockney, British. As a whole, then, the crew of the *Glencairn* is a microcosm for the world and the sea as Fate. The theme of unalterable fate is a recurring one throughout O'Neill's work, but it is especially relevant in his plays concerning the sea. In *Chris Christophersen* (1919), "*The Ole Devil*" revised into *Anna Christie* (1920), and his little known one-act adaptation of *The Ancient Mariner* (1923), the theme of human beings being buffeted by destiny is one on which O'Neill was able to construct his tragic world vision.

The Film

A lifelong passion for sailing and the sea made John Ford an appropriate choice to film the *Glencairn* plays. Many of Ford's early films for Fox studios depicted seamen under strained circumstances. Such films as *Men Without Women* (1930) and *Seas Beneath* (1931) develop such Fordian themes as camaraderie and sacrifice among men. Scenarist Dudley Nichols began his longtime association with John Ford on both of these films as well. The Nichols/Ford relationship produced such films as *The Lost Patrol* (1934), *The Informer* (1935), and *Stagecoach* (1939), prior to the adaptation of O'Neill's sea plays. *Stagecoach* set up the production team of Walter Wanger, John Ford, and Dudley Nichols under the aegis of Argosy Productions, which made *The Long Voyage Home* in 1940. The team added the technical prowess of cinematographer Gregg Toland, whose previous screen credits included *Dead End* (1937),

Wuthering Heights (1939) and *The Grapes of Wrath* (1940). This combination produced what is generally regarded by many, including the playwright himself, as the best cinematic adaptation of an O'Neill play. A film that, according to John Orlandello, "perfectly captured O'Neill's wistful feelings toward the sea, and the camaraderie, pleasures, and pains of its shipboard inhabitants."

Dudley Nichols' screenplay integrates the four plays into a fluid work taking on as its title and basic theme the final one-act of the series, *The Long Voyage Home*. Following the film's opening credit sequence is a title insert that reads:

> With their hates and desires men are changing the face of the earth—but they cannot change the sea. Men who live on the sea never change—for they live in a lonely world apart as they drift from one rusty tramp steamer to the next, forging the life-lines of nations.

Nichols establishes from the start the theme of the loneliness and immutability of the seafaring life. The opening shot of the film is of a ship (the *Glencairn*) anchored offshore at night. The viewpoint is from land, thus juxtaposing the sensual warmth of the islands with the stasis of life aboard ship. Nichols changes the time setting of O'Neill's plays, from World War I to World War II, thereby providing the film with a greater contemporary appeal for its audience. Although the film is not overtly interventionist (the United States had not yet entered into the European conflict) producer Walter Wanger's anti-isolationist sentiments were well established through such films as *Blockade* (1939) and *Foreign Correspondent* (1940). The film follows the order of the plays with a subtle shift, for continuity, between *In the Zone* and *Bound East for Cardiff*.

What is important about the adaptation, and what pleased O'Neill the most, is the numerous episodes in which the plays are opened up. O'Neill's two favorite films adapted from his work were the silent version of *Anna Christie* (1923) and Ford's film. He especially liked the non-dialogue scenes, which transformed the text from one medium into another. There are several instances in the film that are innovative in their departure from the plays: the opening sequence contrasting the islands with the ship, the storm at sea, the sea burial of Yank, Smitty's attempt to leave ship, the bombardment by German planes, and the final scene when many of the crew return to the *Glencairn* to sign on for another voyage. Rather than a "motley assortment of characters and ethnic types," Ford's film focuses on several characters as major protagonists in the film. Driscoll (Thomas Mitchell) and Olson (John Wayne) expand the dimensions of their limitations in O'Neill's plays. A significant change is made by allowing Olson to escape being shanghaied, with Driscoll being taken instead. But it is learned in a highly poetic scene, where a newspaper floats into the waters off the ship, that the "devil ship" *Amindra*, with Driscoll aboard, has been torpedoed as it was leaving the harbor. Ford and Nichols' screen treatment of O'Neill's one-acts, according to John Orlandello, "transcends both the limitations of the plays themselves and the problems of integrating them into a successful artistic whole."

Gregg Toland's cinematography also adds significantly to the overall tone and atmosphere of the one-acts. This was Toland's last film before he began work on *Citizen Kane* and his use of deep-focus photography and a chiaroscuro lighting style contribute to the "artistic" look of Ford's film. Toland utilizes a 24 mm wide-angle lens to emphasize the claustrophobic life aboard ship. This is especially apparent in scenes in the forecastle, particularly the one in which Smitty is accused of being a German spy and the death of Yank. Deep-focus shots, where many planes are in focus, are also used in order to see different fields of action—a technical device that is also significant to Orson Welles' *Citizen Kane*. Toland's expressionistic, chiaroscuro lighting style also contributes to the sense of confined space and entrapment not only aboard ship but on land as well. According to John Orlandello, "Toland's camera work in *Long Voyage Home* makes it clear that spatial confinement need not necessarily diminish compositional interest of a shot or the visual quality of a film."

REFERENCES

Bogdanovich, Peter, *John Ford* (Berkeley: University of California Press, 1978); Orlandello, John, *O'Neill on Film* (Rutherford, N.J.: Fairleigh Dickinson University Press, 1982); Ranald, Margaret Loftus, *The Eugene O'Neill Companion* (Westport, Conn.: Greenwood Press, 1984).

—*R.W.W.*

LOOK BACK IN ANGER (1956)

JOHN OSBORNE (1929–1994)

Look Back in Anger (1959), U.K., directed by Tony Richardson, adapted by Nigel Kneale; Woodfall Films/Warner Bros.

The Play

The discovery at London's Royal Court Theatre of a struggling 27-year-old playwright named John Osborne is one of the benchmark moments in the history of modern British theatre. His first two plays produced at the Royal Court in 1956–57, *Look Back in Anger* and *The Entertainer*, both directed by young Tony Richardson, changed the face of contemporary drama and established him within months as a member of that generation derisively dubbed as "Angry Young Men." If the first play introduced Jimmy Porter, that emblem of his "angry" generation, the second presented an even more colorful character, Archie Rice, a fading song-and-dance man who epitomized a vanishing tradition of music hall theatre.

George Devine and Tony Richardson, two of the founders of the refurbished Royal Court and its performing organization, the English Stage Company, had placed a notice in *The Stage* announcing a search for new writers. Among the hundreds of submissions that arrived in the post was John Osborne's *Look Back in Anger*. Osborne was a virtual unknown at the time, a struggling actor and untried playwright living humbly in Chiswick on a barge in Cubitt's Yacht Basin. "Both George and Tony were completely unknown quantities to me," recalled Osborne, "and, of course, I was to them. We were all out there in an unknown world. Nobody knew at all what anyone's real intentions were. For them to support people like myself, as they did, was a great act of faith, and they both expressed that faith openly." According to Osborne, *Look Back in Anger* grew out of a perceived general malaise across England: "The country was tired, not merely from the sacrifice of two back-breaking wars but from the defeat and misery between them." *Look Back in Anger* premiered at the Royal Court on May 8, 1956, as part of the Court's first season. It ran for 151 performances with a cast including Kenneth Haigh as Jimmy Porter, Mary Ure (who later married Osborne) as Alison, Alan Bates as Cliff, and Helena Hughes (as Helena). After a second run at the Court, beginning in March 1957 (with the same cast), it opened in New York that fall at the Lyceum Theatre with only one casting change, Vivienne Drummond as Helena. It was chosen best foreign play of the season by the New York Drama Critics' Circle.

The character of Jimmy Porter gave form and voice to England's "angry young man," a term concocted by the ESC's publicist, George Fearon. He spoke for the anger, frustration, and isolation of his generation. Jimmy was a product of the postwar Education Act, which opened high schools and university to those working-class children of limited aspirations who had formerly been confined to menial jobs. According to critic Alexander Walker, people like Jimmy had developed an "articulate contempt for [society's] outworn institutions and class-bound attitudes, but saw no means of changing and replacing them. *Look Back in Anger* didn't provide the means, but it gave their rage its release." As Jimmy says in the play, "I suppose people of our generation aren't able to die for good causes any longer. We had all that done for us, in the thirties and forties, when we were still kids. There aren't any good, brave causes left."

The three-act, one-set play is set in a dreary Midland town of the fifties. Squeezed into a tiny one-room flat is Jimmy, a tall, slender man of 25, his long-suffering wife of three years, Alison, and Jimmy's mate and business partner, Cliff Lewis. Although Jimmy has attended a university and is obviously well educated, he has subsequently drifted through a succession of temporary jobs—journalism, advertising, selling vacuum cleaners—before finally settling in to run a market stall. In the first act, Jimmy and Cliff read the Sunday newspapers and unleash a fusillade of scorn at the politics and society of the day. Even his wife Alison is not spared criticism for her timidity and clumsiness. This volley of invective is interrupted when her ironing board is accidentally overturned and the hot iron burns her arm. It is then that Alison confides in Cliff that she is pregnant, but that she's afraid to tell Jimmy for fear of his hostile reaction. The first act concludes as news arrives that Alison's friend, Helena Charles, an actress, is coming for an indefinite stay.

Act Two begins two weeks later. Helena has moved in. Aristocratic and a bit aloof, she intensely dislikes Jimmy, and he hates her right back. News arrives that Jimmy's dear friend, Ma Tanner—who years before had staked him to his market stall—is dying. While he is away attending to her, Alison's father, a retired military man, arrives, and their ensuing dialogue reveals some of the past history behind her decision to marry Jimmy, a man considered beneath her class. When Jimmy returns to the apartment, only Helena is present, and she informs him that Alison is going to have his baby and that she has decided to leave him. Stung by the death of Ma Tanner and now angered by this additional piece of news, Jimmy lashes out: "I don't care. I don't care if she's going to have a baby. I don't care if it has two heads!" Helena strikes him. But then, after a few moments of mutual shock, the two fall into a passionate embrace.

Act Three transpires several months later. Now it is Helena who stands at the ironing board while Jimmy and Cliff scan the Sunday newspapers. At length, Cliff

John Osborne

announces that he is leaving his partnership with Jimmy. There is a knock at the door. It is Alison, come to bring Helena news of her miscarriage. Both women feel they are not right for Jimmy. "He wants something quite different from us," says Helena. "What it is, exactly, I don't know—a kind of cross between a mother and a Greek courtesan, a henchwoman, a mixture of Cleopatra and Boswell." When Helena announces to Jimmy that she, too, will leave him, he launches into the most famous speech of the play. He says that everyone wants to escape from the pain of being alive: "It's no good trying to fool yourself about love. You can't fall into it like a soft job, without dirtying up your hands. It takes muscle and guts. And if you can't bear the thought—of messing up your nice, clean soul—you'd better give up the whole idea of life, and become a saint—because you'll never make it as a human being. It's either this world or the next." In the

Richard Burton as Jimmy Porter was the "angry young man" in Tony Richardson's screen version of John Osborne's Look Back in Anger, *costarring Claire Bloom.* (COURTESY WARNER BROS.)

drift towards anarchy, the instinctive leftishness, the automatic rejection of 'official' attitudes, the surrealist sense of humor. . . ."

The Film

In bringing *Look Back in Anger* to the screen, Tony Richardson wanted to attain nothing less than the revitalization of what he regarded as a moribund British cinema: "I should certainly like British films to be different from what many of them have been in the past. . . . It is absolutely vital to get into British films the same sort of impact and sense of life that, what you loosely call the Angry Young Man cult has had in the theatre and literary worlds. It is a desperate need." Accordingly, Richardson helped form the Woodfall Films production company, the name deriving from the street off King's Road where Osborne had rented a little house. Enter producer Harry Saltzman, a Quebec-born American and an entrepreneur in vaudeville, circuses, advertising, and television. He interested Associated British-Pathé, a British distribution company in which Warner Brothers had a part interest, in financing the film. His determination to cast Richard Burton as Jimmy was, in Osborne's words, "a calculated move on his part to reverse the tide of [Burton's] career [since] his most recent films, which had concentrated in Cinemascope on his splendid knees beneath Roman kilts, had failed to establish his surety as an international star." Mary Ure repeated her stage role as Alison. And Claire Bloom and Edith Evans, the only other "name" actors, were signed on as Helena and Ma Tanner, respectively.

Shooting began in the autumn of 1958 at Elstree studios, where a set was constructed, consisting of a street market standing against a background of shop fronts. Although Richardson realized that the story's power stemmed from the sense that the characters were trapped in the claustrophobic attic, he agreed with scenarist Nigel Kneale that the play should "open up" much of its action to locations outside the Porter flat, to the pub where Jimmy plays his trumpet, the market stalls, the Alison family home in the country, the theatre where Helena is performing, the cemetery visited by Ma Tanner and Jimmy, and the train station where Jimmy and Alison are reconciled. Richardson was making, he said at the time, an important discovery about the filmmaking process: "Miracles happen on location which you could never ever conceive of or imagine when you are writing the script. Life is always more daring and extravagant than art."

The film sprints nimbly out of the blocks. It opens with a blare of jazz by the Chris Barber Jazz Band and

final tableau, Helena has left, and Alison collapses at Jimmy's feet. As if in a trance, they embrace each other, reconciled—temporarily, at least—for the moment. They lapse into a childish word game they frequently play about the "bears and squirrels." "There are cruel steel traps lying about everywhere," he intones, "just waiting for rather mad, slightly satanic, and very timid little animals." She replies sweetly, "Poor squirrels." He adds, softly, "Oh, poor, poor bears!"

The first reviews of *Look Back in Anger* were generally poor. The *Evening Standard* declared that it "sets up a wailing wall for the latest post-generation of the under-thirties. It aims at being a despairing cry but achieves only the stature of a self-pitying snivel." Osborne was dismayed, but Tony Richardson said, "But what on earth did you *expect?* You didn't expect them to *like* it, did you?" However, critic Kenneth Tynan's review in the *Sunday Times*, dated May 13, 1956, helped save the day: "[It] presents post-war youth as it really is. . . . To have done this at all would be a signal achievement; to have done it in a first play is a minor miracle. All the qualities are there, qualities one had despaired of ever seeing on the stage—the

a flurry of tight close-ups of banjos, horns, and dancing feet. Minutes later, Jimmy leaves and wanders down the night streets, a solitary figure blowing a trumpet riff. He climbs the stairs to his flat, where he silently regards the sleeping form of Alison. He bends over her and awakens her with a kiss—first tentative, then passionate. Fade out. The effect of first presenting Jimmy as a sensitive soul, only later revealing his cruelty, is the exact opposite of the play, which first showcased his angry snarl, and only later revealed the wounded vulnerability beneath. After an extended sequence in the flat, a virtual copy of Act One of the play, three scenes (scripted by Osborne himself) are added to further emphasize Jimmy's sympathetic nature: In the first he shares a drink with Ma Tanner. In the second, he takes her to her husband's grave ("We had lots of fun, him and me; being alive. You know—just being alive."). And in the third, he visits her in the hospital where she lies dying. After trying to listen to her inarticulate speech, he cries out, "Hell, *Hell, Hell!*"—at which point director Richardson cuts from his scream to the cries of children playing in the streets outside. Jimmy's impotent rage and frustration in this terrifying scene are as affecting as in any other moment of the film. More added scenes reinforce our sympathy for Jimmy. In the marketplace he tries to thwart the racist bigotry behind an attempt to oust an Indian trader. In another scene, which transpires during a theatre rehearsal of Helena's play, he explodes in contempt at the whole claptrap of Victorian stagecraft: "The bloke who wrote that was never in a woman's bedroom; not even his mother's when she found out the truth about him." And later, when he and Helena attend a movie, a Korda-esque patriotic saga of English colonialism in India, he hoots derisively at the British lancers on screen.

Many of the play's memorable speeches are rendered virtually intact, although they are taken out of the context of Jimmy's flat and redistributed into a variety of other locales. For example, Jimmy's soliloquy on Colonel Redfern's "long days in the sun," which originally appeared in Act One, appears midway through the film during a jazz club scene. Alison's suggestion that she end her pregnancy with an abortion, also from Act One, transpires with her doctor (George Devine in a cameo appearance) in his examining room. Jimmy's savage confrontation with Helena ("I have no public school scruples about hitting girls . . .") occurs in her theatre dressing room after his denunciation of her play. And the concluding scenes in the train station provide the opportunity for a succession of several of the play's key dialogues, including Jimmy's affectionate farewell to Cliff and Jimmy's "bears and squirrels" game with Alison.

The film was released with an "X" certificate, a potential kiss of death at the box office. However, it did respectable business and effectively launched a series of British "angry young man" films, including Karel Reisz' *Saturday Night and Sunday Morning* (1960) and Tony Richardson's *The Loneliness of the Long Distance Runner* (1961). Fans of the play may quibble about Burton's strong performance. It is perhaps *too* strong—after all, here is someone, unlike the original stage Jimmy, who seems capable of handling any adversity. And at the age of 38, he looks a bit old for the part. As for Osborne, he had his share of reservations about the screen version. "The final effect of the film is a softer-edge, more sympathetic portrait free of the claustrophobic confines of the Porter apartment."

REFERENCES

Findlater, Richard, *At the Royal Court* (Derbyshire: Amber Lane Press, 1981); Gomez, Joseph, *"The Entertainer:* From Play to Film," *Film Heritage,* 8 (1973), 19–26; Osborne, John, *Almost a Gentleman: An Autobiography* (London: Faber and Faber, 1991); Richardson, Tony, *The Long Distance Runner: A Memoir* (New York: William Morrow, 1993); Welsh, James M., and John C. Tibbetts, eds., *The Cinema of Tony Richardson: Essays and Interviews* (Albany: State University of New York Press, 1999).

—*J.C.T.*

LOST IN YONKERS (1991)

NEIL SIMON (1927–)

Lost in Yonkers (1993), U.S.A., directed by Martha Coolidge, adapted by Neil Simon; Columbia.

The Play

This Tony Award and Pulitzer Prize–winning play premiered on February 21, 1991, in New York City. Set in Yonkers, New York, in 1942, the story revolves around the Kurnitz family, specifically, two brothers (Arty, age 13, and Jay, 15) who are left under their grandmother's care for 10 long months. Their father (Eddie) leaves them with his mother because he needs to raise $9,000 to pay off a loan shark for his dead wife's medical bills. The boys work at their grandmother's candy shop and also get involved in the lives of their relatives, most notably their Aunt Bella and Uncle Louie, a renegade "bag man" for the mafia. Much of the play's tension is built around the boys' fear and antipathy for their grandmother and Bella's desire to become more independent due to her love for a movie usher named Johnny. In a crucial scene Bella proclaims her desire to marry Johnny, start a restaurant with him, and "have babies," but her mother is unwilling to give her approval or lend the money needed—she allegedly has thousands of dollars stashed away somewhere. The play ends with Bella coming back home because Johnny is afraid of leaving the security of his family, and the boys' father returns for Jay and Arty. The boys leave having learned lessons on how to be "tough," and having developed a meager but fruitful connection with their grandmother. *Lost in Yonkers* is, according to producer Ray Stark, "a human comedy that observes life through the prism of a family that is barely functioning."

The Film

Playwright Neil Simon adapted the play into a film by putting many of the critical scenes into different environments. Conscious of what a moviegoing audience wanted, because of his experience writing more than 10 film adaptations, Simon took many scenes out of Grandma Kurnitz' apartment and placed them into the candy store and its neighborhood. This accentuated the drastic difference between the energy of the outside world and the prison-like atmosphere of the upstairs apartment. Simon did this right from the start and carried it throughout the movie. For example, Act One, Scene One of the play, which is comprised of the boys and their father sitting inside grandma's stuffy apartment, is divided among different settings. The movie begins with the drive to grandmother's in Eddie's beat-up car, and proceeds to a gas station stop, a delay in the candy store as Bella fixes ice cream sundaes, and, finally, a scene in grandma's dimly lit apartment as she determines whether or not they can stay. In a second example, the crucial scene where Bella returns home for her final confrontation with her mother, is distributed among various locations—the back porch, the staircase up to the apartment, and the apartment interior.

The film replaced five of the seven original Broadway actors but used the original stage stars for the roles of Bella and Grandma Kurnitz. The changes are as follows: Jamie Marsh's Jay was replaced with Brad Stoll, Danny Gerard's Arty with Mike Damus, Mark Blum's Eddie with Jack Laufer, Kevin Spacey's Louie with Richard Dreyfuss, and Lauren Klein's Gert with Susan Merson. The boys' perspective on events is maintained via Jay's voice-over narrative. Viewers also get to see (and hear through the narration) Eddie's travels around the South as he sells scrap iron for the war effort. Our sense of the boys' fear of grandma is intensified because the roles of Jay and Arty were given to younger actors than had appeared on stage.

The roles of Aunt Bella (Mercedes Ruehl) and Uncle Louie are amplified in the film. Bella becomes a focal character with the addition of new material. We get to see her interaction with Johnny and the evolution of their courtship. Johnny (David Strathairn), who is never actually seen in the play, is here a supporting character who serves to throw Bella's desire for freedom into high relief. The script accentuates Louie's avoidance of Hollywood Harry (Robert Guy Miranda) and his sidekick by showing the two gangsters constantly monitoring Louie's whereabouts. Their bright yellow convertible always seems to be parked on the corner across from the apartment, and Harry is shown asking the boys about their uncle (an event only alluded to in the play). Two major episodes were added. In the first, Louie sneaks out of the house with the kids by way of a secret passage he dug when he was a kid. In the second, during Bella's confrontation with the family about her plans for the future, Jay helps Uncle Louie escape by dressing up like him, serving as a decoy for Hollywood Harry. As Harry hits Jay and points a gun in his face, Louie escapes in their convertible, and the gangsters give fruitless chase.

A major change from the play is when the film ends with Jay's narration that Bella finally left her mother's apartment to be on her own; moreover, Bella's narration picks up the thread and relates the circumstances of her life in Florida. This ending depicts Bella as a figure of empowerment, rather than the "emotionally arrested" character in the play.

REFERENCES

Coolidge, Martha, "On Directing Neil Simon's *Lost in Yonkers*," in *Neil Simon's Lost in Yonkers: The Illustrated Screenplay of the Film* (New York: New Market, 1993); Lipton, James, "Neil Simon: The Art of Theater X," *The Paris Review*, 125 (Winter 1992); Simon, Neil, *The Play Goes On: A Memoir* (New York: Simon and Schuster, 1999); Stark, Ray, "Producer's Foreword on Neil Simon's *Lost in Yonkers*," in *Neil Simon's Lost in Yonkers. The Illustrated Screenplay of the Film* (New York: New Market, 1993).

—*T.N.T.*

M

MAD WOMAN OF CHAILLOT, THE

See *LA FOLLE DE CHAILLOT*

THE MADNESS OF GEORGE III (1991)

ALAN BENNETT (1934–   )

The Madness of King George (1994), U.S.A./U.K., directed by Nicholas Hytner, adapted by Alan Bennett; Samuel Goldwyn Co./Channel Four Films.

The Play

The Madness of George III premiered at London's Royal National Theatre on November 28, 1991, in a production directed by Nicholas Hytner, who would later be called upon to direct the film adaptation. The play is set in 1788, nearly 30 years into the reign of King George III (r. 1760–1820). As John Lahr wrote in his *New Yorker* review, the play "begins just after the monarch loses his [American] colonies and just before he loses his mind." The hyperactive king (played by Nigel Hawthorne on both stage and screen) babbles constantly about the loss of his North American colonies but also demonstrates other signs of odd and bizarre behavior. In fact, the king, presumably afflicted and diagnosed with porphyria, a metabolic imbalance

that reproduces all the symptoms of mental illness, spent the last decade of his reign "isolated and insane, far from the seat of government," as Peter Wolfe has written, so "his recovery at the end of the Bennett scripts was merely temporary." The malady was to recur for short periods throughout the rest of his life. Only later, after the emergence of the journals of Dr. Willis and the diaries of Sir George Baker, the physicians who treated him, were historians able to piece together the full extent of the king's baffling illness.

Playwright Alan Bennett, popular for his crowd-pleasing National Theatre adaptation of *The Wind in the Willows*, also had screenplay credits, including *A Private Function* (1985) and *Prick Up Your Ears* (1987), a dramatization of the flamboyant life of playwright Joe Orton, directed by Stephen Frears. In *The Madness of George III*, Bennett took his cue from Shakespeare's *King Lear*, which becomes a significant metaphor involved in the king's temporary recovery at the end of the play. The well-being of the nation depends upon the health of the monarch, as Prime Minister William Pitt suggests: "An ailing King means an ailing Government." The ambitious Prince of Wales orchestrates a plot to become regent and replace his ailing father in order to get the government back on track as the stock market falls and the economy declines; but the prince is a ruthless opportunist, who would place his father under house arrest in a "remote hideaway from which reports about his health could be screened carefully before reaching the public," as Peter Wolfe explains in his book *Understanding Alan Bennett* (1999). The play reflected upon contemporary problems in England, especially in the way it presented the royal family as being dysfunctional. Parallels to the current royal family's problems and what Queen Elizabeth II called the "annus horribilis" were quickly noticed and paved the way for the later film adaptation. "The parallels with today's monarchy were largely unsought," Bennett explained in his introduction to the published screenplay, "but they become more obvious as the film proceeds, the final shot of St Paul's consciously recalling the television coverage of the marriage of the Prince and Princess of Wales." The play's royal dilemma seemed both timely and topical by the time the film was made.

The Film

The film adaptation involved the playwright and other London theatrical talents as well. Nigel Hawthorne was cast to play the lead role he had introduced on the London stage and Nicholas Hytner, associate director of the Royal National Theatre when he first directed the National Theatre production, was assigned to direct the film as well. Hytner's stage credits included the enormously successful musical *Miss Saigon*, starring Jonathan Pryce, which premiered in 1989 and enjoyed a long run at the Drury Lane Theatre in London's West End. Nigel Hawthorne had played the role of King George on stage for nearly three years when he was cast for the film. "The role is a bit of a roller coaster," he noted in a press release, "but as I have the experience of having done the play, I do know the journey."

Hawthorne led a distinguished British cast that included Ian Holm as the unconventional Dr. Willis, the psychotherapist who successfully treated the king's ailment. Holm, famous for his Shakespearean roles on stage and screen, had been nominated for an Academy Award in 1981 for his performance in *Chariots of Fire*. Amanda Donohoe played the Countess of Pembroke, the queen's lady-in-waiting who first invited Dr. Willis to the royal court to minister to the king. Queen Charlotte was played by Helen Mirren, best known to American audiences for her Emmy-nominated performances as Inspector Jane Tennison on the BBC television series *Prime Suspect*. She had also played the lead in the stage and screen versions of William Mastrosimone's *Extremities* (1983) and had other screen roles, including *O Lucky Man!* for Lindsay Anderson, *Savage Messiah* for Ken Russell, and *The Cook, the Thief, His Wife, and Her Lover* for Peter Greenaway in 1989. The opportunistic Prince of Wales was played by Rupert Everett, who began his career on the repertory stage of the Glasgow Citizens Theatre. His role in Hytner's film helped to transform him into a major Hollywood star.

The title of Bennett's play was changed so as not to confuse American audiences, who, the Hollywood producers feared, might otherwise regard the film as a sequel on the order of *Psycho II* or *Terminator III*. Nonetheless, the adaptation was reasonably close to the original play. In addition to adapting his play for the screen, Alan Bennett also played the role of a member of Parliament in the film. Following the action of the play, Prime Minister Pitt (Julian Wadham) attempts to calm the House of Commons with false assurances of the king's good health while doctors attempt to diagnose the king's illness with no success. The Prince of Wales, who conspires to have his father declared unfit to rule, does not even permit the queen access to her own husband. Isolated by this conspiracy, the king's only sympathetic friend is his new equerry, Captain Greville (Rupert Graves).

The king's health does not improve until Dr. Willis is brought in from his asylum in Lincolnshire. Under Dr. Willis's therapy, the king enacts scenes from Shakespeare's *King Lear*, which enables the king to recognize parallels between himself and Shakespeare's mad monarch. Even as the king begins to improve, however, Parliament prepares a bill that would enable the Prince of Wales to become regent. Shocked into action, the king recovers his wits and dignified demeanor and races to Westminster to demonstrate that he is in fact qualified to rule. He arrives in the nick of time at Westminster as the film cross-cuts his journey with the parliamentary debate. This is a dramatic ornamentation added to the film. "Had Nicholas Hytner at the outset suggested bringing the King from Kew to Westminster to confront the MPs, I would have been outraged at this adjustment to what actually happened," Bennett explained. But after plodding through three drafts of the screenplay, he confessed, "I would have taken the King to Blackpool if I thought it would have helped."

The film was a critical success, garnering multiple Academy Award nominations for best actor (Hawthorne), best supporting actress (Helen Mirren), and best adapted screenplay, and it eventually won an Oscar for best art direction. Helen Mirren's sensitive portrayal of Queen Charlotte earned her the best actress award at the Cannes Film Festival of 1995. Bennett noted that "the Prince of Wales is more forceful and more of a villain in the film than he was on the stage or in life." Although he was anxious to be made regent, "he was more careful of appearances than I have made him and was more governed too by that fellow-feeling all royals have for each other." In general, however, Hytner's film effectively preserved the play's delightful blend of tragedy and farce and was brilliantly acted and adapted.

REFERENCES

Bennett, Alan, *The Madness of King George* (New York: Random House, 1995); Lahr, John, "The Theatre: Majesty," *The New Yorker* (October 11, 1993): 124–126; Royce, Brenda Scott, "*The Madness of King George*," *Magill's Cinema Annual 1995*, ed. Beth A. Fhaner (Detroit: Gale Research VideoHound Reference, 1996): 372–374; Schiff, Stephen, "The Poet of Embarrassment," *The New Yorker* (September 6, 1993): 92–101; Wolfe, Peter, *Understanding Alan Bennett* (Columbia: University of South Carolina Press, 1999).

—*J.M.W.*

MAJOR BARBARA (1905)

GEORGE BERNARD SHAW (1856–1950)

Major Barbara (1941), U.K., directed by Gabriel Pascal, adapted by Pascal and George Bernard Shaw; General Films/United Artists.

The Play

After George Bernard Shaw wrote several "thesis" plays, such as *Widower's Houses* (1892), *Arms and the Man* (1893), and *Mrs. Warren's Profession* (1899), he then achieved his greatest critical and popular successes with later plays, notably *Man and Superman* (1903), *Major Barbara* (1905), and *Pygmalion* (1913). As Eric Bentley has observed, Shaw frequently depended upon the form of "discussion drama" to air out his views on social and philosophical matters. "Shaw was expert at writing verbal duels in which the acerbity and the interest derive not from the questions discussed but from situation and character." *Major Barbara* is such a play.

Andrew Undershaft is a successful munitions manufacturer. After being separated from his snobbish wife, Lady Britomart, and family for several years, he returns to find that his daughter, Barbara, has become an officer in the Salvation Army. Her fiancé, Professor Adolphus Cusins, has also joined the Army to be near her. Determined to get Barbara out of the Army, Undershaft shows her that the Army can be "bought" by donating to it a large sum of money. Barbara, who disapproves of her father's actions, leaves the Army and goes to visit her father's factory, where she is astonished to see a charitably run institution with a model town attached for the worker inhabitants. Cusins is also impressed, and he joins Undershaft's business so that he can help the poor help themselves. Barbara, meanwhile, contin-

ues her own good work by spreading the gospel among the company employees

The three central characters, Undershaft, Barbara, and Cusins, all represent varying philosophical and political attitudes. Undershaft is a typically Shavian hero, vital and wise. Barbara is the idealistic heroine, but not so far gone in her illusions that she cannot be jolted back to reality at the end of the play. And Cusins, who is to be Undershaft's successor, will unite realism and idealism, practicality and wisdom, in "an almost superhuman union." Undershaft was originally conceived as a sort of monster. But, as Bentley points out, he so bestrides the play that his sermons about the power of money tend to override the normally Shavian attitudes about its corrupting influence—"Like so many other writers, [Shaw] makes his monster so impressive that no good man can match him." Among Shaw's heroines, Barbara emerges as something new, a girlish type, innocent, refined by civilization, yet on fire with ideals.

The Film

Early on, Shaw was skeptical of motion pictures: "Many of them are full of the stupidest errors of judgment," he wrote in 1924. "Overdone and foolishly repeated strokes of expression, hideous make-ups, close-ups that an angel's face would not bear. . . . Conceit is rampant among your film makers; and good sense is about nonexistent." Indeed, before the movies learned to talk, Shaw refused to allow any of his plays to be adapted to the screen. "I repeat that a play with the words left out is a play spoiled; and all those filmings of plays written to be spoken as well as seen are boresome blunders. . . ."

The first Shavian adaptation to hit the screen was *How He Lied to Her Husband* (1931), directed by Cecil Lewis in a virtually unaltered piece of canned theatre. Both it and the next venture, *Arms and the Man* (1932), were tediously static, and they flopped at the box office. But the arrival of one Gabriel Pascal, a self-styled film producer, would change all that. His adaptations of Shaw's *Pygmalion* (1938), *Major Barbara* (1941), and *Caesar and Cleopatra* (1944)—for his own production company, General Films, and examined exhaustively in Donald Costello's invaluable study of the subject, *The Serpent's Eye* (1965)—would not only be successes, but would also represent a more enlightened attitude on Shaw's part toward the recognition of a more "cinematic" union of play text and camera.

The success of *Pygmalion* ensured that the Shaw-Pascal combination would produce another play adaptation. *Major Barbara* was just the thing, and Shaw determined to write the entire screenplay himself and maintain a vigilant presence on the set. However, although the names of Shaw and actress Wendy Hiller brought the financiers running, all was not smooth with the actual production. Wartime conditions forced frequent shut-downs and alterations in the casting (Rex Harrison replaced Andrew Osborn in the role of Adolphus Cusins when Osborn was drafted). Of the 19 new scenes Shaw added to his original text, a few were quite substantial and significant. These included a 10-minute "Prologue" in which Barbara meets Professor Cusins at a Salvation Army street gathering in the East End—all of which transpired before the rise of the curtain in the play—and, most spectacularly, a climactic sequence involving Cusins' tour of the Undershaft factory. Commentator Costello maintains that this final scene was extremely important to the theme and effect of the film: "It must convince the viewer, intellectually and emotionally, that the might and power controlled by Undershaft can lead to a social reorganization in which poverty and injustice are eliminated. Pascal unleashes here the power of the cinema—he uses . . . cutting and camera motion and sound, the dynamism of the cinema, to create a visual and aural impression." Other interpolations depict offstage events (like a wrestling match or an Army march to Albert Hall or, most spectacularly, the climactic depiction of the great Undershaft factory); others are merely transitional scenes that cover gaps in narrative continuity.

Compared to the movie of *Pygmalion* a year before, *Major Barbara* seems more a literary than a pictorial translation to the screen. To the degree that it remained true to the concept of the original play, it was pictorially dull. Moreover, for all Shaw's efforts, the film inevitably simplified certain issues in the play, most obviously in the Shavian social attack on contemporary England. Although Undershaft remains Shaw's Superman, many of his scenes are shortened, his dialogue is abbreviated, and his central position in the play—notably his philosophy of power—is weakened. "What remains," writes Costello, "after a good deal of omission and addition, is a clear, uncomplicated and unparadoxical story of the conversion of Barbara to her father's belief in the utter morality of a power which is strong enough to reorganize society so as to eliminate the one real evil—poverty."

REFERENCES

Bentley, Eric, *Bernard Shaw* (New York: Limelight Editions, 1985); Costello, Donald P., *The Serpent's Eye: Shaw and the Cinema* (Notre Dame, Ind.: University of Notre Dame Press, 1965); Pascal, Valerie, *The Disciple and His Devil: Gabriel Pascal and Bernard Shaw* (New York: McGraw-Hill, 1970).

—*J.C.T.*

A MAN FOR ALL SEASONS (1960)

ROBERT BOLT (1927–   )

A Man for All Seasons (1966), U.S.A., directed by Fred Zinnemann, adapted by Robert Bolt; Columbia.

A Man for All Seasons (1988), U.S.A., directed and adapted by Charlton Heston; Turner Television.

The Play

Robert Bolt's plays, especially *Flowering Cherry* (1957), *The Tiger and the Horse* (1960), and *State of Revolution* (1977), deal with the conflicts between the ideal and the real, between man's dream of perfection and the inevitability of his failure. While repudiating Brecht's marxist beliefs, he pursues issues, ideas, and controversies with the zeal of a platform orator. His *A Man for All Seasons* (1960), a two-act drama that premiered in London in 1960 and came to Broadway at the ANTA Theatre on November 22, 1961, effectively exploits the drama of history and is loaded with religious and moral conflicts—between King Henry VIII (Keith Baxter in the New York production) and the Roman Catholic Church; and between the king and his friend and mentor, Sir Thomas More (Paul Scofield), a devoted Roman Catholic who will not support the king's intention to divorce his wife, Catherine of Aragon (described in the play as being "as barren as a brick") in order to marry Anne Boleyn, whom he believes may bear him a son and heir. More was the author of *Utopia* and was a major figure of the English Renaissance. Because the king wants and needs More's support, he appoints him lord chancellor; but More proves to be a man of conscience who is torn between loyalty to his king and his God. More is placed in a political minefield when he is appointed chancellor to replace the ailing Cardinal Wolsey. Waiting in the wings is his political enemy Thomas Cromwell (Thomas Gomez), who manipulates More's fall from royal favor; then, later, his imprisonment in the Tower of London; and, finally, his trial for treason and execution. He is aided in his Machiavellian scheme by the politically ambitious Richard Rich (William Redfield), an opportunist willing to perjure himself in order to seal More's death warrant. Rich's reward for this betrayal is his appointment as attorney general for Wales.

When Henry's petition to the pope to annul his marriage to Catherine of Aragon is declined, he declares himself supreme head of the Church of England and breaks with the Church of Rome. More resigns the chancellorship, against the advice of his friend the duke of Norfolk, and retires to his country home, at great expense to his family, since he can no longer afford his servants. When an act of Parliament is passed in 1534 requiring all subjects to acknowledge the supremacy of the English king over all foreign sovereigns, including the pope, More, unwilling to take the mandated oath, is sent to the Tower. Possessed of a keen legal mind, More believes that he will be protected by his silence. He says nothing in public that would bring his sovereign's actions or authority into question. More's only flaw is that he is not a cynical pragmatist and that he assumes the world is honest and the law will protect him. He does not calculate that his former student, Richard Rich, would be so eager to advance himself and so unprincipled that he would lie under oath.

The opposition of the ideal to the politics of the state implies that love is the only thing that can rescue people from their despair and isolation. More's superb confidence in his own sense of right empowers him against all odds. As he says to Cromwell, "Yes, a man's soul is his self!" He warns Cromwell: "What you have hunted me for is not my actions, but the thoughts of my heart. It is a long road you have opened. For first men will disclaim their hearts and presently they will have no hearts. God help the people whose Statesmen walk your road." Bolt said of More, "This is why people like the play. They think, 'Thank Christ, somebody can do it. I may not be able to, but life *can* be that perfect.' And he didn't do anything you or I couldn't have done."

The Films

The two films based on this play both define and challenge the notion of what constitutes a "good" cinematic adaptation. If fidelity to the original play text is the measuring rod, then the low-budget Charlton Heston television production of 1988 would seem to be the better adaptation, though it is certainly not the better film. Heston retains Bolt's key theatrical device, a character identified as the "Common Man" (Roy Kinnear), who serves as both narrator and chorus from beginning to end, appearing in several roles as the play traces the political destiny of its protagonist. Closely following the play in this version, the Common Man is first given a name, Matthew, the servant of Sir Thomas who chooses to forsake his master after Sir Thomas resigns as lord chancellor. The Common Man then resurfaces in several other roles, serving Cromwell, then Rich, and as a "publican" (pubkeeper), a boatman on the Thames, and, later, Sir Thomas's jailer at the Tower of London, the foreman of the jury, and, at the end, the "headsman" and executioner.

As in the play, the Common Man steps forward to explain the historical context of the years 1529 to 1535,

the king's desire to have his marriage to Catherine of Aragon annulled so he would be at liberty to marry his mistress, Anne Boleyn, and his break with the Roman Catholic Church over this issue. The strength of this adaptation is the casting of Benjamin Whitrow as Thomas Cromwell, Vanessa Redgrave as More's wife, Lady Alice, and Sir John Gielgud as the beleaguered Cardinal Wolsey. The cast also includes Nicholas Amor as Signor Chapuys, the Spanish ambassador, who considers More an ally of his sovereign. Heston's adaptation retains Bolt's characters and structure but falls a bit short of absolute fidelity. Although some lines are cut and others slightly changed and rearranged, Bolt's theatrical design remains intact. The problem is that the viewer never quite forgets that this is filmed theatre.

The Academy Award–winning film Fred Zinnemann directed in 1966 was adapted by Robert Bolt himself and indulges in a lavish historical spectacle. Zinnemann dispenses with the Common Man chorus, whose functions are covered in the film by several actors, none of whom provides exposition or commentary on the action. Also missing is Signor Chapuys, the Spanish ambassador, who brings Sir Thomas a personal letter of support from the king of Spain in the play, a letter that Sir Thomas returns, unopened. Because these characters are removed, it is surprising that Robert Bolt would have won the Academy Award for best adapted screenplay, unless one considers that the story, though significantly changed and restructured, is brilliantly adapted to the screen in a way that opens up the action for a gorgeous spectacle of historical reconstruction.

As in the play, the king pays Sir Thomas a visit in Chelsea to put pressure on him to approve the pending divorce. In the film, Zinnemann shows the king, flamboyantly played by Robert Shaw, barging down the River Thames from Richmond in regal splendor, accompanied by courtiers and musicians (Georges Delerue composed a wonderfully nuanced period score). Sir Thomas is superbly played by Paul Scofield in a perfectly nuanced, Oscar-winning performance that Charlton Heston could never hope to match. Zinnemann's cast is consistently impressive. Wendy Hiller is wonderfully grumpy as Lady Alice; Susannah York is appealingly perky as More's educated daughter Margaret, whose Latin is better than that of the king; John Hurt is convincingly sleazy as Richard Rich; and Orson Welles quite fills the room as Cardinal Wolsey. Vanessa Redgrave, who was not available in 1966 to play Margaret More, is briefly seen in a cameo as a seductive Anne Boleyn. Leo McKern's Thomas Cromwell functions well enough but lacks the sinister edge Benjamin Whitrow brought to the role in the later adaptation.

Impressed by Ted Moore's cinematography in his *New Yorker* review (December 17, 1966), Brendon Gill considered Zinnemann's adaptation "one of the most beautiful movies ever made." Despite Bolt's restructuring of the text, Hollis Alpert of *The Saturday Review* (December 17) could not imagine a more competent, tasteful, and pleasing adaptation," and, writing for the *The New Republic* (February 25, 1967), Pauline Kael praised Zinnemann's "faithful, respectful interpretation of the play," which would have more accurately been called Bolt's transformation and *re*interpretation of the play. The film won six Oscars, including best director and best picture, as well as best screenplay. To claim the play was not well adapted on the niggling basis of fidelity would be both pedantic and stupid. The awkwardness of a more "literal" approach is well demonstrated by the Heston treatment.

REFERENCES

Ackroyd, Peter, *The Life of Thomas More* (New York: Doubleday, 1998); Matlaw, Myron, *Modern World Drama* (New York: Dutton, 1972); Zinnemann, Fred, *An Autobiography* (London: Bloomsbury, 1992).

—*J.M.W.*

George S. Kaufman

MAN WHO CAME TO DINNER, THE (1939)

GEORGE S. KAUFMAN (1889–1961) AND MOSS HART (1904–1961)

The Man Who Came to Dinner (1942), U.S.A., directed by William Keighley, adapted by Julius and Philip Epstein; Warner Bros.

The Play

The team of Kaufman and Hart was the most successful writing duo on the Broadway stage in the 1930s. The caustic Kaufman and the amiable Hart co-wrote nine plays, beginning with *Once in a Lifetime* in 1930 (the subject of Hart's memoir, *Act One*), a Hollywood spoof that was adapted to the screen in 1931; and including *Merrily We Roll Along* (1934), which told the story of a playwright in reverse chronology; *You Can't Take It With You* (1936), which won the 1936 Pulitzer Prize; *I'd Rather Be Right* (1937), which brought the semiretired George M. Cohan back to the stage as President Franklin D. Roosevelt; *The Man Who Came to Dinner* (1939), written for and about Alexander Woollcott, and filmed in 1941 with Monty Woolley; and

George Washington Slept Here (1940), brought to the screen a year later with Jack Benny and Ann Sheridan. Although they wrote no more plays together after 1941, they remained close friends. They died within a few months of each other in 1961.

The three-act *The Man Who Came to Dinner* premiered in New York at the Music Box Theatre on October 16, 1939, and ran for a spectacular 739 performances. The setting is Mesalia, Ohio, on a late December day in the 1930s. When the celebrated but cantankerous writer Sheridan Whiteside (Monty Woolley) slips on the ice outside the doorstep of the home of Ernest and Daisy Stanley, he determines while convalescing in a wheelchair to make life uncomfortable for the family. He is so disagreeable that he alienates the Stanley children from their parents and turns his nurse, Miss Preen (Mary Wickes), into such a sourpuss that she takes a job at a munitions factory in hopes of destroying mankind. Moreover, he intervenes in the romance between his secretary, Maggie Cutler (Edith Atwater) and a local newsman, Bert Jefferson (Theodore Newton), by conspiring with actress Lorraine Sheldon (Carol Goodner) to break up the relationship; and he even blackmails the Stanleys by threatening to reveal that Mr. Stanley's sister was once suspected of being an ax murderer. Meanwhile, he entertains convicts, greets the press, accepts gifts of penguins, monopolizes the telephone, smuggles a body out of the house in a mummy case, and broadcasts his customary sentimental Christmas radio program for the Cream of Mush Company. Finally, when Whiteside is well enough to leave, everyone heaves a sigh of relief—until he slips and falls again during his departure. At the curtain's fall, he is back in the house bellowing his intentions to wreak six more weeks of havoc.

Kaufman and Hart made no secret of the fact that Whiteside was modeled after their friend, the celebrated critic and humorist, Alexander Woollcott, and that Lorraine Sheldon was patterned after Gertrude Lawrence. Whiteside remains one of the most enduring comic characters in American theatre. Of him, critic John Anderson wrote: "No one [could be] so full of the carbolic acid of human kindness; no one with the enthusiasm, the ruthless wit, the wayward taste, disarming prejudice, and relentless sentimentality of the man so carefully undisguised as the hero." Woollcott himself played the role on tour; and occasionally playwright Moss Hart took the role in revivals. Commentator Ima Honaker Herron in her book, *The Small Town in American Drama*, describes *The Man Who Came to Dinner* as the "most brilliant" of the Kaufman and Hart satires. This "masterpiece of invective," she concludes, is worthy to stand alongside Restoration comedies.

The Film

The production history of the Warner Bros. film was full of false starts. Kaufman and Hart intended to produce their own adaptation for RKO in 1940. They changed their minds when Warner Bros. made the team a counteroffer, a percentage of the film's profits. Director Howard Hawks and actors Cary Grant and Mary Astor were originally slotted as Mr. Stanley and Lorraine, respectively, though all three were ultimately replaced; and among the actors considered for Whiteside were Fredric March, Charles Laughton, Robert Benchley, and John Barrymore. Yet, perhaps inevitably, the final nod went toward former Yale drama professor Monty Woolley, who created the role of Whiteside on Broadway (and who had been appearing in small movie roles since 1937). Another actress, Mary Wickes, reprised her stage character of Miss Preen. Veteran Warners director William Keighley, responsible for such 1930s gangster classics as *G-Men* (1935) and *Each Dawn I Die* (1939), took the helm.

The film followed the play's basic outline. Whiteside is confined to a wheelchair with a broken hip and tortures his hosts, the Stanleys (Grant Mitchell and Billie

Burke), and his visiting friends with a variety of fiendish schemes: He tries to wreck the romance of his loyal secretary, Maggie Cutler (Bette Davis), interferes with the lives of the Stanley children, and tortures his nurse, Miss Preen (Wickes), with numerous wicked verbal barbs (examples: he calls her "Miss Bedpan" and critiques her plain appearance with lines like, "My great-aunt Jennifer ate a whole box of candy every day of her life. She lived to be a hundred and two, and when she had been dead *three days*, she looked better than you do now!"). Critics generally praised the film. Bosley Crowther in the *New York Times* called it "unquestionably the most vicious but hilarious cat-clawing exhibition ever put on the screen, a delicious wicked character portrait and a helter-skelter satire." In his book, *Lunatics and Lovers*, Ted Sennett writes: "As directed by William Keighley, the film is played in the familiar Warners' style of overstating every situation, and racing through the lines as if the police are in hot pursuit of the actors, but it still draws many laughs."

REFERENCES

Herron, Ima Honaker, *The Small Town in American Drama* (Dallas: Southern Methodist University Press, 1969); Sennett, Ted, *Lunatics and Lovers* (New Rochelle, N.Y.: Arlington House, 1973).

—*J.C.T.*

MARIUS (1929)

MARCEL PAGNOL (1895–1974)

Marius (1931), France, directed by Alexander Korda, screenplay by Marcel Pagnol; French Paramount.

The Play

Pagnol's hugely successful 1929 romantic comedy ran for over a thousand performances at the Théâtre de Paris and established his reputation as a dramatist. The action takes place in and around the Bar de la Marine in the Vieux Port of Marseilles. César, a charismatic widower, runs the bar with his son Marius, whose secret ambition is to sail the seas. Fanny has loved Marius since childhood and to make him jealous flirts with Panisse, a wealthy and recently widowed sail-maker who enjoys the support of Honorine, Fanny's mother. Marius, jealous at seeing the middle-aged Panisse and Fanny together, picks a quarrel with his presumed rival. Fanny is delighted, but her schemes appear frustrated when Marius is offered a berth on a ship. Unaware, Fanny declares herself to Marius who is now torn between his childhood sweetheart and the sea. All seems resolved when the offer of a berth falls through and the couple become lovers. However, recognizing that Marius must follow his seafaring ambition, Fanny nobly sacrifices her own happiness to his freedom and resigns herself to marrying Panisse.

If the romantic plot is decidedly slight, Pagnol's play is conversely rich in memorable characters, witty dialogue, and atmosphere. The bar is a natural location for his colorful individuals: Panisse, the rotund sail-maker; Monsieur Brun, the dapper customs inspector; and Escartefigue, the local cuckold and self-promoting ferryboat skipper. Presiding over his customers is the charismatic figure of César, in turn irascible, sentimental, and domineering but essentially good-humored and generous. Particularly memorable scenes are those between father and son and the card games, with excited players slipping into their native Provençal. The success of such scenes derives from Pagnol working closely with his cast of local actors and readily incorporating their suggestions, in particular those of Raimu, whose extraordinary personality shaped the evolution of César's role. Apart from establishing Raimu with Parisian audiences, the play also confirmed the outstanding talents of Charpin as Panisse, Pierre Fresnay as Marius, Orane Demazis as Fanny, and Alida Rouffe as Honorine. Following the success of *Marius*, Pagnol wrote two sequels, *Fanny* (1931) and *César* (1936), to form what is popularly known as his "Marseilles" trilogy.

The Film

Described as the first French masterwork of the sound era, the screen version was directed by Alexander Korda for Paramount at their new St. Maurice studios outside Paris. For Pagnol, this first experience of film production was a brutal revelation, when his views were all but ignored by the studios. Nevertheless his apprenticeship with Korda proved invaluable for his later career as producer and director. Pagnol believed passionately in the importance of text itself and in good acting, suggesting that the value of the film version was "to place the spectator in the best seat in the house." He nevertheless rejected the definition of screen adaptations of his plays as merely "canned theatre"; and certainly in Korda's hands, the added value of the film medium is much in evidence. The play is opened up economically with establishing shots of the port, while the action's dynamic is sustained in smooth transitions between locations. The camera-work provides telling close-ups in the emotionally charged scenes between César and Marius and those between Marius and Fanny, while the

celebrated card game is brought to life in the close shots of the players' faces. Sound, for this early period of sound cinema, is used not merely for realistic effect, but for psychological impact when, for example, Marius hears the haunting call of the ships' sirens. Korda's use of the "close-up in sound" provides a new access to Pagnol's witty throwaway lines, and identification with Marius is established as he eavesdrops on Panisse's intimacies with Fanny. Sound and camera combine to particular effect in capturing Marius's difficult choice between Fanny or the sea: As she declares her love, Marius is seen in close-up looking wistfully toward the port as ships' sirens compete for his attention. Similarly, while his voice is heard promising Fanny his undivided love, images of oceangoing ships fill the screen to contradict his words. Korda's version of Pagnol's play is much more than filmed theatre, but his achievement nevertheless rests on the fundamentals of an excellent play and the exceptional talents of the original stage cast headed by the outstanding Raimu as César.

REFERENCES

Beylie, Claude, *Marcel Pagnol ou le cinéma en liberté* (Paris: Editions de Fallois, 1995); Caldicot, C.E.J., *Marcel Pagnol* (Boston: Twayne, 1977); Pompa, Dany, *Marcel Pagnol* (Paris: Henri Veyrier, 1986).

—R.F.C.

MEDEA [MEDEIA] (431 B.C.)

EURIPIDES (480?–406? B.C.)

Medea (1970), Italy/France/West Germany, directed and adapted by Pier Paolo Pasolini; San Marco (Rome), Les Films Number One (Paris), Janus Film (Frankfurt).

A Dream of Passion (1978), Switzerland/Greece, directed by Jules Dassin, adapted from the modern Greek version of Euripides' *Medea* by Minos Volonakis; Bren film (Geneva)/Melinafilm (Athen's)

The Play

Using witchcraft and betraying her father, Medea saved the life of the Greek adventurer Jason and enabled him to win the golden fleece, whereupon Jason brought her home to Greece as his wife. Jason later decides to divorce her so that he may marry the daughter of King Creon of Corinth. Afraid of her powers, Creon decides to exile Medea and the two children she bore Jason, but Creon underestimates Medea's skills as *pharmakis*, an expert in love charms, drugs, and poisons. Aegeus, the king of Athens, offers Medea sanctuary in his kingdom if she agrees to use her sorcery to enable him to have children.

Medea seeks revenge on Jason and sends their two children with gifts for Creon and his daughter in order to avoid being exiled, but the gifts, a crown and a robe, are poisoned and bring about the death of Creon and Jason's intended bride. Medea then murders her two children, whom she loves, her singular quest for vengeance overcoming her maternal instincts. At the end of this grim tragedy, Medea flies off to Athens in a chariot drawn by dragons.

The Films

According to Kenneth MacKinnon, the conclusion to be drawn from Pasolini's *Medea* is that "Greek tragedy in anything like its original context is indeed dead." Pasolini's treatment serves "to defamiliarize" Euripides, and his film, along with Jules Dassin's *A Dream of Paradise*, represents a "return to the roots of these plays' narratives, to reinvestigate the significance of these with a freedom that the ancient tragedians themselves habitually enjoyed in the dramatization of heroic myth."

Pasolini's film, credited as being "based on the play by Euripides," is in fact loosely based and would appear to be as much Pasolini's *Medea* as Euripides'. Liberties were taken with the text, and the director's signature approach was personalized, eclectic in its music, costuming, and settings: Turkey appropriately for Cappadocia, for example, a composite of Pisa in Italy and Alep in Syria for Corinth. Liberties were also taken with the text, but by 1970 that sort of license was expected of Pasolini. Jason's betrayal of Medea (Maria Callas; Jason is played by Giuseppe Gentile) in Corinth and her revenge—the central action of the play—is eclipsed by extra-textual sequences concerning Jason's early education by Chiron (Laurent Terzieff), for example, and Medea's life in Colchis, which is only alluded to in the play.

The consensus is that both Pasolini's *Medea* and *Edipo Re* (Oedipus the King) are "about Greek tragedy in a broad sense," though it might be argued that nothing seems further from the truth. A case can be made for Pasolini as a creative adapter of ancient tragedy by demonstrating his imaginative skill in finding cinematic analogies for what Ruth Padel accurately describes as the Greek theatre's "dialectics of inside and outside"— that central conflicting spatiality created by the actors' exits and entrances through the door of the wooden skein building upon which the Attic tragedians base their tragic characterizations. Pasolini recreates filmi-

cally what might be termed the Euripidean "skene-self" not by resorting to such a facile device as filming in an actual amphitheater, as Philip Saville did by shooting most of the action in his *Oedipus the King* at Dodona, but by opting for the more aesthetically demanding challenge of rooting his *Medea* in the spatial dialectics of Euripidean drama by re-creating its inside/outside skene-self in the film's non-theatrical space.

Borrowing from Seneca's *Medea*, Pasolini shows Medea's butchering of her brother Absyrtus, filmed in close-up so as not to show any blood, but effectively illustrating Medea's lines in Euripides: "O my father, my city, you I deserted;/My brother I shamefully murdered!" This is Medea's skene-self—the murderous self that she publicly unmasks when, facing the female Corinthian Chorus in the *orchestra*, she confesses her shattering decision to murder her own children. Pasolini masks Medea's dismemberment of Absyrtus by staging it in a partly covered chariot and clearly creating in spatial terms a cinematic situation analogous to that of ancient Greek theatre. For the tragic action of Greek plays almost always occurs, as Padel notes, "unseen and mostly within," which does not mean offstage, but "within-stage," in other words, inside the skene building, which was always before the Athenian audience's eyes but into which those eyes could never pry. Pasolini places the film spectator in an equivalent visual position, using the chariot as a kind of theatrical skene.

Pasolini's handling of the climactic filicide incident is also bloodless. A shot of Medea hugging her first child-victim is followed by a sudden close-up of a knife. Pasolini then reworks the knife image when, after showing Medea cuddling her second child-victim, he cuts to a close-up of her hand grasping the blood-smeared weapon. The blood-stained knife makes us suddenly realize that, though this time we are undoubtedly within the skene building, we are still outside the skene space reserved specifically for the two ritual killings, a private kind of Helios sacrifice. This follows the lyrical moment when Medea bathes her two young children and dons their innocence in ceremonial white tunics. The sacrificial nature of the subsequent unseen murders, which occur ominously at sunset, becomes even more evident with Medea's sunrise burning of the skene, which transforms Jason's Corinthian home into a fiery altar.

While there is no skene-pyre in Euripides, the play's penultimate stage directions deliver the *ekkuklema* or final tragic revelation in the form of a *mekhane*, the divine intervention usually known as the deus ex machina: "Jason batters at the doors. Medea appears above the roof, sitting in a chariot drawn by dragons, with the bodies of the two children beside her."

Pasolini's skene-pyre functions as a suggestive equivalent to the sun god's chariot in Euripides, which similarly seems to transport the now skene-less Medea to the ultimate skene—the underworld, the realm of Hades.

Jules Dassin's *Dream of Passion* seems to move from Greek tragedy toward contemporary melodrama. In fact, the story of *Medea* is embedded into the melodramatic contemporary story that frames the film and play. Dassin got the idea for the film when he saw Melina Mercouri play Medea after having attended in Italy the trial of a woman who had murdered her children.

In the film a Greek actress named Maya (Mercouri) is summoned to Athens to play the role of Medea in a revival of the play to be staged at Delphi, but Maya and her director, Kostas (Andreas Voutsinas), have a creative falling-out because she believes that the play and her performance "should be anchored in a modern context." She finds a way of doing this existentially when she meets, as a publicity stunt to promote the production, Brenda Collins (Ellen Burstyn), whom the Greek tabloids have called "the Medea of Glyfada." Brenda, an American transported to Greece, murdered three children fathered by her husband, Roy, on Father's Day. Maya's performance will be informed by her identification with Brenda, who does not want merely to be considered insane.

The two women characters therefore bond and mesh as Maya creates her persona. MacKinnon quotes French critic Claude-Marie Tremois, who claims that "the film makes us suddenly aware of something that the ancients knew well—that fate is nothing else but the passion and despair which inhabit a person." MacKinnon concludes that if the film seems "close to melodrama today, this may be because melodrama holds the place in cinema which tragedy once occupied in theatre." Even if the film is inherently melodramatic, it still may have something to teach us about the tragic experience.

REFERENCES

Cantina, Saviour, "Cinematizing the Euripidean and Sophoclean Spatial Dialectics: On the 'Skene-Self' in Pasolini's *Medea* and *Edipo Re*," *Literature/Film Quarterly*, 28:3 (2000), 170–182; Gassner, John, and Edward Quinn, *The Reader's Encyclopedia of World Drama* (New York: Thomas Y. Crowell, 1969); MacKinnon, Kenneth, *Greek Tragedy into Film* (London: Croom Helm, 1986); Padel, Ruth, "Making Space Speak," in *Nothing to Do with Dionysos? Athenian Drama in Its Social Context*, ed. John Winkler and Froma I. Zeiten (Princeton, N.J.: Princeton University Press, 1990), 336–365; Viano, Maurizio, *A Certain Realism: Making Use of Pasolini's Film Theory and Practice* (Berkeley: University of California Press, 1993).

—*S.V.C. AND J.M.W.*

MEET JOE BLACK

See *DEATH TAKES A HOLIDAY*

THE MILK TRAIN DOESN'T STOP HERE ANYMORE (1962)

TENNESSEE WILLIAMS (1911–1983)

Boom! (1968), U.K./U.S.A., directed by Joseph Losey, adapted by Tennessee Williams; Universal.

The Play

This has always been one of Tennessee Williams's most problematical plays. It was first produced on Broadway by Roger L. Stevens in January 1962, with Hermione Baddeley, Paul Roebling, and Mildred Dunnock in the leading roles. It ran for only 69 performances, the critics pronouncing the work as shallow, pretentious, and lacking in dramatic energy. Williams revised the play and there was a further attempt at a successful Broadway production in 1964, when director Tony Richardson, having failed to persuade Katharine Hepburn and Anthony Perkins to head the cast, mounted a version starring Tallulah Bankhead and Tab Hunter. Even by Richardson's own admission, it was an unmitigated disaster, closing after two performances.

Williams described the play as an allegory and sophisticated fairy tale, whose heroine, Flora Goforth is, in the playwright's words, a "legendary beauty, a woman of enormous wealth inherited from five kings of industry whom she has survived." Isolated on a remote Mediterranean island with only her secretary, doctor, servants, and bodyguard for company, she occupies herself by dictating her memoirs, unaware that she is suffering from a terminal illness. She is visited one day by her neighbor, the Witch of Capri, who tells her that Mrs. Goforth's guest, a young poet, Christopher Flanders, "has the bad habit of coming to call on a lady just a step or two ahead of the undertaker," and for that reason has earned the nickname of "Angel of Death." Mrs. Goforth is terrified by this presence. But she and Flanders will talk—of "the shock of each moment of still being alive," of Death as "one moment," and life as "so many of them." Mrs. Goforth will come to terms, at first apprehensively, but finally resignedly, with the inevitability of her mortality.

The Film

"I wanted to make a visually lyrical film about the welcome and the terror a person can give to death," said director Joseph Losey. He shot the film on location in Sardinia and cast Noel Coward in the role of the Witch of Capri, to add wit and interest to a part that otherwise was just an expository gossip. When Simone Signoret and Sean Connery proved unavailable for the parts of Flora and Christopher, he cast Elizabeth Taylor and Richard Burton, which immediately had the effect of making the widow younger than in the play and the Angel of Death older. Although Tennessee Williams objected to this, a Universal executive exclaimed, "We've got *Virginia Woolf* in color!"; and Losey declared it gave the piece the style of "Elizabeth Taylor in real life playing herself in opera." Against the background of wind, expressive decor, and the sea's "boom," characters converse in a highly charged discourse that is essentially a set of variations on a single theme—the inescapability of one's mortality. Losey's usual themes—struggles for power, contrasting life-styles, spiritual emptiness—are all here, but they are rendered not in terms of narrative or character development so much as visual and even architectural metaphor. Sadly, this film-poem about the acceptance of dying was greeted with as much critical derision and audience incomprehension as the play, but Williams eventually was to describe it as "a beautiful film, the best ever made of one of my plays."

REFERENCES

Caute, David, *Joseph Losey: A Revenge on Life* (London: Faber and Faber, 1993); Ciment, Michel, *Conversations with Losey* (London: Methuen, 1985); Spoto, Donald, *The Kindness of Strangers: The Life of Tennessee Williams* (London: The Bodley Head, 1985); Williams, Tennessee, *Memoirs* (New York: Doubleday, 1975).

—*N.S.*

THE MIRACLE WORKER (1959)

WILLIAM GIBSON (1914–)

The Miracle Worker (1962), U.S.A., directed by Arthur Penn, adapted by William Gibson; United Artists.

The Play

William Gibson had already scored with his stage success, *Two for the Seesaw* (1958), a two-character drama about a lonely lawyer's affair with a dancer—the first of several collaborations between Gibson and actress Anne Bancroft—when he set to work on a dramatization of the formative years of the relationship between Helen Keller and her teacher, Annie Sullivan. Originally a television drama, *The Miracle Worker* premiered in New York at the Playhouse on October 19, 1959, and ran for an impressive 719 performances. Twenty-year-old Sullivan (Anne Bancroft), a recent graduate of Boston's Perkins Institute for the Blind, arrives at the Alabama home of Captain Keller (Torin Thatcher), where she is employed to be a teacher-companion to his deaf, dumb, and blind daughter, Helen (Patty Duke). Only through Sullivan's tough disciplinary actions is the child's wild and uncontrollable behavior tamed; and Helen begins to learn rudimentary spelling. But her ability to associate between words and objects comes only after a long struggle between teacher and student. At last, after the famous scene at the water pump—when Annie drenches Helen with water and Helen spells out the word "water" in her palm—is Helen able to establish a link between herself and the outside world. Robert Coleman of the *Daily Mirror* wrote: "Gibson's words are terse and eloquent, highly dramatic, but it is the frightening, harrowing, physical conflicts of his drama that terrify and grip you." In 1982 Gibson wrote a sequel, *Monday after the Miracle*, which focuses on the lively courtship and marriage of Sullivan, still Helen's companion and protector 17 years later, to a journalist. It enjoyed only a brief Broadway run.

The Film

Playwright Gibson collaborated with director Arthur Penn (who had directed both the stage and television versions) on the 1962 screen adaptation. The basic structure and dialogue were retained, although commentator Jean-Pierre Coursodon complains that Penn's mandate to bring a Broadway hit to the screen stifled his cinematic vision: "Penn did not realize that much of what may have been necessary on stage could be dispensed with on screen." There is no doubting, however, that by means of powerful close-ups Penn was able to enhance visually the intensity and intimacy of the scenes between Sullivan and Keller. Critic Robin Wood attributes this to Penn's "intense awareness of, and emphasis on, physical expression." This is entirely in keeping with the thematic concerns of the play, i.e., conceptualization through physical contact. For example, when Sullivan first introduces herself to Helen, she slams down her trunk on the step on which Helen is sitting. Helen feels the vibration, and Penn cuts to a close-up of Helen grasping Sullivan's hands and raising them to her nose to smell. In the climactic sequence at the water pump, close-ups intensify Helen's urgency as she taps out the word "W-A-T-E-R" into Sullivan's palm. The emotional impact of this latter scene is overwhelming. As Coursodon says, "Woman, child, and water pump are a closed-circuit system through which meaning suddenly starts running, as though a switch had been thrown, and Helen's mouthing of the word, combined with the spurting of the water and the convulsive, passionate clasp of hand upon clenched fist is truly an orgasmic moment, dimly linking the scene to ancient myths of the creation as the ejaculation of a god." Wow. Both Patty Duke and Anne Bancroft, as Keller and Sullivan, respectively, received Academy Awards for their roles.

REFERENCES

Coursodon, Jean-Pierre, *American Directors*, vol. 2 (New York: McGraw-Hill, 1983); Hochman, Stanley, ed., *American Film Directors* (New York: Frederick Ungar, 1974); Kirkpatrick, D.L., *Contemporary Dramatists* (Chicago: St. James Press, 1988).

—*J.C.T.*

THE MISS FIRECRACKER CONTEST (1984)

BETH HENLEY (1952–)

Miss Firecracker (1989), U.S.A., directed by Thomas Schlamme, adapted by Beth Henley; Corsair Pictures.

The Play

The Miss Firecracker Contest was presented by the Manhattan Theatre Club, in New York City, on May 1, 1984. Holly Hunter was cast as Carnelle Scott; Belita Moreno as Popeye Johnson; Patricia Richardson as Elain Rutledge; Mark Linn-Baker as Delmount Williams; Budge Threlkeld as Mac Sam; and Margo Martindale as Terry Mahoney. Set in the small southern town of Brookhaven, Mississippi, the play opens with Carnelle (Holly Hunter) practicing her star-spangled tap-dancing "skit" for the talent component of the upcoming Miss Firecracker Contest. Hunter, the star in at least six Henley plays, has been a "longtime collaborator" mainly because she, as Henley confirms, "knows how to walk the edge between truth and humor. Holly hears the music of what I write." In the main, the play revolves around the actions (and reactions) of the orphaned Carnelle, a woman who manages to maintain her wide-eyed girlhood innocence despite the manipu-

lative and chaotic world around her. Through her Sisyphean struggle to belong (symbolized by the Miss Firecracker contest saga) and be considered beautiful, we learn some nasty secrets about the characters lurking in Carnelle's shadow: There's a jealous ex-beauty queen (cousin Elain), an emphysemic and alcoholic balloon salesman with a venereal disease (boyfriend Mac Sam); an idealistic seamstress who can "hear voices through her eyes" (Popeye); the town "ugly girl" (Tessy); and an insane asylum fugitive turned Romeo (cousin Delmount). Full of dialogue that, in the opinion of Stanley Kauffmann, "probe[s] the grotesquely comic vein of horror in a small town," *The Miss Firecracker Contest* is a good fusion of rural slapstick humor with humanistic didacticism.

The Film

With Holly Hunter cast as Carnelle for the movie, much of the humor and spunk from the play spills over onto the screen. Added to the screen cast are Tim Robbins (Delmount); Alfre Woodard (Popeye); Mary Steenburgen (Elain); and Scott Glenn (Mac Sam). Like the play, Hunter is a vivacious redhead (read: obnoxiously violet red) who spends her entire life trying to fit in to Yazoo City (Brookhaven in the play) society. The ultimate test of cultural acceptance—winning the Miss Firecracker Contest—slips through Carnelle's fingers with a fifth-place thud. Elain (Steenburgen) is still the wicked cousin who refuses to allow Carnelle to wear the winning Miss Firecracker red dress. One of the most poignant and final scenes in the film shows Carnelle, devastated from her loss in the beauty contest, discovering Elain's red dress at the bottom of her suitcase (Elain had lied and had told Carnelle that she couldn't find it). Carnelle puts on the dress and descends her home's stairs, and just at that moment, Elain enters. A look of shock and then shame covers her face. When asked by Carnelle why she wouldn't let her wear the red dress, Elain jealously retorts: "Because it's *mine*." This intense scene, along with the frame narrative of Carnelle as an orphaned child (complete with dirty clothes and a nappy yellow hat), is missing from the play version. Also, Mac Sam is no longer a VD carrier. In the closing moments, when Carnelle once again places her childhood "ugly hat" on her head, we finally see a Carnelle that has learned to love herself for who she is, not who she keeps trying to be (a beauty queen like Elain). For Carnelle, notes commentator Billy Harbin, "redemptive grace that comes through self-knowledge, spiritual enlightenment or nourishing bonds with others can be but dimly glimpsed and only partially realized." Carnelle's self-love overshadows Delmount's first date with Popeye, an African-American woman who "is not black" in the play, and makes Elain's decision to return to her rich husband all the more an empty gesture.

REFERENCES

Harbin, Billy J., "Familial Bonds in the Plays of Beth Henley," *Southern Quarterly*, 25:3 (Spring 1987); Kauffmann, Stanley, "Two Cheers for Two Plays," *Saturday Review* 9:1 (January 1982); Kauffmann, Stanley, "Films Worth Seeing," *The New Republic*, 200:24 (June 12, 1989); Renner, Pamela, "The Mellowing of 'Miss Firecracker': Beth Henley—and Her Impetuous Characters—Are Undergoing Transformations," *American Theatre*, 15:9 (November 1998).

—*N.A.*

August Strindberg

MISS JULIE (FRÖKEN JULIE/ COUNTESS JULIE) (1889)

JOHAN AUGUST STRINDBERG (1849–1912)

Miss Julie (1950), Sweden, directed and adapted by Alf Sjöberg; Svensk.

Miss Julie (1999), U.S.A., directed by Mike Figgis, adapted by Helen Cooper and Mike Figgis; Moonstone Entertainment-MGM/UA.

The Play

Strindberg considered his one-act tragedy the first naturalistic play written in Scandinavia, and it is in fact a benchmark in theatre history. This psychological study of a woman shaped by her childhood experiences with her dominant, reckless mother and weak-willed, aristocratic father foreshadowed both the methods of expressionist theatre and the class tensions and sexual conflicts represented a quarter-century later, in the novels of D.H. Lawrence. In his preface, Strindberg wrote: "I find 'the joy of life' in life's cruel and mighty conflicts." He intended to create "modern characters, living in an age of transition more urgently hysterical, at any rate, than the age which preceded it." His characters "are agglomerations of past and present cultures," who were "split and vacillating, a mixture of the old and the new." The play has been considered a bitter diatribe against Sweden's class system.

Strindberg lived a notoriously controversial, Bohemian existence, and issues of scandal and censorship plagued the reception of his innovative play. In 1877 the playwright had married Baroness Siri von

Essen, an ambitious actress who had divorced her husband and was one of the aristocratic models for Countess Julie, whom she played on stage. Publisher Karl Otto Bonnier considered *Miss Julie* "too risky" and "too 'naturalistic,'" as he advised Strindberg: "We therefore dare not publish the play," further predicting that Strindberg would "find difficulty in getting it produced," as, indeed, was the case. In November of 1888 Strindberg had founded the Scandinavian Experimental Theatre. Siri von Essen was appointed artistic director and was cast to play Miss Julie. On March 1 of the following year, police, armed with a censorship ban, raided the Theatre Dagmar as the play was being rehearsed. Nonetheless, a way was found to circumvent the censorship ban when the play was premiered for a private performance on March 14, 1889, staged in the Copenhagen University Student Union before an audience of

250 students. Initially, the play was banned in several countries. In 1906 it was produced in Stockholm, the city where Strindberg was born, by the actor-manager August Falk, 17 years after it had been written.

The action is set on Saint John's night, inside an aristocrat's kitchen, while outside midsummer festivities, "surviving from pagan times," are in progress. Miss Julie, the 25-year-old daughter of the count, and her servants are the main characters. The continuous action of the play is interrupted only by an interlude involving a dramatic ballet. Jean, the valet, was once engaged to Kristen, the cook. He is led away by Miss Julie, whom he considers "absolutely mad," to the "pagan" festivities in the barn. When they return, the overworked Kristen falls asleep and Julie flirts with Jean, who admits that as a young boy he had fallen in love with his mistress: "a horse may be caressed by a lady's hand, but [not] a servant," Jean confides, bitterly. Julie orders Jean to kiss her slipper, but then slaps him when he makes advances beyond his station. Finally, they withdraw to Jean's room, where a seduction takes place offstage while the audience is entertained by a folk ballet.

After the seduction, Jean proposes that they elope to Switzerland and open a hotel. Seeming to agree to his scheme, Julie steals money from her father's desk and prepares to elope, but she is conflicted. Fearing the return of the count, Jean tells Julie to make haste, but she refuses to leave without her pet canary, which Jean calmly kills at the chopping block. Julie then goes berserk, takes Jean's razor, and exits, presumably intending to commit suicide.

The Film

The play's kitchen setting is utterly stagebound, so the first challenge for director-adapter Alf Sjöberg (Ingmar Bergman's mentor) was to open up the play's confined setting, indoors and out. Sjöberg extends the action to the drawing room, for example, where a portrait of Julie's mother dominates the mise-en-scène. The drawing room serves as a convenient means for introducing the film's flashback structure that both dramatizes and summarizes Julie's scandalous family history. Julie (Anita Bjork) certainly inherited dominant traits from her mother, a selfish commoner who fancied herself a reformer and an advocate of women's rights. She refused to marry the count and agreed only to become his mistress. When Julie speaks of her mother, the camera zooms into her mother's portrait, then, when the camera pulls back to show the whole room, the viewer has been cinematically transported into her past. Sjöberg presents characters who are not seen in the play, notably the count (Anders Henrikson), her father,

and her fiancé (Kurt-Olof Sundstrom).

The count's "marriage" was troubled and scandalous. Through her extravagant habits, Julie's mother had bankrupted Julie's father and, then, when the count finally asserted his authority, Julie's mother burned the house down. Next, she arranged an interest-free loan from her friend—unbeknownst to the count, her lover—ultimately reducing the count to a position of dependence and servitude. Cruel and deceitful, and apparently incapable of love, she showed little affection or compassion for her daughter. This "backstory," necessary for understanding Julie's fragmented character, is more clearly conveyed in the film than in the play. The viewer can better understand her divided loyalties and her confusion about her place in society. Sjöberg presents her reality clearly dominated by a troubled childhood, as one sees past and present characters intermingling within the confines of the same frame. Thus Sjöberg's inventive flashback structure and mise-en-scène create a compelling sense of psychological realism.

Two extended flashbacks represent the childhood experiences of Jean (Ulf Palme) and Julie. The first of these contextualizes Jean's social conditioning and explains his habitual servitude, while the second helps the viewer to understand Julie as a divided character, torn between the common people and the aristocracy as well as between her father and mother, who taught her to torment men. Sjöberg expands the play by dramatizing the past as his camera makes fluid and unobtrusive transitions between past and present events. Sjöberg also extend the play's action by moving his camera out of doors in order to capture the spirit of midsummer's eve, making Julie's infatuation with her servant Jean all the more plausible in an atmosphere of reckless abandon and midsummer madness.

Miss Julie has inherited traits from both of her parents—from her father the tendency toward suicide, and from her mother the resolution necessary to get on with it. Julie fears that her father will "have a stroke and die," after he discovers she has broken into his desk, stolen his money, and eloped with his servant, which Sjöberg represents in a hypothetical flash-forward. When Julie "goes out resolutely," razor in hand, at the end, spectators are spared her suicide and its aftermath in the play, whereas Sjöberg shows the count discovering Julie's slumped body in the film's coda, as the camera then moves to the razor she has dropped on the floor, under the cold gaze of her mother's portrait. This perfectly acted, well-executed film won the Grand Prize at the Cannes Film Festival of 1951.

Alf Sjöberg's beautifully cinematic transformation became a "classic" adaptation that stood unchallenged for nearly 50 years. In 1999, however, British director Mike Figgis was drawn to the play's erotic content. Figgis moved the action forward to 1894 and kept the focus upon the play's three main characters, Miss Julie (Saffron Burrows), Jean (Peter Mullan), and Kristen the cook (Maria Doyle Kennedy, called Christine in the credits). Figgis prefers to concentrate upon the present, ignoring the flashback structure Sjöberg used so brilliantly to contextualize the childhood of Julie as an unwanted child trained by her mother to frustrate men and her first encounter with Jean as a boy, humiliated and made to accept his inferior status.

Following the play, Miss Julie flirts with her footman, then orders him to wear her father's formal wear in order to dance with her. Figgis uses a split screen to show the seduction scene, which, for *Variety* reviewer Emanuel Levy, amounted to "borderline rape," and worked against "the claustrophobic intensity of the play." The seduction takes place "in a hidden corner of the kitchen," Stephen Holden wrote, with the lovers fully clothed and standing up, "face to face, looking each other in the eye and all but denying the joyless,

perfunctory intercourse taking place." For Levy, Strindberg's "misogynistic and misanthropic ideas" and even the sexual business of the play seemed outdated, though the class warfare still seemed to him potentially relevant. Neither Peter Mullan nor Saffron Burrows could match the performances of Anita Bjork and Ulf Palme in Sjöberg's more definitive treatment, which managed to retain all of the essential elements of the play while expanding it and liberating it from Strindberg's absolutely confined setting.

REFERENCES

Gassner, John, and Edward Quinn, eds., *The Reader's Encyclopedia of World Drama* (New York: Thomas Y. Crowell, 1969); Holden, Stephen, "The Joylessness of Sex in Class-Riven 1890s Sweden," *The New York Times*, December 10, 1999, B19; Langercrantz, Olof, *August Strindberg*, tr. Anselm Hollo (New York: Farrar, Straus, and Giroux, 1984); Levy, Emanuel, "*Miss Julie*," *Variety*, September 20–26, 1999, 82; Matlaw, Myron, *Modern World Drama* (New York: E.P. Dutton, 1972); Meyer, Michael, *Strindberg* (New York: Random House, 1985); Sinyard, Neil, *Filming Literature: The Art of Screen Adaptation* (London: Croom Helm, 1986).

—*J.M.W.*

'NIGHT, MOTHER (1982)

MARSHA NORMAN (1947–)

'Night, Mother (1986), U.S.A., directed by Tom Moore, adapted by Marsha Norman; Universal.

The Play

Winner of a Pulitzer Prize in 1983, *'Night, Mother* also won the Dramatists Guild's prestigious Hull-Warriner Award, the Susan Smith Blackburn Prize, and four Tony nominations. The play's first reading was at the Circle Repertory Company in New York in November 1981; the American Repertory Theatre in Cambridge, Massachusetts, first produced it in December 1982. Kathy Bates was cast as Jessie Cates and Anne Pitoniak played Thelma Cates, Jessie's mother. Later, on March 31, 1983, the play was moved to the John Golden Theatre in New York City, with Bates and Pitoniak cast in the same roles. The tragedy chronicles the conversation between mother and daughter during the last 90 minutes of the daughter's life.

After contemplating suicide for 10 years, Jessie Cates decides to take her own life with a gun. She plans out the entire evening prior to her suicide, including a special message to her mother; instead of a suicide note, Jessie decides it would be best to verbally inform her mother of her suicide plans. Living with her widowed mother in a relatively new house built way out on a country road, the epileptic and divorced Jessie embodies all the despair and discord reminiscent of T.S. Eliot's plays and poems, particularly "The Hollow Men." The final hours of communication with her mother are void of a call for help; they are instead a sterile reminder that there is no hope for a decision change. Jessie lives in a space of worthless domestic work and its aesthetic invisibility, and, like Kate Chopin's Edna Pontellier, she is a woman who ultimately says "no" to life and chooses to leave because she is unhappy with her lack of choices. However, Jessie's deaf ear to her mother's desperate pleas for her not to commit suicide may mark her, in the opinion of Stanley Kauffmann, "as a vengeful neurotic, not a tragic heroine." Toward the end, Jessie only partially denies that her suicide has nothing to do with her mother.

The Film

The stage play received mostly rave reviews; the film adaptation, however, was criticized despite the use of well-known actors Sissy Spacek as Jessie and Anne Bancroft as Thelma. The movie opens and closes with lengthy still shots of the outside of the Cates home, creating an eerie mood and a sense of domestic doom. During the course of the film, the camera moves around the small, middle-class house, following Jessie from room to room as she arranges her final chores before her suicide: canceling the newspaper delivery, donating clothes to Goodwill, folding laundry, checking items off of the pad of paper she compulsively removes from her sweater pocket. Perhaps because of the size of the house and the focus on just a few rooms (or maybe just the content), the camera angles create a feeling of audience invasiveness, and at times, according to a critic writing in *Time* magazine, the "realism of camera close-ups turns probability into utter implausibility." Nevertheless, the movie provides a window into this desperate mother-daughter relationship at the 11th hour.

REFERENCES

Hart, Lynda, "Doing Time: Hunger for Power in Marsha Norman's Plays," *Southern Quarterly*, 25:3 (Spring 1987); Kauffmann, Stanley, "More Trick than Tragedy." *Saturday Night Review*, 9:10 (September–October 1983); Kintz, Linda, *The Subjects Tragedy: Political Poetics, Feminist Theory, and Drama* (Ann Arbor: University of Michigan Press, 1992); "'Night, Mother," *Time*, 128 (October 6, 1986).

—*N.A.*

THE NIGHT OF THE IGUANA (1961)

TENNESSEE WILLIAMS (1911–1983)

The Night of the Iguana (1964), U.S.A., directed by John Huston, adapted by John Huston and Anthony Veiller; Metro-Goldwyn-Mayer.

The Play

The play, which premiered on Broadway in 1961, centers on an American named T. Lawrence Shannon, a defrocked Episcopal clergyman, who has been forced to leave the ministry because of his scandalous personal behavior. He now conducts bus tours throughout Mexico as "a man of God on vacation." Shannon delivers a busload of Texas tourists to the tawdry Costa Verde Hotel on the outskirts of nowhere, run by Fred and Maxine Faulk, who are old friends of his. The hotel's clientele are basically a group of dropouts from society.

Shannon had hoped to find true solace in talking with Fred for a while; but he learns upon his arrival that Fred has recently died. Maxine would like him to remain at the hotel as her co-proprietor and resident lover, but Shannon is put off by Maxine's advances. One of the hotel guests is Hannah Jelkes, a sedate spinster who supports herself by drawing character sketches of the hotel guests. Although she lives what she terms a life of "refined vagrancy," she seems to face life with a serenity that eludes Shannon.

Looking about him, the despairing ex-cleric finds man as God made him, struggling and suffering in a world God never made. Esther Jackson sees Shannon as something of a failed Christ figure: He is a "negative saint, the great sinner toiling up the steep ascent to God." In short, Shannon struggles to make atonement for his own transgressions, and by play's end passes from sin to expiation to redemption. The New York Drama Critics conferred on Williams their best American play award, and Hollywood beckoned.

The Film

John Huston had just finished acting in *The Cardinal* when producer Ray Stark brought him the project, scripted by Gavin Lambert. Huston promptly dismissed the script's emphasis on sex and commissioned another, more thoughtful version by Anthony Veiller (Williams was also brought in for some contributions). Most of the exteriors were shot in Mismaloya, a peninsula just south of Puerto Vallarta. Plans to shoot it in color were abandoned, to Huston's later regret.

The film begins in the steamy, suffocating tropical world of the shabby hotel and its environs. Because the world of the play is a circumscribed one, Huston rightly stays close to the stifling confines of the hotel setting.

The iguana, which gives the story its title, is a reptile common to the Mexican wilds. During the movie, some Mexican boys capture an iguana and tie it under the hotel porch to fatten it up for the table. Shannon (Richard Burton) himself presents a symbolic parallel to the captive iguana. For he is entangled in a number of unresolved emotional problems; and, like the iguana tied up underneath the porch, he has reached the end of his rope—at least for the time being.

The most pronounced parallel between the captive iguana and Shannon occurs when Shannon goes to pieces and has to be literally tied down to a hammock, until his suicidal impulse subsides. He gets through his dark night of the soul mostly with the help of the soothing conversation and poppy seed tea supplied by Hannah Jelkes (Deborah Kerr). When Shannon mentions his sinful past to Hannah, she replies, "Nothing human disgusts me, unless it is unkind or violent." Furthermore, Hannah reminds Shannon, at their age one has to settle for some compromises in life and accept situations that one is powerless to improve. She implicitly suggests that he should leave the past behind and get on with his life.

Shannon repays her kindness by acceding to her request to set the iguana free. He does so, as he explains, "because God won't do it; and we are going to play God here tonight." His point is that God expects us to help others to liberate themselves from the painful problems in which they find themselves entangled in life. This is what Shannon had done when he was active as a minister, and he hopes to do so again.

In the wake of Fred Faulk's death, the blowzy, frowzy Maxine (Ava Gardner, in an impeccable performance) asks Shannon to stay on as co-proprietor of the ramshackle hotel with her; and he eventually decides to do so. This sympathetic treatment of Maxine created a conflict with Williams, who saw her as a kind of predatory female spider. Huston overrode Williams's arguments, declaring, "Tennessee, I think you've got it in for women; you don't want to see a man and a woman in a love relationship, and that's at the bottom of it." Huston won the argument.

Huston was also careful to indicate the better side of Shannon's character in order to foreshadow the fact that Shannon will stay on at the hotel not only to be Maxine's consort but also to assume Fred Faulk's role as sympathetic councillor to the outsiders and misfits who often fill its guest list. The verbal imagery about Shannon's filling Fred's shoes for Maxine is present in the play; but in the movie it is extended to encompass how the defrocked priest will also be the comforter of the lonesome and flawed people who happen upon Maxine's jungle outpost. Moreover, Huston makes this imagery visual as well as verbal in the motion picture by photographing Shannon wearing Fred's shoes (given to him by Maxine) with his feet in the foreground on a desk. In effect Shannon's new ministry will be to help others as Fred helped him. Shannon has thus decided to minister to the lonesome and the flawed human beings that have taken refuge from the world at large in Maxine's outpost in the wilderness. In doing so, he will no longer be "a man of God on vacation."

So pleased was Huston with his collaboration with scenarist Tony Veiller that he signed him on for his next literary adaptation, *The Man Who Would Be King*.

In appraising the film, commentators Gerald Mast and Bruce Kawin confirmed that *Night of the Iguana* is a strong movie on its own terms, but "shares enough of the tone, power, and intent of the original work to be considered a valid, intriguing adaptation" of Williams's play.

REFERENCES

Grobel, Lawrence, *The Hustons* (New York: Charles Scribner's Sons, 1989); Jackson, Esther, *The Broken World of Tennessee Williams* (Madison: University of Wisconsin Press, 1961); Mast, Gerald, and Bruce Kawin, *A Short History of the Movies* (Boston: Allyn and Bacon, 1996).

—G.D.P.

NOISES OFF (1982)

MICHAEL FRAYN (1933–)

Noises Off (1992), U.S.A., directed by Peter Bogdanovich, adapted by Marty Kaplan; Touchstone Pictures.

The Play

Michael Frayn's highly successful 1982 comedy *Noises Off* is a play-within-a-play or, more specifically, a farce-within-a-farce. This English farce depicts actors rehearsing and performing in a touring production of a show called *Nothing On*. By using theater as the backdrop for his play, Frayn is able to poke fun at the late-night rehearsals and rigid professional demands placed upon the cast and crew in order to create an effective theatrical illusion. As Katharine Worth points out, "However trivial the piece, the players who are performing it must take rehearsals, deadlines, all the business of the stage with the same seriousness as if it were Shakespeare. *The show must go on* is a real categorical imperative." This fast-paced play is all about entrances and exits, mistaken identities, and comedic timing. As Lloyd Dallas, the director of the inevitably doomed *Nothing On*, states, "That's what it's all about. Doors and sardines. Getting on—getting off. Getting the sardines on—getting the sardines off. That's farce. That's the theatre. That's life. . . . So just keep going. Bang, bang, bang. Bang, you're on. Bang, you've said it. Bang, you're off." The play was a rousing success on stage and was first performed in London in 1982 and made its New York debut the following year.

In Frayn's play, Act One begins with a late-night dress rehearsal as the frazzled director, Lloyd Dallas, attempts to coax one final performance from an exhausted cast and crew before opening night. Our view of the set is from the front as the actors perform onstage while Lloyd shouts out instructions from offstage. As props and memory begin to fail Lloyd storms the stage and begins to appeal to those involved to pull together long enough to make it through the first act (which is all we ever see of *Nothing On*). Act Two catches up to the production after it's been on the road for several weeks and things have begun to disintegrate at an alarming rate. We are now privy to the backstage view of the set that has been turned 180 degrees. As in Act One, we are seeing a performance of the first act of our play-within-a-play, *Nothing On*, and the personal lives of the cast begin to have a decidedly negative impact on the performance as lines are flubbed and cues missed all around. An always troublesome plate of sardines, a bottle of whiskey, and an ever dwindling bouquet of flowers are passed around in a bit of perfectly timed physical comedy. In the final act, some three months into the tour, we are once again presented with a front stage view of the set as the play spirals completely out of control when "behind the scenes" conflicts between cast and crew members spill over into the onstage action. All sense of a professional attitude is abandoned as the cast literally hangs from the curtain in an attempt to end the scene and salvage whatever dignity remains.

The Film

Noises Off made an entertaining transition to screen in Peter Bogdanovich's 1992 release of the same name. Although Frayn had previously written for film (*Clockwise*, 1986, starring John Cleese), Marty Kaplan (*The Distinguished Gentleman*, 1992, and *Striking Distance*, 1993) adapted the play for the screen. While Americanizing some of the names and references, Kaplan retains most of the dialogue and action and Bogdanovich's direction keeps the pace fast and sharp, taking full advantage of the stage sets. As Armond White points out, "*Noises Off* was an ode to the theater (and to valiant, resilient actors) made by a cineaste appreciative of the theatrical essence (human labor) at the heart of the cinema he loves." The only real deviation between the play and film is Michael Caine's voice-over (as the director) leading up to the Broadway premiere. The final scene in the film, depicting a successful Broadway performance, does not appear in the original play and seems curiously out of place. Certainly nothing in the play or the film up to this point has given us any indi-

cation that the performance will be anything but a failure. One critic who took exception to the film's treatment of the play is John Baxter who states that although the film "has moments that recall Bogdanovich's earlier success with fast-paced farce (the delightful *What's Up Doc?*), . . . the film's only virtues derive from Frayn's play, whose commercial productions are far superior to this screen version." For this reviewer, the film successfully translates Frayn's insights into the theatrical world with the proper energy and an insider's sense of humor. As Karen Blansfield notes, the play "delves into the world of actors and theater personnel both on stage and behind the scenes, showing the demands and refinements of this profession, the precision and timing required in farce, and the comic embroilment of the characters' private lives with their fictional public ones." Certainly the film's cast, led by Caine, Carol Burnett, John Ritter, Christopher Reeve, and Denholm Elliott seem up to the challenge as they enthusiastically tackle the subject matter. The film *Noises Off*, as directed by Bogdanovich, succeeds in bringing an entertaining stage farce to the screen.

REFERENCES

Blansfield, Karen C., "Michael Frayn and the World of Work," *South Atlantic Review*, 60:4 (November 1995); Hillstrom, Laurie Collier, ed., *International Dictionary of Films and Filmmakers*, vol. 2 (Detroit: St. James Press, 1997); White, Armond, "Directed by Peter Bogdanovich," *Film Comment*, 29:2 (March–April 1993), 61–64; Worth, Katharine, "Farce and Michael Frayn," *Modern Drama*, 29:1 (March 1983).

—*M.G.*

OEDIPUS THE KING [OEDIPUS TYRANNUS] (CA. 425 B.C.)

SOPHOCLES (CA. 495–406 B.C.)

Oedipus Rex (1956), Canada, directed by Tyrone Guthrie, adapted by William B. Yeats; Irving M. Lesser.

Oedipus the King (1967), U.K., directed by Philip Saville, adapted by Michael Luke and Philip Saville; Crossroads/Universal.

Oedipus Rex [Edipo Re] (1967), Italy, directed and adapted by Pier Paolo Pasolini; Arco Film.

The Play

Written by one of the most celebrated and recognizable of Greek tragedians, when Athens was the dominant power in the ancient world, *Oedipus the King* is a cultural cornerstone of what used to be called Western Civilization. The story has become a well-known cultural icon of universal significance. Tremendously successful in Athens in his time, Sophocles began as an actor performing in his own plays but gave up acting early on, setting a precedent for later dramatists such as Euripides, who were able to avoid on-stage appearances. As a dramatic innovator, Sophocles increased the number of speaking roles in his plays to six in *Oedi-*

pus, twice as many as Aeschylus employed in *The Suppliant Maidens*, which also reduced the number of choral odes in order to expand the dramatic action. But, as Henry W. Wells wrote in *The Reader's Encyclopedia of World Drama*, Sophoclean drama represented more than simply technical innovation: "it reflected an entirely new view of human action and suffering."

The action is set in Thebes, beset by plague, which Oedipus, the king, hopes to end. Creon, who has been sent to the oracle at Delphi, returns with Apollo's injunction that Oedipus must discover the murderer of the late king Laius and purge Theban society by either executing the assassin or banishing him. Oedipus then sends for the blind soothsayer Tiresias, who is reluctant to tell what he knows but finally reveals that Oedipus himself is the culprit. Infuriated by this news, Oedipus accuses Tiresias of working in league with Creon to discredit him. When Jocasta, the queen, is told of what has transpired, she attempts to comfort Oedipus by telling him of a prophecy that Laius would be killed by his own son, but, instead, he is terrified. Oedipus explains that he had once killed a man at a crossroad, just as Laius had been killed, but Laius had reportedly been set upon by several assailants.

A shepherd brings news from Corinth that Polybus, thought to be the father of Oedipus, has died, and summons Oedipus to return to Corinth to become king. But the messenger brings further disturbing news when he tells Oedipus that Polybus was not, in fact, his father. As a child Oedipus had been given to the child-

Pier Paolo Pasolini's adaptation of Oedipus Rex (Edipo Re) *cast Franco Citti as the blind Oedipus.* (COURTESY MUSEUM OF MODERN ART)

less royal couple by another shepherd from Thebes. Oedipus is then determined to unravel the mystery of his true parentage, even though Jocasta implores him not to, because she now senses the truth—that Oedipus was her own son. The second shepherd is reluctant to tell what he knows, but gives in, under the threat of torture. After discovering that he is both the son and husband of Jocasta, Oedipus then learns that she has committed suicide by hanging. Devastated with remorse, Oedipus blinds himself (offstage) and is sent into banishment by Creon, who now rules Thebes.

The Films

The first film under consideration began as a stage production mounted at the Stratford Ontario Festivals of 1954 and 1955 by Tyrone Guthrie, with all of the characters wearing masks. Although archaeological evidence from the fifth century B.C. suggests that in ancient Greece, masks would have been notably "naturalistic," Guthrie chose to emphasize the artificiality of the oversized masks and to individualize each mask to the character wearing it. The golden mask worn by the actor playing Oedipus (Douglas Campbell), for example, sported a golden crown. Oedipus is also dressed in a gold gown until after his self-mutilation, when he reappears wearing a red robe. Being part of the royal family, Creon (Robert Goodier) also wore a golden mask. Excepting the Chorus, all of the actors wore elevated footwear.

The acting, like the costuming, was designed to achieve maximum stylization. At the appropriate times the Chorus bobs and weaves in what Kenneth MacKinnon called "a ballet of grief." When Tiresias (Donald Davis) responds in anger to Oedipus to warn him not to pursue the issue of who killed Laius, the Chorus moans in agony. MacKinnon explains that the film makes no "concessions to traditional methods of 'theatrical' filming. Thus, there is no audience within the film for this utterly stage-bound event." Camera angles and set-ups "often defy realist convention," as Guthrie uses overhead shots of the Chorus arranged around Oedipus when Jocasta (Eleanor Stuart) first enters, and, again, when she leaves the stage. For MacKinnon, the film's greatest success "is its achievement in defamiliarizing the familiar."

Philip Saville's 1967 adaptation of the play was shot in the amphitheater at Dodona in an acting space that resembles what might have applied in ancient Greece. Saville has chosen to film the action without masks in a realistic mode rather than in the highly stylized manner of Tyrone Guthrie. The logic of this mimetic approach is to unite the theatrical world with the outside world. The plague-ridden citizens of Thebes enter the amphitheater from the outside world to ask Oedipus (Christopher Plummer) for assistance and relief. Saville films events taking place outside the theatrical space, such as when Tiresias (Orson Welles) descends to the court from his mountainside abode. However, Saville was criticized for "attempting to steer a middle course between formalism and naturalism."

On the other hand, the film was praised by theatre critic John Russell Taylor, writing for *The Times* of London (July 1, 1968) for its use of the Paul Roche translation, the fidelity of the screenplay to Sophocles, and the way Saville presented the Chorus in filmic terms. Kenneth MacKinnon questions the way Saville utilized the amphitheater by placing the confrontations between Oedipus and Tiresias and the Shepherd (Roger Livesey) at the top of the seating area. Likewise, the Chorus enters from the top of the amphitheater, sometimes used as a mere archaeological ruin rather than an actual playing space.

As played by Lilli Palmer in Saville's film, Jocasta appears to be appropriately seductive but not exactly the right age to be Oedipus's mother. Saville adds sequences to suggest that Jocasta is haunted by the ghost of Laius, and she seems to be driven to suicide by guilt over her union with her son. She bears the burden of the incestuous relationship, which drives her to suicide. The cast, which includes Cyril Cusack as the Messenger and Donald Sutherland as the Chorus Leader, is gifted. For some, the approach might have been more cohesive. Because of the way the countryside is filmed and the action edged outside the natural amphitheater,

MacKinnon places the adaptation in "the realistic tradition of filming Greek tragedy," rather than the theatrical, "despite superficial evidence to the contrary."

Pasolini's *Oedipus Rex* resembles neither of the adaptations previously discussed. The action is structured in four movements: 1) a prologue set in Italy during the 1930s that is unabashedly autobiographical and Freudian; 2) the "backstory" of the Oedipus myth, his birth and abandonment, his marriage to Jocasta (Silvana Mangano), and the visitation of the plague in Thebes; 3) the action of the play, from the suppliants to the blind departure of Oedipus (Franco Citti) from Thebes; 4) an epilogue, showing blind Oedipus in Italy during the 1960s, revisiting the scene of his childhood.

Pasolini took some pride in the way the central sections were authentic to the text of Sophocles, but he fractures geographical continuity by filming those sections in Morocco, remote from the "civilized" associations with Greece. The costumes are suggestive of Aztec, Sumerian, and black African cultures, while the Romanian folk tunes Pasolini favored, "half-way between Slav, Greek and Arab songs," as Pasolini described them, "are indefinable: it is unlikely that anyone who didn't have a specialized knowledge could locate them; they are a bit outside history." In attempting "to make *Oedipus* a myth," Pasolini "wanted music which was ahistorical [and] atemporal." One might answer that the Oedipus story was a myth long before Pasolini exploited it.

Film critics found this adaptation a thrilling and evocative intellectual playground where they could romp with Freudian, Jungian, and Marxist notions, finding all sorts of "interesting" interpretative ideas. In the epilogue, for example, blind Oedipus plays a pipe, which, Oswald Stack claims, means that "metaphorically, he is a poet," even a "Marxist poet," since he plays "a Russian revolutionary air on his flute." All of this may seem a considerable stretch from Sophocles.

REFERENCES

Gassner, John, and Edward Quinn, eds., *The Reader's Encyclopedia of World Drama* (New York: Thomas Y. Crowell, 1969); MacKinnon, Kenneth, *Greek Tragedy into Film* (London: Croom Helm, 1986); Stack, Oswald, *Pasolini on Pasolini* (London: Thames and Hudson, 1969).

—*J.M.W.*

David Mamet

Oleanna (1995), U.S.A./U.K., directed and adapted by David Mamet; Samuel Goldwyn Productions.

OLEANNA (1992)

DAVID MAMET (1947–)

The Play

First staged on May 1, 1992, at Cambridge, Massachusetts, by the Bay Theater Company, David Mamet's *Oleanna* is a three-act play featuring two characters, John, a college professor, and Carol, a student. All the action transpires in John's office. The original theatrical presentation used two epigraphs absent from the film version. While the first, quoting from Samuel Butler's *The Way of All Flesh*, dealt with the negative effects of an environment on impressionable young people, the second, derived from a Pete Seeger folk song, described a failed 19th-century Norwegian-American utopian colony, which gives the play its title. Shortly after the play's opening Mamet stated at a question-and-answer session that *Oleanna* "is a play about failed Utopia—particularly, the failed Utopia of Academia."

In Act One Carol meets John in his office to discuss her paper assignment. John is condescending and pre-occupied with his own affairs, including the impending purchase of a new house, often breaking off the dialogue with Carol to engage in phone conversations, and never reaching out to establish proper communication with his student. In Act Two, when John refuses to comply with Carol's request for a passing grade, she shifts the blame for her failures onto him. With the aid of an unseen support group, she accuses him of sexual harassment. The dynamics of power are shifting. He's no longer completely in charge; conversely, she's no longer just a supplicant but has assumed a position of power. In their last meeting, the roles are completely reversed. He's lost his tenure bid, lost his job, and lost his house. Once elegantly dressed, he is now haggard and sloppily attired. She, on the other hand, is prim and cool and conservative. As she is about to leave, she offers him a way out: If he will accept her "group's" list of books to be banned (including his own text), she will drop the charges. After a brief instant of possible communication between the two, John assaults Carol.

In Mamet's original script, the action ends with a defeated and humiliated John reading out a public statement confessing the error of his ways. However, as Mamet re-wrote the climax for the New York production, after John has assaulted Carol and realized the violent pattern of behavior she has forced him into, then comes the bombshell. She accuses him of rape. In a fury, he lashes out and strikes her. He continues the assault. Finally, while raising a chair above his head, he pauses and slumps to his desk. "What have I done?" he moans.

Although *Oleanna* has been criticized as an anti-feminist play and an attack upon political correctness, Mamet's concerns are much more subtle, and they are related to his other works. As critics such as Steven Ryan note, "*Oleanna* is developed around one of Mamet's most basic themes: The never-ending battle of people to dominate one another." Mamet told one interviewer that the play "is not about sexual harassment. It's about power." Verna Foster notes that *Oleanna* is really "an indictment of an educational culture in which, in Mamet's view, power-roles and power-games played by both professors and students make teaching destructive and learning impossible." In this sense, Academia is now the 20th-century equivalent of the failed Norwegian-American community. A once noble ideal has degenerated into a battle involving power, hierarchy, and the control of language in which issues of communication no longer count.

The Film

In the cast are William H. Macy as John and Debra Eisenstadt as Carol. Mamet extends some of the action beyond John's office to adjoining rooms and corridors. He also keeps the camera mobile and the editing sharp and percussive, imparting a measure of kinetic energy to the dialogue exchanges. Shot compositions reflect the shifts in the power dynamics. For example, the camera emphasizes John's dominant position in the frame in Act One and in Act Two turns the balance toward Carol. Act Three aims at a more complementary approach, showing both equally positioned within the frame—until John's final act of violence disrupts the balance.

Academia becomes just another version of Mamet's dark vision of a debased American "House of Games," seen also in other works such as *American Buffalo* and *Sexual Perversity in Chicago*. The soundtrack begins with a male singer praising the value of college education, "Honor and joy reside in our school name." This song acts as an intermission device between the three acts, with the male voice gradually diminishing in power. Ironically, the film concludes with a female voice singing the same song, thus intimating that the same power mechanisms prevail despite the change in gender.

REFERENCES

Bechtel, Roger, "P.C. Power Play: Language and Representation in David Mamet's *Oleanna*," *Theatre Studies*, 41 (1996), 29–48; Foster, Verna, "Sex, Power, and Pedagogy in Mamet's *Oleanna* and Ionesco's *The Lesson*," *American Drama*, 5:1 (1995), 36–50; Goggans, Thomas H., "Laying Blame: Gender and Subtext in David Mamet's *Oleanna*," *Modern Drama*, 40 (1997), 433–441; McCleaod, Christine, "The Politics of Gender, Language and Hierarchy in Mamet's *Oleanna*," *Journal of American Studies*, 29 (1995), 199–213.

—*T.W.*

ON GOLDEN POND (1978)

ERNEST THOMPSON (1949–)

On Golden Pond (1981), U.S.A., directed by Mark Rydell, adapted by Ernest Thompson; Universal Pictures.

The Play

New England playwright Ernest Thompson, born in Vermont, wrote the play in California, remembering

Hail and Farewell. . . . Katharine Hepburn and Henry Fonda in the screen version of On Golden Pond. (COURTESY UNIVERSAL PICTURES)

the lake in Maine where his grandparents had settled in 1903 and where he had spent his summers growing up. The play was first produced by the Hudson Guild Theatre in New York City on September 13, 1978, as directed by Craig Anderson, starring Tom Aldredge as Norman Thayer, Jr., and Frances Sternhagen as his wife, Ethel, for a limited run of 36 performances. On February 28, 1979, it opened at the New Apollo Theatre in New York with Tom Aldredge and Frances Sternhagen again playing the leads. The play was eventually selected for *The Best Plays of 1979–1980* anthology. Thompson described his characters as "lakeside visitors who spend their summers, year after year, in New England. Life along the lake changes, but they remain the same, even while they're taken over by events." The somewhat crusty, 79-year-old Norman Thayer is "flirting with senility, but he knows it and he plays it to the hilt," as the play opens, "on Golden Pond, in the state of Maine."

Norman and his 69-year-old wife Ethel have been married for well over 40 years. When the play begins in June, they are awaiting the arrival of their 42-year-old, divorced daughter Chelsea, Bill Ray, a dentist from California and Chelsea's lover, and Bill's 13-year-old son, Billy. They are all coming to celebrate Norman's birthday in July. In Scene One when Ethel remarks that this will be their 48th summer on Golden Pond, Norman responds grumpily that it will "probably be our last," a statement of some ironic resonance, as events transpire. In Scene Two, set in mid-July, they are visited by Charlie, the mailman, who comes by boat, and with whom they discuss daughter Chelsea and her dentist boyfriend. At the end of the scene Norman tells Ethel that he walked to the end of the lane and got lost: "It scared me half to death," so he came running back to feel safe, to feel "That I was still me."

Chelsea arrives for Norman's 80th birthday party in Scene Three with their grandson and her companion, Bill Ray, described as "having a good sense of humor, when he remembers to use it." While Chelsea and her mother and young Billy go down to the lake, Norman does his best to engage Bill in awkward conversation, especially when Bill asks that he and Chelsea be permitted to sleep together. To increase Bill's embarrassment, Norman says "I'd be delighted to have you abusing my daughter under my own roof." Norman amuses himself by making Bill feel uncomfortable but he really enjoys the company of 13-year-old Billy. Chelsea and Bill depart for a European vacation and leave Billy with Chelsea's parents for a few weeks.

Act Two moves the action to the middle of August, when Chelsea comes back to pick up Billy. She tells her parents that she and Bill got married in Brussels and that Bill has gone back to California to make the necessary arrangements so that they can live together with Billy as a family. The last scene of the play, set in mid-September, belongs to Norman and Ethel. As they are packing to leave, Norman has an angina attack and, of course, Ethel is worried; but Norman attempts to make light of his problem after she gives him a nitroglycerin capsule. This could well be their last summer together on Golden Pond.

The Film

As a play involving generational conflicts, *On Golden Pond* was a natural vehicle for Jane Fonda to develop as a tribute to her father, who, like Norman, was in failing health. As Chelsea remarks to her mother about Norman, "Maybe someday we can try to be friends." Mark Rydell's film fully exploits this sentimental play about lovable old codgers in love and becoming increasingly aware of their mortality. The film adds a strongly developed subtext concerning reconciliation, between Chelsea and her father, and between Jane Fonda, who plays Chelsea, and her father, Henry Fonda, from whom she had become alienated during her political years and over her dissenting position on the war in Vietnam.

The sentimental relationships of the play are further enhanced by adding an element of movie nostalgia, since old-timers Henry Fonda and Katharine Hepburn were working together on screen for the first time ever in this film. Intending from the start to costar with her father, Jane Fonda bought the rights to the play and was the driving force behind the production, which was filmed on location in Vermont. Ernest Thompson's adaptation opened up the play to enable the camera to follow Norman and Billy on their bonding fishing expeditions. Thompson also tightened the structure of the play in order to sharpen the focus on Norman and Chelsea's reconciliation by adding an out-of-doors sequence near the end. While in college, Norman had been a competitive diver. While she was growing up, Chelsea had disappointed Norman because she was

afraid to attempt a difficult back flip. Before she leaves Golden Pond in the film, she swims out to the float and executes her back flip perfectly in order to please her father. Later, upon their departure, Norman presents Chelsea with his college diving medal and Billy with a casting rod to complete the reconciliation motif.

Following the play to the end, the film's conclusion concentrates on Norman and Ethel, but it is more upbeat. Since Norman has already given Billy the fishing rod, the film removes the play's telephone conversation with Chelsea and Billy in California, tightening up the action and leaving a stronger and more positive impression that because of Chelsea's reformation and the gift of a grandson in Billy, Norman now has more of a reason to go on living. The adaptation had tremendous potential as a sentimental crowd-pleaser. Henry Fonda, who died in August of 1982, consequently won a well-deserved and long overdue Academy Award for his portrayal of Norman. Thompson also won an Oscar for best adapted screenplay. Even though some of the play's details are changed a bit, the playwright was himself in charge of the script, and certainly the spirit of the play is splendidly sustained.

REFERENCES

Anderson, Christopher, *Citizen Jane: The Turbulent Life of Jane Fonda* (New York: Holt, 1990); Canby, Vincent, "Henry Fonda's 'Effortless' Art," *The New York Times*, August 22, 1982, H1, H17; Davidson, Bill, *Jane Fonda: An Intimate Biography* (New York: Dutton, 1990); Guiles, Fred Lawrence, *Jane Fonda: The Actress in Her Time* (Garden City, N.Y.: Doubleday, 1982).

—J.M.W.

ORPHÉE (1926)

JEAN COCTEAU (1891–1963)

Orphée (1950), France, directed by Jean Cocteau from his play; Palais-Royal Films.

The Play

Cocteau's reworking of the Orpheus myth as an "episodic and gratuitous tragifarce" in one act opened for a controversial two-week run at the Théâtre des Arts in Paris in 1926, with the director Georges Pitoëff as Orphée and his wife Ludmilla as Eurydice. Set in the poet's Thrace, the action begins with a domestic quarrel: Eurydice feels neglected by Orphée for a white horse that taps out poetry. A window broken in anger brings Heurtebise, the glazier. Orphée leaves to enter a

Jean Cocteau

lic accuse Orphée of composing obscenities and cut off his head. Eurydice leads the headless Orphée back through the mirror where Death's henchmen investigate events. The interrogated severed head gives its name as Jean Cocteau. The head is returned to Orphée who, accompanied by Heurtebise, lives happily again with Eurydice.

Cocteau's personal version of the Opheus myth, with his innovatory inspirational horse and Heurtebise, confounded both traditional critics and surrealists alike. His reworking derided the false psychology of contemporary boulevard plays by deliberately portraying one-dimensional characters and, with his eclectic mixture of bizarre happenings, jokes, puns, and music-hall routines (the pantomime horse), he mocked the stultifying conventions of the well-made play. Thematically, the play anticipates Cocteau's enduring preoccupations with creativity, public indifference, the artist's problematic destiny, and Death.

The Film

In form and detail Cocteau's film masterpiece bears little resemblance to his early stage version. The personal concerns with creativity, immortality, and the artist's destiny remain, but Cocteau the film director presents a darker interpretation with a deeper sense of tragedy, perhaps reflecting his own sense of public rejection. Using a contemporary setting, the film opens dramatically at the Café des Poètes, where Orphée witnesses Cégeste's death in a road accident. Shocked, he accompanies the body in a Rolls Royce belonging to a mysterious Princess (Death) whose chauffeur is Heurtebise. Orphée, fascinated by strange messages on the car radio, resolves to discover their source and neglects Eurydice. She joins a feminist group (the Bacchantes), but the Princess, in love with Orphée, has her killed. However, Heurtebise takes Orphée to the Underworld where the Supreme Court punishes the guilty Princess and returns Eurydice to Orphée, but only on condition he does not look at her. Eurydice decides to die a second time by forcing her husband's attention but the belligerent Bacchantes arrive and Orphée is shot dead. The Princess awaits Orphée, but realizing that he will never be hers, she orders Heurtebise to return him to Eurydice.

Cocteau's beautifully evocative film, moving magically between the real and unreal, was largely created in the ruins of the Saint-Cyr military academy, with additional studio sets by Jean d'Eaubonne. With its shadowy figures from the Underworld, where interrogations are only too reminiscent of Gestapo methods, the film borrows from the detective genre to build a compelling investigative mystery. Cocteau stressed this intention,

competition with a poem dictated by the horse, but the first line, "Madame Eurydice reviendra des enfers (Madame Eurydice will return from Hell)" is contentious, because the initial letters spell "Merde." In his absence, Eurydice considers killing the horse with a poisoned sugar lump, but her nerve fails. Ironically it is she who dies after licking an envelope poisoned by her ex-friends the Bacchantes. Death arrives and, having first killed the horse, takes Eurydice to the Underworld through a mirror. Orphée is heartbroken at the loss of his wife and horse, but Heurtebise reveals how to retrieve Eurydice. Orphée succeeds but is banned from looking at her. The Bacchantes and the Thracian pub-

describing his film as "a detective story bathed on one side in myth, and on the other is the supernatural." Drawing on the traditions of early trick films, notably the magical tricks of Méliès, Cocteau delights with characters diving through mirrors (tanks of mercury) or coming back to life (reverse projection). Georges Auric reinforces the sense of myth and mystery with his own suggestive score, but also through the haunting theme from Gluck's *Orfeo ed Eurydice*. Cocteau cast his favorite actors in key roles, with Jean Marais as Orphée and the young Edouard Dermithe as Cégeste. François Périer is also excellent as Heurtebise, looking after Eurydice (Marie Déa). But it is particularly the elegant imposing figure of Maria Casarès as Death, commuting to the Underworld in her black Rolls Royce, that particularly haunts the film.

Orphée is the second of three Cocteau films exploring the Orpheus myth. In 1930 he initiated the trilogy with *Le Sang d'un poète*, and in 1960 he concluded it with *Le Testament d'Orphée*.

REFERENCES

Gilson René, *Jean Cocteau* (Paris: Seghers, 1972); Fraigneau, André, *Cocteau on the Film* (New York: Dover Publications, 1972); Freeman, E., ed., *Orphée: The Play and the Film* (Oxford: Basil Blackwell, 1972).

—*R.F.C.*

ORPHEUS DESCENDING (1957)

TENNESSEE WILLIAMS (1911–1983)

The Fugitive Kind (1960), U.S.A., directed by Sidney Lumet, adapted by Tennesee Williams and Meade Roberts; United Artists.

The Play

Early in his career, Tennessee Williams wrote a play entitled *Battle of Angels*, which closed in Boston in 1940. A substantially revised version of the play, retitled *Orpheus Descending*, finally made it to the Great White Way in 1957. The hero, Val Xavier, is implicitly related to the eponymous Orpheus, since he tries to liberate his beloved Eurydice (Lady Torrence in the play) from the clutches of Pluto, the ruler of the Kingdom of Death (Jabe, Lady's invalid husband), in order that he and Lady can start a new life together. But Val fails just as Orpheus failed before him.

The rewritten play failed to satisfy the critics. Henry Hewes, for example, was convinced that Williams had

been ill-advised to try to pump new blood into a tired old play: "Every writer feels that he could write his early works better now that he knows so much more about his craft. But the fact is that the writer is no longer the same person. All the experiences that went into the original work have been rearranged and re-evaluated" in the intervening years. As a result, the new writing that he imposes on the old does not mesh into a satisfying whole. The play closed after a meager 68 performances.

The Film

Williams was afforded another opportunity to vindicate his belief in the play when director Sidney Lumet, noted for his many screen adaptations of plays (notably *Twelve Angry Men* and *Long Day's Journey into Night*) brought it to the screen as *The Fugitive Kind* (1960). The stellar cast included Academy Award–winners Marlon Brando (Val), Anna Magnani (Lady), and Joanne Woodward (Carol, a wayward girl enamored with Val). Williams, who collaborated on the screenplay with Meade Roberts, added a pre-credit sequence set in New Orleans, which is solidly based on references within the play's exposition about how Val's wild existence in New Orleans had forced him to leave there. Val then moves on to the little town of Marigold, Mississippi, where the play begins.

Val soon falls in love with Lady, and their adulterous love affair stirs up the antipathy of the townsfolk. With Val's assistance, Lady opens a confectionery store, which is decorated like an orchard in full bloom. On the day of the grand opening Lady embraces Val in the store; they happen to look upward and see Jabe (Victor Jory). Like an Angel of Death, Jabe descends the stairs from his sickroom over the store with a gun and kills his unfaithful wife. Then he sets a match to the tinsel and streamers and other decorations, and they immediately burst into flames.

After Jabe dies in the blaze, a maddened mob forces Val back into the burning building with fire hoses, to die with Lady. In the play Val is lynched on a tree and blowtorched. But having him together with Lady in death amid the conflagration is more symbolically right, because it visualizes in stunning images the ruined edifice, which they had erected to give substance to their romantic illusions, crashing down around them.

Some critics maintained that the film, like the play, was littered with too many corpses and catastrophes and populated with unsympathetic riff-raff with whom the filmgoer could not be expected to identify. They felt that *The Fugitive Kind* was a mediocre transposition of the Williams play, even though it was co-scripted by the playwright and featured Marlon Brando (*A Streetcar*

Named Desire) and Anna Magnani (*The Rose Tattoo*) as its stars.

Still the film has some admirers. David Thomson contends that "*The Fugitive Kind* was faithful to Tennessee Williams; it kept Brando and Magnani in intriguing balance, and used Boris Kaufman's black-and-white photography poetically." Moreover, the film presents the "fugitive kind" of the title as doomed creatures like Val and Lady, struggling to regain their footing in a hostile world, which offers them no support or encouragement to be better than they are. As such, the film is worth the attention of serious viewers.

REFERENCES

Crandell, George, ed., *The Critical Response to Tennessee Williams* (Westport, Conn.: Greenwood Press, 1996); Phillips, Gene D., *The Films of Tennessee Williams* (Cranbury, N.J.: Associated University Presses, 1980); Thomson, David, "Sidney Lumet," in *A Biographical Dictionary of Film*, rev. ed. (New York: Knopf, 1994), 459–60.

—*G.D.P.*

OSCAR (1958)

CLAUDE MAGNIER

Oscar (1967), France, directed by Edouard Molinaro, adapted by Louis De Funes, Jean Halain, and Edouard Molinaro; Gaumont.

Oscar (1991), U.S.A., directed by John Landis, adapted by Michael Barrie and Jim Mulholland; Touchstone.

The Play

Claude Magnier's successful French farce *Oscar* (1958) deals with a day in the life of a wealthy businessman who is confronted by an employee who has embezzled money from his company, a daughter who is pregnant, and a maid who resigns in order to marry a wealthy neighbor. Mistaken identity and disappearing luggage are central to the plot in this fast-paced comedy of errors.

Magnier's play was adapted for the English stage in 1960 by Robin Maugham (1916–   ) under the title *It's in the Bag* (Maugham also adapted another of Magnier's plays in 1957, a farce called *Odd Man In*). The American stage adaptation was written by Jerome Chodorov (1911–   ) and was performed under the title *3 Bags Full*. Chodorov is perhaps best known for his collaborative works with Joseph Fields, which included *My Sister*

Eileen (1940) and *Wonderful Town* (1953). *3 Bags Full* premiered at the Henry Miller Theatre in March of 1966. The cast included Paul Ford and Nancy Marchand as the businessman and his wife, Bascom and Genevieve Barlow. In the New York production of Chodorov's adaptation, Paul Ford attempts to marry off his daughter and regain possession of the embezzled money, by sorting out three identical bags that contain cash, diamonds, and the maid's undergarments. Writing for the *New York Times*, Stanley Kauffmann complained of the play's pacing and lack of energy. Kauffmann faulted Gower Champion's direction, pointing out that "the performance—in speed, invention, and a sense of dogged pursuit of demented ends—is generally short of the script's demands." Critics generally faulted the casting of the production along with its languid pacing for not delivering the energy necessary to successfully pull off this adapted French farce.

The Films

The 1967 French film version was considered a success at the box office. The film features Louis De Funes, a popular French comedian, as Bertrand Barnier, the successful businessman who must deal with the complicated story line. De Funes also cowrote the screen adaptation along with Jean Halain and director Edouard Molinaro. Although popular with moviegoers, according to a review in *Variety*, "Only De Funes gets some spirit into this forced farce by his sheer madcap shenanigans." Otherwise, the film suffers from a talky script and erratic pacing, which does little to provide the proper timing necessary for such a stage farce to be successful on film.

The same might be said about the 1991 American remake directed by John Landis and starring Sylvester Stallone. Landis is probably best known for his early comedic efforts such as *Animal House* (1978), *The Blues Brothers* (1980), and *Trading Places* (1983), while Stallone has certainly been identified more as an action star than a comedian (see *Rhinestone* [1984] or *Stop! Or My Mom Will Shoot* [1992] for examples of his forays into comedy). In this mildly amusing film adaptation, Stallone plays "Snaps" Provolone, a gangster who decides to go legit to honor the dying wish of his father (Kirk Douglas). The adaptation is by Michael Barrie and Jim Mullholland, cowriters of *Bad Boys* (1995) and *Amazon Women on the Moon* (1987), and the story has been placed within the stylish 1930s gangster genre. Although the general plot structure of the play is intact, this slick Hollywood gangster film is not entirely successful. As one critic pointedly states, "Without any emotional attachments or cultural sense, this type of comedy becomes colorless and lifeless, . . . But when the film is also straining under an inconsistent, badly developed script and a heartless, ill-humored star turn, it becomes an expensive exercise in futility." Although some blame can be placed on Stallone's performance, one cannot help but appreciate his attempt to play contrary to type and take on the demanding physical comedy of the piece. As with both the French film and the American stage adaptation, the pacing of Landis' *Oscar* is at times languid and never seems to capture the urgency necessary to energize the proceedings properly. Stallone certainly benefits from an all-star supporting cast led by Peter Riegert, Chazz Palminteri, and Marisa Tomei, all of whom labor competently, but the laughs remain few and far between and the film is never completely satisfying.

REFERENCES

Kauffmann, Stanley, "Theater Review: *3 Bags Full*," *New York Times*, March 7, 1966; Miller-Monzon, John, ed., *The Motion Picture Guide: 1992 Annual* (New York: Baseline, 1992); "Film Review: *Oscar*," *Variety*, November 1, 1967.

—M.D.G.

Thornton Wilder

OUR TOWN (1938)

THORNTON WILDER (1897–1975)

Our Town (1940), U.S.A., directed by Sam Wood, adapted by Thornton Wilder/Frank Craven/Harry Chantlee; Principal Artists/United Artists.

The Play

Thornton Wilder had already won fame for novels like the Pulitzer Prize–winning *The Bridge of San Luis Rey* (1927) before he turned to writing plays. After a series of one-act works like *The Long Christmas Dinner* and *The Happy Journey to Trenton and Camden* (1931), in which he first worked in a colloquial style with American characters of unpretentious origin, he produced the three full-length works upon which his stage reputation rests: *Our Town* (1938), *The Skin of Our Teeth* (1942), and *The Matchmaker* (1954). They were deliberate affronts to the conventional "fourth wall" style; and his purpose, as he stated it, was to "make the opaque matters of everyday transparent, with a view . . . to discovering something.

Our Town was very much a play for its times, appearing when, as biographer Rex J. Burbank notes, "Americans were beginning to rediscover their democratic heritage after their disillusionment with the shabby materialism and the subsequent economic paralysis the nation had fallen into in the twenties and thirties." Nonetheless, Wilder protested that the play was to be regarded as a more universal, than particular, attitude and perspective on life: "*Our Town* is not offered as a picture of life in a New Hampshire village; or as a speculation about conditions of life after death (that element I merely took from Dante's *Purgatory*). It is an attempt to find a value above all price for the smallest events of our daily life. I have made the claim as preposterous as possible, for I have set the village against the largest dimensions of time and place." Hence the episode at the close of Act One when George's sister, Rebecca, recites the most famous mailing address in the history of American theatre: "Jane Crofut; the Crofut Farm; Grover's Corner; Sutton County; New Hampshire; United States of America; Continent of North America; Western Hemisphere; the Earth; the Solar System; the Universe; the Mind of God. . . ." Indeed, as Burbank says, "By relating the ordinary events in the lives of these ordinary people to a metaphysical framework that broadens with each act, [Wilder] is able to portray life as being at once significant and trivial, noble and absurd, miraculous and humdrum."

Our Town was given its first performance in Princeton, New Jersey, on January 22, 1938; a month later it opened in New York at Henry Miller's Theatre and ran for an impressive 336 performances. The action is set in Grover's Corner, New Hampshire, on specific days in the years between 1901 and 1913, and it portrays events in the lives of George Gibbs (John Craven) and Emily Webb (Martha Scott) and their families. In a series of scenes—enacted on a relatively bare stage with a minimum of props—Act One depicts in a series of flashbacks and blackout sketches a complete day in the town when George and Emily are youngsters; and Acts Two and Three balance family and street scenes as a backdrop to the courtship and marriage of George and Emily. The last act concludes with Emily's death during childbirth after nine years of marriage. The Dead are seated on one side of the stage, while Emily's funeral takes place on the other. Her spirit joins the mourners at her funeral and then revisits scenes of her life as a 12-year-old girl. Her anguished observation of scenes of her childhood produces the most moving lines in the play: "Oh, Mama, just look at me for one minute as though you really saw me. Mama, fourteen years have gone by. I'm dead. You're a grandmother, Mama. I married George Gibbs, Mama. . . . But just for a moment now we're all together. Mama, just for a moment we're happy. Let's look at one another." After returning to her grave, Emily is saddened by how inadequately the living appreciate their lives: "Do any human beings ever realize life while they live it?—every, every minute?" With that, the Stage Manager sends everybody home.

The Stage Manager is a crucial presence in the play; he is the personification of the spirit of the town. He addresses his ongoing commentary on the proceedings directly to the audience (at one point even answering questions from actors "planted" in the audience) and arranges the props for the changing stage settings.

Critics were generally impressed with the play. Richard Lockridge of the *Evening Sun*, for example, praised its "rare simplicity and truth" and its sense of "something way down deep that's eternal about every human being."

The Film

Wilder himself participated in adapting the play to film and agreed (albeit reluctantly) to make many substantial changes. Consequently, the bare-stage abstractions and minimal use of props yielded to an opulently detailed set, designed by William Cameron Menzies and photographed in deep-focus by Bert Glennon. The simple wedding sequence was inflated into a more sumptuous affair. And, most importantly, the character of Emily was allowed to live (her death and ghostly visitation to the scenes of her youth were revealed at the end to be a dream suffered during the birth of her second child). Those exceptions aside, however, the screenplay succeeds to a remarkable degree in preserving the basic structure and style of the original play. Frank Craven and Martha Scott repeat their roles as the Stage Manager (here called "Mr. Morgan") and Emily, respectively. As in the play, the action is spread over 12 years, from 1901 to 1913, and is divided into three acts: the introduction of the Gibbs and Webb families, the marriage between George (William Holden) and Emily, and the graveyard scenes. Again, as in the play, Craven addresses the viewer directly and at one point solicits questions from an unseen "audience." Occasionally, voice-overs illuminate the inner thoughts of the characters, especially during the wedding scene. The penultimate graveyard scene abandons naturalistic staging and resorts to a more severely abstract conception as the characters stand stiffly in a featureless void, illuminated by only two shafts of light. At the end, Craven reappears and, after wishing the viewer good night, departs. In sum, *Our Town* occupies an uneasy position between the naturalistic staging suited to the film medium and the stark abstractions more typical of experimental drama. Most critics were ecstatic. Welford Beaton in *Hollywood Spectator* wrote, "Greatly human, artistically presented, brilliantly directed, superbly acted, *Our Town* comes to us as one of the finest bits of screen entertainment Hollywood ever sent out to the world." Among its Academy Award nominations were a best picture nomination and nominations to Martha Scott for best actress and to Aaron Copland for best musical score.

REFERENCES

Burbank, Rex, *Thornton Wilder* (Boston: Twayne Publishers, 1961); Castronovo, David, *Thornton Wilder* (New York: Ungar Publishing Company, 1986); Herron, Ima Honaker, *The Small Town in American Drama* (Dallas: Southern Methodist University Press, 1969).

—*J.C.T.*

PANDORA'S BOX (*DER ERDGEIST*, 1893; *DIE BUECHSE DER PANDORA*, 1894)

FRANK WEDEKIND (1864–1918)

Erdgeist [Earth spirit] (1923), Germany, directed by Leopold Jessner, adapted by Carl Mayer; Leopold Jessner-Film.

Pandora's Box (1928), Germany, directed by G.W. Pabst, adapted by Ladislaus Vadja; Nero Films.

The Plays

In Greek mythology, Pandora is a mortal woman endowed by the gods with the gifts of female skills, beauty, and a desire to please. She possesses a box containing all human ills; and when she finally succumbs to temptation and opens it, all hell literally breaks loose. Only the emerging spirit of Hope holds out the promise of redemption. In his dramas *Der Erdgeist* (Earth Spirit, 1993) and *Die Buechse der Pandora* (Pandora's Box, 1894), Swiss-German playwright Frank Wedekind immortalized Pandora as the amoral free spirit Lulu, a character who exists beyond good and evil. She is a creature of her appetites who inspires self-destructive idolatry in her paramours and embraces eros and thanatos with equal avidity.

Wedekind himself appears to have been compulsively attracted for more than dramatic reasons to the sexual subject matter of his plays. For one thing, he and his contemporary, Arthur Schnitzler, were products of the prevailing fascination with Nietzchean theories of the primary nature of power and sex, and Freud's writings about psychoanalysis, sexual repression, and the relativity of moral truths. Moreover, Wedekind's life was as traumatic as the affairs of his protagonists. The product of parents embroiled in political turmoil in Europe, he rejected politics to pursue a literary career. In Munich, his home throughout his adulthood, Wedekind met a group of writers, including Gerhart Hauptmann, who urged him to try his hand at plays. His first major work, *Spring's Awakening*, was produced in 1891. Due to its controversial treatment of emerging sexuality in puberty, it was censored and not produced until a bowdlerized version appeared in 1906 at the Kammerspiele in Berlin.

Undaunted by these obstacles, Wedekind's plays about the dissolute Lulu took his preoccupation with sexuality a step further. She is ruled by her passions as her various lovers fall to the wayside before her voracious appetites. She plays father against son and attracts both male and female lovers. She demonstrates what the lesbian countess Geschwitz had declared: "Men and women are like animals; not one of them knows what he's doing." In the prologue to *Erdgeist* she is introduced by an animal trainer in the guise of a snake. During the course of the play she takes and rids herself of several lovers, including Dr. Schoen, Herr Schigolch, and Herr Rodrigo. In the sequel, *Pandora's Box*—with one act each in German, French, and English—Lulu continues her decline into total degradation. She is convicted of murder but breaks out of prison to flee to Paris with her lover, Alva (Dr. Schoen's son). Their next stop is London, where she is forced to resort to prostitution. Unfortunately, one of her "tricks" is none other than Jack the Ripper, who fatally stabs her.

Because the two plays were denied a license, they were not seen until a private performance was staged in Vienna in 1905. Disaffected with the German theatre of his day, Wedekind turned increasingly to acting in the later years of his career. His 21 dramas, in the opinion of historians Oscar Brockett and Robert Findlay, were "a major influence on the German expressionists, who were attracted both by his dramatic techniques and by his rebellion against conventional values. At the turn of the century, however, Wedekind made his greatest impact through his frank treatment of sex and his mixture of several stylistic modes within single works."

The Film

G.W. Pabst had already had a distinguished career in theatre and film when he turned to Wedekind's "Lulu" plays. Indeed, his celebrated films, *Geheimnisse einer Seele* (Secrets of a Soul, 1925) and *Die Liebe der Jeanne Ney* (The Loves of Jeanne Ney, 1927), and his stage production of *Earth Spirit* demonstrated his affinity with and sympathy to Wedekind's subjects and preoccupations, especially psychoanalysis and sex. *Erdgeist* had already been filmed in 1923 by Leopold Jessner, starring Asta Nielsen as Lulu. But Pabst was dissatisfied by its rather bland, conventional interpretation, and he determined to take a more psychologically complex, yet realistic approach. His search for a "Lulu" led first to Marlene Dietrich, but her sultry persona lacked the fresh innocence (read that, amorality) he wanted. Upon seeing a young American actress in Howard Hawks' *A Girl in Every Port* (1928) and William Wellman's *Beggars of Life* (1928), he decided he had found his leading lady. Her name was Louise Brooks, and she was a Kansas-born ingénue who had danced and acted her way into second-rung stardom in Hollywood. According to Pabst's biographer, Lee Atwell, Pabst perceived in her an actress "whose sense of movement and gesture, instinctive, yet intelligent, fused with a naturally erotic, yet tantalizingly innocent allure that was precisely right for the fatal attractiveness of his Lulu." Brooks, in turn, saw in the opportunity a chance to break out of the "pretty flibbertigibbet" roles she had had in Hollywood.

The two plays are condensed into a single narrative. The prologue to *Erdgeist* was jettisoned, and the subse-quent action was reduced to Lulu's relationship with Dr. Schoen and his son, Alva (the characters of Schigolch, Rodrigo, Countess Geschwitz drift sporadically in and out of the action). The film begins in medias res, as we find Lulu installed in the apartment of the elderly Schigolch (Karl Goetz). He rebukes her for deserting him for a newspaper tycoon, Schoen (Fritz Koertner). When Schoen arrives unexpectedly, Lulu conceals Schigolch. After submitting to her advances, Schoen discovers Schigolch's presence and leaves in a temper. Meanwhile, Rodrigo (Kraft-Raschig), an athlete, puts in a brief appearance and, to Lulu's delight, invites her to join him in his trapeze act. In the next sequence, Schoen, who is about to be married, is rebuked by his daughter because of the rumors circulating about his affair with Lulu. As if on cue, Lulu arrives. Shoen's son, a musical revue producer, Alva (Francis Lederer), is instantly smitten. Schoen warns him not to get involved with Lulu, but Alva considers her for a part in his new revue. After a scene in which Lulu appears in the musical revue and Schoen visits her backstage, she succeeds in marrying the old man. At the marriage reception, however, it is Alva to whom she makes love. When Dr. Schoen discovers them, he produces a revolver and in the ensuing struggle with Lulu, he is shot dead.

Charged with murder, Lulu is convicted to five years' servitude for manslaughter. She escapes and returns to Schoen's residence, where she and Alva soon make love and prepare to travel abroad. In Paris, they take to the gaming tables in a waterfront gambling den, where they encounter Lulu's old consorts, Rodrigo, Schigolch, and the lesbian countess Geschwitz (Alice Roberts). The final scenes of the film transpire in London at Christmas time. As the poverty-stricken Lulu and Alva settle into their sordid attic room, a strange, cloaked figure of a man is seen stalking the fog-bound streets. One night Lulu, now reduced to prostitution, accosts the stranger. Reluctantly at first, he follows her up to her room. Unbeknownst to her, he is concealing a knife. As Lulu's trusting nature calms him, he drops the weapon, momentarily free of the desire to kill. In the attic room, they embrace, and the man gives her a branch of mistletoe. But the sight of a bread knife on the table renews his resolve, and he fatally stabs her. In the story's epilogue, a Salvation Army band marches through the streets, singing carols, while the man passes into the night. In truth, he is Jack the Ripper.

Because Pabst's film was silent, some critics were quick to criticize any attempt to portray Lulu without benefit of her "eternally passion-laden, eruptive, indiscriminating, hard, sentimental, and unaffected words," as commentator A. Kraszna-Krausz put it. Biographer

Atwell responds by pointing out that "whereas Wedekind intended to depict a woman's body by the words she speaks, Pabst uses the body of Louise Brooks as the focal point of expression, employing his talent for revealing psychic states and relationships through camera angles and editing." The film is masterfully constructed, photographed, and edited, moving from the flippant erotic tease of the opening sequence in Schigolch's rooms, to the glitter of the music hall (the entire stage performance is seen only from a backstage vantage point—a brilliant tour de force of cinematography and editing), the darkening tone of Schoen's murder scene, the fast-moving pace of the gambling den riot, and finally the darkling chiaroscuro of the London fogs. Whereas frenetic editing prevails in the gambling den scenes, the penultimate scene with Jack the Ripper is conveyed in prolonged, carefully composed close-ups of Jack and Lulu that slow down the pace and stretch to the breaking point the suspenseful anticipation of her death.

Atwell reports that in some release versions of *Pandora's Box* censorship altered the film radically. Schigolch became Lulu's adopted father, Alva an orphan with no relation to Schoen, Geschwitz merely a devoted friend instead of a lesbian lover. It has only been in recent years that the Cinémathèque Française in Paris and the Cinémathèque Suisse in Lausanne have restored a complete print from available fragments and according to Pabst's original shooting script.

REFERENCES

Atwell, Lee, *G.W. Pabst* (Boston: Twayne Publishers, 1977); Brockett, Oscar G., and Robert R. Findlay, *Century of Innovation* (Englewood Cliffs, N.J.: Prentice-Hall, 1973).

—D.S. AND J.C.T.

LES PARENTS TERRIBLES (1938)

JEAN COCTEAU (1891–1963)

Les Parents Terribles (1948), France, directed by Jean Cocteau from his play of the same name; Sirius.

The Play

First performed at the subsidized Théâtre des Ambassadeurs on November 14, 1938, Cocteau's three-act melodrama of possessive maternal love and infidelity was forced to move to the independent Bouffes Parisiennes following a public outcry and charges of immorality. The action is set in a respectable middle-class Parisian family household whose peace is shattered when Michel confesses to his domineering mother Yvonne that he has a girlfriend called Madeleine. His doting mother cannot cope with the sudden appearance of a rival, but her husband Georges and her sister Léonie (secretly in love with Georges) support Michel's move to independence. This is made worse when Georges realizes that his son's girlfriend is none other than his mistress. Unaware of this potentially explosive situation Michel invites the family to meet his girlfriend at her apartment. Both parents, for their own selfish reasons, seek to destroy their son's relationship, and Georges forces Madeleine to tell Michel she has other lovers. An incredulous and heart-broken Michel returns home with his scheming parents. However, a final twist brings the reconciliation of the young lovers and the suicide of the manipulative, dispossessed Yvonne. Michel, distraught at his mother's death, is left to face a difficult future with Madeleine, as are Georges and Léonie.

Cocteau's powerful study of a mother's destructive love and the hypocrisies of middle-class respectability moves relentlessly toward its tragic conclusion. Tension mounts steadily as his emotionally damaged individuals, condemned to coexist in the closed family setting, are subjected to increasing and ultimately fatal pressures. The enormous success of the play was due in no small part to the exceptional lead performances of Cocteau's protégé Jean Marais as Michel and Yvonne de Bray as his possessive mother, with Marcel André as his father Georges and Gabrielle Dorzat as Léonie offering powerful support.

The Film

Described by André Bazin as "pure cinema," Cocteau's film version of his play seeks to retain "its theatrical flavor even though adopting a filmic one." To preserve the essential claustrophobic intimacy of the original, Cocteau resisted the natural temptations of the film medium to open out his material with transitional scenes or additional everyday characters. For the author/director, the process of adaptation would move precisely in the opposite direction: "Instead of expanding the play, I drew it in, I condensed it . . . On the screen the play regained the strength of writing, and that blackness of ink that is watered down by the footlights." The success of the transposition is in part due to Bérard's decors, with their telling contrast between the dark, cluttered, and oppressive family home and its unhealthy lack of personal space, and the airy, brightly lit, and altogether more open atmosphere of Madeleine's apartment.

However, it is through the excellence of Michel Kelber's fluid camerawork that the qualities of this mise-en-scène and the outstanding acting of the original stage cast are completely realized. Full weight is given to Cocteau's dialogue as the camera moves discreetly and easily between and around characters. There are few elaborate camera angles, but judicious close-ups and editing serve to emphasize the power of the original text. The distant spectator in the theatre becomes a privileged, close observer of human duplicities "able to move among the characters and look them full in the face." The camera constantly links characters in two- or three-shots and occasionally in rapid pans, though more often than not it moves discreetly, almost imperceptibly to adopt the viewpoint of a given character or the interlocutor. The percentage of close-ups is relatively small, but these are all the more striking because of that. Particularly effective is the sequence in which Michel admits his love affair to his mother. The growing drama of the situation is captured as the camera, working in perfect unity with the text, registers in a close two-shot the sheer happiness of Michel and the consternation of his mother, while Georges Auric's musical score powerfully reinforces this crucial emotional moment. The camerawork is again decisive in the powerful final sequence when Yvonne decides to take her own life. Here the retreating camera adopts her point of view as she abandons the reunited lovers before recording in powerful detail her chosen death. Described both as a "triumph of reactionary film technique" but also as "pure cinema," Cocteau's screen version of his popular melodrama presents the case for a restrained, unobtrusive film style that gives due prominence to the taught dialogue and respects the essential theatrical flavor of the original.

REFERENCES

Ashton, Doré, ed., *Jean Cocteau and the French Scene* (New York: Abbeville Press, 1984); Fraigneau, André, *Cocteau on the Film* (New York: Dover Publications, 1972); Gilson, René, *Jean Cocteau* (Paris: Editions Seghers, 1969).

—*R.F.C.*

PARFUMERIE (THE SHOP AROUND THE CORNER) (1937)

MIKLOS LASZLO

The Shop Around the Corner (1940), U.S.A., directed by Ernst Lubitsch, adapted by Samson Raphaelson; MGM.

You've Got Mail (1999), U.S.A., directed by Nora Ephron, adapted by Nora and Delia Ephron; Warner Bros.

The Play

Miklos Laszlo's 1937 play, *Parfumerie*, was set in the late 1920s in a novelty shop in Old World Budapest. Two lovers correspond through a "Lonely Hearts" newspaper column, not realizing until they meet that they are coworkers in the shop. Little is remembered about the play, save for its popular incarnations on film.

The Films

Film director Ernst Lubitsch bought the rights to Laszlo's play for a mere $16,500. MGM in turn purchased it from Lubitsch for more than $62,000, thus making a tidy profit for the famed director. Retitled *The Shop Around the Corner*, it was sandwiched between two of Lubitsch's most successful satiric comedies, *Ninotchka* (1939) and *To Be or Not to Be* (1942). A native of Berlin, Lubitsch was attracted to the play's Old World sensibilities, its setting of a gift and leather goods store in Budapest, Hungary (which reminded him of his father's clothing store in Berlin), and the opportunities it afforded for intimate ensemble casting. This was not the privileged world of aristocrats and the wealthy, as Lubitsch had depicted in his previous films, like *The Love Parade* (1929) and *The Merry Widow* (1935), but a cozy milieu of "everyday" folks—what biographer Herman Weinberg describes as "an evangel, lowly and wistful, of little people, their woes and happinesses, as it concerned the shop which employed them, and their sorrows and joys outside of business." According to historian James Harvey, who regards the film as one of Lubitsch's masterpieces, it is remarkably free of Lubitsch's penchant for double entendres, risque lines, and gags. Rather, "We are always being surprised by affection in this movie—surprised at the tenderness of feeling lurking in a joke that we've taken to be merely clever in a way, those elaborate permutations of witty contrivance that Lubitsch and Raphaelson are so adept at involving us in. These scenes and situations achieve benignity in the same way that the characters do—gradually and at length, after going through and past the resentments and vanities that make them laughable."

Head clerk Alfred Kralik (James Stewart) has been corresponding anonymously in a "Lonely Hearts" newspaper column with a mysterious young lady (Margaret Sullavan). Little does he know that the new clerk in the store, Klara Novak—with whom he conceives an instant aversion—is that very person. They bicker and squabble

Tom Hanks and Meg Ryan starred in an updated version of the play, Parfumerie *(Shop Around the Corner).* (COURTESY WARNER BROS.)

at first, each regarding the other as a competitive threat. But, shortly after Alfred is fired from the store (due to a misunderstanding with his boss), he meets his mystery woman at an arranged rendezvous over coffee and cake. Their identities revealed, antagonisms melt away, and, after Alfred returns to the shop, they settle in for a happy marriage and prosperous business career. Historian Scott Eyman applauds the film's stage-like intimacy—no one and nothing is depicted outside the immediate confines of the shop: "[Lubitsch] gives the people at Matuschek and Company the full measure of his respect and affection. Through the dignity with which he treats them, the film becomes a celebration of the ordinary, gently honoring the extraordinary qualities that lie within the most common of us."

Nora Ephron updated *The Shop Around the Corner* in 1999 as a vehicle for Tom Hanks and Meg Ryan. Only the bare outlines of the play and the Lubitsch version are retained. Joe Fox (Hanks) and Kathleen Kelly (Ryan) are rival book store proprietors. Joe's mammoth discount store has just opened, and it threatens to run Kathleen's little "Shop Around the Corner" out of busi-

ness. Little do these two antagonists know that each is in reality the "mystery person" with whom they've been corresponding anonymously on the internet. It is not until they meet in a prearranged rendezvous over coffee and cake (a scene lifted right out of the play) that they realize each other's true identity. Joe and Kathleen carry on their mutual seduction by tapping away at their respective keyboards in "dialogue" that is bright and literate, sprinkled with numerous fleeting references to books, particularly *Pride and Prejudice* (plainly alluding to Jane Austen's quirky romance between Darcy and Elizabeth).

Whereas the Lubitsch version was a tribute to quaint old Budapest, Ephron's film takes to the streets of Old New York's lovable Upper West Side—with its picturesque shop fronts and homey brownstones, rainy streets, corner markets, and bustling shoppers. Unfortunately, we grow a little annoyed at Tom and Meg's dunderheaded antagonism toward each other; and it takes far too long for hardhearted Tom to soften up and for sweet Meg to get some moxie. Meanwhile, Meg's Shop Around the Corner falls victim to Joe's big bad chain store. That's not quite the happy ending we were looking for.

REFERENCES

Eyman, Scott, *Ernst Lubitsch: Laughter in Paradise* (New York: Simon and Schuster, 1993); Harvey, James, *Romantic Comedy in Hollywood, from Lubitsch to Sturges* (New York: Alfred A. Knopf, 1987); Schwarzbaum, Lisa, "The Yule Tide," *Entertainment Weekly*, 463 (December 18, 1998), 45–46; Weinberg, Herman G., *The Lubitsch Touch: A Critical Study* (New York: Dover, 1977).

—*J.C.T.*

PERFECT CRIME, THE

See *DIAL M FOR MURDER*

EL PERRO DEL HORTELANO (DOG IN THE MANGER) (1618)

LOPE DE FÉLIX VEGA (1562–1635)

El Perro del Hortelano (1995), Spain, directed by Pilar Miró, adapted by Miro and Rafael Perez Sierra; Cartel S.A., Lola Films, Enrique Cerezo P.C.

The Play

Lope de Vega wrote more than 300 comedies, a large number of which have been termed "comedies of manners." They deal with simple episodes and depict characters derived from Lope's observation of the world and of his own circle of acquaintances. One such comedy is *El perro del hortelano* (Dog in the manger). Centered around the topics of love, honor, and jealousy, the action takes place in 17th-century Naples and portrays the complexities of love across social classes in a strongly hierarchical society.

In the first act, Teodoro, secretary to Diana, countess of Belflor, courts Marcela, her servant. Diana offers Teodoro her help to achieve the "fair and honest" goal of marriage. But immediately the countess begins to feel an attraction toward her secretary, though she acknowledges that their difference in class forbids this love. Teodoro is in love with Marcela but as soon as he discovers her mistress's interest, he rejects the commoner. However, the countess's feelings cannot be expressed openly because this goes against decorum. Instead, she uses various stratagems. For instance, she pretends to have a friend on behalf of whom she has written a letter to a lover and asks Teodoro to do the same with a sonnet.

Act Two begins with Count Federico and Marquis Ricardo waiting for Diana. The countess has to choose between her two suitors and asks Teodoro for advice. His answer favors the marquis and Teodoro feels he has been deceived so he intends to return to Marcela, his equal, though shortly before he had denied this love on account of the risks for his post as secretary. In the meantime, Marcela blames another servant, Anarda, for her misfortune, because she disclosed her love to the countess. She takes revenge by stealing Anarda's suitor Flavio. Marcela will not easily be convinced of Teodoro's repentance and renewed love. She apparently continues her plan of vengeance against Anarda and demands that Teodoro insult Diana. The countess, who was eavesdropping, breaks into the scene and, driven by jealousy, dictates a letter to Teodoro, the addressee of the letter, whose hope is again aroused. The act ends with Marquis Ricardo running to express his thanks for having been chosen—only to find that all has been a misunderstanding of the servants. When Teodoro enters and complains about Diana's attitude "like a dog in the manger," and threatens to go back to Marcela, she slaps him twice.

At the beginning of the third act, Ricardo and Federico are planning the death of the secretary. For them, Diana's anger toward the secretary can only mean love, a love that violates the rules of decorum and honor. The killer they hire is Tristan, who happens to be Teodoro's servant and who immediately warns his master. But Teodoro is so overcome by the obstacles to his love that he now wishes to die. Tristan plans a solution: to have

Teodoro pass himself off as the son of old count Ludovico, whose only son was kidnapped years before. The secretary is not persuaded and decides to go to Spain. Marcela asks to go with Teodoro but Diana orders her to marry Flavio. When the countess of Belflor is saying goodbye, Count Ludovico appears to disclose the noble birth of the secretary. Yet, Teodoro insists on going to Spain and confesses the truth to Diana but she accepts the false identity. At the end, Diana marries Teodoro, Marcela marries Flavio, and Dorotea, another servant, marries Tristan.

The Film

Pilar Miró was a 1970s "enfant terrible" who has shown an ability to switch moods and genres. Her last two films were the 1996 thriller, *Tu nombre envenena mis suenos* (Your name poisons my dreams) and *El perro del hortelano* (1996). She died shortly after their release. She set out to make this film inspired by the success of numerous adaptations of plays by Shakespeare. However, the project went through financial difficulties while filming in Lisbon and the team had to halt production until a new producer was found. The choice of a 17th-century play in verse was risky and unusual in a period of film adaptations of contemporary classics or best-sellers. The text was adapted by Rafael Perez Sierra, a former director of the Spanish National Theatre, though Miró was responsible for the screenplay.

All the action takes place inside the countess' palace in Naples and the text provides few stage directions apart from entries and exits. The play presents few problems for a stage performance because there is little action and not many changes of scene. Instead, the plot develops through the masterly dialogue. All this is hardly suitable for the screen as it stands, but Miró's main achievement has been to break the proscenium and present an open staging. Interior and exterior scenes alternate and frame dialogues in various chambers in the palace and gardens. Notably, in the scene on board a boat drifting along the canal that surrounds the palace, the bright red gown worn by the countess stands out against a light green background as a metaphor of her awakening passion.

Most of the text has been maintained in the screenplay. Seventeenth-century Spanish presents few differences in grammar and vocabulary with present-day Spanish, so no adaptation of the text is required for a modern audience. Puns, humor, and irony have all been understood by the public, though attention is necessary to follow the quick rhythm of the verse. There are some cuts, mostly in Teodoro's speeches, to avoid lengthy and rhetorical comparisons. The exchange between Ricardo and Federico at the beginning of Act Three, where Lope de Vega mocks the excess of rhetoric, has also been suppressed.

With this film the late Pilar Miró set an example of how Spanish cinema can go back to the classics and produce results that appeal to large audiences. It won best film at the Mar del Plata Film Festival. Writing in *El pais*, A. Fernandez-Santos noted, "It is a quick, amusing and most clever comedy that keeps the spectator smiling until the last scene."

REFERENCES

Rossetti, Guy, "*El perro del hortelano:* Love, Honor and the *Burla*," *Hispanic Journal*, 1 (1979): 37–46; Fernandezj-Santos, A., "El perro del hortelano," *El pais*, November 29, 1997; Lope de Vega, Félix, *El perro del hortelano*, ed. Mauro Armiño (Madrid: Cátedra, 1998).

—M.M-C.

Betty Bronson portrayed Peter Pan and Mary Brian played Wendy in the Herbert Brenon 1924 production. (COURTESY KINO INTERNATIONAL)

PETER PAN (1904)

JAMES M. BARRIE (1860–1937)

Peter Pan (1924), U.S.A., directed by Herbert Brenon, adapted by Willis Goldbeck; Famous Players-Lasky/Paramount.

Peter Pan (1953), U.S.A., supervised and adapted by Ben Sharpsteen, Hamilton Luske, and Wilfrid Jackson; Walt Disney.

Hook (1991), U.S.A., directed by Steven Spielberg, adapted by Jim V. Hart and Malia Scotch Marmo; Amblin/Columbia Tri-Star.

The Play

The character of Peter Pan has been called the most famous person who never lived. The genesis of James M. Barrie's play is long and complex, drawing characters and incidents from Barrie's boyhood in Kirriemuir, Scotland; his relationships with the four children of Arthur and Sylvia Davies (whom he had met in 1898 in Kensington Gardens and with whom he remained closely associated the rest of his life); and two of his adult novels, *Tommy and Grizel* (1900) and *The Little White Bird* (1901). The story of a boy who refused to grow up and ran away to a life of adventure in the Never-Never Land premiered in London on December 27, 1904, with Nina Boucicault in the title role; and in

America on November 6, 1905, with Maude Adams. It has been estimated that in its first half-century in England alone it was presented over 10,000 times. In 1911 Barrie rewrote the play into novel form with a new title, *Peter and Wendy*. That Barrie himself felt close to the character can be seen from a quotation from his early novel, *Margaret Ogilvey* (1896), in which he describes his own youth: "The horror of my boyhood was that I knew a time would come when I also must give up the games, and how it was to be done I saw not. . . . I felt I must continue playing in secret."

In the original play's first act the spritely Peter Pan arrives at the nursery of the Darling children—Wendy, John, Michael—and flies away with them to Never-Never Land. In the second, the Lost Boys accept Wendy as their mother and build her a house. In the third, the villainous Captain Hook and his pirate gang abduct the children. Peter comes to the rescue in Act Four and feeds Hook to a crocodile. And in Act Five, all the children return to the nursery while Peter remains in Never-Never Land, occasionally visiting the nursery as the years pass.

The Films

Director Herbert Brenon made the first and only silent film version, and with scenarist Willis Goldbeck he took pains to retain the flavor of a stage production. Apart from a magical special-effects shot of Peter tipping out a pillowcase full of fairies (a suggestion from Barrie himself) and a few shots of a real pirate ship and a real sea (including a lovely image of sea gulls gently circling around the ship's mast and shots of mermaids disporting about a beach), most of the action has a stagebound quality (the parts of Nana the dog and the crocodile were obviously played by humans in animal costumes). A few of Barrie's lines were utilized in the intertitles, and he personally endorsed the casting of young Betty Bronson as Peter (continuing the English stage tradition that a girl play the title role). Equally appealing was Ernest Torrence's Captain Hook who, according to Joe Franklin in *Classics of the Silent Screen*, delightfully indulged himself in "grimaces, eyeball-rollings, and other attention-getting gestures that have to be seen to be believed." Barrie, however, was disappointed at the results. "It is only repeating what is done on the stage," he declared, "and the only reason for a film should be that it does the things the stage can't do." His own scenario, amounting to 15,000 words, which he sold to Paramount, was never used. It is reprinted in Roger Lancelyn Green's *Fifty Years of Peter Pan* (1954).

Walt Disney had wanted to make an animated version of Sir James M. Barrie's classic play as early as 1939, when he arranged with the Great Ormond Street Hospital in London (to whom Barrie had bequeathed rights to the play) to produce a film. But it wasn't until near the end of 1949 that actual production began. Including the costs for a live-action version, which was used as a model for the animators (in which dancer Roland Dupree portrayed Pan), it was to be one of his most expensive films to date, coming in at $4 million. The basic outlines of Barrie's play were retained, with the action beginning in the nursery of the Darling family; continuing with Pan's arrival; his teaching of the children—Wendy, Michael, and John—to fly; their departure to Never-Never Land; their encounters with mermaids, Indians, and the villainous Captain Hook; Hook's abduction of the children; and Pan's exciting last-minute rescue of the children and Hook's fate in the jaws of the crocodile. In a striking departure from the play—which brings the children back to the nursery, to be visited sporadically over the years by Pan—Hook's ship is sprinkled with Tinkerbell's pixie dust and, now captained by Peter, it flies across the moon over London to the wondering eyes of the Darling household. As he gazes on the apparition, Mr. Darling gently murmurs that he seems to remember having seen it himself . . . long, long ago. Surprisingly, as historian Leonard Maltin points out, Disney's film was the first enactment of the play in which Pan was *not* played by a girl, where Nana was depicted as a real dog (as opposed to the theatrical tradition of a person in an animal suit), and where Tinkerbell was pictured as a

tiny girlish sprite (as opposed to a mirror's reflected point of light). Moreover, one of the play's most famous moments was discarded—when Pan requests viewers to clap their hands to revive the dying Tinkerbell.

The film did not do well at the box office, and Walt himself was displeased at its performance. Commentator Richard Schickel complains, perhaps with justification, that *Peter Pan* was another example of the "Disneyfication" process. It was Disney's name, not Barrie's, that appeared over the title. Here, noted Schickel, was another example wherein Walt appropriated another person's work in order to gag it up and sentimentalize it: "The egotism that insists on making another man's work your own through wanton tampering and by advertising claim is not an attractive form of egotism, however it is rationalized." To less jaundiced eyes, the film wears well and there are many delightful moments, including the gags built around the relationship between Hook and Smee; the musical score by Oliver Wallace and songs by Sammy Cahn and Sammy Fain (especially "You Can Fly, You Can Fly," "Never Smile at a Crocodile," and "A Pirate's Life"); and the spectacular renderings of the London scenes, particularly when Pan and the children fly across night-shrouded London, the cityscape appearing through a break in the clouds below them.

As a filmmaker and artist who, in the opinion of some of his more acerbic critics, has never grown up, director Steven Spielberg might have seemed the ideal choice to make a full-scale screen adaptation of Sir James M. Barrie's five-act classic. In the Spielberg adaptation, Barrie's original plot outline was retained in only one flashback section of the film, while the rest of the picture revealed that Pan had grown up to become Peter Banning (Robin Williams), a corporate lawyer too busy with his career to pay much attention to his own children, Jack and Maggie. Among his clients is "Gran-Wendy" (Maggie Smith), the lady who had adopted him as a baby and now lives in a picturesque old Victorian mansion with a servant and a strange old man named "Toodles." As Peter and his wife join Wendy for dinner one night, they discover the kids have been kidnapped. A note signed "Jas. Hook" is left behind. Wendy informs the startled Peter that once upon a time he was Peter Pan and she was his Wendy; that Peter had married her daughter, grown up, and forgotten his boyish legend; and that this "Jas. Hook" is none other than the legendary villain, Captain Hook (Dustin Hoffman), returned to steal Peter's children.

Tinkerbell later arrives and conducts the reluctant Peter to Never-Never Land. Once there, Peter is humiliated at his inability to rescue his children, because, as a grown-up, he has forgotten how to be Peter Pan. The Lost Boys' help him remember his past youth and, gradually, he regains his ability to fly. His strength renewed, Peter emerges as the Pan of old and returns to the pirate ship, defeating Hook, who is killed when an enormous statue of a crocodile topples over and crushes him. Triumphant, Peter flies home with the children for a tearful reunion with his wife and Gran-Wendy. At the end, he wakes up in Kensington Gardens from what he thinks is a dream. On his way home he fails to vault the garden wall. "I'm out of pixie dust," he muses sardonically. Adopting the more mundane method of climbing the drain pipe, he clambers through the window and rejoins his waiting family.

There is no denying that Spielberg's film is deeply personal and allusive, involving—an autobiographical allusion to Spielberg's own experiences as a father, an allegorical warning against false father figures, and a complex and challenging postmodern meditation on the whole Peter Pan myth (today referred to rather cynically as a "syndrome"). Despite the fact that *all* of it was shot on soundstages, it is packed with delicious moments and effects, including aerial shots of the island lagoon with two large moons swimming in the hazy sky, Peter's first flying scene, Hook's embarrassment when his wig is knocked askew (didn't we always wonder if he weren't bald?), and, especially, the wonderful flashback sequence chronicling the story of the real Peter Pan (quite one of the finest things in all the Spielberg oeuvre). And yet, like the statue of the crocodile, the whole thing collapses under its own pretentious weight. This Pan has feet of clay. He has been allowed to grow up, which Barrie surely would have found unconscionable. Worse, after the adult Peter regains his lost boyhood and survives his adventures in Never-Never Land, we are to believe that he can now resume his adult responsibilities and function as *both* father and child to his family. The original Pan's tragedy was that he could not—or, more precisely, *would not*—grow up. Here, Spielberg implies that both boy and man can commingle in some happy, fuzzy balance—doubtless an appealing notion to Spielberg but surely an appalling one to the tougher, more insightful, yet more sensitive Barrie.

Other postmodernist attempts to inject modern elements and politically correct agendas into the story—and to erase the boundaries between imagination and reality—include a baseball game (with one team called "The Pirates"), references to pop culture icons like the Beatles, a troupe of skateboarding Lost Boys (who indulge in an *Animal House*–like food fight), the silly business with the crocodile statue, and a full-sized Julia Roberts as Tinkerbell. There are no Indians in sight (do

Dustin Hoffman brought his own unique swagger to the role of Captain Hook in Spielberg's Hook, *an updated version of* Peter Pan. (COURTESY NATIONAL FILM SOCIETY ARCHIVES)

we have to dispense with them now out of fear of racial caricaturing?), and Hook is no villain but merely a frustrated father figure who wants to make Peter's children love him. Similarly, Peter is another frustrated father who must cavort about in tights to regain his kids' love. This is errant nonsense: Those kids know something he doesn't—that parents are no longer children and can never be so again; any attempts to try would provoke only ridicule. In the end, this Pan declares that "to live must be an awfully big adventure," a reversal of the original play's most famous line. So be it. This Pan will live on as an adult-child (a tribute to actor Robin Williams?), even if it means that the play must die in the process.

The film's box-office performance was disappointing, and critics were generally unkind. David Ansen of *Newsweek* complained that "*Hook* is a huge party cake of a movie with too much frosting. After the first delicious bite, sugar shock sets in."

For the record, Mike Newell's film, *An Awfully Big Adventure* (1995), based on the novel by Beryl Bainbridge, is a dark melodrama of incest and corruption surrounding the rehearsal and production of *Peter Pan* in Liverpool in 1947. Although the play itself is depicted only in a few brief scenes, its themes of the incursions of experience and disillusionment upon the precious dream of innocence are central to the film.

REFERENCES

Birkin, Andrew, *J.M. Barrie and the Lost Boys* (New York: Clarkson Potter, 1979); Brode, Douglas, *The Films of Steven Spielberg* (New York: Citadel Press, 1995); Franklin, Joe, *Classics of the Silent Screen* (New York: Citadel Press, 1959); Green, Roger Lancelyn, *Fifty Years of Peter Pan* (London: Peter Davies, 1954); Maltin, Leonard, *The Disney Films* (New York: Bonanza Books, 1973); Schickel, Richard, *The Disney Version* (New York: Simon and Schuster, 1968).

—*J.C.T.*

PETRIFIED FOREST, THE (1935)

ROBERT SHERWOOD (1896–1955)

The Petrified Forest (1936), U.S.A., directed by Archie Mayo, adapted by Charles Kenyon and Delmer Daves; Warner Bros.

The Play

A film critic in the 1920s, Robert Sherwood turned to playwriting with *The Road to Rome* in 1927, an antiwar comedy set in ancient times. The 1930s brought his greatest successes, including *Waterloo Bridge* (1930), a love story set during the Great War; *Reunion in Vienna* (1931), about the relationship between an exiled prince and his mistress; *Idiot's Delight* (1936), a Pulitzer Prize–winning drama about a theatrical troupe in an Austrian hotel on the eve of war; and *Abe Lincoln in Illinois* (1938), recounting the years leading up to Honest Abe's presidency. *The Petrified Forest* premiered in New York at the Broadhurst Theatre on January 7, 1935, and ran for a successful 197 performances.

The year is 1934 and the setting is the Black Mesa Filling Station and Bar-B-Q in the eastern Arizona desert, near the Petrified Forest. A mixed collection of strangers gathers there one autumn afternoon. There's Alan Squier (Leslie Howard), a writer, a world-weary idealist whose travels have brought him to Arizona.

Gabby Maple (Peggy Conklin), the daughter of the lunchroom proprietor, yearns for romance and the study of art in Paris. And Duke Mantee (Humphrey Bogart) is a gangster on the lam with his gang. The love-starved Gabby is enamored of the sophisticated Squier, a feeling he reciprocates. Squier confesses his own disillusionment with humanity: "I belong to a vanishing race," he says, "the intellectuals, who thought they'd conquered Nature" but who find that Nature is reclaiming the world for "the apes." Mantee, by contrast, is a man of action. He commandeers the place and waits for the arrival of his girlfriend. Everyone sits around drinking and talking of their lives. Squier is impressed by Mantee's rough individualism, and he suggests that some day he and Mantee should be buried in the nearby Petrified Forest, which represents "the world of outmoded ideas . . . all so many dead stumps in the desert." Events come to a head when Mantee's girlfriend betrays him to the police. Longing to die, Squier asks Mantee to shoot him before making his escape. Squier dies in Gabby's arms. She agrees to bury him in the Forest, as he had asked her to do. At curtain's fall, she eulogizes him with words from a poem by François Villon:

> Thus in your field my seed of harvestry
> Will thrive—
> For the fruit is like me that I set—
> God bids me tend it with good husbandry;
> This is the end for which we twain are met.

Commentator Joseph Wood Krutch describes Sherwood's play as a "didactic vaudeville," i.e., a melodrama with a moral. It captures the despair common to the Depression period and the rise of pre-World War II totalitarianism. Writing in the *New York Herald Tribune*, critic Percy Hammond lauded the play's "delightful improbability" and concluded it "made probable by [Leslie] Howard and his accomplices."

The Film

Reprising their stage roles were Leslie Howard and Humphrey Bogart, with Bette Davis playing Gabby and Porter Hall playing her father. Edward G. Robinson was the first choice for the role of Mantee, but Howard insisted on Bogart. The role effectively launched Bogie's screen career. (Robinson finally played the part on a *Lux Radio Theatre* broadcast on February 8, 1943.) Veteran director Archie Mayo (*Bordertown*, 1934; *Black Legion*, 1937) was signed on. The play's outlines are retained intact. Alan Squire (note the different spelling) is a disillusioned and destitute intellectual who arrives at the Black Mesa Bar-B-Q, where he strikes up an affec-

Sherwood Anderson

and the characters are confined to one set. While duly noting its staginess, critic Welford Beaton in *Hollywood Spectator* noted that the screen, through the device of the close-up, "can place each member of the audience at the elbow of each character in the photoplay, thereby giving the screen a greater degree of intimacy than is possible for the stage to attain." Moreover, Beaton continued, although the "rowdiness" of the play has been cleaned up, "*The Petrified Forest*, more than any other picture I have seen, demonstrates that the screen is a more powerful medium for the presentation of a stage play than is the stage itself. I cannot believe the play in New York evoked the emotional reaction the audience accorded the screen version." In their study of gangster films, James Parrish and Michael Pitts gave *The Petrified Forest* high marks: "With interesting, offbeat characters and the background of the desert, the film exemplifies the best of Warner Brothers' picturemaking of the decade. While a very stagey production, it is still widely popular today."

In 1945 Warners remade the play as *Escape in the Desert*, a wartime tale about an escaped Nazi flier (Helmut Dantine) caught in the desert. Bogart later reprised the role in a television version of *The Petrified Forest* in 1955, costarring Lauren Bacall and Henry Fonda and directed by Delbert Mann.

REFERENCES

Beaton, Welford, "The Petrified Forest," reprinted in Anthony Slide, ed., *Selected Film Criticism, 1931–1940* (Metuchen, N.J.: Scarecrow Press, 1992); Parrish, James Robert, and Michael R. Pitts, *The Great Gangster Pictures* (Metuchen, N.J.: Scarecrow Press, 1976).

—*J.C.T.*

tionate relationship with the naively idealistic Gabby Maple. Their idyll is cut short by the intrusion of Duke Mantee and his gang. Under the strain of their enforced captivity, all the characters reveal their innermost fears and desires. True to the play, Alan openly admires Mantee. "You're a man of imagination," he says. "You're not afraid to do outlandish things." By contrast, Alan ruefully says of himself: "I doubt if you could find a more likely candidate for extinction." He strikes a deal with Mantee: He will sign his life insurance over to Gabby if Mantee will agree to shoot him. Gabby, ignorant of Alan's sacrifice, inherits the money. Mantee escapes, although he is destined to meet his death at the hands of the pursuing lawmen. This downbeat ending, similar to the play's conclusion, was adopted only after a debate over substituting a happy ending in which Squire lives.

The Petrified Forest is basically a static film, except for a lively shootout with the law at the café, and the action

THE PHILADELPHIA STORY (1939)

PHILIP BARRY (1896–1949)

The Philadelphia Story (1940), U.S.A., directed by George Cukor, adapted by Donald Ogden Stewart; MGM.

High Society (1956), U.S.A., directed by Charles Walrens, adapted by John Patrick; MGM.

The Play

Philip Barry's first plays were written and produced at Yale. Emboldened by their success, he enrolled in George Pierce Baker's famed 47 Workshop at Harvard.

The Philadelphia Story *(1940) starred a matchless trio of actors, Cary Grant, Katharine Hepburn, and James Stewart.* (COURTESY NATIONAL FILM SOCIETY ARCHIVES)

The Youngest was his first Broadway-produced play, and it possessed the hallmarks of his mature work, razor-sharp wit, keen observations of social manners, and an underlying disenchantment with life. His best-known plays today are his social comedies, *Holiday* (1928) and *The Philadelphia Story* (1939), in which groups of upwardly mobile people battle for advantage over circumstances, careers, and individual freedoms.

The Philadelphia Story premiered in New York at the Shubert Theatre on March 28, 1939, and ran for a successful 417 performances. The setting is a mansion outside Philadelphia in late June 1939. When vivacious but willful socialite Tracy Lord (Katharine Hepburn) announces her marriage to the self-made but snobbish George Kitteredge (Frank Fenton), a news frenzy ensues. A magazine reporter, Mike Connor (Van Heflin), and a wisecracking photographer, Elizabeth Imbrie (Shirley Booth), are dispatched to the pre-wedding festivities. Meanwhile, Tracy's doubts about the marriage are exacerbated by the appearance of her first husband, C.K. Dexter Haven (Joseph Cotten) and her own growing attraction to Mike. Tracy drinks too much and winds up swimming nude with Mike Connor in the family pool. Dexter Haven blames her behavior and his own drinking on her high-toned manner and egotistical demands, observing, "She is a goddess, without patience for any kind of human imperfection," to whom a husband should be "a kind of high priest." His critiques of her are echoed by her own father, who had left

the family earlier for an affair. Appalled at recent events, aware of the terminal smugness of her fiancé, and newly awakened to her love for Dexter Haven, Tracy breaks off the marriage at the last minute. George leaves. The marriage does go on, although the new groom is Dexter Haven. Barry does not attack the sophisticated world of his characters; rather, he celebrates it, wondering all the while if it is not possible to enjoy social privileges while retaining individual identity. As Mike Connor observes, "The prettiest sight in this fine, pretty world is the privileged class enjoying its privileges."

The Films

The film version of Barry's play is one of the most successful and best-loved screwball comedies of Hollywood's "golden era." The role of Tracy was written for Hepburn, and its great success brought her back to the movies after a two-year hiatus. Hepburn owned the rights to the play, ensuring that she would not only reprise her role as Tracy Lord for the film version but would also choose her director and costars. After the failures of *Holiday* (1937) and *Bringing up Baby* (1938), she had been voted "box-office poison" by the Independent Theatre Owners Association the year before and was carefully preparing for her "comeback" (this would be her first film at MGM). Cary Grant portrayed Dexter Haven, and James Stewart and Ruth Hussey took on the roles of the reporter, Connor, and the photographer, Elizabeth Imbrie. The play was transferred virtually intact to the screen. Following his earlier success in the film adaptation of Barry's *Holiday* (also starring Grant and Hepburn), director George Cukor foregrounded the banter between the two romantic leads, rather than indulging in their romantic moments. They are introduced in characteristically combative fashion—Tracy throws Dexter Haven out of her house and breaks his golf clubs, only to have him retaliate and shove her back through the open door. Another classic scene reveals a tipsy Tracy and Connor at the pool in the moonlight. After Connor dances with Tracy by the pool's edge, he says, "There's a magnificence in you, Tracy, you're lit from within." A little later, Tracy draped unceremoniously over Connor's shoulder, they confront her outraged fiancé and a highly amused Dexter Haven. "How art the mighty fallen," declares Dexter. Hepburn's image as rather coldly arrogant was cleverly played off here; and she achieves a needed vulnerability when her egotism is exposed. As playwright Barry had originally intended, the view of upper-crust society was never abrasive, but gently ironic. Historian Ted Sennett notes, "[If] its view of the idle rich is far kinder than any film of the thirties (even the rich can learn love and humanity), it is couched in witty terms, and the idle rich never had a lovelier representative than Hepburn."

The Philadelphia Story broke attendance records at the Radio City Music Hall in New York City. James Stewart won his only Oscar in the role of the sensitive Connor, and Donald Ogden Stewart received an Oscar for his screen adaptation. The film recently was designated by the American Film Institute as one of the 100 Greatest Movies of All Time. A delightful remake was to follow in 1956, *High Society*, wonderfully enhanced by the music and lyrics of Cole Porter as performed by Bing Crosby, Frank Sinatra, and Louis Armstrong and further graced by the presence of Grace Kelly and Celeste Holm. In this remake The Main Line setting became The Newport Jazz Festival. Boasting a "swell party" atmosphere, the remake's most famous song, "True Love," was a tribute to the original in its reference to the boat Tracy and Dexter owned together.

REFERENCES

Roppolo, Joseph P., *Philip Barry* (New York: 1965); Sennett, Ted, *Lunatics and Lovers* (New Rochelle, N.Y.: Arlington House, 1973).

—D.S. AND J.A. AND J.C.T. AND J.M.W.

THE PIANO LESSON (1987)

AUGUST WILSON (1945–)

The Piano Lesson (1994), U.S.A., directed by Lloyd Richards, adapted by August Wilson; Republic Pictures.

The Play

First performed as a staged reading for the 1987 National Playwrights Conference at the Eugene O'Neill Theatre, the play opened on November 26, 1987, at the Yale Repertory Theatre in New Haven, Connecticut, in a production directed by Lloyd Richards, with a cast that featured Samuel L. Jackson as Boy Willie Charles, who comes with his friend Lymon (Rocky Carroll) to take away and sell the ornately carved family heirloom piano; but his sister Berniece (Starletta DuPois) is opposed to the idea and refuses to give up the piano, which is symbolic of generations of heartbreak. This is the play's central conflict, "the battle over the piano, its meaning as both legacy and opportunity," in the words of Mary L. Bogumil, "a silent testament to American racism" that is constantly present on the stage. Boy Willie's Uncle Doaker tells

his nephew that Berniece will never agree to sell the piano, although she is afraid to play it, lest the music awaken her ancestral spirits.

Boy Willie plans to purchase land from the Sutter family with the money he would earn from selling the piano. The piano is also linked to the Sutters, erstwhile slaveowners. The current Mr. Sutter was found drowned in a well. Boy Willie blames the Ghosts of Yellow Dog—four black men who were burned alive in a Yellow Dog Railroad boxcar on July 4, 1911—for Sutter's death, but Berniece suspects that Boy Willie shoved Sutter into the well. She also holds him responsible for the death of her late husband, Crawley. The brother and sister represent two very different positions regarding the past and its relationship to the present: Berniece "wants to hide from history and Boy Willie wants to get rid of it," whereas Wilson, according to Alan Nadel, "wants to rewrite it."

The ever-present piano evokes the legacy of racism. Boy Willie's presence in the house, as Bogumil points out, "seems to awaken the dead," Sutter's ghost in particular, which is seen by Berniece at the top of the stairs. Sutter is linked to the piano because his grandfather, Robert, had originally purchased it for his wife, Ophelia. Robert Sutter also owned the Charles family as slaves and had traded two of those slaves for the piano. Boy Willie's Uncle Doaker tells the story of the piano and how the Charles family history had come to be carved into it. Boy Willie sees the piano merely as a means of funding a land investment, but the piano is protected by Sutter's ghost when Boy Willie and Lymon attempt to move it. Avery, a preacher who hopes to marry Berniece, attempts to exorcise the ghost, but the exorcism fails until Berniece, who has not touched the piano since her mother died, plays it "as an exorcism and a dressing for battle." The conflict is finally resolved when Boy Willie gives up and decides to leave town. His final words are ambiguous, however, and may suggest a more profound reconciliation. The play was a critical success and won both the New York Drama Critics' Circle Award and the Pulitzer Prize for drama in 1990.

The Film

Lloyd Richards, who had brought the play to the stage, was also chosen to direct the television film, and August Wilson was asked to write the screenplay adaptation. Moreover, Richards, who had also brought Lorraine Hansberry's *A Raisin in the Sun* to Broadway in 1959—the first Broadway production written by an African-American woman—was able to employ several of the actors who had initially made the play a success at Yale and later at the Walter Kerr Theatre on Broadway: Charles S. Dutton as Boy Willie, Carl Gordon as Doaker, Tommy Hollis as Avery, and Lou Myers as Wining Boy. Alfre Woodard was cast to play Berniece, and Courtney B. Vance to play Lymon. The result was a very high quality production, far better than could ordinarily be expected on commercial television.

Wilson was able to retain the play's original dialogue, for the most part, and Richards was able to open up the play, though not, perhaps, to the extent that the audience would forget that they were watching a play. Willie Boy and Lymon arrive with a watermelon truck, and the film shows them selling watermelons in such a way that Willie Boy appears to be more appealing and not simply the opportunistic materialist he seemed in the play. Some of the other exterior scenes, such as showing Avery at his job as elevator operator, do not really add substance to the drama. More importantly the film dramatizes the family history that the carved piano represents. The film ends with Berniece and her daughter Maretha (Zelda Harris) at the piano, an appropriate closure, since Berniece has wanted to keep the piano so that Maretha could learn to play it.

In general the characters as seen in the film are not as hard-edged as they first seemed in the play. Willie Boy emerges as a more genial and comic character in the film. As Willie Boy says at the end of the play, "Hey Berniece . . . if you and Maretha don't keep playing on that piano . . . ain't no telling . . . me and Sutter both liable to be back." Willie Boy's words reflect a kind of comic bravado that indicates his acceptance of the need for this reconciliation not only with the family, but also with the past. The "lesson" this piano has to teach therefore goes far beyond music. It is a lesson of hardship, travail, endurance, and reconciliation, a lesson that is appropriately taught by the adapted film and one that all viewers could learn from.

REFERENCES

Bogumil, Mary L., *Understanding August Wilson* (Columbia: University of South Carolina Press, 1999); Nadel, Alan, ed., *May All Your Fences Have Gates: Essays on the Drama of August Wilson* (Iowa City: University of Iowa Press, 1994); Pereira, Kim, *August Wilson and the African-American Odyssey* (Urbana: University of Illinois Press, 1995).

—*J.M.W. AND T.L.E.*

PICNIC (1953)

WILLIAM INGE (1913–1973)

Picnic (1955), U.S.A., directed by Joshua Logan, adapted by Daniel Taradash; Columbia Pictures.

Picnic (2000), U.S.A., directed by Ivan Passer, adapted by Shelly Evans; CBS Television.

The Play

Picnic was playwright William Inge's second Broadway hit, following the success of *Come Back, Little Sheba* in 1950. Inge was born in Independence, Kansas, and educated at the University of Kansas in Lawrence. On his way to New York, he worked as drama critic for the St. Louis *Star-Times* from 1943 to 1947. He certainly understood the loneliness and frustration his characters might have experienced in rural Kansas, which was to become the material of his dramatic art. *Picnic* tells the story of Flo Owens (Peggy Conklin), the matriarch of a fatherless family, who wants only the best for her daughters Millie (Kim Stanley) and Madge (Janice Rule). Millie, a sort of tomboy, still in high school, is a good student who is clearly bound for college, but she is eclipsed by her beautiful sister, Madge, who works at the dime store in the small Kansas town where the family lives. Millie, "the smart one," is jealous and resentful of Madge, "the pretty one," winner of a local beauty pageant at the Labor Day picnic that stands at the center of the play.

If the Labor Day picnic is the central event here, the action of the play is a bit off-center, since it is set entirely at the Owens house. Flo's fantasy is that Madge will marry Alan Seymour (Paul Newman), the son of a wealthy local businessman, but the problem is that Madge is not in love with Alan. Flo's plans for Madge are further complicated when Hal Carter (Ralph Meeker), a muscle-headed drifter who had known Alan at college, comes to town in hopes that Alan will help him find work. Madge soon falls in love with Hal, who is therefore alienated from Alan. The action is structured before and after the picnic, which is not dramatized on stage. Act One begins the morning of Labor Day. Act Two continues through the "late afternoon," as the picnic outing is being organized by Flo; her neighbor, Mrs. Potts; spinster schoolmarm, Rosemary Sydney (Eileen Heckart), who boards with the Owens family; and her escort Howard Bevans, who runs "a little shop over in Cheeryville."

Alan plans to take Madge to the picnic. Hal will escort Millie. Alan claims that his father "found a place for Hal on the pipeline." Rosemary, the self-proclaimed "old-maid schoolteacher" who has had too much to drink before the act is over, makes a pass at Hal and rips his shirt. Madge comforts him and the act ends with a romantic embrace and the suggestion that they will not be attending the picnic. Act Three takes place after midnight and during "the morning after" Madge has lost her virginity to Hal, who wants her to go with him to Tulsa, against her mother's wishes, and Madge accepts his offer. Meanwhile, Rosemary has coerced Howard into making an honest woman of her, as the play reaches a conclusion that is more comic than tragic.

The play, then, is about lonely and frustrated women living without men in a rural setting. Madge takes the opportunity to escape with Hal to Tulsa, which was not the sort of ending Inge first imagined. This play and film had a curious history, as its making and unmaking was described by stage and film director Joshua Logan, who, in his memoirs, takes credit for shaping the vehicle into a Broadway success that ran 477 performances after opening at the Music Box Theatre on February 19, 1953. *Picnic* won both the Pulitzer Prize and the New York Critics Circle Award. As Logan remembers the process, William Inge kept rewriting the play's conclusion, right up until the opening night. Inge wanted the play to be utterly realistic in such a way that the ending would not have been a happy one. Logan campaigned for an open-ended and potentially rosy conclusion, and ultimately had his way.

The Films

In the first film adaptation, also directed by Joshua Logan, the emphasis shifts from loneliness, isolation, and sexual frustration to romance, with the relationship between Madge (Kim Novak) and Hal (William Holden) being romantically highlighted at the picnic, which becomes the centerpiece of the film. Inge wanted the play to have a downbeat ending, with Hal leaving Madge behind, her reputation soiled. Logan had convinced Inge to change the ending so that Madge would elope with Hal, arguing that Hal was such a potential loser that Madge's future in Tulsa would be doubtful. But the film nudges the ending even more toward Hollywood happiness. As played by William Holden, Hal is not so rough a rogue as he seemed in the play and seems to embody more decency and potential. Logan opened up the play to include a spectacle of a Labor Day picnic that would reflect the imagined hometown values of rural America. In the film Hal and Madge actually attend the picnic, elaborately filmed on location in Salinas, Kansas, where Hal is embarrassed by Rosemary (Rosalind Russell), before driving off with Madge. Enraged by their behavior, Alan (Cliff Robertson) reports to the police that Hal has stolen the car he loaned to Hal.

In the film Alan's father owns the local grain elevator and storage operation, which Hal visits with Alan before the picnic and where Hal might be hired to scoop wheat. In other action invented for the film, Hal and Alan have a showdown at Alan's home after the picnic when Hal attempts to return Alan's car, and Hal escapes from the police, taking refuge later at the apartment of Howard Bevans (Arthur O'Connell), who lives above his store, which is now conveniently located downtown, and who helps Hal clarify his plans. Daniel Taradash wrote the screenplay that effectively extended the action and substituted romance for realism. The picture's success was reflected by Academy Award nominations for best supporting actor (Arthur O'Connell), best direction, and best picture; but the standout performance was Rosalind Russell's portrayal of the drunken and sexually frustrated Rosemary Sydney. The film is longer than the play and arguably more entertaining, but the edge is dulled.

The Josh Logan adaptation seems a model of fidelity, however, if one compares it to the CBS television adaptation directed by Ivan Passer. This extremely loose adaptation scripted by Shelly Evans updates the action to 1966, for no apparent reason other than to make the story seem relevant to viewers with short memories. It adds a new and different opening from the play or Logan's film by showing Hal Carter (Josh Brolin) walking down a country road into town, while Madge (Gretchen Mol) is doing a photoshoot at the dime store in the town of Elgin, as it's called. Howard Bevans (Chad Morgan) owns the store in this version. Millie (Jay O. Sanders) chases Bomber (Christopher Bills) out of town, and notices Hal washing himself up in a creek on the outskirts of town. Millie, a chipper hippie in this updated version, brings Hal into town and, although a suspicious Mrs. Evans (Bonnie Bedelia) has no work for him, Mrs. Potts (Marietta Marich) gives Hal yard work to do and feeds him, as in the Logan version. Explaining that he is from Staten Island, Hal claims that his wallet has been stolen on the road, probably a lame excuse for his indigence, but this time Hal carries fresh clothes in his duffel bag.

The action roughly parallels the play and the Josh Logan film. Hal meets Alan Benson (Ben Caswell) when Alan comes to visit Madge, and Alan takes Hal to the grain elevators, where Cliff Robertson took William Holden in the original film. In this version Alan's father has decided that Alan should go to law school. Rosemary (Mary Steenburgen) introduces herself to Hal as an "old maid schoolteacher," gets drunk at the Picnic, and tears Hal's shirt on cue at the dance, but Steenburgen's performance is not nearly as dramatic as Rosalind Russell's in Logan's film. Afterward

Rosemary clearly goes off with Howard to a motel, whereas in the earlier film exactly what had transpired between them was left ambiguous. When Howard takes her home later, her pathetic "Marry me, Howard!" plea is considerably downplayed, though she does ask the question. This film does not show Rosemary's schoolteacher chums.

When Hal and Madge dance together to the "Moonlight" theme (the only piece of music taken directly from the Logan film), they are by themselves, and when Madge leaves with Hal, he gives her new information about Alan. Hal explains that he was expelled from school because of a fight caused by Alan. Alan had wanted to use Hal's room for some privacy with a girl. The girl's boyfriend picked a fight with Hal, mistakenly blaming Hal for what Alan had done. So if Hal expects a favor from Alan in this film, it is because Alan owes him one. Hal has a similar argument with Alan after his escape with Madge, when he attempts to return Hal's car and is then pursued by the police. The next morning Howard is his messenger to Madge, who goes to see him at the shack where they had spent the night before, but she refuses to leave town with him at that point. Hal jumps a freight out of town, but does not seem to know where he is going. When Madge returns home, Alan comes by to offer her a wedding ring, but she refuses him, telling him she knows he had lied to the police about Hal. Madge then packs her bag and takes the first bus out of town, even though she does not know in this version where to find Hal. The Inge play has been almost entirely rewritten by Shelly Evans for this television dramatization and restructured after the model of the Logan film rather than the play itself. Although the acting is competent, it pales in comparison to the earlier Academy Award–winning picture.

REFERENCES

Logan, Joshua, *Josh: My Up and Down, In and Out Life* (New York: Delacourt, 1976); Voss, Ralph F., *A Life of William Inge: The Strains of Triumph* (Lawrence: University of Kansas Press, 1989).

—*J.M.W. AND J.C.T.*

PLAY IT AGAIN, SAM (1969)

WOODY ALLEN (1935–)

Play It Again, Sam (1972), U.S.A., directed by Herbert Ross, adapted by Woody Allen; Apjac/Rollins-Joffe/Paramount.

The Play

In the follow-up to his successful Broadway writing debut, *Don't Drink the Water* (1966), comic Woody Allen returned to the Great White Way in 1969 with *Play It Again, Sam*. This time, however, Allen had the confidence to write the leading role for himself. In a case of art imitating life (and also, perhaps, the reverse), the comic playwright-star used his protagonist, film buff Allan Felix, to parse out themes pertinent to both Allan *and* Allen. Neurotic, insecure, and unlucky in love, Allan, a timid film fan, is himself only when he's at the movies. In what passes for his "real" rather than "reel" life, Allan is a klutz, a nebbish, an awkwardly hyper-tense misfit who, although craving the company of women, can't get to first base. In fact, as the play opens, Allan's wife is walking out on him. "You're one of life's great watchers," she hisses. "I'm not like that, I'm a doer." Stung by the marital defection, Allan, as he sucks on unfrosted TV dinners, turns to Hollywood-inspired fantasies. As alluded to in the play's title, the most substantive of these emanations takes the form of Humphrey Bogart (Jerry Lacy). In the ensuing tussle between fantasy and reality, Bogart takes on the job of mentoring Allan in matters pertaining to both women and life.

Things get complicated when Allan's married friends, Linda (Diane Keaton) and Dick Christie (Tony Roberts), try to cheer up the hapless movie fan with a series of what prove to be comic-tragic dates. In the process, Allan and Linda become romantically involved for a night when Dick is out of town on business. It's a defining moment for both characters. Linda realizes that she really loves Dick, even though he seems more married to his job than to Linda. Allan, wracked by guilt, knows that he must press on and learn to stand on his own. Riffing on the end of *Casablanca* (1942), Bogart says: "You don't need me anymore. There's nothing I can show you, you don't already know." Allan responds: "I guess that's right. The secret's not being you, it's being me." In the play's upbeat coda, Allan meets Barbara, also an avid film fan. In contrast to his previous dates, Barbara is impressed with Allan for what he is, a film critic: "You're not *the* Allan Felix who writes for *Film Quarterly*, are you?" Of course, he is. And, with that, the curtain falls with romance and optimism in the air.

One of the most entertaining and insightful views of the modern antihero, *Play It Again, Sam*, a David Merrick production, opened successfully at the Broadhurst Theatre on February 12, 1969, and ran for 453 performances.

The Film

Although Woody Allen had already directed the movies *Take the Money and Run* (1969) and *Bananas* (1971), for the adaptation of *Play It Again, Sam*, Allen turned to Herbert Ross to lens his play. Thus, while the film's overall coherence and tight organization can be attributed in part to Ross, in terms of theme and comic invention, from beginning to end, *Play It Again, Sam* is a Woody Allen picture. The adaptation follows the play's script closely. With Allen, Keaton, Roberts, and Lacy reprising their stage roles, the rapport established among the principals on Broadway bloomed again in the reincarnation of the story for the big screen. The only real oddity, at least for Allen film fans, was the switch in location from New York to San Francisco, a geographical transposition imposed by a strike in the Big Apple.

In the film, the play's cinematic references are drawn with even greater detail. Allan's apartment is crammed with movie memorabilia. As Roger Ebert notes: "[Allan] sleeps beneath a poster for *Across the Pacific*, shaves with *Casablanca* reflected in the mirror, and fries his eggs across from *The Big Sleep*. There is no place in the apartment from which the names Mary Astor and Sydney Greenstreet cannot be read. He is a Humphrey Bogart fan. He is more than that. He is a Humphrey Bogart pupil." As in the play, whenever Allan confronts a crisis, Bogie appears, his trenchcoat collar turned up, the brim of his hat creased down over his eyes, and a Chesterfield dangling from his mug.

Still, Bogart's coaching has minimal impact. When Linda and Dick (Keaton and Roberts) fix him up with a nymphomaniac (Viva), Allan somehow manages to turn her off. With the genuinely sweet Sharon (Jennifer Salt), Allan's macho posturing brings the date to a quick end. And so it goes. Then, when Allan and Linda spend a night together, guilt is the result. There's also fear, fear that Dick will discover his wife's dalliance. In each of these crises, Bogart's advice comes to naught. In resolving the tortured romantic triangle, the intrinsic powers of the film medium come to the fore as Allan, Linda, and Dick play out a fantasy scene taken directly from *Casablanca*'s conclusion. Here, the image of the fog-shrouded runway is as vital, and poignantly comedic, as the paraphrases of *Casablanca*'s dialogue. As Allan departs, restored by a new sense of confidence, Bogart delivers his immortal line, "Here's looking at you, kid." Interestingly, the film deletes the play's final scene in which Allan meets Barbara, the young film fan. So, instead of the play's romantic solution, in the film, Allen moves to a loftier register where love is sacrificed to loyalty, and selfishness to honor.

Play It Again, Sam still strikes responsive chords, and not just for movie buffs appreciative of Allen's reflexively "inside" references to filmdom. Along with the arcane allusions to Erich von Stroheim, François Truffaut, and Ida Lupino, there is a more universal appeal based on the public's fascination with movie stars and their heroic larger-than-life adventures. Also, like Chaplin's Little Tramp, Allen's Allan is a protagonist who moves us through pathos. In Allen/Allan, as with Chaplin, we see ourselves as well as the character on the screen.

REFERENCES

Brode, Douglas, *Woody Allen: His Films and Career*, 2nd ed. (Secaucus, N.J.: Citadel Press, 1987); Girgus, Sam B., *The Films of Woody Allen* (Cambridge: Cambridge University Press, 1993); Jacobs, Diane, *. . . But We Need the Eggs: The Magic of Woody Allen* (New York: St. Martin's Press, 1982).

—C.M.B.

THE PLAYBOY OF THE WESTERN WORLD (1907)

JOHN MILLINGTON SYNGE (1871–1909)

The Playboy of the Western World (1962), Ireland, directed and adapted by Brian Desmond Hurst; Thorn/EMI.

The Play

Now considered modern Ireland's first great playwright, J. M. Synge, encouraged by the poet William Butler Yeats, went to the Aran Islands, off the west coast of Ireland in 1898 to study the folk culture and vernacular of the islanders. He later became a leader of the Irish Renaissance with Yeats and stood at the forefront of the Celtic Revival. The Aran Islands gave him the material and the distinctive language of his two greatest plays, first *Riders to the Sea* (1903), "perhaps the finest one-act play in English," according to Myron Matlaw, and his later masterpiece, *Playboy of the Western World* (1907). For four years (1898–1901) Synge spent his summers on the Aran Islands and the rest of the year in Paris. In 1902 he moved to Dublin to work with the Irish National Theatre Society, and later with the Abbey Theatre, after its founding in 1904. *Playboy of the Western World* was premiered by the Abbey and occasioned riots by Irishmen upset by Synge's national stereotyping.

"Everybody know about the *Playboy* riots of 1907," Irish scholar Harold Orel wrote in 1970, "a joyous Irish free-for-all, with uproars in the theatres, fist-fights, police arresting members of the audience, vigorous denunciations in the press ('Synge is the evil genius of the Abbey'), much shaking of heads, increased pressure of censorship; and then the whole business all over again when the Abbey players toured England and the United States. The play has since become one of the glories of the modern theatre, and its stage history is certainly one of the most fascinating stories of the century."

The action of the play is set "near a village, on the wild coast of Mayo." Act One begins on an autumn evening. Acts Two and Three take place the following day. The play is considered a tragicomedy because of its satirical treatment of the "heroism" of Christy Mahon, the main character, later berated and humiliated by the citizens of Mayo. The play begins in the "rough and untidy" public-house (pub) of Michael James Flaherty. Flaherty's daughter Margaret (called Pegeen Mike) is unhappily betrothed to her fool of a cousin, Shawn Keogh. Excitement comes into her life when Christy Mahon stumbles into the pub claiming to have killed his father with a spade. His bold deed captures the imagination of the locals. Flaherty hires Christy to work at the pub and to protect Pegeen. Synge satirizes the mythology and hero-worship that builds up around Christy. Pegeen and the Widow Quinn compete for his affection, and Christy is pleased to have "two fine women fighting for the likes of me."

All of this collapses the next day when Old Mahon, very much alive, with a bandage on his head, comes looking for his son in Act Two. Christy meanwhile successfully competes in village sports, further enhancing his "heroic" nature. Filled with confidence as "the champion Playboy of the Western World," Christy proposes marriage to Pegeen, who accepts, with the blessing of her soused father. At the top of his game, Christy's reputation quickly falls when Old Mahon finds him and beats and belittles him. Armed with another spade, Christy goes after his father again to finish the job he believed he had accomplished the day before, but now the crowd, including Pegeen, turns against him, intending to turn him over to the police. Like a bad penny, Old Mahon turns up again, alive, and frees his son so that the two of them can return home, saying "we'll have great times from this out telling stories of the villainy of Mayo, and the fools is here." At the end Pegeen laments, "I've lost the only Playboy of the Western World."

The Film

Irish director Brian Desmond Hurst (1900–86) had worked in Hollywood as an assistant to the Irish-Amer-

ican director John Ford for 10 years (1925–34) before returning to England to direct Synge's *Riders to the Sea* (1935), 28 years before he completed *The Playboy of the Western World*, starring Siobhan McKenna, perhaps the most famous Irish actress of her era. Pegeen Mike had been "one of her most celebrated stage roles," but by the time the film was made in 1962, she was too old to play a wild girl in her 20s. Jerry Vermilye defended her performance as an older and more mature woman, who might be exactly what the motherless Christy needs, but for Stanley Kauffmann she seemed "the coeval of the Widow Quinn, which badly unbalances the drama."

The film effectively opens up the play to visualize the mountains and sea coast of the West country. Christy Mahon (Gary Raymond) is first seen stumbling over the rocky shore of County Mayo at twilight. Stanley Kauffmann described the Irish as "the most word-intoxicated" speakers of the English language but regretted that "film is not primarily a verbal medium." He objected to what he considered the "dull" direction, protesting that Synge's dialogue "could not be much condensed for the picture because the plot would be meaningless without the fullness of the context, which means the fullness of the language. It would be like cutting to the plot of an opera," and, as with opera, "it is comfortable on the stage, uncongenial on the screen." Kauffmann, who is generally on target in his assessment of screen acting, considered Niall McGinnis the best of the cast as mad Old Mahon but complained that the English actor Gary Raymond was "so worried about his Irish accent" that he was unable to achieve the "ebullience and vigor" the role required.

Harold Orel was more positive. "Like many other Anglo-Irish plays, it needs an Irish cast for full flavoring," he wrote in 1970, "and the 1962 movie version is, praise be, almost entirely all-Irish. One ungallant suggestion: that Siobhan McKenna is too old to play Pegeen Mike, the young girl who falls for the poetic speeches of the playboy Christy Mahon, may safely be disregarded. Siobhan McKenna's plain, work-lined face comes fairly close to the kind of closed-in desperation of a young woman who fears she will never know romance. The rest of the cast is more than competent, but Elspeth March, as Widow Quinn, deserves particular mention. It is a joy to hear Synge's lines delivered as colloquial and ordinary speech by Irish actors who may not talk very differently off-camera from the characters they portray. And all of this is set against the breath-taking natural scenery of Ireland, handsomely photographed and directed as an opened-up stage play, with racing scenes on the beach, by Brian Desmond Hurst."

Orel considered the film version "enormously helpful to those who have difficulty imagining what Irish rhetoric *sounds* like, as well as to those who have been debating for years the identity of Synge's primary target. Is it, in fact, 'an unmitigated, protracted libel upon Irish peasant men and, worse still, upon Irish girlhood'—as a contemporary reviewer thought? Is it about Ireland at all, at all (since so many have emphasized its use of mythic elements)? At any rate," he concluded, the film "has not been widely shown in [America], and many persons who love the play may not realize that a first-rate film has been made from it." Harold Orel's defense offsets the withering criticism of others less in tune with Irish culture.

REFERENCES

Caughie, John, *The Companion to British and Irish Cinema* (London: Cassell/BFI, 1996); Gassner, John, and Edward Quinn, eds. *The Reader's Encyclopedia of World Drama* (New York: Thomas Y. Crowell, 1969); Kauffmann, Stanley, *A World on Film: Criticism and Comment* (New York: Delta, 1966); Matlaw, Myron, *Modern World Drama* (New York: E.P. Dutton, 1972); Orel, Harold, "K.U. Film Society Notes" (University of Kansas, May 11, 1970); Vermilye, Jerry, ed., *500 Best British and Foreign Films* (New York: William Morrow/Quill, 1988).

—*J.M.W.*

PLENTY (1978)

DAVID HARE (1947–)

Plenty (1985), U.S.A., directed by Fred Schepisi, adapted by David Hare; 20th Century-Fox.

The Play

Plenty premiered at the Lyttelton Theatre, London, on April 7, 1978, with production directed by playwright David Hare and starring Kate Nelligan as Susan Traherne, the lead character, who also played the lead in the New York Shakespeare Festival production that opened at the Public Theater on October 21, 1982. The latter production subsequently was moved to the Plymouth Theatre, opening on Broadway on January 6, 1983. In 1999 the play was revived in London, with Cate Blanchett playing the lead role. In a manner reminiscent of German expressionist drama, the story progresses in 12 brief scenes, or vignettes. Susan declines from innocent optimism to apparent insanity as the world changes around her. She keeps talking about a need to "move on," but she is constantly maladjusted.

The action begins in Easter 1962 with the breakup of her marriage to career diplomat Raymond Brock in

their Knightsbridge apartment in London. Scene Two propels the action backward in time to November 1943, when a 17-year-old Susan was serving as a Special Operations Executive Courier in occupied France during World War II, assisting a British operative known to her only by his code name, Lazar, who narrowly escapes being captured by the Germans. Susan's character is defined by her wartime service with the French Resistance. After the war is over, Susan has difficulty adjusting to civilian life.

In Scene Three (Brussels, 1947) Susan meets her future husband, Raymond Brock, and Sir Leonard Darwin at the British Embassy. She was having an affair with a fellow Resistance worker named Tony, who died, and they are tending after the details of returning Tony's body to England. Susan poses as the man's wife to Darwin, but counts on Brock's discretion to see that Tony's wife will not know that the two of them were traveling together. Later in 1947, Brock follows her to England, where she is sharing a flat with her Bohemian friend Alice Parks and is bored to death working for a shipping company. By Scene Five, set in 1951, Susan is working with the Coronation Committee and strikes up an affair with a working-class fellow named Mick, whom she wants to father her child, though she desires no lasting relationship. Susan is defined by her restlessness. Mick is unable to give her what she wants, and, having been rejected by Susan, complains, "It feels very bad to be used."

By Scene Seven (October 1956) Susan is married to Brock, hosting a dinner party for a Burmese diplomat and his wife and Darwin in the midst of the Suez Crisis. Darwin is about to resign from the Foreign Service because he was not properly informed about his government's policy in the Middle East and feels embarrassed and betrayed. Susan goes out of control and embarrasses her husband by confronting Darwin about his dilemma. In Scene Eight (July 1961) Brock and Susan have returned to London from Iran, where Brock has been assigned, in order to attend Darwin's funeral. (In the film Brock serves in Jordan, not Iran, and Alice visits Susan there.) By Scene Nine (January 1962), Brock has been recalled from Iran, and Susan indiscreetly visits Sir Andrew Charleston, Brock's superior at Whitehall, intending to advance Brock's career. She makes a terrible scene, however, and threatens to commit suicide if her wishes are not granted. As a consequence she destroys Brock's career. Scene 11 finds Susan at Blackpool, a shoddy resort city (July 1962), having an affair in a cheap hotel room with "Lazar," who managed to contact her as a result of a radio interview she had had. Scene 12 concludes the play by springing back in time to Susan in France in August

Meryl Streep starred in Fred Schepisi's adaptation of David Hare's play Plenty. (COURTESY TWENTIETH CENTURY-FOX)

1944, expressing her optimism to a farmer about the future: "We will improve the world," she says. Ironically she will not find fulfillment in Britain during the postwar era of "plenty" and eventual prosperity.

The Film

The challenge of this play, Hare explained in "A Note on Performance," is to maintain "a balance of sympathy for Susan" (Meryl Streep in Fred Schepisi's film). Brock (Charles Dance), he adds, a serious bureaucrat devoted to his work and to Susan, should not be "played as a fool." The film permits fluid transitions from scene to scene, though Hare did change the play's structure for the screenplay, removing the play's opening scene in Knightsbridge and opening and closing the film in France, 1944. In France Susan felt alive and vibrant in a way that would not continue after the war was over. Hare explains that 75 percent of the women flown behind the lines for the Special Operations Executive during the war "were subsequently divorced after the war," and the play dramatizes Susan's restlessness in this context. "Mental illness is it?" Darwin asks Brock after Susan's outburst at the dinner party, but Susan is not insane, merely bored with the life she finds in postwar England. Even Lazar seems transformed and ordinary when she is reunited with him in Blackpool, and she is not at all interested in his later life, the details of his career or his marriage.

The film's casting is splendid. Outstanding performances include John Gielgud as the betrayed diplomat Darwin, Ian McKellen as the chilly and formal diplomat Sir Andrew, Tracey Ullman as Susan's Bohemian friend Alice Parks, and Sting as Mick, who asks "I'd really like to know why you chose me," after Susan asks him to father her child. Brock had earlier asked her the same question, "Why did you choose me?" to notify Tony's wife that her husband had died of a heart attack in Brussels. Hare warns that it would be a mistake to play Brock as a fool. Rather, he is a decent man who sincerely cares for his disturbed wife but cannot hold their marriage together. Hare's political interpretation suggests that Brock is ruined by his dedication to an unworthy career in the Foreign Service, which becomes the Establishment paradigm for superficiality, stagnation, and hypocrisy. Colin Ludlow observed that "by relating Susan's experience to major historical events, Hare is able to suggest that her disillusion is representative rather than merely individual, and thus the play becomes a form of social commentary." The play consisted of 12 scenes out of chronological order, spanning nearly 19 years and tracing Susan's progression from optimism and idealism to bitterness and cynicism. Although the film establishes a less confusing chronological order and excises a few scenes, it is remarkably true to the spirit and intent of the original work.

REFERENCES

Ansen, David, "A Woman Against Her Time," *Newsweek* (September 23, 1985), 68; Kauffmann, Stanley "Revised Version," *The New Republic* (September 30, 1985), 26–28; Lawson, Steve, "Hare Apparent," *Film Comment*, 21:5 (1985), 18–22; Ludlow, Colin, "Hare and Others," *London Magazine*, 18 (July 1978), 76–81; Millar, Gavin, "The Habit of Lying," *Sight and Sound*, 54:4 (1985), 299–300.

—*J.M.W.*

THE POOR LITTLE RICH GIRL (1913)

ELEANOR GATES (1875–1951)

The Poor Little Rich Girl (1917), U.S.A., directed by Maurice Tourneur, adapted by Frances Marion; Artcraft/Paramount.

The Play

Eleanor Gates began a dramatization of her novel, *The Poor Little Rich Girl*, a year after its publication in 1912. It proved to be one of many "growing girl" plays on stage at the time. Reporting in *Everybody's Magazine*, Clayton Hamilton wrote, "Although we have had many plays for children in the past, most of them have been produced singly and have been regarded as unusual events; but in this season, for the first time, a concerted effort has been made by several different managers to develop in the rising generation a habit of going regularly to the theater."

Gates's original novel is a remarkable cautionary tale of the consequences of adult and parental neglect of children, told entirely through the viewpoint of seven-year-old Gwendolyn. The miracle is that the reader, while cognizant only of what Gwendolyn sees and hears, is able to construct a reality quite beyond the child's understanding. Little Gwendolyn lives in a gilded cage of a house, in an upper room kept well away from her parents and the adult activities downstairs. She is not allowed to attend public school, but is instead tutored at home by a retinue of private teachers. Her mother is preoccupied with her social functions, and her father is buried in his downtown business deals. The servants offer little solace or company. Miss Royle, the governess, is bossy and cold; Thomas the butler is preoccupied with his love life; and Jane the nurse would rather go shopping. They refuse her wish to wear ordinary clothes and to go barefoot outdoors; instead, they confine her to the shuttered limousine during outings. These restrictions are not so much for Gwendolyn's own good as to allow the servants more time for their own activities.

As a result of an accidental overdose of medicine, Gwendolyn lapses into a dangerous coma. She falls into a series of dreams that occupy the entire second half of the narrative. All the things she has overheard—but not understood—come to literal life. Metaphors assume shape and substance—like Jane having "eyes in the back of her head," like the policeman being "head over heels" in love with Jane, like her mother's "bee in the bonnet," like her father's "burning the candle at both ends," and like Miss Royle being a "snake in the grass."

Accompanied by the friendly Organ Grinder, Gwendolyn embarks on a search for her parents. Finally, after besting her enemies, including the deceitful, selfish servants, she awakens to the ministrations of her anxious parents and the family doctor. With the assurance that the wicked servants will be banished, the father pledges to put the family business aside long enough to take them all on a long trip to the country. Gwendolyn happily sinks back to sleep.

When Eleanor Gates adapted the novel into a three-act play version, subtitled "A Play of Fact and Fancy," she conflated the narrative of weeks into the hours just before, during, and after Gwendolyn's seventh birthday dinner. It premiered at the Hudson Theatre in New York on January 22, 1913. The characters of the friendly Organ Grinder and the Plumber are fleshed out; and the Wall Street woes of the father are depicted in greater detail. The metaphors-come-to-life, like the "snake-in-the-grass" governess and the "two-faced" nurse, lose the subtlety they enjoyed on the printed page, although on stage they gain a charm of their own as frankly artificial costumes and props. The entire second act is devoted to the dream sequence. It garnered special praise from the critics. "This psychological idea, which is at once surprisingly original and profoundly true, is developed by the author in innumerable fanciful details," wrote critic Clayton Hamilton. "It would be impossible to praise this second act too highly; for it is the greatest contribution to the literature of dreams that has been effected since Rudyard Kipling wrote 'The Brushwood Boy.'"

The Film

Although she had probably not read the novel, actress Mary Pickford had certainly seen the stage production at the time she was appearing on Broadway in David Belasco's production of *The Good Little Devil*. Doubtless she was struck by the healthy contrast little Gwendolyn presented in comparison with her current role as the saintly little blind girl, Juliet. The product of a difficult childhood herself, Pickford must have related to Gwendolyn's use of her imaginative gifts to cope with, rather than escape from, the complexities, cruelties, and betrayals of the adult world. Pickford's choice of her friend, Frances Marion, to adapt the play to the screen was most fortuitous. Like Mary, Frances was tough, self-reliant, and self-supporting since childhood. She knew the classics of literature, and with her feminist sensibilities, saw in works like *The Poor Little Rich Girl* the chance to present a protagonist of unusual intelligence, vivacity, and individuality. Pickford and Marion would collaborate on many other successful films in the

Mary Pickford appeared on screen for the first time as a little girl in her adaptation of Eleanor Gates' play The Poor Little Rich Girl *in 1917.* (COURTESY MARY PICKFORD FOUNDATION/TIMELINE FILMS/MILESTONE FILMS)

next six years, including *A Little Princess* (1917), *Stella Maris* (1917), and *Pollyanna* (1920).

The Poor Little Rich Girl was filmed in Fort Lee, New Jersey, under the direction of Maurice Tourneur. Marion's scenario aged Gwendolyn by four years. A series of concise title cards quickly establish the setting and characters. For example, views of the family mansion are prefaced by a title card, reading, "In the Home of Everything—except for the Love she longed for, dwells Gwendolyn, the Poor Little Rich Girl." The two tall footmen in charge are "The Tyrants of Modern Civilization—by Position, Servants, by disposition, Masters." The dour governess and teacher are described as "Grim Wisdom's Teachers." And framed in long shot, flanked by tall doors, she plays alone with her toys, as a title card proclaims: "Empty Hearts. Empty Lives. Empty Homes. Poor Little Rich Girl." Reinforcing the child's size and limited viewpoint are oversized sets and props designed by Ben Carre, a supporting cast of tall children and adult performers, and a consistent use of low-angle camera positions. Here is a world that, in

Gwendolyn's eyes—and ours—seems outsized and strange. Her fanciful distortions of the adult vernacular are conveyed through a series of metaphors come to literal life. If Wall Street is referred to as "full of bears," she promptly visualizes an attack on her father by huge, bear-like creatures. Added scenes emphasize Gwendolyn's sturdy individuality, such as the long sequence when she battles the spoiled brat Susie May, and the mud fight in the garden with the neighborhood gang of boys.

The elaborate dream sequence contains some of the most charming fantasy work ever seen on screen. Staged with ingenuous simplicity rather than technical sophistication, it relies on painted sets and costumed creatures—just as on stage. However, the entire sequence is lensed in a wholly cinematic fashion. The sequence is initiated by skewed camera angles that function as a visual correlative to her mental imbalance. Subsequent adventures in the dream world are cross-cut with Gwendolyn in her sick bed, reinforcing the connections between the materialized metaphors of the dream and real-life events of the waking world. In a striking departure from both novel and play, Gwendolyn ventures beyond the dark forest to the towering gates of Wall Street, where she finds her father grinding out money from a machine-like contraption that prefigures the "Moloch" of Fritz Lang's *Metropolis* 10 years later. In another added bit of action, Gwendolyn, nearing death, meets a shrouded figure in a cemetery who offers her "eternal sleep." But, after a moment's hesitation, she refuses the invitation, turning instead toward the sunlit image of a young girl who offers her renewed life. Struggling back to consciousness, Gwendolyn greets her anxious parents, while a succession of quick shots flash-forward to a vision of their family life together in the country.

A 25-year-old woman's transformation into an 11-year-old girl was no mean achievement, but in facial expression and physical posture, Pickford is utterly convincing. The scene where she indulges her tomboy attitude is especially memorable. Gwendolyn's father has punished her by dressing her in boy's clothes. Sulkily, she regards herself in the mirror. Surprised by the agreeable image, she tosses her curls, poses and struts, adjusts her cap, and enjoys the luxury of trouser pockets. This delicious piece of cross-dressing humor—not to mention Pickford's delightful pantomiming of a quick succession of childlike mannerisms—is more incisively satiric and convincing than all 10 reels of her later impersonation of the boy Cedric in *Little Lord Fauntleroy* (1921).

The Poor Little Rich Girl was released by Artcraft/Paramount on March 5, 1917. It was, as biographer Scott Eyman declared, "a landmark film for [Pickford], one that exercised a major influence over the rest of her career." Her 11-year-old Gwendolyn marked her first attempt on screen to portray a girl so young, but it would hardly be her last. Audiences loved Pickford and they loved Gwendolyn. To Pickford's growing dismay, they began to confuse the two. "Every now and then," she recalled, "as the years went by and I continued to play children's roles, it would worry me that I was becoming a personality instead of an actress. I would suddenly resent the fact that I had allowed myself to be hypnotized by the public into remaining a little girl."

REFERENCES

Beauchamp, Cari, *Without Lying Down: Frances Marion and the Powerful Women of Early Hollywood* (New York: Scribner's, 1996); Dodge, Wendall Phillips, "The Maude Adams of the 'Movies,'" *The Theatre Magazine*, 18 (June 1913), 176–178; Eyman, Scott, *Mary Pickford: America's Sweetheart* (New York: Donald I. Fine, 1990); Hamilton, Clayton, "The Players," *Everybody's Magazine*, 27:4 (April 1913), 513–515; Pickford, Mary, "The Greatest Business in the World," *Colliers*, June 10, 1922, 22–23; "Poor Little Rich Girl—Something New in the Drama," *Current Opinion*, 54:3 (March 1913), 291–295.

—*J.C.T.*

PRIVATE LIVES OF ELIZABETH AND ESSEX, THE

See *ELIZABETH THE QUEEN*

PYGMALION (1913)

GEORGE BERNARD SHAW (1856–1950)

Pygmalion (1938), U.K., directed by Anthony Asquith and Leslie Howard, adapted by W.P. Lipscomb and Cecil Lewis; General Films/MGM.

The Play

Pygmalion is the best known play of England's greatest playwright since Shakespeare, Dublin-born George Bernard Shaw. The five-act *Pygmalion* updates the Greek myth about a sculptor who rejects all women in favor of the perfectly formed creature of his own creation. When she comes to life, they marry. In the first act of Shaw's version, Professor Higgins, a linguist (the Pygmalion figure), and Eliza Doolittle, a Cockney

George Bernard Shaw

flower girl (the Galatea figure), meet in Covent Garden. In Act Two Eliza comes to Higgins' digs and asks him to teach her how to speak like a "lady." In Act Three Higgins and his genial colleague, Colonel Pickering, transform Eliza's speech, manners, and behavior so much that she convinces another linguist that she is a Hungarian princess. In Act Four, Eliza, who has successfully passed herself off as a duchess, leaves Higgins when he begins to treat her as a possession. Acts Four and Five constitute a "discussion" of the consequences of her actions. Eliza talks to free herself, and Higgins talks to maintain his domination over her. The verbal sparring between Eliza and Higgins is one of the glories of the contemporary theatre. As commentator Eric Bentley notes, "Higgins will never marry. He wants to remain in the relation of God the Creator as far as Eliza is concerned. For her part Eliza will marry. But she won't marry Higgins." Thus, at the end of the play, Eliza returns to Higgins, but vows to marry Freddy (a development Shaw defends in the play's postscript). Shaw has ultimately inverted the Greek myth: Instead of Pygmalion turning a statue into a human being, Shaw's Higgins has attempted to turn a human being into a statue (like a mechanical doll in the role of a duchess).

Eric Bentley maintains that *Pygmalion* is one of Shaw's most "personal" plays. "It is Shavian," he writes, "not in being made of political or philosophic discussions, but in being based on the standard conflict of vitality and system, in working out this conflict through an inversion of romance, in bringing matters to a head in a battle of wills and words, in having an inner psychological action in counterpoint to the outer romantic action, in existing on two contrasted levels of mentality, both of which are related to the main theme, in delighting and surprising us with a constant flow of verbal music and more than verbal wit."

The Film

Though at first distrustful of "movies," Shaw had long been interested in photography and eventually recognized the film medium as a potentially revolutionary social force. Gabriel Pascal, a self-styled film producer, met Shaw in 1935 and persuaded the playwright to permit him to produce his plays on film. "I said that I would make no picture with box-office compromises. And I think the old man believed in my love of art, that's all. There's no mystery about it." Shaw later admitted he had been quite taken with Pascal's charm: "A delightful creature, but quite outside all ordinary rules." Pascal's three adaptations of Shaw—*Pygmalion* (1938), *Major Barbara* (1941), and *Caesar and Cleopatra* (1944)—for his own production company, General Films, would not only be successes, but they would also represent a more enlightened attitude on Shaw's part toward the recognition of a more "cinematic" union of play text and camera.

Despite his lack of experience—and Shaw's notorious insistence that his text remain inviolable—Pascal was able to secure enough backing to set to work on *Pygmalion* at the Pinewood Studios, near London. Shaw had seen a new young actress named Wendy Hiller in a comic play called *Love on the Dole*, and he determined that she was the perfect Eliza. He objected at first to Pascal's choice of Leslie Howard as Higgins, charging that the audience would like him and want him to marry Eliza—"Which is just what I don't want"—but he eventually capitulated. In all, 14 new scenes were either

written by Shaw or approved by him. The opening scene establishes in purely visual terms the feel and atmosphere of Covent Garden. At the end of what was Act One, the movie adds a second new scene that establishes the details of Eliza's home neighborhood in Angel Court. At the beginning of what was Act Two, there is additional business regarding Higgins' elaborate phonetic equipment. Shortly thereafter, Eliza's bath scene is considerably amplified with a montage of shots, as is the ordeal of her "lesson" with Higgins. Immediately afterward there is an elaborate, 10-minute Embassy Ball scene, which had been merely an offstage garden party in the play. Here, Eliza's triumph is communicated in purely visual terms, with tracking shots, alternating close-ups and long-shots of the ballroom and the dancers, and a fair amount of quick cutting to denote the passage of time.

Other additional scenes include a street scene that establishes continuity between Acts Four and Five, wherein Freddy first kisses Eliza; a dialogue between the now-ladylike Eliza and a flower girl in Covent Garden; scenes in which Higgins sounds the alarm for the errant Eliza; and, most startling of all, a two-minute scene in which Higgins and Eliza are reunited, although somewhat ambiguously. Shaw originally had wanted the film to end with an epilogue where Eliza and Freddy are married and run a flower shop. That Shaw capitulated at all is nonetheless a mystery: "What kind of hypnotic powers Pascal, Asquith, and Howard used over Shaw to get him to leave out his flower shop and to approve the final ending of the film only the gods now can tell us," notes commentator Costello. Nonetheless, as Costello adds, it is likely that Shaw never intended this new ending to imply that they were to be permanently united.

Despite these concessions, Shaw did maintain close supervision of the project. "I showed him the still photos weekly," Pascal recalled, "and he immediately recognized with his critical eye the development of the characters by the players. He saw the slightest faults in their makeup or in their portrayal, or the slightest error in sets and décor, and he became my second artistic conscience."

Even if the social dimension of *Pygmalion* is weakened in favor of the romantic Cinderella-like story, the finished film is a triumphant union of Shavian satire and cinematic effect. "The film combines elements of spectacle and movement, speed and surprise, and musical and lighting virtuosity to create a visual excitement which parallels the emotional and intellectual excitement at such climactic scenes as Eliza's lessons and Eliza's triumph at the Ball," concludes Costello. "But the film also creates a visual excitement throughout, at less climactic moments, as the camera races about, often blurring in its speed, as it tries to keep with a restless Higgins who is often chasing after a fearful Eliza . . . The cinema's increased powers of visualization accompanying the dialogue are used in *Pygmalion* for increased humor as well as for increased dynamism." The music by Arthur Honegger likewise enhances background mood and the viewer's emotional reactions, whether romantic in the ballroom, exciting in the laboratory scenes, or nostalgic in the repetition of the ballroom waltz when Eliza returns to Higgins. Viewers responded. The film opened at the Leicester Square Theatre in London on October 6, 1938, to popular and critical enthusiasm. In America, the film broke box-office records, to the astonishment of *Variety* (which trotted out its usual boffo adjectives like "hot" and "smash").

In 1941 Shaw published a new Penguin edition of *Pygmalion* that contained seven of the new scenes that had been incorporated into the screenplay. He referred to these additions as "technically possible only on the cinema screen or on stages furnished with exceptionally elaborate machinery."

REFERENCES

Bentley, Eric, *Bernard Shaw* (New York: Limelight Editions, 1985); Costello, Donald P., *The Serpent's Eye: Shaw and the Cinema* (Notre Dame, Ind.: University of Notre Dame Press, 1965); Pascal, Valerie, *The Disciple and His Devil: Gabriel Pascal and Bernard Shaw* (New York: McGraw-Hill, 1970).

—*J.C.T.*

QUEEN ELIZABETH (1911)

EMILE MOREAU (1852–)

Queen Elizabeth (1912), France, directed and adapted by Louis Mercanton; Film d'Art/Famous Players.

The Play

The legendary, 68-year-old Sarah Bernhardt brought her new stage vehicle, *Queen Elizabeth*, costarring her current consort, 27-year-old Lou Tellegen, to America in 1912. These were years fraught with a strange mixture of triumph and failure for the "Divine Sarah." After her past stage successes like *La Tosca*, *La Dame aux Camelias*, and *L'Aiglon*, it was now becoming increasingly difficult for her devotees (and herself) to ignore her advancing age. A chronic knee problem was worsening and would soon lead to a leg amputation. Moreover, her association/affair with Tellegen had brought her a measure of public and private embarrassment. They had been lovers since 1910, when they toured the United States together for her second "farewell" tour. If the handsome but inept Tellegen's notices were generally negative, hers at least included some generous encomiums. Critic Channing Pollock enthused, "If Bernhardt's fires are burning out, they are burning out brightly and the departing flare, if it be a departing flare, is something approaching a blaze of glory. She represents the highest reaches of her art, thus far, and perhaps even for all times."

Bernhardt and Tellegen's last American tour ended at the Palace Theatre in New York in 1913. It was then that they parted company. "Every moment I worked with her I knew the best that the theatre can give," wrote Tellegen a few years later; "and, remembering the most glorious four years of my life, my eyes fill with tears and my heart again cries out 'Madame! Grande Madame! I am so alone without you!" In 1916 in America, Tellegen married the celebrated opera and film star, Geraldine Farrar, and achieved some success of his own in silent films. But after they parted two years later, his career began a long decline, ending in suicide in 1934. As for Bernhardt, with the war in Europe and the amputation of her leg, she slipped into retirement, appearing only sporadically on stage until her death on March 26, 1923.

Queen Elizabeth, playwright Emile Moreau's story of the presumed affair between Elizabeth I of England (Bernhardt) and Robert Devereaux, earl of Essex (Tellegen), was a fictionalized treatment of historical incidents. The play begins with the young Elizabeth's triumph over the Spanish Armada and concludes with the old queen's disillusionment and death. The main dramatic action concerns the unfaithful earl's betrayal of Elizabeth. He is subsequently marched off to the headsman's ax. Elizabeth, old, sick, and heartbroken, dutifully expires and falls lifeless onto a pile of cushions.

Sarah Bernhardt's Queen Elizabeth, *released by Famous Players in America in 1912, was one of the screen's first feature-length theatrical films.* (COURTESY NATIONAL FILM SOCIETY ARCHIVES)

The Film

While a curiosity piece to today's viewers, the theatrical film of Bernhardt's *Queen Elizabeth* is nonetheless a milestone in the history of the theatrical film. Its exhibition in America not only fueled the growing interest in feature-length films—spearheaded by D.W. Griffith, Thomas Ince, and others—but it also brought a new "legitimacy" to the film medium by playing in theatre houses and attracting the attention of prominent dramatic critics. The four-reel film also sparked a controversy in debating what constitutes the "proper" adaptation of stage to screen that persists to this day. It was filmed in France by the prestigious Film d'Art company, organized in 1908 for the express purpose of aligning theatre and film personnel to bring famous plays to the screen "to raise the prestige of the cinema and erase the memory of its lowly past." It was distributed in America by movie theatre exhibitor Adolph Zukor and theatrical entrepreneur Daniel Frohman

through their newly-formed Famous Players company, after first "premiering" at Frohman's Lyceum Theatre on Broadway on July 12, 1912. Frohman is a key figure in this story, inasmuch as he was one of the few leaders in the American theatre establishment willing to have his name publicly linked with motion pictures. The *New York Dramatic Mirror* reported that Frohman was one of those visionaries who "have become fully convinced that the time for the amalgamation of the legitimate stage and the motion picture has come. . . . It is felt that the last barrier has been removed between the picture and the stage. . . . The films will comprise for the most part past and present successes of the European and American stage."

Contrary to popular belief, *Queen Elizabeth* was *not* Bernhardt's first appearance on screen. She had made several other films, beginning in 1900 with *Le Duel d'Hamlet* and continuing with *La Tosca* in 1906 and *Camille* and *La Dame aux Camelias* in 1911 (with Tellegen as her costar). "I have conquered a new world," she told her American manager, William F. Connor. "I never thought, my dear William, that I would ever be in a film but now . . . I rely for my immortality on these records." Her current American tour of the play of *Queen Elizabeth* sparked unusually lively interest in the film version, and Zukor and Frohman negotiated a $35,000 purchase of the American exhibition rights from the Rex Company. Although the film did brisk box-office, it looked positively creaky compared to the sturdy outdoor dramas of Griffith and Ince. This is not to say that the filmmakers were primitives working in an untried medium. Rather, they set out to make a *theatrical* film, and that is exactly what they did. Like a program book, title cards introduce each "scene," or tableau—i.e., an uncut length of film encompassing a single piece of stage business. The static camera placements keep the players in frontal alignment, full-figure, approximating a viewer's vantage point from third-row center. The exaggerated acting style is an example of what commentator Montrose Moses once described as "strenuous acting in a mechanical age." Actors enter and exit from the "wings" of the frame. Painted backdrops and artificial props are employed. And at the end, each of the players reappear for a final "bow" to the viewer. In his book, *The Gilded Stage*, Henry Knepler claims that the film employed the original stage sets. He also confirms the suspicion that Bernhardt could not have cared less about the "immortality" the screen might grant her; rather, her appearance was an attempt to recoup some of the 200,000 francs she had lost mounting the stage production and tour.

The initial success of the film convinced Zukor and Frohman to make more feature-length theatrical films that would frankly imitate a proscenium stage illusion. Joining the artistic staff at the Famous Players New York studios, located in the top two stories of an old armory on West 26th Street, were veteran directors Edwin S. Porter and J. Searle Dawley and stage producer Hugh Ford. Over the next few years, they produced more Famous Players theatrical features, including James O'Neill's *The Count of Monte Cristo* (1913), Minnie Maddern Fiske's *Tess of the d'Urbervilles* (1913), and James K. Hackett's *The Prisoner of Zenda* (1913).

Almost immediately these films aroused a critical controversy. Some critics, like W. Stephen Bush in *The Moving Picture World*, gushed that *Queen Elizabeth* was "a rare and most creditable achievement" and praised its "accuracy in historical detail," notwithstanding its painted sets and backdrops. In sum, "When motion pictures present such a faithful study in history no praise can be too great for them." By contrast, commentator Robert Grau found the theatrical artifice of it and other Famous Players releases irritating: "A majority of those who had seen these pictures on the screen would emphatically state that they did not wish to renew the experience." A year later, Louis Reeves Harrison implored filmmakers to cease these frankly theatrical illusions: "Screen visualization is an entirely different art, at its best when freed from the artificial limitations imposed by dramatic construction for stage performance." Not surprisingly, D.W. Griffith greeted it and others of its ilk with displeasure. "The conditions of the [stage and screen] being so different," he said, "it follows that the requirements are equally dissimilar. Stage craft and stage people are out of place in the intense realism of motion picture expression."

REFERENCES

Bush, W. Stephen, "Queen Elizabeth," *The Moving Picture World*, 13:5 (August 3, 1912), 428–429; Gold, Arthur, and Robert Fizdale, *The Divine Sarah: A Life of Sarah Bernhardt* (New York: Alfred A. Knopf, 1991); Grau, Robert, *The Stage in the Twentieth Century* (New York: Broadway Publishing Co., 1912); Tibbetts, John C., *The American Theatrical Film* (Bowling Green, Ohio: Bowling Green University Press, 1985).

—*J.C.T.*

A RAISIN IN THE SUN (1959)

LORRAINE HANSBERRY (1930–1965)

A Raisin in the Sun (1961), U.S.A., directed by Daniel Petrie, adapted by Lorraine Hansberry; Columbia Pictures.

The Play

This groundbreaking three-act play was the first Broadway production written by an African-American woman. Directed by Lloyd Richards, it premiered on March 11, 1959, at the Ethel Barrymore Theatre, with Ruby Dee and Sidney Poitier as Ruth Younger and Walter Lee Younger. The action is set "in Chicago's Southside, sometime between World War II and the present" in an overcrowded apartment originally "arranged with taste and pride" but now marked by a certain "weariness" and "depressing uniformity."

Lena Younger (Claudia McNeil) is a widow who lives with her extended family, Walter Lee and his wife Ruth and their son Travis and Walter Lee's sister, Beneatha (Diana Sands), who hopes to become a doctor and is being courted by two men, the well-connected and prosperous George Murchison (Louis Gossett, Jr.) and a Nigerian suitor named Joseph Asagai (Ivan Dixon). Walter works as a chauffeur and desperately wants to improve his station.

Hansberry imagined the home and the play as being ruled by dominant matriarch Lena Younger. Sid-

ney Poitier was at odds with the playwright because he felt Walter Lee should not be depicted as a weakling unable to recover from a devastating loss. Poitier believed the play should evolve from Walter Lee's point of view rather than Mama's, which would have broken the stereotype of the matriarchal black family.

At issue is a $10,000 life-insurance payment owed to Lena as a consequence of her husband's death. She dreams of making a down payment on a house for her family in Clybourne Park, a mainly white neighborhood in the integrated suburbs; but Walter has other plans and hopes to establish a liquor store; unfortunately, he loses money on the scheme. One complication comes when a representative of the Clybourne Park Neighborhood Association visits the family to dissuade them from integrating the neighborhood by buying the house. The play may be seen as emblematic of the changing times and is made especially effective by its resounding human resonance.

The Film

Daniel Petrie's film was another breakthrough, since Columbia Pictures, the same studio that later financed Charles Fuller's *A Soldier's Play* in 1984, risked making a "race" picture about African-American family problems. Most of the Broadway cast made the transfer to the motion picture: Ruby Dee (Ruth), Sidney Poitier (Walter Lee), Claudia McNeil (Mama Lena), Diana Sands (Beneatha), Ivan Dixon (Asagai), and Louis Gossett, Jr. (George), who, like Poitier, was to become a

Hollywood star, though not of quite the same magnitude. In general, the cast was outstanding.

Although the confinement of the stage setting was metaphorically atmospheric, the film opened up the play by showing Walter at work as a chauffeur ("Mama, that ain't no kind of a job!") and at a bar, as well as on a family trip to the Clybourne Park neighborhood, when the grandson offers a gift of garden tools to Lena, who has somehow managed to nourish a plant that was doing poorly but has managed to survive, much like the family itself. Although he admits that the performances were "at times overblown," Donald Bogle praised the work of Poitier, Ruby Dee, and Diana Sands in particular. Bogle was less enthusiastic about Claudia McNeil, however, despite the "glowing reviews" she enjoyed in 1959: "Seen today," Bogle wrote in 1973, "McNeil seems grossly like the mammy of Hattie McDaniel vintage, but without the humor and spontaneity," adding that "she had the power but not the pathos required." The film was a successful integrationist drama, ahead of its times, showing American audiences the "grime and grit of the ghetto as never seen before" on the screen. The National Board of Review voted it one of the Ten Best Films of the Year.

REFERENCES

Bogle, Donald, *Toms, Coons, Mulattoes, Mammies, and Bucks: An Interpretive History of Blacks in American Films* (New York: Viking, 1973); Cheney, Anne, *Lorraine Hansberry* (Boston: G.K. Hall, 1984); Hansberry, Lorraine, *To Be Young, Gifted, and Black: An Informal Biography* (New York: New American Library, 1970); Poitier, Sidney, *The Measure of a Man: A Spiritual Autobiography* (San Francisco: Harper, 2000).

—*T.L.E. AND J.M.W.*

REIGEN (1897)

ARTHUR SCHNITZLER (1862–1931)

La Ronde (1950), France, directed by Max Ophuls, adapted by Jacques Natanson and Max Ophuls; Sacha Gordine.

La Ronde (1965), France, directed by Roger Vadim, adapted by Jean Anouilh; Paris Film Production.

The Play

Though published privately in Vienna in 1897, it was not until 1921 that Schnitzler's frank study of sexual mores received its first public performance in Berlin, where it provoked political riots and was judged obscene for "displaying the basest and most objectionable of human impulses." Set in Vienna at the turn of the century, the play explores attitudes toward sex through encounters between five men (a soldier, a young gentleman, a husband, a poet, and an aristocrat) and five women (a prostitute, a maid, a wife, a young woman, and an actress), with each character representing a different social class and paired in two different relationships. Each encounter serves to reveal the discrepancies between private and public morality, romantic and sexual desire. Though characters talk of love, sexual fulfillment is their goal, but since this desire can never be fully satisfied, new experiences are sought with alternative partners of a different social status. The unusual circular dramatic structure gives the play its title, with the action evolving through 10 self-contained but linked scenes in settings determined by the character pairings. The play opens with a soldier having sex with a prostitute on the banks of the Danube, followed by a scene at a dance-hall where he seeks satisfaction with a chambermaid; the maid is then seen with a young gentleman who in turn seeks pleasure with a married woman in her apartment; the adulterous wife is subsequently found in her bourgeois home with her husband pontificating on marital fidelity. This pattern of linked character situations continues with the hypocritical husband partnered with a young woman who in turn sleeps with a self-important poet. He is then paired with a celebrated actress who later entertains the aristocrat, who in the final scene is found waking from a night of excess with the prostitute of the opening scene. The circle is now complete.

The Films

Though essentially respecting Schnitzler's original narrative development in their reworking for the screen, Max Ophuls and his co-scenarist Jacques Natanson have nevertheless introduced a number of changes. The most significant is the addition of a master of ceremonies who addresses the film audience, prefaces each new episode with pointed verses from the theme song and, in various disguises, takes part in the action, whether simply talking to the characters or occasionally leading them from one experience to another. His presence constantly fractures the illusion of reality normally associated with the cinema, from the moment he is witnessed donning his master of ceremonies costume on what is clearly a film set, to his regular participation in the action and observations to the film audience. He uses a clapper board to introduce the episode between the chambermaid and the young man, intervenes to censor footage of the love scene between the count and the actress, and comments on changes in social attitudes toward sexual mores. The concept of the circle is made concrete in the form of a carousel he controls and which, like a revolving stage, permits both change of character and scene. The last three episodes (arguably the least successful in the play) have been reworked, with the scenes between the actress and the poet now located in the theatre, the meeting between the actress and the count shortened, while a flashback and voice-over are deployed in an abbreviated final episode. Throughout there is a toning down of language, especially in the early episodes where the play's references to sexual activity and sexual dysfunction are explicit and crudely stated.

For Ophuls, turn-of-the-century Vienna is transformed into a romantic city of dreams. The magnificent sets designed by Jean d'Eaubonne, with their atmospheric streets, glittering cafés, and sumptuous intimate apartments, are bathed in the gentle nostalgia of Christian Matras' black-and-white photography, through elaborate and characteristically fluid tracking shots; while the mood is confirmed in the evocative waltz theme of Oscar Strauss that punctuates the episodes. Whereas Schnitzler's view was primarily critical and cynical in tone, Ophuls is more indulgent toward his characters in order to provide a witty, more understanding satire of their human failings. As Karl Reiz notes, "In *La Ronde*, Ophuls' predilection for romanticizing grim, realistic material reaches its extreme . . . The script gives the episodes a framework of indulgent satire."

Given the nature of the narrative and the star cast he assembled, it is not surprising that *La Ronde* was Ophuls' most commercially successful film. The quality of performance from his highly talented cast was, apart from a rather disappointing Gérard Philipe as the Count, outstanding, particularly Simone Signoret as Léocadie, the prostitute, Serge Reggiani as Franz, the soldier, Daniel Gelin as Alfred, the young man, Danielle Darrieux as Emma Bretkopf, the married woman, and Simone Simon as Marie, the chambermaid. Among the most successful episodes were those that paired Gelin with Simone Simon and Danielle Darrieux. However, it was in Anton Walbrook, as the worldly-wise master of ceremonies invented by Ophuls, that the most electrifying and commanding performance is to be found.

Roger Vadim's remake, from a script by the playwright Jean Anouilh, updates the action to a decadent Paris of 1914 and, in the spirit of a more open sixties society, treats the sexual encounters much more explicitly and without the sophisticated subtleties that distin-

guished Ophuls' earlier version. The tone is comic rather than ironic, with additional emphasis on visual humor as eager but clumsy lovers are inclined to trip over each other. There is considerable strength in the re-creation of the prewar period, and Henri Decae's masterful Cinemascope photography in luxuriant color conjures up a decadent atmosphere. Particularly successful is the dance hall sequence where a craning camera looks down through suffused lighting at the dancers on the floor, with Michel Magne's romantic score completing the mood. Vadim is well served by Marie Dubois as the prostitute, Anna Karina as the maid, and Jean-Claude Brialy as the young gentleman; but he brings the most memorable performances from Catherine Spaak as the available young woman, Francine Bergé as the liberated actress, and from his own wife, Jane Fonda, as a beguiling, and seemingly innocent, adulterous partner to Maurice Ronet as the hypocritical husband.

REFERENCES

Beylie, Claude, *Max Ophuls* (Paris: Lherminier, 1984); Roud, Richard, *Max Ophuls* (London: British Film Institute, 1958); Williams, Alan, *Max Ophuls and the Cinema of Desire* (New York: Arno Press, 1980).

—*R.F.C.*

THE RISE AND FALL OF LITTLE VOICE (1992)

JIM CARTWRIGHT

Little Voice (1998), U.K., directed and adapted by Mark Herman.

The Play

Jim Cartwright's 1992 cabaret play, *The Rise and Fall of Little Voice*, brought actress and voice impersonator Jane Horrocks stardom on the London stage in the role of Laura Voss, or "L.V." ("Little Voice"). The action is divided between two locations, a sleazy cabaret platform and the tiny attic room of a sad, withdrawn young woman who barricades herself away from the outside world to worship in solitude the memory of her dead father by imitating the song styling of his favorite singers—Marilyn Monroe, Judy Garland, Shirley Bassey, and others. Alternating with L.V.'s song renditions are conversations and monologues among the members of the cabaret audience that advance L.V.'s backstory and the various subplots. The play came to

Broadway without Horrocks, who went on to a successful career in film, including Mike Leigh's *Life Is Sweet*, and on television, in the series *Absolutely Fabulous*.

The Film

In adapting the play to the screen, Mark Herman's first priority was to get Horrocks to reprise her stage role; and, second, to reconfigure the cabaret, revue-style show into a more traditional linear narrative. The characters and subplots are thus amplified and the action "opened up" to reveal the details of life in a dingy northern English town (Scarborough served as the location). L.V. is surrounded by a loud, frowsy mother who lives downstairs (Brenda Blethyn), a sweet but terminally shy boyfriend who's a telephone repairman and carrier pigeon trainer (Ewan McGregor), and a brash and rather seedy small-time talent promoter named Ray Say (Michael Caine). While conducting a tawdry romance with L.V.'s mother, Ray overhears the girl singing a Judy Garland song. Convinced he has a goldmine of talent on his hands, he pushes her into performing at a local cabaret called "Mr. Boo's." Although her singing creates a sensation, she lapses into a semicoma shortly thereafter, and Ray is unable to get her to repeat the performance. Instead, L.V.'s house is destroyed in a fire and she is rescued by Billy, with whom she has fallen in love. They reunite at the end and, together, tend his prized pigeons. Despite strong performances by all concerned, the movie scants Horrocks in her singing sequences. Only in one scene, when she has her big night at the cabaret—the setpiece of the film—is she permitted to cut loose and belt out a brief medly of Garland/Monroe/Bassey songs. Director Herman was determined to record the sound of this scene "live," eschewing the usual practice of lip-synching the songs to a playback. The results are electrifying, a tantalizing hint of how effective Horrocks must have been in the original stage presentation. In the narrow constrictions of a small stage, this offbeat fable of a timid, insecure woman finding her "voice" was quite engaging; but on the big screen, the fantasy is tied too securely to the trappings of reality, and the results are labored and strained.

REFERENCES

Schwarzbaum, Lisa, "Sing Out, Sister," *Entertainment Weekly*, 462 (December 11, 1998): 48, 50.

—*J.C.T.*

THE RITZ

TERRENCE MCNALLY (1939–)

The Ritz (1976), U.K., directed by Richard Lester, adapted by Terrence McNally; Columbia-Warner Bros.

The Play

The Ritz was originally developed at the Yale Repertory Theatre and opened on Broadway on January 20, 1975, at the Longacre Theatre, where it ran for a spectacular 400 performances. It was much admired for its set design and costumes by Michael H. Yeargan and Lawrence King. Rita Moreno was recognized for her performance as a next-to-talentless bathhouse singer, Googie Gomez. McNally's two-act play is a farce set in the Ritz, a steam bath catering to homosexuals. It is the story of an attempt by Cleveland garbage collector, Gaetano Proclo (Jack Weston), to escape from the hit man sent out by his brother-in-law Carmine Vespucci (Jerry Stiller). Gaetano, married to Carmine's sister Vivian (Ruth Jaroslow), is a fat and hapless man, who believes he has been marked for death on the orders of Old Man Vespucci. Gaetano flees, and his New York City taxi takes him to a gay bathhouse, where he tries to hide, since he presumes it to be an unlikely place for anyone to look for him. But he is pursued there by an old World War II service buddy, Claude Perkins (Paul B. Price), the "chubby chaser," who still has designs on the pudgy Gaetano. And he encounters another man, Chris (F. Murray Abraham), who sees him as a possible date or brief encounter.

A series of mix-ups is provoked by the entry on the scene of Michael Brick (Stephen Collins), an innocent detective hired by Carmine to track down Gaetano. Carmine arrives to meet up with Brick to get Gaetano. A crazy set of chases follows as Vivian comes on the scene to try to help her husband. Meanwhile, the entertainer Googie Gomez (Rita Moreno) falls under the misconception that Gaetano is a producer who can further her career as a singer. At a poolside talent show Gaetano does an Andrews Sisters–type routine with Claude and Chris to escape detection. Carmine orders everyone into the pool, but the bookkeeper casually recognizes Carmine as her employer. He owns the bathhouse, which explains how a taxi just happened to take Gaetano there in the first place. Carmine, threatened with public exposure for his involvement in the bathhouse by Vivian, is taken to jail at the end of the play. Thus Gaetano leaves with his life and his wife.

The Film

The film version was shot on a tight schedule at Twickenham Studios in England. It retained many of the leads from the Broadway cast, including Jack Weston as Gaetano, Paul B. Price as Claude Perkins, F. Murray Abraham as Chris, Rita Moreno as Googie Gomez, and Jerry Stiller as Carmine Vespucci. Treat Williams, who replaced Stephen Collins as Brick, stole the show with his unnaturally blonde hair and squeaky, high-pitched voice. Kaye Ballard took over for the lesser-known Ruth Jaroslow as Vivian. The production design by Philip Harrison and the costumes by Vangie Harrison were excellent, as was Paul Wilson's color cinematography.

A comedy set in a gay bathhouse is bound to be more troubling to audiences of today than to one in 1975, given the AIDS epidemic and the current controversies in the gay community about the advisability of closing and/or policing gay bathhouses. Fortunately, the play and the film of *The Ritz* are so lighthearted and frothy that it is still possible to enjoy this French-style farce set in Manhattan without feeling deeply distressed. The film is tastefully done, and much more attention is paid to the chase antics than to the goings on in the steam bath itself (which remains unseen behind a door). What remains vital in the film is the suggestion that sexual identity is fluid. The many mistakes in the plot made by characters concerning not only their sexual orientation but also the gender identities of the people they meet tend to support the position that sexual orientation is not so much natural as constructed. For example, Jack Weston's assumption that Rita Moreno is a transvestite retains its appeal since she *does* look like a female impersonator. The film also zeroes in on the tendencies of many gay men to assume that some heterosexual men they know are "really gay," even though they themselves do not know it yet. It also plays amusingly with the stereotypical notion that men of a certain physical build simply cannot be "gay." Neil Sinyard finds an undercurrent of sadness in the film through the juxtaposition of the bathhouse, which looks like nothing less than an ocean liner that has seen better days, and the dreary rainy atmosphere of the street outside. For him, it is a world in which people are living in fantasies, but whose dream world could come apart at any moment.

The film has not received much critical discussion, even among gay critics reevaluating gay cinema. Neil Sinyard's book on Richard Lester quotes him as saying that it was a "slight film," not as central to his work as his films for the Beatles, his two *The Three Musketeers* films, and his *Superman* films. Nevertheless, the film version is a better adaptation of a McNally's play than the later, more serious *Frankie and Johnnie at the Claire de Lune* and *Love! Valor! Compassion!*

REFERENCES

Roseneldt, Diane, *Richard Lester: A Guide to References and Resources* (Boston: G.K. Hall, 1978); Sinyard, Neil, *The Films of Richard Lester* (London: Croom Helm, 1985).

—P.C.

LA RONDE

See *REIGEN*

ROPE (1929)

PATRICK HAMILTON (1892–1977)

Rope (1948), U.S.A., directed by Alfred Hitchcock, adapted by Arthur Laurents; Warner Bros.

The Play

Inspired by the infamous Loeb-Leopold murder case, British playwright Patrick Hamilton's stage melodrama, which premiered in London in 1929, opens with two homosexuals, Wyndham Brandon and Charles Granillo, who have just strangled young Ronald Kentley, an acquaintance from their prep school days, just for the thrill of it. After stowing the lad's corpse in an ornate antique chest, they prepare to use it as a buffet table for an elaborate supper for Ronald's relatives and friends, including Ronald's father, Sir Johnstone Kentley, his aunt Mrs. Debenham, and ex-student friend Rupert Cadell, a foppish poet. Gradually, Cadell's suspicions are aroused by the mysterious absence of Ronald. After everyone leaves, Cadell returns and confronts the murderers, forcing them to open the trunk. Although Brandon pleads as justification his Nietzschean philosophy of "living dangerously," the unimpressed Cadell turns him and Granillo in to the police.

Amy Lawrence points out that Rupert is "a character straight out of Oscar Wilde"—foppish in dress and affected in speech, whose affectations border on effeminacy. Besides these suggestions that he is homosexual, Rupert is, in addition, named for the allegedly homosexual British poet Rupert Brooke. Lawrence concludes that Rupert accordingly gives the drama an "arch British drawing room quality" that "dates the play."

The Film

Alfred Hitchcock's film of *Rope* (1948) transplants the play's setting to New York City; more importantly, there is nothing of the effeminate fop in the character of Rupert Cadell as played in the film by the stalwart James Stewart. The action of *Rope* unfolds not only in a single setting but also in a single evening, so that the time span covered by the story corresponds to the running time of the finished film.

To emphasize the plot's uncompromising unity of time and place, Alfred Hitchcock committed himself to shooting the 80-minute movie in 10 unbroken takes of approximately 10 minutes apiece (the duration of a single reel of 35 mm film). Because each 10-minute reel was not broken up into a series of several individual shots, there was ultimately little need to edit the picture once it was shot. The overall effect of this cinematic sleight-of-hand would give the impression that the action moves along fluidly from beginning to end, without any discernible break, in one extended shot that runs the length of the entire movie; and, moreover, that the film viewer is duplicating the experience of watching a stage play.

However, since the action never strays from the suite of Brandon (John Dahl) and Philip (Farley Granger), Hitchcock saw to it that the movie did not turn into a static photographed stage play by keeping his camera perpetually on the go. It unobtrusively glides from one group of characters to another, closing in at times to capture a key gesture or remark, then falling back for a medium or long shot as the action and dialogue continue. Thus, by allowing the camera to draw the filmgoer into the scene and explore the action at close range, the director was, in effect, allowing the viewer to feel as if he were another guest at the ghoulish dinner party and not simply a remote observer watching the action from a distance like a spectator at a stage play.

At the film's climax Rupert returns to the boys' flat after all the other guests have gone and asks enough probing questions to give the two amateur murderers enough rope with which to hang themselves. When the moment of truth is finally at hand, Rupert throws open the chest to peer down on the corpse that he now assumes he will find there. He then opens a window to summon the police with a gunshot.

Rope was a pace-setter in its treatment of homosexuality in a way that was relatively forthright for American movies at the time. Scriptwriter Arthur Laurents remembers that, while the industry film censor allowed the homosexual implications of some of the dialogue to slip by him undetected, he demanded the deletion of some innocuous phrases in the dialogue that Laurents

had in fact brought over from the original English play. Expressions such as "dear boy" are commonly used by teachers and students in British boarding schools, and do not necessarily carry homosexual connotations at all.

Nonetheless, in spite of some censorial interference, Hitchcock depicted the homosexual ambience of the story in a satisfactory fashion. The two young men's over-decorated apartment, their "sympathetic" housekeeper, and their mutually resentful relationship with the dead lad's girlfriend all testify to the sexual orientation of the pair. Still, commentator Vito Russo notes that Jean Renoir, accustomed to the franker portrayal of homosexuality in European films, still thought that Hitchcock had skirted the issue too timidly in *Rope*. "I thought it was supposed to be about homosexuals," he remarked, "and you don't even see the boys kiss each other." Be that as it may, *Rope* is a finely crafted film, worthy of a respected place in the Hitchcock canon.

REFERENCES

Lawrence, Amy, "American Shame: *Rope*," in *Hitchcock's America*, ed. Jonathan Freedman and Richard Millington (New York: Oxford University Press, 1999), 55–76; Russo, Vito, *The Celluloid Closet: Homosexuality in the Movies*, rev. ed. (New York: Harper and Row, 1987); Sarris, Andrew, *"You Ain't Heard Nothin' Yet": The American Talking Film, 1927–49* (New York: Oxford University Press, 1998).

—G.D.P.

THE ROSE TATTOO (1951)

TENNESSEE WILLIAMS (1911–1983)

The Rose Tattoo (1955), U.S.A., directed by Daniel Mann, adapted by Tennessee Williams and Hal Kanter; Paramount.

The Play

The Rose Tattoo, which premiered in New York at the Martin Beck Theatre on February 3, 1951, is a toast to the resilience of the human spirit, as embodied in the heroine, Serafina Della Rosa (Maureen Stapleton). Serafina lives in a colony of Sicilian immigrants in the southern United States. When she is crushed by learning about the infidelity of her deceased husband, Rosario, she is rejuvenated by another, younger Sicilian, Alvaro Mangiacavallo (Eli Wallach)—whose last name literally means "Eat a horse" (suggesting his stallion-like virility). He is a happy-go-lucky, if not terribly intelligent, young man. Alvaro helps to restore Serafina's native warmth and affection, after her world had grown lonely and cold in the wake of her husband's demise and her subsequent disillusionment about him. "Everybody is nothing until you love them," says her daughter Rosa (Phyllis Love), a line that applies as much to Serafina as it does to Alvaro, and states the thesis of the play.

As the play progresses we learn that Rosario had a rose tattooed on his chest and that on the night on which Serafina conceived her daughter Rosa, a burning rose appeared mystically on her own breast for a moment. Not since the War of the Roses, comments John Mason Brown in his review of *The Rose Tattoo*, have roses been employed so significantly as a symbol: "To Mr. Williams roses are mystical signs, proofs of passion, symbols of devotion, and buds no less than thorns in the flesh." The Tony Award–winning play had a respectable run of more than 300 performances on Broadway.

The Film

Tennessee Williams collaborated on the script for the film with screenwriter Hal Kanter. Directed by Daniel Mann, who also directed the play, and photographed by the legendary James Wong Howe (who won an Oscar for his work), it was made largely on location in Key West, Florida, in the very same neighborhood where Williams himself lived at the time.

Howe's camera caught the bright sunlight of the outdoor settings, which represents the warm, exuberant vitality of the Sicilian villagers. He contrasted the exteriors with the murky shadows of the interiors in Serafina's home, which represent the deathly cold, melancholy turn that her temperament has taken in her excessively prolonged mourning over the loss of Rosario.

Some of the revisions of the play that Williams and his co-adapter made involved utilizing visual imagery to enhance the thematic meaning of the story. There is, for example, the player piano in the living room of Serafina (Anna Magnani in an Academy Award–winning performance). The piano, which is closely associated with Rosario, bursts into a joyous rendition of "The Sheik of Araby" at the least provocation. This light-hearted song recalls the gaiety of Serafina's bygone days when she cherished her relationship with Rosario. When Alvaro (Burt Lancaster) tries to liven up their first date by switching on the piano, Serafina quickly shuts it off to keep it from intruding on the atmosphere of mourning that she has maintained since her husband's death. Besides, the song points up that Alvaro is no "Sheik of Araby" à la Rudolph Valentino, as Serafina has always fancied Rosario to be; and she does not want

to be reminded that Alvaro in her mind represents quite a comedown from Rosario.

At the close of the picture, however, she effectively accepts Alvaro as the replacement of Rosario in her home and heart not only by giving him Rosario's rose-colored shirt, but also by turning on the piano to play the tune in Alvaro's honor. They laugh boisterously together while the spirited music plays and she invites him to stay a while "to go on with our conversation." This is her way of saying that they have at last learned to communicate with one another. In accepting Alvaro as he is, she is implicitly admitting that, if the boyish and clumsy Alvaro is no Latin lover such as the song praises, neither was the tawdry and deceptive Rosario.

The care that Howe lavished on photographing the film was rewarded by the intensity and beauty of the images that he created for the picture. An important visual metaphor, which he worked out in consultation with Daniel Mann, centered around the conflict of light and darkness in the story. This light-darkness motif is maintained when Alvaro, who is several years younger than Serafina, comes courting. The first time he visits her home he throws the shutters open to brighten the room, an early indication that he will be a source of sunlight and warmth in her life.

Michael Barson somewhat flippantly but nonetheless accurately characterizes the picture as a praiseworthy adaptation of Williams's play, which presents Magnani as a "repressed widow and Lancaster as the hunky truck driver whose elemental passion gets her motor started again." All in all, *The Rose Tattoo* is one of Williams's most optimistic works, both as a play and as a film.

REFERENCES

Barson, Michael, "Daniel Mann," in *Hollywood Directors of the Sound Era* (New York: Farrar, Straus, and Giroux, 1995), 494; Brown, John Mason, "The Rose Tattoo," *Saturday Review* (March 10, 1951), 23.

—*G.D.P.*

ROXANNE

See *CYRANO DE BERGERAC*

THE RULING CLASS (1968)

PETER BARNES (1931–)

The Ruling Class (1972), U.K., directed by Peter Medak, adapted by Peter Barnes; Avco Embassy.

The Play

The regional Nottingham Playhouse saw the first performance of *The Ruling Class* on November 6, 1968. It subsequently transferred to The Piccadilly Theatre, London, on February 26, 1969, and was acclaimed an astounding success. The usually staid *Sunday Times* drama critic Harold Hobson praised it as one of three major theatrical events of postwar British theatre, the others being John Osborne's *Look Back in Anger* and Harold Pinter's *The Birthday Party*. He described the play as a revelation containing "wit, pathos, exciting melodrama, brilliant satire, double-edged philosophy, horror, cynicism, and sentiment, all combined in a perfect unity." Barnes regarded his first play as the beginning of his attempts to "write a roller coaster drama of hairpin bends; a drama of expertise and ecstasy balanced on a tight-rope between the comic and tragic with a multi-faceted fly-like vision where every line was dramatic and every scene a play in itself." The playwright also regarded *The Ruling Class* as the first of many "repeated bayonet attacks on naturalism," as an attempt to "help create a people who are skeptical, rational, critical, not impressed or fooled." In a word, free, and in the literal sense, ungovernable. It is an attempt also followed by Peter Medak in the film version.

The play opens with a prologue depicting the accidental death of the 13th earl of Gurnsey after his usual sadomasochistic activities, involving the wearing of a three-cornered cocked hat, a sword in a scabbard, and a white tutu ballet skirt. Act One deals with the Gurnsey family discovering his heir, Jack, to be a lunatic who thinks of himself as Jesus Christ. As a pacifist following the philosophy of "God is Love," Jack is everything antithetical to both British imperialism and the English class structure. His Aunt Grace engages a Dr. Herder to cure Jack in the final scene at the same time as his wife gives birth to the required heir to the Gurnsey estate. In Act Two, the now-cured Jack behaves and dresses like a perfect English gentleman but acts out the murderous fantasies of Jack the Ripper. The play closes with his maiden speech praising the bloodthirsty values of British imperialism to the House of Lords, mostly populated by decaying corpses and skeletons. An epilogue concludes with Jack murdering his wife, Grace, in true Ripper fashion.

The Film

British filmmaker Peter Medak had only two feature films behind him—*Negatives* (1968) and *A Day in the Death of Joe Egg* (1970)—when he and playwright/scenarist Peter Barnes took on the play. The screen version closely follows the play's original structure. Virtually all the cast members perform different variations of British class stereotypes, employing every conceivable form of acting mannerism, ranging from Coral Browne's snooty Lady Claire Gurnsey and Arthur Lowe's Bolshevik butler Tucker, to James Villiers's idiosyncratic Dinsdale Gurnsey. Medak generally reproduces Barnes's original stage dialogue but often opens out the play cinematically to include extra exterior scenes such as those situated in the Gurnsey stately home garden, Dr. Herder's clinic, and a reconstructed House of Lords set for the climactic scene in the film. Medak retains the "Varsity Drag" musical number of Act One, Scene Five, with Peter O'Toole's Jack leading the church fair ladies in a number that would have made Busby Berkeley proud. When Dr. Herder attempts to prove that Jack is sane, Medak contrasts the normal view of Jack's behavior with scenes revealing Jack's perception of wrestling an eight-foot Victorian beast who "cures" him of any benevolent pacifism. When Jack first fantasizes his Jack the Ripper act on Aunt Claire, Medak visualizes the 1888 Whitechapel environment only suggested in the original stage production. Jack makes his terrifying speech about torture and capital punishment at a fox hunting meeting rather than the original play's drawing room. This links his speech with one of the most brutal upper-class countryside activities still present today, in an England that has now abolished the hereditary peer system characterizing the House of Lords in Barnes's day.

Finally, Medak extends the symbolic significance of Jack's maiden speech to his peers by cutting back and forth between the House of Lords and Jack's perception of an Upper House totally populated by skeletons and decaying corpses. This not only improves the original play's use of two tiers of decaying, cobwebbed dummies and three lords, one dragging a skeleton behind him, but also cinematically parallels the concluding scene of Act One, which involved a visual contrast between reality and insane perception. The film also uses the play's epilogue with Jack murdering his loving wife, formerly his uncle's mistress. However, Medak employs his own cinematic form of epilogue by concluding the film with an overhead shot of the Gurnsey Manor, Grace's scream, and the voice of the next (male) heir proclaiming "I'm Jack!"

REFERENCES

Barker, Clive, "On Class, Christianity and Questions of Comedy," *New Theatre Quarterly*, 6:21 (1990), 5–24; Barnes, Peter, *Collected Plays* (London: Heinemann, 1981).

—*T.W.*

SABRINA

See *SABRINA FAIR*

SABRINA FAIR; OR, A WOMAN OF THE WORLD: A ROMANTIC COMEDY (1953)

SAMUEL TAYLOR (1912–2000)

Sabrina (1954), U.S.A., directed by Billy Wilder, adapted by Billy Wilder, Samuel Taylor, and Ernest Lehman; Paramount.

Sabrina (1995), U.S.A., directed by Sydney Pollack, adapted by Barbara Benedek and David Rayfiel; Paramount.

The Play

Titled from a line in John Milton's masque *Comus*, ("Sabrina fair,/Listen where thou art sitting . . .") *Sabrina Fair* was first presented by the Playwrights' Company at the National Theatre, New York City, on November 11, 1953. H.C. Potter directed the opening and the set was designed by Donald Oenslager, with Margaret Sullavan as "Sabrina Fairchild" and Russell Collins as "Fairchild," her chauffeur father. The patriarch of the Larrabee clan, Linus Larrabee, Sr., was played by John Cromwell; his wife, "Maude Larrabee" by Cathleen Nesbitt; sons "Linus Larrabee, Jr." by

Joseph Cotten and "David Larrabee" by Scott McKay; Luella Gear plays "Aunt Julia Ward McKinlock," the family friend. After five years working as a U.S. government agency secretary in Paris, the chauffeur's-daughter-turned-Pygmalion leaves a French amour and returns "home" to the Larrabee mansion, located on the North Shore of Long Island. However, despite her education at a woman's college and her French awakenings to love and culture, Sabrina finds herself trapped in the age-old love triangle between two men: the Frenchman, Paul D'Argenson (played by Robert Duke), and David Larrabee, a thrice-wed playboy whom she has loved desperately since childhood. In the end, denying both rich suitors her hand in marriage, Sabrina asserts, "[E]veryone takes it for granted that Cinderella will marry Prince Charming when he comes knocking on her door with that diamond-studded slipper. Nobody considers Cinderella." The twist is that the chauffeur, due to wise investing, is a millionaire. With this knowledge, Sabrina chooses to marry Linus, the elder Larrabee brother, an unmarried bachelor 10 years her senior and her intellectual match. Overall, the tone of *Sabrina Fair* is very much in line with a comedy of manners; according to critic Brooks Atkinson, it is "an artificial comedy about civilized people."

The Films

Both film versions differ greatly from the play; however, the plots of the two films are very similar, a fact not surprising considering that the 1995 version was

Sabrina was made for the second time with Harrison Ford as Linus and Julia Ormond as Sabrina. (COURTESY PARAMOUNT PICTURES)

Audrey Hepburn is a dumbed-down version of the confrontational and quite outspoken Sabrina of *Sabrina Fair*. Perhaps Taylor was aware that a 1950s screen audience might not respond positively to an unmarried young woman claiming, "I would like to decide for myself!" or "I wanted you very much to make love to me last night, did you know that?" While the original Sabrina works in a U.S. government agency for five years in Paris, Hepburn is shipped there for just two years by her father, who hopes that the cooking school she attends will cure her of her hopeless, romantic ambitions. Hepburn resists being domesticated so much so that she tries to commit suicide via carbon monoxide poisoning the night before leaving for Paris. She fails when Linus (Bogart) hears the cars running in the garage; it is this rescue scene that foreshadows the final moments of the film, where Bogart saves himself from an endless life as a hard-driving mogul by falling in love and running off to Paris with Sabrina.

The chauffeur's cooking daughter becomes a budding photographer (Ormond) in the 1996 version. But even though Samuel Taylor gave Sydney Pollack the go-ahead to overhaul the earlier film, the only relevant plot changes were the missing suicide scene and a 20-minute "fashion-photography sequence" of Sabrina's (French) *Vogue* magazine apprenticeship. The Bildungsroman theme remains, however, and Sabrina grows up to have a mind of her own, albeit not one as bright as in the play version. For example, Linus (Bogart; Ford) in both films manages to befuddle a naïve Sabrina into thinking that she is the object of both brothers affections. However, Linus's only goal in charming Sabrina is to lure her away from David so that the unmarried playboy can finally settle down with the daughter of a rich plastics manufacturer. Sabrina takes the bait, dumping David's advances for a wiser and more stable older brother, only to hear Linus confess that it was all a game to get her out of the picture. David does decide to marry the tycoon's daughter, allowing a business merger between the two families, but not before convincing his brother to fulfill the modern day fairy tale by going (back) to Paris with Sabrina.

based on the 1954 film, not the original play. Gone is "Aunt Julia," the intrusive and gossipy family friend who frames much of the dialogue topics in Taylor's play, and, in the 1995 version, Linus Larrabee, Sr., is long dead, making room for Linus, Jr. (Harrison Ford), to be all the more a grumpy workaholic of Larrabee enterprises. Significantly absent from both film versions is the French suitor; he has been replaced by an elderly baron in the 1954 version, and a French photographer, who is briefly her love interest but never a strong enough one to pull her far from her David Larrabee crush, in the 1995 film. Without the French suitor, the love triangle players are now Sabrina (Audrey Hepburn, 1954; Julia Ormond, 1995), David Larrabee (William Holden, 1954; Greg Kinnear, 1995), and Linus Larrabee (Humphrey Bogart, 1954; Harrison Ford, 1995).

Although Samuel Taylor was one of the three screenwriters for the 1954 film, the Sabrina played by

REFERENCES

Atkinson, Brooks, "Review of *Sabrina Fair*," *New York Times Theatre Reviews, 1920–1970*, vol. 6 (New York: Arno Press, 1971); Buckley, Christopher, "Sabrina pere," *The New Yorker*, 71:38 (November 27, 1995); Donaldson, Leslie, "Sabrina," *Magill's Survey of Cinema*, vol. 3, ed. Frank N. Magill (Englewood Cliffs, N.J.: Salem Press, 1980); Rozen, Leah, "Review of *Sabrina*," *People Weekly*, 44:25 (December 18, 1995); Schickel, Richard, "Review of *Sabrina*," *Time*, 146:25 (December 18, 1995); Simon,

John, "Review of *Sabrina,*" *National Review,* 48:1 (January 29, 1996).

—N.A.

SAINT JOAN (1923)

GEORGE BERNARD SHAW (1856–1950)

Saint Joan (1957), U.S.A., directed by Otto Preminger, adapted by Graham Greene; United Artists/Preminger.

The Play

George Bernard Shaw's earliest plays—*Widower's Houses* (1892), *Arms and the Man* (1893), and *Mrs. Warren's Profession* (1899)—were controversial. Noted for his injection of social issues and polemics into his work, his reputation grew with his later plays, most notably *Man and Superman* (1903), *Major Barbara* (1905), *Pygmalion* (1913), and *Saint Joan* (1923). Acclaimed as one of the great dramas of the 20th century—certainly it is Shaw's biggest and longest—*Saint Joan* is a "Chronicle Play in Six Scenes and an Epilogue" that attempts, in Shaw's words, to overturn the "romantic poppycock" and creaky melodrama of previous dramatic interpretations, including those by Shakespeare, Schiller, and Mark Twain. In his preface, written shortly after the canonization of Joan in 1921, he maintained that the Church conducted a fairer trial of Joan than any civil court would today in a comparable case. Moreover, he continued—notwithstanding Joan's sainthood, merely a technicality of Church classification—what is important is that she was a founder of Protestantism and of the modern state, and that she thought of God and King without the intervention of Church and feudal peerage. Her confrontation with the Church embodied the perennial conflict between those essential but incompatible forces, social institutions and individual genius.

The play traces Joan's short-lived military career, trial, execution, and subsequent canonization in 1921, centuries after her death. The action of Scene One begins in 1429 in the castle of Vaucouleurs. The Maid of Lorraine appears to Robert de Baudricourt, castle commander, and demonstrates her control over the egg-laying abilities of the castle's chickens. "You are to give me a horse and armor and some soldiers, and send me to the Dauphin," she announces to the astonished Baudricourt. "Those are your orders from my Lord." When he objects to the validity of her supposed "voices," she declares, "Of course, that is how the messages of God come to us." In Scene Two, Charles VII—"a poor creature physically . . . accustomed to being kicked, yet incorrigible and irrepressible"—agrees to receive Joan. She spots him amongst a crowd of pretenders and announces her mission: "I am sent to you to drive the English away from Orleans and from France, and to crown you king in the cathedral at Rheims." Impressed with her demeanor and sage advice, he gives command of the army to Joan. In Scene Three, six weeks later at the south bank of the Loire, her prayers bring a badly needed west wind and the commander, Dunois, kneels before her and gives her his commander's baton. Scene Four is the only scene in which Joan is not physically present, and it presents a turning point from Shavian romance to tragedy. In a tent in the English camp, the earl of Warwick, the chaplain John de Stogumber, and Cauchon, the bishop of Beauvais, discuss ways of coping with Joan's "heresies," her recent victories over the English, and the imminent coronation of Charles. Warwick and Cauchon agree that Joan is their "common enemy" and a threat both to the Church (because of heresy) and to feudalism (because of the threat she represents to the prevailing social structure).

Scene Five begins in the cathedral of Rheims, just after Charles's coronation. Dunois tells Joan that her victories have made her many enemies. Undaunted, Joan declares that the French forces should not make a peace treaty but resume the battle of Paris. Dunois and the archbishop of Rheims both warn her that her pride and disobedience will result in her capture and death at the stake. Scene Six finds Joan at the Inquisition in the Rouen Bishop's Court. The inquisitor, Cauchon, and the prosecutor, Canon John D'Estivet, are determined to give Joan a fair hearing against charges of heresy. Describing the allegations against her, the Inquisitor notes that although Joan may seem a simple peasant girl, her simplicity may found "a heresy that will wreck both Church and Empire." Joan argues that her acts are natural, not heretical. When asked whose judgment is to decide what constitutes the will of God, hers or that of the Church, she answers, "What other judgment can I judge by but my own?" However, upon realizing that her death at the stake is imminent, she denies her "voices" and signs a document of recantation. Upon hearing that she will be instead imprisoned for life, she tears up the paper: "Light your fire: do you think I dread it as much as the life of a rat in a hole? My voices were right."

Joan's death occurs offstage. The chaplain rushes in with his report of the execution, that Joan died courageously. The play concludes with an epilogue that takes place 25 years later in Charles' royal chamber. After learning that Joan's sentence has been annulled, Charles is visited by visions of many players in the drama, including Dunoir, Cauchon, the executioner, and Joan herself. They apologize to the amused Joan that the burning was "purely political." Finally a clergyman in 1920s garb enters to proclaim Joan's canonization. As they all kneel before her, she asks if she should return to them alive. They depart in hasty confusion, declaring that they would all act the same way again. Joan is left alone as the hour of midnight strikes. She prays: "O God, that madest this beautiful earth, when will it be ready to receive Thy saints? How long, O Lord, how long?"

Commentator Eric Bentley argues that the character of Joan unites many of the qualities seen individually in Shaw's previous heroines, down-to-earth practicality, activist vitality, and spirituality. "Shaw must have realized that here was an opportunity to study and recreate a person who united in herself so much that he had divided between his practical and idealistic characters. It almost seems that if Joan had never existed Shaw would have had to invent her."

The Film

"I shall not be surprised," Shaw remarked as early as 1915, "if the cinematograph and phonograph turn out to be the most revolutionary inventions since writing and printing." He later predicted that cinema would "kill the theatres which are doing what film does better, and bring to life the dying theatre, which does what the film cannot do at all." G.B. Shaw was no fan of the movies, however, particularly American movies. "The huge polynational audience makes mediocrity compulsory," he asserted in 1924. "Many of them are full of the stupidest errors of judgment." Before sound technology came in 1927, Shaw refused to allow any of his plays to be adapted to the screen. "I repeat that a play with the words left out is a play spoiled; and all those filmings of plays written to be spoken as well as seen are boresome blunders. . . ." Yet, eventually Shaw was willing to admit that he saw the film medium as a potentially revolutionary social force. With the advent of the talking picture in the late 1920s he saw the possibility of bringing his plays to the screen. "My shop is open," he told the public in 1928, "and people can come and negotiate with me." However, he still insisted that a cinematic adaptation should be nothing more than a filmed play, that it was the dialogue that mattered, not the techniques of editing and camera.

The subsequent history of Shavian theatrical films is not a happy one. *Androcles and the Lion* (1952) was transformed into a Victor Mature-Jean Simmons love story set against the orgies of pagan Rome. The Hecht-Hill-Lancaster version of *The Devil's Disciple* in 1959 changed the play into a romantic melodrama dubbed by *Films in Review* "a filmic abortion of Shaw's play." Somewhat better received were two Technicolor versions of *The Doctor's Dilemma* (1958) and *The Millionairess* (1961).

Otto Preminger's film of *Saint Joan*, scripted by Graham Greene, was a pageantlike, severely shortened adaptation that drastically cut most of Shaw's lengthy speeches and displayed rather more a comic than a serious tone. As Bernard Dukore notes, Shaw himself reduced Joan's indictment from 64 counts to 12: "If we persist in trying The Maid on Trumpery issues," Shaw wrote of his own screen treatment, "she may escape us on the great main issue." Shaw had encountered stiff resistance from the Roman Catholic Church. Preminger's Catholic screenwriter Graham Greene altered Shaw's work to appease the Church in his screen treatment. It drew a fair share of critical invective: "An awkward, obtunded, and torpid bastardization of a great play," cried *The New Yorker*. Jean Seberg played Saint Joan, Richard Widmark was the Dauphin, Richard Todd was Dunois, and John Gielgud was the earl of Warwick. Green's script begins as the play ends, 25 years after Joan's death, in Charles' royal chambers. Two extensive flashbacks relate prior events. The first flashback depicts Joan's meetings with Robert de Baudricourt, the Dauphin, and Dunois, and then her rejection by the newly crowned Charles. The second is a recounting by the earl of Warwick of Joan's interrogation, her exposure to the instruments of torture, the charges and the trial, the political strife between the French and the English, and then her burning at the stake. Back in the "present," additional characters appear, Cauchon, who describes his excommunication; Dunois, who justifies his decision to back Charles; and "a saint from Hell," the English soldier who gave her the makeshift wooden cross. As the play had concluded, the film ends with the observation that a dead saint is safer for the Church than a live one; and a high-angle shot reveals Charles, covering his head with his bedding, while Joan asks, "How long, oh Lord?"

REFERENCES

Bentley, Eric, *Bernard Shaw*, rev. ed. (New York: Limelight Editions, 1985); Costello, Donald P., *The Serpent's Eye: Shaw and the Cinema* (Notre Dame, Ind.: University of Notre Dame Press, 1965); Dukore, Bernard F., ed. *The Collected Screenplays of George Bernard Shaw* (Athens: University of Georgia Press, 1980); Pratley, Gerald, *The Cinema of Otto Preminger* (New York: A.S. Barnes, 1971).

—J.C.T.

THE SCARECROW (1910)

PERCY MACKAYE (1875–1956)

Feathertop (1916), U.K., directed by Henry Vernot, adapted by Paul M. Bryan; Gaumont/Mutual Film Corporation.

The Play

Percy MacKaye adapted Nathaniel Hawthorne's story "Feathertop: A Moralized Legend" to the stage as a play in four acts. Renamed *The Scarecrow*, the play was first presented by the Harvard Dramatic Club in 1909, two years before being mounted at the Garrick Theatre on January 17, 1911. By that time the original Hawthorne story had already been adapted to the screen several times, first by Edison in 1908 under the title *Lord Feathertop*; the Edison adaptation was then followed by two other short films, *Feather Top* (Éclair, 1912) and *Feathertop* (Kinemacolor, 1913). In the Hawthorne story a witch creates a finely dressed scarecrow and is so delighted that she uses a magical pipe to breathe life into her creation and gives him a three-cornered hat, naming him Feathertop. Her creation then goes into town and meets Polly Gookin, who falls in love with him, until she looks into a mirror and sees what he really is, a pumpkin-headed dummy. Feathertop then returns to the witch, removes the pipe, and collapses into a heap of straw. In MacKaye's adaptation, Feathertop becomes Lord Ravensbane. Acting out of malice and revenge to spite an erstwhile lover, Justice Merton, the witch, Goody Rickby, sends her creation to Merton's home to court Merton's niece, Rachel, but Ravensbane is exposed by Richard Talbot, Rachel's former fiancé. Distraught, and having developed a conscience, Ravensbane commits suicide by destroying the magical pipe that has given him life. Though a commercial failure, the play became popular with amateur groups and earned an off-Broadway revival in 1953.

The Film

In the five-reel Henry Vernot film, Elsie Green (Marguerite Courtot), a country girl, goes to the city to visit her wealthy uncle and falls for playboy Percy Morleigh (John Reinhard). Disenchanted with high society, Elsie's uncle feigns death and bequeaths his estate to his brother, and a copy of Hawthorne's "Feathertop" to Elsie. After reading the story, Elsie has a dream that reenacts the story with herself in the role of Polly Gookin and Morleigh as Feathertop. Waking up, she realizes that Morleigh is as empty of substance as Hawthorne's scarecrow. She then returns home, a wiser person, to her country sweetheart, and learns that her uncle is in fact alive and well. The film, therefore, is freely adapted from both Hawthorne's story and Percy MacKaye's play.

REFERENCES

Hayes, Kevin J., "American Literature, Silent Film, and the Story-within-a-Story," *Literature/Film Quarterly*, 27:1 (1999): 33–38.

—*J.M.W.*

THE SEAGULL (1895)

ANTON CHEKHOV (1860–1904)

The Sea Gull (1968), U.S.A., directed by Sidney Lumet, adapted by Mour Budberg; Warner Bros.-Seven Arts.

Chaika (1972), USSR, directed and adapted by Yuli Karasik; Mosfilm Studios.

The Play

By all accounts, the first production of Chekhov's *The Seagull* (October 17, 1896) was disastrous. Most of the audience, expecting a typical Chekhovian vaudeville, were vastly disappointed in what they saw. It was not until the play's second premiere on December 17, 1898, by the Moscow Art Theatre under the direction of Konstantin Stanislavski that the play became successful and stood on its own merits. That production, in the words of Carol Racomora, forged a relationship "that was to influence the canon of Chekhov's major plays as well as a company which would have a major presence in twentieth century theatre." The play is set on Sorin's estate, which is being visited by his sister, Arkadina, a famous actress. Her son Konstantin Treplev, an aspiring writer, presents an outdoor performance of his new play, in which the single character is played by Nina, a neighbor's daughter, with whom Konstantin is in love. When his mother makes fun of the play, Konstantin stops the performance. Nina becomes infatuated with the writer Trigorin, who is also Arkadina's lover. When both Arkadina and Trigorin move to Moscow, Nina follows them, hoping to become a famous actress. Nina consequently has an affair with Trigorin. A parallel to this relationship is that of Masha, the daughter of the family steward, who is in love with Konstantin (who does not reciprocate her ardor). In order to try to forget her passion for Konstantin she marries Medvedenko, the local schoolmaster.

Two years pass between Acts Three and Four, Konstantin is garnishing some success as a writer and lives at the estate. Arkadina and Trigorin have returned, as has Nina, whose aspiring career as an actress has not been successful. When Nina rejects Treplev's offer of affection he tears up his manuscripts and commits suicide. Chekhov once described his play as "a comedy with . . . a landscape, lots of talk about literature, little action and a ton of love." The play has a classic Chekhovian quadrangle, Konstantin loves Nina, who is in love with Trigorin, who is the lover of Konstantin's mother, Arkadina. As Chekhov promised we have "a ton of love," but it is unrequited love, false love, or as the character Masha describes it, "love without hope." Early in the play, Treplev kills a seagull and presents it to Nina. This action serves as a metaphor for Chekhov's theme of lost ideals and hopes. Chekhov's intended comic vision has not transferred successfully to the screen.

The Films

In 1968 Sidney Lumet directed a film version of *The Seagull* that starred James Mason as Trigorin, Vanessa Redgrave as Nina, Simone Signoret as Arkadina, and David Warner as Konstantin. Lumet, whose previous artistic triumph was an exceptional film adaptation of Eugene O'Neill's autobiographical drama *A Long Day's Journey into Night* (1962), hoped to build on that success with his adaptation of Chekhov. The results were mixed, according to most reviews. Many critics commented on the lack of comedy in the film. Peter Cowie, for instance, stated that, "The wit of Chekhov's play eludes Lumet, for all his worthy, competent rendering of the major scenes and his respectful camera style." Likewise, the reviewer for *Time* magazine noted that Lumet's "lumbering technique" effectively stripped the play of any humor. The critical response notwithstanding, Lumet has often referred to it as one of his favorite films, "The only two films I've made in which I wouldn't change a thing are *Long Day's Journey* and *The Sea Gull*."

Lumet retained the entire text of the play and opened the play up by shooting much of it outdoors (location photography was shot in Sweden). The first five minutes of the film are without dialogue and the camera follows Nina. As she rides her horse toward the estate, we witness Arkadina and Trigorin getting out of bed, and Masha and Medvedenko strolling together in a field. The result is to provide the audience with a pastoral sense of space. All of the interior shots, however, were based on theatrical compositions. Lumet indulges in focusing on wealthy indolence by providing a rather impressionistic view of country life on the estate. A croquet game on the lawn of the estate and the lotto game in the final act become ritual metaphors for the stasis of the upper class. Lumet utilizes the long take often in his films. Examples abound from the opening shot of *The Fugitive Kind* (1960) to *Fail Safe* (1964). The long take is used effectively in *The Sea Gull*, and this may be part of the "lumbering technique" referred to by the *Time* critic. Lumet's camera often follows the characters in a single movement rather than utilizing traditional editing strategy, fragmenting the action into separate shots. The screenplay for the film was based on a recent translation of the play by Mour Budberg, which effectively captures the tragicomic pathos of Chekhov's characters.

Yuli Karasik's 1972 film *Chaika* cuts the play drastically (Karasik's film runs 95 minutes compared to Lumet's full-text version of 141 minutes), streamlining the text into a more plotted narrative by eliminating many "talky" irrelevancies. The film has been described by H. Peter Stowell as one of the most "oppressively static of all Chekhov adaptations." Again, as with Lumet's version, the director has chosen the dramatic/tragic elements of the play at the expense of Chekhov's intended comedy. Karasik utilizes wide-screen aspect ratio and combines lengthy takes with close-ups and medium shots, ultimately to no avail, because of the somber tone that he has injected into the film.

REFERENCES

Bowles, Stephen E., *Sidney Lumet: A Guide to References and Resources* (Boston: G.K. Hall, 1998); Cunningham, Frank R., *Sidney Lumet: Film and Literary Vision* (Lexington: University of Kentucky Press, 1991); Stowell, Peter H., "Chekhov into Film" in *A Chekhov Companion*, ed. Toby W. Clyman (Westport, Conn.: Greenwood Press, 1985).

—R.W.W.

THE SEARCH FOR SIGNS OF INTELLIGENT LIFE IN THE UNIVERSE (1985)

JANE WAGNER (1927–) AND LILY TOMLIN (1939–)

The Search for Signs of Intelligent Life in the Universe (1991), U.S.A., directed by John Bailey, adapted by Jane Wagner; Orion Classics.

The Play

This comedic collaboration marked the high point in the partnership of comic actress Lily Tomlin and writer Jane Wagner. The two had previously written and mounted productions of *Appearing Nitely* and *Moment by Moment*, each a one-woman show highlighting Tomlin's talents at comic characterization. The final Broadway production of *The Search for Signs* was the result of a lengthy process of trial and error, revision, and "work shows" in which the women refined their ideas in front of paying and nonpaying audiences. The efforts paid off, as Tomlin was awarded the 1986 best actress Tony for her multicharacter performance. *The Search for Signs* is an extended monologue with Tomlin shifting among a dozen separate male and female characters. A homeless woman named Trudy is the primary character, with her channeling abilities forming a dramatic conceit for the presentation of the other characters. These include Agnus Angst, a rebellious and belligerent young teen; Agnus' grandparents Lud and Marie; Chrissy, an anxious young exercise aficionado; Kate, a bored socialite; and the trio of Lyn, Edie, and Marge, feminist friends whose reminiscences of the late 1960s and 1970s form the core of the play. Without costume changes, Tomlin used only voice and gesture to differentiate among the several characters.

The Film

The adaptation of *The Search for Signs* to film was preceded by a 1986 documentary entitled *Lily Tomlin*, which highlighted the play's pre-production process and included several onstage segments of the play itself. The documentary, directed by Joan Churchill and Nicholas Broomfield, attempted "to capture a behind-the-scenes view of the creative process of putting a play together." The film ended up as the object of a vicious legal battle between its producers and Tomlin's management, reportedly because the latter saw the documentary as a threat to any potential feature film adaptation of *The Search for Signs*. That adaptation was finally made in 1991, but was considered to be a largely unsuccessful cinematic translation of Tomlin's landmark performance and Wagner's brilliant script. Where in the play Tomlin's character interpretations had been purely vocal and gestural, with much left to the viewer's imagination, in the film each character was made concrete through makeup and costume. In the adaptation, director John Bailey chose to use the capabilities of film to place the characters into more realistic settings, and the result was a disruption of the seamless flow of Tomlin's performance.

These changes affected the adaptation adversely according to most accounts. Critic Mary E. Belles said "the filmmakers did not recognize that the cosmic glue holding the nebulous work together resides in Tomlin's instantaneous transformations . . . everything designed to open [the play] up to the screen is more distracting than enhancing." Belles also stated that "reviewers were understandably more impressed by [the film's] themes than by the overall production." Tomlin followed up the film version of *The Search for Signs* by continuing her successful film and television acting career, appearing in films such as *Short Cuts* (1993) and *Tea with Mussolini* (1999) and the TV shows *The Magic School Bus* (1994) and *Murphy Brown* (1996–98).

REFERENCES

Belles, Mary E., "The Search for Signs of Intelligent Life in the Universe," in *Magill's Cinema Annual 1992*, Frank Magill, ed. (Pasadena: Salem Press, 1992); Sorenson, Jeff, *Lily Tomlin: Woman of a Thousand Faces* (New York: St. Martin's Press, 1989).

—C.M.

SECRET HONOR (1983)

DONALD FREED AND ARNOLD M. STONE

Secret Honor (1984), U.S.A., directed by Robert Altman, adapted by Donald Freed and Arnold M. Stone; Sandcastle 5 Productions in association with the University of Michigan.

The Play

Cowritten by political activist and conspiracy theorist Donald Freed and an ex-government attorney named Arnold Stone, *Secret Honor* was a one-man play about the secret life and public shame of former president Richard Nixon. Originally produced at the Los Angeles Actors' Theatre, the play starred Philip Baker Hall as Nixon, the sole character in the drama. Film director Robert Altman saw the play and proved instrumental in helping it move to an off-Broadway run. The play was an extended monologue in which a drunken, distraught Nixon tape records a series of soliloquies intended to be his self-defense for Watergate and the turmoil it caused the nation. In the course of the drama, shocking revelations emerge: that Nixon had worked as a carnival barker in his youth, that he had originally gotten involved in politics by answering a classified ad in California, and most importantly that his entire political career (including his election as president and the open-

Robert Altman

rounding its production: Altman took the theatrical company to the University of Michigan, where he filmed the play as a "teaching exercise" involving his own crew and local students. A more realistic and cluttered set (of Nixon's study) was created, and the director of the stage production, Robert Harders, served as a dialogue coach for actor Philip Baker Hall. Accounts concur as to the changes in and effectiveness of the transfer from stage to screen: Altman biographer Patrick McGilligan claims that the film in comparison to the play "remained substantially the same . . . Altman never had to add or change a word"; Freed concurred by saying that the primary resource Altman brought to the play was "the courage of filming it."

The film made expert and efficient use of cinematic techniques. By "highlighting key aspects of the script through effective uses of camera and sound," Thomas Monsell found the Altman production of *Secret Honor* to be "one of those rare instances in which a film rendering is considered superior to its stage antecedent." Apart from issues of adaptation, critics tended to receive the film according to their personal feelings about Nixon. Playwright Harold Pinter, impressed with the film's use of pauses, broken phrases, and menacing tone, called *Secret Honor* "the best film that's ever been made." After *Secret Honor*, Altman went on to produce a few more cinematic adaptations of plays (including Sam Shepard's *Fool for Love*) before returning to more mainstream filmmaking in the 1990s.

REFERENCES:

Keyssar, Helene, *Robert Altman's America* (New York: Oxford University Press, 1991); McGilligan, Patrick, *Robert Altman: Jumping Off the Cliff* (New York: St. Martin's Press, 1989); Monsell, Thomas, *Nixon on Stage and Screen: The Thirty-seventh President as Depicted in Films, Television, Plays and Opera* (Jefferson, N.C.: McFarland, 1998).

—C.M.

ing of China) had been orchestrated by a mysterious cabal of wealthy power brokers known as the Committee of One Hundred. By the end of his soliloquy, Nixon is despondent and decides to finally stand up to the committee, which wants him to run for president yet again. The play ends with Nixon chanting obscenities as an unseen crowd calls for "four more years."

The Film

The adaptation of *Secret Honor* was conceived under unique circumstances, as Altman was involved with the play at a very early point in its life. In the early 1980s, Altman had just entered a phase of his career in which he concentrated primarily on filming adaptations of stage productions. By 1983, he had directed adaptations of both *Come Back to the Five and Dime, Jimmy Dean, Jimmy Dean* and *Streamers*. The film of *Secret Honor* was even more unique because of the circumstances sur-

THE SEVEN YEAR ITCH (1952)

GEORGE AXELROD (1922–)

The Seven Year Itch (1955), U.S.A., directed by Billy Wilder, adapted by Billy Wilder and George Axelrod; Twentieth Century-Fox.

The Play

George Axelrod's audacious exposition of the restless libido of a long-time married man was first presented

on Broadway at the Fulton Theatre on November 20, 1952, where it had a spectacular run of 1,141 performances. Completed the previous July after 15 one-hour writing sessions, *The Seven Year Itch* became an instant hit under the direction of John Gerstad and the watchful eyes of Axelrod. Stage and screen actor Tom Ewell played Richard Sherman, the male animal who, when his wife and children leave the City for the summer, finds himself in the arms of the Girl, first played by Vanessa Brown, who is summer-subletting the apartment directly above.

Perhaps partially explaining its phenomenal success, Axelrod's play dug deep into the desires and dreams of its so-called hero: the bored, wedded everyman who is tempted by the forbidden fruit of another woman. The language was smart, at times vulgar; even the title met with some objection from the show's producer Elliot Nugent. (Nugent was Axelrod's first choice to play Sherman but declined, saying he was too old for the part. He came to regret that decision when the show became a hit.) Remarkably, Axelrod and Gerstad in Axelrod's words, "managed to bring the play in unscathed," including keeping the depiction of the extramarital affair. In fact, it is the guilt that Sherman feels because of his tryst that is the primary source of the play's comedy. "The guilt is *funny*," Axelrod once remarked. Yet it was that same guilt, and the reasons for it, that ultimately suffered most when it came time to adapt the play to film. Axelrod wrote only one other popular play, *Will Success Spoil Rock Hunter?* in 1955. He was also co-producer of *Visit to a Small Planet* (1957) and later directed several comedies.

The Film

Axelrod had wanted Billy Wilder to direct *Itch* as soon as the possibility of its film adaptation became known. Despite the play's smash success on Broadway, Axelrod was still considered an unknown writer in Hollywood circles, where MGM was negotiating the play's purchase. So when he requested Wilder as director, he was quickly ignored by MGM. Swifter, however, was Irving "Swifty" Lazar, who, having overheard at a cocktail party of the impending sale of the script to MGM and Axelrod's preference for Wilder, went directly to Wilder and asked if he'd like to direct a film version of the play. Wilder said yes, purchased the play himself, and agreed to let Lazar be his agent in the deal. Lazar then approached Axelrod. When Marilyn Monroe's agent, Charles K. Feldman, then told Lazar that his client wanted to play the Girl, Lazar arranged for Wilder to sell the play to Twentieth Century-Fox, Monroe's studio. Lazar then suggested Feldman pro-

Billy Wilder

duce the picture, with Lazar representing Feldman's producer deal. Once all the behind the scenes workings were sorted out, Wilder and Axelrod got down to business—and Lazar found himself considerably richer.

When Axelrod and Wilder met for the first time, Axelrod handed Wilder the stage script, only to be told by Wilder promptly to throw it out—or possibly use it as a doorstop. Indeed, adapting the play for film proved a harrowing exercise given what Axelrod later termed the "mysteries" of Hollywood narrative formulas. Moreover, censorship problems were considerable. As Axelrod later stated about the numerous sex comedies he penned during the '50s, "The bulk of my sex comedy career was done with this enormous handicap: not being allowed to have any sex. I was trying to write these so-called sex comedies . . . when we had to deal with the Breen Office [the organized censorship body for Hollywood studios]." So while the stage version allowed its protagonist to indulge in adultery, the film offered "fantasy sequences" depicting softer indiscretions. Wilder had a predilection for suggestive references and sexual innuendo, however, so the script passed the censors while still able to offer moments of risqué dialogue and behavior. Indeed, at close inspection, in many ways the visuals and narrative of *Itch* tell two different stories.

Tom Ewell certainly helped the film's success, reprising his stage role, albeit with one hand tied behind his back. For example, while the stage version allowed the flirtation between the two dwellers to consummate as an affair, in the film the girl sleeps in his apartment when her air conditioning breaks and Sherman, seized by propriety, sleeps on the couch. The next day he runs off to his wife's arms and the film closes, leaving the audience to only dream of another ending.

But there is more to Sherman than his fantasies about other women. The character, a typical one in Wilder's oeuvre, is a loner male who is anxious and yet eager to become a respectable, productive, and proud man in his society. His vision of himself is confused and unclear (Wilder's frequent use of mirrors literally conveys this theme), but he knows that young, sexy women are irrefutable status symbols. In many ways, this aspect of the film—the neurotic and tortured male—spoke to larger cultural trends in the fifties: from the embrace of psychoanalysis to the domestic rigidity of the model family and its masculine provider. Both the play and the film comically explore Freud's ideas about repression and the unconscious, exploiting the psychological tension many men were experiencing—or simply the efforts to define it.

Interestingly, some critics noted that the Girl seemed more sympathetic in the film than in the play. And it is paradoxical that by reducing the character to her physicality as Wilder did with Monroe in the part, the director stripped her of threat. Certainly, her form was hardly an innocent vision. But Wilder respected her physique, and adopted, like Sherman, a distant, admiring stance. In the film's most famous and iconic moment, Monroe's skirt billows up as she stands over a subway grate. The cameras, however, never get so close to offend. Additionally, just as Sherman is a Wilder archetype, so is the Girl—a desired woman who is incapable of scheming and somewhat dense. Because her physicality defines her, she is sexual but not emotional. Film scholar Bernard Dick, however, sees in Monroe's Girl a Wilder rarity: a woman who understands men. The primary evidence for this is a sympathetic speech Monroe delivers to Sherman that, in fact, does not appear in the original play. It is interesting to speculate how the needs of the censors and the needs of the male psyche converged in this moment where the sexual woman is simultaneously a maternal figure.

As it turned out, the challenges presented to Wilder weren't limited to the film's content. A new era in Hollywood filmmaking demanded novelties of form. The aforementioned taming of the itch was one thing—using Cinemascope, Stereophonic sound, and DeLuxe color was quite another, especially for a story set almost entirely in an apartment. Improved filmmaking technology had been developed to counter the explosive success of TV. Moreover, while plays had always been sought-after as film properties, many such as *Itch* were chosen expressly because of their sensational and adult subject matter. Dick continues, "While this kind of material usually was rendered innocuous by the time it eventually reached the big screen, it was promoted in such a way to give audiences the impression that they were going to get the kind of viewing experience that they could not get from the small screen." Wilder used Cinemascope to great effect with the "acceptable" fantasy sequences, and while the use of widescreen led some critics to call the film visually static, it did refer to the qualities of social distance permeating the film.

Indeed, one interpretation of the overarching theme of the film is that disillusionment with society can lead to escapism and fantasy. In escaping to the movies, the audience, like Sherman in his home, escaped to a fantasy of Monroe. Wilder used his penchant for self-reflexi-vity to further aid the process: When Sherman is asked who the girl in the kitchen is, he replies "Wouldn't you like to know? Maybe it's Marilyn Monroe." Thus, when Axelrod's play went Hollywood, it was ultimately Monroe's image that became the subject and object of the *Itch*.

REFERENCES

Dick, Bernard F., *Billy Wilder* (Boston: Twayne, 1980); McGilligan, Patrick, "Irony," *Film Comment*, 31:6 (November–December 1995); Seideman, Steve, *The Film Career of Billy Wilder* (Pleasantville, N.Y.: Redgrave, 1977); Zolotow, Maurice, *Billy Wilder in Hollywood* (New York: G.P. Putnam's Sons, 1998); Review, "The Seven Year Itch," *New York Times*, June 4, 1955, Review, "The Seven Year Itch," *Variety*, June 8, 1955.

—R.E.

SHADOWLANDS (1990)

WILLIAM NICHOLSON (1948–)

Shadowlands [aka *C.S. Lewis through the Shadowlands*] (1984), U.K., directed by Norman Stone; BBC.

Shadowlands (1993), U.K., directed by Sir Richard Attenborough; Shadowlands Productions.

The Play

Revising his earlier 1984 BBC teleplay for the stage and premiering it in London in 1989, William Nicholson personalizes the issues of suffering and death by focusing on the life of Clive Staples Lewis and his courtship and marriage to Joy Davidman Gresham, and her death by cancer. The plot focuses entirely on the noted Christian writer's relationship with the American Jewish poet, whom he met and married—less to live as man and wife than to enable her and her children by a prior marriage to stay in England—after 50 years of bachelorhood. Critics found the script far more graphic about her symptoms than about whether this marriage of convenience ripened into sexual love. However, Nicholson finds a wealth of delicate metaphor in the imagery of the title—a reference to Lewis's assertion that true life is inner life or afterlife and what happens on Earth is a mere shadow existence. On the English stage and on Broadway, Nigel Hawthorne's wry performance brought theological abstractions to emotional life as he portrayed Lewis as an embodiment of an older, surer England coming to grips with a new world that is not so much demanding bravery as demanding of bravery. Jane Lapotaire portrayed Joy on the British stage and Jane Alexander meticulously and brilliantly underplayed the role on Broadway. The stage play centers on the quietly developed relationship of two adults and has more dialogue devoted to Lewis's Christian thought as well as a fuller exposition of Joy's life and conversion before she met Lewis. In essence, Nicholson admitted that, given Lewis's reticence, he had to imagine much of what went on in the relationship with Gresham.

What separated *Shadowlands* from typical "romances" was its emphasis on Eros rather than erotica as Lewis and Gresham slowly discover one another as human beings. Onstage, they developed a chaste friendship based first on mutual respect, then on sacrifice. When they marry and finally acknowledge their love, it is not a "relationship" that binds them, but a great love. According to Nicholson, Lewis was a man who, until Joy came along when he was in late middle age, was "afraid of commitments" and quite unable to make any. The play rightly sees pain and pleasure as two significant themes for C.S. Lewis. Yet, apart from redemption, these themes at times stand as more a threat to his faith than its cornerstone.

The Films

Nicholson's quiet teleplay *Shadowlands* first appeared on BBC television in 1984 with Joss Ackland in the role of Lewis and Claire Bloom as Joy. The BBC had originally rejected an earlier screenplay by Brian Sibley (who later turned it into a book in 1985) as "too documentary" and selected Nicholson's version. Ackland's performance was quite bookish and commanding while Bloom's performance is less confrontational. The truncated, small-screen version captures the sidelong glances of two souls forming deep bonds. However, it does not lend itself to condensation and disregards the humor and complexity that arise from the pairing of the circumspect Lewis and the freewheeling Gresham. The telefilm also keeps mostly to tight close-ups and is mostly about dying. A final distinction is that in both the telefilm and the stage play, Oxford is represented almost wholly through Lewis's colleagues, without the ceremonial occasions, fewer student scenes, and the subplot of the student who drops out.

Director Richard Attenborough's 1993 theatrical version adds more texture to Nicholson's play and focuses on living. The film sets up the problem of a comfortable academic who talks about love and pain, but seems to have neither. He's also a fantasist who insists on "magic" as a significant force against the rational analysis of his colleagues. He needs emotional experience, a close relationship with someone other than his brother, Warnie (excellently played by Edward Hardwick), or the memory of his mother (who died of cancer when Lewis was nine), to fulfill what God would make of him. He needs Joy Gresham's love to understand love as more than a courtly allegory or Aristotelian plot motive. He needs it to become a better teacher and more fully human. If his wife's anguish and death become the means of his renewal, the loss of her vital presence makes every evidence of renewal seem commemorative. One of the film's central moments occurs in the attic scene where Lewis (Anthony Hopkins) emotionally bonds with Joy's son, Douglas (Joseph Mazzello), following her death. Douglas, as a double of the young Lewis, faces the death of his mother and cries, which Lewis could not do at his age. This, and the concluding stroll they take in the country, represents a commitment of self to another, a continuance of Joy's (Debra Winger) good influence. Through lighting, backgrounds, shot distances, and angles, the film version de-glamorizes its settings to keep the human scale. Further, a careful structuring of imagery, scenic drama, and color tones helps embody the themes of the plot.

The theme of Attenborough's version develops different meanings: It is a dimension of experience in which emotional involvement, intuition, and imagination take precedence over knowing. But the term also refers to the Neoplatonic Christian tradition: Joy asserts, and Lewis remembers at the end, that human beings live in a shadowland—the future is unknowable and the real is elsewhere. According to William Hagen, the honeymoon scene joins these two meanings—the nonrational experience of life and the sense of unknown reality—together with the traditional sense that death brings humans into the shadows, to become souls without bodies. This scene also manifests the solution to its thematic challenge: What is seen of this life cannot be so vivid or picturesque as to overshadow the hoped-for "real life" beyond; yet, in this life, the "real life" must be glimpsed through the vivid colors of happiness and dark colors of pain.

In the BBC production and the stage play, Nicholson used Douglas to access what the stage play calls the "Other World"—the fantasy world Lewis called Narnia, and a metonymy for an adult belief in heaven. The film version is more limited by expectations of physical verisimilitude. Thus, the essentially realistic theatrical film must project another world through dialogue, plot, and lighting. This world is in the area of what is seen—its light and imagery, its colors and tones—and it is there that the film achieves an integration with its theme. As a result, it is a fine film, although quite different from its television and stage predecessors. It is a more dramatic film in which less reserved and genuinely emotional characters are more in conflict with themselves, with others, and with English conventionality before they face death. In this version, Lewis deals with his own suffering, not through theology—as he does in the opening scene where he says that "the blows of God's chisel, which hurt us so much, are what make us perfect"—but by becoming a real father to Douglas.

Another significant moment—possibly the most tearfully affecting moment—occurs in the proposal scene in the hospital and captures the film's deepest insight, the paradoxical truth that, while Lewis was unable to surrender himself when Joy was well and could have made him happy, he gives himself to her utterly in her dying, when she has nothing to offer but total need and care.

Generally, critics praised both Hopkins and Winger's performances and Attenborough's directorial hand. However, Attenborough's version is not without its detractors. Calling it "untranscendent" though "artfully directed, photographed, and acted," some complain that Attenborough and Nicholson diminish the spiritual aspect of the story. For them, the film version is no longer the story of the romantic union of two equally life-perplexed, God-seeking individuals, perfectly matched in intellect and high spirits. Now, it is the story of an overgrown teddy bear, lovably bookish, who is rescued from emotional suffocation by a warmhearted, tough-tender mother who shatters his routine. Stanley Kauffmann remarked that "Nicholson writes the way Attenborough directs; it's a perfect match. Each looks for the kitschiest approach, the most Hallmark-apt expression of the matter in hand." As a result, the film is relentlessly simplified. The central critical fault lies in the film's highly romanticized treatment that fails to uncover the couple's real theological core.

The film is praised, though, in revealing Lewis' devastation at losing Joy. He rails against the God he describes now as not a master sculptor chiseling humans into shape, but a crude smith hammering them into pieces. But, ultimately, it is the memory of Eros—the true binding of two human beings in love—that sustains Lewis in his grief. The central question addressed by the film is whether it is better to live safely or to risk all for transcendent love. The love affair is a reflection of the Christian life. Great faith must exist in tension with great doubt. The film suggests that belief without the specter of doubt is not really faith, because nothing is at risk. Though close to abandoning his Christian theodicy, Lewis and Douglas are, in the end, united in a human communion of shared grief and love. The film, like Lewis, suggests that, though happiness includes pain and life is filled with suffering, we dwell in a world of shadows—a world that is a reflection of the eternal world whose Light seeks to pierce and perfect it.

REFERENCES

Aleva, Richard, "Yanked Down to Earth: Attenborough's C.S. Lewis," *Commonweal* (January 28, 1994): 22–24; Como, James, "Land of Shadows," *The National Review* (February 7, 1994): 72–75; Hagen, W.M., "*Shadowlands* and the Redemption of Light," *Literature/Film Quarterly* 26:1 (1998): 10–16; Henry, William A., III, "In Search of Healing Magic," *Time* (November 19, 1990), 106; Kauffmann, Stanley, "Soft Focus," *The New Republic* (February 7, 1994), 26; O'Toole, Lawrence, "Pros and Cons: Two 'Shadowlands' Shed Different Lights on a Romance," *Entertainment Weekly* (July 8, 1994): 61; Ullstein, Stefan, "*Shadowlands* Portrays Lewis With Poignance," *Christianity Today* (February 7, 1994), 50; Wood, Ralph C., "The Tears of Things," *Christian Century* (February 23, 1994), 200–203.

—*J.N.Y.*

SHIRLEY VALENTINE (1986)

WILLY RUSSELL (1947–)

Shirley Valentine (1989), U.K., directed by Lewis Gilbert, adapted by Willy Russell; Paramount Pictures.

The Play

By the time *Shirley Valentine* opened in May of 1985 with Pauline Collins in the lead at London's Vaudeville Theatre, Willy Russell had established himself as a major playwright. He followed the considerable success of *Educating Rita* (1980) with *Blood Brothers* (1983), his highly acclaimed mixed-genre musical that ended with a double murder, a play that really hit its stride when it was revived in the West End during the 1990s. In comparison to the theatrical spectacle of *Blood Brothers*, *Shirley Valentine* is about as scaled down and simple as a play can be. It takes the form of an extended monologue. Russell was lucky enough to find in Pauline Collins, born in Devon and raised in Wallasey, near Russell's native Liverpool, an actress capable of bringing the play to life. The play has two sets. The first act shows Shirley cooking her husband's supper in her kitchen while dreaming about a vacation to the Greek islands. The second act places her on a rock, sunning herself in Greece, while explaining to the audience how she got there and how she rediscovered herself. In Act One, she is Shirley Bradshaw, housewife. In Act Two she has transformed herself into Shirley Valentine, the woman she was before taking on the drudgery of raising a family and slaving for her thankless husband. The transformation closely parallels that of Rita into Susan White in his early hit play *Educating Rita*, except that Shirley is transformed by sheer will power and not as a consequence of being formally "educated."

Like Rita, Shirley Bradshaw wants more out of life than her humdrum existence as homemaker for her overworked husband, Joe, and longs to visit Greece, but Joe does not share her fantasy. Shirley desperately wants to escape, but by the end of the first act Joe makes it clear that she will have to do it alone. In Act Two, while relaxing on a rock on the Greek coast, Shirley explains how she got there with the help of her friend Jane, how she had an affair with a local gigolo named Costas, and how she found a job as a waitress, intending to stay there rather than returning home to a husband who does not appreciate her. She wonders how she might react if her husband comes looking for her, now that she has found her place in the sun. The play is about transformation and liberation.

"I first wrote *Shirley Valentine* as a one-woman play, as opposed to a one-woman show," Russell explained. "It has other characters; even though they don't appear on stage, you feel that you've seen them. I didn't want to write what is normally perceived as being a monologue but, instead, a fully plotted play that happened to have only one character in it." Discussing her character, Pauline Collins explained, "I have known many

Pauline Collins reprised on screen her stage role in Shirley Valentine, *opposite Bernard Hill as Joe.* (COURTESY PARAMOUNT PICTURES)

people like Shirley. Her dilemma is a universal one. Who doesn't feel that they haven't fulfilled all of their dreams? This is, of course, true of men as well as women." Collins fully understood the character and how to portray her believably. Her West End performances in London brought Collins the Olivier Award for actress of the year in a new play and *Drama* magazine's 1988 Award for best actress in a stage production. When the play transferred to Broadway, Collins also won the Tony Award for best actress. So astonishing was her success that there was little doubt as to who might be cast to play Shirley in the film adaptation.

The Film

After the considerable Columbia Pictures success of *Educating Rita* (1983), it was only logical that playwright Willy Russell would collaborate again with director Lewis Gilbert in an even more challenging project, converting a play that was an extended monologue into a feature film. Of course, the film involves more than a single actress. Collins begins her monologue in the kitchen, as in the play, but as she tells about her life, the film utilizes a flashback structure to dramatize and visualize her dealings with her husband (Bernard Hill), her children Milandra (Tracie Bennett) and Brian (Gareth Jefferson), and her friends and neighbors, all of whom are represented, both in the present and in past flashbacks. The extended cast features Alison Steadman as Shirley's friend Jane, who talks her into going to Greece; Joanna Lumley as Marjorie, her over-achieving classmate who now works in London as a successful prostitute, Shirley is shocked to learn; and Julia McKenzie as Gillian, Shirley's nosy and demanding neighbor. Tom Conti provides an effective cameo as Costas, the Greek gigolo who seduces her as he does any other willing female visitor to his island. The film does create rather more sympathy for Shirley's husband, seen stranded, lonely, and miserable in rainy England while Shirley has her fling.

The film succeeds, however, mainly because of the brilliance of Pauline Collins. "Theatre is an engagement between the actor and the audience," Collins told the *New York Times* (August 27, 1989). "Film is a different sort of medium. It's not immediate, but in some ways it's more involving. I think you can lose yourself more easily in a film than in theatre." Collins enjoyed the novelty of playing her role with an extended cast when the film was made between her London engagement and her New York opening of the play. It was "lovely," she said, to have "other people to react off [of], so I didn't have to provide all the initial energy myself." The play was effectively transformed by the film, which managed to create a strong sense of place, contrasting rain-drenched England with sunny Mediterranean warmth, once the setting shifts south to Mykonos, Greece. The spirit of the play is appropriately captured as Shirley rediscovers herself in an exotic setting and liberates herself from her kitchen and her unreasonably demanding family. The trick is to literalize the fantasy world of Shirley's imagination and its inhabitants, without reducing the fantasy appeal. In this, the film succeeds and excels.

REFERENCES

Brown, Georgia, "Grecian Formula," *The Village Voice* (September 5, 1989), 75; Kempley, Rita, "Sweetheart Shirley Valentine," *The Washington Post* (September 15, 1989): C1 and C9; Rothstein, Mervyn, "Now Pauline Collins Puts Her Valentine's Message on Film," *The New York Times* (August 27, 1989), 15.

—*J.M.W.*

THE SHOP AROUND THE CORNER

See *PARFUMERIE*

A SOLDIER'S PLAY (1981)

CHARLES FULLER (1939–)

A Soldier's Story (1984), U.S.A., directed by Norman Jewison, adapted by Charles Fuller; Columbia Pictures.

The Play

Directed by Douglas Turner Ward for the Negro Ensemble Company, *A Soldier's Play* was first performed on November 10, 1981, at Theatre Four in New York City and was so successful that it went on to win the Pulitzer Prize for drama in 1982. The action is set on an army base in Louisiana in 1944 where an African-American non-commissioned officer, Sergeant Vernon C. Waters, has been murdered "in the woods, out by the Junction." The other black soldiers in the barracks assume Waters was killed by the Ku Klux Klan, and Captain Taylor, who has reported the incident to Washington, warns the soldiers at Fort Neal not to go into the town of Tynan "looking for red-necks." Washington sends Captain Richard Davenport, a black military lawyer trained at Howard University, to investigate the murder. In the Deep South, Davenport is an outsider, set apart by his color and rank (in January of 1940 there were only five Negro officers in the regular army). Because he is a captain, the black enlisted men are reluctant to confide in Davenport.

Davenport goes about his task in a methodical and professional way, knowing full well that the white officers at Fort Neal believe that he intends to stir up trouble. In fact, he just wants to discover the truth. He gets wind of a possible cover-up when he learns that two white officers encountered Waters on the road, drunk, and one of them, Lt. Byrd, roughed him up because Waters was uppity and insulting; but the other officer, Captain Wilcox, tells Davenport that Colonel Nivens had their weapons checked, and "ballistics cleared them." In order to clear up the mystery, Davenport needs to search elsewhere. He discovers that Waters was psychotic, conflicted by self-hatred caused by his "recognition of the bankruptcy of his efforts to please whites," in the words of Frank Rich, his realization that, no matter what he achieves, in his own words, "They still hate you."

Davenport learns that Waters was not well liked by his men because of the way he bullied them. One soldier in particular Waters harassed because he was embarrassed by the way the soldier, a country boy from the South named C.J. Memphis, acted around white people. C.J. was defined by his athletic ability as a star baseball player, by his musical ability, picking guitar and singing, and by his good nature. Intending to "teach him a lesson," Waters has him framed for a shooting incident and imprisoned, saying "Now I got you—one less fool for the race to be ashamed of." This turns out to be a tragic mistake, however, since C.J., who is physically strong, is psychologically weak; he cannot stand to be imprisoned, and he commits suicide.

Waters, who knows he is responsible for C.J.'s death, takes to drinking. All of the men, with the possible exception of Wilkie, Waters's accomplice and lackey, hate Waters for what he has done. One of them, Private First Class Melvin Peterson, on guard duty the night Waters was killed, along with Private Tony Smalls, turns out to be the murderer(s). By the time Davenport figures it all out, Smalls and Peterson have gone AWOL, but Smalls is apprehended, and, as Davenport explains in his final monologue, Peterson was captured a week later in Alabama. All of the black soldiers get shipped to Europe, an apparent victory for them, until Davenport explains bitterly in his final monologue: "The entire outfit—officers and enlisted men—was wiped out in the Ruhr Valley during a German advance."

The play is a tragedy disguised as a murder mystery. Waters is a tragic figure, but so is Peterson, who challenges Waters at one point by asking "What kinda colored man are you?" Waters represents an older generation, a career army man who served with distinction in World War I. He believes that African Americans can succeed only by imitating the white majority. Peterson embraces his blackness rather than trying to disguise it. Both presume to know how blacks should behave in white America. Even C.J., who is ultimately victimized by Waters's reverse racism, understands Waters perfectly well, exclaiming at one point, "Any man don't know where he belong must be in a whole lot of pain." Waters makes an error in judgment, reaches a point of recognition or discovery, then is killed as a consequence of his fatal flaw. The main theme of the tragic play is Justice, racial justice and criminal justice.

The Film

Director Norman Jewison made several smart decisions in approaching the film production, casting several actors from the original Negro Ensemble stage production (Adolph Caesar as Waters, Larry Riley as Memphis, Denzel Washington as Peterson, but not Samuel L. Jackson, who played Private Henson on stage) and recruiting Charles Fuller to reshape his play as a screenplay. The film opens up the play effectively from the opening credits, when the audience sees Waters getting drunk at a bar in town before stumbling out to the Junction where he will be shot. The screenplay injects humor for Robert Townsend as Corporal Ellis, who meets Davenport (Howard E. Rollins, Jr.) at the bus depot in Tynan. The flashback structure of the play works very well for the film, as Davenport questions the soldiers and their memories are then dramatized. Scenes are added involving Davenport and Colonel

Adolph Caesar as Sgt. Waters in A Soldier's Story. (COLUMBIA PICTURES / LFQ ARCHIVES)

Nivens (Trey Wilson) both in his office and at home with his wife, Ida (Patricia Brandkamp), with Davenport demanding cooperation and permission to interview the white officers Byrd (Wings Hauser) and Wilcox (Scott Paulin). For the most part, however, the film follows the play closely until the end, when both Smalls (David Harris) and Peterson are apprehended. The drama almost demands a confrontation between Davenport and Peterson, and the film effectively delivers one. In the film Peterson is captured and brought before Davenport, who asks him a question that drives home the moral point of the drama: "Who gave you the right to judge, to decide who is fit to be a Negro, and who is not?" The film then ends with the Negro troops marching off to war.

Fuller got rid of Davenport's final monologue, a wise decision since the conflicting irony of the concluding monologue is potentially distracting and tends to obscure the main point of the drama. To have retained it would have given a bitter tone to the film's conclusion and that might have upset the film's mass audience. "Hundreds of movies have white soldiers marching off with joy and fervor," Fuller told Aljean Harmitz of the *New York Times*, but "this is the first time in Hollywood history that anybody has seen black troops marching off to war at the end of a movie." The film showed unexpected strength with a white cross-over audience. Working from a $5 million budget, the film grossed over $30 million and earned three Academy Award nominations, for best supporting actor (Adolph Caesar), best adapted screenplay, and best picture. It lost out mainly because it was competing against another splendid drama adaptation, *Amadeus*, crafted by playwright Peter Shaffer for the screen. But it certainly demonstrated what Charles Fuller said was the whole point of *A Soldier's Play:* "that black people are Americans."

REFERENCES

Cooper, Carol, "*Soldier's Story* Salute," *Film Comment* (December 1984), 17–19; Harmetz, Aljean, "How Endings Have Effected Two Recent Movies," *The New York Times*, October 8, 1984, C13; Rich, Frank, "Stage: Negro Ensemble Presents 'Soldier's Play,'" *The New York Times*, December 6, 1981, sec. 2, 3; Welsh, Jim, "*A Soldier's Story:* A Paradigm for Justice," in *Columbia Pictures: Portrait of a Studio*, ed. Bernard F. Dick (Lexington: University Press of Kentucky, 1992), 208–217.

—*J.M.W.*

SOMEONE WAITING (1954)

(GEORGE) EMLYN WILLIAMS (1905–1987)

Time Without Pity (1957), U.K., directed by Joseph Losey, adapted by Ben Barzman; Harlequin Productions.

The Play

Taking its inspiration from England's infamous Julia Wallace murder case of the early 1930s, *Someone Waiting* has been regarded as one of Emlyn Williams' most tautly constructed thrillers. Williams, a Welshman, developed a style for writing plays in reverse—he would start with the climax so that the action flowed backward in time and "led up to" the initial scene. Such was the case with *Someone Waiting*, which also opens by setting up all the relationships among characters and their respective motivations. Most notably, the beginning of the play introduces Walter Fenn, a law exam tutor who is out to avenge the execution of his son for a murder the boy didn't commit. He arrives at the home of Mr. and Mrs. John Nedlow under the auspices of educating their son, Martin, whom he immediately befriends, and

together they seek to expose John Nedlow as the true murderer. Playwright Williams, also a reputable actor, played the role of Fenn in the first stage production of the show in Liverpool in 1953. The character was one the author crafted as artfully on paper as in performance: Fenn is a timid, unsure man whose sinister capabilities gradually emerge as his obsession with making the true murderer known spirals into madness and his own willingness to kill.

Someone Waiting first appeared on Broadway in 1956. Williams did not reprise his performance for the show's American debut, however; instead, Leo G. Carroll played the part of Fenn. Howard St. John took the role of Nedlow, the murderous automotive magnate, and Jessie Royce Landis played his manipulated wife, Vera. Robert Hardy performed as Martin, the couple's adopted son, whom Fenn schools in the ways of law, as well as in the workings of a vengeful, deviant mind.

Suspenseful and chilling, the "whodunit" play became one of Williams's first self-penned commercial successes. The work did carry an underlying indictment of capital punishment, although critics have debated the severity of its attack. Williams, in fact, tempered this aspect of the play when the show was revived in England in the 1980s, given that the death penalty had long been abolished by that time.

The Film

Joseph Losey was involved with experimental theater in the United States before applying his interests to Hollywood filmmaking. Most likely, Losey saw in *Someone Waiting* a story and structure that suited his own inclination for untraditional narratives; the director once described the play as a "straight thriller which [scenarist Ben] Barzman and I . . . turned on its head." From the outset, Losey's *Time without Pity* ran counter to Hollywood films: It revealed the identity of the murderer even before the titles rolled. Losey followed in Williams's footsteps by wanting his opening to anticipate a narrative about the process of unmasking the true criminal's identity. And, as in the play, the main character is a stranger who enters into and disrupts the distorted equilibrium of the other characters' relationships. But there are also crucial differences between the two versions and their treatment of the lead character. While in the play Mr. Fenn invades the Nedlows' (dis)order, *Time Without Pity* employs his literary equivalent, David Graham (Michael Redgrave), an alcoholic writer who returns home from a sanitarium in order to save his son who is due to be—but has not yet been—executed. The result of this change is significant: In the play, Fenn becomes increasingly unsympathetic as the agony of his son's wrongful death drives him to kill. In the film, however, Graham, truly pathetic in his seeming inability to write, think clearly, or stay free of drink, is ultimately redeemed when he gives his own life to save his son's.

Another significant variation between the two versions of the work is that, while both Losey and Williams pointedly express their characters' spiritual and moral vindictiveness, Losey grafts on class and social critique. As film scholar Colin Gardner states, the director intended to show "that British justice *is itself a form* of class violence." Losey commonly coded social issues in his films, as he did in *Time* with his concerns about capital punishment. But these references often went beyond what was outwardly political; in Losey's hands they touched upon the core of human existence. He saw himself as a humanist and attempted through his films to "say something" about human nature, its social conditions, and its psychological discontents. As he told Tom Milne, "I felt—and feel—that the killing of human beings, whether by the State in capital punishment, or by society in inquisitions, or by misunderstanding of diseased mentalities, or by war, whatever the forces, means that there is not really very much purpose in life unless these forces are understood, unless they are presented in some way so as to make them at least subject to examination by other people." In addition, in *Time* Losey fiercely extrapolates from Williams's template in order to show a set of relationships that violate traditional hierarchies associated with class, gender, and sexual orientation. This, too, serves to embellish his point about the failings of the social order—and to expose them through film.

Most of Losey's films over his career also reveal an interest in mutating expected temporality. It is fitting, then, that he should have chosen to adapt a play that lent itself to ideas about racing against, or running counter to, time. As Gardner notes, "Everyone in the film is trying, in their various ways, to transcend, appropriate, outrun or stave off time." Whereas the play is set over a period of four months, Losey and Barzman turned the film into a document of 24 hours—the time left before Graham's son, Alec (Alec McCowen), is due to be executed for the crime Robert Stanford (Leo McKern) committed. He also connects the effective use of time with the production of art and the notion of disease; as novelist Graham fights against time, he is unable to write or think clearly in his alcoholic haze.

Losey also exploited visual effects in ways impossible for a stage performance. The filmmaker's enduring collaboration with Richard MacDonald, design consultant, production designer, or art director on 17 of Losey's films, helped bring an extraordinary aesthetic texture to the film. One of MacDonald's primary approaches to film design was to find a painter whose work embodied the spirit of the narrative. He chose Francisco de Goya for *Time*. As a result, Goya's painting *Echan perros al toro*, in which a bull is being baited by wild dogs, becomes the centerpiece of the set. The painting literally hangs over the scene of the murder, immediately—although obliquely—connecting the theme of the painting to the action. Then, throughout the film, Stanford gradually emerges as that bull, aggressively charging through his life with lies as he desperately tries to gratify his social ambitions and sexual ego amidst a furious crowd. In essence, Goya's work "frames" the action, at once a status symbol of high taste and a visual metaphor of Stanford's true self.

Stanford's multileveled house furthers the film's layers of visual complexity. Indeed, Losey, with MacDonald's help, frequently set his films in houses encrusted with the *objets d'art* and the splendid interiors of wealthy sophisticates. In this way, class and society become visual, confining constructs. The interior items also indicate the illusory nature of an identity established through external criteria such as wealth, acquisitions, and social appearances. Losey used mirrors, in particular, to make both aesthetic and social points, and here they serve to reflect the distance between Graham's mental and bodily selves, especially in light of his alcoholism and his tortured relationship with his son. But Stanford remains the primary outlet for Losey's criticisms. Again to Milne, "In *Time Without Pity*, I was talking about men who are tyrants in their own families or in their businesses, about human beings who walk over other people to make fortunes, about people who go along with hypocrisies which they dress up in all sorts of trappings as their own—and who are perhaps madmen, the kind of madmen who make wars, although not recognized as being mad, and who have totally disproportionate power over their sons, their wives, the society they live in." (This statement partially justifies Losey's demeaning treatment of women in the film, although his oeuvre consistently depicts women less sensitively than men.)

Losey was blacklisted in the early fifties due to his failure to appear at a hearing held by the House Un-American Activities Committee. He had been in Italy making a film at the time, but his absence at the hearing raised questions about his political leanings and left him exiled in Europe and using the name Joseph Walton on his films. This experience undoubtedly contributed to his need to voice his distaste for social intolerance. With its cool reception in the United

States, however, *Time Without Pity* seemed at first an unremarkable way to announce the return of Losey's name to his films. His untraditional rendering of a suspenseful thriller confused many audiences. Reviews found favor with the performances but were frustrated with the deliberate tension and obfuscated action, observing the film as bursting with cinematic nonsequiturs and performative excess. Moreover, the film's overarching rebuke of capital punishment, in addition to its psychological explication of social power and dominance, seemed to many critics to overload the film, leaving it fairly superficial. With little promotion and support from its American distributor, *Time* quickly vanished from theaters.

Three years later a cinephile movement in France embraced the film for its highly expressive gestures and theatrical histrionics. It granted the film an appreciation even Losey found slightly excessive. The director admitted that the film was "overloaded, overpacked, overdense . . . dense in the sense of trying to say too much directly instead of through people and behavior and . . . well, with less skill." And yet without question that density yields an increasing, brilliant intensity that culminates in the final scene. As Graham dies at the hands of Stanford, Stanford is caught red-handed in his living room (the site of the initial murder) minutes before Alec Graham is due to be executed. Suddenly all the elements of the film are brought full circle in the sublime final shot: the Goya painting, the décor, the multileveled house, the shattering of appearances, the overblown performances, the weary characters. Even the last piece of sound resembles a clock's steady—indeed, maddening—tick.

REFERENCES

Caute, David, *Joseph Losey: A Revenge on Life* (London: Faber and Faber, 1994); Gardner, Colin Raymond, *Time Without Pity: Immanence and Contradiction in the Films of Joseph Losey* (unpublished dissertation, UCLA Department of Film and Television, 1997); Harding, James, *Emlyn Williams: A Life* (London: Weidenfeld and Nicolson, 1993); Leahy, James, *The Cinema of Joseph Losey* (London: A. Zwemmer, 1967); Milne, Tom, *Losey on Losey* (Garden City, N.Y.: Doubleday, 1968); Review, "Time Without Pity," *The New York Times*, November 23, 1957, 11:2.; Review, "Time Without Pity," *Variety*, April 2, 1957.

—R.E.

SORRY WRONG NUMBER (1948)

LUCILLE FLETCHER (1912–)

Sorry Wrong Number (1948), U.S.A., directed by Anatole Litvak, adapted by Lucille Fletcher; Paramount.

The Play

Lucille Fletcher originally wrote *Sorry Wrong Number* as a 22-minute radio script in 1943 for *Suspense*. It is set in New York and centers around a bed-ridden woman, Mrs. Stevenson, who accidentally hears a phone call concerning the plotting of a woman's murder. In the horrific finale, she learns that she is the intended victim. It was a tour de force performance for Agnes Moorehead, and she reprised the role in seven broadcasts between 1943 and 1948. *Sorry Wrong Number* was also staged as a 14-page theatrical production in which the stage was divided up into several sections. In the center area was the expensive bedroom of Mrs. Stevenson; in the flanking areas were spaces for, variously, a telephone operator, a Western Union clerk, police headquarters, and the two assassins planning the murder.

The play begins with Mrs. Stevenson attempting to reach her husband by phone in his office where he is working late at night. But the telephonist accidentally connects her to another phone conversation transpiring between two men. A killer type, George, has apparently received a call in a phone booth giving him a contract assignment to murder a woman and make it look like a robbery. Mrs. Stevenson attempts to alert the telephone operator and the police department. She then learns that her husband, Elbert, who has scarcely left her side since she became an invalid 12 years ago, has left for Boston on "urgent business," not to return until the following afternoon. The play moves toward its exciting climax with the phone operator listening to the frantic last moments of Mrs. Stevenson as she realizes that the killer is in her own house. Her murder takes place as the stage darkens and the roar of a passing train drowns out her screams. Meanwhile, police sergeant Duffy is attempting to reach Mrs. Stevenson. The killer picks up the phone and says, "Sorry, wrong number," before hanging up. The curtain falls.

The Film

Playwright Fletcher conceived of her script "as an experiment in sound with the telephone as the principal protagonist." It was not just a murder story, she said, "I wanted to write something that by its very nature should, for maximum effectiveness, be heard rather than seen." However, as a result of Moorehead's performance and various stage, television, and film versions, Fletcher found that her original script took on "wider horizons than I had imagined for it." She intuitively understood the broader parameters that would affect her originally conceived sound drama. Fletcher also noted that "in the hands of a fine actress like Agnes Moorehead, the script turned out to be more the character study of a woman than a technical experiment, and the plot itself, with its O. Henry twist at the end, fell into the thriller category."

The author's comments also apply to the film version, which relies upon a strong performance by Barbara Stanwyck as the neurotically possessive Leona Stevenson as well as the visual extensions provided by appropriate *film noir* chiaroscuro cinematography, complex camera moves (particularly the circling camera that encloses Leona and her bed), and a typically convoluted time track. These devices emphasize her alienation and also link her with forties "femme fatale" spider women. Leona Stevenson belongs to that "noir" category of the domineering American wife described in Stephen Farber's 1974 essay "Violence and the Bitch Goddess," a figure also seen in *Double Indemnity, Mildred Pierce*, and *The Postman Always Rings Twice*—one whose materialistic characteristics cause disaster for all concerned.

Anatole Litvak's version naturally extends Fletcher's original radio drama by moving beyond the tightly constructed chronological framework to provide via elaborate flashbacks details about Leona's past, as well as information on the supplementary characters, such as her father, family doctor, and Henry's former working-class girlfriend. Although radio listeners could only assume that Elbert may have been responsible for the plot, the film version explicitly assigns the guilt to Leona's emasculated husband, Henry, played by Burt Lancaster. Like the play, the film ends with the conscience-stricken Henry vainly attempting at the last minute to warn Leona before her murder. However, the movie provides a final twist. After the contract killer has murdered Leona offscreen, he picks up her phone and replies "Sorry, wrong number." The police later arrest Henry as he leaves a telephone booth similar to the one in which stage audiences originally saw George in the theatrical version.

REFERENCES

Fletcher, Lucille, *Sorry Wrong Number* and *The Hitchhiker* (New York: Dramatist's Play Service, 1980); Solomon, Matthew, "Adapting 'Radio's Perfect Script': 'Sorry Wrong Number' and *Sorry Wrong Number*," *Quarterly Review of Film Studies*, 16:1 (1995): 23–39; Farber, Stephen, "Violence and the Bitch Goddess," *Film Noir Reader 2*, eds. Alain Silver and James Ursini (New York: Limelight Editions, 1999), 45–56.

—*T.W.*

SQUAW MAN, THE (1905)

EDWIN MILTON ROYLE (1862–1942)

The Squaw Man (1913), U.S.A., directed by Cecil B. DeMille, adapted by Edwin Milton Royle; Jesse L. Lasky Feature Play Company.

The Squaw Man (1918), U.S.A., directed by Cecil B. DeMille, adapted by Beulah Marie Dix; Famous Players-Lasky.

The Squaw Man (1931), U.S.A., directed by Cecil B. DeMille, adapted by Lucien Hubbard and Lenore Coffee; MGM.

The Play

Edwin Milton Royle's most popular play was a shrewd blend of contradictory elements. It demonstrated some aspects of late 19th-century naturalism, utilized plot devices and situations that derived from traditional melodrama, and flung its wild western locales into the teeth of the stiff-upper-lip school of the well-made English play. The play premiered in New York at Wallack's Theatre on October 23, 1905, and ran for a successful 222 performances. Appearing in the role of James Wynnegate/Jim Carston was William Faversham. Dustin Farnum replaced Faversham for the play's revival at the Broadway Theatre in 1911. In the original run, William S. Hart portrayed Wynnegate's nemesis, Cash Hawkins.

The first act is set in England on the estate of the earl of Kerhill. Charity money contributed by the men of the Sixteenth Lancers has mysteriously disappeared. Captain James Wynnegate, in order to protect the culprit, his cousin, assumes the blame and is subsequently forced to leave England in disgrace. In the second act the fugitive Wynnegate, now under the name of "Jim Carston," has assumed the ownership of a ranch in Utah. Opposing him is the villainous rustler, Cash Hawkins. Wynnegate is saved from Hawkins's ambush by an Indian girl, Nat-U-Rich (Mabel Morrison), who shoots Hawkins dead. The third act begins years afterward. Jim has married Nat-U-Rich out of a sense of duty. Now a "squaw man" outcast because of his interracial marriage, he raises his son Hal with dignity while fighting to keep his ranch in operation. When members of the English branch of the Wynnegate family, including Lady Diana (with whom he is in love), visit the ranch to inform him that his name has been cleared and that the way is open for him to return to England as the new earl of Kerhill, he sadly realizes that his ties to Nat-U-Rich must hold him back. He decides to send Hal back to England in his stead. In the fourth and final act, Nat-U-Rich commits suicide, freeing Jim to go to England with his son.

Based on his own experiences out West, Royle was determined to put the "real Indian" on the stage. In casting for the Indian characters, for example, he secured the services of at least one authentic Ute Indian to ensure the proper dialect and speech inflections. The play attacked racist attitudes toward Indians. "I don't think we ever do these primitive races justice," Wynnegate tells a visitor from England. "Here I am a 'Squaw Man'—that is, socially ostracized. You see, we have our social distinctions, even out here." And when he prevents the local sheriff from arresting Nat-U-Rich for the shooting of Cash Hawkins, he declares, "There are cases, sheriff, where justice is superior to the law. And a white man's court is a bad place for justice to the Indian." Also under attack were the pretensions of the English aristocracy. In the first act, titled aristocrats who marry wealthy Americans in an exchange of money for pedigree are ridiculed: "Please examine these first-class specimens of the British aristocracy," jokes one character in the first act in reference to Wynnegate. "He has blue ribbons, medals, and a pedigree longer than your purses. He's for sale." And when Jim reaches Utah and is promptly swindled by a canny cattleman, one of the locals comments, "The prosperity of our beloved country would go plumb to Gehenna if an all-wise Providence did not enable us to sell an Englishman a mine or a ranch now and then."

Although the action of the play was, for the most part, set in wide-open western locales, playwright Royle made little attempt to exploit them, as his contemporary, David Belasco, was doing in works like *The Girl of the Golden West*. Most of the action—including Jim's discovery that Hawkins is a rustler, his rescue by Nat-U-Rich from a fall down a mountain ravine, and Nat-U-Rich's suicide—takes place offstage and is conveyed entirely by expository dialogue. Yet, the *implications* of regional color and open-air romance were there, and the play did not have to wait long for an enterprising film production company to adapt it to the screen.

The Films

Dissatisfied with an unsuccessful career in the theatre as actor and writer, Cecil B. DeMille joined forces with former vaudevillian Jesse L. Lasky and glove salesman Samuel Goldfish (later changed to Goldwyn) to form the Jesse L. Lasky Feature Play Company in 1913. Excited by the successful release a year before of Sarah Bernhardt's film adaptation of her play, *Queen Elizabeth*, they too sought out a popular stage property to bring to the screen. How this group of tyros managed to make a film that would alter the course of American film history is a story worth telling. They bought the rights to Royle's *The Squaw Man*, contracted with Royle himself to write the scenario, contracted with Dustin Farnum to duplicate his stage role as Wynnegate, cast the Indian actress Redwing as Nat-U-Rich, hired veteran film director Oscar Apfel to co-direct with the unseasoned DeMille, and set out for Flagstaff, Arizona, to begin shooting. Disappointed with the locations, the crew continued westward to a small, straggling township 10 miles north of Los Angeles, where they established a barn studio on the corner of Selma Avenue and Vine Street. (From this modest acorn would eventually grow the mighty oak of Paramount Pictures.) By some miracle the film that emerged lays claim to a number of "firsts": It established tiny Hollywood as the future site of the American film industry. It was one of the first—perhaps *the* first—American six-reel feature-length film to be made from a Broadway play. It employed indoor lighting to an extent never before attempted. It was the first to carry a list of acting credits. And it brought a degree of cinematic savvy to the practice of stage adaptations never before attempted.

Indeed, the Lasky Feature Play Company was dedicated in the years 1913–16 to bringing a "fresh-air" approach to its theatrical films, by contrast to the "canned theatre" of *Queen Elizabeth*. Plays by David Belasco and others were exploited for their western locales and physical action. "We can do novel and unusual things on the screen that are impossible on the stage," said Lasky. "We have adopted the motto, 'The World Is Our Studio.' As an earnest of that, we are sending the present company to Southern California and Wyoming for the atmosphere of the story. We will not hesitate to go wherever the best interests of any production require. If necessary, we will send companies abroad. We intend to erect outdoor stages in different parts of the country."

Playwright Royle apparently agreed with this attitude. "The weakest part of the melodrama is its dialogue," he wrote in 1914, "and that's why we let them say as little as possible in the [film] melodrama. The situations are told better by actions than by words." At the same time, he continued, when a play like *The Squaw Man* called for "vision," or "memory" scenes—best executed on the stage by dual staging and lighting effects—the dissolves and vignetting effects possible through photography are infinitely superior in their results. In one scene Wynnegate (the spelling of the name is simplified To Wyngate for the film) quietly relaxes in his ranch house while scanning the illustrated papers looking for news of his native England. A society page with a drawing of a lady of fashion dissolves into a portrait of the woman Jim left behind at Maudsley Towers. In another scene, when Jim has been told that he can return to England with honor, he stands at the right side of the frame and pantomimes his nostalgia for England, while the left half of the frame dissolves into views of his former life in England—including a dinner table scene and a view of a formation of Lancers.

The Squaw Man was one of the first theatrical films to make more than minimal use of natural locations. Many events only alluded to in the play's dialogue were visualized on screen without the insistence upon shallow-depth playing areas and painted scenery. Three examples are Jim Wynnegate's capture of Cash Hawkins, Nat-U-Rich's rescue of Wynnegate during a roundup in the mountain snows, and Jim's passage from England to America. In the first, a quick succession of long shots depict Wynnegate and other horsemen chasing down the rustlers. In the second, Wynnegate, after falling from his horse during the roundup, wanders aimlessly through the thickening snows before being rescued by Nat-U-Rich. By means of cross-cutting, the shots shift from one character to the other as they both wander through the snows. This editing strategy binds together the two principal characters, symbolic of the bonds that will hold them together until her self-sacrifice at the play's conclusion. Finally, Wynnegate's passage from England constitutes an elaborate sequence wherein Wynnegate boards ship and survives a disastrous fire at sea. The shots of the heaving ocean, the burning decks, the hysteria of the jostling passengers fighting for room on the lifeboats, create an epic excitement that DeMille in subsequent films would claim as his own.

This is not to say that the stifling confines of the proscenium stage are not imitated at other times. Throughout, the camera maintains a medium shot position that keeps the characters visible from head to toe. The western saloon, which is pictured exactly as it was described in the play's second act—even down to the double-doors at the rear of the set through which the arrival of the Overland Limited can be seen—is photographed in shallow depth, with the borders of the frame functioning as the side wings of a stage. The acting styles of Dustin Farnum and the other cast members reveal the declamatory style prevalent in stage melodramas. This is most apparent in the scenes that correspond to Acts Three and Four, where the action transpires in the dooryard of the Carston Ranch. The dialogue exchanges between Wynnegate and an English

lawyer (wherein Jim confesses nostalgia for England) consist of prolonged, static shots and broad gestures and posed postures. Unfortunately, only a scant few explanatory titles accompany the histrionics. The longest "take" in the film occurs when the cowboys bid farewell to Carston's little boy. In this scene, faithfully transcribed from the play, several cowboys advance "downstage" in single file, each presenting the child with a gift. The action lasts a full two minutes, without benefit of cutting or camera movement. The film's concluding scene duplicates the play's final tableau: Nat-U-Rich's body has been found and is brought onstage by the cowboys while Carston sits and broods downstage. Farnum's exaggerated pantomime is at its most strenuous here as, echoing the play's original words, he says, "Poor little mother!"

The play's attacks on racism and society cant, and its use of regional dialects, have been largely omitted. However, the film's use of double-exposure affirms the dominant theme of the clash between East and West. And the jarring juxtapositions of natural exteriors and artificial interiors in their own clumsy way affirm Royle's original intention of depicting the confusion of an Englishman, with his rules and artificial codes of conduct, adrift in a boundless country that acknowledge no such restrictions.

The Squaw Man scored big at the box office, taking in a then-generous $250,000, and launching the career of Cecil B. DeMille. While acknowledging the film's stage origins, reviewers were quick to point out its more cinematic achievement. Writing in *The Moving Picture World*, Louis Reeves Harrison praised "the compelling beauty and nobility of actual scenery as compared to stage affectations," noting also that "the fire scenes aboard ship are made plausible by using an actual vessel, sailing in the open, and there is a delightful fidelity to . . . the escape of crew and passengers in the boats." Perhaps, Reeves concluded, the film medium will prove generally superior to the stage as a storytelling medium: "[Royle and DeMille] may perceive that this new method of thought transmission has a grander scope than the boxed-in stage presentation. . . . Its directness, the lack of intervening utterance, its very silence, all contribute to a fascination long proven to exist, not only for the mixed audience, but for those familiar with superior examples of the older arts."

That Cecil B. DeMille had an unusually close relationship with *The Squaw Man* is borne out by his two subsequent remakes, in 1918 and 1931. Both are faithful to the basic plot line, although DeMille, clearly a more seasoned director by then, fleshes out the characters and strays further from the story's stagebound origins. In the first, adapted by Beulah Marie Dix, Elliott

Dexter portrays Jim, Ann Little is Naturich (the name's spelling is altered here), and Jack Holt is Cash Hawkins. In the second, adapted by Lucien Hubbard and Lenore Coffee—the first and only talking version of the play—Warner Baxter is Jim, Lupe Velez is Naturich, and Charles Bickford is Cash Hawkins. Ironically, most of the latter film was shot in the very location that DeMille had once considered, and rejected, for the 1914 version—Hot Springs Junction, Arizona. Its poor box office signaled an end to DeMille's mostly unhappy three-picture association with MGM (which had included *Dynamite* [1929] and *Madame Satan* [1930]). Despite a few good reviews—Mordaunt Hall in the *New York Times* said that although "the seams of age shine through," it was an "agreeable and expert melodrama"—some critics were beginning to regard his work as a quaint holdover from the silent era. Ever resilient, his next feature, *Sign of the Cross* (1932), launched a successful series of historical/biblical epics for which he is still best known.

REFERENCES

"Edwin Milton Royle," *The Moving Picture World*, February 21, 1914, 930; Higashi, Sumiko, *Cecil B. DeMille and American Culture: The Silent Era* (Berkeley: University of California Press, 1994); "Jesse L. Lasky in Pictures," *Moving Picture World*, January 3, 1914, 35; Ringgold, Gene, and DeWitt Bodeen, *The Films of Cecil B. DeMille* (New York: Cadillac Publishing Co., 1969); Tibbetts, John C., *The American Theatrical Film* (Bowling Green, Ohio: Popular Press, 1985).

—*J.C.T.*

STAGE DOOR (1936)

EDNA FERBER (1887–1968) AND GEORGE S. KAUFMAN (1889–1961)

Stage Door (1937), U.S.A., directed by Gregory La Cava, adapted by Morrie Riskind and Anthony Veiller; RKO.

The Play

While not as enduringly popular as other Kaufman and Ferber collaborations, like *The Royal Family* and *Dinner at Eight*, *Stage Door* has plenty of backstage savvy and contains, in the character of Keith Burgess, a wicked satire of Clifford Odets. *Stage Door* premiered in New York at the Music Box Theatre on October 22, 1936, featuring Margaret Sullavan and Phyllis Brooks in the leading roles of Terry Randall and Jean Maitland. The play ran for a respectable 159 performances. With one

exception (occurring in one of the bedrooms), the action of this three-act play transpired entirely in the main room of the Footlights Club in New York's West Fifties. Ferber and Kaufman modeled the story on a real-life boarding house for aspiring actresses, "The Rehearsal Club," which opened in 1913. Many future stars such as Margaret Sullavan and Sandy Duncan actually resided there during the early stages of their careers.

Among a group of budding actresses is Terry Randall, who steps into the shoes of the tragic Kaye Hamilton after Hamilton's suicide. Terry has also lost her boyfriend, former left-wing playwright Keith Burgess (Richard Kendrick), who has dropped her and gone to Hollywood after Terry helped him rewrite a play that has achieved success on Broadway. (Burgess is described as "one of those fellows who started out on a soapbox and ended up in a swimming pool.") But at least Terry finds her career ambitions encouraged by David Kingsley (Onslow Stevens)—a character obviously modeled on Kaufman himself—who has forsaken Hollywood to return to his first love, the theater. In Act Two, Scene Two, Kingsley succinctly articulates the difference between Broadway and Hollywood. "Look at Katharine Cornell, and Lynn Fontanne, and Alfred Lunt. They tramped Broadway in their day. They've worked like horses, trouped the country, and stuck to it. And now they've got something that nothing in the world can take away from them. And what's John Barrymore got? A yacht!" Indeed, the play's idealization of the world of the theatre comes at the expense of several withering critiques of Hollywood, doubtless reflecting the prejudice of coauthor Kaufman.

The play ends with Terry, radiant after rejecting Hollywood values, declaiming, "Now that I am Queen, I wish in future to have a bed, and a room of my own."

The Film

According to certain sources, director Gregory La Cava participated in providing "an entirely new plot" for the film version. Quite naturally, Kaufman's anti-Hollywood diatribes disappear from the new version along with the characters of Burgess and Kingsley. Prior to shooting, La Cava had the cast improvise several scenes and encouraged them to mingle together as if they actually lived in the same boarding house. Katharine Hepburn also jotted down lines following each day's filming and discussed them at length with the director before using them the next day. La Cava, meanwhile, kept rewriting the script daily. Terry and Jean's rivalry still remains until a final reconciliation after she pays homage on stage to the dead Kaye Hamilton. As in the play, Terry does gain the role Kaye originally wanted, but the film also touchingly reveals her sublimation of the latter's spirit into her performance after she learns of her tragic death. Although she becomes a Broadway star, Terry decides to remain at the Footlights Club with her fellow actresses.

The glamorous star personae of Katharine Hepburn and Ginger Rogers contributed significantly to screenplay alterations. While the former entered Hollywood after some theatrical experience, the latter actress was totally identified with a studio system, which, ironically, did not appreciate the more theatrically savvy talents of actors like Hepburn. Class differences become the initial focus of rivalry between them in the film, as Hepburn's upper-middle-class tastes irritate the more down-to-earth Ginger. Adolphe Menjou's casting as theatrical producer Tony Powell recalls a similar role in the 1933 film, *Morning Glory*, which had garnered Hepburn an Academy Award. He gained the part after Burgess Meredith and Douglas Fairbanks, Jr., were eliminated from consideration.

As in the play, the actresses all support struggling actress Kaye Hamilton (Gail Patrick) in affirmative ways. But the film also stresses female solidarity amongst all the women in the boarding house, culminating in the final union between Jean and Terry.

In a footnote to all this, the screenplay adds a play-within-a-play. Terry's father hopes that Terry will so disgrace herself in this production that she will return home. The rehearsals not only reveal Terry's lack of proper stage experience but ironically emphasize the artificial aspects of a performance style both theatrical and cinematic that sometimes passes for "realism."

Despite the radical alterations to the original stage play, the film version operates much more effectively in affirming female solidarity. As historian James Harvey notes, the Ferber-Kaufman original had a conventional boy-gets-girl romantic ending, while the film reveals Hepburn and Rogers explicitly *without* men, and explicitly resigned to being so. "It's interesting that the movie should not only be much better than the play (even Kaufman admitted it was) but bolder and more unconventional, too." Many critics at the time agreed. The *New York Times* review commented that the screenplay was "wittier than the original, more dramatic than the original, more cogent than the original, as well as lacking anti-Hollywood bias."

REFERENCES

Britton, Andrew, *Katharine Hepburn: The Thirties and After* (Newcastle upon Tyne: Tyneside Cinema Publications, 1984); Ferber, Edna, and George S. Kaufman, *Stage Door* (New York: Doubleday, Doran, 1936); Harvey, James, *Romantic Comedy in Hollywood: From Lubitsch to Sturges* (New York: Alfred A. Knopf, 1987).

—*T.W.*

STALAG 17 (1951)

DONALD BEVAN (1920–) AND EDMUND TRZCINSKI (1921–)

Stalag 17 (1953), U.S.A., directed by Billy Wilder, adapted by Billy Wilder and Edwin Blum; Paramount.

The Play

Based in part on their own experiences as prisoners of war, Bevan and Trzcinski wrote *Stalag 17* as a self-described "comedy melodrama." While the stage seemed an unlikely venue for a story of heroism on the grand scale of a battlefield, it proved perfect for a tale of three days in the lives of prisoners of war living in a bleak and crowded barracks, which turns out to be inhabited by an unknown enemy informant. The play premiered in Philadelphia on April 6, 1949, under the title *Stalag XVII-B*. The Broadway version was produced and directed by Jose Ferrer, premiering May 8, 1951, and running for 472 performances. The action takes place within a primitive wood-plank barracks located "somewhere in Germany" during the three days leading up to Christmas 1944. The American prisoners find that an informant is telling the Germans of their escape plans and of the sabotage carried out by a new prisoner. They suspect Sefton (John Ericson), an American prisoner already disliked and distrusted by the others for his profiteering and his isolation. The drama has some comic dialogue and plays out like a whodunit; there are hints to the informant's identity in the dialogue, and the tension builds as the new prisoner's peril grows. As part of their plan to free the threatened prisoner, the others use otherwise useless Red Cross-supplied hockey sticks to grind up cascara pills and gain an advantage by spiking the guards' Christmas drink. Finally, as the prisoners say, it takes the crafty "Sefton to smarten us up" as the isolated, self-interested pariah reveals the informant, Price (Laurence Hugo), and becomes a hero. The play was very popular right after the war when Americans wanted to celebrate their heroes. But this play made the point that "it's a private war" where some soldiers wanted to "leave that honor stuff for the history books." In his *New York Times* review, Brooks Atkinson wrote "Mr. Bevan and Mr.

Trzcinski have made a turbulent and gutsy play out of a haunting experience." *Stalag 17* was their only successful play.

The Film

Billy Wilder took an immediate interest in the story and by 1953 had adapted the play, along with Edwin Blum, and directed the film version. It was the first of four Broadway hits that Wilder directed in the 1950s, along with *Sabrina* (from *Sabrina Fair*), *The Seven Year Itch*, and *Witness for the Prosecution*. Doubtless he was attracted to the play because of its unlikely mix of intrigue and comedy. In the film, he introduces a voice-over narration by a character new to the cast, Stratton, a prisoner who is close to Sefton (William Holden) but still allowed to fraternize with the other prisoners; he understands both. His narration is all after-the-fact and includes recollections of instances of Sefton's barracks businessman acumen and episodes such as "Animal" (Robert Strauss) and Harry's (Harvey Lembeck) short-lived adventure to the compound housing Russian women prisoners. The stories develop the characters and provide the film's comedy.

The film expands the setting beyond the one-room barracks but retains the dreary closed-in feeling of the prison compound. This allows a look into the personality of the German commandant, Scherbach (Otto Preminger). One scene has Commandant Von Scherbach putting his cumbersome black boots on so he can stand at attention in his office, having a telephone conversation with his superior in Berlin. The movie allows Sefton to be clever in uncovering the informant, Price (Peter Graves). The audience learns the informant's identity as Sefton does, so the tension then becomes how the ostracized Sefton will be able to convince the other American prisoners of this before the informant tells the Germans the details of the sabotage carried out by the new prisoner, Dunbar (Don Taylor). Sefton is also portrayed as a reluctant hero; he dislikes Dunbar whom he sees as the privileged son of a wealthy American family. He has reason to allow his fellow prisoners, who recently beat him severely, to suffer the consequences of ignoring him. Still, he orchestrates the expulsion of the informant and, in personally escorting Dunbar safely out of the camp, Sefton himself escapes to freedom. (In the play, an overheard conversation leads to the exposure of Price; in the film, the means are visual, a light cord and a chess piece used by Price as a signal to Corporal Schulz.) After the Christmas party, the men close in on Price and hurl him into the compound where he is killed by his fellow Germans. The film ends as it began, with the music of "When Johnny Comes Marching Home." Whether Sefton is motivated by self-interest or by the "honor stuff" derided by his character in the play is the question Wilder leaves for the viewer.

Wilder biographer Bernard F. Dick cites many scenes and visuals that display Wilder's genius. The film has the prisoners demonstrate American ingenuity in employing otherwise useless Red Cross supplies to aid their plan. The ruse is bigger than a stage play would permit. Here, ping pong balls are ground into powder, which is ignited to create a smoke screen allowing the prisoners to hide Dunbar. Sefton's discovery of the spy's identity ingeniously foregrounds the chess table and the light cord. And the Christmas party displays Wilder's penchant for emotional sexual ambiguity: "Despite the horseplay and the low humor, there is an understated poignancy about a party where bearded men dance together without eye contact, swaying dreamily and sexlessly as if closeness were all that mattered."

Still, the dialogue is what drives the story and much has been written on Wilder's strict control over the dialogue in the adaptation with Blum and in the direction of the film. The colorful characters, most notably "Animal" and Harry, translate very well from stage to screen. Robert Strauss as "Animal" and Harvey Lembeck as Harry played in both the play and film. Play author Edmund Trzcinski appears in the film as himself, as one of the American prisoners.

The film was a great success, earning William Holden an Oscar for his portrayal of Sefton and Robert Strauss a nomination for best supporting actor. It reportedly grossed $10 million in the first six months of its release. It remains popular as a tight, suspenseful story combining elements of comedy and suspense in a study of heroism.

REFERENCES

Dick, Bernard F., *Billy Wilder* (Boston: Twayne Publishers, 1980); Madsen, Axel, *Billy Wilder* (Bloomington: Indiana University Press, 1969); Meyers, Jeffrey, *Stalag 17: Billy Wilder* (Berkeley: University of California Press, 1999); Zolotow, Maurice, *Billy Wilder in Hollywood* (New York: Putnam, 1977).

—S.C.C.

STEEL MAGNOLIAS (1988)

ROBERT HARLING (1951–)

Steel Magnolias (1989), U.S.A., directed by Herbert Ross, adapted by Robert Harling; Tri-Star Pictures.

The Play

Based on the real-life tragedy of his 32-year-old diabetic sister, Susan, Harling's semi-autobiographical *Steel Magnolias* was originally presented at the WPA Theatre in New York City on March 22, 1987. The cast of six women consisted of Margo Martindale (Truvy Jones); Constance Shulman (Annelle Dupuy-Desoto); Kate Wilkinson (Clairee Belcher); Blanche Baker (Shelby Eatenton-Latcherie); Rosemary Prinz (M'Lynn Eatenton); and Mary Fogarty (Ouiser Boudreaux). The cast performed, according to commentator Thomas Disch, "with the ensemble intimacy of an established sitcom team, blending their brassy voices in madrigals of wisecracking humor." On June 19, 1987, the WPA Theatre production of the play was transferred to the Lucille Lortel Theatre; the cast members were the same, except for Betsy Aidem replacing Blanche Baker as Shelby. Set in Chinquapin, Louisiana, the entire play takes place in Truvy's beauty shop. The plot is driven by rites of passage: 25-year-old Shelby Eatenton's marriage to Jackson Latcherie; the birth of their son, Jack Jr.; Shelby's death from kidney failure (resulting from complications of Type I diabetes); and finally the birth of Annelle's baby "Shelby." Even the drama's timeline follows the seasonal chronology (Act One, Scene One = April; Act One, Scene Two = December; Act Two, Scene One = June, 18 months later; Act Two, Scene Two = November), reinforcing the circular themes of life, love, death, and rebirth throughout the play. Undercutting the serious realities of everyday life is Harling's humor, released through the one-liners and sarcastic diatribes of the six female members in this "special kind of 'regional' comedy," as critic Clive Barnes observed.

The Film

The WPA Theatre and the Lucille Lortel Theatre female casts were replaced by the star-studded entourage of Dolly Parton (Truvy Jones); Daryl Hannah (Annelle Dupuy-Desoto); Olympia Dukakis (Clairee Belcher); Julia Roberts (Shelby Eatenton-Latcherie); Sally Field (M'Lynn Eatenton); and Shirley MacLaine (Ouiser Boudreaux) for the movie. Filmed in Harling's hometown of Natchitoches, Louisiana, the movie takes some small departures from the play. No longer limited to the dimensional constraints of the stage, Harling and producer Ray Stark take us outside of the beauty shop in the movie: We are allowed to witness Shelby's wedding, her home in New Orleans with Jackson, the hospital where she dies, and the cemetery where she is buried—all places that are only

Steel Magnolias *reached the screen with Sally Field and* Julia Roberts. (COURTESY TRI-STAR PICTURES)

inferred during the written play's dialogue. The most notable disparity from stage to screen (and the one most reviewers and critics have pointed out) was Harling's decision to develop the minor male characters alluded to in the play's beauty shop talks. Tom Skerritt joins the cast as M'Lynn's husband, Drum Eatenton; one of the opening scenes in the movie finds Drum and his two teenage boys terrorizing the neighborhood by shooting up into the trees to disperse the birds before the outdoor wedding begins. Sam Shepard (Spud Jones) is also a laughable character, a depressed couch potato of a husband who doesn't do anything romantic for his wife until he buys her a second beauty shop, "Truvy's West," as a result of having an emotional enlightenment over the loss of Jackson's young wife, Shelby (a transformation also not in the original play). Finally, Dylan McDermott, who plays "the crucial role of Roberts's [Shelby's] husband, couldn't be less of a presence if he were invisible," according to critic Ralph Novak. The male characters are present, but, like the play, are still relegated to peripheral roles in the film.

Although written by a man, Harling's play is, according to critic David Richards, a chance for men to "see what they've been missing" about who women are as people. The focus of this local-color drama is not meant to be on men, of course, but on the lives of this group of Louisiana women. Despite their diverse backgrounds, ages, and personalities, all six women maintain

---

a close bond through celebrations and hardships. Truvy's salon serves as "a little lodge hall for women," according to commentator Richard Schickel, a place where they can shoot the breeze, share their soul stories, and still get their hair done.

REFERENCES

Barnes, Clive, "Humor & Hair Spray," *New York Post*, March 24, 1987; Disch, Thomas M., "Too Many Girls," *The Nation*, 244 (April 11, 1987); Novak, Ralph, "Steel Magnolias," *People Weekly*, 32:23 (December 4, 1989); Richards, David, "Short Cut to the Big Tease," *New York Post*, September 2, 1987; Schickel, Richard, "Steel Magnolias," *Time*, 134:21 (November 20, 1989); Lisa Tyler, "Mother-Daughter Myth and the Marriage of Death in *Steel Magnolias*," *Literature/Film Quarterly*, 22:1 (1994).

—N.A.

STILL LIFE (BRIEF ENCOUNTER) (1935)

NOËL COWARD (1899–1973)

Brief Encounter (1945), U.K., directed by David Lean, adapted by David Lean and Ronald Neame; Eagle-Lion/Cineguild.

The Play

In 1935–36 Noël Coward wrote a cycle of 12 one-act plays under the collective title *Tonight at 8:30*. *Still Life*—soon to be retitled *Brief Encounter* for the movies—told in five brief scenes the story of two people, Alec Harvey and Laura Jesson, who meet by chance in a railway station. Despite the fact that each is married, they meet several times over the course of a year and fall in love, sharing a few fleeting moments of happiness before they part. In the original production, which premiered on May 22, 1936, at London's Phoenix Theatre, Coward and Gertrude Lawrence assumed the leading roles.

The Film

The genesis of *Brief Encounter*, one of the most famous and fondly remembered of all British films, began when MGM bought the rights to the entire cycle, then sold them to British producer Sydney Box, who in turn sold them to J. Arthur Rank. When Cineguild wanted the rights to *Still Life*, it had to pay for all 12 plays—£60,000. Director David Lean, on the heels of another Coward stage adaptation, *Blithe Spirit*, took on *Still Life* with the help of two co-scenarists, Anthony Have-

David Lean

lock-Allan and Ronald Neame (Coward himself participated in some of the rewriting). They had to fill out the story and invent additional scenes to expand the play's running time from 55 to 85 minutes. Lean compressed the original time structure, which had originally occurred chronologically over almost an entire year, to six successive Thursdays over five weeks, presenting most of the action via two flashbacks remembered by Laura from her fireside at home. As commentator Antonia Lant recognizes, this cinematic reorganization of theatrical time is highly significant: "This temporal reduction accentuates both the brevity of the encounter and the couple's relative innocence by comparison with their stage predecessors. Time is further manipulated in the film by the use of two flashbacks and a fantasy sequence. These make it structurally more convoluted than the temporally linear play." The film also employs a variety of timetables and watches to signify at every step of the proceedings the inexorable passage of time.

Whereas the original play was set entirely in a railway refreshment room of Milford Junction Station, the film opens out the action to include scenes of the outside world: Milford, Laura's home, the lovers' countryside outing, and the apartment of Alec's friend. The characters of Laura's husband and Alec's disapproving friend—unseen in the play—are fleshed out. Although made and released in 1945, before the war had ended, the film is set earlier, in the play's original temporal setting of the late thirties. Thus, its theme of romance/adultery, all too taboo in wartime England, is rendered more acceptable. By evoking subdued performances from his actors, including Trevor Howard in a "breakthrough" role as Alec and Celia Johnson as Laura, Lean aptly contrasts their turbulent inner emotions with their repressed external appearances.

The film was an instant hit. C.A. Lejeune, writing in *The Listener*, declared she would choose it as a desert-island film, "because it seems to me to catch, in words and pictures, so many things that are penetratingly true. The whole colour, the spring, the almost magical feeling of the discovery that someone's in love with you; that someone feels it's exciting to be with you; that is something so tenuous that it's hardly ever been put on the screen." Among the many subsequent critical interpretations of this story is Richard Dyer and Andy Medhurst's argument that *Brief Encounter* has claims for being understood as a "gay text," not only in relation to its original author but as a work "which explores the pain and grief caused by having one's desires destroyed by the pressures of social convention; and it is this set of emotions which has sustained its reputation in gay subcultures."

REFERENCES

Brownlow, Kevin, *David Lean* (New York: St. Martin's Press, 1996); Dyer, Richard, *Brief Encounter* (London: BFI Publishing, 1993); Lant, Antonia, *Blackout: Reinventing Woman for Wartime British Cinema* (Princeton, N.J.: Princeton University Press, 1991); Medhurst, Andy, "That Special Thrill: *Brief Encounter*, Homosexuality and Authorship," *Screen*, 32:2 (1991), 197–208.

—*T.W.*

STRANGE INTERLUDE (1928)

EUGENE O'NEILL (1888–1953)

Strange Interlude (1932), U.S.A., directed by Robert Z. Leonard, screenplay adaptation by Bess Meredith, C. Gardner Sullivan, and Robert Z. Leonard; Metro-Goldwyn-Mayer.

The Play

One of the most popular dramas of its decade, this mammoth-length nine-act play received the 1927–28 Pulitzer Prize and was chosen as the best play of the year by the New York dramatic critics. In it O'Neill attempted to portray the "modern" woman and the "modern" temperament by utilizing "interior monologues" and asides that revealed the characters' innermost thoughts. Perhaps dated and too theatrical by today's standards, this Freudian exercise was the most successful of O'Neill's works in his lifetime.

Strange Interlude chronicles the lives and events surrounding Nina Leeds, daughter of Professor Leeds. Nina, still upset over the death of her fiancé, aviator Gordon Shaw, during World War I, blames her father, and against the objections of both her father and her friend, Charles Marsden (who is in love with her), decides to work as a nurse in a veterans hospital. There she meets a young doctor, Ned Darrell, and Sam Evans. Upon the advice of Ned and Charles she marries Sam Evans in the hope of fulfilling her life. Pregnant with Sam's child (of which he is yet unaware) she learns from Sam's mother of the family history of congenital insanity. Mrs. Evans urges Nina to have a child outside her marriage by breeding with a "healthy male," without Sam's knowledge, in order to produce a healthy child that they can be happy with. Several months following her abortion Nina convinces Ned Darrell of a "scientific" conception in order to provide for both her and Sam's happiness. Throughout the remaining acts Nina juggles her relationships with the three men in her life: her lover and the biological father of her child, Ned Darrell; her husband, Sam Evans; and her childhood friend and surrogate father figure, Charles Marsden. Gordon Evans, her son, becomes as sportsmanlike and independently minded as both his namesake and his "real" father. At play's end Nina alone (following the death of Sam) agrees to marry Charles, "who, passed beyond desire, has all the luck at last."

The soap opera machinations of the plot notwithstanding, the play's primary appeal to its initial audience was no doubt due to both its "novelty" status and the postwar interest in Sigmund Freud. The play achieved an event-like status on the New York stage because of its length. It was performed in two parts, requiring a dinner break in between. The performance began at 5:15 in the afternoon, the dinner break lasted from 7:40

to 9:00 P.M., and the play lasted until 11:00 P.M. Humorist and critic Robert Benchley, who disliked O'Neill, referred to the production as "just another nine-act play." The original production was staged by the Theatre Guild and directed by Philip Moeller at the John Golden Theatre in New York. Lynn Fontanne performed the role of Nina Leeds in a total of 426 performances, unprecedented for an O'Neill production in his lifetime.

According to Ronald Wainscott, O'Neill's working notes during the play's composition revealed that "aloud conscious thinking" was "more important and dynamic to the piece than speech." However, O'Neill himself did not suggest how this device was to be accomplished on the stage. Philip Moeller, in the play's original production, stopped the action of other characters ("arrested motion") whenever the asides and interior monologues were given. The speaking actor was allowed to move and gesture freely. O'Neill often told the Theatre Guild, which mounted most of his major productions that "The audience will stand for anything provided we do it well enough."

The Film

There are two major problems in MGM's 1932 screen adaptation of *Strange Interlude*: the condensation of O'Neill's massive five-hour play into a 110-minute film and the enigma of how to deal with the "interior monologues." In 1932 it would have been unthinkable to attempt to exhibit a film with a running time in excess of two hours, thus making the adaptation of O'Neill's play problematic from the start. The condensation written by Bess Meredith, C. Gardner Sullivan, and the film's director, Robert Z. Leonard, as John Orlandello states, "becomes merely a skeletal plot outline." Further it highlights the melodramatic, soap opera–like qualities inherent in the work by means of reduction, "stripping the play of most of its complexity, its reverberation of themes, and most of its poetry." Large portions of plot and motivation have been excised in order to accommodate both motion picture exhibitors and censorship forces. For example, all references to Nina's abortion are absent in the film, as well as her use of cosmic imagery concerning birth, the womb, and maternity. Her central metaphor concerning "God the Mother" is also lost in the adaptation. As John Orlandello notes, "The play is essentially a sexual biography of the character Nina, and the psychologically connecting roles of daughter, wife, mistress, and mother. . . . In the film the Freudian aspects of these relationships are greatly diminished, weakening the psychological core of the work." The

relationships referred to are the ones between Nina and the five men in her life: Gordon Shaw (her deceased lover); her father, Professor Leeds; her friend, Charles Marsden; her husband, Sam Evans; and her lover, Ned Darrell. These multifaceted, psychologically dense, interconnected relationships are reduced to a conventional lover's triangle in the film, thus diminishing much of the impact of O'Neill's drama.

Burton L. Cooper has suggested that one of the challenges in adapting O'Neill from stage to screen is in finding "visual equivalents" for O'Neill's discursive language. "The size of the movie screen contributes to the sense of overwrought melodrama if there is no compensating visual distraction." Nowhere is this more apparent than in the treatment Robert Z. Leonard gives to the asides and "interior monologues" in *Strange Interlude*. Whereas in the original stage production the technique of "arrested motion" contributed to the theatricality of the drama and actually focused attention on the speaker, Leonard uses voice-over in the film. Initially the effect works, but in its prolonged use and the drastic nature of the adaptation, much of their effectiveness is lost. According to John Orlandello, "Nearly all of the interesting, poetic, and provocative asides were excised, and the ones retained lack both the self-examining and self-revealing qualities which is their only raison d'etre in the work." This, coupled with the uninspired performances of the lead actors, Norma Shearer as Nina Leeds and Clark Gable as Ned Darrell, severely debilitates O'Neill's massive, psychologically motivated drama.

REFERENCES

Cooper, Burton L., "Some Problems in Adapting O'Neill for Film," in *Eugene O'Neill's Century: Centennial Views on America's Foremost Tragic Dramatist*, ed. Richard F. Morton, Jr. (Westport, Conn.: Greenwood Press, 1991); Leiter, Samuel L., ed., *The Encyclopedia of the New York Stage, 1920–1930* (Westport, Conn.: Greenwood Press, 1985); Orlandello, John, *O'Neill on Film* (Rutherford, N.J.: Fairleigh Dickinson University Press, 1982); Wainscott, Ronald H., *Staging O'Neill: The Experimental Years, 1920–1934* (New Haven, Conn.: Yale University Press, 1988).

—R.W.W.

STREAMERS (1976)

DAVID RABE (1940–)

Streamers (1983), U.S.A., directed by Robert Altman, adapted by David Rabe; Mileti Productions/United Artists Classics.

The Play

Streamers was the final installment in what came to be known as Rabe's "Vietnam trilogy" of plays, following *Sticks and Bones* and *The Basic Training of Pavlo Hummel*. The first two, however, were written and initially produced between 1969 and 1971, at the height of the Vietnam War, while *Streamers*, written and first produced in 1976, came after the war's end. Further, *Streamers* came after an interim during which Rabe explored other subject matter. Familiar Rabe themes such as the nature of masculinity and cultural attitudes toward racial and sexual roles permeate this Vietnam drama in which the war itself is relegated to the backstory. The play centers upon a group of soldiers in their boot-camp barracks as they grapple with the specter of being sent to fight in Vietnam. As the play opens, one soldier, Martin, attempts suicide by slitting his wrists rather than face the horrors of combat. His bunkmates, Billy, Roger, and Richie, thwart the suicide but reflect upon their own fears and apprehensions at being sent into a potentially fatal situation. Another soldier, the black Carlyle, erupts with anger at his predicament and taunts Richie, an emerging homosexual, and Roger, a fellow black man. Non-commissioned officers Rooney and Cokes reassure the soldiers with stories of combat, but it turns out that Rooney is as green as the soldiers and Cokes has been recalled as a victim of leukemia. The play climaxes as Carlyle snaps and stabs Billy and Rooney to death before being apprehended by the MPs.

The Film

After directing the disastrous *Popeye* in 1980, Robert Altman retreated from mainstream filmmaking and concentrated on making films adapted from stage plays. His production of *Streamers* was his second effort in this area (following *Come Back to the Five and Dime, Jimmy Dean, Jimmy Dean* in 1982). Rabe was reportedly convinced to write the screenplay for the film when it became clear that Altman was interested in remaining faithful to the play's central concepts. With this, the pattern was set for most of Altman's remaining 1980s theatrical adaptations: a screenplay written by the playwright, modest production values, and an adaptation that exercised a nearly complete fidelity to the original. In the case of *Streamers*, this fidelity extended to the use of a single setting (the barracks) and to little or no "opening up" of the play, a tactic used so often in cinematic adaptations of stage plays. Thus, *Streamers* became one in Altman's series of "filmed plays" (following *Jimmy Dean* and preceding *Secret Honor* and *Fool for Love*). The film adaptation of *Streamers* did not entirely

eschew the virtues of cinematic style, though; according to N. Bradley Christie, motifs such as Richie's aversion to the sight of blood, the camerawork during Carlyle's angry speeches, and the performance of George Dzundza as Cokes all act as potent elements in the story's adaptation to the screen.

Besides the laudable performance of Dzundza, the film version of *Streamers* features Matthew Modine as Billy, Mitchell Lichenstein as Richie, David Alan Grier as Roger, and Michael Wright as Carlyle. The cast is rounded out with Guy Boyd (Rooney) and Albert Macklin (Martin). Rabe would go on to write the screenplay for the Vietnam war picture *Casualties of War* (1989), as well as additional plays such as *Hurlyburly* (adapted by Rabe for film in 1998). Altman continued with his "filmed plays" throughout the 1980s before returning to more mainstream filmmaking in the 1990s.

REFERENCES

Beidler, Philip D., *Re-writing America: Vietnam Authors in Their Generation* (Athens: University of Georgia Press, 1991); Carroll, Dennis, "David Rabe," in *International Dictionary of Theatre*, vol. 2, ed. Mark Hawkins-Dady (London: St. James Press, 1994); Christie, N. Bradley, "David Rabe's Theatre of War and Remembering," in *Search and Clear: Critical Responses to Selected Literature and Films of the Vietnam War*, William J. Searle, ed. (Bowling Green, Ohio: Bowling Green State University Popular Press, 1988).

—C.M.

STREET SCENE (1928)

ELMER RICE (1892–1967)

Street Scene (1931), U.S.A., directed by King Vidor, adapted by Elmer Rice; Samuel Goldwyn/United Artists.

The Play

In a career that lasted more than 40 years, playwright/novelist Elmer Rice had at least 24 plays produced on Broadway, ranging from courtroom drama, *On Trial* (1914) and *Counsellor at Law* (1931), to expressionist fantasy, *The Adding Machine* (1923), to "slice-of-life" realism, *Street Scene* (1928). His authentic concern for social, political, and moral issues, and his skill in plot construction and characterizations, qualified him as one of America's first major playwrights. *Street Scene*, a Pulitzer Prize–winner, was a three-act drama that premiered in New York at the Playhouse on January

10, 1929, and ran for a spectacular 601 performances. Its romance and melodramatic plot elements combine with a naturalistic tenement setting and the portrayal of some 50 characters representing many ethnic types. Among them are an Irish couple, Frank and Anna Maurant (Robert Kelly and Mary Servoss), their daughter Rose (Erin O'Brien-Moore), and younger son Willie (Russell Griffin). Two men are courting the attractive Rose, the flashy Harry Easter (Glenn Coulter) and her amiable Jewish neighbor, Sam Kaplan (Horace Braham). When Frank discovers his wife is having an affair with the milkman, Steve Sankey (Joseph Baird), he kills them both. After he is apprehended, Frank pleads with Rose to take care of her younger brother. Left alone, Rose rejects her suitors. "I don't think people ought to belong to anybody but themselves," she says. "[Father and mother] were always depending on somebody else for what they ought to have had inside themselves." Determined to take her brother out of the slum, she vacates the apartment. The play ends as a shabby couple arrives to inquire about the apartment. In 1947 Rice and Langston Hughes adapted the drama into a musical, with music by Kurt Weill. In the *New York Evening Journal* John Anderson wrote, "It is a play which builds engrossing trivialities into a drama that is rich and compelling and catches in the wide reaches of its curbside panorama the comedy and heartbreak that lie a few steps up from the sidewalks of New York."

The Film

Producer Samuel Goldwyn purchased the rights to the play for $157,000. Screen actors Estelle Taylor and Sylvia Sidney played Anna and Rose Maurrant, David Landau portrayed Frank Maurrant, and William Collier, Jr., was Sam Kaplan. Reprising their roles from the Broadway production were stage players Beulah Bondi (in her screen debut), Matt McHugh, Eleanor Wesselhoeft, T. H. Manning, Conway Washburne, John Qualen, Anna Konstant, and George Humbert. Several controversies followed the production from stage to screen: The character of a social worker, Miss Simpson, was deemed by the Hollywood Studio Relations Office as objectionable (she is seen assisting in the eviction of an unfortunate family); and the adulterous Anna Maurrant was regarded as entirely too sympathetic a character. Rice, who adapted his own play, resisted pressures to make alterations in the characters. Director King Vidor had already proven his versatility with several highly successful pictures, including the war epic, *The Big Parade* (1925), a fable of urban life, *The Crowd* (1928), a satiric Hollywood comedy, *Show People* (1928),

a western, *Billy the Kid* (1930), and an all-black musical, *Hallelujah!* (1930). In *Street Scene* his canvas was ambitious.

Thirty-four characters were retained from the play, including Emma Jones, the chief gossip of the block, and a central "chorus" for the events on and off screen, played in a standout performance by Beulah Bondi. The action is closely patterned after the play and confined to the single set of a street and the front façade of a brownstone apartment built on the Goldwyn backlot. Vidor breaks up any potential monotony by photographing the action from a considerable variety of vantage points. Indeed, he and cinematographer George Barnes determined not to duplicate any of the setups from shot to shot. "I wanted to try to not get away from that one façade," Vidor explained in an interview late in his life. "In the theatre all the audience saw was a sidewalk. They didn't even see the street. I hoped I could enlarge it to include scenes in the street, and further down the block. . . . I tried to make each set-up look different. I also worked out a system with the camera following anyone going out of a door, then picking up the next actor and the next extra just entering through the same door. This gave a flow to it, and it was challenging to see how much movement we could put in one static set in front of the building. I think it worked out. I think the constant change of composition makes it very interesting."

Although a great deal of screen time is devoted to the various plot strands, the characters of Anna, Frank, Rose, and Sam, are foregrounded somewhat by their being given more medium shots and close-ups than the other characters.

The main object of the block's gossip is the ongoing affair between the sadly romantic Anna Maurrant and the married milkman, Steve Sankey. Other plot strands and characters include the Hildebrand family, which faces eviction; Abe Kaplan, a socialist who argues against the capitalist system; Abe's son, Sam, who must escape the tenements to go to college; Rose's relationship with her married office manager and with her best friend, Sam, a Jew; Frank's discovery of his wife's infidelity; and Rose's acceptance of the care of her brother after her father's incarceration. At the end, she leaves her home, prepared to begin a new life away from the tenement. Critical reception was enthusiastic. The critic in *Photoplay* magazine opined that it was "an almost perfectly produced and acted picture," the "pinnacle" of Vidor's directorial career. "Here are the humor, the pathos, the gripping drama which comes to just one street of one city," the critic continued. "You've seen it again and again; you've read it as reported in your daily paper." Vidor's biographers, Raymond Durgnat and Scott Simmon, are less enthusiastic: "The film has the effect of being both direct and sidelong, deeply moving yet never quite memorable, neorealist in theme, yet profoundly anti-neorealist, almost anti-populist, in spirit. It's everything that irritates us about smart American art."

REFERENCES

Dowd, Nancy, and David Shepard, *King Vidor* (Metuchen, N.J.: Directors Guild of America and the Scarecrow Press, 1988); Durgnat, Raymond, and Scott Simmon, *King Vidor, American* (Berkeley: University of California Press, 1988); Wood Krutch, Joseph, *The American Drama Since 1918* (New York: Random House, 1939); "Street Scene," *Photoplay*, 40:5 (October 1931), 49.

—J.C.T.

A STREETCAR NAMED DESIRE (1947)

TENNESSEE WILLIAMS (1911–1983)

A Streetcar Named Desire (1952), U.S.A., directed by Elia Kazan, adapted by Tennessee Williams; Warner Bros.

The Play

Following the success of *The Glass Menagerie* (1944), *A Streetcar Named Desire* (1947) consolidated the position of Tennessee Williams as one of America's leading playwrights. *Streetcar* immortalized for all time two of Williams's favorite character types, the fragile and neurotic southern woman (Blanche Dubois) and the hell-raising stud (Stanley Kowalski). Elia Kazan directed the stage premiere at New York's Barrymore Theatre on December 3, 1947, with Jessica Tandy and Marlon Brando (in his last stage appearance) in the roles of Blanche Dubois and Stanley Kowalski. Irene Selznick, the estranged wife of the famous Hollywood magnate, produced the play. It ran for a successful 855 performances.

Williams broke with the usual three-act dramatic structure and divided the play into 11 separate scenes located in a rundown tenement area of New Orleans incongruously named Elysian Fields. Intermissions occurred after Scenes Four and Six. The action of the play takes place in the spring, summer, and fall. Williams uses a quotation from "The Broken Tower" to open the published edition of his play. This poem by the self-destructive, alcoholic, and tormented Hart Crane significantly alerts the reader to the real issues concealed behind the play's manifest content. It is particularly apt for an era hostile to both the explicit life-style of its author as well as any direct representation of the actual sexual tensions depicted in the fatal attraction between Blanche and Stanley.

The time is the late 1940s. Blanche Dubois arrives in Elysian Fields—the French Quarter of New Orleans—on a dark May evening to stay with her sister, Stella (Kim Hunter), now married to loutish proletarian Stanley Kowalski. "They told me to take a streetcar named Desire," says the bewildered Blanche, "and then transfer to one called Cemeteries and ride six blocks and get off at Elysian Fields!" Living in a dream world of southern gentility, Blanche gradually attracts and infuriates Stanley who eventually destroys her both mentally and physically through a brutal act of rape. Despite Blanche's claims to a now-defunct life-style, Stanley uncovers the truth behind her genteel façade by unearthing the facts behind the suicide of her youthful husband—whose homosexuality had been discovered—and the life of prostitution she has followed. Blanche, in the meantime, possesses a fierce integrity toward her own special sensibilities. Upon learning that her sister is pregnant, Blanche disgustedly tells her that she will live like the local streetcar that travels only through the seediest, most narrow of streets.

The play concludes with the now hopelessly insane Blanche led away to a mental asylum and Stella again succumbing to the repentant Stanley's primal sexual lure. "There are things that happen between a man and a woman in the dark," says Stella, "—that sort of make everything else seem—unimportant." Blanche's last lines to the doctor who comes to take her away are memorable: "Whoever you are—I have always depended on the kindness of strangers." The play attracted instant celebrity and acclaim for its cast and its playwright. Critic Brooks Atkinson wrote, "Out of poetic imagination and ordinary compassion, [Williams] has spun a poignant and luminous story."

The famous "Method" style of acting, derived from Stanislavsky, achieved notoriety in the preparation of this production. By contrast to the classic style, which involved acting "from the outside in"—where the actor remains separated from the character and bases his performance on the observation of people or on the conventions of stagecraft—the Method encouraged acting "from the inside out"—where the actor's inner feelings are employed in combination with the demands of the character. In effect, actor and character merge.

The Film

Elia Kazan's film version is a landmark in American cinema. It made Marlon Brando a star, introduced

Marlon Brando repeated his role as Kowalski opposite Vivien Leigh in Elia Kazan's adaptation of Tennessee Williams' A Streetcar Named Desire. (COURTESY NATIONAL FILM SOCIETY ARCHIVES)

"Method" acting to a mass audience, utilized a musical score by Alex North that incorporated elements of jazz, and forced Hollywood censors to broaden the Production Code. Although Vivien Leigh replaced Jessica Tandy in the film version, largely due to her celebrity and the fact that she had played Blanche in the London production directed by Laurence Olivier, Kazan managed to hire several actors from the original stage production to repeat their roles. Kim Hunter, Karl Malden, and Nick Dennis again appeared in the respective performances of Stella Kowalski, Harold Mitchell (Mitch), and Pablo Gonzales.

As a veiled depiction of the playwright's personal demons containing highly erotic implications, *A Streetcar Named Desire* naturally faced issues concerning contemporary censorship codes that would normally have prevented any faithful film adaptation. Kazan and Williams surmounted these problems both by toning down the original radical content of the play while, at the same time, presenting its latent message by indirect visual codes easily available to both alert viewers and members of the gay community. For example, Kazan opens out the theatrical location of the original play in the introductory sequence to show Blanche arriving by train in New Orleans. She then asks directions

from a handsome young sailor. Neither this character nor location appear in the opening scene of the play, which begins with Stanley and Mitch returning to Elysian Fields after work and being introduced to Blanche by Stella. However, the young sailor operates as one of many sexual signifiers existing in the film to alert readers to the fictional dark secret in Stella's past as well as being a coded reference to the playwright's sexuality.

The sailor image had functioned as a gay signifier within what commentator Vito Russo has termed the "celluloid closet" well before it became a recognizable icon in later theatrical and cinematic productions, such as Fassbinder's *Querelle* (1982) and Derek Jarman's *The Tempest* (1979). Shakespeare's line by actress Toyah Wilcox's Miranda in the latter production, accompanying a dance by sailors, "Oh brave new world, That has such people in't," is but one of many knowing devices designed to alert viewers to the real significance of the text. Although operating in a much more restrictive era, Kazan and Williams also indirectly resort to such playful imagery. For example, one scene in the film contains a sexually charged, coded shot of Brando's Stanley wearing a singlet and smeared with grime from his day's work, a shot not only representing gay magazine imagery but also prefiguring a scene showing Brad Davis in *Querelle* some decades later.

However, the film version had to keep these references covert. For example, in the film's version of Scene Seven, the explicit homosexual characteristics of Blanche's lost love contained in her confession to Mitch, become altered in the generalized, substituted lines "You are weak. I've no respect for you. I despise you." Also, Kazan uses the mobile camera to reflect Blanche's memory concerning her earlier losses by panning along a misty lakeside area when she speaks to Mitch. This not only replaces the limited theatrical confines of the original set but also reproduces the original location where her sexually tormented husband committed suicide. After Stella witnesses Blanche's departure at the end of the film, she does not return to Stanley with "inhuman abandon" as in the play, but with more restraint. Hays Code and Legion of Decency standards intervene here. However, although Kazan had to remove a sexually charged shot of Stanley and Stella's primal attraction toward each other from the original theatrical release (one restored in the director's cut), past and present viewers may speculate as to how firm her resolution will be. Also, the film cannot admit the fact that Stanley does rape Blanche as in the play. Stanley thus utters the line, "I never touched her," after he pushes Mitch back in Scene 11. However, the looks on the faces of his card-playing friends visually contradict Stanley's protestation of innocence. This reaction does not occur in the original play, where Stanley's friends simply ignore what has happened.

Kazan also cinematically extends the play in certain key scenes. Stanley reveals Blanche's past to Mitch in a factory location not in the original play. Factory workers hold Mitch back from assaulting Stanley. This foreshadows the final scene when Mitch hits Stanley for what he has done to Blanche. Kazan visually depicts the consequences of Stanley's rape of Blanche by using the metaphoric device of a mirror cracking. The film achieved a limited theatrical release in the early '90s with certain scenes restored to the film. Thus Stella's return to Stanley after their argument at the end of Scene Three exhibits the clear signs of animal sexuality seen in the stage production but thought taboo for fifties audiences.

Streetcar was a popular and critical success. It won five Academy Awards, including acting nods to Vivien Leigh, Kim Hunter, and Karl Malden. Marlon Brando lost out as best actor to Humphrey Bogart in *The African Queen*.

REFERENCES

Kolin, Philip C., ed., *Confronting Tennessee Williams's A Streetcar Named Desire: Essays in Cultural Pluralism* (Westport, Conn.: Greenwood Press, 1993); Kazin, Elia, *Elia Kazan: A Life* (New York: Alfred A. Knopf, 1988).

—*T.W.*

SUDDENLY LAST SUMMER (1958)

TENNESSEE WILLIAMS (1911–1983)

Suddenly Last Summer (1958), U.S.A., directed by Joseph L. Mankiewicz, adapted by Mankiewicz, Tennessee Williams, and Gore Vidal; Columbia.

The Play

Suddenly Last Summer is a one-act play in four scenes that was produced in 1958 Off-Broadway as part of a double bill, which also included the short play, *Something Unspoken*. His most shocking play to date, it stemmed from Williams' own experiences under psychoanalysis. Its treatment of perversions and cannibalism is relatively restrained and is infused with the poetry of the long narrative by Catherine Holly. The story line involves three principal characters, Catherine Holly, Violet Venable, and Dr. Cukrowicz. Catherine Holly has returned from an extended tour of Europe, where she had been a companion to her poet cousin Sebastian. In a long monologue, Catherine reveals all the sordid details of her summer with Sebastian in Amalfi—that he was a corrupted idealist and a hedonistic homosexual who used Catherine to procure male partners for him at a public beach. When his activities got out of hand, the island youths attacked him, mutilated him, and partially devoured his body. When Catherine discovered his corpse, "it looked like a big white-paper-wrapped bunch of red roses." Catherine's Aunt Violet, who lives amidst her fantastic jungle garden of carnivorous plants, does not want the truth about her son's homosexuality and his ugly death. She hires Dr. Cukrowicz to perform a lobotomy on Catherine and promises in return to fund a medical center. Ultimately, Violet goes insane, and the good doctor is left where he was at the beginning—but with the possibility of a relationship with Catherine.

The play is a tour de force for the actresses playing Catherine and Violet. It also presents scenes containing some of Tennessee Williams' strongest, darkest language and imagery. Catherine's revelations about her cousin's death are singularly graphic and horrific. In sum, the themes of bestiality, homosexuality, and insanity may seem excessive, but they nonetheless fit securely within the Williams canon.

The Film

Joseph L. Mankiewicz directed a black-and-white film version of the play in 1959, starring Elizabeth Taylor, Katharine Hepburn, and Montgomery Clift. The script, written mostly by Mankiewicz and Gore Vidal, confronted three problems in the transference to the screen: the sensational elements of the drama, including homosexuality, nymphomania, rape, and cannibalism; the allegorical nature of the drama; and the need to expand the dimensions of the original one-act play. In the first place, the film "opened up" the play by transplanting the action to several different locations. Violet's New Orleans mansion figures in two major scenes—at the beginning, when a huge elevator lowers Violet into a wild garden full of exotic flowers and other vegetation, and at the end when Catherine delivers her long monologue after being administered a truth serum by Dr. Cukrowicz. Elsewhere, the confrontation between Catherine and her family with Dr. Cukrowicz is set in the asylum; and Catherine's flashback is set in a Spanish Mediterranean village. In the latter instance, the stark black-and-white photography and the harsh Mediterranean sun provide an eerie backdrop for the action with Sebastian and the hungry children.

The harsh savagery of the play is softened by alterations in the character of Dr. Cukrowicz (Montgomery Clift), who is changed from a quiet, cerebral type to a hypersensitive man who now has a romance with Catherine (Elizabeth Taylor). Their bonding as a couple contrasts with the isolated nature of the other individuals in the family and the sterile narcissism of Violet Venable (Katharine Hepburn). Commentator Maurice Yacowar defends this added romance against charges of its being a "box-office concession"; rather, it provides a "love story that comes as a moral corrective and as a breath of fresh air" to the rest of the story. Morever, contends Yacowar, "When the film closes with a shot of the lovers embracing in the garden, their love has turned Sebastian's savage wilderness positively Edenic." Catherine's long, climactic monologue is handled in a series of flashbacks. As Catherine struggles to keep her balance between past and present—or between fantasy and reality—a split screen keeps Catherine in focus in the lower right corner while images of the related events occupy the rest of the screen. The surreal nature of these scenes hints that Catherine may be relating a fantasy as much, if not more, than a memory (implicit in the play, where her monologue on stage is unaccompanied by other images). This confirms Mankiewicz's insistence that the play itself is a "strange mixture of poetry, drama and analytic free-association. It isn't real, it isn't unreal. It doesn't happen but it doesn't not happen."

Unlike the play, the film's conclusion reveals that Mrs. Venable goes quietly and peacefully mad after the monologue, a pathetic note absent from the play. In sum, says Yacowar, *Suddenly Last Summer* is "one of the best 'free' adaptations of modern drama that we have on film. Nor would any new production gain from the current permissiveness; the controversial subject matter was handled with suggestive discretion."

REFERENCES

Welsh, James M., "Dream Doctors As Healers in Drama and Film: A Paradigm, an Antecedent, and an Imitation," *Literature & Medicine* 6 (1987), 117–127; Yacowar, Maurice, *Tennessee Williams and Film* (New York: Frederick Ungar, 1977).

—*J.M.W. AND J.C.T.*

SUMMER AND SMOKE (1948)

TENNESSEE WILLIAMS (1911–1983)

Summer and Smoke (1961), U.S.A., directed by Peter Glenville, adapted by James Poe and Meade Roberts; Paramount.

The Play

Summer and Smoke opened in a theatre-in-the-round format in Dallas before having a brief run on Broadway in 1948. It was revived off-Broadway by Jose Quintero in 1952, but it failed before the spectacular success of *A Streetcar Named Desire*, which had opened the year before. Consisting of a prologue and two parts, it deals with the relationship between two neighbors, John Buchanan, a doctor's son, a pleasure-seeking sensualist, and Alma Winemiller, the prissy daughter of a minister (her names means "soul"). Before the town park's fountain statue of the Angel of Eternity, they discover their mutual affection. As they grow older, John attempts to induct her into the pleasures of physical love, which she rejects in favor of a more spiritual expression. John reaches a turning point when, in a drunken fit of frustration over Alma, he agrees to marry Rosa, the daughter of a tavern keeper. Alarmed, Alma alerts John's father to block the wedding, but in ensuing events he is killed by Rosa's father. At first, John attacks Alma for meddling in his life, but he gradually mellows as he assumes his father's medical responsibilities. Alma, in turn, realizes her own life has become a sterile vacuum. But it is too late to marry John. He has fallen in love with one of her music students, Nellie.

The play ends with the distraught Alma, newly awakened to her carnal side, attempting to pick up a traveling salesman in the park (overseen by the omnipresent Angel of Eternity). Presumably, this will be but the first in a long line of temporary affairs as she searches for the love she has never really known. As reported by Maurice Yacowar in his study of Williams, the play is not intended as a piece of realism, but as a frankly expressionist work. The play's setting is as schematic as the characters. There is the fountain of the Angel of Eternity, and there are two interiors, suggested only by fragments of wall, the doctor's office (with its anatomy chart representing the physicality of man), and Reverend Winemiller's drawing room. Overhead is a "pure and intense blue" sky, suggesting a higher unity over the distinction of body and soul.

The Film

Director Peter Glenville had directed the play in London before turning to a screen adaptation. Abandoning the abstract staging conception, he shot the film in natural settings, including park concerts, outdoor walks, casinos, even adding a cockfight sequence ("I'm hunting an elusive bird, Miss Alma," Buchanan says, "the bird of satisfaction"). The street exteriors were shot on the old MGM sets for Minnelli's musical film, *Meet Me in St. Louis,* providing, says Yacowar, "the starched brightness of an idealized America, just the right abstraction for a debate between body and soul." Producer Hal B. Wallis originally wanted to cast Montgomery Clift as John Buchanan; but he eventually settled on Laurence Harvey, who brought to the role of John Buchanan the sense of dangerous charm and moral weakness that had marked his screen role in *Room at the Top.* Geraldine Page had played the role of Alma in Quintero's revival, and she reprised the role on screen. Each is photographed in a distinctive way, to emphasize their differences. Cinematographer Charles Lang envelops Alma in soft-focus lighting, while he casts a harsher cross-light on John. Just as a statue representing Eternity had brooded over the stage set, so on screen there are intermittent scenes in which the statue appears, by turns suggesting both the coldness of spiritual aspirations, the antithesis of mortal flesh, and the beneficence of the lover's gaze. But the metaphor from the play most fully developed is that of the smoke of the title. The pre-credit scene between the childish John and Alma opens on a smoke-filled Halloween. Later, as adults, John and Alma are seen in the smoke-filled air of a Fourth of July. Still later, when John attacks her for her meddling, the rectory is swathed in the smoke from burning leaves. This is poetic effect, but one that derives from natural sources. Alma describes her spirituality as something that "suffocated in smoke from something on fire" inside her. And John describes his newly found soulful side as "an immaterial something—as thin as smoke." All in all, concludes Yacowar, "as an image of both substance and insubstantiality, the smoke embodies the essential duality of man, the physical and spiritual aspects that together form the human being."

An unfortunate result of the Panavision, wide-screen format is that the characters are too often confined to the center of the screen, surrounded (and buried) by the décor. Not so much a metaphor of their isolation, it may be all too indicative of a failure in film technique.

REFERENCES

Phillips, Gene, *The Films of Tennessee Williams* (East Brunswick, N.J.: Associated University Presses, 1980); Yacowar, Maurice, *Tennessee Williams and Film* (New York: Frederick Ungar, 1977).

—*J.C.T.*

SUMMER HOLIDAY

See *AH, WILDERNESS*

SUMMERTIME

See *TIME OF THE CUCKOO*

SUNRISE AT CAMPOBELLO (1958)

DORE SCHARY (1905–1980)

Sunrise at Campobello (1960), U.S.A., directed by Vincent J. Donehue, adapted by Dore Schary; Warner Bros.

The Play

Following a notable career as a Hollywood film producer and screenwriter, Dore Schary moved to New York to pursue an old ambition—to write for the Broadway stage. Schary, a liberal New Deal Democrat, focused his dramatic and political interests on the real-life crisis faced by Franklin Delano Roosevelt when the president-to-be contracted polio. The result was a poignant theatrical docu-drama, the three-act *Sunrise at Campobello.* Produced by Schary and the Theatre Guild, the play opened at the Cort Theatre on January 30, 1958. Scoring with the public as well as with the critics, Schary's dramatic hit ran for over two years, won five Tony Awards, and received the prestigious Antoinette Perry Award.

Set in 1921, the play takes us to Campobello, a small isle off the Maine coast—but a part of New Brunswick, Canada—where the Roosevelts are vacationing. As we meet various members of the patrician clan, the Roosevelts have no apparent worries. The young, vigorous Franklin D. Roosevelt, assistant secretary of the U.S. Navy, has his sights set on a career in public service. The only conflict, and a small one at that, arises when we learn that his mother wishes that he would lead a more private life and be content to shuttle back and forth between Campobello and the family estate at Hyde Park, New York. The serenity of the idyll is broken when Roosevelt, after a day of sailing, takes to bed complaining of a "chill." Suddenly, his legs are paralyzed. He is rushed to a hospital where he is diagnosed with polio. The doctor tells him that he will never walk again. At this point, his mother insists that he give up his political ambitions. However, Louis Howe, his behind-the-scenes confidant and friend, believes that Roosevelt will be able to best recover if he gets on with life and rekindles his political aspirations. The play concludes three years later, when Roosevelt returns to New York City to nominate Al Smith for president at the

Democratic National Convention, an act signifying FDR's spiritual-psychological rebirth and renewed political resolve.

The Film

In adapting his play for Warner Brothers, Schary, who served as the film's producer, used key members of his original Broadway team. Foremost among these was the justly lauded Ralph Bellamy, the well-known stage and screen actor whose warm re-creation of FDR on Broadway had won him well-earned plaudits, including the Tony and New York Drama Critics awards. Director Vincent J. Donehue was another significant carry-over from the Broadway troupe. There were two other key casting decisions, Greer Garson as Eleanor Roosevelt and Hume Cronyn as Louis Howe, FDR's long-time political adviser.

Closely following Schary's play, the film opens in 1921. We are introduced to the Roosevelts as they loll leisurely about the family retreat at Campobello. Life is easy, although Sara (Ann Shoemaker), FDR's mother, wishes that her son (Bellamy) would pursue a career less demanding than politics. Then, with no warning, tragedy strikes. The hearty FDR, exhausted following a day of sailing, uncharacteristically retreats to bed. When he discovers that his legs won't move, a doctor is called. The symptoms are unmistakable. He has poliomyelitis, and will be paralyzed for life. The rest of the film chronicles FDR's hard-won and personal victories over depression and disability. With the help of family and friends, Roosevelt pulls himself up by the psychological bootstraps. At the film's dramatic conclusion, with his zest for life and political ambition restored, a triumphant FDR stands on crutches at Madison Square Garden to place Al Smith's name in nomination for president of the United States.

Critical and box-office responses were both positive. Again, Bellamy won well-deserved raves as FDR. Greer Garson, fitted with prosthetic teeth to more accurately depict Eleanor Roosevelt, earned an Oscar nomination for best actress. The film also made the *New York Times* "Ten Best" list. Because *Sunrise at Campobello* had been released in September 1960 just as the Kennedy-Nixon race for the U.S. presidency was heating up, and Schary had made the anti-Catholic sentiment faced by Al Smith a central part of his screenplay, the film was credited with having minimalized the issue of Kennedy's Catholicism in the 1960 presidential contest. Significantly, *Sunrise at Campobello* was one of the last Hollywood films to view politics in a positive light, as a worthy pursuit in which good people fight to overcome personal adversity in order to serve the public good.

Indeed, the film is a profile in courage of the man who later, in the midst of the crises created by the Great Depression and World War II, would serve an unprecedented four terms as one of the most admired and distinguished U.S. presidents.

By virtue of its central subject, *Sunrise at Campobello* is also among Hollywood's most poignant and inspirational treatments of the handicapped.

REFERENCES

Bordman, Gerald, *The Concise Oxford Companion to American Theatre* (New York: Oxford University Press, 1987); Monaco, James, *The Movie Guide* (New York: Putnam, 1992); Schary, Dore, *Heyday* (Boston: Little, Brown, 1979).

—C.M.B.

SWEET BIRD OF YOUTH (1959)

TENNESSEE WILLIAMS (1911–1983)

Sweet Bird of Youth (1962), U.S.A., directed and adapted by Richard Brooks; MGM.

Sweet Bird of Youth (1989), U.S.A., directed by Nicolas Roeg, adapted by Gavin Lambert; The Sweet Bird Company (cable television).

The Play

Sweet Bird of Youth was premiered at the Martin Beck Theatre in New York on March 10, 1959, in a production directed by Williams' long-time collaborator, Elia Kazan. Paul Newman and Geraldine Page assumed the leading roles of Chance Wayne and Alexandra Del Lago. Although Page's performance received unanimous acclaim, the critics tended to give the play a lukewarm reception. It was generally felt that it was poorly constructed, with a weak second act; that it was stylistically uneven, marred by curious direct addresses to the audience by the characters; and that the content was lurid, even by Williams' standards. Nevertheless, the play was given 383 performances and ran for almost a year.

A gigolo, Chance Wayne, has returned to his home town, St. Cloud, in the company of a fading movie queen, Alexandra Del Lago, who is taking refuge in drink, drugs, and sex from what she believes has been a disastrous premiere of her comeback film. By blackmailing her with a taped conversation about her drug dependency, Chance is intending to use her influence to procure him a Hollywood contract. At the same time, he wants to reclaim his childhood sweetheart, Heavenly, who is the daughter of the vicious and powerful politician, Boss Finley. Unbeknownst to Chance, however, Heavenly has contracted a sexual disease from her lovemaking with him; and the subsequent operation has left her barren. Consequently, the Finleys have vowed to castrate Chance if he ever turns up in the town again. During the play's concentrated time-span, which is on an Easter Sunday from early morning to late night, Finley's political hypocrisy will be exposed, Alexandra Del Lago will discover that her comeback has been a triumph and that she can face a new future without encumbrances like Chance, and Chance will have to face the promised retribution by the Finleys.

The Films

Having scripted and directed a successful film version of Williams's *Cat on a Hot Tin Roof* for MGM, Richard Brooks was a natural choice to direct this film. Many of the cast were from the original New York production: Paul Newman as Chance, Geraldine Page as Alexandra, Rip Torn as Boss Finley's sadistic son, and Madeleine Sherwood as Finley's mistress, Miss Lucy. Inevitably, the harshness of the play was toned down for a cinema audience. In particular the ending was softened: Chance is badly beaten up rather than castrated as in the play, and he leaves town reunited with Heavenly. Although Brooks claimed the romantic finale was foisted on him by the studio, he did defend his decision to change the nature of Chance's punishment. "No man waits to be castrated. He might think intellectually he is going to be, but he doesn't stand and wait for it." Elsewhere, Brooks dramatized incidents that are part of the play's backstory—for example, Chance's early romance with Heavenly and the scene where Boss Finley crushes Miss Lucy's fingers. With a narrative propulsion that deftly papered over the play's structural and stylistic weaknesses, Brooks fashioned an uneven but sometimes potent critique of political demagoguery, artistic egomania, and the desperation and delusion lurking behind

the American Dream of wealth and fame. Ed Begley won an Oscar for his performance as Boss Finley, though the star turn comes from Geraldine Page, whose display of glitzy grandeur and monstrous ego had not been seen on the screen since Gloria Swanson in *Sunset Boulevard* (an acknowledged influence on the Williams play). Always a big fan of Richard Brooks, Jean-Luc Godard thought the film one of the ten best of 1962.

Made for cable television, Nicolas Roeg's version has much less panache than Brooks'; and in contrast to Brooks's individual and imaginative way with adaptation, Gavin Lambert's screenplay is too fragmented. At least there is no cop-out at the end, and the casting is inspired: Rip Torn, formerly Finley Junior in both the original play and 1962 film, now gets the chance to play Boss Finley. Opposite Mark Harmon's Chance, who convincingly suggests an aging stud who recognizes his time has gone, is a mountainous Elizabeth Taylor as Alexandra Del Lago. She has none of Geraldine Page's vocal and histrionic bravura, but this fine Williams interpreter brings a poignancy to the role that is very much her own. When she asks Chance his age and he replies that he is 31, she says, "By the time I was your age I was already a legend." Page's Alexandra would have delivered the line with swagger and hauteur, but Taylor's says it almost sadly, as if the line is not about Del Lago anymore but about Liz Taylor.

REFERENCES
Kazan, Elia, *A Life* (London: Andre Deutsch, 1988); Spoto, Donald, *The Kindness of Strangers: The Life of Tennessee Williams* (London: The Bodley Head, 1985); Williams, Tennessee, *Memoirs* (New York: Doubleday, 1975).

—N.S.

SWITCHING CHANNELS

See *FRONT PAGE, THE*

TALK RADIO (1985)

ERIC BOGOSIAN (1953–)

Talk Radio (1988), U.S.A., directed by Oliver Stone, adapted by Stone and Eric Bogosian; 20th Century-Fox.

The Play

Monologist Eric Bogosian and artist Tad Savinar first staged *Talk Radio* in 1985 in Portland, Oregon. An expanded version with rear-projected images counterpointing the "shock jock's" monologues opened in New York a year later. The play transpires in 90 minutes of real time in a stripped-down version of a radio studio. Aside from occasional contributions from secondary characters—Dan Woodruff, the executive producer, Stu Noonan, the board operator, Linda MacArthur, an assistant—the action consists entirely of an evening in the life of "shock jock" Barry Champlain, whose *Night Talk* program is about to go nationwide. Among the assortment of crackpots and losers is a young man named Kent, who subsequently appears at the station to join Barry at the microphone. But when Kent gives a caller advice to commit suicide, Barry throws him out. Barry himself is a gaping wound of cynicism and vitriol. "The worst news is three out of four people in this country say they'd rather watch TV than have sex with their spouse," he declaims. "The second worst news is some kids needed money for crack, so they stuck a knife in an 80-year-old grandmother's throat. . . . A country where culture means pornography, ethics means payoffs, integrity means lying. . . . This country is in deep trouble, people, this country is rotten to the core. . . . Tell me what to do about the mess this country's in." By the end of the evening, Barry has confronted many of his own problems, in addition to those of his listeners. "I despise each and every one of you," he says, "The only thing you believe in is me." Bogosian appeared in the role of Barry.

The Film

Oliver Stone had just finished making *Wall Street* in 1987 when *Talk Radio* came to his attention. Ironically, Stone had just lost heavily in stocks and he was looking for some ready money. Producer Ed Pressman appeared with the Bogosian play and an offer for Stone to collaborate with Bogosian on a screen version. Fresh impetus appeared in the form of a book, Stephen Singular's *Talked to Death: The Life and Murder of Alan Berg* (1984), which chronicled the death of a real Denver talk-show host who had been assassinated by neo-Nazis on June 18, 1984. From it came the idea of providing a backstory involving the shock jock's ex-wife, Ellen, and of concluding the film with the assassination of the jock in a parking lot. "Oliver wanted the shooting death," remembers Bogosian. "I said . . . it should be like the way John Lennon died, in that your celebrity is what causes you to be killed."

From the start it was determined that Bogosian would recreate his stage role. The film begins with night shots of Dallas (a city already associated with assassination), its buildings and towers looming up like monolithic forms amidst the blaze of lights. That vast maw of dark and light is contrasted with the narrow, darkened confines of Barry's glassed-in radio studio. Ex-wife Ellen has come to Dallas to visit Barry and winds up being one of his callers. She tells Barry she loves him, but he is so self-destructive that he cynically rejects her love. This triggers a flashback of prior events in their lives. Other changes from play to film include a flashback showing Barry's start as a salesman and radio-show guest and his rise to program host; new character callers—some based on the career of Alan Berg—including a Nazi and a serial rapist; a scene in which Barry is booed at an athletic event (based on a Berg experience). To keep the film from becoming too static, Barry was permitted to wear a headset so he could walk freely about the studio, the camera swooping and encircling him as he talked. The sound ambience of the fictional KGAB—station Ids, commercials, promos, newscasts—were all provided by familiar Dallas radio voices.

Talk Radio was released in December 1988 and was well promoted. Nonetheless, it died quickly at the box office. Although most critics applauded Bogosian's performance, which won him a Golden Bear at the Berlin Film Festival—"He gives the impression of being inhabited by demons," wrote J. Hoberman, "flitting from one persona to another, juggling hate mail, death threats, and packaged bombs all the while"—many reviews were mixed about the film in general. While David Denby called it "a scary ride on a roller coaster that goes faster and faster until it finally flies off the rails," Owen Gleiberman referred to it as "a bit of a stunt, really, but then so is the new trash media culture, which revels in an outrage that's part show biz, part pure American innocence: the parading of everyday madness." Vincent Canby deplored the alterations made in the original play text, transforming the film into a drama "complete with a conventional beginning, middle and end, and long, spongy flashbacks." Moreover, "[It's] a nearly perfect example of how not to make a movie from a play [fancied up] with empty narrative asides [and] idiotic camera work. A lot of Mr. Bogosian's sharper lines remain in the script, but its nihilism now seems unearned. It is also at odds with the orderliness of the new narrative." Stone biographer Norman Kagan writes: "*Talk Radio*'s view of society is a sophisticated if bleak vision—we see endless skyscrapers and apartment towers, lit but symbolically lifeless except for their telephone voices, and see only the talk-show team—society is a great technologized void, real feelings and personalities erased and isolated into faint abstractions, as well as made secret, shameful, and cruel."

REFERENCES

Kagan, Norman, *The Cinema of Oliver Stone* (New York: Continuum, 1995); Riordan, James, *Stone* (New York: Hyperion, 1995).

—*J.C.T.*

TARTUFFE (1669)

JEAN-BAPTISTE POQUELIN [MOLIÈRE] (1622–1673)

Tartüff (1926), Germany, directed by F.W. Murnau, adapted by Carl Meyer; UFA.

Tartuffe (1963), France, directed by Jean Meyer; Europe No 1-Télécompagnie.

Le Tartuffe (1984), France, directed by Gérard Depardieu; Films de Losange, Gaumont, T.F.1. Films Production.

The Play

Initially performed for Louis XIV at the court of Versailles, Molière's verse comedy attacking religious hypocrisy provoked such strong condemnation from the Catholic Church that the play was effectively banned until 1669. The action is set in the home of the well-meaning but credulous Orgon who has been totally taken in by Tartuffe, a sanctimonious hypocrite who, it seems to Orgon, can do no wrong. Despite vigorous objections from his wife Elmire, his level-headed brother-in-law Cléante, and the family's outspoken servant Dorine, Orgon decides to break off the engagement between his daughter Mariane and Valère and marry her to the ingratiating Tartuffe. The wealthy courtier even goes so far as to assign all his property to the impostor. However, Orgon's family set a trap for Tartuffe and he is enticed into attempting to seduce Elmire while the disbelieving Orgon is concealed under a table. Now that Tartuffe has been exposed, Orgon orders him to leave, but the impostor asserts his rights over the property Orgon has foolishly given to him, and he cynically seeks the eviction of the family. The king, however, learning of this fraud appears as a deus ex machina, sends Tartuffe to prison, and restores Orgon's property to him. A much chastened Orgon readily agrees to the marriage of Mariane to Valère.

Molière's satire of religious obsession and hypocrisy sets the folly of the master against the common sense of his immediate family and of his outspoken servant. The comic scenes exposing Orgon's blindness testify to the playwright's command both of verbal and visual humor. When told of his wife's indisposition, Orgon shows concern only for Tartuffe's health, so that his frequently repeated "Et Tartuffe?" or "Le pauvre homme" become revealing tragicomic tags, readily mocked by Dorine. His folly is conclusively exposed in the highly visual scene of the trap set for Tartuffe, when he is persuaded to hide beneath the table to witness for himself the impostor's immoral intentions. As with other Molière studies in obsession, the line between comedy and tragedy is finely drawn.

The Films

The three screen versions contrast sharply in approach. Jean Meyer's Comédie Française production is essentially a filmed theatrical performance, graced by superlative acting in a highly traditional style, which draws on few cinematic resources. Here the camera is little more than a recording instrument providing an invaluable historical document of a highly traditional, benchmark production, with Jean Parédès as Tartuffe, Anne Vernon as Elmire, and Jean Meyer as Orgon.

Depardieu's presentation, on the other hand, uses the film medium to greater effect, shaping the audience's vision through medium close-up or close-up shots and cutting between characters' speeches. Though this version may still be regarded as traditional classical theatre, with its sparely furnished sets and focus on the text itself, a different interpretation of the play is offered that emphasizes human frailty rather than innate deviousness. For Depardieu in his directorial debut, Tartuffe is "above all in love with a woman. He is neither scheming nor unworthy; he is simply overtaken by his emotions."

The most cinematic version is the silent super-production directed by F.W. Murnau from an adaptation by Carl Meyer, which inaugurated the Gloria Palast in 1926. The conventions of silent cinema are in evidence with an emphasis on the visual and the text itself much curtailed and summarized as intertitles. Understandably, several changes are brought to Molière's play, with the action more tightly focused on Tartuffe's hypocrisy and his attempted seduction of Elmire. The subplot involving Mariane and Valère as young lovers is discarded and the cast reduced to the principal characters:

Tartuffe (Emil Jannings); Orgon (Werner Krauss); Elmire (Lil Dagover); Dorine (Lucie Hoflich). However, to suggest the timeless importance of Molière's satire and the need for constant vigilance against hypocrisy in every era (i.e., the present) the film deploys a contentious framing device to introduce additional characters. Murnau's version opens with a prologue in which a wealthy old man (Hermann Opicha) is seen to be completely taken in by a scheming housekeeper (Rosa Valetti) and, with her prompting, he disowns his grandson who has become an actor. Vowing to the film audience to open his grandfather's eyes, the actor grandson returns in disguise and presents a traveling film version of Tartuffe

This film within a film emphasizes the impostor's venal nature when Dorine reveals that he has kept money destined for the poor, while his power over the doting Orgon is demonstrated in a garden scene where he is gently rocked in a hammock by his master. Notable dramatic sequences include the repeated attempts by Elmire to reveal Tartuffe's lustful nature. In the first scene she persuades him to take tea in her boudoir while a reluctant Orgon hides behind a curtain. However, the lecherous Tartuffe catches sight of his master reflected in the silver teapot and he quickly reverts to his cloak of piety. Feeling guilty at misjudging Tartuffe, Orgon turns all his property over to him. Despairing, Elmire then entices Tartuffe to her bedroom where, now slightly the worse for drink, the impostor succumbs to temptation and reveals that he is an ex-convict. Dorine informs Orgon of this development and he expels Tartuffe and reclaims his property.

The point of this little filmic demonstration is not lost on the duped grandfather who now dismisses his housekeeper and reinstates his grandson. In an epilogue, the grandson warns the audience that hypocrisy is found everywhere in all eras. This Hamlet-like device, with a film within a film to reveal a character's deviousness, was both innovative and contentious. To make a clear distinction between the frame and the main body of the play, two contrastive styles were deployed. For the frame a naturalistic mode is deployed in which the actors appear without makeup, whereas in the presentation of Molière's text, the grand theatrical tradition is deployed from makeup and costume to staging and acting style. Robert Herlth's black-and-white set with its shadows and shafts of light suggests dark deception and the potential illumination of hidden intentions, while Karl Freund's camerawork is used expressively to convey mood and character through subjective shots and facial close-ups. Particularly effective is the scene in which the drooling Tartuffe creeps down the darkened stairs intent on

Elmire's seduction, his desire registered in a close-up of his open mouth caught in a shaft of light. Throughout, the acting is of a high order with Emil Jennings alarmingly persuasive as the sensually repressed, religious impostor.

REFERENCES

Eisner, Lotte, *F.W. Murnau* (London: Secker and Warburg, 1973); Jameux, Charles, *F.W. Murnau* (Paris: Editions Universitaires, 1965); Kracauer, Siegfried, *From Caligari to Hitler* (Princeton, N.J.: Princeton University Press, 1974).

—*R.F.C.*

A TASTE OF HONEY (1958)

SHELAGH DELANEY (1939–)

A Taste of Honey (1961), U.K., directed by Tony Richardson, adapted by Richardson and Shelagh Delaney; Woodfall Films/British Lion.

The Play

Shelagh Delaney was only 19 when her first play, *A Taste of Honey*, was produced by Joan Littlewood at the Theatre Workshop at the Stratford East. A self-taught artist, she was born in Salford, Lancashire, where she left school at 16 and worked at various odd jobs before deciding to pursue a playwrighting career. Her play is set in her native Salford. Partly a music-hall piece and partly a naturalistic drama, it tells the story of 18-year-old Jo, who constantly battles with her mother, Helen, whom she calls a "semi-whore." The mother leaves her to marry one of her "customers" and Jo finds temporary solace with a Negro sailor. When she becomes pregnant, the sailor disappears and a gentle young homosexual, Geoff, moves in and takes care of her. Helen, in the meantime, leaves her marriage and arrives at Jo's flat, where she throws out Geoff, calling him a "pansified little freak." Helen is further shocked when she learns that the baby will be half-Negro, and she flees the scene in search of a drink. However, she does promise to return and take care of Jo and the baby. The problematic relationship between Jo and her mother remains unresolved. Curiosities about the play's production include the use of asides, in which the characters address directly the audience, and music and dance interludes during the scene transitions.

Commentator William L. Horne contends that the play, while undeniably brilliant, suffers from problems typical of first plays: "Its structure is arbitrary at best

Tony Richardson

and capricious at worst. Characters are slight, and actions are improbable. One also feels that a number of elements are self-consciously devised to shock." Why, for example, did the sailor have to be black, and why did the roommate have to be a homosexual?

The Film

The chance to direct a screen adaptation of Delaney's play came at a high point in Tony Richardson's career, and he referred to his work on it as "an experience without problems." He had already established himself as a gifted and productive stage director at the Royal Court Theatre in London, and an accomplished filmmaker for his own company, Woodfall Films. With the play and film versions of John Osborne's *Look Back in Anger* and *The Entertainer* behind him, Richardson saw an opportunity to realize a long-standing ambition, film a story entirely—interiors as well as exteriors—in natural surroundings corresponding exactly to those of the play. In this wise, he was following the aims of the Italian neorealists, filmmakers Roberto Rossellini and Vittorio De Sica. Accordingly, he abandoned the self-reflexivity of the play and the musical interludes. Scenes were shot on the back streets, the canals, the smokestacks, and the docks of Salford. Special film stocks were utilized for shooting in low light. Moreover, according to this tradition, Richardson cast relative unknowns, including 17-year-old Rita Tushingham as Jo—against advice to consider instead Audrey Hepburn!

Added bits of story flesh out the bare bones of the play. Details depict how Jo meets the black sailor (he offers to carry her suitcases as she gets off a bus to move into a new flat); Jo's departure from school and how she finds her first job and moves into her first flat; and the ways in which Geoff (Murray Melvin) takes care of Jo ("You need somebody to love you *while* you're looking for someone to love"). The story's ending acquires a deeper resonance when, after an exchange of added dialogue, Helen talks to Jo about childhood memories of Guy Fawkes Day (being celebrated at that moment) while Jo roams about the apartment cataloguing the signs of Geoff's departure. At last, she finds a note that reads, simply, "Tr'ra Jo, Good luck, Geoff." Jo tearfully murmurs to herself, "You clown, Geoff, you clown." (Compare that with Geoff's note in the original play: "Yes, the one thing civilisation couldn't do anything about—women. Goodbye Jo, and good luck.") The final images are poignant. Jo comes down the apartment steps looking for Geoff. He watches her from a hidden vantage point. Just as he begins to move toward her, Helen appears. "I'll make you a cup of tea," she says to Jo as she goes up the stairs. A closeup of Geoff reveals his sorrow and loss as he turns and walks away. Jo is left behind. She turns to a child and lights a fireworks candle. "It is a highly telling image," comments Horne, "for it contains a sense of hope, of new life and vitality, of a baby soon to be born, and yet it also resonates with an indefinable sense of loss." Delaney and Richardson both won the British Film Academy Award for the best screenplay of 1961.

REFERENCES

Horne, William, "Greatest Pleasures: *A Taste of Honey*," in James M. Welsh and John C. Tibbetts, *The Cinema of Tony Richardson: Essay and Interviews* (Albany: State University of New York Press, 1999); Richardson, Tony, *The Long Distance Runner: An Autobiography* (New York: Morrow, 1993); Wiseman, Thomas, "Mr. Richardson Shoots It Rough . . . and Keeps the Bite in That *Taste of Honey*," *Evening Standard*, April 7, 1961.

—*J.C.T.*

TEA AND SYMPATHY (1953)

ROBERT ANDERSON (1917–   )

Tea and Sympathy (1956), U.S.A., directed by Vincente Minnelli, adapted by Robert Anderson; MGM.

The Play

Robert Anderson was born in New York and graduated from Harvard University. He first won recognition as a playwright while serving in the navy during World War II. His play, *Come Marching Home* (1945), won a prize for the best play written by a serviceman. He received a Rockefeller Fellowship to study playwrighting and subsequently taught at the American Theatre Wing. *Tea and Sympathy* (1953) was his first successful Broadway-produced play. It was followed by *Silent Night, Holy Night* (1959), about an unhappy middle-aged couple whose Christmas-time affair enables them to return to and reconcile with their respective mates; *I Never Sang for My Father* (1968), an autobiographical drama; and *You Know I Can't Hear You When the Water's Running* (1967), a comedy.

Tea and Sympathy premiered in New York at the Ethel Barrymore Theatre on September 30, 1953, where it ran for a successful 712 performances. Set in a New England boy's school, it is the story of Tom Lee (John Kerr), a sensitive and lonely boy, wrongly accused of homosexuality. Mocked by his classmates and pressured by his father, Tom's only source of support is Laura Reynolds (Deborah Kerr), the housemaster's wife. Recently married, Laura is appalled at the cruelty of the other boys and her husband's overt hostility to Tom. As the play opens, Tom is obviously deeply in love with Laura. Tom has also developed a friendship with his music professor, Mr. Harris, who encourages Tom's ambition to become a folk singer. When Mr. Harris invites Tom to go swimming, he innocently accepts the invitation in lieu of attending the Varsity Club's beach outing. While swimming in the nude, the two are observed and reported to the dean. Harris, rumored to be gay, is set for discharge and rumors begin to circulate about Tom. Suddenly Tom's non-conforming physical and personal attributes become the focus of peer harassment, giving his nickname, "Grace," a new implication. In an attempt to prove his manhood, Tom makes plans to meet Ellie, the town whore. Intercepting Tom on his way out of the house, Laura tries to divert him from the rendezvous with Ellie. An emotionally charged scene ends with Tom suddenly and awkwardly kissing Laura. When she rejects his further advances, Tom bolts from the room and leaves the house for Ellie's. In a confrontation between Tom and Bill (Leif Erickson), Laura's husband, we learn the following day that Tom had attempted suicide after he was unable to have sex with Ellie. Outraged by the treatment of Tom, particularly the cruel behavior of her husband, Laura tells Bill of her attempt to keep Tom with her and expresses regret for stopping Tom's advances. Laura charges that Bill's "hatred" of Tom stems from his own feelings of repressed homosexuality. The heated exchange ends with Laura announcing her intent to leave Bill. The marriage at an end, Bill storms out of the house. Seeking Tom, Laura finds him alone lying on his bed. She tries to convince him that not being able to have sex with Ellie did not prove him less of a man, but Tom rejects her assurances. Laura starts to leave the room, but turns back and moves to Tom's side. Reaching down for Tom's hand, she unbuttons the top of her blouse and the stage goes dark.

The Film

In 1953, when *Tea and Sympathy* opened, Hollywood immediately exhibited interest in a film adaptation of the Broadway hit. But the play arrived at a time of transition in American culture and society, a period of contradictions, particularly for society's attitudes toward sex.

The film industry's self-imposed censorship, administered by the Production Code Administration (PCA), posed serious obstacles to such an adaptation. The Code prohibited or severely restricted screen portrayal of homosexuality or adultery, both key elements in the play. Moreover the Catholic Church's involvement in the film industry, via the Legion of Decency, added to the problems of the adaptation. Various studios explored a potential film, but MGM acquired the screen rights, hiring Anderson to adapt his own play.

Working to maintain the play's integrity in the face of Hollywood's restrictions, Anderson framed the basic story with a prologue and epilogue. The PCA's objection regarding the issue of homosexuality was addressed first. All terms such as "homosexual," "queer," or "fairy" were purged, and replaced with dialogue referring to "sissy behavior." Tom's nickname "Grace" was con-

verted to "Sister Boy." Structured as a flashback, the prologue shows Tom returning to Chilton for his 10-year class reunion. As he arrives on campus, the reactions of other alumni hint at some past problem, but the camera quickly focuses on Tom and his gold wedding band. In the first scene Tom is established as a "regular fellow." The swimming scene with Tom and Professor Harris was totally eliminated. The character of Professor Harris disappeared completely from the film. A beach scene where Tom is observed sewing with Laura and two other faculty wives replaces the swimming incident. This was now the inciting event causing Tom's persecution.

The second key area was the adulterous affair between the woman and boy. As the prologue provided a foundation for resolving the homosexuality problem, the epilogue was designed to provide the moral compensation for the adultery. The epilogue returns Tom to the present where he visits the housemaster, Bill Reynolds. Separated from Laura, Bill indicates that he has no idea of what has happened to her. He gives Tom an unmailed letter Laura had written him. As Tom reads the letter, the audience hears a voice-over of Laura talking about what they had done and her guilt. It is strongly implied from the letter that she has found nothing but unhappiness. With these major changes the PCA approved the adaptation.

Besides the changes to accommodate the censors, other significant additions were made, which opened up the play. The interaction between Tom and Ellie, previously only reported, became a major dramatic scene in the film. The less restrictive medium of film also allowed Anderson to add a bonfire scene and to move the last scene between Laura and Tom from his bedroom to a secluded wooded area. All of these added visually to the original story.

The original Broadway cast, Deborah Kerr, John Kerr (no relation), and Leif Erickson reprised their roles as Laura, Tom, and Bill, respectively. Vincente Minnelli directed.

Despite the approval of the PCA, the Legion of Decency continued to oppose the film adaptation. In an 11th hour showdown just days before the premiere, the Legion finally relented. The film, like the play, was a box-office success.

REFERENCES

Black, Gregory D., *The Catholic Crusade against the Movies, 1940–1975* (Cambridge: Cambridge University Press, 1996); Black, Gregory D., *Hollywood Censored* (Cambridge: Cambridge University Press, 1994); Walsh, Frank, *Sin and Censorship* (New Haven: Yale University Press, 1996).

—N.I.

THAT CHAMPIONSHIP SEASON (1972)

JASON MILLER (1940–)

That Championship Season (1982), U.S.A., directed and adapted by Jason Miller; Cannon/Golan-Globus.

The Play

Actor-playwright Jason Miller's only Broadway success, *That Championship Season*, was produced by the New York Shakespeare Festival and premiered in New York at the Public Theater on May 2, 1972. The Pulitzer Prize–winning play ran for a total of 844 performances. Four members of a champion high school basketball team of 20 years ago have come to Scranton, Pennsylvania, to the home of their former coach (Richard A. Dysart) for a reunion. Once their lives had been full of promise, but during the course of the evening each reveals his life has been full of failures and thwarted hopes. George (Charles Durning) is a corrupt politician. Phil (Paul Sorvino) is a ruthless lecher not above sleeping with George's wife. James (Michael McGuire) is a failed high school principal. Tom (Walter McGinn) is a cynical alcoholic. And the coach, retired for striking one of his players, is a racist who has abandoned basketball because it is no longer a sport for whites. Throughout the three-act play he serves as a surrogate "father" who has a series of confessional confrontations with his "boys." It is clear that, caught in the grip of memory and the past, the four players and their coach have failed to age gracefully. They are unable to confront and recognize the adultery, betrayal, loss, and racist bigotry that continue to dominate their lives. Absent is a fifth player, Martin, who had been instructed by the coach to break the ribs of a black player on an opposing team. Although this action had won the Big Game for coach, the guilt-ridden Martin was unable to celebrate the victory. "The play uncovers the dark underside . . . and the abject failure beneath any gloss of current success," writes commentator Thomas J. McCormack. "The figures are not cardboard—Miller fills in their dimension with the rich detail of an orthodox novelist."

The Film

When he adapted his play to the screen, playwright Miller retained most of the dialogue, including obscenities, ethnic slurs, anti-Semitic barbs, and the long political speeches. At the same time, he "opened up" the story with extensive location footage of his hometown of Scranton, Pennsylvania. The deteriorating streets reflect the erosion of the moral fabric of the characters. Indeed, the entire city seems to come under indictment. Additional scenes include George's mayoral political rally, complete with cheerleaders, speeches, and the gift to the city of Tilly the elephant; and a scene in the old high school gymnasium, which has been closed (like the rest of Scranton). Reprising his stage role of Phil is Paul Sorvino. Other cast members include Bruce Dern as George, Stacy Keach as James, Martin Sheen as Tom, and Robert Mitchum as Coach Delaney.

REFERENCES

Atkinson, Brooks, *Broadway*, rev. ed. (New York: Limelight, 1985); Denby, David, "Movies: One of the Boys Is One of the Girls," *New York Magazine* (December 27, 1981–January 3, 1982), 76–78; McCormack, Thomas, *Contemporary Dramatists* (Chicago: St. James Press, 1988).

—*J.C.T.*

THESE THREE

See CHILDREN'S HOUR, THE

THIS HAPPY BREED (1943)

NOËL COWARD (1899–1973)

This Happy Breed (1945), U.K., directed by David Lean, adapted by David Lean, Ronald Neame, and Anthony Havelock-Allen; Two Cities.

The Play

Noël Coward wrote *This Happy Breed* in May 1939 as Britain faced another world war. He began rehearsals for the play but disbanded his cast when Neville Chamberlain declared a state of war in September 1939. It gained its first theatrical production on April 30, 1943, at London's Haymarket Theatre, with Noël Coward and Judy Campbell in the leading roles of Frank and Ethel Gibbons. The original play is a three-act, three-scene production, which takes place in the dining room of the Gibbons home at Number 17 Sycamore Road on Clapham Common. It begins in June 1919 when the Gibbons family moves into their new home and concludes 20 years later when Frank and Ethel finish their preparations for their eventual retirement to the country. The play's chronology covers key events in British history such as the end of World War I, the 1926 General Strike, the Great Depression, the abdication of

Noël Coward

Edward VIII, the 1938 Munich crisis, and Britain's eventual drift toward another world war. All these events are viewed through the eyes of the lower-middle-class Gibbons family.

Ironically evoking Shakespeare's "happy breed of men" by focusing on lower-class domestic melodrama, Coward intended to recapture the patriotic impact of his *Cavalcade* (1931), which dealt with an upper-class family affected by key events in British history. The play basically affirms conservative British values, particularly those stressing that the lower orders should know their place. As Robert F. Kiernan notes, "By the late 1930s, Coward was sentimentally a royalist, economically a

capitalist, and emotionally divided between worshipping the aristocracy and keeping faith with the middle class. It is not surprising that he came to mistrust any political development that threatened a social order in which he found such latitude." Not surprisingly, Orson Welles accused Coward of "perpetuating an anachronistic, British public school snobbery" in his 1944 *New York Post* column.

The Film

Noël Coward was so pleased with the success of his wartime propaganda film, *In Which We Serve* (1943), which had been directed by David Lean, that he encouraged the team of Lean, Anthony Havelock-Allan, and Ronald Neame to film his plays. The production company of Cineguild Productions was formed. It would quickly become one of a handful of British film companies, like the Powell-Pressburger The Archers, that was respected for its quality films. Its first production was *This Happy Breed*. Since Lean had had no experience adapting stage plays, he was concerned. "You've got to bring in so many ideas to make it a screenplay," he said. "A film demands an intimate look at the scene that one cannot do on the stage." He was also concerned about the decision to use Technicolor. The Hollywood style of color was brash and vivid; by contrast, Lean's agenda was to mute the palette to both enhance and moderate the period "feel." Lean also decided to replace Coward with Robert Newton in the role of Frank Gibbons (a decision, reports Lean's biographer, Kevin Brownlow, that did not sit well with Coward).

Lean cinematically broadens out Coward's play in several ways. He begins the film with a shot of the Thames before dissolving to terraced houses and then moving into the interior hallway of the Gibbons family's Number 17. He concludes the film by reversing the image chronology: The camera retreats up the stairs, through the window, and the scene dissolves to long shots of South London, with Coward's new song, "London Pride," welling up on the sound track. Lean obviously believes that a future Gibbons family will easily resist the utopian dreams of a postwar Labour government. The major domestic sequences usually conclude with the camera tracking out as the scene fades—the cinematic equivalent of the theatrical transitions of dimming lights and the rise or fall of the curtain. Many external scenes are added to amplify certain historical events only referred to in the course of the play. For example, Lean includes a lavish scene involving a pageant of British military glory when Frank, Ethel, and their neighbor Bob celebrate Empire Day in 1924.

Several scenes show images of the 1926 General Strike, with Frank and Bob "naturally" helping the government as opposed to Frank's son, Reg, and his Bolshevik-inclined friend Sam Leadbitter, who will eventually marry Vi Gibbons and settle down into a life of stagnant domesticity. In 1933, Frank and Ethel briefly listen to a Fascist orator in Hyde Park, loosely modeled on Sir Oswald Mosley, who led the British Union of Fascists during the thirties. They then sit down to a refreshing and ideologically reassuring British cup of tea. After the Gibbons family finishes listening to Edward VIII's abdication speech, Lean emphasizes Ethel's action in Act Three, Scene One, when she removes a calendar displaying the king's image from the wall. Like the Gibbons's errant daughter, Queenie, the king has let down the nation by preferring sexual freedom to the nation's needs.

Other additions include a scene in 1937, when Frank and Bob appear in a crowd witnessing Stanley Baldwin's election victory. The prime minister's poster displays a non-rearmament promise, one regarded as fatal in terms of denying the ongoing Fascist military buildup to the approaching war. Bob also comments in a line added to the screenplay, "That's the face of a man you can trust." Baldwin later became added to the gallery of those "Ten Guilty Men" such as the Bank of England's governor Montagu Norman and Foreign Secretary Lord Halifax, whom many held responsible for ignoring danger signs leading to the future conflict. Before Frank later criticizes Chamberlain's appeasement policy, Lean includes a shot of the prime minister waving the infamous Munich peace agreement before cheering crowds outside Number 10 Downing Street. The film also includes a scene of repentant daughter Queenie leaving for Singapore to join her husband, Billy, the son of Frank's neighbor Bob, who has returned her back to family life after she ran away with a married man several years before. Irony lies in the fact that "good time girl" Queenie may receive further punishment in a Japanese POW camp after 1941.

Like the stage version, the film is highly patronizing to the lower-middle class, thereby affirming the values of a static society in which everyone knows their place. As Clive Fisher points out, Coward secretly detested his "happy breed," as his diaries show. Both play (and film) may be regarded as "a curiosity, a relic of the wartime spirit, and of Coward's class sense; and if it is ever performed, it would be in the interests of historical study rather than entertainment." The film proved to be Britain's top moneymaking film for 1944. The team of Coward and David Lean, meanwhile, went on to make *Blithe Spirit* the next year.

REFERENCES

Brownlow, Kevin, *David Lean: A Biography* (New York: St. Martin's Press, 1996); Fisher, Clive, *Noël Coward* (New York: St. Martin's Press, 1992); Higson, Andrew, *Waving the Flag: Constructing a National Identity in Britain* (Oxford: Clarendon Press, 1995); Kiernan, Robert F., *Noël Coward* (New York: Ungar, 1986).

—T.W.

THIS PROPERTY IS CONDEMNED (1943)

TENNESSEE WILLIAMS (1911–1983)

This Property Is Condemned (1966), directed by Sydney Pollack, adapted by Francis Ford Coppola, Fred Coe, and Edith Sommer; Paramount.

The Play

This Property Is Condemned is a one-act play by Tennessee Williams, which can be acted on the stage in about 20 minutes. The play simply presents a 13-year-old girl named Willie Starr, who has been deserted by her parents. Willie recounts for a lad named Tom the sad story of her sister Alva, who took care of her until Alva's untimely death from lung cancer. And so it is Alva whom Willie idolizes and wants to imitate. Unfortunately, since Alva was a prostitute in her mother's boarding house-brothel for railroad men, Willie naively but firmly believes that the kind of life that Alva led is the only truly glamorous existence for any girl. Consequently, there is little doubt by play's end that Willie is condemned to take up her sister's sordid way of life.

Commentator Philip Weismann notes that Willie seeks solace in reconstructing her unhappy existence into the ideal of an attractive southern belle with many prospects for an enviable life with any number of handsome, well-to-do Gentlemen Callers. She is bereft of family and friends and clings to the image of a family homestead, which recalls better days; in Willie's case it is the family boarding house. She looks for rescue by some prosperous male admirer; for Willie it is Mr. Johnson, the railroad superintendent whom she is convinced will unquestionably transfer his once strong attachment for Alva to her. In short and at play's end, Weismann sees Willie as damned to a dreadful existence like Alva.

The Film

An enormous amount of expansion was imposed on the play's slender plot to bloat it into nearly two hours of screen time. It has been said that inside every fat man there is a thin man struggling to get out, and in *This Property Is Condemned* one senses the original playlet likewise struggling to come across on the screen as it did on the stage. The three principal authors of the 1966 film version—including screenwriter Francis Ford Coppola (later the director of the *Godfather* trilogy)—elaborated Williams's slender little tale far beyond his original conception. The basic format that the screenwriters hit upon was to make Williams's play into a framing device for the rest of the picture. Accordingly they broke the one-acter roughly in half, presenting the first portion as a prologue to the film and the remaining segment as an epilogue. In this way they utilized almost all of the play's original dialogue in their screenplay. In the prologue of the film Willie, played by Mary Badham (*To Kill a Mockingbird*), describes her family and present situation to the boy Tom, and in the epilogue she wraps things up by telling Tom what happened to each of them. The scriptwriters then had to devise a full-blown story told in flashback to fit between the prologue and the epilogue. Several of the characters in the picture are derived from people to whom Willie refers in the one-act play.

The one character who has no discernible counterpart in the play is Owen Legate (Robert Redford). He is a railroad inspector who stays long enough in the Starr boarding house to make Alva (Natalie Wood) dissatisfied with her dead-end existence there and to beckon her to a cleaner life in New Orleans as his wife. But before Owen can make an honest woman of Alva, her life is tragically cut short by lung cancer. The film then closes with the epilogue in which Willie is left with the grim prospect of coping with life alone.

This Property was directed by Sidney Pollack and shot by cinematographer James Wong Howe in locations in rural Mississippi and New Orleans. Williams was understandably disappointed in the finished product. Indeed, he accurately assessed the film as a "vastly expanded and hardly related film with the title taken from a very delicate one-act play." Nonetheless, a few critics find some merit in the movie. David Thomson notes that it is packed with atmosphere and has one of Robert Redford's more committed performances.

REFERENCES

Cowie, Peter, *Coppola: A Biography*, rev. ed. (New York: Da Capo, 1994); Phillips, Gene D., *The Films of Tennessee Williams* (Cranbury, N.J.: Associated University Presses, 1980); Thomson, David, "Sydney Pollack," in *A Biographical Dictionary of Film*, rev. ed. (New York: Knopf, 1994), 592–593.

—G.D.P.

THOUSAND CLOWNS, A (1962)

HERB GARDNER (1934–)

A Thousand Clowns (1965), U.S.A., directed by Fred Coe, adapted by Herb Gardner; United Artists.

The Play

Despite critical attempts to prove the contrary, Herb Gardner has maintained his only interest is to entertain and amuse his audiences. Plays like *The Goodbye People*, *Thieves*, and *I'm Not Rappaport* illuminate through comic techniques the sad conditions of old people and disenfranchised mavericks. Sometimes called the "laureate of losers," Gardner nonetheless insists that his characters remain ever hopeful no matter how difficult the odds, survivors in a bitter world. *A Thousand Clowns* was his second produced play. The three-act seriocomedy premiered in New York at the Eugene O'Neill Theatre on April 5, 1962, and ran for a successful 428 performances. The setting is the incredibly messy room of Murray Burns (Jason Robards, Jr.), who writes television scripts for a show about "Chuckles the Chipmunk." Needless to say, he hates his job. But then, everything about Murray's life seems to be in disarray. It's bad enough when he is fired from his job, but when the Child Welfare Bureau threatens to take away his young nephew Nick (Barry Gordon), things look desperate. He is informed that he will lose Nick unless he can get a job. Murray would rather be a professional unemployed madcap and lean out the window and shout things like "Everybody on stage for the Hawaiian number, please." At the same time, he is intelligent enough that he can articulate the unquiet desperation of millions like him. The outlook brightens when one of the social workers, Sandra (Sandy Dennis), falls in love with Murray; moreover, the star of the "Chuckles" show, Leo Herman (Gene Saks), admits his error in firing Murray and offers to rehire him. "Within this grand expression of comic theatre," writes commentator Walter J. Meserve, "where dreams cannot be answered but believing in dreams is deemed necessary, Gardner presents his characters. . . . Then, he stops; conclusions are not his métier."

The Film

The transfer of play to film was felicitously accomplished by retaining many of the original principals. Director Fred Coe was retained to direct the film. Cast members Jason Robards, Jr., and Barry Gordon reprised their roles. Oddly, Sandy Dennis, who had won a Tony Award as the social worker, was passed over for Barbara

Harris. New to the film's cast was Martin Balsam, who won an Oscar for best supporting actor as Murray's older brother, Arnold. The setting of Murray's apartment is "opened up" by adding several rambles through Manhattan, including locations at Lincoln Center (then under construction) and in Central Park. A new piece of business is a pre-credit prologue, wherein Murray and the nephew look on in mock horror as the early-morning city comes alive. To the beat of "The Union Forever (Hurrah, boys, hurrah!)," the great city hustles, shoves, and elbows its way to the workplace. The film was a hit at the box office and took its place along with other "dropout" comedies of the day, like Brian DePalma's *Greetings* and *Get to Know Your Rabbit* and the Neil Simon comedy *Barefoot in the Park*. Critic Pauline Kael was unimpressed and regarded it as a copout. "Basically, it was about as nonconformist as Mom's apple pie," she sniffed, labeling it as a piece of harmless "romantic crackpotism."

REFERENCES

Kael, Pauline, "A Thousand Clowns," in Pauline Kael, *For Keeps* (New York: Dutton, 1994); Meserve, Walter J., "Herbert Gardner," in D.L. Kirkpatrick, ed., *Contemporary Dramatists* (Chicago: St. James Press, 1988), 186–187; Mordden, Ethan, *Medium Cool: The Movies of the 1960s* (New York: Alfred A. Knopf, 1990).

—*J.C.T.*

George Abbott

THREE MEN ON A HORSE (1936)

JOHN CECIL HOLM (1906–) AND GEORGE ABBOTT (1887–1995)

Three Men on a Horse (1937), U.S.A., directed by Mervyn LeRoy, adapted by Laird Doyle; Warner Bros.

The Play

Three Men on a Horse premiered at New York's Playhouse Theater on January 30, 1935, where it ran for 835 performances. Its action is confined to the Trowbridge home in New Jersey's fictional suburb of Ozone Heights and to the basement bar and rooms of New York's Lavilliere Hotel. Henpecked husband Erwin Trowbridge (William Lynn) has accidentally discovered a system of picking winners in horse races, an activity he does for fun in reaction to his mundane job of writing Mother's Day verses and his dull life with a demanding wife, Audrey (Joyce Arling), and overbearing brother-in-law Clarence. He accidentally falls into the hands of a group of shady characters, Patsy, Charlie, and Frankie,

who use his talents to pick winners. Aided by Patsy's ex-chorus girlfriend, Mabel (Shirley Booth), they keep him overnight in the Lavilliere Hotel while Erwin's boss, J. G. Carver, threatens to fire him. Eventually, Erwin loses his ability to predict winners when Patsy forces him to gamble his own money rather than engage in the activity for fun. After finally asserting his manhood against Patsy, Clarence, and Audrey, as well as gaining a raise in salary and new respect from his boss, Erwin turns to writing Father's Day verses.

The Film

The film version represents a compromise between fidelity to the original play and the demands of the Warner Bros. studio. Director LeRoy attempted to open out the play cinematically by using standard, classic Hollywood devices of varied shot ratios, camera movements, and editing techniques such as dissolves. The film begins with an external shot of a New Jersey street sign before the camera pans left to reveal the bland landscape of Ozone Heights. (Ironically, the opening music is the same time later used in the 1950s television comedy *The Burns and Allen Show*.) Although the film uses much of the original play's dialogue, scenarist Laird Doyle often prunes superfluous lines to the extent that it resembles a Warner Bros. Jimmy Cagney vehicle. Unfortunately, the talents of leading players Frank McHugh and Joan Blondell are better suited to their usual supporting character roles in Warner productions. McHugh is weak as Erwin and Blondell as Mabel mugs in an inappropriately theatrical manner.

The film also suffered from the censorship of the Production Code. Lines such as "go to hell" are changed to "go soak his head." Also, although the Jewish name of Patsy's executive friend, Liebowitch, remains in the film, references to his daughter having a baby at the Beth Israel Hospital and his son's "confirmation at the synagogue" are dropped. The film includes an extra scene of Frankie seeing the baby at the unnamed hospital, but the "confirmation" now takes place at a church. These practices reflect a period when studios realized that urban Jewish references and the performance style of New York favorites such as Eddie Cantor and Fanny Brice would not appeal to less sophisticated outside audiences. Ironically, when Frankie puts on a gown to see baby Liebowitch, he may be indirectly referring to censorship when he remarks, "What is this? A Ku Klux Klan hospital?" (a line that does not appear in the original play).

Among the scenes that Doyle and LeRoy visualize from the bare bones of the play's dialogue are a visit to the racetrack and a comic scene where Patsy, Mabel, and Frankie attempt to inspire Erwin by improvising the effect of him being on a bus.

REFERENCES

Abbott, George, *Mister Abbott* (New York: Random House, 1963); LeRoy, Mervyn, as told to Dick Kleiner, *Mervyn LeRoy: Take One* (New York: Hawthorn Books, 1974).

—T.W.

THE THREEPENNY OPERA/DIE DREIGROSCHENOPER (1928)

BERTOLT BRECHT (1891–1956) AND KURT WEILL (1900–1950)

The Threepenny Opera (1931), Germany, directed by G.W. Pabst, adapted by Leo Lania/Bela Balasz/Ladislas Vajda; Warner Bros./First National (U.S.A.) and Tobis Klang-Film/Nero-Film (Germany).

The Play

The Threepenny Opera (1928) was inspired by *The Beggar's Opera* (1728). Set by Johann Christopher Pepusch (1667–1752) to a libretto by John Gay (1685–1732), the three-act *Beggar's Opera* interspersed spoken dialogue with a pastiche of 69 thematically related tunes taken largely from folk and popular sources of the period. Gay, in the process of creating new lyrics to many of the songs, told a brightly paced story of thieves and highwaymen that poked fun at the corruption of contemporary society as well as the conventions of Italian opera. Taking London's theatrical world by storm, *The Beggar's Opera* inspired playing cards, porcelain figurines, and illustrations, including a well-known and eponymously named set by William Hogarth. The craze continued with a new production staged in London every season for the duration of the century.

The Beggar's Opera also stirred controversy. Indeed, historians believe that when it was first offered to the Drury Lane Theatre, the theatre's manager, Colley Cibber, turned it down because of its stinging references to Whig prime minister Robert Walpole. John Rich, manager of Lincoln's Inn Fields, had no such qualms. The unprecedented vogue for *The Beggar's Opera* made Pepusch, Gay, and Rich wealthy men. Soon, there were highly touted productions throughout Great Britain and the United States. Although its popularity waned during the 19th century, *The Beggar's Opera* once again became a hit in 1920, due to an influential revival at the Lyric Theatre, Hammersmith, England, which ran for an extraordinary 1,463 performances. This was the production that inspired Bertolt Brecht.

During the winter of 1927–28, dramatist Brecht commissioned a translation of the English-language *Beggar's Opera* into German. The project took on urgency when Brecht was approached by entrepreneur Ernst Josef Aufricht to create a new work for the debut of the Theater am Schiffbauerdamm in Berlin. With a tight deadline, the playwright and composer Kurt Weill premiered their "play with music," *The Threepenny Opera (Die Dreigroschenoper)*, on August 31, 1928. Given the chaotic final month of tumultuous rehearsals and revisions, prospects for success seemed bleak. To everyone's astonishment, *The Threepenny Opera* was a hit. With Brecht's sharp-edged political satire and Weill's appealingly jazzed-up score, *The Threepenny*

Opera, which became the Weimar Republic's biggest theatrical success, ran for over two years. The charismatic Lotte Lenya, Weill's wife, and the brash, jazz-inflected playing of Lewis Ruth's pit band were other key elements in the play's success.

Transposing the setting of Gay's *The Beggar's Opera* to the mean streets of late-19th-century London, Brecht and Weill unfolded their parodistic tale of urban low-lifes—pimps, prostitutes, and politicians—with the intent of prodding German playgoers to reflect on the economic and political upheavals of 1928, and with them, the fate of the Weimar Republic.

The Film

Although Brecht and Weill were included at the onset of the adaptation process, artistic differences with noted German film director G.W. Pabst arose almost immediately. While holding onto the play's social satire with its assumption that criminals and politicians have more in common than not, Pabst muted Brecht's political critique by shifting greater weight to the story's romance. Many of Brecht's famed "alienation" devices, designed to provoke audiences to progressive political action, were either marginalized or eliminated. Stylistically, the play's hard-edged and self-consciously theatrical decor was made more realistic by Pabst's naturalistic mise-en-scène, which made effective atmospheric use of billowing clouds of tobacco smoke and swirling banks of London fog. Weill's trenchant pop-inflected songs, so critical to Brecht's strategy of spectatorial estrangement, were reduced in the film to the status of decoration. Pabst, in fact, discarded three of Weill's most pivotal plaints, "Ballad of Sexual Dependency," "The Tango Ballad," and "The Ballad for the Hangman." Still, the film included a moving version of "Moritat," which in 1957 became famous as the hit song, "Mack the Knife." Given the extent of Pabst's alterations, it is not surprising that Brecht and Weill, in separate cases, sued the director as well as the coproducers, Tobis Klang-Film, Nero Films, and Warner Bros./First National. The suits came to naught, and Pabst continued filming.

When released in 1931, it was clear that the film bore the realistic mark of Pabst as well as the theatrical expressionism of Brecht and Weill. That it crackled with Brecht's sharp sarcasm was in part due to the dynamic presence of Carola Neher (Polly Peachum) and Lotte Lenya (Jenny), holdovers from the 1928 theatrical cast. Despite artistic differences, the film ultimately bears witness to Pabst's essential agreement with Brecht and Weill's leftist politics. Indeed, as a work in Pabst's oeuvre, it should be thematically grouped with

the director's similarly anti-capitalist, pro-everyman *Westfront 1918* (1930) and *Kameradschaft* (1931). *The Threepenny Opera* was shot simultaneously in German and French with different casts. A planned English-language version was never completed. In Paris, the French version of *The Threepenny Opera* became a critical and box-office success. In Berlin, with the ascent of the Third Reich, all German prints were seized and destroyed, a testament to the power of Pabst's portrayal of the zeitgeist making Hitler possible. Today, it is the restored German-language version that stands as the work's most definitive and therefore authoritative edition.

A forgettable German remake of *The Threepenny Opera* appeared in 1964, with Curt Jurgens, Hildegarde Neff, and Sammy Davis, Jr., who makes periodic appearances as a sort of "chorus" commenting on the action.

REFERENCES

Eisner, Lotte H., *The Haunted Screen: Expressionism in the German Cinema and the Influence of Max Reinhardt* (Berkeley: University of California Press, 1969); Manvell, Roger, and Heinrich Fraenkel, *The German Cinema* (New York: Praeger, 1971).

—C.M.B.

TIME OF THE CUCKOO (1952) (SUMMERTIME)

ARTHUR LAURENTS (1918–   )

Summertime (1955), U.K., directed by David Lean, adapted by Lean and H.E. Bates; London Films/United Artists.

The Play

The play premiered in New York at the Empire Theatre on October 15, 1952, and ran for a successful 263 performances. A lonely American spinster, Leona Samish (Shirley Booth), arrives in Venice to view the Old-World sights and pursue romance. She meets the suave, handsome Italian, Renato de Rossi (Dino Di Luca), and love blossoms. However, their idyll is shattered when Renato reveals himself to be not only an opportunist, but also a married man. Leona returns, disillusioned, to America. Critic Louis Kronenberger regarded this slender drama as "one with shrewd comments and effective scenes, one where, in terms of love, there is much to be said on both sides; or where—in line with Hebbel's requirement for sound drama—*all* the people seem in the right." The play was later translated into a musical, *Do I Hear a Waltz* (1965), also by Laurents, with music by Richard Rodgers and lyrics by Stephen Sondheim.

The Film

The play's title was the first thing to go. The cuckoo may be a summer visitor to Europe, like Leona, but it was feared that the reference might be too precious for general audiences. Moreover, the original title did not suggest the bittersweet love story that the film became; the more abstract *Summertime* was chosen. Director David Lean took advantage of the Venetian locales to film it on location. The results smack of a travelogue at times, but it does provide a sustained counterpoint to the disillusionment of Leona Samish, here renamed Jane Hudson (Katharine Hepburn). Instead of rejecting Rossi (Rossano Brazzi) when she learns he is married, she continues the affair, which she describes as "the happiest time in my life"—even though she realizes it will "end in nothing." There is a wonderfully symbolic scene in which the white flower, which Rossi has given Jane, drifts slowly away on the water into the distance. Omitted from the screenplay are some of Jane's suspicions regarding Rossi, like an incident involving her being overcharged for the purchase of a goblet. At the end, the expression on the face of the departing Jane, alone again, is not one of sorrow, but happiness.

The film received its world premiere in Venice on May 29, 1955. Critic C.A. Lejeune described it as a combination of *Brief Encounter* and *Three Coins in the Fountain*: "This dubiously moral heroine is brought to glowing life by Katharine Hepburn, whose wide awake face and probing fingers give the effect of receiving and storing up memories more delicately than I have seen the trick done since Garbo did it in the bedroom scene of *Queen Christina*." Playwright Laurents demurred: "I didn't like it at all. They jettisoned most of the play. It was an homage to Kate Hepburn who shed more water than there is in Venice. . . . I knew Kate. When it was all over, she told me, 'You won't like it. But I'm brilliant.'" Both Hepburn and director Lean were nominated for Oscars.

Historian Kevin Brownlow reports that *Summertime* (retitled *Summer Madness* in England) was David Lean's favorite film: "I've put more of myself in that film than in any other I've ever made." It was his third film in color, a coproduction between Alexander Korda's London Films and United Artists in America. Playwright Laurents came to London in 1953 to work on the screenplay, but Lean quickly objected to his rigid adherence to the original play text. Other writers were called in, including Donald Ogden Stewart, S.N. Behrman, and, finally, H.E. Bates. The production itself was shot in Venice, where Lean depended heavily on local technicians and actors.

REFERENCES

Brownlow, Kevin, *David Lean: A Biography* (New York: St. Martin's Press, 1996); Pratley, Gerald, *The Cinema of David Lean* (South Brunswick, N.J.: A.S. Barnes, 1973).

—*J.C.T.*

TOPAZE (1928)

MARCEL PAGNOL (1895–1974)

Topaze (1932), France, directed by Louis Gasnier, adapted by Léopold Marchand and Louis Gasnier; French Paramount.

Topaze (1933), U.S.A., directed by Harry d'Abbadie d'Arrast, adapted by Benn W. Levy; RKO Radio Pictures.

Topaze (1936), France, directed by Marcel Pagnol, from his own play; Société des Films Marcel Pagnol.

Topaze (1951), France, directed by Marcel Pagnol from his own play; Société des Films Marcel Pagnol.

Mr. Topaze (1961), U.K., directed by Peter Sellers, adapted by Pierre Rouve; Twentieth Century-Fox. (U.S.A. release title: *I Like Money*).

The Play

First staged by Max Maurey at the Théâtre des Variétés in 1928, Pagnol's highly successful satirical comedy ran for nearly three years. The action is set in a seedy private boarding school, where Topaze, a naïve but dedicated teacher, makes the cardinal mistake of giving a zero to a rich pupil, the son of Baroness Pitart-Vergniolles. Muche, the headmaster, dismisses him and warns him to keep away from his daughter Ernestine, with whom he is infatuated. Topaze earns a living giving private lessons to the son of Madame Suzy Courtois, who is the mistress of Castel-Bénac, a local politician and crooked financier. He arranges for the town council to buy goods from companies he sets up, which are headed by his own men. The innocent Topaze is duped into becoming one of Castel-Bénac's pawns and is duly outraged when he discovers the fraud. He realizes that all the moral nostrums he taught at school are as nothing in the corrupt world of business and local politics. He decides to quit, but Suzy charms him into staying on to learn from the crooked politician before exposing him to justice and rescuing her from his clutches. Topaze's apparent business acumen wins the admiration of his former employer Muche, who now offers his daughter to him; but the newly assertive Topaze, with Suzy in mind, refuses the invitation. Ironically, the now socially successful Topaze is awarded a teaching accolade formerly denied him, providing yet further confirmation of society's inherent hypocrisy. Warming to his new role, the once mild schoolmaster is now decisive and authoritarian. He turns the tables on Castel-Bénac, asserts his legal position as nominated head of the politician's companies, and drives him out before claiming Suzy for himself. To a surprised former colleague Tamise, Topaze explains, in his new cynicism, that happiness can be bought.

With its tight structure, well-drawn characters, and aphoristic dialogue, Pagnol's ironical social satire succeeds as a piece of well-crafted theatre, with the challenging role of Topaze at its center. For the lead actor the part demands a considerable range as the once gentle, morally correct schoolmaster committed to social values is transformed into an astute, cynical operator, taking on and defeating the newly discovered, corrupt worlds of finance and politics. With its echoes of recent financial scandals and its pungent comment on social hypocrisies, Pagnol's play reflects a widespread disillusionment with politics and big business, thus combining contemporary immediacy with an enduring study of innocence transformed. With the influence of Antoine still dominant in Parisian theatre of the day, the staging was heavily naturalistic in concept, with the classroom re-created in every detail. Here, for example, the moral aphorisms so beloved of Topaze, such as "Money does not buy happiness," adorn the walls only to become an ironically pointed commentary on subsequent events. The scenes at the school, doubtless in part deriving from Pagnol's own experiences as a former teacher, have an engaging authenticity as the naïve Topaze seeks to control his rowdy pupils or exchanges views on teaching with a sympathetic colleague. If the sentimental scenes are rather conventional, the ex-schoolmaster's transformation to a sharp-tongued financier, now smartly dressed and minus his beard, are memorable. The original cast, comprising André Lefaur as Topaze, Marcel Vallée as Muche, Paul Pauley as Castel-Bénac, Pierre Larquey as Tamise, and Jeanne Provost as Suzy Courtois eventually appeared in one or more of the film versions.

The Films

Five screen versions of Pagnol's play have been produced, two of which were directed by the author himself. Each testifies to a particular creative vision of the stage text, though not surprisingly the author's own versions lay claim to most fidelity. The first version, directed by Louis Gasnier for Paramount, was made without consultation and subsequently disowned by Pagnol. The studio had decided that the play needed "a cinematic treatment" and employed Léopold Marchand, a fellow dramatist with film experience, to rework the stage text. The play was duly "opened up" with more frequent changes of location and exterior settings, with some of the essentially static scenes heavily truncated. In the same vein, much of Pagnol's original dialogue is rewritten, with the longer speeches broken into sharper exchanges. It is in the play's initial depiction of Topaze as a teacher that a paring down is most readily observed. The discussions on pedagogy are truncated and the key scene in which unruly pupils disrupt Topaze's class on citizenship is lost, much to the detriment of the message in the play's second half when Topaze becomes anything but a model citizen. Pagnol's satire of contemporary political and financial corruption is diminished by playing down allusions to the Panama Canal scandal, while the humor is coarser, particularly in the addition of visual close-ups, such as those involving the foul-smelling portable toilets left outside cafés to extort money from the owners, or Castel-Bénac's enormous buttocks when out riding in the woods. In a disparaging comparison with the play, one film reviewer noted, "Vulgar, crude humor has replaced barbed wit and observation. If the stage play has all the elements of a bitter farce with credible characters, in the film these characters become caricatures and there is not a ray of hope or generosity to be discovered." The film is redeemed visually by some striking art-deco sets and is notable for the quality of its acting, and, in particular, for Louis Jouvet's cinema début in the role of Topaze. He brings a disturbing quality to the part with his magnetic presence and typically narrowing eyes, now captured in close-up, making Topaze a much more sinister reincarnation as a duplicitous financier. Excellent support was provided by Edwige Feuillère as Suzy Courtois, Paul Pauley as Castel-Bénac, and Marcel Vallée as Muche.

With this unhappy experience of seeing his play betrayed both in spirit and detail, four years later Pagnol decided to make his own version with the original dialogue restored and the original structure respected. To reinforce this authenticity he engaged actors who had previously performed in his plays, casting Arnaudy as Topaze, Leon Brouzet as Muche, and Alida Rouffe as

Pitart-Vergniolles. Despite flattering reviews this version did not measure up to Gasnier's contentious reworking, and after six months Pagnol withdrew all copies of the film. However, in the fifties he returned to his play a third time to direct Fernandel, the celebrated comic actor, as his new Topaze. This version is typical of the early fifties emphasis on high production values and respect for the text. Technically the most ambitious and the most reverential, there is rather too much emphasis on the visual, with Philippe Agostini's self-consciously artistic camera work a distraction. However, Fernandel provides arguably the most successful interpretation of Topaze, conveying with persuasive conviction the change from the unassertive, over-conscientious schoolmaster to the cynical, self-assured, and corrupt businessman.

Two English-language versions have also been made. Following a successful adaptation of the play for the New York stage by Benn W. Levy with Frank Morgan in the title role, the same adaptation became the basis for a screen version directed by Harry d'Abbadie d'Arrast for the RKO studios. In this reworked version, the biting contemporary satire has been abandoned to produce a well-crafted romantic comedy, with Topaze (played by John Barrymore) as the "lovable scoundrel," charming his female friends by his unworldly innocence. As the fall guy he heads up the Latour Chemical Company, which markets a mineral water, "Sparkling Topaze," a concoction that is anything but pure; as a romantic innocent, he sees his first movie *Women of Passion*, but fails to see the point of the title. Myrna Loy plays the enticing Coco (Suzy) and Reginald Mason the dubious Baron de Latour-Latour (Castel-Bénac).

The sixties saw the versatile comic actor Peter Sellers make his directorial debut with his version, *Mr. Topaze*, casting himself in the lead role. Pierre Rouve's script follows Pagnol closely and the French atmosphere is reinforced by theme music by Georges van Parys. The school scenes are handled well and Topaze's attempts to woo Ernestine (Billie Whitelaw) are touchingly funny, but Sellers lacks the discipline to direct himself successfully, and though a competent Topaze, the full complexity of the role is not brought out. Despite a strong supporting cast, notably Nadia Gray as Suzy, Leo McKern as Muche, and Michael Gough as an excellent Tamise, the film never reaches its full potential and proved to be Sellers only attempt at direction.

REFERENCES

Beylie, Claude, *Marcel Pagnol ou le cinéma en liberté* (Paris: Editions de Fallois, 1995); Caldicot, C.E.J., *Marcel Pagnol* (Boston: Twayne, 1977); Pompa, Dany, *Marcel Pagnol* (Paris: Henri Veyrier, 1986).

—R.F.C.

TORCH SONG TRILOGY (1981)

HARVEY FIERSTEIN (1954–   )

Torch Song Trilogy (1988), U.S.A., directed by Paul Bogart, adapted by Harvey Fierstein; New Line Cinema.

The Play

Actually a collection of three one-act plays, *Torch Song Trilogy* gained notice as one of the first works of homosexual drama to have widespread cross-over appeal to heterosexual audiences. In addition, it established Fierstein as one of the premiere gay male playwrights of the late 20th century. Critic Frances Gray has said that Fierstein's appeal is due to "his use of forms already familiar from heterosexual romance. . . . Fierstein uses situations that would, but for the sexuality of the protagonists, be the most bewhiskered of cliches." By populating these romantic clichés with homosexual or bisexual characters, in *Torch Song Trilogy* Fierstein manages to comment on both homosexual culture and the romantic situations used in both straight and gay drama. The three one-act sections of *Torch Song Trilogy* (all produced individually prior to their combination in 1981) shared only their drag-queen protagonist, Arnold. *The International Stud*, the first of the three one-acts, takes place in the early 1970s and centers on the relationship between Arnold, known in his drag persona as Virginia Hamm, and his sexually ambivalent friend Ed, who is flirting with homosexuality. The second part, *Fugue in a Nursery*, returns to examine the relationship between Arnold and Ed a year later; by this time, Ed—still experimenting with his sexuality—has married his girlfriend and Arnold has begun a serious relationship with another man named Alan. The final part of the trilogy, *Widows and Children First!* jumps to the late 1970s as Arnold attempts to simultaneously deal with the murderous death of Alan, a visit from his mother, and a growing parental relationship with a gay teen named David.

The Film

The cinematic adaptation of *Torch Song Trilogy* came seven years after the original stage production, and the

Harvey Fierstein (center) appeared in his own screen adaptation of Torch Song Trilogy. (COURTESY NEW LINE CINEMA)

changes in gay culture that had transpired in the interim profoundly affected the meanings and nuances of the story. By the late 1980s, the AIDS crisis had transformed almost all homosexual artistic expression, and although *Torch Song Trilogy* had initially been produced before the epidemic, the film adaptation was nonetheless colored by its impact. The adaptation—written by and starring Fierstein—had to explicitly frame itself as a pre-AIDS parable in order for its characters to behave as homosexuals really had in the 1970s. Whereas the stage production had been hailed as a major element of the early-1980s Gay Pride artistic movement, the film was seen as a belated and beleaguered "curiosity piece" aimed, due to Fierstein's growing mainstream popularity, at an exclusively heterosexual audience.

The changes made to *Torch Song Trilogy* in the process of adaptation were substantial. The individual acts of the stage production were each given unique visual and dramatic treatment: *The International Stud* had consisted mainly of soliloquies, the action of *Fugue in a Nursery* was confined to a huge, stylized bed, and

Widows and Children First! was staged as a TV sitcom. In the film, Fierstein and director Paul Bogart decided to make the three acts a seamless whole and give the entire story a more realistic style. Besides Fierstein as Arnold, the film's cast included Anne Bancroft as Ma (assuming the role from Estelle Getty), Matthew Broderick as Alan (transferring from his role as David in the play), Eddie Castrodad as David, and Brian Kerwin as Ed. Since the film of *Torch Song Trilogy*, Fierstein has gone on to become a popular character actor in mainstream films, most notably as the brother of Robin Williams in *Mrs. Doubtfire* (1993).

REFERENCES

Gray, Frances, "Harvey Fierstein," in *International Dictionary of Theatre*, vol. 2, ed. Mark Hawkins-Dady (London: St. James Press, 1994); Gray, Frances, "Torch Song Trilogy," in *International Dictionary of Theatre*, vol. 1, Mark Hawkins-Dady, ed. (London: St. James Press, 1992); Parish, James, *Gays and Lesbians in Mainstream Cinema* (Jefferson, N.C.: McFarland, 1993).

—*C.M.*

TWENTY-SEVEN WAGONS FULL OF COTTON (1943)

TENNESSEE WILLIAMS (1911–1983)

Baby Doll (1956), directed by Elia Kazan, adapted by Tennessee Williams; Warner Bros.

The Play

Elia Kazan's film *Baby Doll* was derived principally from one of Tennessee Williams' one-act plays, *Twenty-seven Wagons Full of Cotton*, with some additional material supplied from another one-act play, *The Unsatisfactory Supper* (1939). In the first play the heroine is the voluptuous wife of a seedy cotton gin owner many years her senior. The man burns down the cotton gin owned by Silva Vacarro, in order to force Vacarro to use his facilities instead. In reviewing *Twenty-seven Wagons Full of Cotton*, drama critic Walter Kerr congratulated Williams on the deftness with which he could employ melodrama to propel a play vigorously forward toward emotionally revealing scenes in a way that was neither florid nor forced.

The other one-act play is a much less substantial character sketch of Aunt Rose, an elderly spinster who has worn out her welcome with her niece, Baby Doll, and the latter's husband Archie Lee (the counterpart of the husband and wife in *Twenty-Seven*).

The Film

Williams melded the two one-acters into a single, coherent story for the screen at the behest of film director Elia Kazan (*A Streetcar Named Desire*). Just how firmly the two one-acters solidified into one unified work of art is evidenced by the substantial amount of dialogue that Williams was able to retain from the two plays. In the film, Baby Doll (Carroll Baker) is attracted to Vacarro (Eli Wallach) because he treats her less like a child—which is the approach Archie Lee (Karl Malden) takes to her—and more and more like the young woman she really is.

In the film's finale Archie Lee becomes hysterical when Vacarro informs him that he has wheedled evidence of the arson from Baby Doll and suggests that he has coaxed other favors from her as well. Archie Lee runs around the property drunkenly, firing off his shotgun wildly and indiscriminately, and is finally hauled off by the sheriff to spend the night in jail. Vacarro gal-lantly offers to take Aunt Rose in as his housekeeper, and Baby Doll decides to leave Archie Lee for Vacarro. (Since her May–December marriage to Archie Lee was never consummated, it will not be difficult for her to obtain an annulment.) The movie's conclusion reflects a note of hope and optimism that is nowhere in sight in either of the two source plays.

"I think of *Baby Doll* as a quiet little black comedy," Kazan told this writer; "and I've never been able to understand what all the fuss was about at the time of its release." In fact, Francis Cardinal Spellman, archbishop of New York, in an unprecedented action, denounced the picture from the pulpit of St. Patrick's Cathedral as a corruptive influence on American society. Presumably Spellman and other church leaders who subsequently followed his lead mistakenly thought that some of the movie's images had a sexual intent, when in fact they did not. For example, Baby Doll's sucking her thumb and licking an ice cream cone were not meant to depict the young girl's subconscious longing for fellatio, as some of the film's critics contended, but to show, as Kazan himself said, that "she's still a baby. She's not grown up. That's all I had in mind: arrested development."

Still, some reviewers at the time of the film's release found that *Baby Doll* resembled a lurid potboiler by southern novelist Erskine Caldwell (*Tobacco Road*), rather than the previous work of the author of *The Glass Menagerie*. Making this point, one critic dismissed the movie as "The Crass Menagerie."

Nevertheless, *Baby Doll* had its defenders, even within the Catholic Church. Father John Burke, who reviewed films for the Catholic press in England, did not think *Baby Doll* a prurient picture at all. According to film historian Gregory Black, Burke believed that the film was a serious psychological study of the lives of some poor whites in the backwoods of the American South; as such it was something for "thoughtful adults" to see. Perhaps Kazan said it all when he concluded, "If you see *Baby Doll* today, now that the controversy has long since died down, you can see that it is a charming comedy, poetic and funny; and that is all it ever was."

REFERENCES

Black, Gregory, *The Catholic Crusade Against the Movies, 1940–75* (New York: Cambridge University Press, 1998); Phillips, Gene D., *The Films of Tennessee Williams* (Cranbury, N.J.: Associated University Presses, 1980); Walsh, Frank, *Sin and Censorship: The Catholic Church and the Motion Picture Industry* (New Haven: Yale University Press, 1997).

—G.D.P.

UNCLE VANYA (1897)

ANTON CHEKHOV (1860–1904)

Uncle Vanya (1958), U.S.A., directed by John Goetz and Franchot Tone, adapted by Stark Young; Continental.

Uncle Vanya (1963), U.K., directed and adapted by Stuart Burge; British Home Entertainments.

Dyadya Vanya (1971), USSR, directed by and adapted by Andrei Konchalovsky; Mosfilm Studios.

Country Life (1994), Australia, directed by Michael Blakemore, adapted by Robin Dalton; Miramax Films.

Vanya on 42nd Street (1994), U.S.A., directed and adapted by Louis Malle and Andre Gregory; Sony Pictures Classics.

August (1996), U.K., directed by Anthony Hopkins, adapted by Julian Mitchell; Granada Film Productions/Majestic Films.

The Play

Chekhov's four-act play, *Uncle Vanya*, was written between November 1895 and December 1896. The play was a revision of an earlier, less successful work titled *The Wood Demon* (1889), which closed after only three performances. *Uncle Vanya* was first produced in 1897 in the provinces at Odessa, Kiev, Saratov, and Tbilisi to generally favorable reviews. The play was produced at the Moscow Art Theatre, under the direction of Konstantin Stanislavski, on October 26, 1899. Subtitled "Scenes from Country Life in Four Acts," after Russian dramatist Alexander Ostrovsky, Chekhov's play takes place on a dilapidated country estate. Serebryakov, a retired art professor, has overstayed his welcome at the home of Voynitskaya, the mother of the professor's deceased first wife, who worships and dotes on the scholar. Also living on the estate are Sonya, the professor's daughter from his first marriage, and Voynitsky (Vanya), Voynitskaya's son and Sonya's uncle. In addition the professor is accompanied by his young wife, Yelena Andreevna, whom both Vanya and Dr. Astrov, the country doctor who is interested in conservation and forestry, are in love with. Fleshing out the minor characters in Chekhov's work are Telegin "Waffles," an impoverished landowner who also lives on the estate, and Marina, an old nurse.

Chekhov emphasizes the boredom and inactivity that has come over the household following the arrival of the professor. According to J.L. Styan, "This play above all others presents a group of trivial people in order to show the dullness of life in provincial Russia. The challenge for the playwright is to prove that even if they are dull, an audience need not find them uninteresting." Chekhov's realistic dialogue captures this inactivity, which develops through the play's simple style. We think of Chekhov's characters rather than his plots, because they are so succinctly drawn.

The Films

Of all Chekhov's plays *Uncle Vanya* has received the most film treatments. This perhaps attests to the universality of the play's themes of loneliness, boredom, unrequited love, and missed opportunities. The adaptations of *Uncle Vanya* range from the unabashedly theatrical, retaining the full text of the play and simply recording a stage production, to the truly cinematic, in which the play is adapted and shaped into another artistic medium through cinematic expression via editing, camera angles, film stock, lenses. In 1958 John Goetz and Franchot Tone directed Stark Young's translation of *Uncle Vanya*. The film was independently produced. Franchot Tone used his own money to mount this treatment of his successful stage production of 1956. Much of the original cast was retained and although there are very theatrical sets, the acting of the film is exceptional. Tone portrays Dr. Astrov; George Voskovec, Uncle Vanya; Dolores Dorn, Elena; and Peggy McCay, Sofia. Although the film was made in 1958 it did not receive general release until 1960. Laurence Olivier and Stuart Burge directed the 1963 film version of the Chichester Festival stage production of *Uncle Vanya*. The film was simply a recording of the production and starred Olivier as Dr. Astrov, Michael Redgrave as Vanya, Rosemary Harris as Yelena, and Joan Plowright as Sonya (Sofia). Again the film is exceptional primarily because of its cast of first-rate actors.

The first truly cinematic working of Chekhov's play was made by Andrei Konchalovsky in the Soviet Union in 1971. Konchalovsky made his directorial feature film debut in 1965 with *The First Teacher*. Throughout the 1970s he received numerous prizes and accolades for his films, culminating in the Special Jury Prize at the 1979 Cannes Festival for his epic *Siberiade*. In America Konchalovsky directed such films as *Runaway Train* (1985), *Duet for One* (1986), *Tango and Cash* (1989), and *The Inner Circle* (1991). According to H. Peter Stowell in regard to *Uncle Vanya*, "Konchalovsky clearly thought out the relationship of form to content and made a firm commitment to a style. . . . Konchalovsky realized that editing, framing, and composition are more purely filmic and that it was possible to film a play emphasizing these elements rather than the traditional common denominators (i.e., moving camera, outdoor locations)." Utilizing cinematic means of expression such as editing, color, lighting, composition, and framing, Konchalovsky was able to convey "the ideas of isolation between people, the labyrinth of the house, the half-

Anton Chekhov

hidden qualities of these people's lives, and their sameness and individuality."

Most of the film is set inside the household, and the sense of labyrinthine space becomes a key metaphor for the play itself. In Act Three Serebryakov states, "I don't like this house. It's like a maze. Twenty-six enormous rooms, everybody's scattered all over the place, you can't find anyone." This becomes a metaphor for both personal and psychological dislocation in Chekhov's play, which Konchalovsky is able to convey through editing and composition. Off-screen space is often utilized as well, further fragmenting the space and the characters of the play. Konchalovsky's *Uncle Vanya* is faithful to the spirit of Chekhov without being anchored to the theatrical form itself.

In the 1990s three film versions of *Uncle Vanya* were produced, each distinct in the nature of their adaptations and expression. Two of these films, Michael Blakemore's *Country Life* and Anthony Hopkins's *August*, transpose Chekhov's play to a different setting. In much the same manner as Kurosawa's adaptations of Shakespeare and Dostoyevsky, these films, by dislocating the piece to another culture, emphasize in the process the universality of the author's themes. Blakemore's film is placed in post–World War I Australia, during a transitional period when the Australians were breaking away from England. Michael Blakemore plays former dramatic critic Alexander Voysey (Serebryakov) who arrives at the run-down family estate (named the Canterbury estate) accompanied by his young wife Deborah (Yelena). Both Jack Dickens (Vanya) played by John Hargreaves, and the local doctor Max Askey (Astrov) played by Sam Neill, fall in love with Deborah. Blakemore is quite successful in showing the longings, frustrations, and sense of ennui that are inherent in Chekhov's characters. The director also opens up the play through location photography to display the wonderful landscape of the Australian countryside, especially the opening sequence showing the arrival of Alexander at the train station.

August (1996) was the directorial debut of actor Anthony Hopkins, who also portrayed Ieuan Davies (Vanya). This version of Chekhov's play is transposed to turn-of-the-century South Wales, Hopkins's native homeland. The screenplay by Julian Mitchell successfully transfers Chekhov's basic themes to another location—as isolated and confined as Blakemore's Australian setting. In addition to directing and starring in the film, Anthony Hopkins composed the music score. Both of these films utilized outdoor locations to provide a sense of dislocation as a metaphor for Chekhov's characters. On the opposite extreme is Louis Malle's *Vanya on 42nd Street* (1994).

In 1989 theatrical director Andre Gregory began rehearsing a group of friends and actors with a new translation of *Uncle Vanya* by David Mamet. No performance of the play was planned, Gregory's motive was simply to explore the beauty and construction of Chekhov's play. Off and on for four years the group rehearsed together and provided impromptu performances for select groups. Both Gregory and Wallace Shawn approached film director Louis Malle (whose previous collaboration with Gregory and Shawn was *My Dinner with Andre*) about filming the production. The result was perhaps the most interesting of the many cinematic adaptations of Chekhov's work. Malle's version is basically a filming of the actors as they perform a run-through of the play in an abandoned, run-down theatre (the New Amsterdam Theatre on 42nd Street). Stripped of all theatrical artifice (there are no sets or costumes) Malle relies almost entirely on close-ups, thereby stressing the importance of the actor's performance as well as the author's dialogue. This adaptation is clearly a chamber piece and succeeds entirely on its well-assembled ensemble cast, which includes Wallace Shawn as Vanya, Julianne Moore as Yelena, Larry Pine as Dr. Astrov, George Gaynes as Serebryakov, and Brooke Smith as Sonya.

REFERENCES

Chekhov: Four Plays, tr. Carol Rocamora (Lyme, N.H.: Smith and Kraus, 1996); Stowell, H. Peter, "Chekhov Into Film" in *A Chekhov Companion*, ed. Toby W. Clyman (Westport, Conn.: Greenwood Press, 1985); Styan, J.L., "Chekhov's Dramatic Technique" in *A Chekhov Companion*, ed. Toby W. Clyman (Westport, Conn.: Greenwood Press, 1985).

—*R.W.W.*

THE VIRGINIAN (1904)

KIRKE LA SHELLE (1863–1905) AND OWEN WISTER (1860–1938)

The Virginian (1914), U.S.A., directed by Cecil B. DeMille, adapted by Jesse L. Lasky Feature Play Company.

The Virginian (1923), U.S.A., directed by Tom Foreman, adapted by Hope Loring and Louis D. Lighton; B.P. Schulberg Productions/Preferred Pictures.

The Virginian (1929), U.S.A., directed by Victor Fleming, adapted by Edward E. Paramore, Jr., and Howard Estabrook; Paramount.

The Virginian (1946), U.S.A., directed by Stuart Gilmore, adapted by Frances Goodrich and Albert Hackett; Paramount.

The Play

There have been four filmed versions of Owen Wister's classic 1902 novel, *The Virginian*. The working model for these films has not been so much the original novel as the dramatization cowritten in 1904 by Wister and Kirke La Shelle. The story owed little to the standard western dime thrillers of Ned Buntline and Prentiss Ingraham. As Loren D. Estleman has pointed out in his study of the work, neither the heroes nor the villains were professional gunmen, there was little bloodshed, and scenes of unexpected prankish humor alternated with philosophical musings on the nature of the West and the cowboys who moved across its vast spaces. The nameless protagonist was a mysterious frontiersman with a pragmatic view of life and his fellows—"a man has got to prove himself my equal before I'll believe him." His opposite number was Trampas, a cowardly rustler (to whom the Virginian uttered the classic line, "When you call me that, *smile*"). Even the love story between the Virginian and the schoolmarm was more concerned with delineating the contrasts between Western experience and Eastern culture than anything else. And among the incidents in the book was the climactic shootout between the Virginian and Trampas—the first of its kind in fiction—which became the paradigm for all subsequent western stories. "*The Virginian* is not only the most widely read of western novels," claims Donald E. Houghton in his study of the book, "it may well be the most widely read American novel ever published."

The play version of *The Virginian* premiered in New York at the Manhattan Theatre on January 5, 1904, where it ran for 138 performances. The play's four acts and five scenes smelted down the sprawling novel into a series of episodes located in a ranch house interior, a patch of ground between Judge Henry's ranch and the cowboys' quarters, the interior of Molly Wood's (Agnes Ardeck) home, and a street corner intersecting the hotel and the saloon (in only one scene was an actual range locale suggested, the campfire scene wherein the rustlers are apprehended by the Virginian and his men). The cattle roundups, runaway stage-coaches, and mounted pursuits were conveyed by reported action and descriptive dialogue. The basic theme of the clash between the moral codes of Eastern culture and Western experience—as exemplified in the lynching of the rustler, Steve, and the climactic gunfight between the Virginian (Dustin Farnum) and the villain-ous Trampas—was teased out in extended discussions between the Virginian and the newly arrived school-teacher, Molly. There was very little overt action. Events were confined to a few sets; otherwise, the action is related through dialogue—such as the Virgin-ian's discovery of Steve's rustling and his rescue of Molly from the runaway stagecoach, the "baby-switch-ing" episode, the cattle roundup that precipitates the deadly clash between the Virginian and Trampas, and the trackdown of the rustlers.

The Films

The first film version, released by the Jesse L. Lasky Feature Play Company in 1914, established its theatri-cal connections at the outset: "Jesse L. Lasky Presents Dustin Farnum in 'The Virginian' by Kirke La Shelle and Owen Wister." The story of the Lasky company is sadly forgotten today, yet it brought to the screen adap-tations of many of the most popular stage plays of the day, including Milton Royle's *The Squaw Man* (1913), Booth Tarkington's *Cameo Kirby* (1914), William de Mille's *The Warrens of Virginia* (1915), and David Belasco's *The Girl of the Golden West* (1915). Unlike many theatrical adaptations, then and now, these films revealed remarkably little of their stagebound origins; they presented naturalistic acting styles; and they broke the proscenium to locate their subjects in real exterior locations. Director-general Cecil B. DeMille said it best: "Imagine, the horizon is your stage limit, and the sky your gridiron. No height limit, no close-fitting exits, no conserving of stage space, just the whole world open to you as a stage and a thousand people in a scene does not crowd your accommodations." Thus, while this 1914 *Virginian* retains the basic structure of the play, it also reveals in its photography, acting, deep-focus frame, and cutting, a distinctly cinematic charac-ter. Actor Dustin Farnum duplicated the eponymous stage role. He is a cowpuncher recently appointed the foreman of a large ranch. Also newly arrived in the nearby town of Bear Creek, Wyoming, is Molly Wood, the new schoolmarm. Their blooming romance is threatened by his allegiance to Western codes of per-

Gary Cooper and Mary Brian starred in Victor Fleming's 1929 adaptation of Owen Wister's The Virginian. (COURTESY NATIONAL FILM SOCIETY'S ARCHIVES)

sonal honor, which demand the hanging of his best friend, Steve, when he is caught rustling cattle, and the necessity of a final shootout with Trampas. More than any other theatrical film of its time, *The Virginian* cre-ates a genuine sense of cinematic space, time, and place. Its techniques of parallel editing, for example, graphi-cally contrasted the play's theme of the clash of East and West (the first reel is devoted to extensive cross-cutting between Molly's home in Vermont and the range locales of the Virginian, events that occurred before Act One in the play); and heightened suspense by alternating shots of the Virginian and Trampas before the climax of the gunfight. Lost in this translation to the screen, however, are the play's extensive discussions of the fundamental philosophical conflicts between East and West. At the end, as the Virginian prepares to confront Trampas, only broad pantomiming and two dialogue titles suffice

THE VISIT/THE VISIT OF THE OLD LADY

to convey these issues. The first title has Molly saying, "I can't marry a man with blood on his hands; come away with me right now"; and the second has the Virginian responding, "Trampas put Steve's head in the noose. Now he's after me and I must be ready for him." Unfortunately, the film is not available commercially, although it can be screened at the Library of Congress film collection.

The 1923 and 1946 adaptations are of negligible interest. The first is a "lost" film about which little information is available. The latter picture is, according to western historian Brian Garfield, a "routine oater," a "lethargic remake" that adds little, other than Technicolor, to the earlier versions. Moreover, the cast of Joel McCrea and Brian Donlevy, as the Virginian and Trampas, is "inadequate" and the photography marred by excessive rear-screen process work.

By far the best-known—and arguably the finest—of the film adaptations is the 1929 version directed by Victor Fleming, starring Gary Cooper (in his first talkie) and Mary Brian as the lovers. Although it is an early talkie and suffers a bit from the sort of sound-recording problems all too typical of the day, like an occasional muffling of the dialogue, it is nonetheless quite sophisticated technically. There is no soundtrack musical score; the sounds of a cattle drive underpin the opening credits, snatches of cowboy songs punctuate the dialogue exchanges, and a quail's call becomes a recurring leitmotif representing the bond between the Virginian and his pal, Steve (Richard Arlen). The reported action of the original play—including the Virginian's rescue of Molly in the runaway stagecoach, the capture and hanging of Steve, Trampas' ambush of the Virginian, and the final gunfight—is "opened out," and the Sierra Nevada serves as a wonderful backdrop to the story. The scenes between the graceful, laconic Cooper and the bullying, brash Huston (as Trampas) are particularly enjoyable to watch. The climactic gunfight is stark and spare, yet as effective in its way as any of the many imitations to follow (such as Cooper's reprise of the scene in *High Noon* [1951]). Commentator Garfield praises the picture's "rich characterizations," adding, *"The Virginian* is fun, and very good; possibly we may never come nearer to the ultimate Western."

REFERENCES

Estleman, Loren D., *The Wister Trace: Classic Novels of the American Frontier* (Ottawa, Ill.: Jameson Books, 1987); Garfield, Brian, *Western Films* (New York: Rawson Associates, 1982); Parish, James Robert, and Michael R. Pitts, *The Great Western Pictures* (Metuchen, N.J.: Scarecrow Press, 1976); Tibbetts, John C., "The Stage Goes West: Routes to *The Virginian,*" *Indiana Social Studies Quarterly,* 34:2 (Autumn 1981), 26–37; Trimmer, Joseph H., "*The Virginian:* Novel and Films," *Illinois Quarterly,* 35:2 (December 1972), 5–18.

—*J.C.T.*

THE VISIT/THE VISIT OF THE OLD LADY (DER BESUCH DER ALTEN DAME) (1956)

FRIEDRICH DÜRRENMATT (1921–1990)

The Visit (1964), U.S.A., directed by Bernhard Wicki, adapted by Ben Barzman; 20th Century-Fox.

Hyenas (1992), Senegal, directed and adapted by Djibril Diop Mambety; Domirev.

The Play

Clearly influenced by Bertolt Brecht, the German-Swiss writer Friedrich Dürrenmatt has been called the most important dramatist of the postwar German-speaking world. *Der Besuch der alten Dame,* considered Dürrenmatt's best play, was first produced in Zurich on January 29, 1956. The play opens at the railway station in the impoverished city of Güllen ("liquid manure" is the literal translation), where everyone is on welfare. The local economy is defunct and the desperate citizens are keenly awaiting the arrival of the nearly 70-year-old Claire Zachanassian, a fabulously wealthy heiress, born and raised in Güllen, who later married the richest man in the world. Hoping that Madame Zachanassian will somehow improve the local economy, the townspeople appoint Alfred Ill, her erstwhile suitor, to be their spokesman. They do not understand the motive for her "visit."

The people of Güllen will soon discover that Claire's visit is not benign and that she has returned to take her revenge on the community that wronged her as a young woman. Alfred Ill got her pregnant 50 years before the play begins and saw to her disgrace and exile. Ill bribed two false witnesses to throw the paternity of her child in question, and both claimed that they, too, had been intimate with Claire, who was proclaimed a whore and went off to Hamburg to work as a prostitute. Alfred then married a stupid woman of means in Güllen, who bore him two thankless children.

Claire's arrival is mysterious and grotesque. She leads a strange entourage of servants and reporters and is accompanied by a caged panther and a coffin, carried in a weirdly ritualistic train. She demands justice and is willing to pay a hundred million francs to achieve it.

She could make everyone in town rich, but at what cost? She expects the citizens to kill Ill. At first no one thinks ill of Ill, but since everyone believes they will eventually inherit Claire's money, they indulge themselves in a spending frenzy, buying on credit. As their debts spiral out of control, they eventually decide that Ill must die. Alfred Ill is merely symptomatic of the sickness that infects Güllen. As critic Armin Arnold explains, the whole town is guilty: "The town made her into a whore and now she is turning the townspeople into murderers." In brief, "she punishes Ill through the townspeople and the townspeople through Ill."

Claire is utterly in control. She has purchased all the town's industries, then closed them down: "Without her good will, Güllen has no chance ever to prosper again. With Ill dead, on the other hand, Güllen will at once become an industrial center again." Eventually, Arnold observes, like a tragic hero, Ill "begins to believe in his own guilt" and bears the responsibility "for the grotesque human being that Claire has become." At the conclusion, Ill is given his death sentence and murdered by the townspeople, who mob around him ritualistically on stage. His body goes into the coffin Claire has brought. She leaves Güllen with her trophy, contemptuously tossing her check to the mayor.

The play was first introduced to American audiences in an English version translated by Maurice Valency and successfully produced in New York under the direction of Peter Brook, with Lynn Fontanne and Alfred Lunt in the leading roles. Valency considered the play "a tragedy that ends in satire." Harold Prince revived the play in 1973 on Broadway in the New Phoenix Repertory Company production starring Rachel Roberts and John McMartin. It was again revived in New York in 1992 by the Roundabout Theatre Company at the Criterion Center, with Jane Alexander in the lead, directed by Edwin Sherin.

New York Times drama critic Frank Rich, reviewing the English adaptation of the play by Maurice Valency, called it "a small masterpiece of misanthropy," a "grotesque fable whose icy laughter and bizarre fantastical sideshows"—a freak show that includes a mutilated Claire who has a wooden leg and a hand made of ivory, her blind, guitar-strumming eunuchs (the false witnesses, punished for their deceptions), and her black panther that stalks the characters—reflect the "Swiss author's proximity to both the Holocaust and the accompanying absurdist revolution in theatre."

Operating as moral allegory, this bizarre play resides in the outer limits of bitter satire, on the frontier of tragedy. *Washington Post* drama critic Lloyd Rose called it a "deformed fairy-tale," a *Wizard of Oz* for grown-ups, in which the Yellow Brick Road, paved with bad intentions, takes us eventually to hell, as black comedy is transformed into "a queasy, nasty parable." Dürrenmatt's earlier plays had foreshadowed the cynicism of *The Visit*. *Der Blinde* (The Blind Man, 1948) suggested that "one has to be blind to be able to believe in God," as Arnold described it, and, as one character says, "For one who sees, there is no mercy." Claire is another merciless God-image. Ill "has long since done penance through his miserable life," Arnold notes, and his fate is merely "an extension of the actions of the sadistic, revengeful God of Dürrenmatt's early works."

The Films

The first film adaptation, directed by Bernhard Wicki in 1964 (a German director who had established his credentials with *The Bridge* [1960]), is something of a hybrid, an adaptation of an adaptation, since it follows the English version of Maurice Valency, who changed the name of Alfred Ill to Anton Schill, who wronged Clara Wascher, who later became Claire Zachanassian. Valency described the play as "a tragedy that ends in satire," and it is certainly not a satire that ends in tragedy, since there is some justice in Ill's punishment. Ironically, at the banquet the town gives in her honor, the mayor praises Claire for her love of justice as well as her renowned generosity. Of course, Valency's stage adaptation retains Dürrenmatt's basic plot and action but makes a number of significant modifications in the characters of Claire and Ill, changing the overall spirit of the play.

In Dürrenmatt's play Claire is a kind of inhuman, enigmatic, grotesque goddess of fate who never becomes emotionally involved, even when she sees her former lover for the last time on the night before his death. She is unreal and detached from the world around her. Valency's portrait of Claire, on the other hand, makes her a plausible woman who is determined to have her pound of flesh. Her ruthless, fate-like nature is almost completely removed, her grotesqueness is played down, and she is much less enigmatic and more sympathetic than in the original. Instead of being 63, she is in her fifties, and instead of having a parade of husbands during the course of the play, she has only one (her eighth). She is less humorous and more serious than in Dürrenmatt's original, and the reunion in Güllen with Ill is more tender and even compassionate, as shown in the long kiss that she gives her former lover on the night before the trial.

When Valency's Claire first meets Anton Schill, she does not even recognize him. Schill is not horrified by Claire's wooden leg and ivory hand, but merely patronizing about her injury. In the scene when Schill attempts to leave town at the train station, he becomes paranoid, fearing that although no one actually inhibits his departure, the people are all out to get him and that someone will push him under the wheels when he starts to board the train. Consequently, he never gets on the train, but when a truck driver who just happens to be passing by offers him a ride, he refuses, stating with "strange new dignity," as the stage directions note, that he has changed his mind and is staying because Güllen is his home. Ill also decides not to leave, but there is no truck driver in Dürrenmatt's play to emphasize the issue. Valency's alteration apparently intends to show that Schill has somehow ennobled himself by staying, perhaps so that his eventual and now certain death will be a more compelling tragedy. Ill's decision not to leave does not indicate any kind of newly acquired nobility on his part, but simply that he has accepted his fate. In Dürrenmatt's play, Ill's death is a senseless parody of a genuine tragic death.

The Valency adaptation is still effective theatre, but his modifications reduce the grotesque humor and incisive irony, shifting the focus of the play from the world of Güllen with its contradictions, its moral ineptitude, and its facile sense of justice to a more studied focus on the tragic fall and yet paradoxical triumph of Schill as both the scapegoat for, and the savior of, the now prosperous but guilt-ridden town. Ben Barzman's screenplay, an adaptation twice-removed, based on Valency's adaptation rather than the original, is not especially effective. It completely eliminates the grotesque quality of the original: Ingrid Bergman's Claire (named Karla in the film) is not a half-artificial, grotesque, enigmatic fate goddess but merely a weird woman who wants some kind of retribution for the injustice she has suffered. Her entourage is strange, but not grotesque, and she has no husband at all. At one point she claims that no man since Serge Miller (Anthony Quinn), as Ill is called in the film, has been able to satisfy her. There is no suggestion that she has had the two false witnesses, who appear as her bodyguards, castrated. Seeing Serge the night before his trial, she becomes sentimental and compassionate and engages in a wild embrace

The filmmakers were apparently banking on the star power of Bergman and Quinn, but Quinn's performance seems uninspired. The film adds its own detrimental alterations, such as a subplot involving a hotel maid named Anya, who is having an affair with a married police lieutenant. The central trial scene is almost completely eliminated, except for the summation of Karla's lawyer and the final unanimous vote. Serge's wife kills Karla's escaped panther and later warns the town that her husband is trying to escape. The most damaging change, however, is the ending. After Serge

has been condemned to death and Karla's lawyer has paid the mayor his blood money, Karla intercedes to ask if any of the Gülleners think the verdict is unjust. For fear of losing their reward, no one responds, whereupon Karla reprimands the town by explaining that Serge will be spared in order to live among them as a constant reminder that they condemned him for money and allowed her to buy justice for a price. Hence, her desire for revenge is satisfied by her humiliation of both Serge and the townspeople. Such a contrived ending reduced the dramatic force of both the original and of Valency's adaptation. It is an utter distortion that reduced a forceful and distinctive play to empty melodrama.

To attempt a transformation through the illusionistic and essentially realistic medium of film would present grave and insurmountable problems for the screen adapter, but in 1992 yet another film adaptation of the play appeared out of Africa, directed by Djibril Diop Mambety, with the actors (Mansour Diouf as Dramaan Drameh, the Alfred Ill character, and Ami Diakhate as Linguere Ramatou, the Claire Zachanassian character) speaking in the Wolof language. The desert town of Colobane on the edge of the Saarha is destitute. Its most popular resident is a married grocer, Dramaan Drameh. Linguere Ramatou, who left town 30 years before, is staging a homecoming as the world's richest woman. The townspeople stage a banquet in her honor, at which time she offers "one hundred thousand millions" if the townspeople will put Dramaan to death for having disgraced her and denying the paternity of her child. She has brought along witnesses who swear that Dramaan paid them to testify that they had slept with her. At first the town sides with Dramaan, then turns against him.

Reviewing the film for the 1992 New York Film Festival in the *New York Times*, Stephen Holden wrote that although director Mambety followed the outline of Dürrenmatt's play "the change of locale lends the tale a new political dimension," since the "irresistible Western paraphernalia" the world's richest woman offers the villagers "will eradicate the area's tribal culture." Holden did not find the performances very gripping because of the film's "carnival humor." Though "imposingly grotesque," Diakhate's vengeful character was "something less than the fearsome apotheosis of revenge." The transcultural transformation none the less demonstrates the play's archetypal grasp of human behavior.

REFERENCES

Arnold, Armin, *Friedrich Dürrenmatt* (New York: Frederick Ungar, 1972); Brock, D. Heyward, "Dürrenmatt's *Der Besuch der alten Dame:* Stage and Screen Adaptations," *Literature/Film Quar-*

terly, 4:1 (1976): 60–67; Holden, Stephen, "Buying a Whole Town and a Death Sentence," *The New York Times*, June 18, 1995, C6; Rich, Frank, "Revenge and Common Greed as the Root of Much Evil," *The New York Times*, January 24, 1992, C1; Peppard, Murray B., *Friedrich Dürrenmatt* (New York: Twayne, 1969); Rose, Lloyd, "Düerrenmatt's Vengeful 'Visit,'" *The Washington Post*, May 15, 1991, B1–2.

—D.H.B. AND J.M.W.

VOLPONE (1607)

BEN JONSON (1573–1637)

Volpone (1940), France, directed by Maurice Tourneur, adapted by Jules Romains and Stefan Zweig; Isle de France.

The Play

First performed by the King's Men at London's Globe Theatre in 1606, Jonson's verse comedy in five acts is acknowledged as an innovative Jacobean masterpiece, heralding a transition from pure comedy to comedy with a moral purpose. The action is set in Venice where a wealthy, childless merchant, Volpone, feigns terminal illness to discover which of his friends (Corvino, a merchant, Corbaccio, a miser, and Voltore, a lawyer) is worthy of inheriting his fortune. His servant Mosca persuades each one he is favored and, taking the bait, each seeks to seal the advantage with gifts for Volpone or, in Corvino's case, sexual favors. When Mosca indicates his master's need for a lusty young woman "full of vice," the usually possessive merchant offers his dutiful wife Celia. She is saved by the timely intervention of Corbaccio's son, Bonario. A court case ensues. The old miser disinherits his son in favor of Volpone and at the trial, it is Celia and Bonario who are branded the transgressors thanks to the venal Voltore's corruption and perjury by Corvino and Corbaccio.

Volpone's deception has exposed the immoral depths of his friends' cupidity but, in a final test, he overreaches himself by simulating death and assigning his property to Mosca. The servant turns on his master and claims his rights, but Voltore, thinking he has lost out, initiates a second court case. Volpone is duly condemned and his fortune confiscated, while Mosca is sent to the galleys. A humorous subplot involves an English envoy, Sir Politik-Would-Be, attempting to sell red herrings to the Venetians and to rid ships of plague with bellows and onions.

Jonson's sardonic attack on the venality of his age is delivered through his engaging mixture of visual comedy, witty satire, and moral observation. Drawing on traditional morality plays, he signals a character's nature by a revealing name: Volpone, the fox; Mosca, the fly; Voltore, the vulture; Corbaccio, the crow; Corvino, the raven. With his sardonic exposure of human vices, Jonson extended the accepted purpose of traditional comedy as pure entertainment by raising moral issues.

The Film

The transformation of Jonson's play into Maurice Tourneur's screen version has an unusual genesis, with the jointly credited adapters forming links in a creative chain. Zweig began the process in 1926 with a freely reworked German version for the Viennese stage, which inspired Jules Romains to turn Jonson into French. However, finding the original text too demanding, Romains worked from Zweig's version, introducing several changes: He shortened scenes, eliminated minor characters, and emphasized the Mosca-Volpone relationship. Charles Dullin, who also played Volpone, staged the play in Paris at the Théâtre de l'Atelier in 1928, and it was this version, twice removed from Jonson, that Tourneur used.

The Tourneur/Romains version contains several changes: The subplot involving Sir Politik-Would-Be is discarded, and the film's opening and closure is altered. The narrative now begins with Volpone thrown into prison for defaulting on trading agreements after the apparent loss of his ship. His cellmate is the streetwise Mosca, whom Volpone retains as a servant when the safe arrival of his treasure-laden ship brings his release. These additional scenes establish Volpone's partnership with Mosca and explain his subsequent exposure of his money-grabbing friends. Thereafter, the film follows Jonson closely, except for the introduction of a potential wife for Volpone (Canina) who serves to bring further pressure on the fortune hunters. The most significant reworking comes at the end, where Mosca triumphs over Volpone and philanthropically returns his new fortune to the people of Venice. Name changes turn Celia into Colomba and Bonario into Leone.

The film, with sets by Léon Barsacq, retains a theatrical flavor, particularly in the acting style of Harry Baur as Volpone and the excellent Louis Jouvet as the scheming Mosca. In general, Armand Thirard's camerawork provides a front-of-the house view of events while also successfully creating atmosphere—the fog-bound port, the canals at sunset, busy streets. The action is successfully opened up with additional locations (the gambling den, harbor office, prison, and church), while streets and market scenes provide transitions. Romains's reworked dialogue curtails Jonson's frequent monologues and substitutes shorter exchanges more in keeping with the medium. Notable sequences are the trial, prefaced by Michel Delannoy's suitably lugubrious score, where close-up and rhythmic cutting bring out the humor of the sharp exchanges, and Volpone's attempted seduction of Colomba, which ends in a farcical chase round the bedroom.

REFERENCES

Creaser, John W., ed., *Ben Jonson: Volpone, or The Fox* (London: Hodder and Stoughton, 1978); Dessen, Alan C., *Jonson's Moral Comedy* (Chicago: Northwestern University Press, 1971); Tourneur, Maurice, "Volpone," *L'Avant-Scène du Cinéma*, 189, (1977).

—R.F.C.

WATCH ON THE RHINE (1940)

LILLIAN HELLMAN (1905–1984)

Watch on the Rhine (1943), U.S.A., directed by Herman Shumlin, adapted by Dashiell Hammett; Warner Bros.

The Play

An American icon, Lillian Hellman began her writing career by writing book reviews for the *New York Herald Tribune*. Her first play, *The Children's Hour*, was set in a private girl's school and, in 1934, was considered quite daring for dealing with lesbianism. Hellman followed with *Days to Come* (1936), which dealt with a labor strike, and then *The Little Foxes* (1939), a play that detailed the hatred and greed of a southern family.

A committed leftist, Hellman went to Spain in the 1930s to witness the Spanish Civil War, and smuggled $50,000 to her childhood friend "Julia," which she later recounted in her book *Pentimento* (1973). Hellman earned the admiration of millions of Americans when she stood before the House Un-American Activities Committee in the early 1950s and flatly refused to testify against her friends. It was, perhaps, her finest hour.

Watch on the Rhine, directed by Herman Shumlin, premiered at the Martin Beck Theatre on April 1, 1941, and ran for 378 performances. The setting is Washington, D.C., in the spring of 1940. World War II was being fought in Europe and Asia while Ameri-

cans hotly debated whether or not to become involved. Act One begins as Fanney Farrelly (Lucile Watson) eagerly awaits the return from Europe of Sara Muller, her daughter. Sara has not been home in more than 20 years. She is married to Kurt Muller (Paul Lukas) and has three children: Joshua (Peter Fernandez), Babette (Ann Blyth), and Bobo (Eric Roberts). Fanney is the widow of a former Supreme Court justice and her son David (John Lodge) is a prominent Washington attorney. Staying with the Farrellys as houseguests are the Count and Countess De Brancovis—Tech (George Coulouris) and Marthe (Helen Trenholme). Marthe is an old family friend, and she and her husband are refugees from Rumania who have fallen on hard times. Their marriage has fallen apart and Tech suspects, correctly, that his wife has fallen in love with David Farrelly. The count is desperate to return to Europe, but he needs money and the blessing of the German Embassy in Washington before he can return to the Continent. While the Farrellys are rich, it is soon apparent that the Mullers are not. They are poorly dressed and the children are overwhelmed by the Farrelly home. As the story unfolds, Kurt no longer works as an engineer. He is a leader in the anti-Nazi, German underground. A man with bullet scars on his face, broken bones in his hands, and a price on his head. A man that Tech immediately recognizes may be his ticket back to Fascist Rumania.

Act Two opens 10 days later. Fanney is busily planning the Mullers' future—she is going to build a new

As they leave Tech says the "new world has left the room." But Kurt knows that Tech will doublecross him. As they discuss politics over a drink, Kurt suddenly knocks Tech down and drags him out into the garden where he kills him.

The play ends as Kurt explains to his children that murder is wrong but that he had no choice. When he apologizes to Fanney, she is understanding and mutters, "Well, here we are shaken out of the magnolias."

And so, Hellman hoped, would be the Americans who saw the play in 1940. Critical reaction to the play was glowing and Hellman was awarded the Drama Critics' Circle Award for the best American play in 1940. In January 1942 a special "command performance" was given at the National Theatre in Washington for President Franklin D. Roosevelt. But not everyone liked *Watch on the Rhine*. The politics of the play were circumspect. It was not exactly clear whether or not Kurt was a "radical" or, in the parlance of the day, a communist. When Fanney asks him if he is "a radical," he replies that he would have to know what she means by the term. Kurt had all the trappings of a communist—he fought for the Loyalists in Spain—but it was never made clear what his political beliefs were other than antifascist. The play was set in the spring of 1940 during the period of the Nazi-Soviet Non-Aggression Pact. *The Daily Worker* review complained that Hellman avoided dealing with the exploitation of the working class, and Alvah Bessie (one of the Hollywood Ten) wrote in *The New Masses* that the play was a call to force workers into an "imperialst war under the banner of fighting fascism in Germany." But Hellman was not easily intimidated by Fascists or communists. She ignored political criticism of the play, including that of Dashiell Hammett, her companion, lover, editor, and sometime critic, who told her the play contained too much "antifascist sentimentalism."

The Film

Antifascist sentimentalism is exactly what Warner Bros. wanted when they bought the film rights to the play and paid Dashiell Hammett $30,000 to craft the screenplay. Hammett's major contribution was to bring the play out of the proscenium. He opened the film with the Mullers arriving in the United States from Mexico, added scenes at the train station in Washington, and a scene of Tech playing cards at the German embassy. Hellman thought this scene was wonderful and told her friends that she would have given anything to have written it. But, for the most part, the play was transferred to the screen with much of its original dialogue and its politics intact.

Lillian Hellman

wing on the house for them and David has been told to find Kurt a job as an engineer. But European politics are going to overwhelm Fanney's plans. Kurt learns that the head of an anti-Nazi underground movement, Max Freidank, has been captured. Kurt must return to Germany immediately. He has collected $23,000 for the resistance movement and will use it to try to bribe German guards to free Freidank.

In Act Three the political intrigue continues. Tech has figured out Kurt's true identity and demands $10,000 from Kurt for his silence. Kurt refuses. The Farellys are dumbfounded that this discussion of bribery and international intrigue is taking place in their living room. David asks Sara "is it true that if this swine talks, you and the others will be—?" Sara finishes, "Caught and killed." David and Fanney agree to give Tech his blood money and go upstairs to get the money.

Lillian Hellman's wartime play, Watch on the Rhine, *was brought to the screen in 1944 with Bette Davis and Beulah Bondi.* (COURTESY NATIONAL FILM SOCIETY ARCHIVES)

Warner Bros. brought five members of the stage play to Hollywood for the film version: Paul Lukas (Kurt), Lucile Watson (Fanney), George Coulouris (Teck), Eric Roberts (Bobo), and Frank Wilson (Joseph, the butler). The major casting change in the film was that of Warner Bros. star Bette Davis as Sara. The biggest problem the film encountered in Hollywood was with Joseph Breen, head of the Production Code Administration (PCA), who demanded that Kurt Muller be punished for murdering Tech. He could not "go off scot-free" even for killing a Nazi. When Hellman was informed that her play was going to be censored she was outraged. She threatened to write an expose of the PCA if Breen altered her play. But the threat was more bluster than reality. The film version of *Watch on the Rhine* ends in a scene with Sara and her oldest son, Joshua. It has been several months since Kurt left Washington and no one has heard a word from him. Joshua is studying maps and preparing to return to Europe to take up the fight his father had begun. When

Sara discovers what he is doing she is distraught. She refuses to allow him to go. But Joshua calmly tells her he will soon be of age and will go. She quietly relents. The movie ends.

Kurt's fate is not clear to the audience. One could assume that he was captured and killed by the Nazis. Or perhaps he is in hiding.

The critics praised the film and it won the best movie award from the New York Film Critics. It was also nominated for an Academy Award for best picture. Paul Lukas won the Academy Award for best actor for his performance as Kurt.

REFERENCES

Mellen, Joan, *Hellman and Hammett* (New York: HarperCollins, 1996); Rollyson, Carl, *Lillian Hellman: Her Legend and Her Legacy* (New York: St. Martin's Press, 1998).

—G.B.

WHAT PRICE GLORY? (1924)

MAXWELL ANDERSON (1888–1959) AND LAURENCE STALLINGS (1894–1968)

What Price Glory? (1926), U.S.A., directed by Raoul Walsh, adapted by J.T. Donahue; Fox.

What Price Glory? (1952), U.S.A., directed by John Ford, adapted by Phoebe and Henry Ephron; Twentieth Century-Fox.

The Play

Premiering in New York at the Plymouth Theatre on September 5, 1924, *What Price Glory?* was an instant success, and it ran for 435 performances. Its occasionally gritty realism bespoke Stallings' own wartime experiences. After graduating from Annapolis, Stallings had entered the war and lost a leg at the battle of Château-Thierry. After scoring a big success with the screenplay for *The Big Parade* (1925), Stallings went on to collaborate with Maxwell Anderson on *What Price Glory?* which is generally regarded as the greatest play to come out of World War I. Captain Flagg (Louis Wolheim) and First Sergeant Quirt (William Boyd) of the U.S. Marine Corps are longtime friends and rivals. During Flagg's absence Quirt is put in charge of his company, and he has a fling with the lovely French village girl, Charmaine (Leyla Georgie). She becomes pregnant, and Flagg, who also loves her, orders Quirt to marry her. But orders to the front interrupt the plan and the company departs for battle. Quirt returns, wounded, and renews his affair with Charmaine. Again, war beckons, and Quirt and Flagg leave for the front—apparently unconcerned about the fate of the baby.

The Films

What Price Glory? has been filmed twice. The unforeseen box-office success of another war film, King Vidor's *The Big Parade* (1925), encouraged Fox to adapt the Anderson/Stallings play and place it in the hands of veteran director Raoul Walsh. The basic plotline remained intact, along with some of its antiwar fervor. The grim imagery of the opening scenes is accompanied by the caption, "Civilization—dedicated to destruction, fields of production, drained with blood and fire." Such scenes shocked contemporary audiences, whose memories of the Great War were still all too painful. Other aspects of the film are just as blunt. The character of Charmaine, for example, is little better than a prostitute servicing different armies while her father, Cognac Pete, is a war profiteer and a pimp for his daughter (about whom he says, "Where else could one see some of the best roses that bloom in Picardy?"). Pete's cynical remarks not only play upon one of the most popular Great War songs, "Roses are blooming in Picardy," but also evoke the bucolic imagery employed by poets and writers of that lost generation who contrasted the idyllic world of an agrarian Eden with the mechanical slaughter of the war.

As in the play, the dying Private Lewishon appeals to Captain Flagg to "stop the blood" while shellshocked Lieutenant Moore mocks his superior officer with the lines, "What price glory?" This antiwar message is, at times, diluted by the ribald comedy of the rivalry between Flagg and Quirt and the essentially patriotic spirit that constitutes the heart of the film. Flagg states, "This war and glory racket is something like a religion. When the bugle sounds we will answer." Omitted is the famous concluding line of the play, "What a lot of God damn fools it takes to make a war!" As film historian Larry Suid notes, Walsh turned an essentially pacifistic play into "the archetypal celebration of war as a game played by roistering comrades." Benefiting from a cinematic sweep, the battle scenes were staged with a degree of detail and realism impossible to the stage. The film's box-office success inspired a host of imitations, including an all-talkie sequel, *The Cockeyed World* (1929). "It confirmed the fact that audiences would pay to see war films," writes Suid. "It also demonstrated that

John Ford

moviegoers wanted to see them not because of any antiwar sentiment they might contain, but simply to watch great battle scenes, scenes of men fighting and dying, of plays flying, and of men loving on their time away from combat."

After the success of *The Quiet Man* (1951) John Ford's next assignment was a remake of Raoul Walsh's silent classic. Obviously, the wry militarism and rowdy farce appealed to him, although this new adaptation ultimately lacks the poignancy and zest of Walsh's version. Although it begins with a stunning sound-stage re-creation of trench warfare, too much of the rest of the picture relies heavily upon "John Ford stock company business," especially the tedious ritual brawls between an overweight James Cagney and his military rival played by Dan Dailey. Unlike Walsh's film, which appeared within a decade after American entry into World War I, Ford's *What Price Glory?* is clearly an old man's film exhibiting premature signs of the director's fatigue. Furthermore, it adds a tedious romantic subplot between young Private Lewishon (Robert Wagner) and convent schoolgirl Nicole, the latter performing a love song more suited to an MGM musical than a serious war film. Despite the emphasis in the original play on Lt. Moore's serious accusation "What price glory?" Ford downplays this line, ending the sequence with the shellshocked officer attempting to stumble back to the conflict outside. Similarly, Robert Wagner's weak performance and Ford's apathetic direction both diminish the tragic intensity of Lewishon's dying plea to Captain Flagg, "Stop the blood." Although Ford had to tone down the sexual antics of Charmaine for a '50s audience, he still manages to imply her method of servicing troops of all nations when she returns the wrong-sized officer's cap to one of her "clients." Ford enthusiast, film director Lindsay Anderson, declares it a "bizarre" and "strange" picture, complaining of its musical intrusions and citing its botched blending of knockabout farce and antiquated sentiments. Footnote: Ford casts Hispanic actor Barry Norton, Walsh's original Lewishon, in two brief scenes as a village priest.

REFERENCES

Anderson, Lindsay, *About John Ford* (New York: McGraw-Hill Book Company, 1981); Suid, Lawrence, *Guts and Glory: Great American War Movies* (Reading, Mass.: Addison-Wesley, 1978).

—*T.W.*

WHO'S AFRAID OF VIRGINIA WOOLF? (1962)

EDWARD ALBEE (1928–   )

Who's Afraid of Virginia Woolf? (1967), U.S.A., directed by Mike Nichols, adapted by Nichols and Ernest Lehman; Warner Bros.

The Play

Edward Albee is the adopted grandson of the vaudeville magnate, E.F. Albee. Before his success with his first full-length play, *Who's Afraid of Virginia Woolf?* in 1962, Albee had written several short plays, including *The Zoo*

Story (1959), *The Death of Bessie Smith* (1959), and *The American Dream* (1960). Experimental in form and baffling in content, they provoked controversy and debate. By contrast, *Who's Afraid of Virginia Woolf?* had a relatively conventional surface that attacked—in his words—the hypocrisies of conventional marriage and family and the horrors of "complacency, cruelty, emasculation, and vacuity." In that respect, it has been compared to an important earlier prototype of its kind, Strindberg's *The Dance of Death*. The play premiered in New York at the Billy Rose Theatre on October 13, 1962, and ran for a spectacular 664 performances.

The setting is the living room of a house on the campus of a small New England college. Act One, called "Fun and Games," begins early in the morning as George (Arthur Hill), a professor in the college's history department, and his wife Martha (Uta Hagen) return from a party given by her father, the college president. To George's disgust, Martha confesses that she has invited home Nick (George Grizzard) and Honey (Melinda Dillon), a young couple just arrived on campus. While George promptly launches a vicious verbal attack on Nick's profession as a biologist, Martha is in the kitchen telling Honey about their son, whose 21st birthday is the next day. In the ensuing conversations a number of the play's themes arise, including George's frustration about not being chairperson of his history department, Martha's seductive behavior toward Nick, Nick and Honey's ambivalence about having a child, and the mystery surrounding the very existence of George and Martha's son. Finally, George drowns out Martha's incessant talking by loudly singing a song, "Who's Afraid of Virginia Woolf" (a parody of the Oscar-winning song from Walt Disney's 1932 cartoon, *The Three Little Pigs*).

Act Two, called "Walpurgisnacht," presents several revelations: Nick confesses that he married Honey because she had had what he calls a "hysterical pregnancy." He and George both admit that they married for money. Martha reveals that her father prevented George from publishing a book (about a boy who kills his parents). Arguments and recriminations break out as they begin playing a succession of games, called "Humiliate the Host" and "Hump the Hostess." The action ends as Martha attempts to seduce Nick, Honey implies that she had aborted her unborn child, and George announces that his son is dead.

In Act Three, "The Exorcism," Martha accuses Nick of impotency, and she and George decide to engage in one more game, "Bringing up Baby." The rules consist of Martha's recounting of the upbringing of their son, while George contradicts her on every detail. Finally, George declares that their son died in a car accident.

Martha furiously yells at him: "I will not let you decide these things!" George responds that he has a right to kill their boy, for "you broke our rule, baby. You mentioned him . . . you mentioned him to somebody else." At this point it is clear that there never was a child at all. Nick and Honey depart. George tells Martha it was time to do what he did. He gently puts his hand on her shoulder and softly sings, "Who's afraid of Virginia Woolf?" And she replies, "I am, George . . . I am."

A vital aspect of this mutually destructive duel of sexual politics is its savage humor. In their incessant bickering and attacks on one another, George and Martha veer wildly, sometimes unpredictably, from physical abuse to the deployment of wicked whimsies and deadly games. Caught in this dangerous battle of wits are references to sterility and lust, reality and illusion, and personal and professional failure. What skewers and cauterizes them all is a healing, comic energy. As commentator Walter Kerr suggests, it is this spirit of comedy that has helped destroy all illusions: "Over the dead bones of dreams [George and Martha] sit down together, last survivors in a slaughterhouse. From a serious point of view, this last image does not promise much. It does not promise that when man's last illusion has been shattered he will be any happier or more confident or more at home in his surroundings. It simply promises that he will be free of lies, however dry his mouth may seem to him." There is no question that Albee's play is a benchmark in the history of American drama. As commentator John MacNicholas writes, "In its vigor, precision, and range of emotion, the humor of *Who's Afraid of Virginia Woolf?* is extraordinary. No other comic work in the American tradition has so effectively rendered both the conciliatory and destructive appetites in the human soul."

The play received the New York Drama Critics Circle Award as well as two Tony Awards and one Outer Circle Award. When the Pulitzer Prize jury refused to recognize Albee, John Gassner and John Mason Brown resigned in protest (no prize was given that year).

The Film

Who's Afraid of Virginia Woolf? was theatre director Mike Nichols first film, and he was given relatively free rein in the adaptation process. "How lucky to get a chance to do the movie," he said, "especially since I felt I understood it quite well. How lucky to get a chance to protect it, to some extent. To protect it from being turned into God knows what—'the child was real, but had committed suicide' or whatever else might have been done with it." Nonetheless, the production was fraught with tension. The play's profanity-laden dia-

Mike Nichols

logue would surely be a problem for the film censors. Elizabeth Taylor used her clout to insist not only that newcomer Nichols be given the opportunity but also that husband Richard Burton be cast against type as her costar. Moreover, predictably, the tabloids gossiped about the celebrity couple's fabled rows and shouting matches during the shooting; and a lot of ink was spilled questioning whether Burton could transform his macho image into the provincial, castrated character of George, and whether Taylor could survive the role of the fat, sluttish Martha.

Shot on location on a college campus in Northampton, Massachusetts, and superbly lensed in black and white by cinematographer Haskell Wexler, the story acquired a special immediacy, astringency, and bite.

The film's only significant change, which Albee deplored, was to move the dance scene in Act Two to a roadside café. Other than that, apart from the opening scene when George and Martha walk home through the autumnal night of blowing leaves and full moon, and some dialogue scenes transplanted to the lawn and the car, the action is restricted to the house interiors. Nonetheless, these small changes are effective in their own way. The opening scene's autumnal flavor suggests the ending of a cycle of seasons—perhaps the death of illusion in the lives of George and Martha. In the lawn scene George recalls his childhood while sitting on a swing, a visual metaphor for his lost youth. In the road-house scene, the flashing lights and signs complement George and Martha's physical combat. Commentator H. Wayne Schuth contends that, whereas the play gave equal attention to both George and Martha, the film concentrates on George, the camera staying with him most of the time and viewing things from his vantage point. Frequently the camera becomes George's "eyes"—as he swings Honey around with his arms, as he gazes at the shadows on the bedroom window of Martha and Nick making love, as he approaches Martha with a toy gun. The parts are effectively cast. Burton's George looks the part of the stereotyped college professor with his rumpled tweed coat, unpressed pants, vest sweater, and glasses. George Segal's Nick, by contrast, is the clean-cut young academic. Taylor's Martha is frowsy and overripe. And Sandy Dennis's Honey is appropriately pinch-faced and fraught with nervous mannerisms.

The film was a breakthrough for artistic freedom. After trying at first to "launder" the play's profanity with "clean but suggestive phrases," as Nichols put it, he and scenarist Ernest Lehman reverted to most of the play's original dialogue. By refusing to shoot alternative dialogue scenes as a hedge against censorship, Nichols tried to protect the integrity of his film. Accordingly, on May 25, 1966, Jack L. Warner, president of Warner Bros., announced that *Who's Afraid of Virginia Woolf?* would be released for adults only. Anyone under the age of 18 would not be admitted unless accompanied by an adult. This was the first-ever such policy adopted by Warner Bros. Nonetheless, the Production Code Administration threatened not to grant the film its seal unless some of the dialogue was removed. Jack Warner held his ground. Finally, the 11-man Code Review Committee relented and exempted the film from its standard proscriptions against profanity, granting it an "SMA" rating (suggested for mature audiences) and declaring that the film was "not designed to be prurient" and that it was "largely a reproduction of the play that won the New York Drama Critics Award of 1963

and played throughout the country." Likewise, the Catholic Legion of Decency ultimately approved the film, granting it an "A-4" rating as "morally unobjectionable for adults, with reservations." In sum, *Who's Afraid of Virginia Woolf?* did for freedom of dialogue what another film two years previously, *The Pawnbroker*, did for freedom of images. Elizabeth Taylor and Sandy Dennis both won Academy Awards for their performances (Taylor's second). Richard Burton was nominated, but he lost out to Paul Scofield in *A Man for All Seasons*.

REFERENCES

Bragg, Melvyn, *Richard Burton: A Life* (Boston: Little, Brown, 1988); Downer, Alan S., "Interview with Edward Albee," in Downer, ed., *The American Theater Today* (New York: Basic Books, 1967); Kerr, Walter, *Tragedy and Comedy* (New York: Simon and Schuster, 1967); MacNicholas, John, "Edward Albee," in *Twentieth-century Dramatists* (Detroit: Gale Research Company, 1981); Schuth, H. Wayne *Mike Nichols* (Boston: G.K. Hall, 1978).

—*J.C.T. AND J.M.W. AND K.N.*

THE WILD DUCK [*VILDANDEN*] (1884)

HENRIK IBSEN (1828–1906)

Haus der Lüge [House of Lies] (1925), Germany, directed by Lupu Pick, adapted by Lupu Pick and Fanny Carlsen; Rex-Film der UFA.

Vildanden (1963), Norway, directed and adapted by Tancred Ibsen; Teamfilm A/S.

The Wild Duck [*Die Wildente*] (1976), Germany/Austria, directed and adapted by Hans W. Geissendörfer; Solaris/Sascha.

The Wild Duck (1983), Australia, directed by Henri Safron, adapted by Safron, Tutti Lemkov and Dido Merwin.

The Play

This naturalistic tragicomedy came from Henrik Ibsen's "middle period"—the late 1870s through the 1880s—when he had already written his most influential plays, *A Doll's House* (1879), *Ghosts* (1881), and *An Enemy of the People* (1882). Set in Norway, it begins with a dinner party given by the wealthy industrialist Hakon Werle to celebrate the homecoming of his son Gregers, an idealist who disapproves of his father's unscrupulousness and blames him for the way Old Werle swindled his former business partner, Old Ekdal, now a broken old man employed charitably, but surely out of guilt, by Werle. Ekdal's son, Hjalmar, a photographer and a friend of Gregers, is invited to the homecoming party and is so embarrassed to see his father at work in the Werle household that he ignores him. Gregers learns through Hjalmar that his marriage to his loving wife Gina has been arranged by Old Werle, but Hjalmar does not realize that Gina had been not only Werle's house-keeper but also his mistress. Old Werle is going blind, and so is Gina's daughter, Hedvig, because of an unstated inherited disease.

Gregers hates his unscrupulous father and is appalled that Hjalmar is living in blissful ignorance of the true history of his family. Taking the moral high ground, Gregers refuses his father's offer of a business partnership, leaves him, and rents a spare room at Hjalmar's studio. He decides that Hjalmar must know the truth. But Hjalmar, a simple and sentimental man, finds happiness in illusion and nurtures it at home. He has turned the family loft into an imaginary "forest" where he and his father, once a woodsman, "hunt" caged prey (pigeons, poultry, rabbits, and a wild duck Old Werle had wounded, captured, and given to the Ekdals). Hjalmar is, moreover, a dreamer who imagines that he will some day complete a remarkable invention, which will make his family wealthy. Fourteen-year-old Hedvig adores her father and loves the duck, rescued from "the briny deep."

After Gregers moves in with the Ekdals, he discovers that Hjalmar is so far immersed in his dream world that the more practical Gina is the true family bread-winner and mainly responsible for the photographic work Hjalmar pretends to do. Gregers is determined to tell Hjalmar the truth, despite warnings from his father, from Gina, and from Dr. Relling, a family friend, and despite Hjalmar's own admission that "in my house people never talk to me about unpleasant things." Temperamentally, Hjalmar simply cannot deal with the truth. A newly informed Hjalmar confronts Gina about her past in Act Four, refuses his dinner, and threatens to wring the neck of the wild duck Old Werle gave them. The truth makes him angry and bitter, rather than free. Then Hjalmar discovers that Old Werle is going blind and has given Old Ekdal a pension that will revert to Hedvig once the old man dies. The now suspicious Hjalmar questions Gina about Hedvig's paternity and then rejects his illegitimate daughter, breaking her heart. Gregers comes up with the utterly perverse suggestion that if Hedvig will sacrifice her beloved wild duck, she may regain her father's love. In Act Five Hedvig goes up to the loft intending to sacrifice the duck,

but, confused and conflicted, she shoots herself instead. Dr. Relling clearly states the "message" of this thesis play: "Take away the life-illusion from the average man and straight away you take away his happiness." Gregers' well-intentioned truth-telling destroys the family. The play was published late in 1884 and first performed in January of 1885 in Bergen, Christiania, and Stockholm.

According to commentators Oscar G. Brockett and Robert R. Findlay, *The Wild Duck* is Ibsen's most satiric play: "Many have seen in it a repudiation by Ibsen of his earlier work. More probably it was intended as a message to his militant followers, who considered him to be a social reformer rather than an artist. But it marked a change from his previous plays, for it placed considerable emphasis upon a central symbol, here the wild duck, a device that he was to develop more fully thereafter."

The Films

There were two lost American silent film versions entitled *The Wild Duck* released in 1915 and 1918. The latter starring Alla Nazimova. In 1925 in Germany Lupu Pick adapted the play under the title *Haus der Lüge*, starring Werner Kraus (Hjalmar) and Mary Johnson (Hedvig). The first sound production, *Vildanden*, was directed and adapted in Norway in 1963 by Tancred Ibsen.

The best available adaptation, by Hans W. Geissendörfer, starring Bruno Ganz as Gregers, Peter Kern as Hjalmar, and Anne Bennett as Hedvig, begins like a movie, not like a play. All of the verbal exposition provided first by the servants, Peterson and Jensen, then by the guests at the Werle dinner party, is changed and transformed. The film opens with Gregers arriving at his father's house. He dotes upon a photograph of his mother. He then instructs Peterson to take a dinner invitation to his old friend Hjalmar, who delivers it to Hedvig, who rouses her sleeping father to tell him about it. Since Hjalmar does not have a decent suit to wear, Hedvig goes to borrow one from Molvik (Robert Werner), an erstwhile theology student, passing through Dr. Relling's waiting room to find him. After finding and then being unable to rouse the sleeping Molvik, Hedvig fetches the suit out of Molvik's closet and takes it to her father. The play merely mentions in passing that the suit was borrowed from Molvik.

After this visual exposition, which introduces both Hjalmar and Hedvig, the action cuts abruptly to the Werle dinner party. This opening sequence offers a wealth of telling detail for the attentive viewer. Gregers's attachment to his mother and her memory, for example, is shown in visual terms. When Hedvig

Ibsen's The Wild Duck *reached the screen in Hans W. Giessendörfer's screen adaptation.* (COURTESY NEW YORKER FILMS)

receives the invitation, she has to hold it very close to her face in order to read it, clearly indicating that her vision is impaired. Anne Bennett is younger than Hedvig in the play, and her age is given in the film as 12, not 14. It certainly makes symbolic sense that she should be about to celebrate her 13th birthday. It's an unlucky number, as Gregers, who was 13th at table, later gives testimony. But the most brilliant touch of this opening sequence is the way in which the two characters who live the "life-lie" are linked. It is daytime, yet both Hjalmar and Molvik are sound asleep. Molvik, the more useless of the two, cannot be roused by Hedvig. Hjalmar awakens, and rather than admit to being asleep, claims to have been working on his "invention." Dr. Relling (Heinz Bennett), by contrast, is awake, alert, busy, and active.

Anne Bennett makes a remarkable Hedvig. Her youth makes her more fragile and enhances her sense of innocence. It also makes more plausible her devotion to her father. Being two years younger, she is less likely to understand his flaws. Peter Kern is physically perfect for Hjalmar. He is stout, as a man of Hjalmar's listless and sedentary ways might be. Bruno Ganz as Gregers is a bit of a surprise and a contradiction, since the character is said to be ugly in the play, yet this is the same actor who played the angelic Russian prince in Rohmer's *The Marquise of O. . . .* The actor's benign good looks and

serenity belie his absurd preoccupations with the "claim of the ideal" and his tragically mistaken pursuit of the blissfully ignorant and ultimately ignoble Hjalmar. Jean Seberg plays the loving Gina in her last film role (she died in 1979). John Simon criticized the adaptation for opening up the play to show the attic, "where the wild duck and other animals live," since Ibsen meant this "to be a symbolic realm, the unnatural domicile of natural forces man cannot fully harness." He praised the performance of Heinz Moog as Werle Senior and the cinematography.

The adaptation changes the ending of the play. The final exchanges between Relling and Gregers, with its suicidal implications for the latter, is not included in the film, which brilliantly reveals the death of Hedvig, but then races to its conclusion. Hjalmar's lines signaling recognition ("I drove her away from me like an animal!") are gone, as are the lines Gina speaks to comfort him. Hedvig's lifeless body is discovered by the parents. In the film Gina calls out frantically for Dr. Relling (as a practical-minded woman might do), while Hjalmar sobs and caresses the body. The film also extends the play by a tavern episode in which Relling and Molvik get Hjalmar drunk to enable him to forget his troubles. Gregers attempts to rescue Hjalmar but is chastised by Relling, who is obviously not drunk himself.

The Henri Safron adaptation not only adds dialogue and opens up the text but also updates the action by more than 20 years, for no apparent reason. The story is also Anglicized, so that the Ekdal family becomes the Ackland family, Hedvig becomes Henrietta (Lucinda Jones), Hjalmar becomes Harold (Jeremy Irons), Gregers becomes Gregory (Arthur Dignam), Relling becomes Roland (Rhys McConnochie), Werle becomes Wardle (Michael Pate), and Molvik becomes Mollison (Colin Croft). Only Gina (Liv Ullmann) retains her name from the play. Verna Foster has criticized the adaptation for placing its focus on the play's pathos rather than its comic potential and objects to a "grotesque" drunken spree that follows Gregers's walk with Hjalmar in Act Four and concludes with Hjalmar attempting suicide by throwing himself into a river, though held back by Relling. The film ends with Hedvig's funeral and omits Hjalmar's banal, self-serving rhetoric. Though Verna Foster praised Safron's adaptation as intelligent and moving, others have found it "pretentious" and a "horrid adaptation" of the classic play.

REFERENCES

Brockett, Oscar G. and Robert R. Findlay, *Century of Innovation: A History of European and American Theatre and Drama Since 1870*

(Englewood Cliffs, N.J.: Prentice-Hall, 1973); Hansen, Karin Synnøve, *Henrik Ibsen, 1828–1978: A Filmography* (Oslo: Norsk Film Institutt, 1978); Foster, Verna A., "Ibsen's Tragicomedy: *The Wild Duck*," *Modern Drama*, 38 (1995): 287–297; Richards, David, *Played Out: The Jean Seberg Story* (New York: Random House, 1981); Simon, John, "Well-intentioned, Ill-conceived," *New York*, 10:19 (May 9, 1977): 70–71.

—*J.M.W.*

THE WINSLOW BOY (1946)

TERENCE RATTIGAN (1911–1977)

The Winslow Boy (1948), U.K., directed by Anthony Asquith, adapted by Terence Rattigan; British Lion/London Films.

The Winslow Boy (1999), U.S.A., directed and adapted by David Mamet; Sony Pictures.

The Play

Terence Rattigan's 1946 two-act play was based on a true story: In 1908 a 13-year-old boy was expelled from a British naval academy on the charge that he had forged a friend's signature on a five-shilling postal order and then cashed the order. The cadet's father, a Bristol bank agent, exhausted the family's finances in clearing his name.

The play's action begins in England, 1912. Fourteen-year-old Ronnie Winslow is accused of stealing and forging a postal order and is expelled from Osbourne Naval Academy. Convinced of Ronnie's innocence, his father, Arthur Winslow, a banker, fights to prove his innocence. The case creates a nationwide controversy. When Arthur employs a top barrister, Sir Robert Morton, the family is torn by dissension. Mrs. Winslow fears that her son's name will be irrevocably besmirched by the trial, no matter what the outcome. The eldest son, Dickie, has to withdraw from Oxford because of the high legal fees. Daughter Kate supports her father, but her loyalty causes her to lose her fiancé, who fears his association with her will result in his disinheritance. Consequently, Arthur, whose physical infirmities are exacerbated by the stresses of the case, wavers in his determination to pursue the case. But after talking with Kate, he resolves to push on. Meanwhile, barrister Morton has problems of his own: Public resentment is growing because the case is taking up the time and attention that should otherwise be devoted to more pressing public problems. Morton turns the tide

David Mamet adapted and directed Terence Rattigan's play The Winslow Boy, *with Guy Edwards as Ronnie Winslow.* (COURTESY SONY PICTURES CLASSICS)

when he enlists public support by playing up the slogan, "Never support the powerful against the defenseless." Ronnie's name is cleared. Kate revises her negative judgment of Morton after learning he had turned down the post of lord chief justice to take on the Winslow case. They part, the nature of their future relationship left unclear.

The Films

The first film version was directed by Anthony Asquith in 1948, and it starred Cedric Hardwicke as Arthur, Robert Donat as Morton, and Margaret Leighton as Kate. Asquith, a veteran of the British cinema since the silent days, enjoyed a long and fruitful collaboration with playwright Rattigan, including films made from Rattigan's original scripts (*The Way to the Stars*, 1945; *The VIPs*, 1963; *The Yellow Rolls-Royce*, 1964) and from adaptations of his plays (*While the Sun Shines*, 1947; *The Winslow Boy*, 1948; *The Browning Version*, 1951). Rattigan himself adapted *The Winslow Boy*, and he took care to "open up" the play by adding several dramatic courtroom sequences.

The second film version was adapted and directed by playwright/filmmaker David Mamet. Much of Rattigan's original dialogue is retained, although it is slyly inflected with Mamet's own distinctive "voice." Ironically, his screenplay is more scrupulously faithful to the original playscript than was Rattigan's own adaptation. David Denby's review in the *The New Yorker* appraises this fidelity with some caution, labeling it "a fidelity so profound that one doesn't know whether to be amazed or depressed by it." Mamet also restores the story's theatricality by confining the legal disputes and debates to a handful of brief scenes glimpsed in the House of Commons from the perspective of an open side door and from the visitors' gallery. Many incidents, like the trial itself and the gathering throngs of journalists outside the house, are relegated to reported action. Generally, he avoids long-shots and exteriors, preferring to keep the characters in center frame, in tight close-ups and medium-distance two- and three-shots. The interior photography by Benoit Delhomme and the production design by Gemma Jackson crisply evoke the cameo lighting style and the period décor of the late 19th-century English society portraits of John Singer Sargent.

In a wonderfully ambiguous ending, Morton and Kate confront each other after the winning verdict. She reproaches him for not revealing the compassion and sense of justice that he has so vigorously concealed beneath his rigidly proper exterior. He ripostes that he had pursued right, not justice. "Justice is easy to win," he says sardonically; "it is the right that is difficult." As they part, he reproaches her for continuing to pursue her feminist causes, which surely are doomed to failure. "Then you don't know women," she says. He in turn declares that he hopes to see her again. When she demurs, he replies, "Then you don't know men."

Not so unexpectedly, the story turns out to be a romance, a revelation of Morton's true intentions, which have as much to do with Kate as they have with the case itself. As Owen Gleiberman has pointed out, Kate measures Morton's egotism and "peacock brilliance" but fails to divine his true motivation for taking the case. "Only in England, or a David Mamet movie, could the urgency of romantic love turn out to be the ultimate deception."

The cast is uniformly excellent. Nigel Hawthorne's Arthur visibly fails as events wear on, but his sly humor never flags. Rebecca Pidgeon's Kate is torn between her allegiance to her feminist causes and her loyalty to her family and fiancé. Best of all is Jeremy Northam as Morton, whose slightly saturnine aspect fails to hide his true sensitivity to the case and to Kate.

REFERENCES

Armes, Roy, *A Critical History of the British Cinema* (New York: Oxford University Press, 1978); Denby, David, "The Winslow Boy," *The New Yorker* (May 17, 1999), 99; Gleiberman, Owen, "A Very Civil Action," *Entertainment Weekly*, May 7, 1999, 41.

—*J.C.T.*

WITNESS FOR THE PROSECUTION (1953)

AGATHA CHRISTIE (1890–1976)

Witness for the Prosecution (1958), U.S.A., directed by Billy Wilder, adapted by Billy Wilder and Harry Kurnitz; United Artists.

The Play

Agatha Christie's stage adaptation of her short story opened in London in October 1953 and a year later was attracting capacity audiences on Broadway. The story is set in London and concerns a clever bounder named Leonard Vole. Leonard is accused of the fatal stabbing of Mrs. French, a rich widow with whom he had been friendly—so friendly, in fact, that she wrote him into her will shortly before her demise. Sir Wilfrid Robarts, an eminent barrister, is convinced of Leonard's innocence and manages to get him acquitted. After the verdict is announced, however, Leonard's wife admits to his lawyer that she perjured herself on Leonard's behalf. She did so, she explains—not because she thought he was innocent—but precisely because she knew he was guilty. But then Leonard cavalierly announces that he is now free to leave Christine for a younger woman. Maddened by Leonard's betrayal, Christine stabs him to death right in the courtroom.

Commentator Kevin Lally praises the play as an outstanding example of a mystery melodrama with a plot twist so extraordinary that theater audiences at the time were requested not to divulge it.

The Film

The 1958 film of *Witness for the Prosecution* was directed and adapted by Billy Wilder, who had revealed a flair for diabolical comedy in *Double Indemnity* and *A Foreign Affair*. The screenplay retains the basic plot of Christie's whodunit. Christine (Marlene Dietrich), the wife of Leonard Vole (Tyrone Power), is German; she seems devoted to him, as revealed in a lengthy flashback. This flashback sequence, which is based on references in the play's exposition, is Wilder's major contribution to his literary source. The scene shows how Leonard met Christine while he was serving in the British army after World War II and she was singing in a smoke-filled basement café in Hamburg. Christine seems to be grateful to Leonard for his willingness to bring her to London as a war refugee. The flashback concludes just as the ceiling collapses in Christine's bombed-out dressing room at the nightclub—a disaster that subtly fore-shadows how the roof will eventually cave in on both of them before the film is over.

Given Christine's apparent loyalty to Leonard, Sir Wilfrid (Charles Laughton) is flabbergasted when she appears in court as a witness for the prosecution, and gives evidence that undermines Leonard's alibi for the night of the murder. Later that same evening, Sir Wilfrid is summoned to a railway station by a Cockney prostitute. Here, Wilder opens out the play by depicting an event only referred to in the play's dialogue—a scene at a train depot in which the prostitute sells him documentation that plainly indicates that Christine had given false testimony against Leonard, and that she did so because she wanted to see him convicted so that she could go off with another man. Sir Wilfrid accordingly presents this newly acquired evidence in open court. The jury is shocked at Christine's duplicity and votes to acquit Leonard. Once the courtroom is cleared, Christine approaches Sir Wilfrid and lapses into the Cockney accent she had employed when she talked with him the night before, while she was disguised as a prostitute. It seems that Christine herself had fabricated the spurious documentation, which she, in the guise of the prostitute, had then sold to Sir Wilfrid so that he could use it against her in court and win an acquittal for Leonard.

Christine adds that she had concocted the whole masquerade because she was certain of Leonard's guilt. While Sir Wilfrid is still reeling from Christine's disclosure, Leonard casually announces that he is going away with another woman. Christine snatches from the evidence table the knife with which Leonard had murdered Mrs. French and stabs him to death right in the courtroom. Sir Wilfrid now agrees to defend Christine, explaining that she did not murder Leonard: "she executed him."

London's venerable criminal court, the Old Bailey, which is a traditional emblem of British justice, virtually becomes a character in the film. It is fitting that, once the courtroom has witnessed the miscarriage of justice represented by Leonard's acquittal, it should likewise be the scene of his execution for his crime, as carried out by his own wife.

Witness for the Prosecution has rightly been judged one of the great courtroom dramas ever filmed. Roger Rosenblatt lauds "Charles Laughton's cleverness and Marlene Dietrich's poignant duplicity." One critic, however, termed the film a triumph mainly for Agatha Christie. Asked if he thought the film should have been deemed a triumph for the director as well, Wilder told this writer, "Frankly, I have never been interested in

what the critics say of my films. A good review means less to me than, for instance, a comment Agatha Christie made about *Witness for the Prosecution*. Looking back on the films derived from her mysteries, she called *Witness* the best of the lot. That meant a great deal more to me," Wilder concluded, "than anything a critic has ever said of one of my films."

REFERENCES

Lally, Kevin, *Wilder Times: The Life of Billy Wilder* (New York: Holt, 1996); Rosenblatt, Roger, "Trials and Tribulations," *Modern Maturity*, 38:5 (September–October 1995), 42–45; Sikon, Ed, *On Sunset Boulevard: The Life and Times of Billy Wilder* (New York: Hyperion, 1998).

—*G.D.P.*

THE WOMEN (1936)

CLARE BOOTHE (AKA CLARE BOOTHE LUCE) (1903–1987)

The Women (1939), U.S.A., directed by George Cukor, adapted by Anita Loos and Jane Murfin; Metro-Goldwyn-Mayer.

The Opposite Sex (1956), U.S.A., directed by David Miller, adapted by Faye and Michael Kanin, music by Nicholas Brodsky and lyrics by Sammy Cahn; Metro-Goldwyn-Mayer.

The Play

In Clare Boothe's own words, "*The Women* is a satirical play about a numerically small group of ladies native to the Park Avenues of America." More specifically, it is the tale of a society woman's attempt to handle her husband's infidelity while her female friends, relatives, and servants both advise her and talk behind her back.

Boothe wrote her first draft of *The Women* in three days while recovering from a marital split. As a favor to a mutual friend, producer Max Gordon offered to read Boothe's nascent play, only to purchase and develop it in two months for the stage. Directed by Robert Sinclair, *The Women*, with its cast of 44 females, opened December 26, 1936, at the Ethel Barrymore Theatre, where it ran for a successful 657 performances. Boothe had participated in the casting, choosing well-known stage actress Ilka Chase for the role of Sylvia Fowler, the nosey viper on whose gossip the action regularly turns. Margalo Gillmore played Mary Haines, the cheated wife, and Betty

Lawford played Crystal Allen, the mistress. In addition, a young Doris Day had a small part as a saleswoman.

The show was an instant success despite the misgivings of critics who chided the script for its relentless catfights and what seemed a superficial portrayal of the female gender as gold diggers, husband hunters, and conniving bitches. Although the ranch resort upon which the characters descend to obtain divorces was modeled after Boothe's venture to Reno to end her own union, she steadfastly maintained that the play was not a reflection of either her daily life-style or her opinion of her gender. Rather, her subjects were modeled after a particular group of wealthy, New York City gossip-mongers she regularly encountered but blatantly detested, stating, "The women who inspired this play deserve to be smacked across the head with a meat-axe."

Nevertheless, the tendency to discuss the play as if it were meant to mirror the self-indulgence of the fairer sex was relentless. Some of the criticism and misinterpretation of the play seemed to derive from Boothe's own upper-class breeding and widely acknowledged great beauty, as if these attributes would necessarily make her a participant in the world she portrayed. Moreover, many critics interpreted the action as guided by a masculine point of view—a criticism brought despite the absence of even a single male character in the script. In fact, rumors circulated that it was playwright George Kaufman, not Boothe, who actually penned the successful play, thus explaining its "bias." (Boothe readily admitted that Kaufman made a few suggestions to her, but the authorship query persisted until Kaufman counterposed, "If I'd written it, why would I sign it Clare Boothe?")

Fortunately, Boothe always knew there was an audience who would understand her humor and intention, and upon the play's phenomenal success she thanked "the women who are [the play's] staunchest advocates and best customers—the women who do not think all women are like that." Indeed, as her personal friend Wilfred Sheed wrote, Boothe was lucky to have written a play that was "highly commercial without having to try. What was on Clare's mind was on the audience's too; the rich bitches on the stage were playing to their sisters."

The author slightly revised *The Women* in 1966 by updating some of the references and increasing elements of farce, which ultimately smoothed the play's original linguistic edge. The play did not reappear on a major stage until 1973 when Morton Da Costa created a production that Clive Barnes of the *New York Times* called "fast and pounding" and "bitchy rather than brilliant." Indeed, while many critics continued to see the play as a showcase for shrill behavior, the change in America's social climate—especially attitudes toward women's societal roles—since its initial writing, merited an evaluation in terms of feminist critique. So in addition to Barnes, the *New York Times* also sent a female critic to review Da Costa's production in order to provide a "gender-balanced perspective." The result was a review focused on questions of socioeconomic class and Boothe's dedication to feminism (the author, who had remarried to become Clare Boothe Luce, was by then serving in diplomatic capacities for the U. S. government).

Over time, other questions emerged: Was Boothe criticizing the women themselves or the male domination that oppressed them? While some critics accused the play of not aging well and becoming camp, the fact that a group of GIs staged it in drag at their barracks during World War II suggests that this is a work that has always inspired multivalent readings and a variety of audience pleasures. More recently, feminist and media theorist Molly Haskell characterized Sylvia as a "superfemale" who exaggerates the mass of characteristics that women theoretically possess. None of these approaches, however, overshadow *The Women*'s primary quality: rapier, verbal wit.

The Films

George Cukor was assigned to direct the film version of *The Women* just following his removal as director of *Gone With the Wind*. Cukor had been working with independent producer David O. Selznick on developing the Civil War epic for over two years, but as the fight for creative control of the project escalated, Cukor was fired, only to quickly begin a new contract at MGM. These circumstances have led some critics to believe that Cukor's distracted mental state at the time impacted his work on the film, claiming that for all the visual theatrics deriving from Cukor's gift with the camera, the final product was silly and overdone. Just as there was a discrepancy between the popular and critical views of the play, however, Cukor created for the screen a film that met with poor critical reviews but still thrilled audiences.

Although Loos and Murfin are credited with the adaptation, Cukor also enlisted F. Scott Fitzgerald (whom Cukor had met during his work on *GWTW*) to assist with the script. Fitzgerald, who had given lush portraits of an idle leisure class in *The Great Gatsby*, was especially helpful with the references to the women's breeding and background. Additionally, Donald Ogden Stewart contributed some touches of humor. Loos and Murfin, however, were primarily responsible for the success of the script, putting in off-the-cuff remarks piped with double meaning and innuendo. In this way, they put "the laughs in where the censors had taken them out."

The Women ultimately served to showcase several noteworthy performances, but the project began primarily as a vehicle for actress Norma Shearer. Shearer, then widowed from MGM wunderkind Irving Thalberg, still asserted control at the studio and had little trouble securing the part of the impossibly kind and forgiving Mary Haines. Appropriately, Joan Crawford, who had a long-standing resentment toward Shearer and Thalberg based on their view of her as a "pushy, working-class girl," got the part of Mary's nemesis, Crystal. Crawford lobbied hard for the role, going against the advice of MGM publicity executives who thought her present fans, having seen her play primarily good-willed, career-minded women, wouldn't like her as a "cold-hearted bitch." Crawford was also thought to be too big of a star for what seemed a relatively small role. With her take-no-prisoners performance, however, Crawford turned Crystal into a major, memorable player. When it came to casting Sylvia, Cukor envisioned Ilka Chase, the originator of the role on Broadway. Rosalind Russell, however, despite being told she was "too pretty" and unfit for comedic roles, fought for an audition with Cukor and won the part. Indeed, Russell's portrayal became one of the standout performances of her career and gained her recognition as a true comedienne. Also of casting note was Joan Fontaine, whom Cukor had auditioned for *GWTW* and whose breakthrough performance as the sympathetic and winsome Peggy helped her land the lead in Alfred Hitchcock's *Rebecca*, as well as an illustrious film acting career. Despite all these praised performances, *The Women* failed to garner a single Oscar nomination for any of its actresses that year.

To the delight of fan magazine writers who had no romantic pairings on the film set to expose, many of the tensions in what Hedda Hopper termed "that feminine kennel" played out offscreen. In one case, Crawford deliberately interfered with Shearer's rehearsal by loudly clanking her knitting needles while feeding the insecure Shearer her lines. Cukor gave Crawford a swift scolding and the two women never spoke again on the set. When it came to designing the title card, more problems arose, first with Crawford demanding her name alongside Shearer's, then Russell waging a four-day sick leave when her wish to have her name above the title as well was rebuffed. In the end, all three were listed on the card, although Russell's name came out in considerably smaller type.

The Women is an aesthetic delight but much of what appeals about Cukor's film also throws the picture slightly off-balance. MGM costume designer Adrian created lavish, glimmering gowns for the players that were splendid to the average eye but to Cukor were overdone and "perfectly dreadful." "Adrian was trying to knock them dead," Cukor once said, adding, "like the serious parts of the picture, the very bad and flashy clothes were no good." Moreover, a five-minute fashion show sequence in the middle of the film awkwardly disrupts the rhythm and flow, not only for its content but also because it was filmed in color (a novelty at the time). Cukor railed against the fashion show idea, proclaiming that it could not be done well, but the producer insisted and hired another director to film the sequence. Despite these shortcomings, the film's pacing, especially in the opening scene in the beauty salon, is extraordinary; if Loos and Murfin cleaned up the dialogue, Cukor's sensibilities made it sing. He created a "circus atmosphere around the weak central character," which was a highly effective narrative tactic. In addition, the relentless visual sumptuousness, including the excessive costumes, added to the film's appeal to women. Of course, as with the stage reviews, critics remained overly preoccupied with the gender accuracy of the action: One called it the greatest argument for homosexuality while another saw the role of Crystal as poorly written because "no man would fall for this tramp." The reviewer for the *New York Times* expressed his ambivalence slightly differently, stating, "Marvelous, we believe every studio should make at least one thoroughly nasty picture a year." Certainly Cukor's catty opening credits in which he likened each character to a different animal encouraged the film's interpretation as a "female bestiary" composed of female creatures clawing their way without reason or kindness.

In an interview in 1972, Cukor mused that while kept women and marital breakups presented major moral dilemmas in 1939, the changing times proposed that a present-day remake would involve "everybody screwing everybody and everybody would know about it." Although hardly the orgy Cukor envisioned, a remake was attempted in 1956 with *The Opposite Sex*. With musical numbers and (gasp!) men, *The Opposite Sex* managed to retain much of the venom of the first film but failed to have the edge of the original or garner the same excitement. Starring June Allyson, Joan Collins, Ann Miller, Agnes Moorehead, and Leslie Nielsen, the remake did boast a talented cast, all in grand display via Cinemascope. Curiously, Helen Rose's costuming, like Adrian's before her, was criticized in the *New York Times* for its lush extravagance, which, enhanced by the color photography, was "enough to drive distaff viewers to distraction." Perhaps both versions of the film would have been more favorably reviewed had they been called "The Wardrobe."

REFERENCES

Bernardoni, James, *George Cukor: A Critical Study and Filmography* (Jefferson, N.C.: McFarland, 1985); Boothe, Clare, *The Women* (New York: Random House, 1937); Carey, Gary, *Cukor and Co.: The Films of George Cukor and His Collaborators* (New York: Museum of Modern Art, 1971); Clarens, Carlos, *George Cukor* (London: BFI, 1976); Fearnow, Mark, *Clare Boothe Luce: A Research and Production Sourcebook* (Westport, Conn.: Greenwood Press, 1995); Hatch, Alden, *Ambassador Extraordinary: Clare Booth Luce* (New York: Henry Holt, 1956); Lambert, Gavin, *On Cukor* (New York: G.P. Putnam's Sons, 1972); Levy, Emanuel, *George Cukor: Master of Elegance* (New York: Wm. Morrow, 1994); McGilligan, Patrick, *George Cukor: A Double Life* (New York: St. Martin's Press, 1991); Phillips, Gene, *George Cukor* (Boston: Twayne, 1982); Sheed, Wilfred, *Clare Boothe Luce* (New York: E.P. Dutton, 1982); Review, "The Women," *New York Times*, September 22, 1939: 27; review, "The Opposite Sex," *New York Times*, November 16, 1956; review, "The Opposite Sex," *Variety*, September 18, 1956.

—*R.E.*

WOYZECK (1836)

KARL GEORG BÜCHNER (1813–1837)

Woyzeck (1979), Germany, directed and adapted by Werner Herzog; Werner Herzog Filmproduktion.

The Play

Georg Büchner, born in Darmstadt and educated at Strasbourg University and Giessen, has been considered the first genuinely "modern" playwright. Though he died young, of typhus, he wrote three plays, none of which were produced during his lifetime: *Danton's Death* (1835), which foreshadowed modern epic theatre, *Leonce and Lena* (1836), an absurdist comedy, and *Woyzeck* (1836), which anticipates later developments in both naturalism and expressionism. *Woyzeck* survives only as an unpublished fragment, written in exile three months before Büchner's death at the age of 23. Because of its fragmentary nature, the play was not included in the first collection of Büchner's writings, published in 1850. It was first published in the periodical *Mehr Licht* (More Light) in 1875, then, in the first "critical" edition of Büchner's works in 1879, though a philologically accurate version did not appear until the definitive Hamburg Edition of 1967. The play was not staged until 1913 in Munich.

Although the text is relatively complete, the order of the scenes has been much disputed. The play drama-tizes the life of Johann Christian Woyzeck, a soldier who was beheaded in Leipzig in 1821 for murdering his mistress. Thoroughly exploited by an idiotic doctor, Woyzeck is gradually going mad because of an "experimental" subsistence diet of peas he is paid to eat so that the "scientific" effect of this diet can be studied. Physically weakened, he is also psychologically unbalanced. He hears "voices" he does not understand and he hallucinates. The poor fellow is also mad with jealousy because his mistress is having an affair with a dashing drum major. He is bullied and humiliated by the doctor and by the drum major until he finally snaps, buys a cheap knife, and murders his mistress one night by the river.

The Film

Because of the fragmented and unfinished nature of the text, the eccentric, visionary German filmmaker Werner Herzog was free to arrange and sequence the dramatic fragments cinematically. As Stanley Kauffmann noted, "whoever does *Woyzeck* must make his own version of the scenes that were unfinished by the author." He considered the film a "good" version, "except for the superfluous brutal drilling of Woyzeck at the beginning." Jack Kroll of *Newsweek*, on the other hand, thought Herzog's film was "much better" than any staged version of the play he had ever seen. Kroll considered the play a "startling prophecy of Nazism, not least in the Doctor's crazy experiments—travesties of science that prefigure the insane medical horrors of the concentration camps."

This play was a natural vehicle for Herzog, whose films have often focused on madness, presumptive science, and aberrant human behavior. Donald Barthelme praised Herzog for having made "a remarkably selfless version" of the play. Cast as Woyzeck, Klaus Kinski is the perfect embodiment of Büchner's mad protagonist. The temperamental and volatile Kinski was Herzog's favorite actor for roles evocative of madness and evil, such as his remake of F.W. Murnau's *Nosferatu* (1979), his story of an insane Spanish conquistador in *Aguirre: The Wrath of God* (1972), and the obsessed protagonist of *Fitzcarraldo* (1982), whose mad scheme was to bring grand opera into the wilderness of the Amazon. Eva Mattes plays Woyzeck's wife, Marie, and Willy Semmelrogge is the Doctor, the "scientist" in league with the Captain (Wolfgang Reichmann) to exploit Woyzeck. Josef Bierbichler plays the drum major who cuckolds Woyzeck and helps to drive him crazy. All of these actors except Eva Mattes had also worked on previous Herzog pictures. The adaptation is both power-ful and disturbing as it moves relentlessly toward a final, repulsive, slow-motion spectacle of violence and murder. "A man is an abyss," Woyzeck remarks to his friend Andres (Paul Burion): "You get dizzy looking in." The film captures an eerie sense of that insane dizziness.

REFERENCES

Barthelme, Donald, "The Earth as an Overturned Bowl," *The New Yorker*, September 10, 1979, 119–120; Canby, Vincent, "Late for Life," *The New York Times*, August 24, 1979, B12; Hauser, Ronald, *Georg Büchner* (New York: Twayne, 1974); Kauffmann, Stanley, "On Film," *The New Republic* (September 1 & 8, 1979): 22–23; Kroll, Jack, "The Good Soldier," *Newsweek* (September 17, 1979), 102–103.

—*J.M.W.*

YOU CAN'T TAKE IT WITH YOU (1936)

MOSS HART (1904–1961) AND GEORGE S. KAUFMAN (1889–1961)

You Can't Take It With You (1938), U.S.A., directed by Frank Capra, adapted by Robert Riskin; Columbia.

The Play

The team of Kaufman and Hart was the most successful writing duo on the Broadway stage in the 1930s. The caustic Kaufman and the amiable Hart cowrote nine plays, beginning with *Once in a Lifetime* in 1930 (the subject of Hart's memoir, *Act One*), a Hollywood spoof that was adapted to the screen in 1931; and including *Merrily We Roll Along* (1934), which told the story of a playwright in reverse chronology; *I'd Rather Be Right* (1937), which brought the semi-retired George M. Cohan back to the stage as President Franklin D. Roosevelt; *The Man Who Came to Dinner* (1939), written for and about Alexander Woollcott, and filmed in 1941 with Monte Woolley; *George Washington Slept Here* (1940), brought to the screen a year later with Jack Benny and Ann Sheridan; and *You Can't Take It With You* (1936), which won the 1936 Pulitzer Prize. Although they wrote no more plays together after 1941, they remained close friends. They died within a few months of each other in 1961.

The three-act comedy premiered in New York at the Booth Theatre on December 14, 1936, and ran for a spectacular 837 performances. The setting is a large family mansion in New York City in the 1930s. The action revolves around the wacky Sycamore family, who lives by the motto, "You do as you like, and no questions asked." There's the curmudgeonly patriarch, old Martin Vanderhof (Henry Travers), who attends Columbia University convocations; his daughter, Penelope (Josephine Hull), who writes unproduceable plays; Penelope's husband Paul (Frank Wilcox), who manufactures fireworks in the cellar; a granddaughter, Essie (Paula Trueman), who practices ballet in the living room, to the ongoing dismay of her Russian teacher ("confidentially, she stinks"); Essie's husband, Ed (George Heller), who divides his time between playing a xylophone and operating a printing press; and another granddaughter, Alice (Margot Stevenson), newly affianced. Alice, who appears to be the only sane member of the family, invites the parents of her rich fiancé, Tony Kirby (Jess Barker), to dinner. But they arrive a night early, and in the ensuing mayhem, Paul's fireworks are ignited. The whole clan is marched off to jail. Old man Vanderhoff, in the meantime, learns to his dismay that the feds are after him for delinquent income taxes. But when it is learned that through a quirk of circumstances, Vanderhoff was declared legally dead years before, the case is dropped. As for the stuffy Kirby family, Grandpa converts Mr. Kirby to his philosophy: "Life is simple and kind of beautiful if you let it come to you."

The Film

Frank Capra had directed two very different films before bringing *You Can't Take It With You* to the screen in 1938. *Mr. Deeds Goes to Town* (1936) and *Lost Horizon* (1937) were, respectably, parables of democratic action in Depression America and an exotic fantasy of utopia in the lost paradise of Shangri-La. The former was a box-office smash; the latter a failure. Looking for a sure-fire vehicle to make up for his losses, and perhaps still imbued with the idealism of *Lost Horizon*, Capra saw *You Can't Take It With You* in New York and, according to commentator Charles J. Maland, "was so intrigued with the portrayal of a bunch of people pursuing their interests and still living in harmony with those around them that he talked Harry Cohn into paying $200,000 for the film rights." In the characters of Grandpa Vanderhoff (Lionel Barrymore) and young Tony Kirby (James Stewart), Capra found suitable spokespersons for his usual pleas for tolerance, idealism, and individualism. The moral struggle resides in the conflict between Grandpa, sort of the "High Lama" of the household, and Tony's flint-hearted scoundrel of a father, Anthony Kirby, Sr. (Edward Arnold), whose unscrupulous business practices include an attempt to buy out the Sycamore home as part of a real estate deal. Capra aptly described the confrontation as a clash of two philosophies: "Devour thy neighbor versus love thy neighbor." Rounding out the cast was Jean Arthur as Alice, Eddie "Rochester" Anderson and Lillian Yarbo as the family's black servants, Dub Taylor as Ed, Ann Miller as Essie, and Spring Byington as Mrs. Sycamore.

Robert Riskin's script retains and amplifies the basic action and characters. Grandpa is an ex-businessman who dropped out of a successful career because he was not having any fun. While he keeps busy with his stamp collection and playing the harmonica, he encourages everyone to do just as they please. A sturdy pragmatist and patriot, he distrusts cant and "isms"—"Sure, you know, communism, fascism, voodooism . . . when things go a little bad these days, you go out and get yourself an ism, and you're in business." A key scene prefiguring the theme of *It's a Wonderful Life* is the incarceration of the Sycamores and Kirbys after the incident of the exploding fireworks. When Kirby complains about being away from his business deals, Grandpa asks why he is so obsessed with "making more money than you can ever use. You can't take it with you. The only thing you can take with you is the love of your friends." Angrily dismissing Kirby's retort that he is a "lion in the jungle," Grandpa loses his temper, declaring, "You may be a high mogul to yourself, Mr. Kirby, but to me you're a failure as a man, failure as a human being, even

Frank Capra

failure as a father." In the final scene Kirby, having suffered the death of a rival due to his business practices, and smarting under his son's decision to leave the family business, visits Grandpa to make peace with him. The two sit down to play a harmonica duet of "Polly Wolly Doodle." In the opinion of Maland, the forced whimsy of the scene "simply strains our imaginations too much." The film ends as Grandpa and his now enlarged family sit down to the dinner table, and Grandpa intones another in a series of his dinnertime prayers: "Well, sir, here we are again. We been getting on pretty well for a long time now. . . ."

While an admirer of Capra, novelist/critic Graham Greene's reaction to the film was mixed. It is worth quoting at length: "The director emerges as a rather muddled and sentimental idealist who feels—vaguely—that something is wrong with the social system. Mr.

Deeds started distributing his money, and the hero of *Lost Horizon* settled down in a Tibetan monastery—equipped with all the luxury devices of the best American hotels—and Grandpa Vanderhof persuades, in this new picture, the Wall Street magnate who has made the *coup* of his career and cornered the armaments industry to throw everything up and play the harmonica. . . . We may groan and blush as [Capra] cuts his way remorselessly through all finer values to the fallible human heart, but infallibly he makes his appeal—to that great soft organ with its unreliable goodness and easy melancholy and baseless optimism."

You Can't Take It With You was one of the top 15 money-makers in 1938–1939—Capra's most successful film to date—and it won Oscars for best film and best director.

REFERENCES

Hart, Moss, *Act One* (New York: Random House, 1960); Maland, Charles J., *Frank Capra* (Boston: Twayne, 1980); McBride, Joseph, *Frank Capra: The Catastrophe of Success* (New York: Simon and Schuster, 1992); Parkinson, David, ed., *The Graham Greene Film Reader* (New York: Applause Books, 1993).

—*J.C.T.*

YOU'VE GOT MAIL

See *PARFUMERIE*

PART II
Shakespearean Adaptations

Seduced by Shakespeare, Transfixed by Spectacle

Let's begin with some warm, fuzzy assumptions. Shakespeare (1564–1616) was a universal poet and playwright; film is a universal "language." Therefore, had he lived in the 20th century, Shakespeare would surely have written for the cinema, not for the stage. Instead of poetry, he would have written screenplays. He would have won multiple Oscars and basked in the glory of sunny Hollywood, because, after all, Hollywood *loves*, admires, and respects writers. After having written and produced 36 or 37 memorable scripts, he would have retired not to Stratford-upon-Avon but to Palm Springs, where he might have composed sonnets and played golf. Seven years after his death, the First Folio of his screenplays would have been published (in Pasadena, perhaps), and these would be read and studied and analyzed by anxious students for centuries to come. His reputation would eclipse that of Preston Sturges and Mitchell Leisen for comedy and Robert Towne, Herman J. Mankiewicz, and even Ingmar Bergman for melodrama, if not tragedy. And the world, no doubt, would be a far better place because movies would be better than ever.

Now, there is a fantasy beyond belief. It supposes that the semi-literate 20th century is congenial to poetry (as it is not) and exquisitely sensitive to language and wordplay, like, you know, like it most certainly ain't. It supposes that blank verse would easily be adapted to the screen. And the most egregiously wrong assumption of all, it supposes that theatre and film are one and the same, whereas in fact they are, at best, distant cousins who do not really speak the same language. The soliloquy is the highest manifestation of Shakespeare's dramatic art and the most challenging of his dramatic devices to capture on screen. No, Shakespeare did not write for the screen. The best a film director can do is to trick the audience into thinking he might have done so.

And yet, Hollywood has been seduced by Shakespeare and has done its damnedest—if not its best—to exploit him. It has used his plays for star vehicles, first

William Shakespeare

casting America's Sweetheart and the original Zorro, Mary Pickford and Douglas Fairbanks, Sr., as Kate and Petruchio in *The Taming of the Shrew*, and much later, Elizabeth Taylor and Richard Burton—the play being a natural vehicle for celebrity couples who are not quite getting along. Hamlet has been played by Sir Laurence Olivier, by Richard Chamberlain, by Nicol Williamson, by Kenneth Branagh, by Mel Gibson, and even by

action is fabricated to give the actors opportunities to speak and declaim. There is ample reason for anyone who loves Shakespeare to *hate* movies. In significant ways Shakespeare is simply *too good* for the movies. Why, after all, should the very paradigm of elitist art be forced into a mechanical form of mass entertainment?

Let's consider the plays as performance texts. One could regard a screenplay as a performance text, but no one would consider the experience of reading a screenplay the equivalent of seeing a film. A screenplay is a mere sketch, an incomplete verbal framework that is extremely malleable and likely to be changed while the film is in production. In other words, "the script serves the representation," whereas in theatre "the representation serves the play" (Gerdes 14). On stage "the play's the thing," whereas on film the thing's the play, or supposed to be. Because of the poetry and the language, Shakespeare's plays can be read for pleasure. As Peter Gerdes has noted, "The drama text is an independent art work to be read *or* performed" (Gerdes 11). A film script, by contrast, is merely "a preparatory element for a future art work." Notions of Hamlet or Lear or Macbeth or Othello will have been set in the minds of educated readers—ideals hardly to be realized by any given actor or production. For some, Olivier reaches or surpasses the ideal in his film of *Richard III*, stagebound though it may be. For others, Ian McKellen will hit the mark better in his flamboyant cinematic version of 1996, an ahistorical incursion that shoves the play into the Nazi nightmare of the mid-20th century.

In fact, every one of Olivier's "great" movie renderings of Shakespeare had been eclipsed by the end of the century: His loose-lipped, posturing Othello in blackface now seems a mere embarrassment in comparison to Laurence Fishburne's more natural rendering for Oliver Parker. Olivier's wheyfaced, patriotic Henry V reshaped Shakespeare's play into anti-Nazi propaganda and simply excised the antiwar elements in order to do some service to the state, but a disservice to Shakespeare. Nearly 40 years later Kenneth Branagh would show what the play was really about, a calculating and potentially cruel modern ruler rising out of a medieval morass of chivalric pageantry, manipulative and tough when he needed to be, Machiavellian and cynical, a king with a sense of public relations and something more than a windy rhetorician. Olivier's best innovation in his *Henry V* is the way he begins the film in a model of Shakespeare's Globe Theatre, then gradually opens the action out of this stagebound theatrical framework until, by the time the "mirror of all Christian kings" gets to Agincourt, the film has finally moved the action out of the theatre and into "the vasty fields of France"

Laurence Olivier

Arnold Schwarzenegger (spoofing Olivier's Hamlet in *Last Action Hero*). Moreover, who better to handle the language of *Romeo and Juliet* than Claire Danes and that splendid, Italianate *Titanic* boy, Leonardo DiCaprio?

Those who suppose Shakespeare would have written for the screen should consider that cinema is not the same as theatre, that the shot is the basic unit for constructing a film, whereas the scene is the basic unit for dramatic construction, that on stage the actor is the creator, whereas on film the actor is the created, that theatre is an artificial medium but that film is by its very nature a realistic one, that theatre audiences are conditioned to accept the theatrical artifice and attend carefully to the language, whereas moviegoers are increasingly rude, vulgar, and inattentive. Film is laconic: The language is minimal and simplistic and merely supports the action. Theatre is verbal: The

Orson Welles

(though the battle of Agincourt was actually filmed in Ireland, since France was occupied by the Germans when the film was shot).

Olivier's greatest achievement is the way he mounts the play as a meditation on the differences between theatre and film and a demonstration at the climax of how a well-funded cinema spectacle might be used to enhance the play's potential. Shakespeare's history play invites the sort of spectacular treatment Olivier provided, even though it may be framed as a patriotic, medieval fairy tale. Kenneth Branagh offered, by contrast, a far more realistic battle scene and a far more cynical king, who better resembles the sort of modern politician Shakespeare surely had in mind. Branagh's "muse of fire" was able "to write history with lightning" better than Olivier, or D.W. Griffith, for that matter.

Times change, icons fall. Orson Welles's *Macbeth* now seems about as authentic as Jeanette Nolan's zipper (awkwardly in evidence in the film), a mere shadow of the murderous monster so well portrayed by Jon Finch in Roman Polanski's wickedly evil treatment. But

Polanski had seen the world differently, growing up in Poland during World War II, and had been touched by Evil personally. The thugs who murder Lady Macduff and her children and servants in his film behaved like Nazi Storm Troopers he had seen in his youth. His Macbeth was shaped by 20th-century notions of Satanic cults, a Charles Manson with a political agenda who gave a high definition to the witches' imperative: "be bloody, bold, and resolute."

DISTRACTIONS OF SPECTACLE AND THE SHOCK OF THE NEW

We just suggested that in cinema "the screenplay serves the representation." What this has come to mean in filmed Shakespeare is that the screenplay serves the spectacle—in Polanski's *Macbeth*, for example, in Baz Luhrmann's *Romo + Juliet*, in Richard Loncairne's *Richard III*, and, egregiously, in Peter Greenaway's *Prospero's Books*, which cannibalizes the words of *The Tempest* without adapting it, exactly. The tendency of cinema is toward the spectacular, and spectacle can strip poetry of its sense. Baz Luhrmann's characters in *Romeo + Juliet* speak in anachronisms, conversing in language that is Shakespearean but disjunctive, language that is muted by explosive action and all but erased by the visual spectacle.

Shakespeare's contemporary Ben Jonson, who loved language that was "pure and neat . . . yet plain and customary" understood the proper harmony, balance, and proportion between poetry and spectacle and fought to preserve the integrity of his own poetry in his work with the architect Inigo Jones, as they worked together to design court masques that were intended to be spectacular in their visual display, because he knew the spectacle could quite overwhelm the poetry. This is also the case with the filmed Shakespeare. Viewers can be seduced by the visuals rather than being seduced by the poetry of Shakespeare. Add to this the tendency to reinvent the plays, moving the action out of the Renaissance and out of antiquity and nudging it toward modern times to make it seem "relevant."

As Ben Jonson wrote in his commonplace book *Timber, or Discoveries*, "Expectation of the vulgar is more drawn and held with newness than goodness; . . . so it be new, though never so naught and depraved, they run to it, and are taken." *Vide* Baz Luhrmann and Peter Greenaway and Julie Taymor—or even Kenneth Branagh, whose "complete" *Hamlet* was wrenched out of time if not teased out of thought. "I look upon a monstrous giant, as Titus," Jonson wrote, "and mine eye sticks upon every part; the whole that consists of those parts will never be taken in at one entire view." Jonson was not writing about *Titus Andronicus*, but he might have been, had he been able to see Julie Taymor's *Titus* (2000).

BIG SCREEN, SMALL SCREEN?

"Too vast oppresseth the eyes and exceeds the memory," Jonson wrote; "too little scarce admits either." We've had Big Hamlets and Little Hamlets, comprehensive Hamlets and incoherent Hamlets (such as Franco Zeffirelli's). Kenneth Branagh's *Hamlet* is coherent—he certainly respects the language—but it is overlong and overwrought. Conflating the Folio and Quarto texts stretches the play to well over three hours (arguably, too much of a good thing); but Branagh also adds at least a half-hour of visuals and special effects, as Rufus Sewell's Fortinbras draws near to Blenheim's Elsinore to build a smashing and even bloodier conclusion than Shakespeare wrote. The language is not lost, in other words, but the text has to compete with the shattering, "too vast" visuals that may "oppresseth the eyes."

Arguably, Tony Richardson took the better approach back in 1969, even though he trimmed the text to half its length and totally ignored young Fortinbras at the end. Richardson's *Hamlet* was not distracted by the visual splendor of Blenheim Palace. His film works within the more limited framework of filmed theatre, highlighting the verbal skills of his actors, most notably Anthony Hopkins as Claudius and Nicol Williamson as Hamlet. This "performance text," an actual record of the production mounted at the Round House Theatre in London, works perfectly well on the video screen. The actors are framed in medium-shots or close-ups, and the emphasis is placed squarely upon the language, as the spectacle is scaled down. And that, perhaps, is the paradigm of what the filmed Shakespeare should be—barebones cinema, with text and actors front and center.

Of course Richardson's *Hamlet* does not provide absolute textual fidelity, but the text is so cunningly cut that the whole play *seems* to be intact, although it demonstrably is not. Branagh's film is probably closer to what Shakespeare might have intended—lines added or discarded, they're all there in sometimes awkward profusion (the lengthy exposition of Act One, Scene One, for example); the language is for the most part wonderfully conveyed by Branagh's international cast (though one might suppose that Jack Lemmon, an otherwise splendid actor, was not born to play Shakespeare's spear-carrier). No, the problem here is not textual but in the flamboyant nature of the imagined action—the larger-than-life ghost played by Brian Blessed, in particular, and the fantastically staged duel at the end, which recalls the stage spectacle of *The Phantom of the Opera*.

The 1990s experienced a "Bard Boom," as it was called in the popular press, culminating in the tremendous box-office success of no single Shakespeare adaptation (though many were produced, some good, some not) but of a biofantasy fabricated from the imagined early career of *Shakespeare in Love*, patched together by director John Madden and his two scenarists, Marc Norman and Tom Stoppard. They managed to put an appealingly human face on the Droeshout engraving of the balding Bard, indulging in a biographical fantasy that turned Shakespeare into a sexy and energetic young lover who knew how to thrill with his quill. It's an understandable, made-up Shakespeare make-over that presents a young stud (Joseph Fiennes) rather than a balding Bard struck by the blind bow-boy's butt shaft. It's a backstage drama offering the best bits of *Romeo and Juliet* squeezed into a *faux*-biographical framework that turns the boy Bard into slick Willy, a lovesick puppy pining androgynously for blonde bombshell Viola DeLesseps (Gwyneth Paltrow), a poetry groupie who earns her hour on the stage before being sent to Virginia Beach and an arranged marriage in the Brave New World, but only after Queen Elizabeth (Judi Dench) grants her a night of love. The payoff for this slick confection? Thirteen Academy Award nominations and seven Oscars.

Hollywood loved *Shakespeare in Love* because Hollywood loves success. There is no particular respect here for the real Shakespeare and no real interest at all in his early, obscure London years. Just as his plays can be distorted and bent out of shape in the interest of making money, so can his life be falsified. It's Shakespeare made cute and commodified. No doubt the film is entertaining, even though it is biographically challenged, but it is not really very instructive. This is spectacular exploitation. "Though a man be hungry," Ben Jonson wrote, "he should not play the parasite. That hour wherein I would repent me to be honest," Jonson continued, "there were ways enow open for me to be rich." Screenwriters and directors should take note.

FROM ACTUALITY TO ADVERTISEMENT: REDUCED SHAKESPEARE WITHOUT WORDS

The first Shakespeare film ever made was not much to look at and involved only a scrap of one of Shakespeare's lesser known plays, *King John*, about three minutes of British actor Sir Herbert Beerbohm Tree as the king, poisoned and squirming on his throne in the play's death scene. W.K.L. Dickson filmed this scene from *King John* on September 20, 1899, on the same day that Tree's stage production of the play opened at Her Majesty's Theatre in London. Intended to promote the stage production, the film was shown in variety theatres and also released as a Mutoscope "peepshow."

This and five other early Shakespeare films can be seen on the British Film Institute compilation video *Silent Shakespeare*, digitally mastered from original 35 mm nitrate materials made between 1899 and 1911, but none of these are true adaptations. The Percy Stow *Tempest* (1908), for example, offers vignettes showing Prospero's arrival at the island where he will be exiled, Miranda in arms and books in hand, his release of the spirit Ariel from a tree (not exactly a "cloven pine," as in the play), the discovery of Caliban, and other benchmark moments from the play. J. Stuart Blackton and Charles Kent's *Midsummer Night's Dream* (1909) reduces that comedy to a series of skits. The Italian Gerolamo Lo Savio production of *King Lear* (1910) also reproduces and dramatizes some of the play's big moments, but the play is simplified and compressed. The Edgar/Edmund subplot is not included, for example, nor is the storm scene where Lear goes mad.

In 1996, in Oregon, a nitrate print of a "lost" 1912 film was discovered; it is, historically important because it is the first extant "feature" film of the American cinema. Significantly, it is a Shakespeare film, *Richard III*, a silent five-reeler directed by James Keane and starring the British actor Frederick B. Warde (1851–1935) as Shakespeare's villainous Richard, the Duke of Gloucester, who would be king regardless of the odds against his succession. Warde discovered that he could profitably tour America with the film, interpreting the lines and providing commentary during the reel changes, as Kenneth S. Rothwell notes in his *History of Shakespeare on Screen*. Seen under these circumstances, this film was not exactly an example of Shakespeare without words, but Shakespeare without dialogue—not exactly a substitute for a dramatic production of the play, but a means of showing and telling what the play was about. The film ran to 55 minutes.

Such films are of obvious historical importance, but they cannot qualify as true adaptations. The best research on this arcane period of Shakespeare films was done by Robert Hamilton Ball's groundbreaking book *Shakespeare on Silent Film* (1968), which was the definitive work for over 30 years. Ball's work was later updated by Kenneth Rothwell's *History of Shakespeare on Screen* (1999). Anyone interested in such primitive novelties will find them listed and discussed in these two books. But the point is clear that almost from the beginning, from the turn of the cinema century, filmmakers saw the plays of Shakespeare as marketable and exploitable commodities, although such early attempts could do little more than illustrate and mime the texts of the plays. The language and poetry of Shakespeare could not be approached until after the coming of sound in 1929.

SHAKESPEARE SPEAKS! DIALOGUE TRADITIONS IN HOLLYWOOD

After talking pictures had arrived, theatre people themselves wondered about the impact these films would have on real theatre. In 1929 playwright Luigi Pirandello responded in the following way to the question "Will Talkies Abolish the Theatre?" Pirandello claimed that both the classical theatre and the music hall could "rest easy in the certainty that they will not be abolished for one reason: Theatre is not trying to become cinema; cinema is trying to become theatre. The greatest success to which film can aspire, one moving it even farther along the road toward theatre, will be to become theatre's photographic and mechanical copy, and a bad one at that. Like all copies, it must arouse a desire for the original."

With the coming of sound, Hollywood was deluged with an influx of theatrical talent and voice coaches to help the silent stars make the transition to sound. To make Garbo speak would be a triumph for MGM; to make John Gilbert speak in a manner befitting his image was more of a challenge. Early dialogue conventions make speech patterns in early talking pictures extremely awkward. When Fairbanks and Pickford entered the talking arena with *The Taming of the Shrew* in 1929, the text was cut back as much as possible to make way for knockabout farce. In 1936 Elisabeth Bergner's German accent in Paul Czinner's *As You Like It* gave the character of Rosalind a certain charm but was decidedly odd and awkward.

In *Hamlet* the Prince informs the court "we'll *hear* a play." Four hundred years later people think in terms of *seeing* a play, either on stage or at the movies. If a movie presumes to adapt Shakespeare, however, his lines deserve to he *heard* as well as "seen." In Shakespeare's time educated people were more enamored of language than they are today. Shakespeare's plays are verbally intensive, and even if Shakespeare spoke of "the two-hours traffic of our stage," full dramatic productions today would run to three or four hours. That's rather more talk than a movie can bear, even if the language is expertly handled by an authority as gifted as Kenneth Branagh, whose extended *Hamlet* fully seems as long as it is—four hours, plus an intermission.

Linguists have speculated that, because the Renaissance was so language sensitive, English was spoken much more rapidly in Shakespeare's time than it is today, and that audiences were better conditioned to listen closely in order to follow the dialogue. The coming of sound in Hollywood coincided with the burgeoning popularity of radio in America, which surely had a conditioning listening effect. After the movies learned to talk in the 1930s, the dialogue expectations and the tolerance for dialogue of the 1940s differed from what was to follow during the age of television. Consider, for example, Clarence Day's *Life with Father* (1947), first converted to a play and then adapted to a film by Michael Curtiz, very popular in its day, but now hopelessly dated in terms of gender sensitivity and political correctness. The film seems much longer than it is (117 minutes) because it is all talk and little action. That might not have been a problem when the film was originally released, to be seen *and heard* by a radio-conditioned, radio-intensive audience. Viewers conditioned by radio drama would have listening skills far superior to audiences later in the century.

By the end of the century, moreover, stage dialogue had become simpler—brief, snappy, and profane—so that it might register more effectively for audiences unaccustomed to listening carefully. Movie dialogue now works to echo contemporary speech, to be conversational and "natural." In their everyday affairs, people do not speak in complete, fully-formed sentences, as playwright Harold Pinter realized early in his career. Pinter people express themselves in uneven, fragmented cadences, as if they are thinking while they are speaking and have to pause in order to collect their thoughts and complete their utterances. In America David Mamet would later imitate Pinter, translating Pinter patterns into a distinctively profane American idiom. People in general are not "poetic." They tend to resort to clichés as a means of short-circuiting the thinking process. Increasingly such clichés have involved a great deal of profanity in American films, on television (as in *The Sopranos*, where cursing and clichéd swearing are the building blocks of dialogue) and on stage, especially in the drama of David Manet—a profane, American Pinter. Such realistic conventions of language and dialogue are far removed from the poetry of Shakespeare, whose language may seem more dated and complex than ever.

"SOMETHING ROTTEN": POSTMODERN APPROACHES TO THE PLAYS OF SHAKESPEARE

"Suit the action to the word, the word to the action," Hamlet advises the players in Act Three, Scene Two. Michael Almereyda, director of the Ethan Hawke *Hamlet*, took this advice as his mantra, "so smart and simple it's almost stupefying," he told the *New York Times*. But Hamlet also cautions his players not to "O'erstep . . . the modesty of nature," lest it be "overdone," distorting the mirror held up to nature. Defining and visualizing the action is another challenge, however, and the problem with the postmodern spectacle is that it can distort the action. The language of Shakespeare is preserved in the Baz Luhrmann *Romeo + Juliet*, for example, but the

late-20th-century urban setting refigures and recontextualizes the action, twisting and teasing it out of thought. The anachronistic language of Shakespeare floats above the rubble of a contemporary urban setting and the vulgar Capulet mansion with its fishtanks and swimming pool, even above the helicopters that pursue desperate young Romeo into the candlelit cathedral where Juliet lies in state.

When Michael Almereyda described his own contemporary *Hamlet*, he could also have been describing the Luhrmann *Romeo + Juliet*: "Entire scenes were dropped, Shakespeare's text was further trimmed and torn, and the result is, inevitably, an *attempt* at *Hamlet*—not so much a sketch, but a collage, a patchwork of intuitions, images, and ideas." Almereyda claims that *Hamlet* has been filmed at least 43 times, so what can he presume to offer that is new, besides shifting the action to a contemporary urban setting? Despite evidence in the play to the contrary, he opts for a younger prince in his 20s, even though Kenneth Branagh at 35 was just about the right age for the role, on the evidence of what the Gravedigger says about how long poor Yorick has been interred. The mantra in *Entertainment Weekly* is "Shakespeare *has* to be about what we want now," so forget art: The goal is to serve the imagined wishes of consumers. And following the advice from Jan Kott's *Shakespeare Our Contemporary*, Almereyda believed an "ideal *Hamlet* would be one most true to Shakespeare and most modern at the same time," as if Branagh's *Hamlet*, set sometime before the turn of the 20th century, was not "modern" enough.

Almereyda sets the action of his modern-dress *Hamlet* in Times Square, where a power struggle is going on at the "Denmark Corporation." Elsinore is transformed into a luxury hotel. A skeptical David Denby noted that by abbreviating the text, Almereyda "has lost the players, a great deal of wit, and some extraordinary metaphysical speculation," but these losses are compensated by some fresh dimensions. The film, in his opinion, is "not a travesty," but "a ripely melancholy version of the play," and a "gripping" postmodern translation. Almereyda wanted viewers of his *Hamlet* "to recognize the frailty of spiritual values in a material world, and to get a whiff of something rotten in Denmark on the threshold of our self-congratulatory new century." Such an approach deserves to be taken seriously.

No doubt the contemporary setting of the postmodern approaches can be distracting, as is the case in *Romeo + Juliet*, further hyped by its spectacular excesses. The same could be said of the Richard Loncraine *Richard III* (1995), which refigures Shakespeare's history play as a neo-Nazi nightmare that shows Jan Kott's "Grand Mechanism" of history in all its frightening and wicked manifestations; but that postmodern production is sustained through its wartorn wasteland spectacle by its bravura performances, which make the World War II setting seem almost secondary. Similar claims could be made for the Branagh *Hamlet* and possibly for the Julie Taymor *Titus* (1999), though her disgusting and flamboyant spectacle is distracting, as are the shifts in chronology, when the performance is wrenched into the modern-day Roman Coliseum at the end. Taymor effectively makes a point about primitive violence in the modern world, however, and the film is ultimately coherent, though at times it threatens to be otherwise. The plays of Shakespeare are constantly being reimagined and reinvented, as they should be, to demonstrate the universal implications of dramas that have not become dated over the past 400 years.

DERIVATIVE APPROACHES AND "SHAKE-SPEARE-INFLUENCED" FILMS

The approach of this book is intended to be "encyclopedic," but it cannot be utterly comprehensive. If 43 versions of *Hamlet* have been filmed, we simply lack the space and resources to cover *all* of them, though we will attempt to round up the usual suspects. Out of obligation we should include the films of Akira Kurosawa "inspired" by Shakespeare, such as *Throne of Blood* (1957), an international classic that some have considered the best adaptation of *Macbeth* ever filmed, even though the action is set in medieval Japan, the characters reconfigured (one spooky witch instead of three), the message and ending changed, and the original poetry lost. Kurosawa's later film *Ran* (1985) is even looser in its transformation of *King Lear.*

Therefore, a major problem is posed by what Robert F. Willson, Jr., has called "Shakespeare-influenced" movies, some of which are treated in Chapter 4 of his book *Shakespeare in Hollywood, 1929–1956.* Other authorities have long since recognized *Forbidden Planet* (1956) as an "off-shoot" of *The Tempest,* with Walter Pidgeon playing Dr. Morbius, the Prospero figure, who is lost in space. A better candidate might be Paul Mazursky's *Tempest* (1982), which is a less radical transformation and follows the structure if not the dialogue of Shakespeare's play. But if these "derivatives" dispense with Shakespeare's poetry, should they be treated seriously as adaptations? Even more problematic is Peter Greenaway's postmodern transformation entitled *Prospero's Books* (1991), which shows Prospero (John Gielgud) in the process of writing *The Tempest* as the action unfolds around him. The film begins as he scratches out the opening words of the play, and Greenaway reconfigures much of the action, but the film is more a product of Greenaway's imagination than Shakespeare's.

Akira Kurosawa

Willson pays particular attention to *Joe MacBeth* (1955), an updated gangster version of the Scottish play directed by Ken Hughes and set in Chicago, where no one speaks in the cadences of Shakespeare. He also discusses Delmer Daves; *Jubal* (1956) as a "Western *Othello*" and Edward Dmytryk's *Broken Lance* (1954) as a "*King Lear* on Horseback." Another shoot-'em-up "off-shoot" is John Ford's classic *My Darling Clementine* (1946). Well, Victor Mature's Doc Holliday may recite the "to be or not to be" soliloquy with some feeling, but Jack Benny does it better in *To Be or Not to Be* (1942), Shakespeare "touched" by Lubitsch, who uses tragedy for comic purposes in his film and then comedy for tragic purposes, when he has a Jewish actor in Nazi-occupied Poland recite Shylock's "Hath not a Jew eyes?" defense.

Just as *Hamlet* is embedded (so to speak) in the Ernst Lubitsch film, so *Othello* is embedded in George Cukor's *A Double Life* (1947), another "Shakespeare-influenced" film. Of course, "influence" is not adaptation per se, but Willson's chapter indirectly poses a larger question: What exactly constitutes an adaptation? Is *Last Action Hero* (1993) "Shakespeare-influenced" because of its three-minute spoof of the Olivier *Hamlet?* ("So, you killed my fodder," Arnold Schwarzenegger says as he turns Hamlet into an action hero ready to "take out the trash.") Should *A Thousand Acres* (1997) be considered an "adaptation" of *King Lear* because Jane Smiley used *Lear* as a model for the Iowa farmer who goes round the bend in her novel? Smiley exploits *King Lear*, taking Shakespeare's concept for high drama and reducing it to a cornfed soap opera about a drunken and abusive, cantankerous father who turns two of his daughters against him. The film has some emotive power, but the language belongs to Iowa, not Shakespeare.

In his *History of Shakespeare on Screen*, Kenneth Rothwell offers a taxonomy for seven kinds of Shakespeare derivatives: "Those of the first kind (recontextualizations) will keep the plot but move Shakespeare's play into a wholly new era and jettison the Elizabethan language (*Joe MacBeth*); the second kind (mirror movies) will meta-cinematically make the movie's backstage plot about the troubled lives of actors run parallel to the plot of the Shakespearean play that the actors are appearing in (*A Double Life*); the third kind (music/dance) will turn the plays into musicals (*West Side Story*) or ballets and operas such as Zeffirelli's *Otello* (1986) . . . the fourth kind (revues) will use the excuse of a biography (*Prince of Players*), or of a documentary (*Looking for Richard*), or even a horror show (*Theatre of Blood*) to showcase Shakespeare for embellishment, and/or graft brief visual or verbal quotations onto an otherwise unrelated scenario . . . the sixth kind (animations) \!s>. . will put Shakespeare into cartoon images (*The Lion King*); and finally the seventh kind (documentaries and educational films) will make a variety of pedagogical films that in turn may overlap with any of the permutations and combinations in the previous categories."

Rothwell therefore defines a wide variety of the so-called Shakespeare derivatives. To find many such films

discussed in detail, the reader will have to look elsewhere. Some of the "derivatives"—Pacino's *Looking for Richard*, Merchant-Ivory's *Shakespeare Wallah!* Cukor's *A Double Life*, Madden's *Shakespeare in Love*, for example—are examined in Appendix A of our *Encyclopedia*. See also, for example, Ronald Harwood's *The Dresser* (1983) under our non-Shakespearean drama section. Others—but not *all* of them—will be listed under the plays from which they are derived. We have attempted to include most of the titles that readers and playgoers are likely to think of. That was also our guiding principle in selecting the major Shakespeare films covered here. For a more comprehensive listing, readers will want to consult *Shakespeare on Screen: An International Filmography and Videography*, compiled by Kenneth S. Rothwell and Annabelle Henkin Melzer in 1990.

—James M. Welsh

WORKS CONSULTED

Almereyda, Michael, "A Live Wire to the Brain: Hooking Up 'Hamlet,'" *The New York Times* (May 7, 2000), sec. 2, 19–22.

Ball, Robert Hamilton. *Shakespeare on Silent Film: A Strange, Eventful History*. London: George Allen and Unwin, 1968.

Denby, David, "Flesh and Blood," *The New Yorker* (May 15, 2000), 105–107.

Fierman, Daniel, "The Dane Event," *Entertainment Weekly*, 543 (June 2, 2000), 40–42.

Gerdes, Peter R, "Film and/or Theatre: Some Introductory Comments," *The Australian Journal of Screen Theory*, 7 (1980): 1–17.

Jonson, Ben. *Timber, or Discoveries, Being Observations on Men and Manners*. London: J.M. Dent, 1951.

Kott, Jan. *Shakespeare Our Contemporary*, tr. Boleslaw Taborski. Garden City, N.Y.: Doubleday Anchor Books, 1966.

Norman, Marc, and Tom Stoppard. *Shakespeare in Love: A Screenplay*. New York: Hyperion/Miramax, 1998.

Pirandello, Luigi, "Will Talkies Abolish the Theatre?" in *Pirandello & Film*, ed. Nina DaVinci Nichols and Jana O'Keefe Bazzoni. Lincoln: University of Nebraska Press, 1995.

Rothwell, Kenneth S. *A History of Shakespeare on Screen: A Century of Film and Television*. Cambridge, U.K.: Cambridge University Press, 1999.

Rothwell, Kenneth S., and Annabelle Henkin Melzer. *Shakespeare on Screen: An International Filmography and Videography*. New York: Neal-Schuman, 1990.

Silent Shakespeare: Such Stuff As Dreams Are Made on . . ., 1899–1911. British Film Institute National Film and Television Archive, 1999. 88 minutes.

Willson, Robert F., Jr. *Shakespeare in Hollywood, 1929–1956*. Madison, N.J.: Fairleigh Dickinson University Press, 2000.

ANTONY AND CLEOPATRA (1606–07)

Antony and Cleopatra (1972), U.K./Spain, directed by Charlton Heston, adapted by Pamela Davis; Folio Films.

The Play

Antony and Cleopatra is regarded by many critics as Shakespeare's most romantic tragedy, even more moving than *Romeo and Juliet*. Its mature hero and heroine qualify as fascinating figures, marked by many contradictions. In addition, they express their mutual passion in compelling and highly erotic poetry. Shakespeare locates their complex affair on a historical stage that features a struggle between Roman destiny and Egyptian luxury and decadence. This drama of a monumental love brought down by lovers blind to their self-destructive natures has fascinated audiences for centuries.

As the play opens, Antony has spent long days and nights in the arms of the Egyptian queen Cleopatra. Yet with news of his wife Fulvia's death, he suddenly feels the urge to return to Rome; that urge is intensified by reports from Octavius Caesar and Lepidus, who with Antony form the ruling triumvirate, that their power has been challenged by young Pompey. (A peace settlement is reached with Pompey aboard his yacht, but during the celebration it becomes clear that Octavius plans to destroy the upstart.) Upon his depar-

ture from Egypt, Antony confronts an angry, frightened Cleopatra, who worries that Rome and Octavius will keep her lover from returning. While in Rome, Antony agrees to an arranged marriage to Octavia, Caesar's sister, but his longing for Cleopatra prompts him to leave his new bride behind and return to Egypt. Before he arrives, however, Cleopatra learns of the marriage from a messenger whom she soundly whips in her rage. This behavior reveals the queen's petulance and lack of reason, prompting this wise remark from the messenger: "Gracious madam, I that do bring the news made not the match."

Antony's desertion of his new wife outrages Octavius, who now plans to move against Egypt and Antony without delay. But an aroused Antony, reunited with Cleopatra and relying on her navy, vows to fight with the fury that marked his earlier career. However, his greatness was achieved in land battles and not at sea; Antony's blindness to this and other military realities prompts scornful criticism from his chorus-like follower Enobarbus. When, after the first encounter with Caesar's forces, Cleopatra and her sailors desert the battle, Antony rebukes his mistress and harshly attacks himself for falling prey to her wiles. Desperate and stung by guilt, Cleopatra apologizes and wins back an uxorious Antony's love. But when Antony later sees her showing favor to one of Caesar's ambassadors, Antony loses control, orders the beating of the messenger, and accuses Cleopatra of being a whore. Again, the two are somehow reconciled; in that day's battle,

Antony manages to drive back Caesar's land forces. Despite the victory, his loyal follower Enobarbus decides to leave him, convinced that a weakened Antony has lost his ability to lead. When Antony sends his belongings after him, displaying not anger but love, Enobarbus is so moved by this magnanimous act that he dies of a broken heart.

In the final battle, Cleopatra's navy again flees the scene, leaving a shamed, defeated Antony in a suicidal mood. He turns once more on Cleopatra and tells her to rush to the "boy" Caesar, believing that she has betrayed him to save herself. Now despondent and frantic, Cleopatra sends word to Antony that she has killed herself. When Antony receives the dreadful news, he begs his fittingly named servant Eros to dispatch him; after Eros refuses and kills himself instead, Antony falls on his own sword. With Caesar closing in on them, the two lovers find refuge in Cleopatra's monument. Here the wounded Antony expires, describing himself ironically as "a Roman by a Roman/Valiantly vanquished." Left alone, Cleopatra devises a plan to avoid falling into Caesar's hands, to be paraded through the streets of Rome and scorned by gleeful citizens. When a clown brings her a basket of poisonous asps, she takes one and presses it to her breast, dying after her servants have dressed her in royal robes. Caesar enters too late to win his Egyptian prize but seizes the moment to praise Antony and comment on the great "solemnity" of these tragic events.

The Film

Charlton Heston's version of *Antony and Cleopatra* was rehearsed for weeks in London before being shot in Spain; Heston was following the advice of his mentors, Olivier and Welles, in his approach. When it was finished, the film was not widely distributed, perhaps because the actor-director did not feel his product met the demanding standards of his predecessors. One of the reasons for regarding it as a disappointment is the production's derivative quality. It looks much like earlier Hollywood attempts at Roman epics, films like *Quo Vadis?* (1951) and *Ben-Hur* (1959). Indeed, sea-battle scenes from *Ben-Hur* were intercut to represent the Actium encounter—and to save money. Action scenes involving ships ramming other ships and Roman cavalry charging Antony's foot troops likewise dominate the screen. When Antony negotiates his marriage to Octavius's sister, the scene occurs against the backdrop of gladiators struggling on the Colosseum floor below. As one combatant throws down the other, Antony and Octavius conclude their compact, and the crowd her-

alds Caesar's power with a thumbs-up gesture. The musical score by John Scott and Augusto Algero relies heavily on strings to create a Hollywood-style romanticism and to accentuate the film and Cleopatra's many mood changes. The sybaritic atmosphere in Cleopatra's Court, with billowing curtains, seductive servants, and reclining bodies recalls the settings from biblical epics like *David and Bathsheba* (1951) and *The Robe* (1953).

Heston's Antony and Hildegard Neil's Cleopatra lack the fire that we might expect from such passionate characters. Neil in particular fails to achieve the stature of a queen; she seems more the spoiled bad girl striving to seduce the handsome quarterback. Shots of her speaking while being made up or massaged dominate the Egyptian court sequences. Perhaps Heston couldn't escape the god-like identity he had established as Moses in *The Ten Commandments*. Both appear to be acting on a stage, rather than in the naturalistic context of film. Their relationship relies heavily on props as well: To keep her Antony from leaving, Cleopatra loops a long string of pearls over his neck, pulling him slowly toward her. The death scenes likewise appear wooden and staged, with neither actor achieving the mix of pathos and sensuality that Shakespeare's lines call for.

Some notable performances are delivered by John Castle as Octavius and Eric Porter as Enobarbus. Castle manages to catch the equivocal nature of Octavius, a man destined for imperial rule who can also be petty and vengeful. Porter's Enobarbus is forced to deliver his description of Cleopatra's barge to an Athenian servant and to speak the lines of deleted characters, but he looks and sounds like Antony's only true admirer. Jane Lapotaire, who would play Cleopatra in the 1981 BBC-TV production, performs convincingly as Charmian and Roger Delgado enacts his roles as soothsayer and clown with considerable skill. On the whole, however, Heston's attempt at epic Shakespeare in the manner of Olivier and Welles leaves much in the way of verbal and visual power to be desired.

REFERENCES

Crowl, Samuel, "A World Elsewhere: The Roman Plays on Film and Television," in *Shakespeare and the Moving Image: The Plays on Film and Television*, ed. Anthony Davies and Stanley Wells (Cambridge: Cambridge University Press, 1994), 146–162; Rothwell, Kenneth S., *A History of Shakespeare on Screen: A Century of Film and Television* (Cambridge: Cambridge University Press, 1999); Rothwell, Kenneth S., and Annabelle Henkin Melzer, *Shakespeare on Screen: An International Filmography and Videography* (New York: Neal-Schuman, 1990)

—R.F.W.

AS YOU LIKE IT (1599)

As You Like It (1912), U.S.A., directed by Charles Kent, adapted by Margaret Birch; Vitagraph.

As You Like It (1936), U.K., directed by Paul Czinner, adapted by R.J. Culen and J.M. Barrie; Twentieth Century British Fox.

As You Like It (1978), U.K., directed by Basil Coleman, adapted by Alan Shallcross; British Broadcasting Company/Time-Life Television.

As You Like It (1985), Canada, directed by Herb Roland, adapted by John Hirsch; Canadian Broadcasting Corporation.

As You Like It (1992), U.K., directed and adapted by Christine Edzard; Sands Films.

The Play

When Orlando, youngest son of Sir Rowland de Boys, complains to his brother, Oliver, that he is tired of being confined to menial farm work rather than receiving the training appropriate to a gentleman, he is told by Oliver to leave and take with him Oliver's servant, old Adam. Oliver then tries to get the wrestler Charles to injure Orlando in the next day's competition. Best friends Celia, daughter to Duke Frederick, who rules the court, and Rosalind, daughter of the banished duke Senior, who lives in the forest of Arden, "like the old Robin Hood of England," go to the match. Rosalind falls in love with Orlando and tries to persuade him not to fight. When he wins, she gives him a necklace, leaving him tongue-tied but equally smitten. Duke Frederick congratulates Orlando on the victory, but becomes angry when he learns Orlando is the son of Sir Rowland, so angry that he shortly tells Rosalind, whose banished father was a friend of Sir Rowland, that she must leave his court. Not wanting to be separated, the two women decide to disguise themselves and go into the woods. Rosalind will become the young man, Ganymede, and Celia will be Ganymede's sister, Aliena, a name that reflects her state in life. When Duke Frederick finds out that Rosalind, Celia, and Orlando have all left at the same time, he speculates they went together and tells Oliver to bring Orlando back or forfeit his lands.

Meanwhile, the woods are a paradise to Duke Senior and his followers, except for Jaques, a melancholic who moralizes that the duke's men are all "usurpers" and "tyrants" for hunting. Orlando, having arrived in the forest with old Adam, who is exhausted and unable to go on, breaks into the duke's camp, sword drawn and expecting the men to be "savage," and demands food. While Orlando goes to bring Adam, Jaques delivers his "seven ages of man" speech, concluding, ironically, with the image of dismal old age just as Orlando returns carrying Adam into the camp where they are welcomed and fed. At the same time and elsewhere, Rosalind, Celia, and their fool, Touchstone, appear, buy a cottage, and meet Silvius, a shepherd hopelessly in love with Phebe, who barely tolerates him. Rosalind, Celia, and Touchstone all find poems nailed to the trees, poems praising Rosalind. While Touchstone parodies them, Celia realizes that Orlando must be their author, and shortly they encounter him in the forest. Rosalind complains that someone, clearly sick from love, is defacing the trees. When Orlando confesses he is the one, she offers to cure him by taking Rosalind's part and being fickle and demanding. Rosalind also tries to tell the shepherdess, Phebe, to be kinder to poor Silvius, but her scolding only makes Phebe fall in love with the person she knows as Ganymede. When Orlando shows up an hour late, Rosalind scolds him and then has Celia act as priest for a mock wedding. Later, when he is again late, not Orlando but his brother Oliver arrives, saying he has a message from Orlando, who has been injured saving Oliver's life from a lion. Seeing a handkerchief with Orlando's blood, Rosalind faints. Oliver and Celia fall instantly in love.

Reunited with Orlando, Rosalind says she has magical powers and will solve the various love problems. She will satisfy Orlando, Silvius, and Phebe in their separate desires. Meanwhile Touchstone has met, won, and wedded a simple country-woman named Audrey. Rosalind enters dressed now as a woman. Unable to pursue Ganymede, Phebe agrees to marry Silvius; Oliver will marry Celia, and Rosalind will marry Orlando. Duke Senior recognizes Rosalind as his daughter. The group receives word that Duke Frederick, on his way to find and kill Duke Senior, has met a holy man, converted, and renounced the world. Duke Senior is the new ruler. The melancholy Jaques says he will go to find Duke Frederick. The rest of the company dance, and then Rosalind steps forward and delivers an epilogue.

The Films

One of America's first film companies, the Vitagraph Company of America, located in the Flatbush section of Brooklyn, New York, devoted only a small portion of its filmmaking to Shakespeare, but the effort was significant in developing the tradition of filmed Shakespeare. The director of the Vitagraph *As You Like It*, Charles Kent, had earlier filmed outdoor Shakespeare in *A Midsummer Night's Dream* (1909) and *Twelfth Night* (1910), and he made good use of locations for the pastoral elements of this play. *As You Like It* was somewhat longer than earlier Vitagraph Shakespeare films, three reels rather than two, and it was unusual in relying on the celebrity appeal of stage actress Rose Coghlan, who had played the role of Rosalind in the 1880s. Robert Hamilton Ball quotes from a contemporary review that calls her "one of America's most celebrated actresses," but in spite of her energetic performance it is impossible to overlook the fact that she was 60. The Robin Hood motif is apparent in all the woods scenes, and, unlike some versions of the play, this one shows Rosalind making a serious effort at creating a woodsmanly appearance. Coghlan clearly indicates in broad gestures when her actions are intended to show how Orlando's beloved might act. She is playing at being a man imitating a woman rather than being a woman trying to act like a man. At one point, when Rosalind accidentally leans against Orlando's chest, Oliver and Celia laugh at the accidental contact, and Rosalind quickly straightens up.

The film creates an odd tension between its written and visual elements. Ball makes the point that the film uses extensive titles, "472 feet, a total of almost half a reel." The complications of the play, of course, need a certain amount of explaining, but scenarist Margaret Birch's script sometimes invents scenes that Shakespeare only implies through dialogue. For example, the opening of the film shows Duke Frederick banishing Duke Senior but making his daughter, Rosalind, stay in court as companion to Celia. The following scene shows Sir Rowland De Boys, on his death bed, asking his oldest son, Oliver, to take care of the two younger brothers. Only after these scenes does the film reach the point at which Shakespeare opened the play—with Orlando's complaint about his forced rusticity. Another example occurs when the film illustrates Jaques's "seven ages of man" speech by cutting away to shots of characters in each of the seven stages. Rothwell and Melzer say that "The cinematic peak occurs with the use of cross-cutting to illustrate Jacques' Seven Ages speech," and they may be right, but the device seems confusing at first partly because it is not immediately apparent that these shots are intended to illustrate the speech. Finally, it seems as though the sequence could easily stand separate from the rest of the film. A similarly awkward moment occurs when Orlando must rescue the sleeping Oliver from the lion. Shakespeare has

Oliver tell the story briefly in about 20 lines to Celia and Rosalind. The film dramatizes the situation. Orlando first sees Oliver sleeping, then sees a truly ridiculous lion's head sticking out of the bushes, then starts to walk away, realizes he cannot, takes off his jacket, pulls out his sword, and goes into the bushes, presumably to fight the lion. Oliver is apparently awakened by the movement in the bushes, which are shaking violently, and then Orlando comes out injured and bleeding. Ball points out that Vitagraph did not own a lion and did what it could with what it had, but the real problem again seems to be adding scenes that distract from the narrative flow and slow it down.

In discussing Paul Czinner's 1936 *As You Like It*, probably the first thing to get out of the way is the issue of Elisabeth Bergner's Rosalind. Bergner, the wife of director Czinner, had some reputation on the German stage, and it was Bergner who suggested getting Laurence Olivier to play the part of Orlando after she saw him in *Romeo and Juliet*. Olivier himself in an interview before he made the film said "No one can play with Bergner without learning something from her." Some years later, however, in his book, *On Acting*, Olivier said she "crucified the verse with her German accent." Critics who like Bergner's Rosalind find her charming, sprightly, and kittenish, but those who do not like her find her performance irritating, "disastrous," and "anxiously inappropriate." Her accent certainly does affect her reading of the lines. When she gets excited, for example, when she tries to find out who has been nailing poems about Rosalind on the trees in Arden forest, she is extremely difficult to understand.

The core problem with her performance, however, has to do with an issue that would probably not have occurred on Shakespeare's stage. Bergner seems to make absolutely no attempt to develop a pattern of action that could be taken as masculine behavior. Instead she is feminine in a coy, mincing, and effervescent manner. At the end of the mock marriage ceremony, for example, she calls after Orlando, hangs on the long vowel sounds in "Adieu" and "two," as in "two o'clock," hugs and kisses a tree, and then does a somersault to demonstrate her enthusiasm. Not a few critics have complained specifically about the somersault. On the Elizabethan stage, Rosalind would, of course, have been played by a man who was playing a woman playing a man. Perhaps that particular arrangement of societal construction versus stage construction would solve the problem, but Anthony Holden, in his biography of Olivier, says that when Olivier saw that no audience could possibly imagine that this Orlando could mistake this Rosalind for a man, he "tried to make up for it by adding an edge of madness to Orlando's high spirits."

As this dilemma might suggest, in some respects the film often seems unsure of its direction and fluctuates between the real and the artificial. Quite a few of the ribald or more cynical lines have been cut, and the intent seems to have been to make this a pretty play, with real clouds floating in the sky, and real sheep wandering through a somewhat stylized forest—itself a combination of actual and painted elements. The interiors of Duke Frederick's castle have an ornate but very physical quality to them. Celia's room, in particular, is in a very large, late-medieval castle, but it is a mixture of elaborate, almost confectionery effects and solid stone. Likewise, the opening scenes of Olivier in the peasant environment seem to be modeled on earthy characters and compositions from Bruegel, but the first view of Rosalind and Celia, in their pointed hats and wimples, seems to come from French illuminated manuscripts. Rothwell points out that designer Lazare Meerson's "sudden release of genuine sheep, rabbits, and squirrels into the mise-en-scène shattered the fragile world of his imaginary barnyards and woods." These ambiguities of style, along with the gender ambiguity, perhaps explain the ending of the film. Bergner steps outside the gates, which have enclosed the other members of the wedding party, and, in some of the most heavily accented and unintelligible delivery in the film, speaks the epilogue to the play. When she speaks to the women, she appears in men's clothing and waves a stick that she has carried for the last several scenes of the film, but when she speaks to the men, she reappears in her wedding dress and curtsies, as the line requires, when she finishes the speech. Rather than pursue Shakespeare's original emphasis on the ambiguity of roles, the film instead tries to have it both ways, and both images, male and female, appear in a somewhat stylized pair of characterizations.

Christine Edzard's 1992 modern-dress version of *As You Like It* is interesting, at least in part because of its particular emphasis on contrasting the opposing situations and attitudes in the play and underscoring them by clearly paralleling some of its characters. The major difference between Edzard's version and Shakespeare's play, the issue at any rate that most critics seemed to react to, was that while Shakespeare emphasizes the difference between court and country by drawing on the conventions of the romance, and especially on the idealized conventions of the pastoral world, Edzard draws on a very different set of conventions. In her production the opposition seems to be between bankers and homeless people, the haves and the have nots, or, as Kenneth S. Rothwell puts it, "the wretched

of the earth . . . implicitly condemn the callous Thatcherites."

When this film's scruffy looking Orlando is cast out by his pinstriped and over-coated banker brother (both parts played by Andrew Tiernan), he ends up not in Arden forest but in an urban wasteland where a man stands warming his hands over something that is burning in a 50-gallon metal drum. The economic context gives a new shade of meaning to, for example, wrestler Charles' lines when he tells Oliver "I wrestle for my credit," or when he boasts of how he will defeat Orlando and "give him his payment." Adhering effectively to the logic of the economic context Edzard imposes on the play, this Orlando articulates his love for Rosalind by spray-painting graffiti on walls and fences rather than by hanging poems on trees. Another benefit from this approach may be that the contemporary ambiguity in dress and gender roles makes this Rosalind more easily able to function as a young man. In jeans, pea jacket, and watch cap, she is certainly more believable, if that is a valid criterion, than many of the Robin Hood-attired actresses who usually try this role. In addition, Emma Croft emphasizes physical activity in a way that other Rosalinds do not, or, recalling Elizabeth Bergner's somersaulting performance, certainly Croft is more effectively physical than any other Rosalind. She very simply works at being a tomboy. She tends toward under-expressing emotion rather than being coy. In the mock wedding scene, she seizes Tiernan's hand as though she were about to arm wrestle. When he has to leave, she runs after him and they shout their lines as they run together.

Several writers have objected to Edzard's modernization, but while it is true that much of the film simply does not succeed, the concept behind the Rosalind-Orlando characterization seems promising even if it does not quite achieve that promise. An odd logic sometimes seems to control the handling of other parts of the play. The two incidents that might be dangerous to Orlando, for example, are inexplicably muted. The wrestling match at the beginning of the play seems well enough prepared for, but when the time arrives for the bout, the crowd that gathers completely blocks out any view of even the slightest action. This evading of one of the set-pieces of the play mostly calls attention to the scene's absence. Later, when Oliver tells Celia and Rosalind that Orlando was injured while rescuing him, the film cuts to a very dark flashback scene in which Orlando apparently stops a tramp from robbing the sleeping Oliver and is injured in the process. A similar muting seems to occur in some of the other characterizations. The vaguely pained expression on James Fox's face throughout the film suggests, for example, that his Jaques may be more dyspeptic than melancholic, a characterization that is probably not intended as an allusion to the Jaques/jakes pun embedded in the implied pronunciation of this character's name. Finally the visual pairing of characters at the end seems a little forced, so Oliver and Orlando, Duke Frederick and Duke Senior, Corin and LeBeau, among others, all seem to gaze oddly at each other, as though they had just now understood Edzard's true intentions.

The two made-for-television productions of *As You Like It* are in many ways better than most television versions tend to be. Helen Mirren as Rosalind and Richard Pasco as Jaques bring an exceptionally high level of acting to the BBC production, although both tend to play their roles more seriously than one might expect in this play, which is one of Shakespeare's greenest pastorals. The BBC version perhaps should not really be called a taped stage production since it was all shot at Glamis Castle and in the Scottish countryside. In fact, critics who were used to stage presentations and more stylized versions of the play seemed to be struck by the sheer leafiness of the BBC production of the play—real trees in a real forest. Maurice Charney, for example, says this version "evoked all the wish-fulfillment images of pastoral," while Jack Jorgens says "seldom have natural settings been used to less effect." J.C. Bulman probably frames the issue best when he says that "The more realistic the setting, the more we are inclined to apply the criteria of naturalistic drama to the action. Thus, inevitably, we begin to question the logic of the play." The visual impact of the forest is impressive, but there is no question that it sometimes overwhelms the actors by pointing up somehow the artificiality of the entire enterprise. Hence, for example, when Celia (Angharad Rees) comes on carrying one of Orlando's poems, it is apparent that the parchment, which might have worked well on a stage, in this setting looks as though Orlando (Brian Stirner) has been writing his poems on a giant corn chip. An artificial stage setting would have allowed everything to be taken as convention, but the sheer reality of vibrantly green trees blowing against a very blue sky accentuates the contrast. Jorgens says that there is "warfare" between the realistic setting and "a play which is essentially a fairy tale in verse," but Bulman finds several examples where director Basil Coleman manages to use the real setting as a way to "put quotation marks around the pastoral artifice."

The question of how reality intrudes on the artifice of the play perhaps extends to the characterizations as well. Helen Mirren is an exceptionally attractive and buxom Rosalind in this play and could not easily be taken for a young man. The film's Orlando, on the other hand, is slender, seems somewhat younger, and is not, according to most reviewers, someone who might inspire Rosalind's interest. How then is an audience to believe that Orlando does not notice that the character before him is clearly not a young man? Approaching the issue from another way, Bulman says that the actors must play their love scenes as "a game that neither mistakes for reality," but the fact is that the very reality of the setting diminishes the ability to suspend as many levels of disbelief as one must to enjoy all the things that this play tries to do.

Like other films from the Stratford (Ontario) Shakespeare Festival, Herb Roland's film of the John Hirsh production of *As You Like It* records an excellent performance of the play, apparently before a live audience. The staging is imaginative, the characterization very well thought out, and the several levels of comedy operating in this play all seem to work unusually well. Jaques (Nicholas Pennell) is here perhaps more thoughtful than he is sometimes presented. He is certainly not just vituperative, not just a scold who is occasionally funny. Instead he is presented as a clever man whose humor digs at both the pastoral and romantic conventions of the play. Touchstone (Lewis Gordon) is vigorous, with plenty of stage business to flesh out his long speeches. His bantering about the philosophies of court and country, for example, include magic tricks with an egg and some miming of a golf swing and lining up a pool shot. Silvius and Phebe (Mary Haney and John Jarvis) are appropriately daffy in their respective bouts of love sickness. More than these, Rosalind (Roberta Maxwell) and Celia (Rosemary Dunsmore) manage to fill their roles with humor; both seem to operate from a basic sense of decorum that immediately seizes on the peculiarity of many of the situations in the play. Rosalind is especially good at suddenly adopting a hale-and-hearty masculine manner as soon as she realizes that her bubbling affections threaten to create an embarrassing situation with her buddy (and secret love) Orlando. For his part, Orlando (Andrew Gillies) does a good job of demonstrating the silly side of sincerity, a quality that the literary criticism of his sonnets clearly implies, but a quality that is not often explored by actors who take this role.

Visually this production is most striking in its opening scenes where the icy world of the cruel duke Frederick is presented as a real winter, with heavily dressed characters going back and forth in a very palpable representation of cold weather. More metaphorically, Duke Frederick's entourage consists of men and women dressed entirely in black and silver, with some of the men even wearing dark glasses. They are, of course, additions to the play, but they add considerably to the characterization of this world to which the pastoral world of Duke Senior stands in clear contrast. Contrary to some productions, the handling of the scenes in the woods tends here to be somewhat restrained, and, indeed, the effect seems to accumulate. When Orlando first goes into the woods, his poems are stuck on what seem to be branches stuck in stumps. By the end of the play, at the wedding scene, the pillars supporting the upper playing area are trees green with leaves, and the "country copulatives" gather at both levels as a half-dozen women in white dresses dance in a circle holding lighted candelabras. The effect of the green and white and the glowing candles is the visual counter to the darkness of the opening scenes. Rosalind's delivery of the closing lines is, like the production itself, clear, simple, and straightforward.

REFERENCES

Ball, Robert Hamilton, *Shakespeare on Silent Film* (London: George Allen and Unwin, 1968); Bulman, J.C., "'As You Like It' and the Perils of Pastoral," *Shakespeare on Television*, eds. J.C. Bulman and H.R. Coursen (Hanover, N.H.: University Press of New England, 1988), 174–179; Holden, Anthony, *Laurence Olivier* (New York: Atheneum, 1998); Jackson, Russell, "Shakespeare's Comedies on Film," *Shakespeare and the Moving Image*, eds. Anthony Davies and Stanley Wells (Cambridge: Cambridge University Press, 1994), 99–120; Manville, Roger, *Shakespeare and the Film* (New York: Praeger, 1971); Olivier, Laurence, *On Acting* (New York: Simon and Schuster, 1986); Rothwell, Kenneth S., *A History of Shakespeare on Screen* (Cambridge: Cambridge University Press, 1999); Rothwell, Kenneth S., and Annabelle Melzer, *Shakespeare on Screen* (New York: Neal Schuman, 1900); Willis, Susan, *The BBC Shakespeare Plays: Making the Televised Canon* (Chapel Hill: University of North Carolina Press, 1991).

—*R.V.*

CYMBELINE (1609–10)

Cymbeline (1913), U.S.A., directed by Frederick Sullivan; Edwin Thanhouser Films.

Cymbeline (1982), U.K., directed by Elijah Moshinsky, adapted by David Snodin; British Broadcasting Company/Time-Life Films.

The Play

Cymbeline, king of Britain, beguiled by his duplicitous new queen's beauty and angered by his daughter Imogen's refusal to marry the queen's foolish son, Cloten, banishes Posthumus, the "poor but worthy" man Imogen has married. In Rome, Posthumus almost immediately falls into a wager with the crafty Iachimo, who bets that he can easily seduce Imogen, in spite of Posthumus's description of her goodness. In Britain, Iachimo tells Imogen that Posthumus has been untrue and she should sleep with Iachimo to revenge herself. Rebuffed by the virtuous Imogen, Iachimo says it was only a test of her honor and asks to store a treasure for the emperor in her bedroom. Later that night, Iachimo himself leaps out of the trunk, takes note of the room and of Imogen's marks, steals the bracelet Posthumus gave her, and hides back in the trunk. That morning, when Cloten again attempts to convince her to love him, Imogen tells him she loves Posthumus's "meanest garment" more than she could ever love

Cloten. Back in Rome, Iachimo describes the room, shows the bracelet, and, when Posthumus concedes that his wife is unfaithful, Iachimo goes on to describe the mole on Imogen's breast. Having won the bet, Iachimo leaves a disillusioned Posthumus ranting against all women.

When King Cymbeline, urged by the queen and Cloten, rejects Rome's request for tribute, General Caius Lucius threatens war. Meanwhile, Posthumus's servant, Pisanio, has received one letter from Posthumus telling him to kill Imogen and another asking Imogen to meet him at Milford-Haven. Excited by the letter Pisanio shows her, Imogen makes plans to leave disguised. When they reach their destination, Pisanio tells her Posthumus's real plan, promises to lie to Posthumus, and urges her to disguise herself as a boy and serve "the noble" Caius Lucius, who will keep her safe. In Wales, Belarius, the old courtier exiled 20 years before by Cymbeline, has raised the king's sons, Guiderius and Arviragus, as his own and taught them to recognize simple virtue and disdain the devious courtly life. Cloten, in the meantime, has found out about Imogen's flight to Milford-Haven and gets Pisanio to take him there, secretly planning to be dressed in Posthumus's clothing and rape Imogen when he finds her. But Imogen has been found by Belarius and the princes, her brothers, who feel an instant attraction to Fidele, as Imogen is calling herself. Cloten encounters Guiderius, who kills and beheads Cloten. Belarius recognizes Cloten and realizes they now are in danger of discovery. Just then, Arviragus discovers the body of the apparently dead Fidele. Imogen, exhausted and feeling ill, had taken the restorative potion that Pisanio got from the queen. Luckily, rather than the poison the queen thought she had given him, the medicine is only a drug substituted by Cornelius, the court physician, who suspected the queen's intentions. Nonetheless, Fidele seems dead, so the boys sing over the dead bodies of Fidele and Cloten. When she later awakes, Fidele sees the headless body, dressed in her husband's clothing, and believes it is Posthumus. Caius Lucius arrives and takes the mourning Fidele into his service.

While Cymbeline prepares to battle the Romans, a repentant Posthumus, dressed as a Roman, vows to take off "these Italian weeds" and fight dressed as "a Briton peasant," thinking to expiate his crime through battle. So dressed, Posthumus defeats Iachimo, who does not recognize him but takes his defeat as a sign of his own crimes. Belarius, Guiderius, and Arviragus rescue Cymbeline from the Romans, and the ragged Posthumus helps them defend their position. After the battle, Posthumus changes back into Roman clothing and allows himself to be taken by the victorious British. The jailed Posthumus has a dream in which his dead parents and brothers pray for Jupiter to help him, and Jupiter, descending on an eagle and casting lightning bolts, leaves a prophecy to be interpreted later. Posthumus awakens and is brought before Cymbeline.

Gathered before King Cymbeline, the various characters now sort out their stories. Cornelius, the physician, says the queen has died and confessed to her treachery. Lucius asks for mercy for his servant Fidele, and while Fidele and Cymbeline talk, Belarius and the king's sons recognize the visitor they thought dead. Imogen, as Fidele, asks Iachimo where he got the ring he wears. Iachimo confesses his deception and his offense against the king's daughter. Posthumus steps forward, identifies himself, and threatens Iachimo. When Imogen tries to calm him, Posthumus knocks her down. Pisanio then recognizes Imogen and tells Posthumus that he has just struck his wife, who is still alive. Cornelius adds the information about the drug, which explains how Imogen apparently died, and Pisanio tells how he took Cloten to Milford-Haven. At this point, Guiderius confesses to killing Cloten, and is ready to be punished, but Belarius says Guiderius killed someone who was of lesser rank, since he and Aviragus are the king's lost sons, which he proves by showing their birthmarks. King Cymbeline pardons everyone. The Roman soothsayer explicates Jupiter's message to mean that the king's sons are restored and

Rome and Britain can live in peace. Cymbeline agrees to pay a tribute and declares peace.

The Films

Although this play has its enthusiasts and has been produced more often in the last decade than in most of the rest of the century, many people have agreed with Samuel Johnson on "the folly of the fiction, the absurdity of the conduct, the confusion of the names and manners of different times and the impossibility of the events in any system of life." Perhaps not surprisingly then, no modern commercial film of *Cymbeline* has been attempted. Edwin Thanhouser made a silent version in 1913, and the BBC filmed the play in 1982, as part of its series.

Edwin Thanhouser and his wife, Gertrude, brought the benefits of an extensive theatrical background to their filmmaking. Establishing his Thanhouser Film Corporation in New Rochelle, New York, in 1909, Thanhouser used literary sources for several films that he made between 1909 and 1912, when he sold the company. Kenneth S. Rothwell and Annabelle Melzer call him "the supreme *auteur* of the silent Shakespeare film in America" and note particularly his "effective *mise en scène*," "cinematically based exterior action shots," and "sharp even lighting." Recently arrived from England, Frank Sullivan, who directed *Cymbeline*, directed more than a dozen films and toward the end of his career had several uncredited acting parts in Marx Brothers films. James Cruze, later to become famous for directing *The Covered Wagon* (1923), played Posthumus, and Florence LaBadie, the best-known and most popular actress of Thanhouser's group, played Imogen. They had acted together in other Thanhouser films, such as the previous year's *Dr. Jekyll and Mr. Hyde*.

This silent *Cymbeline* has several qualities to recommend it. Among these is the clear emphasis on Imogen as the virtuous heroine who undergoes a series of catastrophic events. This theme of the virtuous heroine beset by multiple misfortunes was a popular melodramatic device of the time, and the Thanhouser script casts the play in that mold. Shakespeare's play is not at all as straightforward in its emphasis, but, although the silent film loses some in accuracy, it gains from the focusing and cutting that was necessary to get it down to about 40 minutes. This film also does a good job of keeping the various groups in the film clearly separated by easily identifiable means. The members of the British Court wear Germanic-looking costumes, with horned helmets and metal breastplates, while Belarius, Guiderius, and Arviragus wear furs and have a more rustic appearance. The Romans wear the traditional togas, but the soldiers invading Britain wear the short tunic under a breastplate. British men have long hair, while the Romans all have short hair.

The film frames the action somewhat differently from Shakespeare's method and opens with a forest scene of Belarius and the king's sons, so the emphasis immediately is on a divided family. The titles indicate that the king's sons are being raised by a courtier who stole them. From here, the scene shifts back to King Cymbeline's Court and follows the sequence of the play with several omissions. In a series of brief scenes, alternating between the Court and a garden area, the film makes clear that Imogen is being coerced to marry Cloten, but loves Posthumus, whom King Cymbeline then exiles. The queen's role as evil stepmother seems perfectly clear, although details of her story, such as her attempt to poison Imogen, are left out of the film. Cloten is introduced as a suitor of Imogen, but the script does not make clear that he is the queen's son, and, later, his pursuit of Imogen, his death in the fight with Guiderius, and the discovery of his body by Imogen are all left out. With the connecting device of the funeral services missing, Imogen is here instead simply captured by Caius's troops. The elaborate dream scene, the prophecy, and the whole connection of Posthumus with his ancestry and with the future of Britain is omitted. Instead the ending of the film consists of a series of confessions and forgivings. Belarius immediately confesses his guilt in having taken the boys, and Cymbeline immediately forgives him. Next Iachimo confesses his crime and gives the ring back to Posthumus. Imogen embraces him, and the brothers embrace their father, King Cymbeline. In this film, the family is reunited, even if all the cosmic and historical forces Shakespeare outlined are largely subordinated or ignored.

The BBC, in its dedication to mount relatively uncut television productions of all the plays, forces its *Cymbeline* into another set of problems and solutions. The changes are less in the lines of the play than in its visual impact. For example, the lines spoken by one of the Gentlemen, a minor character Shakespeare uses to develop background information in the opening and to comment on Cloten's (Paul Jesson) cloddishness later in the play, in this production are given to the physician, Cornelius (Hugh Thomas), another character with, in his case, an important few lines. The effect is to make Cornelius a recognizable character who seems to be commentator and mover behind the scenes throughout the entire play. In Shakespeare's play, he substitutes a non-lethal drug for the poison the queen (Claire Bloom) requests, apparently giving her some-thing like the drug Juliet must have taken in *Romeo and Juliet*. He appears again at the end to tell Cymbeline (Richard Johnson) that the queen died confessing her crimes. In the BBC production he appears in the opening scene and then intermittently to comment and reflect or simply to stand in the background. By the end of the play, when he appears with the news about the queen, the impression is that he is probably the only person in the play who had a clear idea of what was happening underneath all the appearances.

Another visual simplification occurs with the handling of Shakespeare's four separate loci in this play, places that represent values as much or more than actual physical location. Shakespeare was, of course, working on a bare stage, but clearly the world of Cymbeline's Court is contrasted with the woodland world of Belarius and the princes who have retreated to a place where they can find simpler values that have been lost in the more sophisticated but corrupt Court. Rome is also two places; it is both the world of ancient Rome, inhabited by the noble Caius Lucius, and the corrupt world of Renaissance Rome, represented by the treacherous Iachimo. The BBC *Cymbeline* tends to simplify these distinctions into a case of Rome versus Britain. Caius Lucius (Graham Crowden) is dressed in the general soldier costume worn by other Romans. The anachronistic costuming of Thanhouser's silent version is lost. Instead the BBC *Cymbeline* tries to present Renaissance Rome as the evil city that Imogen imagines will ruin Posthumus. In this Rome, for example, the chess players are being served by bare-chested waiters and a dwarf, left over from *A Midsummer Night's Dream*. The impression is meant to convey a dangerous sensuality, and Iachimo's scenes with Imogen (Helen Mirren) carry out the suggestion. In this production, she seems genuinely tempted by Iachimo's offer to betray her husband. Later, in the bedroom scene, Iachimo is, for some unknown reason, bare-chested, and the camera visually links him with the sleeping Imogen, resulting in a scene that Susan Willis calls "lurid."

The suppression of certain physical effects may be part of this same effort at unity. For example, Shakespeare's final act in this play contains some spectacular scenes as well as actions that strain both credulity and convention. J.M. Nosworthy, in the Arden Edition, calls *Cymbeline* "transitional and experimental in style, as in other matters." One of the riskiest of these efforts perhaps is the event the stage directions describe this way: "Jupiter descends in thunder and lightning, sitting upon an eagle: he throws a thunderbolt. The Ghosts fall on their knees." In the BBC version, Jupiter (Michael Hordern) appears, does his business, and disappears. Roger Warren calls the scene "oddly unspectacular," and it may be that Shakespeare's scene would seem silly presented through the more realistic medium of television, but the shift seems to be part of the way the play is being read for this production. Again, Shakespeare merely uses stage directions to describe the fights, but these battles are significant, almost symbolic, shifts of power. First Posthumus (Michael Pennington), disguised as a "poor soldier," defeats Iachimo (Robert Lindsay), who, as a result, reflects that he "belied a lady,/The princess of this country" and thinks this defeat is a judgment on him and a sign of what is to come. Immediately after this, Cymbeline is captured by the Romans and then rescued by Belarius (Michael Gough) and the two princes, with Posthumus joining them to fight off the Roman army. Several characters later comment on the importance of the fight. In the BBC version, Posthumus stands in the foreground with the fires of battle behind him and simply describes what happened. The action is here discussed rather than presented.

When Katherine Duncan-Jones, reviewing the production, notes that the characters often sit, she may be commenting on this approach that makes the play seem more unified but also talkier than the play seems to be when read. Characters in this production do sit when they might easily be doing something. Cymbeline sits at the beginning of the play, as though overhearing what the Gentlemen are saying about the condition of the kingdom. When Posthumus visits Rome, the Romans sit and play chess. When Pisanio introduces Iachimo to the British court, Imogen is sitting and then sits while Iachimo sits next to her. Pisanio is sitting when he reads Posthumus's letter asking him to kill Imogen. At the end of the play, the Soothsayer sits to decipher the message from Jupiter. In addition, lines that Shakespeare has characters speak, here are sometimes delivered as voice-overs, with the camera moving in as if to enter the mind of the speaker, but also filling the screen with a static image of a face that is saying nothing. As a result, the play, in spite of excellent performances from an unusually fine cast, seems more meditative, and, without its battles and its descending Jupiter, somewhat less dynamic than it might have been.

REFERENCES

Ball, Robert Hamilton, *Shakespeare on Silent Film* (London: George Allen and Unwin, 1968); Bowers, Q. David, *Thanhouser Films: An Encyclopedia and History*, Thanhouser Company Film Preservation, Inc., CD-ROM (Lanham, Md.: Scarecrow Press, 1998); Duncan-Jones, Katherine, "Sitting Pretty," *Times Literary Supplement* (July 22, 1983), 773; Nosworthy, J.M., ed. *Cymbeline* (London: Methuen, 1969); Rothwell, Kenneth S., and Annabelle Henkin Melzer, *Shakespeare on Screen: An International Filmography and Videography* (New York: Neal Schuman, 1990); Willis, Susan, *The BBC Shakespeare Plays* (Chapel Hill: University of North Carolina Press, 1991).

—R.V.

HAMLET (1602)

Hamlet (1948), U.K., directed by Laurence Olivier, adapted by Laurence Olivier and Alan Dent; J. Arthur Rank/Two Cities.

Hamlet (1953), U.S.A., directed by George Schaefer and Albert McCleery, adapted by Mildred Freed Alberg and Tom Sand; NBC Hallmark Hall of Fame.

Hamlet (1960), Germany, directed and adapted by Franz Peter Wirth; Bavaria Atelier.

Hamlet (1964), USSR, directed and adapted by Grigori Kozintsev from Boris Pasternak's Russian translation of the play; Lenfilm/Sovexport.

Hamlet (1964), U.S.A., directed by John Gielgud (originally for the stage) and Bill Colleran, adapted by John Gielgud; Electronovision.

Hamlet (1969), U.K., directed and adapted by Tony Richardson; Woodfall.

Hamlet (1970), U.K./U.S.A., directed by Peter Wood and adapted for television by John Barton; NBC Hallmark Hall of Fame.

Hamlet (1990), U.S.A., directed by Franco Zeffirelli, adapted by Franco Zeffirelli and Christopher DeVore; Warner Bros.

Hamlet (1990), U.S.A., directed and adapted by Kevin Kline and Kirk Browning; WNET "Great Performances"/Corporation for Public Broadcasting.

Hamlet (1996), U.K., directed and adapted by Kenneth Branagh; Castle Rock Entertainment/Columbia Pictures.

Hamlet (2000), U.S.A., directed and adapted by Michael Almereyda; Miramax Films.

The Play

Arguably Shakespeare's most famous play, *Hamlet* first appeared in a corrupt, pirated edition, the so-called Bad Quarto of 1603, published by Nicholas Ling and John Trundell, which was later augmented by the corrected Second Quarto of 1604, "Newly imprinted and enlarged to almost as much again as it was, according to the true and perfect copy," as described on the title page. The First Folio edition of the play in 1623, published after Shakespeare's death by John Heminges and Henry Condell, contains approximately 90 lines not published in the Second Quarto, even though the Second Quarto is otherwise the most complete and substantive text. It is a very long play as a consequence.

The action begins with sentries on the castle walls at Elsinore, discussing with Horatio, the friend of Prince Hamlet, visitations by a mute ghost who seems to resemble the dead king. They decide to tell the prince what they have witnessed. In the next scene, set at court, the new king, Claudius, who has married Gertrude, his sister-in-law and Hamlet's mother, seems regal in his rhetoric and attentive to matters of state, particularly the potential foreign policy threat posed to Denmark by young Fortinbras, prince of Norway, who has raised an army and apparently intends to invade Denmark. After sending ambassadors to old Fortinbras, king of Norway, with instructions to keep the young prince in check, Claudius turns to domestic affairs and grants permission to Laertes, son of his councillor, Polonius, to travel to France. Finally, Claudius turns to domestic affairs and addresses Hamlet, who is still dressed in mourning clothes, grieving the death of his father. Claudius seems especially interested in establishing that Hamlet will stay in Denmark and not return to his studies in Wittenberg, presumably because this was an elected monarchy and Hamlet also had a valid claim to the throne. Hamlet's answer is laced with insolence, but, in deference to his mother, he promises to stay.

In the first soliloquy that follows ("O that this too too sullied flesh would melt,/Thaw, and resolve itself into a dew," I.ii.129–159), Hamlet is defined by his melancholy attitude and is extremely resentful of his mother's decision to marry Claudius, especially so soon after his father's death. Horatio and the guards visit him in this melancholy and suicidal state and tell him about the ghost that Hamlet will soon seek out. The ghost tells Hamlet of foul play, claiming that he was murdered while sleeping in his orchard by Claudius, who poured poison into his ear. Hamlet wants to believe what the ghost has told him but questions whether this "disturbed spirit" is truly the ghost of his dead father or a spirit sent from hell to tempt him into murdering his uncle. Hamlet makes Horatio and the guards swear not to divulge what they have seen and tells them of his plans to "put an antic disposition on" in order to give him license to make inappropriate comments under the guise of craziness.

Later, when a troupe of itinerant players arrives at Elsinore, Hamlet devises a way to test the veracity of what the ghost has told him, requesting that they perform a play called "The Murder of Gonzago," the plot of which resembles the scenario of his father's murder. Hamlet inserts a dozen additional lines to make this play more closely resemble what the ghost had told him. Hamlet and Horatio watch Claudius closely to see if he will register guilt when he sees the play. Claudius takes the bait in what Hamlet calls the "mousetrap," and Hamlet then knows that he must kill Claudius to avenge his father's murder.

Meanwhile, Claudius is spying on Hamlet, whom he rightly considers a threat to his Crown. His adviser Polonius offers to "loose his daughter," Ophelia, on Hamlet and to eavesdrop so as to learn more about Hamlet's intentions. By following her father's wishes, Ophelia must betray Hamlet, whom she loves, and Hamlet soon becomes aware of her intentions. Feeling betrayed by her, he turns on her and treats her roughly and indecently. Later still, Polonius hides behind an arras (a tapestry) while Hamlet meets privately with his mother in her bedchamber. Hamlet is so abusive of Gertrude that she calls out, evoking a response from hidden Polonius, whom Hamlet runs through with his sword, thinking it may be Claudius. Outraged by Hamlet's rash action, Claudius sends him to England with Hamlet's false friends, Rosencrantz and Guildenstern, who carry instructions to the English king to have Hamlet put to death upon his arrival there. Hamlet anticipates this villainy, however, and arranges to be rescued at sea by pirates, who will return him to Denmark.

In Hamlet's absence, Ophelia, emotionally disturbed by Hamlet's rejection of her and by the fact that the man she loves has murdered her father, goes quite mad and eventually drowns herself. Her enraged brother Laertes then returns from France, having heard about the death of his father, and finds his sister pathetically insane. Laertes holds Hamlet responsible for the death of his father and his sister. Hamlet arrives back in Denmark and is confronted by Laertes at her gravesite burial. Claudius plots the death of Hamlet with Laertes, arranging a duel between them. Laertes conspires to anoint the tip of his sword with poison so that Hamlet will be killed if scratched by his opponent's sword. Claudius arranges a drugged and poisoned cup of wine for Hamlet at the duel, but his plot backfires when Gertrude drinks the wine intended for Hamlet and dies. Hamlet is a better swordsman than Claudius imagined him to be, however, and after he is scratched by Laertes's sword, he manages to exchange weapons and wound Laertes, whose dying words alert Hamlet to Claudius's villainy. Hamlet kills Claudius, then dies, just before the arrival of the English ambassador and Fortinbras, who has crossed Denmark with his army and who claims the throne.

The Films

Since *Hamlet* has been filmed something like 43 times, this essay cannot be comprehensive and will cover only the best-known adaptations. Oddly enough, two of the earliest silent film treatments presented Hamlet as a cross-gendered Dane. The first film, released in

France in 1900, featured Sarah Bernhardt as Hamlet, but only in the duel scene, lasting a mere five minutes. In a 78-minute film released in Germany in 1920, shaped by Edward P. Vining's book *The Mystery of Hamlet* (1881), the prince (Asta Nielsen) is actually a princess, whom Gertrude had raised in disguise as a man. In 1913 Cecil Hepworth produced a 22-minute version of the play, especially notable because it featured the celebrated Victorian Shakespearean actor Sir Johnston Forbes-Robertson, who was, of course, far too old for the role. We shall pass over such oddities and move on to the sound features.

Laurence Olivier's *Hamlet* (1948) set the standard at mid-century because it was Olivier's interpretation, following upon the critical success of *Henry V*, which established the actor-director as the leading interpreter of the filmed Shakespeare. Olivier's *Hamlet* was honored by two Academy Awards, for Best Actor and for Best Picture. In approaching *Hamlet*, Olivier followed the Freudian interpretation of the play popular among critics in the late 1940s. Hamlet kisses his mother full on the mouth several times, for example, and the Freudian link is also emphasized both at the beginning and at the end, when the camera roams through the castle to the royal bedchamber, then zooms in on the "incestuous sheets." After the murder of Polonius (Felix Aylmer), Hamlet throws Gertrude (Eileen Herlie) down on the incestuous bed, and the sexual appeal of the queen is conveyed by the way she looks at her son. That glance seems to be a come-hither stare, but it also conveys a sense of anguish and concern.

The film now seems mannered and stylistically overdone, far too conscious of its attempt to be "cinematic." One effective touch is the way scene changes are signified by the camera's roving through the castle corridors. Hamlet's means of returning to Denmark after Claudius (Basil Sydney) sends him to England is doubly emphasized, by his words and by the visual enactment of his encounter with the pirates. Hamlet is made out to be the only survivor after having boarded the pirate ship: We see the other ship sinking. There is a general tendency here to sacrifice poetry for spectacle. The camera work is too often self-conscious and draws attention to itself through moving camera shots, zooms, and dissolves. Ophelia's floating on her back, singing, comes near to being ludicrous, while at the same time being eerie and pathetic. Contemporary critic James Agee generally praised Jean Simmons's portrayal of Ophelia, however. Michael Kustow described the ghost as "an out-of-focus vaporous apparition."

Olivier portrays Hamlet as a sensitive, superior, magnificent young man, overly made up to emphasize his Danishness. There are too many shots of Hamlet lolling about on the throne trying "to make up his mind." The rendering also makes Hamlet appear to be distant and aloof, and there is little cause to be much in sympathy with him for that reason. All in all he is too much the delicate Dane. Hamlet is perhaps at his best when he is bantering with Polonius. The way he poses, leaning against a pillar with his elbow and his hand covering his eyes gets an intentional laugh from the audience and helps to set up the "Fishmonger" scene (II.ii.: by calling Polonius a "fishmonger," Hamlet suggests that the "good old man" is a pimp, willing to prostitute his daughter for his own ends).

In general, Hamlet's lines have been cut back. One listens in vain, for example, for the "O what rogue and peasant slave am I" soliloquy (II.ii). With regard to textual fidelity, Charlton Hinman once remarked that Olivier's treatment was not so much one of modernization as of vulgarization. Hinman, a textual scholar and a "purist," would have objected, of course, to the way Olivier cut the play by nearly 1,900 lines, shortening and simplifying the drama and even sacrificing the "What a piece of work is a man" meditation (II.ii). In his defense, just reproducing the text was not his main agenda. Certainly Shakespeare's organization is disrupted, however, and scenes are rearranged or abridged to make the play conform to the conventions of film pacing and film narrative.

The film is simplified by the way the text has been cut to achieve a running time of two and one-half hours and by Olivier's voice-over at the beginning that proclaims "This is the tragedy of a man who could not make up his mind," which puts rather too much emphasis on the issue of Hamlet's alleged procrastination, as if that were a tragic flaw. Fortinbras and the issue of Norway are missing in Olivier's film, which ends with Hamlet's body being carried up the castle wall to the parapet where Hamlet had earlier delivered his "To be or not to be" soliloquy. Also gone are Rosencrantz and Guildenstern, which diminishes the theme of friendship so carefully worked out by Shakespeare. There is no second gravedigger. Reynaldo is not sent to France by Polonius to spy on Laertes.

There are many other omissions and changes. The "mousetrap" is reduced merely to the "dumb show" Hamlet had requested the actors to avoid, which in this production causes Claudius's discomfort and departure from the great hall. The film's "cinematic" flourishes are flamboyantly overdone, as in the "To be or not to be" soliloquy, spoken as an interior voice-over while the camera zooms in on the back of Hamlet's head to a tight close-up, then dissolves to the waves breaking below the castle wall, supposedly taking the viewer into the turmoil of his mind. The film was regarded as a benchmark production but now seems a bit musty and dated.

The next major *Hamlet* was a Hallmark Hall of Fame production for NBC television, directed by George Schaefer and starring Maurice Evans, broadcast on the anniversary of Shakespeare's christening in 1953. It was called a two-hour production, considered at the time "the longest drama ever done on American television," but the running time was only 90 minutes, according to Alice Griffin. Evans, who had played Hamlet on the Broadway stage, wanted to portray "the inner conflict" of a man "caught up in a web of circumstances which sets him to questioning the values and standards by which he has lived." Barry Jones provided good support as Polonius, but Sarah Churchill as Ophelia and Ruth Chatterton as Gertrude were judged "inadequate." Joseph Schildkraut was "adequate" as Claudius, however, as was Wesley Addy as Horatio.

The Maximilian Schell *Hamlet*, directed by Franz Peter Wirth for West German television in 1960, was respected in its day because of Schell's intelligent rendering of the prince. The film begins with an establishing shot of two empty thrones, one of which will be filled by Schell's dying Hamlet at the end, interpreted as a possible political reference to a divided Germany and evoking Jan Kott's Grand Mechanism of history. Schell's prince is notable for his emotional stability, well acted and "most royal," Lillian Wilds contended, in comparison to Hans Caninenberg's one-dimensional Claudius and Wanda Rotha's overacted Gertrude. The film was shot on a low budget, the sets stylized and claustrophobic, the action filmed predominantly in medium and close-up shots. The film might have retained its critical favor had the language been subtitled rather than dubbed into English from the German.

The Russian *Hamlet* directed by Grigori Kozintsev in 1964 is far more successfully cinematic, though it works many substantive changes on the text. The first scene is missing from the beginning, for example, and lines concerning Fortinbras at the end, as well as Horatio's declaration that he will tell Hamlet's story. Kozintsev adds magnificent visual sequences, however, such as Hamlet's passing through a war-torn village on his way back to Elsinore. Writing for *Sight and Sound* (1964), Michael Kustow was transfixed by Kozintsev's ghost, "a giant figure in glinting armour, his black cloak flaming and fluttering like a turbulent storm-cloud, his face shadowed by a vizor." To demonstrate that "Denmark's a prison" (as Hamlet tells Rosencrantz and Guildenstern), Kozintsev packs his mise-en-scène with telling details: "a massive portcullis, a vast draw-

Maximilian Schell's adaptation of Hamlet *was directed by Edward Dmytryk.* (COURTESY NATIONAL FILM SOCIETY ARCHIVES)

bridge, guards with muskets, and a harsh iron corset into which Ophelia is strapped as she dresses to mourn Polonius." Add to this the music of Dmitri Shostakovich, and the style that results was, for Kustow, "realistic-operatic."

Kozintsev dramatizes scenes that are merely narrated in the play, such as Hamlet's changing the death warrants on ship before his "rescue" and Ophelia's body floating in a pool. In the Kozintsev version, a bundle of dried kindlewood is substituted for the wildflowers Ophelia brings to the king and queen to demonstrate the queen's sad comment, "Alas, she's mad." But that point is also made visually by the way Ophelia dances to the tinkling music of Shostakovich, delicately played on a cembalo.

Jack Jorgens described "an incomplete list of omissions and alterations" in his essay on the film in *Literature/Film Quarterly* (1973), including "all mentions of suicide in the first soliloquy" and the last part of the "O what a rogue and peasant slave am I" soliloquy, references questioning the authenticity of the ghost, "nearly all of Hamlet's instructions to the players, Hamlet's praise of Horatio, the dumb show," Polonius informing Claudius that he will "loose" his daughter on Hamlet, the king's prayer scene, "Hamlet's description of the pirate adventure," and "all of the lines between the killing of Claudius and 'the rest is silence.'"

Absolute fidelity is not the only measure of a successful adaptation, however, and Jorgens praises Kozintsev's rendering and interpretation for its focus throughout "on Hamlet's integrity, his refusal to act without understanding his own motives and the meaning of his action, the moment when he takes arms against the sea of troubles represents a narrowing, a reduction in stature, a compromise," creating the impression that "Hamlet is finer than the world he lives in, greater than language or actions could express, and this feeling is confirmed in his death." In comparison to Olivier's film, which captured what Jorgens called "the inner *Hamlet*," Kozintsev's epic treatment emphasized "the outer *Hamlet*." In the Olivier film "the complexity of the central character grows primarily out of [Olivier's] performance," whereas in Kozintsev's film "the fragmented and conflict-ridden personality grows from within" the character as represented by Innokenti Smoktunovski. In this film Hamlet's first soliloquy ("O that this too too solid flesh would melt . . .") is voiced-over as Hamlet walks through a crowd of smiling courtiers. Jorgens rightly praised the film's mise-en-scène, which captures more of the play's "complexity and mystery" because Kozintsev's "visual texture is denser" and "the images and connections more consistently meaningful."

The other filmed *Hamlet* of 1964, directed by John Gielgud in America, was not intended to be "cinematic" at all, but a filmed theatre record of Gielgud's stage production that first opened at Toronto's O'Keefe Center before moving to the Lunt-Fontanne Theatre in New York. It starred Richard Burton as Hamlet, Alfred Drake as Claudius, Hume Cronyn as Polonius, Eileen Herlie as Gertrude, Linda Marsh as Ophelia, and Robert Milli as Horatio, with Gielgud himself providing the voice of the ghost. Although the theatre reviews were mixed, the stage production was immensely popular and ran for 138 performances on Broadway. Gielgud trimmed "only about 500 lines, or approximately 12% of the text," according to Jay Halio, including "Horatio's description of Fortinbras's threatened invasion (I.i.70–112) and Claudius's first admission of guilt" (III.i.46–54), but retained almost all of "The Murder of Gonzago," written "in a purposely archaic dramatic style" more likely to be understood by theatre audiences. The only wholesale unit cut Gielgud made was in Act Four, Scene Four, the scene in

which Horatio reads Hamlet's letter concerning his adventures with pirates at sea and his "most strange return." This was a barebones approach, "stripped of all extraneous trappings" and filmed with the actors in rehearsal clothes. Burton told Gielgud that he was "anxious not to have to wear a period costume with tights." As a consequence, this led Gielgud "to conceive a production of *Hamlet* in modern dress on a stage with bare walls and only a few platforms and essential furniture." Gielgud recalls the production that was filmed as "bleak and unattractive," despite its enormous success on stage. Burton's performance was judged to be "powerful," but "uneven." The action was recorded by a mysterious technological innovation called "Electronovision."

A far more lively production was directed by Tony Richardson in 1969 at the Round House Theatre in London, starring Nicol Williamson as Hamlet and Anthony Hopkins as Claudius. The film captures a defining performance of Williamson, revising and rethinking the character of the prince for a whole generation of viewers. Richardson's filmed-theatre approach, like Gielgud's, was far different from "cinematic" ones of Olivier and Kozintsev. The ghost is heard but not seen, for example. A bright spotlight is used merely to suggest the presence of the ghost, illuminating the faces of those privileged to see it; the voice of the ghost is in fact the voice of Nicol Williamson, electronically enhanced. This low-budget film is innocent of special effects.

The film was spun off from Richardson's stage production and financed by Woodfall Productions, the company Richardson had formed with playwright John Osborne to film *Look Back in Anger* (1959) and *The Entertainer* (1960). Richardson shot the film by day while the play was still being performed nightly. Williamson's Hamlet was as innovative as Olivier's was traditional, angry, and impudent, and was far more relaxed under the camera's scrutiny. The text was reduced by half, but the trimming of the text was done so seamlessly that the play appears to be intact. All of the major characters are in place except for Fortinbras, and when Hamlet dies, "the rest is silence."

Richardson pushes the theme of incest beyond the limits of the play to include Ophelia (pop star and decidedly unvirginal Rolling Stones groupie Marianne Faithfull) and her brother Laertes (Michael Pennington), who seem to kiss on his departure for France in a way a brother and sister never should. The actress does not convey much of a sense of Ophelia's innocence and virginity and seems to be contaminated, since the atmosphere of this film suggests moral rottenness. Since she seems to be an experienced tart rather than a frail innocent, the rationale for Ophelia's madness and suicide is a bit flawed. Gordon Jackson's Horatio, though a little old for the role, is fully in place as Hamlet's friend and confidant, and his loyalty is effectively paired against Rosencrantz (Ben Aris) and Guildenstern (Clive Graham). Judy Parfitt's Gertrude seems to dote upon both Hamlet and her oily and devious husband.

The strength of Richardson's *Hamlet* is what some might have considered its weakness. It was done essentially as filmed theatre and shot in such a way that it would work for the television screen. Most of the setups are two-shots or close-ups, so that the emphasis is always upon the actors and their lines. There are almost no distractions of the mise-en-scène and the focus is always upon language and inflection, expertly rendered by Nicol Williamson, Anthony Hopkins, and their subordinates. Mark Dignam's Polonius is a memorable comic performance, as is that of Roger Livesey as the gravedigger. If, as Hamlet says, the point is to *hear* a play, this production is well worth listening to.

Less successful, perhaps, in cutting and emending the text seamlessly was Peter Wood's 1970 *Hamlet*, starring Richard Chamberlain as the prince, Martin Shaw as Horatio, Richard Johnson as Claudius, Margaret Leighton as Gertrude, Ciaran Madden as Ophelia, and Alan Bennett as Osric, all of them in Regency period costumes. This production cut large blocs of text—something like 2,100 lines—all but the last five lines of Act Four, Scene Two, e.g., and all of the dialogue of the play-within, retaining only the Dumb Show to spring Hamlet's "mousetrap." The Chamberlain version also removes Act Two, Scene One, and, more significantly, Act Four, Scene Four, and therefore Hamlet's last soliloquy: "How all occasions do inform against me." In this film Chamberlain's prince was well supported by Michael Redgrave's Polonius and John Gielgud as the ghost. When Claudius comes to Laertes (IV.vii) to plot Hamlet's death, he interrupts Laertes at his prayers, so that Gertrude's entrance with the news of Ophelia's death seems, as Jay Halio noted, "a retribution against Laertes" for his complicity in Claudius's diabolical scheme. Ophelia was earlier seen at her prayers in the background as Hamlet recites his "To be or not to be" soliloquy before the nunnery scene, as this adaptation emphasizes the Christian morality violated by Claudius and Laertes. Like Olivier's version, the Chamberlain *Hamlet* is agreeable enough, Halio asserts, "taken on its own premises as a romantic version of a passionate, sensitive young prince."

The Mel Gibson *Hamlet*, directed by Franco Zeffirelli and superbly photographed by David Watkin in 1990, is not only lively but cinematic as well. The

Franco Zeffirelli's Hamlet *starred Mel Gibson as Hamlet, Glenn Close as Gertrude, and Alan Bates as Claudius.* (COURTESY ICON PICTURES)

problem is that the screenplay by Zeffirelli and Christopher DeVore makes hash of the text, transposing lines capriciously and removing whole scenes that are necessary for properly contextualizing the action. The opening of the film springs back in time, for example, to the funeral of the old king Hamlet, stealing lines from the court scene in Act One, Scene Two, which is severely and stupidly abridged. "Let the world take note, that you are most immediate to our throne," Alan Bates's Claudius remarks to Mel Gibson's Hamlet as the prince sifts a handful of soil onto his father's bier. Zeffirelli cuts the first scene entirely, and seriously diminishes the role of Horatio. The screenplay also completely ignores Hamlet's fourth soliloquy, in which he states his resolution, finally, to take action against his uncle.

The faults of this adaptation concern the director's strategy. The medieval atmosphere is most pleasing and the acting, in general, is difficult to fault. Mel Gibson encompasses much the same attitude and impudence as Nicol Williamson had 20 years earlier. His Hamlet is energetic and animated, though at times his lunacy seems more real than imagined. Glenn Close is a fawning, sentimental Gertrude, supposedly innocent of the conspiracy that took her first husband's life. Helena Bonham-Carter's Ophelia, obedient to her father's wishes but resentful nonetheless, is among the best Ophelias ever captured on screen. Ian Holm's Polonius is self-consciously aware of his foolishness, more a snoopy busybody than a sinister figure and Claudius's henchman. There is nothing terribly wrong with Stephan Dillane's Horatio other than the fact that he is not given sufficient screen time. Paul Scofield makes a stately ghost. John McEnery, who had played Mercutio brilliantly in Zeffirelli's *Romeo and Juliet*, is truly sinister as Osric, a far cry from Peter Gale's homosexual fop in Richardson's film. Only Alan Bates might be faulted for his rendering of Claudius, something of a meddlesome buffoon rather than a truly dangerous and sinister politician, and certainly not Hamlet's equal intellectually.

Zeffirelli has a flair for staging operatic spectacles, and this talent is put to excellent use in the duel scene, which is well choreographed, though arguably longer than it needs to be. Gibson's acting deserves to be taken seriously and is more than merely a Danish confection. So much of the play has gone missing, however, that the film might be incoherent to those who have not read and studied Shakespeare. Zeffirelli would have done better to study John Dover Wilson's book *What Happens in Hamlet?* (1967) so as to better understand the complexity of the play and the way in which the pieces should fit together. Unfortunately, he restructured the play without regard to the consequences.

Working with veteran television director Kirk Browning, Kevin Kline co-directed a more ephemeral adaptation for American public television, broadcast on November 2, 1990, in which he played the lead opposite Diane Venora's Ophelia. Derived from the New York Shakespeare production for the "Great Performances" series, this presentation was more complete than the Zeffirelli film because Kline, a classically trained actor as well as a movie star, took Shakespeare seriously and argued to keep as much of the text as possible. "In *Hamlet*," he told observer Mary Maher, "every cut bleeds." Cutting only about 15 percent of the text, the production ran to two hours and 50 minutes in comparison to the stage production, which ran three hours and 20 minutes. This was Kline's directorial debut, and he was well supported by the stage players who would not be recognized, by and large, by filmgoers. Although long and relatively "academic" in its filmed-theatre approach, the performance was praised as "elegant and riveting," and provided an interesting alternative to the mass-audience Zeffirelli version.

Likewise, actor-director Kenneth Branagh had a far superior understanding of the play, which he intended to film in all its complexity and wholeness. Running to just over four hours, Branagh's *Hamlet* is a monument of scholarship, taste, and judgment, and the longest Shakespeare film ever made. Branagh conflated the text of the First Folio of 1623 with that of the Second Quarto, the one version containing lines that the other lacked. The length might be a problem for some viewers, but not for those enthralled by Shakespeare's language. In this case, the usual complaints about textual fidelity simply do not apply. In his published screenplay, Branagh explained the "principles" that guided his adaptation: "a commitment to international casting; a speaking style that is as realistic as a proper adherence to the structure will allow; a period setting that attempts to set the story in a historical context that is resonant for a modern audience but allows a heightened language to sit comfortably," and, above all, "a full emotional commitment to the characters, springing from [a] belief that they can be understood in direct, accessible relation to modern life."

Branagh achieves these goals brilliantly. He clearly wants to help his viewers understand lines that may be difficult, such as those of the player king (Charlton Heston), whose words are illustrated as he speaks them by John Gielgud as Priam and Judi Dench as Hecuba in cameo roles. He has assembled an unbelievably strong cast in keeping with his notions about international casting. Although Jack Lemmon fails to impress viewers at the outset as a spear-carrier, later on Billy Crystal is perfect as the comic first gravedigger. Other pleasant surprises include Robin Williams as Osric. Gerard Depardieu plays Reynaldo, sent by Polonius to France to spy on Laertes (Michael Maloney). Julie Christie came out of retirement to play Gertrude. Kate Winslet was on board as Ophelia before her maiden voyage on the *Titanic*. Richard Briers is a sleazy and potentially dangerous Polonius, Nicholas Farrell a dignified and loyal Horatio. And in Derek Jacobi, Branagh landed one of the most distinguished actors in the English-speaking world to play Claudius, and his Claudius is second to none in his villainy and deviousness, a truly worthy opponent for Hamlet.

The action is moved forward in time to the 19th century and filmed at Blenheim Palace rather than in the Middle Ages, for Branagh intends to demonstrate the play's timeliness. The film begins with a statue of the dead king Hamlet (Brian Blessed) coming to life and ends, after the shift of power to Fortinbras, with that statue being pulled down, as heroic statues of Lenin were in Iron Curtain countries after the fall of communism in 1989. Every detail in the film is meant to point up and clarify the text. When Hamlet confronts the ghost, for example, there are strange eruptions in the realm and Hamlet has good reason to be terrified. The final spectacle of the duel scene is arguably overdone in the way Claudius is killed, perhaps, but the arrival of Fortinbras and his army is a crashing success. Students of Shakespeare will be delighted by Branagh's absolutely clear delivery of the soliloquies. His disappointment in Ophelia is complicated by flashbacks that suggest they have been lovers, a visual departure, to be sure, but this detail also helps to explain her suicide and Hamlet's bizarre behavior at her graveside. It is entirely appropriate that *Hamlet* of all plays should have been given such a thorough treatment.

Michael Almereyda directed the first *Hamlet* of the new century in 2000, starring Ethan Hawke as the prince in a version that runs to a mere 112 minutes, nearly two hours shorter than Branagh's full-text adaptation and updated to New York City in the present day. This postmodern adaptation sets the power struggle in the confines of "The Denmark Corporation," where Claudius (Kyle MacLachlan) is now CEO. Elsinore becomes a luxury hotel, and the Hawke-Hamlet in modern dress recites his "To be or not to be" ironically, in the "action" department of a Blockbuster video store. The ghost (Sam Shepard) appears to Hamlet in a laundry room, wearing a leather jacket. One reviewer described Bill Murray's Polonius as "a slick spin doctor who uses wiretaps" on Ophelia (Julia Stiles). Diane Venora plays Gertrude as a social-climbing Manhattan socialite, not too tenderly. Almereyda rose to the challenge of low-budget filmmaking, shooting the picture on Super 16. Although the director discards huge blocs of text, he retains Shakespeare's language.

Reviews were mixed. Elvis Mitchell of the *New York Times* praised the "boldness and veracity" of Almereyda's trimming of the text and the "bemused hollowness" that Bill Murray "first discovered in sketch comedy" and here spun into "a worn, saddened undercurrent." The more theatrically experienced Stanley Kauffmann was more difficult to please, though he thought that Ethan Hawke was "the perfect choice for this Hamlet because his slithering, mum-

Kenneth Branagh directed the first full-text Hamlet.
(COURTESY CASTLE ROCK ENTERTAINMENT)

bling approach fits the essentially off-handed feeling of the film." Kauffmann considered the classically trained Liev Schreiber "out of place" as Laertes because Almereyda otherwise avoided "any touch of the theatre or of classical tradition in the performances." Besides Schreiber, the only actor in the cast capable of giving "some sense of the size of the work that is here being battered is Sam Shepard." The play has survived "because of and through its language," and "to rip out great chunks [of the text] because they do not fit a director's design is like altering a giant's robe for a pygmy." Kauffmann concluded, brutally, that "to mash the language as an obstacle that must be cleared away for the modern audience is to cheat that audience." If Kauffmann finds an adaptation only "mildly entertaining," that does not bode well for the film's critical reception, once the novelty has gone stale.

REFERENCES

Branagh, Kenneth, *Hamlet, by William Shakespeare: Screenplay and Introduction* (New York: W.W. Norton, 1996); Burnett, Mark Thornton, "The 'Very Cunning of the Scene': Kenneth Branagh's *Hamlet*," *Literature/Film Quarterly*, 25:2 (1997), 78–82; Fierman, Daniel, "The Dane Event," *Entertainment*

Weekly, 543 (June 2, 2000), 40–42; Gielgud, John with John Miller, *Shakespeare—Hit or Miss?* (London: Sidgwick and Jackson, 1991); Griffin, Alice, "Shakespeare Through the Camera's Eye," *Shakespeare Quarterly*, 4:3 (1953), 33–34; Halio, Jay, "Three Filmed *Hamlets*," *Literature/Film Quarterly*, 1:4 (1973), 316–320; Jorgens, Jack J., "Image and Meaning in the Kozintsev *Hamlet*," *Literature/Film Quarterly*, 1:4 (1973), 299–315; Jorgens, Jack J., *Shakespeare on Film* (Bloomington: Indiana University Press, 1977); Kliman, Bernice W., *Hamlet: Film, Television, and Audio Performances* (Rutherford, N.J.: Fairleigh Dickinson University Press, 1988); Kustow, Michael, "Hamlet," *Sight and Sound*, 33:3 (1964), 144–145; Maher, Mary Z., "An American Hamlet for Television," *Literature/Film Quarterly*, 20:4 (1992): 301–307; Mullin, Michael, "Tony Richardson's *Hamlet*: Script and Screen," *Literature/Film Quarterly*, 4:2 (1976), 123–133; Welsh, James M. and John C. Tibbetts, *The Cinema of Tony Richardson: Essays and Interviews* (Albany, N.Y.: SUNY Press, 1999); Wilds, Lillian, "Maximilian Schell's Most Royal *Hamlet*," *Literature/Film Quarterly*, 4:2 (1976), 134–140.

—*J.M.W.*

HENRY IV, PART I (1596–97)
HENRY IV, PART II (1598)

Chimes at Midnight/Campanadas a Medianoche/Falstaff (1967), Spain/Switzerland, directed and adapted by Orson Welles; Internacional Films Espagnol (Madrid)/Alpine Films (Basel).

My Own Private Idaho (1991), U.S.A., directed and adapted by Gus Van Sant; New Line Cinema/Fine Line Features.

The Plays

In these two plays, the core of Shakespeare's second tetralogy of history plays that begins with *Richard II* and ends with *Henry V,* Shakespeare dramatizes the education and development of the politician destined to become King Henry V, "the mirror of all Christian kings." But here he is known mainly as Prince Hal, whose father, Henry Bolingbroke, now King Henry IV (r. 1399–1413), assumed the throne after a civil war that usurped the poetic but ineffectual Richard II. The action of *1 Henry IV* begins in the summer of 1402 and concludes a year later during the summer of 1403, after the battle of Shrewsbury, when the royal army defeated a rebellion led by the fierce Welshman, "that great magician" Owen Glendower and the Percy family—Thomas, earl of Worcester, Henry, earl of Northumberland, and Henry's son, called Hotspur.

Although troubled mainly by civil rebellion, the king is also concerned about the dubious behavior of his son, Prince Hal, an apparent playboy who spends much of his time at the Boar's Head tavern in Eastcheap in the company of a fat old rogue, Sir John Falstaff, and his associates Poins, Bardolph, Peto, and Gadshill, indulging in drinking, gambling, wenching, and practical jokes (such as a botched robbery prank, in which Hal and Poins in disguise scare off the boastful Falstaff and Bardolph, averting the planned robbery). Prince Hal's "loose behavior" is not what it seems, however. Rather, it is a calculated ploy at image-making that foreshadows Hal's later "redemption" as King Henry V. Hal clearly states his intentions when he says (I.ii.239–40): "I'll so offend, to make offence a skill/Redeeming time when men least think I will." Hal proves his mettle at the battle of Shrewsbury when he defeats and kills Harry Hotspur in single combat. Later, Falstaff attempts to take credit for the death of the hotheaded Hotspur.

Civil discord continues into *2 Henry IV.* The earl of Northumberland discovers that his son Hotspur is dead and that the royal army under the command of Prince John of Lancaster and the earl of Westmoreland is moving against him. Northumberland takes his wife and daughter-in-law and retreats into Scotland. The earl of Westmoreland urges the remaining rebels, Mowbray and Hastings, to make peace with Prince John, who promises that their grievances shall be redressed, then has them arrested for treason. This news reaches the king after he has learned of the death of Owen Glendower (Act Three) and the defeat of Northumberland in the north (Act Four). In Act Five the king advises his son "to busy giddy minds/With foreign quarrels," as Hal will later do as King Henry V.

In *2 Henry IV* Prince Hal gradually withdraws from Falstaff, who is seen as even more disreputable and conniving and has taken on another boon companion, a "swaggering rascal" named Pistol, whom Shakespeare stereotypes as a braggart soldier, a drunken whore named Doll Tearsheet, and a corrupt country justice, Master Shallow. Owing money to Master Shallow, Falstaff approaches the new king (Henry V) in Act Five expecting favoritism, but is soundly rejected: "I know thee not old man: fall to thy prayers;/How ill white hairs become a fool and jester!" Hal then adds, "Presume not that I am the thing I was" and banishes Falstaff from his presence.

The Films

One could argue that Orson Welles was born to play the role of Falstaff, or that he grew into it as his own career fell onto hard times after the initial brilliance of *Citizen Kane.* For years Welles was obsessed with his

Falstaff project. Early on he had combined and compressed the texts of *Henry IV* Parts I and II and *The Merry Wives of Windsor* on the stage, but he later had difficulty funding the film project. Shakespeare's so-called Henriad introduces Prince Hal as a calculating playboy who proves his valor in *1 Henry IV,* assumes the throne at the end of *2 Henry IV,* and conquers France in *Henry V.* In these three plays Shakespeare dramatizes the growth and development of a Christian prince destined to become England's first modern king and a hugely popular politician.

In *1 Henry IV* Hal's relationship with Sir John Falstaff is playful and affectionate, regarding Falstaff as a sort of surrogate father who teaches the prince to relate to the common man. At the time *Chimes at Midnight* was made, Falstaff had been seen only fleetingly on screen, at the beginning of Laurence Olivier's *Henry V,* as Mistress Quickly tells Pistol, Nym, and Bardolph of how Falstaff died of a broken heart in Act One. Welles considered Falstaff "the most completely good old man in all drama" when he presumed to rewrite Shakespeare's plays as "a dark comedy [and] the story of the betrayal of a friendship." Understandably, then, Welles pulled Falstaff out of the background and thrust him into the foreground as he presented for the first time in cinema Shakespeare's greatest comic creation. The film is a true adaptation that reworks and restructures Shakespeare's dramatic materials into a cinematic narrative that arches over the two plays.

The film begins with Falstaff (Welles) and Justice Shallow (Alan Dent) remembering their younger days (*2 Henry IV,* III.ii), with Falstaff speaking the lines that gave the film its title: "We have heard the chimes at midnight, Master Shallow." The film then cuts to "the Royal Castle" as Ralph Richardson's voice-over narration from Holinshed's *Chronicles* (Shakespeare's major source for the play) provides exposition summarizing the action of *Richard II* and the political circumstances of *1 Henry IV.* The ransom of Edmund Mortimer, held hostage by Owen Glendower, is demanded. However, King Henry IV (John Gielgud) is unwilling to empty his coffers "to redeem the traitor home," to the chagrin of Northumberland (Jose Nieto), his son Hotspur (Norman Rodway), and Worcester (Fernando Rey), setting up the conflict for the play.

Welles divides the narrative into two parts, paralleling the two parts of Shakespeare's original plays, separated by Richardson's voice-overs, which are also used to conclude the film. Welles presents an amalgam intended to showcase Falstaff, and to present the character more sympathetically than he finally appears in Shakespeare, who makes it clear that Prince Hal is finally forced by politics to reject Falstaff, since Falstaff

would surely have exploited his friendship with the king had he been granted a position at Court. The joviality of the character in Part One gives way to a distasteful cynicism in Part Two, but Welles shows that the prince's decision, though arguably necessary, was not an easy one to make.

There is an intuitive stroke of editorial genius in this film in the way that Welles handles the rejection and, finally, the demise of Falstaff. First of all, Welles stages the rejection scene in such a way as to emphasize the utter presumption of Falstaff's approaching the king. Falstaff breaks through the guards to interrupt the royal procession, as no one else there would dare to do. Hal speaks his opening line ("I know thee not, old man") with his back turned; he pauses ever so slightly, but there is no question that he recognizes the voice. After banishing Falstaff "on pain of death . . . Not to come near our person by ten mile," Welles leaves the impression that Falstaff has been imprisoned for his presumption.

Welles then takes us into the beginning of *Henry V* as the new king, about to embark for France, speaks the lines: "Enlarge the man committed yesterday/That railed against our person. We consider/It was excess of wine that set him on,/And on his more advice, we pardon him." Dramatic time and space are here compressed, but it suits Welles's purpose to suggest that the king's mercy is here being granted to Falstaff, which serves to put Hal in a new and perhaps more human and compassionate light. This compaction and shift works very well for the director, and the description of Falstaff's death from *Henry V* (II.iii) follows immediately, with Pistol, Nym, Bardolph, the boy, and Mistress Quickly being grouped around a huge and portly casket.

After the rejection, as Roger Manvell has noted, Falstaff attempts to rally his self-respect: "I shall be sent for in private to him. Look you, he must seem thus to the world." But thereafter the camera isolates Falstaff, walking "the empty streets at night, alone." Mistress Quickly (Margaret Rutherford) gives her account of Falstaff's death from *Henry V,* getting a final tug of sympathy ("the King hath killed his heart") as the coffin is carried off. Pauline Kael considered the film "a near masterpiece" but criticized the "maddening" cutting and the way the actor's voices fail to match the images, producing a "crazy mix" of long shots and Shakespearean dialogue. Given the director's budget constraints, the film is far better than one might have expected and, arguably, his best Shakespeare film.

My Own Private Idaho (1991), Gus Van Sant's updated and loosely adapted remake of *Chimes at Midnight,* was intended as an homage to Orson Welles but is set in the homosexual netherworld of modern Portland, Oregon. The language, of course, is not Shakespeare's, and many liberties have been taken. Prince Hal becomes Scott Favor (Keanu Reeves), the son of Portland's mayor (Tom Troupe plays the King Henry IV figure), who is currently alienated from his father because of his associations with gay street hustlers and drug addicts. The older Bob Pigeon (William Richert), Scott's former lover, mentor, and "true father" (or so Scott proclaims), steps into the role of Falstaff. Budd (a musician named Flea from a band called "The Red Hot Chili Peppers") and company represent Shallow and company. Jane Lightwork (Sally Curtice), who owns the old hotel where the characters spend their time (the film's equivalent of the Boar's Head tavern), assumes the role played by Mistress Quickly, although her name also alludes to Jane Nightwork, an old friend whom Shallow mentions to Falstaff in *2 Henry IV* (III.ii.204) and also at the beginning of *Chimes at Midnight*, as Falstaff and Shallow recall how old they have become.

The central role of Mike Waters (River Phoenix), a narcoleptic hustler who becomes Scott's companion and lover, is more complicated. A literal reading of the film would consider Mike as Ned Poins, Hal's friend and fellow prankster, if Van Sant had created a literal transfer of the story, but the Poins role could also be ascribed to fellow hustler Gary (Rodney Harvey). Mike is also a younger Falstaff figure who cavorted with Hal as a brother in earlier days. Both Mike and Bob have lived in Idaho. The trans-gendering effect replaces Falstaff's connections with Doll Tearsheet. Ultimately Scott rejects both Mike and Bob.

Scott is heterosexual—his attachments to Mike and Bob are mainly a rebellion against his Establishment father—as evidenced when he comes into his inheritance and marries Carmella (Chiara Caselli), breaking with Mike and his former friends. Mike and Bob encounter Scott and Carmella outside a posh Portland restaurant. When Mike and Bob approach Scott, he rejects them, saying "Now that I've changed, and until I change back, don't come near me." Bob dies of a broken heart that night. The next day the hustlers gather for Bob's burial at the same cemetery where Scott's father is also being buried. The film begins and ends with Mike, collapsed in a narcoleptic seizure on an Idaho highway. *My Own Private Idaho* is an adaptation twice removed from Shakespeare and more of a tribute to Orson Welles than to the Bard, whose lines are parodied but seem only marginally appropriate, given Van Sant's harsh urban environment.

REFERENCES

Anderegg, Michael, *Orson Welles, Shakespeare and Popular Culture* (New York: Columbia University Press, 1999); Kael, Pauline, *For Keeps* (New York: Dutton, 1994); Kline, Jim, "My Own Private Idaho," *Magill's Cinema Annual 1992*, ed. Frank N. Magill (Pasadena: Salem Press, 1992); Manvell, Roger, *Shakespeare and the Film* (New York: Praeger, 1971).

—*J.M.W. AND H.H.D.*

HENRY V (1599)

Henry V (1944), U.K., directed by Laurence Olivier, adapted by Olivier, Reginald Beck, Alan Dent, and Dallas Bower; Two Cities/Eagle-Lion.

Henry V (1989), U.K., directed and adapted by Kenneth Branagh; Renaissance Films.

The Play

The Life of Henry the Fifth represents a culmination of the tetralogy of history plays that began with *Richard II* and continued on through the two parts of *Henry IV*, which traced the development of the modern English monarchy from the medieval rule of Richard II, whose arrogance and belief in the divine right of kings led to his downfall and deposition, to his successor, Henry Bolingbroke. Having assumed the title of King Henry IV, Bolingbroke had to put his realm in order and deal with a decidedly disunited kingdom, as well as his rakish and apparently dissolute son, Prince Hal. It is Hal who will become King Henry V, "the mirror of all Christian kings," as Shakespeare's Chorus describes him.

The play begins with the king's seeking advice from his churchmen, the bishop of Ely and the archbishop of Canterbury, concerning his right to wage war on France to reclaim French territory once ruled by Edward, the Black Prince, the mention of whose name strikes fear in the heart of the French king, Charles VI. Canterbury goes into a long-winded exposition about the French succession and "the Salic Law they have in France," until the king finds the bottom line: "May I with right and conscience make this claim?" (I.ii.96) and is then given the archbishop's "blessing," so to speak. The French ambassador then brings Henry an insulting gift of tennis balls from the French dauphin, to which the king responds in dignified rhetorical anger: "We shall in France, by God's grace, play a set/Shall strike his father's crown into the hazard," then sets about his plans to invade France from Southampton.

A parallel subplot is also set in motion at the Boar's Head tavern, where Prince Hal in his youth had disported himself with his low-life friends, Pistol, Nym, Bardolph, and their ringleader, Sir John Falstaff, who is now on his deathbed, presumably dying of a broken heart because Hal had rejected him upon assuming the Crown. "The king hath killed his heart," Mistress Quickly remarks, after describing the death of Sir John to the others, who then prepare themselves to go to war. They are not honorable soldiers, however. Bardolph is executed in France, by order of the king, for stealing from a church. Nym, a cutpurse also interested in pillage, is killed in the battle. Pistol, having been reprimanded by his nemesis, the fierce Welshman, Captain Fluellen, will return home to become a cutpurse: "To England will I steal, and there I'll steal."

The first skirmish of the main plot is fought outside the gates of Harfleur, and the city is captured. King Henry then advances with his army, which is weakened by sickness en route, to meet, in the battle of Agincourt (October 25, 1415), a vastly superior army representing the very flower of French chivalry. The technological superiority of the English longbow, which could propel arrows capable of piercing French armor, results in a great victory against superior odds.

The denouement deals with the aftermath of the victory at the French Court, with King Henry claiming the French princess Katherine as his bride-to-be. The play would seem to be a patriotic celebration of England's greatest victory, but the Epilogue delivered by the Chorus (who comments on the action throughout) calls into question the ultimate significance of this triumph, since Henry's successor, "Henry the Sixth, in infant bands crowned king," so mismanaged his rule that England "lost France, and made his England bleed."

The Films

There are two remarkable adaptations of *Henry V,* the first of which, directed by Laurence Olivier, set the standard for Shakespeare adaptations to come, though it was not entirely faithful to the play nor to the character of the king, who seems to have been far more benevolent and far less calculating than the character Shakespeare created. This is considered Shakespeare's most patriotic play, and for that reason, Olivier was approached by Jack Beddington of the Ministry of Information and given a budget that would allow him to make a spectacular film in Technicolor. Olivier's film was therefore financed as part of the war effort to bolster morale and the spirit of the English people, then under siege by air and sea by Germany during World War II.

As a propaganda film, *Henry V* parallels the intent of *Alexander Nevsky,* directed in the Soviet Union by the great Sergei Eisenstein in 1938, portraying a mythic, unifying Russian hero, whose army drove the invading Teutonic Knights out of Russia. This was clearly intended as a prophetic warning to Nazi Germany, which was later to suffer horrendous losses on the Eastern Front. Like Nevsky, King Henry also had to unify his country before facing the enemy, and he cleverly uses the French campaign to consolidate his power. Olivier's film, with its parallel warning, is oddly critical of the French, whose nobles, as represented in *Henry V,* are indolent, vainglorious fops, and whose king is represented as a senile old man. Perhaps Olivier is unduly critical of the French, who allowed their country to be captured; arguably, his film would seem to insult the French Resistance effort. The weakness of the French nation in Olivier's rendering would seem to undercut the English victory, and this might be considered mistaken strategy in terms of propaganda value.

The film is much more than simply an exercise in propaganda, however. Olivier won a Special Academy Award for his "Outstanding Achievement as an Actor," but his achievement as director is equally noteworthy. What makes the Olivier adaptation still interesting and relevant is the way that Olivier framed the action, as a sort of meditation on the nature of theatre as opposed to film. If any Shakespeare play was designed for a filmed treatment, *Henry V* is the one, built upon a battle spectacle that could not possibly be appropriately mounted on the stage. Although Olivier could not take his camera to "the vasty fields of France" then under German occupation, the film opens up the play gloriously by shooting out of doors in the Irish countryside. Olivier rises to the challenge of the Chorus's injunction at the play's opening—the memorable "Muse of fire" prologue—when he apologizes for the stage's limitations and entreats the audience, "On your imaginary forces work." He then implores the audience to "Suppose within the girdle of these walls/Are now confined two mighty monarchies;" and to "Piece out our imperfections with your thoughts."

Olivier begins his film as if it were a performance of the play in Shakespeare's time at the Globe Theatre. The camera circles in a 360-degree pan of the audience taking their seats. The camera then takes us backstage, where the bishop of Ely (Robert Helpmann) is quaffing a tankard of ale with the king of France (Harcourt Williams). An actor wearing a crown emerges. He clears his throat as he makes himself ready for the stage. He is King Henry V (Olivier). Thus, the film begins as pure filmed theatre, providing a textbook example of what a production at the Globe might have been like.

Some of the potentially boring bits of the text for a mass audience are judiciously pruned, such as the pedantic ecclesiastical "justification" for the war the king wants to wage, given by the archbishop of Canterbury (Felix Aylmer) and turned into a comic routine by Olivier's comedian churchman. Olivier later cuts all of the scene where the king uncovers a plot against his life and orders the execution of the conspirators, Cambridge, Grey, and Scroop, at Southampton (II.ii).

In the first scenes, up to Southampton, the acting is purposely "theatrical" and overstated. At the Boar's Head (II.i), for example, the low comedy is broadly played for the groundlings by Pistol (Robert Newton), Nym (Frederick Cooper), and Bardolph (Roy Emmerton), but the second Boar's Head scene is handled quite differently, for by that time Olivier has begun his gradual transition from the theatricality of the Globe to a more realistic treatment. Certainly, in the second Boar's Head scene the dialogue is delivered in a more natural and "cinematic" style. Gone are the broad gestures and the buffoonery, and the characters seem far more believable when Mistress Quickly (Freda Jackson) gives her account of the death of Falstaff (George Robey), earlier seen on his deathbed, with an offstage voice off repeating Hal's rejection speech from *2 Henry IV*— "Think not I am the man I was." The flamboyant theatricality of Act Two, Scene One, is recalled later in the scenes involving Pistol's dispute with Captain Fluellen (Esmond Knight), another potentially comic figure.

The Chorus (Leslie Banks) no longer takes the stage after Southampton, for the "stage" is gone thereafter until the final moments of the film, when Olivier swings the action back into the Globe Theatre, breaking the dramatic illusion so wonderfully created by the film. As the English fleet moves across the Channel, the Chorus floats, as if hovering over the mise-en-scène. Thereafter, only Chorus' disembodied voice is heard, but by that time it voice is recognizable.

The early scenes in France are wrenched out of the theatrical frame and seem oddly dislocated in an impressionistic medieval mise-en-scène, imitating the design of such illuminated texts as *Les très riches heures du Duc de Berry* and the *Book of Hours of Anne of Cleves*. The French Court is framed in such a flat, one-dimensional setting as Olivier gradually makes his visual transition between filmed theatre and the realism of the final battle. Even so, the battle spectacle has the appearance of a tastefully decorated illustration. In the actual battle setting, rain would have soaked the field; in Olivier's film there is only a token mud puddle in evidence. For a truly "realistic" rendering of the battle of Agincourt, audiences had to wait for the Branagh adaptation of 1989.

For 45 years no one dared to readapt or upstage Olivier's "classic" treatment, but Kenneth Branagh fully understood the limitations and distortions of Olivier's wartime approach and intended to restore the play and the character of the king to Shakespeare's original design, without the burden of Olivier's political agenda. He also intended to make the play as entertaining and accessible as possible. He achieved both of these goals brilliantly in his 1989 adaptation of *Henry V*, which is far different from Olivier's earlier approach in both interpretation and design.

Branagh begins his film with Derek Jacobi's Chorus standing on a soundstage (or possibly in a television studio), surrounded by props that would later be seen in the film. From the beginning, then, there is no question about Branagh's filmed approach. Jacobi, an accomplished Shakespearean actor, was at the time playing the lead in alternating productions of *Richard II* and *Richard III* at the Phoenix Theatre on Charing Cross Road, taking the train from London to Brighton during the day to film the Chorus for Branagh. Jacobi's Chorus is not so well integrated into the action as Olivier's had been, and keeps appearing as a "You-Are-There" sort of interpreter at awkward moments that disrupt the cinematic flow of the narrative. On the other hand, he does help the audience to understand the flow of events, as when he identifies the conspirators, Cambridge, Scroop, and Grey, seen in the background before King Henry (Branagh) accuses them of treason. Branagh restores that scene, as well as the king's fearsome warning to the citizens of Harfleur of what fate may await them if they refuse to surrender their city.

Branagh's king is a far more tough-minded politician and warrior than Olivier's had been and therefore closer to Shakespeare's design. His response to the ambassadors in Act One, Scene Two, is cold and calculating, and far more menacing than Olivier's had been. As Michael Pursell noted in *Literature/Film Quarterly*, his first appearance in silhouette as he enters the Court visually recalls Darth Vader and Batman, and these popular culture allusions clearly suggest that the king has a dark side. Pursell also demonstrates how visual allusions to soccer and rugby in the way the battle of Agincourt is filmed would resonate meaningfully for younger British and European viewers.

Like Olivier, Branagh adds lines from both parts of *Henry IV* that recall Hal's rejection of Falstaff, and later in the film sets up Bardolph (Richard Briers) as another Falstaff figure. Branagh dramatizes the hanging of Bardolph (merely reported action in the play), as further evidence that the king has rejected his earlier raffish ways. Before the noose is tightened, their eyes lock and both of them seem to remember better times at the Boar's Head before Hal became king. Branagh dramatizes this memory by adding lines from *1 Henry IV* in a far more extensive excavation of that earlier play than Olivier had attempted.

The battle scenes are extended and "realistic" (though the death of the constable of France as he is pulled off the battlefield by his troops is recorded in slow-motion, as is the death of the duke of York). Branagh intends to demonstrate the human cost of the victory, further emphasized by a long tracking shot after the battle, in which the king carries a wounded squire (Christian Bale) the length of the battlefield, accompanied by Patrick Doyle's musical rendering of the *Te Deum* and *Non Nobis*, transformed into a victory anthem.

In this film, the French are worthy opponents, with the exception of the dauphin. The French king (Paul Scofield) seems old and weary, but certainly not senile. Nor is Ian Holm's Captain Fluellen the ethnic caricature he appeared to be in the Olivier adaptation. Brian Blessed's Exeter is contemptuously defiant when he appears as ambassador to the French king, and later, on the battlefield, he is a veritable killing machine, who, in full armor, seems to recall Robocop. Such allusions may weaken the film for some purists, but would no doubt help to maintain the interest of younger viewers. Above all, Branagh wants his film to be understood by a mass audience.

The challenge for Branagh was to adapt the play in such a way that it would not seem a mere imitation of Olivier's achievement. The only scene in Branagh's film that clearly seems to recall Olivier is the king's rousing, patriotic speech to his troops on St. Crispin's Day (IV.ii) before the battle of Agincourt: "We few, we happy few, we band of brothers;/For he today that sheds his blood with me/Shall be my brother; be he ne'er so vile,/This day shall gentle his condition." The speech makes a virtue out of what ought to be a military disadvantage (the fact that the English are seriously outnumbered), and Branagh's delivery, as well as his camera movement, starting in tight on the king, then pulling back as the speech builds resonance, would seem a sort of tribute to Olivier. Otherwise, the film stands entirely on its own merits, and launched Branagh's career as a latter-day Olivier among adaptors of Shakespeare.

Kenneth Branagh's Henry V *was the first adaptation of Shakespeare's battle epic since Olivier's version more than 40 years before.* (COURTESY BRITISH FILM INSTITUTE)

REFERENCES

Branagh, Kenneth, *Henry V, by William Shakespeare: A Screen Adaptation* (London: Chatto and Windus, 1989); Geduld, Harry M., *Filmguide to Henry V* (Bloomington: Indiana University Press, 1973); Jorgens, Jack J., *Shakespeare on Film* (Bloomington: Indiana University Press, 1977); Manvell, Roger, *Shakespeare and the Film* (London: J.M. Dent, 1971); Olivier, Laurence, *Confessions of an Actor* (London: Weidenfeld and Nicholson, 1982); Pursell, Michael, "Playing the Game: Branagh's *Henry V*," *Literature/Film Quarterly*, 20:4 (1992), 268–275.

—*J.M.W.*

JULIUS CAESAR (1599)

Julius Caesar (1953), U.S.A., directed and adapted by Joseph L. Mankiewicz; MGM.

The Play

Julius Caesar was one of four Roman plays (the others being *Antony and Cleopatra*, *Coriolanus*, and *Titus Andronicus*) in which Shakespeare explored systems of government and themes of despotism and decadence. In this play, Julius Caesar has just returned to Rome after defeating Pompey in a civil war and is on the point of proclaiming himself absolute dictator. However, a soothsayer has warned him to "beware the ides of March"; and there is indeed a conspiracy afoot, fostered by Cassius, Casca, and others, to depose him. Their cause is strengthened when they win over the noble Brutus to their side. Caesar is assassinated in the Capitol, with Brutus striking the final blow. However, Brutus' attempt to justify the act to the populace by arguing that it was for their political good is negated by the speech of Caesar's friend, Mark Antony, whose impassioned rhetoric rouses the mob into a mood of fury against the assassins. In the subsequent political turmoil, Antony and Caesar's successor, Octavius, unite against the forces of Brutus and Cassius and defeat them at the battle of Philippi. Brutus and Cassius both die a Roman death; and over the body of the former, Antony proclaims that "this was the noblest Roman of them all."

The Film

Julius Caesar was made on a modest budget by MGM, utilizing some of the costumes and sets left over from its 1951 blockbuster, *Quo Vadis?* Producer John Houseman had been closely involved with Orson Welles's legendary 1937 modern-dress production, which had stressed the play's contemporary relevance. A film version, declared Houseman, should translate "Shakespeare's bloody and turbulent melodrama into a medium where both mass emotion and personal conflict can be more closely observed and more fully revealed." Thus, although the film was not set in modern dress, it nonetheless invoked the demagogues and political rallies of the recent past. Accordingly, Houseman, in defiance of MGM's preference for color, reasoned that black-and-white photography was essential to convey the impression of contemporary newsreels. Much to the chagrin of his former colleague, Orson Welles, Houseman chose Joseph Mankiewicz to direct. His direction of such films as *A Letter to Three Wives* (1949) and *All About Eve* (1950) had established him as the best director of civilized dialogue in Hollywood. Together, Houseman and Mankiewicz agreed on an unusual shooting strategy—as far as possible, they eliminated reaction shots in order not to disrupt the rhythm of Shakespeare's lines.

As was characteristic of MGM's Roman epics of the 1950s, such as *Quo Vadis?* and *Ben-Hur* (1959), the cast combined the accents and styles of British and American actors. English players such as James Mason as a thoughtful Brutus and John Gielgud as a volatile Cassius were balanced by Americans Louis Calhern as an imposing Caesar and Edmond O'Brien as a crafty, cynical Casca. The most contentious choice was Marlon Brando as Antony. Associated with the Method-style of naturalistic mumbling, Brando nonetheless gave a performance that attracted an enormous amount of comment and astonished many with its authority and clarity. Brando's charisma shifted the balance of the play away from Brutus' tragedy, in accordance with Mankiewicz' conception of Brutus as an "Adlai Stevenson-type figure," cultured, intelligent, but a bit at sea amid the hurly-burly of opportunistic politics. Oddly, the film made little attempt to exploit the opportunities presented by the play for spectacle and action, and the battle at Philippi emerges as a pretty tepid affair.

More impressive were the small individual touches—the use of chiaroscuro lighting to suggest Brutus's uncertainty and inner torment; the deployment of statues as adornment of, and ironic commentary on, the action; and an electrifying moment when Brutus's speech to the mob is upstaged by Antony's suddenly producing Caesar's body as a bloodcurdlingly effective theatrical prop.

REFERENCES

Geist, Kenneth L., *People Will Talk: The Life and Films of Joseph L. Mankiewicz* (New York: Charles Scribner's Sons, 1978); Houseman, John, *Unfinished Business* (London: Chatto and Windus, 1986); Jorgens, Jack J., *Shakespeare on Film* (Bloomington: Indiana University Press, 1977); Sinyard, Neil, *Filming Literature: The Art of Screen Adaptation* (London: Croom Helm, 1985).

—*N.S.*

KING LEAR (1606)

King Lear (1909), U.S.A., directed by J. Stuart Blackton and William V. Ranous; Vitagraph.

King Lear (1916), U.S.A., directed by Ernest C. Warde; Thanhouser Film Corporation.

The Yiddish King Lear (1934), U.S.A., directed by Harry Thomashefsky; Lear Pictures, Inc.

King Lear (1948), U.K., directed and adapted by Royston Morley; British Broadcasting Corporation.

King Lear (1953), U.S.A., directed and adapted by Andrew McCullough and Peter Brook; CBS Films/Omnibus Productions.

Karol Lir (1970), USSR, directed and adapted by Grigori Kozintsev; Lenfilm Studio.

King Lear (1971), U.K., directed and adapted by Peter Brook; Athena-Laterna Films.

King Lear (1975), U.K., directed and adapted by Jonathan Miller; British Broadcasting Corporation.

King Lear (1977), U.S.A., directed and adapted by Edwin Sherin for Joseph Papp; Theatre in America.

King Lear (1982), U.K./U.S.A., directed by Jonathan Miller; adapted by David Shodin and Patricia Preece; BBC/Time-Life Television Productions, Inc.

King Lear (1983), U.K., directed and adapted by Michael Elliott; Granada Television.

Ran (1985), Japan, directed by Akira Kurosawa, adapted by Kurosawa, Hideo Oguni, and Masato Ide; Nippon Herald Films.

King Lear (1987), France, directed and adapted by Jean-Luc Godard; Cannon Films.

King Lear (1997), U.K., directed and adapted by Richard Eyre; BBC/Chesterfield Ltd./WGBH-Boston.

The Play

With the exception of Shakespeare's other major tragedies (*Hamlet, Othello, Macbeth*), few plays approach *King Lear* in portraying and evoking the wretchedness of human existence, and even those plays are hard-pressed to equal the devastating spectacle of brutality and misery visited upon Lear and the earl of Gloucester, the play's two protagonists. The play's complex double plot provides a rich orchestration like no other Shakespeare play. King Lear misjudges his children; he disinherits his loving daughter Cordelia in favor of the duplicitous Goneril and Regan; Gloucester falls prey to Edmund's deceptions, disinherits his loyal son Edgar. Both are exiled: Lear is turned out into the storm by his false daughters and, in his madness, realizes his fault against Cordelia; Gloucester, branded a traitor by Edmund, is deprived of his eyesight but at last "sees" the truth about Edgar. Both fathers are finally cared for by their loving children and belatedly reconciled to them, but die bereft and brokenhearted. Cordelia's death, in particular, implies a wanton universe and exemplifies despair. In no other Shakespeare play does injustice triumph so ferociously for so long. It is not surprising, then, that *King Lear* has eclipsed *Hamlet* for many critics as Shakespeare's greatest tragedy.

Gloucester and Lear symbolize the plight of the elderly—whether guilt-ridden and dethroned monarchs or powerless, lonely outcasts haunted by memories and facing poverty and imminent death. The story of these two old men distills the experience of growing old—its despair and panic, its desperation for dignity and affection, and its sense of ingratitude and neglect—as the world goes on without them. Add to that plight the devastating pessimism regarding justice in an indifferent universe, and Shakespeare paints a malignancy at the core of the human heart. Enlightenment comes only through suffering; this enlightenment for Lear comes at the expense of his kingdom and the life of his faithful daughter Cordelia; for Gloucester spiritual wisdom arrives at the cost of his own vision. Just as Lear achieves spiritual wisdom when he goes mad, Gloucester achieves it when he is physically blinded.

Yet, to say merely that Lear and Gloucester learn something precious and significant is not to deny that they are broken and devastated by their brutal humiliation. Misery teaches Lear what he never could know as king about other poor wretches who have been pelted by the storm of existence: "O, I have ta'en/Too little care of this! Take physic, pomp;/Expose thyself to feel what wretches feel,/That thou mayest shake the superflux to them/And show the heavens more just" (III.iv.28–36). Both Gloucester and Lear drive virtuous children into exile (Cordelia and Edgar) and place themselves at the mercy of the wicked (Goneril, Regan, and Edmund). By the play's catastrophe, the appearance and the reality of justice have changed places along with folly and wisdom and blindness and seeing. *King Lear* repeatedly questions the existence of heaven only to provide ambiguous answers: "If you do love old men/If your sweet sway/Allow obedience, if you yourselves are old,/Make it your cause" (II.iv.191–193), Lear implores the gods, his exhortations mounting into frenzy before finally the heavens send down an answer—a storm on Lear himself.

Yet good does exist in this malignant universe: Servants obey their better instincts and turn against Cornwall to minister to Gloucester, doomed Cordelia forgives and cherishes her father, and Edgar ministers to Gloucester. These displays go directly against Edmund's amoral view of humanity and his naturalistic view of the universe in which morality, religion, and conscience are empty myths. The play suggests that villainy will indeed destroy itself, not simply because the gods are just but because insatiable ambition leads to violent death. Edmund, Goneril, and Regan all are consumed by their own lust and thus doom themselves. Yet despite this reassurance that villainy eventually undoes itself, *King Lear*, in its appalling devastation, refuses to answer its central questions about justice. Poetic justice and cause and effect do not account for political order or the enormity of personal disaster. Love's power is at last discovered in its very defeat, though it is learned far too late.

Shakespeare wrote *King Lear* no earlier that 1603 or 1604 and probably in 1605, between *Othello* (ca. 1603–04) and *Macbeth* (ca. 1606–07), while at the height of his literary powers. It was performed at Court in December 1606. However, throughout its earlier history, the ancient Lear story always ended happily. The earliest known version of the story appears in Geoffrey of Monmouth's *Historia Regum Britanniae* (ca. 1136) and records that Lear is overthrown by his sons-in-law—more than by his daughters—and restored to the throne by the intervention of the French king. Shakespeare was familiar with 16th-century Tudor versions that retained the happy ending: John Higgin's account in *The First Part of the Mirror for Magistrates* (1574), Raphael Holinshed's *Chronicles* (1587), Edmund Spenser's *The Faerie Queen*, and a play called *The True Chronicle History of King Leir* (1594, though not published until 1605). But Shakespeare's probable source for the tragic pattern and the Gloucester-Edgar-Edmund plot is Sir Philip Sydney's *Arcadia*, in which the Paphlagonian king falls victim to filial deceit and ingratitude. Yet Shakespeare's authority was not enough to overcome the public's craving for a happy resolution. In 1681, Nahum Tate's adaptation—which banished the fool, united Edgar and Cordelia in marriage, and restored Lear to the throne—held the English stage for nearly 150 years. David Garrick restored a portion of Shakespeare's lines, and Edmund Kean restored the tragic ending, but it was not until 1838 that *King Lear* was again performed more or less as Shakespeare had intended.

The Films

Shakespeare's tragedy first appeared on the screen in a handful of forgettable efforts in the Silent period and in the 1930s. In 1909, J. Stuart Blackton and William V. Ranous directed the first film adaptation of *King Lear*, followed in 1916 by Ernest C. Warde's version. In 1934, Harry Thomashefsky brought *The Yiddish King Lear* to American moviehouses, but film adaptations of the play did not appear again until the advent of television. The first television adaptation was produced by the BBC and directed by Royston Morley with William Devlin in the title role and Patrick Troughton as Edmund. In 1953, CBS and Omnibus featured director Andrew McCullough and producer Peter Brook's adaptation starring Orson Welles in the first American television version.

In 1970, Russian filmmaker Grigori Kozintsev released the first major foreign film version of Shakespeare's play with *Karol Lir*, adapted from Boris Pasternak's Russian translation of *King Lear*; it took few liberties with the structure, except, as Nigel Andrews noted, for one "startling omission," Gloucester's "illusory suicide attempt at Dover." Kozintsev's *Lear* is a Christian-Marxist tale of redemption and social renewal that presents the story of an individual's journey from insensitive ignorance to self-knowledge and pity. It follows the New Testament adage: To find oneself, one must first lose oneself. It is a meditation on the nature of reality and stoic endurance after civilization is stripped away. Though there is tremendous suffering and cruelty, there is also a discernable progression from materialistic tyranny to basic questioning and a deepening understanding. For Kozintsev, *King Lear* is a play localized both in cruelty and in mercy. His is a more romantic film. Yuri Jarvet's Lear is a weaker, more pathetic figure than is usually presented. This frailty heightens the sense of injustice in the suffering he endures. This Lear's violent responses become more interior. The end is not meaningless; rather, it is the beginning. Cruelty will still go on, but there are signs of renewal everywhere. For Kozintsev, *Lear* is not merely "a drama of a particular group of people who are linked by plot, but also a stream of history. Whole structures of life and social situations are carried along and tumbled together. Not only single voices are heard in the din of tragedy but combined and mighty ensembles, whole choruses." From Kozintsev's perspective on Russian and Soviet history, absolute dictatorship is both a cultural legacy and a living historical memory.

Kozintsev's film is a superimposition of the Middle Ages and the Renaissance. Visually, it is elaborate.

Musically, Shostakovich's orchestral score moves the film toward a Russian romantic epic style, structurally significant by adding a more ornate, denser texture. Though it romantically builds toward large dramatic moments, Kozintsev's treatment is brutal and animalistic. Technically, the Russian uses associative montage more consistently to generate meaning between shots and uses camera movement to sweep upward at emotional peaks, or restless tracking shots as characters both pursue and are pursued. Kozintsev's central scene is the capture of Lear and Cordelia in which good triumphs over evil, even as evil prepares to destroy it. Here, in the depiction of the love between father and daughter, and in Edmund's uncomprehending hatred of it, lies the film's most powerful confirmation of love's power and it overrides the suffering at the end. Kozintsev's film represents the life of a willful ruler through its reflection in the lives of his subjects. The tragic destiny of Lear expresses at the same time the destiny of a people.

Having once said that Shakespeare was impossible to film, director Peter Brook in 1971 released his major adaptation of *King Lear*. Shot during the winter of 1968–69, on location in North Jutland, Denmark, Brook set the tragedy in a pagan, pre-Christian society that would still be sophisticated enough in its commentary on social relationships as to be viable for both the Elizabethan and the modern audience. Brook's version is a bleak, existential tale of meaningless violence in a cold, empty universe, beginning in silence and ending with civilization left in ruins. He shows the apocalyptic decline and fall of an archetypal kingdom and its rulers. His is a story of lust for power that consumes the bonds of love between parents and children, a story of jealousy, blindness, and vanity. It is a highly violent film, which assaults its audience with mental cruelty. Nature, though amoral and nihilistic, is infused with aggression and brutality. The absence of justice leaves evil destroying both itself and the good with devastation, emptiness, and scarred individuals too stunned to continue. Lear's generalized pain reflects the shattering of Christian humanist values like forgiveness, compassion, and humility.

Brook's interpretive vision duplicates in cinematic terms Shakespeare's blend of stage artifice and imaginative reality. He also avoids sentimentality to heighten the bleakness of the tale and the power of the scenes between Lear (Paul Scofield) and Cordelia (Annelise Gabold) and between Lear and Gloucester (Alan Webb); one effect is the total elimination of Edmund's reformation and attempt to save Lear and Cordelia's lives. (Edmund is played by Ian Hogg, Edgar by Robert Lloyd; Goneril is played by Irene

Opposite Paul Scofield's King Lear was Jack MacGowan as the Fool. (COURTESY NATIONAL FILM SOCIETY ARCHIVES)

Worth, Regan by Susan Engel; Jack MacGowran plays Lear's Fool.)

The central scene in Brook's version is Lear's beach conversation with Gloucester; here, the simplicity of a blind subject meeting his insane king is heightened by the ferocity and expressionism of the rest of the film. This scene's emotional power lies in its adherence to Shakespeare's mixture of the general and the specific. Brook concludes his perspective on *Lear* in the film's final shot. Contrasting with the film's opening darkness, this version ends on a gravel beach bathed in glaring white light with Lear, kneeling over Cordelia's body; surrounded by nothingness, he falls backward in slow motion, disappearing from the screen. This image leaves a sense of unrelieved hopelessness and emptiness.

Brook's interpretation of *King Lear* is raw, primitive, ascetic, and stripped to nothingness. He uses disjointed images, superimpositions, surreal appearances, crude surfaces, washed-out and grainy black-and-white images, close-ups, and shallow depth of field to increase a sense of solipsism. The actors understate their lines in slow, gruff whispers, which are essentially

devoid of music. Much of Shakespeare's exposition is stripped away and the subplot pared to the leanest elements. Though criticized as self-conscious and flashy, Brook's character-centered version is also a minimalist response to the decorative spectacle of previous Shakespeare adaptations.

Adaptations of Shakespeare's tragedy during the remainder of the 1970s and early 1980s were television productions. In 1975, Jonathan Miller directed a BBC adaptation with Michael Hordern as Lear; then, in 1982, Miller directed a joint American-British venture between BBC and Time-Life that also featured Hordern as Lear. In 1977 the Joseph Papp "Theatre in America" series featured the leading African-American actor James Earl Jones as Lear in a New York Shakespeare Festival production that also featured Paul Sorvino (Gloucester), Raul Julia (Edmund), and Rene Auberjonois (Edgar); the production was not successful with the critics. In 1983, Michael Elliot mounted a Granada Television production starring Sir Laurence Olivier as Lear, Dorothy Tutin (Goneril), Diana Rigg (Regan), Leo McKern (Gloucester), Colin Blakely (Kent), and John Hurt as Lear's Fool. Thanks to such an outstanding cast, this production was much praised, though some liberties were taken with the text and perhaps too much emphasis was placed on Lear's enemies rather than on his suffering. (One possible Shakespeare derivative should arguably be mentioned in passing, Paul Mazursky's *Harry and Tonto* [1974], for which Art Carney won an Academy Award; but to consider this otherwise touching story of a 72-year-old English teacher evicted from his New York apartment with his cat, Tonto, as an updating of *King Lear* is perhaps too much of a stretch.)

In 1985, Japanese director Akira Kurosawa relocated *King Lear* to medieval Japan, rendering Lear an aging feudal warlord. In doing so, he offers a variation on legend and history that contradicts orthodox, institutionalized culture. *Ran* (translated as "chaos") ironically represents the historical conditions of samurai power. Though the first inspiration for the movie came through his idea to invert the legend of Motonari Mori (1497–1571), Kurosawa, in scripting *Ran*'s story of a feared but aging ruler deposed by his disloyal sons, noticed the similarities with Shakespeare's tragedy. However, in considering *King Lear* Kurosawa was puzzled that the English dramatist had not given his characters a past: How did Lear acquire the power that, as an old man, he abuses with such disastrous effects and what accounted for his daughters' ferocious response to their father's attempts to step down? Kurosawa answered such questions by creating a past political career for the ruler and setting events in a specific era. Since the setting is medieval Japan, the fictional Great Lord Hidetora Ichimonji's line of descent had to be male—to divide a kingdom among daughters would have contradicted history. Though Kurosawa drew plot elements, significant incidents, and central metaphors from Shakespeare's tragedy, his treatment is controlled by his original intention of inverting Japanese ideals of family and political loyalty.

In Kurosawa's perspective on the era of Japanese history in which he sets the events of *Ran*, absolute power is based on a legacy of ruthlessness. Amidst the suffering and chaos that results from Hidetora's ill-conceived plans for peace through shared power with his three sons, he encounters the survivors of his own savage conquest of the kingdom years earlier. This dramatic movement through the ruins of past ambition and war is distinctly different in structure from the immediacy of the tragedy that follows from King Lear's demand for professions of love and from his rash temper, which theatre audiences directly witness. This aside, *Ran* has a stronger intertextual connection to Shakespeare in terms of the play's figurative language rather than in terms of incident, characterization, or description. The narrower dramatic action eliminates the Gloucester subplot while transposing other elements from it. Kurosawa condenses and intensifies events and character traits. Through its remarkable costumes, sets, scenes, and cinematography, Kurosawa considers his film more hopeful, less pessimistic, and less tragic than Shakespeare's play. While King Lear has no regrets, does not contemplate his past, and needlessly falls, Hidetora reflects on his past and regrets it. *Ran* lacks the archetypal pattern of Western tragedy's sacrifice of the hero and its promise of redemption for his society. However, in creating a detailed past of misdeeds by the main character, Kurosawa renders Hidetora not only less tragic but also less heroic than Lear. In the film's final shot of the blind Tsurumaru (Kurosawa's parallel for Gloucester and Edgar), unattended and moving toward the edge of a castle rampart, a blind and unprotected humanity stands near the edge of a precipice. This is a summation of Kurosawa's vision of what humanity is, in having brought itself to the brink of extinction. This situation is a final indication that human suffering has entirely human origins; thus, the tragedy is historical, existential, and unheroic.

The most recent film versions of *King Lear* are Jean-Luc Godard's ludicrous version, which updates Shakespeare's play to a bizarre, contemporary punk-apocalyptic setting, featuring Burgess Meredith as "Don Learo," Molly Ringwald (Cordelia), Woody Allen as a film editor, Peter Sellers as "Will Shakespeare," Godard himself as a "Professor," and Norman Mailer (for whatever reason) playing himself. This oddity was followed by Richard Eyre's 1997 television adaptation for American Public Television starring Ian Holm as a cranky, imperious Lear and Victoria Hamilton as a high-strung, quivery Cordelia.

REFERENCES

Andrews, Nigel, "King Lear," *Sight and Sound*, 41:3 (1972), 171–172; Bevington, David, ed., *The Complete Works of Shakespeare* (New York: HarperCollins, 1992); Goodwin, James, *Akira Kurosawa and Intertextual Cinema* (Baltimore: Johns Hopkins University Press, 1994); Jorgens, Jack J., *Shakespeare on Film* (Bloomington: Indiana University Press, 1977); Kozintsev, Grigori, *King Lear: The Space of Tragedy* (Berkeley: University of California Press, 1977); Manville, Roger, *Shakespeare and the Film* (New York: Praeger, 1971); Rothwell, Kenneth S., and Annabelle Henkin Melzer, *Shakespeare on Screen: An International Filmography and Videography* (New York: Neal-Schuman, 1990); Welsh, J.M., "'To See It Feelingly': *King Lear* through Russian Eyes," *Literature/Film Quarterly*, 4:2 (1976), 153–158.

—*J.N.Y.*

LOVE'S LABOURS LOST (1594–95)

Love's Labours Lost (2000), U.K., directed and adapted by Kenneth Branagh; Pathe Pictures/Miramax.

The Play

Perhaps written as early as 1593 or 1594, *A Pleasant Conceited Comedie Called Love's Labours Lost* was first published under that full title in the First Quarto edition of 1598 and was the first time that Shakespeare's name appeared on a title page. It was advertised as having been "presented before her Highness [Queen Elizabeth I] this last Christmas." The play is an academic satire about young King Ferdinand of Navarre, who has decided to take his books rather too seriously, removing himself and three courtly gentlemen—Dumain, Longaville, and Berowne—from his Court and from the company of women for a three-year period. His dedication to celibacy and scholarship is challenged, however, by the presence of four attractive noblewomen, embedded in the plot to shake the men's resolve. There is much pedantry and wordplay in evidence here. The king's "little Academe" in the play pokes fun at the pretensions of French and Italian philosophical debating societies, which had become popular among the educated in Shakespeare's time.

Balanced against the high-minded courtly characters are low-comedy types derived from the Italian *commedia dell'arte*—the pedantic schoolmaster Holo-

fernes, for example; the "braggart" Don Adriano de Armado, described as a "fantastical Spaniard"; the quick-witted fool Moth; and the slow-witted one, Costard. By Act Four the king is in love with the visiting princess, Dumain with Katherine, Longaville with Maria, and even Berowne, who ridicules the others for their hypocrisy, with Rosaline. Act Five indulges in a farce of mistaken identities, as the lords disguise themselves as Russians and the ladies don masks. This is followed by a masque of "The Nine Worthies": Pompey (Costard), Alexander (Nathaniel), Judas Maccabaeus (Holofernes), Hercules (Moth), and Hector (Armado). At the end the princess is recalled to France by the news that her father has died. Romantic consummation is therefore to be postponed for a year to test the lovers, secluded in a "forlorn and naked hermitage." Thus "Our wooing doth not end like an old play," Berowne advises the audience: "Jack hath not Jill."

The Film

By no means Shakespeare's most popular comedy, *Love's Labours Lost* was not produced as a feature film until 1999, only to be released to tepid reviews in America in 2000. There were two television treatments, however: in 1965 BBC-2 captured a Bristol Old Vic performance directed by Roger Jenkins and the BBC "Shakespeare Plays" series production in 18th-century costume directed by Elijah Moshinsky in 1984, which was not a critical success. Perhaps a knowledge of these lackluster attempts prompted Kenneth Branagh's oddly flamboyant, oddly adapted, and greatly transformed approach. As *Variety* described it, Shakespeare's play was "hacked down into a faux, old-style Hollywood tuner and given the handle 'A Romantic Musical Comedy.'"

Because of the thinness of the contrived plot, director Kenneth Branagh decided to give the play a postmodern hydraulic life, setting it in the early 20th century (September 1939, to be exact) and striving mightily to turn it into a boulevardish comedy, into a Hollywood musical that would augment the language of Shakespeare with the music and lyrics of George and Ira Gershwin, Jerome Kern, Cole Porter, and Irving Berlin—anything that would make the play amusing for an audience less than attuned to the wordplay. Critics were dubious about whether the cast was up to the challenge of being Shakespearean actors, singers, and dancers. This is not so much an adaptation as a substitution. Stanley Kauffmann estimated that two-thirds of Shakespeare's language had been discarded, all the more surprising since in his previous Shakespeare outing, *Hamlet*, Branagh had produced a four-hour film that was absolutely faithful to every word of every speech in the published record of the play up to 1623. By appropriating the songs of other talents, Branagh had to jettison one of Shakespeare's most famous songs, because, he explained, "It just couldn't be reconciled with the great modern songs we decided to use."

Of course, *Love's Labours Lost* is not *Hamlet* and not the product of Shakespeare's most mature art. Among the comedies, *Love's Labours Lost* pales in comparison to *Twelfth Night* and *A Midsummer Night's Dream*, plays that had been done and redone before Branagh could have a go at them. Trevor Nunn beat him to the punch with *Twelfth Night* and Michael Hoffman with *A Midsummer Night's Dream*. So Branagh apparently opted for the overdone rather than the redone so as to avoid the redundant. As a consequence, Branagh decided to "face the music, and dance."

Branagh's concept seems to have sprung full-blown, not from the brow of Zeus, but from that of Woody Allen when Branagh was involved in another ill-advised project, Allen's *Celebrity*, after Allen had taken what Gary Arnold called "an eccentric swing at musical comedy in *Everyone Says I Love You*." However, Allen was not screwing around with Shakespeare in that film, and Woody Allen has a more finely honed sense of comedy than Kenneth Branagh, *Much Ado About Nothing* notwithstanding. Branagh had played the amorous king of Navarre in his Royal Shakespeare Company production, which, like Branagh's filmed *Hamlet*, had moved the play up in time to the 1870s.

The film moved the time-frame forward by another 70 years so that Branagh could lard it with Schmaltz from the swing era and maybe a touch of *Casablanca*. This pop-culture extravaganza was not likely to impress the purists.

Stanley Kauffmann, a critic who understood theatre as well as anyone reviewing films when *Love's Labours Lost* was released, is not a purist, but he does respect the language of Shakespeare, which Branagh slighted. But Kauffmann was most displeased by the inadequacies of the cast. He found the casting of the two leads—Alessandro Nivola and Alicia Silverstone as the king and princess—"dull or dreadful." As the Spaniard Don Armado, Timothy Spaull—who had played the sleaziness of Eric Lyle brilliantly in Bernardo Bertolucci's *The Sheltering Sky* and who was a fine Guildenstern in Branagh's *Hamlet*—has trouble both dancing and delivering the Cole Porter song given to him to perform.

Of the eight principals, Kauffmann found only Branagh himself "impressive" and dismissed Alessandro Nivola and Alicia Silverstone as being "inadequate in every way," though the *Variety* reviewer claimed that Silverstone was able to "hold her own" in a "sporty" performance. Branagh gave himself the role of Berowne, the most verbal and eloquent of the attendant lords, who, with just under 600 lines, has the play's longest part. Natascha McElhone plays Rosaline to Branagh's Berowne, and Richard Briers, who played a sinister Polonius in Branagh's *Hamlet*, is cast as Nathaniel, a curate. Costard (Nathan Lane) is reimagined as a vaudeville clown, and Dull (Jimmy Yuill) as a police constable.

For Kauffmann the enterprise was "not completely lost," thanks to Geraldine McEwan, who plays the "schoolmistress Holofornia (Shakespeare's Holofornes transgendered) with her imperishable wit and charm," and Nathan Lane, who Kauffmann found impeccable as Costard, the clown who has the honor of singing the showstopper, "There's No Business Like Show Business." Because the 10 songs are so easy, familiar, and listenable, they make what's left of the text seem more difficult than usual. The film ends somewhat awkwardly on the eve of World War II, and the war enforces the postponement of marital bliss for the lovers, providing a grim little twist at the conclusion.

Predicting disgruntled and wicked reviews, *Variety* warned that Branagh would have difficulty selling the concept as an enjoyable, "slightly campy entertainment to the younger crowd" because there were "few recent precedents for such a picture," though one possible precedent may be the work of Dennis Potter, no doubt unknown to most younger viewers. Branagh assumed the mantle of Lord Olivier in 1989 with his spectacularly good treatment of *Henry V* and has gone on to become the world's foremost popularizer of Shakespeare. His previous attempts all hit the mark with varying degrees of accuracy, but *Love's Labours Lost* surely misfired both with audiences and critics.

REFERENCES

Ansen, David, "Shakespeare Less Loved," *Newsweek* (June 12, 2000), 74; Arnold, Gary, "The Bard Keeps Branagh in Business," *The Washington Times*, June 16, 2000, C4; Elley, Derek, "Bold Tuner from Branagh," *Variety*, February 21–27, 2000, 50–51; Kauffmann, Stanley, "Well, Not Completely Lost," *The New Republic* (June 10 & 17, 2000), 32–33; Rothwell, Kenneth S. and Annabelle Henkin Melzer, *Shakespeare on Screen* (New York: Neal-Schuman, 1990).

—*J.M.W.*

MACBETH (1606)

Macbeth (1916), U.S.A., directed and adapted by John Emerson; Fine Arts/Reliance-Majestic.

Macbeth (1948), U.S.A., directed and adapted by Orson Welles; Republic Pictures.

Joe MacBeth (1955), U.K., directed by Ken Hughes, adapted by Philip Yordan; Film Locations/Frankovich/Columbia Pictures.

Throne of Blood/The Castle of the Spider's Web [*Kumonosu-Djo*] (1957), Japan, directed and adapted by Akira Kurosawa; Toho Films.

Macbeth (1972), U.K., directed by Roman Polanski, adapted by Kenneth Tynan and Roman Polanski, Playboy Productions/Columbia-Warner.

Men of Respect (1990), U.S.A., directed and adapted by William Reilly; Central City/Ephraim Goldblatt.

The Play

Next to *Hamlet*, *Macbeth* is Shakespeare's best-known tragedy, a study of ambition's destruction of a man of conscience. First performed in 1606 and based on sources in Raphael Holinshed's *Chronicles*, the play recounts the fall of Macbeth, a military hero first introduced to us as a brave defender of King Duncan, whose reign has been threatened by foreign and native rebels. Returning to his castle and devoted wife following his army's victory, Macbeth and his fellow general Banquo are accosted by three witches who prophesy that the hero will become king, while his companion's children will one day wear the Crown. Banquo is skeptical, but Macbeth secretly embraces the prediction because it conforms to his desire for sovereignty. When Duncan and his train arrive at Macbeth's castle to celebrate, the king takes the occasion to announce that he has delegated his son Malcolm to succeed him. The news perplexes Macbeth, but Lady Macbeth urges him to remain firm and behave "like a man." She spawns a plan to stab Duncan in his sleep and blame the murder on his attendants. Macbeth's conscience troubles him, provoking in his mind's eye the vision of an imaginary dagger.

After their father's murder, Malcolm and his brother Donalbain flee to England, giving Macbeth the opportunity to hint at their guilt and assume Scotland's throne. To solidify his grip, the newly crowned king arranges the assassination of his rival Banquo on the eve of a royal banquet. Fleance, Banquo's son, manages to escape, however, keeping alive the possibility that he or his heirs might one day come to power. During the feast, Banquo's ghost takes Macbeth's place at the table, prompting the distracted host to hurl threats at the specter and declare his manhood to a stunned audience unable to see what he sees. Lady

Macbeth proves incapable of restoring peace and urges the guests to depart in disorder and haste. The disruption of the banquet marks Macbeth's decline into despotism and Lady Macbeth's loss of control over her husband. He becomes more robotic, she more withdrawn and conscience-stricken.

Frantic to know "the future in an instant," Macbeth forces the witches to make clear his fate. They reassure him that "no man of woman born" will defeat him and that he will rule until "Birnam Wood come to Dunsinane [Macbeth's castle]." These pronouncements still his fears but give him unwarranted confidence in his invincibility. That confidence is shaken when Lady Macbeth suddenly dies, following a sleepwalking episode in which she reveals her guilt for Duncan's murder. Her death occurs at just the wrong moment for the besieged Macbeth: Malcolm, backed by loyal Macduff and English forces, leads his army toward Dunsinane under camouflage provided by branches from Birnam's trees. Desperate but undaunted, Macbeth battles the invaders, scorning those he kills as obviously born of women. Yet, when he confronts Macduff, whom he is reluctant to fight because he has already killed the thane's wife and children, Macbeth discovers to his dismay that his opponent was "untimely ripped" from his mother's womb. The play ends with Macduff beheading Macbeth and proudly championing Malcolm's rightful assumption of Scotland's throne. The resumed succession would have been particularly pleasing to James I, who ruled Scotland before becoming England's king and traced his lineage back to Banquo.

The Films

Several films of *Macbeth* appeared in the silent era, foremost of which was Sir Herbert Beerbohm Tree's 1916 production for the Fine Arts company (a component of the three-pronged Triangle Films studio), directed and adapted by John Emerson. (Publicity at the time claimed that the production was supervised by D.W. Griffith but was doubtless greatly exaggerated.) It was a time when stage stars by the dozens were being lured to Hollywood, and Tree's appearance promised to confer legitimacy on the production (indeed, his salary of between $3,000 and $4,000 a week was one of the highest salaries paid to an actor up to that time). Costarring as Lady Macbeth was another stage star, Constance Collier. Because this *Macbeth* is a "lost" film, we have only historians' and contemporary critics' commentary to go on. In his history of the Triangle studio, Kalton Lahue notes that Tree "had no concept of motion pictures and continually moved out

of range or frame, turning his back to the camera and grandly overexaggerating his pantomime." So bad was Tree, Lahue contends, that actor Monte Blue was called in to double many of his scenes. As for the contemporary reviews of the three-hour film, they were varied, to say the least. Writing in *The Moving Picture World* in June 1916, Lynde Denig praised the production as one that "not only visualizes the dramatic incidents completely and convincingly, but makes clear the mental processes of Macbeth and Lady Macbeth." When speech was necessary, Denig continued, "lines from the play are invariably used, and the arrangement of the scenario necessitates few explanatory leaders. It is a treat, indeed, to read so much of Shakespeare on the screen, even if some familiar quotations are slightly altered." Sir Herbert, moreover, was a "virile, compelling Macbeth, possessed of the rare art that makes possible the communication of emotional states." However, critic Julian Johnson demurred in the pages of *Photoplay* a few weeks later. He singled out Tree's performance as stiff and static: "After the first few episodes, this acting consisted, on the part of Sir Herbert, of staring and wobbling, and the staring eye when translated into black and white, becomes extremely monotonous." What is beyond dispute is that *Macbeth* was a failure at the box office. A few months later, Beerbohm Tree's movie career was likewise a footnote in history.

The first major sound production was Orson Welles's 1948 version for the B-movie studio, Republic Pictures. With the box-office failures and budget overruns of *The Lady from Shanghai* (1947) and *The Stranger* (1947) behind him, he determined to bring a film in on time and on a modest budget. Certainly Welles knew his way around Shakespeare's play, having already produced an experimental all-black "voodoo" version on Broadway for the Federal Theatre Project in the mid-1930s. The new film project, based on his production for the Utah Shakespeare Festival, and shot in just 23 days, was a daring effort, but a box-office disaster. The brilliant director of such films as *Citizen Kane* (1941) and *The Magnificent Ambersons* (1942) seemed not to care about the fate of the picture as it went into post-production. "The fact was," as biographer Barbara Leaming has written, "that as far as Orson was concerned, *Macbeth* was in a sense finished—not as a film of course, but as an experiment. In *Macbeth* Orson had never intended to make a great film; just to prove a point, to show what could be shot quickly and cheaply." As for the finished product, it transformed Shakespeare's tragedy into a morality tale about Christian good and pagan evil. This interpretation is evident in the opening sequence, during which the witches shape a mud doll representative of Macbeth that can be controlled by a kind of voodoo-like magic. Welles also created a character named Holy Father (Alan Napier) to oppose the witches; he conducts a general mass aimed at exorcising Satan after Duncan's party arrives at Macbeth's castle. During the action, he carries a cross-topped staff while the witches brandish sticks that look for all the world like television antennas. Macbeth seals his fate when he kills Holy Father with a spear during the siege of Dunsinane.

Working with a meager budget, Welles had to rely on Fred Ritter's cardboard-like sets, which looked more like leaky caves than monumental castles. He also asked his actors, many of whom had worked on his *Mercury Theatre of the Air* radio show, to speak in a Scottish burr, a decision that resulted in a garbled sound track to go along with the generally murky chiaroscuro of the cinematography. A weak performance by Jeanette Nolan as Lady Macbeth and drastic cuts and transpositions further hampered the film. Most telling was, as one critic complained, the director's decision to represent the hero as a "static, two-dimensional creature" capable of villainy from the tragedy's very beginning, which strips the role and the play of their compelling psychological dimension.

An even more problematic translation is Ken Hughes's 1955 *Joe Macbeth*. Hughes and screenwriter Philip Yordan displace the tragedy into the tale of a gangster who kills his way to the top of the mob. Set in Chicago, this genre piece begins with the gunning down of boss Big Duca's (Gregoire Aslan) rival in Tommy's Café. The man behind the hit is Joe (Paul Douglas), who celebrates his newfound status with his wife Lily (Ruth Roman) in another nightclub. During the celebration, a fortune-teller named Rosie (Minerva Pious) announces that Joe will soon become "Lord of Lakeview Drive," then "King of the City." Lily urges her husband to fulfill the prophecy when Big Duca comes to the mansion for a weekend party, accompanied by Bandy (Sid Jones) and Lennie (Bonar Coleano). These two lieutenants correspond to Banquo and his son, Fleance; Joe and Lily will try to pin Big Duca's murder on them. Instead of staying in his bed, however, the boss of bosses takes a late-night swim, forcing Joe to stab and drown him. Lily has to dive into the lake to retrieve the murder weapon when her frightened husband forgets it. Joe tries to consolidate his power by killing Bandy and Lennie's wife and children. During the banquet to confirm his ascension, however, he encounters Banky's ghost and delivers the classic mobster line, "Which one-a you guys done this?"

His paranoia increasing, the hero becomes a prisoner in his own home, where he barricades himself and, in a fit of blind terror, mistakenly guns down Lily when she tries to free him from his office. Lennie finally gains his revenge by shooting Joe, then running out into a hail of bullets from the police. The film ends as another morality tale about the bitter fruits of ambition told in the context of gangster culture. Marred by amateurish acting—Ruth Roman's performance is the sole exception—unintentionally funny dialogue, and pretentious *noirish* sequences, *Joe Macbeth* richly deserves its place at the bottom of the remaindered videos bin.

A more compelling offshoot is Akira Kurosawa's *Throne of Blood* (1957). Bearing the characteristics of a samurai fable and an American western, *Throne* (also translated as *The Castle of the Spider's Web*) traces the career of Washizu (Toshiro Mifune), a medieval Japanese warrior who with his comrade Miki (Minoru Chiaki) defeats the rebels challenging Kuniharu's (Takamaru Sasaki) reign. On the way back from the decisive battle, the two captains lose their way in a fog-shrouded forest and encounter a ghostly figure turning a spinning wheel and singing of Washizu's rise to the position of lord of the Forest Castle. From this point, the film generally follows the *Macbeth* plot, but with some interesting variations: Asaji/Lady Macbeth (Isuzu Yamada) performs a Noh-like ritual dance after Kuniharu's murder; she tells Washizu that she is pregnant to prevent him from tapping Miki's son as his successor; Miki's murder is signaled by the return of his riderless white horse to his castle; Asaji wears a strange-looking mask while sleepwalking; and Washizu, instead of being beheaded in the finale, is pierced by hundreds of arrows that rain down on him from the bows of his own vengeful troops. This ritualized ending, one of the most horrific scenes of violence in the history of film, underscores Kurosawa's morality message that the general's own men are the only proper judges and executioners of one whose ambition transgressed their samurai code.

Roman Polanski's 1971 treatment, financed by Playboy Productions and adapted by Kenneth Tynan, seemed to many reviewers to inscribe onto the story a highly personalized code, one dealing with the life of Polanski himself. His wife, Sharon Tate, and the baby she was carrying had recently been brutally murdered by members of the Manson family. Polanski's obsession with graphically bloody scenes, especially Duncan's murder, appeared to have been prompted by visions of the ritual killing of his wife. The director's obsession with sexuality was thought to be mirrored in Lady Macbeth's (Francesca Annis) nude sleepwalking scene, a gratuitous sequence perhaps bespeaking the *Playboy* underwriting.

Jon Finch portrayed Macbeth in Roman Polanski's screen adaptation. (COURTESY COLUMBIA PICTURES)

Francesca Annis portrayed Lady Macbeth in Roman Polanski's Macbeth. (COURTESY COLUMBIA PICTURES)

The tragedy is marked by numerous references to blood and sex, notwithstanding Polanski's own private obsessions. There's the bloody captain, gore-smeared daggers, the sexually charged relationship between Macbeth (Jon Finch) and his lady—all of which underscore the links between eroticism and power. Polanski also stressed the play's social context by introducing dogs, bears, chickens, and other objects that tend to ground the action in its historical setting. We witness the witches burying a hangman's noose, dagger, and severed hand on the beach, the rebel Cawdor mouthing "long live the king" as he is hanged in chains; a bear-baiting sequence observed closely by a fascinated Lady Macbeth. The film's mise-en-scène has been described as "claustrophobic," creating a mood in which Macbeth and others struggle, like chained bears, to escape a certain, terrible fate. Indeed, Macbeth's severed head is mocked and treated like that of an animal when he is finally brought down. Instead of a morality fable, Polanski sees *Macbeth* as a Marxist tale about the unceasing hunger for power: The final shot is of Donalbain, who, following Malcolm's coronation, seeks shelter from a driving rain and finds him-

self drawn to the siren-like song of the witches in their hut. The wheel of fortune, Polanski suggests, continues to turn.

Unlike Polanski's sociopolitical reading of *Macbeth*, William Reilly's *Men of Respect* (1990) recalls *Joe Macbeth* in its attempt to recontextualize the play in the gangster-movie idiom. John Turturro plays the hero Mike Battaglia as a young, neurotic climber who displays no signs of Macbeth's conscience when, in the opening, slow-motion sequence, he guns down several mafiosi in a New York restaurant. This sequence is preceded by a voice-over chorus declaring, "There is nothing but what has a violent end or violent beginnings." Relying on the success of *The Godfather* trilogy and Martin Scorsese's *GoodFellas*, Reilly transforms Mike into a schemer for whom "respect" means more than conscience or loyalty.

Like *Joe Macbeth* the film uses a fortune-teller (Lilia Skala) instead of witches for prophecies and substitutes New York (as opposed to Chicago) street idioms for Shakespeare's verse. This descent into banality shows up most strikingly when, for example, Mike learns that his boss Charlie D'Amato (Rod Steiger) has promoted him to *capo regime*. The good news is greeted with "Whatever happens, happens." As in *Joe Macbeth*, the best performance is given by the actress—Katherine Borowitz—playing Lady Macbeth, here named Ruth. She displays genuine emotion and psychological depth as she tries to steel Mike's resolve to kill Charlie. To underline her determination, for instance, she reminds the hero that she had an abortion to further his career! Unfortunately, Borowitz's performance is the only bright spot in a disappointing offshoot that ends with a fatally injured Mike observing, "Shit happens."

REFERENCES

Andrews, Nigel, "*Macbeth*," *Sight and Sound*, 41 (Spring 1972), 108; Berlin, Normand, "*Macbeth*, Polanski, and Shakespeare," *Literature/Film Quarterly*, 1:4 (1973), 291–298; Denig, Lynde, "Macbeth," *The Moving Picture World*, 28:13 (June 24, 1916), 2258; Eckert, Charles W., ed., *Focus on Shakespearean Films* (Englewood Cliffs, N.J.: Prentice-Hall, 1972); Johnson, Julian, "Macbeth," *Photoplay*, 10:3 (August 1916), 141; Lahue, Kalton, *Dreams for Sale: The Rise and Fall of the Triangle Film Corporation* (Cranbury, N.J.: A.S. Barnes, 1971); Leaming, Barbara, *Orson Welles: A Biography* (New York: Viking Press, 1985); Willson, Robert F., Jr., *Shakespeare in Hollywood, 1929–1956* (Madison, N.J.: Fairleigh Dickinson University Press, 2000).

—*R.F.W.*

A MIDSUMMER NIGHT'S DREAM (1595)

A Midsummer Night's Dream (1935), U.S.A., directed by Max Reinhardt and William Dieterle, adapted by Charles Kenyon and Mary C. McCall; Warner Bros.

A Midsummer Night's Dream (1969), directed and adapted by Peter Hall; RSC Ent. Warner Bros.

William Shakespeare's A Midsummer Night's Dream (1999), directed and adapted by Michael Hoffman; Fox Searchlight Pictures.

The Play

The play begins in anticipation of the marriage of Theseus and Hippolyta and ends with their wedding celebration, and a comic masque, "A tedious brief scene of young Pyramus and his love Thisbe," involving "very tragical mirth," performed by a troupe of Athenian tradesmen led by Peter Quince and Bottom, the Weaver. But "the course of true love never did run smooth," and that is certainly the case for four young lovers who are unfortunately mismatched. Hermia loves Lysander, but is also loved by Demetrius, who is the choice of her father, Egeus, to marry her. Helena loves Demetrius, who has eyes only for Hermia. When Theseus rules that Hermia must marry Demetrius, Hermia and Lysander decide to elope into the forest and escape the obligations of Athenian law. They are pursued into the forest by Demetrius and Helena and find themselves caught up in a net of enchantment and frustration.

Deep in the forest, they are noticed by Oberon, king of the Fairies, who takes pity on Helena and instructs Puck, his mischief-making henchman, to enchant Demetrius with a love potion so that he will fall in love with Helena. By mistake Puck enchants Lysander instead, who rejects Hermia for Helena. Helena finds herself courted by two randy young men after Demetrius is also put under the spell of the love potion, and confusion ensues, until, toward morning, Puck reverses the spell on Lysander. Puck also works his mischief on Bottom the Weaver as the artisans rehearse their absurd play in the forest, transforming him into a half-beast with the head of an ass. Oberon has demanded that Titania, his Fairy Queen, surrender to him a young Indian boy, a changeling who has been in her service. When she refuses, Oberon tells Puck to work a spell on her while she sleeps that will humiliate her and teach her a lesson of submission. When she awakens, she will fall in love with the first creature she sees, monstrous Bottom, whom she takes for a lover. Bottom takes this all in stride, but after Titania has been humiliated, Puck lifts the spell and Bottom is restored to his former self.

The play ends at court, with multiple marriages: Theseus and Hippolyta, Demetrius and Helena, and Lysander and Hermia, despite her father's objections. The wedding masque is performed, and the rude mechanicals perform their absurd play of Pyramus and Thisbe. Puck concludes the play with his "If we spirits have offended" Epilogue, and all live happily ever after.

The Films

The first film to treat the play in part was a 1909 Vitagraph production directed by the stage actor Charles Kent, shot in Brooklyn's Prospect Park and Flatbush. Italian and German versions were filmed in 1913, and a later German version that appeared in 1925 employed double exposures and a female Puck. But Shakespeare demands sound, and the Warner Bros.' adaptation of Shakespeare's comedy was the first talking adaptation of the play, and certainly one of the most entertaining in its extravagance and silliness. The Austrian impresario Max Reinhardt, who had staged

A group portrait from Warner Bros.'s 1935 production of A Midsummer Night's Dream. (COURTESY NATIONAL FILM SOCIETY ARCHIVES)

the play frequently between 1905 and 1934, directed the film with William Dieterle.

The production overloads the text with non-Shakespearean material. The orchestral music of Felix Mendelssohn and the fairy dance performed by a Russian ballet troupe extend the action and, although decidedly atmospheric, tend to be distracting for those expecting the language of Shakespeare, which is abbreviated and sometimes mangled by the studio contract players, with the exceptions of Ian Hunter (Theseus) and Victor Jory, who plays an imposing and imperious Oberon. Warner Brothers threw all of its resources into the film, including such contract players as Jimmy Cagney as Bottom, Mickey Rooney as Puck, Olivia de Havilland as Hermia, Jean Muir as Helena, Dick Powell as Lysander, Ross Alexander as

Demetrius, and an unforgettable Joe E. Brown as Francis Flute, who is given the role of Thisbe in the masque. The film was nominated for three Academy Awards for 1935, including best picture, best cinematography (Hal Mohr), and best film editing (Ralph Dawson) and won the latter two. The film was designed as an escapist Depression fantasy and is most successful in the farcical action in the "Pyramus and Thisbe" masque, as well as in the confusions of the hexed forest. Its spectacle of enchantment seems artificial and contrived in retrospect, and the farcical action tends to obliterate the poetry.

The Peter Hall film of 1969 was graced by outstanding talent from the Royal Shakespeare Company, most notably Diana Rigg as Hermia, Helen Mirren as Helena, and Judi Dench as a far sexier Tita-

Oberon (Rupert Everett) and his queen, Titania (Michelle Pfeiffer), in a romantic moment in Michael Hoffman's A Midsummer Night's Dream. (COURTESY FOX SEARCHLIGHT PICTURES)

nia than had yet been filmed. The outstanding performance of this production is Ian Holm's panting Puck, whose comings and goings are enhanced by trick photography. The lovers are not interchangeable, as in the 1935 film, thanks to Diana Rigg and Helen Mirren, who sort out the differences between Helena and Hermia. The interpretation had surely been influenced by Jan Kott's *Shakespeare, Our Contemporary* (1964), which had been translated into English in 1966 and which put a nasty spin on a comedy that had hitherto been regarded as "innocent," emphasizing the bestial relationship between Bottom (Paul Rogers) and Titania. Hall manages to dirty-up the action as the lovers muck about in the forest in anger and frustration before Puck finally reverses the love spells. The Hall production took a low-budget approach. The "Athenian" setting appears to be a rural English one (actually filmed by Peter Suschitzky outside of Stratford-upon-Avon), and no attempt was made to dress it up. The costumes were also minimal, Carnaby Street coats with lace collars for the men, mini-skirts for the women, near nudity for the fairies, with green-toned body makeup. Hippolyta (Barbara Jeffords) wears a kinky leather mini-skirt and boots but is not a very forceful Amazon queen. Peter Hall wanted to use "the advantages of the cinema not to make a film in the accepted sense, but to communicate the words." Certainly this production attempts to be faithful to the text; but to include as much of the text as possible, the actors fairly race through their lines, which makes the language difficult to follow, especially since the sound recording is not very good. All in all, this is a competent but generally joyless rendering of the play.

The Michael Hoffman production updates the play by setting it in Tuscany during the late 19th century, making the production "operatic," though the music (Verdi's *La Traviata* and Bellini's *Norma*, combined with Mendelssohn's incidental music) seems mismatched. The director also decided to put his actors on bicycles, which must have seemed to him a good idea. In his *Variety* review (May 10–16, 1999), Emanuel Levy, who found the production inventive, noted that it "suffers from a lack of coherent vision and an incongruous tone." The standout performance here was Kevin Kline as Bottom, played without an ass's head, but given long ears and a snout with facial hair, as Charles Laughton had done in a stage production directed by Peter Hall at Stratford-upon-Avon in 1958. Calista Flockhart plays an appealing Helena against Anna Friel's Hermia, Christian Bale's Demetrius, and Dominic West's Lysander. Friel pouts mightily as the much-abused Hermia, and Bale and West personalize the look-alike *beaux* Demetrius and Lysander. Stanley Tucci plays an adult Puck, following the instructions of Rupert Everett's Oberon; Michelle Pfeiffer is a beautiful Titania.

The cast is fine, but the concept suffers. David Strathairn's Duke Theseus lacks the authority the play demands because his lines have been abridged in keeping with the near-contemporary Italianate setting. He appears to be the maitre d' of a resort hotel rather than a ruler whose nuptials are most central to the plot. Sophie Marceau's Hippolyta is presented as a genteel, aristocratic lady, a highly unlikely Amazon queen. One effective touch in the film is the way in which the fairies seem to interact with the townspeople, as one catches glimpses of them in the town from time to time. Stanley Tucci, gives a carefully modulated and thoroughly professional rendering of Puck, but he seems a bit cumbersome. This *Midsummer Night's Dream* is generally short on comic energy and is something of a snooze, but it is generally entertaining.

REFERENCES

Jorgens, Jack J., *Shakespeare on Film* (Bloomington: Indiana University Press, 1977); Manvell, Roger, *Shakespeare and the Film* (New York: Praeger, 1971); Rothwell, Kenneth, *A History of Shakespeare on Screen* (Cambridge University Press, 1999); Willson, Robert F., Jr., *Shakespeare in Hollywood, 1929–1956* (Madison, N.J.: Fairleigh Dickinson University Press, 2000).

—*J.M.W.*

MUCH ADO ABOUT NOTHING
(1598–99)

Much Ado About Nothing (1973), U.S.A., directed by A.J. Antoon, adapted by A.J. Antoon and Joseph Papp; New York Shakespeare Festival/Columbia Broadcasting System.

Much Ado About Nothing (1984), U. K., directed by Stuart Burge; British Broadcasting Company/Time-Life Television.

Much Ado About Nothing (1993), U.S.A., directed and adapted by Kenneth Branagh; Samuel Goldyn Company.

The Play

With *As You Like It* and *Twelfth Night*, Shakespeare's *Much Ado About Nothing* belongs to a series of "joyous" comedies. There are two primary relationships here. One is a comedy of courtship and the other is a comedy of marriage. The quick courtship nearly results in disaster, and the slow, reluctant marriage is successful. The quarto of 1600, the first published text of the play, notes on the title page that it had been performed publicly "sundry times" by the Lord Chamberlain's Men. The plot source is Lodovico Ariosto's *Orlando Furioso* (1516).

After helping Don Pedro subdue his malcontent brother, Don John, returning soldiers Benedick and Claudio find themselves quickly entangled in amorous wars. Benedick renews his battle of wits with Beatrice (his "Lady Disdain"), the niece of Messina's governor, Leonato, while Claudio, who distinguished himself in battle, realizes that he has been subdued by the beauty of Leonato's daughter, Hero. A confirmed bachelor, Benedick expresses dismay that his young friend is in love, but Don Pedro offers to intercede with Hero and her father, since Claudio himself seems uneasy about declaring his sudden affection. At a masked dance, Don Pedro will woo Hero in Claudio's name. Meanwhile Don John (who describes himself as "a plain-dealing villain") has found out about the affair and decides to get revenge on Don Pedro and Claudio by ruining it. He convinces Claudio that Don Pedro won Hero for himself, but his victory is short-lived since the others convince Claudio that this is not so. With the issue settled, and Claudio and Hero planning marriage, they, Don Pedro, and Leonato decide to find a way to bring Benedick and Beatrice together. The men arrange for Benedick to overhear them talking about Beatrice's great secret love for him, while Hero and the other women will do the same for Beatrice, convincing her that Benedick is also hiding his affection. The plot works and, although formerly well known for their stance against love, both Benedick and Beatrice are soon sure they are deeply in love.

Don John has not, however, given up and instead escalates his villainy with a plan to make Don Pedro and Claudio believe they see Hero being unfaithful. When Hero appears the next day to be married, she and the others are shocked to hear Claudio, with the support of Don Pedro, reject his bride-to-be and say she is unchaste. Hero faints, Leonato is outraged, but the priest suggests gaining time to prove Hero innocent by saying she has died. Beatrice is so angry with Claudio that she takes advantage of Benedick's declaration of love to ask him to kill his friend. Undercutting the seriousness of the broken nuptial, Shakespeare introduces Constable Dogberry and his Watch, who patrol the streets of Messina and have very accidentally overheard Don John's henchmen, Borachio and Conrade, boasting of how they tricked Claudio and Don Pedro. Without really understanding what has happened, Dogberry and his men arrest the conspirators and take them to be interrogated.

Meanwhile Leonato and his brother Antonio accuse Don Pedro and Claudio of having killed Hero. Don Pedro expresses sorrow, but insists the charges against Hero are true. He and Claudio next see Benedick, who calls Claudio a villain and challenges him to a duel. Though they at first think he is jesting, they soon realize Benedick is serious. Just then, Dogberry brings in Borachio, who confesses the whole plot. Suddenly repentant, Claudio tells Leonato to take his own revenge. Leonato tells Claudio to marry, sight-unseen, a niece who is "Almost the copy of my child that's dead." Called back from hiding, Hero, Beatrice, and the other women appear, masked, for a new wedding ceremony. When Claudio humbly agrees to marry this woman whose face he has not even seen, Hero suddenly removes her mask. With all corrected, Benedick and Beatrice try briefly once more to deny their affections, but Claudio and Hero produce love poems written by the reluctant lovers. Benedick concludes that "man is a giddy thing," and tells Don Pedro to marry. As the guests begin to dance, word comes that Don John has been captured.

The Films

The only feature film treatment of *Much Ado About Nothing* is the very popular version by Kenneth Branagh, who transforms Shakespeare's Sicilian city of

Messina into the Tuscany region of sunny central Italy, and structures the film around a light/dark division. He creates a world in which the land and the lovers almost visibly ache for satisfaction, and impediments seem sure to evaporate in the hot sun. Only the villainous Don John and, in this film, the slightly psychotic Dogberry embrace the darkness. The emotional center of this production, as in most, is the relationship between Benedick (Kenneth Branagh) and Beatrice (Emma Thompson), here boosted by their star power and by the fact they were at the time married to each other. Opening the film with Thompson reading the cautionary song, "Sigh no more, ladies, sigh no more, Men were deceivers ever," director Branagh throws the emphasis on Thompson's thoughtful portrayal of Beatrice as a woman whose sense of humor is only one of several weapons against painful vulnerability. From this point of view, the Claudio-Hero story almost becomes an example of what might happen in a love affair of less depth, the kind of affair that this Beatrice would avoid to escape further pain. Branagh does not push this point too far, and yet Thompson conveys this sense of a deeper offense in her charge to "Kill Claudio." Branagh's Benedick, on the other hand, is less the former rake (Leonato jokes that he is confident of being Hero's father because Benedick was then himself a child) than the screwball comedy hero who wonders at how the world is bit by bit taking shape before him. This is not a cynical Benedick but a surprised Benedick. He is innocent in a benign way, whereas his friend Claudio's innocence threatens cruelty. Perhaps only Don John, however, is really allowed to threaten much of anything in this film. As played by Keanu Reeves, Don John is a character composed mainly of scowls. This bastard brother is the negative image of the courtly and amiable Don Pedro (Denzel Washington), a point Branagh underscores by making Don John white and Don Pedro black.

Branagh cut and transposed a considerable portion of the original play, primarily, he says, "where the plot (such as it is) was not advanced" or where he needed "to create a movie pace (quite different from that of the theatre)." One section in which the characters seem most obviously altered are the scenes having to do with Dogberry (Michael Keaton). Branagh introduces Dogberry and the Watch earlier than the play does, placing them, in effect, where they need to be to foil Don John's plot when it unfolds. In addition, Branagh wanted "to amend the ugliness inherent in the wedding scene and in Claudio's behavior afterwards." To do this, he and Michael Keaton reduced Dogberry's verbal malapropisms and made him a "physical malaprop." To do this, they seem to have borrowed from a variety of types of physical comedy. Dogberry's invisible horses, for example, are from the British Monty Python group's film *Monty Python and the Holy Grail* (1975), where the knights ride similar mounts. The physical violence, especially Dogberry's abuse of Verges, seems to come from the Three Stooges.

The effect seems to push the characterization away from sympathy and closer to slapstick. Several of Dogberry's more sympathetic lines have been cut, such as his plaintive "and a rich fellow enough, go to, and a fellow that hath had losses, and on that hath had two gowns, and everything handsome about him." A similarly motivated change in the physicality of the action occurs when Branagh shows Hero's supposed adultery. Shakespeare has Don John tell Claudio that he "shall see her chamber-window entered," and later Borachio says he has "wooed Margaret, the Lady Hero's gentlewoman, by the name of Hero." In Branagh's film, we see the bare back of a woman who is being made love to standing up, leaning back over a balcony. Here too, the effect is very different. Several writers have pointed out that this rendering of the incident makes the viewer more sympathetic toward Claudio and more in a position to understand his later rejection of Hero at the wedding, but it is clearly a violent change from Shakespeare's more oblique description.

Of the two notable filmed performances of *Much Ado About Nothing*, the A.J. Antoon and Joseph Papp version was enjoying a run at the New York Shakespeare Festival when it was prepared for television and broadcast on CBS in 1973. The television performance, apparently to everyone's surprise, effectively killed the Broadway show, which closed within four days. Papp himself said, "I've never seen anything fall so rapidly in my life." Antoon had directed the stage version, but had no television experience. Eventually, he worked primarily with the actors, and assistant Nick Havinga took over the shooting, though Antoon kept final artistic control of the production. Papp, who saw the project as "an attempt to reach a mass audience for plays of quality and content," had shifted the location of the play to turn-of-the-century America. In this version, Don Pedro, Benedick, Claudio, and the others ride into the opening scene wearing post Spanish-American War uniforms and surrounded by brass bands, red-white-and-blue banners, men waving American flags, women wearing long flowing dresses with high collars, and a Keystone Kops-style police force. Critic H.R. Coursen deplored this approach and said that by shifting time periods Antoon "obliterates what Shakespeare may be saying to us with *his* play" and called the result "a cultural disaster." Papp himself had said that "Whenever you put Shakespeare in a

Kenneth Branagh's Much Ado About Nothing *cast himself as Benedick and Emma Thompson as Beatrice.* (COURTESY SAMUEL GOLDWYN COMPANY)

more modern period, it is diminished," and he questioned several of Antoon's choices, including the Keystone Kops chase.

The Papp-Antoon production differs from other versions of the play at least in part because of the selection of the time period, but perhaps more importantly because of the emphasis on the conventions associated with that time period. The effect of making Dogberry (Bernard Hughes) a Keystone Kop, for example, is to provide a context that explains his behavior, but also to draw on the popular understanding of both the early 1900s and silent film conventions. Because its antecedents are more likely to be found in *Meet Me in St. Louis* (1944) and *Abbott and Costello Meet the Keystone Kops* (1955) than in the films of Mack Sennett, the production's use of ragtime music, tubas, and slow waltzes, along with the speeded up chase scenes, freeze frames, and other photographic tricks, are not the product of studying the silent film era, as Coursen correctly points out, but instead of manipulating the late-20th-century expectations of what those conventions were.

Benedick (Sam Waterston) is a cigar-smoking, deliberately old-fashioned man, bemused by the world, but aware of the precariousness of his position in it. Beatrice (Kathleen Widdoes) is a proto-feminist, who takes Benedick's beer and drinks it when she bests him in a verbal battle and later sits on a porch with the other women to sneak a cigarette. In this world, Don John (Jerry Mayo) is a comic villain, rather than the sullen or potentially dangerous force of other productions. The first view of Don John shows him trying to shoot the ducks in the pond, about as threatening as Elmer Fudd. When he finds out that Claudio and Hero will marry, Don John pounds his piano in frustration, and, when he sits in a barber's chair and spreads rumors about Hero, he plops a lollipop in his mouth with childish glee and tells the audience, rather than just Claudio, "O'plague right well prevented! So will you say when you have seen the sequel." In general, this is a world without malice. Borachio and Conrade are visibly saddened when they hear that Hero has died. It is a safe world of Victrolas, gazebos, straw hats, crinoline skirts, and parasols. The most serious moment comes when Don Pedro (Douglas Watson) gets down on one knee at the end of the dance in Act Two and asks Beatrice "Would you have me, lady?" Rather than tongue-in-cheek playfulness, the line suddenly makes Don Pedro into a disappointed but gallant lover, a characterization consistent with Benedick's line at the end of the play "Prince, thou art sad, get thee a wife."

The BBC version of the play, directed by Stuart Burge, makes the play a generally darker experience. Don John himself is dressed all in black and everything is in shadow, as though he were somehow sensitive to the light, although obviously the implication is that his condition is more metaphorical than medical. Later, when Dogberry's men seize the black-cloaked Borachio and Conrade, the visual metaphor seems to suggest two kinds of darkness meeting. While this does not seem to be an inappropriate image, this production gives the connection an emphasis that it seldom has had. Given this pattern of visual signals, however, holding the wedding scene in a darkened room seems to be a somewhat heavy-handed commentary on the state of things. Leonato (Lee Montague) and Beatrice (Cherie Lunghi), for example, the bride's father and cousin, are both dressed in dark clothing. Certainly in close shots their dark figures contrast effectively with Hero's white dress, and later Beatrice's black dress and Benedick's dark red outfit both seem appropriate in the darkened church when their discussion turns to killing Claudio. This dark palette continues until the final wedding scene when the women enter wearing the lighter colored dresses of the earliest scenes in the play.

Burge has said that "the subtleties and sophistications of this play require some kind of stylized setting" and that designer Jan Spoczynski "succeeded very well in merging a stylized background and a real foreground." Perhaps this light/dark patterning is part of the intended stylization, although Susan McCloskey believes that "this production would obscure" the contrast "between the sunlit comedy of Beatrice and Benedick's courtship and the potentially tragic darkening of Claudio's love for Hero." As she points out, Beatrice "is seldom merry" and Benedick (Robert Lindsay) seems to be "in a prickly funk" during the opening scenes of the play. Part of the problem, however, seems to be that the other actors do not respond to the lines, or seldom do. Dogberry (Michael Elphick) rarely gets a reaction from the characters onstage to his malaprop humor. The effect, of course, is to diminish his comic effect in the play. A notable exception, for example, might be Beatrice, who has been somewhat shrewish in her humor in the opening scenes, but suddenly winces, and is caught doing so by a close-up shot, when Benedick says "I cannot endure my Lady Tongue." It is a reading that gives more weight to her next lines, when Don Pedro says ". . . you have lost the heart of Signior Benedick," and she replies "Indeed, my lord, he lent it me awhile, and I gave him use for it, a double heart for his single one." Toward the end of the play, when Benedick asks Beatrice "for which of my good parts did you first suffer love for me?" they again achieve the kind of romantic connection that genuinely suggests that something has been overcome and that they really have reached the level of romance that the play suggests they should.

REFERENCES

Barton, Anne, "Shakespeare in the Sun," *The New York Review*, May 27, 1993, 11–13; Branagh, Kenneth, *Much Ado About Nothing by William Shakespeare: Screenplay, Introduction, and Notes on the Making of the Movie* (New York: W.W. Norton, 1993); Coursen, H.R., "Anachronism and Papp's *Much Ado*," in *Shakespeare on Television*, eds. J.C. Bulman and H.R. Coursen (Hanover, N.H.: University Press of New England, 1988), 151–155; Little, Stuart W., *Enter Joe Papp: In Search of a New American Theater* (New York: Coward, McCann and Geoghegan, 1974); McCloskey, Susan, "*Much Ado About Nothing*," *Shakespeare on Film Newsletter* (April 1985), 5; Shuttleworth, Ian, *Ken and Em: A Biography of Kenneth Branagh and Emma Thompson* (New York: St. Martin's Press, 1995); Weiss, Tanja, *Shakespeare on the Screen: Kenneth Branagh's Adaptations of Henry V, Much Ado About Nothing, and Hamlet* (Frankfurt: Peter Lang, 1999); Willis, Susan, *The BBC Shakespeare Plays* (Chapel Hill: University of North Carolina Press, 1991).

—R.V.

OTHELLO (1603–1604)

A Double Life (1947), U.S.A., directed by George Cukor, adapted by Ruth Gordon and Garson Kanin; Universal-International/Kanin Productions.

Othello (1952), Morocco/Italy, directed and adapted by Orson Welles; Mogador/Mercury Productions.

Othello (1955), USSR, directed by Sergei Yutkevich, adapted by Boris Pasternak; Mosfilm/Universal-International.

Othello (1965), U.K., directed by Stuart Burge, based on National Theatre production directed by John Dexter; BHE Production/Eagle Films Ltd.

Othello (1995), U.K., directed and adapted by Oliver Parker; Dakota Films/Imminent Films/Castle Rock Entertainment.

The Play

Dismissed for many years by classical critics as a "domestic tragedy," *Othello* has received greater attention from modern readers and viewers because of its complex racial and sexual themes. The hero is a Moor serving as leader of the Venetian army who marries the daughter of a senator opposed to the union on the grounds that Othello has used magic to seduce his innocent child. But Desdemona's love for her noble husband proves more than just a passing dalliance, and Othello greets her passion with some of the most powerful romantic poetry in all of Shakespeare.

Their union is destroyed by Othello's jealousy, prompted by his diabolic ensign Iago, and proves compellingly tragic, striking a chord with contemporary audiences attuned to domestic violence. While *Othello* is a sensational story with contrived plot turns—the hero's rage is provoked by Desdemona's supposed gift of a treasured handkerchief to her lover—the drama thoroughly explores the psyches of passionate characters with whom we strongly identify.

The action begins when Desdemona's father, Brabantio, is rudely awakened by her suitor Roderigo, urged on by a disgruntled Iago, who informs the senator that his daughter has eloped with the Moor. Iago uses Roderigo to avenge himself on Othello because the captain promoted Cassio to lieutenant instead of him. When Brabantio doesn't find Desdemona in her bed, he rushes to the duke and senate to demand Othello's arrest. Called upon to explain himself, the composed Moor tells his accusers that he has indeed married Desdemona but that he wooed her with descriptions of his military adventures, not magic spells. The duke overrides Brabantio's complain and orders Othello to Cyprus to defend the island against invading Turks. A frustrated Brabantio directs this parting shot at Othello: "Look to her, Moor, if thou had eyes to see; She has deceived her father, and may thee." Thus the seeds of doubt are planted.

As the Venetian party arrives at Cyprus aboard different ships nearly sunk in a storm, Othello learns that the Turkish fleet has been destroyed in the same storm. No longer required to prepare for invasion, he becomes vulnerable to Iago's innuendoes about an affair between Michael Cassio and Desdemona. He also arranges for Cassio to drink too much wine while on watch, then calls on Roderigo to provoke a noisy street brawl. His sleep disrupted, Othello blames Cassio and demotes him after hearing "honest" Iago's account of the struggle. Appearing to be everyone's friend and confidant, Iago weaves a web out of bits and pieces of volunteered information that eventually ensnares Cassio, Desdemona, and Othello.

When Desdemona vigorously urges that her husband reinstate his friend Cassio, Iago has the opening he has been hoping for. He tells his captain that Cassio has revealed his sexual relationship with Desdemona while talking in his sleep. He also claims he saw Cassio wipe his beard with the special handkerchief given to Desdemona by Othello on their wedding day. For the hero, now in a frenzied state, the gift also signifies the giving away of her body to Cassio. Thus wedded to Iago's will, Othello orders Iago to kill Cassio and assigns him the title of lieutenant. He also vows to stifle Desdemona in her wedding bed. On the fatal night, we first witness Iago's attempt on Cassio's life with Roderigo's help; they manage only to wound him, however, and Iago kills Roderigo to cover up the scheme. When Othello accuses Desdemona, she declares her innocence but is unable to convince her enraged husband, who proceeds to stifle her. As she is about to expire, her attendant Emilia, Iago's wife, rushes into the bedroom, embraces her dying mistress, and accuses Othello of cruel murder. He tells her that her husband has proved Desdemona's unfaithfulness, using the handkerchief as evidence. Emilia then turns on her just-arrived husband, naming him as the cause of these tragic events; in payment for her honesty, she is stabbed to death by her conscienceless husband. Wounded and finally exposed, Iago refuses to give a reason for his plotting; Othello, heartbroken and desperate, commits suicide with a dagger he has hidden from his captors. As Cassio takes over the governorship of the island and Iago is led away, Othello's dying self-description—"one that loved not wisely but too well"—reverberates as a tragic, yet ironic, truth.

The Films

A few silent versions of the tragedy were made in Italy and Germany early in the century; these might be bet-

ter described as "scenes from *Othello*." A 1936 British offshoot, *Men Are Not Gods*, concerns the efforts of a London newspaperman to save the reputation of an actor playing Othello. *A Double Life* (1947) also uses the Othello plot within a frame but in a more unusual, inventive way than *Men Are Not Gods* had done. Ronald Colman plays Broadway star Anthony John, who is urged by his agent to revive the *Othello* production that won him fame. John reluctantly agrees because he hopes to regain the affection of his estranged wife Brita (Signe Hasso), who will reprise her role as Desdemona. As rehearsals commence, the hero begins to confound his stage role with his real-life persona; like Othello, he grows increasingly jealous of his wife. When Tony meets and pursues a waitress (Shelley Winters) who resembles Brita as Desdemona, the siege on his sanity grows more intense. Convinced that the waitress is indeed Desdemona, he murders her in her bed during one of their late-night encounters. Police investigating the murder have no leads until a newspaper reporter talks to the coroner and discovers that the waitress was stifled "with a kiss." This is exactly the way Desdemona is murdered every night in Tony's production. Aided by the show's publicist Bill Friend (Edmond O'Brien), whom Tony suspects as Brita's wooer, police detectives gather behind the scenes of the play, planning to arrest Tony. But he has grown so remorseful that he decides to use a real knife for Othello's onstage suicide. Distinguished by *film noir* elements and superior direction by Hollywood veteran George Cukor, *A Double Life* is an artistic success and won Colman an Academy Award for best actor.

Orson Welles's 1952 version has some of the same *film noir* touches as *A Double Life*, but it is a more faithful, if shortened, treatment of the play. Welles's first Shakespeare film was *Macbeth* (1948), an artistic and box-office failure. Though he brutally cuts the text and overacts in the title role, Welles manages to catch more of the spirit of *Othello* than he did of *Macbeth*. Michael MacLiammoir's Iago first appears suspended in a cage looking down on a funeral procession carrying Othello and Desdemona's bodies. The cage, iron bars, and stone vaults are objects that suggest Othello's imprisonment in a destructive world where he is manipulated by an impotent Iago. Shot in Morocco and Italy, the film is aptly characterized by Jack J. Jorgens as "a mannerist montage of broken continuities, wrenched perspectives, clashing images, and surreal sound." Welles's voice-over narration is extratextual and often distracting; it seems designed chiefly to instruct audiences unfamiliar with the play. Still, he manages to coax strong performances from his actors: Suzanne Cloutier's Desdemona and Michael Lawrence's Cassio

Laurence Olivier's Othello *cast Maggie Smith as Desdemona and Anthony Nicholls as her father.* (COURTESY WARNER BROS.)

prove almost as powerful as MacLiammoir's Iago. Now available in a restored video format, the film deserves reconsideration by audiences and critics alike.

The 1955 Russian *Othello* is, by contrast with Welles's production, a more colorful spectacle with operatic overtones that recall Verdi's *Otello*. Director Yutkevich believed film to be the right medium to represent the expansive lifelikeness of Shakespeare's plays. The crowd scenes, especially in Cyprus, achieve this effect, and the color photography presents a vivid portrait of the characters and action. Though originally made with Russian-speaking actors, a later version was made with dubbed-in voices of British players. Sergei Bondarchuk's Othello and Andrei Popov's Iago are both impressive, although their acting appears melodramatic by comparison with Anglo-American style.

That style is brilliantly demonstrated in Stuart Burge's 1965 *Othello*, featuring Sir Laurence Olivier, Maggie Smith as Desdemona, and Frank Finlay as Iago. A filmed re-creation of the London National Theatre production (directed by John Dexter), this version does seem hemmed in by comparison with the Welles and Yutkevich interpretations. Shot on a stage-like set, the film follows theatrical—rather than realistic—conventions in movement and speech. Olivier plays Othello in blackface and employs a Jamaican accent that seems at times, especially during the great soliloquies, distinctly out of place. But Olivier's speech rhythms contrast interestingly with those of Frank Finlay's Iago, who uses the accent of a Cockney. Maggie Smith's performance as Desdemona strikes just the right note of sincerity and innocence, although the camera tends to bring out a matronly quality in her appearance. Olivier's Othello carries the day, however, especially in Act Three, Scene Three, when Iago persuades him of his wife's infidelity. The riveting murder scene (V.ii) uncovers the hero's ferocity and tenderness in a convincing way. On the whole, Burge's attempt to engage the film audience as a stage director would a theatre audience yields mixed results.

A much more realistic translation of the tragedy is Oliver Parker's 1995 version. Kenneth Branagh as Iago controls the camera and action throughout as he delivers his soliloquies in close-up. His ability to speak Shakespeare's lines with clarity and precision adds to the naturalistic tone of the film; it also means that he

Laurence Fishburne starred as the proud Moor in Oliver Parker's adaptation of Shakespeare's Othello.
(COURTESY CASTLE ROCK ENTERTAINMENT)

holds our attention in ensemble scenes. Laurence Fishburne's Othello is likewise a powerful presence (though perhaps eclipsed by Branagh's Iago), his youth and dynamism suggesting a hero still in his prime. His relationship with Desdemona (Irene Jacobs) is convincingly portrayed, stressing her modesty and straightforward innocence. Yet when Fishburne's Othello begins to doubt, Parker has him visualizing a seductress entwining a naked Cassio in her arms. Sequences like this one suggest a parallel with MTV music videos, hinting at Parker's attempt to attract a younger audience to his film. While Branagh's riveting Iago and Fishburne's menacing Othello offer the viewer much to enjoy, the film cuts many lines of Othello's poetry and tends to focus more on the trappings of his world than on the tortured psyche of the hero.

REFERENCES

Crowl, Samuel, "Othello," *Shakespeare Bulletin*, 41 (Winter 1996), 41–42; Donaldson, Peter S., *Shakespearean Films/Shakespearean Directors* (Boston: Unwin Hyman, 1990); Eckert, Charles W,, ed., *Focus on Shakespearean Films* (Englewood Cliffs, N.J.: Prentice-Hall, 1972); Jorgens, Jack J., *Shakespeare on Film* (Bloomington: Indiana University Press, 1977); Manvell, Roger, *Shakespeare and the Film*, rev. ed. (Cranbury, N.J.: A.S. Barnes, 1979); Rothwell, Kenneth S., and Annabelle Henkin Melzer, *Shakespeare on Screen: An International Filmography and Videography* (New York: Neal Schuman, 1990).

—*R.F.W.*

RAN

See *KING LEAR*

RICHARD III (1592)

Richard III (1912), U.S.A., directed by James Keane, adapted by Frederick Warde; M.B. Dudley Amusement Company.

Richard III (1955), U.K., directed by Laurence Olivier, adapted by Olivier and Alan Dent; London Films.

Richard III (1995), U.S.A., directed by Richard Loncraine, adapted by Loncraine and Ian McKellen; United Artists.

Looking for Richard (1996), U.S.A., directed by Al Pacino; Twentieth Century-Fox.

The Play

Although the play dates to 1592, the Quarto edition was not published until 1597. The Quarto's title page pretty well describes the action as follows: *The Tragedy of King Richard the Third, containing his treacherous plots against his brother Clarence; the pitiful murder of his innocent nephews; his tyrannical usurpation; with the whole course of his detested life, and most deserved death.* Though the title page lists this history play as a tragedy, it is only "tragic" in the medieval sense, in that it deals with the fall of a king. Shakespeare's source was Raphael Holinshed's *Chronicles* and Sir Thomas More's *History of King Richard the Third*, not a very flattering portrait, written circa 1514 but not published until 1557. Tudor historians tended to demonize Richard of Gloucester, and, following their lead, Shakespeare makes him deformed in body (the dowager queen Margaret, who has his number, calls Richard a "poisonous bunch-backed toad") and in mind. He is the equal of Othello's ensign Iago in his malice, though his villainy has a more apparent purpose.

Richard seeks the Crown and methodically goes about destroying those who stand in his way. This "elfish-marked, abortive, rooting hog" intends to usurp his dying brother, Edward IV, and cheerfully plots to dispose of George, duke of Clarence, his elder brother, who is framed by Richard, put in prison, and then drowned in a butt (cask) of malmsey wine, on Richard's orders. Informed of Clarence's death, King Edward IV dies of grief, but Richard has to overcome yet another obstacle. He thereupon orders the murder of the little princes, Edward, prince of Wales, and his brother Richard, duke of York, both of whom Gloucester, ironically their protector, has imprisoned in the Tower of London. He has already seen to the death of Edward, prince of Wales, the son and heir of King Henry VI and, outrageously, "woo'd and won" Edward's widow, the Lady Anne, who should despise him and yet succumbs to his poisonous charm.

Richard is constantly pleased with himself and his wicked plotting, and enjoys taking the audience into his confidence, but the spider king weaves a seductive verbal web as one evil scheme is eclipsed by the next, each increasingly more flamboyant, until Richard finally overreaches himself and alienates his henchman, the duke of Buckingham, whom he underestimates and stupidly slights. Buckingham then turns against Richard and joins his sworn enemy Henry, the earl of Richmond, who finally kills Gloucester at the battle of Bosworth Field.

The Films

This survey must begin in May of 1912, when a film of *Richard III*, starring the popular Shakespearean actor Frederick Warde, was released—and is most significant because it is now believed by archivists to be the oldest extant American feature film. (Film archivists define "feature" length as being at least four reels, or 40 minutes long; *Richard III* runs to 55 minutes.) The surviving print was donated to the American Film Institute in 1996 by William Buffum of Portland, Oregon, a retired flour mill manager who acquired the film in 1960 and carefully preserved the 35 mm print for 35 years but without understanding its historical importance. Archivist and historian Kevin Brownlow remarked to the *New York Times* that to find such a lost film that had been "expunged from the memory" but "complete in its original print is really astounding," because "over 70 percent of all feature films produced before the 1920s no longer exist."

According to Bernard Weinraub of the *New York Times*, the film was made in Westchester County and at City Island in the Bronx at a cost of $30,000 and is remarkable for its "lavish battle scenes," filmed with a cast of hundreds. Interviewed by *The Brooklyn Daily Eagle* in November of 1912, Frederick Warde expressed amazement at the "staging and methods of the moving-picture people," especially the way in which the director would tell "the other actors what to do, telling them when to look glad or sorry, when to shout and when to fight, without telling them why they did any of these things." The 1912 film was not the first film treatment, however. A one-reel Vitagraph abridgment was made in 1908 under the supervision of J. Stuart Blackton, and in 1911 a 27-minute abridgment was made in Britain, starring F.R. Benson.

The first major sound film to treat *Richard III* as a play—discounting the derivative *Tower of London* directed by Rowland V. Lee and scripted by Robert N.

"My Kingdom for a horse!" shouts Laurence Olivier in the title role of Shakespeare's Richard III. (COURTESY NATIONAL FILM SOCIETY ARCHIVES)

Lee in 1939—was Laurence Olivier's film made at Shepperton Studios, London, and shot in Technicolor and VistaVision. Again, Olivier set the standard, transforming himself into a bent and twisted stage villain, whose asides to the camera are used to hypnotize the viewers and lure them into his evil mentality. The credentials of the supporting cast are impeccable: John Gielgud (Clarence), Ralph Richardson (Buckingham), Cedric Hardwicke (Edward IV), Stanley Baker (Richmond), and Claire Bloom (Lady Anne).

Just as Olivier's *Henry V* had incorporated contextualizing material from *2 Henry IV*, Alan Dent's screenplay for *Richard III* incorporated portions of *3 Henry VI* as indicated by the film's full title: *Richard the Third, by William Shakespeare, with Some Interpolations by David Garrick, Colly Cibber, etc.* Such "interpolations" are in evidence from the play's opening "Now is the winter of our discontent" soliloquy that establishes Olivier's character unforgettably. The film offers none of the lavish spectacle of *Henry V*, but its inventive deployment of intimate stage settings suggestive of medieval woodcuts (designed by Roger Furse and Carmen Dillon) as well as Olivier's stark facial makeup—producing a pasty white face crowned by coiling black curls—contrasts sharply with the film's muted pastel color palette

Ian McKellen portrayed Richard III as a fascist dictator in the 1930s in Shakespeare's play. (COURTESY
UNITED ARTISTS)

and is distinctive in its stylization. The film's artful design allows Olivier's bravura acting performance to come to the fore.

Richard III, which Olivier first played on stage in 1944, was one of Olivier's defining roles, and for many years his interpretation was considered definitive. His achievement was so daunting that no one attempted another feature film treatment for 40 years, though there were two video interpretations. The first of these was produced in Georgia in the Soviet Union in 1980, directed by Robert Sturua, featuring Ramaz Chkhikvadze as Gloucester, and produced at the Rustaveli Theatre in Tbilisi. In 1983 Jane Howell directed a video interpretation for the BBC Shakespeare Series, adapted by David Snodin and starring Ron Cook as Gloucester.

In 1995 the play was given an astonishing postmodern fascist spin by director Richard Loncraine, who broke Olivier's spell by updating the action to the 20th century. Ian McKellen played the lead role of Richard,

supported by Jim Broadbent (Buckingham), Maggie Smith (the duchess of York), Nigel Hawthorne (Clarence), Annette Bening (Queen Elizabeth), and Kristin Scott Thomas (Lady Anne). The film's design operates on the supposition that England had gone Fascist during the 1930s and that Richard was a fascist dictator.

The Court scenes take place in elegant cafés, where a jazz baby sings a musical rendering of Christopher Marlowe's famous lyric, "The Passionate Shepherd's Reply." Chronology is fractured and the play is considerably streamlined and simplified, but the language is still Shakespeare's. At the stylized Victory Ball that begins the film, McKellen's Richard steps up to a microphone to begin his "Now is the winter of our discontent" monologue, then pisses away the rest of its more sinister implications in a urinal.

One derivative film that should not be ignored here is Al Pacino's *Looking for Richard* (1996), a sort of skewered documentary that might just as easily have been titled "Looking for Shakespeare." While trying to make sense of what may be Shakespeare's most frequently performed play, Pacino and his company also question the relevance of Shakespeare for today's audiences. (He might have saved some of this agonizing by looking carefully at Ian McKellen's political performance.) His man-on-the-street interview approach demonstrates only that the man on the street is not necessarily well informed about Shakespeare or history.

Establishing a proper focus seems to be a major challenge here, and it is not entirely clear what Pacino intends to document: the relevance of Shakespeare today? Behind-the-scenes preparations for a play performance? The shooting of a motion picture adaptation? Pacino himself seems not to be entirely certain. The film includes a pilgrimage to Shakespeare's Birthplace Museum in Stratford-upon-Avon, a visit to the site of the Globe Theatre reconstruction on the South Bank, and interviews with remarkable actors and directors, such as Sir John Gielgud, Vanessa Redgrave, Peter Brook, and Kenneth Branagh.

With his own cast (Alex Baldwin as Clarence, Winona Ryder as Lady Anne, Aidan Quinn as Richmond, Kevin Spacey as Buckingham) Pacino questions why American actors should be intimidated by the Bard, whether Richard and Buckingham should be treated as gangsters, the proper use of iambic pentameter, and the riddles of Shakespeare's densely packed rhetoric and the ambiguous motivation of his characters. He even brings in an educator, Frederick Kimball, for scholarly advice, whose advice he ends up rejecting.

Rehearsals, finished performances, and video replays of several scenes (Richard's seduction of the Lady Anne, for example, the arrest of Hastings, Gloucester's vexed nightmares and his death under Richmond's sword) are combined in a fascinating, seamless flow. Pacino will begin a line in his apartment, continue it on stage in costume, then review the finished product on a video monitor in the studio. Pacino creates a very interesting Richard, compounded of diffidence and deadly authority. What is the point? To show a serious actor attempting to find his character and attempting to perfect his craft. The questions raised about the play are well worth listening to.

REFERENCES

Colley, Scott, *Richard's Himself Again: A Stage History of Richard III* (Westport, Conn.: Greenwood Press, 1992); Manvell, Roger, *Shakespeare and the Film* (New York: Praeger, 1971); Mitchell, Deborah, *"Richard III*: Tonypandy in the Twentieth Century," *Literature/Film Quarterly*, 25:2 (1997), 133–145; Rothwell, Kenneth S., and Annabelle Henkin Melzer, *Shakespeare on Screen: An International Filmography and Videography* (New York: Neal Schuman, 1990); Weinraub, Bernard, "Movie History Emerges from a Basement," *The New York Times*, September 17, 1996, A1, B2.

—*J.M.W. AND J.C.T.*

ROMEO AND JULIET

See *TRAGEDY OF ROMEO AND JULIET, THE*

THE TAMING OF THE SHREW
(1593–94)

The Taming of the Shrew (1929), U.S.A., directed and adapted by Sam Taylor; United Artists.

Kiss Me Kate (1953), U.S.A., directed by George Sidney, adapted by Dorothy Kingsley; MGM.

The Taming of the Shrew (1966), U.S.A./Italy, directed by Franco Zeffirelli, adapted by Zeffirelli, Suso Cecci D'Amico, Paul Dehn; Royal Films International, F.A.I.

10 Things I Hate about You (1999), U.S.A., directed by Gil Junger, adapted by Karen McCullah Lutz; Touchstone Pictures.

The Play

The general reader may be surprised to know that *The Taming of the Shrew* does not immediately begin with the familiar story of Kate and Petruchio; rather, one of Shakespeare's earliest comedies begins with an extended "Induction" (prologue), involving a practical joke played upon a drunken tinker, Christopher Sly, who awakens to find himself treated like a lord, much to his amazement. Unaware of the joke being played on him, Sly assumes the lordly role and allows himself to be entertained by men employed by the true lord, who is the initiator of the joke. The performance for Sly becomes the core of Shakespeare's play, though, oddly, the Sly character disappears completely after the first act. The main plot of the play Sly is watching involves two sisters, Katharina and Bianca, the daughters of Baptista Minola. Baptista will not allow Bianca, the younger and more conventional, to marry until a husband has been found for her cantankerous older sister. The eligible bachelors of Padua prize the beautiful and docile Bianca, but none is interested in Katharina. Bianca's rivals, Hortensio, Lucentio, and Gremio, hire Petruchio, a gentleman from Verona, to woo Kate in order to clear the way for their courtship of Bianca. Upon hearing of Baptista's wealth, Petruchio seems mainly interested in Kate's dowry. Baptista readily accepts Petruchio's offer of marriage. Meanwhile, Lucentio and Hortensio disguise themselves as instructors to Bianca so as to woo her without her father's interference.

Petruchio arrives at his wedding outrageously garbed in beggar's clothing and insists Kate marry him as he is. This is merely his ploy to begin the process of Kate's "taming." Throughout the next several scenes, Petruchio denies Kate food, sleep, and a suitable wardrobe, as he attempts to establish himself as her "lord and master"; but although he humbles and humiliates her constantly until she blindly agrees to whatever he says, Petruchio never breaks her spirit. In contrast, Lucentio, disguised as Cambio, a tutor, woos and wins Bianca's love only after she is assured of his father's wealth; then they marry, secretly. Unaware that Cambio is really Lucentio, Hortensio, disgusted by

Bianca's favoritism of a lowly tutor, withdraws his offer of marriage to Bianca and instead proposes to a wealthy widow. The final scene has Petruchio, Kate, Lucentio, Bianca, Hortensio, and his new wife all celebrating their nuptials. During the wedding feast, the men wager on the obedience of their wives, but, surprisingly, Petruchio wins the wager. Kate not only shows obedience to her husband but is also extremely critical of the other wives for their neglect. As Cordelia will later do in *King Lear*, Kate pledges her love according to her bond, on condition that Petruchio remain loving and honest. She proclaims Petruchio "her loving lord" and proves submissive to "his honest will." She even offers to place her hands beneath his feet, an offer that Petruchio does not accept. Instead, he kisses Kate, proclaiming her his equal, not his servant.

The Films

Among the first screen treatments of *The Taming of the Shrew* is the abbreviated version made by D.W. Griffith in 1908, which reduced the entire play to one reel of running time. Much later, the Sam Taylor adaptation was the first complete Shakespeare play to be filmed as a Hollywood talkie. It was a benchmark United Artists production that established the trend of a celebrity husband-and-wife team in the central roles that would be followed three decades later by Richard Burton and Elizabeth Taylor. The play was used as a vehicle to showcase the talents of Hollywood's most famous couple, Mary Pickford and Douglas Fairbanks, Sr. Mary, celebrated as "America's Sweetheart" for most of her career, essayed her second "mature" role (after having won the second best actress Oscar for *Coquette* in 1929) as Kate; and Douglas Fairbanks, the matinee idol who had built his reputation during the 1920s with several highly entertaining swashbuckling roles, starting with *The Mark of Zorro* (1920), drew upon his own Shakespearean experience (with the Frederick Warde Company) as Petruchio.

The sophistication of the talking picture technique is remarkable for its time. The broadly farcical action was influenced by conventions of silent comedy, and the "talk" was kept to a minimum (the wedding ceremony is nearly wordless, for example, as the scene is driven by Fairbanks's pantomimic comic talent). The action is certainly pared down, and there is no evidence of a screen credit alluding to "additional dialogue by Sam Taylor." The screenplay dispenses with the Sly Induction and most of the Bianca subplot so that the stars can shine immediately. Act One was considerably compressed in order to get Fairbanks on camera as quickly as possible (the camera tracking

Mary Pickford and Douglas Fairbanks, as Kate and Petruchio, brought Shakespeare to the talkies for the first time, in The Taming of the Shrew *(1929).* (MARY PICKFORD FOUNDATION)

back before his broad stride down the streets of Verona is a nice touch), and the characters of Lucentio and Hortensio are conflated into a single suitor for Bianca. The movie really hits its stride with the wedding scene and its aftermath in Act Three. In the play Kate is deprived of food and sleep for days until she learns her lesson, but in the film this ordeal is compressed into a single night of comic abuse (perhaps reflecting something of the stormy relationship Fairbanks and Pickford were experiencing at the time of the production). The ending is simplified; the 100-crown wager is cut; the text is arguably corrupted, but the meaning is clear—reconciliation comes as the result of mutual respect and understanding. In 1954 the film, slightly abbreviated, was re-released with a new soundtrack. Long out of print, it is being replaced at this writing with a restored version of its original state.

Franco Zeffirelli's 1966 adaptation is far more traditional and complete (nearly twice as long as the 1929 version), incorporating lush sets and lavish costumes in

Real-life husband and wife Richard Burton and Elizabeth Taylor starred as Petruchio and Kate in Franco Zeffirelli's The Taming of the Shrew (COURTESY ROYAL FILMS INTERNATIONAL)

an attempt to place the play in an appropriate Italianate setting. Even so, Zeffirelli does not incorporate the Induction scene, which introduces the motif of disguise and trickery. The film does clearly portray that Bianca (Natasha Pyne) only plays at being the dutiful daughter, hiding a shrewish nature that might rival her sister's. Richard Burton's Petruchio shows little artful finesse in his manipulation of Kate (Elizabeth Taylor); he is merely bigger and more bullying than the shrew he courts. Elizabeth Taylor's Kate, although humble and suitably submissive in her final speech, leaves the celebration feast at the end, leaving Petruchio to chase after her, perhaps implying that theirs is not the marriage of equal wit and passion suggested by Shakespeare, but merely a childish tug-of-war for power. Burton's Petruchio at first pretends not to notice Kate's hostility when he chases her with oblivious gusto over the rooftops of the Minola mansion, until they tumble into the woolstack, as Zeffirelli visualizes their initial sparring. This Petruchio first seems to be merely a vul-

gar, boorish, drunken lout; but these traits are countered by his verbal dexterity and diction, which suggest that this is not an utterly crude man.

The couple is not entirely mismatched since the two have a great deal in common and seem to arrive at a mutual understanding. Zeffirelli's Kate is more spirited, interesting, and appealing than her devious sister. From behind a stained-glass window, she watches Petruchio with longing and interest. Zeffirelli takes far more time to humanize the character of Petruchio than Sam Taylor had done and provides a better reason for Katharine's astonishing transformation. Her absolute loyalty to a domineering husband is mainly a matter of gamesmanship, as romantic comedy displaces the earlier farcical action. The film is made even more entertaining by the able supporting cast, including Michael Hordern's Baptista, Michael York's Lucentio, and Cyril Cusack's Gremio. The film was important in the way it reestablished the marketability and accessibility of Shakespeare for a mass audience.

The other titles listed above as adaptations represent more of a stretch. Cole Porter's masterful *Kiss Me Kate* premiered on Broadway in 1948 and is mainly a backstage musical rather than a true adaptation of Shakespeare's play. (See also the entry under "Musicals.") In the framing story a once happily married couple, now bitterly divorced, each still knowing the other's weak spots, exploit their past personal knowledge onstage and off as they rehearse a musical version of *The Taming of the Shrew*. Unlike Christopher Sly in Shakespeare's "Induction" scene, Lilli Vanessi (Kathryn Grayson) and Fred Graham (Howard Keel) do not merely watch the play-within-a-play but are its main participants. The imbedded play provides a rationale for role-changing as the actors compete for the limelight. Fred uses Lilli's vanity to manipulate her into accepting the part of Katharina before Lilli is at all sure that she really wants to play the role. Lilli flaunts gifts from her new fiancé, Tex, in order to make Fred jealous, but Lilli is herself jealous of Fred's offstage romance with Lois Lane (Ann Miller), the actress playing the part of Bianca. This offstage battle of the sexes parallels and compliments the onstage contest between Petruchio and Kate.

The actor playing Lucentio has accumulated a gambling debt under a false name and signed an I.O.U. using Fred Graham's name as his own. When gangsters come to the theatre to collect on the debt, Fred gains an advantage by playing along with the gangsters and insisting that they use their brute charm to keep Lilli from running out mid-show. Being forced to stay with the production and perform only increases Lilli's hostility, which is carried over to her performance as Kate. When Lilli receives flowers from Fred, she thinks he has remembered the one-year anniversary of their divorce, but is later enraged to learn the flowers were intended for Miss Lane and delivered to Lilli by mistake. Lilli threatens to walk out of the theatre and never return. The gangsters threaten her, but Fred allows her to leave with her fiancé and orders the understudy to complete the production for Lilli.

The final scene of the movie takes place onstage, the scene where Kate berates the other wives for their lack of service to their husbands. When Petruchio calls for Kate, Kate does not come onstage. When he calls again, whispering orders to the stage manager to find the understudy, Kate, played by Lilli Vanessi, returns to appear onstage. Both Kate and Lilli become willing captives of love, willing to assist their husbands, showing that the heart and not merely the taming method is truly the rationale behind their speech of obedience and devotion.

10 Things I Hate about You *translated* The Taming of the Shrew *into contemporary teen-speak.* (COURTESY TOUCHSTONE PICTURES)

The last film, *10 Things I Hate about You*, is even more of a stretch, reducing Shakespeare's play to a teenpic, set at Padua High School. Cameron Jones (Joseph Gordon-Levitt), an updated Lucentio, is a new transfer student who falls for the lovely Bianca Stratford (Larisa Oleynik), but in order to date her he has to pay off somebody foolish enough to date her formidable older sister, Kat (Julia Stiles). Here, the edict that Bianca cannot date until Kat does stems from Kat's basic unwillingness to date, not because her father fears that he will not otherwise be rid of his daughter. Enter Patrick Verona (Heath Ledger), the Petruchio figure, an Aussie with a reputation for being a Bad Boy. Patrick pockets the money and courts Kat. After a rocky start, including a party scene where Kat loosens up, gets drunk, and throws up on Patrick, the two find true romance at the senior prom. Cameron, meanwhile, finds bliss in Bianca's arms. At the prom Bianca defends Kat and the sisters actually reconcile their differences, a plot twist utterly alien to Shakespeare. At the end the wifely obedience speech is transformed into a reworked sonnet, assigned as a homework assignment, that Kat reads in front of the class, stating that her love for Patrick is greater than her humiliation at finding out that he was paid to date her. Her emotional honesty shows clearly what Shakespeare only hinted at, that love is greater than pride.

All the kids are freshly scrubbed, look great in their chic clothes, live in upscale homes, and go to a school that looks like a storybook castle. It is interesting to see a New Age spin on the traditional concept of a lusty, sexist beast of a Petruchio, and of a kittenish, bitchy Kate. He is now just a lovable hunk, and she is a feminist icon. In other words, the edges of both are dulled for the sake of political correctness. This is one twisted *Shrew* stripped of its language, elegance, and spirit. Purists may be justifiably horrified.

REFERENCES

Brownlow, Kevin, *Mary Pickford Rediscovered* (New York: Abrams, 1999); Manvell, Roger, *Shakespeare & the Film* (New York: Praeger, 1971); Tibbetts, John C., and James M. Welsh, *His Majesty the American: The Cinema of Douglas Fairbanks, Sr.* (Cranbury, N.J.: A.S. Barnes, 1977); Zeffirelli, Franco, *Zeffirelli: An Autobiography* (New York: Weidenfeld and Nicholson, 1986).

—*J.C.T. AND J.M.W. AND H.O.*

THE TEMPEST (1611)

The Tempest (1908), U.K., directed and adapted by Percy Stow; Clarendon Film Co.

Tempest (1939), U.K., directed and adapted by Dallas Bower; BBC-TV.

Forbidden Planet (1956), U.S.A., directed by Fred McLeod Wilcox, adapted by Cyril Hume from a story by Irving Black and Allen Adler; MGM.

The Tempest (1956), U.K., directed and adapted by Robert and Ian Atkins; BBC-TV.

The Tempest (1960), U.S.A., directed and adapted by George Schaefer; Hallmark Hall of Fame/NBC-TV.

The Tempest (1968), U.K., directed by Basil Coleman, adapted by Cedric Messina; BBC-TV.

The Tempest (1979), U.K., directed by John Gorrie, adapted by Alan Shallcross; "The Shakespeare Plays" Series/BBC-TV.

The Tempest: by William Shakespeare, as seen through the eyes of Derek Jarman (1980), U.K., directed and adapted by Derek Jarman; British Film Now.

Tempest (1982), U.S.A., directed by Paul Mazursky, adapted by Mazursky and Leon Capetanos; Columbia Pictures.

Prospero's Books (1991), U.K./France, directed and freely adapted by Peter Greenaway; Allarts-Cinea/Camera One-Penta Co-Production/Miramax.

The Tempest (1999), U.S.A., directed by Jack Bender, adapted by James Henderson; NBC Studios/Trimark Pictures.

The Play

The play, believed to be Shakespeare's last before his retirement to Stratford-upon-Avon, was given special treatment in the First Folio of 1623, placed first among all the plays printed therein. It is possible that Shakespeare collaborated with John Fletcher on a later play entitled *The Two Noble Kinsmen* in 1613, but that play was not included in the Folio or in any other subsequent 17th-century editions. Strikingly original in its substance and execution, *The Tempest* later inspired artists outside the theatre, such musical treatments as those by Hector Berlioz ("Dramatic Fantasy," 1830), Tchaikovsky ("Fantasy," 1873), the incidental music Sir Arthur Sullivan composed in 1872, as well as an opera, *Der Sturm* (1956), by the Swiss composer Frank Martin. Two of the filmmakers drawn to this play were trained artists as well: Derek Jarman was a painter and designer trained at the Slade School of Art in the late 1960s; Peter Greenaway was a trained draughtsman, illustrator, and mural painter, an artist who happened to make films.

Prospero, the scholar-sorcerer and central character of *The Tempest*, was betrayed by his brother Antonio, who, aided by Alonso, the king of Naples, usurped Prospero to become duke of Milan 12 years before the plot begins, sending Prospero and his three-year-old daughter Miranda into exile. Adrift at sea in a leaky boat, Prospero eventually finds himself beached on a remote island. His only resources are his books on magic, given to him by his loyal friend Gonzalo. He puts these books to good use on the island. His knowledge gives him dominance over the native Caliban, the misshapen son of the dead witch Sycorax, who had claimed to rule the island. Prospero intends to educate Caliban, but after Caliban attempts to rape Miranda, Prospero makes Caliban his slave. He also uses his power to release the spirit Ariel, whom Sycorax had imprisoned in a cloven pine. Ariel becomes his faithful fairy servant.

Prospero conjures up a tempest that shipwrecks his former antagonists on the island—Antonio, Alonso, Alonso's son Ferdinand, and Alonzo's brother, Sebastian. Ariel takes Ferdinand, who landed apart from the others, to Prospero's lodgings, where Ferdinand meets and falls in love with Miranda. Prospero puts Ferdinand to work bearing logs to test the young man's mettle. Meanwhile, Ferdinand's father, Alonso, is grieving because be thinks his son has been drowned.

On its strange trajectory toward forgiveness and reconciliation, the play has sinister implications. Antonio and Sebastian conspire to murder Alonso, for example, but their plans are foiled by Ariel. This plot is paralleled by a comic subplot involving two lowlife characters, Alonso's butler Trinculo and his colleague Stephano, who introduce Caliban to alcohol, getting him drunk, then conspire with Caliban to kill Prospero so that Trinculo can rule the island with Miranda as his queen. These characters are stupid, however, and no match for Prospero's power, as Ariel distracts them and leads them away to a stagnant pond, where they sink chin-deep into the muck.

Ariel tells Alonso that the gods have taken his son in punishment for his previous crimes. Bewitched into contrition, Alonso, Antonio, and Sebastian become conscience-ridden, desperate men. Satisfied by the worthiness of Ferdinand, meanwhile, Prospero consents to his betrothal to Miranda and conjures up a masque in celebration in Act Four. In Act Five Ariel has imprisoned the castaways in a grove of lime trees and indicates that he feels sorry for them, which makes Prospero question his motives for revenge. Moved by compassion to forgive his enemies, Prospero reveals himself to them, dressed in the regalia of the duke of Milan and demands that his dukedom be restored. He shows Alonso his son, playing chess with Miranda, and explains to his guests how they were brought magically to the island.

Ariel appears with the ship's captain and boatswain and the news that the ship has been magically transformed, repaired, and made seaworthy. Ariel is instructed to release Caliban, Trinculo, and Stephano. Ariel is then given his freedom in reward for his service, and Prospero decides to break his staff, since he no longer needs his magic. He plans to return to Milan after stopping in Naples, where Ferdinand and Miranda will be married. Thus Prospero is restored and virtue is rewarded.

Critics have described the play as Shakespeare's fantasy meditation on the New World, with European seafarers discovering an exotic island populated by strange creatures who are transformed into servants and slaves by the superior colonist. Caliban's name has been recognized as an anagram of the word "cannibal." Coming at the end of Shakespeare's dramatic career, the play has also been discussed as an allegory in which Prospero is seen as a symbolic representation of Shakespeare himself. John Russell Brown writes that unlike a "straightforward valediction" (or leave-taking), the play "is packed with innovations." Although Shakespeare "may well have intended it to be his last play," Brown adds, "nothing is shirked." It was premiered in a command performance for King James I in the Banqueting House at Whitehall by Shakespeare's company, the King's Majesty's Servants, on Hallowmas (All Saints' Day), November 1, 1611.

The Films

The Tempest, a magical and enchanted play, has had a rich and imaginative history of media productions. Because *The Tempest* is one of the shortest plays in the Shakespeare canon, and one of the most interesting, it is more easily adaptable to the screen, though directors and adaptors have taken incredible liberties with Shakespeare's text, stripping away its poetry and transforming it into a science fiction space epic, as in *The Forbidden Planet* (1956), or into a modern fable, as in the Paul Mazursky transformation of 1982.

The first *Tempest* on film was made in 1908, directed by Percy Stow for the Clarendon Film Company in Britain. An unidentified cast sketches the action of Shakespeare's play in this one-reeler through vignettes such as Prospero's arrival at the island after his exile, Miranda in arms and books in hand, the release of the spirit Ariel from a tree, which is clearly not a "cloven pine," the discovery and taming of Caliban, the conjuring of the tempest. Although it is only 11 minutes long, the film attempts to follow Shakespeare's design. An American *Tempest*, no longer extant, was released by Thanhouser in 1911, and a French version was released by Eclair in 1912. The first extended sound adaptation would not come until 37 years later, surprisingly, through the medium of early television.

Arguably, the play has fared better on television than film, depending on one's reaction to the distinctive and peculiar treatments of Derek Jarman and Peter Greenaway. The first television treatment came as early as 1939, a low-budget BBC production with a high-profile cast, notably Peggy Ashcroft as Miranda, George Devine (later famous for his work at the Royal Court Theatre) as Caliban, and John Abbott as Prospero. The play was later produced for BBC in 1956 by the father-son team of Robert and Ian Atkins, with Robert Atkins playing Caliban as a monstrously deformed creature. A notably ethereal television adaptation was directed in America in 1960 by George Schaefer for the Hallmark Hall of Fame NBC television series, graced with a talented cast that included Maurice Evans (Prospero), Lee Remick (Miranda), Roddy McDowall (Ariel), and Richard Burton as "an unforgettable Caliban," in the words of Kenneth Rothwell. Shortened to a 90-minute performance, Schaefer's lighthearted treatment has been considered one of the most successful television adaptations.

According to Kenneth S. Rothwell and Annabelle Henkin Melzer, the Cedric Messina BBC television production of 1968 should be considered a benchmark in the "modern era" of BBC Shakespeare productions, since later, in 1976, Messina was named first producer of the ambitious BBC "Shakespeare Plays" series. Though prints are unavailable, the cast was impressive, featuring Michael Redgrave as Prospero, Ronald Pickup as Ariel, Tessa Wyatt as Miranda, Keith Michell as Caliban, and Douglas Rain as Stephano. Messina later produced the adaptation for "The Shakespeare Plays" series, directed by John Gorrie that featured Michael Hordern as Prospero, Warren Clarke as Caliban, Pippa Guard as Miranda, David Dixon as Ariel, and Nigel Hawthorne as Stephano. Kenneth Rothwell notes that the production follows the text faithfully: "there are no gross excesses." The play is enhanced by a spectacle of music and dance, performed by a "balletic fairy troupe."

There is simply no conventional film adaptation for this play, which seems a magnet for eccentric talents such as Derek Jarman, whose inventive and unconventional adaptation comes the nearest to the play itself, even if the betrothal masque is oddly imagined and the text restructured and abridged. Prospero's long expository monologues providing the backstory of his exile (I.ii) are broken up and patched in *passim* in order to avoid stagebound business that is inherently uncinematic.

Jarman first imagined "a mad Prospero, rightly imprisoned by his brother," and considered having Prospero speak all the lines, as Peter Greenaway was later to do; but this concept was later modified. Heathcote Williams plays a younger Prospero than is usual, preoccupied by "curious" knowledge. As a consequence, Miranda (Toyah Wilcox) is a neglected child, used to entertaining herself, adventuresome and curious about sex. Caliban (blind actor Jack Birkett) is merely a "voyeuristic nuisance," more "mooncalf" than "monster," and not a serious sexual threat to Miranda. "He is like a giant baby," as Diana Harris and MacDonald Jackson have written, "so that the bizarre flashback showing him sucking at the breast of his grotesque mother, the hookah-smoking Sycorax, seems strangely appropriate." On the other hand, Kenneth Rothwell, from an earlier generation of critics, found "the breast-feeding of a full-grown Caliban by his sow of a mother, Sycorax," surely "one of the most revolting spectacles ever filmed."

Karl Johnson's Ariel, according to Harris and Jackson, "fits Jan Kott's conception of the character" as resembling "a laboratory assistant working on an atomic reactor," hence, "the technician for Prospero's research." Wearing a pearl in his left earlobe, and "without the least suggestion of stereotypical homosexual mannerisms or the conventional androgyny," Harris and Jackson contend, "he comes across as knowingly and securely gay." They also discern an "ambiguous, homoerotically charged and sometimes tortuous" relationship between this Ariel and Prospero.

In this adaptation, Ferdinand (David Meyer) finds his way to Prospero's castle and sleeps naked in Caliban's lair, where he is discovered by Ariel, then humiliated by Prospero, who provides him with a white uniform and then manacles him to the wall, suggestive, perhaps, of bondage. An atmosphere of "carnivalesque gaity" is then established as Caliban "grinds out a merry tune on a hurdy-gurdy," as Harris and Jackson describe the scene. That atmosphere extends into the nuptial masque, done up as a high-camp extravaganza that combines elements of Gilbert and Sullivan's *H.M.S. Pinafore* and Busby Berkley's confections, as a troupe of Balkan sailor boys dance to the hornpipe, which Harris and Jackson describe as a "gay in-joke": "In his autobiography Jarman describes a party for Sir Francis Rose, where Jean Cocteau brought twenty-one sailor boys as a gift to Francis for his twenty-first birthday." Caliban then enters with Trinculo, garbed as a drag-queen, and this spectacle is then topped by the entrance of blues singer Elisabeth Welch—"Iris, Ceres, and Juno rolled into one"—who does a knockout rendering of Harold Arlen's "Stormy Weather." The treatment is astonishing; some purists may object to its campy extravagance, but its originality cannot be denied.

Shakespeare's play has spawned a number of entertaining derivative features, the most famous of which is probably *Forbidden Planet* (1956). In this loosely adapted, futuristic science fiction rendering of the play set in the year 2257, Dr. Morbius (Walter Pidgeon), the Prospero figure, lives in exile with his daughter Altaira (Anne Francis) on a remote planet, Altair-4. They are assisted by Robby the Robot, a mechanical Ariel. They are visited by a United Planets Cruiser mission led by Commander Adams (Leslie Nielsen), who comes to take Dr. Morbius and his daughter back to Earth, but Morbius refuses and orders the crew to leave. Dr. Morbius's magic involves the "Krell" technology he discovered on the planet and mastered, but the technology gets out of control and Morbius is killed in the process. Altaira (Miranda) and Adams (Ferdinand) and his crew escape the planet, which is destroyed as they depart. The Shakespeare connection may seem a bit remote here, but the film is a popular science fiction "classic."

Another displaced derivative that was not so successful was Jack Bender's *The Tempest*, produced for

Director Paul Mazursky retold Shakespeare's The Tempest *in contemporary terms.* (COURTESY COLUMBIA PICTURES)

NBC television in 1999. Set before and during the American Civil War, it tells the story of Gideon Prosper (Peter Fonda), who is more interested in the voodoo magic and sorcery known to his slaves than he is in the business of running his plantation. In a voice-over he explains that he was born into wealth and had no way of predicting the coming tempest, involving both the Civil War and a power struggle instigated by his brother. Gideon has given over the running of the plantation to his younger brother, Anthony (John Glover), who challenges Gideon's authority and accuses him of freeing a slave named Ariel (Harold Perrineau, Jr.), who earlier was seen being horsewhipped, while the white owners dance in the elegant plantation house. Anthony demands that Gideon be executed. Gideon escapes, however, with his young daughter (Katherine Heigl) to a Mississippi bayou, where Ariel helps him to start a new life. Twelve years later, while the Civil War rages around them, Gideon is forced to confront his murderous brother and give up his grown daughter and his ex-slave, releasing them to true freedom. This is a Civil War story of feuding brothers hung upon the framework of Shakespeare's play and stripped of Shakespeare's poetry. Without the language of Shakespeare, can it seriously be considered an adaptation?

Paul Mazursky's film updates and reconfigures the play as a contemporary comedy with a successful, 50-year-old American architect named Philip (John Cas-

savetes) as the Prospero figure, experiencing a mid-life crisis. Philip is fed up with his career, his life, and his wife Antonia (Gena Rowlands), an actress mainly interested in resurrecting her neglected career. Philip's employer, Alonzo (Vittorio Gassman), is a real estate tycoon. Although Shakespeare's Prospero was deposed of his dukedom and driven into exile, Philip leaves his profession by choice, forsaking Manhattan island for a Greek island in the Aegean Sea, where he takes his daughter Miranda (Molly Ringwald). Philip merely wants to escape a tempestuous marriage and to find himself. On his way to Greece, Philip meets a modernized version of Ariel, the twice-divorced Aretha (Susan Sarandon), who gives up her job singing in an Athens nightclub to accompany Philip to his island.

One problem is that there is hardly any magic in the modern world. Instead of a staff, Philip has a telescope, a poor substitution. Before he leaves New York, Philip observes a storm from his apartment window and says to himself "Show me the magic," but there is little to suggest that Philip is in control or has true magical powers until he arrives in Greece, where he is more in tune with Nature. There a storm has been forecast, so one has to take on faith the idea that Philip is able to conjure it up.

The Greek island is inhabited by a lusty goatherder named Kalibanos (Raul Julia) who has his lustful eye on Miranda but he is too foolish to pose much of a serious threat to her. His bestial nature is suggested only by his lust for Miranda, and this Caliban figure is humorously transformed into a banal materialist, obsessed with watching television. Philip lives at peace with himself until the tempest brings to the island the very people Philip had sought to escape from, when Alonzo's yacht is marooned there. With Alonzo is his son Freddie, played by Sam Robards (the son of Jason Robards, Jr., and Lauren Bacall).

This is a well-made and well-conceived film, but Shakespeare, it isn't. "I was originally going to try to do Shakespeare's play on film," Mazursky told the *New York Times*, but after 10 years, the project was languishing. "I found that it just wasn't right for me to do it," Mazursky explained. "The poetry of Shakespeare's language was so fabulous that somebody who was an expert on Shakespeare should do it—not me. But a couple of years ago, my friend Leon Capetanos and I came up with a way we felt we could modernize the story and use our language, rather than Shakespeare's language. The play is filled with a lot of mixtures of crazy things; at one point I was even going to do a sort of Marx Brothers version. Now it's probably a strange cross between some kind of lunacy and some kind of seriousness."

Mazursky was blocked for 10 years because he knew Shakespeare's language would not work for a contemporary story and mass audience. He finally realized that what appealed to him most was the plot: "A man and his daughter on an island. A man consumed with negative feelings about his past. A man who felt that terrible things had been done to him and who in the end would put down his magic and forgive." Capetanos explained that "Philip doesn't really have any power." No one does: "You only have the power to forgive people for their mistakes and become friends with them and see them as human beings and see yourself as a human being."

Consequently, the main focus was shifted to the father-daughter relationship. They decided the play was not about magic but about "a person who people believe has magic." Like Philip, Mazursky "loved the magic," however, and "loved the idea of forgiveness." Although the film is not exactly Shakespeare, it is awfully close in its way to Shakespeare's denouement of reconciliation, forgiveness, and sacrifice, as Philip gives up his hold on Miranda to Freddy, Aretha (Ariel) is "released," and Antonia and Alonzo are forgiven. The benign enchantment of this film is perhaps closer in spirit to Shakespeare's *A Midsummer Night's Dream* than to *The Tempest*. It is a derivative hybrid transformation, but the palimpsest of Shakespeare's play is still discernible.

The most astonishingly inventive adaptation of *The Tempest* is Peter Greenaway's *Prospero's Books*, starring John Gielgud as Prospero in a signature performance by one of England's most respected actors. Gielgud interpreted the role of Prospero three times on stage: at the Old Vic (1940), Stratford and Drury Lane (1957), and at the National Theatre (1974), and was Greenaway's natural choice to play Prospero, seen in his tub at the beginning of the film beginning to write a play called *The Tempest* and composing it as the action unfolds in a bizarre spectacle of nudity and revenge. The first word Gielgud utters—"Boatswain!"—is the first word of the play, and the text is both written and spoken throughout the film derivative.

Added to the recited text of Shakespeare are colorful and odd digressions concerning the books in Prospero's library, 24 of which are explained and defined, such as "The Book of Water" (vol. one), "The Book of Mirrors" (vol. two), "Architecture and Other Music" (vol. three), and so on, each serving to illustrate the Renaissance worldview in microcosm. The whole film involves a process of illustration, in fact. The only actor to act and speak is the awesome John Gielgud as Prospero; the other "actors" are there only to illustrate the text. As Greenaway once wrote: "Film is far too rich and capable a medium to be merely left to the storytellers." *Prospero's Books* is not for the narratively challenged, and Greenaway expects his audience to know and understand the text as a prerequisite for viewing the film.

As surely as Prospero controls his island in the play, John Gielgud controls the film through his distinctive, mellifluous voice and his command of language in diction and inflection. At the age of 87 when the film was made, Sir John Gielgud was the last of a line of knighted and titled actors, including Sir Laurence Olivier and Sir Ralph Richardson and Dame Peggy Ashcroft, who had conquered the London stage. According to Peter Conrad, the casting of Prospero "was intended by the director as an homage to the actor and to his 'mastery of illusion.' Sir John's Prospero is Shakespeare, and having rehearsed the action inside his head, speaking the lines of all the other characters, he concludes the film by sitting down to write *The Tempest*." After quitting the stage Sir John considered *Prospero's Books* "a summary of his career" as well as a formal valediction.

Although the other players may be non-actors in this "illustrated" classic, they are not without impressive credentials. Erland Josephson, who plays Prospero's faithful friend Gonzalo and provides Prospero with his precious books, worked on many a film project with Ingmar Bergman. Mark Rylance came to the role of Ferdinand from the Royal Shakespeare Company. Kenneth Cranham (Sebastian) had acted for the Royal Shakespeare Company, the National Theatre, and the Royal Court Theatre in London. Michel Blanc (Alonso) had won the best actor prize at the 1986 Cannes Film Festival for his work in Bertrand Blier's *Menage*. Tom Bell (Antonio) had extensive experience in film and television. Isabelle Pasco (Miranda) began as a model but had acted in several French- and English-language films. Perhaps the only true non-actor in the film was Michael Clark (Caliban), a dancer and choreographer trained by the Royal Ballet School—but that should qualify for "theatrical" experience.

Of course, some reviewers were alienated or offended by Greenaway's "lavishly ornamental ordeal [that] smothers *The Tempest* with an illustrative gloss so prurient [that] it defeats the pleasures of the original material," as Gary Arnold protested: Greenaway "prefers manipulating actors as puppets or decor himself, so the idea of Prospero as the inventor and mouthpiece for the entire ensemble must have seemed irresistible. Sir John could be treated like royalty and the remainder of the cast like Mardi Gras flotsam." Against this tirade, is the more measured evaluation of Brian McFarlane, who thought the film gave "new meaning to the idea of film adaptation," taking "a great text in another medium" and altering, modifying, and reimagining "it in such a way that it becomes unthinkable as anything other than a film." *Prospero's Books* is "not just a matter of turning the original inside out or upside down, but rather, a dazzling tour de force in which the play has been shaken in the manner of a kaleidoscope. In the process, the eye is assailed with gorgeous imagery and the mind is kept panting with the effort to reconstruct the glittering pieces as they fall." Perhaps no critic has better defined the method behind Greenaway's alleged madness.

REFERENCES

Arnold, Gary, "Stormy Weather for Greenaway's Purient 'Prospero,'" *Washington Times*, November 27, 1991, E2; Bennetts, Leslie, "Paul Mazursky Brews a 'Tempest,'" *New York Times*, August 30, 1981, D19, D24; Brown, John Russell, *Shakespeare's The Tempest* (London: Edward Arnold, 1969); Cavecchi, Mariacristina, "Peter Greenaway's *Prospero's Books*: A Tempest between Word and Image," *Literature/Film Quarterly* 25:2 (1997), 83–89; Conrad, Peter, "From a Vigorous Prospero, A Farewell Without Tears," *The New York Times*, November 17, 1991, II:1, 18; Coppedge, Walter, "Derek Jarman's *The Tempest*," *Creative Screenwriting* (April 1998), 12–15; Harris, Diana, and MacDonald Jackson, "Stormy Weather: Derek Jarman's *The Tempest*," *Literature/Film Quarterly*, 25:2 (1997), 90–98; Jarman, Derek, *Dancing Ledge* (London: Quartet, 1984), 186–206; McFarlane, Brian, "*Prospero's Books*," *Cinema Papers*, 86 (1992), 57–58; Mazursky, Paul, and Leon Capetanos, *Tempest: A Screenplay* (New York: Performing Arts Journal Publications, 1982); Rothwell, Kenneth S., and Annabelle Henkin Melzer, *Shakespeare on Screen: An International Filmography and Videography* (New York: Neal Schuman, 1990); Stenmetz, Leon, and Peter Greenaway, *The World of Peter Greenaway* (Boston: Journey Editions, 1995); Sonnabend, Yolanda, "Designing *The Tempest* with Derek Jarman," in *Derek Jarman: A Portrait* (London: Thames and Hudson, 1996): 77–79; Taylor, Geoffrey, *Paul Mazursky's Tempest* (New York: New York Zoetrope, 1982); Vaughan, Virginia Mason, and Alden T. Vaughan, "Tampering with *The Tempest*," *Shakespeare Bulletin*, 10:1 (1992), 16–17; Woods, Alan, *Being Naked Playing Dead: The Art of Peter Greenaway* (Manchester, U.K.: Manchester University Press, 1996).

—*J.M.W.*

10 THINGS I HATE ABOUT YOU

See *TAMING OF THE SHREW, THE*

THRONE OF BLOOD

See *MACBETH*

TITUS ANDRONICUS (1594)

Titus (1999), directed and adapted by Julie Taymor; Fox Searchlight Pictures.

The Play

Shakespeare's early tragedy was staged on January 24, 1594, by the Earl of Sussex's men at the Rose Theatre. It was published later that year, then reprinted in 1600 and 1611. The 1611 quarto was reprinted in the First Folio of 1623. Dating its composition is problematic. Some scholars have questioned whether Shakespeare wrote all of it. As one of his earliest works, it has all the faults to be expected from an inexperienced, 30-year-old playwright. Its violence and butchery were clearly modeled after that exemplar of classical tragedy, Seneca, whose works include the story of Thyestes, in which the protagonist is served a banquet of his children's flesh. *Titus Andronicus* begins in Rome where the eponymous general has just returned from his victory over the Goths. Two of his captives are Aaron, a Moor, and Tamora, queen of the Goths. Titus orders that Tamora's eldest son is to be butchered in retribution for the deaths of two of his own sons. Seeking her own revenge, Tamora enlists the aid of Aaron and her two remaining sons to bring about the deaths of Titus's son-in-law (by stabbing) and two of his sons (by beheading). Moreover, Aaron tricks Titus into cutting off one of Titus's hands after his daughter Lavinia has been raped and mutilated and her tongue torn out. Unable to communicate to Titus the persons responsible for these outrages, Lavinia scratches out their names in the sand with a stick.

Now it is Titus's turn for vengeance. First he slays Tamora's sons, grinds up their bones into a pie, which he feeds to Tamora, and then he kills Tamora. For his actions, Titus is killed by the emperor (who in the meantime had married Tamora), and subsequently Titus's surviving son, Lucius, kills the emperor. As one of the only surviving nobles, Lucius assumes governorship of Rome, punishes Aaron, buries the growing pile of the dead, and instills peace at last over the city. Commentator Marchette Chute argues that rather than presume that Shakespeare was "carried away by his desire to please his audience" with "witless atrocities," Shakespeare was "trying to write a 'noble Roman history' and conform to the best standards of the clas-

sical drama as they were understood in his day." Chute seems to be writing as an apologist for what is generally considered an atrocious play.

The Film

Titus is too much of a bad thing, without question Shakespeare's cruelest and crudest play. As an unrelenting revenge tragedy repulsive in its grotesquerie, it is fair game for the sort of postmodern interpretation that Julie Taymor lends to it, giving an astonishingly high-tech, low-concept spin to the play's post-Senecan horrors. The film begins with a boy, identified as "Young Lucius," in a contemporary setting, playing cruel games with his toy soldiers. He is then transported back into a postmodern version of ancient Rome to witness the story of Titus as a bystander, incorporated into the action, witnessing it, and, presumably, learning from it. After the final spectacle of revenge and blood sacrifice, the image widens out to indicate that the performance has been enacted before a modern audience, clothed in black, in the Roman Coliseum, with microphones in place so that

Anthony Hopkins played the title role in Julie Taymor's Titus, *an adaptation of Shakespeare's* Titus Andronicus.
(COURTESY FOX SEARCHLIGHT PICTURES)

Lucius, the surviving son of Titus (not to be confused with the invented character of Young Lucius), may address the Coliseum audience at the play's conclusion.

The film is splendidly cast. Anthony Hopkins plays Titus, proud, dutiful, soon transformed through grief and madness into a fearsome avenger. Jessica Lange is an overly made-up, stone-hearted Tamora. But the stand-out performances belong to Alan Cumming, looking as though he had stepped out of *Cabaret* and into *Fellini Satyricon*, utterly decadent, self-absorbed, and evil, and, especially, to Harry Lennix as Aaron the Moor, the ultimate emblem of subconscious evil and one of Shakespeare's most powerful creations. The film production is marked by gross indulgence and hideous excess, but it is sometimes shockingly effective and even darkly humorous, as at the play's climax, when Titus scampers around dressed in a chef's uniform and hat at the Thyestian feast served to Saturninus, who finds it tasty, and Tamora, who clearly doesn't know what's cooking.

Taymor's stylization purposely jumbles together ancient and modern elements and motifs, lifting part of her concept from Fellini, not only from *Satyricon*, but also from *Fellini Roma*. "Modern Rome built on the ruins of ancient Rome, offered perfect stratification for the setting of the film," she wrote for a press release, without mentioning Fellini or Carlos Fuentes, both of whom have put the stratification of civilizations to metaphorical use. "I wanted to blend and collide time to create a singular period that juxtaposed elements of ancient barbaric ritual with Familiar, contemporary attitude and style." For her symbolic denouement, Taymor wanted the Roman Coliseum, "the archetypal theatre of cruelty, where violence as entertainment reached its apex."

In the film's prologue, Young Lucius, involved in pretend "violence" with his toy soldiers, "falls through an 'Alice in Wonderland' time-warp, right into the Coliseum," as his toy soldiers are translated into Titus and his army, marching mechanically and in triumph into Rome. Young Lucius himself is transformed into Titus's grandson. The horrors of Shakespeare's play are framed through a coming-of-age metaphor as Young Lucius passes from innocence to experience, "to knowledge, wisdom, compassion, and choice." His final exit from the Coliseum toward the dawning of a new day with evil Aaron's baby in arms symbolically is a journey toward redemption.

REFERENCES

Chute, Marchette, *Shakespeare of London* (New York: E.P. Dutton, 1949); Welsh, J., and J. Tibbets, "'To Sup with Horrors': Julie Taymor's Senecan Feast," *Literature Film Quarterly*, 28:2 (2000), 155–156.

—*J.M.W.*

THE TRAGEDY OF ROMEO AND JULIET (1595–96)

Romeo and Juliet (1936), U.S.A., directed by George Cukor, adapted by Talbot Jennings; Metro-Goldwyn-Mayer.

Giuliete e Romeo/Romeo and Juliet (1954), Italy/U.K., directed and adapted by Renato Castellani; Verona Productions.

West Side Story (1961), U.S.A., directed by Robert Wise, adapted by Jerome Robbins, Arthur Laurents, and Ernest Lehman; United Artists.

Romanoff and Juliet (1961), U.S.A., directed and adapted by Peter Ustinov from his play; Universal-International.

Romeo and Juliet (1968), U.K./Italy, directed by Franco Zeffirelli, adapted by Franco Brusati and Maestro D'Amico; Paramount.

Romeo and Juliet (1978), U.K., directed by Alvin Rakoff, adapted by Alan Shallcross; British Broadcasting Company/Time-Life Television.

Romeo and Juliet (1982), U.S.A., directed and adapted by William Woodman; Bard Productions.

China Girl (1987), U.S.A., directed by Abel Ferrara, written by Nicholas St.John; Vestron Pictures.

Romeo and Juliet (1988), U.K., directed and adapted by Joan Kemp-Welch; Thames Television.

Zebrahead (1992), U.S.A., directed and written by Anthony Drazan; Ixlan Corporation.

Romeo and Juliet (1993), Canada, directed and adapted by Norman Campbell; Canadian Broadcasting Company.

Romeo and Juliet (1994), U.K., directed by Alan Horrox, adapted by Grant Cathro; Thames Television.

William Shakespeare's Romeo + Juliet (1996), U.S.A., directed by Baz Luhrmann, script by Craig Pearce and Baz Luhrmann; Twentieth Century-Fox.

Shakespeare in Love (1998), U.S.A., directed by John Madden, screenplay by Marc Norman and Tom Stoppard; Universal Pictures.

The Play

Romeo and Juliet may be the best known of Shakespeare's works. Its balcony scene has become part of the cultural iconography, and even people who have never read the play know what it means to be called a "Romeo." Opening with a sonnet spoken by the figure of the Chorus who describes the action that will occupy "the two hours traffic of our stage," Shakespeare shows how a quarrel between the servants of opposing families quickly escalates into a fight that stops only when the prince of Verona intervenes. Distanced from the fighting, Romeo suffers from an unrequited love, while elsewhere Paris receives Capulet's permission to woo the 13-year-old Juliet. A party to be held at the Capulets' provides an intersection for these various lines of action. Benvolio believes the party will help his melancholy friend Romeo forget an infatuation with Rosaline, but Romeo is going because he learns Rosaline will be there. Capulet invites Paris, and Lady Capulet urges her daughter, Juliet, to judge the suitor's qualities. At the party, Capulet must calm Juliet's fiery cousin Tybalt, who recognizes Romeo and wants to fight him. Romeo and Juliet, of course, fall in love at first sight, compose a sonnet in their first lines to each other, and later pledge marriage when they meet alone outside Juliet's balcony.

The first half of the play contains many romantic and comic moments. The love between Romeo and Juliet allows Shakespeare the opportunity for some of his most memorable and frequently quoted lines. In addition, Juliet's nurse, who reminisces about Juliet's girlhood, and Romeo's friend, Mercutio, who invents the Queen Mab story, demonstrate a comic ability to spin a long-winded tale. The two later have a wonderful scene of bawdy bantering when the nurse comes to confirm Romeo's intentions. The nurse later pairs with Romeo's confessor, Friar Laurence, to bring the young lovers together, and, just before the middle of the play, the lovers are secretly married.

At this pivotal point, Mercutio and Benvolio encounter the angry Tybalt, who is looking for Romeo. When Romeo refuses to fight, Mercutio instead challenges Tybalt, and when Romeo tries to stop it, he succeeds only in causing Mercutio's death. Saying that his love has made him weak, Romeo goes after Tybalt, kills him, and then flees before the prince arrives to banish him. Meanwhile Juliet, waiting for news from her new husband, learns instead that he has killed her cousin. The lovers manage to spend one night together before Romeo escapes to Mantua. Distraught over the effect of Tybalt's death, Capulet decides to push forward with Juliet's marriage. When Juliet tells the friar she will kill herself rather than marry, he devises a risky plan to reunite the lovers. On the evening that her parents prepare for a second party, this one to celebrate Juliet's wedding, Juliet takes a sleeping potion that will make her appear dead. The next morning the nurse discovers the apparently dead Juliet, and the family must prepare for a funeral rather than a wedding.

In Mantua, Romeo has not received Friar Laurence's message that Juliet is alive, and instead Balthazar tells him that he has seen her buried. In despair, Romeo gets poison from an apothecary and travels to Verona to die next to Juliet. In a confrontation at the tomb, Romeo kills Paris, opens the tomb, weeps over Juliet, and then kills himself. When Friar Laurence arrives, he finds Romeo and Paris dead, and Juliet reviving from the drug-induced sleep. Hearing noises outside, the friar leaves, and Juliet stabs herself with Romeo's dagger. The prince arrives, finds out what has happened, and admonishes the families. Montague promises to raise a gold statue to Juliet, and Capulet promises to raise another of Romeo.

The Films

Next to *Hamlet*, *Romeo and Juliet* is Shakespeare's most often filmed play, and several major silent film companies have tried their hand at it. Robert Hamilton Ball lists a *Burlesque on Romeo and Juliet* (1902) by Thomas Edison and speculates that it may be from an earlier George Méliès short. The largest of the early East Coast studios, Vitagraph, which often used "high-culture" material to gain respectability for the new industry, released a one-reel abridgment of *Romeo and Juliet* in 1908. The next year, Edwin Thanhouser, a theatrical producer before turning to films, made a two-reel *Romeo and Juliet*, of which about half survives. When Metro announced a *Romeo and Juliet*, staring Francis X. Bushman (the reigning matinee idol) and Beverly Bayne, to be released in October of 1916, William Fox hurried to produce a version starring Theda Bara (the original vamp) and Harry Hilliard, which managed to open at the same time.

The first sound version of the play followed the tradition of the prestige film treatment. The Irving Thalberg and George Cukor *Romeo and Juliet* boasted a large budget and a big-name cast. When Louis B. Mayer rejected Thalberg's original suggestion to film in Verona as being too expensive, designer Cedric Gibbons built a massive and elaborate set that eventually occupied more than five acres of the MGM lot. English actors took several key roles, including Leslie Howard as Romeo, Basil Rathbone as Tybalt, and Dame Edith Oliver as the nurse, but Thalberg's wife, Norma Shearer, played Juliet, John Barrymore played Mercutio, and comic actor Andy Devine gave his gravelly, rustic whine to the role of Peter. Agnes de Mille choreographed the Capulet ball, and scholars John Tucker Murray and William Strunk provided scholarly expertise, with Thalberg reportedly telling Strunk, "Your job is to protect Shakespeare from us."

Leslie Howard, who was not Thalberg's first choice among available English actors, was himself reluctant to take the part and wrote that Romeo "seems hardly to be a three dimensional figure since his principal function is little more than to be the object of Juliet's affection." In addition, Howard was 42 and Norma Shearer was 36—hardly budding adolescents. He agreed finally, at least in part, because he decided that the Romeo of the second half of the play, the Romeo banished to Mantua and stunned into suicide by the news of Juliet's death, was, as he put it, "a baby Hamlet," the role for which he wanted to prepare.

The film emphasizes the force of circumstance on individual action even more than the play. Although Shakespeare's play opens with a small incident—the thumb-biting gesture—that rapidly multiplies into a larger conflict, Cukor's film shows how the quarrel between servants grows out of the larger conflict between the families. As the film opens, the entire Capulet household seems to be in procession when they suddenly encounter the Montagues, coming from the opposite direction, in a similar procession. The thumb-biting incident develops as an overflow of the hatred generated by this accidental meeting of the two families. The film's charm, however, lies more in its gestures than in its passions. Examples are not hard to find. Andy Devine's role in the opening fight is immediately undercut by the fact that, in keeping with his slapstick characterization, he cannot get his sword out. Basil Rathbone's controlled performance as Tybalt makes him menacing and glowering, but projects cold-blooded malice rather than passionate fury. However appealing Norma Shearer's Juliet may be in her balcony, one cannot help noticing that she is enshrined in an intricate pulpit-like structure that seems to be about 30 feet above Romeo. Barrymore's wonderfully eccentric Mercutio bows and waves to the ladies of the square, delivers a fanciful and energetic reading of the

Queen Mab speech, and is the only Mercutio that dies laughing, but in the central scene of the film his wounding happens so rapidly it is almost unexpected. The same is true of Romeo's fight with Tybalt, which lasts only 30 seconds, about half as long as the more dramatically staged fight with Paris where their shadows cross and loom against the walls as they fight in the labyrinthine crypt.

The film lost money and was not well received by critics, but seen from today's perspective, it possesses a kind of charm in its very artificiality. It is an example of that midnight-and-silver 1930s photography that makes black-and-white movies glisten, a contrast that is most apparent in the ball scene where Juliet's shimmering white dress and jewels contrast with Romeo's black outfit and white shirt. When he approaches her on the floor, the rest of the dancers fall into a shadow.

Renato Castellani in his *Giuliete e Romeo/Romeo and Juliet*, for which he won an award in the 1954 Venice Film Festival, makes an entirely different set of choices. His stars are less well known, and, in spite of the beautiful photography, Castellani gives the play perhaps the darkest, most enclosed feeling of any of these film versions. Shot in Italy, the film is notable both for its realistic settings and for its use of Renaissance art as pattern and backdrop for several of the costumes and scenes. Indeed, watching the movie can seem a bit like thumbing through a well-illustrated art book as one notices a dress from Botticelli, a fresco from Fra Angelico, the door from San Zeno Maggiore, and others.

More than just providing authenticity, however, Castellani's Renaissance world encloses and isolates his characters. After John Gielgud delivers the prologue, dressed in dark Elizabethan costume, the Italian neorealist camera style leads the viewers into a walled city, through its gate, and up narrow streets whose high walls on either side make the streets seem almost like tunnels. Except for a shot of Romeo on a small finger of land near the water at the beginning of the film and the shots on the road to Mantua, neither the sky nor much else of undomesticated nature appears in this film. The fight scenes at the beginning and middle of the play seem to add to the oppressive atmosphere by cutting off the tops of the buildings. When Romeo (Laurence Harvey) and Juliet (Susan Shentall) meet for the balcony scene, they are framed by the pillars, windows, and walls of the building. Castellani deliberately puts architectural barriers between them at all times, and they are never together in a single unobstructed shot. This frustration extends to the wedding scene, not dramatized in the play itself, where they are married through an iron grille, exchanging a flower, the ring, and a chaste kiss. Romeo has to make his way through the labyrinth of Verona several times. Castellani eliminates Capulet's illiterate servant and the invitation episode, so Romeo and his friends seem accidentally to run into the partygoers. Romeo finds a passage, follows it to a door, and comes out in the middle of the party. Later, when he comes back from Mantua, he must get into the walled city, so he dismounts and sends his horse running up to the entrance. With the guards distracted, Romeo sneaks through the streets. Later, when he gets to the church and finds the doors closed, he again finds a way around and then must move a huge stone covering the entrance to the tomb before he can get to Juliet.

Capulet, as played by Sebastian Cabot, generates tremendous emotional energy both at the party when he restrains Tybalt and later when he threatens Juliet for not wanting to marry Paris, but for the most part Castellani focuses on the two main characters and diminishes the role of Mercutio, whose Queen Mab speech disappears altogether. In the central scene of the play, Romeo meets Tybalt alone and is joined soon after by Mercutio and Benvolio. Castellani also provides some unusual turns at the end of the play. For example, Romeo kills Paris with a huge candlestick rather than with a sword. Then, rather than take poison, Romeo must stab himself, since Castellani has eliminated the apothecary scene. He also adds some minor characters, such as Abraham, a young man killed in the opening fight, and Rosaline, who does not actually appear in Shakespeare's play but in this film attends the Capulet ball and warns Romeo to leave.

By contrast, Franco Zeffirelli's *Romeo and Juliet* seems to be a film about youth and spring, populated with long-haired, beautiful adolescents. Its charm and sexuality captured the youth movement of the late '60s and made this the most popular and lucrative adaptation of any Shakespeare play; it won Academy Awards for cinematography and for costuming. For the title roles, Zeffirelli picked Leonard Whiting and Olivia Hussey, unknown but attractive actors whose looks projected his vision of the play. He pared it down and gave the film a focus that eliminates moments such as Juliet's speech on consummating her marriage, her confusion later in this same scene over who has killed whom, her speech before she takes the potion, the nurse's discovery of Juliet's body, Romeo's visit to the apothecary, and the fight in which Romeo kills Paris. Among several cuts and rearrangements, these choices in particular indicate how Zeffirelli emphasizes the rapid development of the love story and eliminates aspects that might make the characters more reflective or otherwise complicate their image.

Leonard Whiting and Olivia Hussey portrayed the star-crossed lovers in Franco Zeffirelli's Romeo and Juliet. (COURTESY PARAMOUNT PICTURES)

One of the accomplishments of the film is to present a solid and believable world of dimension and substance. Zeffirelli uses some of the same locations that Castellani did, but while Castellani's version is dark and claustrophobic, Zeffirelli's version is light and open and spacious. If Castellani's characters seem oppressed by their environment, Zeffirelli's move through it with comfort. John McEnery's extraordinarily complex Mercutio, for example, not only fights in the square, he also bathes himself and washes his handkerchief in its fountain, climbs its stairs, and dies on one of its tiers. Perhaps following that same logic, this Romeo and Juliet are themselves very real and very attainable lovers. The balcony scene, for example, shows Zeffirelli attempting to balance Shakespeare's poetry against the physical images. While Cukor's lovers touch hands, and Castellani's do not touch at all, this Romeo sees his Juliet in a low-cut gown sitting on the edge of a long and spacious balcony that wraps part way around the building. Framed in the greenery of the Capulet garden, the lovers discover each other, then Romeo rather quickly climbs a tree and is on the balcony with her. Though many of the best-known lines of the play remain, they are punctuated by passionate kissing. Juliet at one point has to stop and catch her breath. When this Romeo asks "Oh wilt thou leave me so unsatisfied?" Juliet's startled face makes clear that she understands the term in its sexual context, and she seems relieved when he explains that the only satisfaction he wants is to exchange vows. She coyly presses her hand toward him, recalling the hand imagery of their first meeting.

Among Zeffirelli's embellishments is the suggestion that Capulet's statement about early marriage marring a woman might refer to Lady Capulet herself. When Capulet says the line to Paris, Lady Capulet appears in a window in the background, glares in his direction and then shuts it. Later she, rather than Capulet himself, calms Tybalt, who has caught sight of Romeo at the party. Finally, as Anthony Davis points out, she seems "devastated by the death of a lover rather than a nephew" when Tybalt dies. Another addition is the song, "What Is a Youth," whose mournful lines, "so dies the rose, so dies the youth," a young man sings as the Capulet guests encircle him, and as Romeo and Juliet are speaking their first words to each other.

However irritating some critics found this and other sentimental additions, the song itself became a popular hit, perhaps underscoring Zeffirelli's accuracy in reaching his intended youthful audience.

William Shakespeare's Romeo + Juliet has been called the version for the Generation X, MTV, or postmodern sensibility, and more than one critic reviewing the film longed for the comparatively milder excesses of Zeffirelli's version. Certainly Baz Luhrmann refracts the Romeo and Juliet story through the conventions of contemporary pop media. A TV anchorwoman speaks the play's prologue and epilogue from the framed confines of a television screen. Characters are introduced through captioned freeze-frames from a news story. Almost immediately after the opening brawl between Montagues and Capulets, newspaper headlines announce it. When Leonardo DiCaprio's Romeo wanders back from his early morning reveries, he sees the video playback of the fight that opened the film. This is a nervous, frenetic film, visually and emotionally intense, characterized by rapid camera movement and fragmentation. Close-ups dissect their subjects, dis-

Baz Luhrman's Romeo + Juliet *brought Shakespeare into the postmodern age.* (COURTESY TWENTIETH CENTURY-FOX)

torting faces and objects, while long shots tend to fill the screen with iconic images of, for example, a huge Christ statue positioned between the Montague and Capulet business towers, or a church interior glowing in the light of hundreds of candles, or the ruined proscenium arch that frames a junk-filled beach. In this world, Romeo and Juliet (Claire Danes) are constantly interrupted. When Juliet first meets Romeo gazing through an aquarium, the nurse immediately pulls her away. When they hold hands and kiss, they must seek refuge in an elevator. In the balcony scene, they evade security cameras by kissing underwater. In the aubade scene, the nurse and Lady Capulet are in the bedroom as Juliet kisses Romeo goodbye, and he once more falls into the pool. In the tomb scene, Romeo fights his way past the police who are searching for him with helicopters and spotlights. He is at the business of drinking the poison when Juliet awakens, and interrupts him too late. He dies in her arms.

Luhrmann, like Zeffirelli, selected young actors for the part, but neither Claire Danes nor Leonardo DiCaprio were unknowns. Both were familiar from television, and both had achieved recognition in coming-of-age films. The division of older and younger generation in this film, however, seems ultimately an illusion. The violence of the younger generation is clearly an extension of parental excesses, most notably Fulgencio Capulet's (Paul Sorvino) angry rebuke of Tybalt in the Fellini-esque party scene or his later fury when he tells Juliet she must marry Dave Paris, the governor's son whose face is on a magazine cover labeled "most eligible bachelor."

Perhaps it is not so much the changes in the actual lines as the unusualness of the accompanying visual images that makes this film so disconcerting. Attempting to reconcile Shakespeare's "swords" with the hip world of Verona Beach, Luhrmann uses a close-up of the characters' guns to show that their brand name is "Sword" (instead of, one might suppose, "Colt"). Romeo and Juliet deliver most of the lines of the balcony scene in the Capulet swimming pool. Mercutio (Harold Perrineau), perhaps exploiting recent critical trends, comes to the party wearing a sequined mini-dress and makeup and then appears as the star of a Las Vegas-style production number. Romeo is unsure of his first vision of Juliet because he is recovering from the Queen Mab drug that Mercutio has given him. Friar Laurence (well played by Pete Postlethwaite) seems to be an advocate of alternative medicine, and other alternative solutions, rather than a well-intentioned confessor. He has a large crucifix tattooed on his back, clearly visible through his transparent guayabera, and has nearly mystical visions of how his intervention

can end the violence. In addition, employing ethnic divisions that are often used in adaptations of this play, Luhrmann makes the Montagues Latin, with Paul Sorvino as Fulgencio Capulet, John Leguizamo as Tybalt, and dark-eyed Claire Danes as Juliet. The Montagues are Anglo, perhaps Irish, with Brian Denehy as Ted Montague and Leonardo DiCaprio as Romeo. Interestingly, from this point of view, Mercutio is black, which gives a somewhat different weight to his dying lines, "a plague o' both your houses."

The several adaptations of the Romeo and Juliet story use various ways to divide their young lovers. Whereas *Romanoff and Juliet*, for example, makes the warring households the diplomatic outposts of the United States and Russia, *West Side Story*, *China Girl*, and *Zebrahead* rely on ethnic and racial differences. Shakespeare himself examined such differences as Christian and Jew in *The Merchant of Venice*, Moor and Venetian in *Othello*, and Egyptian and Roman in *Antony and Cleopatra*, but, in *Romeo and Juliet*, his Montagues and Capulets are feuding families of the same tribe, and seem to be more often paralleled than contrasted.

In filming *West Side Story*, film director Robert Wise used actual street scenes for some of the musical numbers and perhaps drew on his background as an editor to create dynamic and interesting scenes from co-director Jerome Robbins' choreography. Wise managed to improve the genre of musicals just as he had earlier significantly contributed to the western (*Blood on the Moon*, 1948), the fight film (*The Set-Up*, 1949), and the science fiction film (*The Day the Earth Stood Still*, 1951). *West Side Story* won nine Academy Awards, including best director, best picture, best supporting actor (George Chakiris), best actress (Rita Moreno), and best scoring of a musical picture.

Based on the play by Arthur Laurents, with lyrics by Stephen Sondheim and music by Leonard Bernstein, *West Side Story* uses several elements from Shakespeare's play but casts them in a somewhat different context. In this telling of the story, the Capulets become the Puerto Rican gang, the Sharks, and Capulet and Lady Capulet are replaced by a big brother, Bernardo (George Chakiris), who watches out for this story's Juliet, Maria (Natalie Wood), who has recently arrived from Puerto Rico, but who also becomes the Tybalt of the film. Instead of a nurse, Maria has a best friend, Anita (Rita Moreno), and Paris becomes Bernado's fellow gang member, Chino (Jose De Vega). A rival gang, the Jets, show even fewer specific resemblances to the Montagues. Riff (Russ Tamblyn), who is actually the leader of the gang, seems most like Mercutio mainly in that Bernardo kills him.

The Romeo character in the film, Tony (Richard Beymer), is retired from the gang and working in a drugstore for Doc, who resembles Friar Laurence to the extent that the friar is often pictured as being surrounded by alchemical instruments. At the end of the film, Tony, Bernardo, and Riff die, and only Maria remains to articulate the sense of anger and violation that Shakespeare's play gives to the prince.

In her reconstruction of the actual process of writing this play, Bernstein's biographer, Joan Peyser, says that various approaches to the main conflict included opposing Jews and Catholics, Anglos and Latinos in Los Angeles, and blacks and Puerto Ricans in New York, before they settled on the Sharks and the Jets, one gang composed of recently immigrated Puerto Ricans and the other composed largely of first-generation Americans, the children of European immigrants. The play is unusual also in its attention to the question of immigration and the idea of what it means to be an American. For Maria, Anita, Bernardo, and the other recently immigrated members of the Sharks, life in Puerto Rico is not so distant, and they frequently discuss the notion of going back there. Tony, on the other hand, is Polish, and the other members of the Jets are identified as Irish or Italian, members of the previous wave of immigrants. The New York accents of the Jets contrast strongly with the Spanish accents of the Sharks. Lieutenant Schrank, for example, very pointedly identifies himself and the Jets as "American," as opposed to the Sharks.

Peter Ustinov's original play, *Romanoff and Juliet*, focuses more on the quarrel between families than on the fate of the young lovers, and the film version, released the same year as *West Side Story*, reinforces the Shakespearean borrowing. From the beginning, Ustinov made Shakespeare's Montagues and Capulets into cold war–era Russians and Americans, but whereas the play opens with two soldiers who relieve the boredom of their watch by indulging in word games, the film plunges immediately into political comment with a shot of the United Nations building as Ustinov's voice-over explains that the film is dedicated to the UN, while the camera sweeps over rows of bored or sleeping delegates. For Ustinov, the love story of Romanoff and Juliet, the son of the Russian ambassador to Concordia and the daughter of the American ambassador to the same country, only underscores the political divisions. Ustinov himself appears as the leader of the tiny nation, which attracts the attention of the superpowers when he casts an abstention on a crucial UN vote. When both nations realize they must court the tiny country, Concordia finds itself offered aid, grain, and, among other things, performances by the Bolshoi Ballet. Seizing his opportunity, Ustinov's character becomes a more successful version of Shakespeare's friar and manages to get the lovers married, bringing peace and saving the day. Although the film has not received much attention and is not currently available, Ustinov was serious about his critique of governments and "huge supra-national corporations," and, in his autobiography, describes how he was pleased to receive a letter of praise from former president Harry Truman.

Abel Ferrara's *China Girl* retains several motifs from Shakespeare's play but also seems to draw on some of the visual imagery of *West Side Story*. The maze of chainlink fence, the graffiti-covered brick walls, the teen dance scene, the use of the fire escape for Juliet's balcony—all these elements establish the New York City atmosphere for both films. Where *West Side Story* depicted rival street gangs, *China Girl* presents, in effect, a second generation of gangs in which the disruptions caused by the younger gangs upset the carefully negotiated cooperation of the more established Chinese and Italian mobsters. The opening shots of the film make it clear that this is a neighborhood undergoing a significant transition. As a Chinese restaurant owner and his helpers transform an Italian restaurant into a Chinese one, Ferrara shows the angry and dismayed faces of the Italians in the neighborhood. Apparently later that same evening, the Romeo of this story, Tony Monte (Richard Panebianco), notices the film's Juliet, a beautiful Chinese girl named Tyan Hue, but called Tye (Sari Chang), dancing at a local dance club. When, without speaking, he begins to dance with her, their attraction is immediate and apparent, so much so that Tye's cousin and brother break up the dance and chase Tony through the streets. He crosses the Canal Street line between the territories, but the boys hesitate only briefly before following him down an alley to a chainlink fence, recalling one of the opening scenes of *West Side Story*. The Italian boys suddenly come out of the shadows on the other side of the fence and rescue Tony by attacking the Chinese. The fight stops only when the police arrive. Tye's brother, Yung Gan (Russell Wong), very much recalls Bernardo of *West Side Story*, and her cousin, Tsu Shin (Joey Chin), is clearly a Tybalt figure. Tony also has an older brother, Alby (James Russo), who parallels Tye's brother, and it is Alby's death that sets off the final violent action in the film. David Caruso plays a Mercutio, here called Mercury, who is more incendiary than mercurial, more a second Tybalt.

Director Ferrara's flair for urban violence gets ample display in this film as the multiple gangs come into conflict. In an odd travesty of cooperation, at one point a member of the older Chinese mob in a disciplinary raid stabs one of the rebellious young Chinese gang members, and when the young man gets up and moves toward the attacker, a member of the older Italian mob appears from the shadows and kills the young man by running a knife through his back. At the film's conclusion, in the middle of an Italian community celebration that features a procession of men carrying a statue of the Virgin Mary, violence erupts again, and both Tony and Tye are shot and die in the street, lying face up on the wet pavement, their hands touching.

Zebrahead, director Anthony Drazan's first film, and winner of the 1992 Sundance Film Festival's Filmmaker's Award, borrows the broader elements from the Romeo and Juliet story—a couple whose love is complicated if not prevented by family barriers, the death of an innocent friend who tries to break up a fight, a killer with a flammable temper, and a violent and fatalistic atmosphere. One of the recurring images in the film is of a character who drops matches on his lawn to show how pollution is seeping into his land and making everything flammable. This film, however, is less direct in its borrowing from either Shakespeare or other films, such as the influential *West Side Story*. The setting of this film is Detroit. Zach (Michael Rapaport), the Romeo of this film, is a redheaded, Jewish high school senior whose family owns a record store. The Juliet character, Nikki (N'Bushe Wright), is a young black girl who has just transferred from a Brooklyn high school and is the cousin of Zach's best friend Dominic, called Dee (DeShonn Castle). Shakespearean identities seem rather blurred in this film. While Dominic has some elements of Romeo's friend and confidant, Benvolio, he also has a protective role toward the film's Juliet. In this respect, he is like the older brothers in *West Side Story* and *China Girl*, except that he, like Shakespeare's Mercutio, dies in Romeo's place. The film's Tybalt character, named Nut (Ron Johnson), is volatile, but rather than being Juliet's cousin, he wants to date her and says he used to live in the house where she now lives.

While Zach apparently has an unrequited romance with a Rosaline-like character, his breaking up with her seems part of a broader effort to define love. In a scene at the record store, Zach's womanizing father (Ray Sharkey) says sex is a subspecies of rhythm and defines love by playing a Johnny Mathis album. Calling Zach's father a schmuck, Zach's grandfather says instead that love is responsibility. In another scene in the high school, a group of black girls point out different boys in the cafeteria and argue over which ones they would date and whether race would make a difference to them. Zack himself is accused by some of the black characters in the film of being a "wannabe," the word

they spray-paint across his locker. He acts black, listens to black music, and is dating a young black woman. At the end of the film, although Dee has died, Zach and Nikki have survived, and Zach goes over to Nikki and embraces her, but over their shoulder, in the background, a bookish black militant and an Italian boy fight each other.

Shakespeare in Love, written by Tom Stoppard and Marc Norman, and directed by John Madden, is not so much a version of *Romeo and Juliet* as it is a cleverly imagined story of how the play might have been written, recalling somewhat the atmosphere of Anthony Burgess's 1964 novel *Nothing Like the Sun*. Norman has said that the idea for the film began when his son asked him to do a story about young Shakespeare. Stoppard, of course, has written speculatively about Shakespeare's work in *Rosencrantz and Guildenstern Are Dead* (1967) and has often toyed with the notion of the creative process and its relationship to reality in various plays from *The Real Inspector Hound* (1968) to *Arcadia* (1993). Following the logic of the story, and Stoppard's usual practice, the play contains several clever allusions and anachronisms that build a comedy around the construction of the tragic play. This Shakespeare (Joseph Fiennes) goes to see a doctor named Moth whose Freudian practice extends to what, in some future day, will become the traditional psychiatrist's couch. Dr. Moth gives him a serpent-shaped bracelet, obviously phallic, and, seeking amorous inspiration along with the other kind, Shakespeare gives the bracelet to Rosaline. Later, when he goes to Richard Burbage's house looking for Burbage (Martin Clunes), he instead finds his Rosaline in bed with Mr. Tilney (Simon Callow), the master of the revels. Later in the film, Christopher Marlowe (Rupert Everett) goes to the same house and finds Rosaline astride Burbage himself. It is Marlowe himself, in casual bar talk, who suggests the outline of Shakespeare's *Romeo and Juliet*; and Lady Viola De Lesseps (Gwyneth Paltrow), who, as she is leaving to go to America, outlines the plot of *Twelfth Night*.

Shakespeare in Love first constructs a huge log jam of obstacles, including an insolvent theatre owner, Philip Henslowe (Geoffrey Rush), a creatively and sexually blocked Shakespeare, feuding theatrical companies, and an unpromising group of actors, including a Juliet whose voice changes just as the show is going on stage. Breaking through these barriers, however, is Lady Viola De Lesseps, representing the combined inspirations of love, beauty, and sex, who inspires Shakespeare to revise his proposed comedy, *Romeo and Ethyl, The Pirate's Daughter*, into the play we all know. (Stoppard's humor being what it is, it may be worthwhile noting that Ferdinand De Lesseps is the engineer who built the Suez Canal.) Assisting this process at a different level is Queen Elizabeth herself, who seems to represent intuition, good sense, and both practical and imaginative power. In the best tradition of movies about theatrical productions, everything that can go wrong does, but the play goes on and wins over even Viola's cuckolded husband Lord Wessex (Colin Firth), as well as a street preacher who was railing against plays when he was accidentally swept inside, and the hard-nosed money lender, Mr. Fennyman (Thomas Wilkinson), who goes from roasting Henslowe's feet in the opening scene of the film to reveling in the part of the apothecary, which Shakespeare adds for him (or at least says he does). The film won seven Academy Awards, including best picture, best actress for Gwyneth Paltrow, best supporting actress for Judi Dench, and best original screenplay for Norman and Stoppard.

Televised stage productions, although they tend to be more complete than versions prepared as theatrical films, generally suffer in comparison with theatrical films, sometimes regardless of either medium's individual merits or faults. That was perhaps the case with Alvin Rakoff's *Romeo and Juliet* for the BBC Shakespeare series, which Kenneth S. Rothwell says is "dismal . . . a shadowy replica of the dazzling Zeffirelli film," although Anthony Davies finds it "thematically more satisfying in its subtlety." Of historical note, Gielgud again plays the Chorus, though costumed very differently than his appearance 24 years earlier in Castellani's film. Also interesting is the fact that the black eye Rakoff gives to the Capulet servant Gregory is echoed in Luhrmann's film—same eye, same place.

Attempting to overcome the limitations of a filmed stage production, Rakoff uses a set that has several windows, stairways, and other openings. His camera almost never finds a blank wall. Besides the visual differences between Zeffirelli's version and this one, Rakoff attempts to give the complete play and to restore some dignity to Juliet's parents. Here they are more Juliet's concerned parents than Castellani's domestic tyrants or Zeffirelli's unhappily married couple. They often appear together and frequently touch Juliet, demonstrating both care and affection. Michael Hordern's Capulet is amiable and even a bit confused, recalling Hordern's wonderful portrayal of Baptista in Zeffirelli's *The Taming of the Shrew*, an impression oddly reinforced by the line "'Tis gone, 'tis gone, 'tis gone," which echoes the song in the earlier play. While Romeo (Patrick Ryecart) and Juliet (Rebecca Saire) are given back the inner life Shakespeare constructed for them, to look at this Juliet is to recall that 13-year-olds are today middle school children. She seems brighter but also younger and less animated than some other Juliets. Finally, Rakoff sometimes strives too hard to illustrate lines, for example, on the way to the party when Mercutio throws out his hands and kicks up his heels when he tells Romeo to dance. Later Friar Laurence's proverbial "they stumble that run fast" becomes a response to Romeo's actually falling on his way out of the Friar's cell.

Bard Productions uses American actors and advertises on the video jacket that "Unfamiliar English accents, so prevalent in most Shakespearean productions, are absent from this series." In William Woodman's *Romeo and Juliet*, for example, Alex Hyde-White (son of actor Wilfrid Hyde-White) is Romeo, Blanche Baker (daughter of actress Carroll Baker) is Juliet, and black actress Esther Rolle is the nurse. All three had backgrounds in television and some movie experience at the time this play was filmed. Bard also claims the play is "staged as seen in the 16th Century." In fact, this is not Shakespeare's bare stage but a somewhat more ambitiously used two-level stage area, including several props, and some expertise in modern stage design and lighting.

Perhaps to illustrate the play's prologue, William Woodman opens with a close-up of the faces of the dead lovers, and, as a voice-over recites those opening lines, the camera pulls back to reveal a circle of people standing around the platform on which the two lovers lie. Juliet wears what looks very much like a white bridal gown, complete with veil. At the end of the play, Woodman returns to the same shot, almost suggesting the circularity of a tale told. In general, the costumes in this production tend to be bright and ornate, making Zeffirelli's seem comparatively restrained; in fact, the choice of cast and costumes suggests that sexual appeal was an important consideration in assembling this production. There are no unnoticed double entendres, and many of them are rewarded with clarifying gestures. Woodman's *Romeo and Juliet* is also a very physical play. In the opening scene, Gregory and Sampson are playing dice. Later, when Benvolio and Romeo talk, they punctuate their delivery by tossing oranges spilled in the previous fight. Lady Capulet is checking her makeup and adjusting her dress while she waits for Juliet's first appearance. Mercutio is prostrate at the end of both the Queen Mab speech and the conjuration speech. As one might expect, the fights are athletic and well choreographed. Mercutio tweaks Tybalt's nose, taunts him with a hat, and spits in his face. Unique to this production is the fact that Mercutio is stabbed in the back when Romeo spins him around to stop the fight. Occasionally the physicality is distracting, especially when Juliet gives a horsey motion to her reading of "Gallop apace, you fiery-footed steeds," or when Romeo, in the tomb, stands straddling Juliet's prone body just before taking the poison.

Relying frequently on mid-shots and close-ups, Joan Kemp-Welch's version of *Romeo and Juliet*, more than any other, sometimes has a "talking head" effect. Many of the soliloquies are spoken directly into the camera. When characters—such as the nurse, Mercutio, Friar Laurence, Juliet, and Romeo—have long speeches, the camera tends to come closer as they speak and then recede when they finish. On the other hand, scenes that seem to call for a more spacious treatment, such as the two fight scenes, seem a bit cramped, although the skillfully staged fights are lively and inventive, making up for the lack of space. Similarly there are only about a dozen dancers at the Capulet party, but Capulet and Tybalt position themselves immediately in front of the camera, and thus cut off some of the stage space. Verona itself seems to be a city of narrow alleys with sharp twists. In this town, distances seem to go back and forth in space but almost never left to right. Interiors generally seem more spacious, with Juliet's bedroom and the tomb, ironically, the most ample.

Like Zeffirelli and Rakoff, Kemp-Welch selected a very young Juliet, with a success that falls somewhere between the other two. Ann Hanson's Juliet is a pleasant young woman who smiles quite a bit of the time and does a reasonably good job with her lines, but she must be at least a foot shorter than Romeo, who seems uncomfortable as he bends over to give her their first kiss. The high-waisted dress she wears through most of the play unfortunately emphasizes this difference in stature. Positioning the camera below her, as in the balcony scene, seems to help, but too often she is viewed from over Romeo's shoulder. Patrick Mc-Namee's Romeo somehow conveys the more poetic elements of Romeo's character. His features are somewhat delicate, he is inclined to stare off into space or into the camera, and, although he seems athletic enough in the fight scenes with Tybalt and later with Paris, the camera tends to focus more on his face. Mercutio is an introspective and droll man who seems acquainted with disappointment. When Romeo stops his Queen Mab speech, Mercutio rubs his temples and looks down reflectively as he says, "True, I talk of dreams . . . the children of an idle brain."

Norman Campbell's filming of the Stratford, Ontario, *Romeo and Juliet*, as staged by Richard Monette, is in many respects good precisely because it makes no attempt to disguise the fact that it records an excellent stage production, apparently before a live audience. Locations are suggested simply—arranging a few tables and chairs, for example, creates a restaurant; adding a piano and a candelabra makes it the Capulet party; and the grave is simply a pair of open doors in the floor of the stage. The second, smaller upper level, differently lit each time, becomes the platform from which the prince castigates the feuding families, the head of the stairs from which Juliet is presented before descending to the party, and later her balcony, and, finally, with gates around its supporting pillars, the graveyard. While transitions between scenes are conveyed by a fade, stagehands push props off and on. Backgrounds are kept dark, and locations seem to glide from one to the next, while characters are isolated simply by moving to a close-up. In the pauses between acts, the audience applauds, and the camera pulls back to show the full stage. At the end the cast comes out for a bow and the silhouetted figures of the audience stand in the foreground.

Set in Italy during Mussolini's time, this CBC production has the Capulet young men wear black and tan military uniforms, while the Montague men wear light-colored suits. The prince wears a white uniform, with gold epaulets, and a blue sash. Interestingly, when Romeo (Antoni Cimolino), Mercutio (Colm Feore), and Benvolio (Paul Miller) attend the Capulet party, they dress in Renaissance costume, so that the scene visually recalls the period of Shakespeare's play. The cast is almost uniformly excellent. Mercutio is a forceful character, clever, nimble, athletic, and funny. Juliet (Megan Porter Follows) makes a subtle transition from a child to a young woman apparently simply by changing her clothing and hair, although it is really her entire posture that changes. When we first see her, she is a child in a white nautical outfit and pinned up hair. Later, when she appears at the party standing on the upper level, wearing a golden dress, with her red hair combed out, her sparkle easily supports Romeo's comment about her shining like a jewel. The Capulets (Lewis Gordon and Kate Trotter) are also especially strong. Capulet himself is clearly in charge of things; bellowing, glad handing, and hugging, he is the ruler of his family. An interesting bit of characterization occurs when Capulet gets angry with Juliet after she resists the marriage to Paris; the nurse, Lady Capulet, and Juliet huddle together and hug as Capulet rants at all the women in his house.

Alan Horrox's *Romeo and Juliet* is abbreviated to about half the length of the BBC and CBC versions, and, although much is lost, he manages to develop a consistent look without straining the resources of the medium. The world of this production is neither sunny nor bright, and many scenes seem permeated by a smoky haze. The two fight scenes take place in an enclosed area with large pillars, which the duelists use to their advantage, and when Romeo fights Tybalt each holds a torch in one hand and the sword in the other. When the nurse brings Juliet's message to Romeo, she enters a room where Romeo, Benvolio, and Mercutio sit around a long table. The only exterior view in this production is through Juliet's window.

Romeo (Jonathan Firth) and Juliet (Geraldine Somerville) are not here children pitted against an adult world. Juliet, in particular, speaks with her mother (Jenny Agutter) and the nurse (Dearbhla Molloy) as an equal. When she pleads with Capulet not to force her into the marriage with Paris, she is a young woman hoping that she can manipulate her father by acting submissively, rather than a child cowering before him. Her reading of the line, "You kiss by the book," in response to Romeo's second kiss suggests that she has some basis of comparison. Yet her speech in Act Three wishing her marriage to be consummated and her speech before taking the potion are both cut. The cuts generally seem intended to focus the action and speed up the pace of the play. Horrox sacrifices the beginnings and endings of scenes and pretty much all of the extended comparisons. For example, the lines leading up to Mercutio's Queen Mab speech are cut, but Mercutio (Ben Daniels) is allowed to give a particularly animated delivery of the whole thing. When Mercutio dies, rather than have Benvolio lead him out and then return with the news that he has died, Mercutio dies seated with Romeo and Benvolio on either side of him. At the grave, Romeo enters by himself, Paris does not appear, and most of the friar's speech is cut, yet the production retains Montague and Capulet making their offers to build gold statues of the dead lovers.

REFERENCES

Ball, Robert Hamilton, *Shakespeare on Silent Film* (London: George Allen and Unwin, 1968); Courson, H.R., *Shakespeare: The Two Traditions* (Cranbury, N.J.: Associated University Presses, 1999); Davies, Anthony, "The Film Versions of *Romeo and Juliet*," *Shakespeare Survey*, 49 (1996), 153–162; Flamini, Roland, *Thalberg: The Last Tycoon and the World of MGM* (New York: Crown, 1994); Goodale, Gloria, "How They Imagined *Shakespeare in Love*," *Christian Science Monitor*, March 5, 1999, 17; Howard, Leslie, *Trivial Fond Records* (London: William Kimber, 1982); Levy, Emanuel, *George Cukor, Master of Elegance: Hollywood's Legendary Director and His Stars* (New York: William Morrow, 1994); Manvell, Roger, *Shakespeare and the Film* (New York: Praeger, 1971); Payser, Joan, *Bernstein: A Biography*, rev. (New York: Bill Board Books, 1998); Rothwell, Kenneth S., *A History of Shakespeare on Screen* (Cambridge, U.K.: Cambridge University Press, 1999); Thomas, Bob, *Thalberg: Life and Legend* (New York: Doubleday, 1969); Uricchio, William, and Roberta E. Pearson, *Reframing Culture: The Case of Vitagraph Quality Films* (Princeton, N.J.: Princeton University Press, 1993); Ustinov, Peter, *Dear Me* (Boston: Little, Brown, 1977); Willis, Susan, *The BBC Shakespeare Plays: Making the Televised Canon* (Chapel Hill: University of North Carolina Press, 1991); Willson, Robert F., Jr., *Shakespeare in Hollywood, 1929–1956* (London: Associated University Presses, 2000); Zeffirelli, Franco, *Zeffirelli: An Autobiography* (New York: Weidenfeld and Nicholson, 1986).

—*R.V.*

TWELFTH NIGHT, OR WHAT YOU WILL (1600–01)

WILLIAM SHAKESPEARE

Twelfth Night (1996), U.K., directed and adapted by Trevor Nunn; Fine Line Features.

The Play

Recognized as Shakespeare's most stageworthy comedy, *Twelfth Night* entertains with a complex plot and intriguing characters. Yet for all of its ribald fun, this farce also features notes of melancholy that call to mind the mood of the tragedies. Its central figure is Viola, who is shipwrecked on the coast of Illyria as the play begins. Believing that her twin brother Sebastian has been lost in the storm, she disguises herself (with the aid of a sea captain) as a page named Cesario and enters the service of Duke Orsino. She quickly falls in love with him, but he pines for the young countess Olivia, who is in extended mourning for a brother drowned at sea and has repeatedly refused the duke's many advances. Orsino, unfazed by these rebukes, sends Viola-Cesario to Olivia with more entreaties; Olivia finds herself immediately attracted not to the duke's words but to the charms of his young page. When Sebastian, who has also been swept ashore on Illyria, encounters Olivia while searching for his companion Antonio, she mistakes him for Viola-Cesario and persuades him to marry her. Orsino, believing himself betrayed by his page, threatens to kill Viola-Cesario, who stands utterly amazed by the turn of events. But when the twins finally meet and Viola discovers that her brother is alive, all is forgiven. The duke marries Viola and Sebastian, a beneficiary of fortune, wins the beautiful countess Olivia.

The play's subplot is equally diverting and filled with clever comic business. Malvolio, Olivia's steward, believes himself superior to the other members of the household and treats them with contempt. He harbors a desire for Olivia, yearning for the day when he can marry her and punish those who have challenged his rule. These characters include Olivia's drunken uncle Sir Toby Belch, her foppish suitor Sir Andrew Aguecheek, her clown Feste, and her clever gentlewoman Maria. To the delight of the others, Maria devises a plot whereby Malvolio finds a letter, apparently from Olivia, urging him to be bold, approach her smiling and in yellow cross-garters, and express his love for her. When he does so, Malvolio's mad behavior prompts Olivia to have him imprisoned. He is released only after Olivia discovers the plot and reprimands her wayward householders. Although Malvolio vows to seek revenge on all of them, his ambition and pomposity have forever been exposed. Sir Toby proves so enchanted by Maria's wit that he promises to marry her. Thus the madness-tinged story of twins reunited and a household restored to order ends with happy, transforming weddings, even though Feste reminds us in song of the rain that "raineth every day."

The Film

Trevor Nunn's 1996 treatment of *Twelfth Night* is framed by a melancholy Feste's (Ben Kingsley) song "With hey, ho, the wind and the rain." The song nicely catches the complex mood of this version, in which song, both joyous and somber, water, and windy emotions are artfully mixed. Feste's opening words fade as we see a 19th-century galley sailing on a stormy sea. Inside, Sebastian and Viola entertain the travelers in pantaloons and veils; when they remove the veils, both are wearing identical mustaches. This sequence strikes the keynote of gender confusion and its stormy consequences throughout the action. Indeed, Nunn seems to be inviting us to consider the dangerous assumptions underlying gender stereotypes in order to make the point that male and female differences can sometimes collapse into mirror-like similarities.

When the tempest blows up suddenly and wrecks the ship, Viola (Imogen Stubbs) can be seen underwater, struggling to reach the surface, then miraculously reborn on the shores of Illyria. She is a survivor and brings to the place a saving grace. Here she must quickly change her appearance because her country Messaline is at war with Illyria. This modification of Shakespeare's text provides a reason for her disguise but also oversimplifies the plot to no great advantage. It also undercuts the mystery of her rebirth.

Though saved from the sea, Viola-Cesario seems never far from drowning in the emotional tempest that follows. Tony Stephens's Orsino is attracted to her

from the beginning of her service; his mansion, located near the seashore, is fittingly placed to suggest his strong association with love's watery siren-song. Helena Bonham Carter's Olivia sheds salt tears in mourning for her brother lost at sea, although she too finds in Viola-Cesario the means to save her from drowning. Both Stephens and Carter here reveal a kind of world-weariness and despair that often suggests not Shakespeare but Chekhov. Stubbs's Viola manages to keep her balance and the audience's attention throughout, but in the realistic medium of film her disguise proves an all-too-recognizable artifice.

As for the comic subplot, Nigel Hawthorne's Malvolio is depicted as an almost sympathetic character, instead of the hypocritical spoilsport of Shakespeare's text. Indeed, through some ingenious cross-cutting, Nunn suggests a parallel between Feste and Malvolio, characters whose melancholy humor sets them apart from the rest. This interpretation is reinforced by Mel Smith's Toby Belch, who behaves as a boorish fellow guilty of harassing Maria and embarrassing Olivia. The same can be said for Richard E. Grant's annoying Andrew Aguecheek. Nunn's treatment of the subplot might be called politically correct; the result is that these sequences lack the comic energy necessary to balance the more emotional main plot. But because of Nunn's fascination with cross-dressing and its gender-bending implications, the farcical scheme to expose Malvolio created by an ingenious Maria (Imelda Staunton) comes off as little more than a sick prank conducted by drunks and lechers. And while the lovers and siblings are finally joined in a festive wedding scene, Nunn cross-cuts shots of Malvolio, suitcase in hand, Toby and Maria, Aguecheek, Antonio, and Feste all departing Olivia's estate in various stages of disappointment. When, at the close, Kingsley's Feste reprises "With hey, ho, the wind and the rain" at sunset, the song reminds us that the spirit of inclusiveness marking Shakespeare's *Twelfth Night* is perhaps a watery dream not fully achieved at the turn of yet another century.

REFERENCES

Coursen, H.R., "Three Recent Shakespearean Films," *Shakespeare Bulletin*, 17 (Winter 1999), 38–41; Crowl, Samuel, "Twelfth Night," *Shakespeare Bulletin*, 15 (Winter 1997), 36–37; Lane, Anthony, "Tights, Camera, Action!," *The New Yorker*, November 25, 1996, 65–77; Rothwell, Kenneth S., *A History of Shakespeare on Screen: A Century of Film and Television* (Cambridge, U.K.: Cambridge University Press, 1999).

—R.F.W.

PART III
Musical Theatre Adaptations

Musical Theatre

From New York's "naughty, gaudy, bawdy" 42nd Street to the back lots of Hollywood, the journey of stage musicals to movie theatres has a long and complicated history. To be sure, the list of musicals represented in this section is hardly comprehensive—such a documentation would require a book many times this length—but it does represent the best of a very rich and varied tradition that began with the advent of the talking picture in 1927 and continues, albeit sporadically, to this day. Bear in mind as you read (and hopefully watch the film versions of these stage musicals), that the mediums of stage and film are essentially different. Each of the more than 40 theatrical film musicals in these pages represents a distinctive object lesson in the adaptation process; each highlights the strategies, the obstacles, the triumphs, and the failures attendant upon the transfer. The directors of the most successful film musicals knew this all too well. In these pages you will meet such accomplished film directors as Robert Wise, Stanley Donen, Fred Zinnemann, John Huston, George Cukor, Vincente Minnelli, and Gene Kelly; and also those stage directors who have tried their hand at filmmaking with varied degrees of success, most notably Harold Prince, Joshua Logan, George Abbott, and Bob Fosse.

One can argue that the heyday of the mature Broadway musical began in 1943, when the Theatre Guild production of Rodgers and Hammerstein's *Oklahoma!* opened at the St. James Theatre on March 31, changing the face of the Broadway musical forever. As Arthur Jackson writes in his pictorial history, *The Best Musicals*, nothing could at first have seemed less prepossessing: "the curtain rose on almost an empty stage. Stage left, an old woman churning butter. Offstage right, the voice of a lone cowboy singing 'Oh, What a Beautiful Mornin.' From so restrained a beginning sprang not only the most fabulously successful production in theatrical history but an epoch-making musical play that caused a revolution in the progress of the Broadway musical." Historian David Ewen adds that in adapting the play, *Green Grow the Lilacs*, by

Oscar Hammerstein II

Lynn Riggs, to a musical show, "Rodgers and Hammerstein proceeded to break down most of the shopworn concepts, clichés, and rituals of musical comedy to produce a musical play that was a single artistic whole, a musical play in which the text would always dictate their methods and procedures, however iconoclastic." In a way, says Stephen Sondheim, the traditional formula was ruined forever, because what

Richard Rodgers

Rodgers and Hammerstein did was make every song a part of the dramatic action. Musical theatre was now tied to the demands of a specific text. No longer would it be acceptable to have a character sing for no reason. Music and song were to be an integral part of the characterizations and the story.

The heyday of the theatrical musical film lasted from the early 1950s to the early 1970s. It was precisely at this time that Hollywood was thirsty for new product to rival the expanding television market. The styles of the musical films of the 1930s and early 1940s were shopworn, the material thin, the formulas extremely predictable. Just as it had done in the late 1920s, Hollywood again raided the Broadway stage for fresh material, not the musical comedies of the '30s and '40s, but the new, innovative musical "plays" that began with *Oklahoma!* The Broadway theatre was extremely popular at the time, and the eventual appearance of a film version of a stage play could be counted upon to generate much anticipation. Once a given musical had completed its first run and had gone on live tours throughout the United States, the property was finally available to be filmed. In the larger, more deluxe movie theatres, particularly, these theatrical musicals arrived with all the pomp and circumstance of a Broadway opening.

While this study deals essentially with the transfer of stage musicals to the medium of film, it is also necessary to say something about the history of musical films in general. For one thing, as will be noted presently, there was no novelty in hearing recorded speech and song coming from the screen. Jolson's true speaking and singing debut had transpired months before *The Jazz Singer* when he talked and sang three songs, including "Rock-a-Bye Your Baby with a Dixie Melody," in a talking Vitaphone short film, *Al Jolson in a Plantation Act.* Moreover, because so few theatre houses were equipped to show *The Jazz Singer* in its synchronized-sound version, most of its audiences saw it in its alternative version, as a silent film. Six months after the premiere of *The Jazz Singer* there were still more than 12,000 theatres, mostly in the small towns and hinterlands, not yet wired for sound. Even in New York, its box office was unexceptional, eclipsed by silent films like *Wings.* It can even be argued that *The Jazz Singer* technically was not a musical film at all. Rather, it was a part-talkie; and aside from a few singing sequences and a few lines of dialogue, it was a silent film with intertitles and a music track. The same can be said about Jolson's second film, another part-talkie called *The Singing Fool* (1928). Although it was a bona fide smash hit, introducing three song hits interpolated into the story, "Sonny Boy," "There's a Rainbow 'Round My Shoulder," and "I'm Sitting on Top of the World," it shared the same shortcomings as its predecessor. It was not until two all-talkies—*Mammy*, based on Irving Berlin and James Gleason's 1928 show, *Mr. Bones*, and *Big Boy*, based on Harold Atteridge's 1925 musical—that Jolson appeared in films that might be characterized as "musicals" in a stricter sense of the word.

It is all too often forgotten that attempts to bring the musical theatre, vaudeville, and the revue to the screen preceded *The Jazz Singer* by several years.

Warner Bros.' Vitaphone sound-on-disc system was created by Western Electric and put into commercial use in early 1926. For the next two years hundreds of short films recording the music and routines of opera singers and vaudeville performers were produced at the former Vitagraph studios in Brooklyn and at the Manhattan Opera House on West 34th Street in New York. Fox's Movietone system, which was developed at roughly the same time, also recorded the performances of prominent Broadway performers. Unlike Vitaphone, it was a *sound-on-film* process derived from the pioneering work of inventor Lee De Forest. In 1923 De Forest, who worked throughout the decade to develop a system of recording sound on film, argued that sound and image could combine to create an entirely new kind of artistic expression: "An entirely new form of screen drama can be worked out taking advantage of the possibilities of introducing music and voice and appropriate acoustic effects," he predicted, "not necessarily throughout the entire action, but here and there where the effects can be much more startling or theatrical, if you will, or significant, than is possible by pantomime alone." He founded his De Forest Phonofilm Corporation in 1922, with which he presented public screenings of performances by Eddie Cantor, DeWolf Hopper, and Fannie Ward. From the mid-twenties onward, De Forest pursued a doomed ambition to film and exhibit vaudeville and opera acts in theatres especially wired to accommodate his sound-on-film process. More successful were the efforts by two former associates, E.I. Sponable and Theodore Case, to improve a substantially similar system, which became the Fox Movietone system in the late 1920s.

Between 1929 and 1930 Warner Bros. quickly established a pattern of musical film production soon to be followed by all other studios. *On With the Show* was Warners' first Technicolor musical, followed a few months later by *Show of Shows* and the operetta adaptation, *The Desert Song*. Distinctions must be made among these films, distinctions that would mark most musical films in the next decade. *On With the Show* was a "backstage" story that cleverly juggled two narrative lines transpiring on stage and behind the scenes. This formula, sometimes called a "realistic" musical, allowed the musical numbers to flow naturally from the theatrical setting. The story line and the music thus were intertwined. Subsequent backstage musical films, from *42nd Street* (1932) to *The Bandwagon* (1953)—and more recently, Bob Fosse's *Cabaret* (1966) and Richard Attenborough's *A Chorus Line* (1985)—have elaborated on this formula. *Show of Shows* brought the standard stage revue to the screen, complete with a master of ceremonies, curtain divisions for each "act," a stage

orchestra, and a roster of Broadway stars already familiar to popular audiences. *The Desert Song*, on the other hand, was an example of the "formalist" musical, where song and dance need not be plausibly derived from a theatrical setting, but are allowed to emerge as spontaneous actions from the story and the characters. Faithfully based on the popular 1926 operetta by Otto Harbach, Oscar Hammerstein II, and Sigmund Romberg, it was one of the first full-scale stage musicals transferred to the screen.

Other studios quickly followed the Warners formula. Paramount released its own revues, like *Glorifying the American Girl* and *Paramount on Parade*, and adapted popular backstage and formalist musicals, bringing the Marx Brothers to the screen in *Cocoanuts* (George S. Kaufman and Irving Berlin) and Dennis King and Jeanette MacDonald in an adaptation of

Al Jolson appeared in blackface in his Warner Bros. musicals in the late 1920s, including The Jazz Singer *and* The Singing Fool. (COURTESY NATIONAL FILM SOCIETY ARCHIVES)

Rudolph Friml's *The Vagabond King*. Fox's revues were *William Fox Movietone Follies*, and its stage adaptations included an adaptation of George Kelly's stage hit, *Love, Live, and Laugh*. MGM's big revue was *The Hollywood Revue of 1929*, which featured Jack Benny and Conrad Nagel as masters of ceremonies. Samuel Goldwyn and United Artists, in conjunction with Florenz Ziegfeld, adapted the popular stage hit *Whoopee!* to the screen, featuring members of its original cast. Universal added a talking and singing prologue to its adaptation of another Ziegfeld stage hit, the Kern-Hammerstein *Show Boat*. RKO released yet another Ziegfeld adaptation, the operetta *Rio Rita*, as well as an adaptation of *Hit the Deck*, based on the show by Herbert Fields and Vincent Youmans.

At the same time, a trend in musical films was beginning that would continue to run parallel to the stage adaptations and the revue formulas for the next half-century. Writers and composers were writing *original* musicals directly for the screen. MGM's backstage story, *The Broadway Melody* (1929) was a smash hit. For Warner Bros., Sigmund Romberg wrote an original operetta, *Viennese Nights* (1930), that foreshadowed the Nelson Eddy/Jeanette MacDonald cycle of operettas

The four Marx Brothers brought their Broadway stage musicals to the screen with the advent of talking pictures.
(COURTESY NATIONAL FILM SOCIETY ARCHIVES)

of the 1930s, especially *Maytime* (which could almost pass as a remake). Fox produced *Sunny Side Up*, which as a novelty located much of its action and musical sequences—the songs were by the Broadway team of DeSylva, Brown, and Henderson—in a New York tenement district setting. It was innovative in other ways. The songs were integrated into the plot, and the special effects-laden "If I Had a Talking Picture of You" and the highly eroticized "Turn on the Heat" number (with scantily clad chorus girls doffing their eskimo togs while they writhed and danced away the northern chill) would inspire ever more imaginative and exotic numbers in Busby Berkeley's Eddie Cantor films and the Warner Bros. "Gold Digger" cycle of the 1930s. Universal's *King of Jazz* (1930) was nominally a revue, but it strayed so far from the standard formula as to achieve a cinematic character all its own (interpolating animation, special effects-like superimpositions and double printings, and dizzy montage sequences).

And Paramount's *Applause*, directed by Rouben Mamoulian, was a benchmark effort in the search for a kind of movie musical that was relatively independent—in technique and effect, if not in setting—from its theatrical precedents. Thus, while *Applause* had a routine backstage story, with stage star Helen Morgan as a down-and-out burlesque performer trying to hide the circumstances of her life from her grown daughter, its achievement in the asynchronous union of image, sound, and music was wholly cinematic. This precedent was developed further by Mamoulian in his masterpiece, *Love Me Tonight* (1932), with songs and lyrics by Rodgers and Hart; and by Busby Berkeley and the songwriting team of Al Dubin and Harry Warren in the Warner Bros. cycle of musical films, beginning with *42nd Street* and continuing on through the *Gold Diggers* series. Original material like this, contends historian Richard Barrios, "offered a modicum of potential for cinematic life, the sense that these songs and characters and situations were based in celluloid independence rather than stage constriction. It was hardly true on a regular basis, yet some of the early originals were among the most interesting films of the time, and the most successful." However, inasmuch as these kinds of musical films do not stem directly from stage shows, they are not directly relevant to this study.

As popular as this first surge in musical films from 1927 to 1932 seems to have been—at least in the larger urban districts—there were problems nonetheless. Image-sound synchronization, or the lack thereof, was a constant worry. The Vitaphone system risked the needle jumping a groove in the record or a momentary jam in the projector. Even the sound-on-film system

Florenz Ziegfeld

had its hazards. If the film lost its "loop," the frames and soundtrack were thrown out of synch. Lest the dilemmas depicted in MGM's classic *Singin' in the Rain* be considered exaggerated, here is a typical problem reported by a journalist during a screening of *The Broadway Melody*: "The reproduction was fairly passable until the final reel began, when the synchronization suddenly went bad, the spoken words being several seconds behind the lip movement on the screen." After the projectionist stopped the show, rewound the reel, and resumed the film, the problems cropped up again. "[The action was repeated that] we had seen before. A girl behind me giggled and said—referring to the entry of Charles King into a room, 'I guess he went out and came back in.' After fifteen seconds, it was obvious that synchronization was again off, the picture was stopped, and, shortly thereafter, begun for the third time."

By 1932 the sound-on-film optical process had all but replaced the disc system. It is worth noting, however, that 60 years later a system known as DTS (Digital Theater Sound) provided for off-the-shelf, mass-produced CD drives to be adapted so that CDs with the film sound track encoded on them could run in interlock with the film—a spinning disc in synch with the projector. The addition of a time code on the film itself that corresponded to the correct sound for that frame meant that synchronization now was assured, as opposed to the hit-and-miss method of the Vitaphone system. The resulting sound is noticeably richer and fuller than conventional optical sound.

Second, it should not be presumed that musical shows "played" with equal success in all parts of the country. Historian Henry Jenkins has pointed out that pictures like *Glorifying the American Girl* failed to "educate" filmgoers in the sticks toward the more "sophisticated taste" required to appreciate the Broadway show. They were being made for the "classes" and not "the masses." Signs of resistance to talking pictures, particularly musicals, were everywhere in evidence, writes Jenkins: "Film fans frequently cited 'confusion' or distaste over the 'stage formulas included in new talkers' as a key factor behind their dislike of sound pictures." More and more theatre exhibitors demanded that Hollywood abandon the Broadway show and return to traditional screen genres, like westerns and farce comedies. A Florida theatre owner even cited *The Desert Song* as an offensive example of "all this 'Broadway' stagey stuff' that 'cluttered' up the theatres." A picture like *Sunny Side Up*, with its freedom from the Broadway "taint" and its emphasis on middle-class working characters seemed to hold out a better prospect for these audiences.

Regardless of whether they are adapted from the stage or written originally for film, one fact remains and is the deciding factor for all production decisions: *musicals are expensive*. The musical theatre is popular art, and consequently, big business. Over the years, most successful musicals have become merchandising machines. With *Oklahoma!* Broadway was introduced to the "long-run" syndrome. Long lines at the box office meant a demand for products associated with the shows. Like the merchandising of films today, the producers of musicals for the stage created companies for the sole purpose of selling products associated with their shows. And not just sheet music, posters, souvenir programs, and recordings (*Oklahoma!* was the first Broadway show to have an "original cast album"), but clothing lines, toys, dolls, and various other trinkets with the name of the show embossed everywhere.

The popular stage musicals or, as we say in the theatre, the war-horses (those strong enough to survive the critics and the test of time) continue to be produced all over the world. From amateur and academic to professional productions, the musical is the most popular show in a season, often helping theatres break even financially.

So how does the transfer from popular stage show to blockbuster film take place? What are the considerations, besides economic and more specifically musical, that seem to be consistent with most screen adaptations?

The best musical adaptations are exactly that, adaptations. Rather than filming the play as if it were a play, with all the conventions of the proscenium, most good film musicals are opened up scenically to various locales that are impossible to realize on the stage. After all, the stage is fundamentally an auditory experience taking place in an auditorium where people go to "hear" the dialogue and music. In the movie theatre people go to "see" a film. Witness the brilliant opening sequences in *West Side Story* (1961) and *The Sound of Music* (1965), both directed by Robert Wise. Each establishes the natural locations of the story, first by a long shot and then by a zoom in to the characters in action. Julie Andrews stretching out her arms to welcome the morning on the top of the Austrian Alps, as she sings "the hills are alive," is now a quintessential icon in musical films.

Film also has the capacity to break up a song into temporal and spatial components. Some films are more successful than others at using this technique. It takes a skilled director and editor to make dramatic sense of all these cuts. An especially brilliant example is the "Isn't It Romantic" sequence in Mamoulian's *Love Me Tonight* (1932). And Robert Wise utilized the technique beautifully in his rendition of "Do, Re, Mi" for *The Sound of Music*. The number starts on a hillside and as the song develops and the children begin to learn to harmonize, they are seen all over Salzburg, on bikes, in a car, in a canoe on the river, skipping in the streets, dancing up and down marble stairs.

As is common with most film versions, at least one of the leading characters from the stage is paired with a big Hollywood star with little or no stage experience. In some cases, the entire stage cast is replaced by film actors. Thus, the casting of a musical film often brings with it controversy. While some Hollywood casting is acceptable, and even desirable—Julie Andrews in *The Sound of Music*, Fred Astaire in *Finian's Rainbow* (1970), Doris Day in *The Pajama Game* (1957), Tab Hunter in *Damn Yankees* (1957), Debbie Reynolds in *The Unsinkable Molly Brown* (1964), John Travolta in *Grease*

(1978), and even Madonna in *Evita* (1997)—other choices will never be fully explained, reasoned, or justified, like Barbra Streisand over Carol Channing in *Hello, Dolly!* (1969), Audrey Hepburn over Julie Andrews in *My Fair Lady* (1964), Rosalind Russell over Ethel Merman in *Gypsy* (1960), and again, Vanessa Redgrave in place of Julie Andrews in *Camelot* (1967). As Gerald Mast states in his book *Can't Help Singin': The American Musical on Stage and Screen*, "the danger of playing mix and match with Hollywood stars and Broadway performers [is] to find no musical style where the two could meet." This certainly was the case with the difference in styles between Judy Holliday and Dean Martin in the film of *Bells Are Ringing* (1960).

But most of the time, the star is not why the movie audience flocks to musicals. Musicals tend to do well at the box office if they tell a good story through exciting acting and choreography, if they deal with controversial subject matter, if they are colorful and enjoyable to watch and, ultimately, if they are entertaining.

We are truly indebted to the producers of film versions who wisely preserved the original stage performances of many leading players, including Eddie Cantor in Ziegfeld's *Whoopee!* (1930), Helen Morgan in the James Whale version of *Show Boat* (1936), Vivian Blaine as Adelaide in *Guys and Dolls* (1955), Ellen Greene as Audrey in *Little Shop of Horrors*, Joel Grey as the Emcee in *Cabaret*, Rex Harrison and Stanley Holloway in *My Fair Lady*, Judy Holliday as Ella in *Bells Are Ringing*, Robert Morse in *How to Succeed in Business Without Really Trying* (1967), Zero Mostel in *A Funny Thing Happened on the Way to the Forum* (1966), Robert Preston as Harold Hill in *The Music Man* (1962), Barbra Streisand as Fanny Brice in *Funny Girl* (1968), and Gwen Verdon as Lola and Ray Walston as Mr. Applegate in *Damn Yankees*.

And there are instances where a performance of a single song has been an invaluable gift to posterity. Mary Martin's rendition of "My Heart Belongs to Daddy" is a memorable highlight from the otherwise intolerable Cole Porter biopic, *Night and Day* (1946). When she introduced the song in Cole Porter's *Leave it to Me!* clad in an Eskimo parka, tastefully stripping to Porter's naughty lyrics about a young girl's gratitude to her "sugar daddy," the song made Martin an instant star.

Films have also preserved the brilliant choreographic work of Michael Kidd, Bob Fosse, Onna White, Jerome Robbins, Peter Gennaro, Agnes De Mille, and Michael Bennett. As Rick Altman writes in his thoughtful study, *American Musical Film*, "the filming of dance has come a long way since the early days of filmed vaudeville, when the camera remained bolted to the center seat of the fifth row of the orchestra. . . . and

Cole Porter

Hollywood's directors have become unusually adept at making the camera dance along with the actors."

When you watch a musical on stage or film, there are specific facts to keep in mind about the formula itself. The basic structure of almost any text is boy meets girl, boy wins girl, boy loses girl, and boy wins girl back. The order of the wording is correct, boy to girl. The most popular examples of musical theatre, and the musical film for that matter, are inherently sexist and predominantly heterosexual. For the most part, the man and woman play the traditional roles in society: Man is the breadwinner and woman is the homemaker. There are, of course, exceptions to this rule, but the basic principle remains the same. The characters are pursuing the American Dream, the ideal, and the comfortable. For this reason, Rosemary from *How to Succeed in Business Without Really Trying* is "Happy to Keep His Dinner Warm," and Audrey from *Little Shop*

Barbra Streisand

entertainment to film, we are condemned to banishment from the immediacy of the original event by an intermediary, by the mediation of the medium itself. No longer are we in the presence of real human beings, but of actors instead, of shadows rather than flesh and blood. Where once the space of the show was total space, participatory space, 360-degree space, now it is restricted to the field of the camera. Where once the time of the show was total time, continuous time, now the process of editing fragments of time imposes on the spectator the perceptions of another."

Whether the medium is stage or screen, the act of singing falls into several categories. The solo, duet, and production number are usually organized in the text using three specific techniques. These techniques require different focuses on the part of the actor, and specific decisions to be made by the director. The first technique, specifically used for solo singing, is the soliloquy, a device frequently encountered in formalist musicals. In this kind of song we experience the character's innermost feelings and desires. Like a Shakespearean soliloquy, the character is alone and expressing his or her thoughts aloud. There are two approaches to this style of song. The actor can either address himself/herself or the audience, or a combination of the two, usually starting internally with himself/herself, and then opening up externally to include the audience as a confidant on the journey. Examples of this style of singing in musical theatre are too numerous to mention; they are a part of every score since *Oklahoma!*

In film, because there is no audience interaction, the camera must connect the character with the viewer by means of visual correlatives of the character's vulnerable state. A notable example is the filming of the song "Don't Rain on My Parade" from *Funny Girl*, where we see Barbra Streisand, as Fanny Brice, chasing after Nick Arnstein (Omar Sharif), using every possible mode of transportation in order to reach her lover. This sequence is a brilliant transfer of the soliloquy song from stage to film. What had been a soliloquy on the stage becomes on film a journey from Brice's thoughts to her external actions. The final shot of Barbra Streisand on a tugboat, arms outstretched for the entire world to see, belting out her final notes, "Hey Mr. Arnstein, here I am!" is now the stuff of legend. This soliloquy technique on film exists today, even in the non-musical film, most notably in the recent *Magnolia* (1999), where each of the primary characters is shot alone in the "act of singing," while they confront their situation and express their emotional state.

The second style of singing involves a character in the actual *state* or *act* of singing, i.e., either performing

of Horrors would be thrilled to "look like Donna Reed." These are examples of the theatre of romance, where characters fall in love, live happily ever after, or die trying. They are about life, not as it is, but as it should be. Theirs is a message of hope, of uplift beyond the drudgery of everyday existence.

In musical theatre, the main means of communication between two characters is song. Yet, unlike the dialogue of the straight drama on stage or film, it is important to understand that the composer fixes the lyric in the mature musical play (which we call the dialogue of the song) in time. What this means is that the actor/singer is bound by the time allotted from the chosen configuration of notes. Therefore, the performer has only a specific amount of time in which to convey his or her thoughts and feelings. Thus, the performance itself *lives in time.*

When the song is transferred to film, there is a more fluid, discontinuous sense of time than in the theatre. As Rick Altman writes, "In moving from live

in front of an audience in order to entertain them (the realistic musical), or actually crooning to another character as part of the dramatic action (the formalist musical). This technique is also used for duet singing and production numbers and is often referred to as the "show-within-a-show" number. Yet, even when the characters are actually in the state of singing, there are still significant connections being made to the themes of the story. Examples of this include most of the Emcee's numbers in *Cabaret*, Adelaide's songs at the club in *Guys and Dolls*, and many of the production numbers in *Funny Girl*. Film is especially kind to this style of song, as the actor looks more natural (or realistic) when the singing plausibly derives from the dramatic context.

The third type of song is directed toward another character or group of characters. In this style of song, the character *needs* the help of another person (or persons) to sort through a particular problem, seek advice, or explain himself or herself. Examples of this kind of solo number are also numerous, and include Ado Annie's lament to Laurey as she sings "I Cain't Say No" in *Oklahoma!*; "Without You," Eliza Doolittle's declaration of independence to Professor Higgins in *My Fair Lady*; "Cockeyed Optimist," Nellie Forbush's opening song from *South Pacific*; and Eva Peron's speech to the masses, "Don't Cry for Me Argentina," from *Evita*. Love duets are often sung this way and include Laurey and Curley's "People Will Say We're in Love," again from *Oklahoma!*; "Shall We Dance" from *The King and I*; and "I Loved You Once in Silence" from *Camelot*.

One technique that is unique to the film musical is the singing "voice-over." In this style of song, the singer's voice is heard on the soundtrack while images of action and scene unfold before our eyes. This technique—a mainstay of music videos and a variant of the soliloquy—is often very effective for film as the character is not actually singing to another character, but sharing with the audience their innermost thoughts and feelings. This was used in the filming of the "You Are Woman, I Am Man" sequence from *Funny Girl*. The director will frequently vary the strategy, sometimes allowing the audience to see the character in the act of singing, at other times just to hear their "interior" voice.

One style of song that always seems to transfer smoothly from stage to film is the production number. These numbers are usually reserved for the moments in the story when a large group of people, usually in a state of celebration, at a party or large gathering, expresses their collective community spirit about an idea or issue. The setup may be realistic, i.e., they are singing in church or at a social function; or it may be

formalistic, as they suddenly burst into song when their emotions collectively explode. Most musicals include this kind of number in their score. Examples include the barn dance from *Oklahoma!* ("The Farmer and the Cowman"); "You're the One That I Want" performed at the Spring Fair in *Grease*; the "Ascot Gavotte" from *My Fair Lady*; "June is Bustin' Out All Over" from *Carousel*; "The Lusty Month of May" from *Camelot*; "A Lotta Livin' to Do" from *Bye, Bye, Birdie*; and the "Once a Year Day" company picnic from *The Pajama Game*. Somehow, when every character is singing, the very act of singing seems less forced and more spontaneous. Keep in mind, however, that these types of numbers are also written for dramatic purposes, specifically for when the tension has risen to a point in the action where a collective song becomes necessary, such as the "Tonight Quintet" from *West Side Story* or "Guenevere" from *Camelot*.

Most of the musicals represented in this section are more than 20 years old. With the exception of *Evita* there has not been one major studio release of a musical in the last 20 years. When James L. Brooks attempted to bring back the integrated musical with *I'll Do Anything* (1992), it aroused such negative pre-release criticism that he deleted all the songs before exhibiting it nationwide. Although the near-future might bring a few restorations of old musical films to theatres or presentations of new works to television, there is reason for continued pessimism. Stephen Sondheim has lamented the present state of things in a recent article in the *New York Times Magazine*: "You have two kinds of shows on Broadway—revivals and the same kind of musicals over and over again, all spectacles. You get your tickets for *The Lion King* a year in advance, and essentially a family comes as if to a picnic, and they pass on to their children the idea that that's what the theater is—a spectacular musical you see once a year, a stage version of a movie. It has nothing to do with theater at all. It has to do with seeing what is familiar. We live in a recycled culture."

Indeed, talk of a new hit show, such as *Ragtime* or *Titanic: The Musical*, becoming a blockbuster film is rare these days. The trend now is almost the opposite of what it used to be. Once upon a time a hit play or musical would eventually be made into a film. Now, the thinking is reversed: First you make a hit film and then retool it as a live stage show. Witness Disney's spectacular success on Broadway with *Beauty and the Beast* and *The Lion King* or musical versions of the films *The Goodbye Girl*, *Big*, *My Favorite Year*, *Fame*, *Saturday Night Fever*, and *The Full Monty*.

In the final analysis, come rain or shine, many of us can't help but cling to the sentiments expressed by

Wendy Wasserstein, when she wrote in the *New York Times* about Branagh's musical adaptation of Shakespeare's *Love's Labours Lost:* "I thought perhaps Mr. Branagh shares with me a desire to musicalize even the classics simply because movie musicals are among the top ten reasons to live."

Amen to that.

—JOHN STANIUNAS
WITH JOHN C. TIBBETS

REFERENCES AND WORKS CITED

Altman, Rick, *American Film Musical* (Bloomington: Indiana University Press, 1987); Babington, Bruce, and Peter William Evans, *Blue Skies and Silver Linings* (Manchester: Manchester University Press, 1985); Barrios, Richard, *A Song in the Dark* (New York: Oxford University Press, 1995); Ewen, David, *New Complete Book of the American Musical Theater* (New York: Holt, Rinehart, Winston, 1958); Jackson, Arthur, *The Best Musicals* (New York: Crown, 1977); Jenkins, Henry, *What Made Pistachio Nuts? Early Sound Comedy and the Vaudeville Aesthetic* (New York: Columbia University Press, 1992); Kobol, John, *Gotta Sing Gotta Dance* (London: Hamlyn, 1970); Rich, Frank, "Conversations With Sondheim," *The New York Times Magazine*, March 12, 2000; Secrest, Meryle, *Stephen Sondheim: A Life* (New York: Alfred Knopf, 1998); Sennett, Ted, *Hollywood Musicals* (New York: Harry Abrams, 1981); Wasserstein, Wendy, "Where I Seem to Find the Happiness I Seek," *The New York Times*, June 4, 2000.

ANNIE (1977)

MUSIC: CHARLES STROUSE (1928–)
LYRICS: MARTIN CHARNIN (1934–)
BOOK: THOMAS MEEHAN (DATES?)

Annie (1982), U.S.A., directed by John Huston, screenplay by Carol Sobieski; Columbia Pictures.

The Play

At first, director-lyricist Martin Charnin had trouble convincing collaborators that his idea of basing a musical on Harold Gray's successful comic strip *Little Orphan Annie* was a good idea. Conventional wisdom said that a cartoon musical was sure to fail. But once assured that Charnin was not interested in camp, Charles Strouse and Thomas Meehan signed on, and the three partners set out to develop an original story using only the central characters of Gray's strip. During its tryout at the Goodspeed Opera House in Connecticut, Mike Nichols joined up as one of the show's producers, which immediately brought the project more prestige. It opened at the Alvin Theatre on April 21, 1977.

It is 1933 and the middle of the Great Depression. Annie (Andrea McArdle), an 11-year-old orphan, dreams of being united with her long-lost parents and leaving mean-spirited Miss Hannigan (Dorothy Loudon) who runs the New York Municipal Orphan-age. Grace Farrell (Sandy Faison), secretary to the billionaire Oliver Warbucks (Reid Shelton), comes seeking an orphan to stay with her employer for the Christmas holidays. Despite Miss Hannigan's objections, Annie is selected and soon she wins her way into Warbucks's heart, so much so that he plans to adopt her. Annie, however, is still interested in meeting her real parents, so Warbucks mounts a massive campaign to find them. Enter Rooster, Miss Hannigan's brother, and Rooster's girlfriend Lily with a plan to outsmart Warbucks and collect a $50,000 reward. Rooster and Lily disguise themselves as Annie's parents, armed with secret information about Annie's origins provided by Miss Hannigan. It takes help from President Roosevelt and the FBI to expose the ruse. Annie, her dog Sandy, and Warbucks celebrate Christmas as a family and look forward to the New Deal and prosperity for America.

Despite its simplistic themes and storyline, *Annie* still emerges as a satisfying entertainment. It is fun, upbeat, and easy to watch. With an optimistic viewpoint, a hummable score, charming orphans, and a dog, it has no difficulty appealing to families and adults longing for happy endings. A huge hit on Broadway, it garnered seven Tony Awards including best musical, best actress in a musical (Dorothy Loudon), best score, and best book. Critics generally recognized its warmhearted spirit, but some attacked its sentimentality. Clive Barnes of the *New York Times* called it "an intensely likable musical" and Meg Greenfield of *Newsweek* thought it was "spectacular on every count."

Martin Gottfried of the *New York Post* proclaimed "It has hit stamped all over it!" "despite its mawkishness," "cheap nostalgia," and "unabashed corniness."

The Film

Columbia paid a record $9.5 million for the movie rights to *Annie*, and spent $39 million more for a lavish production. Although Carol Sobieski's screenplay maintains the general plot structure of the Broadway script, the dialogue has been extensively rewritten. There are additional scenes, additional characters (most notably Mrs. Roosevelt and Warbucks's bodyguards Punjab and the Asp, drawn from the comic strip), as well as some significant omissions. The number of changes in the score reflects the vast nature of the revisions: five new songs appear ("Dumb Dog," "Sandy," "Let's Go to the Movies," "We Got Annie," and "Sign") and six songs from the Broadway version are eliminated ("Hooverville," "NYC," "You Won't Be an Orphan for Long," "Something Was Missing," "A

Annie reached the screen with Aileen Quinn in the title role and Albert Finney as Daddy Warbucks. (COURTESY COLUMBIA PICTURES)

New Deal for Christmas," and "Annie"). Big production numbers and multiple locations characterize the extravagant nature of the film. Acrobatic choreography is performed by both orphans and Warbucks's servants. On her night on the town, Annie (Aileen Quinn) is taken to Radio City Music Hall where she is treated to the precision dancing of the Rockettes. The final scene is the most opulent, a Fourth of July celebration with circus acts, elephants, tap dancing, and fireworks. The role of Grace Farrell (Ann Reinking) was expanded for the film, allowing the romantic potential between Farrell and Warbucks (Albert Finney) to receive some focus, though the idea is not pursued. Annie even attempts to play matchmaker in one scene. The bonding between Annie and Warbucks is not emphasized, in part due to the elimination of Warbucks's song to Annie ("Something Was Missing"). Miss Hannigan is played with drunken finesse by Carol Burnett, and her character appears far more man-hungry than in the stage play. Also interesting to note is that the film gives Sandy a much larger role.

Since the movie removes the song "Hooverville" and never visits a shantytown, the historical backdrop of the Depression is less prominent. Also gone is the scene with President Roosevelt's cabinet, which highlighted the economic issues of the time. Discovering the villains' trickery is a fairly quick task on stage, but in the film this episode is far more elaborate. Annie is kidnapped by Miss Hannigan, Rooster, and Lily, and her life is placed in danger. A harrowing chase sequence ensues, involving the girls in the orphanage, Sandy, multiple cars, and a finale with Punjab in a helicopter rescuing Annie (who has ended up hanging by her fingertips off an open railroad drawbridge). Though in this version Miss Hannigan has known all along that Annie's parents are dead and has kept this fact secret, she has a turn of heart toward Annie, and in the end, tries to protect her when she fears Rooster will really kill the little girl.

The box-office returns were disappointing, and critics were not always kind. Richard Corliss of *Time* found the "production numbers full of empty extravagance" and Pauline Kael of *The New Yorker* thought "the movie has the feel of a manufactured romp." David Ansen of *Newsweek* said, "something essential has been lost in the story's simple, all-American warmth," though he conceded "the lovableness of Annie is probably built in." Director John Huston, angered by the critics, denounced them publicly at a seminar of his films. In 1999, Disney produced a television version of Annie for ABC, starring Kathy Bates (Miss Hannigan), Victor Garber (Warbucks), and a number of Broadway veterans.

REFERENCES

Charnin, Martin, *Annie: A Theatre Memoir* (New York: E.P. Dutton, 1977); Green, Stanley, *Broadway Musicals: Show by Show* (Milwaukee: Hal Leonard Books, 1985); Green, Stanley, *The World of Musical Comedy* (San Diego: A.S. Barnes, 1980); Magill, Frank N., ed., *Magill's Cinema Annual 1983* (Englewood Cliffs, N.J.: Salem Press, 1983); Ansen, David, "Here Comes Annie Again," *Newsweek*, 99:21 (May 24, 1982), 82–83.

—*M.R.*

ANNIE GET YOUR GUN (1946)

MUSIC: IRVING BERLIN (1888–1989)
LYRICS: IRVING BERLIN
BOOK: HERBERT (1897–1958) AND DOROTHY FIELDS (1905–1974)

Annie Get Your Gun (1950), U.S.A., directed by George Sidney, adapted by Sidney Sheldon; MGM.

The Play

A musical biography of a late 19th-century female sharpshooter, *Annie Get Your Gun* tells the story of hillbilly Annie Oakley and her romance with Frank Butler, the featured marksman in Buffalo Bill's Wild West Show. Troubles arise when Annie is hired as a second sharpshooter for the traveling show, and her popularity with the crowd exceeds that of Frank's, doing little to encourage their otherwise growing romance. In the end, Chief Sitting Bull counsels Annie to let Frank win a shooting contest, and by losing the match, win the man—fulfilling the prophecy of the first-act song, "You Can't Get a Man with a Gun."

The only show produced by Rodgers and Hammerstein without a score written by them, the musical was originally slated for composer Jerome Kern and lyricist Dorothy Fields. The untimely death of Kern led them to approach Irving Berlin, with Hammerstein insisting he was the only one who could do the job. Berlin had doubts about his capabilities for such a score, but went away for a week-long retreat to Atlantic City to consider the proposition. He returned still doubtful, wanting to "audition" with a few new songs: "Doin' What Comes Natur'lly," "There's No Business Like Show Business," and "They Say It's Wonderful." He got the job and all three songs remained in the show.

Annie Get Your Gun opened May 16, 1946 at the Imperial Theatre in New York with a mixed bag of critical notices. All agreed with the star power of Ethel

Irving Berlin

Merman and her powerhouse singing, and several commented on her blossoming comic ability. "She is a better comedienne than she ever was before, with some of the earthy humor of Fanny Brice," exclaimed John Chapman in the *New York Daily News*, while Louis Kronenberger described her comedic gifts as "raising an oak of a laugh out of an acorn of a joke." Kronenberger also complained that "Irving Berlin's score is musically not exciting—of the real songs, only one or two are tuneful." Chapman called it "a good, standard, lavish, big musical . . . but it isn't the greatest show in the world." And Ward Morehouse in the *New York Sun* described the book as "flimsy" and "witless." Nevertheless, *Annie Get Your Gun* was a smash at the box office running 1,147 performances, making it the third-longest-running musical of the 1940s. Irving Berlin, Joshua Logan (director), and Merman all won Donaldson Awards for their work.

The Film

The film adaptation had a problematic early production. Producer Arthur Freed assigned the directorship to Busby Berkeley, while Judy Garland was cast in the role of Annie. The fact that neither one had much affection for the other going into production did not help matters. In the opinion of Garland's biographer, Gerald Clarke, the intense Berkeley had so bullied and harassed Garland in the "Babes in Arms" cycle of films that "Freed could not have made a worse choice, or one more puzzling and perverse." He treated her with the same sadistic condescension that he had 12 years before when she was just a teenager. Moreover, Garland was in the last stages of her disastrous marriage to Vincente Minnelli, and unsuccessfully battling her addiction to pills. Nevertheless, Garland and Howard Keel, a newcomer who came from the London production of *Oklahoma!*, forged ahead and recorded the songs in the studio. During these studio sessions, however, Garland had difficulty recapturing the magic of her earlier singing, and there was a growing concern about her appropriateness for the role. "As shooting began," reports Clarke, "she seemed unsure of herself, tiptoeing around the character rather than jumping into her role as she usually did. Portraying the blustery, gun-toting Annie was a stretch for her, different from any part she had ever before attempted, and she seemed uncertain how to proceed." After 12 days of filming, Freed took a look at the film and fired Berkeley, accusing him of shooting it like a stage play. He was immediately replaced by Charles Walters who convinced Garland to stay with the picture in spite of her reservations. Ultimately, Garland was fired for her erratic habits. Moreover, Frank Morgan, who was to have played Buffalo Bill, died. As if this weren't

enough, during the second day of shooting, Howard Keel fell from his horse, broke his ankle, and was confined in a cast for three months. It turned out that Keel's rehabilitation provided the beleaguered production some well-needed time to regroup and recast. In the end, George Sidney replaced Walters as director, Betty Hutton, under contract with Paramount, was put on loan to MGM to play Annie, and Louis Calhern assumed the role of Buffalo Bill. The other original cast members remained: J. Carroll Naish as Sitting Bull, Edward Arnold as Pawnee Bill, Keenan Wynn as Charlie Davenport, Benay Venuta as Dolly Tate. Filming started anew on October 10, 1949.

Screenwriter Sidney Sheldon was charged with adapting Herbert and Dorothy Fields's book. As is customary, he opened it up to include a greater number of physical locations, and reduced the musical numbers to 10 in order to keep the running time under two hours. As part of her contract, Hutton demanded that comedy be stressed over dance numbers, so Sheldon wrote yet another revision when she was hired. Finally, to meet social mores of the times and minimize sexual inferences, changes were made in the lyrics of "Doin' What Comes Natur'lly," "You Can't Get a Man with a Gun," and "My Defenses Are Down."

The film had a successful run at the box office, making it the fifth-highest-grossing film of the year. It was nominated for four Academy Awards: cinematography, art direction, film editing, and scoring of a musical picture, winning the last two. Bosley Crowther (*New York Times*) called the film "a whale of a motion picture," with *Variety* describing it as "socko musical entertainment." Due to legal problems *Annie Get Your Gun* was the most famous MGM musical to remain unavailable on videotape or laserdisc—until the year 2000.

REFERENCES

Clarke, Gerald, *Get Happy: The Life of Judy Garland* (New York: Random House, 2000); Druxman, Michael B., *The Musical: From Broadway to Hollywood* (New York: A.S. Barnes, 1980); Fordin, Hugh, *The World of Entertainment: Hollywood's Greatest Musicals* (New York: Doubleday, 1975).

—T.J.F.

BABES IN ARMS (1937)

MUSIC, BOOK, AND LYRICS: RICHARD RODGERS
(1902–1979) AND LORENZ HART (1895–1943)

Babes in Arms (1939), U.S.A., directed by Busby Berkeley, adapted by Jack McGowan and Kay Van Riper;
MGM.

The Play

Babes in Arms was the first musical for which the team
of Richard Rodgers and Lorenz Hart wrote not only
the music and lyrics but the book as well. The show
marked the team's return to Broadway after a stint in
Hollywood, where they wrote songs for several Hollywood musicals, including *Love Me Tonight* (1932) and
Mississippi (1935). *Babes in Arms* opened at the Shubert
Theatre on April 14, 1937, and ran for a successful
289 performances. The cast was comprised principally
of young performers, many of whom—Robert Rounseville, Dan Dailey, Alfred Drake, Mitzi Green,
Wynne Murray, among others—went on to successful
careers.

The story begins when the offspring of touring
vaudevillians are left behind to shift for themselves in
Eastport, Long Island, while their parents go on tour.
The local sheriff appears and threatens to transfer
them to a work camp unless their parents return to
take charge of them. Seeking to make enough money
to resolve their problem, the kids decide to put on a
show of their own, called "Lee Calhoun's Follies." The
talents of the young performers are obvious, but the
show is a failure and the kids are sent to the farm. At
the last minute, however, a French transatlantic flyer,
Rene Flambeau, makes a forced landing in their farmyard and comes to their aid. The remarkable score
included such standards as "Where or When" (sung by
Mitzi Green and Ray Heatherton), "I Wish I Were in
Love Again" (Grace McDonald and Rolly Poickert),
"Johnny One Note" (Wynn Murray), and "The Lady
Is a Tramp" and "My Funny Valentine" (both by Mitzi
Green). (It is interesting to note that the latter song
was not a Valentine's Day song, but a tune sung to a
boy named Valentine.) And there was a dream ballet,
"Peter's Dream," in which the children meet the mag-
ical stars of Hollywood, including impersonations of
Greta Garbo, Marlene Dietrich, and Clark Gable.
Critic John Mason Brown was enthusiastic, calling it
"a zestful, tuneful, and brilliantly danced affair . . .
filled with talented striplings and bubbling over with
the freshness and energy of youth."

The Film

Many key elements came together to make the film
version of *Babes in Arms* not only one of MGM's most
successful pictures but also one that marked a conflu-
ence of talent that for the next decade would mark

many of the studio's best musical films. Young actress/singer Judy Garland was the newest element in the mix. No sooner had she scored a success in *The Wizard of Oz*, than MGM rushed her into the projected adaptation. Costarring was Mickey Rooney, already a veteran of the movies and one of MGM's top stars. He and Garland had already appeared together in two films, *Thoroughbreds Don't Cry* (1937) and *Love Finds Andy Hardy* (1938). But it was *Babes on Broadway* that proved to the MGM bosses what a potent combination they had in the two stars. Two other key figures came into play. The imaginative director/choreographer Busby Berkeley was signed on to direct. He had come to Hollywood from Broadway to direct the dance sequences in *Whoopee!* in 1930; thereafter, he had made his mark in a series of Warner Bros. musicals (*42nd Street, Gold Diggers of 1933, Footlight Parade*, among others) and a cycle of Goldwyn vehicles for Eddie Cantor (*Roman Scandals, Palmy Days*). Assuming the role of producer for the first time was Arthur Freed, a lyricist at MGM since the dawn of the talkies. Freed would go on to helm most of MGM's most successful musicals, including the "Babes" cycle and many productions in the 1940s and 1950s directed by Vincente Minnelli, Stanley Donen, Gene Kelly, and others.

For the film version Freed retained only two of the original songs, "Babes in Arms" and "Where or When" ("The Lady Is a Tramp" was heard occasionally only in the background instrumental music score). Freed and his longtime collaborator, composer Nacio Brown, added a new number, "Good Morning," along with two of their old hits, "You Are My Lucky Star" and "I Cried for You." E.Y. Harburg and Harold Arlen added yet another song, "God's Country." The original story line was altered to beef up Rooney's part. He plays Mickey Moran, energetic son of veteran vaudeville hoofers Joe and Florrie Moran (Charles Winninger and Grace Hayes). The film's prologue opens in 1921 at the Palace Theatre as Joe is winding up the act while Florrie gives birth to Mickey backstage. Joe toasts the event with his fellow vaudevillians and promises that vaudeville will live forever. Years pass and talking motion pictures arrive. A brief montage of scenes from *Broadway Melody* and *Hollywood Revue of 1929* illustrate how wrong Joe is. Now, in the present and out of work, he and his wife join up with their friends in a desperate attempt to launch one last vaudeville tour. Mickey, in the meantime, is busily writing songs to support the family. He and his pal, Patsy (Judy Garland), successfully "put over" his newest, "Good Mornin,'" and make a sale. While the old folks hit the road, Mickey and his young friends pledge to put on their own show: "Most of us were born in the theatre;

greasepaint is in our veins." Blocking their efforts is the head of the Welfare Board (Margaret Hamilton), who is determined to place this mongrel bunch of kids in a work camp. But Mickey has the support of the local judge (Guy Kibbee), and the kids march out into the night, singing "Babes in Arms." "They call us Babes in Arms," they chant, "but we are Babes in Armor. . . ."

Money is tight, of course, so Mickey takes advantage of the "comeback" attempt by rich kid, Baby Rosalie (June Preisser), to secure her financial backing. But there is a catch to the arrangement. Baby Rosalie insists on headlining the show, much to the disappointment and outrage of Patsy (who sings out her hurt in a solo soliloquy, "I'll Cry for You"). Opening night arrives, and several disasters beset the production. First, Baby Rosalie's irate father pulls her out of the show. Second, a hurricane hits the town and drowns out the opening "Minstrel Show" number. Things look bleak. The kids are out of money, and their parents have returned home in utter failure. Joe, especially, bitterly denounces show business and settles for a job as an elevator operator. He even agrees with the Welfare Board that the children should go to a work camp. At the eleventh hour, an "angel" appears with new hope. A producer who had been present at the kids' disastrous show opening decides to bring the production to Broadway. He enlists Joe to help out, reminding him that the kids badly need his show-biz savvy: "Old fashioned sentiment's not taboo any more," he tells Joe. "Those kids have got their eyes on you." Then the producer turns to Mickey, ordering him to bring a new spirit to Broadway—and to America. "Gee," responds Mickey breathlessly, "it's bigger than a show!"

The production, called *Babes in Arms*, goes on, and it concludes with a big production number, "God's Country." As he conducts the orchestra, Mickey turns around to face the audience and exhorts them (and us) to share in a new spirit of America. He and his cast members file into the audience, chanting lines like, "We've got no Duce/We've got no Fuehrer/But we've got Garbo and Norma Shearer." As they climb the steps to the stage platform, they sing, "We've got no goosestep/But we've got a Suzy-Q step." The full ensemble now launches into a swing dance against the backdrop of the Capitol Dome. The peroration is nothing less than a musical call to arms for America to join hands with the nations of the world.

The irrepressible Mickey Rooney, as usual, wears on the nerves. But his protean talents are amply on display. He's all over the map, banging away at the piano, stroking a cello like a bass fiddle, badgering his cast members, berating his parents, beating up a member of the Welfare Board, cajoling money out of Baby Rosalie, laughing and crying all the while (sometimes at the same time). Some of his best moments come during a show rehearsal when, in an impromptu manner, he mimics Clark Gable and Lionel Barrymore. Nothing could be simpler, and more effective, than his sparkling duet with Judy Garland, "Good Mornin.'" Garland, in the meantime, is considerably more restrained. Perhaps her finest moment is the quietly poignant "I'll Cry for You" number, sung and spoken while clasping in her hands a photo of Mickey. She also has a chance to vamp her way through a jazzy pastiche of the operatic aria, the "Largo al Factotum" from Rossini's *Barber of Seville*. Busby Berkeley's big musical numbers are more naturalistic, more realistic, if you will, than his earlier dance abstractions for Warner Bros. The marching ranks of kids that patrol the neighborhood in the "Babes in Arms" number at the beginning and the formations that invade the aisles of the theatre in the concluding "God's Country" sequence bespeak his background in World War I as a military instructor.

Babes in Arms was a sensation. "[It] has a sort of awkward, frantic-to-please, you-can't-beat-youth quality which makes one capitulate easily," enthused critic Richard Sheridan Ames. "Its freshness and sauciness and ceaseless activity provide a shot in the arm for the world-weary and cynical, and no picture released in recent months, unless it was *Wizard of Oz*, is so likely to make one forget the importunate war news and other distressing manifestations of civilized existence—for which we may be thankful." It surpassed *The Wizard of Oz* at the box office and ended up as MGM's biggest grosser of the year. Garland and Rooney teamed up with Berkeley three more times for the sequels, *Strike Up the Band* (1940), *Babes on Broadway* (1942), and *Girl Crazy* (1943). Garland biographer Gerald Clarke argues that together they constitute a cycle of films related to the "Andy Hardy" series: "A genealogist might argue that the *Babes in Arms* pictures were not really a new series, but an offshoot of the [Andy] Hardys. Mickey is still the central character, concocting schemes, issuing orders and getting himself in and out of trouble. Judy is his right hand, his chief adviser and his conscience, the not-so-gentle voice that informs him when he is breaking [a] strict code of honesty, integrity, and small-town piety." Indeed, the only difference between the "Andy Hardy" series and the "Babes" series was the music. In each of the Babes installments, Mickey and Judy have to "put on a show" to raise money for a worthy cause. "Obstacles arise and disaster looms," says Clarke, "but ten or fifteen minutes before the film ends, they put on a show that Ziegfeld would have cheered."

REFERENCES

Ames, Richard Sheridan, "Babes in Arms," in Anthony Slide, ed., *Selected Film Criticism, 1931–1940* (Metuchen, N.J.: Scarecrow Press, 1982); Clarke, Gerald, *Get Happy: The Life of Judy Garland* (New York: Random House, 2000); Thomas, Tony, and Jim Terry, *The Busby Berkeley Book* (Greenwich, Conn.: New York Graphic Society, 1973).

—*J.C.T.*

BELLS ARE RINGING (1956)

MUSIC: JULE STYNE (1905–1994)
BOOK AND LYRICS: BETTY COMDEN (1915–), ADOLPH GREEN (1915–)

Bells Are Ringing (1958), U.S.A., directed by Vincente Minnelli, adapted for the screen by Betty Comden and Adolph Green; Metro-Goldwyn-Mayer.

The Play

"It's Machiavelli with a heart of gold," quipped Walter Kerr in the *Herald Tribune*. He was describing the altogether engaging performance of the late, great Judy Holliday as Ella Peterson (aka "Mom, aka "Millicente Scott") in the charming romantic comedy with music, *Bells Are Ringing*. When the show opened, Ms. Holliday was a well-known comedienne and Academy Award–winning actress, for her priceless performance as Billie Dawn in *Born Yesterday* and for subsequent film hits *The Marrying Kind, Solid Gold Cadillac*, and *It Should Happen to You*. But no one knew what a good singing voice she had, or just how unique her comic talents were, until Ms. Holliday triumphed in *Bells Are Ringing* on Broadway and together with her costar Sydney Chaplin won the Tony awards for best performance of the season.

Bells Are Ringing opened at the Shubert Theatre on November 29, 1956. The plot, though somewhat antiquated today, revolves around an answering service operator at "Susanswerphone." Ella Peterson (Holliday) is hopelessly in love with her answering service customer (Plaza 0, Double 0, Double 3) down-on-his-luck playwright Jeff Moss (Chaplin). Posing as the voice of "mom," a helpful older woman who treats him just like a son, Ella takes on the responsibility of getting Jeff back on his feet. Her boss and cousin, Sue (Jean Stapleton), has warned her not to get involved with the customers, but Ella's big heart just can't seem to stand people who are unhappy or in trouble. Her other customers include a dentist who really wants to be a Gershwin, an actor who just can't seem to land a part, a mother who needs her little boy to eat his spinach, and an opera singer who, because of Ella's generous spirit, sends her a dress from *Traviata*. Indeed, Ella states, "if she'd been on the switchboard when Romeo and Juliet were dating, those two kids would be alive today." On the phone, she is outgoing and funny, but in person she is painfully shy. When she finally meets the man of her dreams face to face, posing as Millicente Scott, the attraction is mutual. She helps him start to write again and, to thank her, he takes her out on the town to various parties and nightclubs. Ella is hopelessly smitten but can't let him know that she is not who he thinks she is, and she feels she is living in a fantasy world. In the end, Jeff discovers who she really is through a chance meeting of the dentist and the actor (also being helped by Ella over the phone) at a nightclub. He comes to Susanswerphone and professes his love. Ella falls into his arms and all ends happily.

The subplot centers around Sue's love interest, a shady dealer named Sandor (Eddie Lawrence) who has set up a business called Titanic Records in Sue's shop. The record business is really a front for his illegal gambling operation. Customers ring to place an order (really a bet) and the order is transferred to the shipping department (another phone that is a direct line to the track). When Ella unwittingly interferes, the entire gambling ring is exposed and Sue's business and reputation is saved. The plot is unrealistic and too romantic, but as Walter Kerr said in his review in the *Herald Tribune*, "The quality that most distinguishes *Bells Are Ringing* is its homey, comfortable, old-shoe belief in its attractive people and its wide-eyed plot." Some of the hit songs of Jule Styne's brilliant score included "The Party's Over," "Just in Time," "Long Before I Knew You," and "I Met a Girl." The only major thing criticized about the show was the lack of dance numbers, choreographed by Peter Gennaro.

The Film

The simple problem with the Comden and Green script was that it did not lend itself easily to a screen adaptation. With Vincente Minnelli directing his 12th major screen musical, Dean Martin was hired to play the Sydney Chaplin role, and he fared rather well opposite Judy Holliday reprising her great success on Broadway. "Adding Martin's star's persona to the Judy Holliday vehicle produced another close match of movie star to musical role," notes commentator Gerald Mast. "Even those who don't care for the liquid Martin style find him charming in this musical." Minnelli

uses his signature method to open (or close) a scene by either beginning with a medium shot of a small detail that is appropriate to the dramatic action (like Dean Martin waking up on the sofa, in hangover position) or starting with an overall shot of the big picture followed by a closing in on the action (such as the "Hello" sequence on the streets of New York, cutting to Holliday waiting on the street for Martin, outside his producer's office).

"The plot and dialogue by Betty [Comden] and Adolph [Green] afford Holliday many fine comic-pathetic opportunities," writes commentator Douglas McVay, "and she turns the heroine's resolve to revert to her old post with the Bonjour Tristesse Brassiere Company, 'I'm Goin' Back,' into the film's happiest number." But in the end, the film was overly talky and under-choreographed. There are some fine additions to the score and some sad deletions. Minnelli's sure hand with the camera is seen in a very funny spoof on the rich and famous with the new number "Drop That Name," with Judy Holliday looking appropriately uncomfortable in her "Traviata" red dress, surrounded by the jet set of New York all clad in fancy black and white garb. The supporting cast is, for the most part, on the money. Frank Gorshin scores as the beatnik Blake "Brando" Barton, Jean Stapleton is funny and sincere as Sue, Eddie Foy, Jr., is all accent and style (especially in the show-stopping number "A Simple Little System") as Sue's gangster boyfriend Otto, and Bernie West (direct from the Broadway show) as Dr. Joe Kitchell, the song-composing dentist, is appropriately manic about his desire to create songs rather than the perfect smile.

REFERENCES

Casper, Joseph Andrew, *Vincente Minnelli and the Film Musical* (New York: A.S. Barnes, 1977); Kennedy, Michael Patrick, and John Muir, *Musicals* (Glasgow: HarperCollins Publishers, 1997); Mast, Gerald, *Can't Help Singin'* (Woodstock, N.Y.: Overlook Press, 1987); McVay, Douglas, *The Musical Film* (New York: A.S. Barnes, 1967); Suskin, Steven, *Opening Night on Broadway* (New York: Schirmer, 1990).

—J.S.

THE BOY FRIEND (1954)

MUSIC, LYRICS, AND BOOK: SANDY WILSON (1924–)

The Boy Friend (1971), U.K., directed and adapted by Ken Russell; MGM.

The Play

Originally, composer/lyricist/librettist Sandy Wilson was commissioned to write a one-hour revue that was to be an homage to the 1920s. Favorable response led to a three-act version, which opened in London's West End on January 14, 1954. Eight months later, on September 30, 1954, *The Boy Friend* debuted on Broadway, with almost half of its British cast intact. "The very special virtue of the new spoof at the Royale," wrote Walter Kerr in the *New York Herald Tribune*, "is that is has taken one more look at the bobbing ankles, the bathing bandanas, and the bee-stung lips of a time gone by—and done it with open admiration, with unconcealed affection, with simple good humor, even with kindness. The pastiche that Sandy Wilson has written and composed, and that Vida Hope has directed, isn't really a parody at all. It's a romantic adolescent's love letter to a girl in a cloche hat."

The setting is 1926 on the French Riviera. Rich demoiselle Polly Browne attends Mme. Dubonnet's French finishing school. Polly has invented a boyfriend for the upcoming Carnival ball, because her father fears every eligible bachelor will chase her for her millions. Her ball costume is delivered by a messenger boy, Tony, who she instantly determines to be the boy of her dreams ("I Could Be Happy with You"). Lest Tony prove to be a fortune hunter, however, Polly pretends to be a poor working girl, the secretary to Mme. Dubonnet. Later that night at the ball, Polly confesses her real identity. To her astonishment, so does Tony, who turns out to be a wealthy young aristocrat, the son of Lord and Lady Brockhurst. All ends well. Even Polly's father is happy, since he has in the meantime launched into an affair with Mme. Dubonnet.

Wilson's witty music and book mimic the stylings of Noël Coward, Jerome Kern, George Gershwin, and Rodgers and Hart. Indeed, the title song, "The Boy Friend," so closely imitated Rodgers and Hart's song, "The Girl Friend," that the New York producers requested a rewrite to ward off a potential lawsuit. Not to fear; Rodgers was pleased with the musical tribute. The show has enjoyed a remarkable longevity. The 1954 West End version played over five years, numbering 2,084 performances. The Broadway show, which launched 19-year-old Julie Andrews, enjoyed 485 performances. In 1958 an off-Broadway revival accounted for 763 more shows; and Broadway snagged it again in 1970, featuring Sandy Duncan. In 1997 Sandy Wilson's sequel, *Divorce Me, Darling!* took his "Boy Friend" characters joyfully tapping into the milieu of the 1930s.

The Film

Despite the admonition of director Vida Hope that *The Boy Friend* be performed in a "witty, elegant, charming and tender" manner—above all, *not* be overplayed—filmmaker Ken Russell tossed restraint to the winds and produced in 1971 a lush, tropical hot-house version. Dissatisfied with the plot outline, he decided to relegate Wilson's story to a play-within-a-film, framing it with the backstage world of a "real-life" touring theatrical company. "[Wilson's] old show itself was nice enough but I felt it needed another dimension, and my backstage sub-plots seemed to fit very well," explained Russell. He found a derelict theatre in Portsmouth to use for his locations. "The place was a shambles," Russell recounted. "All the seats had gone, rain dripped on to the stage, doves fluttered through holes in the roof and all the basins and loos had been irrevocably smashed by vandals. . . . Anyway, it was just what we wanted for our tatty touring company and with a few bob spent on it and some dark lighting by David Watkin we soon made it look as good as it needed to."

As the film opens, we are backstage at Portsmouth's seedy Theatre Royal, well outside London. A second-class company is performing *The Boy Friend* to a dreadfully small house. The star, Rita (Glenda Jackson), has sprained her ankle and the shy assistant stage manager, Polly Browne (Twiggy), must appear in her stead. Under Rita's last-minute tutelage—as an inside joke, she quotes Bebe Daniels's lines from the Warner Bros. backstage classic, *42nd Street*—Polly struggles at the last minute to learn her song and dance numbers. She is also shy about working with the leading man, Tony (Chris Gable), with whom she is secretly, desperately in love. And everyone's anxiety is compounded by the fact that famed Hollywood director, Cecil B. DeThrill (Vladek Sheybal), has just arrived at the matinee to scout for talent for his forthcoming movie version of their play. The play does not begin well—Polly is awkward and tentative in her first scene. Worse, the cast members try to upstage one another to capture DeThrill's attention. And worst of all, dancer Tommy seems to be paying more attention to a flashy chorine than to the play. As DeThrill looks on, he begins to imagine how his film will stage these shabby routines in a glittering, Busby Berkeley–like manner. Moreover, he fantasizes the scenes between Tony and Polly in terms of Astaire-Rogers routines on fantastic Art Deco sets. (These scenes allow director Ken Russell to indulge himself in spectacular dance routines to the song standards, "All I Do Is Dream of You" and "You Are My Lucky Star.")

At last the play ends. Offstage, Tommy (Tommy Tune), who has just learned that he is the long-lost son of DeThrill, departs with his father while Tony declares his love for Polly. Everyone is happy, although DeThrill by now has decided *not* to make a film of *The Boy Friend* but to make *Singin' in the Rain* instead.

Sandy Wilson was outraged at Russell's film version. He considered it an "accomplished travesty," and added that it was a willfully messy and at times incomprehensible mélange of twenties and thirties camp, through which poor Twiggy—making her film debut—barely twittered and pranced. He was appalled, moreover, that the whole was almost suffocated by the welter of grotesque décor and noise. The critics generally agreed. Yet the film has achieved something of a cult status in subsequent years. In 1987 an uncut version was released. "It's a delight, gushed critic Kevin Thomas in the *Los Angeles Times*, calling it one of the high points of the extravagant career of bad-boy Ken Russell.

REFERENCES

Baxter, John, *An Appalling Talent, Ken Russell* (London: Michael Joseph, 1973); Druxman, Michael B., *The Musical: From Broadway to Hollywood* (New York: A.S. Barnes, 1980); Rosenfeldt, Diane, *Ken Russell: A Guide to References and Resources* (Boston: G.K. Hall, 1978); Thomas, Kevin, "The Boy Friend," *The Los Angeles Times,* June 19, 1987; Windeler, Robert, *Julie Andrews: A Life on Stage and Screen* (Secaucus, N.J.: Birch Lane Press, 1997).

—*K.P.*

BRIGADOON (1947)

MUSIC: FREDERICK LOEWE (1904–1988)
LYRICS: ALAN JAY LERNER (1918–1986)
BOOK: ALAN JAY LERNER

Brigadoon (1954), U.S.A., directed by Vincente Minnelli, Screenplay by Frederick Loewe and Alan Jay Lerner; MGM.

The Play

During the Broadway season of 1946–47, two fantasy musicals were playing on Broadway, one Gaelic and one Scottish. *Finian's Rainbow* was already a hit when Lerner and Loewe's *Brigadoon* finally opened at the Ziegfeld Theatre on March 13, 1947. Coming off a string of non-hits, Lerner and Loewe had found the perfect vehicle for collaboration in a fantasy about a little village that comes alive for only one day each 100 years.

They had a difficult time finding a producer, however, and worked even harder at raising money for the production costs. After peddling the script and score to Billy Rose, who wanted the right to bring in another composer or authors and have final say on casting, Lerner and Loewe turned to Cheryl Crawford. She brought in Robert Lewis as director and Agnes de Mille agreed to do the choreography.

Loosely inspired by *Germelshausen*, a German story by Friedrich Gerstaecker, *Brigadoon* tells the story of two Americans, Tommy Albright (David Brooks) and Jeff Douglas (George Keene), who find themselves lost overnight in the Scottish highlands while on a hunting trip. As the morning mist clears, they see the village of Brigadoon, which does not appear on the map and whose inhabitants dress and act as though they were in the middle of the 18th century. Tommy and Jeff are puzzled but charmed by the villagers who are in the middle of preparations for the wedding of Jeannie MacLaren (Virginia Bosler) and Charlie Dalrymple (Lee Sullivan). While Jeff is preoccupied by the man-hungry Meg Brockie (Pamela Britton), Tommy spends the day with Fiona MacLaren (Marion Bell), Jeannie's older sister, and finds himself falling in love with her. Both men are confused by the circumstances of the town's appearance and the behavior of the villagers, and when Tommy sees that the date of Jeannie and Charlie's wedding is entered into the family Bible as May 24, 1746, he confronts Fiona, demanding an answer. So she takes them to the schoolmaster, Mr. Lundie (William Hansen), who explains that the village minister, Mr. Forsythe, was worried that the people of Brigadoon would be set upon by witches and devils. So he prayed for a miracle. God answered his prayer that the village disappear and be visible for only one day every 100 years. The only condition was that all the people stay within the village boundaries. If anyone leaves, Brigadoon will disappear forever. An outsider may stay in the village only if he or she truly loves one of the inhabitants.

This day is the second of their 100-year sleeps, and the villagers are ready for Jeannie and Charlie's wedding celebration. The only citizen unhappy about the festivities is Harry Beaton, who is in love with Jeannie and jealous of Charlie. He confronts Charlie at the wedding party; they fight, and Harry flees from the village, cursing its inhabitants. Intending to cross the boundary of the village and cause its disappearance, Harry is chased through the woods by the entire town. During the chase, Harry is tripped by Jeff Douglas, hits his head on a rock, and dies. As the day draws to a close, Tommy struggles with the prospect of either leaving Fiona, whom he now loves, or leaving his own world behind. His doubts assail him, and he decides he must leave. Jeff and Tommy walk out of the village just as it disappears in the mists. They return to New York, but Tommy is restless and dissatisfied. All he can think of is Fiona and Brigadoon. He decides he must return to Scotland at least to see that it was not all a dream.

As he and Jeff wander about in the woods, they suddenly see the village again and Mr. Lundie coming across the bridge. Mr. Lundie explains that Tommy's love was strong enough to bring the village back into his time. Tommy then crosses the bridge and enters Brigadoon forever.

Opening in the wake of World War II, the Scottish fantasy may have seemed slightly unpromising. But as Steven Suskin suggests, "*Brigadoon's* setting was incidental to its message; and the writing . . . was not only unhackneyed but completely enchanting. The theme of life and eternal love after death was not only universal, but almost painfully timely." The essence of *Brigadoon's* popularity is its appeal to a universal desire for the perfect place. Like Shangri-La, Brigadoon is a place where people have found contentment in their lives and with themselves. Here that contentment is a consequence of their unabiding faith in the reality of the "miracle." Simple values and honest emotions like true love are the keys to participation in the miracle. Tommy must do exactly what Mr. Lundie suggests: He must give up everything in order to gain everything. He must take a leap of faith.

Lerner and Loewe's music captured a faintly Scottish flavor and the score contains some of the most well-known and popular songs of the musical theatre. "It's Almost Like Being in Love" has become a standard. The choreography by Agnes de Mille is especially noteworthy in its reflection of highland dance and in the chase sequence in the second act: "A kind of idyllic rhythm flows through the whole pattern of the production, and Miss de Mille has dipped again into the Pandora's box where she keeps her dance designs," said Brooks Atkinson in *Time*.

Brigadoon ran for 581 performances and won the New York Drama Critics Circle best musical award: "Because it is an altogether original and inventive blending of words, music and dance," wrote Howard Barnes of the *New York Herald Tribune;* "because its taste, discretion and thoughtful beauty mark a high note in any season; and because it finds the lyric theatre at its best . . . [It is] a bonny thing for Broadway, a scintillating song and dance fantasy that has given theatregoers reason to toss tamoshanters in air."

The Film

The 1954 film was to be shot in Cinemascope, and director Vincente Minnelli was determined to create a faithful piece of the Scottish highlands. The weather in Scotland was too unpredictable, however, so Minnelli planned to shoot the film on three separate MGM sound stages. Art director Preston Ames suggested to Minnelli that they create the entire set on one stage, creating a wide panorama of the hills and the village. "We tried to do it so that in every place you looked, there was a different aspect—a cavern or a river, a bridge or hills. And I got as good a replica of Scotland as we could get," said Minnelli. Covering 40,000 square feet on Stage 15, the set reportedly cost $382,280. However, the biggest problem seemed to be with the heather. "I want lots of heather," said Minnelli. The trouble was that the texture of real heather is too fine to register well on camera. "So," said backdrop painter George Gibson, "we wound up painting sumac purple to represent purple heather, which we placed against the backing."

One of the challenges was the opening scene in which the fog lifts slowly to reveal the village lying in the valley. The difficulty lay in the fact that the scene had to be timed to the music of the prologue. The fog must clear just as the musical prologue ends, and fog just doesn't take direction well. So Minnelli had the music precisely timed, turned on the fog machines and began the filming with the village *in the clear* and the fog rolling in. Then he reversed the film making it appear as though the fog was clearing, leaving the village in view at precisely the right time. Another tour de force bit of filming involved the chase sequence. Hugh Fordin describes the filming: "Minnelli and [Joseph] Ruttenberg shot the entire chase, with its dispersed group of hunters, in one setup, without a cut. It was a highly complex affair; the whole sequence was shot to a prerecorded music track; deer were running through the landscape; the hunters were thrashing around carrying torches. 'It was marvelous,' [said] Minnelli, 'because it was all so nervous and wild.'" The shooting took 17 days and cost $442,898.

The film starred Gene Kelly, Cyd Charisse, and Van Johnson in the title roles. As a result, the dance element of the musical (already very strong in the stage show) is emphasized over the singing element. Lerner even modified the first draft of the screenplay, making Tommy Albright a dancer, thus tailoring the character to Kelly's particular talents. Since Loewe's music was written for trained voices, Gene Kelly had a hard time preparing the vocals. As a result, the musical relies even more on the dance choreography to convey the emotions of the musical scenes. Kelly's choreography succeeds splendidly, and he and Cyd Charisse do some of the most beautiful, if not the most technically demanding, dancing of their careers (Charisse's voice was dubbed by Carole Richards). She is less convincing in her non-dancing scenes, and her characterization of Fiona is a bit stiff. Van Johnson was the second choice as Jeff Douglas. The part was to be offered to Donald O'Conner, but he was committed elsewhere. Johnson's sardonic portrayal of the jaded New Yorker is often very funny, but he tries a bit too hard, and becomes annoying after a while. No doubt, Johnson was hampered by the fact that Douglas's role was meant to be paired in subplot with Meg Brockie. Because Meg's role is almost entirely eliminated from the film (both of her comic musical numbers, "The Love of My Life" and "My Mother's Wedding Day" are cut), their scenes together are necessarily truncated. So Johnson's screen time is limited mostly to ironic commentary on his friend's love affair. Kelly and Johnson do have one extended soft shoe routine during the "I'll Go Home with Bonnie Jean" number.

An interesting script change involving Jeff Douglas is associated with the death of Harry Beaton. In the stage script, Douglas confesses that he tripped Harry in an attempt to stop him and had no intent to hurt him. In the film, Jeff is ignoring the chase for Harry and is instead sitting out in the woods with his rifle drinking rather heavily. He's had enough of Brigadoon and wants to leave. As he sits in the darkening woods, he sees a grouse and raises his rifle to shoot at it. He misses and shoots Harry who has taken refuge in a tree. Surprisingly, the verdict by the villagers is still the same: Harry fell and hit his head. (The villagers apparently can't tell the difference between a gunshot wound and a hole in the head.)

The Lerner and Loewe score also suffered the elimination of "Come to Me, Bend to Me," "There but for You Go I" (both recorded and on the soundtrack album), and "The Sword Dance." Added are more extensive dance numbers in the remaining musical tracks. In essence, the musical becomes a dancer rather than a singer's vehicle. This was wise, given the vocal limitations of its stars, and Gene Kelly's choreography succeeds in almost every case. The costumes, Ames's set, and the musical arrangements are highlights, but the movie was only moderately successful. The film cost $2,352,625 to make and it grossed $3,385,000 in its first release.

REFERENCES

Casper, Joseph Andrew, *Vincente Minnelli and the Film Musical* (South Brunswick, N.J.: A.S. Barnes, 1977); Druxman, Michael B., *The Musical: From Broadway to Hollywood* (South Brunswick, N.J.: A.S. Barnes, 1980); Fordin, Hugh, *The World of Entertainment* (New York: Doubleday, 1975); Ganzl, Kurt, *The Encyclopedia of Musical Theatre* (New York: Schirmer, 1994); Kennedy, Michael Patrick, and John Muir, *Musicals* (Glasgow: Harper-Collins, 1997); Lerner, Alan J., *The Musical Theatre: A Celebration* (New York: McGraw-Hill, 1986); Parish, James Robert, and Michael R. Pitts *The Great Hollywood Musical Pictures* (Metuchen, N.J.: Scarecrow Press, 1992); Schickel, Richard, *The Men Who Made the Movies* (New York: Atheneum, 1975); Suskin, Steven, *Opening Nights on Broadway* (New York: Schirmer, 1990).

—S.L.Y.

BYE, BYE, BIRDIE (1960)

MUSIC: CHARLES STROUSE (1928–)
LYRICS: LEE ADAMS (1924–)
BOOK: MICHAEL STEWART (1929–1987)

Bye, Bye, Birdie (1963), U.S.A., directed by George Sidney, adapted by Irving Brecher; Columbia.

The Play

The musical *Bye, Bye, Birdie* ushered in the era of the rock musical on Broadway. The premise of the story was a spoof on the over-the-top media coverage of two major events in the career of Elvis Presley, his being drafted into the army and his scandalous hip-swinging appearances on *The Ed Sullivan Show*. The show premiered in New York on April 24, 1960, and ran for a successful 607 performances. Conrad Birdie (Dick Gautier) is an Elvis-type rock star who must sign up for duty and serve his country, like every other good American. His manager, Albert Peterson (Dick Van Dyke), and Albert's faithful secretary, the long-suffering Rose Grant (Chita Rivera), who has been engaged to Albert for years, cook up a scheme to publicize the event and hopefully keep Birdie out of the army. If Birdie goes, Peterson will lose all his commissions and not be able to afford to marry Rose. The idea is to go to small-town America (Sweet Apple, Ohio) and have Birdie sing a song, "One Last Kiss" to a young girl on *The Ed Sullivan Show*. If the song sticks, Albert and Rose will have enough money to marry and live on, until Birdie is discharged from the army. Kim MacAfee (Susan Watson), Birdie's number-one fan in Sweet Apple, is selected as the girl, much to the chagrin of her boyfriend, Hugo (Michael J. Pollard). Albert's mother is dead-set against him marrying Rose (or any woman) and tries to break up the couple by continually feigning illness. In the end, all works out: Kim grows tired of Birdie's ego and makes up with Hugo, and Albert, hand in hand with Rose, leaves his overbearing mother and the pop-music business for a small-town teaching job.

The musical was the sleeper hit of the season, garnering Tony awards for best musical, best book, and best supporting actor for Dick Van Dyke. The authors, virtually unknown at the time, went on to become famous Broadway writers. John Chapman in the *Daily News* wrote "*Bye Bye Birdie* is the funniest, most captivating, and most expert musical comedy one could hope to see in several seasons of showgoing." Though the plot is somewhat thin, the score is charming (with songs like "Put on a Happy Face," "Lotta Livin' to Do," and "One Boy") and the musical has been a staple of high school and community theatres for many years. There was a successful revival in the mid-80s that toured the country starring Tommy Tune (Albert) and Ann Reinking (Rose).

The Film

MGM's George Sidney, known for his work on musicals like *Pal Joey* and *The Harvey Girls*, directed the film. Sidney was known for his sometimes unusual sense of casting. Whether it was intentional or not, both Ann-Margret as the young, innocent Kim MacAfee and Janet Leigh as Rose (in a ridiculous dark wig) seem to be miscast in this film. There's irony in almost every scene. When Ann-Margret is changing clothes in her bedroom, singing "How Lovely to Be a Woman," the innocence of her lyric belies her fetching figure. What does work is when Margret as Kim, virginal and wholesome and very much in love with her boyfriend Hugo (Bobby Rydell), listens to the music of Conrad Birdie—she goes into an appropriately gyrating, rock-and-roll frenzy. Janet Leigh isn't really given much to do in the movie and she is unconvincing as a

hot-tempered Spanish beauty. Her only solo is "Spanish Rose," where, after a heated argument with Albert, she invades a Shriner's meeting and winds up letting go to frenzied rhythms.

Ed Sullivan plays himself and the backstage scenes involving his television show constitute something of a document of this important chapter in 1950s television history. Dick Van Dyke reprises his Tony-winning performance, hot off the success of his newly created and eventually highly successful situation comedy. Paul Lynde as Kim's father, obsessed with being on *The Ed Sullivan Show*, also reprised his Broadway role. Newcomer Jesse Pearson suitably conveyed the sensuous nature of the Elvis role. A new song for Ann-Margret, "Bye, Bye, Birdie," brackets the film's main action, and most of the other songs were either enlarged for, altered for, or reassigned to her and the "younger" cast members. Much of the material for Albert and Rose, the starring roles in the Broadway show, was cut from the picture. Thus, the focus of the story was changed, from a satiric comment on teenagers obsessed with rock-and-roll and their pubescent problems, to a celebration of youthful exuberance.

Director Sidney's penchant for trick effects occasionally overwhelms the picture. The opening "Telephone Gossip" number is conveyed with a complicated split-screen scheme, and the "Kids" song has added touches of animation.

REFERENCES

Altman, Rick, ed., *Genre: The Musical* (London: Routledge and Kegan Paul, 1981); Bordman, Gerald, *American Musical Theatre: A Chronicle* (New York: Oxford University Press, 1978); Druxman, Michael B., *The Musical from Broadway to Hollywood* (South Brunswick, N.J.: A.S. Barnes, 1980); Mast, Gerald, *Can't Help Singin'* (Woodstock, N.Y.: Overlook Press, 1987); Suskin, Steven, *Opening Night on Broadway* (New York: Schirmer, 1990).

—*J.S.*

CABARET (1966)

MUSIC: JOHN KANDER (1927–)
LYRICS: FRED EBB (1932–)
BOOK: JOE MASTEROFF (1919–)

Cabaret (1972), U.S.A., directed by Bob Fosse, adapted by Jay Presson Allen; Allied Artists.

The Play

When *Cabaret* opened at New York's Broadhurst Theatre on November 20, 1966, it changed the course of the American musical theatre. Guided by director Harold Prince, composed and written by the relatively untried team of Kander and Ebb, the show juxtaposed a serious story set in the milieu of the decadent late 1920s of Weimar Germany against a cabaret setting. In the words of Prince, "We wanted to present a challenge to audiences conditioned to the jolly predictability of musical theatre." It was adapted from Christopher Isherwood's autobiographical *Berlin Stories* and John Van Druten's dramatization, *I Am a Camera*. The original production featured accomplished performances by Jack Gilford, Bert Convy, the inimitable Lotte Lenya, and a breakout turn by Joel Grey as the Master of Ceremonies.

At the sleazy Kit Kat Klub, the Master of Ceremonies invites us to leave our troubles outside and enjoy a few hours of entertainment. Offstage, American writer Cliff Bradshaw (Convy) arrives in Berlin and arranges lodgings at the boarding house of Fraulein Schneider (Lotte Lenya). He earns a precarious living by giving English lessons to his newfound friend, Ernst Ludwig (Edward Winter). Back at the cabaret, Cliff meets vivacious singer Sally Bowles (Jill Haworth), who promptly moves in with him. Fraulein Schneider, too, finds love when she allows herself to be courted by the gentle Jewish grocer, Herr Schultz (Gilford). When Sally announces she is pregnant, neither she nor Cliff are sure who the father is. Later, at the engagement party for Schneider and Herr Schultz, Ernst reveals his anti-Semitism when he leads his friends in a Nazi anthem. Shocked, Cliff realizes that he has been an unwitting accomplice to Cliff's anti-Semitic activities. Sally, in the meantime, has an abortion and leaves Cliff to return to the Kit Kat Klub. Cliff leaves for America, accompanied by Herr Schultz. Throughout these proceedings, the MC at the cabaret periodically returns, leading the ensemble in song routines like "Cabaret" and "The Money Song" that ironically comment on the story. After asserting that "life is beautiful," he bids us good night.

The Kit Kat Klub is a buffer zone that stands between the internal chaos of the characters' lives and the overall turmoil of the rise of the Nazi regime. From its stage platform the MC regards the world swirling without and within with a cool, sardonic humor. The world may be going to hell, but not without a rude swash of greasepaint painted on its cold lips.

Cabaret opened to almost universal critical acclaim and garnered eight Tony Awards. Walter Kerr in the *New York Times* called it "a stirring musical, brilliantly conceived. It opens the door to a fresh notion of the bizarre . . . and yet beguiling uses that can be made of song and dance." Since its initial 1,165-performance run, it has been revived often. A revival in London in 1993, brilliantly directed by Sam Mendes and Rob Marshall, combines the music of both the stage and film versions with a newly revised book. It brings the audience into the action in an environmental staging inside a real nightclub. It puts *all* the story into the Kit Kat Klub stage and set new standards for future productions.

The Film

"That show did everything for us," recalls John Kander. "Fred Ebb and I were accepted as professionals. Although we wrote something like 60 songs for *Cabaret*, many were left out of the film. We had no control on it at all. Our one stipulation was that if anything new were written for the film, Fred and I would be the ones to do it. We never went to Hollywood, nor were we involved with the film that much." Indeed, in many ways the film version is a completely different work from the stage original—more faithful in its way to the play, *I Am a Camera*, than to the Kander and Ebb original. An entirely new script focuses more on the trials and tribulations of Brian (Michael York) and Sally. The affair of the elderly couple is replaced with the relationship between a young Jewish heiress and her German suitor. Only Joel Grey returns from the original cast. In this, his second film, director Bob Fosse decided that film audiences would not accept characters bursting into song, so he relegated musical sequences only to the Kit Kat Klub (except for "Tomorrow Belongs to Me"). Songs that were cut include "So What?" "Don't Tell Mama," "The Telephone Song," "Perfectly Marvelous," "The Pineapple Song," "Why Should I Wake Up?" "Married," and "What Would You Do?" Only five songs were retained, "Willkommen," "Two Ladies," "Tomorrow Belongs to Me," "If You Could See Her," and "Cabaret." Three songs were written especially for the film in order to give Sally (Liza Minnelli) more time on the cabaret stage, "Mein Herr," "Money, Money," and "Maybe This Time." The only song not performed at the cabaret is a haunting German anthem sung by a Nazi Youth in a beer garden, one of the most chillingly memorable moments in the film. "It is not at all usual in American musicals," says historian John Kobal, "or any other musicals, to find that

what you are seeing and hearing is beautiful but in which the *meaning* is awful. It sounds good; it looks good, but the meaning is terrible. That is the artist, through his art, pulling the blinkers off our eyes." The links between the dramatic action and the stage performances are more firmly delineated. Musical numbers reveal the slow rise of Nazism: A mud wrestling act between two women is capped when the MC steps forward and gives himself a Hitler mustache with some of the mud; a beer barrel dance is intercut with shots of a Jewish businessman being viciously beaten by soldiers. The bolder sexuality of the film bespeaks the cultural changes between 1966 and 1972. In the film it is revealed that Cliff is bisexual, confused by his attraction to wealthy playboy Maximillian and to Sally.

Cabaret was filmed in West Berlin, Bavaria, and at studios in Munich. Its success put Fosse and Minnelli on the map. Fosse was uniquely attuned to the sordid world of the Kit Kat Klub. His signature stamp on the choreography provides the film's finest moments. For Minnelli, the film was a veritable showcase. Her childlike vulnerability and idiosyncratic personality perfectly fit Sally's clumsy search for individual and sexual fulfillment. The production was showered with Oscars, including best director (Fosse), best cinematography (Geoffrey Unsworth), best actress (Liza Minnelli), and best supporting actor (Joel Grey).

REFERENCES

Kobal, John, *Gotta Sing Gotta Dance* (London: Spring Books, 1983); Tibbetts, John C., "New York, New York: An Interview with John Kander," *New York*, 1996–1997, 226–225.

—*D.S.G.*

CAMELOT (1960)

MUSIC: FREDRICK LOEWE (1904–1988)
BOOK AND LYRICS: ALAN JAY LERNER (1918–1986)

Camelot (1967), U.S.A., directed by Joshua Logan, screenplay by Alan Jay Lerner; Warner Bros.-Seven Arts.

The Play

Based on *The Once and Future King* by T. H. White, *Camelot* was the second major triumph of Lerner and Loewe on Broadway. The show opened at the Majestic Theatre on December 3, 1960. It was directed by Moss Hart and choreographed by Hanya Holm with scenery by Oliver Smith and costumes by Adrian (who died before the opening) and Tony Duquette.

"The Arthur legend deals with love, loyalty, idealism, war and peace, perfection, and the ultimate in good versus evil. That's a tall order for a novel, but it's a *very* tall order for a musical," writes commentator Scott Miller. The story begins on the eve of King Arthur's (Richard Burton) marriage to Guenevere (Julie Andrews), a young princess he has never met. Arthur has stolen away from the castle to sneak a peek at his bride. Instead, he gets some much-needed advice from his teacher Merlyn (David Hurst). Arthur is a boyish young man in his twenties at the start of the play and does not feel ready for marriage. Much to his surprise, the 17-year-old Guenevere rushes into the wood, having stolen away from her entourage. She prays to St. Genevieve for strength as Arthur hides in a tree watching her. When she discovers she is being watched, she immediately asks the stranger to take her away from her awful fate as queen of Camelot. Without letting her know who he is, Arthur proceeds to tell Guenevere of the beauty and majesty of the enchanting castle and land called Camelot. When guards rush in they immediately bow to Arthur and Guenevere suddenly realizes she has been talking to her future husband. She too bows but Arthur takes her by the hand and they are quickly married.

The opening scene establishes the characters not as a king and queen, but as two vulnerable young people who meet in the woods and fall in love. Just as in the opening of Rodgers and Hammerstein's *South Pacific* and in their own musical, *My Fair Lady*, the authors are unafraid to introduce the main characters in the very first moments of the show. By having Arthur and Guenevere meet in this way, their love for each other is never in question throughout the rest of the story.

Years pass and Arthur has established his famous Round Table. Yet, Arthur's Round Table is a flawed idea from the beginning. He sees a world where Might is Right, where the knights can do as they please because they have the money, the power, and the armor. So, he dedicates himself to changing things, to using Might *for* Right. Into the picture walks the virtuous and perfect Lancelot (Robert Goulet) who has dreamt of being a knight of the Round Table his entire life. Together with Lancelot, Arthur begins to institute his changes. Of course, Guenevere does not approve of the self-aggrandizing Lancelot; and there is jealousy between the two over their love for and devotion to Arthur. She quickly plots to see his downfall in a jousting match. When Lancelot successfully beats all the knights in the match and even accidentally kills one, he

is very shaken. With his pure heart he prays over the fallen knight and miraculously breathes life back into him. Guenevere is immediately drawn to the inner power and outer strength of the handsome young knight and as the first act closes, the ill-fated love affair between the two begins.

In the second act Mordred (Roddy McDowall), Arthur's illegitimate son, arrives at Camelot to make trouble. He has designs on the throne, and by exposing Guenevere and Lancelot's adulterous behavior, he succeeds in getting Arthur to arrest them and burn Guenevere at the stake. At the last possible hour, Lancelot, who has escaped from prison, returns to save Guenevere, and immediately Arthur must now make war against France. With the collapse of Camelot and the loss of both his wife and best friend, Arthur looks over the battlefield and encounters a young lad who wishes to become a knight. Renewed by the boy's idealism, Arthur sings to him of the land that will never be forgot, "for one brief shining moment that was known as Camelot."

Reviews for the show were mixed. John McClain of the *Journal-American* noted, "it would be impossible to top *My Fair Lady* and indeed it is . . . Great Holy Grail!, it is the most beautiful and resplendent show in the world . . . [but] the splendor of the surroundings overpowers everything else." John Chapman in the *Daily News* thought the play was "magnificent. Its songs are lovely and unfailingly right. Its cast is superb." But "despite its shortcomings . . . there's . . . an underlying subtext of great violence and unfettered sexuality that gives the show a very rich texture," writes Scott Miller, and *Camelot* has gone on to become one of the most widely produced shows in revival today. Sadly, one major reason the show has survived is due in part to the assassination of President John F. Kennedy in 1963. The show and its ideals will be forever linked to his presidency and his memory.

The Film

If there was ever a musical that could have worked better on film than on stage, it was *Camelot*. There are 20 scenes in the play, and moving the story along without having to change the scenery is what slows down any stage production. Film also has the capability of creating a magical and mystical world that can only be hinted at in the theatre. Indeed, the marriage scene between Arthur and Guenevere in the film is breathtaking. There was also the opportunity to film two offstage scenes, the joust and the rescue of Guenevere by Lancelot from being burned at the stake—

which were impossible to do on stage—and make them exciting film sequences. Unfortunately, Joshua Logan as director was just not up to the task. Though he had worked on two previous attempts to bring a stage musical to life on the screen (*South Pacific* and *Fanny*), Logan was far more successful with his transfer of nonmusical dramas like *Picnic* and *Ensign Pulver*. In his book *Can't Help Singin',* Gerald Mast writes, "Logan's ponderous *Camelot* spread Lerner and Loewe's trademark talk-songs to an entire cast of mumblers, supporting the postcard scenery." Indeed, the film musical does not have great singers, but to give them credit, they were all fine actors, just horribly miscast. Both Richard Harris and Vanessa Redgrave did their own singing, but French heartthrob Franco Nero was dubbed by Gene Merlino. "The man who sings 'C'est Moi,' 'If Ever I Would Leave You,' and 'I Loved You Once in Silence' is supposed to know why those songs are there; Nero clearly doesn't" quips Ethan Mordden. Though his song "The Seven Deadly Virtues" was cut from the film, David Hemmings turns in a deliciously wicked performance as Arthur's illegitimate son, Mordred, and Lionel Jeffries makes for a very winning and bumbling Pellinore. Richard Harris, whose Arthur in the film rants his songs and lines, did go on to play the role on stage to critical acclaim in London and America.

REFERENCES

Lerner, Alan Jay, *The Street Where I Live* (New York: De Capo Press, 1994); Logan, Joshua, *Josh: My Up and Down, In and Out Life* (New York: Delacorte Press, 1976); Mast, Gerald, *Can't Help Singin'* (Woodstock, N.Y.: Overlook Press, 1987); Miller, Scott, *Deconstructing Harold Hill* (Portsmouth, N.H.: Heinemann, 2000); Mordden, Ethan, *The Hollywood Musical* (New York: St. Martin's Press, 1981); Parish, James Robert, and Michael R. Pitts, *The Great Hollywood Musical Pictures* (Metuchen, N.J.: Scarecrow Press, 1992); Suskin, Steven, *Opening Night on Broadway* (New York: Schirmer Books, 1990).

—J.S.

CAROUSEL (1945)

MUSIC: RICHARD RODGERS (1902–1979)
LYRICS: OSCAR HAMMERSTEIN II (1895–1960)
STORY: OSCAR HAMMERSTEIN II, BASED ON FERENC MOLNAR'S PLAY *LILIOM*.

Carousel (1956), U.S.A., directed by Henry King, adapted by Phoebe and Henry Ephron; Twentieth Century-Fox.

The Play

Near the end of January 1944, Theresa Helburn of the Theatre Guild approached Oscar Hammerstein and Richard Rodgers about reworking Ferenc Molnar's fantasy drama, *Liliom*, into a musical. The Theatre Guild had just collaborated with Rodgers and Hammerstein on the successful production of *Oklahoma!* and was looking for its next project. The Molnar play about a shiftless carousel barker's seduction of a young factory girl in Hungary had been produced by the Theatre Guild in 1921 with Joseph Schildkraut and Eva Le Gallienne. Hammerstein was rather dubious about the musical appeal of a European setting and with the ending, which leaves Liliom suffering in purgatory after he has failed in completing his good deed back on Earth. In an interview with the *New York Times*, Hammerstein said, "We knew we wouldn't wind up with a conventional musical comedy. It was obvious that we would have to mix in values from the dramatic stage and opera. The idea that really opened the way to it all was suggested by Dick. This was to transplant the play to the New England coast."

Molnar, who had denied even Puccini the permission to use his play for an opera, saw the Rodgers and Hammerstein work on *Oklahoma!* and readily gave his permission for *Liliom*'s adaptation to musical theatre. He also agreed that the bitter and unhopeful ending must be changed in order for the show to appeal to the musical theatre audience. Rodgers and Hammerstein brought back the successful team from *Oklahoma!*—Rouben Mamoulian as director and Agnes de Mille as choreographer.

The plot is simple enough. A young girl, Julie Jordan (Jan Clayton), falls in love with the carnival barker, Billy Bigelow (John Raitt). Bigelow's jealous employer (Jean Casto) fires him, and Julie also loses her job at the mill. Julie and Billy settle down, living primarily on the largess of Julie's Aunt Nettie (Christine Johnson). Frustrated at his lack of prospects, Billy beats Julie. In the meantime, Julie's friend Carrie (Jean Darling) confides that she is engaged to the up-and-coming herringboat owner, Mr. Snow (Eric Mattson). As the young men and women prepare for the spring clambake, Jigger Craigin, a ne'er-do-well sailor, tries to persuade Billy to assist him in a robbery. Billy refuses, but then Julie tells him that she is pregnant, and Billy comes face-to-face with the responsibilities of fatherhood. Desperate, because he has no way to support a family, Billy agrees to help in the robbery. The plan goes awry, however. Jigger runs off and Billy, faced with imminent capture, stabs himself and dies calling out "Julie!" Billy then finds himself in a kind of purgatory with the "Starkeeper" (Russell Collins), who offers him the chance to return to Earth to help his now teenaged daughter. Louise (Bambi Linn) is as much a rebel and outcast as her father had been. Billy brings down a star to give her, but she distrusts him and refuses to take it. In frustration, Billy slaps her. Once again, he can communicate only through violence. He is given one more chance to attend Louise's graduation as an invisible presence. Finally he is able to tell both his wife and daughter that he loves them, and though they do not see him, they are able to accept the hope he wishes to impart to them. Billy can now leave and ascend to a better place.

Carousel's plot source created a need for Rodgers and Hammerstein to reconsider the conventions of the musical theater piece. In their hands, the story becomes largely metaphoric, and the score attempts to achieve that kind of complexity. There is no overture; instead, the curtain opens on the extended "Carousel Waltz" during which the characters and their conflicts are revealed in pantomime. "Because of the almost operatic theme of the play, the orchestra used more instruments than had ever been used before for a Broadway musical," writes Stanley Green. The score serves to reveal character and explain motivations. Dialogue tends to meld seamlessly into music or sometimes the music underscores the dialogue throughout a scene as the characters learn about one another. The first example occurs in the early scene between Julie and Carrie. The music is a background to their conversation until suddenly the two are conversing in song, first "You're a Queer One, Julie Jordan," and then "When I Marry Mr. Snow." Billy's "Soliloquy" is the most consciously operatic number of the score. It carries Billy through several emotional states and realizations as he ruminates on the possibilities and responsibilities of being a father. As he considers the idea that the baby might be a girl, he suddenly realizes that he has nothing to give her, no security to offer. This realization directly motivates him to participate in the robbery with Jigger.

The musical continues the technique used in *Oklahoma!* of dance to advance the plot and add to characterization. Agnes de Mille's work was particularly notable in the second act opening ballet. This fantasy ballet number serves to reveal Louise's status as an outcast in her community as well as her tendencies to repeat her father's rebellious behavior. De Mille's choreography was restaged by Rod Alexander and also used in the 1956 film.

Carousel opened across the street from the long-running *Oklahoma!* and Rodgers and Hammerstein became their own competitors. *Carousel* did not have as wide an appeal, however, and it opened and closed within *Oklahoma!*'s long run. However, it had a very respectable run of 890 performances and won the New York Drama Critics Circle and Donaldson Awards. In 1993, it won four Olivier Awards, including best musical revival. In 1994, it won five Tony Awards, including best musical revival.

The Film

Directed by Henry King, the film was produced by Twentieth Century-Fox and was to be filmed both in the new, widescreen Cinemascope 55 and regular anomorphic Cinemascope. Frank Sinatra was first hired to play Billy Bigelow, but he argued that because each scene must be shot twice—once for each format—he would be doing two films for the price of one. After Sinatra departed, the studio dropped the dual filming because the effect could be achieved more inexpensively in the laboratory. Gordon MacRae and Shirley Jones, fresh from the film version of *Oklahoma!* were then cast as Billy and Julie. Barbara Ruick as Carrie, Cameron Mitchell as Jigger, Robert Rounseville as Mr. Snow, and Claramae Turner as Nettie were also cast.

The film has earned a dubious reputation for various reasons. Henry King chose to set the entire story in a flashback. In the first scene, Billy is already "up there," polishing stars and awaiting his fate. In addition to this rearrangement, several musical numbers are cut, including "You're a Queer One, Julie Jordan," "Blow High, Blow Low," "Geraniums in the Winder," "The Highest Judge of All," and some introductory and incidental music. Minor changes were made in the lyrics to smooth over slightly risqué phrases or vulgar language. There is also an awkward juxtaposition of actual exterior shots and obvious sound-stage sets. In another interesting change, Billy's death occurs as an accident during the robbery rather than a suicide. Evidently suicide would not have played well to a middle-class American audience.

Carousel explores the dark side of love and marriage. Unlike Curly and Laurey in *Oklahoma!* Billy and Julie do not overcome their troubles after finally marrying. In fact, this is not the story of a courtship; it is the story about what can come after marriage: poverty, abuse, heartache, and death. One of the most disturbing elements of the story is Julie's response to Billy's abuse. As his wife, she excuses him because he is unhappy and frustrated. As his widow, she tells her daughter that "it is possible . . . fer someone to hit you—hit you hard—and not hurt at all." Even the "successful" marriage of Carrie and Mr. Snow is not without its darkly ironic undertones. The high-spirited Carrie has settled down with the respectable Mr. Snow to the detriment of her own personality and interests. Their comfortable family life comes at a price that includes intolerant and snobbish children. "Their differences have not proved mutually beneficial: instead they seem wholly apart. . . . If Billy has too little virtue . . . Mr. Snow has too much," write commentators Babington and Evans. Although Julie and Billy's impulsive and passionate relationship brings heartache, Hammerstein does not seem inclined to hold up the marriage of the Snows as a viable alternative. The fruits of love are tinged with bitterness. Accompanying that bitterness, however, is a belief in the hope offered by that love as well as by an abiding faith. The final scene relies on Louise and Julie remembering that love and trusting that they will "never walk alone" either in this world or the next.

Carousel is "a beautifully turned out film, crisply played and richly sung by a fine cast that is fully worthy of the original musical show," wrote Bosley Crowther in the *New York Times*. It is "a distinct technical advance in the field of projection. . . . The screenplay does no violence to the essentials of the stage play . . . solely for the story it tells in narrative and beautiful song, it is extremely touching," said Archer Winsten of the *New York Post*.

REFERENCES

Babington, Bruce, and Peter William Evans, *Blue Skies and Silver Linings: Aspects of the Hollywood Musical* (Manchester, U.K.: Manchester University Press, 1985); Druxman, Michael B., *The Musical: From Broadway to Hollywood* (New York: A.S. Barnes, 1980); Ganzl, Kurt, *The Encyclopedia of Musical Theatre* (New York: Schirmer, 1994); Green, Stanley, *The Rodgers and Hammerstein Story* (New York: John Day, 1963); Hammerstein, Oscar II, "Turns on a Carousel," *The New York Times*, April 15, 1945; Kennedy, Michael Patrick, *Musicals* (Glasgow: HarperCollins, 1997); Mordden, Ethan, *Rodgers and Hammerstein*, (New York: Harry N. Abrams, 1992); *Richard Rodgers Fact Book* (New York: Lynn Farnol Group, 1968).

—*S.L.Y.*

A CHORUS LINE (1975)

LYRICS: EDWARD KLEBAN (1939–1987)
MUSIC: MARVIN HAMLISCH (1944–   )
BOOK: JAMES KIRKWOOD (1930–1989) AND NICHOLAS DANTE (1941–1991), FROM A CONCEPT BY MICHAEL BENNETT (1943–1987)

A Chorus Line (1985), U.S.A., directed by Richard Attenborough, adapted by Arnold Schulman; Embassy/Polygram.

The Play

New York, January 29, 1974. A group of dancers converge on the Nicholas Exercise Center on the Lower East Side. It is midnight. The curtain has come down on most of the shows in town for the night. The group has been called together by dancers Michon Peacock and Tony Stevens. There is talk of starting a "dancers company." There is a lot of frustration with the treatment dancers are getting now. After warm-ups and a series of dance combinations, Michael Bennett arrives with Donna McKechnie on his arm. The questions begin, the tape recorder is turned on.

A Chorus Line was the product of this historic 12-hour-long meeting of dancers talking together about their lives, their hopes, and their dreams. After more interviews and more meetings it was apparent that a show was emerging and that the show was in need of a venue. Bennett approached Joseph Papp, a logical choice as Papp's company had produced many successful experimental pieces in its long history. Bennett had no script, no music, no well-known dancers, he had only hours of taped interviews to offer to Papp as a proposal. Papp agreed. With space and backing from Papp, Bennett moved into high gear. The project evolved from collective dreams about a dancer's company into a professional off-Broadway production. Bennett wasted no time in assembling a staff to synthesize the book, write the lyrics and music, and most importantly, work out the legalities of using the interview material from the meetings. Out of the childhoods, trials, and aspirations of the group of dancers came the script for *A Chorus Line*, written by one of the group's members, Nicholas Dante. Marvin Hamlisch, winner of awards for *The Way We Were* and *The Sting*, was hired to write music, Ed Kleban for lyrics. It premiered in New York at the Public Theater on April 15, 1975, and moved to Broadway at the Shubert Theatre on July 25, 1975.

Bennett began to think about casting. Papp's theatre would pay $100.00 a week. Auditions were scheduled. Many of the dancers were stunned to discover that they were requested to audition for parts that were made from their own lives. For the dancers who were cast, the process of reading text from their own mouths was both strange and thrilling. It was odd to be auditioning with your own life story, as one dancer noted in a book by Danny Flinn: "He gave me this piece of paper to read, and here I'm reading verbatim what I had said on the tape, including the little spaces where I normally take a breath." It was also exciting for some to feel like their stories were important enough to be made into a musical. It was not so interesting or exciting for those from the original group who did not get cast.

As rehearsals progressed and the show began to take shape, Bennett tried to create situations for the dancers that would expose them to conditions and feelings he felt would be useful to the development of the story. Since Dante was working on the script, another dancer, Sammy Williams, was brought in to play the part created from Dante's life (Paul). Bennett reportedly ignored Williams at first to get him to feel what it was like to be ostracized. In another instance, Bennett faked being seriously injured to force the cast to reflect on what it might be like to be faced with the prospect of never dancing again. This was the basis for the "Alternatives" scene preceding the song "What I Did for Love." The techniques Bennett employed are illustrative of popular ideas about acting in the late 1960s and '70s. Analogous to many of the ideas about trust and openness that came with the encounter group movement, were concepts of acting that involved putting your true self on stage. As in an encounter group, there was pressure for actors to reveal the core of their being in order to present performances that were real. *A Chorus Line* was a real story about real dancers sharing their innermost feelings—jazzed up and polished by a staff of professionals who knew how to make a winning product.

But this musical is not just a testimony to ideas and feelings of the 1970s. In performance, it becomes a sort of encounter for both the performers and the audience. And yet, it is not real life on stage. In the encounter that takes place between Zach and the dancers the audience is complicit, complicit in the judging of these men and women whose lives hang on the audition event, and complicit in the revealing of the dancers' personal experiences. The dancer, presented as both an especially gifted performer and an identifiable "everyman," becomes the mirror for the audience. Along with the recognition of shortcomings and life frustrations is also the hope for the fulfillment of dreams. The musical finale "One" becomes a tribute not only to the absent leading-lady but also to the chorus and, ultimately, to the audience. *A Chorus Line* became the musical that spoke to anyone who had ever put himself or herself "on the line."

The story was simple. We are at an audition for an upcoming Broadway show. The director/choreographer Zach (Robert LuPone) is auditioning dancers for the chorus. He eventually eliminates them down to a group of 20 in the hope of finding four boys and four girls who can handle not only the dancing but the singing and acting as well. His choices are pivotal to the success of the show. One of the dancers in the line is Zach's old girlfriend, Cassie (McKechnie), who has just returned to New York after trying to seek stardom in Hollywood. Things have not gone well for her in L.A. and she pleads with Zach to give her a chance back in the chorus. He is very reluctant to oblige, as they broke up when she left him to move to the coast. As the grueling audition wears on, Zach asks each of the dancers to step forward and tell him something about their past, about who they are, where they came from, and what they want in life. The result is at times a heart-wrenching exploration of personal triumphs over everything from rejection to sexual awakening. After one of the dancers falls and breaks his ankle during a routine, Zach asks them what they would do if they could not dance anymore. Their response is summed up in the very moving "What I Did for Love." Finally, the eight dancers are chosen and the rest are dismissed. The bows for the evening are perhaps the most exciting part of the show as each dancer returns, bedecked in gold and sequins to dance together in a chorus line that will go on forever and ever.

A Chorus Line became the longest-running show on Broadway, until the show was superseded by the British import *Cats*. Because the show was so successful, the profits helped to support Joseph Papp's other projects, including the free Shakespeare in the Park series, for years. It finally closed at the Shubert Theater on April 28, 1990, after 6,137 performances. On that final night, over 100 cast members returned to the stage to perform the finale. It was an ending like Broadway had never seen before.

The Film

Richard Attenborough's film version of the show was much anticipated and many young performers lobbied for auditions. As happens with most Broadway shows, no film would be made until the show closed in New York. Many thought that making a film of what is so clearly a theatrical event was pointless. Gerald Mast writes, "Although the line of masking tape absolutely separates the onstage performer from the audience observer, the mirror that reflects the audience at the show's conclusion leaps the gulf to put us onstage with the dancers. No matter how many games the plodding . . . film found to play with mirrors, it was unable to connect the onstage and offstage choruses so literally." Of course, the starring role of Zach the director was given to Hollywood box-office star Michael Douglas, and while he was a good enough actor, no one found him convincing as a Broadway director or choreographer. Moreover, much of his mystery was lost by constantly cutting away to him from the stage action. (In the stage original, the director is merely an unseen voice, a godlike presence, if you will.) Other cross-cutting techniques were equally distressing and distracting. The backstory and subsequent developments in the relationship between Cassie and Zach, for example—which emerged simply as reported action in the original play's dialogue—constantly intruded into the main action, draining it of its cumulative power. Many changes were made to the original score, taking out the entire puberty sequence "Hello Twelve," for something more suitable to the virginal ears of middle-class America. Cassie's big number, "The Music and the Mirror," was replaced with something far inferior to the original. In the end, the film should probably never have been made. There is a current trend to film stage versions of current Broadway shows. Stephen Sondheim has been documenting his shows ever sense the live video performance of *Sweeney Todd* starring Angela Lansbury was released to critical acclaim. Perhaps *A Chorus Line* may one day be filmed in this manner. Until then, it will need to live in live performances across the country.

REFERENCES

Flinn, Denny Martin, *What They Did for Love: The Untold Story Behind the Making of A Chorus Line* (New York: Bantam Books, 1989); Kennedy, Michael Patrick, and John Muir, *Musicals* (Glasgow: HarperCollins Publishers, 1997); Mast, Gerald, *Can't Help Singin'* (Woodstock, N.Y.: Overlook Press, 1987); Suskin, Steven, *More Opening Nights on Broadway* (New York: MacMillan, 1997).

—*J.S.*

THE COCOANUTS (1929)

BOOK: GEORGE S. KAUFMAN (1889–1961), MUSIC AND LYRICS BY IRVING BERLIN (1888–1989)

The Cocoanuts (1929), U.S.A., directed by Robert Florey, adapted by George S. Kaufman and Morrie Ryskind; Paramount.

The Play

This classic Marx Brothers stage farce went through many changes as it moved from its Boston tryout to its New York premiere at the Lyric Theatre on December 8, 1925. As historian David Ewen notes, "any resemblance of dialogue and plot to the original concept of the authors is purely coincidental." The action of the Kaufman-Ryskind-Berlin Broadway hit is set in Florida during the real estate boom of the 1920s. Henry W. Schlemmer (Groucho) is in charge of the Hotel de Cocoanut, whose only paying guest is the wealthy and haughty Mrs. Potter (Margaret Dumont). Naturally, she is the target of fortune hunters, including Schlemmer himself. Meanwhile, the conventional love story asks the questions: Will Polly Potter marry Bob Adams, and will Mrs. Potter's stolen necklace ever be recovered? Among the songs by Irving Berlin were "A Little Bungalow," "We Should Care," and "Monkey Doodle Doo."

The Film

The coming of sound brought a throng of vaudevillians and revue stars to the movies. Hollywood invested heavily in the assumption that New York–style entertainment could be marketed to mass audiences. Paramount's Astoria Studios, located in Queens (just a short subway ride away from Broadway), became a mecca for this influx of stage talent. The physical antics and verbal pyrotechnics of the Brothers seemed ready-made for a talking picture, and Paramount chose *Cocoanuts* for its first musical comedy talkie. During the four-week shoot in the autumn of 1929 the Brothers found themselves doing double-duty—performing *Cocoanuts* at Astoria before the cameras by day and playing their newest show, *Animal Crackers*, on Broadway by night. Stage director Joseph Santley collaborated with film director Robert Florey to produce what historians Paul D. Zimmerman and Burt Goldblatt have described as "the best record we have of [the Marxes] vaudeville style," a record of the brothers "at the height of their stage art rather than [at] their film beginnings." Joining the Brothers from the original stage cast was Margaret Dumont, who would remain with them as their perennial foil in the years to come. Two songs from the original score were retained, "Florida by the Sea" and "Monkey Doodle Doo"; and Berlin contributed a new song, "When My Dreams Come True," as the movie's recurring theme.

Rarely do the results seem anything but a canned stage performance: Played out against painted flats and shallow-depth playing spaces, interminable monologues alternate with static tableaux and an occasional song and/or dance number. Yet, just as they had done on stage, the Brothers unleash such furious energy that they triumph over the otherwise mediocre material. It is also worth noting that one dance number introduces a uniquely cinematic device: Cameraman George Folsey shot the sequence looking *straight down* from the rafters. "It is this brief moment," says historian Miles Kreuger, "that marks the emancipation of the screen musical from its theatrical roots; for the first time the camera offered the moviegoer a new perspective on a theatrical event." It would soon be imitated and brought to perfection by a newcomer on the scene—Busby Berkeley. As historian Henry Jenkins notes, delighted viewers at the time cared little about the plots to gag-oriented pictures like *The Cocoanuts*, "rather, they went to see a succession of performances by the Marx Brothers—a series of gags, jokes, wisecracks, and other comic bits—that gain minimal coherence by being attached to a flat and predictable plot. Critics who admired them praised their inventiveness and the subversiveness of their gags while those who disliked them emphasized the gags' poor integration into the plot or argued that constant disruptions and

interruptions made it impossible to follow the narrative."

REFERENCES

Ewen, David, *The Complete Book of the American Musical Theater* (New York: Holt, Rinehart and Winston, 1970); Jenkins, Henry, *What Made Pistachio Nuts? Early Sound Comedy and the Vaudeville Aesthetic* (New York: Columbia University Press, 1992); Tibbetts, John C., *The American Theatrical Film* (Bowling Green, Ohio: Popular Press, 1985); Zimmerman, Paul D., and Burt Goldblatt, *The Marx Brothers at the Movies* (New York: Putnam's, 1968).

—*J.C.T.*

DAMN YANKEES (1955)

MUSIC AND LYRICS: RICHARD ADLER (1921–) AND JERRY ROSS (1926–1955)

BOOK: GEORGE ABBOTT (1887–1999) AND DOUGLAS WALLOP (1920–1985)

Damn Yankees [Whatever Lola Wants] (1958), U.S.A., directed by Stanley Donen and George Abbott, adapted by George Abbott; Warner Bros.

The Play

"As shiny as a new baseball and almost as smooth" wrote Lewis Funke in the *Times*. "The new song-and-dance sockeroo. Baseball is the great national pastime, and we predict that *Damn Yankees* will become a great national entertainment," quipped Robert Coleman in the *Daily Mirror*. Based on the novel *The Year the Yankees Lost the Pennant* and more loosely on the *Faust* legend, *Damn Yankees* is the single most successful musical centered on and around a sporting event, namely, baseball. The story revolves around Joe Boyd (Robert Shafer), a die-hard Washington Senators fan who for six months out of every year ignores his wife Meg (Shannon Bolin) while he glues himself to the television. In a moment of weakness, Joe states that he would "sell his soul" for the chance to help the Senators win the pennant for once. Enter Mr. Applegate—

Ray Walston, aka the devil. (Notice the clever name, "apple" to signify that nasty biblical temptation fruit and "gate" to signify the gates that Adam and Eve walked out of after being expelled from the Garden of Eden.) Applegate successfully gets Joe to sell his soul, but not before he agrees to an escape clause, Joe being a pretty good salesman himself. If Joe wants out, he has until September 24 to do so. What he finds out, of course, is that the race for the pennant does not end until September 25. Nevertheless, Joe Boyd is transformed into handsome young Joe Hardy (Stephen Douglass) and proceeds to give the Senators their first winning streak in decades.

But Joe is getting restless and misses his wife so he moves back into his old home as a boarder. To alleviate the situation and the potential danger of Joe using his escape clause, Applegate enlists the aid of the temptress Lola (Gwen Verdon) to steer young Joe Hardy away from his long-suffering wife. But Lola fails to tempt Joe away, and Applegate is about to run out of time and ideas. As the baseball season closes, Applegate plants two rumors to ensure his control over Joe. One is that Joe is secretly having an affair with his landlady (really his wife), and he is forced to move out. The second is that Joe is really "Shifty McCoy," the Mexican baseball player who took bribes to throw a number of games. But despite the use of every trick in Applegate's evil book, Joe successfully helps the Senators to win the pennant and returns to the arms of his loving wife.

The musical opened on May 5, 1955, and ran for 1,019 performances. Critics like William Hawkins especially enjoyed Gwen Verdon's "seductive, impertinent, subtle, luscious, and talented" performance. It won the Tony awards for best musical, for its composer and lyricist, for libretto, choreography, best actor (Ray Walston), best actress (Gwen Verdon), best supporting actor (Russ Brown), and musical director. *Damn Yankees* was successfully revived (and only marginally rewritten) on Broadway in 1994, starring Victor Garber as Mr. Applegate and Bebe Neuwirth as Lola (Jerry Lewis stepped into the cast later as Applegate). The writing team of Richard Adler and Jerry Ross, who also gave us the wonderful *Pajama Game*, another musical about America's working class, was tragically cut short when Ross died at a young age.

The Film

What had worked on stage fell somewhat flat on the screen. Most of the original cast reprised their roles, but while they may have been mesmerizing on stage, both Walston and Verdon shamelessly mugged for the screen. Ironically, it is Tab Hunter, the one true movie star in the picture, who seems to know what he is doing. "Hunter had amassed a teenaged following after a spate of action and romantic melodramas," writes Donen biographer Joseph Casper; "and it was argued he would sell tickets. In this career switch Hunter brings presence to the part, and his playing is a right blend of ingenuousness and confusion, nervous earnestness and energy." Although Hunter's Joe Hardy is sweetly charming, his singing was inadequate and parts of his role were dubbed.

Always fascinated by the screen's potential for technical wizardry, director Stanley Donen opened the film with a split-screen sequence for the song "Six Months Out of Every Year." He also staged "Shoeless Joe from Hannibal Mo" in an elaborate 30-shot montage of steadily accelerating tempo. Bob Fosse's choreography, on the other hand, looks like it belongs more on the stage than on a baseball field. The one number that is a choreographic standout is "Who's Got the Pain," danced by Gwen Verdon and Bob Fosse. It actually takes place *on a stage*. Indeed, the whole film looks as if it were done on a shoestring budget, and the baseball sequences seem stinted and lack the necessary excitement and tension. Nonetheless, the film is worth a look if only for a chance to sample how Gwen Verdon's Lola must have come off onstage, particularly in the show-stopping "Whatever Lola Wants, Lola Gets."

REFERENCES

Casper, Joseph Andrew, *Stanley Donen* (Metuchen, N.J.: Scarecrow Press, 1983); Kennedy, Michael Patrick, and John Muir, *Musicals* (Glasgow: HarperCollins, 1997); Mast, Gerald, *Can't Help Singin'* (Woodstock, N.Y.: Overlook Press, 1987); Suskin, Steven, *Opening Night on Broadway* (New York: Schirmer, 1990).

—*J.S.*

EVERGREEN

See *EVER GREEN*

EVER GREEN (1931)

MUSIC AND LYRICS: RICHARD RODGERS (1902–1979)
AND LORENZ HART (1895–1943)
BOOK: BENN LEVY (1900–1974)

Evergreen (1934), U.K., directed by Victor Saville, adapted by Emlyn Williams and Marjorie Gaffney; Gaumont-British.

The Play

References to the stage musical, *Ever Green*, and its film adaptation, *Evergreen*, are conspicuously absent in most histories of the musical theatre of the 1930s. This is most unfortunate. If the play is today only a footnote in the careers of the songwriting team of Richard Rodgers and Lorenz Hart, the film version wears well and, in its time, constituted the high-water mark of the British musical film and launched the international celebrity of the redoubtable Jessie Matthews. In 1931 young Matthews, a singer/dancer just out of the chorus and coming into her own, was under contract to C. B. Cochran, a revue producer. Cochran had just

commissioned Rodgers and Hart to write a musical show to premiere in London. It told the story of a young stage aspirant who takes on the guise of her late mother—who had mysteriously left the stage 20 years before and vanished without a trace—in order to make a splash on the London stage. When the news breaks about the girl's ruse, she confronts her audience, doffs her granny clothes, and proclaims her true identity.

In her memoirs, Matthews writes at length about the preparation of the show, and she remembers that Richard Rodgers was difficult to work with. They argued, for example, about the proper interpretation of the show's hit song, "Dancing on the Ceiling." It had been written originally for a Ziegfeld show, *Simple Simon*, starring Ed Wynn, but had been discarded. Now, in its new incarnation, it would soon create a sensation on both sides of the Atlantic and become a Rodgers and Hart standard. Insisting on an impassioned interpretation, instead of the coy delicacy Rodgers demanded, she auditioned the song with characteristic verve:

> He dances overhead, on the ceiling near my
>   bed,
> In my sight, through the night.
> I try to hide in vain, underneath my counter-
>   pane,
> There's my love, up above.

Inevitably, she says, she had to bow to the dictates of Rodgers and his colleagues: "Of course I knew I must do as they said in the end. *Ever Green* was their creation and even if I thought the storyline was corny and the character a mess, I was paid to play it." The song garnered a measure of notoriety when Matthews brought it to the stage. Required to wear filmy chiffon pajamas and a flesh-colored silk leotard underneath, she was shocked when she learned that the lights cut straight through the lining, to the obvious delight of the male audience members. She took corrective measures immediately.

Ever Green premiered at the Adelphi Theatre to an enthusiastic public and press. "The most lavish and sumptuous production Cochran ever put on the British stage," gushed one critic. "Theatrical history was made last night," wrote another. The reality was that the show was regarded as something of an oddball production, and it never made the transition across the Atlantic to Broadway.

The Film

While performing in the stage version of *Ever Green*, Jessie Matthews began to eye the movie medium. Although her first two experiences in films with director Albert Pierre de Courville (*Out of the Blue* and *Here Comes the Bride*) proved to be frustrating—she found him tyrannical and bullying—her next projects, *Waltzes from Vienna* (1933) for Alfred Hitchcock and *The Good Companions* for Victor Saville, were more encouraging. It was Saville, the one British director whose musicals rivaled at the time the work of René Clair in France and Ernst Lubitsch in America, who would go on to direct her best musical films, including the gem of them all, *Evergreen*. Joining the ensemble was cinematographer Glen MacWilliams, an American who had come to England to make Hitchcock's *Waltzes in Vienna*. His role in the picture and in Matthews's subsequent films cannot be overestimated. The ever-temperamental Matthews had complained that the lighting used in her first films was unflattering. By her own account, MacWilliams devised a new technique that saved the day: "He looked at me and said, 'Anybody who says they can't photograph you, baby, is alibi-ing their own damn bad photography!'" He adjusted her makeup and employed baby spots to bring out her eyes. The results were magical. "I wouldn't move in any film after that, unless I had Glen MacWilliams as my photographer," Matthews recalled.

While it was a foregone conclusion that Matthews would reprise on film her role of Harriet Green, the selection of a leading man to play the character of publicist Tommy Thompson was a different matter. Initially, Fred Astaire seemed the perfect choice. He was currently playing at the Palace in London, and his new musical film, *Flying Down to Rio*, had just opened. But RKO in Hollywood rejected the offer, ordering Astaire home to begin shooting *The Gay Divorcee* (ironically, he would return to England in 1937 to make *Damsel in Distress*). The role went instead to a handsome newcomer, Barry Mackay. Another key role, the hard-driving show director, went to Sonnie Hale, Matthews' husband. Meanwhile, Harry Woods was called in to supplement the Rodgers and Hart score—with their permission, of course—with additional songs. To Woods goes the everlasting credit for concocting the show-stopping number that was to become Matthews' signature song (and the title of her autobiography), "Over My Shoulder." Director Saville had felt that a new number was needed for the denouement, wherein the heroine reveals to the audience that she is not her mother but a young and attractive girl. "Over My Shoulder" gave Matthews the opportunity to punch up the scene by tearing off her "granny" clothes and appearing, as if newborn, half-naked before her stunned audience. Another of Woods's contributions was "When You've Got a Little Springtime in Your Heart," which not only was performed by Matthews three times in the film, but was also showcased in an elaborate dance number and in the ongoing background score.

The action begins with a prologue, "YESTERDAY." It is 1909 and Harriet Green is concluding her farewell performance at the Tivoli Music Hall with her popular ditty, "Daddy Wouldn't Buy Me a Bow-Wow." After a post-show farewell party, Harriet is accosted by a man claiming to be her former husband (Hartley Power) and the father of her baby daughter. He threatens to spill these secrets to the public unless she submits to blackmail. She refuses. Defiantly declaring she will go away and live her own life, she departs, leaving the child in the care of her maid. The scene now shifts to "TODAY," 24 years later. A brief montage of shots of modern London concludes with a view of the facade of the Adelphi Theatre (the site of the real-life production of *Ever Green*). A young lady, on the point of fainting from hunger, enters the theatre looking for a part in the new show. She is immediately recognized by a middle-aged actress as "Harrriet Green"—or, as the girl hastens to correct her, the *daughter* of Harriet Green.

Publicist Tommy Thompson (Barry Mackay), who has been looking for a publicity "stunt," looks on and hits upon a scheme to present her as the *real* Harriet Green returned from a long retirement. He brings stage director Leslie Benn to see her. For a few moments, as she sings "When You've Got a Little

Springtime in Your Heart," Benn is fooled into thinking she is Harriet Green. Convinced that Thompson's scheme can succeed, Benn agrees to bill the girl in his new show as "Harriet Green, Sixty-Years Young, Out of Retirement." (Indeed, so convincing is she as her mother—now wearing a white wig—that she even gulls her mother's former beau.) The show premieres and creates a sensation. In her new incarnation, Harriet falls in love with Thompson; but she has to pass him off as her son in order to forestall the certain gossip that would attend a seemingly older woman going about with a younger man. All seems well until the real Harriet Green's former husband shows up again, this time with fresh plans to blackmail young Harriet. Sick of the impersonation, heedless of the punishment sure to attend her larceny, and anxious to declare her love for Thompson, Harriet now displays the fierce independence she has inherited from her mother. She impulsively runs on stage and, like a veritable whirlwind, scatters the dancers. As she spins and gyrates to the music of "Over My Shoulder," she strips off her bonnet and skirt. She tears off her white wig and defiantly shakes loose her dark hair. Everyone on stage and in the audience recoils in shock. Harriet stops, then, uncertainly. "Now you know what I've been wanting to tell you for weeks," she laughs bitterly. "A woman of sixty. . . ." Her mocking laughter trails off on the verge of hysteria.

The audience begins to jeer and catcall, angry their beloved "Harriet Green" is a fraud. The curtain falls. To the rescue comes Leslie Benn who steps forward to address the outraged audience. He admits the hoax and appeals to "the sporting English public" to forgive him and Harriet. Harriet reappears and everyone bursts into spontaneous applause. In a clever scene transition, a close-up of the stage spotlight dissolves into the high window of an English courtroom. Now on trial for larceny, Harriet's case looks bad until her lawyer hits upon a clever scheme. In order to prove that Harriet is indeed the rightful daughter of the late Harriet Green—that she is, in effect, *Harriet Green*—he cranks up a phonograph of one of the late actress' recordings. One more time we hear "When You've Got a Little Springtime in Your Heart"; and after a few moments, young Harriet blends her voice with her mother's. It's a perfect duet. There's not a dry eye in the courtroom. The case is won. In the epilogue, the entire cast comes onstage to sing a reprise of "Over My Shoulder."

Evergreen is an important British musical for several reasons, not the least of which is the fact that it was the first musical to be a hit not just in England but also in America, granting the Gaumont-British studio an important foothold in America. As a result, MGM flourished a tempting contract before Matthews's eyes. But Gaumont-British said no. Just as Astaire had been forbidden to appear in England, so now was Matthews not allowed to make a movie in America (indeed, all her subsequent films, including *It's Love Again* and *Sailing Along*, were British-made). *Evergreen* also displays a fascinating blend of English music hall stylings with the more brash chorus numbers and precision routines of Hollywood musicals, especially *42nd Street* and *Gold Diggers of 1933*. This is most apparent in the numbers staged by Buddy Bradley, like the precision tap dancing of "Tinkle, Tinkle," which Leslie Benn rehearses with his chorus, and the climactic "Over My Shoulder" number, whose dancers rather clumsily attempt to imitate the style of a Busby Berkeley routine.

Defying description is the most ambitious of the production numbers, titled simply "Springtime in Your Heart." It is nothing less than a history of popular dance, backtracking in increments of 10 years, from 1934 to 1924 to 1914 and finally 1904. Each segment, demarcated by a spinning hourglass, presents a variant on "When You've Got a Little Springtime in Your Heart," first as a ballad sung by Harriet, then as a Charleston dance, a percussive war chant, and finally a polka and quadrille danced by the entire company. Strangest of the episodes in this sequence is the 1914 number, with its weirdly garbed chorines in futuristic robot-like costumes moving through a mechanistic assembly line straight out of Fritz Lang's *Metropolis*.

Overall, *Evergreen* achieves a successful balance and integration of song, dance, and story rare in any musical film, before or since. The delicious "Dear, Dear, This Is Much Too Nice," one of the original Rodgers and Hart tunes, is casually tossed off in a wonderful impromptu rehearsal sequence with Matthews and Mackay. So disarming is the interplay of dialogue and song, accompanied by a "pick-up" combo of piano and trumpet, that its charm and intimacy remain fresh after more than 66 years. Strains from that number bleed over into the subsequent "Dancing on the Ceiling" sequence—to many, the highlight not just of this film but of the entire oeuvre of the British musical film. A self-contained romantic story in itself, it begins with an elaborate series of cross-cuts as Harriet and Thompson, alone in their huge mansion and forced to continue their "roles" as mother and son, prepare separately for bed. Unable to sleep, Harriet comes back downstairs and sits at the piano to sing a couple of verses of "Dancing on the Ceiling." The orchestral backup continues as she moves away from the piano and leans into a graceful stride, then a balletic glide, then a full-bodied dance routine that steadily mounts in intensity as she moves from room to room, up the staircase, then finally into her bed. Matthews's lithe body and high kicks make the routine into a wordless soliloquy of love and yearning. Hollywood never did anything better.

REFERENCES

Kobal, John, *Gotta Sing Gotta Dance* (London: Spring Books, 1988); Matthews, Jessie, *Over My Shoulder: An Autobiography* (New Rochelle, N.Y.: Arlington House, 1974); Tibbetts, John C., "Glen MacWilliams: Following the Sun with a Veteran Hollywood Cameraman," *American Classic Screen*, 3:3 (January–February 1979), 32–39.

—*J.C.T.*

EVITA (1979)

BOOK AND LYRICS: TIM RICE (1944–   )
MUSIC: ANDREW LLOYD WEBBER (1948   )

Evita (1997), U.S.A., directed by Alan Parker, screenplay by Alan Parker and Oliver Stone; Disney Studios.

The Play

A tradition that started in the 1930s was to write a hit tune for an established singer, record it, and release it before the musical in which it appeared opened on Broadway. Having some familiarity with the score, audiences would thus feel more "at home" with the stage performance. Andrew Lloyd Webber and Tim Rice took this tradition one step further by recording entire shows before they even had a stage venue. Such was the case with *Jesus Christ Superstar* and *Evita*. Both albums were unquestionable hits, and they guaranteed an audience who wanted to see the rock operas performed live.

The "live" version of the Webber and Rice musical *Evita* opened in London at the Prince Edward Theatre on June 21, 1978, and ran for 2,900 performances. Patti Lupone scored a triumph on Broadway when the show opened the next year in New York—significantly changed to reflect more radical politics—at the Broadway Theatre on September 25, 1979.

The story, due to its political roots, is somewhat complicated. It is based on the life of Eva Duarte Perón (Evita), controversial yet world-famous wife of Argentina's Fascist dictator Juan Perón. Eva tragically died at 33. Though the two people's lives are extremely different, their treatment by Webber and Rice subjects them to history as seen through the medium of show business. Their view is that Evita was essentially a media celebrity, and should be understood in that context. The plot centers around the rags-to-riches story of Eva Duarte: from poverty and prostitution, to fame and fortune, to virtual sainthood. The show opens in a cinema in Buenos Aires where on July 26, 1952, it is announced that the first lady of Argentina, Evita, has died. She is mourned by the entire country and at the funeral we meet Che (modeled after the revolutionary Che Guevara) who, chorus-like, periodically appears to relate and comment on the story of Eva's life, and who himself has a love/hate relationship with Eva. We then travel backward in time to when Eva Perón was Eva Duarte, a 15-year-old prostitute who attaches herself to the tango singer Magaldi. She gains some success as an actress, mostly on radio. Years later, she meets the politician Juan Perón and proceeds to become his mistress, eliminating his former mistress of 16 years. She quickly marries Perón and pushes his political ambitions even further than he thought possible. In 1946, Perón makes a bid for the presidency of Argentina and wins.

Eva becomes Perón's propaganda machine, a mouthpiece to the working classes and the poor of Argentina. She tells them of Perón's (and hers) plan to tax (i.e., rob) the rich and give to the poor, much like Robin Hood. She becomes extremely popular in her own land, but her ambitions are great; she wants to be known worldwide. She embarks on a "Rainbow Tour" of the world, as Argentina's official ambassador and even has a meeting with the pope (Argentina is predominantly and faithfully Catholic). Though snubbed by many, she nonetheless returns triumphantly to Argentina and creates the Eva Perón Foundation for the poor. Still wanting more, she asks her husband to make her vice president, but for political reasons he is unable to oblige. In the meantime, Eva falls ill. She goes on the radio to turn down the vice presidency, which was never offered to her in the first place, and sings the now-famous "Don't Cry for Me Argentina," displaying her mesmeric hold over her people. Soon after, she dies, having accomplished her greatest goal, wanting to be remembered.

Despite mixed reviews from the critics, it was extremely popular with the public and ran for 1,568 performances, winning the Tony Awards for best musical, best director (Harold Prince), best featured actor (Mandy Patinkin), and best actress (Lupone, a breakout role). Clive Barnes wrote in the *New York Post*, "The performances are etched in the blood of expertise, and the masterly ingenuity of the staging will deservedly become a classic Broadway memory."

Alan Parker's Evita *starred Madonna as Eva Perón.* (COURTESY CINERGI PICTURES ENTERTAINMENT)

The Film

It took 20 years for the film adaptation to be made, which in itself is ironic since the subject is so attuned to "Hollywood." After all, the story offers passion, politics, glamour, conflict, and an undeniably juicy role for a female star. But filming was stalled for many complicated reasons, and by the time it was ready to be produced, Elaine Page (who originated it in London) and Patti Lupone were too old to play the role of Eva Duarte. There were also rumors that Meryl Streep, Faye Dunaway, Liza Minnelli, Michelle Pfeiffer, and even Barbra Streisand were interested in the coveted role. Pop star Madonna campaigned successfully and won the part. The casting of Latin sex symbol Antonio Banderas as Che and pop artist Madonna in the two leads was supposed to make the film of *Evita* a lucrative venture. Instead, the people who flocked to the stage play, stayed away. It is worth noting that Madonna had a fairly interesting connection to the personna of Eva Duarte. Both had similar life backgrounds. They both understood ambition, the use of sex as a powerful tool, and both had unconventional fixations on religion. But she could not necessarily translate that to her playing of the role. She did take voice lessons in order to come up to the challenges of the score, and succeeded in

almost every instance to make her voice a more rich and textured blend of emotion and intelligence. In his review in the *Chicago Sun-Times*, Roger Ebert notes "She is convincing as Evita . . . there is a certain opaque quality in Madonna's Evita; what you see is not exactly what you get."

The pivotal role of Che, the narrator of the story, was entrusted to first-time singer Antonio Banderas. Consequently, when he is singing, which is most of the time, he looks extremely uncomfortable. But he is undeniably charismatic, and his singing voice is more than adequate. In the end, he steals the movie away from both Madonna and Jonathan Pryce (as Evita's husband, General Perón). Pryce, the only cast member with significant musical theatre experience, is wasted in the film. But, as Roger Ebert has noted, "There is a quiet little scene where he knocks on [Evita's] locked bedroom door and then shuffles back to his own room; and that scene speaks volumes for the haunted look in his eyes." Unfortunately, this is the only time the camera focuses directly on Pryce's performance and Perón's emotional core.

Director Alan Parker (*Fame* and *Mississippi Burning*) is certainly up to the challenges of this enormous undertaking. No expense was spared and the production values are stunning. Madonna's wardrobe in the film is almost more opulent than that of the character she portrays, and she wears it well. The crowd scenes are appropriately large, but the camera manages to spend time on individual faces long enough to see and feel their emotional reactions to their adored St. Evita. Cinematographer Darius Khondji's images are both sharp and haunting. In the end, perhaps the general movie-going public was not interested in an all-sung rock opera. But the insertion of the occasional word of dialogue almost seems intrusive to the style of the film, and ultimately, the movie plays as a 160-minute music video.

Note: Nowadays a musical's songs are not eligible for Academy Awards if they have been previously composed and sung in another medium. Therefore, many Broadway composers write new songs for the film versions of their musicals. Following that custom, com-poser Andrew Lloyd Webber and lyricist Tim Rice, professionally separated for many years, reunited to write a new song for the score. "You Must Love Me" went on to win the Academy Award for best song, become a pop single hit for Madonna, and a very popular music video.

REFERENCES

Ganzl, Kurt, *The Encyclopedia of Musical Theatre* (New York: Schirmer, 1994); Kennedy, Michael Patrick, and John Muir, *Musicals* (Glasgow: HarperCollins, 1997); Mast, Gerald, *Can't Help Singin'* (Woodstock, N.Y.: Overlook Press, 1987); McKnight, Gerald, *Andrew Lloyd Webber: A Biography* (New York: St. Martin's Press, 1984); Ostrow, Stuart, *A Producer's Broadway Journey* (Westport, Conn.: Praeger, 1999); Suskin, Steven, *More Opening Nights on Broadway* (New York: MacMillan, 1997); Ebert, Roger, "Evita," *Chicago Sun Times*, January 1, 1997.

—*J.S.*

FIDDLER ON THE ROOF (1964)

MUSIC: JERRY BOCK (1928–)
LYRICS: SHELDON HARNICK (1924–)
BOOK: JOSEPH STEIN (1912–)

Fiddler on the Roof (1971), U.S.A., directed by Norman Jewison, adapted by Joseph Stein; United Artists and Mirisch.

The Play

Fiddler on the Roof is the story of a community of Jews who find the traditions they live by challenged in a changing world. It opened on September 22, 1964, at New York's Imperial Theatre and went on to win the New York Drama Critics Circle award and 10 Tony awards, including best musical, and was, for a time, the longest-running musical in Broadway history. *Fiddler on the Roof* is often considered the last great master-work of the American musical theatre. The universality of its themes, its seriousness, originality, and sheer artistry propelled it to international success and a special place in the heart of the public.

In 1905, in Anatevka, a village in czarist Russia, a small Jewish community works hard to keep their families together amidst poverty, prejudice, and revolutionary upheaval. The pious dairyman Tevye (Zero Mostel) and his wife Golde (Maria Karnilova) have five daughters, three of marrying age. They have arranged for Yenta (Beatrice Arthur), the matchmaker, to find a mate for their eldest, Tzeitel (Joanna Merlin). An older well-to-do butcher, Lazar Wolf, asks for Tzeitel's hand, but she has fallen in love with Motel (Austin Pendleton), the tailor. Tevye convinces his wife to accept a poor son-in-law by describing a nightmare omen. The wedding celebration is interrupted by a pogrom, an officially sanctioned ransacking of the village. Against his better judgment, Tevye consents to a marriage between his second daughter, Hovel (Julia Migenes), and a radical teacher, Perchik (Bert Convy). Perchik is arrested and sent to Siberia and Hodel soon follows him. When his third daughter, Chava, elopes with a Christian, Tevye is heartbroken and disowns her. Finally, the Jews are forced to leave Anatevka. Tevye and his family plan to join a relative in America. As they leave, a fiddler is seen playing in the street. Tevye beckons to him, and he tucks the fiddle under his arm and joins the journey.

Fiddler on the Roof is based on the stories of Yiddish writer Sholem Aleichem. Born Solomon J. Rabinowitz (1859–1916) in the Ukraine, he wrote deceptively simple tales of late-19th-century Jewish life in Russia. This stage adaptation is a testament to the original creative team's collaborative vision and skill. Joseph Stein's book manages to achieve the delicate balance of humor and pathos apparent in the original stories. The character of Tevye is infused with complex emotions, resourcefulness, and devotion to his family, an intimate relationship with his God, and a profound sense of his place in the world. The music of Jerry Bock and the lyrics of Sheldon Harnick, while breaking no new ground, are consistent in establishing themes, developing the story, expressing character, and are marked by a memorable simplicity. Boris Aronson's evocative sets and Patricia Zipprodt's realistic costumes established time, place, and ethnicity. The physical production as well as the musical's title were inspired by the paintings of Marc Chagall. The entire original production was dominated by the demanding imagination of director Jerome Robbins whose obsessive attention to thematic truth shaped an ungainly musical into a cohesive whole. The production was completed by a dynamic cast lead by the eccentrically talented Zero Mostel. The strong personalities of the cast buoyed the production above the dreariness of its main journey.

The show was greeted with generally positive reviews, with special praise for the imaginative production and exalted notices for Zero Mostel. John Chapman of the *Daily News* wrote, "[It is] one of the great works of the American musical theatre. It is darling, touching, beautiful, warm, funny, and inspiring." After praising Mostel's Tevye, the *Herald Tribune*'s critic Walter Kerr wrote, "I think it might be an altogether charming musical if only the people of Anatevka did not pause now and then to give their regards to Broadway . . . a very-near-miss, and I very much miss what it might have been." According to John McClain of the *Journal-American*: "The show has a fine folksy style, with exceptional direction by Jerome Robbins. . . . There are arid areas in the book . . . and it seemed to me there was an overabundance of self-pity displayed. But . . . the show has taste and humor and style."

The Film

With Joseph Stein transferring his script to a screenplay, the film of *Fiddler on the Roof* is remarkably faithful to the stage version. Directed by Norman Jewison with visual flair, it was filmed in Yugoslavia and at London's Pinewood Studios. The film achieves a consistent approach to a sprawling tale, balancing plot, character, and song against a sweeping landscape. The screen is filled with lively details of the community's daily life. According to Jewison, "Musical plays are indigenous to the theatre, not to film. In the theatre it is easier to accept a stylized unreal atmosphere; film introduces the real world, with real scenery and real sound. . . . In film today, it is very difficult to use music and poetry and to suspend audiences' disbelief." One of the last of

the grand, mammoth, widescreen, Technicolor movie musicals, at times the sheer size of it threatens to overwhelm the relatively straightforward storyline, and its pace slackens occasionally. Minor script adjustments serve to eliminate what can be visualized, to soften some declaratory statements, to flesh out relationships, and to finesse comic moments. The relationship between Golde and Motel is more developed. Perchik's revolutionary activities and arrest are shown. And the official sanctioning of the pogroms is made clear. There is a particularly effective sequence of Golde searching for Chava at the Russian Orthodox Church. Lazar Wolf's fancy home establishes both his high status in the community, and Tevye's low one. The songs "I Just Heard" and "Now I Have Everything" were deleted. The high points of the film match those of the stage version, particularly the Chagall-influenced nightmare, "To Life," and the wedding celebration. The film preserves Jerome Robbins's thrilling choreography. Isaac Stern lends his special gifts to the fiddler's music.

Israeli actor Chaim Topol, who played Tevye in Israel and London, was tapped for the film version. A charismatic presence, and an energetic and enthusiastic performer, his Tevye is sometimes over-performed, turning the simple dairyman into a bombastic orator. Topol is at his best in the serious moments, dealing with the weight of difficult decisions. Norma Crane's Golde tends toward a singular note of sternness. Molly Picon's matchmaker seems to have dropped in from another more lively community. Leonard Frey's Motel and Paul Mann's Lazar Wolf are particularly vivid creations. The one holdover from the original production, Zvee Scooler, has been promoted to the role of the Rabbi.

For millions of people of widely differing cultures and religions, age groups, and ethnic backgrounds, *Fiddler on the Roof*'s story of a family's struggle with persecution and poverty while trying to hold on to their beliefs struck a deeply personal chord.

REFERENCES

Altman, Richard, *The Making of a Musical: Fiddler on the Roof* (New York: Crown Publishers, 1971); Engel, Lehman, *The Making of a Musical* (New York: MacMillan, 1977); Bordman, Gerald, *American Musical Theatre* (New York: Oxford University Press, 1978); Citron, Stephen, *The Musical, From the Inside Out* (Chicago: Ivan R. Dee, 1991); Flinn, Denny Martin, *Musical!, a Grand Tour* (New York: Schirmer Books, 1997); Kennedy, Michael Patrick, and John Muir, *Musicals* (Glasgow: HarperCollins, 1997).

—D.S.G.

FINIAN'S RAINBOW (1949)

MUSIC: BURTON LANE (1912–1997)
LYRICS: E.Y. HARBURG (1898–1981)
BOOK: E.Y. HARBURG AND FRED SAIDY (1907–1982)

Finian's Rainbow (1968), U.S.A., directed by Francis Ford Coppola, adapted by E.Y. Harburg and Fred Saidy; Warner Bros.

The Play

The story is a fantasy-filled satirization of an economic system based on the burying of U.S. gold reserves at Fort Knox. With its topical bent and left-wing leanings, *Finian's Rainbow* features "politics tempered by wit, melody and [a] fundamentally sunny disposition" writes Gerald Bordman.

The mythical southern town of Rainbow Valley, Missitucky, is the setting for *Finian's Rainbow*. Finian McLonergan (Albert Sharpe) and his daughter Sharon (Ella Logan) have fled their native Glocca Mora to escape Og the leprechaun, from whom Finian has stolen a pot of gold. Og (David Wayne) has followed in pursuit of the gold, since it has the magic power to grant three wishes. Finian purchases a plot of land from sharecropper Woody Mahoney (Donald Richards), and buries the gold in hopes that it will grow. Sharon falls for Woody, and Og falls for Woody's deaf-mute sister Susan (Anita Alvarez). Og must become human, however, to have a relationship with her. This makes his search for the gold even more urgent.

The play boasts a true villain, the bigoted senator Billboard Rawkins whom Sharon, in a fit of anger, turns into a black man while she is standing over the crock of gold. Senator Rawkins is wiser and more liberal at the play's end for having had to walk a mile in another man's shoes. Woody discovers a method for growing menthol tobacco, assuring financial security for Rainbow Valley; Og becomes human; and Susan gains her hearing and speech. Since the crock has lost its magic, Finian decides to go on alone after Woody and Sharon are married. What is the moral of this story? "[That] gold is a base metal and people constitute the world's true wealth" writes critic Clive Hirschhorn.

Directed by Bretaigne Windust and choreographed by Michael Kidd, the production opened in New York at the 46th Street Theatre in January of 1947 and ran for 725 performances. It received the Donaldson Award for best musical of the season and Michael Kidd and David Wayne garnered Tony Awards.

Brooks Atkinson wrote, "*Finian's Rainbow*'s political satire and comic caprice helped to redeem Broadway from drudgery." *New York Daily News* writer John Chapman called *Finian's Rainbow* "captivating whimsy." Overall the reviews were favorable, though some critics took issue with the blatant political comments and occasional bathroom humor. "How Are Things in Glocca Mora?" "Old Devil Moon," "Look to the Rainbow," and "If This Isn't Love" enjoyed success in the world of popular music as well.

The Film

Producer Joseph Landon discussed with the *Los Angeles Times* the reasons why it took so long to adapt and produce the film. Among the contributing factors for the delay were Harburg's demand of $1 million for the film rights, and perhaps more important, the somewhat radical and racial overtones, unusual in a musical show. An animated film version of *Finian's Rainbow* was begun and the soundtrack recorded, featuring the talents of Frank Sinatra, Ella Fitzgerald, Louis Armstrong, and Judy Garland. Distributors Corporation of America ditched the project after spending $1 million. Other talents considered for a possible live-action film included Dick Van Dyke, Debbie Reynolds, Mickey Rooney, and Burt Lancaster.

Eventually Warner Brothers agreed to make the film, which starred Fred Astaire as Finian, Petula Clark as Sharon, Tommy Steele as Og, Keenan Wynn as Rawkins, Barbara Hancock as Susan, and Don Francks as Woody. So as not to let Astaire's talents go unfeatured, Harburg and Saidy adjusted the script so that the non-singing, non-dancing Finian could participate in several numbers in the film. Another difference between the stage and film versions is that the role of Howard (Woody's friend and partner) was expanded in the film for actor Al Freeman, Jr. All of the songs from the stage remained in the film with the exception of "Necessity."

Produced 21 years after it first opened on Broadway, "[t]he film couldn't decide whether is was romantic story or biting satire, and settled for neither" writes commentators Kennedy and Muir. "Its unique blend of blarney, social comment and sheer Broadway know-how was a decidedly difficult substance to capture on film and it eluded Francis Ford Coppola," writes Clive Hirschhorn. Performances by Astaire and Clark were appealing, as were wonderful visual moments such as the opening credits picturing Sharon and Finian walking across the countryside while the chorus sings "Look to the Rainbow." Coppola capitalized on his medium and deployed a savvy visual style and editing to enhance Hermes Pan's choreography. Some critics felt Steele's portrayal of Og was over the top, while others were disturbed by the imbalance of indoor and outdoor settings. *Boston After Dark* wrote, "Filming *Finian's Rainbow* in wide screen diminishes the musical rather than enlarging it and the gaiety and the underlying sadness that tugged at the corner of one's mind simply disappears under the onslaught of the movie's stupendous technology."

REFERENCES

Bordman, Gerald, *American Musical Theater: A Chronicle* (New York: Boston University Press, 1992); Druxman, Michael B., *The Musical: From Broadway to Hollywood* (South Brunswick, N.J.: A.S. Barnes, 1980); Mast, Gerald, *Can't Help Singin': The American Musical on Stage and Screen* (New York: Overlook Press, 1987); Suskin, Steven, *Opening Night on Broadway* (New York: Shirmer Books, 1990).

—L.M.F.

FUNNY GIRL (1964)

MUSIC: JULE STYNE (1905–1994)
LYRICS: BOB MERRILL (1921–1998)
BOOK: ISOBEL LENNART (1915–1971)

Funny Girl (1968), U.S.A., directed by William Wyler, adapted by Isobel Lennart; Columbia Pictures and Rastar Productions.

The Play

Based on the career and romance of the vaudeville comedienne Fanny Brice, *Funny Girl* explores the era of theatrical vaudeville and revue, circa World War I. First produced by Ray Stark to celebrate his mother-in-law's unique theatrical contributions, *Funny Girl* instantly became a star vehicle for Barbra Streisand. When it opened in New York City's Winter Garden Theatre on March 26, 1964, the oft-rewritten script could boast adverse out-of-town tryouts and a New York premiere postponed five times. Among other troubling hurdles, real-life mobster Nicky Arnstein, Fanny's great love, threatened lawsuits if treated slanderously in the show. Not only that, but the producers failed to obtain rights to any of Brice's most popular songs, including her signature, "My Man." Thus, the score's success credits Jule Styne and Bob Merrill entirely.

The curtain rises backstage at the Ziegfeld Follies as Ziegfeld is waiting to talk to his star, Fanny Brice. In flashback, Fanny recalls her rise to stardom. With teenage determination, she relentlessly practices a dance routine for her chorus girl debut. However, it is when Brice sings that her audience is entranced, as is Nicky Arnstein who congratulates—and captivates—her. Their rocky affair exploits her passion for work and his compulsion to gamble. From her colorful parody of Follies girls in "His Love Makes Me Beautiful," Fanny enjoys a collaboration with Ziegfeld that lasts throughout her career. Meanwhile, gambler Arnstein embezzles Wall St. securities and incurs an 18-month prison sentence. The flashback over, the action resumes in the present as Fanny talks about Arnstein's imminent release from prison. It is clear that despite Fanny's wish of marital bliss, their union is over.

The tale of Fanny Brice touches the prototypic dream of success. Her aspiration, spiced with comic innuendo, has universal appeal. The talented comedienne points up her decidedly ethnic characteristics as physical flaws, but fashions them to fuel her ambitions. Although buoyed by support from her mother, her community, and hoofer Eddie Ryan, it is Brice's strength of character that sustains her through her troubled romance. Styne and Merrill's refreshing music and haunting lyrics transport a slightly saccharine story to a level of pungent emotion. Their powerful score includes: "People," "Don't Rain on My Parade," and "I'm the Greatest Star."

After a rough start, *Funny Girl* resided on Broadway for 1,348 performances. The show endured three directors, four title changes, two choreographers, different producers and numerous rewrites, but was a major financial success. However, to date no revivals of *Funny Girl* have graced Broadway's stages.

The Film

The film concentrates exclusively on Fanny Brice, as if its sole intent is to be a star vehicle for Barbra Streisand. Gone are the stage version's references to the world at war, and mostly absent are allusions to Fanny's Lower East Side community. Several songs are abandoned, including the show-stopping militaristic ditty, "Rat-Tat-Tat-Tat." In fact, the 1968 film includes only seven of the original 16 songs. On the positive side, the film producers obtained rights to three Brice songs, "I'd Rather Be Blue Over You," "Second Hand Rose," and her torch song "My Man." Among the new Styne-Merrill tunes are "Roller Skate Rag" and "The Swan," both highlighting Brice's abilities as a satirist. However, the film tends to whitewash con man Nicky Arnstein, played by Omar Sharif. Kay Medford who plays Fanny's mother is underutilized, much to the film's detriment. Yet the film takes advantage of daz-zling Follies numbers, and the finale "My Man" is galvanized by Streisand's singing live to tape. All other numbers suffer from lip-synching.

Most reviewers found flaws with the film. Some thought it drawn out. "Almost every shot is held too long, every pointless scene is interminable, sometimes shots are held just to let you know the scene has come to an end," writes reviewer Renata Adler for the *New York Times*. Unfortunately, the film indulges in a garish procession of outfits and shots of Barbra in different glamour coiffeurs but never resolves the relentless self-deprecating jokes about having an imposing nose. Commentator Michael Druxman writes, "[William] Wyler, directing a musical for the first time, created in *Funny Girl* some of the most exciting sequences in memory, witness the helicopter tracking Streisand as she sang, 'Don't Rain on My Parade.'"

Funny Girl was a box office triumph, placing fourth among all movies in the 1960s. A sequel, *Funny Lady*, takes over where *Funny Girl* ends and explores Brice's marriage to Billy Rose. This was actually Brice's third marriage, but Lennart's script takes poetic license and ignores a first marriage to barber Frank White. The film *Funny Girl* won an Academy Award for best actress (Streisand) and was nominated for best picture, best supporting actress (Kay Medford), cinematography, sound, film editing, best song, and best score of a musical picture.

REFERENCES

Druxman, Michael B., *The Musical: From Broadway to Hollywood* (South Brunswick, N.J.: A.S. Barnes, 1980); Edwards, Anne, *Streisand: A Biography* (Boston: Little, Brown, 1997); Suskind, Steven, *Opening Night on Broadway: A Critical Quotebook of the Golden Era of the Musical Theatre, Oklahoma! (1943) to Fiddler on the Roof (1964)* (New York: Schirmer Books, 1990); Taylor, Theodore, *Jule: The Story of Composer Jule Styne* (New York: Random House, 1979).

—K.P.

A FUNNY THING HAPPENED ON THE WAY TO THE FORUM (1962)

MUSIC AND LYRICS: STEPHEN SONDHEIM (1930–)
BOOK: BURT SHEVELOVE (1915–1982) AND LARRY GELBART (1923–)

A Funny Thing Happened on the Way to the Forum (1966), U.S.A., directed by Richard Lester, screenplay by Frank and Michael Pertwee; MGM.

The Play

Winner of the Tony for best musical of 1962 and the most produced of all Stephen Sondheim shows, *A Funny Thing Happened on the Way to the Forum* opened at the Alvin Theatre on May 8, 1962, starring Zero Mostel as Pseudolus and ran for 964 performances. It was successfully revived in 1972 starring Phil Silvers and again in1996 starring Nathan Lane (his role being taken over by the first female and African/American Pseudolus, Whoopi Goldberg, after Lane left the show). The original received mostly favorable reviews, especially for Zero Mostel, but Sondheim was lauded more for his witty lyrics than his music and was not even nominated for any awards. In his review, Clive Barnes wrote "This is the funniest, bawdiest and most enchanting Broadway musical that Plautus, with a little help from Stephen Sondheim, Burt Shevelove and Larry Gelbart ever wrote." "You won't find anything more hilarious" wrote Robert Coleman of the *Mirror*.

The story is simple. The slave Pseudolus (Mostel) wishes to buy his freedom and sees a chance when his young master Hero (Brian Davies) falls for the courtesan next door, Philia (Peshy Marker). With his mother Domina (Ruth Kobart) and father Senex (David Burns) out of town, Hero enlists Pseudolus to find a way to buy the girl for him; if he can do it, Hero will set the slave free. What follows is organized confusion: a series of jokes, gags, mistaken identities, incest, cross-dressing, sex, and general mayhem as Pseudolus lies, cheats, steals, and connives in any way he can to achieve his freedom. Sondheim writes: "The style of the dialogue is very elegant . . . the phrasings and grace of that dialogue are better than most of the writing of the musical or nonmusical theater of the last twenty years." And the finale of the show is a chase scene beyond description. By no means incidentally, the opening number was changed many times until Jerome Robbins was brought in as a doctor. He suggested that what the show needed was a hummable opening number that told the audience exactly what they were going to see that night, a low comedy where you were encouraged to laugh from the get go. The result was perhaps one of Sondheim's most oft-produced numbers, "Comedy Tonight."

The Film

In contrast to the play, the film of *Forum* is perhaps one of the most unfunny comedies ever made. Directed by Richard Lester, who was known for his frenetic comedies, like the Beatles' *A Hard Day's Night*, the making of the film became more of a farce than the farce itself. Even Zero Mostel, re-creating his Broadway triumph, who suggested Lester as director, became disenchanted with the filming. Mostel said, "The great thing about the piece on stage was that it was one set, sixteen characters, three houses, and you did it very simply." Lester's direction was extremely busy and complicated with its arsenal of trick effects, like jump cuts, rapid editing, and variable motion speeds. Ethan Mordden writes, "applying the fast-cut wacky style he had developed for the first two Beatles films, Lester let Zero Mostel, Phil Silvers, Jack Gilford, and Michael Hordern do their stuff against a sarcastically naturalistic ancient Rome of brutality, oppression, and buzzing flies." Somehow this mix of zany comedy and harsh reality just didn't mix. Larry Gelbart admitted, "Any film in which Buster Keaton is an embarrassment says a lot for how unfunny it is." The plot was somewhat changed so the role of Lycus, played by Phil Silvers, was increased to equal Mostel's. A number of songs were cut from the score, including many solos for the leading characters: Hero's "Love, I Hear," Domina's "That Dirty Old Man," Hysterium's "I'm Calm," and Philia's "That'll Show Him," as well as the trio "Pretty Little Picture." The finale was changed to a riotous chariot race rather than a foot race.

REFERENCES

Kael, Pauline, *Kiss Kiss Bang Bang* (Boston: Little, Brown, 1968); Mordden, Ethan, *The Hollywood Musical* (New York: St. Martin's Press, 1981); Parish, James Robert, and Michael R. Pitts, *The Great Hollywood Musical Pictures* (Metuchen, N.J.: Scarecrow Press, 1992); Secrest, Meryle, *Stephen Sondheim: A Life* (New York: Alfred A. Knopf, 1998); Zadan, Craig, *Sondheim and Co.*, 2nd ed., rev. (New York: Harper and Row, 1989).

—*J.S.*

GLORIFYING THE AMERICAN GIRL (1929)

ADAPTED FROM THE ZIEGFELD FOLLIES AND PRO-
DUCED BY FLORENZ ZIEGFELD (1867–1932)

Glorifying the American Girl (1929), U.S.A., directed by
Millard Webb, adapted by J.P. McEvoy; Paramount.

The Play

No one in the history of the American theatre was
more dedicated to "glorifying the American girl" than
Florenz Ziegfeld. He was born in Chicago, where his
father ran a musical conservatory. When the elder
Ziegfeld took charge of directing musical events for
the 1893 Columbian Exposition, he sent his son to
Europe to sign up talent. Florenz used the opportunity
to hire music-hall performers and circus acts. Three
years later he produced his first Broadway show, *A
Parlor Match*, which featured his first wife, Anna Held.
Throughout the next decade Held appeared in many
Ziegfeld shows, most of which offered a chorus line of
beautiful girls. His first *Follies* was staged in 1907, and
it set the pattern for the distinctive Ziegfeld style. He
added his name to the *Follies* in 1911 and produced
them annually in New York's New Amsterdam Theatre until 1925. From 1922 on they were advertised as
"Glorifying the American Girl." After his death in
1932, the Shuberts continued to produce annual editions in his name. Ziegfeld was a starmaker of the first
order. Among his discoveries were Nora Bayes, Fanny
Brice, Eddie Cantor, W.C. Fields, Marilyn Miller, Bert
Williams, and Will Rogers.

Born out of a combination of opulent exoticism and
studied elegance, the "Ziegfeld Girl" was a more "respectable" stage creation than the standard, commonplace "chorus girl." Even if she did little more than
strike "sculptural" poses and wear elaborate (and
revealing) costumes, she was an essential element in
some of the most imaginatively staged musical revues
in the history of the American musical theatre. Critic
George Jean Nathan wrote of these productions: "Out
of the vulgar leg-show, Ziegfeld has fashioned a thing
of grace and beauty, of loveliness and charm; he knows
quality and mood. He has lifted, with sensitive skill, a
thing that was mere food for smirking baldheads and
downy college boys out of its low estate and into a
thing of symmetry and bloom."

The Film

As the talking picture boom picked up steam in
1928–29, the New York–based theatre establishment
was suffering some setbacks. Roadshow productions
had declined from a high of 339 in 1900 to just 61.
Vaudeville was dying. Film industry executives saw an
opportunity to broaden their entertainment empire
and bring Broadway and vaudeville productions and

stars under their corporate control and offer them to mass audiences at popular prices. Indeed, the competition for Broadway plays became so intense that studios began financing productions in return for a reduced purchase price of their eventual screen rights. Warner Bros., Metro, and Paramount opened New York–based studios so that stage stars could work in the movies while continuing their performances on Broadway. The Paramount Astoria Studio in Queens, particularly, became a mecca for theatrical films of the period.

Florenz Ziegfeld, meanwhile, had had his eye on the movies as early as 1926. His idea to showcase his revues in a film called *Glorifying the American Girl* went through a complex gestation of more than two years before it was made at Astoria and finally released in 1929. On the one hand, it is a typical backstage musical of the period—it has been estimated that one in four of the films from the major studios at that time were musical comedies—about a young chorus girl who moves from the five-a-day circuit to success as a "Ziegfeld Girl." The "backstage" settings of musicals like this, according to historian Henry Jenkins, "allowed [producers] to reproduce or mimic established stage performances and to foreground their 'Broadwayness' as a major part of their appeal to urban consumers." *Glorifying the American Girl* conveys the essential Ziegfeld style in a weird extravaganza that is uncertainly poised between "canned theater" and "cinematic" spectacle. However, as a fascinating document of the Ziegfeld revue, it is invaluable.

After the backstage business is fairly wrapped up, the last third of the picture is entirely taken up with a mini-revue, a duplication of the 1929 stage *Follies*. It opens with a *Variety* headline, "Ziegfeld gets $25 per Ticket as Revue Opens," followed by a close-up of theatre tickets and a program brochure that flips open to reveal Ziegfeld's name and a cast list. A mock newsreel sequence depicts a radiocaster announcing an opening night gala at the Ziegfeld Theatre with attending luminaries like Ziegfeld, Billie Burke, Fanny Brice, Texas Guinan, Mayor James J. Walker, and Paramount mogul Adolph Zukor, including several lavishly staged Ziegfeld-style *tableaux vivants*, or "living pictures" (shot in two-color Technicolor)—including a nautical scene with the show girls immobilized within frames of fishnets, starfish, and sea shells; and a "butterfly" scene featuring Mary Eaton atop a high column, attended by show girls wearing giant butterfly wings. Ziegfeld stars Eddie Cantor, Rudy Vallee, and Helen Morgan also perform. The entire sequence appears to have been shot on a real proscenium stage—or its duplicate at the Astoria Studios.

Framing the action are close-ups of audience members examining the program and shots of curtains opening and closing. The stage is seen only from the audience's vantage point; and several overhead perspectives and shifts in camera angle merely serve to approximate a variety of perspectives from different seats in the house. This is not to say that there are not effective cinematic moments. The most outstanding example is the imaginative two-minute sequence that opens the picture: Superimposed over a series of titles are images of "glorified" Ziegfeld girls. Shots of women in various "domestic poses"—ironing, washing, etc.—rapidly dissolve and transform into images of dazzling show girls with fantastic headdresses and flowing gowns. Fragments of Ziegfeld songs—such as "A Pretty Girl Is Like a Melody"—blend in an aural montage on the soundtrack. In sum, as Henry Jenkins notes, "The film never lets the audience forget that they are getting glimpses of a show that others have paid considerably more to see on Broadway."

Nonetheless, the film bombed at the box office, possibly because the "backstage musical" cycle was on the wane by the time it was released. Some of today's commentators have not been kind to the film: "*Glorifying the American Girl* remains a glittery wreck," opines historian Richard Barrios, "a strange and sad fricassee of story lines and revue bits that collapses completely during its final reels."

REFERENCES

Barrios, Richard, *A Song in the Dark: The Birth of the Musical Film* (New York: Oxford University Press, 1995); Carter, Randolph, *The World of Flo Ziegfeld* (New York: Praeger, 1974); Jenkins, Henry, *What Made Pistachio Nuts? Early Sound Comedy and the Vaudeville Aesthetic* (New York: Columbia University Press, 1992); Tibbetts, John C., *The American Theatrical Film* (Bowling Green, Ohio: Popular Press, 1985).

—J.C.T.

GODSPELL (1971)

MUSIC AND LYRICS: STEPHEN SCHWARTZ (1948–)
BOOK: JOHN-MICHAEL TEBELAK, BASED ON THE GOSPEL ACCORDING TO ST. MATTHEW

Godspell (1973), U.S.A., directed by David Greene, adapted by David Greene and John-Michael Tebelak; Columbia.

The Play

The stage musical *Godspell* has had a rich and varied history worldwide. The show began as a class project for John-Michael Tebelak while attending Carnegie Tech. It was first presented professionally in New York at Ellen Stewart's experimental haven, La Mama E.T.C. Music was added to the script by Stephen Schwartz (who went on to write music and lyrics for *Pippin*, *The Magic Show*, and *Children of Eden*) and the show had a very successful off-Broadway run (2,651 performances) at the Cherry Lane Theater. Before officially opening on Broadway at the Broadhurst Theater on June 22, 1976, the show had a number of successful national and international productions and was translated into many languages, including German, French, Spanish, Danish, and Swedish. Of note is the very successful London version of the show, which ran for 1,128 performances at the Wyndham Theatre and starred such now notable British actors as Jeremy Irons, Robert Lindsay, Julie Covington, and pop and film star David Essex.

Based on the life of Jesus according to the Gospel of St. Matthew (but really Mark, Luke, and John as well), the show is a modern retelling of the adult life of Jesus. The show begins with a rather complex musical round called "The Tower of Babble" (often cut from the show, but really the most interesting piece musically and lyrically in the entire score), where a number of philosophers (really young men and women posing as them) meet to disagree about the existence of God and the meaning of religion in their lives and the life of man. The list of philosophers includes Socrates, Leonardo Da Vinci, Martin Luther, Sir Isaac Newton, Nietzsche, Jean-Paul Sartre, Gibbon, and Buckminster Fuller. As the argument gets heated, from a distance they hear the sound of a horn. A stranger appears and baptizes them and then relays to them a speech of hellfire and brimstone. In walks a young man dressed in a Superman T-shirt and looking very much like a clown. He also wishes to be baptized. He begins to teach the other young members of the now-formed performing troupe about God and love. His message is simple, love one another and do unto others what you would have them do unto you. But the manner in which this message is delivered is far different from the writings in the Bible. Jesus' parables are reenacted by the young troupe through a mixture of pop-culture styles of the 1960s, including parodies of comic strips, television shows, circus, and children's theatre techniques. The second act shifts the focus somewhat from the more playful antics of the first, as the leader, now called "master," takes on a more active performance of Jesus' life. He confronts the Pharisees, storms the temple, and is ultimately crucified. As his loyal followers carry the body out high above their heads, they sing once again the cry "Prepare Ye the Way of the Lord/Long Live God." But the show is not over until the actors come out to take their bows, including the actor who played Jesus, as a metaphor for the Resurrection, singing the popular favorite from the score "Day by Day."

The original setting for the show was the back of a schoolyard, surrounded by a chain metal fence that the character of Jesus was tied to during the crucifixion. The score was a mixture of pop-rock, rock, and country and western tunes. Gerald Mast, in his book *Can't Help Singin'*, makes a distinction between the composer Steven Schwartz and others of his generation: "Successful rock composers, attracted by the prestigious idea of Broadway, want a hit there. But . . . conscientious craftsmanship for the musical theater requires a specific commitment to musical theater. Steven Schwartz . . . is the rare exception who combines rock sounds and rhythms, traditional American song structures, and a commitment to theater."

The Film

Gleaming photography and a very charming and clever opening sequence save this film from becoming yet another Hollywood version of a stage musical. There are no stars in the cast, and a number of original cast members from the Cherry Lane Theater production reprise their roles. Victor Garber, who would go on to achieve fame in a number of hits on Broadway, was cast as Jesus. The tone of the film is gentle and quiet. A new song was added to the score, "Beautiful City," which does not add or detract from the story. The movie was set in New York where a number of professional looking young people, all in working attire, converge on the outskirts of the city to band together for a sort of hippie group retreat. At the end of the film, they cross the bridge back into the city, carrying the now dead body of Victor Garber. There is a wonderfully metaphoric moment during the crucifixion when the police (or establishment) show up and light the body with the headlights from their cars. It is a wonderful juxtaposition of ancient and modern allusions. Perhaps owing to its unconventional mode and its lack of star power, the reviews were generally mildly favorable, at best.

REFERENCES

Ganzl, Kurt, *The Encyclopedia of Musical Theatre* (New York: Schirmer, 1994); Kennedy, Michael Patrick, and John Muir,

Musicals (Glasgow: HarperCollins, 1997); Kinnard, Roy, and Tim Davis, *Divine Images: A History of Jesus on the Screen* (New York: Carol Publishing Group, 1992); Mast, Gerald, *Can't Help Singin'* (Woodstock, N.Y.: Overlook Press, 1987); Suskin, Steven, *More Opening Nights on Broadway* (New York: MacMillan, 1997).

—*J.S.*

GREASE (1972)

BOOK, MUSIC AND LYRICS: JIM JACOBS AND WARREN CASEY (D. 1988)

Grease (1978), U.S.A., directed by Randal Kleiser, adapted by Alan Carr and Bronte Woodard; Paramount.

The Play

Billed as "the new 1950's rock 'n' roll musical," *Grease* opened at the Eden Theatre in New York on February 14, 1972, and moved to the Broadhurst Theatre on June 7, 1972. The title referred to the grease that young men used in their hair to slick it back or sculpt it into "duck tails." The story centers around Danny Zuko (Barry Bostwick), the leader of the Burger Palace Boys at Rydell High School. Danny spent the previous summer holding hands with the squeaky-clean Sandy Dumbrowski (Carole Demas). It is now the first day of the new school year and unbeknownst to Danny, Sandy has transferred to his school. He brags of the adventure he had with the cool chick who "put out" for him over the summer; simultaneously, on a split stage, Sandy tells the girls of the sweet and gentle boy she met and fell in love with over summer vacation. When the two of them meet in the schoolyard, Danny, not wanting to look like a wimp in front of all his friends, snubs Sandy until he can meet and talk to her later. Sandy is hurt by his behavior and refuses to talk to him.

The rest of the show is a series of scenes where Danny and Sandy try to work things out and get back together. She is thought of as un-cool by his friends, especially Rizzo (Adrienne Barbeau), the leader of the girls' gang, the Pink Ladies. Danny winds up taking someone else to the big school dance and Sandy stays home crying over her lack of popularity and self-confidence. Rizzo continues to mock Sandy throughout the course of the play, until she discovers that she has missed her period after having sex with her boyfriend, Kenickie (Timothy Meyers). Danny and Sandy go to the drive-in movie, but she leaves when he gets fresh.

Danny tries to change, and joins an athletic team, but he can't take the ribbing from his friends, and in the end drops out. Sandy sees that there is only one thing to do if she is to get her man, so with the help of her friend Frenchy, a "beauty school dropout," she gets a make-over and, in skin-tight jeans, learns how to swear like the best of them. Rizzo is not pregnant after all and everyone winds up happy as they celebrate the coming graduation and life in the real world.

Bostwick was singled out for his James Dean mannerisms and struts when he had to act "cool," as well as his sincerity and vulnerability when he was alone with Sandy. Adrienne Barbeau also scored as the tough-talking Rizzo, and her ballad "There Are Worse Things I Could Do" was a bona fide show-stopper. Barbeau was the only one of the actors nominated for a Tony Award, but she lost to Linda Hopkins of the musical *Inner City*. The critics were mixed about the score. Some liked its bounce and brightness, but others found it to be monotonous and derivative.

For a time, the musical was the longest-running show in New York, second only to *The Fantasticks* off-Broadway, and closed after 3,388 performances. The show was retooled and revived in the early 1990s with additions from the film version. In order to ensure a loyal following and numerous "come backs" to the show, the producers borrowed an old Hollywood trick and cast famous television and movie stars in the roles of Rizzo and Johnny Fontaine, including Rosie O'Donnell, Brooke Shields, and Lucy Lawless (TV's *Xena: Warrior Princess*). The London production starred Richard Gere as Danny Zuko in his pre-screen-stardom days.

The Film

Just six years after the show opened on Broadway, Paramount released its movie version, which has gone on to be the single most successful filmed stage musical in history. Many of the songs from the movie hit the top of the charts, including "Summer Nights," "Greased Lightnin'," "Grease Is the Word," and "Hopelessly Devoted," the latter two written expressly for the film. The film starred John Travolta as Danny and Olivia Newton-John as Sandy. Travolta, hot off his Academy Award–nominated performance in *Saturday Night Fever*, had some musical theatre experience, having performed on stage with the Andrews Sisters in *Over Here!* He exuded charm and became a teeny-bopper idol. The part of Sandy was rewritten for Newton-John so she could use her Australian accent rather than struggle to sound like an American. This added a new dimension to the plot. Rather than Sandy conforming to peer pressure, she looks as though she is really learning how to fit in as a foreigner. Either way, the ending of the show and film is problematic: Sandy gives in and becomes Danny's ideal woman, a leather jacket, hoop-earringed, chewing gum, cigarette-smoking rebel without a cause. Other notable performances are turned in by Stockard Channing as Rizzo, Eve Arden as Principal McGee, Sid Caesar as the coach, Alice Ghostly as Mrs. Murdoch, Joan Blondell as an understanding waitress at the diner, Jeff Conaway as Kenickie, and Didi Conn as Frenchy. Frankie Avalon recorded the title song and made a special guest appearance as the "teen angel."

REFERENCES

Kennedy, Michael Patrick, and John Muir, *Musicals* (Glasgow: HarperCollins, 1997); Parish, James R., and Michael R. Pitts, *The Great Hollywood Musical Pictures* (Metuchen, N.J.: Scarecrow Press, 1992); Suskin, Steven, *More Opening Nights on Broadway* (New York: MacMillan, 1997).

—*J.S.*

GUYS AND DOLLS (1950)

MUSIC AND LYRICS: FRANK LOESSER (1910–1969)
BOOK: ABE BURROWS (1910–1985) (JO SWERLING, CREDIT PER CONTRACT BUT CONTRIBUTION); BASED ON STORIES AND CHARACTERS OF DAMON RUNYAN.

Guys and Dolls (1955), U.S.A., directed and adapted by Joseph L. Mankiewicz; Samuel Goldwyn/ MGM.

The Play

Guys and Dolls celebrates New York City in all its idiosyncratic, low-life wonders. The characters, drawn from the stories of Damon Runyan (particularly, "The Idyll of Miss Sarah Brown"), revel in their underworld milieu and disdain the conventionally moral-minded. In short, *Guys and Dolls* brought Broadway to Broadway. The mega-hit opened at the Forty-sixth Street Theatre on November 24, 1950, and ran for a spectacular 1,200 performances. Typical of the rave reviews was this notice in the *New York Post* by Richard Watts, Jr.: "*Guys and Dolls* is just what it should be to celebrate the Runyan spirit, vigorous, noisy, humorous, tough on the surface and shamelessly sentimental underneath, filled with salty characters and richly original language sacred to the memory of the Master, and a pleasure to all beholders."

Two plot lines interweave. The main intrigue concerns a bet between gamblers Sky Masterson (Robert Alda) and Nathan Detroit (Sam Levene), who runs the oldest established permanent floating crap game in New York. Needing money to rent space for a dice game, Nathan bets high-roller Masterson that Masterson cannot persuade the next doll he sees to accompany him to Havana for an evening. Enter Sarah Brown (Isabel Bigley), a beautiful but strictly virtuous Salvation Army sergeant. Ordinarily Sky might not stand a chance with the missionary, but he pledges her a dozen sinners for a critical meeting at the Salvation Army headquarters if she accompanies him. The counter-plot deals with Detroit's 14-year-old courtship with Adelaide (Vivian Blaine), who has been "waiting around for that plain little band of gold," and is a perfect foil for Masterson's Cuban excursion. Nathan is stalling on his affair with Adelaide—she, in turn, suffers psychosomatic symptoms while impatiently waiting to wed. The minor characters of this musical fable have flamboyant names and create the proper, slightly skewed urban ambience: Harry the Horse, Nicely-Nicely Johnson, Angie the Ox, Benny Southstreet, and Big Jule (likely reference to songwriter Jule Styne). These endearing mobsters retain a moral code all their own. True, they might use marked dice, but they would never welsh on a deal. Indeed, Sky is eventually converted to a more virtuous life and Nathan is wed by the persistent Adelaide. The music, in the meanwhile, was brash and romantic, by turns, including such standards as "Luck Be a Lady," "I've Never Been in Love Before," "A Bushel and a Peck," and the show-stopper, "Sit Down, You're Rockin' the Boat."

Originally, producers Cy Feuer and Ernest Martin had sought to finance a romantic musical, based on Runyan's stories, and commissioned Frank Loesser and a string of 11 librettists before they realized that a comedy was the better venue. Critics universally thought it a smash. "The Runyan milieu is rich in startling types, and *Guys and Dolls* has the most flamboyant population of any show in town," wrote Brooks Atkinson in the *New York Times*. "In all departments 'Guys and Dolls' is a perfect musical comedy," opined John Chapman of the *Daily News*. While kudos for "a superlative job" went to director George S. Kaufman, from William Hawkins of the *New York World-Telegram:* "the most startling contributions are the affectionately witty idea and musical vernacular of Frank Loesser's score, and Michael Kidd's sharply staged dances."

Guys and Dolls won the Antoinette Perry, Donaldson, and New York Drama Critics Circle awards for best musical. In addition to the 1953 London run, *Guys and Dolls* has enjoyed two full-fledged Broadway revivals. The first, in 1976, featured an all-black cast and played 239 performances. The 1992 revival, restaged under the direction of Jerry Zaks, starred Nathan Lane, Peter Gallagher, Josie de Guzman, Faith Prince, and played 1,143 shows.

The Film

A Hollywood bidding war ensued for the coveted show. Paramount owned the rights and wanted to procure the musical for Bing Crosby. MGM thought Gene Kelly ideal, while Columbia envisioned Clark Gable. However, once librettist Abe Burrows surfaced on the studio blacklist, Paramount bowed out. In the end, Samuel Goldwyn outbid all others with a stunning $1 million offer and gave the project to Oscar-winner Joseph L. Mankiewicz. Mankiewicz wrote the film's screenplay, Michael Kidd designed the choreography, and Loesser added three new songs ("Pet Me, Poppa," "Adelaide," and "A Woman in Love"), and dropped five tunes ("My Time of Day," "I've Never Been in Love Before," "A Bushel and a Peck," "More I Could Not Wish You," and "Marry the Man Today").

The film capitalizes on the caricatured elements of New York City life. Its inventive opening dance sequence immortalizes the Broadway version—as the film credits roll, riffraff pickpockets fleece the tourists and cleverly elude the police. Rather than try for photographic realism, Mankiewicz wisely chose to depict the Broadway milieu in a stylized manner—with billboards and buildings colorfully painted on a cyclorama. Sadly, logical casting in Hollywood means using box-office names, which translates into who is currently hot, not who is best for a role. While Vivian Blaine and Stubby Kaye successfully reprised their Broadway roles as Adelaide and Nicely-Nicely, it was Marlon Brando's Sky Masterson, Frank Sinatra's Nathan Detroit, and Jean Simmons's Sarah Brown who drew mixed reviews. Apparently, no one checked in advance to see if Brando could sing. He ruined take after take, and his songs ultimately were the result of the splicing together of the better portions of each recording. Mankiewicz biographer Kenneth Geist writes: "By consenting to the miscasting of Brando and Sinatra, Mankiewicz killed any chance of his *Guys and Dolls* equaling the impact of George S. Kaufman's masterful Broadway production." However, the 1955 film garnered four Oscar nominations, and was among the most financially successful films Goldwyn ever produced.

REFERENCES

Druxman, Michael B., *The Musical: From Broadway to Hollywood* (South Brunswick, N.J.: A.S. Barnes, 1980); Geist, Kenneth L., *Pictures Will Talk: The Life and Films of Joseph L. Mankiewicz* (New York: Scribner's, 1978); Loesser, Susan, *A Most Remarkable Fella: Frank Loesser and the Guys and Dolls in His Life* (New York: Donald I. Fine, 1993); Suskind, Steven, *Opening Night on Broadway: A Critical Quotebook of the Golden Era of the Musical Theatre, Oklahoma! (1943) to Fiddler on the Roof (1964)* (New York: Schirmer Books, 1990).

—K.P.

GYPSY (1959)

MUSIC: JULE STYNE (1905–)
LYRICS: STEPHEN SONDHEIM (1930–)
BOOK: ARTHUR LAURENTS (1918–) BASED ON GYPSY ROSE LEE'S AUTOBIOGRAPHY

Gypsy (1962), U.S.A., directed by Mervyn LeRoy, adapted by Leonard Spigelgass; Warner Bros.

The Play

The stage mother is always a dependable character type in any stage or movie production about the entertainment business. She has become a cliché only because there is so much truth in the caricature. Perhaps the most fabled stage mother of them all was Mama Rose, the mother of burlesque queen, Gypsy Rose Lee. Lee's autobiography *Gypsy* gave her mother a prominent and infamous place in theatre history. As commentator Scott Miller suggests, "Though Rose is a very real and believable character . . . she is truly Bigger Than Life. It is her grotesque yet captivating personality that drives this 'musical fable.' . . . Rose is a monster of mythic proportions who exploits and torments everyone around her, yet we actually *like* her for some reason."

Based on Lee's book, the musical by Arthur Laurents, Jule Styne, and Stephen Sondheim opened at the Broadway Theatre on May 21, 1959. It tells the story of Mama Rose (Ethel Merman) and her two daughters, "Baby" June (Lane Bradbury and Jacqueline Mayro) and Louise (Sandra Church) and their attempts to make a success on the vaudeville circuit. Mama Rose is obsessed with making June (who would find success on stage and film as June Havoc) the star of the biggest act in vaudeville. Convinced of her daughter's talent, Mama fixes contests, lies, and manipulates in order to get June into the spotlight. Louise, however, is largely ignored since she appears to have no talent at all. Both girls would rather their mother marry Herbie (Jack Klugman), their erstwhile agent, and settle down, forgetting the whole stage scene. June finally tires of her mother's interference and runs away with Tulsa (Paul Wallace), one of the boys in the act. Now Mama Rose, deserted by June, decides to set her sights on fame for Louise. Their act has fallen so far down the vaudeville hierarchy, however, that they find themselves booked in a burlesque house in Wichita, Kansas. There, Louise learns from the other strippers that success in their business depends on having a "gimmick." One night the star stripper is arrested and Mama sees their chance. She convinces Louise to go on in the stripper's place. Louise teases the audience by not stripping, and Louise's insouciance and innocent appearance are a huge hit. Louise has found her gimmick and Mama has found her star.

As the years pass, Louise (now Gypsy Rose Lee) becomes an even greater success, and her mother's monomaniacal tendencies become even more pronounced. Gypsy can't get rid of her, and she is ashamed of her mother's over-the-top personality. Rose is annoyed by her daughter's attitude, and the two quarrel. In the best "eleven-o-clock number" in Broadway history, Rose shows the audience what she could have done if she were the star. Imitating her daughter's strip act, Rose slowly begins to succumb to the nervous breakdown that has been threatening to occur for years. Frank Aston of the *New York World-Telegram & Sun* recorded the show-stopping moment: "To close the proceedings, Jerome Robbins puts her in a spot, with the whole stage open about her. Jo Mielziner's lamps paint changing letters against the background. And Miss Merman lets go in the best song Jule Styne and Stephen Sondheim have prepared for the evening, 'Rose's Turn.'" It is an epiphany for Louise, who watches from the wings and realizes that her mother's ambitions to be a star herself were thwarted by Rose's own mother and the circumstances of her life. Louise realizes that Mama Rose had needed to live vicariously through her daughter's success.

Directed and choreographed by Jerome Robbins, *Gypsy* contained some of the greatest of Jule Styne's compositions. With lyrics by Stephen Sondheim (a protégé of Oscar Hammerstein fresh off his success in *West Side Story*), *Gypsy* was one of the most psychologically complicated scores of its time. The songs included "Everything's Coming up Roses," "Small World," "Together," and "Rose's Turn." As Laurents finished each scene, Sondheim would bring it to Styne, who would compose the music, often without a full lyric. In his biography, Jule Styne says of Sondheim:

"Marvelous lyrics came to me from Steve. When you write with him, you actually feel good as a composer. He places value on the music, what kind of word fits each note. . . . The thought is the main thing with Steve. In most cases, I wrote the music first, and then he wrote the lyrics. Steve said that the music must set the character as well as the words." Indeed, Styne had never written this way before, and *Gypsy* is his true masterpiece, due in part to Sondheim's insistence that the song must reveal character.

As Mama Rose, Ethel Merman gave one of her greatest performances. She had insisted that Jule Styne write the music, even though Sondheim had been approached to do both music and lyrics. Merman was unsure of the young composer's ability to write well for her voice and powerhouse style: "This is not denying Steve's musical talent," said Styne, "but to write for Ethel Merman was a kind of bag he didn't know much about." As it turned out, the team of Styne and Sondheim was an unexpected success.

An interesting event on the road to dramatizing Lee's book was the attempt of producers Leland Hayward and David Merrick to get June Havoc's release for the portrayal of her character. As reported in Styne's biography, they went with Arthur Laurents to meet with her. She asked Laurents why he wanted to write a play based on her sister's book. "I find it touching," he said. "I'm touching," said June Havoc. "Not her. She's cheap. She eats out of tin cans." Havoc never did sign that release.

Gypsy was a smash hit. It ran for 702 performances and was later successfully revived in London in 1973 with Angela Lansbury. But it will be forever associated with Merman's performance. "This musical is a great deal more than a flashy accommodation for Miss Merman's grand and well-known talent for playing and singing high, wide, and handsome," wrote John Chapman of the *New York Daily News*. "It is a story—a real story, and, funny though it seems to be, a touching story. It needs more than a musical comedy star to play it; it needs an actress—and Miss Merman turns out to be just the actress. Walter Kerr of the *New York Herald Tribune* called it "the best damn musical I've seen in years. . . . *Gypsy* has one of the strongest musical comedy finishes I ever saw—and it doesn't even need it. Its generous authors have provided it with a great beginning, a great middle, and a great future."

Despite its virtues, *Gypsy* lost out on the major awards that season to *Fiorello!* and *The Sound of Music*. Ethel Merman lost the Tony Award for best actress to Mary Martin. In the 1973 London revival, Angela Lansbury's performance was hailed as brilliant, and Laurents allowed her to play on her strengths as a dramatic actress instead of forcing her into a reliance upon a singing performance. She won the *Plays and Players* Award as best actress and then won the Tony Award in 1975 when the revival came to Broadway. Many other great actresses have gone on to play the coveted role of Mama Rose, and in the early 1980s Tyne Daly made a splash on Broadway in a somewhat more sympathetic rendition of the role.

The Film

The film version of *Gypsy* was produced and directed by Mervyn LeRoy. A veteran of backstage film musicals himself (he had directed Warner Brothers' classic *Gold Diggers of 1933*), he saw the musical on Broadway and was determined to bring it to the screen. He talked Jack L. Warner into buying the rights and began to consider the casting. According to commentator Scott Miller, Freddie Brisson was responsible for the casting of Rosalind Russell as Mama Rose. Brisson, who was married to Russell, had purchased the rights to *A Majority of One* for her. He agreed to let Warner Brothers produce it if Russell could get the green light to play Rose. According to commentator Michael Druxman, Mervyn LeRoy indicated that Merman never was under serious consideration: "Ethel Merman is a great talent," [he said], "and I love her. She, of course, was dying to do the role, but we had to turn her down. No matter how big a star she is on Broadway, her name means very little at the movie box office. *Gypsy* was going to be too important a project to gamble on anything less than a major film star with a proven track record." Russell was signed and Merman joined the long, distinguished list of Broadway stars who originated roles on the stage that were denied them on film. Russell was not a singer, however, and Lisa Kirk dubbed some of her vocals. Natalie Wood gained the coveted role of Louise, Karl Malden did a turn as Herbie Sommers, and Paul Wallace re-created his role for the film. Marni Nixon did high-note singing for Wood.

While not altering the basic structure of the stage production, Mervyn LeRoy opened it up into 48 sets built especially for the film. The backstage milieu of Depression America was carefully observed, with its cramped dressing rooms, late-night deserted railroad stations, back alleys, and seedy lodging houses. "Together" was finally cut from the film because preview audiences indicated it made the picture too long.

The reviews of the picture were mixed. Although LeRoy thought that only Russell could have played Rose on screen, the audience and the critics were not kind to her performance. Ethel Merman had left too big a footprint. Whether Merman could have made the transition from stage to screen has been a subject of much debate. Michael Druxman does note that "Mama Rose is a complex character, requiring the talents of a sensitive actress in order to avoid caricature. Whether Miss Merman could have toned down her brassy personality to achieve the proper effect *on camera* is questionable." He considered Russell's performance "a truly compelling characterization." Said the *New York Times:* "That tornado of a stage mother (and perfectly abominable woman) played and sung on Broadway by Ethel Merman is little more than a big wind now in the brassy, fiercely energetic and often amusing person of Rosalind Russell . . . there are too many dull intervals when the band snoozes and Miss Russell, an unappetizing Karl Malden and young Natalie Wood, who is charming throughout, simply talk. The real fire and lubricant here is the excellent Jule Styne score, most of it intact." The popularity of the score is supported by the fact that the soundtrack appeared on *Billboard's* chart for 13 weeks, and did reach the top ten.

After Tyne Daly's acclaimed performance in the early 1990s, Barbra Streisand indicated a desire to star as Rose in a film remake with Madonna as Gypsy. The creators firmly denied permission. According to James Parish and Michael Pitts, Arthur Laurents declared, "Not for all the money in the world will we let them make another film version of *Gypsy*." Jule Styne agreed, saying, "The show was dead in stock. It took almost 30 years to offset that lousy picture." Nevertheless, *Gypsy* did come to the small screen in 1993 in a mini-series movie staring Bette Midler, which remained very faithful to the stage show. Midler's performance was well received.

REFERENCES

Druxman, Michael, *The Musical: From Broadway to Hollywood* (South Brunswick, N.J.: A.S. Barnes, 1980); Garebian, Keith, *The Making of Gypsy* (Toronto: ECW Press, 1993); Miller, Scott, *From Assassins to West Side Story* (Portsmouth, N.H.: Heineman, 1996); Parish, James Robert, and Michael R. Pitts, *The Great Hollywood Musical Pictures* (Metuchen, N.J.: Scarecrow Press, 1992); Taylor, Theodore, *Jule: The Story of Composer Jule Styne* (New York: Random House, 1979).

—*S.L.Y. AND J.S.*

HAIR (1967)

BOOK AND LYRICS: GEROME RAGNI (1930–1991) AND
JAMES RADO
MUSIC: GALT MACDERMOT (1928–)

Hair (1979), U.S.A., directed by Milos Forman,
screenplay by Michael Weller; United Artists.

The Play

The anti-establishment, hippie, tribal love-rock musical *Hair* opened at the New York Public Theater on
October 29, 1967, and subsequently transferred to the
Biltmore Theatre on April 29, 1968, for a successful
Broadway run of 1,742 performances. The critics were
unanimous in their praise for this "epochal" musical,
referring to the show as new and inventive, creative,
exciting, and revisionist theatre. As Stanley Richards
writes in his editor's notes for the play script: "*Hair*
became the archetypal musical of the sixties, the love
song of the flower-children generation." Clive Barnes
in the *New York Times* wrote that the show is "so likeable, so new, so fresh and so unassuming, even in its
pretensions. It is the first Broadway musical in some
time to have the authentic voice of today rather than
the day before yesterday."

   Set mostly in and around the East Village in New
York City, the central conflict of the plot revolves
around the military draft, specifically, the conscription
into the army of Claude (Gerome Ragni), one of the
shows three central characters. Berger is the second
major character. He is Claude's friend, the head of the
hippie tribe, and something of a counterculture hero, if
you will. The third character completes the "romantic"
triangle. Sheila (Lynn Kellogg), an NYU college student, is in love with both Berger and Claude. Berger
and Sheila are very much involved in the "protest
movement," agitating against the draft and America's
involvement in the Vietnam conflict. Claude, meanwhile, vacillates in the question of duty over principle.
Should he burn his draft card in defiance of the establishment and the war, or report and serve his country
with honor? In the end, Claude decides to be con-
scripted, doles out his possessions to his friends, and in
a final act of conformity, cuts off his hair. He joins the
army and goes off to war. Though we never find out
conclusively, it is more than likely that he will be killed.
The musical is driven more by its energy than by its
plot. The show is a pastiche of songs and sketches, a
celebration of free love, "harmony and understanding"
over hatred, violence, drugs, antiwar protests, racial
inequality, conflicts with the older generation, and of
course profane love.

   Hair has the distinction of being the first (and perhaps only, with the exception of *Oh, Calcutta!*) Broadway musical to incorporate full frontal nudity, both
male and female, into its story line. Full frontal nudity
was indeed something new. Attracted by the notoriety,
audiences flocked to the show to experience the sensa-

tionalistic "Be-In," to decide for themselves whether the nudity was gratuitous or not. "In keeping with the author's vision, [director Tom] O'Horgan saw the act as a symbolic act of freedom, honesty, and openness, a gentle defiance of another of society's taboos. People frequently took off their clothes at Be-In's. It was part of the gesture of the times," writes Barbara Lee Horn in her definitive work, *The Age of "Hair."*

The creators of *Hair*, Gerome Ragni and James Rado, were both actors before becoming playwrights, and the composer Galt MacDermot also wrote the score for *Two Gentlemen of Verona*, which went on to win the Tony Award for the best musical of 1972. The show was revived on Broadway in 1977 and directed once again by Tom O'Horgan. But times had changed and the critics were not kind. Richard Ader wrote in the *New York Times*, "nothing ages worse than graffiti. . . . *Hair* . . . is too far gone to be timely, too recently gone to be history or even nostalgia." And Douglas Watt wrote in the *New York Daily News*, "*Hair*, like long undisciplined hair for hair's sake, has gone out of style . . . at least at the moment . . . lost in a marijuana cloud as we tiptoe uncertainly through the saintly 70's." Perhaps the show had not been closed long enough (only five years before the revival opened) and needed a good long rest before taking its place as a thing of the past. Today the show is extremely popular in revivals on college campuses across the country, but most of the young performers were born long after the time when "love . . . [steered] the stars" and the show takes on more of the quality of a history lesson. The hit song from the score, "Age of Aquarius/Let the Sunshine In," was recorded by the Fifth Dimension in the early 1970s, and became one of their only hit singles. The London production ran even longer than the American, 1,997 performances. In 1988, a gala concert dinner version of the show was presented in New York at the United Nations, to mark the musical's 20th anniversary. Among the guest artists were Bea Arthur singing "Black Boys" and Dr. Ruth Westheimer playing Margaret Mead.

The Film

With the failure of the revival on Broadway, it is a wonder that the film version of *Hair* ever made it into theatres. Directed by Milos Forman, with astounding choreography by modern dancers Twyla Tharp and Kenneth Rinker, the plot was retooled somewhat for the film by screenwriter and playwright Michael Weller. First, Weller had to take out all references in the script to the story taking place in a theatre house. Second, Forman insisted on a more coherent plot with a clear line of action and a dramatic ending.

Unlike the stage play, Claude (John Savage) is a young man from the Midwest, who goes to New York to receive his induction physical (his decision to join the army has already been made). In New York, he encounters the hippies in Central Park and joins their tribe. They encourage him to seduce his lover, debutante Sheila (Beverly D'Angelo). Sheila then becomes a member of the tribe, rebelling against her proper upbringing. When Claude leaves for Nevada for basic training, the tribe chases after him, including Sheila, as they all sing "Good Morning Starshine." But there is a mix-up when Berger (Treat Williams) substitutes for Claude so he can spend his final night in the States with Sheila. Berger, rather than Claude, is sent overseas. A year later, the tribe meets at a cemetery to mourn the loss of Berger, who was killed in action. Though the ending is contrived, one element common to both the stage show and the film is the prominence of "antiwar feelings" in its characters and situation. The film even goes so far as to redirect the focus on the Vietnam War to include a protest against the coming Armageddon and nuclear war. About two-thirds of the musical's score was retained, and two songs were written specifically for the film, "Somebody to Love" and "Party Music."

REFERENCES

Babington, Bruce, and Peter William Evans, *Blue Skies and Silver Linings: Aspects of the Hollywood Musical* (Manchester, Eng.: Manchester University Press, 1985); Horn, Barbara Lee, *The Age of Hair: Evolution and Impact of Broadway's First Rock Musical* (New York: Greenwood Press, 1991); Richards, Stanley, ed., *Great Rock Musicals* (New York: Stein and Day, 1979).

—*J.S.*

HELLO, DOLLY! (1964)

MUSIC AND LYRICS: JERRY HERMAN (1932–)
BOOK: MICHAEL STEWART, BASED ON THORTON WILDER'S PLAY *THE MATCHMAKER*.

Hello, Dolly! (1969), U.S.A., directed by Gene Kelly, adapted by Ernest Lehman; Twentieth Century-Fox.

The Play

Composer/lyricist Jerry Herman's adaptation of Thornton Wilder's play *The Matchmaker* (rewritten from his earlier work *The Merchant of Yonkers*) has a longer than usual stage history. The story is based on a play by John Oxenford called *A Day Well Spent*, which was adapted from the classic Austrian farce *Einen Jux will er sich machen* by Johann Nestroy. The British playwright Tom Stoppard also wrote a version of the play, called *On the Razzle*, which was more an adaptation of Nestroy's work than of Wilder's plays. The musical, which opened at the St. James Theatre in New York on January 16, 1964, starring Carol Channing, was an instant classic. "A pot-walloping hit" declared John McClain of the *Journal-American*, "The best musical of the season" said Howard Tubman of the *New York Times*. "[It is] big, bouncing, handsome, rapidly-paced and filled with the shrewdest ingredients of successful showmanship, provid[ing] Carol Channing with a cheerfully flamboyant role," raved Richard Watts of the *Post*.

Under the expert direction and with energetic choreography by Gower Champion, the musical takes place around the turn of the 20th century and tells the story of a busy-body matchmaker's (Channing) clandestine plan of matching millionaire Horace Vandergelder (David Burns) with a new wife. Dolly sets Horace up with a pretty young Irish widow, Mrs. Irene Malloy (Eileen Brennan), as a means of getting him to New York for dinner at the Harmonia Gardens. She actually wants to marry Horace herself, and so she gets Mrs. Malloy out of the way by pairing her up with Vandergelder's chief clerk at the feed store, Cornelius Hackl (Charles Nelson Reilly), who is out on a razzle to find girls and get kissed. Along with his assistant Barnaby Tucker (Jerry Dodge) and Mrs. Malloy's cohort Minnie Fay (Sondra Lee), the two inexperienced clerks find themselves also at the Harmonia Gardens restaurant having a splendid dinner (for which they cannot pay) until they unwittingly stumble upon a purse belonging to Mr. Vandergelder. The police raid the restaurant and everyone is taken to jail. All the characters are released through Dolly's expert handling of a rather emotionally romantic judge, all, that is, except Horace, who has to spend the night in jail in order to see the error of his ways. The next morning, Horace is back at the feed store mooning over Dolly. Her plan to capture a new husband has worked and the musical ends in a series of romantic alliances between Horace and Dolly, Mrs. Malloy and Cornelius, Barnaby and Minnie Fay, and Horace's niece Ermengarde and her artist beau, Ambrose Kemper.

The musical garnered a number of awards and won the Tony and New York Drama Critics awards for best musical of the season. A copyright infringement suit was brought against Jerry Herman by Mack David, who thought his 1948 hit "Sunflower" sounded too

much like the title song "Hello, Dolly!" The case was settled out of court to the tune of $275,000 and Jerry Herman retained the rights to the song. The character of Dolly Gallagher Levi is the sole invention of Thornton Wilder and does not appear in any other version of the story but his. It is a much coveted role and has been played by everyone from Ethel Merman to Pearl Bailey (in an all-black version of the show that scored a huge success in a revival on Broadway). Many thought that Carol Channing was robbed of the film role, but to her credit she continued to play the part on stage well into her 70s.

The Film

"'She's too young for Dolly!' they screamed," writes Ethan Mordden in his book *The Hollywood Musical*. The controversy over casting Barbra Streisand as Dolly is still a bone of contention with many critics. But Hollywood needed a big name in the starring role and Ms. Streisand, though her first film, *Funny Girl*, had get to be released, was nonetheless a star on the rise. Gene Kelly found it difficult to direct the temperamental star and was unable to help her develop a clear characterization. The result was a "Dolly made up of ill-assimilated parts of Jewish wiseguy, crypto-glamour girl, and Mae West," quips Mordden. Ernest Lehman was the producer and wrote the screenplay. He retained most of the original dialogue, adding only occasional new lines more suited to Ms. Streisand's particular comedic gifts. Director Gene Kelly created a big, expansive, pictorially opulent production, which featured a $2 million re-creation of 14th Street in New York City, and a parade of thousands of gaily costumed extras. The lack of chemistry on the set between Walter Matthau and Barbra Streisand is now the stuff of legend. Though he was perfectly suited to play the part of Horace Vandergelder and turned in a brilliant performance, it is somewhat unbelievable that Streisand's Dolly was ever in love with the old curmudgeon Matthau. Kelly tried to take the characters seriously and even added a beautiful romantic ballad for Ms. Streisand, "Love Is Only Love." In this very touching scene, Mrs. Levi gets ready for her big evening on the town with Horace, while exploring in song the possibility of marrying again.

Ultimately, though, the film comes off as a mixture of acting styles and somehow doesn't quite have the vivacity and freshness of the stage show. Shirley MacLaine who had played Irene Malloy in the movie version of *The Matchmaker*, tested for the role but lost out to newcomer Marianne McAndrew (perhaps in hindsight a mistake on the part of director Gene Kelly). Other cast members included Michael Crawford as Cornelius, E.J. Peaker as Minnie Fay, and a young Tommy Tune as Ambrose Kemper, artist-turned-professional dancer. Louis Armstrong, who had earlier made a recording of the title song, was enlisted to sing a verse of it with Ms. Streisand in the film, calling to mind his earlier performance in the musical film *High Society*. It is a highlight of an otherwise dry rendition of the stage play. Most disappointing is the obvious studio singing dubbed in after the fact and the canned singing of the chorus, who are so busy dancing that Mr. Kelly forgot to tell them to move their mouths. "The Fox studio was convinced that Gene ha[d] brought forth a winner," writes Kelly biographer Michael Yudkoff, "but the box-office returns were instructive. In the era of the Vietnam War and the hippie counterculture, a sea of change was taking place. Despite the youthful admirers who had mobbed Streisand at the New York premiere, the under-thirty mass audience that year had gravitated even more to gritty realistic films such as United Artists' *Midnight Cowboy* . . . and Columbia's *Easy Rider*." Perhaps with so much going on in the world at the time, audiences were just not willing to be entertained by a piece of "fluff." Ironically, the G-rated film was nominated that year as best picture, losing out to the X-rated *Midnight Cowboy*.

REFERENCES

Druxman, Michael B., *The Musical: From Broadway to Hollywood* (South Brunswick, N.J.: A.S. Barnes, 1980); Mordden, Ethan, *The Hollywood Musical* (New York: St. Martin's Press, 1981); Suskin, Steven, *Opening Night on Broadway* (New York: Schirmer Books, 1990); Yudkoff, Alvin, *Gene Kelly: A Life of Dance and Dreams* (New York: Back Stage Books, 1999).

—*J.S.*

HOW TO SUCCEED IN BUSINESS WITHOUT REALLY TRYING (1961)

MUSIC AND LYRICS: FRANK LOESSER (1910–1969)
BOOK: ABE BURROWS (1910–1985), JACK WEINSTEIN, WILLIE GILBERT, BASED ON SHEPHERD MEAD'S BOOK.

How to Succeed in Business Without Really Trying (1967), U.S.A., directed and adapted by David Swift; United Artists/Mirisch.

The Play

The fourth musical to be awarded the Pulitzer Prize in drama, *How to Succeed in Business Without Really Trying* is based on the 1952 satirical book by Shepherd Mead, titled *How to Succeed in Business Without Really Trying: The Dastard's Guide to Fame and Fortune*. The book for the musical brought back together the writing team that scored such a huge success with *Guys and Dolls*, Abe Burrows and Frank Loesser. The show opened in New York on October 14, 1961, at the 46th Street Theatre, directed by Abe Burrows and with choreography by Bob Fosse.

The central character, J. Pierpont Finch (Robert Morse) or Ponty, is a window-washer with aspirations. He happens upon a book, *How to Succeed in Business Without Really Trying*, which is a manual for success in the corporate world. He keeps it with him through the entire show, referring to it as his bible for success. But rather than reading the book in its entirety, before embarking on the next logical step up the ladder, Ponty reads the book chapter by chapter. This will eventually get him into a pickle that becomes almost impossible to get out of, until it is discovered that the chairman of the board also began his career as a window washer.

The story begins 20 floors up; outside the corporate headquarters of the World Wide Wickets Company (appropriately named, as the company produces people caught in a series of sticky wickets). Finch, reading his trusty book, learns that in order to get on the fast track in the corporate world, you have to start at the bottom and work your way up. Thus, he gets a job in the mailroom. There he meets his archenemy, Bud Frump (Charles Nelson Reilly), nephew of the president of the company, also working his way to the top.

As instructed by his trusty bible, Finch is warned that once in the mailroom, forever in the mailroom. He befriends the head of the mailroom, is offered the job of his successor, but knowing that it is a dead-end position, he cleverly turns it down, recommending Bud instead. He quickly works his charm and lands a junior executive decision in systems and planning. There he meets up again with the pretty secretary, Rosemary (Bonnie Scott), with whom he has fallen in love earlier in the show.

Rosemary is frustrated with Finch's desire for success, but nothing will stop him from achieving his goal. As instructed by the book, he cleverly comes in early on Saturday morning and pretends to be asleep, hard at work at his desk. He is discovered by the president of the company, Mr. Biggley (Rudy Vallee), who, after learning that Finch attended his alma mater (which is a lie) and that, like Mr. Biggley, he loves to knit, promotes him to vice president of advertising. Finch is also assigned a new secretary, Hedy La Rue (Virginia Martin), who is secretly having an affair with Biggley. Biggley is being pressured by his wife to get rid of Hedy as his own secretary, so he keeps her near by giving her to Finch. But soon Bud catches Hedy and Finch in an innocent but compromising position and starts to cause trouble.

Ponty, who now has a key to the executive washroom, must come up with an idea in order to keep his job. Back into the story comes Bud Frump, who slyly suggests to Ponty the idea of a treasure hunt. Bud had tried to sell the idea to his uncle months ago, but Mr. Biggley hated it; now, Finch manages to sell the idea to Biggley by making Hedy the World Wide Wickets Treasure Girl. This solves two problems; it gives Hedy a new job and allows Rosemary to become Ponty's secretary. On the eve of the announcement of the winner of the Treasure Hunt on national television, everything falls apart. Only Finch and Biggley are supposed to know where the treasure is hidden, but Biggley has accidentally told his girlfriend Hedy while they were in bed together and she must now swear on the Bible that she does not know the whereabouts of the treasure.

The broadcast is a disaster and Ponty is in serious trouble. Enter the chairman of the board, Mr. Whopper. In a rousing finale, Finch persuades the chairman that we are all part of the "brotherhood of man" and learns that Whopper also started his corporate career as a window washer. Whopper marries Hedy and Ponty takes over as chairman of the board, marries Rosemary, and looks toward his future with optimism: first the White House, then the world.

The central character in *How to Succeed in Business Without Really Trying* is not your typical musical theatre leading man. He is not tall and good looking, with a rich baritone voice and sexy demeanor. J. Pierpont Finch, as played by Robert Morse (and then Matthew Broderick in the 1995 revival), is an average guy, really a boy more than a man. He is cute more than handsome, none too tall, and singing in the tenor range. And his best feature is his smile. In truth, he is very much a "dastard" where his career is concerned. Nothing will stop him from achieving success, even the love of a good woman. As Howard Tubman wrote in the *New York Times*, "Imagine a combination of Horatio Alger and Machiavelli and you have Finch. . . . as played with unfaltering bravura and wit by Robert Morse, he is a rumpled, dimpled angel with a streak of Lucifer."

Ponty is on the fast track, and he climbs all over people, rung by rung up the corporate ladder. In essence, when it comes to business, he is conniving, deceitful, manipulative, and, in certain instances, evil. And yet, just like Rosemary, you fall in love with him. Why? Because deep down, underneath all that boyish charm and the winning smile, behind the twinkle in his eye and the smoothness of his talk, he is a vulnerable human being, with a childlike outlook toward the world. And, because the other characters who surround him are even more dastardly than he is, so you always root for the underdog.

In addition to the Pulitzer Prize, *How to Succeed in Business Without Really Trying* received seven Tony Awards, including one for best musical and one for best actor, Robert Morse (Matthew Broderick also received the Tony for his performance of the role in 1995). The show was also voted best musical by the New York Drama Critics Circle and received the Theater Club Award for the best play of the season by an American, only the second musical at the time to receive this honor. The show became the sixth-longest-running show on Broadway during its run. Sadly, this was to be Frank Loesser's last original score. He died of cancer at the age of 59, only a few months after the show opened on Broadway.

The New York critics were unanimous in their praise for the witty and satirical show. At the core of this musical lurks its vision of backstabbing ambition, somewhere on a par with *Macbeth*, yet told with humor and celebration rather than bloodshed and tears. As John Chapman wrote in the *New York Daily News*, "what goes on up here is murder—murder by stiletto, by poison, by decapitation. This splendidly sardonic account of Big Business is an example of perfect musical comedy construction, swift, sharp, jam-packed with characters and incident and clear-headed as it moves unerringly through an interesting and funny story." In the *New York Herald Tribune*, Walter Kerr wrote, "*How to Succeed* is crafty, conniving, sneaky, cynical, irreverent, impertinent, sly, malicious, and lovely, just lovely."

The Film

Both Robert Morse and Rudy Vallee reprised their roles for the film version of *How to Succeed in Business Without Really Trying*, which also starred the lovely Michele Lee as Rosemary (who had replaced Bonnie Scott in the original run on Broadway). Directed by David Swift, the film is remarkably faithful to the original stage production. As happens with most films, the locales are opened up to accommodate the story. But unlike other screen adaptations, the satiric bite and blatant sexual situations of the story are not toned down for a general public audience. Most of Rosemary's songs were cut from the score, which is a disappointment, but Ms. Lee was given the song "I Believe in You" to compensate. Also cut from the score are "Paris Original," "Coffee Break," "Cinderella Darling," and "Love from a Heart of Gold." Bob Fosse recreated most of his choreography from the original. The *New York Times* reported that "David Swift has done nothing to diminish the wit, sparkle and the zing of the musical show in transferring it into the movie," and the *Hollywood Reporter* determined it to be "bristling with humor, romance and song, and busting with bright stars."

More critical of the film is Rick Altman, who, in his book *The American Film Musical*, believes the musical was transferred too literally from the stage to film. "The . . . film manages to shoot 'I Believe in You' without a single camera movement, and without the least cut. Worse than a return to the common early thirties camera-in-the-fifth-row-of-the-orchestra technique, this arrangement puts the camera in a head brace," says Altman. Perhaps David Swift's filming is rather mechanical and uninventive, tied too much to the proscenium, but the performances of the major players are nonetheless very charming.

REFERENCES

Altman, Rick, *The American Film Musical* (Bloomington: Indiana University Press, 1987); Ewen, David, *New Complete Book of the American Musical Theatre* (New York: Holt, Rinehart and Winston, 1970); Kennedy, Michael Patrick, and John Muir, *Musicals* (Glasgow: HarperCollins Publishers, 1997); Lerner, Alan Jay, *The Musical Theatre* (New York: McGraw-Hill, 1986); Suskin, Steven, *Opening Night on Broadway* (New York: Schirmer, 1990).

—*J.S.*

JESUS CHRIST SUPERSTAR (1971)

MUSIC: ANDREW LLOYD WEBBER (1948–)
BOOK AND LYRICS: TIM RICE (1944–) BASED ON THE
NEW TESTAMENT

Jesus Christ Superstar (1973), U.S.A., directed by Norman Jewison, screenplay by Jewison and Melvyn Bragg; Universal Pictures.

The Play

Jesus Christ Superstar tells the story of the last seven days of Christ in the style of a rock opera. Following the overture, Judas Iscariot shares with the audience his discovery that Jesus is no longer committed to his original humanitarian goals, but has now allowed himself to become a cult personality. After several efforts to persuade Jesus out of his misguided behavior, Judas separates himself from Jesus and the apostles and colludes with the Priests and Pharisees in the hope of forcing Jesus back to his original mission. As a result of his betrayal, Jesus is arrested and passed from the Priests to Herod, and finally Pilate, where he receives the sentence of death by crucifixion. In despair over a plan gone wrong, Judas hangs himself, and the rest of Jesus' followers disband.

Unable to find a producer, *Jesus Christ Superstar* first gained public popularity as a gold-record-selling double album. The musical was controversial because it combined a through-composed rock music score (no dialogue) with the familiar passion story, portraying Christ, seen through the eyes of Judas, as someone as much human, if not more so, than divine. When it finally reached the stage, directed by Tom O'Horgan (*Hair*), the reviews were mixed: Doug Watt of the *New York Daily News* gave it a rave, describing it as "so stunningly effective a theatrical experience that I am still finding it difficult to compose my thoughts about it. It is, in short, a triumph." On the other hand, Clive Barnes of the *New York Times* compared it with one's first visit to the Empire State Building: "not at all uninteresting, but somewhat unsurprising and of minimal artistic value . . . Christ is updated, but hardly, I felt, renewed." Although Christian religious groups protested its performance as blasphemous, and many in the Jewish community perceived it as anti-Semitic, the musical had a respectable New York run of 720 performances at the Mark Hellinger Theatre, opening October 12, 1971. Jeff Fenholt played the title role, with Ben Vereen as Judas, Yvonne Elliman as Mary Magdalene, Barry Dennen as Pilate, and Bob Bingham as Caiaphas. Although it won no awards at the 1972 Tonys, it received five nominations, including best supporting or featured actor in a musical for Ben Vereen, best score, best scenic design, best costume design, and best lighting design. A London production opened at the Palace Theatre on August 9, 1972, and ran for 3,358 performances; until overtaken by *Cats*, it was the longest-running West End musical of all time.

Although Rice and Webber had previously collaborated on *Joseph and the Amazing Technicolor Dreamcoat* as a 15-minute children's cantata, *Jesus Christ Superstar* marks the true beginning of the successful musical writing team.

The Film

As movie musicals go, the film version is exceptionally faithful to the original score and lyrics, although it does include a few changes doubtless intended to broaden the appeal to a larger Christian audience. An additional scene was added for Caiaphas and Annas, which serves to place the blame for killing Jesus more specifically on Caiaphas, due to his paranoia, rather than on the Jewish Priests as a whole. There is an additional verse for "Hosanna" in which Jesus instructs his followers to "Sing me your songs but not for me alone. Sing out for yourselves for you are blessed. There is not one of you who cannot win the kingdom." This appeal to the larger Christian community now assumes its place among the play's central themes. Another small deviation from the text comes during "Trial by Pilate": Jesus responds to Pilate, saying "There may be a kingdom for me somewhere if you [replacing *I*] only knew." Perhaps it was thought that the portrayal of Jesus having doubts—to the degree depicted in the original show—was too disconcerting for a broader public.

The film was produced by Norman Jewison and Robert Stigwood, with the screenplay by Jewison and Melvyn Bragg. Jewison's direction begins the film as a contemporary (1973) pageant wagon—a troupe of players arriving in the Israeli desert (filmed on location) on a bus loaded with props and costumes. The players then reenact the passion play in a hybrid of biblical and early '70s attire. In "Damned for All Time," the roles of the tormentors are either eliminated from their scenes or replaced by some menacing army tanks and fighter jets. The final scene, titled "John 19:41" in the score, departs significantly from the suggestion of its title, which would be for Jesus to be wrapped in sheets and placed in a tomb. Instead, the players leave their colleague on the cross, remove their costumes, and return to the bus and drive off; the final image remaining was a silhouetted empty cross in front of a sunset.

Perhaps what has most endured from the film is the popularity of Ted Neeley and his portrayal of Jesus, which he has subsequently reprised in revivals. Also popular is Carl Anderson's Judas. Both individuals were understudies for the original New York production. Original cast members that appeared in the film include Yvonne Elliman as Mary Magdalene, Barry Dennen as Pilate, and Bob Bingham as Caiaphas. Joshua Mostel, Zero Mostel's son, played the role of King Herod. Although popular at the box office, *Variety* described the film as veering "from elegantly simple through forced metaphor to outright synthetic in dramatic impact." Ted Neeley's portrayal of Jesus was noted as "uneven," but Carl Anderson's Judas was "outstanding." The film received one Oscar nomination for best score, with orchestrations and conducting by Andre Previn.

REFERENCES

Green, Stanley, *Broadway Musicals: Show by Show* (Milwaukee: Hal Leonard Books, 1985); Nassour, Ellis, *Rock Opera: The Creation of Jesus Christ Superstar from Record Album to Broadway Show and Motion Picture* (New York: Hawthorn Books, 1973); Walsh, Michael, *Andrew Lloyd Webber: His Life and Works* (New York: Harry N. Abrams, 1989).

—*T.J.F.*

THE KING AND I (1951)

MUSIC: RICHARD RODGERS (1902–1979)
LYRICS: OSCAR HAMMERSTEIN II (1895–1960)
BOOK: OSCAR HAMMERSTEIN II, BASED ON MARGARET
LANDON'S NOVEL *ANNA AND THE KING OF SIAM*,
AND THE SCREENPLAY OF TALBOT JENNINGS AND
SALLY BENSON.

The King and I (1956), U.S.A., directed by Walter
Lang, adapted by Ernest Lehman; Twentieth Century-Fox.

The King and I (1999, animated), U.S.A., directed by
Richard Rich, adapted by Peter Bakalian, Jacqueline Feather, and David Seidler; Warner Bros.

The Play

Rodgers and Hammerstein followed the phenomenal
success of *South Pacific* with *The King and I*, which
opened on Broadway at the St. James Theatre on
March 29, 1951, and ran for a spectacular 1,246 performances. The musical was conceived as a vehicle for
Broadway star Gertrude Lawrence. Margaret Landon's
book, *Anna and the King of Siam*, and the 1946 Twentieth Century-Fox film of the same name, starring Rex
Harrison and Irene Dunne, had charmed Lawrence.
Lawrence suggested that Rodgers and Hammerstein
turn the story into a musical in which she would play

the British governess to the children of King Mongkut
of Siam.

Anna Leonowens' experiences in Siam (now Thailand) in the mid-19th century were very well known,
both through her own diaries published as *The English
Governess at the Siamese Court* and from Landon's semi-
biographical novel. Mrs. Leonowens lived at the Court
with her two children as governess to the king's numerous progeny and was witness to the conflicts engen-
dered by the increasing interaction between Eastern
and Western cultures and value systems. Her influence
at Court in terms of social and political matters is likely
to have been less than she might have had led her readers to believe, and certainly she had no romantic
involvement with King Mongkut; however, the basic
elements of her story—the exotic locale, the strangely
"barbaric" king, and the prim British widow who came
to teach his children—created fertile ground for
romantic imaginings.

By the time Rodgers and Hammerstein came to the
story, the tensions created by an unrequited (or even
unrecognized) affection between these diametrically
opposed characters were perfect for the musical stage.
The composing team was intrigued by the idea in part
because it presented a variation of the conventional
musical theatre love story. "The intangibility of their
strange union was a challenge to us as librettist and
composer," recalled Richard Rodgers. "In dealing with
them musically, we could not write songs which said 'I
love you' or even 'I love him' or 'I love her.' We were

dealing with two characters who could indulge themselves only in oblique expressions of their feelings for each other, since they themselves do not realize exactly what these feelings mean."

The musical's story brings Anna (Gertrude Lawrence) and her son Louis (her daughter was excised from the screenplay) to Bangkok in the early 1860s. Once she arrives, she discovers to her dismay that the king (Yul Brynner) has broken his promise to her about giving her a house of her own and now wishes her to live in the palace. Anna is appalled at being required to live under the watchful eye of the palace guard just as if she were one of the king's many wives. Although she is persuaded to stay after meeting the children, the house disagreement initiates a tug of war between her and the king. The king's chief wife, Lady Thiang, touchingly acted and sung by Dorothy Sarnoff, helps Anna to understand the king's stubborn but sincere character in "Something Wonderful." Nevertheless, despite the objections of the Kralahome (John Juliano), Anna slowly becomes an unofficial adviser to the king as he struggles with the dilemmas placed before him as a result of his own desire to understand the world outside his kingdom. Siam is in a dangerous position as the countries surrounding it are colonized by Western nations. When he discovers that the British are considering making Siam a protectorate, the king and Anna decide to host a dinner in the Western tradition for British emissaries, to show them that Siam and its king are not barbaric.

The subplot of the musical involves Tuptim (Doretta Morrow), a young woman sent to the king as a new concubine. However, Tuptim is in love with Lun Tha (Larry Douglas), the young emissary who escorted her from Burma. During the entertainment for the dinner, Tuptim presents her Siamese retelling of *Uncle Tom's Cabin*, not very subtly castigating the king for his patronage of slavery. The "Small House of Uncle Thomas" ballet required an entirely new composition rather than an arrangement of other Rodgers tunes from throughout the musical. The choreography was put into place by Jerome Robbins, and, according to historian Ethan Mordden, "its almost over-the-top theatre-of-gesture is studded with some of the show's most evocative moments, including 'King Simon of Legree' chasing Eliza with 'scientific dogs who sniff and smell' (dancers in ferocious masks); the freezing and liquidizing of the river presented by means of a giant silk scarf; and, of course, Tuptim's climactic loss of composure when she starts to beg the king for her freedom." Indeed, the "Uncle Thomas" sequence is a moment when East meets West, and the result is new, inspiring, and beautiful. Another such moment directly

follows when the king is puzzled by the European style of dance in which men are holding women. In the most touching but exuberant musical number of the show, "Shall We Dance," Anna teaches the king to polka. This scene serves to hint at the depth of their feelings for one another.

The happy scene is shattered by the news that Tuptim has fled the palace with Lun Tha. The king orders them captured and plans to whip Tuptim himself as punishment. Anna begs him to forgive, to realize that the girl has "hurt his vanity" not his heart. Then Anna calls him a barbarian. Feeling betrayed, the king seizes upon that moment to reassert his authority in the face of his growing uncertainties: "I am King, as I was born to be, and Siam to be governed in my way! Not English way, not French way, not Chinese way. My way!" But he cannot beat the girl in front of Anna, and he turns away in shame. Deeply wounded, Anna plans to leave Siam. When the next boat arrives, Anna and her son make ready to leave, but she is called back to Court because the king is dying—his spirit and his health broken. As she sits by his deathbed, she realizes that she cannot leave and promises to remain in Siam to help guide the young crown prince as he struggles to continue his father's quest to bring Siam into peaceful and autonomous step with the rest of the world.

The King and I won five Tony Awards including best musical, best actress (Lawrence), and best supporting actor (Brynner). Louis Kronenberger of *Time* thought it could "do better with a less solemn ending"; however, he also called it "musicomedy at its most charming." Brooks Atkinson of the *New York Times* called it an original and beautiful excursion into the rich splendors of the Far East, done with impeccable taste by two artists and brought to life with a warm, romantic score, idiomatic lyrics and some exquisite dancing." Atkinson did feel, however, that the show could not compare to its predecessor, *South Pacific*. On the other hand, Richard Watts, Jr., of the *New York Post* called it "a beautiful and fascinating musical play, a splendid successor to *South Pacific*. . . . [with] a remarkably believable performance by Yul Brynner, and the magic of Gertrude Lawrence. . . . [I]t is a show of rare quality."

Sadly, Gertrude Lawrence's brilliant performance was all too short-lived. She died of cancer during the show's run, and, after a temporary substitution by Celeste Holm, she was replaced by Constance Carpenter. Brynner's king became his signature role, especially after he brought it to the screen. He returned to Broadway as the king in 1977 with his role now the center of attention and gave a "much broader and barnstorming characterization" writes commentator Kurt Ganzl. He toured with the show around America and to the London Palladium (with Virginia McKenna as Anna) and then back to Broadway for a second season. Like his first leading lady, he died of cancer during the show's run.

The Films

There was no doubt that the new Rodgers and Hammerstein hit would be brought to the screen. Twentieth Century-Fox hired Walter Lang to direct and Yul Brynner reprised his role as the king. Deborah Kerr was perfect as the ladylike governess with the spine of steel. Although Marni Nixon did her singing, Kerr's performance in her dubbed numbers was perfectly timed and acted. Rita Moreno as Tuptim, Martin Benson as the Kralahome, Terry Saunders as Lady Thiang, and Carlos Rivas (sung by Reuben Fuentes) as Lun Tha rounded out the cast.

The problems of screen adaptation that plagued the earlier Rodgers and Hammerstein shows also affected the production of The King and I; however, as Gerald Mast suggests, this film was better at performing the "original script and score with as much visual and cinematic adornment as possible." Although the filming was studio-bound, the production numbers filled the screen with the lush sights and sounds of Siam. Mast calls the "Small House of Uncle Thomas" number "the greatest single musical number in any Rodgers and Hammerstein film." Directed, according to rumor by an uncredited Vincente Minnelli with costumes by Irene Sharaff, "the piece offers a blazing display of radiant orange and yellow in an abstracted black metal space, a brilliant synthesis of Eastern theatrical convention and Western cinematic dance."

The film succeeds despite a rather truncated and rearranged script and score. Tuptim's soliloquy, "My Lord and Master," and Anna's soliloquy, "Shall I Tell You What I Think of You," were filmed but excised from the final release. Tuptim and Lun Tha's ballad "I Have Dreamed" was used only as background music. (All of these songs appear on the soundtrack album.) The most spectacularly successful number is "Shall We Dance." Cinematographer Lang made full use of the camera's ability to follow the exuberant dancers around the great ballroom. Its success makes the subsequent scene where the king prepares to beat the prostrate Tuptim even more horrific as we realize that the tenuous connection we've just seen created between the king and the governess is broken.

The film was a success both in the United States and abroad. It won several Academy Awards, including best actor for Brynner. Archer Winston of the New York Post called the film "extraordinarily beautiful,"

although he felt that "it fell short of expectation. . . . The real weakness stems from the negative relationship of the king and Anna." However, Saul Levinson in the New York World-Telegram and Sun said, "Surely one of the most beautiful pictures ever put on film, it is further enhanced by an excellent cast."

In 1999, Warner Brothers produced an animated version of the Rodgers and Hammerstein score. Mike Cidoni of ABC-TV says of this film: "At long last a King and I for the whole family!" A film "for the whole family" apparently means making a farcical attempt to appeal to a child audience with every animated film cliché in the book. Thus the Kralahome is an evil sorcerer assisted by the requisite bumbling sidekick. All of the characters have anthropomorphized animal companions, who offer assistance to the humans. The king has only one wife and five or six children, and the crown prince is a young man of 17 or 18 whose favorite pastime is kickboxing. It is he who falls in love with Tuptim, brought to the palace as a "servant," not a slave or concubine. They flee from the palace, assisted by friendly white elephants that the politically incorrect Kralahome intends to breed and kill for their tusks. In addition, the king's scientific explorations have expanded to rockets on top of the palace and a hot air balloon, in which he chases his son and Tuptim. He rescues them from a raging river created by the Kralahome's magic, but falls apparently to his death when the sorcerer shoots down the balloon with the rockets. One can not have sad endings in films "for the whole family," so the king returns to life in time to bless his son's marriage to the worthy servant girl and dance with Anna in the "Shall We Dance" number, which closes the picture on a nice happy note. The score may be pure Rodgers and Hammerstein, but the script is perfectly ridiculous. Even the animation, supposed to be the most innovative computer technology available, is sloppy and uninspired.

On a final note, there is merit in the charge against The King and I's historical accuracy and its depiction of the culture of Siam, but those arguments seem to overlook the subtleties of Oscar Hammerstein's lyrics. Chalermsri Chantasingh suggests that "the musical depicts [the king] as a savage, whose promise of enlightened character and nobility is manifested only when he agrees to embrace Western cultures, ethics, manners, and language." This criticism seems too harsh, for the source of the audience's sympathy for the king lies squarely in Hammerstein's creation of the character. For example, in the king's soliloquy "A Puzzlement," he articulates his constant struggle over how to be a good king, how to reconcile what he has believed to be true with what he suspects might be true, and how to be a father and teacher to a son he hopes will carry on his legacy. His solutions do not lie with a wholehearted acceptance of Western values; they lie in being true to his desire to be a good king. Nevertheless, the stage musical and its film, the 1945 film, Landon's book, and Anna Leonowens' published diaries are banned in Thailand because they are considered disrespectful and hint too strongly of a romantic relationship between the king and his governess. In fact, Thailand's National Film Board also denied Twentieth Century Fox's request to film on location for the 1999 version of *Anna and the King of Siam*, produced by and starring Jodie Foster.

REFERENCES

Chantasingh, Chalermsri, "Musical Not an Accurate Portrayal of Siam," *Topeka Capitol-Journal*, November 29, 1998; Green, Stanley, *The World of Musical Comedy* (London: Tantivy Press, 1980); Mast, Gerald, *Can't Help Singing* (New York: Overlook Press, 1987); Mordden, Ethan, *Rodgers and Hammerstein* (New York: Harry N. Abrams, 1992); Ostrow, Stuart, *A Producer's Broadway Journey* (Westport, Conn.: Praeger, 1999).

—*S.L.Y.*

KISS ME, KATE (1948)

BOOK: SAMUEL (1899–1971) AND BELLA SPEWACK, (1899–1990)
MUSIC AND LYRICS: COLE PORTER (1892–1964)

Kiss Me, Kate (1953), U.S.A., directed by George Sidney, adapted by Dorothy Kingsley; MGM.

The Play

Cole Porter's late masterpiece premiered at the New Century Theatre on December 30, 1948, and ran for a spectacular 1,077 performances, winning a Tony Award along the way for the season's best musical. *Kiss Me, Kate* was Porter's resounding response to those critics who had considered him washed up since a crippling horseback riding accident 10 years before. Its success was something of a surprise, since it was a musical derived from Shakespeare, something rarely attempted before (Rodgers and Hart's *The Boys from Syracuse* is an example). Moreover, not one of the principal performers in the cast had box-office appeal; and Porter himself had not had a successful stage production for a number of years and not one durable song hit in over a decade. Yet the finished product, in the opinion of historian David Ewen, turned out to be "an inte-

grated masterwork, distinguished in every single department—and with the best score Porter ever wrote, and one of the best ever written for the American musical stage. And it also boasted one of the best texts ever written for Broadway."

This play-within-a-play begins with actors Fred Graham (Alfred Drake) and his ex-wife, Lilli Vanessi (Patricia Morison), preparing for the opening night in Baltimore of their musical version of Shakespeare's *The Taming of the Shrew*. Their romantic squabbles offstage complement the action between Petruchio and Kate onstage (most of which is contained in Act Two). Book and music join in a seamless union, and the songs— "Another Op'nin', Another Show," "Wunderbar," "So in Love," "Brush Up Your Shakespeare," etc.—are witty and sophisticated. Many derive directly from Shakespeare's lines; "I Am Ashamed That Women Are So Simple" musically transcribes Katherine's final capitulation speech. And "Where Is the Life That Late I Led?" derives from one of Petruchio's "catalog" speeches. Writing in the *New York Post*, Richard Watts, Jr., applauded the show: "To Mr. Porter, the new musical comedy must be a particularly gratifying success, since there had been dark rumors abroad that the eminent composer had lost some of his old-time power. There is no sign of any such decline in either the music or the lyrics of *Kiss Me, Kate*."

The Film

Kiss Me Kate was released in 1953, when MGM was at the zenith of its reputation for producing extravagant musical films borrowed from Broadway. *On the Town* (1949), *Annie Get Your Gun* (1950), and *Show Boat* (1951) were recent hits, and soon to come were *Kismet* and *Brigadoon* (both 1953). All stops were pulled out for the Porter hit. MGM's top stars Howard Keel and Kathryn Grayson replaced Alfred Drake and Patricia Morrison as Fred Graham and Lilli Vanessi, respectively. George Sidney directed. Hermes Pan and Bob Fosse took on the choreography. Charles Rosher handled the cinematography and Walter Plunkett the costume design. The action of the modern story was transported from its Baltimore setting to New York City. A prologue was added, in which Cole Porter himself (portrayed by actor Ron Randell) talks Fred and Lilli into doing his play. Song lyrics thought to be too risqué for the Hollywood censors were altered. Porter himself added an important new number for Ann Miller, who, in the secondary role of Lois Lane, fairly stole the show out from under the principles—the classic "From This Moment On" sequence, which he had previously dropped from another stage show, *Out of*

Cole Porter's Kiss Me Kate *starred Howard Keel and Katharine Grayson in an updated, (backstage) version of Shakespeare's play.* (COURTESY MGM)

This World (1950). *Kiss Me Kate* was the only major Hollywood musical to be filmed in the then-novel technique of 3-D. MGM tested the 3-D version against the "flat" version in six cities, and the public clearly expressed a preference for the former. However, when Radio City Music Hall chose the flat version for the New York premiere, citing the "shady reputation of 3-D in the public's mind," the die was cast for subsequent flat screenings. Among the favorable reviews, the *Hollywood Reporter* opined, "In this picture [MGM has] blended wonderful, colorful sets into optical orgies, using them as backgrounds for gay musical numbers enacted by artists who have no comparable values out of this studio." Despite the press approval, *Kiss Me Kate* did not do as well as expected at the box office. "Maybe, back in 1953 when it was first released, the idea of Shakespeare in any form was just too highbrow to attract a mass audience," writes historian Michael B. Druxman, "particularly when television was still a novelty and, of course, free."

REFERENCES

Bordman, Gerald, *American Musical Theatre: A Chronicle* (New York: Oxford University Press, 1978); Druxman, Michael B., *The Musical: From Broadway to Hollywood* (New York: A.S. Barnes, 1980); Ewen, David, *New Complete Book of the American Musical Theater* (New York: Holt, Rinehart and Winston, 1970); Mast, Gerald, *Can't Help Singin'* (New York: Overlook Press, 1987).

—*J.C.T.*

A LITTLE NIGHT MUSIC (1973)

MUSIC AND LYRICS: STEPHEN SONDHEIM (1930–)
BOOK: HUGH WHEELER, (1912–1987) BASED ON THE
1956 SCREENPLAY BY INGMAR BERGMAN FOR HIS
FILM *SMILES OF A SUMMER NIGHT*

A Little Night Music (1977), Austria/West Germany,
directed by Harold Prince, screenplay by Hugh
Wheeler; New World.

The Play

"At last a new operetta. At last resonances and ele-
gances in a Broadway musical," wrote Clive Barnes in
the *New York Times*. On February 25, 1973, *A Little
Night Music* opened to critical acclaim at the Shubert
Theatre. The setting is Sweden at the turn of the century. It is summer. The show begins with a quintet of
ghostly figures, lieder singers in beautiful period costume, singing a lilting waltz like human musical instruments. The ghosts beckon us to "remember" as the
leading characters enter in pairs and join them in a
romantic waltz of life, continually exchanging partners
as they dance. Sondheim's entire score is written in
multiples of three-quarter or waltz time to evoke mood
and period, and it is at times as complicated as the
emotional lives of the central characters. The ghosts
act as a chamber chorus, often singing aloud the

thoughts and feelings of the central characters
throughout the play.

The plot is reminiscent of Anton Chekhov. Many
years ago, the lawyer Fredrik Egerman had an affair
with the actress Desiree Armfeldt (Glynis Johns). The
result was a child that Desiree kept secret from
Fredrik, though she named her Fredrika (Judy Kahan).
Fredrik has just married his second wife, the very
young and virginal Anne (Victoria Mallory), but he has
been unable as yet to consummate their relationship.
He also has a grown son, Henrik (Mark Lambert), who
is studying for the clergy but is hopelessly in love with
Anne. As it happens, Desiree is playing at a theatre in
town and Fredrik has decided to drop in on her as he
has contractual business with her mother, the wealthy
Madame Armfeldt (Hermione Gingold). While visiting her in her dressing room, the old flame is kindled
once again and they make love. The next morning, her
present lover, the dragoon Count Carl-Magnus Malcolm (Laurence Guittard), visits Desiree. Though they
make up some excuse about why Fredrik is in a
bathrobe, Carl-Magnus nonetheless suspects Fredrik
and Desiree of foul play. He retreats to discuss the
matter with his long-suffering wife, Charlotte (Patricia
Elliott). Charlotte in turn informs Anne of the clandestine meeting of her husband and the other woman.
The end of Act One is a complex and very satisfying
musical scene where all the characters get ready to
retreat to the country for a weekend at Madame Armfeldt's estate (whether they were invited or not).

Act Two opens as Desiree greets her guests at her mother's estate. There is an awkward moment as she meets the wives (Anne and Charlotte) of both her lovers (Fredrik and Carl-Magnus). Everyone retires to get ready for what turns into an awkward dinner where no one has a good time. Carl-Magnus challenges Fredrik to a duel over Desiree, but he is only slightly grazed. One of Sondheim's only palpable hit songs, "Send in the Clowns," is sung by Desiree to her love Fredrik. It recounts very winsomely, the foolishness of their past together as well as their current situation. The final scene takes place all over the estate as the summer night smiles: once for the young (as Anne and Henrik run off together), once for the old (as Madame Armfeldt closes her eyes for the last time), and once for the foolish (as Fredrik, left by his wife Anne, renews his love for Desiree).

The Film

Harold Prince has always thought of his stage direction as being very cinematic: "I once again utilized certain movie techniques as I did with *Company* and *Follies*. The last scene in *Night Music*, which takes place *everywhere* on the estate, appears to be happening only on the lawn." But for Prince, who is a master of stage technique, transferring his stage play to film was a disaster. The opening scene of the film actually takes place in a theatre. The turn-of-the-century audience take their seats and as the curtain rises we see the principal characters dancing on a stage to a new song written by Sondheim, "Lecture in Love." Though Prince is trying to make the transition easier for the audience, why is there a need when filming a musical to apologize for the fact that the central characters will be singing their emotions and innermost thoughts? Is this a movie or a filming of a stage performance? Perhaps Prince was indeed using stage rather than cinema technique when he originally staged the final scene of *Night Music*. After all, the audience *has* to use their imagination when in the theatre and a scene that takes place "everywhere" on the estate, must be magically imagined. Just because you go from place to place on the stage does not necessarily mean you are utilizing film technique. In the end, the story was "too static to lend itself to film . . . it's all about savoring moments," recounts Sondheim biographer Meryle Secrest. "As a director of musicals, he [Prince] had been extremely influential in furthering the idea of staging that jumped from scene to scene effortlessly. But, paradoxically, once he went to work behind a camera his theatrical instincts took charge, and what ought to have been fluid became still and lifeless."

In the *New York Times*, Vincent Canby wrote, "It's something more than a shock that the film adaptation of the Broadway show not only fails to raise the spirits; it also tramples on them . . . the movie pursues disaster in the manner of someone who, with mindless self-confidence, saws off the limb he's sitting on." The movie suffers for a number of other reasons. First and foremost, the Greek chorus, so much a part of the stage production, was excised from the film, resulting in long stretches of dramatic action sans music. Second, its leading actress, movie queen Elizabeth Taylor, could not sing and was at the time suffering from endless physical ailments and weight problems. Desiree as a character is a great stage actress and Taylor, whose stage experience was limited, was really more of a movie actress. Consequently, her acting does not match with the rather overdrawn performances of her counterparts. Lesley-Ann Down, however, is sumptuous as Fredrik's young wife Anne, and Diana Rigg is perfectly suited for the long-suffering countess Charlotte Malcolm. Sondheim included a new version of the song "Glamorous Life" for Fredrika (Chloe Franks), replacing the one from the play (which is *really meant* for the stage). Along with the brilliant filming of the musical number "A Weekend in the Country," it is perhaps one of the only truly cinematic pieces in the movie. As she daydreams on her grandmother's estate, young Fredrika envisions what life must be like for her mother on the road. While she conjures up visions of elegance and chivalry, the movie cuts to the reality (or drudgery) of what her mother's life is actually like. In the end, one thought comes to mind. If her mother is so wealthy, why does she continue to lead the *not so* "glamorous life" of a stage actress? It is a tender moment of a young girl longing for the love of her absent mother, and blaming herself for being the reason she stays away. Perhaps Desiree cannot bear to see Fredrika grow up, looking so much like her father. One conjures up memories of Chekhov's characters, the actress Madame Arkadina and her son Constantin, from *The Seagull*. In the *Hollywood Reporter*, Ron Pennington wrote "In spite of the flaws, however, it is not really a bad movie. It's just a disappointing one, especially in consideration of Prince's innovative stage work."

REFERENCES

Druxman, Michael, *The Musical: From Broadway to Hollywood* (New York: A.S. Barnes, 1980); Mast, Gerald, *Can't Help Singin'* (Woodstock, N.Y.: Overlook Press, 1987); Secrest, Meryle, *Stephen Sondheim: A Life* (New York: Alfred A. Knopf, 1998); Suskin, Steven, *More Opening Nights on Broadway* (New York:

MacMillan, 1997); Zadan, Craig, *Sondheim and Co.*, 2nd ed., rev. (New York: Harper and Row, 1989).

—*J.S.*

LITTLE SHOP OF HORRORS (1982)

MUSIC: ALAN MENKEN (1950–)
LYRICS: HOWARD ASHMAN (1951–1991)
BOOK: HOWARD ASHMAN

Little Shop of Horrors (1986), U.S.A., directed by Frank Oz, screenplay by Howard Ashman; Warner Bros.

The Play

Though a killer Venus flytrap from outer space is an unlikely subject for a musical comedy, Alan Menken and Howard Ashman fashioned a charming concoction that has delighted audiences. *Little Shop of Horrors* is based on Charles Griffith's screenplay for the 1960 Roger Corman film, featuring Jack Nicholson. The musical opened at New York's Off-Broadway WPA Theatre on May 6, 1982, transferring to the larger Orpheum Theatre on July 27 where it ran for 2,209 performances.

"On the twenty-first day of the month of September, in an early year of a decade not too long before our own, the human race suddenly encountered a deadly threat to its very existence. And this terrifying enemy surfaced—as such enemies often do—in the seemingly most innocent and unlikely of places." So begins our tale of a poor nebbish, Seymour Krelborn (Lee Wilkof), who happens upon a unique Venus flytrap and cares for it at Mr. Mushnick's (Hy Anzell) flower shop on Skid Row, where he is an assistant. He names the plant Audrey II after the sweet girl who works with him, for whom he pines. Audrey's (Ellen Greene) boyfriend is the sadistic dentist, Orin (Franc Luz). She doesn't think she deserves the gentle Seymour. The flower shop hasn't been doing too well, but the plant seems to have a strange attraction for customers. To his astonishment, Seymour realizes that Audrey II needs fresh blood as plant food . . . so Seymour obliges with his own. As the plant grows so does the success of the flower shop and Mr. Mushnick adopts Seymour as a son and partner. Audrey II, who now talks, insists on being fed. Seymour makes a Faustian pact with the plant in order to win the girl he loves. A confrontation in the dentist's office between our hero and Orin goes awry. Due to a helping of laughing gas, Orin laughs himself to death. He then becomes plant food. When Mushnick realizes what's been going on, he becomes the next victim. Seymour tells Audrey the awful truth and she sacrifices herself for his sake. After World Botanical Enterprises offers to take cuttings of Audrey II, Seymour tries to kill the plant, but only succeeds in succumbing himself. Audrey II is now primed to take over the world as its victims plead with us: "Don't feed the plants!"

Roger Corman's threadbare sick-joke comedy was transformed into a musical of near-Greek tragedy proportions, complete with a doo-wop Greek chorus. While the original film was funnier, the musical has wider appeal. It was Menken and Ashman's first success, and is marked by the popular flair of their later work (Disney's *The Little Mermaid, Beauty and the Beast,* and *Aladdin*). The 1950s- and 1960s-influenced rock-tinged score is full of satiric wit and surprising power. It has a classically structured, self-mocking book. The Grand Guignol performance style of the original production suited the material. Ellen Greene's highly skilled and idiosyncratic Audrey won the hearts of audiences in New York, London, and Hollywood.

The Film

With Howard Ashman adapting his own book, and puppeteer extraordinaire Frank Oz at the helm, the film succeeds in capturing the theatrical charm and humor of the musical, at least in its first half. However, in the second half it makes a lefthand turn toward a happy ending and loses its focus. The screenplay is more an adaptation geared to the talents on hand, rather than a direct transfer of the original book. Mr. Mushnick is reduced to a satellite of the main characters. Small roles are padded to satisfy the guest star turns of Christopher Guest, John Candy, James Belushi, and Bill Murray. The latter, reprising Jack Nicholson's role of a masochistic dental patient (missing in the stage musical) performs a gruesomely funny scene with Steve Martin. The role of the dentist is expanded to allow Martin more room for his own brand of broad humor. Though there is admirable comic energy on display, all of the above serve to diminish the role of Seymour, charmingly played by Rick Moranis.

The film loses the stage musical's vitality when it reduces the tragic central couple to a conventionally happy romance. What was to have been the ending of the film is much more in line with the stage version, wherein the plant kills Audrey and Seymour and then takes over the world. This "darker" ending was actually filmed and the attack on New York by several Audrey

IIs is very impressive. The ending was changed against Ashman and Oz's wishes after unsuccessful preview audience reactions. As happens with most movie versions, the material is somehow softened and diluted to suit the temperament of the masses.

About 60 puppeteers manipulate the largest of the plants. In some shots it was necessary to film at a slower speed in order to achieve fluid movements. This meant that Moranis had to lip-synch and act at a slower pace in double shots with the plant. The film preserves the remarkable satiric performance of Ellen Greene as Audrey. Levi Stubbs, Jr., of the Four Tops gives lively voice to Audrey II.

Songs cut from the original include "Don't It Go to Show Ya Never Know" (reworked for the film as a dialogue sequence), "Some Fun Now," "Mushnick and Son" (the concept of father and son never appears in the film at all), "Now (It's Just the Gas)," "Closed for Renovation" (cut because it no longer moved the story forward), and "Don't Feed the Plants." "Mean Green Mother from Outer Space" was written for the screen version to replace the song "Bad" from the original score.

REFERENCES

Citron, Stephen, *The Musical, From the Inside Out* (Chicago: Ivan R. Dee, 1991); Flinn, Denny Martin, *Musical! a Grand Tour* (New York, Schirmer Books, 1997); Kennedy, Michael Patrick, and John Muir, *Musicals* (Glasgow: HarperCollins, 1997); Ganzl, Kurt, *The Musical, a Chronicle* (Boston: Northeastern University Press, 1997).

—*D.S.G.*

LITTLE VOICE

See *RISE AND FALL OF LITTLE VOICE, THE*

MAME (1969)

MUSIC AND LYRICS: JERRY HERMAN (1932)
BOOK: ROBERT E. LEE (1918–1994) AND JEROME LAWRENCE (1915–), BASED ON THEIR PLAY *AUNTIE MAME*, ADAPTED FROM THE NOVEL BY PATRICK DENNIS.

Mame (1974), U.S.A., directed by Gene Saks, adapted by Paul Zandel; Warner Bros.

The Play

With the success of *Hello Dolly!* Jerry Herman began work on a musical version of Jerome Lawrence and Robert E. Lee's *Auntie Mame*. Based on the novel written by Patrick Dennis about his real, larger than life aunt, the play was a huge success for Rosaland Russell. Russell went on to re-create her role in the 1958 movie, recently voted one of the top 100 comedies of all time by the American Film Institute. Angela Lansbury was cast in the musical version and she scored an equally huge success, garnering the Tony Award as best actress. Gene Saks directed and Onna White created the swift and vigorous choreography.

The story takes place over a 20-year span of time and centers around the vicissitudes of the life of Mame Dennis (Lansbury). After her brother and his wife have tragically died, Mame becomes guardian for her 10-year-old nephew, Patrick (Frankie Michaels). The action of Act One begins on December 1, 1928, at No. 3 Beekman Place, where Mame is having another one of her parties for the very rich and very famous. Everyone who is anyone is there, including Mame's very dear friend, the celebrated actress, Vera Charles (Bea Arthur). Patrick arrives with his nanny, Agnes Gooch (Jane Connell). Mame immediately takes to the child and determines to escort him on a wild ride through life. After all, says Mame "life's a banquet and most poor suckers are starving to death . . . so live, live, live." Mame's custody over Patrick is shared with the Knickerbocker Bank, appointed as trustees in her brother's will to make sure Patrick is brought up in a conservative manner. Enter the bank's agent, Mr. Babcock (Willard Waterman).

Mame and Mr. Babcock will have a continual battle over Patrick's upbringing up until the very last moments in the play. In the end, she wins out but not before a series of disasters and catastrophes beset her life. First, the stock market crashes and Mame is suddenly left penniless. To make ends meet, she takes a job on the stage as a supernumerary in one of Vera's productions. But her excessive enthusiasm disrupts the play. Next she tries being a salesclerk at Macy's department store where she runs into a very rich plantation owner by the name of Beauregard Jackson Pickett Burnside (Charles Braswell). They immediately fall in love and Beau invites her to meet his family at Peckerwood. The family does not take too kindly to this Yankee infiltrator, but when Mame—tricked into riding a very unruly horse during a foxhunt—manages to survive as well as bring back the fox alive, all are won over. She and Beau are married and her financial woes are solved.

Act Two opens with a grown-up Patrick writing to his aunt from college. He has been introduced to a young debutante named Gloria Upson. Mame is extremely disturbed by this union but agrees to meet Gloria's arrogant and bigoted parents. In order to break up the couple, Mame foils everyone's plans by buying the land next to the Upson home and starting a home for wayward girls. The home will be established in honor of Patrick's very pregnant and unwed nanny, Agnes. The musical ends with Patrick happily married to Mame's choice for a wife, Pegeen, and Mame taking their young son on a summer trip to Moscow, where they intend to "live, live, live!"

The musical opened on May 24, 1966, at the Winter Garden Theatre to mostly mixed reviews. The show was regarded as somehow too old-fashioned, and Jerry Herman's score was criticized for being cloned, too close in structure to his very successful *Hello, Dolly!* The songs were hummable but nonetheless derivative of other, more famous tunes. Walter Kerr wrote in his review in the *New York Herald-Tribune* that the songs "are not so much directly familiar as atmospherically stock." But Herman was very good at writing hit songs, and the title song, "Mame" was an instant standard and has been recorded by numerous artists; and "We Need a Little Christmas" has become a seasonal standard.

The Film

The advertisements proclaimed, "Everyone's favorite aunt, played by everyone's favorite redhead." But Pauline Kael in *The New Yorker* pointedly asked, "Why did Lucille Ball do *Mame?* The sound is somewhere between a bark, a croak, and a quaver and it doesn't quite match the movement of the lips. Did Lucille Ball sync her own singing . . . or did Dick Cavett dub it for her?" Indeed, there was not much that Ms. Kael—or anyone else, for that matter—liked about this movie. Brought to the screen by director Gene Saks and choreographed by Onna White, the miscasting of Lucille Ball was a grave error on the part of Warner Bros. Robert Preston fared better as Beauregard Burnside, and Kirby Furlong made for a winning young Patrick. Also captured for posterity are the Broadway performances of Bea Arthur as Vera Charles and Jane Connell as Agnes Gooch. "That's How Young I Feel" was dropped from the score for the film and a solo ballad was added for Robert Pre-

ston, "Loving You," to sing to Lucille Ball. But the script, reworked by playwright Paul Zindel, was unabashedly dated and often politically incorrect. The entire production seemed embalmed, wrapped in the haze of the gauzy lens tissues that blurred Ball's ageing face and form. In the opinion of many, *Mame* played a dismal part in the decline ever after of the theatrical film musical.

REFERENCES

Kael, Pauline, *Reeling* (Boston: Little Brown, 1976); Laufe, Abe, *Broadway's Greatest Musicals*, rev. ed. (New York: Funk and Wagnalls, 1977); Ostrow, Stuart, *A Producer's Broadway Journey* (Westport, Conn.: Praeger, 1999); Parish, James Robert, and Michael R. Pitts, *The Great Hollywood Musical Pictures* (Metuchen, N.J.: Scarecrow Press, 1992); Suskin, Steven, *More Opening Nights on Broadway* (New York: MacMillan, 1997).

—*J.S.*

MAN OF LA MANCHA (1965)

MUSIC: MITCH LEIGH
LYRICS: JOE DARION
BOOK: DALE WASSERMAN

Man of La Mancha (1972), U.S.A., directed by Arthur Hiller, adapted by Dale Wasserman; United Artists.

The Play

When playwright Dale Wasserman read an erroneous report in a Madrid newspaper that he had traveled to Spain to conduct research for a play based on Don Quixote, he used it as an excuse to finally tackle the multivolume epic. After learning how Miguel de Cervantes y Saavedra wrote what is considered one of the world's finest novels when, after a lifetime of failure and imprisonment, he was a sick and aging man, Wasserman's interest was truly piqued. He decided to write about Cervantes and his famous character in the same story, celebrating the world of each. First came a television play, then an unproduced stage play, and finally, after the urging of director Albert Marre, a musical version. After a tryout at Connecticut's Goodspeed Opera House, *Man of La Mancha* opened at the ANTA Washington Square Theatre on November 22, 1965.

Cervantes (Richard Kiley), with his manservant (Irving Jacobson), has been thrown into a prison dungeon in Seville, awaiting a summons by the Inquisition. His fellow prisoners make him stand trial in their mock court, and Cervantes defends himself by presenting the story of Don Quixote and Sancho Panza, whom he and his manservant impersonate. The prisoners are persuaded to participate in this entertainment and assume all the other roles. Quixote's escapades range from fighting a windmill to convincing an innkeeper to dub him a knight, but his focus mostly centers on Aldonza (Joan Diener), a serving girl and parttime prostitute. Quixote praises Aldonza's virtues and calls her his lady Dulcinea, much to her chagrin and puzzlement. Disgusted by her uncle's madness and concerned about her own reputation, Quixote's niece Antonia and her fiancé Dr. Carrasco decide to cure the man of his illusions, but fail. But just at the moment when Aldonza begins to believe in Quixote's idealistic world, she is brutally assaulted by a band of lecherous muleteers, which leads her to denounce Quixote. Soon the Knight of the Mirrors appears, in fact a disguised Dr. Carrasco, forcing Quixote to acknowledge reality and to abandon his impassioned dream world. Aldonza visits his bedside and begs him to remember his former idealism, which he does for a moment before he dies. The story now over, the prisoners are deeply affected and Cervantes leaves to face his real trial.

The challenge of bringing one of literature's greatest characters to the musical stage is daunting, but it is handled with style and theatricality by Wasserman. The decision to focus on only a small segment of Quixote's adventures was a wise one, and the story is compact and moving. An effective combination of pathos, humor, and stunning music (especially the now classic "The Impossible Dream"), *Man of La Mancha* is a testament to the power of idealism. Some critics were unhappy with departures from Cervantes' novel and thought the approach romantic and schmaltzy; however, overall the musical was widely praised. Brooks Atkinson of the *New York Times* dubbed it "one of the most imaginative theatre events of the decade," while Howard Taubman of the same paper touted Kiley's performance by saying, "he becomes the amiable visionary, childlike in his pretensions, and oddly, touchingly gallant." The musical went on to win five Tony Awards, including best musical and best actor in a musical (Richard Kiley).

The Film

Prior to the start of shooting, United Artists went through two production teams before landing on the third with director Arthur Hiller at the helm. By this time, certain components of the film had already been decided upon and work on the sets and costumes was

already in progress. So, whether or not he agreed with it, Hiller was handed a visual concept for his film. Hiller hired Wasserman as the writer and the resulting screenplay was very close to the stage version. The sequence of scenes was slightly reordered, a few additions were made, and one song was cut ("To Each His Dulcinea"). The arrest of the leading characters was added to the beginning of the film. It opens in the town square as Cervantes (Peter O'Toole) and his theatre company are entertaining a crowd. Just as a masked Cervantes is about to be burned at the stake by the Spanish Inquisition, real Inquisition guards enter to apprehend him and his servant (James Coco). Escorted down many steps to the depths of the prison, the characters leave the light of day and enter their new dark world. Antonia and Dr. Carrasco are played as sinister schemers. They make an ominous approach looking for Quixote, disguised in black and bringing the shrouded and motionless body of a man they claim has been bewitched by the Great Enchanter, Quixote's proclaimed enemy. With this trick they seduce him into fighting the Knight of the Mirrors.

In the theatre, the audience is asked to use its imagination as Cervantes and the prisoners use simple props and costume pieces to tell their story. This approach gives the play its style. However, since confining the action to a single place is less suitable for the screen, the film jumps between the prison and locations in Cervantes's story. The transition between the two realities is not always smooth. O'Toole's thick, stylized makeup seems more suited to the stage, fine for the scenes in the prison, but a bit odd in the rest of the film. O'Toole and Sophia Loren (Aldonza) are cast for their fine acting talents. However, O'Toole's singing voice is dubbed, and though Loren manages satisfactorily through her songs, singing is not her strongest asset. Some critics questioned why the two leading roles lacked professional singers. If the producers were not entirely happy with this film, the critics were especially vicious. Jay Cocks of *Time* called it an "epically vulgar movie" and Leonard Maltin rated it a "Bomb" as well as a "plodding, abysmal adaptation."

REFERENCES

Chaplin, Saul, *The Golden Age of Movie Musicals and Me* (Norman: University of Oklahoma Press, 1994); Ewen, David, *The Story of America's Musical Theater* (Philadelphia: Chilton, 1968); Green, Stanley, *Broadway Musicals: Show by Show* (Milwaukee: Hal Leonard Books, 1985); Green, Stanley, *The World of Musical Comedy* (San Diego: A.S. Barnes, 1980).

—*M.R.*

THE MIKADO (1885)

MUSIC AND LYRICS: W(illiam) S(chwenck) Gilbert (1836-1911) and Arthur Sullivan (184221900)

Topsy-Turvy (1999), U.K., directed and adapted by Mike Leigh; October Films.

The Play

Premiered on March 14, l885, at the Savoy Theatre in London, *The Mikado* came on the heels of four extremely successful Gilbert and Sullivan comic operas—*H.M.S. Pinafore, The Pirates of Penzance, Patience, Iolanthe*—and one moderately successful production, *Princess Ida*. It is almost a miracle that it was written at all, inasmuch as Gilbert and Sullivan had decided after the lukewarm reception of *Princess Ida* to split up for a time, each determined to pursue other career aims. But when a Japanese exhibition opened in Knightsbridge in 1884—part of the ongoing craze in London for all things Japanese (spurred over the previous two decades by the painters Whistler and Rossetti)—Gilbert was inspired to write a libretto about the perils of love and deception in Old Japan that became *The Mikado*. For his part, Sullivan was delighted to reunite with Gilbert, especially since, as he declared, Gilbert was willing to eschew his customary reliance on supernatural apparatus. As was usual for these Savoy productions, Gilbert handled all the details of staging and rehearsal, and Sullivan was no less exacting in the pit with the orchestral preparations. Assembled for the cast were those stalwart performers already associated with G & S productions, Richard Temple, George Grossmith, Durward Lely, and Leonora Braham. Oddly, one of *The Mikado*'s most popular songs, declaimed by Ko-Ko, the lord high executioner—

> My object all sublime
> I shall achieve in time
> To let the punishment fit the crime—
> The punishment fit the crime. . . .

—was nearly cut by Gilbert at the last minute. It was only through the exhortations of Richard Temple and other cast members that the tune was restored. The show ran for nearly two years, and the whole country went Mikado-mad; it made more money for the partners than any other of their operas. Their subsequent collaborations included *The Yeoman of the Guard* and *The Gondoliers*.

Despite its abandonment of supernatural contrivances, *The Mikado* is as delightfully improbable as anything else the team wrote. The action of Act One begins in Titipu as Nanki-Poo (Durward Lely), son of the "great and virtuous Mikado" (Richard Temple), has fled from court to avoid marriage with the elderly and ugly Katisha ("I have a shoulder-blade that is a miracle of loveliness," she boasts; "people come miles to see it"). Disguising his name and his rank, Nanki-Poo arrives in Titipu and falls in love with the beautiful Yum-Yum (Leonora Braham), even though this act of flirtation is a capital offense—especially dangerous since Yum-Yum's fiancé is her guardian, Ko-Ko (played by George Grossmith), recently elevated to the rank of lord high executioner. Meanwhile, Ko-Ko receives an ultimatum from the Mikado that unless an execution takes place in Titipu within the next year, he will lose his job and the city will be reduced to a lowly village. Understandably unwilling to behead himself, he turns to the lovelorn Nanki-Poo, who agrees to be the next victim only under the condition that he be allowed to marry Yum-Yum first and enjoy his last remaining days in wedded bliss. But to their horror, Nanki-Poo and Yum-Yum both learn that the law demands that upon his death she be buried alive. Nanki-Poo resolves to spare her life by freeing her to marry Ko-Ko. Ko-Ko contrives to draw up a false writ of Nanki-Poo's execution to convince the angry Mikado that his directive has been carried out. Imagine everyone's consternation when it is learned that Nanki-Poo is none other than the Mikado's son. Killing such a luminary carries with it an automatic punishment of being boiled in oil. There is only one thing for it now—Nanki-Poo must come back to life. He agrees only on the condition that Ko-Ko marry Katisha, because only when Katisha is safely married will Nanki-Poo enjoy the bliss coming to him (he has, in the meantime, secretly wedded Yum-Yum). This occasions Ko-Ko's famous duet with Nanki-Poo, "The Flowers That Bloom in the Spring, Tra-La." Ko-Ko does indeed throw himself at Katisha's feet, singing the sad little tale, "Tit-Willow." Finally, the newly "revived" Nanki-Poo presents Yum-Yum to the Mikado as his daughter-in-law elect. As the Mikado himself declares, "Nothing could possibly be more satisfactory."

The Film

Mike Leigh's *Topsy-Turvy* (the title takes its name from satirist W. S. Gilbert's sobriquet as "The King of Topsy-Turvydom") is a backstage portrait of the mounting in 1885 of the premiere of *The Mikado*. The film marks a significant departure from Leigh's previous work, such as his raw, documentary-like views of modern English caste society in *High Hopes* and *Secrets and Lies.* Here, by contrast, is a sunny and delicious confection that beautifully captures not only the quarrelsome relationship between Gilbert and Sullivan but also the painstaking preparations that went into the premiere of the show. Indeed, *Topsy Turvy* ranks among the most fascinating and detailed backstage films ever made.

Librettist and composer are finely drawn in all their contradictory aspects. Gilbert (Jim Broadbent) is as waspish and irascible as Sullivan (Arthur Corduner) is phlegmatic and mild. And Gilbert's marriage is as sexually dysfunctional as Sullivan's affair with his American mistress is flamboyantly sensuous. Where they find commonality, of course, is in their work; and together they supervise every detail of *The Mikado*'s production and rehearsals. Filmmaker Mike Leigh is no less exacting in his depiction of these preparations, all modeled after the historical record. For example, Gilbert was a notoriously careful and exacting producer. After carefully blocking out the action on his miniature model stage, he would run his players through their verbal and physical paces with relentless exactitude. As biographer Hesketh Pearson has noted: "His energy never flagged. He could show the chorus how to dance with the efficiency of a ballet-master and instruct them how to pronounce the words and maintain the rhythm with the skill of a music-master. . . . Whenever he thought that a performer was not trying to obtain the effect he desired, his patience gave way to temper and his sarcasms were relentless. . . . The drilling to which they were exposed was of a military kind. Nothing was left to chance, and the company had to go through its evolutions at the word of command, repeating them, as on a parade-ground, until the process became automatic."

Accordingly, *Topsy-Turvy* lavishes considerable screen time on Gilbert's supervision of text and staging, meticulously coaching every word and syllable and inflection of the dialogue, remonstrating with the men how to wear their costumes, bringing in Japanese women to show the actresses how to hold a fan and walk in their corset-less gowns, etc. Sullivan, by contrast a more amiable, egregious fellow, is no less exacting with his musicians; he knows when to drop his easy manner and excoriate his players for failing to sing triplets with the proper springing rhythm, for arriving late, and for failing to observe their cues. "Every detail is touched by the spirit of a great enterprise carried out with selfless love," observes *New Yorker* critic David Denby. "It turns out that Mike Leigh, the profane poet and rough beast of modernism, adores the discipline and brilliance and elaborate jackanapes of the imperial age."

Seamlessly intercut with these rehearsal preparations are musical moments from the fully staged *The Mikado*, bits and pieces of arias like "A Wand'ring Minstrel, I" and choruses like "Three Little Maids from School Are We." A given scene may begin with the performers rehearsing in street clothes and conclude with a full-dress version of the same number. Significantly, however, none of this coheres enough to present a full picture of what *The Mikado* itself is all about. It is the process of mounting the production, not so much the finished product, that is under scrutiny here. Critic Geoffrey O'Brien suggests that too much familiarity with the show's plot might impede the viewer's sense of the reality of the offstage action. Meanwhile, the theatrical reenactments are captured by the luminous photography of cinematographer Dick Pope, who provides authentic period stage lighting to cast a wonderful golden glow on the painted stage faces. Thus, the film is a feast for the ear as well as the eye. Composer-arranger Carl Davis serves up a potpourri of music from the period. Extracts from three G & S operas figure in the stage action — *Princess Ida*, *The Sorcerer*, and, of course, *The Mikado*. Other scenes include Fanny's rendition of Sullivan's classic song, "The Lost Chord," allusions in the background score to other Sullivan songs, like "The Long Day Closes," and brief stage scenes from *The Yeoman of the Guard* and *The Gondoliers*.

Woven through this amiable fabric of a film are darker threads. "It's clear that this is to be a period film in which the costumes and furnishings do not protect the characters from physical vulnerability," writes critic Geoffrey O'Brien. Director Leigh is not content to allow trivial pleasures to remain uncontested. Members of the Savoy company, dazzling apparitions as they are on stage, reveal their own inner demons off stage. Durward Lely nurses a morphine addiction. Leonora Braham is an alcoholic who guards the secret existence of her illegitimate child. Gilbert's father is quite mad, and in a quietly chilling scene, the infirm old man turns a casual conversation into an inarticulate soliloquy of pain and paranoia. Hours after the spectacular success of *The Mikado*'s opening night, Gilbert sits at his wife's bedside, mutely listening to her free-form fantasy about a woman who strangles newly born babies (an obvious reference to the sterility of their own relationship). The cozy bliss Sullivan enjoys with his mistress, Fanny (Eleanor David), is interrupted by her admission that she is pregnant, and calmly, with heartbreaking casualness, they arrange for an abortion (apparently not for the first time).

In the film's penultimate scene, Leonora Braham sits before her dressing-room mirror, soliloquizing about the bitterness and folly of her beauty; it is only after a few moments that we recognize the lines as belonging to Yum-Yum in the play. Moments later, in the final scene, Braham stands alone on stage declaiming one of G & S's loveliest songs from *The Mikado*'s second act, "The Sun, Whose Rays Are All Ablaze":

Ah, pray make no mistake,
We are not shy;
We're very wide awake,
The Moon and I!

The song begins with a tight close-up of the singer's face. Gradually, slowly, the camera withdraws and spirals up and away in an uncut take that concludes in a long shot of the stage and the woman's tiny figure surrounded by scenery and proscenium. The lines are those of a heartless, utterly vain creature who is transformed by the sublime music into the apotheosis of beauty. The moment also bespeaks the world of Gilbert and Sullivan—of the cold calculation of Gilbert's chilly temperament and the mammalian buoyancy of Sullivan's lyricism. That they could bridge the gulf between them and work together to create their plays says a lot about art and life. Here is the final and most poignant reminder that all the world, indeed, is a stage.

Topsy-Turvy was voted Best Picture of the year by both the New York Film Critics Circle and the National Society of Film Critics. Jim Broadbent won the Best Actor Award at the Venice Film Festival and a similar award from the New York Film Critics' Circle.

REFERENCES

Cannadine, David, "Three Who Made a Revolution," *The New York Review of Books*, March 7, 1991, 38–43; Hyman, Alan, *Sullivan and His Satellites* (London: Chappell and Company, 1978); Lane, Anthony, "Topsy-Turvy," *The New Yorker*, December 27, 1999/January 3, 2000, 131-132; O'Brien, Geoffrey, "Stompin' at the Savoy," *The New York Review of Books*, February 24, 2000, 16–19; Pearson, Hesketh, *Gilbert: His Life and Strife* (New York: Harper & Brothers, 1957); Tibbetts, John C., "Topsy-Turvy," *The American Historical Review*, 105; 3 (June 2000), 1061–1062.

—*J.C.T.*

THE MUSIC MAN (1957)

MUSIC AND LYRICS: MEREDITH WILLSON (1902–1984)
BOOK: MEREDITH WILLSON AND FRANKLIN LACEY (1917–1988)

The Music Man (1962), U.S.A., directed by Morton DaCosta, adapted by Marion Hargrove; Warner Bros.

The Play

Meredith Willson conceived the story for *The Music Man* from tales and experiences of his own small-town Iowa childhood. None other than Frank Loesser suggested the idea to him in 1949 after hearing Willson reminisce about growing up in Mason City, Iowa, at the turn of the century. Willson was a well-known composer and conductor for radio, having graduated from the Institute of Musical Art (now the Juilliard School of Music). He had a distinguished musical background, including playing in John Philip Sousa's band and in the New York Philharmonic under Arturo Toscanini. He was, however, a newcomer to the Broadway stage and struggled to get his script produced. In 1956, after teaming up with Franklin Lacey on the libretto, he pitched the idea to Kermit Bloomgarden, a co-producer of Frank Loesser's *The Most Happy Fella*. According to Stanley Green, on the day after the audition, Bloomgarden called Willson to his office. "Meredith," he asked, "may I have the privilege of producing your beautiful play?"

The show opened at the Majestic Theatre on December 19, 1957. Directed by Morton DaCosta and choreographed by Onna White, the musical starred Robert Preston as Professor Harold Hill in his first Broadway musical role. Preston, known primarily for his work in Hollywood westerns, was far down the list of possible performers. Danny Kaye was the first choice, but he refused. Dan Dailey, Phil Harris, and Gene Kelly also expressed no interest. The story revolves around the appearance in River City, Iowa, of Harold Hill, a traveling salesman and professional con man. Calling himself "Professor" Hill, he sets about convincing the townspeople of their need for a boys' band to combat the sin and licentiousness sure to be generated by the brand new pool table at the local billiard hall. He begins selling instruments and uniforms, and he promises that he will teach the boys music and conduct the band. Of course, Hill has no intention of leading the band. In fact, he knows nothing about music. He plans to collect the money and skip town. The town's mayor, Mr. Shinn (David Burns), is suspicious and continues to insist on seeing Hill's credentials. However, the fast-talking con man manages effectively to side-step the mayor's efforts while turning the bickering school board members into a barbershop quartet (the Buffalo Bills) and the gossipy town matrons into a classical dance troupe, led by the mayor's wife (Helen Raymond).

The principal threat to Harold Hill's con is Marian Paroo (Barbara Cook), the town librarian and music teacher, so Hill begins romancing her in order to "keep her off balance." He also befriends Marian's mother (Pert Kelton) and younger brother Winthrop (Eddie Hodges), who is afflicted by paralyzing timidity and a pronounced lisp. In the meantime, Marian seeks out and finds the evidence to expose Hill's perfidy; however, she too has fallen under his spell, and when she sees Winthrop come out of his shell when presented with his new cornet, she decides to keep the evidence to herself. Of course, Hill's con is soon discovered, and the townspeople band together, planning to tar and feather him. Hill has been quite prepared to skip town, but he discovers that he has fallen in love with Marian and stays too long. Marian sees the good that has come of Harold Hill's presence and points out to the people that even if the boys never played a note, Hill has succeeded in helping to create community unity and pride. When the new band arrives at Town Hall, resplendent in their uniforms and playing something that rather resembles music on their shiny new instruments, the parents of River City swell with pride and gratitude. Harold Hill leads the town in the rousing finale of "Seventy-Six Trombones" and is accepted into the community.

The Music Man ran for 1,375 performances, garnering eight Tony Awards and the New Drama Critics Circle and Outer Circle awards. The reviews were unequivocal in their praise. "Nothing like it has ever been seen on Broadway," said *Variety*. John Chapman of the *Daily News* called it "one of the few great musical comedies of the last 26 years." They were as enthusiastic about the performers: "If all our stack-tenders looked, sang, danced, and acted like Miss Barbara [Cook], this nation's book learning would be overwhelming," said Frank Aston of the *World-Telegram & Sun*. "Kermit Bloomgarden has found the right people to make it as vivid as a Turner sky. He's made a 10-strike in landing Robert Preston for the title role. . . . He paces the piece dynamically, acts ingratiatingly, sings as if he'd been doing it all his life and offers steps that would score on the cards of dance judges. A triumphant performance in a triumphant musical!" said Robert Coleman of the *Daily Mirror*.

The Film

Warner Brothers optioned the film rights to Willson's creation and planned to release it in 1962. Morton DaCosta was tapped to direct the film and Onna White was called on again to choreograph. Susan Luckey (Zaneeta Shinn), Pert Kelton (Mrs. Paroo), and the Buffalo Bills reprised their roles for the film. Shirley Jones was called in to play Marian. Yet, despite his incredible performance, Robert Preston was not

Meredith Wilson's The Music Man *brought Robert Preston to the screen to reprise his role as Harold Hill.* (NATIONAL FILM SOCIETY ARCHIVES)

Warner Brothers' choice as Harold Hill. The studio wanted a younger, more bankable film star. The leading contenders were Cary Grant and Frank Sinatra. They both insisted that Preston be given first refusal and Willson and DaCosta were adamant that Preston be signed. As a result Robert Preston's once-in-a-lifetime performance was captured on film. Paul Ford and Hermione Gingold did hilarious turns as Mayor and Mrs. Shinn, and Buddy Hackett took over from Iggie Wolfington as Hill's pal Marcellus Washington. The role of Winthrop Paroo was picked up by a very young but talented Ronny Howard.

All of the best elements of the stage production were transferred quite successfully to the film. The storyline and score were retained as DaCosta and Onna White repeated their work from the stage to film. His fidelity to the original concept did not keep DaCosta from recognizing the opportunities created by his new project: "Ever since the Broadway show, I've been looking forward to making the film," he said. "The advantages of exterior shooting, creating a small-town atmosphere, open up whole new possibilities. It isn't enough to recreate a stage show on film." Thus he deployed some innovative techniques, including the iris dissolves instead of simple close-up that he had also employed successfully in *Auntie Mame* to highlight the characters. He also devised several split-screen musical numbers; and for Onna White's choreography of "Shipoopi," he used a spectacular overhead shot reminiscent of the work of Busby Berkeley. Michael Druxman suggests that *The Music Man* was a perfect marriage of the stage and screen mediums, asserting that DaCosta seemed to direct the material as if it had been written directly for the screen.

The most significant change in the score occurred with the substitution of "Being in Love" for Marian's love ballad "My White Knight." The change is a little puzzling, although the song suits Shirley Jones's vocal quality quite well. The lead-in to the song, however, was not changed significantly, so Marian still introduces the song by speaking of her dreams of a "white knight." Steven Suskin suggests that Frank Loesser wrote "My White Knight" and calls Willson's substitution in the film "second-rate." However, Michael Druxman claims that the creators may have had an eye on the "best original song" category of the Oscars for that year. At any rate, both songs achieve what is needed: the reassurance that Marian Paroo is not the cold-hearted repressed woman that the town matrons would have us believe. Nor is she the "sadder, but wiser girl" of Harold Hill's estimation. She is an old-fashioned romantic, who has never found the love of her life. Another fascinating and effective element of the film production was the creation of the film's opening credits by Pacific Title. Thousands of miniature music men were painted by hand, arranged and manipulated one at a time, then filmed to form the words of the opening tile sequence.

"Sophisticates may arch an eyebrow again at the Hollywood version of this breezy, broad-beamed and copiously sentimental show lifted more or less intact from Broadway," opined the *New York Times*. "The characters are the same (right out of vaudeville), the sentiments as tall as field-grown corn, the jokes as dependable . . . [and the songs] as thumping and precisely tailored as before." *The Music Man*, however, isn't about sophistication. Its themes are as homespun as homemade ice cream and fireworks on the Fourth of July. It celebrates a time that never really existed, except in the rosy realm of memory, and its portrayal of all those good American values is actually slightly sardonic. However, even as it holds the people of River City up for ridicule, it manages to celebrate the basic power of love and personal integrity even over its own lovable but deeply flawed hero. Sentimental or not, the film was a success. It earned several Oscar nominations and won the award for best scoring of music-adaptation or treatment. The soundtrack album was on *Billboard* magazine's chart for 35 weeks and rose to number

2. The musical was successfully revived on Broadway in 1999.

REFERENCES

Altman, Rick, *The American Musical* (Bloomington: Indiana University Press, 1987); Druxman, Michael B., *The Musical: From Broadway to Hollywood* (London: A.S. Barnes, 1980); Lerner, Alan Jay, *The Musical Theatre: A Celebration* (New York: Schirmer, 1994); Miller, Scott, *Deconstructing Harold Hill: An Insider's Guide to Musical Theatre* (Portsmouth, N.H.: Heinemann, 2000).

—*S.L.Y.*

MY FAIR LADY (1956)

MUSIC: FREDERICK LOEWE (1901–1988)
LYRICS: ALAN JAY LERNER (1918–1986)
BOOK: ALAN JAY LERNER

My Fair Lady (1964), U.S.A., directed by George Cukor, adapted by Alan Jay Lerner; Warner Bros.

The Play

My Fair Lady is adapted from George Bernard Shaw's satiric drama, *Pygmalion*. The musical opened at New York's Mark Hellinger Theatre on March 15, 1956. The 2,717-performance run established it as the longest-running Broadway show, a record held for 10 years until it was surpassed by *Hello, Dolly!* Directed by Moss Hart, *My Fair Lady* was noteworthy for its wit, grace, and definitive performances by Rex Harrison, Julie Andrews, and Stanley Holloway.

The setting is 1912 London. A chance meeting in the bustling Covent Garden flower market between the erudite, egotistical dialectician Henry Higgins (Rex Harrison) and plucky flower-seller Eliza Doolittle (Julie Andrews) sets in motion a series of events that will change their lives. Eliza's desire to "better herself" brings her to Higgins's house, where the professor and his avuncular colleague, Colonel Pickering (Robert Coote), wager whether Higgins can pass Eliza off as a duchess in six weeks time. She is to stay in Higgins's house and endure grueling daily lessons. Eliza's father, Alfred Doolittle (Stanley Holloway), attempts to extort money from Higgins for the unseemly arrangement and succeeds—thanks to his charm and unique reasoning. A trial run at the Ascot races ends disastrously, but at the end of six weeks Eliza is a triumph at a grand ball. Higgins's ingratitude finally sends Eliza from his house into the arms of wealthy Freddy Eynsford-Hill who offers her an unchallenging life of comfort. After a confrontation at Higgins's mother's house, both realize their special attraction to each other and Eliza returns to Higgins.

A hallmark in American musical theatre, *My Fair Lady* set a new standard in the development of the "book" musical. The fierce intelligence of the libretto is based directly on George Bernard Shaw's drama, *Pygmalion*. Shaw had written the ball scene and the happy ending at the insistence of Gabriel Pascal for his 1937 film adaptation of *Pygmalion*. Lerner gave the ending more resonance by pointing up the attraction between these disparate characters and how much they excite and complete each other. The lush and varied score further romanticizes the relationship. *My Fair Lady* broke the mold of romantic musical fable by giving its one love song ("On the Street Where You Live") to a peripheral character, pointing up the struggle of the main characters to find each other. In some ways the romantic underpinning of the musical makes these fascinating characters even more complex than their straight-play counterparts.

The show was greeted with unanimous acclaim, garnering 10 Tony awards, recording the most successful original cast album in history, and continuing the success internationally. Brooks Atkinson of the *New York Times* called it ". . . a wonderful show. To Shaw's agile intelligence it adds the warmth, loveliness, and excitement of a memorable theatre frolic." According to John Chapman of the *Daily News*, "There could be a no more captivating pair of players than Rex Harrison and Julie Andrews. Physically, *My Fair Lady* is splendid and splendorous, with scene designer Oliver Smith and costumer Cecil Beaton collaborating on the quality-rich atmosphere."

The Film

Jack Warner wrangled with Shaw's estate for six years until he acquired the rights to the musical for the record sum of $5.5 million in 1962. Knowing he was going to produce the most expensive musical to date he intended to hedge his bet by gathering a name team to make the film. After Vincente Minnelli asked for too much money and final cut, George Cukor's services were secured. This was to be his 44th film, his last unqualified hit, and the one to bring him a much desired Oscar as best director. Since Julie Andrews had never made a movie, Audrey Hepburn was hired to play Eliza. According to Warner, the former was "just a Broadway name" and the latter was "an international movie star." Ironically, Julie Andrews was awarded the best actress Oscar that year for her first film, *Mary Poppins*. After Cary Grant turned down the role and nego-

tiations with Peter O'Toole foundered, Rex Harrison was set to reprise the character he played for three years on the stage. James Cagney refused to come out of retirement for Doolittle, and Stanley Holloway returned to the role.

With Alan Jay Lerner as scenarist, it adheres closely to the original show, transferring the text and musical numbers (including "I Could Have Danced All Night," "Get Me to the Church on Time," "I've Grown Accustomed to Her Face," and "The Rain in Spain") virtually intact to the screen. George Cukor was determined to keep the strengths of the original production, and the film is marked by his signature elegance, professionalism, taste, and sensitive handling of his actors. Harrison and Holloway clearly revel in returning to these roles, both delivering more detailed and rounded characterizations. In order to achieve performance immediacy, Harrison was allowed more than usual physical freedom in his songs, which are recorded "live on film" rather than pre-recorded. Audrey Hepburn fares less well. After training hard for the role's singing demands, her voice was dubbed by Marni Nixon. Her innate grace and gamine quality serve her well as the lady, but make her flower-seller seem forced by comparison. Originally planned for location shoots, the film was created entirely on sound stages. Cecil Beaton's elaborate sets and costumes are remarkable in their stylization of Edwardian London and give the film a unifying, if overpowering, visual flair.

The critical reception was generally filled with praise, though some noted that the film's style seemed occasionally stiff and distant. *The New Republic* reviewer, Stanley Kaufmann, said "Cukor's direction is like a rich gravy poured over everything, not remotely as delicately right as in the Asquith-Howard 1937 *Pygmalion*." Kaufmann had praise only for Harrison's work, saying, "his first name never seemed more apt." Still, the film was a huge success, was embraced by the public, and won eight Oscars including best picture. The strength of the characters, story, script, and score and the theme of personal transformation have established the film as an enduring classic.

REFERENCES

Levy, Emanuel, *George Cukor, Master of Elegance* (New York: William Morrow, 1994); Ganzl, Kurt, *The Musical, a Chronicle* (Boston: Northeastern University Press, 1997); Citron, Stephen, *The Musical, From the Inside Out* (Chicago: Ivan R. Dee, 1991); Bordman, Gerald, *American Musical Theatre* (New York: Oxford University Press, 1978); Flinn, Denny Martin, *Musical!, a Grand Tour* (New York: Schirmer Books, 1997); Kennedy, Michael Patrick, and John Muir, *Musicals* (Glasgow: HarperCollins, 1997).

—D.S.G.

NAUGHTY MARIETTA (1910)

MUSIC: VICTOR HERBERT (1859–1924)

Naughty Marietta (1935), U.S.A., directed by W.S. Van Dyke; adapted by Albert Hackett and Frances Goodrich; MGM.

The Play

The story of the contemporary American musical theatre begins with Victor Herbert. As historian David Ewen points out, Herbert was the first composer for the popular theatre whose best work has survived; whose best operettas are still revived on occasion; and whose songs remain great favorites to this day. Over a span of almost 40 years, beginning in the 1890s, this born melodist and gifted orchestrator wrote 50 operettas. Works like *The Red Mill* (1906), *Babes in Toyland* (1903), and *Naughty Marietta* (1910) retain the model of the European operetta, i.e., story-book settings, dashing heroes, aristocratic heroines, sentimental romances, and happy endings—all spiced with lovely tunes in the formal verse-chorus format. He belongs in that select company that includes Sir Arthur Sullivan, Johann Strauss II, and Jacques Offenbach.

Linking the form of the operetta—also called opera bouffe, German *Singspiel*, comic opera, and musical romance—with today's musical shows should come as no surprise. Gerald Bordman in *American Operetta* states flatly that modern musical plays, from *Oklahoma!* to *Sweeney Todd*, are the "direct and natural descendants of a distinguished line of operettas" by Gilbert and Sullivan, Franz Lehar, Victor Herbert, and Sigmund Romberg.

Naughty Marietta occupies a special place in Herbert's distinguished oeuvre. As biographer Edward N. Waters writes, "Herbert's great achievement, and one of the greatest of his life, was that classic of American operetta, *Naughty Marietta*, which with its sensuous beauty, romantic charm, and virile energy remains a distinguished landmark in American culture." It premiered in Syracuse, New York, at the Wieting Opera House on October 24, 1910. The New York premiere transpired two weeks later at the New York Theatre on November 7. Originally commissioned by opera impresario Oscar Hammerstein for the Manhattan Opera House, the original title was to be *Little Paris*, with libretto by Rida Johnson Young and starring opera diva Emma Trentini and tenor Orville Harrold. The setting is New Orleans around 1780. The opening scene takes place in the Place d'Armes with the arrival of Captain Richard Warrington (Harrold) and his men, singing the stirring "Tramp! Tramp! Tramp!" Calling themselves Rangers, they sing of their valor and of their far-flung travels. Warrington has come to capture the pirate Bras-Pique, but his heart is instead captured by the vivacious Marietta (Trentini), a Neapolitan girl of noble birth who came here in disguise as part of a group of *casquette* girls on their way to marry planters in Louisiana. In her first song, "Naughty Marietta," she describes herself as a flirtatious and sometimes dangerous lass. She has captured the attentions of another would-be suitor, Etienne Grandet (Edward Martindel), son of the lieutenant governor. In a fit of pique over a misunderstanding with Warrington, Marietta chooses to marry Etienne. Heartsick, Warrington sings the memorable "I'm Falling in Love with Someone." Imagine his astonishment when he discovers that Etienne is in reality the pirate Bras-Pique! Etienne escapes before he can be incarcerated. Warrington, meanwhile, is determined to marry Marietta. He pledges his troth by completing the fragment of a song that has been haunting her, "Ah, Sweet Mystery of Life." Composer Herbert brings off a theatrical coup here, in that this song has been heard only in brief, incomplete snatches previously; now, in the final minutes of the show, it is heard for the first time in its entirety. It may be the first and only time in the history of the American musical theatre that a romantic swain won his suit by virtue of his ability to complete a song. The two lovers flee into the wilderness and all ends well.

The Film

MGM's lavish production of *Naughty Marietta* not only brought Victor Herbert's classic show to the screen, it also set the standard for the many operetta-films to come that featured the team of Jeanette MacDonald and Nelson Eddy. MacDonald had already achieved status as the First Lady of the Hollywood operetta with her performances in *The Love Parade* (1929), songs by Victor Schertzinger and Clifford Grey; *The Vagabond King* (1930), based on Rudolf Friml's production; *Monte Carlo* (1930), with songs by Richard Whiting and W. Franke Harling; and *The Merry Widow* (1934), freely adapted from the Franz Lehar operetta. She was a natural for the part of Marietta. Giving costar billing to the relatively untested Nelson Eddy as Warrington, however, was risky. He had appeared only in brief cameos in several films; moreover, he was ambivalent about a future in Hollywood, preferring the concert stage. But when MacDonald saw his screen test, she was impressed: "I remember seeing Nelson for the first time and thinking he fulfilled most of my requirement in a man: he was tall, blond, good looking—but was awfully self-conscious about his acting." That was enough. Although Louis B. Mayer preferred Allan Jones, MacDonald won out and Eddy was in. MacDonald's generosity to her neophyte costar was incredible; she even gave him Herbert's lovely "'Neath the Southern Moon," a song originally intended for her in the film.

Meanwhile, producer Hunt Stromberg felt that the original libretto was hopelessly outdated, and he demanded a total revision of plot and characters. The husband and wife writing team of Albert Hackett and Frances Goodrich took over. Now the movie told a story of high adventure that begins in Paris under Louis XV and moves through sequences depicting the voyage of the prospective brides to the New World, their capture by pirates (and subsequent rescue), and the romance between Warrington and Princesse Marie de Namours de la Bonfain (MacDonald), an aristocrat masquerading as her serving girl, Marietta, to avoid marriage to a limp-wristed Spanish grandee. The story's spine was further stiffened by bringing in Woody Van Dyke to direct. Van Dyke had been known principally for his tough pictures, like *White Shadows in the South Seas* (1931), *Tarzan, the Ape Man* (1932), and *The Thin Man* (1934). He gave the proceedings a no-nonsense character and a relatively modern sensibility.

The MacDonald-Eddy team worked beautifully on screen. Separately, each had his and her highlights—songs like "The Italian Street Song" gave MacDonald her first chance to sing coloratura on screen, and Eddy's "Tramp! Tramp! Tramp!" immediately established his stalwart, macho presence. Together, however—particularly in their climactic duet of "Ah! Sweet Mystery of Life"—they were pure magic for adoring fans. As MacDonald's biographer, Edward Baron Turk, reports: "Almost everyone who previewed the pictures agreed that its most compelling feature was MacDonald and Eddy's singing—a sensual blend of pulsating voices, the likes of which had never been heard in movies."

The film became one of the most honored productions of the year. It reaped $407,000 in profits, won an Academy nomination for best picture, and garnered the Oscar for best achievement in sound. Moreover, in a poll from *Film Daily* it ranked fourth in the best feature category, placing it above pictures like *Top Hat*, *Broadway Melody of 1936*, and *Roberta*. Perhaps most importantly, it launched the cycle of operetta vehicles for MacDonald and Eddy, including *Rose Marie* (1936), *Maytime* (1937), *The Girl of the Golden West* (1938), *Sweethearts* (1938), *New Moon* (1940), and *Bittersweet* (1940).

Alas, the operetta film, or what historian Rick Altman has described as the "fairytale musical," has fallen into disrepute today (unless one includes the handful of animated musicals from Disney and Dreamworks). Altman theorizes that the very otherworldliness of the genre alienates modern audiences. It sets in stark opposition the spectator's mundane reality with the ideal imagery on the screen. "The fairy tale musical reinforces this opposition by setting its characters in a class, a plot, and a locale which are as far as possible from those familiar to the audience (and known to the audience only through the prettifying lens of travel publicity or society column chatter)." Audiences of the 1930s bought in to this idealization, but now, "what once may have appeared ideal or mysterious now clearly seems to result from misrepresentation." Without the saving grace of irony and sophistication—qualities suffusing the musical films of René Clair and Ernst Lubitsch and Rouben Mamoulian—these movies are doomed to founder on the shoals of today's temper of incredulity and cynicism.

REFERENCES

Altman, Rick, *The American Film Musical* (Bloomington: Indiana University Press, 1987); Baron Turk, Edward, *Hollywood Diva: A Biography of Jeanette MacDonald* (University of California Press, 1998); Bordman, Gerald, *American Operetta: From H.M.S. Pinafore to Sweeney Todd* (New York: Oxford University Press, 1981); Ewen, David, *Panorama of American Popular Music* (Englewood Cliffs, N.J.: Prentice-Hall, 1968); Waters, Edward N., *Victor Herbert: A Life in Music* (New York: Macmillan, 1955).

—*J.C.T.*

OKLAHOMA! (1943)

MUSIC: RICHARD RODGERS (1902–1979)
BOOK AND LYRICS: OSCAR HAMMERSTEIN II (1895–1943)
BASED ON THE PLAY *GREEN GROW THE LILACS* BY
LYNN RIGGS

Oklahoma! (1955), U.S.A., directed by Fred Zinnemann, adapted by Sonia Levien and William Ludwig; Magna/Rodgers and Hammerstein.

The Play

"It is a radiant summer morning several years ago, the
kind of morning which, enveloping the shape of the
earth—men, cattle in the meadows, blades of the
young corn, streams—makes them seem to exist now
for the first time, their images giving off a visible
golden emanation that is partly a trick of imagination
focusing to keep alive a loveliness that may pass away."
These words, from the stage directions of Lynn Riggs'
play *Green Grow the Lilacs,* inspired Oscar Hammerstein to write the opening to the musical *Oklahoma!*
Never before had a musical show opened with a single
voice off in the distance and a lone woman on stage
churning butter and listening to a song of the morning
and the beauty of the land.

   Oklahoma! premiered in New York on March 31,
1943, at the St. James Theatre, where it ran for a spectacular 2,212 performances. It changed the face of
American musical theatre. It was the first musical to
introduce classical ballet and the first to receive recognition as a literary drama. The title song was officially
adopted as Oklahoma's state song in 1953. Its source,
Riggs's *Green Grow the Lilacs,* a portrait of the folkways
of settlers in Oklahoma Territory, had been presented
by the Theatre Guild in 1930. When the Theatre
Guild decided to adapt it to a musical comedy, Rodgers
and Hammerstein were teamed together professionally
for the first time. Heretofore, Rodgers had written
with only one other lyricist, Lorenz Hart, but after *By
Jupiter* (1942) the two had drifted apart. Hammerstein,
who had worked with other composers, had not had a
hit since *Show Boat* and *Desert Song* in the late 1920s.
The new team seemed incompatible at first, since
Rodgers was known for his sophisticated, sassy shows
and Hammerstein was famous for his operettas. Veteran stage and screen director Rouben Mamoulian
(who had brought *Porgy and Bess* to the stage) was
called in to direct, and choreographer Agnes de Mille
was appointed to the dance chores. The show opened
in New Haven under the title, *Away We Go,* where it
did not impress its first audiences. In Boston the title
was changed to *Oklahoma!* and some of the numbers,
especially the title number, were reworked. The
Broadway debut was a smash and soon it was the
hottest ticket in town.

   The action is set in Oklahoma Territory in 1907, the
year of Oklahoma's impending statehood. The curtain
rises on a farmyard, where Aunt Eller (Betty Garde) is

churning butter while Curly (Alfred Drake), a handsome cowboy, sings "Oh, What a Beautiful Mornin'." There's a big box social coming up and Curly wants to take the beautiful Laurey (Joan Roberts). He entices her with "Surrey with the Fringe on Top." Other characters are introduced: the cowboy Will Parker (Lee Dixon), who sings "Everythin's Up to Date in Kansas City"; Ado Annie (Celeste Holm) whose "I Cain't Say No" describes her love life; a peddler named Ali Hakim; and a disreputable farmhand named Judd Fry (Howard da Silva). Laurey impulsively accepts a ride to the dance with Jud, a "growly man" with a questionable character and past. Curly proceeds to convince Jud to stay away from Laurey in the now famous smokehouse scene, but to no avail. He winds up taking Laurey's Aunt Eller to the social in the real "made-up" rig with the fringe on top. The first act ends with a Freudian "dream-ballet" where Laurey, induced by a potion bought from the wily Ali Hakim, tries to decide between the affections of both Curly and Jud.

The second act opens with everyone dancing and singing at the box social. Laurey, who comes late to the party with Jud, is flustered when he and Curly vie for her attention by offering everything they own in the world for the honor of buying her picnic basket (part of a charity auction to put a roof on the school house). Curly wins the bid and, impulsively, Laurey fires Jud as her hired hand. The musical proceeds much as Riggs's original play, with the addition of one character, young Will Parker, the rope spinning, somewhat dimwitted boyfriend of Ado Annie Carnes. This secondary love story is used in the musical specifically as a comic counter-story to that of Laurey and Curly. In the end, all works out and Laurey and Curly are married on the eve of Oklahoma becoming a new state. On their wedding night, Jud arrives back on the farm and threatens Curly's life. When he pulls a knife on Curly, Jud is accidentally stabbed and dies. An impromptu trial is held, led by Aunt Eller, Curly is found not guilty and the couple proceeds on their honeymoon trip.

Even more than the Kern-Hammerstein *Show Boat*, *Oklahoma!* was an "integrated" show, blending its story, music, lyrics, and ballet numbers into a satisfying whole. Agnes de Mille's choreography, particularly in Laurey's dream sequence and the square dance that opens Act Two, brought a western-style zest and kick to traditional ballet forms. In his autobiography *Musical Stages*, Richard Rodgers writes "most of the musical numbers presented no great problems. One, which every songwriter must face over and over again, is how to say 'I love you' in a way that makes the song different from any other romantic ballad ever written. In 'People Will Say We're in Love," Oscar hit on the notion of having the young lovers warn each other against showing any signs of affection so that people won't realize they're in love . . . This song also demonstrates another familiar problem, especially for lyric writers. There are, after all, only so many rhymes for the word 'love,' and when Oscar decided to call the duet 'People Will Say We're in Love,' he was determined to avoid using any of the more obvious ones. After spending days thinking about this one rhyme, he called me up exultantly to announce that he'd solved the problem. His solution: the girl ends the refrain by admonishing the boy: 'Don't start collecting things, give me my rose and my glove, Sweetheart, they're suspecting things—People will say we're in love.'" This was the kind of meticulous thinking that made the musical so winning.

The show opened to rave reviews. "Critics and audiences alike were overwhelmed by [the musical's] innovative blend of song, story and dance," says Steven Suskin. The show established Rodgers and Hammerstein as the top writing team on Broadway. It was one of the first musical comedies to be recorded with its original cast. Touring shows brought it to service people overseas. It broke all existing musical comedy records by running five years and nine weeks for a total of 2,248 consecutive performances, and it became the third-longest-running attraction in the history of the New York theatre (exceeded only by two non-musical plays, *Life with Father* and *Tobacco Road*. Part of the success of the musical was due to timing. In 1943, America was heavily involved in World War II. Rodgers writes, "there was the fact that we were in the midst of a devastating war. People could come to see *Oklahoma!* and derive not only pleasure but also a measure of optimism. It dealt with pioneers in the Southwest, it showed their spirit, and it gave citizens an appreciation of the hardy stock from which they'd sprung. People said to themselves, in effect, 'If this is what our country looked and sounded like at the turn of the century, perhaps once the war is over we can again return to this kind of buoyant, optimistic life.'"

The Film

The film of the stage play was a much anticipated event. Shot in both anamorphic Cinemascope and the newly devised TODD-AO, the opening sequence photographed by Robert Sturges of Curly riding his horse through the corn "as high as an elephant's eye," captured in magnificent beauty the morning that Riggs described at the beginning of his play. From then on, however, the film is somewhat disappointing. Rodgers and Hammerstein had complete control of the film and wanted to be faithful to their stage success. As a result, Zinnemann's hands were often tied when trying to utilize the medium of film in order to tell the story. Two songs were cut from the original, Jud's soliloquy, "Lonely Room," and Ali Hakim's ranting "It's a Scandal, It's an Outrage." Everything else was intact, down to Agnes De Mille's original choreography for the stage. In the cast, Rod Steiger's stolidly powerful psychopath, Jud, was a blot in the otherwise sunny landscape; Shirley Jones and Gordon Macrae had both the looks and pipes to make Laurey and Curly endearing figures; Gene Nelson (Will Parker), in his last screen appearance, had a spectacular time twirling lariats and running atop train cars for his "Everythin's Up to Date" number; and Gloria Grahame and Eddie Albert (perhaps a bit too American to play the Persian peddler) were likewise winning as Ado Annie and Ali Hakim.

REFERENCES

Druxman, Michael B., *The Musical: From Broadway to Hollywood* (New York: A.S. Barnes, 1980); McVay, Douglas, *The Musical Film* (London: A. Zwemmer Limited, 1967); Mordden, Ethan, *Beautiful Mornin'* (New York: Oxford University Press, 1999); Rodgers, Richard, *Musical Stages* (New York: Random House, 1975); Suskin, Steven, *Opening Night on Broadway* (New York: Schirmer Books, 1990); Max Wilk, *OK! The Story of Oklahoma!* (New York: Grove Press, 1993).

—*J.S.*

OLIVER! (1960)

BOOK, MUSIC AND LYRICS: LIONEL BART (1930–1999)

Oliver! (1968), U.K., directed by Sir Carol Reed, adapted by Lionel Bart from Charles Dickens's *Oliver Twist;* Columbia Pictures.

The Play

It is tricky business turning a classic novel about a young boy's grim journey through poverty and crime into a sprightly musical that leaves audiences happily humming. Such was Lionel Bart's task when he converted Charles Dickens's *Oliver Twist* into a musical. Given Bart's intent, villainous characters that haunt the novel's pages are transformed into picaresque charmers in the play. The grimy, opportunistic Fagin becomes a kind of hoodlum den mother, who instructs his gang of street urchins, particularly Bill Sikes and the Artful Dodger, in the arts of larceny. Sikes's woman, Nancy, who sings that her kind "have to sin to eat," loves her

man literally to her distraction. Granted, these characters may be whitewashed, but they still manage to create some semblance of the seedy, Dickensian world of early 19th-century London—a world of child abuse, poverty, street crime, and prostitution, where life is dispensable for the poor, and rewarding for the rich.

The story remains faithful to the novel's basic outline. A wall sampler proclaiming "God Is Love" adorns the workhouse where the underfed and penniless foundlings eke out a meager subsistence (the ironic song, "Food, Glorious Food"). Surely, it's the only sign of love, as orphaned Twist discovers when he draws the fortuitous straw to beg more gruel. With brows raised in disapproval of his outrageous presumption, Oliver is sold ("Boy for Sale"), but soon runs off to London. Once there ("Consider Yourself"), he befriends a group of pickpockets led by Fagin and Bill Sikes ("Pick a Pocket or Two") and promptly lands in court. No sooner does a wealthy gentleman, Mr. Brownlow, come to Oliver's rescue ("Who Will Buy") than he is kidnapped ("As Long As He Needs Me"). In the ensuing violence the gang members are either killed ("Where Is Love?") or survive to go their separate ways ("Reviewing the Situation"). Oliver returns to his rightful home. As it turns out, his benefactor is his own grandfather.

Oliver!, which premiered on June 30, 1960, was wildly popular in London, and played 2,618 performances at the West End's New Theatre. In Britain, the show enjoyed two long-running revivals in 1967 and 1977. Broadway audiences first saw the American production after an extensive tour (Los Angeles, San Francisco, Toronto, and Detroit). *Oliver!* opened at the Imperial Theater on January 6, 1963, with much of the original cast, featuring Clive Revill as Fagin. In a bit of show-business acumen, producer David Merrick released the cast album well before the musical opened ("As Long As He Needs Me" was already a hit). It turned out to be a clever plan, especially with the city in the midst of a newspaper strike. The 1985 revival on Broadway featured Ron Moody re-creating his London Fagin; however, according to Merrick's biographer, Howard Kissel, Moody's stereotypically Jewish portrayal caused the play to be closed immediately.

Reviews for *Oliver!* were nearly all favorable. "Its beauty, melodiousness, humor and occasional pathos are shrewdly combined in a pattern that isn't ashamed to be good fun," wrote the *New York Post*'s Richard Watts, Jr. *Oliver!* secured three Tony awards: best composer-lyricist (Lionel Bart, an exceptional achievement for a man unable to read or write music or play a musical instrument), best musical direction (Donald Pippin), and best scenic designer (Sean Kenny). Kenny's designs won accolades because mobile sets allowed scenes a cinematic flow, as each scene subtly glided into the next. *Oliver!* also garnered seven Tony nominations: best musical play, actor, actress, supporting actor, director, producer, and author of a musical play.

The Film

Productions of a non-musical *Oliver Twist* abound—there are 10 versions! Among others, the list includes five silent films, the classic David Lean 1948 version from Britain, and a made-for-television movie in 1997. In addition, Disney created an animated cartoon, *Oliver and Company.*

Despite Sir Andrew Lloyd Webber's fame, *Oliver!* remains one of the few British musical films that have attracted a wide American following. For a while, it had difficulty finding American backers, even with Peter Sellers signed to play Fagin. Other stars in the wings were Peter O'Toole, Richard Burton and Elizabeth Taylor, Laurence Harvey, and Sean Connery. Signed to direct was Sir Oliver Reed, a director whose career, according to biographer Robert F. Moss, had been considered to be in irreversible decline since the failure of *The Agony and the Ecstasy* (1965), and whose experience with musicals had been limited to a Jessie Matthews vehicle, *Climbing High* (1938). Backed by American money from Columbia studios, Reed set to work. He selected actors not by Hollywood's typical "star system," but using musical theatre veterans like Ron Moody as Fagin. Nepotism also reared its head, as Reed cast his nephew Oliver Reed as Bill Sikes. If Reed's villainy has not the vicious menace of Robert Newton's in the David Lean adaptation of *Great Expectations*, it is doubtless attributable to the fact that this is a musical film and not a "straight" drama. And nine-year-old newcomer Mark Lester, who made a credible impression as an orphan in Jack Clayton's melodrama, *Our Mother's House*, the year before, turns in a pure, winsome performance in the title role, playing a perfect foil to Jack Wild's shrewd and cunning Artful Dodger.

On screen, *Oliver!* differs from the stage play in a number of regards. According to historian John Green, "On stage, *Oliver!* was done in a very stylized manner, but the movie opened up the show considerably and played it on a realistic level. At one point, Bart thought we were destroying his play." In a *Los Angeles Times* interview, Moody said, "I played it very Jewish on the stage, but we changed it for the film." While Shani Wallis (Nancy) reports that director Carol Reed enhanced the musical selections with lots of added stage business, like having Nancy steal Oliver during the "Oom Pah Pah" number, the entire score was transferred to the film virtually intact (save Bill's "My Name," which was dropped at Oliver Reed's request; the duet "I Shall Scream"; and the trio "That's Your Funeral"). The major production numbers in the first half of the film, "Food, Glorious Food" and "Consider Yourself at Home," are choreographed with abundant, old-fashioned Broadway-style energy by Oona White, photographed by the legendary Oswald Morris, and designed by Terence Marsh. The second half of the film opens with the delicious "Who Will Buy?" an entrancing motley of street songs, opening with the *a capella* song by a flower girl in the deserted Bloomsbury Square and building gracefully into a full-blown oratorio.

Most critics praised the film. *Variety* wrote: "It's a bright, shining heartwarming musical, packed with songs and lively production high spots." Pauline Kael, newly installed in the pages of *The New Yorker*, was enthusiastic: "I . . . applaud the commercial heroism of a director who can steer a huge production and keep his sanity and perspective and decent human feelings as beautifully intact as they are in *Oliver!*" Historian Michael Druxman writes, "*Oliver!* is as near perfect as a musical can get. It is a careful blending of realistic and stylized elements into a film that entraps its audience from start to finish." A dissenting note comes from historian John Kobal: "It plays safe, whitewashing anything that might stamp it with Dickens' telling power, leaving it little more than a tepid fairy tale in ornately grim settings. Its dances are hectic, but going nowhere fast, and its likeable songs are orchestrated out of all recognition."

Oliver! swept the Academy Awards, winning best picture, best direction, best art direction, sound, musical score, with a special Oscar for Onna White for choreography, as well as six nominations, including best actor (Moody), and best supporting actor (Wild).

REFERENCES

Druxman, Michael B., *The Musical: From Broadway to Hollywood* (South Brunswick, N.J.: A.S. Barnes, 1980); Davies, Brenda, ed., *Carol Reed* (London: British Film Institute, 1978); Kissel, Howard, *David Merrick: The Abominable Showman* (New York: Applause, 1993; Moss, Robert F., *The Films of Carol Reed* (New York: Columbia University Press, 1987); Reed, Oliver, *Oliver Reed: Read All about Me* (London: W.H. Allen, 1979).

—K.P.

ON A CLEAR DAY YOU CAN SEE FOREVER (1965)

BOOK AND LYRICS: ALAN JAY LERNER (1918–1986)
MUSIC: BURTON LANE (1912–1997)

On a Clear Day You Can See Forever (1969), U.S.A., directed by Vincente Minnelli, adapted by Alan Jay Lerner; Paramount.

The Play

Alan Jay Lerner had been interested in the occult, extrasensory perception, reincarnation, and all things metaphysical ever since he was a child. The result of this penchant for fantasy as subject matter was the 1965 *On a Clear Day You Can See Forever* (previously titled *I Picked a Daisy*), a musical about parapsychology, reincarnation, and hypnotism. Daisy Gamble (Barbara Harris) is a young student of Professor Mark Bruchner (John Cullum). One day in class, Bruchner discovers that Daisy is highly susceptible to hypnosis. He becomes extremely curious as she tells him of her special powers to make flowers grow and know where to find all things lost. Mark convinces Daisy to be hypnotized once again (supposedly to help her quit smoking) and she regresses into the world of the 18th century, calling herself Melinda Wells. When she awakens, Mark informs her that she is indeed very special. He is determined to discover if this Melinda existed or if it is all a figment of her imagination. He files a medical report on Daisy and continues to have sessions with her, recording them on tape for further study. Unbeknownst to Daisy, Mark has fallen in love with the 18th-century Melinda while she has fallen in love with the 20th-century doctor. Mark's sessions with Daisy become more frequent until one day she discovers the secret recordings and finds out that the doctor does not love her, Daisy, but her former self, Melinda. She leaves the office determined to live a normal life with her fiancé Warren (William Daniels), but Mark wills her back with extrasensory powers of his own. In the end they find a common bond in the present and the future looks rosy for the couple.

While the show did not have an extremely long run, it nevertheless fared well at the box office mostly due to the incredible score by Burton Lane and the quirky performance of its leading lady, Barbara Harris. The reviewers were decidedly mixed and most agreed that the idea was innovative for a musical but that the story was "frail and rickety" and a "melodious muddle." John McClain's headline in the *Journal-American* read, "*Clear Day* But Foggy."

The Film

The film was considerably rewritten to highlight the talents of its two stars, Barbra Streisand and Yves Montand and the brilliance of its director, Vincente Minnelli, whose career had been faltering in the 1960s. The reincarnation story allowed for Streisand to play a variety of roles using a variety of accents. The movie is arguably better than the stage play. The story was cleaned up and revised and the ending changed. Rather than Daisy and Mark getting together at the end, as in the play, the doctor hypnotizes her one more time, only to discover that she has regressed not into the past but the future. In this altered ending, Daisy and Marc (spelled the "French" way) will finally live as husband and wife somewhere on a farm in Virginia. The ending of the film works better because it is less about romance (where, traditionally, the boy gets the girl) and more about self-discovery in the central character, a particularly Minnellian touch, which "deepen[ed] the musical's traditional theme of the discovery of a truer self beneath the outer self of inhibition and pretension," in the words of commentators Babington and Evans. A number of songs were added to the score to enhance Streisand's singing presence, and her rendition of "What Did I Have" is a tour de force of combined acting and singing to create a dramatic moment virtually unequalled in the movie musical. The title song became a hit for Streisand; she wound up recording it three times and even sang it as the Act One closer on her 1994 tour.

In his book *Vincente Minnelli and the Film Musical*, Joseph Casper recounts a "shamelessly romantic" use of the camera that details the meeting of Melinda and Robert Tentrees. The scene is more than reminiscent of the famous seduction scene from the film *Tom Jones*, only the dirty deed is done with wine instead of fruit and meat. Minnelli carefully crafts the melding of "time future" into "time present" in a number of beautifully photographed sequences. Streisand gets to play her quirky New York Jewish neurotic character as the modern Daisy Gamble and fumble with a number of different British accents as Melinda Tentrees. Playing her ex-stepbrother Tad Pringle, Jack Nicholson is wasted as a semi-love interest for Streisand.

Missing from the score are any songs that could not be reassigned to the film's two stars, including one song about a Greek tycoon ("When I'm Being Born Again") who wants to fund the doctor's research into ESP so he can find a way to leave all his money to himself. Two cinematic delights are the treatment of the songs "Hurry It's Lovely Up Here" and "Come Back to Me." The first opens the film with the appropriately named Daisy (Streisand) singing to the flowers and beckoning them to quickly grow because the world is so lovely up above and no one should live their life in a hole. The sequence is actualized in the film through time-lapse photography. In the second song, in order to compel Daisy to come back to him, Dr. Chabot sings "Come Back to Me" from the top of the Pan-American building in New York, shot by means of a combination of telephoto lenses and airborne cameras. Minnelli cleverly has Yves Montand assuming the voices of everyone Streisand encounters, including a dog, while continually cutting back to a close-up of him singing from the rooftop. Of special note are the musical arrangements by Nelson Riddle and the ever-famous '60s hairdo worn by Ms. Streisand.

REFERENCES

Babington, Bruce and Peter William Evans, *Blue Skies and Silver Linings* (Manchester, Eng.: Manchester University Press, 1985); Casper, Joseph Andrew, *Vincente Minnelli and the Film Musical* (New York: A.S. Barnes, 1977); Lerner, Alan Jay, *On the Street Where I Live* (New York: De Capo Press, 1994); Pohly, Linda, *The Barbra Streisand Companion* (Westport, Conn.: Greenwood Press, 2000); Suskin, Steven, *More Opening Nights on Broadway* (New York: MacMillan, 1997).

—*J.S.*

RIO RITA (1927)

BOOK: GUY BOLTON AND FRED THOMPSON
MUSIC: HARRY TIERNEY
LYRICS: JOE MCCARTHY

Rio Rita (1929), U.S.A., directed and adapted by Luther Reed; RKO.

Rio Rita (1942), U.S.A., directed by S. Sylvan Simon, adapted by Richard Connell; MGM.

The Play

Showcasing the New York premiere of *Rio Rita* on February 2, 1927, was Ziegfeld's new theatre, the Ziegfeld, located on Sixth Avenue. The show's Mexican setting gave scenic designer Joseph Urban and costume designer John Harkrider an excuse to concoct some of their most extravagant and exotic designs. The plot was merely a vehicle for dashing heroics, fainting heroines, and breakout action. Jim, a Texas Ranger captain (J. Harold Murray), is hunting for a notorious Mexican bandit called "The Kinkajou." He and his band sing the stirring "March of the Rangers." Across the border, he meets the woman he presumes to be the bandit's sister, the beautiful Rio Rita (Ethelind Terry). Their romance is further complicated by the fact that she is also loved by General Esteban (Vincent Serrano). Moreover, Rita is worried that Jim's only inter-

est in her is the capture of her brother Roberto (George Baxter). To everyone's relief, when the bandit is finally captured, he is not related to Rita after all—but is in reality Esteban himself. She and Jim become lovers again, and the show ends with their lavish wedding. There is comedy and sentiment aplenty. The team of Wheeler and Woolsey, brought together for the first time to handle the slapstick chores, play Ed Lovett and Chick Bean, two American visitors to Mexico. On a more romantic note, Jim and Rita's duet, the title song, is one of the loveliest songs from an American musical of that time. The show closely imitated the classic formulas of the standard operetta. Indeed, its plot was virtually a carbon copy of Victor Herbert's classic *Naughty Marietta*. It was a big success and ran for 494 performances.

The Films

The first film version, produced at newly formed RKO, could fairly be described as an historical antique, of primary interest to film history specialists. Nonetheless, it holds a special place in the history of the American musical film in that it was one of the first "talkies" to adapt a contemporary stage musical. "The first age of the filmed Broadway musical begins with *Rio Rita*," writes historian Richard Barrios in his estimable study, *A Song in the Dark: The Birth of the Musical Film*. "One of 1929's most successful and well liked movies, it now requires a willing viewer to don a particularly rosy pair of specs to comprehend its impact." The film neatly divides into three sections. The first is set in and around the hacienda of Rio Rita; the second, in the headquarters of General Ravenant (Esteban in the original play); and the third aboard Ravenant's pirate barge. The last act, shot entirely in two-color Technicolor, concludes with a stage tableau as Ravenant is unmasked as the Kinkajou and the marriage proceeds between Captain Jim Stewart (John Boles) and Rio Rita (Bebe Daniels). Wheeler and Woolsey reprise their comic roles.

Surprisingly, there is a generous amount of location shooting, unusual at a time when films of this ilk were notoriously stagebound. For example, the opening "Rangers' Song" is sung entirely out of doors, the rangers arriving with whoops, shouts, and twirling lariats, to gather in a tight circle around their leader. And in another extended exterior sequence, Bebe Daniels sings "Following the Sun Around" while walking through her outdoor garden. Equally surprising is the occasional use of a background musical score. In Ravenant's headquarters, for example, the tensions among Jim, Rita, and Ravenant are complemented by a steadily increasing crescendo of background music.

For all that, Rio Rita is very much a film of its time. To begin with, its primitive synchronized-sound technique is very wearing on today's viewers. The blend of dialogue and orchestral music is clumsily balanced, with the music usually drowning out the words (the sort of problem satirized years later in the classic musical film, Singin' in the Rain). In addition, a stiffness in the acting and a tedium in the secondary comic routines do not wear well on screen. As bad as John Boles's histrionics are, Wheeler and Woolsey have to be singled out as the prime culprits. Their scenes, digressive, even irrelevant as they are, interrupt the action at increasingly annoying intervals. It seems Wheeler has married a second time without bothering to divorce his first wife. Woolsey in turn falls for the first wife. The two couples attend a nightclub, with subsequent disastrous consequences—a boxing match, a dance routine, a few jokes, a slapstick fall or two. "Wheeler and Woolsey are a taste that many audiences will never wish to acquire," writes historian Barrios, "the kind of standardized Broadway comedy that can't bridge years and changing types of humor." Overall, the film stubbornly plays to the proscenium. Individual scenes are blocked out as if on a stage. The principal characters occupy a foreground plane while the "atmosphere" extras stand tableaux-like in the background, duplicating the stage platform's division between "downstage" and "upstage" areas. Yet it should be remembered that these scenes, irritating and irrelevant as they are—and bad cinema, to boot—are nonetheless an authentic document of the standard staging practices at that time.

Predictably, critics were sharply divided. Writing in The Film Mercury in November 1929, Richard Watts, Jr., praised it as "a faithful screen transcription of the Ziegfeld musical comedy that is careful to follow the original stage production almost scene by scene. . . . Bert Wheeler and Robert Woolsey prove to be more amusing in the film than on the stage." By contrast, writing two months later, James Shelley Hamilton in Cinema noted, "This is another musical spectacle, gorgeously and unimaginatively photographed. It isn't worth while getting all het up over whether this kind of thing couldn't be done a lot better. . . . Spectacle is about all the thing is, and it is probably perfectly sufficient." Audiences in 1929 certainly loved it, despite its more than two-hour length. At year's end it placed high in most "Ten-Best" lists, and it garnered more than $2 million at the box office. Rio Rita would be RKO's biggest hit until King Kong three years later.

The 1942 version from MGM reflects a different set of contexts. The story and most of the songs were scrapped in favor of wartime seriocomedy about Nazi spies. The team of Abbott and Costello, which had come to the screen a year before in Buck Privates, took on the Wheeler and Woolsey roles, relegating the romantic plot between Kathryn Grayson and John Carroll to secondary status. Only two of the stage songs were retained. New numbers were composed by E.Y. Harburg and Harold Arlen.

REFERENCES

Barrios, Richard, *A Song in the Dark: The Birth of the Musical Film* (New York: Oxford University Press, 1995); Carter, Randolph, *The World of Flo Ziegfeld* (New York: Praeger, 1974); Slide, Anthony, *Selected Film Criticism, 1921–1930* (Metuchen, N.J.: Scarecrow Press, 1982); Tibbetts, John C., *The American Theatrical Film* (Bowling Green, Ohio: Popular Press).

—*J.C.T.*

1776 (1969)

MUSIC AND LYRICS: SHERMAN EDWARDS (1919–1981)
BOOK: PETER STONE

1776 (1972), U.S.A, directed by Peter H. Hunt, adapted by Peter Stone; Columbia.

The Play

Sherman Edwards majored in history at New York University, taught American history in high school, played piano in several of the best of the big bands, and composed several moderately successful pop hits. He was obsessed also with writing a musical based on the signing of the Declaration of Independence, but the whole idea of a nearly all-male cast singing about the Declaration of Independence seemed too ridiculous even to contemplate. Edwards persisted, however, and like his good friend (and fellow newcomer to Broadway) Meredith Willson, he was determined to see his story on the stage. After much persuasion and several years of development, he was convinced to allow Peter Stone to rework the book, and the neophyte Broadway composer finally saw his creation open at the 46th Street Theatre on March 16, 1969.

"Everyone discounted us," said Peter Stone. "We didn't have an advance of five beans. We had no real stars, a director who had never worked on Broadway before, a writer whose two previous shows had not done very well, and a composer-lyricist who was even more of an unknown quantity. And there were all kinds of questions about the subject matter." The choreography was done by Onna White, scenery by Jo Mielziner, and the direction by Peter Hunt.

The musical takes place in the chamber of the Continental Congress in Philadelphia during three stiflingly hot months of 1776. Representatives of the 13 colonies are debating several issues related to the ongoing conflict with Great Britain. John Adams (William Daniels), however, is impatient and resolved to declare a motion for independence. Unfortunately, as his good friend Benjamin Franklin (Howard da Silva) puts it, he is "obnoxious and disliked," and no one wants even to debate his proposal. So Adams agrees to Franklin's suggestion that they persuade Richard Henry Lee of Virginia (Ronald Holgate) to make the motion in order to get the idea into debate. As a member of the "Lees of Old Virginia," he carries a great deal of respect in Congress.

The most vociferous opponent to the independence resolution is John Dickinson of Pennsylvania, and to forestall his inevitable "nay" vote, Adams and Franklin propose that a document of some sort be written, outlining the reasons for the resolution. They compel the poor, lovesick, and homesick newlywed Thomas Jefferson (Ken Howard) to postpone his journey home in order to write the declaration of intent.

The power of *1776* lies in part in its commitment to as much historical accuracy as is dramatically possible.

Although the number of members of Congress is diminished for the sake of clarity, each of the 20 representatives as well as the congressional secretary and custodian are completely and particularly defined as characters. Edwards and Stone reveal the men of the Continental Congress in such a way that their historical status as "founding fathers" falls away, and we see them as individuals, some with high-flung ideals, others with feet of clay.

John Adams, however, is the focal point. As David Spencer puts it: "[The others] are satellites who relate to *him*, rather than to the abstraction of 'independence'—more specifically, he personifies the abstraction." Adams rants about alienating everyone, but his character is softened by the scenes with his wife Abigail (Virginia Vestoff). In an often maligned technique of the musical, Abigail appears on the stage in a fantasy sequence responding to the letters her husband writes to her in which he details his various frustrations and loneliness. The friendly and sometimes tender bantering between the two serves to humanize Adams and helps us understand the depth of his feeling for his wife and the cause he so ardently supports. "Till Then" and "Is Anybody There" reveal the high personal price he pays to remain in Philadelphia championing his cause.

The spirited debate in the Congress is punctuated by General Washington's continued dispatches about the desperate situations faced by his men of the Continental Army. A silent, grubby messenger, no more than 15 or 16 years old, delivers the reports from the front. Silent, until a moment when he describes the horrors of the battle at Lexington in "Momma, Look Sharp," he provides another touch of the real cost paid by rebellion. The gloomy dispatches he carries from the general serve to bolster Dickinson's opposition to the independence vote. The final third of the play involves the debate over the document Jefferson has completed. Here Edwards and Stone have taken a bit of historical license. The Declaration of Independence was reported back to the Congress before the July 2nd vote; however, the debate over the revisions did not take place until after the vote on independence. The document received 86 separate changes including one whose significance threatened to kill the independence movement entirely. One of the passages describing the faults of King George III condemned slavery and called for its abolition. The paragraph finally had to be removed in order to maintain the support of the southern colonies, much to Adams and Jefferson's sorrow. "Mark me, Franklin," says Adams, "if we give in on this issue, posterity will never forgive us." Franklin tries to console him, saying "If we don't secure [independence], what difference will the rest make?" So the "offending passage" is removed, and they secure the votes of the southern delegations. According to Peter Stone, Adams's words (spoken actually by his cousin Samuel Adams) were exactly: "If we give in on this issue, *there will be trouble a hundred years hence*; posterity will never forgive us." Stone could not use the phrase in its exact form for fear the audience would believe it to be only dramatic invention. Adams's prophecy, of course, was frighteningly accurate.

The final scene depicting the signing of the document proceeds with one member after another striding to the platform and affixing his name. (In actuality the signing took place over several weeks throughout the summer.) The characters then take up positions reminiscent of the famous Pine-Savage engraving of the occasion, and the Liberty Bell tolls out over the frozen scene.

"It makes even an Englishman's heart beat faster," said the *New York Times*. "A brilliant and remarkably moving work of theatrical art . . . a most exhilarating accomplishment," raved the *New York Post*. *1776* ran for 1,217 performances and was "the first musical ever presented in its entirety at the White House on 22 February 1970 at a command performance for President Nixon and his guests." It was nominated for several Tony Awards and won best musical. There was a splendid revival of *1776* on Broadway in 1997, directed by Scott Ellis and starring Brent Spiner as John Adams.

The Film

Jack L. Warner produced the film for Columbia Pictures and hired Peter Hunt as director. Peter Stone adapted his play for the screen, and Ken Howard, Virginia Vestoff, Ronald Holgate, and several others recreated their roles on film. William Daniels and Howard da Silva also reprised their incomparable performances. As Yul Brynner did with the king of Siam, they so define the roles of Adams and Franklin that the echoes of their performances hover about every production. Hunt also brought in several actors who had played various roles in the touring companies or who had been replacements during the Broadway run. John Cullum was one of the most interesting of these. He had been the third actor to play Edward Rutledge on Broadway, but, according to David Spencer, "the deep South authenticity he brought with him was so perfect and unassailable, and so redefined the role, that it was he who got the screen assignment." Cullum's show-stopping performance of "Molasses to Rum" is riveting.

The film is a faithful (some say too faithful) rendering of the stage production, and Edwards's score again achieves its aim of character definition. Some bright moments are Blythe Danner's charming performance as Martha Jefferson, singing "He Plays the Violin," and Daniels and Vestoff's duet on "Till Then." Da Silva is often hilariously funny as the quip-spouting Franklin, and Ronald Holgate's exuberant performance as Richard Henry Lee takes full advantage of the outdoor locale of "The Lees of Old Virginia" for plenty of slap-stick choreography. The one number that did not appear in the final film edit was "Cool, Cool Consid-erate Men," the piece sung by the conservative mem-bers of Congress. According to David Spencer, its excision was political rather than artistic. In an inter-view with Peter Stone in the early 1970s, Spencer asked him why the number was cut. Stone assured him that it had been shot, but that Jack Warner received a call from the Nixon White House firmly suggesting that the eight minutes be cut from the film. Warner, being of a fairly conservative bent, cut the number and then burned the negatives. He also excised another 40 minutes or so of political debate and two verses of "Piddle, Twiddle, and Resolve." Presumably the seg-ment was lost forever; however, a strange sequence of events of the sort that people think happen only in movies then occurred. The editor's assistant secretly set aside copies of the burned scenes in strips, and they were stored in Columbia's storage facilities in Wiscon-sin and Kansas. In the early 1990s Joseph Caporiccio and Michael Matessino of Pioneer Video set out to find and restore the missing scenes. The strips were cleaned and restored, edited, and synchronized to newly mixed and mastered stereo tracks. Again fortune favored their efforts. Columbia Records had saved the original 16-track master tapes with all the songs, the unreleased reprises, and incidental music. The restored film was released on laser disc and so returned what was an adequate film version of the stage musical to a more cohesive production.

Whether it was the sometimes choppy continuity of the film or not, *1776* failed to gross even $4,000,000 in distributor's domestic film rentals. However, *Newsday* called it "a rarity among movie musicals—literate, fre-quently hilarious, continually engrossing historical drama."

REFERENCES

Frommer, Myrna Katz, and Harry Frommer, *It Happened on Broadway: An Oral History of the Great White Way* (New York: Harcourt Brace, 1998); Ganzl, Kurt, *The Encyclopedia of Musical Theatre* (New York: Schirmer, 1994); Kennedy, Michael Patrick, and John Muir, *Musicals* (Glasgow: HarperCollins, 1997); Parish, James Robert, and Michael R. Pitts, *The Great Hollywood Musical Pictures* (Metuchen, N.J.: Scarecrow Press, 1992); Spencer, David, *Review of 1776. Aisle Say: The Internet Magazine of Stage Reviews and Opinions,* (www.escape.com/~theanet/NY=1776.html) 1997; Stone, Peter, and Sherman Edwards, "Historical Notes," *1776: A Musical Play,* (New York: Viking Press, 1970); Suskin, Steven, *Opening Nights on Broadway* (New York: Schirmer, 1990).

—S.L.Y.

SHOW BOAT (1927)

MUSIC: JEROME KERN (1885–1945)

BOOK AND LYRICS: OSCAR HAMMERSTEIN II (1895–1960)

Show Boat (1929), U.S.A., directed by Harry A. Pollard, adapted by Charles Kenyon; Universal.

Show Boat (1936), U.S.A., directed by James Whale, adapted by Oscar Hammerstein II; Universal.

Show Boat (1951), U.S.A., directed by George Sidney, adapted by John Lee Mahin; MGM.

The Play

Edna Ferber's novel *Show Boat* (1926) has reached the screen three times, but always via the the Kern-Ham-merstein musical production. This landmark of the American musical theatre, with its integrated book and music, its sprawling 50-year time span, and its contro-versial themes of miscegenation and a wife's desertion by her ne'er-do-well husband, premiered in Washing-ton, D.C., at the National Theatre on November 15, 1927, and a month later in New York at the Ziegfeld Theatre (a last-minute switch from the Lyric Theatre), on December 27, 1927, where it ran for a spectacular 575 performances. Jerome Kern had read Ferber's book and, after securing permission from her to adapt it to the stage, sought out librettist Oscar Hammer-stein II to collaborate on the production. The gesta-tion was unusually long—more than a year.

The story begins in the 1880s aboard the riverboat, *Cotton Blossom*, where Cap'n Andy (Charles Win-ninger) and his troupe of performers have arrived in Natchez to put on a show. But when the racist sheriff discovers that the leading lady, Julie (Helen Morgan), is a half-caste, he moves to stop the show. Intervening is Magnolia (Norma Terris), daughter of the ship's cap-tain, and her lover, the handsome gambler Gaylord Ravenal (Howard Marsh). Later, Magnolia and Rave-nal marry and relocate to Chicago, where Gaylord's dissolute life and gambling losses lead to his desertion

Paul Robeson sang "Ol Man River" in James Whale's 1936 adaptation of Kern and Hammerstein's Show Boat.
(COURTESY NATIONAL FILM SOCIETY ARCHIVES)

of his wife and daughter, Kim. Magnolia finds work singing at the Trocadero. Years later, she and her daughter, now radio stars, attend a reunion with the old showboat troupe, including the now-reformed Ravenal. The stellar list of songs includes the classic "Ol' Man River," sung by the black dockhand, Joe (Jules Bledsoe), the "Make Believe" and "Why Do I Love You?" duets by Gaylord and Magnolia, "Bill" and "Can't Help Lovin' Dat Man" by Julie. The 1932 revival brought Paul Robeson to the role of Joe, and a 1946 revival, which opened just after Kern's death, featured his last new song. Among subsequent revivals is the recent restoration by historian/conductor John McGlinn at the Houston Opera and on EMI Records. In sum, *Show Boat* deserves its reputation as a modern classic, as historian Miles Kreuger notes in his definitive history of the show—"a tightly written musical play with devotion to character development, with songs that grew meaningfully out of the plot, with spectacle and dance only when spectacle and dance seemed appropriate to the story . . . something the

American Musical Theatre had never before experienced."

The Films

Universal Studios originally purchased the rights to adapt Ferber's novel-only to the screen, but with the success of the musical stage version, coupled with the advent of the talking picture, it decided to incorporate elements of the Kern-Hammerstein production into its almost-completed part-talkie. Universal stars Laura La Plante, Alma Rubens, and Joseph Schildkraut were brought in. The scenario includes most of the key moments of novel and play, although the theme of miscegenation is dropped. Of particular historical interest is the addition of a filmed prologue featuring original cast members performing numbers from the show— including Helen Morgan singing "Bill" and "Can't Help Lovin' Dat Man"; Jules Bledsoe singing "Ol' Man River," and Tess "Aunt Jemima" Gardella singing "C'mon Folks" and "Hey, Feller!" Some critics were generally unimpressed with the finished film (of which only the picture portion and a partial soundtrack survive today), and they complained that the stagy prologue did not mesh at all well with the more "realistic" treatment of the main story. Welford Beaton in *The Film Spectator*, however, praised the seamless transitions between the talking and sound sequences and the use of musical interpolations on the soundtrack: "Through many of the sequences there is an engaging obligato of Negro voices singing songs of the Mississippi. Several selections from the musical version of the story were used to good effect, both the words and the music of 'Ol' Man River' coming into the production at various times in a most welcome manner."

As early as 1934 Universal Pictures wanted to remake *Show Boat* In an effort to return to the Broadway original, several principals were signed on to re-create their original stage roles, including Helen Morgan (Julie), Charles Winninger (Cap'n Andy), and Sammy White (Frank). Also brought on board were the original conductor Victor Baravalle, orchestrator Robert Russell Bennett, and Oscar Hammerstein himself, who wrote the scenario. From the London premiere came Paul Robeson as Joe. Otherwise, the key roles of Gaylord Ravenal went to newcomer Allan Jones, a classically trained tenor, and Magnolia to Irene Dunne, a veteran of musical comedy. British emigre director James Whale (*Frankenstein, The Invisible Man, The Bride of Frankenstein*) seemed at first an odd choice to helm the project, but, as historian Miles Kreuger notes, "Whale manages to blend perfectly his finely crafted sketch of social mores, architectural and interior decor, costume design, and geographic atmosphere with the inherent conventions of the musical." The film's exposition, sequence by sequence—especially the events of Act One, Scene One, concluding with Robeson's rendition of "Ol Man River"—follows Hammerstein's original 1927 libretto very closely. A radical departure from the play comes at the story's conclusion, however, when a modern-dress sequence alters events and brings Magnolia and Kim to Broadway.

Among the other alterations from the stage production are a new wedding scene to replace the World's Fair scene; the elimination of the song, "Why Do I Love You?"; the addition of an extra song for Robeson; and the reunion of Magnolia and Ravenal, which occurs at Kim's Broadway opening night rather than back at the *Cotton Blossom*. Among the many highlights is the delicious sequence in which Charles Winninger re-creates his original stage business of enacting all the parts in the rehearsal of the showboat's production of the melodrama, *The Parson's Bride*; and when

Joe sings "Ol' Man River" while the camera makes a 360-degree pan around him, moving into a tight close-up as the picture dissolves into a series of expressionist scenes of dock workers laboring under their heavy burdens. Although Helen Morgan appears relatively briefly—a handful of scenes that total barely 20 minutes of screen time—her rendition of "Bill" ranks among the great moments in the history of the musical film. It would be Morgan's last film; she died in 1941 at the age of 41. The film opened to rapturous reviews and has remained ever since an outstanding example of the conjunction of the Broadway musical and the Hollywood film.

The third and, to date, last version of the Kern-Hammerstein stage musical was produced for MGM in 1951 by ace musical impresario Arthur Freed. A great admirer of Jerome Kern, Freed had already incorporated several numbers from the stage show into his lavish screen biography of Kern, *Till the Clouds Roll By* (1946). George Sidney, director of the film's splashy finale, was brought in to helm the new adaptation, freshly conceived by John Lee Mahin. Robert Alton and Charles Rosher provided the dance choreography and the vivid Technicolor photography, respectively. However, despite the all-star cast and lavish production values—and spectacular box office—purists have dismissed the overall results. Mahin reduced the time-span of the sprawling story from 50 years to a mere decade, so that Magnolia and Ravenal are reunited while still young (and their daughter Kim is still just a child). Almost all of Hammerstein's dialogue was scrapped, and a whole new story line is introduced after Magnolia's triumphal debut at the Trocadero. Now, instead of going on to fame in New York, Magnolia (Kathryn Grayson) returns to the *Cotton Blossom* to raise her little girl and wait for the return of Ravenal (Howard Keel). Julie (Ava Gardner), meanwhile, returns to the story just in time to encourage Ravenal to return to the showboat and to his wife and child (of whose existence he is unaware). As Magnolia and Ravenal embrace, the boat pulls away to the sounds of an offscreen choir of "Ol' Man River." Julie, looking pathetically worn and alone, remains on the pier and silently blows them a kiss.

While historian Miles Kreuger applauds the inclusion of one more scene for Julie, he also sarcastically deplores how this vulnerable waif—a role originally intended for Judy Garland—is transformed by Ava Gardner's performance into a sensuous, strapping woman: "She is a glamour queen trying valiantly to break out of her mould to become a serious actress. Yet apparently neither she nor the studio is quite sure how to manage the transition." Gardner's vocalizations can be heard on the MGM soundtrack album, but her singing on screen is dubbed by Annette Warren. Regrettably, continues Kreuger, the film is sadly lacking in humor. All the *Cotton Blossom* stage performances have been excised (including Cap'n Andy's show-stopping rendering of the roles in *The Parson's Bride*), along with the World's Fair scenes and the banter between Joe (William Warfield) and Queenie. "Can't Help Lovin' Dat Man of Mine," rendered authentically onstage and in the 1936 version in a spirited quartet of voices, is here transformed into a slow, mournful soliloquy for Julie. And most of "Ol' Man River," except for its refrain, is eliminated (perhaps, argues Kreuger, because it was felt that the deleted lyrics placed too much emphasis on the toil of the black dockhands). As for the *Cotton Blossom* itself, it was constructed as a steam-driven, back-wheel paddle boat—a grievous error, since all showboats were simply barges with no power whatever of their own (they were pushed along by little towboats). "An ill-informed gaggle of critics and the public alike swallowed this film," laments Kreuger, "its largely inappropriate cast, its musical mutilation, its humorless script, and its empty Technicolored fripperies like a sack of sticky, sweet gumdrops."

REFERENCES

Curtis, James, *James Whale* (Metuchen, N.J.: Scarecrow Press, 1982); Fordin, Hugh, *The World of Entertainment: The Freed Unit at MGM* (Garden City, N.Y.: Doubleday, 1975); Kreuger, Miles, *Show Boat: The Story of a Classic American Musical* (New York: Oxford University Press, 1977); Tibbetts, John, "John McGlinn: Restoring the American Musical Theater," *The World and I*, 10:4 (April 1995): 112–117.

—*J.C.T.*

THE SOUND OF MUSIC (1959)

BOOK: HOWARD LINDSAY (1889–1968)/RUSSEL CROUSE (1893–1966)
MUSIC: RICHARD RODGERS (1902–1979)/LYRICS BY OSCAR HAMMERSTEIN II (1895–1960)

The Sound of Music (1965), U.S.A., directed by Robert Wise, adapted by Ernest Lehman; 20th Century-Fox.

The Play

Rodgers and Hammerstein's *The Sound of Music*, which opened on Broadway on November 16, 1959, was based upon the true story of the Trapp Family Singers, an Austrian family whose success in their own country was cut short when they were forced to flee from the Nazis in the late 1930s. The play followed the story of young Maria Kutschera (Mary Martin), a postulant in an Austrian abbey who is sent to serve as governess for the seven mischievous children of a stern military man, Georg von Trapp (Theodore Bikel). Maria and the captain fall in love and are married, but their new life together is endangered by the Anschluss that joined Austria to Hitler's Third Reich. After performing one last concert, they make their getaway, escaping across the mountains to freedom. Although critics derided the show as excessively sentimental and saccharine, it became an enormous hit and produced several classic songs, including the title tune, "Do-Re-Mi," "Climb Every Mountain," "My Favorite Things," and "Edelweiss." *The Sound of Music* ran for 1,443 performances in New York and 2,385 in London, making it one of the greatest successes of the modern theatre. It won six Antoinette Perry Awards ("Tonys"), including one for best musical.

The Film

Twentieth Century-Fox paid a million dollars for the screen rights to *The Sound of Music* in 1960. It was the highest price ever paid by a film company for a theatrical work, but the investment turned out to be a sound one. Robert Wise's elaborate film version, which opened on March 2, 1965, became one of the biggest blockbusters in cinema history. Although critics weren't much kinder to the film than to the play, audiences adored it; some people saw it dozens of times; others sat through literally hundreds of screenings. If the original play was a success, the film version was a genuine phenomenon. It won Academy Awards for best director, picture, sound, film editing, and scoring of music. It also received many other awards and nominations.

The Sound of Music wasn't the first film version of the story of the Trapp Family Singers: *Die Trapp-Familie* (1956) and *Die Trapp-Familie in Amerika* (1958) were both based on Maria von Trapp's autobiography, "Maria," but were made without her involvement. Both films were very popular and profitable in Germany. They were then edited together and released in the United States in 1961 as *The Trapp Family*, where success was more modest.

William Wyler was originally set to direct the film, but he abruptly resigned from the project after working on it for the better part of a year. Wyler was replaced by Robert Wise, already an Academy Award winner for *West Side Story* (1961), and the acclaimed director of film classics as diverse as *The Day the Earth Stood Still* (1951), *I Want to Live!* (1958) and *The Haunting* (1963). Wise embraced the project because, he said, "I thought it was a chance to do a different kind of musical, one that could entertain all kinds of people and still had serious things to say."

Filmmakers usually attempt to "open up" a play when adapting it to the screen. In an article he wrote at the time for the *Los Angeles Times*, Wise explains that this is done in order to take "some of the action out into the world in order to utilize the flexibility of the camera to emphasize mood and action that, on stage, can only be referred to or implied." Perhaps no adaptation has ever been opened up as magnificently, or to better effect, as *The Sound of Music*. From the opening helicopter shot that locates an exuberant Maria (Julie Andrews) on an Austrian mountaintop, to the breathtaking views of Salzburg, the film is a visual feast.

Even so, in adapting the story from one medium to another, Wise and screenwriter Ernest Lehman tried to keep changes to a minimum. Only two songs from the play were dropped, while two new songs were written specifically for the film: "I Have Confidence" helped to define Maria's uncertainty and hope as she leaves the convent for her new assignment at the von Trapp home; and "Something Good" marked the beginning of romance for the captain (Christopher Plummer) and Maria. Lehman toned down some of the play's more overt sentimentality and added some much needed humor. His script also emphasized the danger that faced the Trapp family. The Nazis had been an offstage presence in the play, but Wise and Lehman felt that the more realistic medium of film demanded a more straightforward presentation of this aspect of the drama.

However, even with more realistic Nazis posing a more palpable threat, *The Sound of Music* never veers toward hard-hitting political or historical drama. It is a "feel good" movie in the best sense of the term, a warm and endearing—and undemanding—film of accessible, yet genuine, emotion. Its themes are simple and its presentation sumptuous. The performances are first-rate and the songs are memorable and, at best, positively inspired. *The Sound of Music* has never garnered much critical respect, but it occupies a major space in the very select cinematic pantheon of films that are genuinely beloved.

REFERENCES

Amoruso, Marino, and Gallagher, John, "Robert Wise: Part One 'The RKO Years,'" *Grand Illusion* (Winter 1977); Aylesworth, Thomas G., *Broadway to Hollywood* (New York: Bison Books, 1985); Hirsch, Julia Antopol, *The Sound of Music: The Making of America's Favorite Movie* (Chicago: Contemporary Books, 1993); Thompson, Frank, *Robert Wise: A Bio-Bibliography* (Westport, Conn.: Greenwood Press, 1995); Wise, Robert, "Why *The Sound of Music* Sounds Differently," *The Los Angeles Times Calendar* (January 24, 1965).

—F.T./D.H.

SOUTH PACIFIC (1949)

LYRICS: OSCAR HAMMERSTEIN II (1895–1960)
MUSIC: RICHARD RODGERS (1902–1979)
BOOK: OSCAR HAMMERSTEIN II AND JOSHUA LOGAN, BASED ON JAMES MICHENER'S *TALES OF THE SOUTH PACIFIC* (SPECIFICALLY, "OUR HEROINE" AND "FO' DOLLA")

South Pacific (1958), U.S.A., directed by Joshua Logan, adapted by Paul Osborn; Twentieth Century-Fox.

The Play

Directed and choreographed by the redoubtable Joshua Logan, Rodgers and Hammerstein's musicalization of James Michener's Pulitzer Prize–winning stories opened to unanimous raves on April 7, 1949, at the Majestic Theatre. Writing in the *New York Daily Mirror*, Robert Coleman opined, "Programmed as a musical play, *South Pacific* is just that. It boasts no ballets and no hot footing. It has no chorus in the conventional sense. Every one in it plays a part. It is likely to establish a new trend in musicals."

The setting is an island in the South Pacific during World War II. Nellie Forbush (Mary Martin, who never missed a single performance of the long run), a bright and cheery U.S. Navy nurse from Arkansas, has just had lunch with a dashing older man, Emile de Becque (Metropolitan Opera basso Ezio Pinza making his straight theatre debut). De Becque is much older than Nellie and has many secrets. He was originally from France but had to leave when he killed a man. He now lives and works on a plantation and, unbeknownst to Nellie, has fathered two children by a Polynesian woman. With advice from her mother (via a letter from back home) Nellie is determined to wash Emile out of her hair, citing too many differences between them. In the meantime, a young marine, Lieutenant Joe Cable (William Tabbert), has just arrived on the island with orders to learn all he can about the French planter and pursue with him a dangerous mission. But Cable gets distracted. Together with Luther Billis (Myron

McCormick), a conniving sailor, they take a launch and leave for a mysterious island named Bali Ha'i, a real dreamland full of riches beyond compare and host to the everything-goes Ceremonial of the Boar's Tooth. On the island, Cable meets a lovely Polynesian girl, Liat (Betta St. John), the daughter of the wise and crafty Bloody Mary (Juanita Hall). Bloody Mary allows Cable to make love to her daughter in the hopes that he will marry her and take her back to the States.

For the first time, the composer and lyricist team dealt openly with a racy, sexy scene. "*South Pacific*'s erotic moment is a lengthy one, and not pre-marital or conjugal sex but sex as pure bliss between two beautiful youngsters," writes historian Ethan Mordden. Back on the main island, Nellie is still disturbed over her relationship with Emile. She is called in by the commander of the naval forces and is asked to use her influence and convince de Becque to undergo a top secret and highly dangerous mission. He refuses the commander, alluding to his love for Nellie as a reason not to go. However, at the close of the first act, Nellie finds out that de Becque fathered two children with a Polynesian woman and this fact disturbs her greatly, bringing forth old, forgotten prejudices from her upbringing. Nellie can't seem to love a man with half-caste children and de Becque, extremely disappointed in her attitude, decides to go on the dangerous mission after all.

Unlike their other musicals, such as *Oklahoma!* and *Carousel*, the subplot of *South Pacific* is not comic but serious. Joe Cable is having the same difficulties with his conscience and learned prejudices as Nellie Forbush. Unfortunately, the only way he can see clear to solve his problem is to take on a suicide mission. Where Joe retreats, Nellie attacks her problem head on, and when Emile returns from the mission safely they create a beautiful picture of family life. Nellie does not run into her lover's arms or even kiss him, but rather invites him to sit down. As they have breakfast with Emile's racially mixed children, the music swells and Nellie and Emile slowly and carefully reach across the table to hold the other's hand. Love overpowers prejudice. It was a picture-perfect moment and beautifully orchestrated by director, composer, librettist, and actors.

Book writers Hammerstein and Logan did not lose sight of the fact that the show, so rich with dramatic situation, still needed some necessary comic relief. "In *South Pacific* we had two serious themes, with the second becoming tragedy when young Cable is killed during the mission," recalled Richard Rodgers. "Breaking the rules didn't bother us, but we did think the show needed comic leavening." Josh Logan adds, "Oscar asked James Michener for more comic material, and Jim wrote him a complete story of the GI's elaborate handling of the laundry. So we went to still a third story for an affable wheeler-dealer named Luther Billis and added him to the cast." The second act opens with a show-stopping "show within a show" as Nellie and Billis cross-dress for the very funny "Honey Bun" number (she wearing a much too large sailor uniform and he in grass skirt and coconut bra).

The musical garnered numerous awards, including 10 Tony awards, the Donaldson Award for best musical, the New York Drama Critics' Outer Circle Award, and the prestigious Pulitzer Prize for drama, only the second in history awarded to a musical and the first to include a composer, Richard Rodgers, as author. The show was so successful that the authors even went into merchandising. "We formed a company called South Pacific Enterprises to produce *South Pacific* scarves, dolls, perfume, underwear, sheets and pillowcases," writes Logan. Once launched, *South Pacific* immediately joined that rare company of such musicals as *Oklahoma!*, *My Fair Lady*, and *Fiddler on the Roof*, which are not only successful stage productions but also major social, theatrical, historical, cultural, and musical events.

The Film

In his book *Can't Help Singin'* Gerald Mast describes the kind of reverential film Rodgers and Hammerstein intended to make of their masterpiece: "In *South Pacific* the sailors sing 'There Is Nothin' Like a Dame' on what appears to be a real beach: a blue sky blazes overhead, waves roll toward the shore, palm trees offer their leafy shade. The wide CinemaScope frame supplies a vast panorama of visual potential—which Joshua Logan's direction proceeds to ignore, duplicating the movements and gestures that might have been performed in his stage production (and probably were)." Mast makes a very good point. Too often, the filming of a stage musical can turn into nothing more than a documentation of what happened in the stage original, a sort of "opera film." Mast continues: "Joshua Logan's sole visual 'idea' for the film was a series of colored filters [and colored gases] to convey the poetic imagery of Hammerstein's lyrics." Striving to create an atmosphere of mystery, the lens filters were a disastrous mistake, marring the beauty of the scenery. Rather than enhancing the emotional mood they wound up distracting the viewer from the story.

John Kerr, looking like a young Jack Kennedy, was cast as the all-American, Philadelphia-born, Princeton graduate Joe Cable. Though Kerr could not sing, Bill

Lee (whose voice did not match with Kerr's personality) awkwardly dubbed his songs. It does seem strange, then, that Rodgers and Hammerstein added to the score an additional song for Cable, "My Girl Back Home," which had been cut from the original stage play. Juanita Hall, reprising her stage role as Bloody Mary, was also dubbed (curiously enough by her London counterpart Muriel Smith), and Rossano Brazzi stiffly assayed the role of Emile de Becque (singing voice dubbed by Giorgio Tozzi). Mitzi Gaynor was a spunky Nellie Forbush, and she was to play the role on stage for many years. Rounding out the cast was Ray Walston as Luther Billis, reprising his role from the London production.

REFERENCES

Altman, Rick, *The American Film Musical* (Bloomington: Indiana University Press, 1987); Block, Geoffrey, *Enchanted Evenings* (New York: Oxford University Press, 1997); Logan, Joshua, *Josh: My Up and Down, In and Out Life* (New York: Delacorte Press, 1976); Mast, Gerald, *Can't Help Singin'* (Woodstock, N.Y.: Overlook Press, 1987); Mordden, Ethan, *Beautiful Mornin'* (New York: Oxford University Press, 1999); Rodgers, Richard, *Musical Stages* (New York: Random House, 1975); Suskin, Steven, *Opening Night on Broadway* (New York: Schirmer, 1990).

—*J.S.*

SWEET CHARITY (1966)

MUSIC: CY COLEMAN (1929–)
LYRICS: DOROTHY FIELDS (1905–1974)
BOOK: NEIL SIMON (1927–)

Sweet Charity (1969), U.S.A., directed and choreographed by Bob Fosse, adapted by Peter Stone; Universal Studios.

The Play

Sweet Charity is based on Federico Fellini's 1956 film *Le Notti di Cabiria* (Nights of Cabiria), written by Fellini, Ennio Flaiano, and Tullio Pinelli. Cabiria, the protagonist of Fellini's film, was a Roman streetwalker, but in Fosse's play she is called Charity Hope Valentine and works as a taxi dancer, largely because Fosse felt that "there is something ugly about a prostitute in this country"; what was essential for him was that Charity sells something for money: "a dance, her understanding, conversation, something," as he put it. To do research for the play, Fosse pretended to be an out-of-towner and patronized a series of dance-halls. He also

had Gwen Verdon, his wife and the star of the show, work as a taxi dancer (at the time, $6.50 would buy you 30 minutes of a dancer's time). Fosse wanted desperately to be known as more than a dancer/choreographer, and he spent a great deal of time and energy writing the script as well as directing the play. Eventually, he admitted that he needed help and asked Neil Simon, who had two plays on Broadway at the time (*Barefoot in the Park* and *The Odd Couple*) and was already known as a "play doctor," to work on the book.

While his impact on the script was less than he had hoped for, Fosse exceeded himself in the choreography. Turning away from the classic ballet-like dances choreographed by Agnes de Mille and Jerome Robbins, Fosse created a new idiom, based on overt sexuality and the rhythms of the street. "If My Friends Could See Me Now," "Hey Big Spender," and "Rhythm of Life" represent major breakthroughs in stage choreography. *Sweet Charity* was not only a turning point in Fosse's career, it also marks a watershed in both Broadway and film musicals in terms of narrative as well as dance style. Previously, musicals were romantic comedies in which the boy eventually got the girl. In *Sweet Charity*, as in *Le Notti di Cabiria*, the ending is downbeat: Charity is dumped a second time, but "lives hopefully ever after."

Advance publicity from the show's out-of-town performances and from the many cover versions of its songs recorded by singers such as Perry Como, Tony Bennett, Peggy Lee, Sarah Vaughan, Robert Goulet, and Barbra Streisand increased public awareness of the production and pre-sold a lot of tickets. The play opened in New York City on January 25, 1966, and ran for 608 performances. John McMartin, who played Oscar, was the only member of the cast to repeat his role in the film version.

In Act One, Charity is robbed and nearly drowned by her "fiancé" in the lake in Central Park. She bumps into Vittorio Vidal, a movie star, and becomes his date for the night, but her romantic fantasies don't come true, and she winds up spending the night in his closet when his girlfriend shows up unexpectedly. Determined to change her life, Charity goes to the 92nd Street "Y" in search of culture, where she meets Oscar. They get stuck in an elevator, and Charity helps Oscar through a claustrophobic crisis. Act Two begins when they are freed from the elevator, and Oscar invites her to a service at the Rhythm of Life Church. She and Oscar begin dating, and Charity's friends, Helene and Nickie, are concerned because Charity hasn't told Oscar what she really does for a living. Eventually, she tells him, but he already knows, having followed her one night. He was angry at first, but still wants to marry her. However, after seeing her in her milieu, he reneges, accidentally pushing her into the lake again. Unlike Cabiria's fate in Fellini's *Nights of Cabiria*, Charity is not robbed of her possessions and the Good Fairy (an advertisement for a TV show) appears and tells her that her dreams will all come true.

The Film

Fellini's film is the last in his *oeuvre* to show touches of neorealism, and the film's tone conforms to that grittiness more closely than the anti-realistic staging of the play does. The essence of *Le Notti di Cabiria* is the spirit of the protagonist and her ability to retain hope for the future, despite the trials that she undergoes. Unlike the play, the film is able to use close-ups, as Fellini did, to communicate the protagonist's longing, innocence, disappointment, and hurt, as she struggles to attain her desire, although the nature of this desire is changed in Fosse's version. Fellini's Cabiria wants love, but even more she wants to become a respected member of the bourgeoisie. This latter aspect is ignored in the play and in the film, if not actively denied. For example, Cabiria's costume becomes much more tasteful when she goes off to meet Oscar, expecting to marry him. Charity's costume in the film, on the other hand, changes from a rather tasteful little black dress to a luridly colored dress with giant daisies on it.

This black dress has consequences for the audience's perceptions of Charity. In Fellini's film, Cabiria wears socks and sandals, a striped jersey, a short skirt, and a fake fur jacket, and always carries an umbrella, a costume that represents her lower-class tastes, her childlike innocence, and her practicality. The little black dress was introduced by Fosse when he developed the play because he felt that a costume that accurately represented Cabiria's peculiar tastes distracted the audience from the dancing. However, the actual result is that, except for the tattoo of a heart with the name "Charlie" on her biceps (smaller in the film than it is on stage), Charity already looks like the bourgeoise that Cabiria aspires to be.

The unhappy ending of the play is made even more poignant and unhappy in the film, since Oscar waits until they are actually at the Registry Office before deciding that he cannot go through with their marriage, although the only thing that goes into the lake is a sign that says "Almost Married," and Fosse uses a Fellini gesture and has a band of hippies console Char-

ity instead of the play's Good Fairy. The executives at Universal resisted this sad ending, but ultimately accepted it, after an alternative ending in which Oscar comes back was shot and rejected. To balance the poignancy of Charity's heartbreak at the end, the tone of the rest of the film has been lightened. For example, several ballads sung on stage were deleted from the film version to avoid slowing the momentum of the plot down and to place the emphasis on the more upbeat musical numbers. This effort went too far in the case of the "Rhythm of Life" number. Originally intended to serve a satirical function comparable to Cabiria's visit to the shrine of the Madonna of Divine Love, where her money is taken and her prayers for a change in her status go unanswered, in the film this number becomes an over-the-top star turn for Sammy Davis, Jr., and loses its cynical punch. On the other hand, presenting "There's Gotta Be Something Better Than This" on a dingy rooftop in the film dramatizes more starkly than the play does exactly what Charity and her friends want to get away from. And the film's setting "I'm a Brass Band" on a Sunday morning in Wall Street creates a dream-like atmosphere not so easily represented on stage, as well as allowing Charity to jump from rooftops to Yankee Stadium through the magic of editing.

Since 1964 there had been a string of highly successful, big-budget blockbuster film versions of Broadway musicals—*My Fair Lady* (1964), *The Sound of Music* (1965), *A Funny Thing Happened on the Way to the Forum* and *How to Succeed in Business* (1966), and *Camelot* (1967)—and Universal Studios agreed to finance the filming of *Sweet Charity* in hopes of cashing in on some of this public interest. Unfortunately, *Sweet Charity* was not successful. Reviewers praised Shirley MacLaine's performance and admired Fosse's choreography and the staging of the musical numbers, but overall found the film overlong and overwrought. (Note: The VHS version of the film reflects this judgment; it uses the letterboxed, widescreen format for the dances while the rest of the film is presented in the cropped, pan-and-scan format.)

REFERENCES

Dyer, Richard, *Only Entertainment* (London: Routledge, 1992); Grubb, Kevin Lloyd, *Razzle Dazzle: The Life and Work of Bob Fosse* (New York: St. Martin's Press, 1989).

—*S.C.*

THE UNSINKABLE MOLLY BROWN (1960)

MUSIC AND LYRICS: MEREDITH WILLSON (1902–1984)
BOOK: RICHARD MORRIS (D.1996)

The Unsinkable Molly Brown (1964), U.S.A., directed by Charles Walters, adapted by Helen Deutsch; Paramount.

The Play

With the success of *The Music Man*, Meredith Willson next tried to put to music the tale of real-life heroine Molly Tobin Brown. Because of her indomitable spirit, the "unsinkable" Mrs. Brown somehow managed to survive the sinking of the *Titanic*. She went on to become a well-respected citizen of Denver, and one of the most famous and outspoken heroines of the new century.

   The story opens with a young Molly Tobin (Tammy Grimes) being teased by her older siblings, all brothers. She is a feisty Irish lass who wants more out of life than to work as a slave in her all-male environment. So she moves from her small shack in Hannibal, Missouri, to the mining town of Leadville, Colorado. There she takes a job as a saloon singer. Then, one night, into her life walks the tall and handsome Johnny Brown (Harve Presnell). Brown is a prospector in the Colorado hills whose mine has, unfortunately, failed to hit the mother lode. She marries Johnny and together they move into his newly built cabin, complete with her very own brass bed. But on their wedding night they argue about money and ambition and Johnny leaves. He arrives back a week later with $300,000, from work he did at his mine. As they finally go to consummate their marriage, Molly hides the money in the stove. The next day, Johnny, not knowing where Molly has hidden the money, lights a fire in the stove, and all the money is burned. This minor setback is no match for Johnny's strength of character; because of his love for Molly, he goes back to the mine and works until he has amassed another fortune. Happy and rich, they move to Denver and set up home in one of the wealthiest neighborhoods in the community. But no matter how hard Molly tries, she just can't seem to fit into the snobbish upper crust of Denver society. So Molly and Johnny go on a tour of Europe, where they become the darlings of the elite. But Johnny misses Colorado and when they finally return, with all of their royal friends in tow, Molly throws a party that enchants the snobbish Denver ladies. Unbeknownst to Molly, Johnny has also invited his friends from Leadville to the society soiree, and the party erupts into an all-out brawl. Molly, disillusioned by the disaster, leaves Johnny and flees to Europe. There she is romanced by a handsome prince, but she cannot go through with the affair. She still loves Johnny, and so she gets on the first boat bound for New York, which just happens to be the ill-fated *Titanic*.

As the ship is sinking in the distance, the confusion in the lifeboat almost causes it to sink as well. Molly immediately takes charge and lifts the spirits of her fellow lifeboat survivors, encouraging them to sing with her an old saloon song, "Belly Up to the Bar Boys." When she returns to Denver, she is the toast of the town. But Johnny is nowhere to be found. She discovers that he has returned to the Rocky Mountains, where they first met. Immediately, she leaves to go find him. In the grove, surrounded by Aspen trees, Molly reunites with Johnny and they collapse into each other's arms. He has built Molly a castle of her own, a majestic lodge made out of the red rock of Colorado, with two stoves, "one for cookin' and one for heatin'." After all their travels and adventures, they are finally home, where they belong.

As stated by historian Gerald Mast, "Willson's score proved to be as unsinkable as Molly Brown." The book of the show had many flaws, notably an incessant use of the "in-one" scene, commonly used in the musical theatre while scenery is being changed behind, which hampers the pace. Even the excessively buoyant Tammy Grimes could not help boost the lack of pace. Harve Presnell was unanimously praised for his rich baritone singing voice. Most of the love songs were given to him, save one, "Dolce Far Niente," which was sung by Prince DeLong, who tries unsuccessfully to woo Molly away from Johnny.

Note: When a new musical, *Titanic*, opened on Broadway in the early 1990s and won the Tony Award for best musical that season, the character of Molly Brown was conspicuously absent.

The Film

The success of James Cameron's movie, *Titanic* (1997) spurred a renewed interest in anything associated with that fatal voyage. Consequently, the movie musical of *The Unsinkable Molly Brown* has found a new audience. The film version is far superior to the stage show, perhaps because the 25 scene changes in the play were more easily accomplished on film than on stage. Director Charles Walters keeps the movie at a crisp pace and the chemistry between the two leads is electric. Debbie Reynolds was cast as the spunky tomboy Molly, and her handsome counterpart was played and sung by Harve Presnell, reprising his Broadway role. Reynolds got an Academy Award nod as best actress for her work, but the award that year went to another performer in a musical film, Julie Andrews in *Mary Poppins*. The *New York Times* reported the film to be "Cheerful, spirited, with the sweet corn-high score from Meredith Willson's Broadway musical, some down-to-earth tomboyish strutting from Debbie Reynolds and fine, manly singing by Harve Presnell. . . . The picture is bountiful and beaming." In 1989, both Debbie Reynolds and Harve Presnell reprised their roles from the film in a national tour of the show.

REFERENCES

Mast, Gerald, *Can't Help Singin'* (Woodstock, N.Y.: Overlook Press, 1987); Parish, James Robert, and Michael R. Pitts, *The Great Hollywood Musical* (Metuchen, N.J.: Scarecrow Press, 1992); Suskin, Steven, *Opening Night on Broadway* (New York: Schirmer, 1990).

—*J.S.*

WEST SIDE STORY (1957)

MUSIC: LEONARD BERNSTEIN (1918–1990)
LYRICS: STEPHEN SONDHEIM (1930–)
BOOK: ARTHUR LAURENTS (1918–), BASED ON AN IDEA BY JEROME ROBBINS AND ON SHAKESPEARE'S *ROMEO AND JULIET*

West Side Story (1961), U.S.A., directed by Robert Wise and Jerome Robbins, adapted by Ernest Lehman; United Artists.

The Play

The seeds for this landmark musical were planted in 1949 when Leonard Bernstein and Jerome Robbins agreed to write a contemporary version of William Shakespeare's *Romeo and Juliet* in the form of a musical based upon a strong social issue or point of view that would have depth and substance. Originally called *East Side Story*, it was to focus upon a Jewish girl and Catholic boy in an interracial romance (much like that 1920s melodramatic classic, *Abie's Irish Rose*). But the years went by and the work had stalled until the mid-1950s, when a migration of Puerto Ricans had gathered in New York and tensions broke out between the young immigrants and white New York gangs. The themes changed to match the social issues of the times and Arthur Laurents and Stephen Sondheim joined the team. It was to be Sondheim's first Broadway

musical play credit and Arthur Laurent's first musical.

West Side Story opened at the Winter Garden Theatre on September 26, 1957, and ran for 732 performances. It was directed with meticulous detail by Jerome Robbins and choreographed by Robbins and Peter Gennaro. It opened at Her Majesty's Theatre in London on December 12, 1958, running for 1,040 performances. The Bernstein score is one of the greatest musical scores of all time with such memorable songs as "Tonight," "Somewhere," "I Feel Pretty," "Maria," and many more. The original cast included Carol Lawrence, Larry Kert, Chita Rivera, Mickey Calin, and Martin Charnin, among other emerging talents.

The entire action takes place in two days. The teenage gang of American boys, the Jets, led by Riff (Calin), are out to destroy the Puerto Rican gang, the Sharks, led by Bernardo (Ken Le Roy), and drive them from the neighborhood. Tony (Kert), a past member of the Jets gang and now trying to refocus his life by working in a local drugstore, is persuaded by Riff to join the Jets one last time to fight against the hated Sharks. Both gangs arrive at a dance and Tony meets and falls in love with Bernardo's sister, Maria (Lawrence). She has just arrived from Puerto Rico to marry a Shark gang member, Chino (Jamie Sanchez). But Tony and Maria's "love at first sight" romance is destined to end in tragedy. While Tony and Maria plan their future in a mock marriage staged in the Bridal Shop where Maria is employed, the Jets and the Sharks meet in a drugstore to make plans for a "big rumble" that will decide who owns the neighborhood. At the rumble, Bernardo, furious about Tony's love for his sister, threatens Tony and an all out "war" ensues as weapons emerge and Riff is killed. Tony, bitter over the loss of his friend, murders Bernardo with Riff's knife. Later, Chino, the new leader of the Sharks, procures a gun and searches for Tony. Anita (Rivera), suppressing her hate, tries to find Tony to warn him of Chino's plans. At the drugstore, Anita is mauled by the Jets and, out of anger, tells them that Chino has killed Maria. Tony hears the news and goes into the streets where he suddenly encounters Maria. In that moment, Chino kills Tony. There is some awareness by both the Jets and the Sharks that what has happened has been senseless. As the two gangs carry Tony's body away, there is a sense that, for the moment, at least, these two worlds must find a way to live together.

The success currently associated with *West Side Story* did not come immediately. *The Music Man* beat it out for all major awards that year. According to historian Steven Suskin, "It wasn't until the 1961 movie version that the *West Side* score entered the public consciousness; since then the show has been properly recognized as a classic blend of music, words, and dance."

The Film

One of the most successful transitions of a musical play to the screen was accomplished with the filming of *West Side Story*. Directed by Robert Wise and Jerome Robbins, the film remained mostly faithful to the stage work. Despite mixed reviews when it was released in 1961, it became one of the greatest box-office hits in the history of stage musicals adapted to screen. It captured ten Academy Awards, including best picture, best direction, and best supporting actor and actress (George Chakiris and Rita Moreno). "Because of the quality of the original materials and of the translation, the result is the best film musical ever made," writes Stanley Kauffmann.

A variety of emerging talent auditioned and were rejected for the screen version, including George Hamilton, Joey Heatherton, Jill St. John, Robert Redford, Keir Dullea (who refused to cut his curly blond hair for the role), Leonard Nimoy, Jack Nicholson, Bobby Darin, and Warren Beatty. In the end, the coveted roles of Maria and Tony went to Natalie Wood and Richard Beymer as Tony, neither of whom could sing. Wood was dubbed by Marni Nixon and Beymer was dubbed entirely by Jimmy Bryant. "Of the large cast only Richard Beymer is inadequate," wrote Kauffmann; "his earnestness does not compensate for his

lack of appeal." Interestingly enough, when a section of the "Tonight Quintet" proved to be too high for Rita Moreno, Marni Nixon was brought in to dub that as well, which means that in the film she is in essence harmonizing with herself. Tucker Smith who played the role of Ice in the film (and sang the song "Cool") had a similar singing voice to that of Russ Tamblyn (playing Riff), so he wound up dubbing Tamblyn's voice for the "Jet Song."

The film version is also remembered for the collaboration of the two directors, Wise and Robbins. Wise was finishing post-production work on his *noir* thriller, *Odds Against Tomorrow*, when he was contacted by producer Harold Mirisch about the project. He agreed to direct but insisted that Robbins join him in a co-directing capacity. Although Robbins left the production near the end, his co-directing credit was retained. "Jerry was involved in all aspects of the film from scripting to music to sets and costumes," asserted Wise. "His contribution was of such stature and such quality that I felt he definitely deserved co-directing credit with me and he got it." From the outset a relatively faithful adaptation was envisioned, even to the degree of opening the film with an overture. Location shooting on the Manhattan streets of the dance numbers was integrated with sound stage photography at the Samuel Goldwyn Studios in Hollywood, creating a blend of *noirish* atmosphere and romantic fantasy. "The principal difficulty that had to be surmounted in transferring *West Side Story* from stage to the screen was one of style," writes Saul Chaplin. "How do you get movie audiences to accept gang members not only dancing but dancing in the street? . . . The only way to solve the problem was for the dancing to start unobtrusively and gradually out of natural movement." For example, Wise opted to begin the action with aerial shots of New York City, which established the city as a real location; however, by shooting straight down at the buildings, patterns and forms gave the site an abstract quality that helped establish the place as an arena of mystery and fantasy as well. The striking dance scene that follows is a model of precision dancing and editing. The Jets lurk around the playground, snapping fingers in jazzy synchronization. Gradually, they break into a dance, which accelerates in swift intensity, breaking into pirouettes and running jumps. They confront the Sharks in a beautifully choreographed piece of balletic violence.

However, after this exciting opening, according to historian Gerald Mast, "The film runs out of visual ideas after its prologue, translating the CinemaScope frame into a stable proscenium arch, within which dances are conceived as purely horizontal, in a relatively flat, open, and static space." The only major change that occurred in the translation to the screen had to do with the placement of two musical numbers. "Gee, Officer Krupke" had originally been in the second act after the boys were killed, and "Cool" had been in the first part of the show. It was agreed that they should be reversed for the film, placing the "comedy number" early and saving "Cool" for the latter half. The dance prologue was also doubled in length from the original stage version. In the end, says Mast, the film strikes a "powerful cultural chord: the first film to sing the spirit of the sixties protest against the Krupkes of American life and politics."

REFERENCES

Bordman, Gerald, *American Musical Theatre* (New York: Oxford University Press, 1986); Chaplin, Saul, *The Golden Age of Movie Musicals and Me* (Norman: University of Oklahoma Press, 1994); Kauffmann, Stanley, *A World on Film: Criticism and Comment* (New York: Delta, 1966); Mast, Gerald, *Can't Help Singin'* (Woodstock, N.Y.: Overlook Press, 1987); Suskin, Steven, *Opening Night on Broadway* (New York: Schirmer, 1990).

—*J.W. AND J.S.*

WHOOPEE! (1928)

BOOK: WILLIAM ANTHONY MCGUIRE
LYRICS: GUS KAHN
MUSIC: WALTER DONALDSON

Whoopee! (1930), U.S.A., directed by Thornton Freeland, adapted by William Counselman; Goldwyn/United Artists.

The Play

Whoopee! was the last of a series of successful shows produced by the redoubtable Florenz Ziegfeld in the late 1920s (preceded by *Show Boat, Rio Rita, Rosalie,* and *The Three Musketeers,* among others). It opened at the New Amsterdam Theatre on December 4, 1928, and ran for a spectacular 407 performances. Audiences enthusiastically acclaimed its headliner, Eddie Cantor, the songs by Gus Kahn and Walter Donaldson, the elaborate choreography by Seymour Felix, and brilliant costume design by John Harkrider. Based on Owen Davis's 1923 satire, *The Nervous Wreck,* it chronicles the seriocomic misadventures of pretty Sally Morgan (Frances Upton). Since she loves the Indian Wanenis (Paul Gregory) and does not want to marry Sheriff Wells (Jack Rutherford), she runs away with the

assistance of the hypochondriacal Henry Williams (Cantor). Their subsequent misadventures out West include a pursuit by a posse, the breakdown of their car, and a romance for Henry with his nurse, Mary Custer (Ethel Shutta). Objections to Sally's romance with Wanenis melt away when it is learned that he is really a white man. Also in the cast was Ruth Etting as Leslie Daws, a movie star, who had little to do but sing her signature song, "Love Me or Leave Me."

But it was Cantor's rendition of the show-stopping "Whoopee" that made the biggest impression with audiences. Meanwhile, taking advantage of the wild western locales, Ziegfeld bedecked his famous chorus beauties with fantastic Indian feathered costumes and paraded them around the stage on horseback. While *Whoopee*'s ethnic slurs, arguably sexist glorification of the American Girl, and exaggerated comic turns by Cantor make it seem dated today, it was in its time, as historian Gerald Bordman notes, an outstanding achievement: "The book's strong, well-motivated story is especially remarkable when it is realized how much of the writing was done with particular performers and not the plot in mind." The play was one of Ziegfeld's biggest musical successes, but it was forced to close when the stock market crash wiped out Ziegfeld's finances.

The Film

Emboldened by its popular success—and anxious to recoup his financial losses after the stock market crash—Ziegfeld contracted in 1929 with film producer Samuel Goldwyn to bring it to the screen. The Ziegfeld-Goldwyn collaboration was stormy; Ziegfeld particularly objected to some of the casting choices and the deletion of many of the original songs. Yet, as historian Miles Kreuger has noted, the film version was "as close as you'll ever get to seeing a Broadway show of that period." Indeed, everyone involved seems to have been determined to transfer the show to the screen as faithfully as possible. Eddie Cantor and Paul Gregory repeated their stage roles as Eddie and Wanenis, respectively; and most of the production was photographed on sound stages in a manner suggestive of a proscenium-based production, wherein the action was photographed from the proverbial third-row-center vantage point. The famed, climactic "Wedding Scene," is a valuable document of the Ziegfeld-style "fashion show": The girls advance in single file toward the camera, each arrayed in elaborate bridal gowns; meanwhile, a few more arrive on horseback, sporting Indian headdresses so enormous and cumbersome they have to be supported by show girls walking alongside. An

The Ziegfeld showgirls donned western garb in United Artists's screen version of Whoopee! *(COURTESY SAMUEL GOLDWYN PICTURES)*

important exception to this pronounced theatricality was the wholly "cinematic" work of dance director Busby Berkeley. For the dance sequences, particularly the "Stetson Dance," he employed the camera and staging techniques that quickly became his signature style—such as photographing the show girls from overhead, arranging them into geometrical formations, and intercutting long shots with successive close-ups of the individuals.

Photographed in two-color Technicolor (the handful of exteriors shot in the desert Southwest were particularly gorgeous), *Whoopee!* made a big splash with critics and audiences alike, earning $2.3 million. One critic, however, grew exasperated with what he called an excess of the "glorification business," i.e., of the endless fashion parades of girls: "Somehow there seem to be too many lovely girls—their maneuvers through long dance routines, their endless parades across the stage in Ziegfeldish cowboy adaptations or elaborately head-dressed with feathers, are not a feast to the eye any more than a kaleidoscope. Individual beauty gets lost in the procession. . . ." Today, historian Richard Barrios writes with more perspective: "[The film] survives today as the summation of filmed musical comedy, vintage 1930."

REFERENCES

Barrios, Richard, *A Song in the Dark: The Birth of the Musical Film* (New York: Oxford University Press, 1995); Tibbetts, John C., *The American Theatrical Film* (Bowling Green, Ohio: Popular Press, 1985); Ziegfeld, Richard and Paulette, *The Ziegfeld Touch* (New York: Harry N. Abrams, 1993).

—*J.C.T.*

Appendix

Appendix

BACKSTAGE WITH THE BARD: OR, BUILDING A BETTER MOUSETRAP

Hamlet, Prince of Denmark, pauses a moment, sword at the ready, and takes the measure of his opponent, Laertes. Suddenly, with a deft stroke, he slices off Laertes' arm. Blood spurts 10 feet in the air as the severed limb falls to the stage. "A hit," declares Oscric. "A palpable hit!" Laertes, in turn, ripostes with a lunge and cuts off Hamlet's arm. Another jet of blood arches across the stage. With a second thrust Laertes stabs Hamlet through the throat. Blood is now gushing everywhere, splashing onto the stage and spilling out into the audience seats. Stunned and horrified, the viewers are transfixed with horror.

Hamlet and Laertes, sans a few limbs and spouting fountains of blood, come down to the stage apron and cheerfully take their bow.

The interpreters of this extraordinary *guignol* version of Shakespeare's play are none other than those wayward children of the notorious Addams Family, Wednesday and Pugsley. They have just brought down the curtain on their school's kiddie talent pageant. More importantly, for our purposes, they have deconstructed every sugar-sweet children's show that parents and kids have ever had to endure.

Surely the Bard would have been pleased.

This moment, this brief play-within-a film, typifies just one of the many ways in which a Shakespearean "moment" may be cited within a motion picture to comment on its surrounding contexts. In the case of *The Addams Family*, it, like Hamlet's "mousetrap" play, creates seismic responses in the play's onlookers, each according to his or her particular disposition. While it outrages the hidebound stuffed shirts in the audience, it delights Wednesday and Pugsley's proud parents, Morticia and Gomez Addams, who rise to their feet, wildly cheering and applauding.

As Hamlet knew, it is all in how you look at it.

STAGING THE MOUSETRAP
Not all theatrical films directly adapt stage plays to the screen. Another category is a form of meta-cinema, that, taking the play-within-a-play in Shakespeare's *Hamlet* as its precedent, employs theatrical allusions as "mousetraps" that "capture the conscience," as it were, of the action and the characters. All too often, unfortunately, films of this kind are neglected in standard studies of theatrical films. But where would we be without masterpieces like George Cukor's *A Double Life* (1947), Jean Renoir's *The Golden Coach* (1952), Merchant-Ivory's *Shakespeare Wallah!* (1975), Kenneth Branagh's *A Midwinter's Tale* (1996), and that greatest of all theatrical films, Marcel Carne's *Children of Paradise* (1944)? These films do not adapt plays so much as they assimilate them into their primary texts. "The theatre as a metaphor for life's madness is hardly new," says Kenneth Branagh, "and movies that use the stories of particular productions to provide a microcosmic view of human nature abound."

Actually, the idea of a play-within-a-play goes back further than *Hamlet*, to Thomas Kyd's *The Spanish Tragedy* (ca. 1583–87), in which the hero Hieronimo stages a play to trap his enemy. His revenge is complete when he substitutes a real dagger for the fake one in the final scene. The situation, it will be remembered, is similar in *Hamlet*. A troupe of traveling players has come to Elsinore. Hamlet asks them to present a play called *The Murder of Gonzago* before his uncle, King Claudius, to which Hamlet will add a few lines. The play, which is about a murder by poison, is designed to be a kind of "mousetrap" (indeed, that is the title Hamlet later gives the play): "The play's the thing wherein I'll catch the conscience of the king," he muses to himself. In this action, which transpires in Act Three, Scene Two, Claudius attends the show only to humor Hamlet. The performance begins with a dumb show, wherein a conspirator pours poison into the ears of the sleeping player-king. He subsequently woos the player-queen, who seems disposed to accept his favors. A dialogue ensues that identifies the dramatis personae as Gonzago, the victim and Lucianus, Gonzago's nephew as the murder/ aspirant to the throne. King

Claudius watches this performance with growing agitation. Hamlet assures him, "We that have free souls, it touches us not. Let the galled jade wince; our withers are unwrung." Nonetheless, Claudius abruptly rises, calls for lights, and stops the play. Hamlet's suspicions are confirmed.

Hamlet's little mousetrap dissolves the barriers between the fictive and the real. On the stage is a play in which an actor is playing a king. He is observed by Claudius, who is also seated on the stage (as was the custom). Attentively observing both of them is Hamlet. And all around them are Gertrude, Rosencrantz, Guildenstern, and Polonius. Lastly, we in the theatre or in the movie house look on at these several tiers of audiences, knowing them all to be players.

THE ROAR OF THE GREASEPAINT

The related activities of those maverick theatrical forms, the circus, the music hall, the commedia dell'arte, the farce, the pantomime, the Grand Guignol, and puppet plays, figure frequently in films. The circus ring becomes an effective arena, a "theatre of cruelty," if you will, to ritualize before a faceless crowd humankind's follies, frustrations, and abuses. Victor Seastrom's *He Who Gets Slapped* (1925), adapted from Leonid Andreyev's expressionist play, features Lon Chaney as a scientist so humiliated and traumatized by the treachery of a rival, that he flees to a circus where, before an hysterically amused audience, he endures the slaps and blows of a contingent of fellow clowns. Among Chaney's other circus pictures the strangest is *The Unknown* (1928), in which he portrays "Alonzo the Armless," a precision knife-thrower and sharpshooter who handles blades and bullets with his bare feet. His disability, however, is an "act." He hides the fact that he has arms from his beautiful assistant, Nanon (Joan Crawford), because she has a phobia, a repulsion to men's upper extremities. In an effort to finally win her love, he actually has his arms amputated, only to learn that she is in love with Malabar (Norman Kerry), the circus strongman. In an insane rage, Alonzo sabotages the strongman's specialty act. He disables the treadmills on which two horses pull in opposite directions the ropes tied to Malabar's arms. In the words of historian David J. Skal, *The Unknown* itself is a "perfectly constructed torture machine." Alejandro Jodorowsky's *Santa Sangre* (1990) may claim to be the most bizarre of all circus pictures. Its collection of strange theatrical rituals and guignol fantasies includes a deranged young magician's apprentice who escapes from an asylum and joins his armless mother in a bizarre circus act in which he slips his arms through her empty sleeves to perform various actions, including, ultimately, murder. Trapeze

pictures like DuPont's *Variety* (1926), Murnau's *The Four Devils* (1928), and Carol Reed's *Trapeze* (1956), to mention only a few, carry the deadly jealousies of the ménage à trois high above the expectant crowds, where the slightest miscue can plunge one of the rival lovers to his or her death. And, of course, there is that unchallenged ringmaster of the circus metaphor, Federico Fellini, whose *Variety Lights* (1950), *La Strada* (1956), *8 1/2* (1963), *Juliet of the Spirits* (1965), and *The Clowns* (1970) smear the whole world with greasepaint and thrust it into the harsh glare of the center-ring spotlight. Nothing less than a book-length volume could hope to do justice to these themes.

A full-scale music-hall revue transpires midway through Renoir's *Rules of the Game* (1939) at the estate of Robert de la Chesnaye, including one character dressed as a bear, another impersonating a gypsy, a "skeleton" dance, and, as the pièce de résistance, a novelty "performance" by a six-foot-high *orchestion*, or mechanical music box. It is at this point in the film, appropriately enough, that as counterpoint to the burlesques, all the frustrations, envies, jealousies, and hatreds of the various pairs of mismatched lovers break out. When shots are fired in earnest, the gathered guests applaud, as if this is all part of the comedy.

The commedia tradition finds its way into many films, including Carlos Diegues' *Bye Bye Brazil* (1980) and Jean Renoir's *The Golden Coach* (1952). In Diegues' film a small troupe of performers travels through the provincial areas of Brazil. The leader, Lord Gypsy, is nothing so much as a medicine show huckster. His assistant is Salome, an exotic beauty who keeps busy with affairs d'amour on the side. Swallow, the strongman, doubles as crew and supporting act. Their truck contains their living quarters, a generator, and the props for their performances. After they pick up two hitchhikers, a musician and his wife, the story tracks the changing interrelationships among the five, on and off stage. Straddling the fault line between backwater, provincial Brazil, and a burgeoning modern civilization, is the world of theatre. The sense of wonder is common currency in both regions. The most memorable moment transpires when a magician climaxes his act by producing a snowfall in the hot, makeshift tent, to the accompaniment on the soundtrack of Bing Crosby singing "White Christmas."

Jean Renoir's *La Carrosse d'or* (1952), one of three theatre-based films he made in the 1950s—along with *French Cancan* and *Elena et les hommes*—is an evocation of the commedia dell'arte tradition. It is based on Prosper Merimee's one-act play, *Le Carrosse du Saint-Sacrament* (which also inspired an episode in Thornton Wilder's *The Bridge of San Luis Rey*). Anna Magnani is

Camilla, the "Columbine" of a troupe of commedia players traveling through 18th-century Peru. These players, by tradition, were great improvisers and freely used their imagination on given, formulaic scenes, broadly pantomiming love's dalliance and love's confounding consequences. The commedia tradition, a junction of spontaneity and classicism, was ideally suited to Renoir's temperament.

The story begins as a commedia troupe arrives in a Spanish colonial town in Peru. Its leading player, Camilla (Anna Magnani), is divided between her love for the Peruvian viceroy, Ramon the matador, and Felipe, a young Spanish soldier. She wears a variety of "faces," in effect, for each of them. Indeed, her "performances" with them differ little from her stage impersonations. When the viceroy offers to give her a golden coach that the people had made for him, she refuses, realizing that her love is unworthy of his. She renounces him and presents the coach to the bishop. The bishop declares that the coach will be used to carry the holy sacrament to the dying, nobles and the commonality alike. "[Camilla] knows no reality but the theatre's," writes biographer Raymond Durgnat; "desires no love but that of the audience." But her profession, continues Durgnat, "which might seem the apotheosis of life's glitter, is finally revealed as a vocation almost as solitary as the Bishop's. All is the vanity game." Finally, she stands alone onstage as the curtain falls. When asked if she misses her three lovers, she answers with a sigh, "Just a little." As her theatre director tells her: "You weren't cut out for what they call real life. Your place is with us, the actors, acrobats, mimes, clowns, and tumblers. You'll only find happiness on the stage every night for the two short hours when you do what an actress does, that is, when you forget yourself. Through the characters that you will embody, perhaps someday you'll discover the real Camilla."

The characters in the story mirror the characters in the commedia. The viceroy recalls Pantalone, Felipe is a blend of Scaramouche and Pierrot, and Ramon is the captain. There is a crucial point in the story when Camilla suddenly announces—to the other players? to the movie viewers?—that the "second act" has ended; suddenly the movie becomes a formalized stage set. Director Renoir doesn't want us to forget that we are watching a *play*, or a *play-within-a-film*. He doesn't just remind us; he proclaims it. Accordingly, he shoots the non-stage sequences in a frontal manner, that, in effect, positions them within the "proscenium" of the camera's viewfinder; and he demands a discreet overacting from his players to give their scene what Durgnat calls "an insidiously theatrical air. . . ."

In the end, she spurns them all for her real love, the theatre. Pauline Kael notes, "The artifice has the simplest of results: we become caught up in a chase through the levels of fantasy, finding ourselves at last with the actress, naked in loneliness as the curtain descends, but awed by the wonders of man's artistic creation of himself. Suddenly, the meaning is restored to a line we have heard and idly discounted a thousand times: 'All the world's a stage.'"

Farce comedy finds its way into René Clair's classic *Le Million* (1931). Adapted from a 1913 play of the same title written by Georges Berr and Marcel Guillemaud, it tells the story of how a jacket containing a valuable lottery ticket has come into the hands of Sopranelli, an Italian tenor. During a production of an opera, *The Bohemians*, Sopranelli wears the coat while singing a romantic duet with his partner, a corpulent soprano named Ravallini. Meanwhile, the rightful owner of the jacket, Michel (René Lefevre), and his girlfriend Beatrice (Annabella) have come to the theatre in pursuit of the coat. Finding themselves inadvertently upstage at the rise of the curtain, they quickly crouch, unseen to the audience, behind a piece of stage scenery.

What transpires for the next few minutes is wholly magical, a scene that, in the opinion of R.C. Dale, constitutes, "the most masterful stroke of ironic genius in all [Clair's] work." While the theatre audience sees the two overstuffed singers trysting in the woods, singing their rather declamatory duet against a wholly artificial backdrop of trees and moon, the movie viewer enjoys a more privileged "backstage" view of the action. A delicious counterpoint is set up between the two performers downstage and the pair of lovers upstage. During the duet—

> At last we are alone tonight
> As everything on earth sleeps tight;
> 'Neath the black heavens are we alone
> Seated on the olden bench of stone—

the quarreling Michel and Beatrice gradually resolve their bickering. Unconsciously at first, they silently act out the singers' words; and by the song's end they have melted into each other's arms. It is they who endow the song with all the authentic meaning it lacked as sung by the two downstage performers. This culminating moment is a delirious confection of romantic love surrounded by fake clouds sailing past a cardboard moon while paper leaves cascade downward. It is capped by a high-angle long-shot revealing both the pair of singers downstage and the two lovers almost lost in the background. The film thus erases the boundary line between public artifice and private romance, between objective and subjective reality. Indeed, one can argue that in Clair's world, only the pronounced artifice of the stage can provoke a moment as tender, and as *real*, as this.

The tradition of the British Christmas pantomime was brought into the 20th century by Sir James M. Barrie's immortal play, *Peter Pan*. This modern fairy tale was put to a poignantly ironic use in Mike Newell's *An Awfully Big Adventure* (1995). Here, the glittering illusions of the pantomime contrast with the harsh realities of life in wartime Liverpool. It is 1941 and nine-year-old Stella Bradshaw delightedly claps her hands at the night bombings and flashing lights. Flash forward to 1947. Stella is now 15 (Georgina Cates in her film debut), abandoned by her mother and now living with her aunt and uncle. She persuades them to allow her to audition at a local theatre. More through pluck than talent, she's chosen to join the company as an intern. During the course of three stage productions, *Dangerous Corner, Caesar and Cleopatra,* and *Peter Pan,* she is initiated into the bitter aspects of life and love. The stage director is Meredith Potter (Hugh Grant), a thoroughly self-centered and despicable character who has a habit of ruining the young boys in his companies. There is also the alcoholic actress who is fired from the company, the stage manager whose selfless adoration for Meredith leads him to clean up the emotional messes he leaves behind him, and P.L. O'Hara, the dashing leading man who comes out of exile to portray Captain Hook in *Peter Pan*.

Stella has problems of her own. The traumas she suffered as a little girl during the German bombardments and the abandonment of her mother have left her a trembling, vulnerable, emotional wreck. First, she turns to Meredith, the director, with blind infatuation, oblivious to his sadistic nature. Then, all too casually, she submits to the seduction of a man she doesn't love, O'Hara. During rehearsals and the production of *Peter Pan* they meet and make love. But it is a cold, detached act devoid of any real feeling.

The film is a concatenation of the intermingled layers of reality and illusion, war and uneasy peace, love and seduction, sanity and obsession. And above it all is the production of *Peter Pan* that parallels and illumines the sad career of Stella. It is Pan's line about death—that it would be "an awfully big adventure" (an allusion never explained in the movie)—that gives the film its title. Stella personifies the innocence of the children in Barrie's play, while the adults around her—particularly Meredith the director and O'Hara the actor—are everything that is wicked in Barrie's adult world, and they ultimately exploit and ruin her. What happens to her is unspeakable: O'Hara learns from a photograph he sees in Stella's home that she is the daughter of a woman he loved years before and who had disappeared. Horrified at his incestuous acts, he stumbles to the docks, the place where he had last seen Stella's mother. Accidentally he stumbles, falls, knocks himself unconscious, and drowns. Stella is left on her own, and when we last see her, she is talking to her mother on the call-box telephone. But we know by now that the conversation is wholly imaginary. The voice recorded on the phone's time clock is that of her mother years before.

Peter Weir's *The Year of Living Dangerously* (1982) introduces us to the tradition of the Indonesian shadow puppet play, the "Wayang." Here is a theatre of ambiguity wrought from the simplest of materials. Yet its implications are profound. "If you want to understand Java, says the character of Billy (Linda Hunt) to Mel Gibson, "you have to understand the 'Wayang.'" She compares the political despot, Sukarno, to the "great puppet master" of the play, a master manipulator. In the Wayang the shadows thrown by the puppets onto the white screen represent souls disporting against the backdrop of heaven. "You must watch the shadows," advises Billy, "not the puppets. The right in constant struggle with the left, the forces of light and darkness in endless balance. In the West we want constants for everything; everything is right or wrong, good or bad. But in the Wayang no such final conclusions exist." This dramatic anecdote exists at the heart of not just *The Year of Living Dangerously* but throughout all of Weir's oeuvre. Ambiguity, not resolution, is Weir's great theme.

PUTTING ON A SHOW—BACKSTAGE DURING THE DEPRESSION

At the heart of any history of the mousetrap film is, of course, the backstage drama and musical. The use of a play-within-a-film or a musical-within-a-film grows organically out of the thematic materials at hand. At no time in the chronicle of modern theatre and film did this kind of theatrical film appear more frequently than in the 1930s, in America and abroad, when the need for relief from life's brutal economic, political, and personal reversals was most prominently and insistently expressed. Such films were the "mousetraps" that captured society's collective struggle against these miseries. If the message was generally muted in one of the finest films of this type, Gregory La Cava's *Stage Door* (1937), in which aspiring actress Katharine Hepburn triumphs as a last-minute replacement in a coveted dramatic role, it sounded out loud and clear in the cycle of backstage musicals. The rallying cry was "Let's put on a show," especially in the MGM cycle of Busby

Berkeley musicals featuring Mickey Rooney and Judy Garland, like *Babes in Arms* (1939) and *Babes on Broadway* (1941). However, because these musicals proliferated in such numbers, any attempt to list and discuss them would require more space than is available here. A few representative examples must suffice.

Although by no means the first backstage musical play-within-a-film—pride of place must go to MGM's archetypal *The Broadway Melody* in 1929—the best known is undoubtedly *42nd Street* (1933). Based on a novel by Bradford Ropes, this prototype of all modern backstage musicals has tough, but down-and-out Broadway director Julian Marsh (Warner Baxter in a pre-Bob Fosse take) preparing *Pretty Lady* as his "comeback." In a very real sense, this musical-within-a-musical is itself a metaphor for the "comeback" of the Hollywood musical, which had been on the ropes since its initial boom time, in the late 1920s and early 1930s. More generally, it is also a metaphor for the "comeback" of an America still reeling from the Depression. Marsh is the Machiavellian presence behind the dance auditions, rehearsals, cast intrigues, and last-minute changes leading to the finished production. He is the puppet master (a stand-in for President Roosevelt?), at once evocative of the extravagant Florenz Ziegfeld, who died the year the film was released, and prophetic of the newer, brasher Bob Fosse type to come.

Pretty Lady is the hard-driving Marsh's last chance to salvage a failing career. "Actors tell you how Marsh drove 'em . . . bullied 'em . . . and tore it out of them," he says, "and maybe a few'll tell you how Marsh really made 'em . . . and they all have something to show for it . . . except Marsh! Well, this is my last shot!" His challenges and exhortations to the show folks are classics of their kind: "You're going to work and sweat and work some more—you're going to work days and you're going to work nights—and you're going to work between times when I think you need it—you're going to dance until your feet fall off. . . . But six weeks from now—we're going to have a SHOW!" Above all, there is his inspirational speech to Peggy Sawyer (Ruby Keeler) as she is about to go onstage as a last-minute replacement for the aging diva, Dorothy Brock (Bebe Daniels). It has been heard in a thousand variations in a thousand subsequent backstage films. It is worth quoting in full:

> Now listen to me—listen hard. Two hundred people—two hundred jobs—two hundred thousand dollars—five weeks of grind—and blood—and sweat—depend on you. It's the life of all these people who have worked with you. You've got to go on—and you've got to give—and give and give—they've GOT

"Let's put on a show!" says Mickey Rooney to Judy Garland in Busby Berkeley's Babes in Arms. (COURTESY NATIONAL FILM SOCIETY ARCHIVES)

to like you—GOT to—you understand. You can't fall down—you *can't*—Your future's in it—my future's in it—and everything that all of us have is staked on you. I'm through. Now keep your feet on the ground—and your head on those shoulders of yours—and go out—and Sawyer—you're going out a youngster—you've GOT to come back a star!

At the film's end, *Pretty Lady* has been a smashing success. Marsh, ill and tired, slumps against a fire escape, listening to the departing theatregoers. "Marsh will probably say he discovered [Peggy Sawyer]," says one excited patron. "Some guys get all the breaks."

It is difficult to determine just what kind of a show *Pretty Lady* really is. Some production numbers, like "Young and Healthy" and "Shuffle off to Buffalo," are light and frothy. The concluding number, "42nd Street," best captures the tone and times of Depression America. Virtually a story-within-a-musical-within-a-film, it depicts vignettes in the lives of several street types, a policeman, a gangster, a cuckolded lover. Busby Berkeley's mobile camera effortlessly envelops the action as the number builds in intensity and scope. Finally, the assembled chorines fill the stage in a massive formation, each carrying a huge billboard image of a skyscraper. The hundreds of pasteboard images meld into one spectacular cityscape, the New York City of

Hollywood fantasies and dreams. If *42nd Street* signaled the apex of the backstage movie, it also looked forward to a wholly cinematic style of theatrical filmmaking that Berkeley continued in subsequent backstage musicals, like *Gold Diggers of 1933*, *Footlight Parade* (1933), and *Dames* (1933). Bewildered movie critics complained that the musical numbers in *Pretty Lady* could never have been staged in a theatre. No one knew that better than Berkeley. As commentator Rocco Fumento notes, "Berkeley had years of stage experience before he ever went to Hollywood. Apparently these critics never stopped to think that Berkeley was the first to know that his numbers could not be performed on any 'real' stage. It is their very liberation from the stage that makes them exciting. From the real, stage-bound world of the rehearsal hall, he plunges us into a fantasy world with no boundaries. His chorus boys and girls are performing for the mobile camera, not for the critic anchored in a third row aisle seat."

Meanwhile, Warner Baxter was back in *Stand Up and Cheer!* (1934), another important Depression backstage musical. As if the metaphor of *Pretty Lady* weren't plain enough, Baxter here is a government official, a "Secretary of Amusement" hired to devise entertainments to defeat Depression woes. It is as if Julian Marsh had recovered from *Pretty Lady* and found a new employer in the Roosevelt administration. Baxter sets to work with typical enthusiasm and extravagance, raising the ire of theatre competitors and legislators alike. Part of his agenda is to organize a Children's Division, which will feature seven-year-old Shirley Dugan (Shirley Temple) in a number called "Baby Take a Bow." Viewers in 1934 must have come away from the film convinced that the Depression had been vanquished, a conviction that surely vanished within minutes after emerging from the darkened precincts of the movie house.

More recently, in his *Bullets Over Broadway* (1994), Woody Allen blends the 1930s backstage musical formula of *42nd Street* with the popular gangster films of the day, like *The Public Enemy* (1931) and *Scarface* (1932). John Cusack is David Shayne, a struggling playwright who, weary of writing plays that never get staged, arranges with a New York gangster to bankroll his next show, *God of Our Fathers*. It gets staged all right, and it is a moderate success, but Shayne inherits lots of problems, on and off stage. The company of performers are a motley lot, a kind of commedia dell'arte cast as filtered through something by Damon Runyan. Jim Broadbent is Wayne, the fading matinee idol imported from England, who is more busy burying his face in the food buffet than in his role. Jennifer Tilly is Olive, the gangster's moll, with a voice like

sandpaper. Chazz Palminteri is Cheech, a deadpan gangster whose unexpected talents at writing transform him from a loutish hood to a temperamental, wannabe playwright. And best of all if Dianne Wiest as Helen Sinclair, the archetypal First Lady, all furs and cigarette holders and flasks filled with paint thinner. "I never play frumps or virgins," she explains to her awestruck cast members. Indeed, no one is more impressed with her than she herself. "Every time the curtain raises, it's like a birth," she declaims. "And then, when it goes down, it's . . . well, it's like a death." Meanwhile, internecine conflicts erupt among the gangsters and the cast and soon Shayne decides to leave the theatre behind him.

A most interesting entry in the Depression-era backstage formula appeared in Germany. Leontine Sagan's *Maedchen in Uniform* (1931) employed a play-within-a-play to "capture the conscience" of a Germany on the verge of falling victim to Fascist tyranny. This extraordinarily prescient film was based on a play, *Yesterday and Today*, by Christine Winsloe, which depicted in grim detail the life of a regimented girl's school in Potsdam in 1911, where the daughters of soldiers are trained to be the mothers of the next generation. The developing love between student Manuela von Meinhardis (Herta Thiele) and the teacher Fraulein von Bernburg (Dorothea Wieck) flies against the school's rules. Homesick Manuela is fixated on Bernburg. Bernburg is at first reluctant to respond to the girl, but gradually she softens and encourages her friendship, even love. The situation comes to a head when Manuela acts the male lead in a romantic costume play. The play allows her to enact her pent-up feelings for Bernburg. Manuela scores a triumph, but later she publicly and rashly declares her love for Bernburg. The Frau Principal punishes Manuela and threatens her with expulsion. Despairing, Manuela tries to throw herself off a high flight of stairs. She is saved in the nick of time by her schoolmates. The film was regarded by Joseph Goebbels as morally unhealthy and later by the women's movement as a radical lesbian film. Allan Silver sees the film, made two years before the Nazis' assumption of power, as an attack on Prussian militarism.

The backstage formula as a mousetrap to capture political realities has continued to proliferate throughout film history. Presently, four outstanding examples will be examined in some detail, Tim Robbins' *The Cradle Will Rock* (1999), an intersection of art, politics, and society in 1930s America; *To Be or Not to Be* (1942), Ernst Lubitsch's classic indictment of Nazi tyranny in wartime Poland; and *Children of Paradise* (1944) and *The Last Metro* (1980), Marcel Carné and François

Truffaut's tributes to the role of the theatre in the wartime Resistance, respectively.

STAGESTRUCK DIRECTORS

Because some film directors have maintained strong ties with the theatre, they have stamped upon their films a particularly indelible theatrical impression. Buster Keaton's long experience in vaudeville left him a legacy of illusions and acrobatic routines that surface constantly in his films, particularly in the entirety of the two-reel comedy, *The Playhouse* (1922), in the film-within-a-film sequence in *Sherlock, Jr.* (1924), the storm sequence in *Steamboat Bill, Jr.* (1928), and the hilarious Civil War drama spoof in *Spite Marriage* (1929). The French masters, Jean Renoir and Marcel Carné, as will be seen presently, derived much of their themes and effects from the stage. The same is true of Orson Welles, so completely a man of the theatre by temperament, from his days at the Gate Theatre in Dublin and the Mercury Theatre in New York City, that he invested a sense of theatricality in virtually every film he made, even those, like *Touch of Evil* (1958), *Mr. Arkadin* (1956), and *Immoral Story* (1968), which were not adapted from stage works—and the same is true of Elia Kazan, whose background in the Group Theatre and on Broadway with Tennessee Williams and William Inge informed his best pictures, like *A Streetcar Named Desire* (1952) and *Splendor in the Grass* (1961).

Parenthetically, Kazan found in the theatre a means for his political and artistic survival. His *Man on a Tightrope* (1952), for example, is truly a piece of living theatre, his response to the complex political and professional situation he found himself in after testifying as a "friendly" witness before the House Un-American Activities Committee. His "naming of names" had thrust him into a vicious crossfire of disapproval, both from the right and the left, that jeopardized his career. Yet, when offered Robert Sherwood's script for *Man on a Tightrope*, based on the true story of how the Cirkus Brumbach, a small, seedy circus troupe, escaped across the heavily guarded border between communist Czechoslovakia and free Austria, he at first hesitated. "Was I still blocked by my own iron curtain against saying anything unfavorable about the Soviet Union?" he recalled in his autobiography. "If I found out that what I'd read in Sherwood's script was true and not pumped-up propaganda, I'd make the film. . . ." Indeed, he acquiesced, if only to convince himself that he "was not afraid to say true things about the Communists or anyone else, that I was still capable of free inquiry, that I was no longer a Party regular in my head." Members of the actual troupe were used in the

Elia Kazan

film, along with the actor Fredric March, who, like Kazan, had suffered from the opprobrium of HUAC. Reality imitated the theatre when on location in Bavaria the circus actors were warned by communist radio broadcasts to leave the set lest their relatives in East Germany be abused. In the film, Fredric March portrayed the troupe's leader, Karel Cernik, who finds himself dispossessed of his circus when the communists take over the country. Against the backdrop of the big top and its animal and aerial acts, he carries out his plan of escape, while matching wits with his lion tamer, a suspected communist sympathizer, and a suave Red investigator (Adolphe Menjou). The film's climax depicts the daring flight to freedom and the unveiling of the actual Red agent.

Born out of his boyhood fascination with music hall turns and lurid melodramas, a strong sense of theatricality suffuses most of Alfred Hitchcock's films. A few examples must suffice: *The 39 Steps* begins and ends in the London Palladium, where a performance by one "Mr. Memory" holds the key to the operations of a spy ring. As the spies are arrested onstage, the curtain falls, signaling a final fusion of the theatre of entertainment with the "theatre" of political subterfuge. *Stage Fright* begins with a rising curtain, signaling the blurring of easy distinctions between theatrical life and street life in its story of a drama student who enacts a real-life role to clear a man of a murder charge. *Rope* and *Under Capricorn* employ long takes in their blatantly artificial imitations of proscenium staging. Likewise, *Rear Window* derives much of its seductive power from the voyeuristic gaze Jimmy Stewart (and we viewers) train upon the private lives of the characters framed by their proscenium-like window openings. And frequently elaborate charades and false impersonations are carefully "stage-managed" to entrap the hapless protagonists (see especially *Vertigo*), just as Hitch carefully developed and promoted—*enacted* is perhaps a better word—for his critics and viewers the "role" of the chubby, saturnine "bad boy" of cinema.

A definitive example of a director who has straddled film and theatre all his life is the Swedish master, Ingmar Bergman. Indeed, it is difficult to fully appreciate his films without understanding his background in, and constant allusions to, the theatre. "The theatre is like a loyal wife," he once said; "film is the great adventure, the costly and demanding mistress—you worship both, each in its own way." His attraction to the stage stems from his boyhood when, at the age of 10, he received his favorite toy, a puppet theatre, for which he made scenery and characters and wrote plays (it is with a toy theatre that the couple in *The Devil's Wanton* relive their childhood). He made his debut staging plays as chairman of the Student Theatre in Stockholm. Later, he supervised the City Theatre in Hälsingborg in the south of Sweden, the Gothenburg City Theatre, and in the early 1950s conducted a six-year directorship at the Malmö City Theatre, one of the most modern playhouses in Europe. His theatrical career culminated in the mid-1960s when he became head of Sweden's national stage, the Royal Dramatic Theatre in Stockholm. During his maturity, he never strayed far from the theatre and from personally directing plays, no matter how successful he was as a film director. Indeed, both worlds frequently interconnected. In his stage production of *The Misanthrope*, for example, one may see the seeds of *The Magician*; in *Don Juan*, his film, *The Devil's Eye*; in *Saga*, the film *The Virgin Spring*; and in *The Merry Widow*, his *Smiles of a Summer Night*.

Theatrical allusions are everywhere. People attend plays in *Smiles of a Summer Night* and *Fanny and Alexander*. Three cabaret actors discuss their profession during the course of *The Ritual*. A toy theatre version of Mozart's *The Magic Flute* appears in *Hour of the Wolf*. Acting troupes figure in the action of *The Seventh Seal* and *The Naked Night*. In the former we have some of Bergman's most benign characters, the juggler Jof and his wife Mia. Yet their performance is interrupted by a rather different kind of spectacle, a theatre of cruelty rather than good humor—the arrival of a band of flagellants. *The Naked Night* is a meditation on the insecurities and vulnerability of show folk, be they circus performers or "legitimate" actors. It juxtaposes both worlds—the shabby, blatantly emotional circus act and the more intellectual, mannered stage play—in its romance between the sensuous but childlike bareback rider, Anna, and the simpering, callous stage actor, Frans. In the end, a disillusioned Anna must return to the only life she really understands, the circus.

Neither kind of theatrical event is better or more "legitimate" than the other for Bergman; rather, they represent the constant struggle in the artist between the emotions and the intellect. The play-within-the-film sequence in *Through a Glass Darkly* likewise expresses the dilemma of choosing to pursue the ideals of his art at the expense of the more sordid practicalities of real life. Early in the film, the troubled adolescent boy, Minus, enacts a little drama with his sister, Karin, on a makeshift stage. The occasion is the return after a long absence of their father. Minus portrays the "artist of purest blood," who considers the temptation of his dead sister to follow her into "the realm of death." She says, "In this way, you will complete your masterpiece and crown your love; ennoble your life and show to those of little faith what a true artist can achieve." But he hesitates. "I am standing on the threshold of an ultimate consummation," he declaims. "I tremble with excitement. Oblivion shall possess me. . . ." But no, he turns away. "What am I about?" he asks at last. "Sacrificing my life! For what? To the perfect masterpiece. . . . Am I out of my mind?" Minus's play is not only about art and artists, it is also a critique of his own father. As Hamlet had done in the play he had enacted before Claudius, Minus stages his play to prick the conscience of his father, David, who had sacrificed bringing up his family for the sake of his career as a novelist. *Persona* (whose title derives from the Latin word for the facial mask that Roman actors used to wear to suggest their character type) has as its central character the actress Elisabet Vogler, who during a performance of Euripedes' *Electra*, has lapsed into a mute state. Shorn of her masks, she has no identity or language. And it is only as a result of her association with her therapist, that we see her acquiring something of a new personality. What results is nothing less than an allegory of the artist as vampire and her audience as victim.

Bergman films as various as *The Magician* and *Fanny and Alexander* demonstrate that no matter how fraudulent the practices of the artist performer, there are still miracles at hand. In the first film, Albert Emanuel Vogler, the eponymous "magician," is dismissed as a simple charlatan and trickster by the rationalist medical doctor, Dr. Vergerus. "Miracles don't happen," scoffs Vergerus. "It's always the apparatus and the Spiel that have to do the work. The clergy have the same sad experience. God is silent and the people chatter." They take each other's measure at once, and find themselves locked in a deadly battle of wits and magic. Vogler is able to scare the wits out of Vergerus in the famous "attic scene" in which a corpse seems to come to life. But of course, it's all a trick—on Bergman's movie viewers as much as on Vergerus. Vogler has contrived his delicious piece of Grand Guignol by the simple deployment of macabre props, including a dissected eyeball and a dismembered hand. And Bergman has seduced his viewers into a lesson in terror by the manipulation of editing, sound, and camera movement. Later, however, Vogler's triumph is rebuked when he has to grovel before Vergerus for a letter of safe conduct. Without his makeup—his mask—Vogler appears a pathetic figure. "I liked *his* face better than yours," says Vergerus, referring to the magician who is now but a shabby charlatan. Nonetheless, Vogler has made his point. As Bergman biographer Birgitta Steene notes about this famous scene, "Bergman seems to say to his spectators: "You may doubt me, but look, I can shake you in your aloofness and skepticism. I can make you tremble and scream. Such is my power, and for once the humiliation is yours, for you have been taken by my simple tricks.""

In *Fanny and Alexander* the most terrifying theatrical moment in all of Bergman transpires when the boy Alexander confronts the figure of God Himself. A large, gaunt shape clicks and rattles as it glides through a doorway. Moments later we realize that it is only a puppet.

All of Bergman's films, in essence, are preoccupied with some aspect of theatrical illusion. As biographer Peter Cowie writes, "The moment of truth is the moment when the mask is torn aside and the real face uncovered. Every Bergman film turns on this process. The mask is shown, examined, and then removed." Moreover, for Bergman, the theatre—with all its shabby illusions and pasteboard characters—can satisfy our deepest hunger and aspiration to move beyond the commonplace and toward the miraculous. It is like the dream of the performer Jof, in *The Seventh Seal*, i.e., that his baby son Mikael will one day be a great juggler and perform an impossible trick—making a ball stand still in the air.

All these topics and techniques are summed up in one of his masterpieces, *The Magic Flute* (1975). Far from being merely canned theatre, it is an interrogation of both mediums very much in the manner and effect of Olivier's *Henry V.*

THE PLAY IS INDEED THE THING

Before moving on to more specific discussion of selected "mousetrap" movies, it is worth noting that many films are in their entirety plays-within-movies. Theatrical events and cinematic realities are virtually indistinguishable. Again, examples are too numerous to catalogue, so a few will have to suffice. German expressionist films like Robert Wiene's *The Cabinet of Dr. Caligari* (1919) and Leopold Jessner's *Hintertreppe* (Backstairs, 1922), while not based on plays, were nonetheless emblematic of expressionist stagecraft and acting style with their stiffly mannered actors' postures, pasteboard sets, props, and painted backdrops. Laurence Olivier's much-discussed *Henry V* is essentially a meditation on the stagecraft of Elizabethan England in contradistinction to the cinematic resources of wartime England in 1944. It begins in the cramped confines of the Globe Theatre as the extras and principals mill about backstage; and it proceeds, bit by bit in gradual fashion, to stretch and finally to "explode" the proscenium until, as events move toward the battle of Agincourt, the play assumes on screen a wholly cinematic character. The concluding third of the film gradually reverses the procedure, until we are back on the Globe stage for Henry's wedding. Julie Taymor's recent *Titus* reveals at the end that the entire production has been staged before a modern audience in the Roman Colosseum. Max Ophuls' *Lola Montez* frames the story of the notorious 19th-century Spanish-Irish cabaret dancer (Martine Carol) inside a mammoth circus ring with Peter Ustinov as the flamboyant ringmaster. Lola is confined in a cage, displayed along with the rest of the vicious beasts of the jungle. Stiff and mute, like a doll, she stands on a pedestal revolving in one direction, while the camera circles around moving in the opposite direction. A short mime show precedes each flashback. Ophuls uses the trope of the circus ring to deconstruct the apparatus of exhibitionism and lurid publicity that too often attends the world of show business. For him the brittle artifice of the theatre can be dangerous, since it destroys through the cruelty of spectacle the personality of the performer.

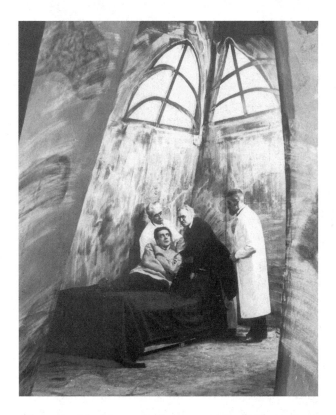

The painted backdrops, shallow stage, and architectural distortions of German expressionist stagecraft found their way into The Cabinet of Dr. Caligari *(1919).*
(COURTESY NATIONAL FILM SOCIETY ARCHIVES)

Eric Rohmer's *Perceval le Galois* (1978) is limned with the glare of footlights and its performers declaim their lines on a shallow-depth stage against painted forced perspective backdrops. Garcia Lorca's play, *Blood Wedding*, is performed as a pantomime flamenco ballet by Antonio Gades' dance troupe in the 1981 film by Carlos Saura. It begins offstage as the troupe arrives at the dance studio, applies makeup, dons costumes, and talks to the camera. After a few practice steps, the performance proper transpires on a bare stage, accompanied by two guitarists and a small combo. After an "intermission" break while the company assembles for a group photograph, the dance continues. At the finish, the dancers silently depart. Peter Bogdanovich's *Noises Off* (1992), adapted from Michael Frayn's play, is a play-within-a-play-within-a film as we see a performance of a farce called *Nothing On* from two vantage points—first from backstage and later from the audience. Peter Weir's *The Truman Show* (1998) places the unwitting Truman Burbank (Jim Carrey) at the center of his own ongoing drama, a 24-hour daily television show. His whole world of Seahaven is nothing but a vast set, a construct of false fronts, lights, scripted actors, and props. Even the horizon turns out to be a cyclorama. Similarly, the virtual realities constructed in *The Thirteenth Floor* (1998), *Dark City* (1997), and *The Game* (1998) surround their protagonists with dramatic constructions to which they are both audience and participant.

SELECTED CLASSICS— BACKSTAGE WITH THE BARD

1. *TO BE OR NOT TO BE* (1942), U.S.A., directed by Ernst Lubitsch

Ernst Lubitsch's *To Be or Not to Be* employs its own "mousetrap" to foil Nazi tyranny in Poland. It belongs to a select company of backstage theatrical films set in World War II that also include Istvan Szabo's *Mephisto* (1981) and Francois Truffaut's *The Last Metro* (1980). Whereas *Mephisto*, adapted from Klaus Mann's long-suppressed novel, is a devastating indictment of artistic compromise in the service of the Nazi Party—the character of Hendrik was based on the opportunistic actor Gustaf Gründgens, who sold his soul, as it were (hence the title *Mephisto*), to curry the favor of Hermann Goering—the Lubitsch and Truffaut films are glorious tributes to the role that theatre plays in the battle for personal and political freedom. (The Truffaut film will be examined presently in these pages.) *To Be or Not to Be* tells the story of the Josef Tura Troupe's involvement in the dangerous politics of World War II. Taking its cue from the title, a production of *Hamlet* is exploited for a variety of seriocomic possibilities. The setting is Poland in 1939. Jack Benny portrays Josef Tura, "that great, *great* Polish actor," as he describes himself on several occasions. A running gag in the film is his intonation of the lines of Hamlet's famous soliloquy—which are always interrupted by the departure from the audience of a handsome, young Polish flyer (principally, Robert Stack as Lieutenant Sobinski). Tura misunderstands the action: He thinks it is a critique of his acting, when in reality, unbeknownst to him, those particular lines are a signal arranged by his wife, Maria (Carole Lombard), for an assignation. It is doubtful if the Bard's words had ever before functioned as a coded message for extramarital dalliance. Those words may also be construed as the burning question that will decide Poland's fate.

But I get ahead of myself. Ernst Lubitsch's classic seriocomedy, written by Edwin Justus Mayer, depicts the adventures of a troupe of actors in war-torn Poland who find themselves utilizing their talents to outwit the Gestapo and support the Resistance. The movie opens with Adolph Hitler striding through the streets of Warsaw. But it is not Hitler. It is Bronski, an actor in Josef Tura's troupe, rehearsing a play called *Gestapo* that satirizes the Nazis. Sent out into the streets to test the effectiveness of his impersonation, he "fails" when a little girl comes up to him and asks him by his stage name for an autograph. Unlike the child, we movie viewers have been fooled at the outset (later in the film, this same impersonation will succeed with the Nazi Gestapo officers). Illusion and reality jostle for our attention. As Robert Willson has pointed out, this opening anecdote establishes at once not only the theme of the film but also the essential parallel between the movie and Shakespeare's *Hamlet*, i.e., "the feared German tyrant" proves to be "nothing more than a bad actor trying to convince us he is more powerful than he is." Hitler, like Claudius, "is little more than a player-king, incapable of ruling himself, let alone the kingdom."

When it is learned that a presumed Polish patriot, Professor Siletsky (Stanley Ridges), is in reality a Nazi agent bent on turning over the names of loyal Poles to the Nazis, the Tura troupe springs into action to intercept him and, at the same time, to effect the escape of the Polish aviator Sobinski. Josef Tura impersonates the Gestapo officer Erhardt (Sig Rumann), and interviews Siletsky. Smelling a rat, Siletsky almost escapes before he is killed by Sobinski. (This moment is one of the highlights of the film: Siletsky flees to Tura's theatre, where he is shot dead on center-stage, a spotlight full upon him.) Tura now turns to his next challenge, impersonating Siletsky ("I'm going to have to do the impossible; I'm going to have to surpass myself"). As Siletsky, he goes to the real Erhardt in order to procure a plane for the fleeing Sobinski. But Erhardt, too, sees through the disguise, although he is unsuccessful in preventing Tura-Siletsky from escaping. The problem remains—Sobinski still has to be spirited out of the country. Now the stage is set, as it were, for the last and most ambitious of the Tura impersonations.

Learning that the real Hitler is coming to Tura's theatre to witness a celebration performed in his honor, Tura contrives to use the occasion to effect Sobinski's escape. He may be motivated by more than just patriotism—after all, his troupe's Nazi satire, *Gestapo*, had been cancelled by the censors, and here is a chance at last to bring the play to the public. Using the uniforms from *Gestapo*, he and his actors invade the lobby *before* the arrival of the real Hitler. One of Tura's actors, Greenberg (Felix Bressart), has in the meantime been planted in the restroom in advance. He rushes out to confront "Hitler" (Bronski again) and commences Shylock's Rialto speech ("Hath not a Jew eyes?") from *The Merchant of Venice* (3.1.55–69). It is Greenberg's

Shakespeare's Hamlet *came to the backstage seriocomedy,* To Be or Not to Be, *which starred Jack Benny and Carole Lombard as members of a Polish theatre troupe.* (COURTESY NATIONAL FILM SOCIETY ARCHIVES)

finest hour, and he recites the lines with poignant simplicity. While the fake Hitler orders the man's arrest, Tura (also in disguise as an SS officer) uses the ruckus as a diversion to spirit away Sobinski along with the rest of the fake soldiers. It is a subtle irony that while Bronski had not fooled the Poles with his Hitler impersonation, he is able to fool the Germans.

That the machinations of an acting troupe are central to the plot resolution and the deception of the villains underscores yet another link between the film and the "mousetrap" of Shakespeare's play. Significantly, as Danny Peary points out, it takes ham-handed actors to "have the tremendous egos that can compete with those of the Nazis"; and it takes their skills in theatrical deception to compete with the spy Siletsky.

The "To Be or Not to Be" words are declaimed one last time at the end of the film. Tura and his troupe have come to England to perform *Hamlet*. To the astonishment of Tura—and of Sobinski seated in the audience—at the utterance of the famous lines, *another* serviceman rises from his seat and heads for the exits! It is the last stroke in a world full of illusion and deception. Or, as Willson suggests, perhaps this last exit is indeed a critical reaction to Tura's performance (his rendition of Hamlet had earlier been criticized as comparable to what the Nazis were doing to Poland). Thus, by extension, "Lubitsch also seems to be suggesting that such poor players or player-kings as Hitler and Mussolini will likewise be exposed and hooted off the world stage."

It is worth noting that in Mel Brooks's remake in 1983 the play being performed by the Polish troupe is not *Hamlet*, but a series of excerpts from a collage play entitled *Highlights from Hamlet*. That in itself is perhaps a commentary upon our modern-day penchant for bowdlerizing Shakespeare and abbreviating him for modern consumption.

2. *A DOUBLE LIFE* (1947), U.S.A., directed by George Cukor

A Double Life is one of many films that utilize theatrical events to illuminate psychological truths about the particular characters involved. To digress a moment, in *The Dresser* (1983), based on Ronald Harwood's 1980 play, a performance of *King Lear* salvages the wreckage of the unstable mental and emotional life of the actor known only as "Sir" (Albert Finney). With the support and urging of his loyal dresser, Norman (Tom Courtenay), Sir, who had earlier confused his lines, is able to pull himself together to deliver the last and definitive performance of his life. Perhaps appropriately, at the curtain's fall, Sir dies. Clearly, the character of Lear is an extension, or reflection, of Sir himself. Thus, the film emerges as a commentary on the excessive degree to which an actor identifies with a role.

More germane to *A Double Life* are the several films that have selected another Shakespeare play, *Othello*, to explore the darker implications of role identification. From the silent era comes *Carnival* (1921), which stars the great Italian Shakespearean actor Silvio Steno who, during a performance of *Othello*, goes crazy with jealousy and nearly strangles his wife to death while she is playing Desdemona. Two films from Britain have similar plot lines. *Men Are Not Gods* (1936) features an actor playing Othello, Edmund Davey (Sebastian Shaw), and his Desdemona, his wife (Gertrude Lawrence), who find themselves in a real-life triangle that nearly results in her murder onstage.

The most famous entry in this list—and one of mainstream Hollywood's finest treatments of Shakespeare—is undoubtedly *A Double Life* (1947), directed by George Cukor and scripted by Garson Kanin and Ruth Gordon. Shakespeare is dragged, all too willingly, one might suspect, into the world of late-1940s *film noir*. Ronald Colman (who won an Oscar for his performance) is Anthony John, an aging Broadway stage star who is currently costarring with his newly

George Cukor

divorced wife, Brita (Signe Hasso), in a drawing-room comedy called *A Gentleman's Gentleman*. As a publicity stunt and a career boost, Tony considers mounting on Broadway a production of *Othello*, which will feature Brita as Desdemona. A gimmick will be that he will not smother Desdemona to death, but stifle her with a kiss. Ex-wife Brita is dubious about his taking on the role of Othello, since she knows all too well that Anthony has a tendency to identify too much with his roles. Sure enough, Tony immediately takes to the streets to ponder the new project, reciting lines from the play as he walks. Stopping at a café, he continues to recite lines to himself while chatting with a waitress named Pat Kroll (Shelley Winters). Throughout their exchange, Tony's interior voice declaims lines like "We do call these delicate creatures ours. . . ." from *Othello*. More lines whirl through his brain as he goes to her apartment and discovers that her bed is partitioned from the rest of the room, just as Desdemona's is in the play. "Have you prayed tonight, Desdemona?" The next morning Tony leaves Pat to begin rehearsals. Tony's interior monologue continues throughout, as he says to himself, "Look within yourself to find the key—jealousy!"

A remarkable montage takes us through the months spanning pre-production preparations to the successful opening night. We catch swift glimpses of the preliminary blocking, the first run-through, adjustments of the script, the costume tryouts, the glitches during technical rehearsals, and the night of the premiere. "The part begins to seep into your life and the battle begins," muses Tony. "Imagination against reality. Keep each in its place. That's the job, if you can do it." Although the production is a success, Tony is increasingly plagued by these interior voices and by the jangling sounds of bells.

The play is now in its second successful year. But as Tony's attempts to reconcile with Brita fail, his acting becomes more agitated, and his murder scenes with Desdemona become increasingly realistic. Things come to a head when Brita refuses Tony's marriage proposal, and he follows her to her rooms. "Yet she must die lest she betray more men," intones his interior voice. "Heaven truly knows that thou art false as hell. Oh, now, forever, farewell the tranquil mind." In a deranged state, he leaves her and staggers out into the night to Pat's room. After asking her repeatedly if she has had other lovers, he murders her. "Put out the light, and then put out the light," he intones. The newspapers are full of the scandal, reporting that the victim was dispatched by a "kiss of death." It's a press agent's dream, aided by Tony's publicist and rival for Brita's affections, Bill Friend (Edmund O'Brien). But when Tony spots the story, he furiously rushes to Bill's flat and unsuccessfully tries to strangle him, shouting lines from the play all the while. Suspicious of Tony's complicity in the murder, Bill determines to set a trap for Tony, a "mousetrap" device. (Bill himself may be acting out of a combination of an altruistic search for justice and jealousy over Tony's relations with Brita.) Bill "auditions" several prospective actresses to impersonate the dead Pat Kroll. After selecting one, he has her made up and dressed like Pat, down to wearing her earrings. He then positions her in a bar where he will contrive to have Tony run into her. Tony's guilty reactions convince Bill he is indeed guilty of Pat's murder. Meanwhile, Tony prepares for the evening's performance of *Othello*. He confesses to Brita that nightmares and distractions are plaguing him. He summons up his strength, however, and goes on. After the murder scene with Desdemona, he speaks the lines, "Speak of me as one who loved not wisely but too well. . . ." Before the police waiting in the wings can capture him, he produces Othello's knife, for which he has substituted a real blade, and fatally stabs himself. While the audience reacts in shock, Tony is dragged backstage where he confesses his crime to Brita, Bill, and the police. At the moment of his death a shadow falls across his face, and at the same time the curtain closes and the spotlight is extinguished.

Veteran stage actor-manager Walter Hampden supervised the generous helping of *Othello* sequences. Cinematographer Milton Krasner photographed many of the exterior scenes in the New York streets and the interior, theatrical sequences in a heavily cloaked chiaroscuro lighting. Miklos Rozsa's music "doubles" as diegetic music for the play and as nondiegetic music to accompany and enhance the offstage action.

There are many levels of reality and illusion, each "doubling" for the other. Indeed, the "double" motif permeates all aspects of the film and the play-within-the film (while Bill's little "mousetrap" device constitutes yet another level, *another* play-within-the film). Just as Shakespeare demonstrated that Othello was himself a divided soul, as capable of noble-hearted generosity as he was of lethal jealousy, Tony John is immediately depicted as a man possessed also of a double personality. When we first see him, he is standing in the foyer of the Empire Theatre before a large painting of himself. Tony turns toward the camera; and before his face blocks out the painting we see two Tonys, the enormous painting towering above and behind him. Moments later he pauses and silently regards his bust, the two faces in a "two-shot," as it were. Later in the street he encounters two actresses. "What a darling," one says. "What a stinker," retorts the other.

Clearly, there are *two* Tony Johns to consider. When he first seriously considers performing in *Othello* he shuffles through some drawings while the image of the bearded, dark-skinned Othello superimposes over his face. "Oh, beware, my lord, of jealousy. It is the green-eyed monster," says a voice in his head. It is our first encounter with another "double"—we realize that Tony has *two* voices. The interior one functions throughout as the equivalent of the Shakespearean soliloquy, i.e., it both enhances and comments upon the action. When Tony first follows Pat to her apartment, he has difficulty telling her his name, his *real* name. Instead, he catalogues the names of many roles he has played. Immediately thereafter as he turns to a mirror and tries on one of her earrings, declaiming Othello's lines, "the bawdy wind that kisses all it meets . . .," the camera pans from his face to the mirror image, positioning the two together within the shot.

Desdemona's deathbed scene is also doubled, finding its real-life counterpart in Pat's bedroom. The scene is depicted four times. The first time we are on the Empire stage for opening night, and the scene is played virtually intact. "Yet I would not shed her blood, yet she must die," declaims Tony. At that same moment his interior voice comments: "You're two men now, grappling for control. You and Othello." He strangles Desdemona, then kisses her intently until her spasms cease. He then stabs himself, saying, "No way but this, killing myself to die upon a kiss." All is played strictly according to the book; but a disturbing moment, a discordant grace note, as it were, polishes off the scene. Tony remains in place, taking his curtain calls, even though the curtain has fallen and the audience departed. Having established the basic outline of the scene, Desdemona's murder is played a second time in more truncated form. A series of views from the wings and backstage, along with several powerful close-ups, give it a more intimate quality. Tony is now somewhat deranged and his strangling of Desdemona is frighteningly real—so real that she has to call for a doctor afterward.

The third replay of the scene occurs in Pat's apartment. Her bed, the curtain partition, even details of the décor echo the stage set. Her blonde hair has tumbled loose, and she is wearing a white nightgown, very much like Desdemona. As she brings him a cup of coffee, he interrogates her about other men in her life. Tony grows more agitated as she asks him to "put out the light." It's a fatal mistake. Her remark reminds him of Desdemona's line, and he responds, now wholly caught up in the play, "If I quench thee, thou flaming minister . . ." He strangles, then kisses her. Her clutching hand grips the partition and draws it across the scene like a closing curtain. For the fourth and final enactment of the scene we are back on the Empire stage. Distraught and anxious, Tony nervously awaits the scene. He is at the end of his rope, and the police are closing in. This time the action begins after the murder, when Othello is about to be taken away by his councillors. Instead of stabbing himself with the prop knife, he procures a real blade (another "double" motif). "Then must you speak of one who loved," he intones brokenly, "not wisely but too well; of one not easily jealous but being wrought perplexed in the extreme." As the interior noises rise in a crescendo in his head, he collapses.

Commentator Robert F. Willson argues persuasively that the role of Othello functioned as an Iago-like device that precipitated Tony's homicidal tendencies and his own death. "*A Double Life* represents Iago as a psychological demon that in the modern world has become internalized; relying on the device, the writers and director explore depths of character that the Freudian age has come to regard as determinate and psychopathic rather than 'tragic.'" Putting it another way, the play—indeed, the acting profession generally—functions as a kind of potion that can stimulate alternate personalities in an actor, just as the elixir of the noble Dr. Jekyll frees Mr. Hyde.

3. *THEATER OF BLOOD* (1973), U.K., directed by Douglas Hickox

Theater of Blood trumps *A Double Life* several times over. An actor chooses not just one, but 10 methods of Shakespearean-inspired homicide. In a brilliant stroke, Vincent Price is cast as the vengeful Edward Lionheart, a most theatrically flamboyant, if ham-handed, serial killer.

Setting the scene is a prologue containing clips of death scenes from several black-and-white Shakespearean silent films. The eerily mute succession of suffocations and stabbings takes on the elegantly Grand Guignol character of drawings by Edward Gorey. The story proper begins on March 15 (appropriately enough, as it turns out) with the savage stabbing death of theatre critic George Maxwell (Michael Hordern). After being lured to an abandoned building, Maxwell finds himself confronting a knife-wielding mob in a scene straight out of *Julius Caesar*. He is brutally attacked and hacked to pieces. Looking on is the costumed character of Mark Antony. "Pardon me, thou bleeding piece of earth," Antony mocks, "that I am meek and gentle with these butchers." Discarding the broken corpse, Antony turns to his bedraggled accomplices and intones his eulogy of the dead Caesar, "Friends, Romans, countrymen, lend me your ears!"

Edward Lionheart, once presumed dead, is very much alive. Assisted by his deranged daughter, Edwina (Diana Rigg), and a motley crew of accomplices, he has begun his vendetta against the critics who savaged his performances. Each murder will be patterned after one of the Shakespearean plays that marked Lionheart's last season on the boards. Like Caesar himself, back from the dead, he is ready to "Cry 'Havoc!' and let slip the dogs of war. . . ."

In *Troilus and Cressida* Achilles slays Hector and lashes his corpse to the tail of a wild horse. Lionheart's second victim, critic Hector Snipe (Dennis Price), suffers the same fate. "Look, Hector, how the sun begins to set, how ugly night comes breathing at his heels," declaims Lionheart, dressed in the armor of Achilles, as he thrusts his spear into Snipe's body. "Even with the violent darkening of the sun to close the day up, Hector's life is done." Lionheart orders his accomplices, "Come tie his body to my tail, along the field I will the Trojan trail . . ."

Just as in *Cymbeline*, Imogen wakes up and finds the headless body of Cloten in the bed with her, so now does Lionheart arrange a like fate for his third victim, critic Horace Sprout (Arthur Lowe). Lionheart and his accomplice (Diana Rigg disguised as a man) invade Sprout's bedchamber, drug him and his wife with a hypodermic, lay out their surgical tools, and proceed to saw off Sprout's head. Jets of blood spurt upward while dreamy music is heard on the soundtrack. Beside her decapitated husband, Mrs. Sprout sleeps on. She is due for a rude awakening.

In *The Merchant of Venice* the vengeful Shylock wants to claim his pound of flesh from Antonio, but his daughter, Portia, dissuades him. Lionheart has worked out his own version of the play for his fourth victim, critic Trevor Dickman (Harry Andrews). Dickman protests that Antonio is spared in the play. "We have revised this script," retorts Lionheart, dressed in the robes of the Jew, as he cuts out Dickman's heart. "You spurned me such a day," recites Lionheart. "Another time you called me dog. . . . But if I am a dog, beware my fangs." He weighs the bleeding tissue on the scales. Two ounces too heavy. He snips off a tiny piece. *Now* he has his pound of flesh. Later, viewing the dead man's remains, another critic quips, "Only Lionheart would have the temerity to rewrite Shakespeare."

In *Richard III* the scheming Richard has his henchmen murder George, the duke of Clarence, by drowning him in a cask of wine. Lionheart duly lures his fifth victim, critic Oliver Larding (Robert Coote) to a fake wine tasting, where he is thrust upside down into a wine cask. "Now is the winter of our discontent," snarls Lionheart, wearing the wig and mincing the walk of Richard, "made glorious summer by this son of York. . . . As I am subtle, false, and treacherous, this day should Clarence be closely mewed up."

The sixth murder attempt is a curiously unfinished affair. Critic Peregrine Devlin (Ian Hendry) goes to his fencing school, where instead of his teacher, he confronts Lionheart, rapier in hand. Like Tybalt and Romeo in *Romeo and Juliet*, they go at it, hurdling barriers and bouncing on trampolines. But then, curiously, Lionheart lets him go, delaying the kill for another day.

Inspired by Othello's deadly jealousy, Lionheart contrives to stage-manage a scene where his sixth victim, critic Solomon Psaltery (Jack Hawkins), finds his wife in bed with a lover (Lionheart disguised as a masseur). Psaltery seizes a pillow and suffocates his wife. Lionheart may not have killed Psaltery, observes

a police detective, but he has managed to consign the poor man to prison for the rest of his life.

Henry VI, Part I has a grisly scene where Joan of Arc is burned at the stake. Lionheart's seventh victim, critic Chloe Moon (Carol Browne), faces a similar fate when she goes to an appointment at a hair salon. Lionheart, affecting a limp-wristed persona, waits on her. He hooks her hair curlers to the electricity and turns on the juice. "Bring forth that sorceress condemned to burn," he intones. "Break thou in pieces and consume to ashes, thou foul, accursed minister of Hell." Chloe is left in the chair, burnt to a cinder.

Titus Andronicus contains Shakespeare's most notorious piece of Grand Guignol revenge as Titus feeds his arch enemy, Queen Tamara, a meat pie consisting of her two sons. This is the fate reserved for Lionheart's eighth victim, critic Meredith Merridew (Robert Morley). Merridew dotes on his two poodle dogs with the same enthusiasm as he relishes a gourmet meal. Lionheart contrives to combine both pleasures. He fakes a live performance of a popular cooking television show, *This Is Your Dish*, where the delighted Merridew is treated to a succulent dish. But the meat pie that Merridew consumes with such pleasure turns out to made from his two dogs. "I will grind your bones to dust and make two pasties of your shameful head," quotes Lionheart as Titus, as he stuffs food down Merridew's throat with a funnel. Moments later, Lionheart smirks, "Pity, he didn't have the stomach for it."

Lionheart reserves critic Peregrine Devlin for the fate of Gloucester in *King Lear*. Devlin is tied to a bench while two red-hot daggers slowly descend toward his eyes. Lionheart offers mercy if Devlin will admit that he is a great actor. Refusing, Devlin gazes at Edwina, who is all too willingly assisting her father. "What have you done to your daughter?" Devlin protests. Edwina, standing in for Lear's loyal daughter, Cordelia, turns toward her father: "Good my lord you have begot me, bred me, loved me," she says, assuming her own role. "I return those duties back as are right fit. Obey you, love you, most honor you." Before Devlin's eyes can be put out, the police burst in. Edwina is injured and Lionheart, clasping her body to his breast, staggers off and sets the theatre on fire. "Come, fire," he moans, "consume this petty world; and in its ashes let my memory lie." He and Edwina exchange their last words. "How does my royal lord," she whispers. "How fares your majesty?" He responds, "You did me wrong to take me out of the grave. Thou art a soul in bliss, but I am bound upon a wheel of fire. Mine own tears do scald like molten lead." She breathes her last, "We are not the first, who best meaning, have incurred the worst."

Both perish in the fire. It remains for Devlin, the only surviving critic, to have the last word: "Yes, it was a fascinating performance, but of course he was madly overacting, as usual. But you must admit, he did know how to make an exit."

If Lionheart identifies with his Shakespearean characters, so surely does Vincent Price empathize with his character of Lionheart. Both, near the end of their careers, suffered critical jibes for their broad-brush theatrics. And in this film both have the chance to wreak revenge most foul. *Theater of Blood* is the most erudite piece of Grand Guignol in film history; and Lionheart/Price is the most articulate of serial killers.

4. *SHAKESPEARE WALLAH* (1965), U.K., directed by James Ivory

The term "wallah" in Hindustani means a small-time operator. Here it refers to a small troupe of touring English players. The film is loosely based on the diaries of actor-manager Geoffrey Kendal while touring India with his "Shakesperiana" troupe in 1947, the year India achieved independence from Britain. When filmmaker James Ivory read the diary, he showed it to novelist Ruth Prawer Jhabvala, who collaborated with him on a screenplay. Kendal and his wife, Laura Liddel, portrayed their fictional counterparts, the Buckinghams. Their daughter Felicity was cast in the key role of Lizzie Buckingham. Popular actor Shashi Kapoor portrayed Sanju, Lizzie's romantic lead. And Madjur Jaffrey played Manjula, a popular Bollywood actress. The film was made on a shoestring budget of $80,000 and shot on locations in the hill station of Kasauli, in the Punjab; in the vice-regal summer capital of Simla; in Alwar, in Rajasthan; in Lucknow; and in Bombay.

The story spins out against the background of the passing of British culture in post-independence India. It is a world too impatient for Shakespearean drama and too preoccupied with the novelties of musical films. The disasters that befall the Buckingham Players exemplify the schisms opening up between worlds old and new, between classical and popular entertainment. The Buckinghams are slow to adapt to these changes. "One is always conscious of them as being constrained by their theatrical calling," notes Patrice Sorace, "which has lost popularity to Indian films that represent the new, indigenous Indian culture."

Indeed, the Buckinghams' tour is marked by disasters of all kinds. At the film's beginning, when they are performing Sheridan's *The Critic* in front of a chateau near Lucknow, a runaway cow stampedes the actors and audience. Their next performance, of Shake-

speare's *Antony and Cleopatra*, transpires in the renovated palace of the maharaja of Betawar, who complains that current conditions have forced him to rent out half his palace as office space. Later, at a private school the troupe learns that they will have to cut back on the usual number of performances. Mr. Buckingham protests: "But surely Shakespeare is still in your curriculum. I mean, our shows are very popular with schools and colleges. We do a kind of package—Hamlet, some comedy, some tragedy, a bit of *Twelfth Night*. . . ." But the department head only shakes him off, citing the importance of allowing time for a game of cricket: "I don't want to put undue stress on our sports activities, but they do take a lot of time. . . ." To Buckingham's dismay, the troupe is dismissed after just one performance. "It all changed, slowly, over these past years," he says bitterly. "I keep thinking about it. I can't help it. We should have gone home in '47 when the others went. But we were too sure of ourselves."

Tensions of a different sort arise when young Lizzie Buckingham meets and falls in love with Sanju, a wealthy young Indian playboy. Sanju conveys his admiration of the troupe's performance of *Hamlet* to his friend, the celebrated Indian actress Manjula. In particular, he extols Lizzie's artistry: "She is a very fine artist. For such people one can have some respect." Manjula, who has no inkling of what classical drama is all about, retorts that she, too, has played "many great dramatic roles in my time." To which Sanju admits, "People don't care for the theatre so much these days. Only for films."

Ignoring Manjula's jealousy, Sanju follows Lizzie when the troupe takes to the road toward Simla. He watches her performance as Maria in *Twelfth Night* and as Desdemona in *Othello*. During the latter performance, Manjula unexpectedly bursts in, and her ostentatious entrance literally stops the show. Mr. Buckingham advances to the footlights and requests silence. Unabashed, Manjula maintains her grand manner and signs autographs during the murder scene. In mock horror at the violence of Desdemona's death, Manjula departs with considerable commotion. "How can you like something like that?" she asks Sanju. "All that moaning and groaning, so bloodthirsty." Later, when Sanju tries to apologize to Buckingham, he shrugs, saying, "Let's just call it the victory of the moving pictures over the theatre." The final humiliation comes during the Buckinghams' performance of *Romeo and Juliet*. Lizzie's entrance onstage as Juliet is greeted with rude whistles and comments from the audience. As she declaims the lines, "But my true love is grown to such excess/I cannot sum up half my wealth," a fight breaks out between Sanju and the offending toughs. A near riot ensues and the performance is halted. Minutes later, Sanju objects to Lizzie's choice of a lifestyle that constantly exposes her to the public. "It's a wonderful life," she replies defensively; "I wouldn't want to be anything else. Acting's my whole life." Yet, it is obvious she is prepared to give it up if Sanju would ask her to marry him. But it is just as obvious that Sanju will never understand her devotion to the theatre, and that he is not prepared to take that final step. The lovers part. In the concluding scene, at the behest of her parents, a saddened Lizzie boards a ship bound for England.

Although the original source material of the film, the Kendal diaries, had depicted the adventures of the troupe as a positive experience, it was decidedly the intention of Ivory and Jhabvala to negate that. The Buckinghams' failure was designed to be emblematic of the larger failure of classical drama in the face of the culture of a New India—a culture at once rooted both in Eastern traditions and in the pop culture of Bollywood. Similarly, Lizzie's devotion to her craft was also out of place in the face of Sanju's traditionalist—some would say "sexist"—attitudes toward a woman's place in society. "The Kendals felt uncomfortable," recalled James Ivory, "were hard put sometimes even to bring out their dialogue, which seemed to give utterance to thoughts which were at variance with everything they believed. It did not help that the stuff of their lives was being used in order to create a drama symbolic of a moment in history."

5. *A MIDWINTER'S TALE* (1995), U.K., directed by Kenneth Branagh (released in the U.K. as *IN THE BLEAK MIDWINTER*)

In *A Midwinter's Tale* (1995) the redoubtable Shakespearean Kenneth Branagh chronicles the glitches, twitches, and occasional glories of a theatrical troupe desperately trying to ready a performance of *Hamlet* for a Christmas Eve opening in an abandoned English country church. Fiction merges with reality in that the actors are drawn from Branagh's own troupe, the Renaissance Theatre Company. Thus, you can believe what you're seeing on screen is the real thing, drawn from their shared experiences. "It was the cumulative experience of this group that informed and changed the script," recalled Branagh. "All the mad audition sequences come from life, as do many of the characters. The film itself was made in the spirit of the story. . . . The spirit of generous collaboration (not without the odd fit of temper) made for a shoot . . . which, as Hamlet would, held 'the mirror up to nature.'" Moreover, Branagh serves it up with quick wit, swift pacing, peppery dialogue, and a no-nonsense camera style. "The more 'serious' the play the more likely rehearsals are to

create amusement," says Branagh, "although the hijinks may not always be intentional and may not always be enjoyed by the people involved. . . . In Shakespeare particularly, the great tragedies tread such a fine line between laughter and tears, that any group working on them can find themselves in the grip of hysteria. . . . It's the very stuff of drama, inside the drama." Critics of the film agreed. "[It] starts off as an amusing free-for-all spoof of the acting profession," wrote Stephen Holden, "and eventually turns into a comic valentine to diehard thespian dedication."

Much of the film is frankly autobiographical, both of the adventures Branagh has experienced on the road, and of his childhood delight in watching Hollywood backstage musicals. In particular, Branagh wanted to emulate the cycle of backstage movies that teamed up director Busby Berkeley with Judy Garland and Mickey Rooney—*Babes in Arms* (1939), *Strike up the Band* (1940), *Babes on Broadway* (1942), and *Girl Crazy* (1943)—wherein the determination of a bunch of squabbling, disparate kids to "put on a show" transforms them into a solidly organized and creatively productive theatrical unit.

A Midwinter's Tale begins as Joe (Michael Maloney) holds auditions for an upcoming production of *Hamlet:* A dancer tap-dances the "To Be or Not to Be" soliloquy. A ventriloquist and his dummy proclaim the "Alas poor Yorick" lines. A madwoman enacts with hand puppets the characters of Mrs. and Mrs. Macbeth. A balding man belts out "Mule Train" while hitting himself on the head with an aluminum tray.

What a mismatched assortment of players is finally brought together! As Kenneth Rothwell says, they are "losers, not glamorous stars, making pathetic efforts to interest the world in their Shakespearean tragedy." There's Michael Maloney as Joe, the intense producer rolling the dice on this production; Julia Sawalha as Nina, his Ophelia, a nearsighted klutz who can't even find a creek to drown in; Nicholas Farrell as Tom Newman, who plays Laertes, slipping in and out of unlikely accents ("from another solar system") and motivations like a shopper trying on suits; John Sessions as Terry Du Bois, a campy gay man who takes on Gertrude (and who will supply his own frocks and breasts for the role); Richard Briers as Henry Wakefield, the company's Claudius (who starchly declares, "The English theatre is dominated by the class system and a bunch of Oxbridge homos"); and Celia Imrie as Fadge, the production designer with singularly inventive ideas, including populating the empty auditorium seats with cardboard cutouts of spectators "just to keep the actors company," she confides to Joe (the sight of these bizarre, stiff forms mixed in with the living

Backstage with the Bard: A theatre troupe prepares their production of Hamlet in Kenneth Branagh's A Midwinter's Tale.
(COURTESY CASTLE ROCK ENTERTAINMENT)

patrons accounts for the funniest scenes in the movie). "If we don't get a natural audience, I want to create a World for you. You should at least have people watching you. Even if they are cardboard."

The company arrives in Joe's car at the village of Hope. They tumble out and admire the picturesque little church situated at the top of a hill. But no, this is the wrong site. The *real* church is down by the village, an "ugly red church" that is damp and cavernous. At the first read-through, Joe admits, "I see it as a very long play." "I see it as a *very* long play, darling," retorts one of the players. "Sally Scissors is going to appear, we hope?" Everybody bickers about what lines are to be cut, details of costuming, who will play multiple roles, what period to set the play in, how to advertise. They worry about attracting the locals to see the play. "Hello kids," mocks Molly. "Do stop watching Mighty Morphin Power Rangers and come and watch a four-hundred-year-old play about a depressed aristocrat. I mean it's something you can really relate to."

The first rehearsals. One actor defends his preposterous "grande dame" accent in Gertrude's opening lines ("They don't talk like they do in the real world—they put on the old cigarette gravel—the tragic thrill—the emotional break in the middle of the line—the operatic cadenzas"). So caught up is she in Ophelia's madness, poor nearsighted Nina shouts "Oh, my lord, I have been so affrighted"—and races right off the edge of the stage. One actor finds himself having to play Rosencrantz and Guildenstern *at the same time*. There are worries about paying the landlord overdue electric bills. And there is not enough time for sufficient rehearsal. "We have set ourselves a challenge there is no doubt," declares Joe. "But at Shakespeare's own theatre, a six-week season would have produced 35 performances of 17 different plays including at times four world premieres. So, as Polonius says, 'Sometimes Brevity can be the soul of wit.' But I don't think we should lose our nerve." The closet scene between Hamlet and Gertrude is interrupted by the revelation that the actor playing Gertrude had abandoned a child years before.

As things keep going wrong and the prospect of additional needed funding looks bleak, Joe at last loses his temper: "What is the point? . . . You're a perfectly decent bunch of people. A group of actors with all the normal insecurities and vanities. But basically I know you want to be here, we all want to do what's best for the show. But look at us. We argue. We're depressed. We've set ourselves too great a target. It is too personal for us all. It's a big play and we keep running up against it and hurting ourselves, and I for one can no longer remember what I'm doing or why I'm doing it." But the next day things look better. The scenes snap into focus. The cast comes up with the extra money.

Now comes the technical rehearsal. Too much smoke. Nobody can see anything. The opening words, "Who's there?" take on extra meaning. Meanwhile, no one (least of all the movie viewers) has a clue as to what is the time period for the play. Relations among the cast are likewise indeterminate, as they keep falling in and out of love with each other.

In a last-minute crisis, Joe's agent, Margaretta (Joan Collins), gets him a lucrative movie job acting in a science fiction trilogy. She arrives on Christmas Eve to announce that the show will have to close and that Joe has to leave that night. The actors, by now united into a family group, protest that the show must go on: "That's what actors do . . . they hang on, they stick it out." Joe's Ophelia reminds him, "You put your whole life into this, Joe. Right from the start. You needed this job. You needed it then and you need it now. It's not about fame or money or so-called wealth and security, it's about nourishing your soul, nourishing your heart." Molly prepares to go on at the last minute as Hamlet. She receives a canny piece of advice: "If I ever forget my lines in Shakespeare, I always say, 'Crouch we here awhile and lurk.' Always seems to do the trick."

At last the performance begins as smoke envelops the stage (and the audience). At the words, "Who's there?" Horatio, clad in a trench coat, fires a machine gun over the heads of the startled audience. From the back of the church comes Hamlet's first words: "A little more than kin and less than kind." It is Joe, to the rescue, clad in his winter coat, returned unexpectedly at the last minute for opening night. Quick onstage scenes intercut with Fadge backstage clinking glasses with Molly. The Nunnery Scene. Nina's Ophelia is clad in a silver turban and glittery dress, making her look for all the world like Theda Bara. Clearly upset with Joe's last-minute grandstanding, Nina concludes her lines—"Rich gifts wax poor when givers prove unkind"—with a hard slap to his face. Quick glimpse of the Mousetrap Scene (with Claudius clad in military tunic and epaulettes). Cut to the Closet Scene, where Hamlet says, "What is a man if his chief good and market of his time be but to sleep and feed, a beast no

more." The sword fight features Hamlet and Laertes, bare-chested, in trousers and suspenders, exchanging lines and blades as they whirl about the room. Hamlet declaims his last lines, "The rest is silence." Fortinbras says: "Go, bid the soldiers shoot." Darkness. Drum. Gong. Wild applause. The whole performance has taken up a mere four minutes of screen time. Tom Stoppard could not have abbreviated the whole thing in a more trenchant and succinct manner. It is the Bard played at top speed.

The theatrical improbabilities spill out into the post-performance sequence with several tearful reunions and last-minute revelations. One of the audience members turns out to be a Hollywood celebrity. After dubbing Joe and Nina "Mickey" and "Judy" ("The whole thing was like a Judy Garland movie"), she offers Tom Newman a leading role and Fadge a job as designer in her new science fiction movie. Another audience member turns out to be Terry's long-lost son; and they reconcile with a tearful embrace as Terry says, "I think you're a wonderful queen, in every way." In the meantime, it is revealed that Joe really has turned down the movie part for the sake of being with the play and with Nina. A mollified Nina falls into his arms and they dance, their future romance assured. Against an exterior night shot of the church, the words of the company are heard: "Merry Christmas!"

The triumph of this performance is nothing less than a Christmas apotheosis for the lowly cast members. "The enchantment of assuming the identities of fabled persons like Hamlet, Gertrude, and Ophelia casts its spell," writes Kenneth Rothwell, "and their play turns into a Christmas miracle in which wretchedness is transfigured into sublimity."

A Midwinter's Tale serves as a comic curtain-raiser for the real treat to come—Branagh's full-scale production of *Hamlet* (1996), which presented the complete play, intact, for the first time on screen. (There's a private joke in *A Midwinter's Tale*, incidentally, when the director reassures his troupe that they'll perform the play with cuts.) For some of us, however, Branagh's *Midwinter* deserves its own privileged place alongside his *Hamlet*.

6. *LOOKING FOR RICHARD* (1996), U.S.A., directed by
   Al Pacino

Al Pacino's *Looking for Richard* (1996) might be subtitled *Looking for Shakespeare*. While trying to make sense of what is probably Shakespeare's most frequently performed play, Pacino and his company also cast about for the relevance of Shakespeare for today's audiences. To make *that* long story short, dozens of

Al Pacino and Winona Ryder embark on a search for Shakespearean relevance in Looking for Richard.
(COURTESY FOX SEARCHLIGHT PICTURES)

brief interviews with "the man in the street" persuade us that he doesn't mean a heck of a lot. As Anthony Lane wrote in *The New Yorker*; "This reaching out to an ideal public is bound to be a disappointment, because the majority of the population doesn't care a whit for Shakespeare and never will."

To be sure, just what Pacino intends this project to be is never made clear. Just what is it documenting: the relevance of Shakespeare today; the behind-the-scenes preparations for a play performance; or the shooting of a motion picture adaptation? Pacino himself is not quite sure, and he drifts through the proceedings like a Shakespearean version of Marcello Mastroianni trying to make sense of his creative vision in Fellini's *8 1/2*. There are discussions of the proper use of iambic pentameter, a trip to Shakespeare's birthplace in Stratford-upon-Avon (where Pacino inadvertently trips the fire alarm), a brief visit to the site of the Globe Theatre (which at the time was beginning its reconstruction), and interviews with stalwart Shakespeareans like Kenneth Branagh, Sir John Gielgud, Vanessa Redgrave, and Peter Brook. Pacino gathers his cast—Alec Baldwin as Clarence, Winona Ryder as Lady Anne, Aidan Quinn as Richmond, Kevin Spacey as Buckingham, and Pacino himself as Richard—and they tussle mightily over issues of why American actors are intimidated by performing the Bard, how to make sense of some of the more densely textured rhetoric, how Richard and Buckingham can be related to today's gangsters (but

"high-class gangsters"), and the riddles of character motivation (just why does Richard feel he has to marry Lady Anne?). Pacino has also brought along an educator, Frederic Kimball, for his scholarly savvy.

Predictably, rarely does anyone agree on anything. "Nobody knows *Richard III*," mutters Pacino in exasperation. "It's very confusing. I don't know why we're doing this [movie] at all." Later, as he begins to settle into his character, Pacino doesn't hesitate to reject the advice of Kimball. Kimball erupts in very real anger. "You hired me as a scholar to explain things," he shouts, "yet you *actors* seem to think your ideas are better than mine." Pacino only smiles and grabs a sword to confer a mock knighthood on the poor man, dubbing him "Sir Ph.D."

Meanwhile, Pacino, who does not exactly enjoy an extensive experience in matters Shakespearean, struggles with the convoluted plot. He is bemused but not abashed at its complexities. "There is something sly and rather Richard-like in the throwaway glee with which [Pacino] approaches matters of grave intent," notes Anthony Lane. He also credits Pacino's experience in the three "Godfather" movies with his understanding of the "diplomatic savagery" that Richard employs to place himself on the English throne. There is the backstory of the War of the Roses and the recent defeat of the house of Lancaster to unravel; the complicated relationships among King Edward's presumptives to the throne; Richard's campaign to eliminate his rivals (in order, Clarence, the two princes, and Hastings); and the circumstances of the battle of Bosworth.

Rehearsals, finished performance, and video replay all combine in a seamless flux and flow. In a series of quick edits, Pacino begins a line in his apartment, continues it on stage in full costume, and then reviews the finished product on the video monitor in the studio. Punctuating the proceedings are a number of brief scenes when Pacino's Richard, clad in black tunic, hair wisping from beneath his black cap, addresses the camera with smarmy familiarity. His pale face emerges from out of the enveloping darkness, and his dissipated eyes flicker warily while his lips curdle in an ever so slight smirk. This is a most interesting Richard, a compound of diffidence and deadly authority. In the second half of the film are several protracted sequences that give us our Shakespeare "straight," as it were. These include, in order, Richard's seduction of Lady Anne ("'Twas thy beauty that provoked me," he suggests softly), his charge to two assassins to murder Clarence, the council meeting and the arrest of Hastings, and his exhortation to Buckingham to kill the two princes, and his nightmarish sleep when he is visited by the specters of his past crimes.

Unimpressed by all this are two filmmakers who protest Pacino's extravagance with the whole thing. Finally, after the battle of Bosworth and Richard's death under Richmond's sword, one of them stands back from the set and asks in deadpan, "Is Richard dead? Is that *it*?" The other retorts sarcastically, "If I had told [Pacino] about that other ten rolls of film, he'd want to use it!"

7. *SHAKESPEARE IN LOVE* (1998), U.K., directed by John Madden

Shakespeare in Love (1998) would have us believe that an ill-starred love affair between young Shakespeare and a beauteous woman named Viola De Lesseps (Joseph Fiennes and Gwyneth Paltrow) directly inspired—and was in turn inspired by—the romantic tragedy, *Romeo and Juliet*. What is backstage comes to the forestage—and returns full circle. This play-within-a-play-within-a-movie is cunningly written by Shakespeare veteran Tom Stoppard (*The Fifteen-Minute Hamlet* and *Rosencrantz and Guildenstern Are Dead*) and Marc Norman; and directed by John Madden (who displayed a deft touch with actress Judi Dench in another historical film, about Queen Victoria, *Mrs. Brown*).

London, 1593. Two theatres are contending for popular (and royal) favor—the Curtain Theatre, which claims the talents of the Chamberlain's company and playwright Kit Marlowe; and the Rose Theatre, with the Admiral's company and young Will Shakespeare. The latter house is deep in debt, and its manager, Philip Henslowe (Geoffrey Rush), must get Shakespeare to write a sensational melodrama to fill the coffers. But poor, scruffy, ink-stained Will is suffering from writer's block and sexual impotence ("I dreamed I was trying to pick a lock with a limp herring," he innocently tells his astrologer/councillor in an early scene). The play that's resisting his pen is a melodrama called *Romeo and Ethel, the Pirate's Daughter*.

But inspiration springs up afresh, so to speak, when Will espies a young man at the play auditions named Thomas Kent, who speaks his lines with extraordinary eloquence. Amazed, Will pursues him and tracks him down to a wealthy estate across the Thames. He does not find Thomas Kent, but he does encounter a dazzling, golden-tressed damsel named Viola. Will is instantly smitten with her and impetuously crashes a dance party to see her. But because Will is from the wrong side of the tracks—from the far shore of the Thames, as it were—he's tossed out by her angry suitor, Lord Wessex (Colin Firth). Back at the Rose Theatre, rehearsals begin for *Romeo and Ethel, the*

Pirate's Daughter. The mysterious Thomas Kent reappears and joins the theatre cast as the character of "Romeo." It's only a little later that Will realizes at last that he has been hoodwinked—that this boy is in actuality his beloved Viola in disguise ("I am theatre mad," she says, "and dream myself into a company of players"). It's a delicious moment, as Will waxes eloquently to the "boy" about Viola's charms, and "he" in response suddenly kisses Will.

Keeping their secret, Will and Viola rehearse by day onstage at the Rose and make love by night in her chambers (her parents are conveniently out of town); and, newly inspired, Will transmutes their tender moments into scenes for the new play. In this way life, love, and the theater blissfully intertwine—until Viola's ruse is discovered by the angry Lord Wessex, who first attacks Will in a sword fight and then has the Master of the Revels close down the Rose Theatre on the grounds of the illegality of having a woman appear on the stage. But Burbage's, the Chamberlain's company, comes to the rescue and offers its Curtain Theatre to put on the play (by now retitled, at the casual suggestion of one of Will's actors, *Romeo and Juliet*). The play commences, but Will is brokenhearted because Viola is now married to Lord Wessex. Little does he know that not only has Viola run away from Wessex to attend the opening day of the play, but that she has also taken the place of the boy portraying Juliet. When she comes on to the stage—a real woman playing Will's real love—she and the character of Juliet have melded into one (just as Will is now a real-life Romeo). After the play ends to tumultuous applause, the Master of the Revels shows up determined to close down the theatre. But who should rebuke him but Queen Elizabeth herself, who emerges from the gallery to closely examine Viola and slyly declare that her "illusion" as a "woman" is very convincing. The queen sends Viola off with Wessex. Will, after a tearful departing scene with Viola, settles down to write *Twelfth Night*, with a heroine named Viola. "Write me well," Viola says, "with a new life beginning on a stranger shore."

Joseph Fiennes' Shakespeare is a portrait of a man on the run. He's an artistic chameleon, alive to the vivid colorations of life on the street. He cadges plot tips from Kit Marlowe and lines of dialogue from street conversations—like "a plague on both your houses," overheard from a local minister fulminating against the wicked stage. And he writes like he makes love—at top speed, the quill pen splattering ink across the snow-white foolscap. Gwyneth Paltrow is certainly an intriguing sight sporting a mustache and dressed in men's clothes, quite at home, ironically, amidst a crowd of men dressed like women! Other memorable touches include the boy who periodically shows up, torturing cats and mice, who says his name is John Webster and that he likes blood and murder (who, of course, will grow up to become the Jacobean author of such blood-and-thunder revenge dramas as *The Duchess of Malfi*). There's some business with Kit Marlowe (Rupert Everett in a subdued mood), whose death from a tavern brawl Shakespeare mistakenly supposes to have been caused by his inference to Wessex that it is Kit, not he, who has been visiting Viola at night. Meanwhile, the show's benefactor, the "money man," as he declares himself, ends up a stagestruck idiot playing the character of the apothecary. Philip Henslowe, the manager of the Rose, has a continuing bit of business wherein he declares that some "mysterious" power always comes to the rescue of even the most disaster-ridden theatrical enterprise (and sure enough, at the last moment the tongue-tied character portraying Chorus miraculously declaims his opening speech perfectly). It is also Henslowe who has the best line: After hearing Will describe the action of the play, Henslowe rolls his eyes and responds sarcastically, "*That'll* have 'em rolling in the aisles." And maybe best of all is Judi Dench, who appears in only a few extended scenes (attending a farce with Will Kemp on stage, conferring her blessing on the marriage between Viola and Wessex, and settling matters after the premiere of *Romeo and Juliet*), who with a flash of an eye or a grimace of the mouth can convey more of Elizabeth's hauteur and sly wit than all the arm-waving histrionics of another actress could have.

The play, *Romeo and Juliet*, indeed permeates the entire film, both on- and off-stage. Many set pieces illustrate the point. First is the long montage sequence wherein scenes of Will and Viola's nocturnal lovemaking are cross-cut with the actions of the daily stage rehearsals. In a seamless interchange, desperate embraces and impassioned speeches begin in the bedchamber, continue onstage, and conclude back in the bed. Similarly, in the extended scene of the play's premiere, Will/Romeo and Viola/Juliet come together to enact their and the play's anguish of frustrated love. As in the play, Will's first declaration of love to Viola is a veritable balcony scene. Again, as in the play, her nurse becomes the accomplice through which they conspire to meet. Throughout, the impossibility of his love against her life of privilege and her arranged marriage parallels the play's "star-crossed" fatalism. Events come to blows between Will and his rival, Wessex, just as they do between Romeo and Tybalt. And there's also the rivalry between his company of players and

Burbage's men, echoing that between the houses of Capulet and Montague.

Love and artifice, private life and public performance are indistinguishable. These lovers are actors in their own lives and participants in their own drama. It's a grand game, one in which they, and the viewers, become willing conspirators. The play-within-the-film functions not just to imitate the offstage action but also to inflect it, to reveal that the true theatrical clichés and artifices reside in the real world, not just on stage. Truly, art has only imitated life.

MORE OF THE USUAL SUSPECTS— A POTPOURRI

1. *WAITING FOR GUFFMAN* (1997), U.S.A., directed by Christopher Guest

Waiting for Guffman is the screen's ultimate tribute to every patriotic pageant that was ever inflicted upon the hapless citizens of Smalltown, U.S.A. The town of Blaine, Missouri, is celebrating its "sesquicentennial"—"that's a century-and-half," explains the mayor—and it wants to put on a show called "Red, White, and Blaine." The local theatre director, one Corky St. Clair (Christopher Guest), takes on the assignment, rounds up the wannabe actors, suffers through the rehearsals, and prepares for opening night. Tension thickens with the news that a big-time Broadway scout will attend the premiere. His name— Mort Guffman.

The first 10 minutes set the stage, as it were, reviewing the history of the town of Blaine: In frontier days a pioneer named Blaine Fabin, bound with his wagon train from Philadelphia for California, pitched camp at the first scent of salt water. Proclaiming the region to be part of California, he established a town in his own name. No matter the region turned out to be Missouri, Blaine's noble history had begun. Years later came a visit from President McKinley, whose delight at the presentation of a locally manufactured footstool assured the town a future in stool-making, establishing its claim as "The Stool Capitol of the World." Then, in 1946, a UFO landed and abducted a local character. Upon the abductee's return, he recalled to anyone who would listen the numberless hours of alien "probing."

Corky's challenge in mounting the pageant is considerable. His own credentials are impressive, like his local production of a stage version of the movie, *Backdraft* ("You can *feel* the heat!"), which almost burned down the theatre house. Now, with *Red, White, and Blaine* set to go, Corky awaits Mr. Guffman with more than the usual anticipation. Maybe, just maybe the show can go to Broadway and Corky will have a chance to make his triumphant return to the Great White Way.

The cast members prepare. The openly gay Corky pouts and lisps his way through a series of outrageously caricatured stereotypes, which manage also to be starkly poignant on occasion. With his "Judy Tenuto" T-shirts and vest-bolero pants ensembles, he's an exotic fish in the humdrum aquarium of Blaine City. Eugene Levy is Allan Pearl, the dentist, who claims a theatrical legacy inherited from his grandfather's Yiddish days. Catherine O'Hara and Fred Willard are Sara and Ron Albertson, actor wannabes and local travel agents who've never ventured beyond Blaine (except for Ron, who once had a penis-reduction operation in Jefferson City). Parker Posey is Libby the Dairy Queen Girl, who's willing to quit ice cream confections like Blizzards and Derbys for the footlights. Bob Balaban is Lloyd the music teacher, terminally timid offstage but a veritable dynamo at the podium. And Lewis Arquette is Clifford, the grizzled town father who's lured out of his trailer and out of retirement. At rehearsals they sing Stephen Foster medleys and whack through "Midnight at the Oasis." My favorite moment was Posey's bump-and-grind rendition of "Teacher's Pet."

The pageant both illumines and alters the lives of Blaine's residents. The dentist and the travel planners leave their jobs and head for showbiz, the former to entertain at a nursing home in Miami, the latter to work as extras in Hollywood. The Dairy Queen Girl leaves town, too, but that's because her father is now out of prison ("on good behavior, since he didn't kill anybody"), and they take to the road together while she dreams of ways to make fat-free Blizzards. As for Corky, well, he returns to New York where he opens up a theatre memorabilia shop, featuring such hot items as *Remains of the Day* lunch boxes and *My Dinner with Andre* action figures.

Waiting for Guffman is a Judy Garland/Mickey Rooney version of *This Is Spinal Tap*, a cross between Busby Berkeley and Samuel Beckett. Shot in pseudo-cinema-verité style, the camera wobbles around the characters, who speak directly into the camera, shamelessly proclaiming who and what they are. Because the cast and credits are reserved for the end of the film, you almost feel like you are viewing a real documentary about small-town life. As for the big musical production itself, you see it in its entirety, replete with pioneers, footstools, and flying saucers.

Beneath the amiable antics of the pageant are hints of pathos. Revelations of Corky's dismal private and professional life counterpoint the comedy. There are references to a non-existent "wife," which presumably was the necessary "straight" cover for his residence as

a gay man in Blaine. And his theatrical past consisted of nothing more than years of off-off-off-off-Broadway theatre in New York. Most moving of all is the town councilman's not-so-subtly concealed infatuation with Corky. At the pageant he gazes with rapt, but unspoken love at Corky's performance. In his hungry stare is the real drama, the play behind the play, the hollow dark that lurks behind the brightly painted sets. That is perhaps the real meaning of Blaine City and the real message behind this film: You can *dream* of California, but you've got to *live* in Blaine.

2. *KING OF MASKS* (1999), CHINA, directed by Wu Tianming

One of the most unusual theatrical films of recent years is Wu Tianming's *King of Masks* (1999). There are two kinds of Chinese theatre here, the virtually lost art of "face changing" and folk drama. The central character, Old Wang (Zhu Xu), is a master at "face changing," a peculiar transformative act in which he dons and discards a variety of face masks with lightning rapidity. He's a street performer, living by his wits and his skills in Sechuan Province in 1930 China. Life is harsh, as the land is wracked by devastating floods and torn by the political instability of the years between the demise of the ruling Manchu dynasty in China in 1912 and the birth of the People's Republic in 1949. Wang's own distresses include the lack of an apprentice to carry on his tradition and his secrets. So when he purchases for $5 a little boy at a black market, things look better. He christens the boy "Doggie" (Zhou Ren-ying) and teaches him to do handstands and hawk for money during his routines. But when he discovers the child is really a little girl, his dream fades. He had wanted a male heir; moreover, women, especially little girls, are forbidden to perform on the stage. Wang rejects her, but the child entreats him to stay. He relents, but no longer will he permit her to call him "grandfather," but simply "boss." Well meaning and devoted as the girl is, she brings more disasters into his life: One night she brings one of his masks too close to the lantern flame, and Wang's boat erupts in flame. Another time, she befriends a little boy who has been kidnapped from a wealthy family, escapes with him to safety, and brings him to the delighted Wang. But the police are looking for the boy, and they arrest Wang on trumped charges. They toss Wang into jail, torture a confession out of him, and consign him to execution in a week. In desperation, Doggie goes to Wang's only friend, a cross-dressing theatre actor named Master Liang (Zhao Zhigang). But even Liang's popularity and influence with the local police fail to win Wang a pardon. So, finally, Doggie hatches a plot: Earlier, she had seen Liang perform in a

Chinese play where a princess dangles from a rope and threatens to cut the rope and fall to her death unless her father is released by his captors. She cuts the rope and falls into the stage pit, out of sight. Doggie was delighted at that, especially when old Wang told her that in this way the princess would achieve a spiritual status. So now here's Doggie doing the same thing, interrupting Liang's play by dangling from a rope tied to the roof, threatening to cut the rope unless the attending police chief releases Wang. And darned if Doggie doesn't cut the rope and take the plunge. She is barely saved by the lunging Master Liang, who cushions her fall. It is Liang who, while carrying the unconscious form of little Doggie, then talks the police chief into releasing Wang. In the epilogue, Wang is told by Liang what had happened. He finds Doggie on the houseboat and embraces her. She calls him "grandfather" again. And they sail off together.

The business about the "dangling woman" in the Chinese play is brilliantly injected into the movie's "real-life" story. It's an agreeable shock when life imitates art as Doggie suddenly drops into view, hanging upside down, declaiming her threats to the police chief. It's just the way a child would have solved the problem, given the circumstances (and given her belief that the action in the play had resulted in the princess's spiritual redemption). Liang knows as an actor that he's at the lowest rung of the social ladder, but, as he tells the police chief, "The world is a cold place but we artists can bring warmth to it."

Master Liang and Wang are alike under the skin—not only are they both men, but they are also both traveling players. Indeed, it is Liang who shows the most obeisance toward Wang. This Liang is a fascinating, charismatic character (played by an actor with the Shaoxing Opera in Shanghai), a man dressed as a woman, since women could not appear on a stage. Like Wang, he has his own mask, and he slips in and out of it effortlessly.

The mystery behind Wang's miraculous face-changing abilities is never really explained. At one point he's exhorted by several soldiers to reveal his secret, but he evades them, mumbling something about eye-hand coordination. Some secrets just resist explanation.

3. *THE LAST METRO* (1980), FRANCE, directed by
   François Truffaut.

Although Truffaut was not generally as disposed to pay tribute to the theatre as he was to the medium of film—see especially *La Nuit Americaine* ("Day for Night," 1973)—his *The Last Metro* did realize a long-held dream to recall his boyhood days during the German Occupation of France in the early 1940s and pay tribute to the role theatres played in bolstering the morale of the French citizens. If the tensions of the Occupation were the subtext of *Children of Paradise*, they are foregrounded here. "My intention was to do for the theater what I had done for the cinema in *Day for Night*," Truffaut recalled, "the chronicle of a troupe at work, within a framework respecting the unities of place, time, and action." Realizing that during the war 15 or more theatres in Paris were run by women, either actresses or former actresses, he determined to place at the center of the story the character of actress-turned-theatre-manager, Catherine Steiner (Catherine Deneuve). Her husband, a Jew trying to escape the pressures of the German censors, was based on playwright Louis Jouvet, who during the Occupation had escaped and fled to South America. And the third of the central characters, the young actor Bernard Granger (Gerard Depardieu), torn between his loyalties to the theatre and to the French Resistance, was based on two people, Louis Jourdan and Jean-Pierre Aumont.

The setting is Paris in 1942. The Nazi Occupation is a year-and-a-half old. Lucas Steiner (Heinz Bennent), a German-Jewish stage director and manager of the prestigious Montmartre Theatre, has fled to safety in South America. Now in charge is his wife, the eminent film actress Marion (Catherine Deneuve). Once happy to let her husband assume the day-to-day duties of the theatre, now she must muster the energy and resourcefulness to keep the operation going. For example, in order to pass the censors and retain her license, she must agree not to hire Jews and to pander to the proper government officials and critics. Currently in pre-production is a new play, *La Disparue* ("The Woman Who Disappeared"), a mildly Ibsenesque chamber drama. A newcomer to the company is actor Bernard Granger (Gerard Depardieu). He is a rather mysterious fellow who has achieved some prior fame in the Theatre Grand-Guignol in such lurid melodramas as *The Skeleton in the Closet*. Although his brusque, philandering ways alienate him from Marion, he is a competent actor, and she accepts him as her new costar.

Behind the pasteboard façade of the Theatre Montmartre reside many secrets. Some are trivial, like the furtive lesbian affair between the costumier, Arlette (Andrea Ferreol), and the ingénue actress, and Marion's own brief tryst with a stranger. And some are more profound: Bernard, for example, is in touch with the Resistance, and he supplies explosives for their missions. Marion is secretly in love with Bernard. And

Lucas Steiner, far from being in exile, is actually hidden in the theatre's cellar where, unbeknownst to anyone but his wife, he monitors the stage rehearsals and relays via Marion his instructions to the play's unsuspecting director. His makeshift apartment is itself like a stage set, appointed with props and furnishings from past productions. At the premiere of *The Woman Who Disappeared* a critic, Daxiat (Jean-Louis Richard), a Nazi sympathizer who denounces Jews in his radio broadcasts and in his newspaper column, condemns the performance as "too effeminate" and "too Jewish." In retaliation, the volatile Bernard roughs him up. Not long afterward, German officials arrive to search the theatre. Lucas quickly dismantles his apartment—"striking the set," as it were—and successfully evades discovery. Bernard, in the meantime, determines to quit the company and join the Resistance. Before he leaves, Marion confesses her love for him. He is astonished. She admits that her position as company manager and leading actress—not to mention her marriage to Lucas—has forced her to disguise her feelings. The two cling together in a passionate embrace. Two years pass. After the Normandy invasion, the political situation begins to change. The Vichy government is in disarray and the British and Americans arrive. Lucas Steiner emerges from the theatre cellar at last, after 813 days of virtual incarceration. What never changes, however, is the need that French theatres satisfy for the entertainment-starved French citizens.

In what the voice-over narrator calls the story's "epilogue," we have a final scene in which Marion finds her lover, Bernard, in a hospital bed. She sits next to him and says, "He's dead now" (presumably a reference to her husband). She admits that she has never stopped loving him, and that she realizes her work in the theatre should never have come between them. He rudely dismisses her protestations and declares that "there was never anything real between us." He can scarcely remember her name now. At that moment, a curtain closes over them. Applause. We are back in the Montmartre Theatre. What we have been watching is a performance by Marion and Bernard of a new play. The director, Lucas Steiner, is called from his box. He joins them on stage and the three clasp hands as they bow. Marion stands between them, radiant, mysterious, looking from one to the other.

On one level *The Last Metro* is a work of historical and autobiographical significance. It depicts in fascinating detail the operation of French theatres during the Occupation as sanctuaries for the citizenry and as arenas for the politics of compromise and resistance (the film takes its title from the fact that theatres had to close before the last subway run at night). Musi-

cians' instrument cases are used to smuggle black-market foods, automobile headlights operate on electrical current supplied by stagehands riding bicycles, German recruiters hang around the stage exits looking for conscripts, and so on. And for Truffaut it recalls a period in which his own personality was shaped. For him, as for so many others, the Occupation was a kind of theatrical event in the broadest sense, fraught with all the ingredients of farce and melodrama. "Everything was paradoxical," he recalled. "We were told to be honest while surrounded by examples of the dishonesty needed to survive. For example, without food tickets, we would have starved. We had false tickets—badly made, obviously—so children were sent to the grocers: 'They'll close their eyes and wouldn't dare send back kids,' we said. I'm sure that my profound wariness of all certitudes stems from this period."

Thus, *The Last Metro*—like Ernst Lubitsch's *To Be or Not to Be*, another film about the exploits of a theatre troupe against the backdrop of World War II—is also a meditation on the role-playing, improvisation, and imagination that enable the human spirit to survive life off and *onstage*. If, at the same time, the film's simple décor and sets seem oddly stylized, and characters and incidents frequently verge on the blatantly theatric—the director a prisoner in his own theatre cellar; the Grand Guignol actor who assists Resistance operations; the absurd dialogue of the play-within-a-play, *The Woman Who Disappeared*; the shameless and bigoted opportunism of the critic, Daxtiat (he does everything but twirl a moustache); the hurried revelations of love and the last desperate clinch between Marion and Bernard—this is most assuredly for a purpose.

All of this snaps into focus in the last, stunningly brilliant scene. Marion visits Bernard in the hospital. She is kept tightly framed as the camera follows her to Bernard's bed. Through the window behind him we see women moving about on their apartment balconies. But after he says, "There was nothing real between us," there is a cut to a medium shot of her seated beside him—and suddenly we realize that the view through the window has now transformed into a scene painting. Marion and Bernard's faces seem to have mysteriously acquired makeup. Marion's husband, Lucas, not dead at all, but very much alive, arrives on stage. The burst of applause completes our epiphany. This is transpiring on a *stage* set and this is merely the conclusion of a theatrical event. What is the applause for? Is it for the play itself, or, as commentator Annette Insdorf suggests, is it for Marion, who managed to save both the Theatre Montmartre and her husband, a Jew? Now, it is true that we can take all this literally, i.e., the war is ending and Bernard has reunited with Marion and Lucas to perform a new play. As Insdorf says, "[When] our three protagonists take a final bow together, the triangle . . . is redeemed: no longer must the woman choose between husband and lover, for each has recognized the existence of the other." But I prefer to believe otherwise: *How much of what has come before is actually a part of this play?* The illusion of reality and the reality of illusion have merged. As in the final moments of Olivier's *Henry V,* we have embarked on a long journey fraught with romance and drama, only to find at the end that we have never left the stage at all. Brief and understated, this moment is nonetheless one of the most magical in all of Truffaut's work.

4. *BEAUMARCHAIS THE SCOUNDREL* (1996), FRANCE, directed by Edouard Molinaro

Beaumarchais the Scoundrel (1996) is an important entry in the biopic category of theatrical films. Included also are *The Royal Box* (1930), wherein Alexander Moissi portrays the celebrated actor Edmund Kean; *Prince of Players* (1955), with Richard Burton as Edwin Booth in scenes with Romeo, Hamlet, and Richard III; and *Wilde* (1997), with Stephen Fray as the immortal Oscar.

When his *The Marriage of Figaro* was first performed in 1784, Beaumarchais appended the subtitle, "A Mad Day." The play's conflation into 24 hours of the multifarious intrigues, deceptions, and loves of Figaro, Count Almaviva, and Cherubino was no less a "mad" enterprise than the attempts by filmmaker Edouard Molinaro to encompass within two hours of screen time a decade in the life of Beaumarchais himself.

The action begins in 1773—a time of "high ideas and low subjects," as an opening title declares. Louis XVI is waiting in the wings to succeed his grandfather. Art and politics are in ferment. France is "dangerously behind the times." It is up to figures like Voltaire and Pierre Caron de Beaumarchais "to set the clocks right."

Well, Beaumarchais was indeed the son of a clockmaker. But his timing was nothing less than erratic. As the ensuing first 15 minutes of the film admirably demonstrate, this gentle playwright, philanderer, intriguer, revolutionary, and swordsman led a hectic and complicated life. In a flurry of brief episodes he's instructing the actors rehearsing his *Barber of Seville* in the art of naturalistic performance; dashing off a pamphlet to his enemy, Goezman; fighting a duel with a man he's cuckolded, the duke de Chaulnes; and cooling his heels in jail on charges of sedition. And so it goes. Beaumarchais accepts it all with perfect equanimity. "I

write better in prison," he says, settling down in his cell to write a new draft of *Barber.*

And that's only the beginning! As Beaumarchais connives, flatters, and protests his way through the theatres and courts of Louis XV and XVI, running through litigious intrigues as frequently as he went through wives (and spending almost as much time in jail as out), he seizes opportunities for adventure as a French spy in London and a gunrunner to the American revolutionaries.

Meanwhile, his plays are helping foment a revolution—in drama. Beaumarchais regarded his *Barber* as too timid a critique of the monarchy and that perhaps Voltaire was right when he quipped, "Beaumarchais will never be another Molière because he values his life too much." Reluctantly, Beaumarchais determines to bring back the character of the wily servant, Figaro, in a tougher play, *The Marriage of Figaro.* It is an astringent political satire that creates considerable sensation and notoriety. Figaro's rebellion against his master may be compared, according to the filmmakers—albeit rather simplistically—to Beaumarchais' own challenge to traditional stagecraft as well as to the institution of the aristocracy. Ironically, in the midst of thunderous audience applause at the play's premiere, Beaumarchais is sent back to prison. But when the king relents and offers his release, Beaumarchais bargains that he'll leave his cell only if the king and his courtiers attend his play's next performance.

As improbable, even bewildering as most of it may seem to the uninitiated viewer (who may be tempted to dismiss it as pure Hollywood-style fabrication), the movie does a remarkable job in touching the requisite historical bases. Granted, at best, this densely packed film can only suggest the complexity of the noisy polemics and endless intrigues, political and artistic, that always surrounded Beaumarchais. Yet several extended scenes nicely convey Beaumarchais' windy legal battles with his bête noire, Goezman; the complex motivations behind his American endeavors (perhaps stimulated as much by a passion for political intrigue and business opportunities as a genuine regard for the American cause); and his ambivalent attitudes toward the aristocracy (wittily conveyed in a number of staged excerpts from *Barber* and *Figaro*).

The crazy-quilt, episodic narrative structure betrays the scattered nature of its source materials, fragments of an unpublished play by Sacha Guitry; but it is, nonetheless, a beautifully mounted and compelling historical drama with an outstanding French cast. Fabrice Luchini's Beaumarchais, particularly, is a wryly genial and charming rascal whose rather bland round face is punctuated with sharply peaked brows and dancing eyes.

Even if Beaumarchais was probably not quite the impassioned revolutionary advocating the overthrow of the monarchy and its institutions that the film ultimately suggests—the concluding title declaims, "The great men of this world applauded Figaro, without realizing they were also applauding the birth of the French Revolution"—there was nonetheless enough historical smoke in the factual record to justify and fuel this cinematic fire. (Wisely, the film concludes at this point, omitting the sad ironies of Beaumarchais' later years, the destruction of his fine home, a narrow brush with the guillotine, and years in exile as an emigré.)

In the final analysis, Beaumarchais is the perfect subject for a vivid, flamboyant pageant—a veritable succession of *tableaux vivants*—such as this; a movie worthy to stand alongside other outstanding and recent French literary and historical films, like Patrice Leconte's comedy of manners and politics in the court of Louis XVI, *Ridicule* (1996); Yves Angelo's adaptation of Balzac's Napoleonic drama, *Colonel Chabert* (1994); and Patrice Chereau's re-creation of the Catholic and Protestant disputes in late 17th-century France, *Queen Margot* (1994). Beaumarchais himself paved the way for *Beaumarchais the Scoundrel*'s dramatic licenses. He knew how to embellish the dry legalities of his numerous *Memoires* with irony and wit, his spy missions with dubious accounts of action and swordplay, his comic plays with song and dance. As one character in the film observes of him, "He's fond of intrigues, as befits a good playwright." If he is caricatured here a bit, it is only just, for he himself was a master of caricature. "When my subject seizes me," he wrote regarding his theatrical endeavors, "I call out all my characters and place them in a situation. . . . What they will say, I know not at all; it's what they will do that concerns me. Then, when they are fully come to life, I write under their rapid dictation."

One suspects that had he the opportunity, Beaumarchais might have written just such a scenario as we have in this film.

REVISITING A CLASSIC
No theatrical film can rival Marcel Carné's classic *The Children of Paradise* (1944) in its variety of theatrical evocations, complex layerings of reality and illusion, and in its enduring charm. "*Les Enfants du Paradis* is a tribute to the theatre," said director Carné in 1944, shortly after completing the film. It generously alludes to many forms of theatrical event, including pantomime, farce, and melodrama; and its central theme, the frustrations and jealousies of love, derives particularly from Shakespeare's *Othello*.

In the words of commentator Edward Baron Turk, Jacques Prevert's screenplay "glorifies the capacity of theatrical fictions to confer coherence upon real-life experience." That applies as much to the film's directly contemporaneous context (it was made during the German Occupation) as it does to the fictions depicted on screen. The setting is Paris, beginning in the year 1827, during Carnival time. The action is framed by the rise and fall of a theatre curtain and begins on the "Boulevard of Crime" (the Boulevard du Temple), Paris' theatre district, which teems with acrobats, clowns, barkers, peepshows, and animal acts. Many of the patrons who come here are from society's lower ranks. They occupy *le paradis*, "the gods," slang for the highest and least expensive gallery seats, where they vent their frustrations and shout their enthusiasms to the actors (the "children of the gods"), disporting themselves on the stage. It is clear that these crowds are a metaphor not just for the oppressed compatriots of the French Occupation (during which time the film was made) but for today's audiences who come to movie theatres seeking relief from worldly burdens. "They're poor people, but I am like them," declares an actor. "I love them, I know them well. Their lives are small, but they have big dreams. And I don't only want to make them laugh, I want to move them, to frighten them, to make them cry."

Two of the principal characters of the story are based on real-life figures—the elegant mime Jean-Gaspard Deburau (played by Jean-Louis Barrault under the altered name of Baptiste Deburau) and the flamboyant Shakespearean performer Frederick Lemaitre (Pierre Brasseur). Each has his own theatre—Baptiste at Les Funambules and Lemaitre at the Grand Theatre. The comedy and farce of the commedia dell'arte (Pierrot, Columbine, Harlequin, and Pantalone) and the tragedy and melodrama of *Othello* (Othello, Desdemona, Iago, and Brabantio), respectively, reflect and govern the actions of these men. What unites them—and links them with the more peripheral characters of the story, the villainous Lacenaire (Marcel Herrand) and the slimy aristocrat Edouard de Montray (Louis Salou)—is their fascination and involvement with the enigmatic beauty, Garance (Arletty). "Jealousy belongs to everyone," says Lemaitre. "Even if women belong to no one!"

Baptiste and Lemaitre must turn to their art to survive. For both the theatre offers not only solace but also a kind of creative whetstone. As Lemaitre observes, "When I act, I am desperately in love, desperately, do you understand? But when the curtain falls, the audience goes away, and takes 'my love' with it. You see, I make the audience a present of my love. The audience is very happy, and so am I. And I become wise and free and calm and sensible, again, like Baptiste!"

Thus, Lemaitre transmutes his murderous jealousy into the role of Othello. Upon learning that Garance is in love with Baptiste, Lemaitre tells her that she is like a "Desdemona." He declares, "Thanks to you . . . I shall be able to play Othello! I have been trying to find the character, but I didn't feel him. He was a stranger. There it is, now he's a friend, he's a brother. I know him . . . I have him in my grasp." Later, while performing *Othello* at the Grand Theatre, we witness a portion of the scene wherein Othello plots with Iago against Desdemona: "Get me some poison, Iago—this night. I'll not expostulate with her, lest her body and beauty unprovide my mind again. . . ." Iago advises him to strangle her instead. Lemaitre/Othello's eyes stray toward one of the boxes, where Garance/Desdemona is seated with her lover, the Count Edouard de Montray. Cut to the count, who is beginning to suspect that Garance has had an affair with Lemaitre. He audibly complains at this point of the play's "debased violence." Onstage, meanwhile, Lemaitre/Othello continues: ". . . for she shall not live. No, my heart is turned to stone: I strike it, and it hurts my hand." Minutes later, while watching the bedroom scene as Lemaitre/Othello prepares to strangle Desdemona, de Montray, by now beside himself, threatens to murder Lemaitre. Cut to the stage, where Lemaitre/Othello is clearly addressing his lines not to his Desdemona on stage, but to his Desdemona in the box beside the count:

> Therefore confess thee freely of thy sin;
> For to deny each article with oath
> Cannot remove nor choke the strong conception
> That I do groan withal.
> Thou art to die.

The theatrics don't end with the curtain, however. Minutes after the performance, the drama continues backstage in the Green Room, when the count angrily confronts Lemaitre. He insults Lemaitre, and in the process tries to insult the whole institution of Shakespearean theatre:

COUNT: Monsieur, you played the part of this simpleminded and bloodthirsty brute as if you found it perfectly natural.

FREDERICK: You are too kind, Monsieur, but I hope that above all I played it as Shakespeare wrote it—as if it was the most natural thing in the world!

COUNT: A very peculiar character, this "Monsieur Shakespeare!"

I have been given to understand that he served his literary apprenticeship . . . chopping meat on a butcher's slab.

FREDERICK: And why not?

COUNT: Which would explain the bestial and savage character of his plays, and why, when he was alive, he was a great favorite among such people as dockers, carters . . .

FREDERICK: And kings!

Before this protracted disquisition can be revealed for what it really is, a deadly exchange between these two rivals for the affections of Garance, it is interrupted by the arrival of Lacenaire, who clearly has something up his sleeve, as it were. In a nifty piece of theatrics of his own, he approaches his enemy, the count, and then wounds him more sorely than if he thrust a sword into his back. "I'm not a character out of a bedroom farce," he tells de Montray, at which point he draws aside a curtain, revealing Garance and Baptiste in a passionate embrace. What the astonished onlookers see is a perfect stage picture, nicely framed by the curtain, calculated to humiliate the count and drive him into a duel with his rival, Lemaitre. Lacenaire has wrought as beautiful a piece of tragically dangerous theatrics as if he had just staged *Othello* himself. Putting it another way, he has played Iago to de Montray's Othello. Whereas Lemaitre was able to purge himself of his deadly jealousies by enacting them on stage, de Montray will inevitably fall victim to them. Before he can duel with Lemaitre, he will be slain by Lacenaire's knife thrust the next morning.

As for the neurotic, lovelorn Baptiste, he, like Lemaitre, also finds in his art both a reflection and an expression of his own frustrations. As his pantomimes become darker and more violent, he observes that there is not really such a great difference between pantomime and tragedy. After all, he says, *Othello* would "make a nice pantomime." Bitterly, he continues: "A man who kills his love, and dies of it. Poor man. A sad and ridiculous story, like so many others. . . ." His great performance, not unlike Lemaitre's aforementioned role as Othello, is a pantomime called "The Rag and Bone Man." It opens with Baptiste, clad in his silken white costume, face masked with makeup, arriving at a sumptuous evening party. His attempts to enter are rejected. Alone, under a street lamp, he encounters a rag merchant. Realizing he must attire himself in suitable evening dress, he tries to purchase the merchant's clothes. When he is unable to come up with the money, Baptiste draws a sword and runs the man through. The audience, startled but delighted at the unexpectedly morbid tone of the performance, applauds wildly.

In the course of these events we realize that the other characters, the non-actors like Garance, Lacenaire, and the count, have likewise donned masks of their own. As Garance has dallied with Lemaitre, Baptiste, and the count, she has donned the twin masks of comedy and tragedy, assuming the "roles" of Columbine and Desdemona. The count has found himself the object of a very deadly piece of theatrics (he ultimately dies at Lacenaire's hands), and Lacenaire himself has assumed the role of *metteur en scène*, or master stage director.

The film is not free of moments of delicious theatrical parody. One of the set pieces is when Lemaitre chafes at having to act in a blood-and-thunder melodrama, *L'Auberge des Adrets*. ("The Brigand's End"). During the rehearsal, which is attended by the play's authors, Lemaitre, as the hero, Robert Macaire, ridicules the absurdities of the play. Example: When the play's heroine, Marie, asks Macaire if it is possible that he has committed many crimes, Lemaitre, as Macaire, replies: "What do you expect, Marie; everyone has their little weaknesses!" The outraged authors protest that the line was not in the text. Lemaitre replies: "Since there's absolutely nothing in your play, it's got to be padded out a little." In retaliation, the authors remind Lemaitre that this is the sort of thing one would expect from "someone who started his career at the Funambules . . . walking on his hands." Lemaitre smiles and retorts, "And why not on my hands? You've certainly managed to write a play with your feet!" Later, on opening night, Lemaitre completes the devastation of the play he had begun in rehearsal. In perhaps the most hilarious moment in the film, Lemaitre quits the stage and mounts to a stage box. Now, as an audience member, he vigorously applauds the play and shouts his "Bravos." Now declaring himself to be not Robert Macaire but "Frederic Lemaitre," he continues to improvise to the consternation of his fellow cast members and the delight of the audience. At last, feigning death, he adlibs that his were not the real crimes of the story; indeed, "the real criminals, the ones who plotted everything . . . are the AUTHORS!" And he rises magnificently to point to the playwrights seated below him. Preposterous as all this is, moments later a rather similar melodrama transpires in Lemaitre's dressing room when the villainous Lacenaire arrives and demands blackmail money from Lemaitre. "Well, I'll be," smiles the actor; "It's exactly like the *Brigand's Inn*."

In the largest sense, *Children of Paradise* is about the enduring legacy of 19th-century French theatre. The casting of Jean-Louis Barrault and Pierre Brasseur as, respectively, Baptiste and Lemaitre, constituted a tribute to those two great traditions of the French theatre, the pantomime and the romantic drama, and their two greatest 19th-century exponents, Deburau and Lemaitre. At the time of the film's release, Barrault, newly elected *societaire* of the Comédie Française, had already initiated a general resurgence of interest in pantomime—for what Antonin Artaud called "the irresistible significance of gesture." His identification with Deburau was unquestioned. Pierre Brasseur was likewise a highly respected actor-playwright. In his excessive energies and self indulgences, he was ideally suited to convey the raw power and fierce individuality of the actor-rebel Lemaitre—who had once been dubbed by Hugo as "the French Kean." In evoking these traditions, says Turk, Barrault and Brasseur contributed to the film's theme that theatre is the proper arena in which to claim one's authentic being. Indeed, it has been demonstrated that theatrical activity, not political action, was France's chief bulwark against the Nazi oppression that gripped Paris during the German Occupation. In the words of Turk, France's theatres were "the 'safe houses' of those collective dreams that take the form of plays and movies [and which] provided a public site for relief from political oppression."

AT THE CURTAIN'S FALL

As commentator Francis Fergusson has noted, the subtlety of Hamlet's "mousetrap" play suggests that it is designed not only to "catch" the conscience of Claudius but also to provoke reaction from any other auditors—and that includes all of us in the audience. Part of that reaction, as critic Anthony Lane has suggested, is that movies like these "perplex a settled theatrical tradition" in altering the contexts in which theatrical events are perceived and measured. They "break a long line of grand performing masters in favor of something not just more sneaky but also, in an odd way, more democratic." And that, in its own way, is a method and consequence of the grandest kind of theatrical endeavor.

—*JOHN C. TIBBETTS*

WORKS CITED

Bertin, Celia, *Jean Renoir: A Life in Pictures* (Baltimore: Johns Hopkins University Press, 1991).

Branagh, Kenneth, *A Midwinter's Tale: The Shooting Script*, with an introduction (New York: Newmarket Press, 1995).

Brooke, Dinah, tr., *Children of Paradise: A Film by Marcel Carne* (New York: Simon and Schuster, 1968).

Cowie, Peter, *Ingmar Bergman: A Critical Biography* (New York: Charles Scribner's Sons, 1982).

Dale, R.C., *The Films of Rene Clair*, vol. I (Metuchen, N.J.: Scarecrow Press, 1986).

Denby, David, "Under the Lights," *The New Yorker*, January 3, 2000, 130–132.

Durgnat, Raymond, *Jean Renoir* (Berkeley: University of California Press, 1974).

Fergusson, Francis, *Shakespeare: The Pattern in His Carpet* (New York: Delacorte Press, 1970).

Fumento, Rocco, ed., *42nd Street* (Madison: University of Wisconsin Press, 1980).

Holden, Stephen, "A Midwinter's Tale," *New York Times*, February 9, 1996, C5:1.

Houseman, John, *Run-Through: A Memoir* (New York: Simon and Schuster, 1972).

Insdorf, Annette, *Francois Truffaut* (New York: Simon and Schuster, 1989).

Ivory, James, "Introduction" to *Shakespeare Wallah* (New York: Grove Press, 1973)

Kael, Pauline, *For Keeps: 30 Years at the Movies* (New York: Dutton, 1994).

Kauffmann, Stanley, "Listening Again," *The New Republic* (January 10, 2000): 26–27.

Kazan, Elia, *A Life* (New York: Alfred A. Knopf, 1988).

Lane, Anthony, "Stagestruck," *The New Yorker*, December 13, 1999, 111–113.

———, "Tights! Camera! Action!" *The New Yorker*, November 25, 1996.

O'Brien, Geoffrey, "Stompin' at the Savoy," *The New York Review of Books*, February 24, 2000, 16, 18–19.

Pearson, Hesketh, *Gilbert: His Life and Strife* (New York: Harper, 1957).

Peary, Danny, *Cult Movies* (New York: Delta Books, 1981).

———, *Cult Movies 2* (New York: Dell, 1983).

Robbins, Tim, *Cradle Will Rock: The Movie and the Moment* (New York: Newmarket Press, 2000).

Rothwell, Kenneth S., *A History of Shakespeare on Screen* (Cambridge, Eng.: Cambridge University Press, 1999), 222.

Silver, Allan, "Maedchen in Uniform," in Arthur Lennig, *Classics of the Film* (Madison: Wisconsin Society Press, 1965), 126–131.

Skal, David J. and Elias Savada, *Dark Carnival: The Secret World of Tod Browning* (New York: Anchor Books, 1995).

Steene, Birgitta, *Ingmar Bergman* (New York: Twayne Publishers, 1968).

Storace, Patricia, "The Poet of Karma," *The New York Review*, October 17, 1999, 26.

Truffaut, François, *Truffaut by Truffaut* (New York: Harry N. Abrams, 1987).

Turk, Edward Baron, *Child of Paradise: Marcel Carné and the Golden Age of French Cinema* (Cambridge: Harvard University Press, 1989).

Willson, Robert F., Jr., *Shakespeare in Hollywood, 1929–1956* (Madison N.J.: Fairleigh Dickinson University Press, 1999).

Wilmington, Michael, "Cradle Will Rock," *Film Comment*, 35:6 (November–December 1999), 79.

Contributors

C.D.—Carol Dole is chair of the English department at Ursinus College, Pennsylvania. She specializes in Jane Austen studies and is a contributing editor of *Literature/Film Quarterly*.

C.M.—Chris Meissner has completed his Ph.D. in film studies at the University of Kansas and is currently researching a book on the history of the multi-cinema theatres.

C.M.B.—Charles M. Berg is a professor of theatre and film at the University of Kansas and author of many articles and several books on music and film. He is also a jazz musician and critic.

D.H.—Dottie Hamilton is a professor of film studies at Avila College in Kansas City, Missouri. She is completing a book on the Ratings Administration.

D.H.B.—D. Heyward Brock is senior associate dean of arts and sciences at the University of Delaware and the author of *A Ben Jonson Companion* (1983) and *Ben Jonson: A Quadricentennial* (1974).

D.S.—David Sanjek is the archive director for Broadcast Music, Inc., in New York. He is the coauthor, with his father, the late Russell Sanjek, of *American Popular Music in the 20th Century* (1991).

D.S.G.—Douglas Scott Glasser is the artistic director of the Madison Repertory Theatre in Wisconsin.

F.T.—Frank Thompson is a redoubtable free-lance writer in Hollywood, whose numerous credits include scripts for the American Movie Classics channel and books *Alamo Movies* (1992), *Lost Movies* (1996), and *Lincoln Movies* (1999).

G.B.—Greg Black is communications professor at the University of Missouri–Kansas City and author of several books on film censorship, including *Hollywood Censored* (1995).

G.D.P.—Gene D. Phillips, S.J., is professor of English and film at Loyola University, Chicago, and author of many articles and books on literature and film, including *Fiction, Film, and Faulkner*. He has just completed a book of interviews about Stanley Kubrick for the University of Mississippi Press.

H.H.D.—Hugh H. Davis teaches English at Chowan College in North Carolina and has contributed to *Literature/Film Quarterly*.

H.O.—Heather Owings has just completed a graduate degree in English at Salisbury State University, Maryland, and received her early training at Kent State University.

J.A.—John Ahearn is completing his Ph.D. in film studies at the University of Kansas. His primary research interest is the American independent film movement.

J.C.T.—John C. Tibbetts is an associate professor of theatre and film at the University of Kansas. His books include *The American Theatrical Film* (1985), *Dvorak in America* (1993), and (with co-editor James M. Welsh) *The Encyclopedia of Novels into Film* (1997) and *The Cinema of Tony Richardson* (1999).

J.M.W.—James M. Welsh is editor-in-chief of *Literature/Film Quarterly* and the founding president of the Literature/Film Association. His books include *Abel Gance* (1978), *The Encyclopedia of Novels into Film* (co-edited with John C. Tibbetts, 1997), and *The Cinema of Tony Richardson: Essays and Interviews* (co-edited with John C. Tibbetts, 1999).

J.W.—Jack Wright is a professor of theatre in the Department of Theatre and Film at the University of Kansas.

J.N.Y.—James N. Yates is associate professor of English at Northwestern Oklahoma State University. He has published in *The Journal of Popular Culture* and is a contributor to the *Columbia Companion to Film and History* (forthcoming).

J.S.—John Staniunas is an associate professor of theatre and film at the University of Kansas and is preparing a book on acting and directing.

K.N.—Kendall Natvig teaches in the language arts department at Iowa Central Community College, Webster City, Iowa.

K.P.—Karen Prager is an actress with extensive experience in New York stage shows.

L.C.C. and S.C.C.—Linda Costanzo Cahir is assistant professor of English at Centenary College, New Jersey, and author of *Solitude and Society in the Works of Herman Melville and Edith Wharton* (1999). Stephen C. Cahir is a civil litigation attorney in New Jersey and a student of literature and film.

L.M.F.—Laurie Merrill Fink teaches at Southern Illinois University, Carbondale.

M.D.G.—Michael Gunther holds a master's degree from the University of Kansas and currently teaches at Georgia State University.

M.M-C.—Miguel Martinez-Cabeza teaches in the department of philosophy and letters at the University of Granada, Spain.

M.R.—Mandy Reese teaches at California State University, Bakersfield. She is currently writing *Between Directing and Acting: Strategies for Effective Performance* with cowriter John Staniunas.

M.V.L.—Maria Van Liew teaches in the Department of Foreign Languages at West Chester University, Pennsylvania.

N.A.—Nicole Ervin Amare is a Ph.D. candidate in rhetoric, composition, and English studies at the University of Alabama. She has published in the *Dictionary of Literary Biography* and *Business Communication Quarterly.*

N.I.—Nancy Ingle received her Ph.D. in film studies at the University of Kansas and is researching the work of playwright Robert Anderson

N.S.—Neil Sinyard teaches literature and film at the University of Hull, England. He is the author of *Filming Literature* and *The Films of Richard Lester.*

P.C.—Peter Christensen is an assistant professor in English at Cardinal Stritch University, Milwaukee.

R.C.—Russell Cousins is a senior lecturer in French studies at the University of Birmingham in England. He has published several essays on French cinema in the *Literature/Film Quarterly.*

R.E.—Rebecca Epstein is a doctoral candidate in the Department of Film and Television at UCLA.

R.F.V.—Ralph Voss is a professor of English at the University of Alabama and has written *A Life of William Inge: The Strains of Triumph* (1989).

R.F.W.—Robert F. Willson is professor of English at the University of Missouri–Kansas City. His books include *Shakespeare: Entering the Maze* (1995) and, most recently, *Shakespeare in Hollywood, 1929–1956* (2000).

R.P.—Renee Pigeon teaches in the Department of English at California State University, San Bernardino.

R.V.—Richard Vela is a professor of English and theatre and language at the University of North Carolina–Pembroke. He has researched extensively Shakespearean cinema and has published in *Postscript* and other journals.

R.W.W.—Ron Wilson has recently completed his Ph.D. in film studies at the University of Kansas. He is currently writing a book on the Interstate Theatre Circuit in Wichita Falls, Texas.

S.C.—Sandra Camargo is a Ph.D. candidate in English at the University of Missouri, Columbia.

S.C.B.—Sheri Chinen Biesen is an independent scholar who has studied at the University of Texas–Austin with Thomas Schatz.

S.L.Y.—Sarah Young teaches at Baker University and has a Ph.D. in English from the University of Kansas. She is both a scholar and a performer of musical theatre.

Sv.C.—Saviour Catania is a senior lecturer at the University of Malta.

T.J.F.—Timothy Fink teaches at Southern Illinois University, Carbondale. His research interests include opera and musical theatre.

T.L.E.—Thomas L. Erskine, professor of English and formerly academic dean at Salisbury State University in Maryland, is the founding editor of *Literature/Film Quarterly.* His most recent book is *Video Versions: Film Adaptations of Plays on Video* (2000).

T.N.T.—Timothy N. Taylor is a graduate student at the University of Alabama.

T.W.—Tony Williams is associate professor of cinema studies at Southern Illinois University at Carbondale and author of books, including *Hearts of Darkness: The Family in the American Horror Film* (1996).

W.W.D.—Wheeler Winston Dixon is professor of English and chairperson of the film studies program, University of Nebraska–Lincoln. Author of *The Exploding Eye: A Re-Visionary History of 1960s American Experimental Cinema* and *The Films of Jean-Luc Godard,* his most recent work is an anthology, *Film Genre 2000* (2000). He is general editor of the State University of New York Press' "Cultural Studies in Cinema/Video" series.

Drama on Film Bibliography

Adler, Thomas P. *American Drama, 1940–1960: A Critical History.* New York: Twayne, 1994.

———. *Robert Anderson.* Boston: Twayne, 1978.

Amacher, Richard. *Edward Albee.* Boston: Twayne, 1982.

Anderegg, Michael A. *David Lean.* Boston: Twayne, 1984.

Atkinson, Brooks. *Broadway,* rev. New York: Limelight Editions, 1985.

Atwell, Lee. *G.W. Pabst.* Boston: Twayne, 1977.

Bacon, Henry. *Continuity and Transformation: The Influence of Literature and Drama on Cinema as a Process of Cultural Continuity and Renewal.* Helsinki, Finland: Soumalainen Tiedeakatemia, 1994.

Baskin, Ellen, and Mandy Hicken. *Enser's Filmed Books and Plays, 1928–1991.* Aldershot, Hants.: Ashgate, 1993.

Bazin, Andre. *What Is Cinema?* tr. Hugh Gray. Berkeley: University of California Press, 1967.

———. *Orson Welles: A Critical View.* New York: Harper & Row, 1972.

Bentley, Eric. *Bernard Shaw.* New York: Limelight Editions, 1985.

———. *What Is Theatre? Incorporating the Dramatic Event and Other Reviews, 1944–1967.* New York: Atheneum, 1968.

Bergman, Ingmar. *The Magic Lantern: An Autobiography,* tr. Joan Tate. New York: Viking, 1988.

Bergman, Paul, and Michael Asimow. *Reel Justice: The Courtroom Goes to the Movies.* Kansas City, Mo.: Andrews and McMeel, 1996.

Bertin, Celia. *Jean Renoir: A Life in Pictures,* tr. Mireille Muellner and Leonard Muellner. Baltimore: Johns Hopkins University Press, 1986.

Billington, Michael. *The Life and Work of Harold Pinter.* London: Faber & Faber, 1996.

Birkin, Andrew. *J.M. Barrie and the Lost Boys.* New York: Clarkson Potter, 1979.

Boggs, Joseph M. *The Art of Watching Films,* 2nd ed. Palo Alto, Calif.: Mayfield, 1985.

Bordman, Gerald. *American Musical Theatre: A Chronicle.* New York: Oxford University Press, 1978.

Bowles, Stephen E. *Sidney Lumet: A Guide to References and Resources.* Boston: G.K. Hall, 1979.

Boyer, Jay. *Sidney Lumet.* New York: Twayne, 1993.

Brewery, Gay. *David Mamet and Film.* Jefferson, N.C.: McFarland, 1993.

Brewster, Ben, and Lea Jacobs. *Theatre to Cinema.* New York: Oxford University Press, 1997.

Brockett, Oscar G., and Robert R. Findlay. *Century of Innovation: A History of European and American Theatre and Drama Since 1870.* Englewood Cliffs, N.J.: Prentice-Hall, 1973.

Brown, John Russell. *A Short Guide to Modern British Drama.* London: Heinemann Educational Books, 1982.

Brownlow, Kevin. *David Lean.* New York: St. Martin's Press, 1996.

Brownlow, Kevin, and John Kobal. *Hollywood: The Pioneers.* New York: Knopf, 1979.

Capra, Frank. *The Name Above the Title.* New York: Macmillan, 1971.

Casper, Joseph Andrew. *Stanley Donen.* Metuchen, N.J.: Scarecrow, 1983

Castronovo, David. *Thornton Wilder.* New York: Frederick Ungar, 1986.

Caute, David. *Joseph Losey: A Revenge on Life.* London: Faber & Faber, 1994.

Charney, Maurice. *Joe Orton.* London: Macmillan, 1984.

Ciment, Michel. *Conversations with Losey.* London: Methuen, 1985.

Cohen, Hubert J. *Ingmar Berman: The Art of Confession.* New York: Twayne, 1993.

Corliss, Richard. *Talking Pictures: Screenwriters in the American Cinema.* Woodstock, N.Y.: Overlook Press, 1974.

Corrigan, Timothy. *Film and Literature: An Introduction and a Reader.* Upper Saddle River, N.J.: Prentice-Hall, 1999.

Costello, Donald P. *The Serpent's Eye: Shaw and the Cinema.* Notre Dame, Ind.: University of Notre Dame Press, 1965.

Cowie, Peter. *The Cinema of Orson Welles.* South Brunswick, N.J.: A.S. Barnes, 1973.

Crafton, Donald. *The Talkies: American Cinema's Transition to Sound, 1926–1931.* New York: Charles Scribner's Sons, 1997.

Crandell, George, ed. *The Critical Response to Tennessee Williams.* Westport, Conn.: Greenwood Press, 1996.

Cunningham, Frank R. *Sidney Lumet: Film and Literary Vision.* Lexington: University Press of Kentucky, 1991.

Curtis, James. *James Whale.* Metuchen, N.J.: Scarecrow Press, 1982.

Dale, R.C. *The Films of Rene Clair*, 2 vols. Metuchen, N.J.: Scarecrow Press, 1986.

Daniels, Robert L. *Laurence Olivier: Theater and Cinema*. San Diego, Calif.: A.S. Barnes, 1980.

Dean, Joan Fitzpatrick. *Tom Stoppard: Comedy as Moral Matrix*. Columbia: University of Missouri Press, 1981.

Delaney, Paul. *Tom Stoppard: The Moral Vision of the Major Plays*. New York: St. Martin's Press, 1990.

DeRose, David J. *Sam Shepard*. New York: Twayne, 1992.

Dick, Bernard F. *Billy Wilder*. Boston: Twayne, 1980.

———, ed. *Columbia Pictures: Portrait of a Studio*. Lexington: University Press of Kentucky, 1992.

———. *Hellman in Hollywood*. Rutherford, N.J.: Fairleigh Dickinson University Press, 1982.

Dowd, Nancy, and David Shepard. *King Vidor*. Metuchen, N.J.: Scarecrow Press, 1988.

Druxman, Michael B. *The Musical: From Broadway to Hollywood*. New York: A.S. Barnes, 1980.

Dukore, Bernard F., ed. *The Collected Screenplays of Bernard Shaw*. Athens: University of Georgia Press, 1980.

———, ed. *Saint Joan: A Screenplay by Bernard Shaw*. Seattle: University of Washington Press, 1968.

Durgnat, Raymond. *Jean Renoir*. Berkeley: University of California Press, 1974.

Durgnat, Raymond, and Scott Simmon. *King Vidor, American*. Berkeley: University of California Press, 1988.

Enser, A.G.S. *Filmed Books and Plays*. London: Deutsch, 1968.

Erskine, Thomas L., and James M. Welsh, eds. *Video Versions: Film Adaptations of Plays on Video*. Westport, Conn.: Greenwood Press, 2000.

Eyman, Scott. *Ernst Lubitsch: Laughter in Paradise*. New York: Simon and Schuster, 1993.

———. *The Speed of Sound: Hollywood and the Talkie Revolution, 1926–1930*. New York: Simon and Schuster, 1997.

Fordin, Hugh. *The World of Entertainment: The Freed Unit at MGM*. Garden City, N.Y.: Doubleday, 1975.

Forman, Milos, and Jan Novak. *Turnaround: A Memoir*. New York: Villard Books, 1994.

Ganzl, Kurt. *The Encyclopedia of Musical Theatre*. New York: Schirmer, 1994.

Garebian, Keith. *The Making of West Side Story*. Toronto: ECS, 1995.

Geduld, Harry M. *The Birth of the Talkies: From Edison to Jolson*. Bloomington: Indiana University Press, 1975.

Geist, Kenneth L. *Pictures Will Talk: The Life and Films of Joseph L. Mankiewicz*. New York: Charles Scribner's Sons, 1978.

Giannetti, Louis. *Understanding Movies*, 3rd ed. Englewood Cliffs, N.J.: Prentice-Hall, 1982.

Gifford, Denis. *Books and Plays in Films, 1896–1915*. Jefferson, N.C.: McFarland, 1991.

Ginter, Linda, ed. *Marsha Norman: A Casebook*. New York: Garland, 1996.

Goldstein, Malcolm. *George S. Kaufman: His Life, His Theater*. New York: Oxford University Press, 1979.

Goodwin, James. *Akira Kurosawa and Intertextual Cinema*. Baltimore: Johns Hopkins University Press, 1994.

Gottlieb, Sidney, ed. *Hitchcock on Hitchcock: Selected Writings and Interviews*. Los Angeles: University of California Press, 1997.

Green, Stanley. *Hollywood Musicals Year by Year*. New York: Hal Leonard, 1990.

Griffin, Alice. *Understanding Arthur Miller*. Columbia: University of South Carolina Press, 1996.

———. *Understanding Tennessee Williams*. Columbia: University of South Carolina Press, 1995.

Griffin, Alice, and Geraldine Thorsten. *Understanding Lillian Hellman*. Columbia: University of South Carolina Press, 1999.

Gunn, Drewey Wayne. *Tennessee Wiliams: A Bibliography*, 2nd ed. Metuchen, N.J.: Scarecrow Press, 1991.

Gussow, Mel. *Conversations with Pinter*. New York: Grove Press, 1994.

Hare, David. *Writing Left-Handed*. London: Faber and Faber, 1991.

Harmetz, Aljean. *Round Up the Usual Suspects*. New York: Hyperion, 1992.

Harrington, John. *Film and/as Literature*. Englewood Cliffs, N.J.: Prentice-Hall, 1977.

Harris, Thomas J. *Courtroom's Finest Hour in American Cinema*. Metuchen, N.J.: Scarecrow Press, 1987.

Hayman, Ronald. *British Theatre since 1955: A Reassessment*. New York: Oxford University Press, 1979.

———. *Harold Pinter*. New York: Frederick Ungar, 1973.

Hewison, Robert. *In Anger: British Culture in the Cold War, 1945–60*. New York: Oxford University Press, 1981.

Higham, Charles. *The Films of Orson Welles*. Berkeley: University of California Press, 1970.

Hinchliffe, Arnold P. *Harold Pinter*. Boston: Twayne, 1967.

Hirsch, Foster. *Joseph Losey*. Boston: Twayne, 1980.

Horton, Andrew. *The Films of George Roy Hill*. New York: Columbia University Press, 1984.

Houseman, John. *Front and Center*. New York: Simon and Schuster, 1979.

———. *Run Through: A Memoir*. New York: Simon and Schuster, 1972.

Hurt, James, ed. *Focus on Film and Theatre*. Englewood Cliffs, N.J.: Prentice-Hall, 1974.

Jenkins, Henry. *What Made Pistachio Nuts? Early Sound Comedy and the Vaudeville Aesthetic*. New York: Columbia University Press, 1992.

Johnson, Robert K. *Neil Simon*. Boston: Twayne, 1983.

Kagan, Norman. *The Cinema of Oliver Stone*. New York: Continuum, 1995.

Karp, Alan. *The Films of Robert Altman*. Metuchen, N.J.: Scarecrow Press, 1981.

Kazin, Elia. *A Life*. New York: Alfred A. Knopf, 1988.

Kennedy, Michael Patrick, and John Muir. *Musicals*. New York: HarperCollins, 1997.

Klein, Dennis A. *Peter Shaffer*. Boston: Twayne, 1979.

Kreuger, Miles. *Show Boat: The Story of a Classic American Musical*. New York: Oxford University Press, 1977.

Lally, Kevin. *Wilder Times: The Life of Billy Wilder*. New York: Henry Holt, 1996.

Lambert, Gavin. *On Cukor.* New York: Capricorn Books, 1972.

Lanza, Joseph. *Fragile Geometry: The Films, Philosophy, and Misadventures of Nicolas Roeg.* New York: PAJ Publications, 1989.

Leaming, Barbara. *Grigori Kozintsev.* Boston: Twayne, 1980.

———. *Orson Welles: A Biography.* New York: Viking, 1985.

Leonard, William Torbert. *Theatre: Stage to Screen to Television.* Metuchen, N.J.: Scarecrow Press, 1981.

Lindsay, Howard, and Russel Crouse. *Clarence Day's Life with Father Made into a Play.* New York: Knopf, 1949.

Lumet, Sidney. *Making Movies.* New York: Alfred A. Knopf, 1995.

MacAdams, William. *Ben Hecht: The Man Behind the Legend.* New York: Charles Scribner's Sons, 1990.

MacCann, Richard Dyer, ed. *Film: A Montage of Theories.* New York: E.P. Dutton, 1966.

MacKinnon, Kenneth. *Greek Tragedy into Film.* London: Croom Helm, 1986.

Madsen, Axel. *Billy Wilder.* Bloomington: Indiana University Press, 1969.

———. *William Wyler.* New York: Thomas Y. Crowell, 1973.

Maland, Charles J. *Frank Capra.* Boston: Twayne, 1980.

Mamet, David. *On Directing Film.* New York: Viking, 1991.

Manvell, Roger. *New Cinema in Britain.* London: Studio Vista, 1969.

———. *Theatre and Film: A Comprehensive Study of the Two Forms of Dramatic Art and of the Problems of Adaptation of Stage Plays into Films.* Rutherford, N.J.: Fairleigh Dickinson University Press, 1979.

Martine, James J., ed. *Critical Essays on Eugene O'Neill.* Boston: G.K. Hall, 1984.

Mast, Gerald. *Can't Help Singin'.* New York: Overlook Press, 1987.

McAuliffe, Jody, ed. *Plays, Movies, and Critics.* Durham, N.C.: Duke University Press, 1993.

McBride, Joseph. *Frank Capra: The Catastrophe of Success.* New York: Simon and Schuster, 1992.

———. *Orson Welles.* New York: Viking Cinema One, 1972.

McDougal, Stuart Y. *Made into Movies: From Literature to Film.* New York: Harcourt Brace Jovanovich, 1985.

McGerr, Celia. *Rene Clair.* Boston: Twayne, 1980.

McGilligan, Patrick. *George Cukor: A Double Life.* New York: St. Martins Griffin, 1991.

———. *Robert Altman: Jumping Off the Cliff.* New York: St. Martin's Press, 1989.

McGovern, Edythe. *Neil Simon: A Critical Study.* New York: Frederick Ungar, 1978.

Mellon, Joan. *Hellman and Hammett: The Legendary Passion of Lillian Hellman and Dashiell Hammett.* New York: HarperCollins, 1996.

Meryman, Richard. *Mank: The Wit, World, and Life of Herman Mankiewicz.* New York: William Morrow, 1978.

Michaels, Lloyd. *Elia Kazan: A Guide to References and Resources.* Boston: G.K. Hall, 1985.

Miller, Arthur. *Timebends.* New York: Grove Press, 1987.

Millichap, Joseph. *Lewis Milestone.* Boston: Twayne, 1981.

Milne, Tom. *Rouben Mamoulian.* London: Thomas Hudson, 1969.

Moffitt, David, ed. *Between Two Silences: Talking with Peter Broo.* Dallas: Southern Methodist University Press, 1999.

Monaco, James. *How to Read a Film.* New York: Oxford University Press, 1981.

Naremore, James. *The Magic World of Orson Welles.* New York: Oxford University Press, 1978.

Nichols, Nina Da Vinci, and Jana O'Keefe Bazzoni. *Pirandello and Film.* Lincoln: University of Nebraska Press, 1995.

Nicoll, Allardyce. *Film and Theatre.* New York: Arno Press, 1972.

Nolletti, Arthur, Jr. *The Films of Fred Zinnemann: Critical Perspectives.* Albany, N.Y.: SUNY Press, 1999.

O'Brien, Daniel. *Robert Altman: Hollywood Survivor.* New York: Continuum, 1995.

Orlandello, John. *O'Neill on Film.* Rutherford, N.J.: Fairleigh Dickinson University Press, 1982.

Osborne, John. *Almost a Gentleman.* London: Faber and Faber, 1991.

Parish, James. *Gays and Lesbians in Mainstream Cinema.* Jefferson, N.C.: McFarland, 1993.

Parker, John. *Polanski.* London: Victor Gollancz, 1993.

Phillips, Gene D. *The Films of Tennessee Williams.* East Brunswick, N.J.: Associated University Presses, 1980.

———. *George Cukor.* Boston: Twayne, 1982.

———. *John Schlesinger.* Boston: Twayne, 1981.

Plecki, Gerard. *Robert Altman.* Boston: Twayne, 1985.

Poague, Leland A. *Howard Hawks.* Boston: Twayne, 1982.

Polanski, Roman. *Roman by Polanski.* New York: William Morrow, 1984.

Pratley, Gerald. *The Cinema of John Huston.* South Brunswick, N.J.: A.S. Barnes, 1977.

———. *The Cinema of Otto Preminger.* New York: A.S. Barnes, 1971.

Preminger, Otto. *Preminger: An Autobiography.* Garden City, N.Y.: Doubleday, 1977.

Radovich, Don. *Tony Richardson: A Bio-Bibliography.* Westport, Conn.: Greenwood Press, 1995.

Richardson, Tony. *The Long-Distance Runner: A Memoir.* London: Faber and Faber, 1993.

Riordan, James. *Stone: The Controversies, Excesses, and Exploits of a Radical Filmmaker.* New York: Hyperion, 1995.

Rogoff, Rosalind Louise. *Sound and Film—The Long Engagement.* Los Angeles: UCLA (Thesis), 1973.

Rosenberg, Bernard, and Ernest Harburg. *The Broadway Musical: Collaboration in Commerce and Art.* New York: New York University Press, 1993.

Roudane, Matthew. *Understanding Edward Albee.* Columbia: University of South Carolina Press, 1987.

Ruskino, Susan. *Joe Orton.* New York: Twayne, 1995.

———. *Tom Stoppard.* Boston: Twayne, 1986.

Schary, Dore. *Heyday.* Boston: Little, Brown, 1979.

Schuster, Mel. *The Contemporary Greek Cinema.* Metuchen, N.J.: Scarecrow Press, 1979.

Schuth, H. Wayne. *Mike Nichols.* Boston: Twayne, 1978.

Segaloff, Nat. *Hurricane Billy: The Stormy Life and Films of William Friedkin.* New York: William Morrow, 1990.

Seidman, Steve. *The Film Career of Billy Wilder*. Pleasantville, N.Y.: Redgrave, 1977.

Selinske, Robert. *Talking about Films: A Discussion Guide*. Menlo Park, Calif.: Filmquest Books, 1983.

Sesonske, Alexander. *Jean Renoir: The French Films, 1924–1939*. Cambridge, Mass.: Harvard University Press, 1980.

Siciliano, Enzo. *Pasolini: A Biography*, tr. John Shepley. New York: Random House, 1982.

Silverman, Stephen M. *Dancing on the Ceiling: Stanley Donen and His Movies*. New York: Knopf, 1996.

Simon, Neil. *The Play Goes On: A Memoir*. New York: Simon and Schuster, 1999.

———. *Rewrites: A Memoir*. New York: Simon and Schuster, 1996.

Sinyard, Neil. *Filming Literature: The Art of Screen Adaptation*. London: Croom Helm, 1986.

———. *The Films of Nicolas Roeg*. London: Charles Letts, 1991.

Sontag, Susan. *Styles of the Radical Will*. New York: Farrar, Straus and Giroux, 1966.

Spoto, Donald. *Stanley Kramer: Film Maker*. New York: G.P. Putnam's Sons, 1978.

Stack, Oswald, ed. *Pasolini on Pasolini: Interviews with Oswald Stack*. Bloomington: Indiana University Press, 1969.

Stoppard, Tom. *Rosencrantz and Guildenstern Are Dead: The Film*. London: Faber and Faber, 1991.

Taylor, John Russell. *Hitch: The Life and Times of Alfred Hitchcock*. New York: Pantheon Books, 1978.

———. *Orson Welles: A Celebration*. Boston: Little, Brown, 1986.

Taylor, William R. *Sydney Pollack*. Boston: Twayne, 1981.

Thompson, Frank. *Robert Wise: A Bio-Bibliography*. Westport, Conn.: Greenwood Press, 1995.

Tibbetts, John C. *The American Theatrical Film: Stages in Development*. Bowling Green, Ohio: Bowling Green State University Popular Press, 1985.

Vardac, A. Nicholas. *Stage to Screen: Theatrical Method from Garrick to Griffith*. Cambridge, Mass.: Harvard University Press, 1949.

Voss, Ralph F. *A Life of William Inge: The Strains of Triumph*. Lawrence: University of Kansas Press, 1989.

Walker, Robert Matthew. *From Broadway to Hollywood: The Musical and the Cinema*. London: Sanctuary Publishing, 1996.

Wansell, Geoffrey. *Terence Rattigan*. New York: St. Martins Press, 1991.

Weinberg, Herman G. *The Lubitsch Touch: A Critical Study*, 3rd ed., rev. New York: Dover, 1977.

Welsh, James M., and John C. Tibbetts, eds. *The Cinema of Tony Richardson*. Albany, N.Y.: SUNY Press, 1999.

Wexman, Virginia Wright, and Gretchen Bispinghoff. *Robert Altman: A Guide to References and Resources*. Boston: G.K. Hall, 1984.

Whitaker, Thomas. *Tom Stoppard*. New York: Grove Press, 1983.

Willis, Donald C. *The Films of Frank Capra*. Metuchen, N.J.: Scarecrow Press, 1974.

———. *The Films of Howard Hawks*. Metuchen, N.J.: Scarecrow Press, 1975.

Wolfe, Charles. *Frank Capra: A Guide to References and Resources*. Boston: G.K. Hall, 1987.

Yacowar, Maurice. *Tennessee Williams and Film*. New York: Frederick Ungar, 1977.

Young, Jeff. *Kazan: The Master Director Discusses His Films*. New York: Newmarket Press, 1999.

Zeffirelli, Franco. *Zeffirelli: The Autobiography of Franco Zeffirelli*. New York: Weidenfeld and Nicholson, 1986.

Zinnemann, Fred. *An Autobiography: A Life in the Movies*. New York: Charles Scribner's Sons, 1992.

Zolotow, Maurice. *Billy Wilder in Hollywood*. New York: Putnam, 1977.

Zucker, Carole. *In the Company of Actors: Reflections on the Craft of Acting*. New York: Theatre Arts Books/Routledge, 1999.

Shakespeare on Film Bibliography

Anderegg, Michael. *Orson Welles, Shakespeare, and Popular Culture.* New York: Columbia University Press, 1999.

Ball, Robert Hamilton. *Shakespeare on Silent Film: A Strange Eventful History.* London: Allen and Unwin, 1968.

Boose, Lynda E., and Richard Bart, eds. *Shakespeare, The Movie: Popularizing the Plays on Film, TV, and Video.* London: Routledge, 1997.

Branagh, Kenneth. *Hamlet, by William Shakespeare: Screenplay and Introduction.* New York: W.W. Norton, 1996.

———. *Henry V, by William Shakespeare: A Screen Adaptation.* London: Chatto and Windus, 1989.

———. *Much Ado About Nothing, by William Shakespeare: Screenplay, Introduction, and Notes on the Making of the Movie.* New York: W.W. Norton, 1993.

Brode, Douglas. *Shakespeare in the Movies: From the Silent Era to Shakespeare in Love.* New York: Oxford University Press, 2000.

Buchman, Lorne M. *Still in Movement: Shakespeare on Screen.* New York: Oxford University Press, 1991.

Bulman, J.C., and H.R. Coursen, eds. *Shakespeare on Television.* Hanover, N.H.: University Press of New England, 1988.

Burt, Richard. *Unspeakable Shaxxxspeare: Queer Theory and American Kiddie Culture.* New York: St. Martin's Press, 1998.

Cartmell, Deborah. *Interpreting Shakespeare on Screen.* New York: St. Martin's Press, 2000.

Coursen, H.R. *Macbeth: A Guide to the Play.* Westport, Conn.: Greenwood Press, 1997.

———. *Shakespeare in Production: Whose History?* Athens: Ohio University Press, 1996.

———. *Shakespearean Performance As Interpretation.* Newark: University of Delaware Press, 1992.

Crowl, Samuel. *Shakespeare Observed: Studies in Performance on Stage and Screen.* Athens: Ohio University Press, 1992.

Davies, Anthony. *Filming Shakespeare's Plays: The Adaptations of Laurence Olivier, Orson Welles, Peter Brook, and Akira Kurosawa.* Cambridge, U.K.: Cambridge University Press, 1988.

Davies, Anthony, and Stanley Wells, eds. *Shakespeare and the Moving Image: The Plays on Film and Television.* Cambridge, U.K.: Cambridge University Press, 1994.

Donaldson, Peter S. *Shakespearean Films/Shakespearean Directors* Boston: Unwin Hyman, 1990.

Eckert, Charles W., ed. *Focus on Shakespearean Films.* Englewood Cliffs, N.J.: Prentice-Hall, 1972.

Ehrens, Patricia. *Akira Kurosawa: A Guide to References and Resources.* Boston: G.K. Hall, 1979.

Forman, Milos, and Jan Novak. *Turnaround: A Memoir.* New York: Villard Books, 1994.

Geduld, Harry M. *Filmguide to Henry V.* Bloomington: Indiana University Press, 1973.

Gielgud, John, and John Miller. *Shakespeare: Hit or Miss?* London: Sidgwick and Jackson, 1991.

Goodwin, James, ed. *Perspectives on Akira Kurosawa.* New York: G.K. Hall, 1994.

Hall, Joan Lord. *Henry V: A Guide to the Play.* Westport, Conn.: Greenwood Press, 1997.

Homan, Sidney, ed. *Shakespeare's More Than Words Can Witness: Essays on Visual and Nonverbal Enactment in the Plays.* Lewisburg, Pa.: Bucknell University Press, 1980.

Howlett, Kathy M. *Framing Shakespeare on Film.* Athens: Ohio University Press, 2000.

Jackson, Russell, ed.. *The Cambridge Companion to Shakespeare on Film.* Cambridge, Eng.: Cambridge University Press, 2000.

Jorgens, Jack J. *Shakespeare on Film.* Bloomington: Indiana University Press, 1977.

Kliman, Bernice W. *Hamlet: Film, Television, and Audio Performance.* Rutherford, N.J.: Fairleigh Dickinson University Press, 1988.

———. *Macbeth: Shakespeare in Performance.* Manchester, U.K.: Manchester University Press, 1992.

Kozintsev, Grigori. "*Hamlet* and *King Lear:* Stage and Film," in *Shakespeare 1971: Proceedings of the World Shakespeare Congress, Vancouver, August 1971,* ed. Clifford Leech and J.M.R. Margeson. Toronto: University of Toronto Press, 1972.

———. *King Lear: The Space of Tragedy. The Diary of a Film Director,* tr. Mary Mackintosh. Berkeley: University of California Press, 1977.

———. *Shakespeare: Time and Conscience,* tr. Joyce Vining. New York: Hill and Wang, 1966.

Lippmann, Max, ed. *Shakespeare in Film.* Wiesbaden: Saaten Verlag, 1964.

Lusardi, James P., and June Schlueter. *Reading Shakespeare in Performance: King Lear.* Rutherford, N.J.: Fairleigh Dickinson University Press, 1991.

————, eds. *Shakespeare Bulletin* (incorporating *Shakespeare on Film Newsletter* since 1972), English Department, Lafayette College, Easton, Pennsylvania.

Maher, Mary Z. *Modern Hamlets & Their Soliloquies.* Iowa City: University of Iowa Press, 1992.

Manvell, Roger. *Shakespeare and the Film.* London: J.M. Dent, 1971.

Mazursky, Paul, and Leon Capetanos. *Tempest: A Screenplay.* New York: Performing Arts Journal Publications, 1982.

Morris, Peter. *Shakespeare on Film.* Ottawa: Canadian Film Institute, 1972.

Parker, Barry M. *The Folger Shakespeare Filmography A Directory of Feature Films Based on the Works of William Shakespeare.* Washington, D.C.: Folger Shakespeare Library, 1979.

Pilkington, Ace G. *Screening Shakespeare from Richard II to Henry V.* Newark: University of Delaware Press, 1991.

Richie, Donald. *The Films of Akira Kurosawa,* rev. Berkeley: University of California Press, 1984.

Rothwell, Kenneth S. *A History of Shakespeare on Screen: A Century of Film and Television.* Cambridge, U.K.: Cambridge University Press, 1999.

Rothwell, Kenneth S., and Bernice W. Kliman, eds. *Shakespeare on Film Newsletter.* Published 1976 to 1992.

Rothwell, Kenneth S., and Annabelle Henkin Melzer. *Shakespeare on Screen: An International Filmography and Videography.* New York: Neal-Schuman, 1990.

Shaughnessy, Robert, ed. *Shakespeare on Film,* New Casebooks Series. New York: St. Martin's Press, 1998.

Silviria, Dale. *Laurence Olivier and the Art of Film Making.* Rutherford, N.J.: Fairleigh Dickinson University Press, 1985.

Skovmand, Michael, ed. *Screen Shakespeare.* Aarhus, Denmark: Aarhus University Press, 1994.

Stalpaert, Christel, ed. *Peter Greenaway's Prospero's Books: Critical Essays.* Ghent: Academia Press, 2000.

Taylor, Geoffrey. *Paul Mazursky's Tempest.* New York: New York Zoetrope, 1982.

Tibbetts, John C., and James M. Welsh. *His Majesty the American: The Films of Douglas Fairbanks, Sr.* South Brunswick, N.J.: A.S. Barnes, 1977.

Welsh, James M., and John C. Tibbetts, eds. *The Cinema of Tony Richardson: Essays and Interviews.* Albany, N.Y.: SUNY Press, 1999.

Welsh, James M., and Thomas L. Erskine, eds. *Literature/Film Quarterly.* Shakespeare Issues: 1:4 (1973), 4:2 (1976), 5:4 (1977), 11:3 (1983), 14:4 (1986), 20:4 (1992), 22:2 (1994), 25:2 (1997), 28:2 (2000).

Willis, Susan. *The BBC Shakespeare Plays.* Chapel Hill: University of North Carolina Press, 1992.

Willson, Robert F., ed. *Shakespeare: Entering the Maze.* New York: Peter Lang, 1995.

Willson, Robert F., Jr. *Shakespeare in Hollywood, 1929–1956.* Madison, N.J.: Fairleigh Dickinson University Press, 2000.

Wollen, Roger. *Derek Jarman: A Portrait; Artist, Film-maker, Designer.* London: Thames and Hudson, 1996.

Woods, Alan. *Being Naked Playing Dead: The Art of Peter Greenaway.* Manchester, U.K.: Manchester University Press, 1996.

Musicals on Film Bibliography

Allen, John. *Vaudeville and Film*. New York: Arno Press, 1980.

Altman, Rick. *American Film Musicals*. Bloomington: Indiana University Press, 1987.

———, ed. *Genre: The Musical*. London: Routledge and Kegan Paul, 1981.

Aylesworth, Thomas G. *Broadway to Hollywood*. New York: Bison Books, 1985.

Babington, Bruce, and Peter William Evans. *Blue Skies and Silver Linings*. Manchester, U.K.: Manchester University Press, 1985.

Baral, Robert. *Revue: The Great Broadway Period*. New York: Fleet Press Corporation, 1962.

Barrios, Richard. *A Song in the Dark*. New York: Oxford University Press, 1995.

Bergreen, Laurence. *As Thousands Cheer: The Life of Irving Berlin*. New York: Viking Press, 1990.

Block, Geoffrey. *Enchanted Evenings*. New York: Oxford University Press, 1997.

Bordman, Gerald. *American Musical Theatre: A Chronicle*. New York: Oxford University Press, 1978.

———. *American Operetta*. New York: Oxford University Press, 1981.

———. *American Musical Revue: From "The Passing Show" to "Sugar Babies"*. New York: Oxford University Press, 1985.

———. *Jerome Kern: His Life and Music*. New York: Oxford University Press, 1980.

Carringer, Robert L., ed. *The Jazz Singer*. Madison: University of Wisconsin Press, 1979.

Carter, Randolph. *The World of Flo Ziegfeld*. New York: Praeger, 1974.

Casper, Joseph Andrew. *Stanley Donen*. Metuchen, N.J.: Scarecrow Press, 1983.

———. *Vincente Minnelli and the Film Musical*. New York: A.S. Barnes, 1977.

Chapin, Saul. *The Golden Age of Movie Musicals and Me*. Norman: University of Oklahoma Press, 1994.

Citron, Stephen. *The Musical, from the Inside Out*. Chicago: Ivan R. Dee, 1991.

Clarke, Gerald. *Get Happy: The Life of Judy Garland*. New York: Random House, 2000.

Condon, Frank, "Over the Bridge to the Movies," *The Saturday Evening Post*, 2104 (January 16, 1932): 31–48.

Druxman, Michael B. *The Musical from Broadway to Hollywood*. New York: Barnes, 1980.

Edwards, Anne. *Streisand: A Biography*. New York: Little, Brown, 1997.

Erenberg, Lewis A. *Steppin' Out: New York Nightlife and the Transformation of American Culture, 1890–1930*. Westport, Conn.: Greenwood Press, 1981.

Ewen, David. *New Complete Book of the American Musical Theater*. New York: Holt, Rinehart, Winston, 1958.

Feuer, Jane. *The Hollywood Musical*. Bloomington: Indiana University Press, 1982.

Flinn, Danny Martin. *What They Did for Love: The Untold Story Behind the Making of "A Chorus Line."* New York: Bantam Books, 1989.

Fordin, Hugh. *The World of Entertainment: Hollywood's Greatest Musicals*. New York: Doubleday, 1975.

Frommer, Myrna Katz, and Harry Frommer. *It Happened on Broadway: An Oral History of the Great White Way*. New York: Harcourt, Brace, 1998.

Ganzl, Kurt. *The Encyclopedia of Musical Theatre*. New York: Schirmer, 1994.

Garebian, Keith. *The Making of "West Side Story."* Toronto: ECS, 1995.

Green, Stanley. *Broadway Musicals: Show by Show*. Milwaukee: Hal Leonard Books, 1985.

Hamm, Charles. *Yesterdays: Popular Song in America*. New York: W.W. Norton, 1979.

Hirsch, Julia Antopol. *The Sound of Music: The Making of America's Favorite Movie*. Chicago: Contemporary Books, 1993.

Hirschhorn, Clive. *The Hollywood Musical*. New York: Crown, 1981.

Jackson, Arthur. *The Best Musicals*. New York: Crown, 1977.

Jason, David A. *Tin Pan Alley*. New York: Donald I. Fine, 1988.

Jenkins, Henry. *What Made Pistachio Nuts? Early Sound Comedy and the Vaudeville Aesthetic*. New York: Columbia University Press, 1992.

Kislan, Richard. *Hoofing on Broadway: A History of Show Dancing*. New York: Prentice-Hall Press, 1987.

Kissel, Howard. *David Merrick: The Abominable Showman*. New York: Applause, 1993.

Kobol, John. *Gotta Sing Gotta Dance*. London: Hamlyn, 1970.

Kreuger, Miles, ed. *The Movie Musical: From Vitaphone to 42nd Street.* New York: Dover Books, 1975.

Kreuger, Miles. *Show Boat: The Story of a Classic American Musical.* New York: Oxford University Press, 1977.

Lerner, Alan Jay. *The Musical Theatre: A Celebration.* New York: Schirmer, 1994.

———. *On the Street Where I Live.* New York: Da Capo Press, 1994.

Levy, Alan Howard, "The Search for Identity in American Music, 1890–1920," *American Music,* 2:2 (Summer 1984), 70–81.

Loesser, Susan. *A Most Remarkable Fella: Frank Loesser and the Guys and Dolls in His Life.* New York: Donald I. Fine, 1993.

Logan, Joshua. *Josh: My Ups and Downs, In and Out of Life.* New York: Delacorte Press, 1976.

Mast, Gerald. *Can't Help Singin': The American Musical on Stage and Screen.* New York: Overlook Press, 1987.

Matthews, Jessie. *Over My Shoulder: An Autobiography.* New Rochelle, N.Y.: Arlington House, 1974.

McVay, Douglas. *The Musical Film.* New York: A.S. Barnes, 1967.

Miller, Scott. *From Assassins to West Side Story.* Portsmouth N.H.: Heinemann, 1996.

Moore, Macdonald Smith. *Yankee Blues: Musical Culture and American Identity.* Bloomington: Indiana University Press, 1985.

Mordden, Ethan. *Rodgers and Hammerstein.* New York: Harry N. Abrams, 1992.

Ostrow, Stuart. *A Producer's Broadway Journey.* Westport, Conn.: Praeger, 1999.

Parish, James Robert, and Michael R. Pitts. *The Great Hollywood Musicals.* Metuchen N.J.: Scarecrow Press, 1992.

Pessen, Edward, "The Great Songwriters of Tin Pan Alley's Golden Age: A Social, Occupational, and Aesthetic Inquiry," *American Music,* 3:2 (Summer 1985), 193–195.

Pitts, Michael R., "Popular Singers and the Early Movie Musicals," *Classic Images,* 72 (November 1980), 10–11.

Rich, Frank, "Conversations with Sondheim," *New York Times Magazine,* March 12, 2000.

Rodgers, Richard. *Musical Stages.* New York: Random House, 1975.

Schwartz, Charles. *Gershwin: His Life and Music.* New York: Bobbs-Merrill, 1973.

———. *Cole Porter.* New York: Da Capo Press, 1979.

Secrest, Meryle. *Stephen Sondheim: A Life.* New York: Alfred Knopf, 1998.

Sennett, Ted. *Hollywood Musicals.* New York: Harry Abrams, 1981.

Suskin, Steven. *Opening Night on Broadway.* New York: Schirmer Books, 1990.

———. *More Opening Nights on Broadway.* New York: Macmillan, 1997.

Thomas, Tony. *That's Dancing!* New York: Harry N. Abrams, 1984.

Thomas, Tony, and Jim Terry. *The Busby Berkeley Book.* New York: New York Graphic Society, 1973.

Tibbetts, John C. *The American Theatrical Film.* Bowling Green, Ohio: Popular Press, 1985.

———, "The New Tin Pan Alley: 1940s Hollywood Looks at American Popular Songwriters," in Michael Saffle, ed., *Perspectives on American Music, 1900–1950.* New York: Garland Publishing, 2000; 349–384.

———. "John McGlinn: Restoring the American Musical Theatre," *The World and I,* 10:4 (April 1995), 112–117.

Turk, Edward Baron. *Hollywood Diva: A Biography of Jeanette MacDonald.* Los Angeles: University of California Press, 1998.

Walker, Alexander. *The Shattered Silents.* New York: Oxford University Press, 1979.

Waters, Edward N. *Victor Herbert: A Life in Music.* New York: Macmillan, 1955.

Wilk, Max. *They're Playing Our Song.* New York: Atheneum, 1973.

———. *OK!: The Story of Oklahoma.* New York: Grove Press, 1993.

Wilson, Edmund, "Movietone and Musical Show," *The New Republic,* 55 (July 18, 1928), 226–227.

Yudkoff, Alvin. *Gene Kelly: A Life of Dance and Dreams.* New York: Back Stage Books, 1999.

Ziegfeld, Richard and Paulette. *The Ziegfeld Touch.* New York: Harry N. Abrams, 1993.

Index

Croft, Colin 330
Croft, Douglas 126
Croft, Emma 355
Cromwell, John 3, 4, 257
Cronyn, Hume 81, 292, 366
Crosby, Bing 6, 59, 233
Crosland, Alan 162, 163
Crouse, Russel 22, 176–177, 527
Crowden, Graham 360
Crowd Roars, The 46
Crowley, Bob 174
Crowley, Jeananne 100
Crowther, Bosley 51–52, 82, 111, 197, 444, 459
Crucible, The **64–67**, *66*
Cruel Intentions 176
Cruikshank, Herbert xviii
Cruise, Tom 113
Cruze, James 359
Crystal, Billy 368
Cukor, George xx, 16, 17, 35, 86, 87, 138, 231, 232, 333–335, 350, 397, 398, 416–418, 509, 510, 552, *552*
Cul-de-Sac 77
Culen, R.J. 353
Culkin, Michael 149
Cullum, John 518, 523
Cumming, Alan 416
Cummings, Robert 86
Cunningham, James P. 150
Curley, Leo 63
Curtice, Sally 372
Curtis, Tony 160
Curtiz, Michael 104, 109, 110, 111, 163, 176, 348
Cusack, Cyril 211, 407
Cusack, John 60, 546
Cuskern, Dominic 121
Cymbeline **358–361**, 555
Cyrano de Bergerac **67–69**, *68*
Czinner, Paul 347, 353, 354

D

DaCosta, Morton 334, 507–509
Dagover, Lil 296
Dahl, John 254
Dailey, Dan 326, 445
Dale, R.C. 543
Dall, John 57, 58
Dalton, Robin 312
D'Amico, Suso Cecci 405
Damn Yankees 436, 437, **463–464**
Damus, Mike 190
Dance, Charles 240

Dancing at Lughnasa **70–72**
Danes, Claire 344, *420*, 421
D'Angelo, Beverly 486
Dangerous Liaisons 174, *175*, 175–176
Daniels, Bebe 58, 521, 545
Daniels, Ben 426
Daniels, William 518, 522, 523
Danner, Blythe 524
Danon, Marcello 42
Dante, Nicholas 459–460
Dantine, Helmut 231
Darby, Ken 38
Darion, Joe 503
Dark at the Top of the Stairs, The **72–73**
Darling, Jean 457
Darlow, Michael 36
Darrieux, Danielle 251
da Silva, Howard 60, 515, 522, 523, 524
Dassin, Jules 198, 199, 200
Daves, Delmer 230, 349
David, Eleanor 506
David, Mack 487
Davies, Anthony 424
Davies, Brian 475
Davies, Howard 174
Davies, Ieuan 314
Davis, Andrew 85, 86
Davis, Anthony 420
Davis, Bette 57, 58, 104–105, 164, 173, 177, 181, 197, 230, 324, *324*
Davis, Carl 506
Davis, Donald 211
Davis, Judy 159
Davis, Owen 163–164
Davis, Pamela 351
Davis, Sammy, Jr. 306, 531
Davison, Bruce 67
Dawley, J. Searle 6, 120, 248
Dawn Patrol, The 46
Dawson, Ralph 391
Day, Clarence Day, Jr. 177, 348
Day, Doris 334
Day, Peter 103
Day, Richard 75
Day-Lewis, Daniel 67
Days of Wine and Roses **73–74**
Déa, Marie 217
Dead End **74–76**, 181
Dean, James 7
Deane, Hamilton 90–91, 119
Death and the Maiden 76, **76–77**

Death of a Salesman 64, **77–79**, *79*
Death Takes a Holiday **79–80**
De Brulier, Nigel 89
Decae, Henri 251
Dee, Ruby 249, 250
De Forest, Lee 433
De Grasse, Joseph 87, 89
de Havilland, Olivia 391
Dehn, Paul 405
De Junes, Louis 218
Delaney, Shelagh 297–298
Delannoy, Michel 321
Delerue, Georges 195
Delgado, Roger 352
Delhomme, Benoit 332
Delicate Balance, A **80–82**
Dell, Gabriel 75
Demas, Carole 480
Demazis, Orane 198
de Mille, Agnes 418, 450, 451, 457, 458, 514, 516, 530
DeMille, Cecil B. xvi, xvii, 61, 62, 275–278, 315, 316
Denby, David 117, 295, 331, 348, 506
Dench, Judi 102, 346, 368, 391, 424, 562
Denehy, Brian 421
Denevue, Catherine 564
Denig, Lynde 387
Denison, Michael 153
Dennen, Barry 491, 492
Dennis, Nick 288
Dennis, Patrick 502
Dennis, Sandy 303, 328
Dent, Alan 362, 371, 372, 401
Depardieu, Gerard *68*, 69, 295, 296, 368, 564
Dermithe, Edouard 217
Dern, Bruce 300
Desert Song, The 433, 436
De Sica, Vittoria 298
Desire Under the Elms **82–83**
Deutsch, Helen 532
De Vega, Jose 421
Devil's Disciple, The **83–85**, 260
Devine, Alan 418
Devine, Andy 418
Devine, George 186, 189, 410
DeVito, Danny 141
Devlin, William 380
DeVore, Christopher 362, 367
Dexter, Elliott 277–278

Dexter, John 108, 397, 399
Diakhate, Ami 319
Dial M for Murder **85–86**
Diamond, I. A. L. 122, 123
Diamond, Neil 163
DiCaprio, Leonardo 344, *420*, 420–421
Dick, Bernard 51, 123, 266, 280
Dickens, Charles 516
Dickinson, Thorold 16–17
Dickson, W. K. L. 346
Diegues, Carlos 542
Diener, Joan 504
Dieterle, William 390, 391
Dietrich, Marlene 222, 332
Digges, Dudley 125, 146
Dighton, John 83, 85
Dignam, Arthur 330
Dignam, Mark 367
Dillane, Stephen 70, 368
Dillon, Carmen 402
Dillon, Melinda 326
Di Luca, Dino 306
Dingle, Charles 126, 180, 181
Dinner at Eight **86–87**
Diouf, Mansour 319
Disch, Thomas 281
Disney, Walt 228
Disraeli xvii
Dix, Beulah Marie 275, 277
Dixon, David 411
Dixon, Ivan 249
Dixon, Jean 125
Dixon, Lee 515
Dmytryk, Edward 349
Doctor's Secret, The xviii
Dodge, Jerry 487
Doel, Frank 101
Dog in the Manger, The 225–227
Doll's House, The **87–90**
Donahue, J. T. 324
Donaldson, Walter 536
Donat, Robert 331
Donehue, Vincent J. 291, 292
Donen, Stanley 463, 464
Donlevy, Brian 317
Donner, Clive 44
Donohoe, Amanda 192
Dorfman, Ariel 76
Dorn, Dolores 313
Dorzat, Gabrielle 223
Dotrice, Roy 13
Double Life, A 350, 397, 398, 552–554
Douglas, Kirk 85, 128, 218